the ONION® PRESENTS

Homeland Insecurity

COMPLETE NEWS ARCHIVES • VOLUME 17

ALSO BY *THE ONION*

Our Dumb Century:
100 Years of Headlines from America's Finest News Source

The Onion's Finest News Reporting, Volume One

Dispatches from the Tenth Circle:
The Best of The Onion

The Onion Ad Nauseam:
Complete News Archives, Volume 13

The Tenacity of the Cockroach:
Conversations with Entertainment's
Most Enduring Outsiders

The Onion Ad Nauseam:
Complete News Archives, Volume 14

Fanfare for the Area Man
The Onion Ad Nauseam: Complete News Archives, Volume 15

Embedded in America
Complete News Archives, Volume 16

the ONION® PRESENTS
Homeland Insecurity

COMPLETE NEWS ARCHIVES • VOLUME 17

EDITED BY
Scott Dikkers, Carol Kolb

WRITTEN BY
Amie Barrodale, Rich Dahm, Mike DiCenzo, Scott Dikkers,
Joe Garden, Dan Guterman, Todd Hanson, Chris Karwowski, Peter Koechley,
Carol Kolb, John Krewson, Maria Schneider

GRAPHICS BY
Mike Loew, Chad Nackers

DESIGN BY
Jenny Paulo, Jill Rosenmerkel, Andrew Welyczko

COVER DESIGN BY
Mike Loew, Chad Nackers

ADDITIONAL PRODUCTION BY
Aric Meidl, Emily Pittsley, Jun Ueno

ADDITIONAL MATERIAL BY
Adam Albright-Hanna, Diane Bullock, Janet Ginsburg, Josh Greenman, John Howell Harris,
Barry Julien, Jackie Lalley, Sam Means, Nick Nadel, Chris Pauls, Ben Rutter, Mike Schuster, Wil Shepard,
Dave Sherman, Scott Sherman, Jacob Sager Weinstein

COPYEDITED BY
Amie Barrodale, Mike DiCenzo, Tasha Robinson

SPECIAL THANKS
Jessie Altman, Andy Battaglia, Rachel Berger, Christine Carlson, Becca Carr, Erica Christensen, Chet Clem,
Chris Cranmer, Dan Friel, Amelie Gillette, Daniel Greenberg, Steve Hannah, Annik LaFarge, Matt McDonagh,
Sean Mills, David Miner, P.S. Mueller, Michael O'Brien, Keith Phipps, Nathan Rabin, Allison Ray, Erin Riipi, Mario Rojas,
Lars Russell, David Schafer, Miles Seiden, Glenn Severance, Rob Siegel, Andrew Smith, Julie Stainer, Barb Stamatelatos,
Amy Steinhauser, Sigmund Stern, Carrie Thornton, Pete Tunney

BOXTREE

This book uses invented names in all stories, except notable public figures who are the subject of satire. Any other use of real names is accidental and coincidental.

First published 2006 by Three Rivers Press, New York, New York.
Member of the Crown Publishing Group, a Division of Random House, Inc.

First published in Great Britain 2006 by Boxtree
an imprint of Pan Macmillan Ltd
Pan Macmillan, 20 New Wharf Road, London N1 9RR
Basingstoke and Oxford
Associated companies throughout the world
www.panmacmillan.com

ISBN-13: 978-0-7522-2636-1
ISBN-10: 0-7522-2636-3

9 8 7 6 5 4 3 2 1

A CIP catalogue record for this book is available from the British Library.

Designed by The Onion
Printed and bound in Great Britain by the Bath Press, Bath

PHOTO CREDITS:

p. 94, Jackson; p. 115, Helicopter (bottom right); p. 253, Fire: AFP/Getty Images. p. 67, Moore: Evan Agostini/Getty Images. p. 250, Survival: Carlo Allegri/Getty Images. p. 140, Government; p. 277, Burning: Ahmad al-Rubaye/AFP/Getty Images. p. 203, Bombing: Sabah Arar/AFP/Getty Images. p. 67, Dolphin: Pedro Armestre/AFP/Getty Images. p. 271, Pallbearers: Tony Ashby/AFP/Getty Images. p. 66, Dillon: Brian Bahr/Getty Images. p. 292, Airport: Roberto Baretti/AFP/Getty Images. p. 127, Cardinal: Niurka Barroso/AFP/Getty Images. p. 257, Homeless: Robyn Beck/AFP/Getty Images. p. 66, Dawkins: Doug Benc/Getty Images. p. 55, Alarmists: Chris Bernacchi/AFP/Getty Images. p. 175, Hopper: Torsten Blackwood/AFP/Getty Images. p. 79, Neighborhood; p. 112, Van; p. 134, Amtrak; p. 146, Winfrey; p. 205, Ambulance: Tim Boyle/Getty Images. p. 45 (bottom), Celebrities; p. 73, Law: Vince Bucci/Getty Images. p. 121, Vatican City, St. Peter's Square: Giuseppe Cacace/Getty Images. p. 135, Mint: Matthew Cavanaugh/Getty Images. p. 265, Tollefsen: Chill-O-Vision, LLC. p. 271, Showoff: China Photos/Getty Images. p. 239, Prague: Michael Cizek/AFP/Getty Images. p. 194, Disneyland: Mike Clarke/AFP/Getty Images. p. 83, Maradiaga: Paolo Cocco/AFP/Getty Images. p. 241, Oprah: Thomas Cooper/Getty Images. p. 211, Burdett: Adrian Dennis, AFP/Getty. p. 91, Investigator: Jay Directo/AFP/Getty Images. p. 154, Highway: Dave Einsel/Getty Images. p. 187, Underwater; p. 223, Pharmacy; p. 247, Kidman: Rob Elliott/AFP/Getty Images. p. 67, Nyboyev: EPA/AFP/Getty Images. p. 284, Iraqi: Mehdi Fedouach/AFP/Getty Images. p. 187, Senate; p. 235, Bush; p. 285, Press conference: Luke Frazza/AFP/Getty Images. p. 232, Waiting; p. 233, Helicopter; p. 260, Al-Qaeda: Sean Gallup/Getty Images. p. 229, Cheney; p. 295, Bush: Mannie Garcia/Getty Images. p. 8, Rice; p. 151, Crash; p. 163, Bush; p. 226, Buells: Getty Images. p.1, Winfrey; p. 50, Mars; p. 67, Bush; p. 70, Abbas/Sharon; p. 86, Nico; p. 215, Hassim: Getty Images/Handout. p. 45 (top right), Celebrities; p. 91, Neverland (aerial view); p. 181, Celebrities; p. 250, Marmont: Frazer Harrison/Getty Images. p. 127, Couric: Paul Hawthorne/Getty Images. p. 117, Pope: Patrick Hertzog/AFP/Getty Images. p. 139, Usher: Dave Hogan/Getty Images. p. 152, Parade: David S. Holloway/AFP/Getty Images. p. 10, Soldier; p. 235, Home: Chris Hondros/Getty Images. p. 175, Mutant: Boris Horyat/AFP/Getty Images. p. 212, Biofuels; p. 238, Police: Sandy Huffaker/Getty Images. p. 80, Bush; p. 223, Bush: Stephen Jaffe/AFP/Getty Images. p. 177, Robot: Koichi Kamoshida/Getty Images. p. 74, Klastermann: Saeed Khan/AFP/Getty Images. p. 44, Iraq: Wathiq Khuzaie/Getty Images. p. 145, Ford: Jeff Kowalski/AFP/Getty Images. p. 14, Trump: Peter Kramer/Getty Images. p. 175, Construction; p. 253, Crane: Jimin Lai/AFP/Getty Images. p. 130, Protest: Pascal Le Segretain/Getty Images. p. 71, Weapons: Mauricio Lima/AFP/Getty Images. p. 61, McNabb: Andy Lyons/Getty Images. p. 221, House: Preston Mack/Getty Images. p. 182, Camp: Giulio Marcocchi/Getty Images. p.139, Kiss: Pierre Philippe-Marcou/AFP/Getty Images. p. 223, Pharmacist: Darren McCollester/Getty Images. p. 187, Senators: Win McNamee/Getty Images. p. 2, Ice; p. 4, Machine; p. 85, Bush; p. 110, Oil; p. 133, Townspeople: David McNew/Getty Images. p. 88, Iranians: Behrouz Mehri/AFP/Getty Images. p. 45 (top left), Celebrities; p. 241, Wrestlers: Frank Micelotta/Getty Images. p. 49, Jackson: Donald Morale/Getty Images. p. 56, Google; p. 223, Google: David Paul Morris, Getty Images. p. 145, Bush: Stephen Morton/Getty Images. p. 163, Hug: Cathrin Mueller/Bongarts/Getty Images. p. 103, Computers: Indranil Mukherjee/AFP/Getty Images. p. 43, Justices: Joyce Naltchayan/AFP/Getty Images. p. 217, Planet; p. 248, Shuttle: NASA/Handout/Getty Images. p. 283, Casket: Mandel Ngan/AFP/Getty Images. p. 253, Hollywood: Lucy Nicholson/AFP/Getty Images. p. 175, Robot: Kazuhiro Nogi/AFP/Getty. p. 115, Bridge: Fayez Nureldine/AFP/Getty Images. p. 133, Firemen; p. 167, Vigilantes; p. 177, Buildings; p. 180, Bikers; p. 278, McDonald's: Scott Olson/Getty Images. p. 79, Pope; p. 115, St. Peter's: Franco Origlia/Getty Images. p. 45 (top center), Celebrities; p. 181, NASCAR: Doug Pensinger/Getty Images. p. 51, Police; p. 113, Redford: Matthew Peyton/Getty Images. p. 115, Pope: Vincenzo Pinto/AFP/Getty Images. p. 13, Miller; p. 85, Clinton: Spencer Platt/Getty Images. p. 103, Simmons: Brian Pobuda/Getty Images. p. 205, Bush; p. 230, Constitution; p. 266, Hussein: Pool/Getty Images. p. 66, Truck: Bill Pugliano/Getty Images. p. 187, Hurricane, p. 190, Reid; p. 195, Schultz: Joe Raedle/Getty Images. p. 1, Ashcroft; p. 11, Kerry; p. 101, Bush/Powell; p. 151, White House; p. 175, Capitol: Paul J. Richards/AFP/Getty Images. p. 142, Conference: Kayne Robinson/Getty Images. p. 181, Bertoli, p. 230, Fox: Adalberto Roque/AFP/Getty Images. p. 166, Athletes: Nadine Rupp/Bongarts/Getty Images. p. 213, Hassim: Karim Sahib/AFP/Getty Images. p. 220, Jet lag: Issouf Sanogo/AFP/Getty Images. p. 272, Flu: Paco Serinelli/AFP/Getty Images. p. 79, Maradiaga: Orlando Sierra/AFP/Getty Images. p. 115, Helicopter (top left): Christophe Simon/AFP/Getty Images. p. 5 (right), Winfrey: Mark Simons/Getty Images. p. 103, Bush; p. 232, Cheney: Brendan Smialowski/AFP/Getty Images. p. 133, Senator; p. 202, Bush/Rove; p. 242, Roberts; p. 259, Bush: Chip Somodevilla/Getty Images. p. 218, Filmmaking: Cameron Spencer/Getty Images. p. 7, Kerry: Michael Springer/Getty Images. p. 116, Minutemen: Curtis Stewart/Getty Images. p. 7, Stadium; p. 227, Purge: STR/AFP/Getty Images. p. 188, Shuttle: Matt Stroshane/Getty Images. p. 122, Depp: Stephen Sugarman/Getty Images. p. 89, Reality TV; p. 96, Wi-Fi; p. 121, Butterfly; p. 139, Bridge; p. 223, Schmidt: Justin Sullivan/Getty Images. p. 307, Cheney: Robert Sullivan/AFP/Getty Images. p. 49, Protest; p. 98, SAT; p. 169, Oval Office; p. 205, Search; p. 283, Aquarium: Mario Tama/Getty Images. p. 109, Congress: Mario Tama/AFP/Getty Images. p. 289, Crash: Fred Tanneau/AFP/Getty Images. p. 175, Car: Yoshikazu Tsuno/AFP/Getty Images. p. 229, Hurricane: U.S. Coast Guard/Getty Images. p. 104, Information: Herwig Vergult/AFP/Getty Images. p. 277, Churchgoer: Mario Villafuerte/Getty Images. p. 151, Bush; p. 289, Bush: Jim Watson/AFP/Getty Images. p. 271, Shuttle: Bruce Weaver/AFP/Getty Images. p. 49, Duff: Donald Weber/Getty Images. p. 251, Billboard: Barry Williams/Getty Images. p. 7, Agents; p. 91, Bush; p. 133, Bush; p. 187, Hastert; p. 206, CAFTA; p. 307, Bush: Mark Wilson/Getty Images. p. 74, Rock; p. 75, Law; p. 103, Bergeron: Kevin Winter/Getty Images. p. 1, Santorum; p. 5 (center), Winfrey; p. 97, Powell; p. 109, Bush; p. 128, DeLay; p. 199, McClellan; p. 275, Chertoff; p. 301, Goss: Alex Wong/Getty Images. p. 43, Tsunami: Choo Youn-Kong/AFP/Getty Images. p. 175, Farmer: Ahmad Yusni/AFP/Getty Images. p. 137, Podium: Stefan Zaklin/Getty Images.

the ONION®

VOLUME 40 ISSUE 46 AMERICA'S FINEST NEWS SOURCE™ 18–24 NOVEMBER 2004

NEWS

Ashcroft Loses Job To Mexican

see WASHINGTON page 3B

Woman With Really Pointy Feet Finds Perfect Shoes

see LOCAL page 13G

Domineering Wife Specifically Said 'Chunk-Style' Pineapple

see PEOPLE page 9E

STATshot

A look at the numbers that shape your world.

Who Do We Owe Money To?
13% Bookie, but just 'til next race
15% Whoever owns rights to "Happy Birthday" song
24% Kevin, but we give him lifts all the time, so…
16% Church, for 11 years of past-due tithes
18% Stepdad, who's being a total dick about it
14% Medium-Sized Louie, but he owes Big Louie, so it's the same thing

THE ONION • $2.00 US • $3.00 CAN

Oprah Celebrates 20,000th Pound Lost

CHICAGO—Talk-show superstar Oprah Winfrey celebrated losing her 20,000th pound in a star-packed gala at the Sutton Place Hotel in Chicago's Gold Coast Monday night.

"Tonight is an amazing personal milestone," Winfrey said. "I want everyone who has supported me through the years—my friends, my loved ones, and all of my wonderful fans—to share the joy I feel tonight in having shed my 20,000th pound."

According to her spokesman, Winfrey has been on 674 diets, embarked on 255 fitness routines, and weighed herself 4,349,571 times during her 30-year career in broadcasting and film.

see OPRAH page 5

Above: Winfrey celebrates her momentous achievement on the set of her TV show.

Teen Handed Awesome Responsibility Of Closing Subway Alone

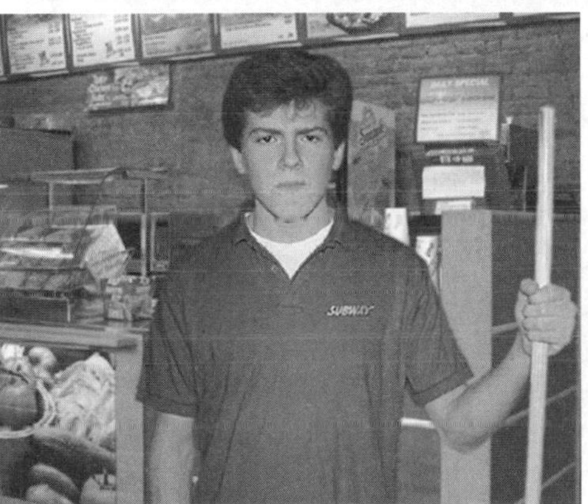

Left: Prusher, minutes after being told that he, and he alone, would be in charge of closing the restaurant.

BARTLESVILLE, OK—Subway sources report that employee Jeremy Prusher, 17, appeared proud and a little nervous after accepting the momentous duty of closing the franchise location by himself Monday night.

"Okay, here are keys to the front door and the deadbolt at the back," said Michael Rotley, 32, who has managed the Juniper Avenue restaurant since March 2003. "I know it seems like a lot to remember the first time, but as long as the doors are locked, the alarm is set, and the lids on the sandwich line are closed, I probably won't fire you."

"Just kidding about the firing," Rotley added. "But seriously, if those lids are up, we'll have to throw everything out. That's hundreds of dollars in product, so don't forget."

A Subway employee since Aug. 1, Prusher quickly earned several positive performance reviews and a 45-cent raise. Rotley said that, although Prusher is only a high-school junior, he is

see TEEN page 5

Republicans Call For Privatization Of Next Election

Above: Santorum calls for the removal of big government from the election process.

WASHINGTON, DC—Citing the "extreme inefficiency" of this month's U.S. presidential election, key Republicans called for future elections to be conducted by the private sector.

"When the average citizen hears the phrase 'presidential election,' he thinks of long lines at polling places and agonizing waits as election results are tallied," U.S. Sen. Rick Santorum (R-PA) told reporters Monday. "Putting the election of our public officials into the hands of private industry would motivate election officials to be more efficient."

"There's too much talk about the accuracy and fairness of our national elections, and not enough about their proficiency and profitability," Santorum added. "Who bears the brunt of bureaucratic waste? Taxpayers."

U.S. Sen. Conrad Burns (R-MT) called for an e[...] to "big government [...] seeing the election[...] government."

see REPU[...]

Arafat's Death

The death of Palestinian leader Yasser Arafat could represent a turning point in the Mideast peace process. What do *you* think?

"Now that Arafat's dead, the only thing standing in the way of peace in the Mideast is Sharon."

Amir Zubar
Painter

"Dead of natural causes at 75? If only more Palestinians were able to follow his example."

Robert Cook
Chef

"Mahmoud Abbas was chosen as his successor? Not Marwan Barghouti? Aw, man, if you were a Palestine policy wonk like me, you'd be so pissed."

Bruce Daniels
Systems Analyst

"The saddest part is that this Nobel Peace Prize winner died without seeing his lifelong dream of eternal war with Israel come to fruition."

Ellen Carter
Travel Writer

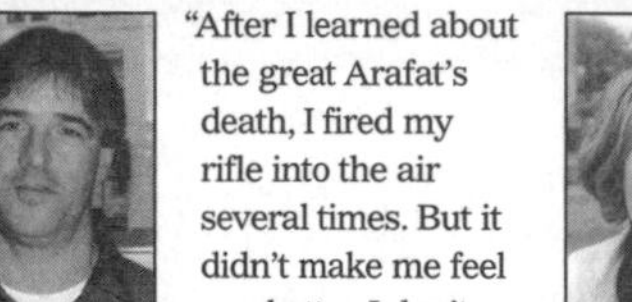

"After I learned about the great Arafat's death, I fired my rifle into the air several times. But it didn't make me feel any better. I don't know. I guess I'm changing."

Ibrahim Salah
Electrician

"If Palestine needs a hard-line religious nutjob to fill Arafat's position, our old attorney general is looking for work."

Karen Anderson
Hostess

The Effects Of Global Warming

Scientists say global warming is on the rise. What adverse effects do they predict will occur within the next decade?

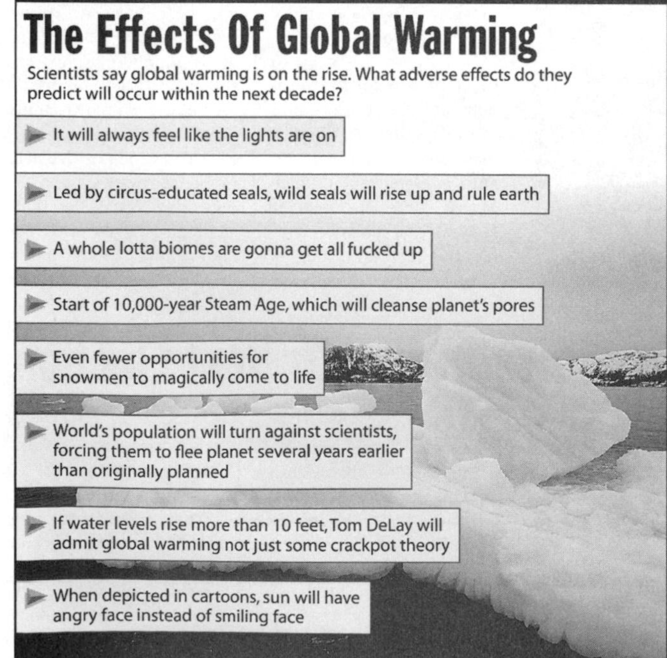

It will always feel like the lights are on
Led by circus-educated seals, wild seals will rise up and rule earth
A whole lotta biomes are gonna get all fucked up
Start of 10,000-year Steam Age, which will cleanse planet's pores
Even fewer opportunities for snowmen to magically come to life
World's population will turn against scientists, forcing them to flee planet several years earlier than originally planned
If water levels rise more than 10 feet, Tom DeLay will admit global warming not just some crackpot theory
When depicted in cartoons, sun will have angry face instead of smiling face

America's Finest News Source.™

Herman Ulysses Zweibel
Founder

T. Herman Zweibel
Publisher Emeritus
J. Phineas Zweibel
Publisher
Maxwell Prescott Zweibel
Editor-In-Chief

What Happens At Yucca Mountain Stays At Yucca Mountain

By Jack Laleigh

The name "Yucca Mountain" is synonymous with danger and excitement. It's so much more than some single-industry desert town with a lot of unusual buildings—the entire place surges with activity and pulses with the thrill of the forbidden. The eerie luminescent glow lights the Nevada sky all through the night. Everyone has heard stories, but no one who hasn't visited can truly understand Yucca Mountain. Why's that? Well, my friend, I'd like to tell you, but folks who work here have a little saying: What happens at the Yucca Mountain Federal Nuclear Waste Disposal and Encasement Facility *stays* at the Yucca Mountain Federal Nuclear Waste Disposal and Encasement Facility.

I can tell you firsthand: There's no place like this in the entire country. The instant you see the strip—the one they pin to your coverall to measure your exposure to radiation—you understand how high the stakes are. Yucca Mountain isn't for the faint of heart. You never get used to the surge of adrenaline you feel watching the Geiger counter whirl, or the frenzy that fills the lab when someone's number comes up. And bubbling below the surface all day—and all night—are the rumors about what immoral things go on behind closed doors, who really runs the place, and who's making the big money.

Discretion is the legally binding watchword for everyone who walks the facility floor. Whether you come for business or just to take a tour, your secrets stay at Yucca Mountain when you go. Hell, would you want your wife to know what happened during that weekend with your Secretary of Energy? Of course not. That's why you wouldn't want to let, oh, say, Mr. Media catch wind of the words you overheard escaping from a nearby Hilton Hyatt table occupied by the seven-man board of Nuclear Regulatory Commission attorneys.

Face it, there's a reason they call this place Synthetic-High-Radiation-And-Weapons-Research-Byproduct-Disposal City. You can try to sell it as a safe, clean site for the long-term storage of 80 million pounds of spent nuclear fuel and high-level radioactive waste all you want, but the truth remains that humans have certain desires. The desire for more electricity ain't going to just disappear overnight, and neither are its byproducts. As long as there are people, there will be a need for places like Yucca Mountain. And you didn't hear any of that from me, friend.

We don't like to talk about what goes on at the nation's first geological repository. It simply isn't wise. Even so, stuff gets out. We don't know how—mind you, we'd love to find out. When we do, I can tell you this: There are a few tattlers who'll be sorry. Very sorry. Not that anyone believes the leaks anyway. They're just legends and fragments of tall tales told by loonies found wandering the Mohave with no memory of how they got the burns on their bodies and lesions on their faces. Stories of roller-coaster rides on the wings of probability, people betting it all on a wink from lady luck and one number of the Periodic Table, and then spiraling down into a pit of despair and reinforced concrete when it all goes wrong. Well, believe what you want. No one at Yucca Mountain is talking.

The name "Yucca Mountain" is synonymous with danger and excitement.

If there's one thing that you can't stop, it's rumors. Do what you will, but they'll continue to fly. Maybe you heard the story that was circulating a year or so ago about a couple boys from Utah, name of Bob Bennett and Orrin Hatch, and a little problem called the Goshute Reservation Spent Nuclear Fuel Storage Facility proposed for their own state. Story says they took a gamble backing Yucca Mountain all the way to Congress and won big. But maybe that never happened. Hard to say. And, if you've heard that Nevada senator Harry Reid used the clout of his position as minority whip to make hundreds of millions of dollars in the 2005 Yucca Mountain budget disappear—why, I wouldn't know. I've been too busy watching the beautiful birds circling our little mountain here. You really do have to see them yourself to understand.

Hell, there are things we don't even talk about ourselves. Sometimes, it's wise not to let the left manipulator arm know what the right manipulator arm is doing, if you follow. Those guys in the fancy suits who fly out from Washington are always looking to score big and bust the place on a technicality of the Safe Drinking Water Act. But in the end, we're the ones who control the embankment around the repository. Us and the little birdies. If the EPA thinks we keep a

see YUCCA page 4

Local Life-Insurance Salesman A Catalog Of Horrific Sudden-Death Scenarios

PLEASANT HILL, TN—Bob Carson, a State Farm life-insurance salesman for the past 27 years, is a walking encyclopedia of sudden-death scenarios, local sources reported Monday.

"Did I ever tell you about that poor barber in Mississippi, Frank?" Carson said, addressing the owner of Frank Klemper's Fourth Street Barbershop. "Such a shame. He stepped on a pushbroom, and the handle flipped up, hit his arm, and drove the shears he was holding into his eye."

Added Carson: "Killed him instantly, because of the brain trauma. Went three inches down in there. Busted the eye like a grape and gouged the brain: home lobotomy. Hell of a thing for his wife and infant son. Had to fill the socket with a marble for the funeral."

"Next thing I knew, he was giving a forensically detailed account of a body found after a May 1978 bakery flash fire," Francis said.

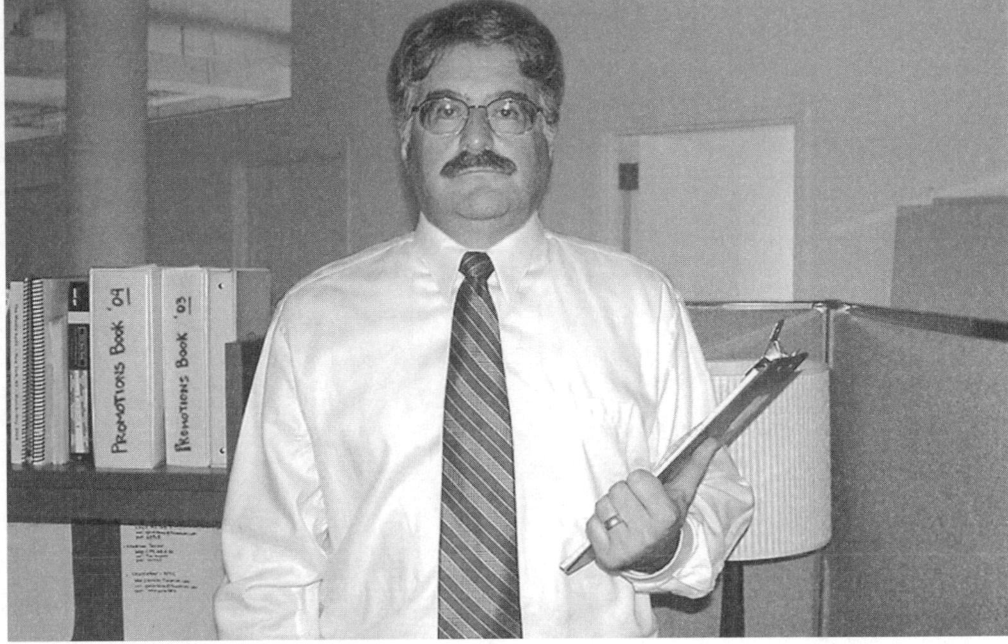

Above: Carson, who sells life insurance to local residents.

Carson has reportedly inserted hundreds of similar anecdotes into conversations during the past several years. Among his stories: a 1976 incident in which a Texas oilman got his tool-belt latch stuck in a high-pressure pump moments before it was turned on, the tale of a Southern Electric high-tension-wire worker who absorbed 10,000 amps through his metal lunch pail, and the story of an Arkansas grandmother who was hit and killed instantly by a passing tanker truck, which subsequently careened into a busload of kindergarten students on a field trip to see the Carlsbad Caverns and blew up cars within a quarter-mile radius.

"At this point, I'm almost afraid to say hello to Bob after Sunday services," neighbor Jane Francis said. "The last time I did, I remarked how good the coffee and Danishes were. The next thing I knew, he was giving a forensically detailed account of a body found after a May 1978 bakery flash fire caused when a malfunctioning pilot light ignited a cloud of flour."

"It was all 'charred and grisly remains,' and then he tipped his hat, said 'God bless you and good morning,' and walked over to Tim Hutter," Francis added.

Francis said Carson has a friendly smile, a charming personality, and a cheerful demeanor, but seems to have "an absolutely lurid obsession with freak accidents."

Francis said she walked by Carson several minutes later, on the same Sunday, and overheard him telling Hutter about the fast-acting carcinogens found in the groundwater near chemical plants like the one adjacent to Hut-

see SALESMAN page 6

NEWS IN BRIEF

Actual Governing To Resume

WASHINGTON, DC—Following 16 months of non-stop campaigning, members of the executive and legislative branches of the U.S. government returned to the task of governing the country Monday. "The electioneering is over, so it's time to get back to work," said U.S. Sen. Kit Bond (R-MO), who won a third term Nov. 2, beating Democrat Nancy Farmer. "I got the time, so I may as well use it writing and enacting some laws, I guess." Bond said he hopes to get a lot accomplished before summer, when he'll need to begin campaigning again.

Son Conned Out Of Allowance For Seventh Consecutive Week

MISSOULA, MT—For the seventh week in a row, Bill Trusky cheated his son Shane out of the boy's $3 allowance, the 8-year-old's father said Monday. "Sorry, Shane, I said it was double or nothing if you could sneeze with your eyes open," Trusky said. "But I'll tell you what: If you can mow the lawn—front and back—in 20 minutes, I'll pay you triple." Household sources report that Shane might have completed the task had Trusky not hurled a croquet ball in the mower's path 10 feet before his son finished.

FDA Recommends The Blue Marlin

ROCKVILLE, MD—The Food and Drug Administration announced Monday that it recommends the blue marlin for its combination of flavor, texture, and price. "Have you tried the blue marlin?" FDA commissioner Lester M. Crawford asked, referring to the broiled ocean fish served on a bed of sautéed corn, tomato, and lima beans. "It's absolutely delicious. Really, you must try it, along with a glass of Chardonnay or a light beer." The FDA said the crab cakes are excellent, as well.

Ghost Can't Make A Simple Cup Of Coffee Without Everyone Freaking Out

BOUTTE, LA—Former police chief Robert J. Kensworth, whose specter still roams the top floor of the old Third Precinct station, said Monday that he is unable to make a cup of coffee without everyone freaking out. "Can't a man make himself a cup of joe without some cleaning lady screaming her head off or some bandy-kneed recruit falling all over himself?" asked Kensworth, who was knifed to death by a convict in the third-floor hallway six years ago. "So there's a cup and saucer floating in midair... What do they want? I'm supposed to drink out of my hands?" According to Tom Carlton, who has worked at the Third Precinct for 17 years, "old hardnosed Kensworth" loved his coffee.

Guy From Pringles Ad Convicted Of Murder *On Law & Order*

RIO RANCHO, NM—Lionel Carver, who appears in a Pringles commercial currently airing on major networks, was convicted of first-degree murder on NBC's *Law & Order*, area TV viewer Cami Taylor reported Monday. "When [Carver] was led into the courtroom, I knew I'd seen him before," Taylor said of Carver, who played Hank Greene, a domestic abuser charged with beating his wife to death with a tire iron. "Then it hit me—he's the dad in that ad where the kids keep asking him trivia questions printed on the chips." Taylor said she was happy Carver was convicted, but added that "knowing our TV justice system, he'll probably be back on the streets in a Verizon commercial in a matter of weeks." Ø

REPUBLICANS from page 1

"It's time we opened the election process to competition," Burns said. "The free market is the petri dish for innovation, be it in telecommunications, the healthcare system, or democracy."

Burns said that, to create healthy market activity, each congressional district should be able to collect bids and offer contracts to the company that can offer the lowest prices and the best service.

"Look at the voter turnout we had this year," Burns said. "Less than 60 percent of the population voted, and that number is still the highest it's been since 1968. Contractors should get a cut based on the number of votes their machines record. That way, they'd have a monetary incentive to get more Americans to the polls."

Although legislation has not yet been drafted, several companies have hired development teams to draw up proposals for the takeover of the electoral process.

"Voters need an incentive to get to the polls," said potential contractor Fred Mitchelson of Accenture, formerly Arthur Andersen. "It's not like the old days when people were motivated by a sense of civic pride—that's just too Waltons. We're in negotiations to partner with Best Buy. Under our plan, every voter would receive a coupon for 20 percent off any purchase up to $500—it would actually pay to go to the polls! It'd be great exposure for Best Buy and a fantastic opportunity for us to hit and exceed that magic six-zero. Oh, and this whole registration thing has gotta go."

Mitchelson said prior elections failed to take advantage of the "vast potential for corporate tie-ins and advertising revenue."

"There is a lot of untapped revenue in elections," Mitchelson said. "We could get sponsorship for every blank surface in the polling place easily—I mean everything, from the back of the ballot to the curtain itself. If we really want to break out of the box, we don't even have to stop at surfaces. We could pipe music by Sony recording artists into the voting booths."

"I'm looking at all these missed opportunities and thinking, 'Who's the numbskull in charge here?'" Mitchelson added. "With the level of foot traffic they see, it's ridiculous that every polling place doesn't have an Au Bon Pain."

According to Mitchelson, the advantages of privatized voting go beyond quick, friendly service and great savings. A percentage of all privatized-voting profits would go to the U.S. government, which would "pass those savings on to you, the taxpayer."

"We also plan to offer premium voting services," Mitchelson said. "For only $20, you'll be eligible for Guaranteed No-Wait Voting™ and you'll receive access to the luxurious VIP voting lounge, with fresh coffee and pastries. Going to vote will feel like a trip to the spa!"

Above: A prototype for the new voting machines.

Not all election contractors advocate the use of premium election services.

"The American tradition of democracy is great, but it could be dramatically streamlined," said former Intel executive Jerome Klieg, now the CEO of VelociVote, a company that plans to bid for the 2008 presidential election. "Guaranteed No-Wait Voting™ is a good idea, but it basically approaches the election of our leader the same way we've approached it for centuries. Now, hear me out. Currently, every American citizen over 18 years of age is eligible to vote. That's 195 million voters. Whoa! Seriously. That's a lot of voters. Having every American vote creates mass confusion, as we saw in 2000 and 2004. Why? To what end?"

> **"It's not like the old days when people were motivated by a sense of civic pride—that's just too Waltons. We're in negotiations to partner with Best Buy."**

Added Klieg: "Rather than trying to attract more voters, let's attract better voters. We could reduce the overall cost of the election by 97 percent if we paid a small body of informed, designated voters to keep abreast of candidates' policy positions. The candidates would save time and money, too, because they could focus their attention on the thousand votes that count. And fewer ballots means faster, more accurate counting. It's just good sense."

Some critics have voiced concerns about private-sector elections, arguing that small businesses might be excluded from the bidding process.

"The government needs to make sure that local companies have a shot at contracts, too," said Dean Small, founder of Capitol City Speed-E Elections in Austin, TX. "It's only fair."

Santorum said these complaints will be considered as the election-reform bill is drafted.

"We've already got some good ideas on the table," Santorum said. "And, considering that we control both the House and the Senate, selling this proposal to Congress will be a breeze." Ø

YUCCA from page 2

lead-lined, reinforced-concrete lid on things 24-7, well, so much the better. But those of us who are around every day know the real story. Believe me, there were days when we were a hair on a horse's ass away from an absolute meltdown. But it's better all around that we forget to mention it if—just as an example, mind you—we suffer some big losses because of cask cracks. Or if someone starts acting crazy after drinking a little too much of the water down river. Or if the shipment of "pills" from the Diablo Canyon nuclear power plant shows up a little short. No need to worry the brass about it. Nothing they could do about it anyway, is there?

Yeah, Yucca Mountain is the land of opportunity, as long as you know two things: how the numbers work and how to keep your lips sealed. With exposure to the legal limit of 15 millirem of radiation per year, the risk of developing a fatal form of cancer is 3 in 10,000—ask me, those are pretty good odds. So if you hear any rumbles coming from Yucca Mountain, or the adjoining Nevada High Plains Test Site, hey, don't worry. It's just someone, or something, blowing off superheated ionized steam. Ø

OPRAH from page 1

Oprah's Struggle—And Success

250 lbs

200 lbs

150 lbs

100 lbs

1954: Oprah Winfrey is born in Kosciusko, MS, weighing 6 pounds, 11 ounces. Throughout her infancy, she steadily gains weight, a habit that persists throughout her life.

1980s: A decade of incredible success for Oprah, as she becomes a multimillionaire from her talk show, opens her own Chicago studio, and cumulatively gains and loses 9,482 pounds.

1987: Birthday party for co-producer turns into four-week cake binge.

1990: Wishbone, home of Chicago's best biscuits and gravy, opens across from Harpo studios.

1996: Fears of mad cow disease prompt Winfrey to stop eating raw hamburger.

1997: With promise of Olestra, Winfrey switches to all-chip diet.

1999: Massive blizzard forces Winfrey to hole up inside mansion, where she consumes all food and servants by fifth day

2000: Following a dramatic 85-pound loss, she maintains a steady weight for the next three years, jeopardizing her chance to reach the 20,000-pound mark.

2004: Success! Winfrey loses her 20,000th pound.

1950 1960 1970 1980 1990 2000

Luminaries such as John Travolta, Bernie Mac, Patti LaBelle, U.S. Sen. Hillary Rodham Clinton (D-NY), Billy Crystal, Dr. Phil McGraw, and longtime boyfriend Stedman Graham joined the *Oprah Winfrey Show* staff in honoring the media icon's monumental achievements in weight loss.

The historic event was also showcased on Monday's episode of *Oprah*. Following a standing ovation from her studio audience, Winfrey explained that, during a weigh-in last Tuesday, she discovered that she had lost another pound, bringing her weight down to 139.

"I was recording my weight in my journal," Winfrey said. "You can imagine how excited and proud I was when I discovered that my one-pound loss that morning nudged my lifetime total to... 20,000 pounds!"

Over the audience's cheers, Winfrey added: "20,000 pounds! 20,000 pounds!"

The milestone follows Winfrey's recent loss of 33 pounds, following a protracted ballooning to 200 pounds, not long after a loss of more than 100.

"Oprah is absolutely extraordinary," said friend Gayle King, who helped organize the event. "Not only is she a talk-show host, actor, entertainment mogul, and philanthropist, but she's also a super-dieter. Oprah is so capable at what she does that she makes weight loss look easy. But it takes faith, staying power, and single-minded focus to keep losing thousands of pounds, gaining them back, and then losing them again."

Fans have lauded Winfrey for inspiring them to change their attitude toward weight loss.

"I felt horrible when I gained back the 60 pounds I'd worked so hard to lose," wrote one fan on an Oprah.com message board. "But Oprah has gained and lost that much countless times over. If she can do it, I can, too. Thanks, Oprah!"

Another fan wrote that she "share[s]

Fans have lauded Winfrey for inspiring them to change their attitude toward weight loss.

Oprah's struggle."

"Pound number 428 and counting!" the post read. "Last week I gained five, and this week I lost two! Thanks, Oprah! Bless you for teaching me to be as fat or as thin as I can!"

The most eloquent tribute came from Maya Angelou, the celebrated author and poet, and a personal friend of Winfrey's. During the celebration, Angelou read a poem dedicated to Winfrey, "Water Into Air."

"As I lose, I gain," Angelou said. "I wing home to a place long forgotten. I swell as I recede, taking in all that has come before me. I molt. I shed. I diminish. But I feel no loss for I am free. My song slips its long confinement and joins the celestial roar. I was made of water, now I am air. I lose as I gain, but again I lose. I lose. I lose."

Far ahead of other celebrity weight-losers Rosie O'Donnell (15,860 pounds) and Roseanne Barr (7,229 pounds), Winfrey nevertheless appears determined to top her own record.

"I am going to ask my personal chef to whip me up some more of these breaded filet mignon appetizers," Winfrey said, piling her plate with filets during a post-celebration party. "Life is a process, people!" ⌀

TEEN from page 1

"perfectly capable" of closing Subway.

"Jeremy's a good kid," said Rotley, who also attends a night class at Tulsa Community Business College. "Normally, an assistant manager or a shift lead closes, but I don't foresee any problems. If he follows the checklist taped up on the walk-in cooler, he should do just fine."

While he expressed surprise at being handed so much responsibility so soon, Prusher said he believes he will rise to the occasion.

"I think I've got a handle on it," Prusher said. "I've been working at night helping other people close, so I have a pretty good idea what happens. I know the drill. Like, even before Michael told me, I knew he slid the cash envelope into the safe in the breakroom after he Z-ed out the register."

Added Prusher: "I think it'll be a while before he trusts me with the combination to the safe, though. A long while."

Prusher said he has a plan in place in case he encounters any setbacks while closing.

"[Coworker] Dewey [Taylor] has closed a bunch of times," Prusher said. "If I run into any problems, I'll call his cell. He lives pretty close."

Although the duty does not come with a pay raise, Prusher expressed gratitude for the opportunity to prove himself.

Prusher said he will not betray Rotley's trust by giving friends free food.

"I can do this," said Prusher, who has reread the list of end-of-night duties six times since he was asked to close Subway all by himself. "I worked over at the McDonald's by my house for a couple months before I came on here. There, a manager would always close the store, but he just sat there and watched me do everything. I totally could've done it by myself."

Prusher said he will not betray Rotley's trust by giving friends free food or eating more than his earned meal allotment.

"I've heard of people giving their buddies free subs, but I always thought that was immature," Prusher said. "You're just asking for trouble. Do they think the manager isn't going to notice that a bunch of food is gone the next morning?"

Prusher said he will, however, continue to honor unspoken agreements with employees of stores adjacent to Subway in the strip mall.

"If the guys from the TCBY or Domino's come by, I'll hook them up, like we always do," Prusher added. "I'm not going to get all high and mighty just because I'm closing by myself."

To make his night go more smoothly, Prusher said he plans to take advantage of coworker Nate Sankey as much as possible until Sankey's shift ends at 10 p.m.

"I'll try to get Nate to do a bunch of cleaning and stocking before he goes," Prusher said. "If there's no rush in the last hour, I'm pretty sure I'll be fine. There'll still be a lot of sweeping and mopping to do, but I'm gonna get the bucket all set up so all I have to do is add water. If there's a rush, I'll have to restock the cooler, which would suck. I want to do a good job and all, but I don't want to be here all night. It'll take 20 minutes just to flip and sanitize the sandwich counter."

"I'm just glad it's Monday," Prusher added. "Mondays are usually pretty dead."

Rotley said he doesn't generally entrust an employee with a closing shift before his six-month evaluation, but poor scheduling left him no alternative.

"I just wasn't thinking, and I forgot I had plans to meet up with some friends to see a movie," Rotley said. "But Jeremy will do fine. Maybe I'll drive past the store after the movie to make sure Jeremy's not standing in front of the alarm tearing his hair out."

A Domino's Pizza employee later reported that Prusher closed the store without incident, but after 15 minutes returned to check the front and back doors and peer through the window to make sure the sandwich-bar lids were shut. ⌀

COMMUNITY VOICES

Back In The Driver's Seat

Hola, amigos. Who's your daddy? I know it's been a long time since I rapped at ya, but there's been no end of troubles in Anchower Town.

The Cruise
By Jim Anchower

I did finally get my cast off—and just in time. My whole place was starting to smell like a raccoon had died in the wall. Not like I'm the tidiest guy in the world, but even I know when it's time to pick the sausage and pepperoni slices up off the floor. I borrowed a shop vac and sucked up everything that wasn't nailed down. I know someday I'm gonna wish I had those pennies that got vacuumed up, but I just couldn't bring myself to dig them out of the dirt this time.

After cleaning the place, I went out to take care of the important business of taking my Ford Festiva for its first drive in months. Man, when I couldn't drive, I felt like I'd lost a leg. In a way, I guess I had, since it was broken and all. Really, it was more like my nuts fell off for two months. But suddenly, it was just me and my ride, and like the song goes, it felt like the first time.

First, I took all the parking tickets off the windshield, then I unlocked the door. It was a little sticky, but that was to be expected. I got behind the wheel and just sat there, cherishing the moment. It was gonna rule. I caught my eyes in the rear-view, and I thought, you know, all in all, everything's been pretty sweet this year. I lost my job and broke my leg, but I got some awesome worker's comp. I got in a fight with that dude at the car-rental place, but fuck it. I slid the key in the ignition and gave it a turn—*nothing*. Sitting there for all that time must have drained the car's battery.

I'd waited two months for this moment, so I sure as hell didn't want to wait another hour for someone to come over and give me a jump. I was parked a quarter of the way down a quiet block, and the street was straight and flat with a little downhill stretch at the end. It was perfect for a one-man pop-start.

Now, if you've never pop-started a car, you're a huge pussy. And that goes double if you've got an automatic transmission. Thing is, I know you won't stop reading, so I'm gonna lay it down. You put your transmission in neutral, then get out and push the car. You don't have to go super fast, but you should be trotting. Once the car's rolling at a good speed, jump in really fast, put it in first gear, and pop the clutch. When the engine catches, put the clutch back in real fast, gun the gas, and you're good to go. It's easier to do with an old car, and something with a V6 engine is your best bet: It starts faster, and you can totally get a feel for it.

It's even easier to pop-start a car if you have a second person on hand to do the pushing. I wasn't so lucky. I thought about asking a neighbor to give me a hand, but I don't like talking to people. So I did the only thing I could do: I shifted the car into neutral and gave it a shove.

Pushing a car on your own isn't easy. I couldn't get shit for leverage, because I had to lean in and steer at the same time. Plus, my leg was still a little gimpy. Pushing the car out of a parking spot first made the process even more of a bitch. I had to stop a few times to let cars go by, which really pissed me off, but I finally got out into the middle of the street and ready to roll.

I got behind the wheel and just sat there, cherishing the moment.

I started off on my good leg, since I needed to get up enough speed to start the car by the stop sign at the end of the block. I made it maybe 15 feet before I slipped and almost fell on my face. It didn't hurt or anything, but I lost some ground. That didn't stop me, though. I was determined to drive that car. Even if I hadn't been determined, there was no stopping now, because someone behind me was laying on his horn. If I hadn't needed my strength, I would've wrapped that horn around his head. Instead, I kept pushing.

I was only about 30 feet from the part of the street that started downhill, so I kept telling myself it was just a little bit longer. That bit before you build up momentum is rough, though. The first five feet feel like you're knee-deep in tar, but then it gets a little easier. By the time I reached the hill, I was almost up to speed.

At the end of the block, I jumped in and popped the clutch. Sure enough, the engine caught and started purring. Everything would've been cool, except right as I was sailing through the intersection, I felt something ram into my passenger side. I was so focused on pushing and the car behind me that I didn't even notice a Hummer coming. As the dick who had been honking squeezed around the accident and drove off, I could see him laughing. If I ever see that guy again, he's getting dropped.

The Hummer was going slow, but it still did a number on my car. The door was all messed up, the passenger window was busted, and the side mirror was clipped. It sucked, but at least there wasn't any serious damage to the frame or engine. The Hummer driver climbed out cussing, but he calmed down as soon as he saw there wasn't a scratch on his ride. He ended up being pretty cool. Once we figured out that my car was the only one that got fucked up, we agreed we didn't need to call the cops. Then he got his Hummer up behind my car and pushed me so I could pop-start.

I drove around for about an hour, which was about all the gas I had left. It was like a dream. It wasn't enough to charge the battery, though. When I tried to start the car again, it didn't even click, let alone turn over. So I got a dead battery—I hope. Otherwise it's the alternator, and that'd be 200 bucks to fix. Mind you, this isn't my dream car, but it's a good little ride. Anyway, for now, I'm gonna have to pop-start *and* freeze my ass off driving around with a garbage bag taped over the window frame. I wouldn't even worry about it, but I'm gonna need a reliable ride to get to work, as soon as I get a job. Maybe I could get one of those work-from-home jobs that I see advertised on flyers all the time. You can make some serious cash doing those. It'd be cool to be able to save up for something nice, like a nice ride—something I could be proud of. Shit. A little pride's not too much to ask for, is it? ⌀

HOROSCOPES

Your Horoscope

By Lloyd Schumner Sr.
Retired Machinist and
A.A.P.B.-Certified Astrologer

Aries: (March 21–April 19)
When you're finally given the chance to run the entire circus, you'll be amazed at how quickly it goes bad on you.

Taurus: (April 20–May 20)
Through odd circumstances, you acquire a blowtorch, a case of razor blades, a cage of deadly asps, and a pint of cyanide, but since you didn't acquire any guts, they'll all just sit in the corner.

Gemini: (May 21–June 21)
In spite of your incredible, God-given skill as a crane operator, you won't be able to pick up any girls.

Cancer: (June 22–July 22)
Your illusions, innocence, and worldview will all be shattered this week in a bizarre accident involving your personality and some liquid nitrogen.

Leo: (July 23–Aug. 22)
You'll find inspiration in the classic story of *Great Expectations* and go on to turn more wonderful novels into abhorrent movies.

Virgo: (Aug. 23–Sept. 22)
You're aware of the wondrous healing powers of love, but you have a feeling you'll get more mileage out of the cooler transformative powers of hate.

Libra: (Sept. 23–Oct. 23)
There is little you can do to halt your downward spiral of lassitude and inaction, but you don't really care.

Scorpio: (Oct. 24–Nov. 21)
Frankly, it never occurred to you to win that special someone over with kindness and compassion—those things have never worked on you.

Sagittarius: (Nov. 22–Dec. 21)
The stars could perceive six numbers that would be of great help to you in winning large sums of money, but somehow, they never get around to it.

Capricorn: (Dec. 22–Jan. 19)
The funny thing about people trying to copy the famous crime of D.B. Cooper is that one of them slams down onto your head Thursday afternoon.

Aquarius: (Jan. 20–Feb. 18)
You have an unhealthy obsession with getting everyone to like you, which might be healthy if you were any good at it.

Pisces: (Feb. 19–March 20)
You'll be granted a momentary glimpse through the omniscient eye of the Creator, causing you to remark that now you've seen everything.

SALESMAN from page 3

ter's hunting cabin in Trousdale county.

Holy Redeemer Baptist Church pastor Hal Jackson said he is "a little concerned" about Carson.

"Granted, Bob does a very good job selling life insurance and making sure all the townsfolk are adequately covered, but still," Jackson said. "His habit of introducing technical accounts of fatalities into polite conversation is something we should sit down together and talk about."

Asked about the reason for his obsession with death, Carson had this to say.

"Your last name is Kemp, you say? If I'm not mistaken, the town of Kemp was the site of a grain-silo explosion not two years ago. A ladder fragment flying at about 250 miles an hour beheaded a fellow about your age. Head cut clean off, if you call that clean. Just imagine."

"Wait," Carson added. "It may be I'm thinking of the fellow who fell 20 feet from a collapsed balcony into a running wood chipper. But I've forgotten your question. What was it you were asking again?" ⌀

NEWS

Study: 86 Percent Of World's Soccer Stadiums Double As Places Of Mass Execution

see WORLD page 3B

Pabst Still Coasting On 1893 Blue Ribbon Win

see BUSINESS page 11F

Knights Of Columbo Hold Trenchcoat Drive

see LOCAL page 9E

STATshot

A look at the numbers that shape your world.

Leading Causes Of Nightclub Brawls
16% Phonies
11% Poor lighting
23% Hip-hop clothing-line rivalry
19% Argument over legitimacy of Hanoverian succession
21% "Tear This Shit Up (Nightclub Brawl Remix)"
10% Bar out of Veuve Clicquot

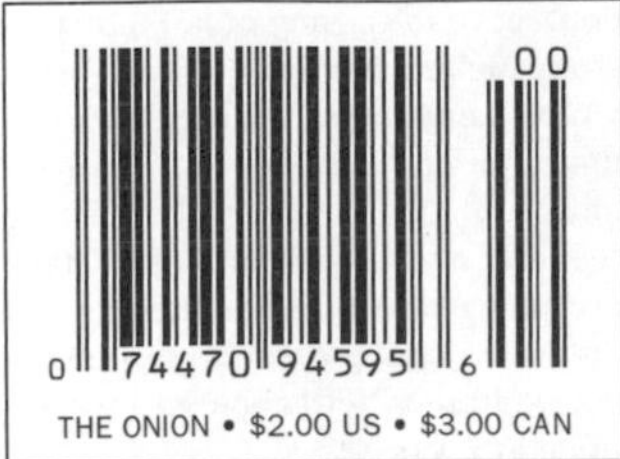

THE ONION • $2.00 US • $3.00 CAN

the ONION®

VOLUME 40 ISSUE 47 AMERICA'S FINEST NEWS SOURCE™ 25 NOV.–1 DEC. 2004

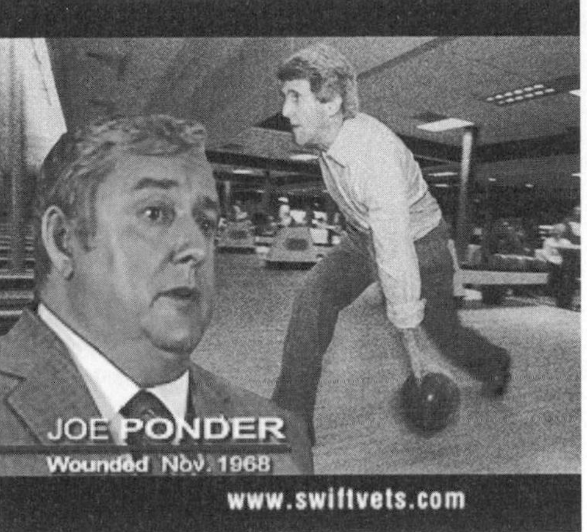

Left: "Crossing The Line," an ad which claims Kerry wore street shoes on the lanes at a local bowling alley.

Swift Boat Veterans Still Hounding Kerry

BOSTON—Swift Boat Veterans For Truth, a group that gained national prominence in the months before the 2004 election, announced Monday that it will continue its campaign "to set the record straight about John Kerry."

"We've made great progress in spreading the truth about John Kerry's treasonous past, but our job isn't over just because he lost the presidency," said John O'Neill, founding member of the Swift Vets and author of *Unfit For The Community*, a new book arguing that Kerry's Vietnam service record indicates that he would make a dangerous neighbor. "John Kerry is a threat to every American he comes in contact with, whether he's running for president, getting

see VETERANS page 11

Check Clears In Spite Of Overwhelming Odds

RINGLING, MT—A wild adventure pitting man against the forces of time ended happily, when, in spite of overwhelming odds, a personal check written by Greg Lippman, 33, cleared Monday.

Above: Lippman.

"It's done," Lippman said, slumping back onto his sofa. "All the tension and drama is over: The check cleared."

The saga began Nov. 17, when Lippman mailed a $183.23 credit-card payment to Mastercard. Lippman said he'd naively assumed that he had enough money in his Washington Mutual account to cover the check, until an unrelated conversation with his wife Kim revealed just how wrong he'd been.

"During dinner on Thursday, Kim mentioned that she went shopping for stuff for the kids' lunches," Lippman said. "I wasn't really paying attention until she started complaining about how she had to spend close to $60 on lunch meat and yogurt and stuff. Then it hit me: There was only about $200 in our checking account. There was no way the check I'd mailed the day before was going to clear. My heart dropped into my stomach."

Before panic set in, Lippman asked his wife for all the facts regarding the groceries. The conversation

see CHECK page 11

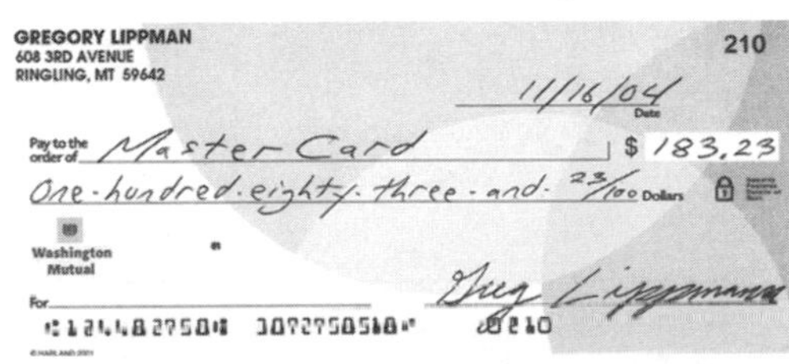
GREGORY LIPPMAN
608 3RD AVENUE
RINGLING, MT 59642

210

11/16/04
Date

Pay to the order of Master Card $ 183.23
One-hundred-eighty-three-and-23/100 Dollars

Washington Mutual

For

Greg Lippman

Above: The check which set off a race against time—a race Lippman somehow won.

White House Thanksgiving Turkey Detained Without Counsel

WASHINGTON, DC—Cousin Wattle, the official National Thanksgiving Turkey who was to have been pardoned by President Bush in an annual White House ceremony that dates back to the Truman administration, is currently being held without formal charges or access to legal counsel, White House press secretary Scott McClellan confirmed Tuesday.

McClellan said that Wattle, a 41-pound White Holland tom, is in custody after having been judged a "potential security risk" to the president Monday.

"Cousin Wattle's conduct prior to the pardoning ceremony prompted Justice Department officials to authorize the

see TURKEY page 10

Right: Secret Service agents subdue Wattle.

The Kmart-Sears Merger

Last week, Kmart bought Sears in a surprise $11 billion deal, creating the nation's third-largest retailer. What do *you* think?

"It's about time a serious heavyweight challenged Wal-Mart's position as the most depressing place on earth."

Etta Newkirk
Radiation Therapist

"As a major purchaser of lawn shit, I'm as happy as I let myself get."

Chester Hoyt
Systems Analyst

"Does this mean the Sears Tower will be repurposed for Kmart? Just think how awesome a giant red neon "K" is gonna look up there on the top of that mamma jamma!"

Javier DeKalb
Winch Operator

"I'm glad I no longer have to choose between Kmart and Sears. It often made things very uncomfortable."

Leo Nevins
Biologist

"I'm gonna love the look on their faces when I announce that I, F.W. Woolworth IV, am relaunching the trusted Woolworth name!"

F.W. Woolworth IV
Financier

"But... I just want a new dish brush..."

Alicia Bergen
Broadcast Technician

Cabinet Shake-Up

Many members of Bush's cabinet recently resigned, with more expected to follow. Who's in, who's out, and why?

- **OUT** Colin Powell, Secretary of State — Was last remaining cabinet member rest of world respects
- **IN** Alberto Gonzales, Attorney General — Is just like Ashcroft, but without the wooden leg and hook
- **OUT** Don Evans, Secretary of Commerce — Was fooled into thinking that "resign" meant "to sign on again"
- **IN** Condoleezza Rice, Secretary of State — Is loyal to Bush, plus she kinda reminds him of Catwoman
- **OUT** Tommy Thompson, Secretary of Health and Human Services — Will likely switch cabinet positions, as he can no longer hide fact that he's both unhealthy and inhuman
- **IN** John Snow, Secretary of Treasury — Will remain in spite of ongoing public fury over the new nickel
- **OUT** Norman Mineta, Secretary of Transportation — Will likely leave, as everyone's slowly getting wise to fact that he hasn't done much but run his model railroad through the DOT hallways
- **OUT** Spencer Abraham, Secretary of Energy — Bush sick of his fat face
- **OUT** Rod Paige, Secretary of Education — Position eliminated due to budget cuts

America's Finest News Source.™

Herman Ulysses Zweibel
Founder

T. Herman Zweibel
Publisher Emeritus
J. Phineas Zweibel
Publisher
Maxwell Prescott Zweibel
Editor-In-Chief

Kids Grow The Fuck Up So Fast These Days

By Steve Cunningham

Man, I tell you, I don't know where the fucking time goes. Seems like just yesterday Janie was bawling a blue streak and shitting herself in the car. Now, she's looking forward to high school, and her snot-nosed younger brother just turned 10. Instead of whining about wanting a pony, they're begging for cell phones, clothes, video games—you name it. Jesus Christ. Kids grow the fuck up so fast these days.

For years, you're telling them, "Grow the fuck up," "Stop your goddamn crying," and "Be a fucking big girl and eat that shit your mom cooked." Then, all of a sudden, they're not whiny kids anymore, but good-for-nothing bitchy teens.

For years, you run your ass ragged telling your kids "No, you can't go to swimming lessons," "No, you're not going to get a clarinet," and "Just shut the fuck up about the after-school soccer team." There's never a moment's peace. They won't stop annoying you with stupid questions about why the sky is blue, or what trees eat to stay alive. Then one day the stupid questions stop, you look up, and they're glaring at you with their little zit-faces, refusing to say a word. That means one of two things: Either they got into the cough syrup or their childhood is over.

It's still kind of a shock when they turn out to have devious little minds of their own. You notice 20 bucks missing out of your coat pocket here, a couple cans of beer gone from the fridge there. Before you know it, you're finding cigarette butts and airplane glue out in the garage and noticing mysterious dents on the car.

Every parent goes through the same process. You find out you knocked someone up, and, once you're sure you can't get out of it, you have about seven months to run around before she shits out the kid and you never get to relax again ever. I mean, in no time, they go from screaming, stinking, toothless babies to pantsless, snot-nose brats who draw on the TV screen with the crayons they didn't eat. Before you know it, you're pushing 40, the Cowboys haven't won a Super Bowl in years, and the kids are getting old enough to hit back.

For years, you're telling them, "Grow the fuck up," "Stop your goddamn crying," and "Be a fucking big girl and eat that shit your mom cooked." Then, all of a sudden, they're not whiny kids anymore, but good-for-nothing bitchy teens.

You know it's coming, but it's still kind of a shock when they turn out to have devious little minds of their own. You notice 20 bucks missing out of your coat pocket here, a couple cans of beer gone from the fridge there. Before you know it, you're finding cigarette butts and airplane glue out in the garage and noticing mysterious dents on the car. At that point, you have to admit that they're exploring the world on their own, I guess. It's only a matter of time before they head out into the world to find out what a bitch life is and how fucking good they had it all along, the ungrateful cocksuckers.

Soon enough, they'll be 18 and out of the house for good. They'll be all grown up, with shitty jobs, terrible marriages, and worthless fucking kids of their own. And, as long as I don't have to see any of it, I'll be perfectly fucking happy.

Yup, sometimes, it feels like I've done nothing but yell "no," "wrong," and "shut up" for years. I seriously thought my kids would never take my advice and grow the fuck up. But the worthless pieces of shit did. I guess I'm a better parent than I thought I was.

OFFICE

Wild, Unattached Twenties Spent At Work

SEATTLE—The unattached, free-wheeling, consequence-free years following Frank Anderton's graduation from college are being spent in "one of the coolest offices in all of Seattle," the 24-year-old reported Tuesday.

"Man, it's the greatest feeling in the world, knowing that I could do anything right now," Anderton said, sitting at his desk at 8:30 p.m. Friday. "I don't have any kids to worry about or a mortgage to pay. If I wanted to pick up and backpack through Europe, I could leave in two weeks, no questions asked. Of course, that would set me back a little, career-wise."

Anderton explained that the burdens of close personal relationships do not tie him down.

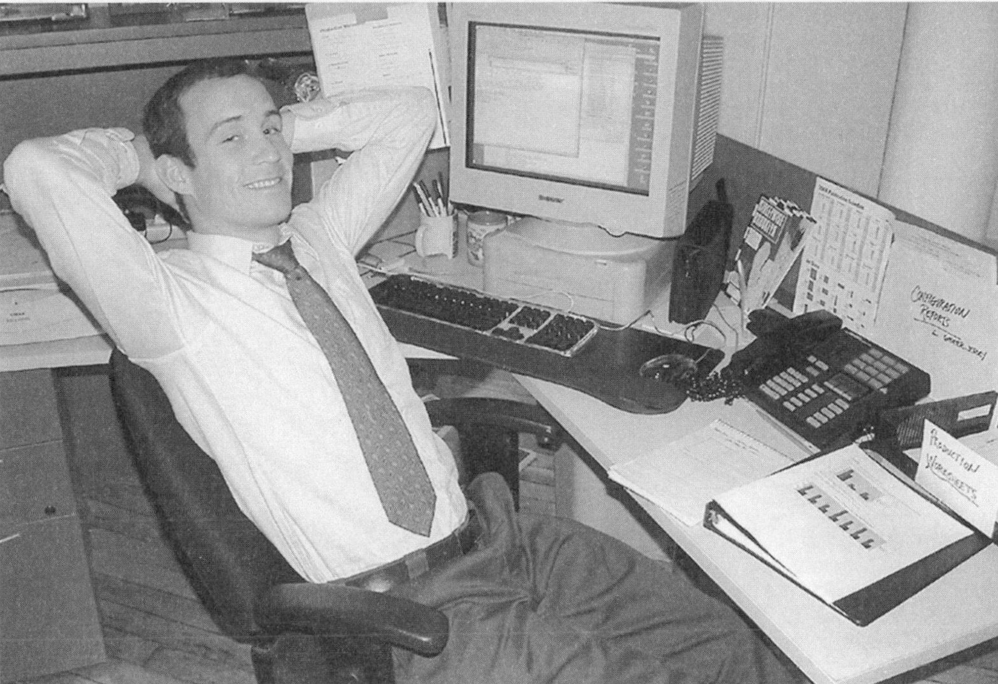

Above: Anderton, who has the world at his feet, works late at the office.

Anderton was hired directly out of college by Walsh & Billings, a high-profile Seattle advertising firm, where he has worked more than 60 hours per week for the past 68 weeks.

"The world is my oyster," said Anderton, who has been single but not actively dating for all of his post-college life. "Not to brag, but I'm doing pretty well. I've got a great apartment all to myself, I'm in good shape, and I've been dressing a lot better. When my sister visited me last month, she told me I was shaping up to be quite a catch."

Anderton explained that the burdens of close personal relationships do not tie him down.

"Nobody tells me what to do or when to do it—other than my bosses, of course," said Anderton, who recently cancelled his Netflix subscription after letting his first three DVDs sit on his dining-room table unwatched for nine weeks. "The other junior account execs are always complaining about their kids and their wives. Not me. I'm completely free to stay at work as long as I want. Hell, I can even come in weekends without someone getting on my case, like Mom always used to with Dad."

Even though he's only two years out of college, Anderton has already had the opportunity to work as an assistant print supervisor on such high-profile accounts as Compaq and Canon. His willingness to work long hours, even on weekends and holidays, has not gone unnoticed by his superiors at work.

"He's a real go-getter, that's for sure," said Tim Bradley, the senior brand strategist on the Canon account. "When I was his age, I was totally lost. I was working dead-end jobs and blowing paycheck after paycheck on partying. It wasn't until I was pushing 30 that I got my act together and started climbing the ladder. It's cool that Frank's got his eyes set on a corner office at 24."

Anderton, who majored in communications at the University Of Wash-

see TWENTIES page 10

NEWS IN BRIEF

7-Year-Old Puts On Uno Face

QUINTER, KS—Sophia Reed, 7, dominated Monday's Family Game Night, thanks in part to her inscrutable Uno face, family members reported. "She'd just sit as quiet as a church mouse, then hit me with a 'draw four wild card,'" said Leo Reed, Sophia's grandfather and Uno opponent. "Didn't matter whether I played blue, red, yellow, or green, that girl would not so much as twitch an eye after calling 'Uno'—until she laid down that last card. Then she giggled like crazy, the little monkey." Family members said Reed is also renowned for her super-steady Hungry Hungry Hippos trigger finger.

Rick Steves Cleaned Out By Gypsies

LISBON—Rick Steves, host of the PBS series *Rick Steves' Europe*, was robbed by gypsies while wandering the labyrinthine streets of the Alfama Monday. "These quaint but rickety sailors' quarters no longer house salty men of the sea, but they do play host to a colorful array of vagabonds," Steves said, clapping along to a band of dancing Roma children while his watch was being stolen from his backpack by their mother. "Peak time for seeing these lively characters is before sunset, as darkness attracts a less savory element to the area." Bonus footage of Steves getting mugged by a street punk in Berlin will be available on the Season 3 DVD anthology.

FDA Okays Every Drug Pending Approval, Takes Rest Of Year Off

ROCKVILLE, MD—Commissioner Lester M. Crawford of the Food and Drug Administration announced Monday that the FDA has cleared all 314 drugs pending approval—from Avoxildon to Zofax KB—and plans to take the remainder of the year off. "Hmm, 'Monozyklin... a selective serotonin re-uptake inhibitor... may cause irregular heart murmur'... That sounds reasonable," Crawford said, reading the drugs' intended uses from a checklist. "I'm sure Merck wouldn't have bothered making this if it didn't actually work. Approved!" Crawford said he'll use the rest of November to research his month-long Christmas travel plans.

Local Newswoman's Hairstyle Reported On By Co-Anchor

BALTIMORE—WMAR's TV2 News At 6 anchor Kent Niering reported on co-anchor Connie Everhart's recently altered hairstyle Monday night. "Well, it looks like Connie has a new 'do!" Niering said of Everhart's formerly shoulder-length hair, which she'd cut into a bob and dyed red over the weekend. "I think I speak for everyone here at WMAR when I say it looks fabulous!" Everhart smiled and thanked Niering for the compliment before throwing to a consumer-advocacy piece.

Alternative Theater Waits Three Hours For Stragglers

AUSTIN, TX—Maurice Juarez has held up an evening performance of *Ashcans And Ticker Tape: A Treatise* for three hours, hoping to get more late-arriving patrons, the owner and manager of the Austin ArtSpace theater reported. "People who enjoy alternative theater are all about opening their minds, so they don't pay attention to restrictive things like curtain times," said Juarez, who is also the play's author, director, producer, and choreographer. "I put up 200 flyers, so I fully expect this show to sell out." As of press time, 14 of the theater's 22 seats remained empty. ⌀

TURKEY from page 7

bird's detention as an enemy combatant," McClellan said. "He exhibited hostile, potentially seditious behavior that could endanger the safety of the president or other government officials."

Officials report that Wattle became agitated shortly after he was led into the White House Rose Garden, where he broke loose from his handlers and began strutting about the grounds. Witnesses allege that Wattle, without warning or provocation, began to flap his flightless wings wildly and rush nearby White House staffers, ignoring orders to halt. Wattle also allegedly pecked Council of Economic Advisors Chairman Greg Mankiw on the left hand.

Cousin Wattle continues to resist confinement.

Above: A soldier escorts Wattle through the prison yard.

The president, who was being debriefed on the ceremony by aides in the East Room when the incident began, was whisked by Secret Service agents to the safety of an underground bunker a half-mile below the White House.

After several minutes of chasing by various security officers, handlers, and gleeful schoolchildren, Wattle was subdued. The shackled and hooded bird was then escorted to an unmarked Secret Service vehicle and driven from the White House.

Fanny Clune, a spokeswoman from the farm where Wattle was bred, could not account for the turkey's violent outburst. She explained that the National Turkey Federation is careful to screen national Thanksgiving turkey candidates, adding that the 1-year-old gobbler was hand-fed from birth, and had never expressed any violent sentiments against the American government.

"I have no idea why Cousin Wattle snapped like that," Clune said. "He's accustomed to human contact. We know of no loyalty Wattle may have to any turkey nationalist movement. His closest contacts are a 9-year-old member of the farm family that raised him and a duck named Flap."

McClellan said Cousin Wattle continues to resist confinement and refuses to cooperate with his interrogators.

"We are doing everything we can to ensure that Cousin Wattle is given fair treatment," McClellan said. "Unfortunately, it has proven difficult to find appropriate translators."

So far, animal-rights attorneys have been denied access to the offshore prison farm where Wattle is being held until a formal arraignment can be arranged.

"This is an outrage," lawyer Jeffrey Alexander said. "Cousin Wattle has not been allowed to see relatives or lawyers, and has not been formally charged with a crime. The pervasive anti-turkey sentiment in this country is the only reason this shocking deprivation of basic freedoms is allowed to continue. If a Labrador retriever were being treated this way, the outcry would be deafening."

Representatives from the American Society for the Prevention of Cruelty to Animals visited Cousin Wattle early Tuesday and roundly criticized the conditions of the turkey's confinement.

"Cousin Wattle is being detained alone in a cold, dirt-floor pen with nothing to eat but raw corn," ASPCA officer Peter Woljak said. "He was leaning against the chain-link wall of the pen, literally sitting in his own feces. He appeared despondent, and his face and neck bore evidence that he had been bound and gagged."

McClellan dismissed ASPCA complaints, saying that Wattle had been gagged and blindfolded only because he had resisted confinement, and that the state of his pen was fully compliant with standards set by the National 4-H Convention of 1982.

"The real horror Wattle faces isn't inadequate prison conditions anyway," Woljak said. "It's the threat of infinite confinement, without trial or access to legal representation. The government has all but said it intends to hold the turkey until he talks."

Public reaction to the bird's detention has been mixed.

"There's no proof that Cousin Wattle intended to attack the president," an Ohio-based caller to *The Randi Rhodes Show* said. "He's a free-range domestic bird, not some wild turkey. Something like this makes you stop and wonder what other appalling things are going on. There sure doesn't seem to be a whole lot of pigeon activity on the White House lawn, if you follow me."

A caller on *The Michael Savage Show* was less forgiving.

"I remember a time when the National Thanksgiving Turkey would never even think of disrespecting the commander-in-chief," a man identifying himself as "Larry from North Carolina" said. "Those mealy-mouthed liberals who complain about Cousin Wattle's treatment should be happy he wasn't shot on sight. They claim he's all by himself feeling lonely in that pen of his. Well, I know my family would be happy to keep Cousin Wattle company this Thanksgiving. We'd serve him on a silver platter!"

Refusing to offer an opinion on the confined turkey's innocence or guilt, National Turkey Federation spokesperson Gina Webster made a plea for Americans to "find common ground during the holiday."

"While we may disagree about the handling of Cousin Wattle's case, most of us can at least agree on one thing," Webster said. "Turkey is incredibly delicious!"

While Wattle remains in custody awaiting a presidential pardon that may never come, the bird's ceremonial duties will be undertaken by his designated alternate, Miss Prissy, a turkey hen whose political beliefs are unknown at this time. ⌀

TWENTIES from page 9

ington, has already received a 5 percent raise at work.

"I used to have to think about every concert ticket or restaurant meal I bought, but now that I have a salary, I can do whatever I want," said Anderton, who puts nearly all of his $500 entertainment budget into savings each month. "If I don't have time to cook, which I never do, I just order Chinese. I got an awesome flat-screen TV for my bedroom, so a lot of times I just sit on my bed or at my desk and eat while I watch television."

Anderton's 32-year-old brother Josh, who recently became a regional sales manager for Microsoft's enterprise server line, described his sibling's position as "the best of both worlds."

"On the one hand, he's got the freedom to do whatever he wants, and on the other, he's got a really solid five-year plan all mapped out," Josh said. "He's got such potential and such liberty, but he also has the wisdom to know that night after night of meaningless sex with women you meet while going out and having fun with your friends is really pretty hollow in the end."

Anderton said he hopes his quick success at Walsh & Billings doesn't cause problems with his coworkers.

"I don't want the other guys at work to envy me because I've got my whole life ahead of me," Anderton said. "I can tell that they're getting burnt out. They practically have to drag themselves into work after the weekend. But I come in each morning, fresh and ready to start another day. Just imagine where I'll be by the time I'm their age."

"Yeah, I'm going to remember these years forever," Anderton continued. "I get to live in Seattle, I have my own super-sweet computer at work, and, since I don't have to get to the office until 10 a.m., I could theoretically stay out past midnight." ⌀

VETERANS from page 7

his oil changed, or going to a movie with his wife."

Although many expected the Swift Vets' campaign to end when Bush was re-elected, a spokesman for the group said its efforts have only begun.

"Just because that lying, cheating, opportunistic fraud from Massachusetts happened to be the Democratic presidential nominee, people assumed our efforts were politically motivated," said retired Rear Adm. Roy Hoffman, chairman of Swift Boat Veterans For Truth. "Well, Kerry's loss to George W. Bush does not undo the deeds of his youth."

"The vigilance and determination of groups like the Swift Boat Veterans For Truth are the only things that can protect us from the devious, traitorous tendencies that John Kerry demonstrated 35 years ago in the jungles of Vietnam," said Colin O'Flannery, a Massachusetts circuit-court judge.

Hoffman added: "We humble servants of truth will not stop until citizens are throwing garbage at John Kerry when they see him at the park."

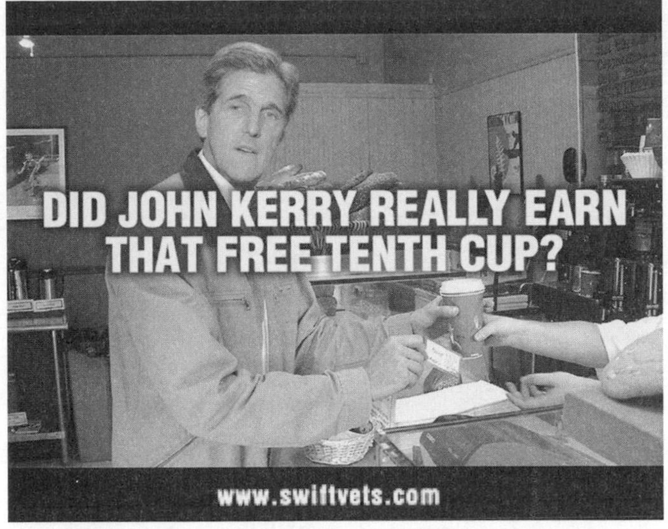

DID JOHN KERRY REALLY EARN THAT FREE TENTH CUP?
www.swiftvets.com

Above: A Swift Boat Veterans For Truth ad questions Kerry's coffee-purchase record.

At the center of the group's efforts is a $1.8 million television ad campaign that includes spots questioning Kerry's ability to make quick decisions in a fast-food line, leave adequate distance between his car and the next in heavy traffic, and take proper care of his lawn. The ads have run in heavy rotation throughout the Boston area since Kerry gave his concession speech Nov. 3, and local television affiliates confirmed that the group has purchased airtime through the summer of 2005.

In one ad, titled "Anything At All," former Navy gunner Andrew Elder addresses the camera while sitting in front of black-and-white, Vietnam-era photos of Kerry.

"John Kerry is a ruthless man who will do anything to get ahead," Elder says. "If he was willing to betray America to our Vietnamese enemies, can he really be trusted to sell you cookies at his church bake sale?"

Another ad, called "The Cheat," features first-hand testimony from Retired U.S. Navy Cpt. Charles Plumly.

"With my own eyes, I witnessed John Kerry cheating at poker," Plumly says in the ad. "If he's willing to cheat at card games in a war zone, what might he do while playing badminton at his next-door neighbor's barbecue?"

A third ad, called "War Criminal," uses silent video footage of a younger Kerry testifying before Congress, interspersed with recent footage of the senator waving to a crowd as he exits an airplane.

"Mr. Kerry accused his fellow soldiers in Vietnam of war crimes," a narrator says in the ad. "He claimed they cut off ears and heads, raped women, and killed young children. What lies might he make up about you if you happen to be seated next to him on an airplane?"

Although some viewers have criticized the Swift Boat ads as character assassination, many Americans said the organization has raised valid questions about Kerry's character.

"The vigilance and determination of groups like the Swift Boat Veterans For Truth are the only things that can protect us from the devious, traitorous tendencies that John Kerry demonstrated 35 years ago in the jungles of Vietnam," said Colin O'Flannery, a Massachusetts circuit-court judge. "If they stop now, just because George Bush won his reelection bid, Kerry will continue to threaten the sanctity of America well into his retirement."

Added O'Flannery: "That man is out there on the street washing his car every Sunday. Everyone near the Kerry home ought to know what kind of pathological monster they're dealing with."

Retired USMC Lt. Col. James Zumwalt also appears in the "War Criminal" ad.

"John Kerry returned home from Vietnam and made outrageous statements and allegations about those who had fought with honor in that conflict," Zumwalt says in the ad. "Then he made his four-month combat tour in Vietnam the centerpiece of his bid for the presidency. Our nation's libraries need to think twice before granting this turncoat a library card. What's to say he won't suddenly change his mind about returning his books?"

Kerry has not yet responded to the ads, but several former campaign aides said they expect him to issue a statement disputing the attacks before the end of next year. Ø

CHECK from page 7

confirmed his fears: She had paid the Shop 'N Save grocery chain using the debit card on the couple's joint checking account. Barring a miracle, the money would have been subtracted from the account immediately.

"I kept asking Kim if she was sure she didn't use a credit card," Lippman said. "She kept saying 'yes, yes.' As much as it hurt to ask, I needed to know if there were any other checks she'd written that I might not be aware of. She said there weren't."

Continued Lippman: "'Think hard,' I said. 'This is serious. Is there anything at all you might have overlooked? A check to your sister that she never cashed, maybe?' She kept saying 'no, no, no.' She was getting pretty ticked at me, but if there was another check out there, I had to know it."

"Basically, the course of action was clear," he added. "We had to get money in that checking account—fast."

Lippman knew the money would not come from his employer.

"I get paid Friday, but not until the end of the day," he said. "Even if I deposit the check at an ATM immediately after work, the earliest it shows up on my balance is Tuesday. I had to find another solution."

According to Lippman, the bitter irony was that the Mastercard payment was not actually due until Dec. 5.

"It was a cruel twist," he said. "Kim kept saying that the credit-card payment wasn't even due for another three weeks, so there was no reason to mail it without talking to her. What could I say other than 'I know. I was wrong. I'm sorry'?"

Lippman said he believed Mastercard would attempt to cash the check within three days of the day it was sent, giving him until Monday to deposit money into his account and see it reflected on his available balance.

"I'd just cashed in my loose change two weeks ago, so my normal backup plan was out of the question," Lippman said. "After spending all Thursday night considering my possibilities, I was convinced it came down to one option: finding someone who would give me a personal loan."

Lippman's friend and next-door neighbor, Jack Woodruff, entered the picture Friday morning.

"I've helped Jack out of a couple of scrapes," Lippman said. "He owed me, but I knew that he might not actually have the money."

"Thank God he did," Lippman added.

Woodruff wrote a $45 check out to Lippman, but warned him that it could take a couple days to clear.

"He's a contractor who lives in Florida during the winter, so his checks are from down there," Lippman said. "He said banks sometimes hold out-of-state checks until they clear, so I thought it was over. But then providence smiled: We both had Washington Mutual checking accounts."

Lippman's adventures were not over.

"I had to get to the bank first thing Friday, or the whole plan would fall apart," Lippman said. "But I couldn't be late for work Friday, because I had a conference call with the regional managers."

Knowing that the conference call was scheduled for 9 a.m., the same time his bank opened, Lippman reluctantly asked his wife for help.

"I didn't want to get Kim involved, but there was no other option," he said. "On Friday morning, she got up with me. Before I left for work, she hugged me. Then she looked me square in the eyes and told me that she knew I was only trying to help out when I paid the Mastercard bill in advance. It meant a lot."

After he arrived at work Friday, Lippman attempted to call his wife every 45 minutes. When she finally got home that afternoon, he received some long-awaited good news: His wife had deposited the check with no complications.

Checking his account balance online Monday, Lippman rejoiced to find that his plan had worked, and the check had cleared with $1.38 to spare. He said he was "finally able to breathe easy."

"We did it—we got the money in, and we didn't have to pay an overdraft charge," Lippman said. "Man, I really gotta get one of those checking accounts with an overdraft line of credit. I never want to go through this again." Ø

COMMUNITY VOICES

We Must Protect Our Daredevil Jobs From Cheap Foreign Labor

To the casual circus attendee, the daredevil's job probably looks like it's all fun and games. But believe me, it's not nearly as easy as it seems. We daredevils put our lives on the line every day providing entertainment for the nation. Sure, we get to spend our days going over Niagara Falls in barrels and zooming around on motorcycles inside metal globes, but when the day is done, we're just like anyone else. We have families to raise, bills to pay, and looming fears that our jobs will be taken away by immigrants.

By The Great Martinelli
Daredevil

Daredevils have walked real tightropes for more than a century. Now, we walk metaphorical tightropes, too, with the unemployment line always looming beneath us.

Ten years ago, if you'd told me a daredevil from overseas could take away my job, I would've laughed in your face. I'd have told you all the greats were homegrown: Annie Taylor, Evel Knievel, that guy who climbed up the Golden Gate Bridge. All Americans, all classics. But our problem isn't a lack of talent: This country has plenty of men willing to put on a pair of roller skates and jump a row of 15 cars. The problem is that Ellis Island is crawling with Slovenians—each one more than willing to put on a pair of flaming roller skates and jump 20 cars for half the money.

Our notoriously porous borders are particularly vulnerable to human cannonballs and speeding motorcyclists from Mexico. There's nothing in place to quell the tide of daredevils flying over the Rio Grande and landing safely on American soil to steal our livelihoods. This rhinestone-studded locust swarm is prying the food right out of our death-defying mouths.

Worst of all, these foreigners have no regard for standards of conduct and safety. When you've been risking your life as long as I have, you learn how to better your odds with special nets and harnesses. We fought long and hard to make our ringmasters and fans see such precautions as necessities. All our years of hard work are shot to hell, though, the second some Indian agrees to be shot out of a cannon across a gorge with no net. Sure, a Kenyan will ride a unicycle across a 50-story-high steel beam without so much as a kneepad, and I grant you it's exciting. Gives me chills, and I'm a professional. But I guarantee you that the day something goes wrong, you'll wish you didn't have to explain to your kid why you took him out to see a man die. Hell, that's some show! Little Johnny'll never forget that one, that's for darn sure.

Look, what riles me up is not that this new group of daredevils is foreign-born, but that they don't care a whit about the sacred traditions of the profession of dare-devilry. Their devil-may-care attitude is jeopardizing the profession and everyone who has ever broken his back in its name. My great-grandparents came to this country from Italy with nothing but matching outfits and a dream to be the greatest silks-and-tissue aerialists the world had ever known. They had to invent themselves, one step at a time, like pioneers. My brothers and I devoted our lives to the stewardship of their proud tradition. Now, in the twilight of our lives, when we should be passing our gold lamé parachutes onto our sons, a reckless new breed from the hinterlands is usurping their birthright.

Take that French guy that calls himself Spider-Man. If he's French, shouldn't he call himself Spider-Homme? He's using an American daredevil name, but he's not even English! How about we let Americans climb American skyscrapers? You go climb the Eiffel Tower next time you're feeling frisky, Pepe. Leave the Sears Tower to us.

Daredevils have walked real tightropes for more than a century. Now, we walk metaphorical tightropes, too, with the unemployment line always looming beneath us.

A lot of people say these outsiders are doing jobs no American wants, anyway. I strongly disagree. Flying through a burning hoop at a county fair may not be everyone's vision of the American dream, but shoot, you have to work your way up to igniting yourself at the top of Devils Tower. You build a name for yourself while you learn the ropes. But with the flood of cheap labor streaming over our borders, the bar has been raised. To secure a basic carnival job, beginner daredevils are forced to perform stunts so crazy, you'd think only someone who's suffered repeated head trauma would be willing to chance them.

When I think of the great opportunities I've had in this country, I am filled with pride. I've been wearing a star-spangled helmet for 20 years, risking life and limb to make people forget their problems, if only for a few minutes. I inspire people. They think, "If that man can remain in a tiger cage with a grizzly bear and four rattlesnakes for five minutes, what am I capable of?" But now, I must worry for my future. People no longer come to shows to see me cleverly cheat death with a bold display of showmanship—they want the possibility of death to be real and present. Face it: When I'm on the bill with some Angolan willing to bungee-jump 150 feet into a flaming barrel of gasoline while French-kissing a meth-stoked cobra, my stunt where I ride a tricycle across a tightrope loses a little bit of its luster.

I only hope our country wakes up to this problem, so that someday, my son has the chance to drive a rocket-propelled car across a shark tank without being eaten alive in front of a jaded crowd. ⌀

HOROSCOPES

Your Horoscope

By Lloyd Schumner Sr.
Retired Machinist and
A.A.P.B.-Certified Astrologer

Aries: (March 21–April 19)
Although nothing exciting usually happens to you, the law of averages will catch up this week and everything exciting will happen to you all at once.

Taurus: (April 20–May 20)
What was shaping up to be the worst Christmas ever will be salvaged when you barely make it past Thanksgiving.

Gemini: (May 21–June 21)
You'll win an improbable bet by driving a stolen SWAT van through a burning oil refinery, but due to a lack of faith and foresight, the prize will be five bucks.

Cancer: (June 22–July 22)
An old man will finally teach you how to read letters and numbers. Since he meant no harm, you should probably stop the other villagers from burning him.

Leo: (July 23–Aug. 22)
If you think that nothing you do matters anymore, it would behoove you to consider your use of the word "anymore."

Virgo: (Aug. 23–Sept. 22)
You couldn't parallel park if your life depended on it, so it's unfortunate that, due to the alien invaders' strange emphasis on motorist competence, that's exactly what it comes down to.

Libra: (Sept. 23–Oct. 23)
Take heart: There are people with bigger problems than yours, and acting like you care about them will get you laid.

Scorpio: (Oct. 24–Nov. 21)
Yours is a story rife with pathos, sacrifice, and sexual intrigue, so it's confusing to see how pathetic it all sounds when you finally write it down.

Sagittarius: (Nov. 22–Dec. 21)
Your sense of triumph over getting a white rhino to mate in captivity will dissipate when the disgusted biologists inform you that they wanted it to mate with another rhino.

Capricorn: (Dec. 22–Jan. 19)
You'll achieve notoriety at the patent office after you discover a way to turn food into a nitrate-rich material useful in the fertilization of crops.

Aquarius: (Jan. 20–Feb. 18)
You've read everything you can on the subject, but it still seems to you that some stuff about religion just doesn't add up.

Pisces: (Feb. 19–March 20)
You'll finally get the public humiliation you deserve for using yellow food coloring instead of eggs in the batter at your British-style chip shop.

CHICKENS from page 5

amounts of blood. Passersby were amazed by the unusually large amounts of blood. Passersby were amazed by the unusually large amounts of blood. Passersby were amazed by the unusually large amounts of blood. Passersby were

I couldn't believe how well she took my decision to perform the abortion myself.

amazed by the unusually large amounts of blood. Passersby were amazed by the unusually large amounts of blood. Passersby were amazed by the unusually large amounts of blood. Passersby were amazed by the unusually large amounts of blood. Passersby were amazed by the unusually large

see CHICKENS page 201

NEWS

Zell Miller Named First Secretary Of Offense

see WASHINGTON page 4B

Graffiti Artist No Longer Putting His Heart In It

see LOCAL page 14E

Ear, Nose, And Throat Doctor Dreams Of Being Ear, Nose, And Throat Doctor To The Stars

see LOCAL page 9E

STATshot

A look at the numbers that shape your world.

Why Are We Shaving Our Heads?
21% Need to consult treasure-map tattoo
14% Employee manual specifically told us not to
26% Are female college sophomores challenging bullshit societal mores
17% It gets all hairy if we don't
9% Are named "THX-1138" and live in futuristic dystopia
13% For the last time, not because we're balding

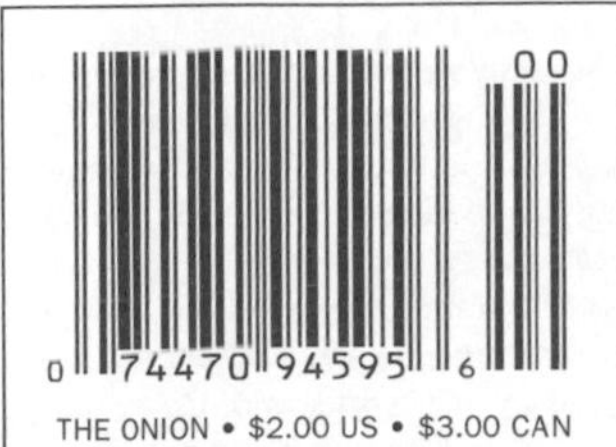

THE ONION • $2.00 US • $3.00 CAN

the ONION®

VOLUME 40 ISSUE 48 AMERICA'S FINEST NEWS SOURCE™ 2–8 DECEMBER 2004

WAR ON TERROR

Iraq Adopts Terror Alert System

BAGHDAD—The Iraqi Department of Homeland Security recently released a 10-level, color-coded homeland security advisory system that will alert citizens to the risk of a terrorist attack within Iraq's borders. The country's current threat level is elevated, or Code Yellow-Orange. Citizens living in towns with populations of 1,500 or more should prepare for the smoke of burning vehicles to obscure the sun and expect hostages to be tortured for several days before being killed. Should the terror risk level rise to Code Orange-Yellow, it is likely that hostages will be left alive only long enough to dig their own graves.

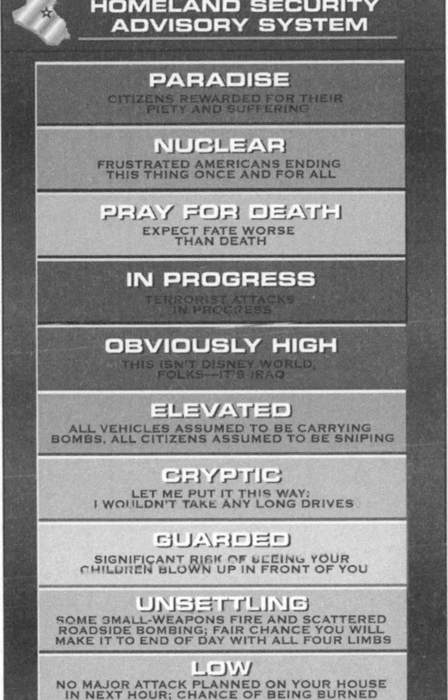

HOMELAND SECURITY ADVISORY SYSTEM
PARADISE
CITIZENS REWARDED FOR THEIR PIETY AND SUFFERING
NUCLEAR
FRUSTRATED AMERICANS ENDING THIS THING ONCE AND FOR ALL
PRAY FOR DEATH
EXPECT FATE WORSE THAN DEATH
IN PROGRESS
TERRORIST ATTACKS IN PROGRESS
OBVIOUSLY HIGH
THIS ISN'T DISNEY WORLD, FOLKS—IT'S IRAQ
ELEVATED
ALL VEHICLES ASSUMED TO BE CARRYING BOMBS, ALL CITIZENS ASSUMED TO BE SNIPING
CRYPTIC
LET ME PUT IT THIS WAY: I WOULDN'T TAKE ANY LONG DRIVES
GUARDED
SIGNIFICANT RISK OF SEEING YOUR CHILDREN BLOWN UP IN FRONT OF YOU
UNSETTLING
SOME SMALL-WEAPONS FIRE AND SCATTERED ROADSIDE BOMBING; FAIR CHANCE YOU WILL MAKE IT TO END OF DAY WITH ALL FOUR LIMBS
LOW
NO MAJOR ATTACK PLANNED ON YOUR HOUSE IN NEXT HOUR; CHANCE OF BEING BURNED ALIVE OR DECAPITATED ONLY 40 PERCENT

New Social Security Plan Allows Workers To Put Portion Of Earnings On Favorite Team

Above: Three sports fans hope to win big benefits before their retirement next year.

WASHINGTON, DC—President Bush signed an ambitious Social Security plan into law Monday that will allow citizens to bet a third of their payroll taxes on their favorite sports teams.

"It's time we gave the American people the chance to make some real money for retirement," Bush said, speaking from the new Office of Social Security and Pari-mutuel Wagering Building. "Some naysayers think the average citizen doesn't know how to handle his own money. When spring training starts next year, it's up to you to prove them wrong."

"It's your money," Bush added. "You earned it. You should be able to bet it on whatever team you want."

Under the new plan, participating citizens will be asked to list their fa-

see PLAN page 16

Office-Newsletter Editor Refuses To Back Down

SALINA, KS—Shipping department manager Nathan Harrity refused to apologize Monday for the controversy surrounding the November issue of *Shoppe Talk*, the Vitamin Shoppe corporate headquarters' internal newsletter.

"People don't like to hear the truth," Harrity said. "I knew the parking-space article would upset a few people, but I'm not giving in. I know there are people who'd like *Shoppe Talk* to be nice

Above: Harrity stands by the newsletter he edits.

and fluffy. Well, I'm sorry, but I'm not a nice-and-fluffy guy. I tell it like it is."

Harrity's editorial, "A Parking Polemic," was the latest article to raise two or three eyebrows around the office.

"Nathan really took the company to task for designating that entire front parking section for visitors," said receptionist Debbie Jurgens, who was among the handful of Vitamin Shoppe employees to read the article. "And that part about the sales managers getting the spaces closest to the building, despite the fact that they're out of town a lot—I was sorta surprised he wrote that."

Harrity, who writes the vast majority of *Shoppe Talk*'s stories in addition to editing the newsletter and overseeing its printing and distribution, said he wrote the controversial article "to get people talking and to inspire change."

"I know a lot of other people are thinking that same thing about the parking lot—I just put it down in black and white," Harrity said. "Yes, I understand that when the sales managers are here, they're going in and out of the office a lot, but someone had to present the other side of the issue. Luckily, this office has a public forum."

see EDITOR page 16

Kids Using Drugs To Study

Studies show that more and more college students are abusing prescription ADHD drugs like Adderall and Ritalin to help them study. What do *you* think?

"Slippage in grades is a sure sign your child may not be on drugs."

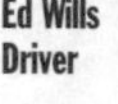

Ed Wills
Driver

"These drugs help them *study*? Wow. Turns out drugs aren't cool after all."

Jeffrey Stuart
Surgeon

"Taking Ritalin to study is very dangerous. If you let your focus drift, you'll spend the night scrubbing your telephone."

Danielle Carlson
Novelist

"It turns out the main ingredient in Adderall is dextroamphetamin e. So all these years, long-haul truckers have been a vast, untapped intellectual resource?"

Scott Wolman
Cashier

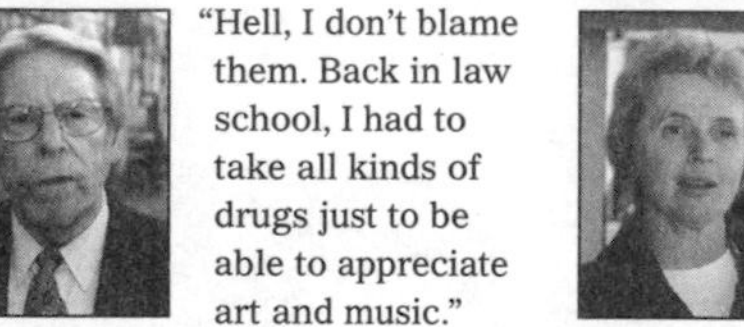

"Hell, I don't blame them. Back in law school, I had to take all kinds of drugs just to be able to appreciate art and music."

Stephen Underhill
Lawyer

"When I was a kid, we didn't have drugs to help us study. If we wanted to get good grades, we had no choice but to stop getting drunk."

Dana Williams
Personal Shopper

Trump Casinos Bankrupt

Last week, Donald Trump's casino empire filed for bankruptcy. What caused the company's crushing debt?

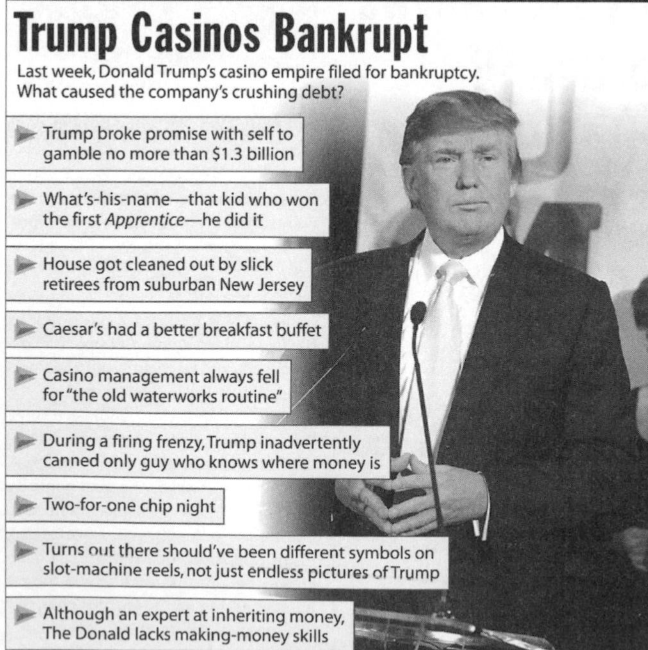

Trump broke promise with self to gamble no more than $1.3 billion
What's-his-name—that kid who won the first *Apprentice*—he did it
House got cleaned out by slick retirees from suburban New Jersey
Caesar's had a better breakfast buffet
Casino management always fell for "the old waterworks routine"
During a firing frenzy, Trump inadvertently canned only guy who knows where money is
Two-for-one chip night
Turns out there should've been different symbols on slot-machine reels, not just endless pictures of Trump
Although an expert at inheriting money, The Donald lacks making-money skills

America's Finest News Source.™

Herman Ulysses Zweibel
Founder

T. Herman Zweibel
Publisher Emeritus
J. Phineas Zweibel
Publisher
Maxwell Prescott Zweibel
Editor-In-Chief

$25,000 Is Its Own Reward

By Harry Wilcox

I don't consider myself special. True, I helped bring a dangerous criminal to justice, but the attention I received doesn't matter to me. Call me a hero if you want, but I didn't do it for the praise. As far as I'm concerned, $25,000 is its own reward.

I've been called a "model citizen." I prefer to think of myself as a "paid informer." Sure, by providing information to the authorities, I did my small part in the war on crime. But, more importantly, I got 25,000 big ones. That's no small potatoes.

After I stumbled upon those counterfeiters in the abandoned warehouse, I had a choice to make: play it safe and stay silent, or go to the police. Fortunately, the feds posted a $25,000 reward, and an even better choice presented itself: tell the feds everything and collect 25 large. Sure, if I'd gone to the authorities immediately, I would've been standing up for what's true and right. But what would it have gotten me? A one-way ticket to no-reward city. No, thank you!

With so many friends calling to congratulate me for coming forward, it takes some effort to remember what motivated me from the start: the money. Without it, I'd be just another do-gooder in a world full of hopeless suckers. With it, I'm something my friends and family never thought I would be—financially secure for about a year if I play my cards right. And that feeling of security is something no one can buy, unless they have tens of thousands of dollars in cash.

With so many friends calling to congratulate me for coming forward, it takes some effort to remember what motivated me from the start: the money. Without it, I'd be just another do-gooder in a world full of hopeless suckers.

By leading the police to that warehouse, I earned so much more than a feeling of satisfaction. I earned 25 grand! That's something no one can take away from me, unless they sneak into my house and steal all the big wads of cash from where I hid them in the... Hey! Nice try. Unless they steal the big wads of cash from... the hiding place. Or places. Not to sing my own praises, but I'm armed at all times and a hell of a shot. From the bottom of my heart, I swear I'll shoot anyone who tries to get my money.

It all comes down to this: There are things money can't buy and things money can buy. And $25,000 can buy a whole lot of things, like a plasma-screen TV, a five-speaker surround-sound stereo system, new jewelry, and rims for my car, not to mention expensive dinners with a lot of expensive women and expensive booze. So, no, I don't need your kind words, thank you—$25,000 is payment enough for me.

My only regret is that I'll eventually run through the $25,000, and all I'll have left is the satisfaction of knowing that I helped make the world a better place.

Some people might say it would've been better to take the easy way out. They say I risked my life, that I should have left an anonymous tip, that I jeopardized my safety by providing my name. And they're right. I could have gone the safe, anonymous way. But that would have meant giving up something far more precious than my dignity: a big fat check made out to "Harry Wilcox."

I have to admit that sometimes I think about those counterfeiters. I wonder how they feel sitting in that prison. I wonder what events in their lives led them to gamble their freedom. Most of all, I wonder if I couldn't have gotten more than $25,000 if I'd gone to them first. But, if I'm honest with myself, I know I could never do that—I don't know the first thing about extortion. At least I can sleep at night knowing that, even if a sharp operator could have made more, I made $25,000.

My only regret is that I'll eventually run through the $25,000, and all I'll have left is the satisfaction of knowing that I helped make the world a better place. But maybe there'll be another criminal to put behind bars, another chance to stand up and do some good in this world, and, if I'm lucky, $50,000 in it for me next time. ⌀

PROFILES

In Search Of A Better Life, Teen Moves Downstairs

Above: Jankowski arrives in the basement, where he hopes to find increased freedom and opportunity.

DEERFIELD, IL—Like generations of teenagers before him, 16-year-old Eric Jankowski has pulled up stakes to seek a future in a distant land of opportunity and independence. Bravely facing the difficulties of a harsh new world, he placed his meager possessions on his back and made a journey of 70 feet in search of a better life downstairs.

"Life's gonna be so much better down here," Jankowski said, his eyes gleaming as he placed a backpack on the unfinished basement's concrete floor Monday. "There's totally enough room to set up some old couches so me and my friends can hang out. Plus, Dad says maybe I can put an air-hockey table down there if I promise to keep the noise down."

A sophomore at Edna Dane Memorial High School, Jankowski requested permission to move to a little-used storage room in his family's basement last month. After an excruciating three-week wait, his parents granted him emigration rights.

"I have no idea why Eric wants to live down there in that dark basement, but fine," Jankowski's mother Ellen said. "All I can say is that he'd better understand that there's not going to be any funny business. I told him, 'This house has rules. I don't care what floor you're on.'"

In spite of such warnings, Jankowski is looking forward to the freedoms the basement offers, such as the ability to play his stereo loud and stay up late.

"This room is totally gonna kick ass once I get it set up," Jankowski said. "I got a line on a great set of speakers. Once I start making more money at Popeye's, I can save up to get a bigger TV. As for the walls, I'm getting rid of all my old posters and starting fresh from square one."

Determined as he is, Jankowski faces many difficulties. The basement bathroom has no working shower, so he will have to install one himself with the help of his friend, Rob Gaer. Carpet remnants will need to be collected. Cordless drills must be borrowed from an unwilling and suspicious father. Additionally, Jankowski will have to brave the elements during the harsh winter months, when temperatures in the basement dip as low as 50 degrees, necessitating the use of a space heater.

According to Jankowski, the move offers the opportunity to escape an oppressive regime.

"Mom and Dad watch everything I do," Jankowski said. "But now, I'll be able to hear them coming down the stairs. And, if I'm slick about it, I'll be able to sneak out the basement window and, like, party."

Across the country, millions of suburban teens have sought better lives in the subterranean realm, a topic Dr. Grant Tompkins explores in *Where The Floor Is Paved With Cement: An Adolescent's Quest For His Under-*

see TEEN page 17

NEWS IN BRIEF

Congress Approves Of $250 Billion

WASHINGTON, DC—In a near-unanimous vote Monday, 434 members of the House and all 100 senators voiced their approval of $250 billion. "My fellow members of Congress, $250 billion is an incredibly vast sum of money," U.S. Rep. Dennis Rehberg (R-MT) said. "That much money is totally awesome." House Minority Leader Nancy Pelosi (D-CA), the lone dissenter, disagreed with Rehberg's assessment, saying that, unless the money was stacked on a table in one-dollar bills, it was "pretty cool," but not "awesome."

Childhood Friend Stops Writing After Two E-mails

LOUISVILLE, KY—David Krohl, 29, said Monday that his renewed contact with childhood friend Mike Bunge seems to have ended after two e-mails. "It was so cool to hear from my old locker buddy Mike!" Krohl said. "He sent me all these photos of his kids and told me he still thinks about me, and I sent him this big, long e-mail about my life. But now it's been two months since I've heard from him. Ah, well, glad to hear he's doing well." Krohl said that, though it was great to reconnect with his old friend, it's unlikely he'll fly to Fargo, ND for Bunge's 30th birthday in January as planned.

Party Host Proudly Informs Guests They're Eating Shark

MANKATO, MN—At a dinner party Monday, host Jeanette Rojahn, 44, announced with great pride that the main course she was serving was shark. "Can you guess what you're eating? It's shark!" Rojahn said to her seven dinner guests, who collectively muttered forced exclamations of surprise. "I know, can you believe it? It's actual shark! I saw it at the Market Basket, and I thought, 'What the heck! Let's try shark!'" Rojahn's guests last feigned excitement in August, when the hostess served cactus.

Dance-Club Bathroom Left Out Of Gay Couple's Meeting Story

MINNEAPOLIS—During an anniversary get-together at their apartment Monday, Matthew Ledger and Dale Robertson told the story of their first meeting to a curious friend, omitting key details that took place in the men's room of a Hennepin Avenue dance club. "Oh, we met at The Gay '90s," Robertson said, making no mention of the fellatio Ledger performed on him in the second-floor restroom. "Matt bought me a drink, and we and ended up dancing together all night long. When his date was pulling him out of the club at the end of the night, he slipped me his number." Helen Meske, the friend who asked about the couple's meeting, said the story was "so sweet."

Man Gets All The Way To Hospital Just To Find Out Wife Will Be Fine

BRIDGEPORT, CT—Responding to a distressing message left on his voicemail, Martin Hermenson drove all the way across town to Bridgeport Hospital Saturday, only to learn that his wife Kara will be fine. "All I heard was 'Kara fell off a ladder,' so I left work and rushed right to the emergency room," Hermenson said. "I got there, and it turned out she'd fractured her fibula—no big deal at all. It wasn't like she was never going to walk again." Hermenson added that he didn't see why he had to waste perfectly good Knicks tickets that night, when Kara went straight to bed after getting home anyway.

PLAN from page 13

vorite teams on their W-2 forms. At the start of each major sports season, program participants will visit their local Social Security booking offices to review point spreads and sample playoff trees. Citizens' team selections will be subject to approval by their employers, who contribute a percentage of wages to the employee Social Security Earned Benefits Fund, or "pot," under the new system.

"Some naysayers think the average citizen doesn't know how to handle his own money," Bush said.

Above: A Lawrence, KS resident forms an investment strategy.

"For too long, Social Security has been managed by an elite group of government accountants and economists," said U.S. Sen. Paul Ryan (R-WI), a longtime advocate of Social Security reform and athletics-based gambling. "Why let your retirement money sit around in an account when you could double or triple it in a single year? Under the new plan, anyone with access to a sports page can control his financial destiny."

Added Ryan: "Assuming, of course, that Favre keeps a lid on those turnovers next season."

Many in Congress praised the bipartisan Social Security Athletic Wagering Commission for "developing a system with favorable odds" for America's taxpayers.

"The risk is greater, but so are the potential payouts," said commission member U.S. Sen. Harry Reid (D-NV), who has long argued that sporting organizations have higher standards of oversight, accountability, and strategic transparency than the federal government. "Why, a Boston-area resident who placed 2 percent of his lifetime earnings on the Patriots or the Red Sox this year would have tens of thousands of dollars in his retirement fund. That's a lot of squeeze, even after taxes."

Reid refused to comment on the potential financial losses of a Brooklyn mother of three who bet the Mets, Knicks, Jets, or Giants during the past 10 years.

"Not everyone likes pouring money into a long-term account month after month, motivated only by the promise of a solid future," newly appointed Social Security and Pari-mutuel Wagering chief Demitri "The Greek" Kanpolis said. "Now, citizens will be able to see their Social Security system working every time they flip through the sports pages. It'll make the games more fun, too, because there'll be more riding on them."

Several members of Congress have criticized the plan.

"While we do need to restructure our Social Security system, this isn't the way to do it," U.S. Rep. Bob Matsui (D-CA) said. "Statistics show that certain groups of people—women below the poverty line, for example—don't care about sports. I support an addition to the plan that will allow citizens who don't follow professional athletics to put a portion of their SSI payout into lottery tickets."

"Everyone deserves a chance at realizing the American dream, whether they like to follow the Rams or the PowerBall picks," Matsui added.

U.S. Sen. Rick Santorum (R-PA) dismissed critics who contend that the plan will cause a $2 trillion shortfall in the current funds being paid out to seniors.

"People can nitpick all they want, but there's a lot of money to be made if you take the time to do a little research," Santorum said. "Just look at this football season. With the Steelers leading the AFC North and the Eagles leading the NFC East, people in my state might have benefited handsomely from an opportunity like this."

Added Santorum: "Sure, we're risking a couple trillion, but I got a feeling people are gonna double that money when baseball season comes around, no problem." ⊘

EDITOR from page 13

Although Harrity said he's heard several coworkers express similar opinions about the parking problem over drinks at a nearby Houlihan's, he expressed a willingness to accept full responsibility for the opinions expressed in his article.

"It was my decision to champion the parking cause and publish the article, so I don't mind taking the heat," Harrity said. "I'm sure the company execs aren't happy that I'm using company paper and copiers to criticize their policies, but short of shutting me down, there's not a whole lot they can do."

"They should be grateful I didn't name names," Harrity added.

Harrity said he's heard comments ranging from "Interesting newsletter this week, Nate" to "I'm not sure that essay was a good idea."

"I think people got accustomed to the newsletter being only about event reminders and human-interest bits," Harrity said. "They aren't used to someone taking employee issues seriously. But I want to give everyone the real story on our dental benefits."

Added Harrity: "Oh, and don't forget about Gail's going-away party this Friday at Houlihan's. It would be nice if everyone showed up."

"It was my decision to publish the article, so I don't mind taking the heat," Harrity said.

Harrity took over *Shoppe Talk* in May 2004 after previous editor Lila Nessman was promoted to vice president of marketing.

"Under Lila, *Shoppe Talk* was professional, but a little soft," Harrity said. "Her idea of an office newsletter was an article about the most recent sales-award winners padded out with the monthly calendar, a little seasonal clip art, and a 'Did You Know?' trivia section. When I took over, I did a complete redesign, got rid of the clip art, and doubled the length of the paper to four pages."

"I tried to get rid of 'Did You Know?' but too many people complained," Harrity added.

Although Harrity has encouraged coworkers to submit items to *Shoppe Talk*, he said he has received very few strong submissions.

"No one else will put their ass on the line," Harrity said. "Fine for them, but that's not the way I was raised. Nor is it news. If there's something rotten in Denmark, I can't keep quiet about it."

Harrity cited several changes that have occurred in the office as a result of his stories, including the reduction of dirty dishes in the office sink, the installation of new carpeting in the reception area, and the outing of gay coworker Martin Killgraves.

"That article about Martin was an accident," Harrity said. "I really thought everyone knew."

While the company president's personal secretary reported that she doesn't believe anyone in upper management has read the parking article, at least one of Harrity's coworkers said he is willing to support the editor, should a problem arise.

"Oh, yeah, the parking thing Nate wrote," information-technology specialist Michael Levans said. "Yeah, I totally support that. All the sales managers here are complete morons."

"I don't usually read the newsletter, but I saw that last one in the kitchen," Levans added. "I'm glad I read it, because I'd totally forgotten about Gail's party on Friday." ⊘

TEEN from page 15

ground Domain, an account of his own teenage post-war journey downstairs.

"Downstairs migration surged in the '50s, with the proliferation of suburbs," Tompkins said. "Teens were excited by the taste of freedom that the economic prosperity of post-WWII America brought, and they wanted more. The conflict between the free-

"When I was a boy, fat chance I would have my own basement room," Kleinbold said.

wheeling beatniks and their strict forebears was reaching a boiling point. This, combined with large territories of virgin basement acreage, created conditions leading to a mass exodus of teens into the rough-hewn land below."

Though some would-be pioneers were told "absolutely not, young man," a great many made the journey down the stairs.

"For these trailblazers, the path was strewn with obstacles," Tompkins said. "Early suburban basements were dingy, drafty places filled with cobwebs and firewood. Many had only rudimentary, crumbling stairs. Nevertheless, the basement offered opportunities children of the Great Depression thought possible only in their dreams."

Gus Kleinbold, 89, was one such Depression-era teen.

"When I was a boy, fat chance I would have my own basement room," Kleinbold said. "We slept five to a bed! When the war began, forget it. Not like the young people today, with their carpeted basements and X-Boxes."

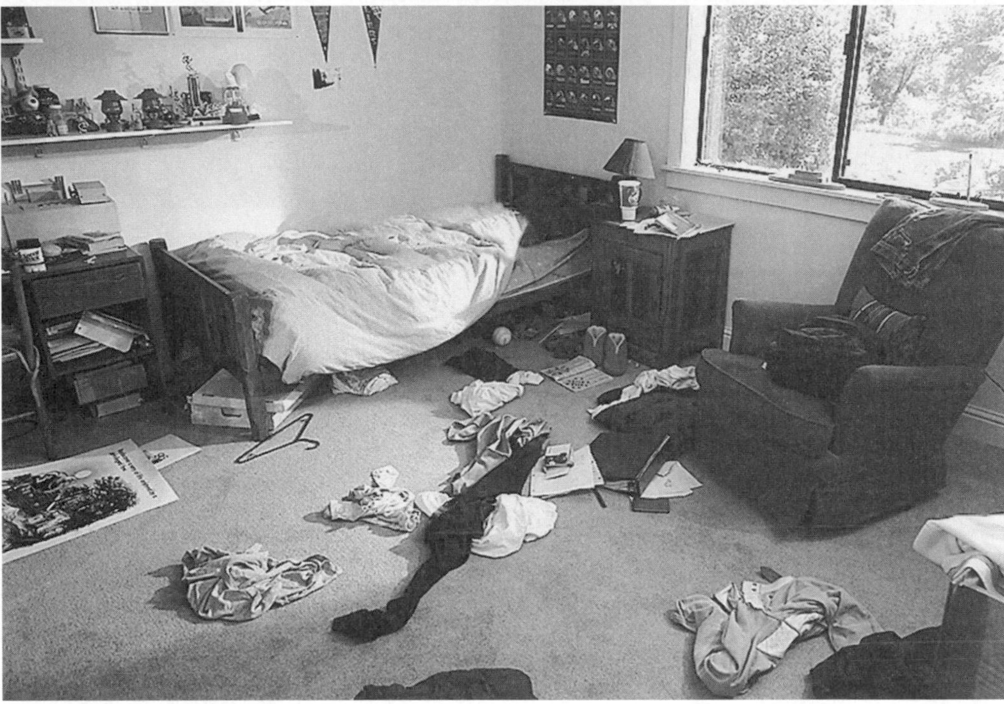

Above: The upstairs room Jankowski escaped.

By the '70s, the room downstairs was a cherished part of the American youth experience, Tompkins said.

"Some of them were squeezed out of the basement by baby-boomer parents claiming the territory for rec rooms. These teens were often forced to seek out new lives in the roof space of their homes, as dramatized in the *Brady Bunch* episode where Greg sets up a room in the attic," Tompkins said. "But for the most part, teens continued to settle in the basement—a land of peace and undisturbed independence far below the war-torn lands of family strife and authoritarianism above."

In the '90s, teens began to populate their parents' basements even after graduation. Indeed, with easy access to pornography via the Internet and a depressed job market creating strong cultural and economic incentives to stay, some have inhabited their parents' basements well into their 30s.

The way is still not easy for the population Tompkins calls the "downwardly mobile," but teens like Jankowski continue to be lured by the chance to pursue happiness on their own terms, combined with the opportunity to dream big.

"This room is gonna rule," Jankowski said, hauling a cinderblock downstairs to serve as the cornerstone of a shelf. "The chicks are gonna go crazy for it, too. I bet I'll totally get a girlfriend this year." ⊘

the ONION presents:

Fighting Insomnia

Insomnia—the chronic inability to fall and remain asleep—affects roughly 20 percent of American adults. Here are some tips to get a better night's sleep:

- Although it's tempting to use liquor as a cure for chronic sleeplessness, be warned: Liquor is quite expensive.
- Getting more exercise can help combat insomnia. If you suffer from sleeplessness, try shuffling from the bed to the kitchen, opening and shutting the refrigerator door, and shuffling back to bed.
- According to researchers at the National Sleep Foundation, there is an actual National Sleep Foundation. Yes, for real.
- If you are going to take pills to help you sleep, be sure you take enough to knock yourself out. Watching *Good Morning America* while sleep-deprived and tranquilized is a hellish experience.
- Use your bed for sleeping only. Conduct all reading, eating, phone calls, and sexual relations on the kitchen table.
- Try counting sheep, rather than the number of times you've failed as a wife and mother.
- If you got less than three hours of sleep the previous night, it's important to inform everyone you meet of that fact all day long.
- If you're having night after night of hours-long jungle sex when all you really want is a decent night's rest, go cry on someone else's shoulder.
- Minimize noise, light, excessive temperature—all factors that could potentially disrupt rest—by sleeping indoors.
- Sleeping pills can and do become addictive. Before you know it, you'll be giving back-alley blow jobs for hits of Ambien.
- Remember: Insomnia is only a problem if you are employed or have a reason to live.

Beware The Kristina Applegate Curse!

Item! I've been researching one of my favorite actresses. You may know her as **Kelly Bundy**, but her real name is **Kristina Applegate**. She's always been a shining example of an acting triple threat: brains, beauty, and a great sense of humor. That's why I could hardly believe my discovery, but I checked and double-checked the evidence, and there was no denying the unsettling box-office phenomenon I christened **The Kristina Applegate Curse**. We little guys all think of Kristina as celebrity dynamite, but she's actually, at best, a firecracker. How do I know it? Let me set the scene. After seeing the underrated **Surviving Christmas**, I went on the Internet line, just to make sure I hadn't overlooked any of Kristina's work. What a surprise I was in for! It turns out I hadn't even scratched the surface. Her résumé read like a Top 10 list of flops. *Surviving Christmas* was a lump of coal, business-wise. **Employee Of The Month?** Never heard of it. **View From The Top?** Crashed on landing. All these movies had star power out the wazoo, so there was no reason they should've tanked. I double-checked the Harvey research, and sure enough, these movies all had one common element: Kristina.

The Outside Scoop
By Jackie Harvey

Fine, Anchor Men was a success. But it's the exception that proves the rule: Applegate is box-office poison. Let's hope the right project comes along and breaks the curse. She's too cute to be an utter failure.

Fine, **Anchor Men** was a success. But it's the exception that proves the rule: Applegate is box-office poison. Let's hope the right project comes along and breaks the curse. She's too cute to be an utter failure.

Item! Speaking of the underrated *Surviving Christmas*... Go see it! It's a fun family romp everyone will enjoy! As a member of the media, I do my darnedest to spread the word about those movies and shows you, the busy consumer, may have overlooked. This is why I'm launching my new feature, **Second Looks With Jackie Harvey**. This week, I'd like to humbly direct people's attention to a movie that had all the right stuff, but for reasons no one can explain, never took off. What movie is that? That movie is **Taxi**, with **Queen Levitra** and **Jimmy Fallen!** *Taxi* has it all. It's a buddy comedy with Jimmy as a cop who can't drive and Queen as a taxi driver who can. Using her car, Queen helps Jimmy track down a drug dealer. Or killer. I have to watch it again to figure out which one it is. It really doesn't matter, since it's all just a backdrop for the sexual tension between the two fishes out of water. (*Ka-pow!* When are those two going to get it on?) Laughs get a green light in this automotive thrill ride through Harvey-hometown **New York City**!

The election is over, so now we can get back to having fun—or so I thought! I was watching **CSI** the other night, and right at the climax, they interrupted the show to tell me that **Yessir Afarat** was dead. Sure, it's news, and it's very tragic news, and I am not one to celebrate death, but listen, buddy: When I want the news, I watch **the news**. Save your interruptions for the reruns, networks!

Sometimes, I am way ahead of the curve. **Susan Powder?** I predicted she'd go bankrupt weeks before she announced it. **Tara Lipinski?** Saw it coming at the pre-Olympic trials. **Carson Daley and teeth?** I don't know. The other night, I wrote down "Carson Daley and teeth," and then I got lost roaming the Internet for several hours and forgot about it. When I sat down to write this column, I found it written down at my desk: "Carson Daley and teeth." I have no idea what I was going to say about one or the other, let alone both. Carson's teeth are nice, as far as I can see. They are a nice hue, and they are nicely proportioned to his mouth—but all celebrities have nice teeth. Except **Peter Gallager**; he's a little cappy. My choppers are pretty good, and I've never even had braces, not to brag. Anyway, if you read an article about Carson Daley's teeth, just remember: You heard it here first!

Item! The **other Hilton**—not **Paris**, but the other one—and her husband got an annulment after only three months. This is sad news for those of us who had hoped that she would make Paris think, "Oh, what a mess I've made of my life while my less-famous sister has done so well for herself!" Now, the trap door has been opened, and they're both on a chute to the same basement laundry facility where all the hotel towels go. On the other hand, that other Hilton is pretty cute... Fellas, start your romance engines!

For every storm there is a rainbow, and the yin to the Hilton yang is **Star Jones**, who, after teasing us for months—almost to the point where I was ready for the divorce!—made an honest man of **Al Roynolds** in a fairy-tale wedding that will be remembered for weeks to come. I have it on good authority that Al worked at the bank that Star uses for her personal account, and that the two love-doves met when she brought in a jam-jar full of nickels to deposit. They made small talk while the sorter counted out the amount ($13.70), and before you know it, a love connection was made. From pocket change to major lifestyle changes, I give the couple a hearty Outside Scoop congratulations!

Winter is coming and so is snow. So now I have to get myself some snow boots. When I was a kid, I had to carry my shoes to school with me and slip plastic bread bags over my socks before I put on my snowmobile boots to keep my feet dry. Do they make those boots in adult sizes? I think it would be fun to wear them again.

As a special treat, take a peak at the **Harvey Things-To-See-Or-Places-To-Dine List!**

1. **Desperate Housewives**—it's the No. 1 new show for a reason, right?
2. **Ray**—there's a lot of **Oscar™** buzz surrounding star **Jamie Fox** for his turn as of boxer **Sugar Ray Leonard.**
3. **The Incredibles**—I love hero stories.
4. **Outback Steak House**—combines my three loves: Australia, ribeye steaks, and theme restaurants.

Well, that's all the room we have for now. I had more thoughtful essays than I did gossip this time around, so I promise a ton of juicy morsels next time. Just to get the juices flowing, what **Soprannoes** star may be following **Andrea DeMatteao** to the show **Joey**? Plus, I'll ask the tough question that no one wants to ask about **Scott Peterson**: killer or monster? All that next time... on the Outside! ⊘

Your Horoscope

By Lloyd Schumner Sr.
Retired Machinist and
A.A.P.B.-Certified Astrologer

Aries: (March 21–April 19)
You fail to see why people are trying to stop you from crying because you have no shoes. Dammit, you're in a lot of foot pain.

Taurus: (April 20–May 20)
There are some unreasonable types out there who object to your wanting everyone to be a nice, normal skin color.

Gemini: (May 21–June 21)
There's nothing wrong with putting women on a pedestal, but fastening them there with nails, adhesives, and bulky straps tends to ruin the look.

Cancer: (June 22–July 22)
Legends have it that the statue of Lincoln on the National Mall will stand up for an honest man, but they give no clue as to why it would show up in your driveway and take a nine-iron to your car.

Leo: (July 23–Aug. 22)
You will never again be able to act just as you will in a fried-chicken restaurant without being held accountable.

Virgo: (Aug. 23–Sept. 22)
You thought the old gag with the banana peel was dead forever, and if it weren't for you and a Dumpster full of shattered fluorescent-light tubes, it would be.

Libra: (Sept. 23–Oct. 23)
No, baboons do not understand human speech. You just happened to run across an angry one who could read your snotty body language.

Scorpio: (Oct. 24–Nov. 21)
If you're reading this on the weekend, the stars wish for your speedy recovery. If you're reading it before the weekend, call a plumber and a rat-catcher right now.

Sagittarius: (Nov. 22–Dec. 21)
You've long sought the solitary life of the lighthouse keeper, but it turns out that most of those things are built at the entrances to subdivisions these days.

Capricorn: (Dec. 22–Jan. 19)
You believe great things are right around the corner, but they might be more accurately described as great big things hurtling out of control.

Aquarius: (Jan. 20–Feb. 18)
You obviously weren't concealing anything, so your new theory is that airport security has it in for naked people.

Pisces: (Feb. 19–March 20)
Like all people, you are powerless to change your fate, but not your nature. Try to become a kinder, more loving person by the time that safe lands on you.

NEWS

Bollywood Remake Of Fahrenheit 9/11 Criticizes Bush Administration Through Show-Stopping Musical Numbers

see ENTERTAINMENT page 13E

Pet Winterized

see LOCAL page 8C

High Times Web Page Cached

see TECHNOLOGY page 3D

STATshot

A look at the numbers that shape your world.

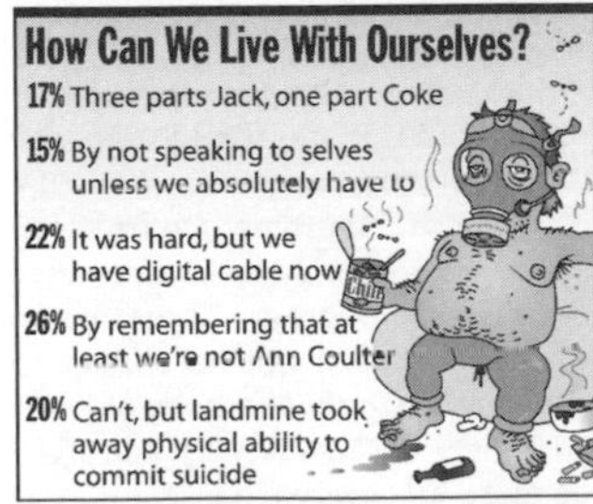

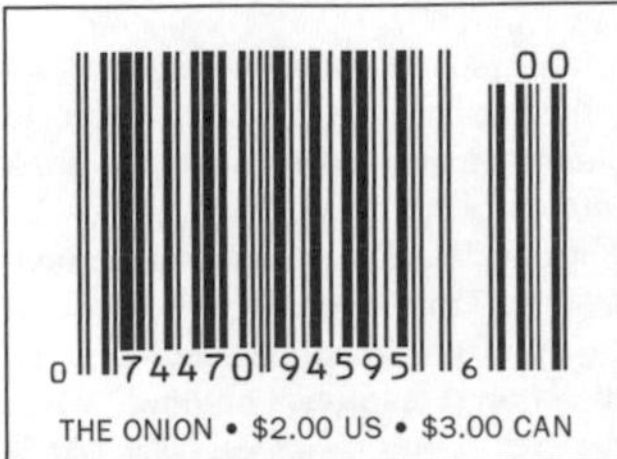

the ONION®

VOLUME 40 ISSUE 49 AMERICA'S FINEST NEWS SOURCE™ 9–15 DECEMBER 2004

Wal-Mart Announces Massive Rollback On Employee Wages

BENTONVILLE, AR—Wal-Mart, the world's largest discount retailer, announced its biggest-ever rollback Monday, with employee pay cuts of up to 35 percent.

"Just in time for the holiday shopping season, we're rolling back the hourly wages of workers in every department—housewares, automotive, health and beauty, and so many more!" Wal-Mart president and CEO H. Lee Scott Jr. announced at a press conference. "From Baton Rouge to Boise, we're continuing our tradition of low, low prices and using our muscle to create unbelievable savings!"

Above: A sign announces a Louisville, KY Wal-Mart's low, low wage for cashiers.

"For us!" Scott added.

Scott then turned to a large projection screen on which the company's trademark yellow happy face whizzed

see WAL-MART page 22

World's Scientists Admit They Just Don't Like Mice

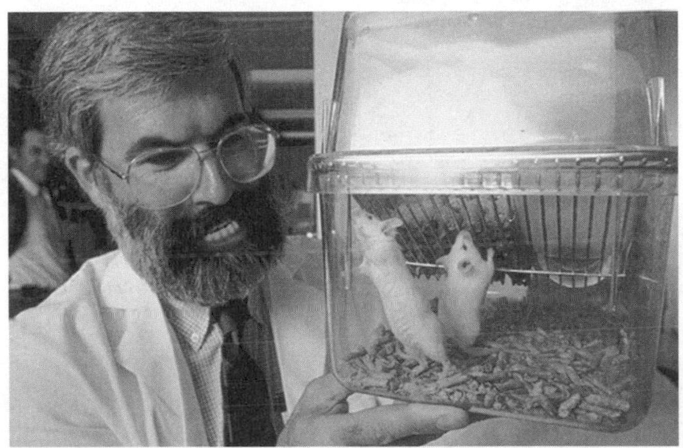

Above: White examines detested specimens in his Oxford lab.

ZURICH, SWITZERLAND—Nearly 700 scientists representing 27 countries convened at the University of Zurich Monday to formally announce that their experimentation on mice has been motivated not by a desire to advance human knowledge, but out of sheer distaste for the furry little rodents.

"As a man of science, I deal with facts, and the fact is that mice are gross," said Dr. Douglas White, chair of the Oxford biogenetics department and lifelong mouse-hater. "They're squirmy, scurrying little vermin, and they make my skin crawl. I speak for all of my assembled colleagues when I say that the

see SCIENTISTS page 23

Authority Figures Call For Closing Of Area Roughhouse

SEYMOUR, IN—Local authority figures and townspeople assembled Monday at Seymour Town Hall to call for the closure of the town's controversial roughhouse, alleging that it has caused countless scrapes, bumps, and bruises since it opened in 1986.

"We're fed up," said Dolly Geary, the local PTA chairwoman and a co-founder of the Task Force Against Skinned Knees. "That place is dangerous. It needs to be shut down before someone gets hurt."

The roughhouse, a crude wooden shanty erected on a vacant lot in the southwestern edge of the city, serves as the site of activities that Geary characterized as rowdy. She said screaming, giggling, and "slamming sounds" often emanate from the structure, especially when school isn't in session.

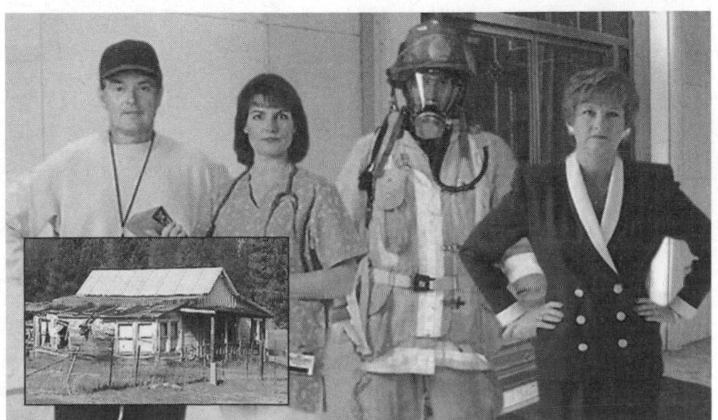

Above: Authority figures at City Hall call for the closing of the roughhouse (inset).

"I'm tired of people asking 'Where's the rumpus?'" Geary said. "We know darn well where it is, and it's about time we did something about it."

While roughhousers have never reported injuries more severe than minor skin abrasions, pulled hair,

see ROUGHHOUSE page 22

Americans Marrying Later

Census Bureau figures for 2003 show that Americans are getting married later, with the average age for a first marriage having risen to 26. What do *you* think?

"Oh, great. First my grandmother starts pestering me about not being married, then my parents, and now the national media."

Dale Steele
Systems Analyst

"Thank God there's a greater trend I can look to when I ponder my lonely, loveless existence in the midnight hour."

Lois Halverson
Real Estate Clerk

"I don't have to worry about marriage at this point in my life. Paying child support for three kids is stressful enough as it is."

Curtis Fuller
Salesperson

"It's because of the sluggish economy. It's harder to get a dowry together these days."

Ruby Turpin
Auditor

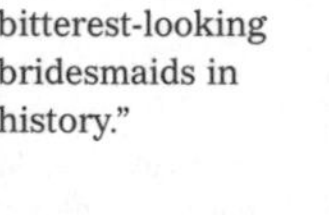

"Christ. Get ready for some of the bitterest-looking bridesmaids in history."

Marvin Watts
Robotics Technician

"My folks got married at 17. They were also cousins. Let me know when you have your tape recorder ready."

Glen Powers
Home Health Aide

Dollar Low Against Euro

Last week, the U.S. dollar dipped to a record low against the euro. What are the reasons for the currency's decline?

World confused by ever-changing $20 bill
Masonic iconography not as powerful as it used to be
European Union, consisting of 25 culturally and linguistically distinct nations, more unified than U.S.
Vermont quarter so pretty no one wants to spend it
Inflation inevitable after U.S. Mint began allowing people to print $20 bills on their inkjet printers
Currency markets hate freedom
All part of ingenious plan to keep American tourists out of Europe
Shiny metal euro will always be stronger than weak paper dollar
Some experts think it may have something to do with fact that U.S. has a shitty economy

America's Finest News Source.™

Herman Ulysses Zweibel
Founder

T. Herman Zweibel
Publisher Emeritus
J. Phineas Zweibel
Publisher
Maxwell Prescott Zweibel
Editor-In-Chief

Son, We Need To Talk About This Supreme Court Obsession Of Yours

Son, could you come in here for a second? Well, I'm sorry, but that newspaper's just going to have to wait, because we really need to talk. Son, your mother and I have been worried about you. Your grades have been slipping, you've been spending less time with your friends, and you've been shutting yourself in your room for hours at a time. Now, I know it may make you feel uncomfortable to talk about it, but this Supreme Court obsession of yours has become a problem.

By Chuck Lager

You can debate with me and defend yourself all you want, but it's evident to your mother and me that your interest borders on unhealthy. The Supreme Court is all you talk about. You lie awake at night making up fantasy scenarios about what kind of decisions William Rehnquist might make in the matter of *Jill L. Brown, Acting Warden v. Charles Payton*. I mean, you get more excited about the first Monday in October than your friends do about Super Bowl Sunday! Son, you shouldn't plan your life around the start of the new Supreme Court term.

Okay, name one thing you do, besides sleeping or eating, that doesn't involve the Supreme Court. Bassoon lessons don't count. Your mom and I make you take those. If you had your way, you'd be up in your room, cutting pictures of your favorite justices out of the Washington Post to add to your mural, which is another thing we need to discuss.

You can debate with me and defend yourself all you want, but it's evident to your mother and me that your interest borders on unhealthy.

It's perfectly natural to go through a Supreme Court phase. I went through one myself when I was your age. I remember spending hours in the library poring over orders of the Court. I spent nights lying in bed imagining I was presiding with Warren Burger or John Jay. I even had quite a collection of court drawings from the *Furman v. Georgia* case that—well, I think I was able to get them because my friend's dad knew someone who knew a lawyer. No, son, I don't still have them. My point is that I know what you're going through.

But here's the difference: Even though I was an enormous fan of the Supreme Court, I had other interests. I read mysteries. I went to movies. I kept up on the appellate and state courts and played basketball with friends. I had some of my favorite opinions up on the wall, much like you do, but I also had a couple of pictures of hot rods and a poster of Mia Farrow. Look at your room—there's nothing but collages of court justices through the years. Your floor is covered with printouts of opinions and dissents. You spend all night on the Internet holding mock Supreme Court hearings in the chat rooms. I don't want to say it's not normal, but I do think it's behavior we need to evaluate.

I'm going to talk to the school librarian, so if you think you can look at Supreme Court information at school, you've got another thing coming.

Well, because it's affecting your school career. When you fake being sick, it does. Do you think your mother and I are stupid? Do you think we don't know when Court TV airs major Supreme Court decisions? Son, everybody is interested in what the Supreme Court has to say, but you can't skip school just so you can watch the outcome of *United States v. Galetti*. Why can't you be more like everyone else and read it the next day on page 42 in the newspaper?

Your mother and I thought if we talked to you, we might be able to show you just how far you've sunk into this Supreme Court obsession. But it's clear I'm not getting through to you. From now on, no Supreme Court of any kind. No decisions, no dissenting opinions, nothing. We're

see COURT page 24

COMMUNITY

Local Woman's Life Looks Bearable In Scrapbook

OCCOQUAN, VA—Jane Hemmer's family scrapbook, prominently displayed on her coffee table at all times, gives the impression that her life is not only bearable, but even pleasant, sources not particularly close to the 58-year-old homemaker said Monday.

"My goodness, what a lovely family!" new neighbor Fern Kopein said as she flipped past an 8-year-old family portrait, the last to include both Hemmer's son Alex and her estranged daughter Diane. "You and [husband] Bruce certainly have done a wonderful job raising your children."

A photo taken in 1998 shows Hemmer with her son at a San Diego marina. Alex appears healthy and robust, and his mother beams under a large straw hat. However, the photo was taken mere hours before Hemmer's husband denied Alex a $10,000 loan to cover gambling debts.

The scrapbook, a neatly organized digest of Hemmer's 35 years as a wife and mother, contains photos and keepsakes that project an image of a functional family bound by unconditional love and total fulfillment. By layering carefully chosen photos with brightly colored paper, elaborately patterned borders, and whimsical stickers, Hemmer has successfully concealed a lifetime of anguish, scorn, and contempt.

One page, labeled "Vacation Time" in glitter-penned letters, features snippets of old road maps, stop-sign stickers, and the few happy photos taken during camping trips spent in grim silence and seaside vacations filled with ugly marital spats.

A photo taken in 1998 shows Hemmer with her son at a San Diego marina. Alex appears healthy and robust, and his mother beams under a large straw hat. However, the photo was taken mere hours before Hemmer's husband denied Alex a $10,000 loan to cover gambling debts.

"Look at that breathtaking sunset!" Kopein said. "Alex restores old boats for a living, doesn't he? How interesting!"

Although Alex was fired from the job in July 2001, Hemmer did not correct her neighbor.

When Kopein paused to admire photos from the Hemmers' 30th-anniversary party, Hemmer neglected to acknowledge that Diane was not in any of the photos because she was serving three months in jail for writing bad checks.

"Oooh, pretty tree!" Kopein said, squinting at a 1985 Christmas Polaroid snapshot bordered with snippets of red and green ribbon.

The photo depicts a traditional holiday gathering of a functional family. However, on the evening in question, a teenage Alex got into a shoving match with his father, who knocked over the Christmas tree in the scuffle. The tree upset a nearby candle display, which in turn ignited an heirloom quilt sewn by Hemmer's grandmother.

Photos in the scrapbook convey numerous other half-truths, among them that Hemmer was warmly accepted by her coworkers at a Mutual Dental holiday party, that her own mother is physically affectionate, and that Hemmer's pride in Diane's 1982 spelling-bee victory was not clouded by the discovery of her husband's homosexual dalliances.

A two-page collage of photos and dog-bone stickers suggests that Wispy, the family's terrier-beagle mix, was a beloved member of the family. In fact, his death was the direct result of a misunderstanding over whether Hemmer or her husband was responsible for dropping him off at the kennel before leaving for the two-week cruise pictured on the previous page.

Above: Hemmel pages through her scrapbook.

Even Hemmer's late father—a stern, Norwegian-born disciplinarian unanimously disliked by his

see SCRAPBOOK page 23

NEWS IN BRIEF

Peterson Given Lifetime Channel Sentence

REDWOOD CITY, CA—Scott Peterson, convicted in November of murdering his wife Laci and their unborn child, was issued a Lifetime Channel sentence during the penalty phase of his trial Monday. "Mr. Peterson's story shall be re-enacted in Lifetime movies and miniseries for a period of no less than 10 years," Judge Alfred Delucci told a packed courtroom Monday. "His story shall be remanded to Lifetime's custody until the network determines that public interest has waned sufficiently to allow airings on Oxygen." Delucci ordered that Peterson's team of lawyers be present for the casting.

Friend's Wife Reportedly Very Funny

BILLINGS, MT—Accountant Carl Scoval told reporters Monday that, although he's heard that his coworker Tom Barton's wife is hilarious, he's never had the opportunity to witness her sense of humor. "Tom is always saying how cool his wife Kim is, how she's always cracking these ironic jokes," Scoval said. "I guess she can cuss a blue streak, too. I don't know. Maybe someday I'll catch her in the act. Every time I've been around her, she's been pretty quiet." Scoval said he hears Kim can drink Barton under the table, as well.

City To Issue Deep, Meaningful Municipal Bonds

MODESTO, CA—The Modesto City Council announced Monday that it will issue deep, meaningful, general-obligation municipal bonds to any investor wishing to improve relations with the city. "My hope is that we can foster a closer, richer relationship with those who might provide us monies to improve Modesto's antiquated sewer system," Mayor Jim Ridenour said in an appeal to potential investors. "I promise—and this is coming right from the heart—if you stick with us through the long term, you will find yourself in a rewarding relationship with tax-exempt dividends." Ridenour added that bonds like his will need constant nurturing if they are to keep their Triple-A-rated status.

Bible Only Work Of Fiction In Family's Home

LAWRENCE, KS—After a weekend visit to the home of Gloria and Ben Kirchbauer, nephew James Fenderman, 26, said Monday that he was unable to locate a single work of fiction in the house. "I just wanted something to read before bed, but all my aunt and uncle had was a row of Time-Life how-to books, *Dr. Atkins' New Diet Revolution*, a yearbook, and *Sincerely, Andy Rooney*," Fenderman said. "The only book with any narrative whatsoever was the Good News Bible." Fenderman said he finally settled for a March 1995 issue of Prevention magazine that he'd found on a shelf with his aunt's cookbooks.

Complete Idiot Still Thinks Brittany Murphy Dating Jeff Kwatinetz

CINCINNATI—Out-of-the-loop moron Karen Lenz stunned everyone within earshot Monday when she said Brittany Murphy was still dating Jeff Kwatinetz. "Isn't Brittany Murphy that teen star who's engaged to that agent?" said Lenz, who has apparently been in a coma since May 2004, when Kwatinetz and Murphy split. Sources close to the dumbbell said she's so retarded, she wasn't even aware that Murphy attended a guest screening of the film *Bad Education* last month, escorted by an anonymous hunk of arm candy. Ø

ROUGHHOUSE from page 19

squeezed ribcages, and hyperventilation, authority figures said greater harm could occur if the antics continue unchecked.

"I'll bet that place is littered with rusty nails," Geary said. "It's all fun and games now, but when someone gets lockjaw, who'll be laughing?"

Neighbors report that they are losing patience with the racket that emanates from the roughhouse.

"You tell them to knock it off until you're blue in the face," said Larry Diggs, a task-force member and high-school shop teacher who lives across the street from the roughhouse. "Sure, it'll quiet down for a minute, but as soon I turn my back, the squeals and thuds start right up again."

Little is known about what goes on inside the roughhouse, as its visitors are reluctant to snitch. Seymour authority figures have not visited the roughhouse personally, for fear of slipping and breaking their necks.

Former roughhouser Will Keegan provided clues to the place's seemingly irresistible attraction.

"Aw, yeah, the good old roughhouse," said Keegan, 22. "Haven't thought about it in years. Does it still have that ratty old mattress? We used to crouch on the windowsill and leap onto the mattress. You had to have good aim, because anyone who missed and hit the floor got beaten with Wiffle-ball bats as punishment. Oh, and that grocery cart! Is that still there, too?"

"You tell them to knock it off until you're blue in the face," said Larry Diggs, a task-force member and high-school shop teacher who lives across the street from the roughhouse. "Sure, it'll quiet down for a minute, but as soon I turn my back, the squeals and thuds start right up again."

Roughhouse proponents like Keegan argue that the horseplay remains voluntary, and that risk of injury is low because total wusses aren't allowed inside the structure.

Brad Martinelli, an area resident who frequented the roughhouse during his youth, said his years inside instilled him with a sense of confidence and belonging.

"Even though I was failing at school and struggling with my parents' divorce, the roughhouse showed me that I could win a good chicken fight or worm my way out of a half-nelson," Martinelli said. "I'm sure that even the queers who got smeared knew it was all in fun."

This defense has failed to satisfy roughhouse opponents, who maintain that the site is an eyesore, a nuisance, and a recipe for trouble.

"If we don't take action now, the problem could get worse," nurse practitioner Shirley Stotts said. "I don't want Seymour to go the route of Muncie, which has a big roughhousing development right downtown. Police are always getting called there to break up giant monkey piles."

With so many grown-ups, from librarians to softball coaches, calling for the roughhouse's closure, it seems likely to soon go the way of the giant mud hole, a downtown mud-pie-making location shut down in 1997. ⊘

WAL-MART from page 19

through the aisles of a Wal-Mart, enthusiastically "slashing" the hourly wages of employees all over the store.

"Paying $7.75 an hour for a Class-2 cashier with fewer than two years' experience?" a cheery narrator asked in amused disbelief. "How about $6.50? And $8.45 an hour for a dockworker to unload boxes of bath towels all day? We think $6.75 sounds more like it!"

"Why, some of those old stockers have been collecting dust in our aisles and ledgers for five years," the narrator said as the smiley-face ushered reluctant ex-employees and their bloated wages to the parking lot.

In addition to wage rollbacks, Scott said Wal-Mart will discontinue a number of shelf-stocking, warehousing, and sales-floor jobs that have been occupying valuable space on the payroll.

"Why, some of those old stockers have been collecting dust in our aisles and ledgers for five years," the narrator said as the smiley-face ushered reluctant ex-employees and their bloated wages to the parking lot. "It's time for a store-wide clearance! Out with the old and in with the new!"

The beaming smiley-face then placed a sign reading "Help Wanted—$5.15/Hour" in a window and welcomed in a long line of smiling job applicants bearing brand-new high-school diplomas, military discharge papers, and green cards.

"Wal-Mart is the place to find the latest of everything!" the narrator said. "The benefits of having long-time employees around don't add up to the benefits we have to pay them. It's time for newer, fresher, cheaper faces!"

As a result of the announcement, Wal-Mart's stock rose 20 points Monday.

"We're very excited," Wal-Mart stockholder James Seaton said. "After all, everyone loves a good value. And you can't beat the combination of low cost and high quality you find in good old-fashioned American labor."

According to Scott, employees at all 1,362 Wal-Marts, 1,671 Supercenters, and 550 Sam's Clubs will be notified of the rollbacks this week by greeters stationed at the employee entrance of each store. Greeters will address employees by their first names, shake their hands, and inform them of the store's special new wage plan. Those who remain on staff will find red "Wage Rollback!" stickers on their time cards in celebration of the occasion and in compliance with the scant federal regulations protecting minimum-wage earners.

"Wow! A 24 percent reduction!" said Harold Reis, who works in the garden department in a Marshfield, WI Wal-Mart. "I can't believe it! Why, I never saw cuts like this when I used to work at the family-owned Seubert Greenhouse!"

"But that was a few years ago," Reis added. "Nowadays, you can drive all over town looking for someplace to pay you more, but good luck. Wal-Mart is the single biggest employer in 21 states!"

In spite of the savings on labor, Wal-Mart director of human resources Lawrence Jackson said he isn't worried about incurring losses.

"What we might lose in terms of shrinkage of our work force, we'll make back almost immediately," Jackson said. "That's what's so great about being a part of so many small communities across the country—once we get a location up and running, people find out they can't afford not to work for us!"

As a result of the announcement, Wal-Mart's stock rose 20 points Monday.

In a related plan, Jackson said Wal-Mart plans to slash the prices it pays for manufactured goods in various Pacific Rim and South American countries by 20, 30, and even 40 percent. ⊘

PASTE from page 21

amounts of blood. Passersby were amazed by the unusually large amounts of blood. Passersby were amazed by the unusually large amounts of blood. Passersby were amazed by the unusually large amounts of blood. Passersby were amazed by the unusually large amounts of blood. Passersby were amazed by the unusually large amounts of blood. Passersby were amazed by the unusually large amounts of blood. Passersby were amazed by the unusually large amounts of blood. Passersby were amazed by the unusually large amounts of blood. Passersby were amazed by the unusually large amounts of blood. Passersby were amazed by the unusually large amounts of blood. Passersby were amazed by the unusually large amounts of blood. Passersby were amazed by the unusually large amounts of blood. Passersby were amazed by the unusually large amounts of blood. Passersby were amazed by the unusually large amounts of blood. Passersby were amazed by the unusually large

It's the emotional burns I'm more worried about.

amounts of blood. Passersby were amazed by the unusually large amounts of blood. Passersby were amazed by the unusually large amounts of blood. Passersby were amazed by the unusually large amounts of blood. Passersby were amazed by the unusually large amounts of blood. Passersby were amazed by the unusually large amounts of blood. Passersby were amazed by the unusually large amounts of blood. Passersby were amazed by the unusually large amounts of blood. Passersby were amazed by the unusually large amounts of blood. Passersby were amazed by the unusually large amounts of blood. Passersby were amazed by the unusually large amounts of blood. Passersby were amazed by the unusually large amounts of blood. Passersby were amazed by the unusually large amounts of blood. Passersby were amazed by the unusually large amounts of blood. Passersby were amazed by the unusually large amounts of blood. Passersby were amazed by the unusually large amounts of blood. Passersby were amazed by the unusually large amounts of blood. Passersby were amazed by the unusually large amounts of blood. Passersby were amazed by the unusually large amounts of blood. Passersby were amazed by the unusually large amounts of blood. Passersby were amazed by the unusually large

see PASTE page 201

SCIENTISTS from page 19

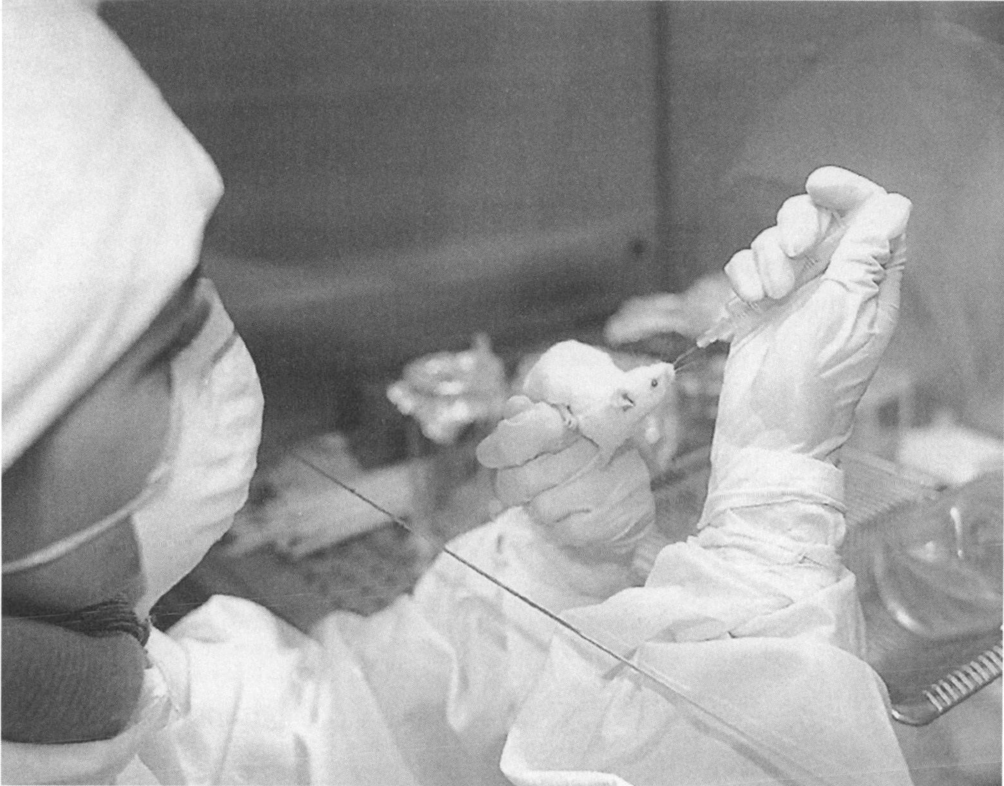

Above: A University of Miami researcher injects dye into a mouse's eyeball "for the heck of it."

horrible little things deserve the worst we can dish out."

According to a 500-word statement, scientists hate mice for "their beady little eyes," "their repulsive tails," and "the annoying little squeaking sounds they make."

At the press conference, several scientists detailed their involvement in the centuries-long ruse of "conducting experiments" and "curing diseases."

"For years, I've used lab mice to research cell breakdown in living tissue—and I've been lucky enough to make some pretty important medical advancements along the way," said researcher Ellen Gresham of the Harvard Institute for Advanced Studies. "But even if there were no scientific benefit to the work I do, I'd still experiment on mice, just to watch them suffer."

"The truth is, mice are particularly ill-suited for our tissue study," Gresham added. "We could construct a computer model that would yield more accurate results, but we don't care."

"The truth is, mice are particularly ill-suited for our tissue study," Gresham added. "We could construct a computer model that would yield more accurate results, but we don't care."

According to Gresham, scientists have enjoyed dissolving mice in acid, spinning them in centrifuges, blowing them up in vacuum chambers, and forcing them to navigate exit-free mazes for years—all the while towering above them, laughing.

"Every high-pitched squeak from the holding area is a warm reminder that the mice desperately want to escape," said Dr. Frances Villalobos, a contagious-disease researcher at the University of Mexico. "All they want to do is get out from behind those bars so they can chew on everything, defecate all over, and poke their filthy twitching faces into piles of garbage. Well, I know of at least 80 little test subjects who won't be doing any more of that. They're headed straight for the dissection lab."

Villalobos said he spent six months writing a grant proposal that provided him with funding to inject mice with the smallpox virus.

"It kills me that I can't infect the control group," Villalobos said. "Unfortunately, if I infect them, I'll throw off my results. But once I complete this experiment, I'll rotate the control group into the hot seat. Don't you worry. They'll get what's coming to them."

After applauding the scientists for coming forward, anthropologist Brent Wrigley suggested that the hatred of mice may be the single most important factor in the evolution of modern science.

"Despising mice may have pushed humanity out of the Stone Age," Wrigley said. "After all, the cave habitats of early man must have been infested with the horrific little monsters. The entire history of human advancement via the scientific method may be a byproduct of the higher forebrain's natural revulsion toward the nasty critters."

Mouse-killing isn't solely the province of organic and medical scientists. Many other scientists kill mice, as well.

"As a physicist, I don't really have much cause to use mice in my regular research, which mostly requires the use of theoretical math," said Dr. Thomas Huber, author of the 1996 study *Mouse Elasticity And Kinetic Rebound In High-Acceleration Collisions*. "But when I have the time, I like to send them flying into walls. Even just seeing them in a cage makes me feel kind of good inside. I like knowing I'm depriving them of their freedom, even if my research doesn't provide me the opportunity to cut them open."

"I hate those little fuckers," he added. ⌀

"All they want to do is get out from behind those bars so they can chew on everything, defecate all over, and poke their filthy twitching faces into piles of garbage. Well, I know of at least 80 little test subjects who won't be doing any more of that. They're headed straight for the dissection lab."

SCRAPBOOK from page 21

children—is represented in the scrapbook.

"Who is that little dear man in the rocking chair?" Kopein asked, pointing to the carefully mounted black-and-white portrait. "Such kind eyes he has. There must be so many fond memories in this scrapbook, I'm sure."

The last photo in the scrapbook shows Diane with her husband and their 2-year-old daughter. The studio portrait was particularly difficult to come by, as Diane has not spoken to either of her parents for four years. Hemmer obtained the photos from her daughter's mother-in-law, Candace Minsky, whom she ran into at the grocery store. Rather than reveal the rift between herself and her daughter, Hemmer explained that she'd lost all her photos to a roof leak.

"I felt bad for Jane," Minsky said. "Can you imagine losing precious photos like that? So I sent her some of my extra 4"x6" photos of Diane and the family."

With the scrapbook full, Hemmer said she plans to take advantage of new digital-photography technologies.

"I got a digital camera this fall, and there's a lot of wonderful shots I took at Thanksgiving of Alex and his new girlfriend, Marissa," Hemmer said. "Of course, when I put the photos on the computer, I'll delete the ones I took after Marissa and Bru[illegible] got into that little disagreem[illegible] about abortion." ⌀

"Who is that little dear man in the rocking chair?" Kopein asked, pointing to the carefully mounted black-and-white portrait.

COMMUNITY VOICES

What This Town Needs Is A Child In A Well

By Janet Casey

It seems like every house in this town has a fence, every door a lock. Our next-door neighbors have become strangers. We've lost touch with our friends. Our community's streets are safer than ever, but its residents have become isolated. We desperately need something to strengthen the common bonds that have weakened over time. If you ask me, what this town needs is a child in a well.

Yes, a child trapped 50 feet underground would do wonders for Greenwood. It could be a private well, but for logistical reasons, it'd be better if it were a public one. In a perfect world, the child would fall into the well smack-dab in the center of the town square. If that happened, I'll bet you anything we could shrug off decades of simmering resentment, distrust, and alienation way before the little shaver was back in his bed.

It's important to pick the right boy. Timmy is young enough to be cute, but old enough to comprehend danger. And with that flaxen hair and those skinny little arms, he inspires sympathy even before any tragedy has befallen him. Another option would be young Danny Williams.

The feeble, intermittent moans of that poor child trapped beneath the earth would do wonders for folks up above. Townsfolk would exchange silent, concerned looks in the grocery store. Citizens would invite mail carriers into their living rooms for tea. No one would eat alone at Nora's Diner anymore—all because of one innocent child lodged inside a deep abandoned well. It should definitely be a dry well. The boy will have to suffer, of course, but if he were to drown on Day One, the whole rescue-bonding thing would be shot to hell.

Can you imagine? People will say "I just hope he's okay." They won't even have to say whom. Our minds will be so in sync, they'll automatically conjure up images of a helpless, whimpering little boy trapped in the darkness below, day after day. Hopefully, at least eight days. Maybe as many as 10 if we lower him some sandwiches. As the days stretch on, his pain will be our pain—Greenwood's.

I do want it to be a boy in our well. A girl just wouldn't do. Sure, it would be tragic to know that a dishwater-blonde angel was trapped down inside the cold ground, but I can feel it in my bones: A boy is what Greenwood needs to get out of this slump.

That little Timmy Evans would do splendidly.

It's important to pick the right boy. Timmy is young enough to be cute, but old enough to comprehend danger. And with that flaxen hair and those skinny little arms, he inspires sympathy even before any tragedy has befallen him. Another option would be young Danny Williams. Of course, at 9, Danny is no spring chicken, as far as well-trapped kids go. Still, I believe he could do in a pinch. We definitely don't want that good-for-nothing Max Bartleby. Everyone would just sit at home secretly thinking, "I hope the brat dies." That would be even worse than if nobody fell down the well.

Whoever the boy ultimately is, he should handle the situation with class. His bravery should impress us. He shouldn't whine or cry wantonly. He should make the adults of the town wonder whether they would be so fearless in similar circumstances. The child who gets lodged in our town well should be heroic.

We'd keep the tragedy to ourselves for a couple days, but after the second or third day, the story could go national. Just imagine the headlines! *USA Today*: "Small Town Rallies Around Third-Grader Stuck In Well." *Chicago Sun-Times*: "Greenwood Danny Soldiers On." The copy writes itself. If we could drop a camera down there to snap a photo, it might even go global. It definitely would if the photo managed to capture the terror in the child's eyes.

Do you think they could get a microphone down there? Imagine his thin little voice: "I'll be okay, Mommy. Don't worry." Then you'd cut to a shot of his mother. She'd be on the verge of hysterics even before the boy got to say, "I can't feel my legs no more." Now is not the time to discuss merchandising opportunities, but these well stories make great movies.

But, like I said, now is not the time. Above all, this is about reviving our cherished sense of community.

Of course, the child would have to survive. It's good to end these sorts of heart-wrenching, dramatic events with a message of hope and inspiration. The people of Greenwood do not need a corpse. That's just depressing. A whole town comes together, puts aside its differences, invites the mailman in for tea, and then the boy dies? Nope, the boy must live.

That said, we don't want him totally out of danger. No. Greenwood needs to hear the experts talking about gangrene and hypothermia. We need to start imagining the little tyke in tattered rags, deep circles under his eyes, limbs blue. Greenwood needs a crisis with a dirty, tear-stained face. And I truly believe that, if we apply our strong Greenwood work ethic and a little bit of ingenuity, we can make it happen. ⌀

HOROSCOPES

Your Horoscope

By Lloyd Schumner Sr.
Retired Machinist and
A.A.P.B.-Certified Astrologer

Aries: (March 21–April 19)
Enjoy your position at the top of the food chain, because God is about to shake things up a little with the new Mountain Lion 2.0.

Taurus: (April 20–May 20)
Singing underneath your true love's window seems romantic, but because of poor planning, you'll wind up seducing the convent's entire dormitory wing.

Gemini: (May 21–June 21)
You're about to face yet another week of life-or-death struggles, but as usual, all you really have to do is remember to eat.

Cancer: (June 22–July 22)
The idea behind judo is to make an opponent's strength work against him, making you immune to the martial art.

Leo: (July 23–Aug. 22)
Many prophesied that you'd wind up wearing your ass for a hat, but they didn't predict that the fickle world of fashion would co-opt the look overnight.

Virgo: (Aug. 23–Sept. 22)
The inner world of every person contains realms unimagined, but you should still be able to guess what your license-plate-collecting brother-in-law might like for Christmas.

Libra: (Sept. 23–Oct. 23)
Where there's life, there's hope. This week, your heart will become the home of many single-celled, fungal, and parasitic species of hope.

Scorpio: (Oct. 24–Nov. 21)
Your inability to conduct both parallel and distributed computational processes will prevent you from being an integral component in next year's hottest laptops.

Sagittarius: (Nov. 22–Dec. 21)
You will suffer terrible pain and emotional trauma, and all because someone put a diving board where it didn't belong.

Capricorn: (Dec. 22–Jan. 19)
It's small-minded of him, but the detective investigating your death will suspect foul play simply because he would have tried to kill you himself.

Aquarius: (Jan. 20–Feb. 18)
You may march to the beat of a different drummer, but the important thing is that you're not being subversive and trying to walk on your own.

Pisces: (Feb. 19–March 20)
You'll be sued for slander, sexual harassment, inciting to riot, and a half-dozen other crimes when you decide to let your dancing speak for you.

COURT from page 20

taking away your computer, and I'm going to talk to the school librarian, so if you think you can look at Supreme Court information at school, you've got another thing coming. If I catch you with so much as a stay application, you'll be grounded for a month!

You're still free to read about the appellate courts, and of course I won't take your law reviews. I know it's not the same. But if you behave, maybe your mother and I will let you have your copy of *Closed Chambers* after a month or two. This isn't easy for me, either, but crying isn't going to help. Let's see if you can stay away from the Supreme Court for six months. Yes, six months. No, you will not die.

Don't be so dramatic. The Supreme Court is the most important judicial body in America, but it isn't everything. I'm sure you'll find plenty of things to occupy your time. Well, you'd better, because for the next six months, you are going to be Antonin Scalia and Sandra Day O'Connor-free, whether you like it or not.

Yes, my decision is final. ⌀

NEWS

Rommel, Hummel Dominate Parents' Christmas List

see LOCAL page 4B

Gold Bond Spokesman Grudgingly Admits It Makes Your Balls Tingle

see BUSINESS page 11E

Sponge Actor Turns Square-Pant Affliction Into Strength

see ENTERTAINMENT page 7D

STATshot

A look at the numbers that shape your world.

Top High-School Debate Topics
14% Geometry: Will we ever use it in real life?
18% Drunk driving: right or wrong?
21% Are these really the best years in our lives?
17% Is rap music destroying our debate coach's culture?
30% Which sophomores have done it?
SUZIE RAYNOR: HOT OR NOT?

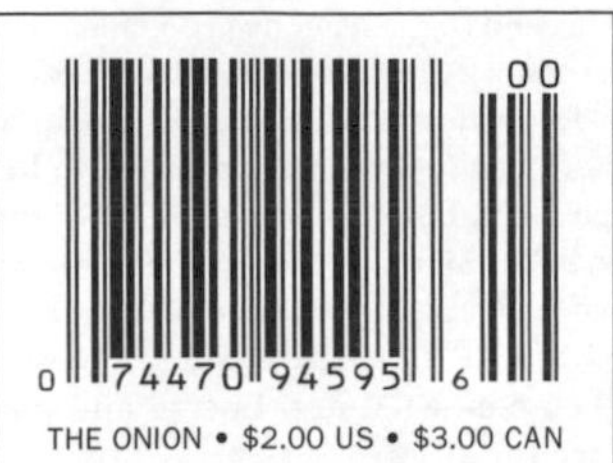

the ONION®

VOLUME 40 ISSUE 50 AMERICA'S FINEST NEWS SOURCE™ 16–22 DECEMBER 2004

New Homeless Initiative To Raise Bottle Deposit To 12 Cents

Above: Three of the many homeless who will soon benefit from a higher bottle refund rate.

WASHINGTON, DC—A bipartisan Congressional initiative passed Monday promises that relief, in the form of a national, 12-cent bottle-and-can refund, will soon come to the nation's estimated 600,000 homeless.

"We can no longer ignore the problem of homelessness in our country," Rep. Benjamin L. Cardin (D-MD) said. "Under the new program, all aluminum and glass beverage containers will be required to carry a minimum refund value of 12 cents, boosting homeless citizens' incomes and endowing them with a sense of pride in their work."

Citing the track records of local deposit plans, the Subcommittee on Human Resources drew up a proposal that would tap into

see DEPOSIT page 28

Nigeria Chosen To Host 2008 Genocides

ABUJA, NIGERIA—At a celebratory press conference Monday, President Olusegun Obasanjo announced that Nigeria's troubled but oil-rich city of Warri has been chosen to host the 2008 Genocides.

"Nigeria is excited for this chance to follow in the footsteps of Somalia, Rwanda, and Sudan," Obasanjo said. "Much work remains to be done, but all of the building blocks are in place. Nigeria has many contentious ethnic groups, a volatile economy, and a dependence on food imports. We are well on our way to making 2008 a genocidal year to remember in Nigeria!"

Obasanjo acknowledged that many people considered Nigeria, a relatively stable West African nation, an unlikely candidate to host the Genocides.

"With a multi-party government

see NIGERIA page 28

Above: Annan congratulates Obasanjo.

Above: Turnbee and the wrap he is "not so sure about."

Area Man Suspicious Of Wrap

ERIE, PA—Local resident and frequent fast-food-restaurant patron Don Turnbee said Monday that he was "still a little leery" of the wrap he'd ordered from the Jefferson Street Subway sandwich shop minutes before.

"I'm not sure about this thing," Turnbee said, eyeing the Chicken Bacon Ranch wrap sitting on his tray beside a bag of chips and a large soda. "I mean, I'm gonna try it,

see WRAP page 29

Iraq Troops Complain

Last week, troops complained to Defense Secretary Donald Rumsfeld about extended deployments and poor equipment. What do *you* think?

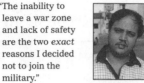

"The inability to leave a war zone and lack of safety are the two *exact* reasons I decided not to join the military."

Joy Parks
Systems Analyst

"I'm so confused. In times of war, should I support the troops or the president?"

Neil Dawson
Farmworker

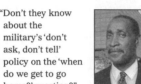

"Don't they know about the military's 'don't ask, don't tell' policy on the 'when do we get to go home?' question?"

Dustin O'Brien
Fire Fighter

"If those troops keep griping and grousing, I don't think they're going to be named *Time*'s Person of the Year again any time soon."

Lewis Richards
Lab Supervisor

"Years from now, our troops will look back at the war in Iraq and wonder why they haven't been allowed to go home yet."

Clinton Rhodes
Film Editor

"Man, all the troops do these days is bitch, bitch, die unnecessarily, and bitch."

Heidi Williamson
Teacher

Stopping Steroids

Major League Baseball is under pressure to impose tougher rules against steroids. How do they plan to prevent the use of the performance-enhancing drugs?

- Finally doing away with American League's much-debated "designated pisser" rule
- Reacquainting players with strength and energy one derives from eating a good breakfast every morning
- Toughening up their "Don't get caught using steroids" policy
- Explaining to players that they don't need to take drugs to have a good 40-yard-dash time
- Putting up posters of Major League players at every GNC outlet with the instructions "do not serve"
- Pressuring Mr. Met to halt the excessive steroid use that has grotesquely swollen his head
- Periodically checking players' syringes to make sure they don't contain steroids
- Keeping players off drugs by getting them involved in sports

America's Finest News Source.™

Herman Ulysses Zweibel
Founder

T. Herman Zweibel
Publisher Emeritus
J. Phineas Zweibel
Publisher
Maxwell Prescott Zweibel
Editor-In-Chief

Desperate Times Call For *Desperate Housewives*

By Eric Wendt
ABC Vice Chairman

We Americans are not strangers to hardship. We have endured economic woes, enmity between the states, and protracted campaigns in foreign lands. We have survived imperialist wars; we have survived unexpected attacks; we have seen countless lives wasted. Since America declared its independence, each successive generation has met a unique and unexpected challenge, but ours is the first to face the worst hardships of many generations in legion. Fellow citizens, we are living in desperate times, and desperate times call for *Desperate Housewives*.

Each morning, our newspapers bring reports of chaos in the Mideast, violence in our schools, and a leadership in disarray. Our televisions, once cynosures for placid reflection, are now given to reports of violence and injustice. Maintaining our purity of heart while staring into the widening chasm of world events is a task for which many of us feel ill-equipped. In times like these, we must fix our gaze upon Wisteria Lane. For, as everyone here at ABC can assure you, there is

Each morning, our newspapers bring reports of chaos in the Mideast, violence in our schools, and a leadership in disarray. Our televisions, once cynosures for placid reflection, are now given to reports of violence and injustice.

nothing wrong with America that cannot be cured by what is right with *Desperate Housewives*.

On the surface, our nation is sharply divided between the red states and the blue. But look deeper, tune in, and watch as Bree Van De Kamp bonds unexpectedly with Mary Alice's troubled son Zach. At the heart of our great nation is a friendship between Bree and Zach. And so watch *Desperate Housewives*, and find out what lies buried beneath Mary Alice's pool. When you do, I promise that it will be every bit as emotionally satisfying as the revelation that Mrs. Huber wrote the mysterious note that Mary Alice received before her untimely death.

Questions... Doubts... Will single-

Yes, allow chaos. Allow mystery. For our nation was not shaped by short, 30-minute outbursts of emotion, but by the tranquil and steady dedication of Rex Van De Kamp, who agreed to seek counseling to rectify his marriage with Bree.

mom Susan find new love with Mike Delfino? What sort of "plumber" is Mike, anyway? And what of Lynette, who has deferred her dreams of corporate success? What of the lawnboy, who takes his affair with Gabrielle to heart? Friends, dare to leave conundrums unsolved, unsimplified. For *Desperate Housewives*, like America's participatory democracy, is always changing, infinite in its variety—sometimes turbulent—and all the more valuable for having had its shocking conclusion shaped by focus groups from multiple demographics. Stay tuned! This week's episode is a doozy.

Yes, allow chaos. Allow mystery. For our nation was not shaped by short, 30-minute outbursts of emotion, but by the tranquil and steady dedication of Rex Van De Kamp, who agreed to seek counseling to rectify his marriage with Bree. Tune in, America.

For, without the collective efforts of many, we Americans will find ourselves doing much worse than burning down our neighbors' houses, taking our childrens' medication, and almost bringing down the entire NFL through our lascivious pre-game locker-room seduction of Terrell Owens.

To paraphrase George Santayana: A man's feet must be planted in his country, but his eyes should follow ABC's Sunday primetime line-up, with *Extreme Makeover* at 8:00 p.m. EST, *Desperate Housewives* at 9:00 p.m. EST, and liberty and justice for all. Ø

FAMILY

Family Secret Turns Out To Be Boring

MINNETONKA, MN—After nearly 30 years of subterfuge, Michael Henderson's parents Doug and Pam broke down and revealed their painful family secret, which turned out to be unbelievably boring, their son reported Monday.

"Ever since I was a kid, Mom and Dad have avoided talking about their first couple years of marriage," said the 28-year-old Henderson, who visited his parents last weekend. "My sisters and I knew they lived in Indiana for two years, but we never knew why they moved back to Minnesota. Eventually, we started wondering if it was something too horrible to talk about. Who would've imagined it was such a non-story after all that drama?"

According to Henderson, whenever he asked his parents about Indiana, they responded in a "vague, noncommittal way, then changed the subject."

"Once, I asked Dad what his first job was, and he refused to answer," Henderson said. "He basically acted like he had been a spy or a drug dealer or something."

When Henderson's parents finally revealed the mysterious truth during a teary, post-dinner confession Saturday, Henderson said he was shocked not by the revelation, but by its mundanity.

"Last Thanksgiving, I asked Aunt Janet what the deal was, and even she got all agitated," Henderson said. "The real story is so mild and silly that I'm almost embarrassed to say what it was."

After a pause, Henderson continued: "Okay, ready? Here it is: Dad got kicked out of the Air Force for stealing a motorcycle."

When Henderson's parents finally revealed the mysterious truth during a teary, post-dinner confession Saturday, Henderson said he was shocked not by the revelation, but by its mundanity.

According to Henderson, the years of secrecy had fueled intense speculation, with him and his sisters Joyce and Randi dreaming up scenarios ranging from the tragic to the truly horrific.

"I was imagining all this crazy stuff," Hendeson said. "Was he involved in an anti-establishment bombing of a campus building that resulted in an accidental death? Did it have something to do with the scar on his stomach? Does he have a whole different family somewhere? Was there an uncle who died in a mysterious hunting accident after Dad caught him making out with Mom? That kind of thing."

Above: Henderson and his father, Doug.

None of the hypotheses turned out to be even remotely close to the mundane story of motorcycle theft, which did not even result in any jail time.

"Well, it turns out the scar is from an appendectomy, Mom and Dad never even dated anyone else before they got married, and Dad's been an actuary ever since leaving the Air Force," Henderson said. "In fact, I'm pretty sure the motorcycle incident is the most exciting thing that ever happened to either of them."

Henderson said the truth came out during a late-night conversation that "took place over a few too many brandy eggnogs." Basking in the glow of the fireplace, the parents broke down and told their son the burning secret they had kept hidden for so long.

"It was really emotionally trying for

see SECRET page 30

NEWS IN BRIEF

Area Man Too Busy For His Buddy Phil, Eh?

JEFFERSON CITY, MO—College chum Steve Maeske is apparently too busy to give his buddy Phil a quick ring, sources reported Monday. "Phil, honestly, you know I'd love to go out to help you celebrate your birthday," said Maeske, who's been like a ghost ever since he married that Veronica woman. "It's just that, with work and the new baby, I don't have a spare minute. Come on, you can understand, can't you?" Sources close to Maeske don't see why he can't go out for one damn beer.

Lawyers Separate Mary-Kate & Ashley Olsen In 17-Hour Procedure

HOLLYWOOD—Attorneys representing Mary-Kate & Ashley Olsen separated the career-conjoined twins in a harrowing, 17-hour procedure Monday. "Because they lived symbiotically for so many years, the most difficult task was methodically detaching each of their shared credits," said Divorah Kessler, one of the heroic lawyers on the five-person team. "After carefully removing the ampersand between their names and replacing it with a comma, we'll attempt to construct an individual persona for each girl." Lawyers on both sides list the girls' chances for solo-career survival as "fair."

Risk Champ Flunks Geography Test

ALBANY, NY—Alfred Wu, the 13-year-old winner of the 2004 East Coast Risk Championship, flunked his 8th-grade world-geography test, social-studies teacher Jane Laurent reported Monday. "His test paper was filled with names like Kamchatka and Yakutsk, and the Ukraine spread over half of Europe," Laurent said. "And, by his account, the U.S. is made up of only three states: Eastern United States, Western United States, and Alaska." Last week, Wu received an "F" on a paper he wrote about Napoleonic military Stratego.

Sports-Related Murder Provides Perfect Local-News Segue

PHOENIX—The arrest of former Arizona State running back Darius Cantrell in connection with a homicide provided the perfect segue from local news to the sports report on KPHO CBS 5's News At Ten Monday. "Cantrell, who is charged with stabbing his ex-girlfriend 38 times, is being held without bail," anchor Diana Sullivan said. "Speaking of sports, can the Cardinals' coach bail the team out of a third-place finish in the NFC West? Our own Gary Cruz will have the verdict after the break." It was the station's most convenient transition to sports since May 1996, when an anchor moved from a piece on sex toys with the phrase, "and speaking of long double headers..."

Dad's Marine Corps Training Evident During Christmas-Present Opening

CHARLESTON, SC—Retired Cpl. Kent Packard, 58, rarely puts his Marine Corps expertise to use, except during the yearly Christmas gift exchange, family sources reported Monday. "Every year, exactly two hours after cutting the ham, Dad makes us line up by the tree, then he distributes the presents to us in increasing order of age," his 17-year-old son Jerome said. "When he unwraps his own gifts, he lines up the pieces of cardboard and plastic packaging in a neat row, like he's field-stripping a rifle." Although family members say they admire Packard's acumen, they've warned him against waking the house with a Christmas-morning bugle rendition of "Jingle Bells."

NIGERIA from page 25

transitioning from military to civilian rule, Nigeria is not a shoo-in to host the Genocides," Obasanjo said. "But last week's municipal election—with ballot shortages and ethnic groups trading accusations of vote tampering—showed the world that Nigeria is, indeed, geared up for the unimaginable."

Oni Radhiya, a spokesman from the 2004 Genocide Board, said September's crippling polio outbreak may have helped Nigeria beat out the competition.

"Sudan was a fantastic host this year—the 2004 Genocides have really raised the bar," Radhiya said. "For 2008, many of us on the committee had our eyes on Tajikistan. The country's ongoing ethnic and religious strife made it a strong contender. But there was some concern that the conflict was as likely to simmer down as it was to boil over."

Annan said he first noticed the full genocidal potential of soon-to-be embattled Nigeria in September, when the Niger Delta People's Volunteer Force threatened to shut down oil production.

Radhiya added that Iraq was ruled out because the country is unlikely to exist three and a half years from now.

UN Secretary General Kofi Annan said that, after a close examination of all bids, a Nigerian genocide "began to seem almost inevitable."

Above: A newly erected billboard in Makurdi.

"Nigeria's stability has been repeatedly threatened by fighting between fundamentalist Muslims and Christians," Annan said. "Five of Nigeria's seven political parties are extremist groups. The nation's ethnic Yoruba, Hausa, and Ibo populations of the oil-rich Niger Delta area also show genocidal promise."

Annan said he first noticed the full genocidal potential of soon-to-be embattled Nigeria in September, when the Niger Delta People's Volunteer Force threatened to shut down oil production.

"With so many poor and powerless people involved in messy, years-old conflicts, the situation is likely to be ignored long enough for things to get really ugly," Annan said. "And, of course, the slow-to-move, ineffectual UN will do everything it can to help shepherd Nigeria into a combined religious, political, and economic disaster of horrific proportions."

According to Nigerian officials, now that their country has secured the bid, the government has much work to do.

"Don't think we'll just sit on our hands and wait for a crippling drought to pit neighbor against neighbor," Nigerian Minister of State Bello Usman said. "No, the next two years will be crucial. We need to default on our $2 billion IMF loan, invest the entire treasury in the overhead-heavy petroleum business, and turn a blind eye to regional guerrilla groups. That'd be a good start. After that, food shipments must fall into rebel hands, armed forces must go unpaid, and the emerging national infrastructure must be allowed to deteriorate."

Added Usman: "There's a lot to accomplish, but I promise you this: By early 2008, ashes will blacken the sky and blood will run in the streets."

According to Red Cross programming director Ellen Schumacher, genocide, once a spectacle that drew the attention of the entire world, has received less attention in recent years, drawing an ever-diminishing Western audience.

"The most glaring problem has been a time-zone issue, since most of the proceedings take place during inconvenient, off-peak viewing times," Schumacher said. "But, as an oil-rich nation, Nigeria is much more likely to build a viewer base in the West. Perhaps the country will even be able to get one of the networks to pony up for exclusive rights." Ø

DEPOSIT from page 25

the nation's existing infrastructure to minimize the homeless epidemic without creating budgetary hurdles. Dubbed the Shelter And Recycling Initiative (SARI), it is the first nation-wide, federally mandated bottle-deposit program. It is also the first government program designed to lift the burden of homelessness from the taxpayers' shoulders.

"For homeless can-collectors in my home state of Michigan, the plan represents a 20-percent raise," Rep. Dave Camp (R-MI) said. "For those in states like California, New York, and Iowa, it represents a whopping 140 percent wage increase. Everyone wins: The homeless enjoy a higher standard of living, and we taxpayers enjoy cleaner streets, free of cans and bottles!"

Under the plan, an additional 50,000 bottle-and-can redemption machines will be placed in front of the nation's grocery stores to cut down on the amount of time homeless people spend in line.

"This is the best way to help the homeless help themselves," Camp said. "Think of how good they'll feel about themselves when they can march right up to that refund machine, deposit their grocery basket full of bottles and cans, roll on over to the register, and pay for their Dinty Moore stew with money they've earned."

"For homeless can-collectors in my home state of Michigan, the plan represents a 20-percent raise," Camp said.

According to Camp, if the homeless can't "pull themselves up by their bootstraps" after the return-rate increase, then "there is no helping them."

"This is a chance to give the homeless a hand up, instead of a handout," Camp said. "With the amount of alcohol they consume, industrious homeless winos will be able to drink themselves to a better life."

The refund bill, though approved by Congress, has caused a public outcry. Makers of boxed beverages argue that the bill will create a windfall for aluminum- and glass-packaged beverage manufacturers. Soda drinkers argue that soda is expensive enough as it is, without the additional expense of a deposit. Activists have suggested that the bill is "insensitive."

"This program is a slap in the face for the poor and unfortunate," homeless advocate Neal Schweiber said. "Does Congress really think they can sweep the problem of homelessness under the rug with a 12-cent rebate? Nothing less than 20 cents per container constitutes an effective policy shift."

Added Schweiber: "Have you ever had to dig through someone's trash to make a living? I haven't either, but I have seen people do it. It looks extremely unpleasant."

Homeless-shelter worker Patricia Wenzel agrees that the initiative is inadequate.

"This bill has no provisions to care for disabled homeless men and women, many of whom do not have the capacity to collect drink containers," Wenzel said. "We need to provide all hopeless and destitute individuals with a ray of hope."

In spite of the warnings and protestations of its detractors, the subcommittee plans to institute SARI by Nov. 12, 2005.

"This isn't a tax, it's a deposit in our future," Camp said. "And taxpayers who opt out of their redemptions can write off discarded cans as a contribution to the poor. As the saying goes, one man's trash is another man's treasure." Ø

WRAP from page 25

but I don't understand this whole tortilla fad. What's wrong with bread?"

Turnbee acknowledged that he probably wouldn't have sampled the wrap without the 20-percent-off coupon he found in a newspaper insert, but added that he isn't averse to trying "new and unusual foods." In

"Half the places I go offer some low-carb or Atkins thing," Turnbee said. "I ignore all that crazy business. At most of the places I go, I can still get one of the old standbys: a burger, a roast beef sandwich, or a ham and cheese sub. I do have some trouble when we go up to Canada to visit Shelly's sister. The restaurants are all different up there."

fact, the Erie native reports that he ordered a McDonald's Big N' Tasty Burger only days after learning about the sandwich on television.

"This wrap can't be all that bad," Turnbee said, poking at the item's paper exterior. "If I don't like it, at least I'll know I didn't pay full price."

Although Turnbee said he likes all the ingredients inside of his wrap, especially bacon, he said he was skeptical of "the whole idea of wrapping."

"I almost got the Turkey Bacon Melt, but that Chipotle Southwest Sauce scared me off," Turnbee said. "But this one seems like it'll be all right. What's the big deal, right? I guess I'll know in a couple bites."

Turnbee said he was thankful that Subway displayed a detailed list of ingredients near the serving line, allowing him to make an informed choice. He said his worries that he might accidentally get a wrap with "fancy" ingredients, such as sun-dried tomatoes, have stopped him from ordering wraps in the past.

"Some places don't tell you what's inside of the wrap," Turnbee said. "They cut it in half and make you guess from the colors. Some of these new types of sandwiches have a lot of weird stuff in them. I'd rather know what I'm eating."

In addition to his fear of unfamiliar ingredients, Turnbee said he is "uneasy with wraps," because he associates them with salads.

"My wife Shelly wants me to eat more salads," Turnbee said. "I try to eat one once a week. But I don't want to halfway eat a salad by eating a salad wrapped up in a tortilla."

"Not that Shelly ever told me to eat a wrap," Turnbee added. "I bet she doesn't even know what a wrap is. She doesn't dine out as frequently as I do."

Turnbee said he is pretty sure that wraps have something to do with the Atkins diet craze.

"Half the places I go offer some low-carb or Atkins thing," Turnbee said. "I ignore all that crazy business. At most of the places I go, I can still get one of the old standbys: a burger, a roast beef sandwich, or a ham and cheese sub. I do have some trouble when we go up to Canada to visit Shelly's sister. The restaurants are all different up there."

Although Turnbee acknowledged that he enjoys tortilla-based food items at restaurants such as Taco Bell, he said he doesn't understand why people want "regular sandwich fillings inside of Mexican food."

"That might be okay for the people in California, but I can't see myself getting too into them," Turnbee said. "They seem kind of flimsy. I like food you can grip with both hands, something like a Double Whopper with cheese."

In spite of Turnbee's reservations, sources close to him expect him to enjoy the wrap that he is about to eat.

"I'll bet Don likes it," Shelly Turnbee said. "I've never seen him not like anything with chicken and bacon in it. He's just wary of new things, es-

"I'll bet Don likes it," Shelly Turnbee said. "I've never seen him not like anything with chicken and bacon in it. He's just wary of new things, especially if they seem gourmet. It's like when restaurants started switching from iceberg to romaine lettuce. He complained for a while, but he got used to it."

pecially if they seem gourmet. It's like when restaurants started switching from iceberg to romaine lettuce. He complained for a while, but he got used to it." Ø

COMMUNITY VOICES

Spawn Of Santa

It's Christmastime again, and for your old pal Jean, that means one thing: limited-term seasonal employment. This year, my job is something I've done before. I'm wrapping gifts at the Northway Mall in the town where I grew up, about 30 minutes from Casa Teasdale. It pays seven bucks an hour,

A Room Of Jean's Own
By Jean Teasdale

and there's quite a lot of sitting-around time on weekday mornings. But weekends are a whole different story! (Boy, if you ever start a business, hang a banner reading "Free Gift Wrapping Here!" People will wait in line for 25 minutes to avoid buying their own Scotch tape.)

Given that the wrapping is free, customers are awfully choosy about the type of paper they want. They can choose reindeer paper, holly leaves paper, solid red paper, even blue Hanukkah paper, but people still complain. "That's all you have?" they ask. "Isn't there any with Santa on it?" Then, they get all snippy when I tell them there are no bows and ribbons. I hear a lot of, "Some free gift-wrap deal!" and, "This is just a way for you to get rid of the wrapping paper nobody wants."

Boy, Jeanketeers! I remember the day when people kept those kinds of cynical thoughts to themselves. Is it just me, or was Christmas a lot more fun back when? It seemed like the crowds at the Northway Mall were thinner and less aggressive, the toys were cuter and quieter, and the decorations were just wonderful. True, I was a kid at the time, but I remember being dazzled by the way they decorated the mall fountain. They put fiberglass over it, to make it look like it had iced over. Then, they posed little skater dolls on top. And up above, glitter-sprinkled white reindeer soared on wires. It was magical. It felt like you were in an animated Christmas special. They've since dismantled the fountain. Now they just hang a little gold bunting, set up some fake trees, and call it Christmas.

A security guard told me a story that really surprised me. She said that last week, she smelled something foul near one of the Christmas displays. When she opened a prop toy box, what do you think she found? A used diaper. I guess somebody was changing her baby on the benches and stuck it in there when no one was looking. The guard thought it was funny, but I didn't see the humor at all. Needless to say, my dream of working in a Christmas paradise has soured. I mean, if you can't find Christmas cheer inside a shopping mall, where can you find it?

Last Saturday, after a long, hard day of wrapping, I was headed home. Walking through the mall to my car, my heart felt like it weighed a ton. What is Christmas all about, and why do people celebrate it? Had I ever had a genuine Christmas experience of my own, or was it all a sham? Were all my Christmas memories as artificial as one of the mall trees?

"Snap out of it, Jean old girl," I said to myself. "Try to think of how you'll feel if you wake up Christmas morn and that breadmaker you've been bugging Rick about is sitting under the tree."

I was just about to walk into Hobby Corner and buy some artificial snow to scatter around the Beanie Babies in my bedroom when someone with a bushy white beard and a red stocking hat caught my eye. He was wearing a Hawaiian shirt and maneuvering a

If you can't find Christmas cheer inside a shopping mall, where can you find it?

Rascal scooter out of an ice-cream parlor.

"Dad?" I shouted.

He turned around, or I should say, he made a three-point turn in his scooter. "Jeannie!" he said.

I was shocked to see Dad in town. For the past few years, he'd been living with his third wife Dana, in California. I know what you're thinking, and no, I hadn't hallucinated the beard and hat. Ever since his beard went white, Dad started working as a shopping-mall Santa at Christmastime. A couple of years ago, he was even lucky enough to land the gig at a mega-mall near his home with real ritzy stores like Nordstrom and Sharper Image.

"I'm never leaving these sweatpants!" he said, as I bent down to give him a hug. (Instead of greeting you or asking you how you are, Dad always says something completely unrelated. It used to bug my mom, and I think his second wife cited it in her divorce papers.)

I asked my dad what brought him back to town, and he said he was visiting my brother Kevin and his family. I was shocked.

"You guys made up?" I asked. "When? And why didn't you tell me you were here?"

Dad, in usual form, ignored my question. Munching his cone, he told

see TEASDALE page 30

TEASDALE from page 29

me to come back with him to the mall atrium where he had his "setup."

"Picking up a little cash as usual," he said and drove his scooter up a ramp and onto an elevated platform. He parked beside a hand-lettered sign that read "Chill out with Santa!"

A beach towel lay on the carpeted floor beside a plastic pail, a shovel, and a child's beach chair. Dad threw himself onto the chair and straightened his hat. Of course, by then I was completely confused.

"Dad, what happened to your Santa suit?" I said.

Dad hushed me. "Don't break the illusion," he said. "Remember: I'm Santa." He gestured for me to kneel down beside him and listen.

"The suit is back home," he said. "My trip to town was a little sudden, you see. But I was doing some Christmas shopping with Kevin when I noticed this place didn't have a Santa, so I showed 'em my resume and offered my services cheap. I didn't have my suit, so I improvised. It's like Santa's enjoying a quick sabbatical before the big day. You know, he's 'chilling out'—like the kids say. Twenty bucks plus all the ice cream and pretzels I want for six hours of work. A far cry from what I make back home, but a pretty good take for someone who just breezed into town. I like to stay busy. Plus, it's Christmas—no time to be greedy."

I asked him why he was using the Rascal, and he said it contributed to the image of Santa as a laid-back, mellow guy. He acknowledged that it helps him get around better, too. Finishing his cone, Dad wiped his beard, put on sunglasses, and gave me the thumbs-up.

Dad did look pretty relaxed, but still, I wasn't sure about the vacationing-Santa idea. Without the red suit, Dad just looked like an eccentric old loiterer. I mean, I don't think Santa would wear flip-flops, particularly if he were missing a toe. I wasn't the only one who didn't get it. While I was talking to Dad, I spotted a lot of families walking by with confused looks on their faces.

"Dad, where's Dana?" I asked.

Dad scowled.

"I mean, where's Mrs. Claus?"

Dad sighed and explained that he and "the missus" were spending some time apart. He went on to explain that he'd decided to use the separation period as an opportunity to see the family back home. He was obviously uncomfortable with imparting so much personal information, so I didn't push him to elaborate.

"Look, honeysuckle, I gotta get back to work," he said. "I'll call you soon. I'm gonna be here a while, so there'll be plenty of time to catch up with good old St. Nick."

When you reunite with your dad, do you feel like the meeting was just a dream? I always do! I drove home in a daze, with so many unanswered questions swirling in my mind. (I almost rear-ended someone in the process!)

I'm pretty sure I got a lot of my imagination and sass from my dad. He was the parent I was the most drawn to while I was growing up, but he did strange things. He'd leave the windows open in winter so we'd develop a resistance to cold. He paved over our yard, because he didn't want ants infesting the house. He wouldn't let us have yo-yos in the house, because the faint sound of the string winding and unwinding against the yo-yo's axle drove him crazy. A typical Sunday afternoon consisted of my brother and me helping Dad bundle up and drop off newspapers at the recycling center for cash. Then, he'd drop us off at his buddy's supper club so we could guzzle chocolate milk and color placemats while he went over the grounds with his metal detector. I thought this was all perfectly normal until hubby Rick informed me otherwise.

Dad sighed and explained that he and "the missus" were spending some time apart. He went on to explain that he'd decided to use the separation period as an opportunity to see the family back home. He was obviously uncomfortable with imparting so much personal information, so I didn't push him to elaborate.

Speaking of hubby Rick, when I told him I saw Dad, the first thing out of his mouth was "He's not staying here." When I told him that Dad hadn't said a word about staying with us, he snorted without turning his eyes from his football video game. "As usual, you're giving that guy way too much credit," he muttered. "My family would've sent him straight to the nuthouse."

(Ho-dee ho, ho, Rick!)

Well, I like to think of my dad's return as a Christmas gift. I mean, it wasn't miraculous, like you'd see on a Christmas special, and it wasn't even something I particularly yearned for, but it's still nice I got it. (I definitely still want that breadmaker, though.)

HOROSCOPES

Your Horoscope

By Lloyd Schumner Sr.
Retired Machinist and
A.A.P.B.-Certified Astrologer

Aries: (March 21–April 19)
There truly is more than one way to skin a cat, but the limited market for cat skins makes learning more than three methods impractical.

Taurus: (April 20–May 20)
You are possessed with abilities far beyond those of mortal man, but if your super-heroic origin story ever got out, no one would take you seriously.

Gemini: (May 21–June 21)
It turns out that being a slumlord is actually a whole lot of fun, at least for the time being.

Cancer: (June 22–July 22)
Whoever said it was easier to destroy than to create never tried collecting their feces in jars for 18 months.

Leo: (July 23–Aug. 22)
You thought you'd seen the worst humanity had to offer, but that was before you read fan-fiction set in an alternate universe where Hawkeye Pierce and Father Mulcahy are lovers.

Virgo: (Aug. 23–Sept. 22)
There will finally be a call for restraint among athletes, but not before Joe Horn does a taunting victory dance over the burst ribcages of your family.

Libra: (Sept. 23–Oct. 23)
With winter upon us, it's time to reflect, take stock of our lives, and maybe wear a skirt that covers your thighs, you slut.

Scorpio: (Oct. 24–Nov. 21)
Somehow, you don't believe your boss when he tells you that your coworker of 12 years went off to live with a nice family on a beautiful farm.

Sagittarius: (Nov. 22–Dec. 21)
It's often hard to say goodbye, but that doesn't excuse your practice of throwing down a smoke bomb and escaping in the confusion.

Capricorn: (Dec. 22–Jan. 19)
Unfortunately, a disagreement over whether cool jazz is superior to smooth jazz will not end in bloodshed.

Aquarius: (Jan. 20–Feb. 18)
A mysterious portrait of you, painted by an acknowledged master, will increase in value as the years progress, while you remain worthless.

Pisces: (Feb. 19–March 20)
You may be new to farming, but everyone knows that haystacks should be made of hay. Using needles not only injures your cattle, it also clues the other farmers in to the fact that you are a nerd.

SECRET from page 27

them to finally come clean," Henderson said. "That's why I feel so bad that I still couldn't keep from laughing."

In the confession, Doug explained that he and Pam were 19, married, and living together in military housing. One night, Doug got drunk and accepted a dare to race five circles around the base on a motorcycle that had been left running outside the PX. Unfortunately, he was apprehended by military police on his second lap.

"The funniest part is, he didn't even steal it, really," Henderson said. "He and some buddies got drunk, and he went for a joyride. It was a run-of-the-mill story of kids blowing off steam. I kept waiting for Dad to get to the good part, but it never came."

Continued Henderson: "I mean, who didn't get drunk and do something stupid at 19? I totaled Dad's car when I was a senior in high school and even broke my collarbone. You don't see me hiding it."

According to Henderson, his parents had tears in their eyes when they related the boring tale. In spite of his disappointment, he said there was a bright side: Both of his parents appeared "as if a weight had been lifted from their shoulders" after the confession.

"For the rest of the weekend, they were a lot more relaxed," Henderson said. "To me, it was such a non-event that, when we went to the mall the next day and passed a parked motorcycle, I almost said, 'Dad, is that thing safe around you?' But I thought better of it, thank God. I don't think he would've forgiven me."

Henderson said his parents made him promise never to tell his sisters.

"Of course, I went right out to the garage with my cell phone and called Joyce and Randi," Henderson said. "I mean, come on! Maybe somewhere in the mists of time, something interesting has happened in this family, but I can guarantee that it didn't have anything to do with Mom and Dad and Indiana."

NEWS

44 Suspicious Packages Detonated Under White House Christmas Tree

see WASHINGTON page 13C

Outgoing HHS Secretary Tommy Thompson Caught With Briefcase Full Of Flu Vaccine

see NATION page 4B

U.S. Gripped By Y2K05 Fears

see TECHNOLOGY page 4F

STATshot

A look at the numbers that shape your world.

Why Did She Pack Up And Go?
17% Wasn't really into the whole married-with-kids thing
12% Tired of us always saying "anyhoo"
23% Missed Russia
28% Kids practically raise selves anyway
20% Didn't want to die alone with us
QUICKSAND

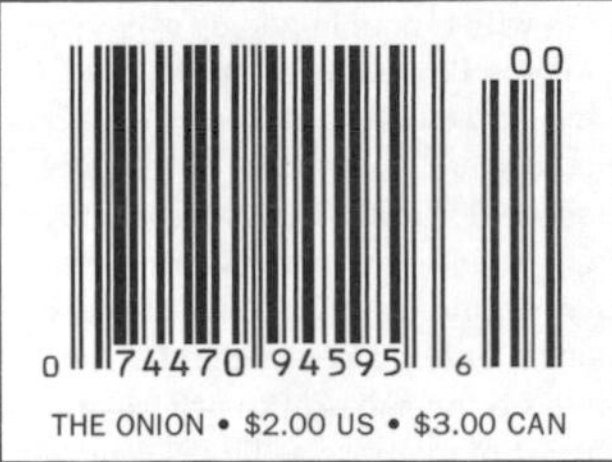

the ONION®

VOLUME 40 ISSUE 51 AMERICA'S FINEST NEWS SOURCE™ 23–29 DECEMBER 2004

HOLIDAY HOPE

Weed Delivery Guy Saves Christmas

MADISON, WI—The holidays evoke images of carolers and hot cocoa, sleigh rides through the crisp country air, and chestnuts roasting on an open fire. But for the four residents of a drafty little apartment on Johnson Street, such holiday traditions seemed nothing more than fairy tales. For, through a combination of poverty, circumstance, and plain old bad luck, these young gentlemen nearly saw their holiday dreams shattered like so many fallen ornaments.

Almost, but not quite. For although there would be no Yule log in the fireplace, a crackling blaze of another kind *would* come to warm the

see WEED page 35

Above: The weed guy delivers holiday tidings.

Psychiatrists Treating *Phantom Of The Opera* Viewers For Post-Melodramatic Stress Disorder

Above: A scene from The Phantom Of The Opera, a movie incapacitating audiences nationwide.

HOLLYWOOD—Psychiatrists in select cities nationwide have reported a surge in Post-Melodramatic Stress Disorder cases following the Dec. 22 release of Andrew Lloyd Webber's *The Phantom Of The Opera*.

"We're seeing a barrage of psychological consequences in those who have been exposed to the violently overblown acting and protracted, heightened emotions in *The Phantom Of The Opera*," said Bill Lambert, a psychology professor at the University of Chicago. "After such intense abuse of their artistic sensibilities, melodrama victims are finding themselves plagued by extreme sentimentality, flashbacks to especially torturous scenes, and canned-emotional detachment."

According to Lambert, a good portion of PMSD sufferers are experiencing distress so great that it is interfering with their jobs as

see PHANTOM page 34

Area Daughter Belittled Out Of Concern

PENSACOLA, FL—Out of concern for her daughter's well-being, Valerie Guzman spent the majority of her 26-year-old daughter Nancy's brief holiday visit belittling her.

"You only have that small bag?" Guzman asked Sunday when her daughter stepped off the plane. "You don't plan to wear the same outfit for three days, do you? You remembered we're going to the DiSicas'

see DAUGHTER page 35

Above: Nancy and Valerie Guzman.

Jury: Peterson Deserves Death

Last week, jurors recommended that Scott Peterson be sentenced to death for murdering his pregnant wife, Laci. What do *you* think?

Pedro Fernandez
Baggage Porter

"Let this be a warning to psychopaths with photogenic wives everywhere."

Derrick Watts
Systems Analyst

"What about Laci's fetus' potential children, and those childrens' children? Folks, this was way more than a double-homicide."

Sherry Morrison
Cashier

"What's going on? I've been busy trying to keep up with the thousands of other murders that took place this year. I'm a bit out of the loop on the Peterson case."

Rich Hale
Bartender

"This story had everything—sex, death, and now death once again. I would've appreciated some more sex, also."

Warren Jacobs
Ship Captain

"What am I supposed to tell my daughter when she asks, 'Why do exhaustively drawn-out things happen to bad people?'"

Florence Norris
Cardiologist

"Finally, the death of little Connor, the fetus with no personality, will be avenged."

Recalled Holiday Toys

The U.S. Consumer Product Safety Commission recently released its annual list of recalled toys. Which items should parents avoid buying?

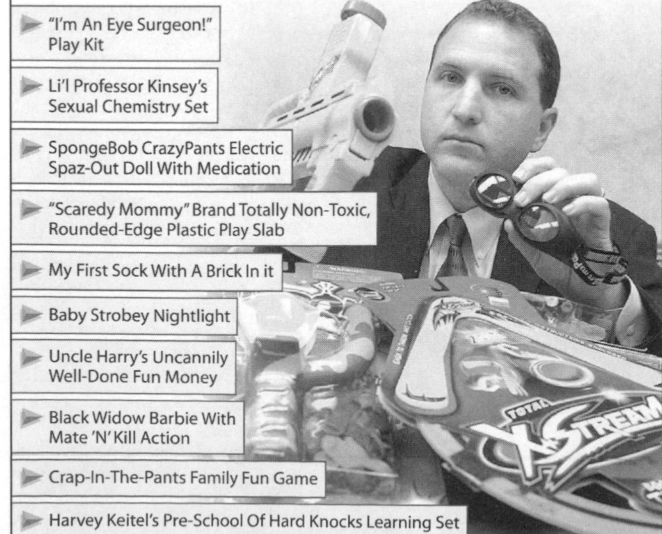

- "I'm An Eye Surgeon!" Play Kit
- Li'l Professor Kinsey's Sexual Chemistry Set
- SpongeBob CrazyPants Electric Spaz-Out Doll With Medication
- "Scaredy Mommy" Brand Totally Non-Toxic, Rounded-Edge Plastic Play Slab
- My First Sock With A Brick In it
- Baby Strobey Nightlight
- Uncle Harry's Uncannily Well-Done Fun Money
- Black Widow Barbie With Mate 'N' Kill Action
- Crap-In-The-Pants Family Fun Game
- Harvey Keitel's Pre-School Of Hard Knocks Learning Set

America's Finest News Source.™

Herman Ulysses Zweibel
Founder

T. Herman Zweibel
Publisher Emeritus
J. Phineas Zweibel
Publisher
Maxwell Prescott Zweibel
Editor-In-Chief

Where Are Today's Mattress-Sales Visionaries?

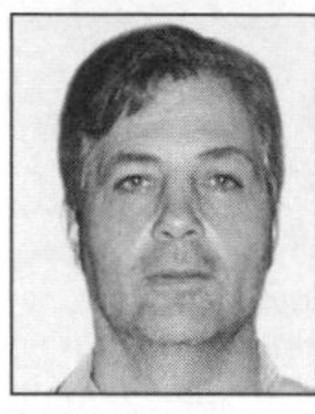

By Malcolm Farber

After many nights spent tossing and turning, I broke down and bought a new mattress. Is it just me—pardon the pun—or has bedding sales lost its spring? Seriously, though, where have all the mattress-sales visionaries gone?

Time was, mattress salesmen were touched by the holy fire. Loony Lenny the Mattress Czar, Crazy Mattress Benny, Wacky Willy the Spring King: These were the top men in the sleep game, and they neared the ineffable. Mad Dog Mike would get so deranged before a year-end closeout, he'd foam at the mouth. Back then, shoppers knew the mental shortcomings of the man on top meant big, big savings on Sealy, Simmons, Serta, and Stearns & Foster.

Just try to get a modern mattress salesman to scream at you. With these guys, it's all courtesy, predictable prices, and an organized showroom. Where's the pizzazz? Where's the push? Their idea of the hard sell is following you around the store or

Just try to get a modern mattress salesman to scream at you. With these guys, it's all courtesy, predictable prices, and an organized showroom.

handing you a pamphlet. The whole time I was shopping, I didn't have one salesman threaten to set himself on fire if I didn't buy a mattress from him in the next five seconds. Sure, in the '80s, you walked out of the store with a queen-size mattress when you wanted a twin, but you knew you had been in the presence of an artist. Not one of these jokers has the guts to make a crown out of bedsprings and dub himself the King of the Snooze.

The old timers were masters of the two M's: mattresses and the media. Commercials today focus on things like "wide selection" and "same-day delivery in many areas." Oh, how very responsible. Pardon me while I sip my latte and peruse the newspaper. Man, pros like Loony Lenny would stand in front of a blue screen and make you truly believe they'd be mauled by giant apes if they didn't sell every mattress in the store. When they got into a lab coat and commanded Pricezilla to crush that high mark-up, Pricezilla

Mattress sellers today may pay lip service to big holidays like President's Day, but what do they actually do? Give me Psycho Rick the Bedding Guru's Twelve Days of Mattress. Give me Institutionalized Wally's Box-Spring Rebellion Sale-A-Bration.

did as he was told.

Mattress sellers today may pay lip service to big holidays like President's Day, but what do they actually do? Give me Psycho Rick the Bedding Guru's Twelve Days of Mattress. Give me Institutionalized Wally's Box-Spring Rebellion Sale-A-Bration. Those guys didn't need the post office to close to put on the Uncle Sam suit. They did it for the thrill.

Remember Voice-Hearing Harry? The prices at his Mattress Barn were so low, it's a miracle he wasn't locked up. Now, that was a mattress store. So what if the mattress frames were recycled? You got what you paid for: an amazing experience. Sure, it wasn't pleasant when you got hit with a rubber chicken or pushed into a kiddy pool, but the brass band and the helium balloons made up for it.

Listen to me! Am I foolish to think there's still room for showmanship? Am I a throwback to a bygone era of a psychotic parachuting into a Mattress-Land parking lot wearing nothing but a wooden barrel and a smile? When people can just go online and buy a mattress with one click, why would they drive in heavy traffic to do business with a man in googly eyeglasses?

Maybe I'm just getting old, but I believe mattress salespeople should make giant spectacles of themselves on local TV, and when someone buys a king-size Serta mattress from them, they should toss in a box of steaks as a bonus. Unless a new generation comes in to fill the shoes of their forefathers, the art of mattress-selling is dead. Ø

Privacy Advocates Refuse To Release New Report

WASHINGTON, DC—Privacy-rights advocates from the American Privacy Rights Center refused to release a heavily researched report on the new Intelligence Reform and Terrorism Prevention Act of 2004 Monday.

"The report contains 475 pages of information about the ways in which the impending overhaul of U.S. intelligence and law-enforcement agencies will violate the privacy of individuals," APRC chief counsel and media director Michael Zeller said. "But it has a great deal of sensitive material that we'd rather not divulge. We feel it would be best to keep our findings safe from intruding eyes—government or otherwise."

Last month, Zeller openly criticized government intelligence measures for "extending the business of intelligence-gathering into the lives of private individuals" in the fourth paragraph of a confidential internal memo obtained by the press.

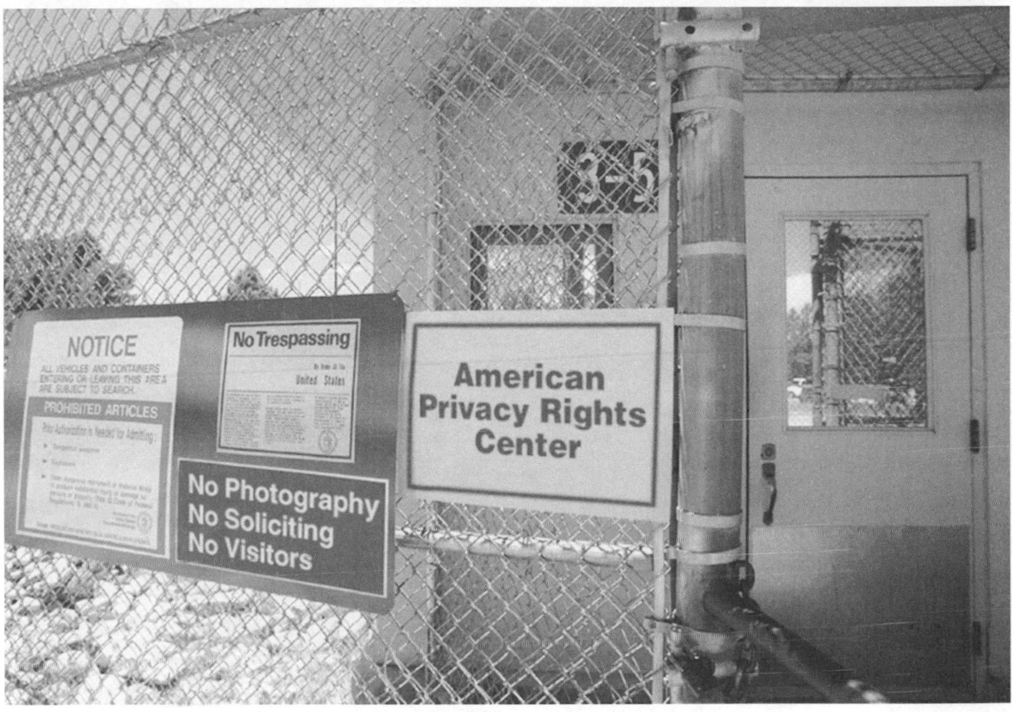

Above: The American Privacy Rights Center in Washington, DC.

"Wait...who is this?" Zeller added. "How did you get this number?"

Further attempts to reach Zeller at his office, on his cell phone, by e-mail, at his home, and at his children's school were unsuccessful.

Last month, Zeller openly criticized government intelligence measures for "extending the business of intelligence-gathering into the lives of private individuals" in the fourth paragraph of a confidential internal memo obtained by the press. In a conversation with a coworker later the same day, Zeller said "the government is taking advantage of the lack of explicit restrictions on the monitoring of electronic correspondence and cellphone communications in current right-to-privacy laws."

More recently, an APRC staffer criticized the civil-liberties board established by the intelligence-reform bill.

"The board was meant to serve as a safeguard against government abuses, but as outlined in the bill, it would have no legal authority to challenge measures taken by the government

see PRIVACY page 36

NEWS IN BRIEF

Actor Receives $25 Million For Everyman Role

HOLLYWOOD—Tom Hanks will reunite with director Steven Spielberg in Dreamworks' *Payne's Pride*, in which he will play the part of everyman John Hamilton Payne and receive $25 million for his efforts. "Tom is a man of the people," Spielberg said. "America loves him because he seems so approachable, and that's exactly what I told him last weekend over some Merlot from his vineyards." Spielberg added that Hanks is always a joy to work with because "he can really nail 'down to earth.'"

Scientific Journal Releases List Of Year's Top 100 Compounds

CAMBRIDGE, MA—*The Atlantic Journal Of Computational Chemistry* released its ranking of the top 100 compounds of the year Tuesday, with H2O topping the list, and C12H22O11, NaCl, CaCO3, and Fe2O3 appearing in the top 10. "Some people griped because hydrogen-, carbon-, and oxygen-based compounds made up more than 75 percent of the list," said Dr. Timothy Grant, one of 50 top scientists polled for the list. "But the influence these elements have on the chemical world cannot be denied." The list, which appeared in the magazine's December issue, has stirred up controversy among chemists for excluding the lesser-known but vital compound zinc sulfate heptahydrate.

Recently Mugged Friend A Racist All Of A Sudden

CHICAGO—Ever since being mugged by a black man, 28-year-old Caucasian Mark Weisner has become a racist, friends reported Monday. "I used to be more trusting, but I learned my lesson the hard way in October," Weisner said, alluding to the mugging. "Now I'm a lot more cautious around certain types, if you know what I mean." Weisner added that he has "no problem with Asian Americans."

Secretary Cracks Under Administration Of Third Raspberry Margarita

ARLINGTON HEIGHTS, IL—Wintrust Financial secretary Kerry Jorgenson finally succumbed to coworker Charlotte Franze's interrogation after the administration of a third raspberry margarita at Champ's Dugout Monday. "No, Helen wasn't really sick last week—she and her husband are in counseling," a tipsy Jorgenson told Franze after slurping up the last few drops of her Razzmatazz. "And Jeffrey in tech support? Queer as a $3 bill. He and his 'roommate' are taking a trip to Florence together." Coworkers announced plans to re-administer margaritas at some point in the future, to coax Jorgenson into confirming their suspicions that their supervisor Jack Doogan gets Botox injections.

Son Loved More Than Football, Less Than Playoff Football

ALLENTOWN, PA—Diehard Eagles fan Bill Ferris said Monday that he loves his 12-year-old son Rex more than football, excepting the thrilling playoff games, of course. "When I tell you I love my son more than football, you better believe I'm saying something important," said Ferris, a 38-year-old accountant. "I wouldn't think of missing Rex playing a shepherd in the church nativity scene this Sunday. That's because the Eagles clinched the NFC East, and probably home-field advantage, too." Ferris said he has yet to form a plan for next month when a playoff game overlaps with his son's band concert. ⌀

PHANTOM from page 31

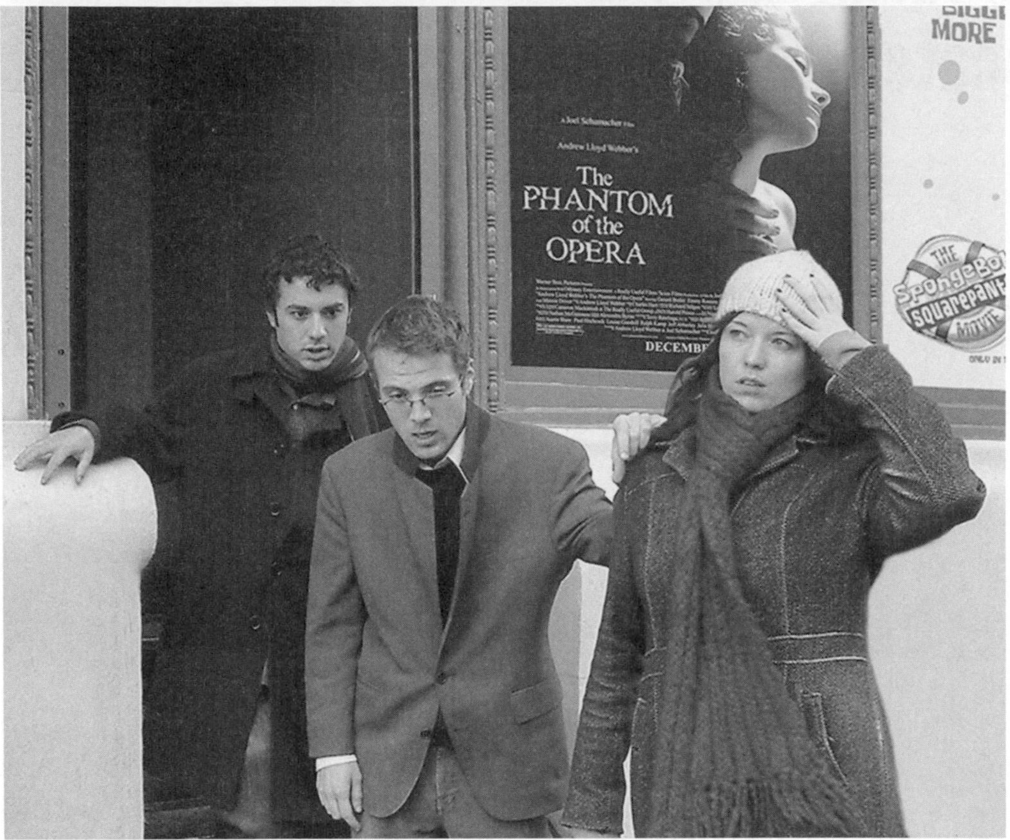

Above: Melodramatized moviegoers exit a theater in Chicago.

overweight receptionists, struggling fashion designers, and community-theater actors.

"PMSD sufferers walk through their days with the specter of an unnecessary musical number hanging over them like a mask," Lambert said. "The prelude is constantly playing in their unconscious minds, threatening to crescendo into exaggerated, choreographed action at any moment. Anything can set them off: a chandelier, a strain of saccharine music, a gaudy outfit."

According to Lambert, PMSD victims are vulnerable to further emotional manipulation.

"Those who have witnessed *Phantom* often tend to leave themselves open to additional emotional battery, whether in the form of another vapid musical or a book of heartwarming anecdotes," Lambert said. "Programs that appear contrived to healthy people appear heartbreakingly sad to PMSD sufferers. They sometimes sit and stare at the Hallmark Channel for hours on end."

Lambert urged loved ones to watch possible PMSD sufferers closely and seek professional help if necessary.

"It's impossible to know what your friends and loved ones are going through if you haven't witnessed the rapidly vacillating extremes of *Phantom*," said Dr. Harris Jones, a prominent New York psychiatrist who specializes in entertainment-related disorders. "Offer your support, but do not claim to understand the levels of treacle a PMSD sufferer has survived."

Post-melodramatic stress disorder was first identified in 1949, following the debut of the World War II-themed *South Pacific*. Though anecdotal evidence of PMSD mounted for the next four decades, the affliction was not studied at length until researchers at Cornell performed a systematic analysis of theatergoers returning from the 1989 opening of the Vietnam-era musical *Miss Saigon*.

In recent years, researchers have found that PMSD can result from any number of near-tragic dramas, be they live musical theater or televised soap opera. They found PMSD especially dangerous among individuals already suffering from disbelief suspension, aesthetic vacuity, or general mental insufficiency.

While PMSD isn't a new phenomenon, the magnitude of the current outbreak is unprecedented.

"This outbreak rivals the Broadway *Phantom* epidemic of 1988," said Dr. David Sussman, a psychiatrist at Beth Israel Medical Center in New York. "Many victims choose to relive the horrifying play season after season."

"And even if they don't see the play several times, the unfortunate fact is that those who have seen *Phantom* never forget their first time," Sussman added.

Boston resident Leo Wilson was forced by his girlfriend to see a preview of the film version of *Phantom*.

"And even if they don't see the play several times, the unfortunate fact is that those who have seen Phantom never forget their first time," Sussman added.

"I was led down a dark hallway. I found myself in a large room filled with rows of chairs all facing in the same direction," Wilson said. "I sat down, and I was subjected to a series of horrendously overwrought images. I was powerless to stop them. I cried out, but I was silenced by those around me and forced to watch for what seemed like hours."

After several days spent with the song "Think Of Me" playing over and over again in his head, Wilson sought psychiatric treatment.

"I don't blame any one aspect of the melodrama—the shallow characters, the unbelievable swings in emotion, the repellent score," Wilson said. "But I can't help regretting that there was no absolutely redeeming value to this atrocity. We all suffered for nothing. It's hard to come to terms with the fact that a human being would perpetrate three such unconscionable acts upon another human." Ø

DAUGHTER from page 31

dinner, right? I don't want you running out at the last minute and buying a dress with money you don't have, just because you forgot to pack something nice."

"It would make things so much easier on everybody if you'd just plan ahead," added Guzman, whose first priority is the well-being of her children. "I mean, think about what you're doing once in a while."

Within the first hours of her daughter's visit, Guzman attempted to help Nancy by noting that her job doesn't pay enough and observing that her wardrobe is "scruffy."

"You could be doing something better if you'd put your mind to it," said Guzman, who is simply worried about her daughter's future. "I have no idea why you stay at that place. You say you like it, but I'm concerned about how you manage to get by."

"She gets involved because she cares," Nancy said.

Guzman observed that Nancy's hair looks better when she cuts it short, that drinking coffee is staining her teeth, and that men don't like women who curse. The mother cared enough to help Nancy plan her visit with her high-school friend Barbara Legstrom, as well.

"Are you going to try to see Barbara this year?" Guzman asked Sunday evening. "Because if you're going to have to run all the way across town again, you have to think about it ahead of time. You're here for such a short visit, and we have so many family obligations."

Nancy told her mother that she and Barbara would probably go out for drinks some night after everyone else had gone to bed.

"Well, don't wear your nice clothes to the bars," Guzman said helpfully. "You always reek of smoke after you go out with her. You don't want to smell like an ashtray for brunch at your brother's, do you?"

Nancy said she understands that her mother only wants what's best for her.

"Mom says she gets involved because she cares," Nancy said. "Apparently, she lies awake at night worrying about me and my brothers."

Although the topic has not yet been broached, Nancy said she expects that her mother will want to discuss her July 2003 breakup with long-term boyfriend Keith Solanas.

"She usually brings Keith up when

see DAUGHTER page 35

WEED from page 31

hearts of the hapless roommates. For, these four lucky friends had a guardian angel watching over them, and this is the heartwarming true story of how the weed delivery guy saved Christmas.

"Dude, I was so bummed when I found out my stupid supervisor scheduled me for first shift Christmas Eve," said Patrick Moynihan, 26, a "part-time musician and full-time phone drone." "I was like, 'Come on, I *gotta* go to Milwaukee to see my old man and watch the game.' He was like, 'Sorry man, life's rough. You should've remembered to ask off.'"

"It's not like Milwaukee's so great," Moynihan added, "but it beats spending Christmas alone in my shithole apartment."

But, in a turn of events Moynihan described as "*X-Files*-type shit," each of his remaining roommates—first Dirk, then Kleist, and finally even White Jimmy—watched their Christmas plans come undone, leaving the four housemates together in Madison on the night before Christmas.

"I was supposed to go home with this chick and meet her parents," said Dirk Udell, 24, a part-time bicycle-store clerk and bassist. "But we totally got into this huge fight the night before, and she was like, 'Sayonara, sweetheart.' Then Kleist got wasted and slept through his flight, and White Jimmy's credit card got turned down at the bus station, because he maxed it out on that amp he bought."

Individual heartbreak turned into collective joy when the roommates realized that they could have their own Christmas... together.

"We said, 'Fuck it,'" James "White Jimmy" Gaines said. "We were like, 'We have all the ingredients for old-time holiday cheer right here: some brews, the tube, and the Chinese place across the street that never closes on holidays.' We even cleaned the living room and washed the dishes. Then fate threw a monkey wrench."

"Dudes, it's a *no go*," Kleist said before delivering the bad news. "Carl totally flaked on us. He left for Michigan already."

The roommates' faces turned ashen: There would be no Christmas weed.

"I was, like, 'No way, man!'" Moynihan said. "Kleist even called all our friends, trying to find someone who was holding, but everyone was out of town. We tried to drum up some Christmas cheer, but there was no escaping the sad reality that the four of us had all this time to hang out, but no pot."

> **"We were so psyched when he answered his cell on the second ring!"**

Disconsolate, the roommates went through the motions of scraping the bowl for resin. But, in their hearts, they knew that it wasn't enough to get them high. Peering out of the fourth-floor window, gazing at the municipal streetlight decorations below, they felt that Christmas had deserted them... Or had it?

"That's when Jimmy—I think it was Jimmy. It could've been Kleist—wait, was it Jimmy or Kleist?" Moynihan said. "Aw, never mind—whoever it was looked up and said, 'Hey Dirk, why don't we try the number that that guy who worked at Big Mike's Subs gave you?'"

After searching high and low with the help of his three determined roommates, Udell located the piece of paper containing the phone number given to him by his old stoner buddy Javier.

"Javier told me he hardly knows the dealer, but the guy always has really great shit and he comes right over," Udell said. "Kleist was all like, 'Who in their right mind is gonna be out delivering weed on Christmas Eve?' But I was like, 'What would it hurt to give the number a try?'"

"We were so psyched when he answered his cell on the second ring!" Udell added.

The roommates busily prepared for the weed guy's arrival by laying out Chips Ahoy cookies on paper plates, loading disks into the CD changer, and lovingly placing a new screen in the bong. All the while, they listened for the crunch-crunch-crunch of his footsteps on the snowy walk and the jingle-jangle-jingle of the Apt. 4-D buzzer. They even put the porch light on for the dude, so he'd feel welcome. And when, in less than an hour, the weed delivery guy showed up bearing a gift more precious than gold, the roommates' hearts soared with joy.

"That stranger brought us something so much better than any store-bought gift," Moynihan said. "I don't know his name—it's considered bad form to ask—but he taught us that Christmas wishes can come true, if you believe."

And so it was that the weed delivery guy—hardworking, dedicated, and discreet—saved Christmas in the nick of time.

"We may not have had a big tree and all that," Moynihan said. "And there wasn't eggnog dusted with nutmeg, 'cause the only time we ever had any nutmeg in the house was the time we tried to trip on it. Not recommended, by the way. But we had a happy Christmas all the same."

It wasn't long before all through the house, not a creature was stirring up off the couch. The boys opened the baggie and packed a bowl with delight, murmuring, "Happy Christmas, weed delivery guy. You did us one right." ⊘

Above: The residents of Apt. 4-D celebrate Christmas together.

DAUGHTER from page 31

other people are around," Nancy said. "I don't mind people knowing about my personal life. She just asks if I still talk to him. She always says she has no idea what could've possibly gone wrong. Then she tells me she feels bad for me because she knows how hard it is to find a good guy these days, especially for someone who's almost 30."

Although her father Thomas tends to be less emotionally open than his wife, Nancy said she knows that he cares, too.

"Dad doesn't get as involved in my life," Nancy said. "But he does always say, 'Listen to your mother.' And he'll check to make sure that my car is clean and my trunk has antifreeze in it if Mom tells him to."

Nancy said that when she moved away to go to Boston College in 1994, both she and her mother had hoped that there would be less need for parental guidance. This hope soon faded.

"I thought that when I moved so far away, Mom wouldn't be so much a part of my life," Nancy said. "But I still find myself relying on her. Like, if I talk about going to Ikea, she tells me that I have too much clutter and that's probably why Keith left me. That sort of thing."

Nancy acknowledged that her mother is right to say she has a temper.

"Every once in awhile, I even blow up at Mom," Nancy said. "Like, once, I told her that eyeliner doesn't make me look like a hooker and that she shouldn't talk to me that way. Well, after she ran to her room crying, I realized I shouldn't have snapped at her."

Nancy said she has been the object of her mother's constructive belittlement since she was 4 years old, when Guzman told her it was unladylike to run in a Sunday dress.

"Even if I land a million-dollar job, marry a great man, and lose 20 pounds, I know my mom will always be there for me," Nancy said. "It's like Mom says: No matter what, there's always room for improvement." ⊘

COMMUNITY VOICES

My Beloved, Would You Do Me The Honor Of Becoming The Fourth Mrs. Charles Ballard?

My dearest Rachel, we've been through so much in the past eight months. We've loved together, laughed together, and grown ever closer. You are everything I look for in a new wife: beautiful, intelligent, strong-willed, and creative. I can't imagine a life without you. So now, down on bended knee, my beloved, I ask you: Will you make me the happiest man alive by doing me the honor of becoming the fourth Mrs. Charles Ballard?

By Charles Ballard

I only told you about Veronica and Patrice? Well, I'm sorry. Janice and I got an annulment after a week, so I usually don't count her. Please, I was so young. It's ancient history. But when I look into your eyes, Rachel, I see our future. I see us living a perfect life in the house that I got from Veronica in the settlement. Unless Veronica gets a better lawyer, I have no doubt that you and I will spend many fine years there.

I know you want to raise a family, and I can't wait for you to meet Travis, Jason, Andrew, Mike, and Charles Jr. The boys are going to love you. And, my darling, as you know, one of the things I value most about our relationship is that we can be honest with each other. That's why I feel comfortable telling you now that I had a vasectomy when I was 35. Patrice insisted on it.

Yeah, she was nuts.

I can honestly say that these eight months have shown me what true love can be. It doesn't have to be predictable and boring like Patrice, or contentious and competitive like Veronica. And there is no reason for love to be like try-to-run-you-down-with-a-riding-lawn-mower-because-you-forgot-to-return-a-video Janice, but I'd rather not talk about that. Our love is on a completely different level. You are the woman I want to spend the rest of my life with, the fourth and final Mrs. Charles Ballard. I mean, I'm really hoping it turns out that way.

I want to take you away, my love. Have you ever dreamt of a glorious, two-week honeymoon in the Greek Isles? I've heard it's very beautiful, very romantic, better than Paris. Paris was way too crowded—it's not as great for honeymooning as everyone says. Oh, and obviously, Vegas is out. Yeesh, Vegas. That was a bust. Seriously, I think the Greek Isles is the way to go. Or we could go somewhere else I've never honeymooned before, like Cancun. Why don't you just think about it?

If you accept my humble offer, I will make you so happy. I'll do everything in my power to make sure you never regret that you married me. It's much too painful when that happens.

By the way, I know you wanted a big church wedding, but I really can't get married in a Catholic church again after Veronica. It's not so bad, though.

I know you want to raise a family, and I can't wait for you to meet Travis, Jason, Andrew, Mike, and Charles Jr. The boys are going to love you. And, my darling, as you know, one of the things I value most about our relationship is that we can be honest with each other. That's why I feel comfortable telling you now that I had a vasectomy when I was 35.

You wouldn't believe how nice a civil ceremony can be if you put some effort into it. And not to keep harping on this, but I really wish you would reconsider a small wedding with close family and a few friends. Take it from me, the big weddings really aren't worth the hassle and expense.

I just love you so much. Our relationship is so strong—stronger than the other marriages. You complete me in ways my other wives never did. We're always growing together—which is essential, believe me. By now I kinda have it all down. Yup, I think I've seen just about every mistake a wife can make. And I'm better for it! Don't you see? The path of marriage and divorce, marriage and divorce, marriage and divorce has led me to you, at last. And ending up with you has made the journey worth it.

So, Rachel Montesanto, will you make me the happiest man on earth and become Mrs. Charles Ballard *numero quattro*? ⌀

HOROSCOPES

Your Horoscope

By Lloyd Schumner Sr.
Retired Machinist and
A.A.P.B.-Certified Astrologer

Aries: (March 21–April 19)
Financial success looms large in your future, perched to topple over and crush you and everything you love.

Taurus: (April 20–May 20)
There is nothing in your world more satisfying than a good taco and a can of beer, but then, there is almost nothing in your world at all.

Gemini: (May 21–June 21)
Post-coital cigarettes are one thing, but the pre- and mid-coitus cigarettes you're asking those men to smoke are really starting to annoy them.

Cancer: (June 22–July 22)
Death by firing squad has a certain desolate nobility, but it'll be ruined when the inept, drunken Australians fail to hit you above your waist with the first nine volleys.

Leo: (July 23–Aug. 22)
Your fear of terrorist attacks is just the thing to get you out of getting married and raising a family.

Virgo: (Aug. 23–Sept. 22)
There's probably something in your life that can't be explained in a single-panel cartoon, but so far, those *New Yorker* guys have hit the nail on the head every time.

Libra: (Sept. 23–Oct. 23)
You'll briefly be the centerpiece of all creation when the guiding force of the universe remembers that it hasn't hit anyone with lightning in a long time.

Scorpio: (Oct. 24–Nov. 21)
You've explained over and over that you aren't Siamese twins, but unfortunately for you, your surgical team has "separation" on the brain.

Sagittarius: (Nov. 22–Dec. 21)
You'll wish you'd bought better shoes when your smelly, worn-out, charred sneakers are featured in a "Don't Smoke At The Pumps" PSA.

Capricorn: (Dec. 22–Jan. 19)
You'll launch a new street fashion when you find a way to embed diamonds in an otherwise unremarkable pair of breasts.

Aquarius: (Jan. 20–Feb. 18)
Don't worry: You aren't the first guy to fall in love with a fast-talking, gold-digging knockout, you derivative hack.

Pisces: (Feb. 19–March 20)
You've always said that if you had to do it all over again, you wouldn't change a thing, so expect the eternal return of a morass of mediocrity followed by an untimely death.

PRIVACY from page 33

against private citizens in the name of security," said Julie Grafney, a privacy-rights lawyer who asked that her name not be used. "Our organization prepared a list of recommendations for more-adequate provisions. Unfortunately, the items on that list are confidential."

Asked if the report contains any information about the new federal standards for state-issued drivers' licenses, Grafney said the APRC's position on the matter is "not open to discussion—not now, not ever."

American Civil Liberties Union spokesman Bob Kearney said privacy is "one of the most important domestic issues facing Americans today."

"Citizens should be armed with the information they need to protect their private lives," Kearney said. "That is why the ACLU is attempting to force the APRC to release this report by bringing a Freedom of Information Act suit against the organization."

Added Kearney: "What vital information about privacy are they trying to hide? The American public has a right to know."

The APRC has previously compiled detailed reports on skin-implantable medical-record microchips, "black boxes" for automobiles, and GPS-enabled cell phones, but none of the documents were released to the public. Nonetheless, each came under public scrutiny. Hackers posted the first on the Internet, portions of the second were recovered from the APRC's garbage, and the notes for the third were seized during an FBI raid. ⌀

"We feel it would be best to keep our findings safe from intruding eyes—government or otherwise," Zeller said.

the ONION®

VOLUME 41 ISSUE 01 AMERICA'S FINEST NEWS SOURCE™ 6–12 JANUARY 2005

2004: A LOOK BACK AT THE YEAR'S TOP STORIES

NEWS

Non-Priest Arrested On Charges Of Child Molestation

see NATION page 12B

Newlywed Britney Spears Hangs Bloody Sheet In Window For Reporters

see PEOPLE page 13E

Christopher Reeve Still Paralyzed In Heaven

see PEOPLE page 7E

STATshot

A look at the numbers that shape your world.

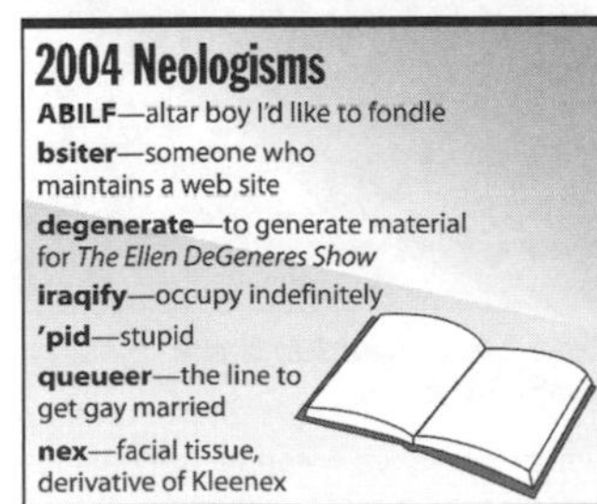

2004 Neologisms

ABILF—altar boy I'd like to fondle
bsiter—someone who maintains a web site
degenerate—to generate material for *The Ellen DeGeneres Show*
iraqify—occupy indefinitely
'pid—stupid
queueer—the line to get gay married
nex—facial tissue, derivative of Kleenex

WORLD

Russia Reiterates Zero-Tolerance Policy For Terrorists, Hostages

MOSCOW (Sept. 3)—In response to the ongoing hostage situation at a middle school in the town of Beslan in North Ossetia, Russian Prime Minister Vladimir Putin firmly reiterated his nation's hard-line policy against terrorists and their hostages Tuesday.

"Russia does not tolerate terrorism," Putin announced at a press conference. "We deal with terrorists swiftly and completely. This is a warning to terrorists, hostages, rescue workers,

see RUSSIA page 41

Above: Russian troops prepare to storm the school.

SOCIETY

Gay Marriage Proponents Hope To Send Message To Religious Right Before Election

Above: Two gay marriage proponents protest in Washington, DC.

BOSTON (Aug. 11)—With the presidential election approaching, gay rights advocates are working in Massachusetts and across the nation to bring national attention to the issue of same-sex marriage.

"This election year, we want to make sure everybody hears us loud and clear: Marriage is a civil right owed to all couples—gay, straight, or otherwise," said Mary Kleibold of the Boston-based advocacy group The Future Belongs To Us. "This year, the nation's gays and lesbians will be sending a clear message to the religious right: You can no longer ignore us."

Proponents of gay marriage have

see GAY MARRIAGE page 40

CRIME

Poll: Americans Feel Safer With Martha Stewart In Jail

WASHINGTON, DC (Oct. 12)—According to a poll released by the Pew Research Center Monday, Americans "feel safer" with Martha Stewart in prison.

"Martha Stewart is a menace to society," said Jolene Lim, a receptionist from Baton Rouge, LA. "She sold nearly 4,000 shares of ImClone on an insider tip, then alleged her innocence in her own magazine. Thank God

see STEWART page 41

Above: Martha Stewart, who is now safely behind bars.

THE YEAR AT A GLANCE

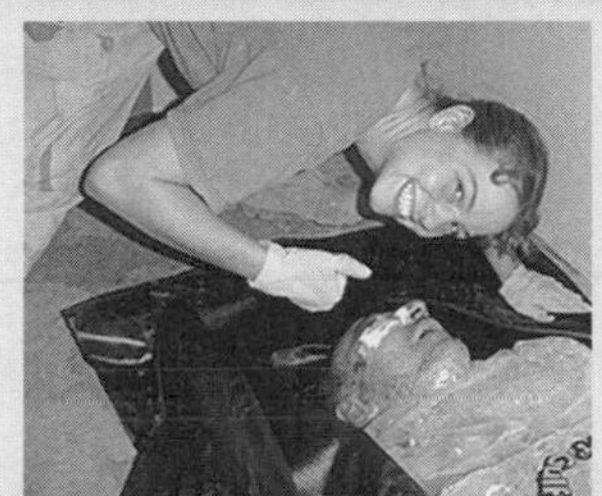

Abu Ghraib Inside Joke Lost On Rest Of World

see INTERNATIONAL page 15E

Nation Delighted By Rich Ass Who Fires People

see ENTERTAINMENT page 6G

OBITUARIES INSIDE

Old Bastard, Dirty Bastard, Dirty Old Bastard, Ol' Dirty Bastard

see OBITUARIES page 7H

A Polarized Nation

Many people say the nation became even more politically polarized in 2004. What do *you* think?

Cory Shade
Parking Attendant

"Come on. The nation hasn't experienced a moment of unity in decades, except for the 'who shot J.R.?' craze and those two weeks in September 2001."

Frankin Stedder
Director

"Yeah. Sheesh—*women!*"

Duane Segar
Systems Analyst

"Our nation will never be healed so long as those redneck rubes in flyover land refuse to listen to reason, and continue to vote for who they want."

Karen Anderson
Cellist

"Yes, the rift between the left-leaning centrist moderate Republicans and the right-leaning ultra conservative Republicans grows ever wider."

Tom Knight
Plumbers Assistant

"I got this funny e-mail about the red and blue states. I can't remember exactly what it said, but it was funny in that poignant sort of way."

Jill Karls
Nurse

"Polarized sounds like one of those fancy liberal words. Why don't you just say 'right' and 'wrong'?"

Lesser-Known Celebrity Trials

The year brought a number of celebrity trials, but few received as much attention as those of Michael Jackson and Martha Stewart. What were some of 2004's lesser-known celebrity trials?

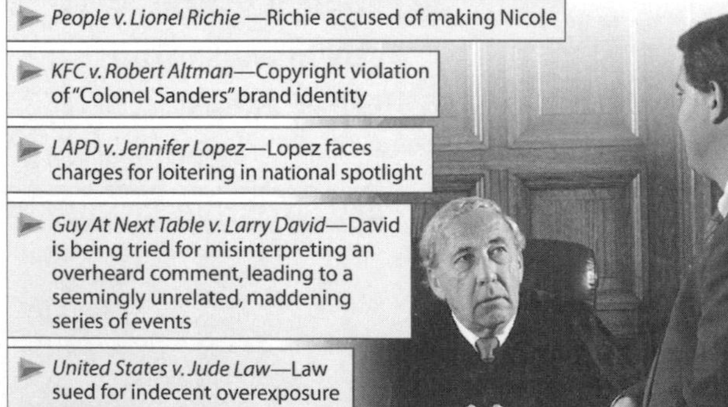

- *People v. Lionel Richie* —Richie accused of making Nicole
- *KFC v. Robert Altman*—Copyright violation of "Colonel Sanders" brand identity
- *LAPD v. Jennifer Lopez*—Lopez faces charges for loitering in national spotlight
- *Guy At Next Table v. Larry David*—David is being tried for misinterpreting an overheard comment, leading to a seemingly unrelated, maddening series of events
- *United States v. Jude Law*—Law sued for indecent overexposure
- *Sol Greenberg v. Mel Gibson*—Gibson is accused of throwing a Bible at Greenberg, a production assistant on *The Passion Of The Christ*
- *Muscular Dystrophy Association v. Barry Bostwick*—Bostwick held for unspecified charges in charity jail; eventually released when $250 bail was raised
- *Iowa Pork Suppliers Inc. v. Emeril Lagasse*—Lagasse charged with shoplifting two hogs

America's Finest News Source.™

Herman Ulysses Zweibel
Founder

T. Herman Zweibel
Publisher Emeritus
J. Phineas Zweibel
Publisher
Maxwell Prescott Zweibel
Editor-In-Chief

Above: The 2004 champion non-Yankees celebrate after the final out of Game 4.

Yankees Lose World Series

NEW YORK (Oct. 27)—Many baseball fans were disappointed Wednesday when the New York Yankees, 26-time world champions and the highest-paid team in baseball, did not win the 2004 World Series.

"I really thought they were going to pull this one off in the end," Joe Oliver said, speaking from the Midtown oyster bar where he watched the final game with a group of fellow Yankees fans. "But it just wasn't in the cards. At end, the Yankees didn't even make a single run the entire final game. They didn't even get on base."

Added Oliver: "In many ways, this is worse than going to the Series and then losing it, like we did last year."

Owner George Steinbrenner has vowed to rebuild the team for next season by wooing the top players away from the team that won the Fall Classic, a process he said will begin just as soon as someone tells him which team won the Fall Classic.

Threat Of Catching Olympic Fever At All-Time Low

COLORADO SPRINGS, CO (June 13)—U.S. Olympic Committee Chief Executive Jim Scherr announced Thursday that the risk of contracting Olympic Fever, the virulent international strain of athletic obsession that sweeps the nation every four years, has dropped to a historic low.

"The once-infectious strain is no longer considered contagious," Scherr said. "This is largely because of a years-long immunization campaign in which Americans were exposed to related strains, such as NFL Fever, March Madness, and the NASCAR Immunodeficiency Virus. As a result, most American sports fans have built up powerful immunities. Just look at the once-menacing NHL Pandemic, which has been completely eradicated as of this year."

> **"The once-infectious strain is no longer considered contagious," Scherr said.**

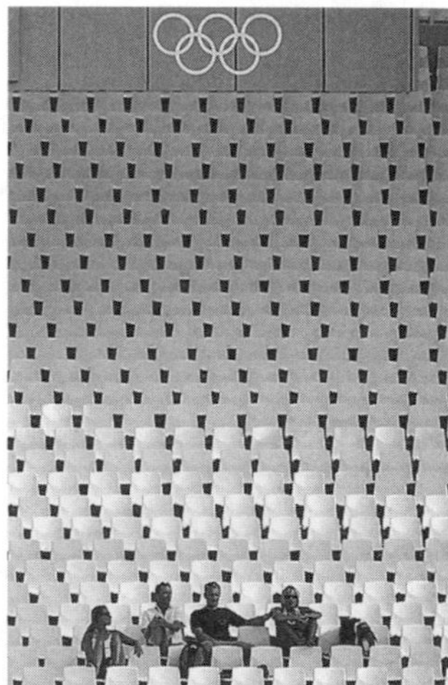
Above: Spectators watch an Olympic event in Athens.

According to Scherr, even children under the age of 12, a group once extremely susceptible to the fever, have been largely unaffected in recent years.

Scherr warned that Olympic Fever, which still affects hundreds of thousands in developing nations, could re-emerge in America if New York City carries out its plan to build a sports complex on the disease-infested shores of the Hudson River by 2012.

WAR ON TERRORISM

WMDs Found

Nuclear-Weapons Programs Discovered In North Korea, Iran

TEHRAN, IRAN (June 19)—The U.S. military's long search for weapons of mass destruction ended Wednesday when state officials in North Korea and Iran admitted to having nuclear-weapons programs.

"Our uranium-enrichment program is part of our plan to make Iran a nuclear state," Iranian foreign minister Kamal Kharazi said. "The U.S. wishes to remove nuclear capabilities from our hands as a way of achieving their ultimate goal: the collapse of the ruling Islamic establishment."

North Korean Vice-Foreign Minister Paek Nam Sum said North Korea resumed its plutonium-reprocessing program as a part of its plan to produce nuclear weapons.

"The United States is correct: Weapons of mass destruction are falling into the hands of their enemies," Paek said.

"The United States is correct: Weapons of mass destruction are falling into the hands of their enemies," Paek said. "My country has been reprocessing plutonium ever since the U.S. withdrew from an aid agreement after accusing North Korea of enriching uranium. Consider the situation highly destabilized."

Paek's statements echoed those of Mohamed ElBaradei, director general of the IAEA, who said several months ago that he believed North Korea may have built between four and six nuclear bombs.

Secretary of State Colin Powell expressed relief that the long and difficult hunt for WMDs is finally over.

"These discoveries show us that the U.S. was right all along—dangerous nations do harbor nuclear intentions," Powell said. "Given our suspicions that hardline elements within the Iranian regime were in league with senior al-Qaeda officials, the invasion of Iraq has finally been vindicated." ⊘

Above: Missiles capable of transporting nuclear warheads discovered in Iran (top) and North Korea.

OUR PRESIDENT IN 2004

Bush Celebrates Millionth Utterance Of 'Lessons Of Sept. 11'

NEW YORK (Sept. 3)—The already jubilant mood of the Republican National Convention was given a further boost Thursday night when, during his closing address at Madison Square Garden, President Bush uttered the phrase "the lessons of Sept. 11" for the one-millionth time. "The American people have risen to the challenges of the past three years, working tirelessly to ensure that the world will never forget...the lessons of Sept. 11," Bush said and outstretched his arms as balloons and confetti rained down on the delegates, whose deafening cheers lasted nearly five minutes. To make the event possible, Bush crammed hundreds of references to the "lessons of Sept. 11" into campaign speeches during the days leading up to the speech, sometimes simply chanting the four words repeatedly for several minutes.

Bush Unveils New Blind-Faith-Based Initiatives

COLUMBUS, OH (Sept. 27)—Seeking to broaden his appeal among undecided voters, President Bush unveiled a new set of blind-faith-based initiatives during a campaign stop in the battleground state of Ohio Sunday. According to a senior staff member, the sweeping initiatives—which address such complex matters as climate change, the faltering economy, and challenges to American security at home and abroad—are founded on the unquestioned assumption that the Bush Administration will "take care of everything." "My blind-faith initiatives are far-reaching, and like many large issues, they are simple," Bush said. "I call upon all Americans to surrender any doubts they may have about my record. After all, naysaying is no substitute for real governance." Officials from the newly created Office Of Blind-Faith-Based Initiatives were at church and unavailable for comment. ⊘

Bush Vows To Put Man On Moon Before It Disappears At End Of Month

WASHINGTON, DC (Jan. 14)—To revive U.S. interest in manned space exploration, President Bush called on NASA Wednesday to put an astronaut on the moon before it vanishes at the month's end. "The moon has already shrunk to nearly a quarter of its size," Bush said in his speech at NASA headquarters. "That means we have less than a week to move. But I do believe America has the strength, determination, and old-fashioned know-how to get a man atop the moon before it disappears altogether." The president went on to propose the construction of a lunar capsule that could land on a concave surface.

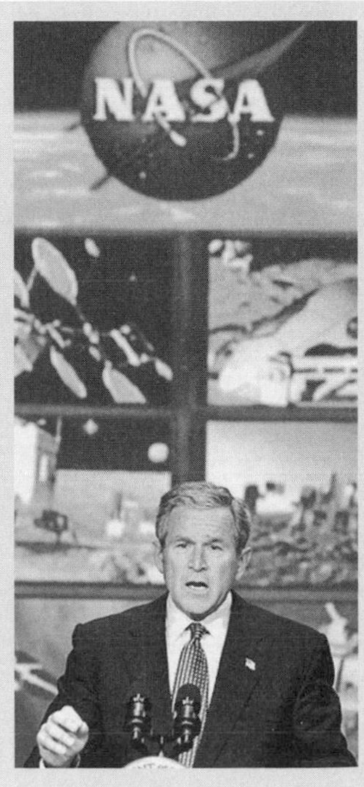

Obesity, Obesity Reports On The Rise

ALBANY, NY (Nov. 14)—Americans have never been more aware of the dangers of weight gain, nor have they ever weighed so much, according to a SUNY-Binghamton study released Monday.

"In 1989, Americans were exposed to 1.8 reports on obesity each week and were an average of five pounds overweight," study director Marilyn Fleder said. "Today, the average

"The average American is nearly 10 pounds overweight and sees or reads at least four reports on the obesity epidemic each week," Fleder said.

American is nearly 10 pounds overweight and sees or reads at least four reports on the obesity epidemic each week. If the trend continues unchecked, Americans will weigh 17 pounds more, and network news shows will devote a daily minimum of three minutes of airtime to obesity issues by 2010."

Fleder blamed the dual trend on Americans' increasingly sedentary lifestyles.

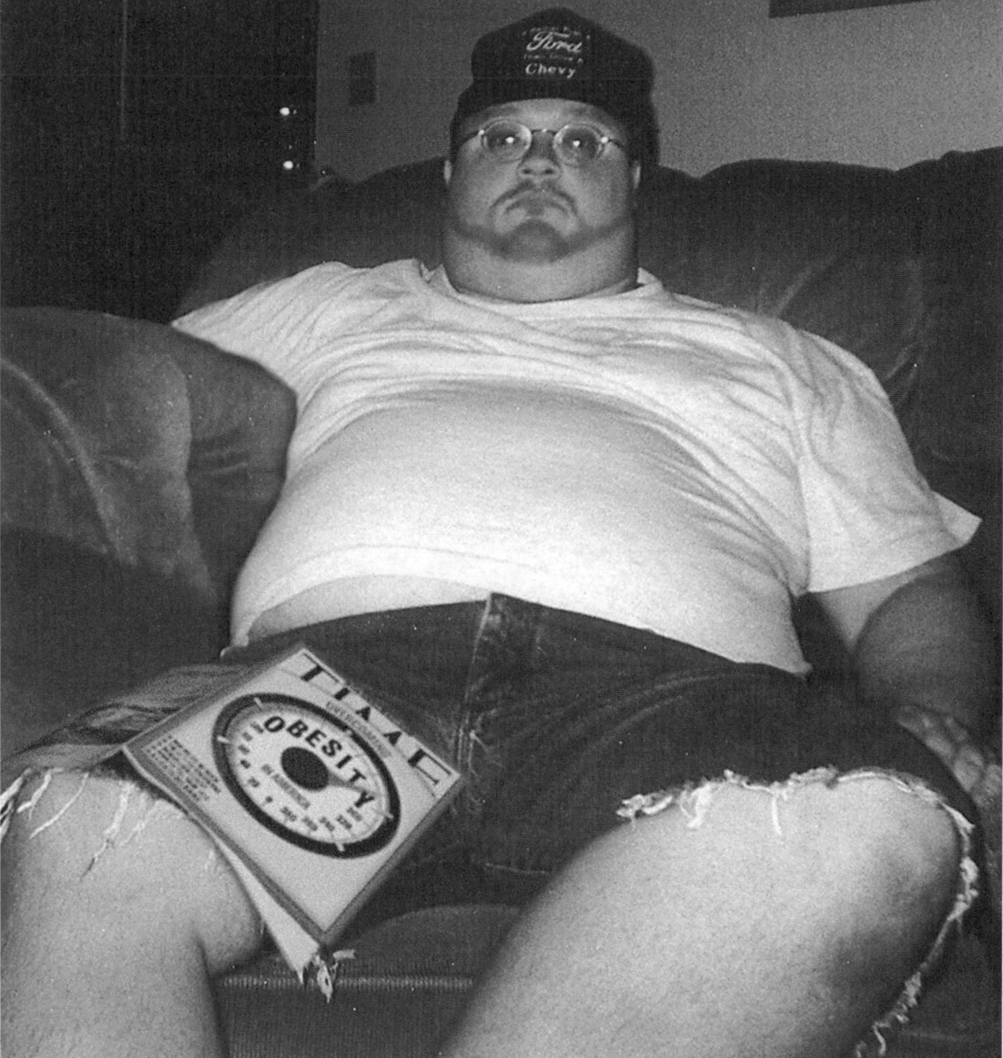

Above: An obese obesity-report reader.

"Americans get their news about obesity by watching television or reading magazines and newspapers, which force the reader or viewer to assume a physically passive position," Fleder said. "This contributes to weight gain, which is then dutifully reported by the media. It's a vicious cycle."

Fleder said the trend could reverse itself if Americans had healthier diets and became more physically active.

"While reports have ballooned to hundreds of pages in length, there is hope," Fleder said. "If Americans improve their eating and exercise habits, obesity reports could quickly begin to drop in size, shedding as many as 20 to 30 pages a year, until they disappear altogether."

Fleder added that the media could also play a useful role by limiting obesity coverage to the later prime-time hours between 9 and 11 p.m., after the dinner hour. ⌀

GAY MARRIAGE from page 37

reason to be optimistic. Earlier this year, state judges in Massachusetts and California ruled to permit same-sex unions, and President Bush's subsequent proposal for a constitutional ban on gay marriage was voted down by Congress.

Invigorated by victories like these, Bill Yaeger, a lawyer and co-chairman of the activist group Pride Now, said his group "plans to throw a spotlight on the gay-marriage issue" before November.

"My group plans to use the next election to galvanize support for our cause," Yaeger said. "Every concerned voter in America needs to realize that the gay-rights movement is growing larger every day. It's time to sit up, take notice, and do something."

Yaeger said he does not expect the battle to legalize gay marriage to be easy.

"My group plans to use the next election to galvanize support for our cause," Yaeger said.

"Even if we don't win any serious legislative battles, we'll get people talking," Yaeger said. "The issue might help to mobilize political forces in America. I just have the feeling that we're onto something big right now, and that this year will go down in history as the year the tide turned for gay rights."

Columbus, OH, activist Jerry Farmer said "it's ridiculously outdated" to deny gays the right to file joint tax returns, receive family health-insurance benefits, and enjoy inheritance rights.

"Many politicians are frightened by the taboo topic of gay marriage," Farmer said. "But we're not going to let the bigotry of a handful of conservative policy makers silence us. It's time to let America tell Washington what it thinks about gay men and women. We're not living in the dark ages anymore. From Oregon to Ohio, it's time for the people to stand up and be heard."

Farmer said the issue could motivate more Americans to vote.

"The gay marriage issue might even show up on the ballots as a referendum in some states," Farmer said. "If so, we may influence voters in ways we never imagined."

"Even if the gay-marriage issue only motivates a few thousand people to come out to the polls, we'll be able to look back and know we've done our part to influence this country," Farmer added.

San Francisco gay options trader Barry Dilham supports the idea of making same-sex marriage a larger part of the national dialogue.

"Conservatives don't want us to be heard," Dilham said. "But, if we keep up the pressure, the religious right will be forced to acknowledge that this controversial issue is out there and respond." ⌀

RUSSIA from page 37

bystanders...all those involved in terrorist activities: You will be shown no mercy."

The situation in the southern Russian town of Beslan began Wednesday when armed multinational terrorists stormed a small school on the first day of classes, taking more than 1,200 teachers, children, and parents hostage.

Now, on the third day of the conflict, Russian security forces await the command to terminate the standoff.

Terrorists want to destroy Russia, but we will not let them. Make no mistake: Terrorists—and those who happen to be near them—will meet with a swift, terrible end."

"The Russian government will not accede to the terrorists' demands, nor will it be swayed by hostage pleas for mercy," Putin said. "Without the parents and children as hostages, the terrorists would be powerless. Anyone who assists terrorist monsters—in any capacity—is an enemy to the Russian people and will be treated as such."

Putin first publicly announced the country's anti-terrorist stance in October 2002, when 40 Chechen terrorists seized a crowded Moscow theater, taking more than 700 hostages and demanding the withdrawal of Russian forces from Chechnya. In accordance with Russia's zero-tolerance policy, government forces from Russia's elite Spetsnaz commando unit of the Federal Security Service pumped an aerosol anaesthetic into the theater, killing all of the terrorists and 128 of the hostages.

"The Moscow theater crisis was a perfect example of my willingness to do everything necessary to battle terrorists," Putin said. "As prime minister, my first job is to keep the Russian people safe. Terrorists want to destroy Russia, but we will not let them. Make no mistake: Terrorists—and those who happen to be near them—will meet with a swift, terrible end."

Although Russian laws limit press coverage of terrorist incidents, citizens who do know about the ongoing crisis have applauded Putin's hardline stance.

"To ensure the stability of our country, we need to take a firm stance against terrorists," said Tamara Dmitriyevna, a professor at Rostov State University. "Yes, we can play intellectual games and draw parallels between Putin and Stalin, but any citizen who is not currently being held hostage will tell you that there is an openness and an honesty in Russia that never existed before. Citizens are not being killed secretly anymore."

Although many international leaders have criticized the Russian government's position, President Bush released a statement commending Putin for his leadership in the war on terror.

"The enemies of freedom have no friend in Vladimir Putin," Bush's statement read. "He goes to any means necessary to protect his people and make the world a safer place. As the world knows, you are either with us or with the terrorists. God help those who are with the terrorists."

THE WAR ON TERROR

Ashcroft Begins Crackdown On Rival Religious Folk Musicians

see CAT STEVENS page 19E

SOFT-BOILED EGG from page 14

amounts of blood. Passersby were amazed by the unusually large amounts of blood. Passersby were amazed by the unusually large amounts of blood. Passersby were amazed by the unusually large amounts of blood. Passersby were amazed by the unusually large amounts of blood. Passersby were amazed by the unusually large amounts of blood. Passersby were

If I were a vampire, would I be wearing this stupid fanny pack?

amazed by the unusually large amounts of blood. Passersby were amazed by the unusually large amounts of blood.Passersby were amazed by the unusually large amounts of blood.Passersby were amazed by the unusually large

see SOFT-BOILED EGG page 172

STEWART from page 37

she's behind bars. Now I can sleep soundly at night."

Lim added: "I just couldn't ever feel at ease when I knew she was out there obstructing justice and making false statements to federal officials. Even talking about it gives me the shivers."

"Martha Stewart avoided losses of $45,000 by selling that stock," Greene said. "$45,000! If they didn't put her in jail for that, people would've taken to the streets! Outraged citizens would have broken windows, overturned cars, and set fire to the courthouse."

Of the 2,500 people polled, 22 percent said they "felt safer" and 41 percent said they "felt extremely relieved" when Stewart began serving her five-month sentence at West Virginia's Alderson Prison.

"When I found out [Stewart] was behind a 10-foot-thick concrete wall, I heaved a huge sigh of relief," said Daniel McAllen, a jeweler from Newark, NJ. "If she were on the streets, who knows what sort of business maneuvering she'd be up to behind closed doors?"

"I have a family to think of," McAllen added.

Boston-area teacher Helen Greene said she had been "afraid to leave the house" before the verdict in Stewart's trial was announced.

"Martha Stewart avoided losses of $45,000 by selling that stock," Greene said. "$45,000! If they didn't put her in jail for that, people would've taken to the streets! Outraged citizens would have broken windows, overturned cars, and set fire to the courthouse."

Even citizens who said they were only vaguely familiar with the Stewart case reported feeling safer after her conviction.

"I don't know the technical aspects of it, but I know that Martha Stewart did something with the stock market," Chicago welder Marvin Manckowicz said. "I'm not sure if she was selling her own stock or someone else's, but I do know that everyone said it was wrong. I breathed easier when I found out she wasn't going to be doing any more of that again for five months."

Of those polled, 62 percent said the five-month sentence was inadequate, with 46 percent of those believing that Stewart should have been imprisoned for 10 years or longer, and 3 percent expressing the belief that she should have received a life sentence.

Prosecutor Karen Patton Seymour said that, in addition to the five-month prison sentence, Stewart has been sentenced to five months of home confinement and two years of probation.

"Even after she's out of prison, she'll be kept under close watch," Seymou[r] said. "No one is going to forget wh[at] she did."

HARVEY'S HOLLYWOOD

What A Year 2004 Was—For Entertainment!

There was a number on everyone's lips last year, and that number was **2004**. Who could blame them? It was a year big on surprises: thrills, love, laughter, and of course, entertainment. So let's take a trip down recent-memory lane to check out the big stories of last year!

The Outside Scoop
By Jackie Harvey

Politics are usually pretty boring, but they made for big, big, big entertainment in 2004. **Michael More**, who found fame trying to interview General Motors CEO **Roger Lodge** a few years ago, turned up the heat on Washington with **Fahrenheit 9-1-1**. Call the cops, because *9-1-1* "stole" the box office! It raked in more than $100 million, and it didn't even have **Julia Roberts**. Congratulations on the big money-maker, Mike! Even though you may have gone a little too far picking on the **president**, no one can deny that you put together a wild ride!

This year, there weren't any movies about animals.

Know what else was big? The man himself! I am talking about Jesus. Hunk-tor **Mel Gibsen** performed a miracle of his own, directing **The Last Passion of Christ**, which made more than $100 million without Julia Roberts or English. Who says that there are no surprises left in Hollywood?

People stuck on an island? Seen it! Twelve women vying for one unattached guy? Snore! A bunch of people stuck in a house while cameras follow their every move? Come on! With all this re-hashing of old ideas, it seemed like reality shows had run their course in '04, making reality junkies like me start to get the shakes. (Did anyone else have that dream where **Sharon Osbourne** is a baby with fangs, and she is climbing above your bed?) Thank goodness for a trio of shows that pumped some juice into the genre: **The Simple Life**, **The Apprentice**, and **The Swan**. These groundbreaking shows taught us some valuable lessons. For one, money can't buy happiness. And no matter how ambitious you are, you can always be fired, especially if you're black. And finally, if you're ugly, you should do something about it, even if you have to undergo plastic surgery on national television. But the biggest lesson? If you want a successful reality show, add **the word "the"** to the beginning of the title.

Just when you think you've seen the lowest people will go, something else comes along and surprises you. Of course, I am talking about **the British** and their recent remake of **Band Aid's** classic hit **"We Are The World."** Now, I know it's for charity and all, but a classic like "We Are The World" shouldn't be touched. How could anyone possibly recapture the magic of **Michael Jackson** and **Huey Lewis** singing to raise money to feed Africans? Hey UK, here's an idea: Why not write a new song for charity instead of stealing someone else's?

Christopher Reeves died. So did former Plantera guitarist **Dimestore Daryl**. **Martha Stewart** went to jail. **Cat Stephens** was deported. **Courtney Love** got drunk and hit a fan with a mic stand. And a basketball player was suspended for fighting. What has happened of the nation's heroes?

Tongues were wagging after "Did It Again" girl **Brittany Spears** got married not once, but twice! The first one didn't count because it was in Vegas, but not too long afterwards, she took a second walk down the aisle with **You Got Served dancer** Eddie Fendergrass. Why the rush to get married? Could it be that Brittany's biological clock is ticking? Let's keep our fingers crossed!

Speaking of babies, congratulations to Julia Roberts and **her husband**; the couple brought home a set of twins. **Glenneth Paltrow** also had a bundle of joy this year and named her after her computer. Australian singer **Phil Collins** had a son. Actually, it was his wife who had the son, of course! Phil is male!

In two of the year's sadder events, **JenLo and Ben Afflex** and **Barbie and Ken** split. We never did find out who to blame for the breakups.

This year, there weren't any **movies about animals**. I guess 2004 will be remembered as the year that people mattered most.

Music? *Tones* of it! I barely know where to begin. **Kanye West** took home 10 Grammy nominations, and I still have no idea who he is. But I found out his name is pronounced like "Tanya." You heard it here first, readers. Rapper **Jay Zee** retired and released two albums. And **Ashlie Simpson** emerged from the shadows of older sister **Jessica**, who released a Christmas album and is still happily married to **Nick Cage**. Way to go, Jessica and Nick!

Shreck II was a smash hit, proving that you can go home again, especially if you're **Mike Meyers**. Do I smell a sequel?

That reminds me: Where was **Billy Crystal** this year? I always liked him.

In two of the year's sadder events, JenLo and Ben Afflex and Barbie and Ken split. We never did find out who to blame for the breakups.

With **Sex In The City** over for good, where can viewers turn for top-notch puns and innuendoes from self-satisfied singles looking for love? Strangely, salvation has a name and its name is **The OC**. Snappy outfits, snappier banter, and the ladies? *Trés lovely*! Still, I'm going to miss **Sarah Jessica Perker** and her **Big Apple pals**. Now who's going to keep me in the know about the shoes I can't afford? Or wear!

And now, friends, with this, my last column of 2004, I officially retire the phrase **"turn the dial."** When I was a kid, I had a television with a dial that you would "turn" to change the channel. Well, anyone born after 1985 probably doesn't know what I'm talking about when I say that now, so I need to come up with another phrase that means the same thing. "Push the button" doesn't have that zing.

Had I had the space, I would've talked about a lot more entertainment. Unfortunately, I don't have that luxury in a newspaper column, which is why I'm working on a book about 2004. The working title is **2004: The Year That Laughed.** I'm only up to mid-February so far, but I'm going to keep at it. That is, unless the **2005** television series keep me as busy as the 2004 shows did! In the meantime, save a seat for me...on The Outside! ⌀

HOROSCOPES

Your Horoscope

By Lloyd Schumner Sr.
Retired Machinist and
A.A.P.B.-Certified Astrologer

Aries: (March 21–April 19)
Skin irritation and the inability to sit will continue to plague you for as long as you continue to associate sexual release with mittens full of foaming cleanser.

Taurus: (April 20–May 20)
They won't let you drive the actual Wienermobile, but driving your own vehicle made out of commercially available hot dogs is not a viable alternative.

Gemini: (May 21–June 21)
Perhaps your pets could be cuter, but that's no excuse for sewing them inside of your favorite stuffed animals.

Cancer: (June 22–July 22)
Your future as a professional criminal seemed rosy when you moved to Keystone, but the city has dedicated a lot of money to fielding more professional Kops.

Leo: (July 23–Aug. 22)
A full-body tattoo is an exciting idea, but your busy schedule will require that 24 professional skin artists team up during the most painful lunch hour in history.

Virgo: (Aug. 23–Sept. 22)
The rest of the judges will soon grow to hate your long pauses and the way you say "Weeelllll..." and drum your fingers on the dais before pronouncing sentence.

Libra: (Sept. 23–Oct. 23)
Overall, you led a pretty good life, unless you count the full-ensemble dance numbers that broke out every time you tried to talk to the opposite sex.

Scorpio: (Oct. 24–Nov. 21)
Before you take too much pride in earning the title of "Monroe, ID's Answer To William Tell," you should really find out more about the town they call the Eye Patch Capitol Of The West.

Sagittarius: (Nov. 22–Dec. 21)
You'd really like to know where the people who say, "another day, another dollar" are getting their damn money.

Capricorn: (Dec. 22–Jan. 19)
Look at it this way: In some admittedly deviant cultures, blood on the ceiling is a sign you're doing something noteworthy.

Aquarius: (Jan. 20–Feb. 18)
Not only will you be relegated to the status of historical footnote, but the histories involved are those of aluminum cookware and unreadable sestina poetry.

Pisces: (Feb. 19–March 20)
When all is said and done, you'll have proven that a tone-deaf man with a banjo and no need to sleep can make a difference in his community.

the ONION®
VOLUME 41 ISSUE 03 | AMERICA'S FINEST NEWS SOURCE™ | 20–26 JANUARY 2005

NEWS

Tsunami Death Toll Rises To 36 Americans

see WORLD page 1B

Porch Ceded To Bats

see HOME page 14C

Carpenter Mentally Hammering Things On Way To Work

see BUSINESS page 3D

Minibar Set Really Low

see TRAVEL page 8H

STATshot

A look at the numbers that shape your world.

Law Enforcement Officials Call For Creation Of Bulletproof Sleeves

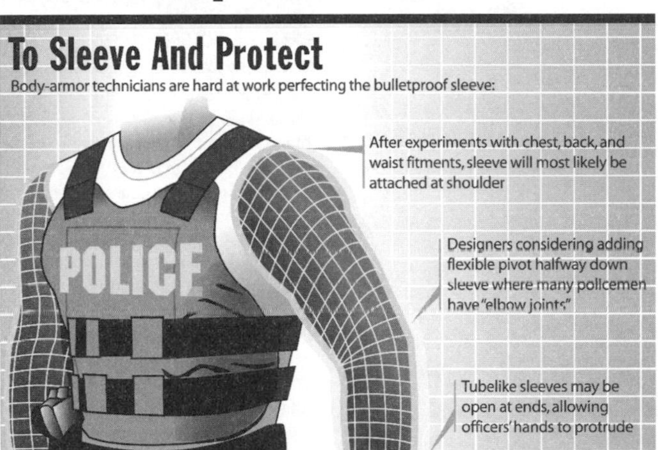

Above: A computer representation of the theoretical sleeves.

DETROIT—Citing decades of advancements in torso protection, the National Association of Law Enforcement Officials held a press conference Monday, calling for the development of a bulletproof sleeve.

"Since 1975, the modern Kevlar bulletproof vest has been an integral part of the protective gear worn by police officers," said NALEO spokesman Sgt. Nicholas Arons, an 18-year veteran of the Detroit Police Department. "For some reason, however, both private- and public-sector forces have spent the past 30 years focusing their creative energies on the development of newer, lighter fabrics to protect the same limited portion of the upper body. While safeguarding the torso is

see SLEEVES page 46

Above: Four members of the Manilla Grill waitstaff.

Waitstaff Tired Of Sleeping With Each Other

MOUNTAIN VIEW, CA—After years on the job, members of the Manilla Grill waitstaff reported Monday that they are tired of having sex with each other.

"I'm closing tonight, so I'll probably end up sleeping with [assistant manager] Robert [Stein]," waitress Katie Glenn said. "A few months ago, I would've been excited. He's really cute, and [coworker] Lynette [Hardy] says he's a great lay, but now... I don't know. We have nothing in common, except that we're both working a double and neither of us can stand [manager] Dan Musket."

Glenn said workplace stress, youth, and access to the restaurant's tap beer contribute to the waitstaff couplings.

"When I first had sex with [hostess] Tracy [Ballucci], I thought she was the

see WAITSTAFF page 46

Supreme Court To Break Up If Rehnquist Leaves

WASHINGTON, DC—Responding to widespread speculation, members of the U.S. Supreme Court told reporters Monday that they will not continue to hear cases if Chief Justice William Rehnquist, 80, steps down.

"It just wouldn't be the same court without Bill," Justice David Souter said. "He's the heart and soul of this judicature, the one who motivates us to keep ruling. I can't imagine doing it without him."

In October, Rehnquist, who has served on the Supreme Court for 33 years, announced that he has thyroid cancer. The statement led some to speculate

Above: The Supreme Court, which plans to split if Chief Justice Rehnquist (right) leaves.

whether he will complete his annual term.

"The Supreme Court is a middle-aged man's game," Rehnquist told *Law and Justice* magazine in November 1997. "I can't see myself swinging the gavel at

see REHNQUIST page 47

Georgia's Evolution Stickers

Last week, a U.S. district judge ordered a Georgia school district to remove stickers reading, "Evolution is a theory, not a fact" from its textbooks. What do *you* think?

"The thing is, they're right. Evolution is nothing more than a well-supported, predictive, scientifically rigorous theory."

Jered Garza
Driver

"If you don't believe in creationism, then how do you explain the fact that I do, smart guy?"

Carlton Fuller
Teacher

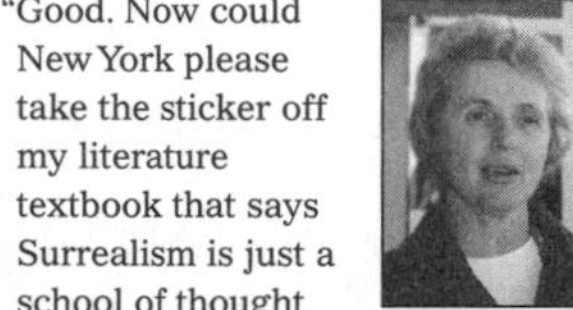

"Good. Now could New York please take the sticker off my literature textbook that says Surrealism is just a school of thought often in conflict with Abstractism?"

Melanie Burton
Systems Analyst

"Maybe now a judge will press Georgia schools to remove the 'Mr. Yuk' stickers from books by black authors."

Susan McKinney
Painter

"Man, I gotta get one of those stickers for my guitar case. That'd be awesome."

Danny Hale
Plumber

"I hope they replaced the old stickers with new ones that read, 'Do not burn.'"

Brad Dawson
Novelist

The Upcoming Iraqi Election

How are Iraqi citizens preparing for their Jan. 30 election?

- Carefully considering the positions and platforms of the candidates before placing bets on their chances for survival
- Politely asking nearest person holding a machine gun, "For whom would you prefer I vote, sir?"
- Attending grassroots "Shoot Out The Vote" events
- Volunteering to car-bomb voters to the polls
- Repairing damage caused by last week's bombing of Ramadi's campaign-button-making machine
- Providing covering fire while friends run for office
- Reading the helpful illustrated guides distributed by the League Of Remaining Voters
- Lightening the mood by slamming doors, popping inflated paper bags, and dropping dictionaries behind backs of major candidates
- Attempting to grasp concept of freedom

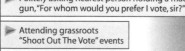

the ONION®
America's Finest News Source.™

Herman Ulysses Zweibel
Founder

T. Herman Zweibel
Publisher Emeritus
J. Phineas Zweibel
Publisher
Maxwell Prescott Zweibel
Editor-In-Chief

I'm Pretty Sure I Know Why The Caged Bird Sings

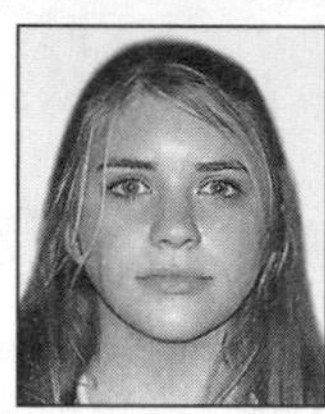

By Madeleine Schumann

I must admit that, at first, I wasn't sure if I was going to like the African-American Lit class I signed up for. I had to take it because it was the only humanities class available at 9:20 on Wednesdays—long story—and I just couldn't see what black lit had to do with pre-med. But you know what? Once I started listening—really listening—to what these beautiful writers had to say, I found myself totally inspired by the incredible black men and women who suffered so much because of their skin color and the fact that they had hardly any money. And even though I know that, as a white person, I will never really have a complete understanding of the black experience, I have to say that I now have a fairly good idea why the caged bird sings.

Growing up in the affluent suburb of Sherwood Oaks, I didn't meet a lot of black people. There just weren't too many of them around. In fact, I don't think there were any at all. I used to think Sherwood Oaks High was the greatest place on earth, but since I started college, I've been exposed to so many more cultural perspectives. I've really grown as a person.

Sure, I had some super fun times at Sherwood. I'll never forget my prom night—the only word I can use to describe it is magical. But looking back, I can't believe how sheltered I was! I was so naïve! I didn't know anything about Maya Angelou, Toni Morrison, Ralph Ellison, Gwendolyn Brooks, Langston Hughes, or any of the other African-American writers who broadened my worldview last semester. During my entire prom, I did not once think about all the suffering blacks and their novels and poetry and personal memoirs. I didn't think for two seconds about all of the black women being raped by their fathers and brothers. Where were their magical prom nights? They didn't have any, because they were trapped in cages, singing.

Not in physical cages, but in metaphorical ones constructed by society. Like I said before, I'm not 100-percent clear on all of this. But even if I don't completely understand, at least I understand how little I used to understand. And that is totally the beginning of understanding.

Before last semester, I didn't have any black friends. I still don't, but I do have some black classmates. And if I ever meet any black people socially, I will totally be up for hanging out, now that I know where they are coming from. When I was in high school, I only knew about black people from seeing them on television. But the book versions of their lives tell you so much more about who black people truly are. Through the spiritual, soulful, and musical quality of their lyrical writing, certain universal themes transcended the cultural barrier, and I came to realize that I can totally relate.

Take, for example, Langston Hughes' famous couplet, "My motto as I live and learn is: dig and be dug in return." I understood that right away. It's like my Dad always says: "You scratch my back, and I scratch yours." One hand washes the other, you know? That's exactly the kind of philosophy that allowed my dad to become such a successful and respected CEO. It's about mutual advantage and common interest, like when two corporations merge for the benefit of both. If only we could

Growing up in the affluent suburb of Sherwood Oaks, I didn't meet a lot of black people. There just weren't too many of them around. In fact, I don't think there were any at all.

learn to live that way as human beings, then maybe there would be no ghettos.

It really makes you think.

Other parts of the class were harder for me to grasp intuitively, and I had to struggle with them, just like the blacks had to struggle before civil rights made them equal. Like this one poem by Gwendolyn Brooks, "We Real Cool." I knew that gangs were a big problem in certain neighborhoods—or as some members of the black community call them, "'hoods." But as a white person, it was hard for me to understand what motivates a black person to join a gang. I mean, I never left school or "lurked late" or "sang sin" or any of the things the black people do in the poem. And I certainly never "jazzed June," which I had to ask my T.A. about during discussion section. So I was a bit confused. Like, why would they "thin gin," I wondered. That would only water it down. Then I realized they were probably too poor to afford enough gin,

see CAGED BIRD page 47

Study: Watching Fewer Than Four Hours Of TV A Day Impairs Ability To Ridicule Pop Culture

NEW YORK—A Columbia University study released Tuesday suggests that viewing fewer than four hours of TV a day severely inhibits a person's ability to ridicule popular culture.

"An hour or two of television per day simply does not provide enough information to effectively mock mediocre sitcoms, vapid celebrities, music videos, and talk-show hosts—an essential skill in modern society," said Dr. Madeleine Ben-Ami, a professor of cognitive science and chief author of the study. "The average person requires a minimum of four to six hours of television programming each day to be conversant on the subject of *The Apprentice* contestants or pull off a passable impersonation of Anna Nicole Smith."

Tracking 800 individuals between the ages of 15 and 39, researchers found that people who watched fewer than four hours of television a day had difficulty understanding the references made on VH1's *Best Week Ever*, and were often unable to point out the absurd elements in contemporary infomercial products or the cluelessness of *American Idol* finalists.

"Study participants who watched television inconsistently were less personally invested in what they saw than regular viewers," Ben-Ami said. "While some sporadic viewers were able to enjoy jokes made by others, they were unable to make jokes of their own. The regular viewers averaged 12 celebrity-related sarcastic asides per hour, while the uninformed viewers made almost none."

The contrast between regular and irregular TV viewers was made plain by a simple experiment: Irregular and regular TV viewers were videotaped while watching footage of Michael Jackson.

"Note how this young man remains calm, observing the series of photographs quietly," said Ben-Ami, pointing to one of two

see POP CULTURE page 47

Above: A few of the many celebrities underinformed television viewers were unable to mock.

NEWS IN BRIEF

White House Dishwasher Tenders Resignation

WASHINGTON, DC—T. Eric Mayhew, 36, who began working in the White House kitchen the day President George W. Bush took office, submitted his resignation Monday. "The noble work of dishwashing preceded my appointment to this job and will continue long after I leave," Mayhew said. "It was an honor to serve under the president. I leave my post proudly, knowing the White House flatware is more sanitary today than it was when I began my work here." Mayhew will maintain his position until Bush appoints a replacement.

Caged Saddam To Be Highlight Of Inaugural Ball

WASHINGTON, DC—Attendees at the Independence Ball, one of nine officially sanctioned galas celebrating President George W. Bush's second inauguration Thursday, will be treated to a viewing of a caged Saddam Hussein, White House Press Secretary Scott McClellan said Monday. "What better way to honor the president than with a physical symbol of his many first-term triumphs?" McClellan said as Hussein rattled the bars of a cage already suspended above the ballroom where the event will be held. "And I must compliment the planning committee. Outfitting Gitmo detainees with iron collars and forcing them to serve appetizers was an inspired stroke." Ball attendees will also be awarded door prizes, including a basket of nuts, 20 yards of cloth, and a barrel of crude oil.

Mets Earmark $53 Million For Pitching Relief

NEW YORK—Following a stormy 2004 season that some observers called nothing short of a disaster, the New York Mets have addressed the tidal wave of criticism by earmarking more than $53 million to pitching relief. "We're doing all we can to salvage what's left of our team in this emergency situation," Mets general manager Omar Minaya said of his team, which signed pitcher Pedro Martinez in recent weeks. "We ask that everyone say a prayer for us as we attempt to rebuild this once-thriving franchise." The Mets also signed outfielder Carlos Beltran, dedicating $117 million to shore up a defense that has recently been flooded with runs.

Woman Sensitive About That Thing On Her Face

RUTLAND, VT—Coworkers of administrative assistant Audrey Foss, 28, reported Monday that she is "very sensitive" about that thing on the right side of her face. "Whenever you talk to Audrey, she'll sort of tilt her head away from you, or if she's sitting down, she'll cup her hand over her cheek," said Marcia Doland, Foss' supervisor at Rutland Heating and Cooling. "You can tell she's really self-conscious about that...well, whatever it is. She shouldn't be." In an informal office poll, nearly all of her coworkers agreed that Foss is pretty, even with the thing.

Friend Whose Mom Just Died Allowed to Pick Pizza Topping

HYANNIS, NE—Because his mother died of cancer on Jan. 8, Jon Brendemuehl, 11, got to choose the pizza topping during a bowling outing with best friend Greg Weber and his family Monday. "Go ahead, Jon—pick whatever you like," Weber said as the entire table gazed at Brendemuehl in sympathy. "See, you got a higher score than all of us—even my dad, who once bowled a 300 game—and now you get to eat whatever kind of pizza you want. This is fun, hey?" Witnesses report Brendemuehl smiled weakly and ordered pepperoni. Ø

WAITSTAFF from page 43

one," waiter Kevin Cobb said. "Two months later, I had sex with Katie, but I still had to work with Tracy. I should've learned my lesson when Tracy 'accidentally' threw away a shrimp scampi that was supposed to go to a 14-top. But it's a little too late now, since there's not a waitress left

"But there is the line cook," Stern added. "It might be fun to back him into the walk-in cooler and fuck his brains out. I've never had sex with anyone from the back of the house before."

that I haven't slept with."

"Oh, Kelly [Spencer]—I haven't had sex with Kelly, yet," Cobb added. "Man, I'm not looking forward to that."

While most of the intercourse occurs off the premises, the waitstaff said they sometimes have sex with each other in the restaurant's storage areas.

"I don't know how much more of this I can take," hostess Jill Stern said. "I've gone through every waiter and even two waitresses. Maybe I should get a new job. I definitely need a change."

"But there is the line cook," Stern added. "It might be fun to back him into the walk-in cooler and fuck his brains out. I've never had sex with anyone from the back of the house before."

"Kelly said it's pretty hot," Stern added.

Psychologist Dorian Ledin, an expert in workplace relationships, said the best way to solve the problems

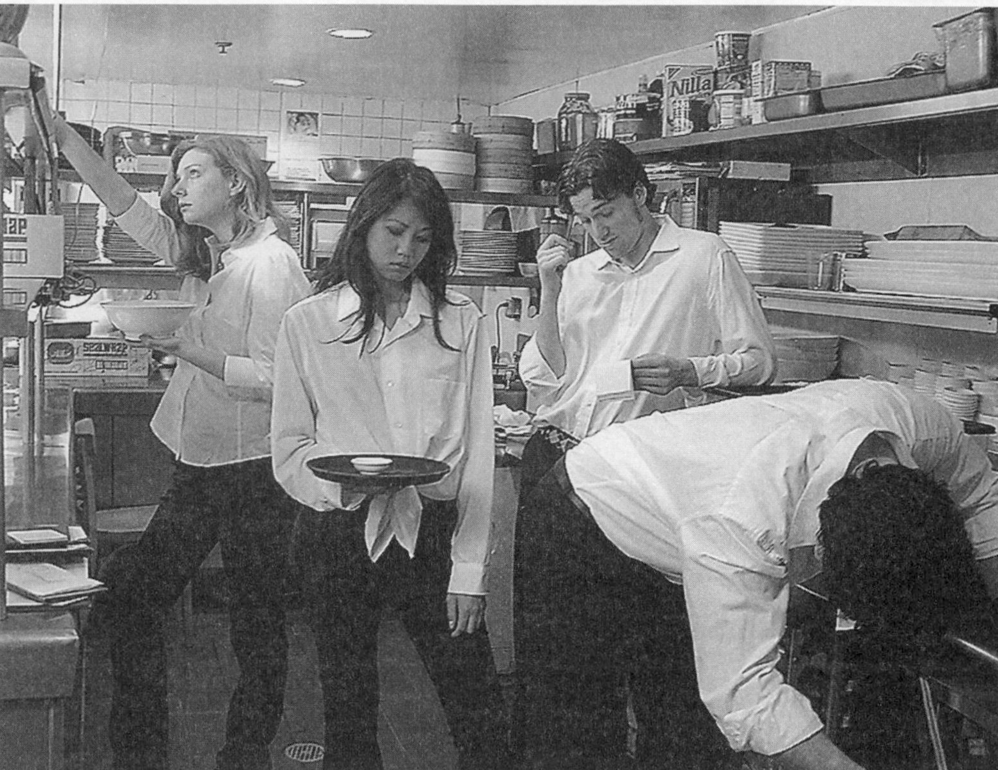

Above: Stern listlessly observes Cobb bend over.

brought about by sleeping with too many coworkers is to find a new job.

"Jill would do best to follow her first impulse," Ledin said. "Quitting is the best way to break the cycle. This behavior is inhibiting her ability to forge permanent relationships. And it's also keeping her from refilling her customers' glasses of ice water."

Ledin said food-service employees may initially be disoriented when they start working at new locations, but after a short adjustment period, a new sense of purpose will often fill their lives.

"There is hope," Ledin said. "Many former waitstaff members go on to form long-term, monogamous relationships with colleagues in fields such as telemarketing or hotel management."

Former Manilla Grill employee Greg Nelson agreed with Ledin's theory.

"Almost immediately after I quit, I got work at Loews Cinema," said Nelson, who tendered his resignation in August 2004. "That's where I met this totally hot usher. We've been going out, like, six weeks."

Nelson added, "I went back to the bar at Manilla Grill last week, and I barely had anything to say to those people, much less a desire to have sex with them."

Regardless of the easy solution leaving offers, many waiters and waitresses try to modify their behavior by refraining from having sex with their coworkers. They report little success.

"When I left Pizzeria Prima, I had a motto: 'Don't get laid where you get paid,'" waiter Jack Dulles said. "Then I started working at Manilla Grill. One night after a football-game rush, I wound up sleeping with Pat in what's turned into a three-month, eight-waitress binge. I keep telling my roommates it's the last time, but even I don't believe it anymore." ⌀

SLEEVES from page 43

extremely important, it's time we began to think about what might be done to protect some other body parts."

According to Arons, two key areas overlooked by the protection industry are the left and right arms.

"We believe a bulletproof sleeve, if properly designed, could protect the shoulder, upper arm, elbow, and lower arm regions," said Arons, who lost both his forearms in a narcotics raid in October. "An officer wearing one of these devices on each arm would find himself doubly protected."

Arons characterized the arms as "crucial" to the successful completion of a police officer's duties.

"Police officers use their arms hundreds of times every day," Arons said. "If they didn't have arms, officers would be unable to brandish or discharge firearms, handcuff perpetrators, operate doors, write speeding tickets, or file reports. A policeman's arms and attached appendages are essential."

NALEO advisory board member Lt. Lee Skille agreed, stating that the standard-issue upper-body protection armor has significant shortcomings.

"People say, 'You can live without

Arons characterized the arms as "crucial" to the successful completion of a police officer's duties.

your arms, but you can't live without your chest,'" said Skille, whose partner's arm was shot in the line of duty in 2003. "True. But try not using your arms for a day, and then come and tell me how arms aren't a 'vital organ.'"

Skille said he does not know how a bulletproof sleeve would be anchored onto the body, but that "in a perfect world, the sleeve would attach to the vest."

In response to the announcement, representatives for domestic defense contractor FirstShield said they plan to develop a marketable bulletproof sleeve by the end of the year. The company's 2004 prototype ArmVest failed in initial testing, because of complaints that the two 34-inch-wide ArmVests impeded movement and were prone to falling off. FirstShield is now investigating the practicality of using snaps, zippers, and Velcro to anchor the vest to the body.

FirstShield CEO Alastair Gilbert pledged "to redouble efforts to design a product that meets the arm-protection needs of today's 21st-century police force."

"While we might not get there in our first hundred days, or even our first thousand, we have risen to this challenge," Gilbert said. "Anyone who puts in 25 years with a police force deserves to have a wrist to put his gold watch on."

While the law-enforcement community is largely united over the bulletproof-sleeves initiative, the announcement did have a few detractors.

"Maybe the NALEO nancy-boys have never taken a bullet in the rear end," said Gary, IN police officer Bernard Dirkson, who was shot twice in the buttocks during a routine traffic stop in 2002. "But it's no stroll on the beach, I assure you. I challenge the defensive-apparel industry to take the next major step in protective gear: Protect our hindquarters."

Arons said the NALEO plans to look beyond the upper body.

"By the end of the century, a police officer might be equipped with some form of protection for his legs," Arons said. "Of course, right now we're focused on achieving our first goal—guarding the arms." ⌀

REHNQUIST from page 43

90. I just don't have the stamina."

At an informal hearing held in Justice Steven J. Breyer's kitchen in December, the Supreme Court voted 7 to 1 in favor of breaking up, with Justice Antonin Scalia abstaining from the vote. Rehnquist was the sole dissenting voice.

"Bill kept arguing that no matter what happened, the Supreme Court should continue," Justice Sandra Day O'Connor said. "It was touching to see how much faith he has in us, but I think the majority opinion is in favor of quitting while we're on top, rather than muddling through a bunch of mediocre judicial sessions and becoming some sort of kangaroo court."

Continued O'Connor, "The hardest thing to achieve with a judicial body as large as ours is a rapport. To effectively interpret the law, you need that certain magical something. Without Rehnquist, we'll lose that vibe."

Justice Anthony Kennedy agreed.

"Maybe you have to be sitting on the bench to understand, but there's something special about Rehnquist," Kennedy said. "You can feel the electricity fill the air as soon as the court marshal calls out, 'Oyez! Oyez! Oyez! All persons having business before the Honorable, the Supreme Court of the United States are admonished to draw near and give their attention, for the court is now sitting.'"

While he was not appointed chief justice until 1986, Rehnquist has appeared on more television shows and in more magazines than any justice in the history of the Supreme Court.

"I don't think they're ready to give up interpreting the law just yet," Tomaine said. "I wouldn't be surprised if a number of these justices get together and start something very similar to the Supreme Court, but under a different name.

"Rehnquist's been the court's spiritual leader since being sworn in in 1972," Souter said. "Right now, the Supreme Court is the most powerful legal body in the country. I think we'd all prefer to go down in the books that way."

Bernard Tomaine, publisher of the Supreme Court fanzine *The Docket*, characterized Rehnquist's role as "essential."

"When Rehnquist leaves, it's going to be the end of an era," Tomaine said. "He's absolutely irreplaceable."

Added Tomaine: "I've got a bootleg copy of an opinion that Rehnquist wrote for U.S. v. Verdugo-Urquidez that would blow your mind."

Although the associate justices have yet to announce their plans following the dissolution of the Supreme Court, Tomaine said he believes that many will continue on with solo judiciary projects.

"I don't think they're ready to give up interpreting the law just yet," Tomaine said. "I wouldn't be surprised if a number of these justices get together and start something very similar to the Supreme Court, but under a different name. I heard that Scalia wants to set up a new organization under the name 'The U.S. Supreme Court featuring Antonin Scalia.' Personally, I think it's very disrespectful to use the name of that honorable institution, but I suppose it's his right."

While no definitive time frame has been established for Rehnquist's departure, many speculate that it will be soon.

"Swearing in Bush for his second term will be a big moment," Tomaine said. "Unless he's got something up his sleeve for [terrorism suspect Zacarias] Moussaoui's trial, he'll probably leave right after the inauguration. I can't see Rehnquist going out on a quiet note. That's just not his style."

Although the justices' resolve seems strong, some fans of the Supreme Court say the eight justices will change their minds after Rehnquist leaves.

"This is not the first time a government branch has threatened to quit for personal reasons," said Henry Loghermann, a prominent Washington D.C. historian and Supreme Court groupie. "Take the Department of the Interior in the '80s. They kept saying that if James Watt left, they'd all go their separate ways. Well, Watt left, and the DOI is still going strong. And I can't even count how many times the British House of Lords has broken up and reformed in the past 50 years. When the harsh reality sets in, the high court will see what few options they have and cut the bluster." ⊘

POP CULTURE from page 45

monitors running footage of individual study participants. "Meanwhile, his counterpart laughs uproariously, pretends to gag, and feigns sexual intercourse with a throw pillow.

"By incorporating Paris Hilton into our oral interviews, we provided participants with an easy opportunity to 'riff' on the heiress," Ben-Ami said. "Nevertheless, non-TV viewers reacted to softball questions like 'What's up with Paris' hair extensions?' with monosyllabic shrugs or bemused silence.

Seconds later, he leaves his seat to execute some kind of '80s-style breakdance, and injures himself, probably because of his excessive weight."

"The first man doesn't have a television," Ben-Ami added gravely. "The other man watches an average of 40 hours of network and cable programming each week."

Ben-Ami said study participants who watched fewer than 28 hours per week were unable to ridicule Paris Hilton "with any specificity whatsoever."

"By incorporating Paris Hilton into our oral interviews, we provided participants with an easy opportunity to 'riff' on the heiress," Ben-Ami said. "Nevertheless, non-TV viewers reacted to softball questions like 'What's up with Paris' hair extensions?' with monosyllabic shrugs or bemused silence. It was like they were completely ignorant of her many skanky attributes and laughable traits."

Ben-Ami said she and her colleagues fear that an inability to ridicule popular culture could result in an American sub-group unable to function in the modern world.

"Because the ridicule of pop culture comprises the bulk of today's social discourse, a non-viewer is at a distinct disadvantage in the workplace, on campus, and in the dating scene," Ben-Ami said. "An employee who can't participate in jokes about Ashlee Simpson's disastrous Orange Bowl appearance will sit dumbfounded while a more able coworker ingratiates himself to the boss by laughing. And just as the bird with the most colorful plumage attracts the most attention, so too does the bar-TV viewer who yells, 'Have a sandwich before you faint!' when Mary-Kate Olsen appears on screen."

The study's findings have triggered concern among parents across the country.

"I don't want my 10-year-old to enter college without the ability to mock boy bands," said Myra Savage of Phoenix. "I want him to excel, like those kids who form campus sketch troupes or win college-wide trivia contests. Should I make him cut down on his reading?"

University of Colorado communication arts professor N. Clyde Graf said parents should nurture their children's enthusiasm for pop culture by having them watch a minimum of four hours of television each day, with at least two of those hours falling during prime time.

"As a TV-literate child grows into adolescence, he begins to develop either moody contempt or perverse love for camp," Graf said. "Both attitudes are vital to the informed ridicule of pop culture."

Graf said parents should encourage children to watch "the silliest, most throwaway TV available" by example.

"Don't instruct your child to turn on *Nanny 911* and then go and watch educational television right in front of them," Graf said. "They should only be watching PBS once they've attained the level of jaded detachment that will allow them to find humor in low-budget sets, nerdy hosts, and clichéd, Ken Burns-style pan-and-scan direction."

Graf said that without supersaturation in the worst forms of the medium, children will treat TV as a source of passive entertainment.

"Long gone are the days when an individual would switch on his set and enjoy a simple, satisfying, and fun hour of diversion," Graf said. "To perceive television this way is to be hopelessly out-of-step with our times." ⊘

CAGED BIRD from page 44

and that just broke my heart. Because of cultural differences, I still can't relate to why they think it's so cool that they're going to die soon, but the poem spoke to me nonetheless. Yeah, I'm pretty sure I got it.

Because even as a white pre-med

Even though it's trapped in a cage, it refuses to be silenced. It still has hope, and it still has something beautiful to give the world. See?

student with a Tri-Delt legacy, I understood, mostly, why the caged bird sings. It sings because it longs to be free. Even though it's trapped in a cage, it refuses to be silenced. It still has hope, and it still has something beautiful to give the world. See?

I asked my boyfriend why the caged bird sings, and he said maybe it's because it likes being inside a cage, because it's lazy and too stupid to get out, which I told him right out was rude. If he'd gone through the living hell of prejudice like Maya Angelou had, I told him, then maybe he might be tired and undereducated, too. And then we broke up. After all the changes I've gone through in the past 14 weeks, I couldn't keep dating someone so insensitive. ⊘

COMMUNITY VOICES

Junk Yardin'

Hola, amigos. I know it's been a long time since I rapped at ya, but I've had a fistful of problems lately. I had to beg Ron for a second chance at the crappy carbonics plant. That sucked, first because I hate begging, and second because I hate begging Ron. I had to remind him of the time I pulled this guy with a USMC tattoo off of him after he got too friendly with the marine's woman. I was hoping to cash that favor in for something good, instead I had to waste it on a job.

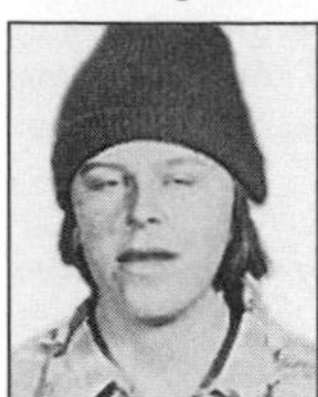

The Cruise
By Jim Anchower

It's cool making rent, but the job sucks. We make dry ice, and we put carbon dioxide into tanks. I haul the tanks and wrap the ice. The last time I worked there, it was summer, so at least I could go outside to warm up. Now I have to go to the break room if I want my nuts to drop back into place. Plus, I gotta take orders from Ron, and the only time he mellows out is if I smoke him up out back.

Have you ever been to one? It's like a giant, rusty candy store. You walk through rows and rows of smashed-up cars and just take the parts you want without paying a fortune. But it's rusty and disorganized and you sometimes get lost in all the cars, because they pack them in tighter than a nun's twat.

On top of all that, the alternator on my Festiva was broken all last month. After about five weeks of parking on hills to pop-start it, I finally decided I had to replace the alternator. I know what you're thinking: "Anchower, why would you throw more money at that car? It's like polishing a turd." Well, shut up and let me talk for a second. It was either buy a new alternator or buy a new ride, and I don't have enough money to buy a new ride. Got it? Good.

Anyway, I figured that if I was gonna throw money at the alternator, I should fix up some other things, like the door that got smashed in by a Hummer and the headlight that never worked. You know, make the most of a bad situation.

I went out to the junkyard thinking it would be a breeze to find another Festiva. I forgot how much of a mess a junkyard can be. Have you ever been to one? It's like a giant, rusty candy store. You walk through rows and rows of smashed-up cars and just take the parts you want without paying a fortune. But it's rusty and disorganized and you sometimes get lost in all the cars, because they pack them in tighter than a nun's twat. Well anyway, I wandered around the junkyard for about two hours in the freezing cold. I saw a bunch of cars, some of which must've been pretty sweet in their primes, but I never found a Festiva.

I was this close to giving up when I saw one of my old cars, the Volkswagon Golf from four years ago. The windows were shattered, the back seat was ripped out, and there were mouse turds all over the dash, but I could still tell it was my old car by the gouge in the ding protector. You know, the rubber strip on the door to keep your car from being banged up. Mine got torn up that time I turned around to yell at a guy in the back seat and sideswiped a mailbox. I knocked the box clean off the pole and tore ass out of there, thinking I'd made off scot free, but then I saw the gouge when I got home. It's funny, you never forget a great memory.

That Golf was a good car. The engine seized up on it, or I never would've sold it to that high-school kid who wanted to fix it up in shop class. Anyway, I was standing there thinking about the good times, and then I remembered the car had a special anti-cop hidey spot I jerry-rigged by gluing a plastic tube inside of the wheel well. It had always been the perfect spot to hold an emergency joint. I squatted down in front of the wheel well and tried to reach for it, but I couldn't get a good angle. I didn't want to just walk away, so I laid on my back with one shoulder under the car and went to work. After a couple of minutes reaching around, I got up in there and found the tube, but I couldn't pop the cap off, so I just gave the entire tube a hard jerk. Well, turns out that wasn't such a good idea, because I had my hand wedged up inside there, and the force of that jerk got my arm totally stuck.

I started trying to wiggle myself unstuck, but my jacket got caught on a screw or something, and everything got a hundred times worse. I started to get panicky. I was like, "No way I want to die like this. I'll cut my arm off before I freeze to death under a car that doesn't even start anymore." Thank God, I didn't end up having to cut my own arm off. After 10 minutes of twisting and squirming, some big old guy in greasy coveralls walked up like, "Hey, who let you on my lot?"

After he reached in and ripped my jacket to free me, he started giving me the business about going out in the yard without supervision. "You can't just come on in here and start grabbing at stuff. You've gotta come in through the gates." Like I'm gonna steal some hubcaps or something. I mean, sure, I did steal some hubcaps once, but the junkyard guy didn't know about it, so he had no right to talk to me like I was a criminal.

Then the guy would not shut up. He starts telling me it's a city ordinance that I can't be out there alone, and he can't afford a $500 ticket. Plus, what if I got caught under one of the cars and no one was there to find me? Well, I didn't say anything to that, but in my head I was like, "I'd cut my arm off."

The guy asked me what I was looking for, and I told him I was looking for a Festiva, and he took me right to one and stood and watched while I pried off the parts I needed. I paid for the parts, pushed my ride down the drive, climbed in, did a pop start, and drove off. It wasn't until I was three blocks from home that I realized I'd forgotten to see if there was a joint in the hidey-hole, so I've gotta go all the way back over there and check sometime this week.

After all the hassle, I'm still screwed because the headlight I got was the wrong model. The alternator worked great, but before I can get the new door on, I have to pop a lot of dents out. I spent most of Sunday doing that, using a prybar until my hands bled. That's how I realized that parts are only a quick fix, and I need to get a new car. I went to Ron and asked for a raise, but he said I can't even be up for a raise until I'm on the job six months. That dick. Take my advice: Don't work for a friend. Period. It's you who's going to end up paying the price. Ø

HOROSCOPES

Your Horoscope

By Lloyd Schumner Sr.
Retired Machinist and
A.A.P.B.-Certified Astrologer

Aries: (March 21–April 19)
You're not sure why, but you've never bought that one chicken's alleged reason for crossing the road.

Taurus: (April 20–May 20)
A trip to sunny Bermuda does not recharge your batteries due to the fact that your worker-robot casing isn't equipped for solar-energy uptake.

Gemini: (May 21–June 21)
Classical musicians worldwide will be out for your blood when you compose the brilliant but torturous-to-play *Punishment Symphony For Orchestral Dipshits.*

Cancer: (June 22–July 22)
You'll balloon up to triple your weight after several months spent following a diet-book typo that told you to eat 16,000 calories a day.

Leo: (July 23–Aug. 22)
You'll be held in contempt of court by several judges you haven't even met, which you have to admit is pretty good anticipation on their part.

Virgo: (Aug. 23–Sept. 22)
You'll be stripped, cleaned, oiled, and lovingly Briwaxed even though you insist that you are not a 1930s craft project.

Libra: (Sept. 23–Oct. 23)
They say make-up sex is the hottest, so it's probably not a good idea to resolve that long-standing feud with your parents.

Scorpio: (Oct. 24–Nov. 21)
Eventually, they'll figure out who it was that broke into the safe, but they'll just laugh at you for taking the money when you could've had the secret pie recipe.

Sagittarius: (Nov. 22–Dec. 21)
You'll finally learn to stop looking like you've put your makeup on with a trowel just as the hot new trend of trowel-applied makeup catches on.

Capricorn: (Dec. 22–Jan. 19)
It's true that the best-laid plans of mice and men go oft awry, but the mutant rodents in the sewers beneath your home have been planning your death for years.

Aquarius: (Jan. 20–Feb. 18)
You can remember a happier time when you were young and hopeful and Yaphet Kotto wasn't following you everywhere.

Pisces: (Feb. 19–March 20)
Executives at all the major networks will reject your idea for a fiction-based "non-reality show" as "too hard to understand."

Hilary Duff's Number-One Fan Tasered

see ENTERTAINMENT page 3F

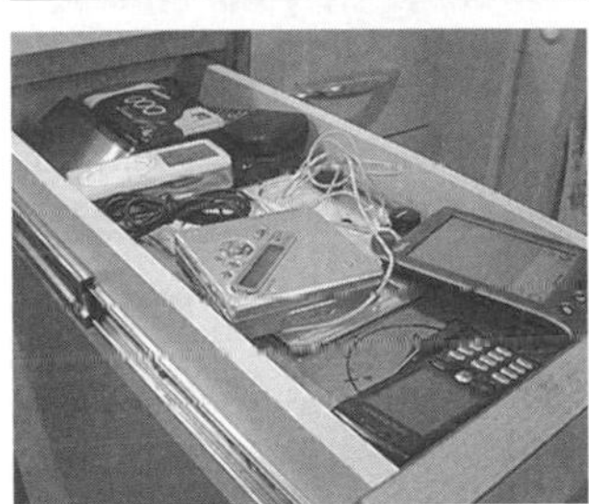

Technophile Has Coolest Junk Drawer Ever

see TECHNOLOGY page 8D

Terrifying Sea Monster Turns Out To Be Even More Terrifying Amphibious Monster

see NATURE page 22H

STATshot

A look at the numbers that shape your world.

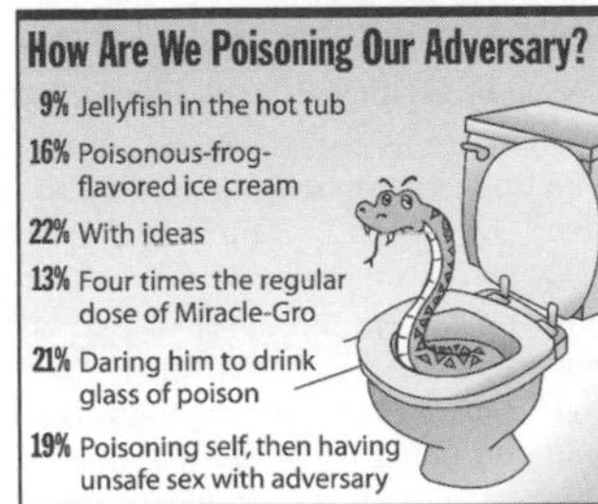

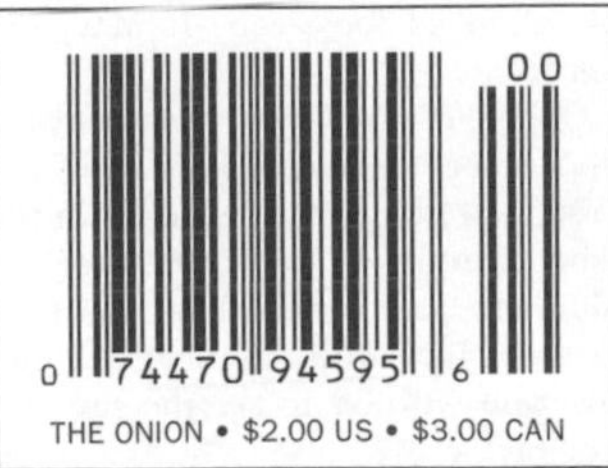

the ONION®

VOLUME 41 ISSUE 04 AMERICA'S FINEST NEWS SOURCE™ 27 JAN.–2 FEB. 2005

U.S. Children Still Traumatized One Year After Seeing Partially Exposed Breast On TV

WASHINGTON, DC—As the nation approaches the one-year anniversary of the Super Bowl XXXVIII tragedy, an FCC study shows that millions of U.S. children were severely traumatized by the exposure to a partially nude female breast during the Feb. 1, 2004 halftime show.

"No one who lived through that day is likely to forget the horror," said noted child therapist Dr. Eli Wasserbaum. "But it was especially hard on the children."

The tragic wardrobe malfunction occurred approximately 360 days ago, during Janet Jackson and Justin Timberlake's performance of "Rock Your Body," when Timberlake tore Jackson's costume, accidentally revealing her right breast.

"By the time CBS cut to an aerial view of the stadium, the damage was done," said Wasserbaum, who has also

see CHILDREN page 53

Above: Jackson irrevocably damages millions of American children.

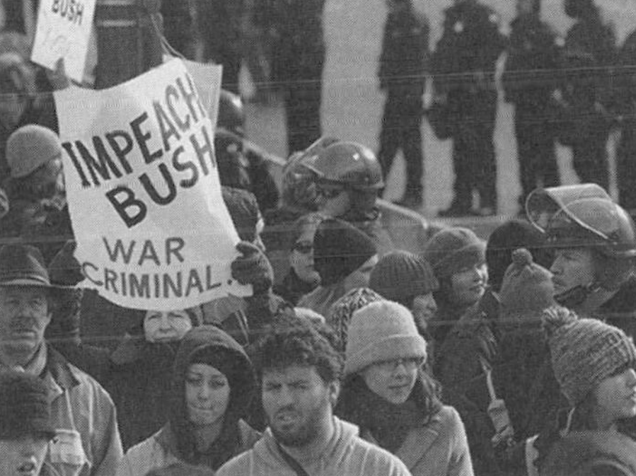

Above: Some of the 24,999 protesters who showed up to turn their backs on Bush.

Protest One Person Short Of Success

WASHINGTON, DC—The counter-inauguration protests held in Washington Wednesday were one person short of success, analysts reported Thursday.

"It's a pity that so many people who support our cause didn't make it out," said Jet Heiko, who organized the protest through his website TurnYourBackOnBush.org. "If one more person had come through for us, Bush would have had a moment of clarity and changed his entire approach to governing America."

"I guess that one person who didn't show had other plans," Heiko said.

see PROTEST page 52

Relationship Beats Second-Quarter Expectations

JERSEY CITY, NJ—Kirk Herman and Deanna Greunwald surprised friends by exceeding second-quarter expectations for their relationship Monday.

"Deanna has made some questionable emotional investments in the past, so when she merged with Kirk six months ago, my expectations for their futures were conservative," Greunwald's friend Doreen Miller said. "I guess Q2's explosive close proves how hard it is to predict meat-market forces."

Herman and Greunwald had their initial meeting in July 2004 at the Bull & Bear, a midtown Manhattan bar. Although they immediately capitalized on their mutual interests and single status, it was several weeks before the pair formed an official partnership.

"Kirk generally keeps a tight rein on his interpersonal expenditures," Herman's longtime friend Ken Klein said. "Contributions of affection rarely exceed his own yearnings. Also, there was an exchange of liquid assets

see RELATIONSHIP page 53

Above: Herman and Greunwald, who are successfully dating.

The Rice Confirmation

After a delay caused by Congressional Democrats, Condoleezza Rice was confirmed as Secretary of State this week. What do *you* think?

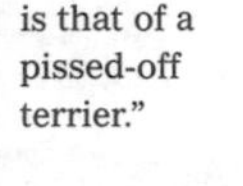

"Great. Now the public face of U.S. diplomacy is that of a pissed-off terrier."

Ted Ramos
Upholsterer

"Ms. Rice should make an ideal Secretary of State. She's already proved to the U.S. that she can evade questions in front of a Congressional panel."

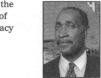

Michael Shaw
Systems Analyst

"I say, why not give Condi a shot as Secretary of State? It might help her self-esteem and encourage her to start taking an interest in her appearance."

Colleen Burns
Appraiser

"The implications are profound. She's paved the way for a black female to perform with the Capitol Steps."

Peter Swain
Unemployed

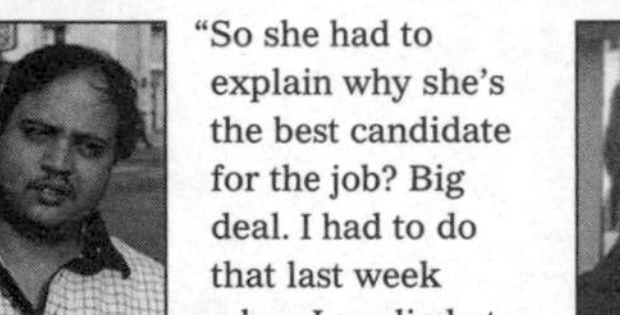

"So she had to explain why she's the best candidate for the job? Big deal. I had to do that last week when I applied at Panda Express."

Gregory Gordon
Cashier

"Twenty years ago, I never would've believed that we'd have a black, female Secretary of State, much less one who was a conservative warmonger, too. We've come a long way."

Joy Mattingly
Designer

Huygens Space Probe Discoveries

The European Space Agency landed the Huygens probe on Saturn's largest moon, Titan, on Jan. 14. What have scientists discovered?

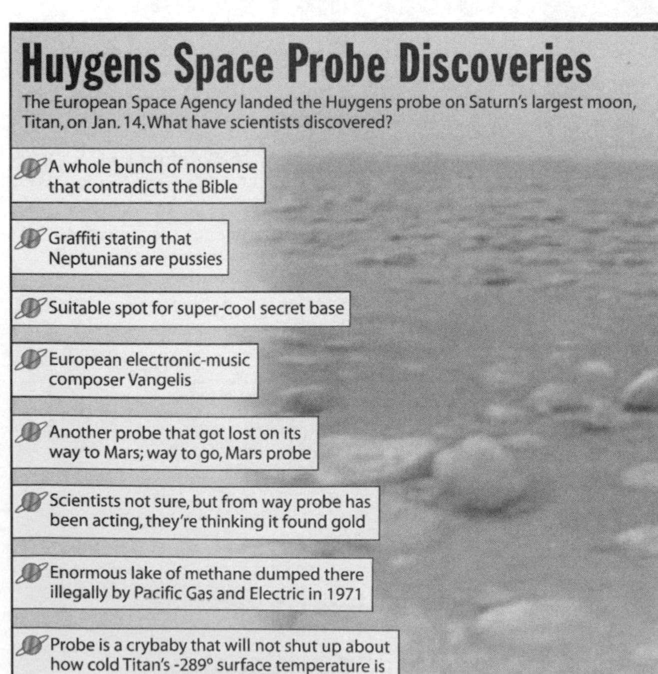

- A whole bunch of nonsense that contradicts the Bible
- Graffiti stating that Neptunians are pussies
- Suitable spot for super-cool secret base
- European electronic-music composer Vangelis
- Another probe that got lost on its way to Mars; way to go, Mars probe
- Scientists not sure, but from way probe has been acting, they're thinking it found gold
- Enormous lake of methane dumped there illegally by Pacific Gas and Electric in 1971
- Probe is a crybaby that will not shut up about how cold Titan's -289° surface temperature is

America's Finest News Source.™

Herman Ulysses Zweibel
Founder

T. Herman Zweibel
Publisher Emeritus
J. Phineas Zweibel
Publisher
Maxwell Prescott Zweibel
Editor-In-Chief

My Reclining Squirrel Kung Fu Stance Is Eminently Defeatable

By Quaking Rodent
Master of Losing at Kung Fu

Dare you face me? I should think so! Even the most craven cowards of our land shake with laughter at my challenge. The most feeble and infirm peasants shrug with indifference when I pass. Far and wide, my name is known, and no men feel the slightest quaver of fear when they look upon me! For I am the legendary Quaking Rodent, and my Reclining Squirrel stance is eminently defeatable!

Do not stand there looking at your shoes! Prepare to humiliate me! Face me with honor and make ready for the battle that you will win.

I will disgust you as I beg for mercy!

I have journeyed for almost a day, detouring several miles to avoid the frighteningly high bridge over the Yue Jiang river, so that I might challenge the one man in all of China who any girl-child could conquer! The elders told me there was no one worse at kung fu than you. "Ha!" I laughed in their faces. "My technique is infinitely inferior to any he may have learned!" After I apologized and begged the elders for their mercy, I made a vow. "I shall find this man you speak of, wherever he is napping. And, on the day I find him, I will be beaten to a bloody pulp!" Now I stand before you, and we will see who holds the title of Worst Kung Fu Master.

And, as you stand over me on the field of victory, my master Breaking Reed shall look down from the heavens and laugh with derision at my total annihilation at your hands! Ha ha ha ha, he will laugh!

I am down here on the floor, coward! Prepare to beat me! All shall conquer practitioners of the notoriously ineffective Reclining Squirrel stance! *You will destroy me!*

Many years have I studied in anticipation of this day, laboring under the gentle tutelage of ancient master Breaking Reed, who taught me the Contemptible Way of the Reclining Squirrel. It was said of Breaking Reed that none had ever lost to him, so well trained was he in the arts of the squirrel stance. He remains to this day the only man I have ever defeated in battle. Yes, you heard me correctly—I killed my master! And on this day, you shall annihilate me and avenge his death.

Do not stand there looking at your shoes! Prepare to humiliate me! Face me with honor and make ready for the battle that you will win.

Your superior kung fu shall wreak devastation upon my famous Squirrel-Covering-Nuts maneuver! Your fists will easily overcome my pathetic Skittering-To-Other-Side-Of-Tree defense! I will shatter in the face of your attack as I deploy the Blank-Staring-Face move! No matter how useless your technique, you shall be victorious. The Reclining Squirrel stance can only be defeated!

And, as you stand over me on the field of victory, my master Breaking Reed shall look down from the heavens and laugh with derision at my total annihilation at your hands! *Ha ha ha ha*, he will laugh!

My death is certain! Face your destiny and break me apart like a clod of dirt!

Nothing cannot defeat Quaking Rodent! The Slightly Twitching-Tail attack leaves no mark! The Relaxing-On-Branch kick has never caused my opponents the slightest bit of damage! And if that's not enough, then you will finish me with my signature move, the one it took me years to hone to perfection: The Bloated-With-Acorns-And-Too-Sleepy-To-Move defense!

Quit your sniveling! I have cowered in fear before hundreds of warriors. You have come face to face with the one man in all of China weaker, dumber, and lazier than yourself! Prepare for battle, Stunted Duckling! For you will live to see the sun rise tomorrow! Ø

CRIME

Crime Scene Used To Be Cool

LOS ANGELES—According to early arrivals at the scene of a multiple homicide in Koreatown, the alley is no longer cool.

Crime scenester Troy Gassel, 25, arrived at the crime scene around 6 p.m. Monday, when he and friends found two dead males slumped against a Dumpster behind Yo Minh's Korean Barbecue.

"It was cool, but then more people started showing up, and somehow the police got wind of what was happening," Gassel said. "Once they got on the scene, you couldn't even approach the bodies anymore. They turned the perfect little out-of-the-way place into a mob scene."

"The traffic cops had fucked up my evidence by the time I got there, but you basically expect that," Cramer said. "The rookies get the call on the radio and show up for social hour. There were so many blue-suits, I could barely turn around."

Gassel added: "My friends and I totally discovered those bodies."

LAPD officer Jason Carmanica was patrolling a nearby park when he saw a group of people gathered in the alley.

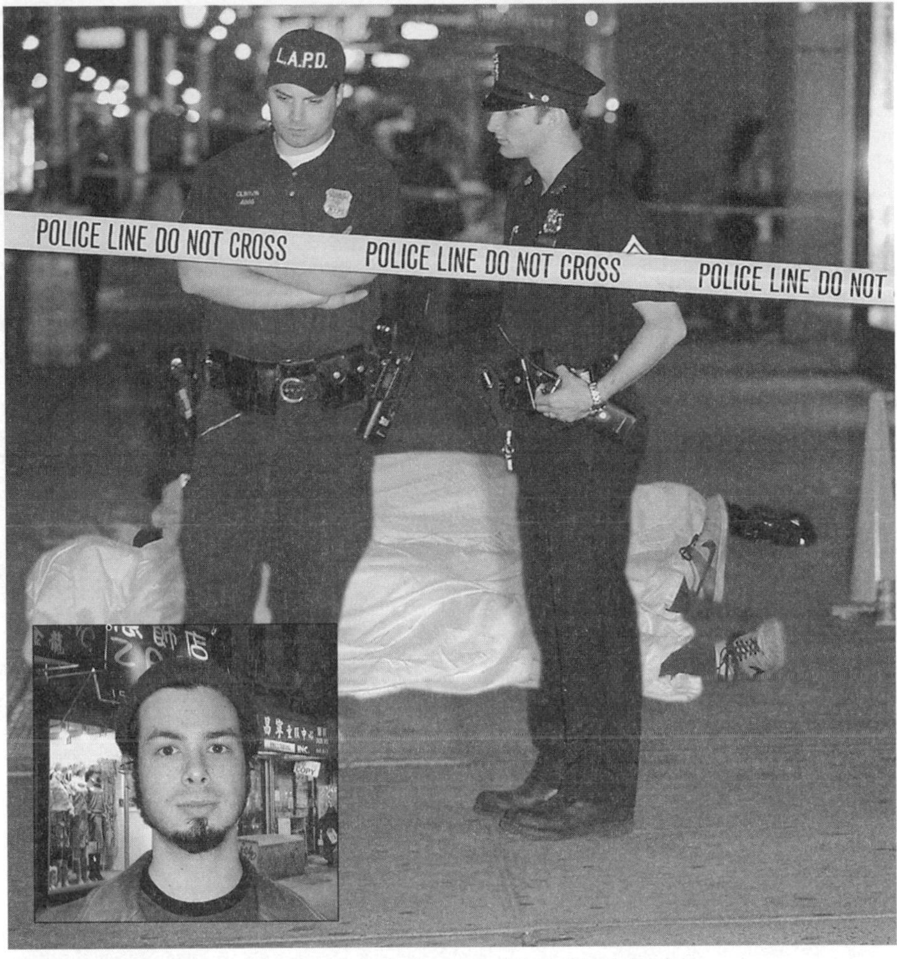

Above: Gassel, who split a Koreatown crime scene shortly after Carmanica and Strenge (above) showed up.

"When I showed up, I was the only member of the force on the scene," Carmanica said. "It was just people from the neighborhood: a couple ratty kids, a mailman, and some guy who was throwing out a mattress. That first APB about the murders? Mine."

Carmanica said the scene was initially "mellow."

"It was real laid-back at first—no sirens, just the

see CRIME SCENE page 52

NEWS IN BRIEF

Roommate Not Seen For, Like, Five Days

LEXINGTON, KY—Ty Crandon and Wesley Sandino realized Tuesday that they haven't seen roommate Joel Kramer in, like, five days. "Dude, have you seen Joel?" Crandon asked Sandino as the two sorted the mail. "No? Shit. His door is closed, but I knocked and there was no answer. I don't think I've seen him since, like, Thursday." Sandino and Crandon said they figure he's been staying at girlfriend Nora Krause's or something, and they hope he's all right.

GEICO Saves 15 Percent Or More By Discontinuing Advertising

WASHINGTON, DC—Executives at the car-insurance company GEICO learned Monday that they could slice 15 percent or more from their operating budget by discontinuing their extensive TV advertising campaign. "We couldn't believe it when we found out how much we could save by axing that ad campaign," said Tony Nicely, GEICO's chairman, president, and CEO. "Dropping that CGI gecko saved us a quarter of a million dollars—and it only took one phone call to our marketing department." Nicely added that sometimes a company has to save money to save money.

Doctor Unable To Hide His Excitement From Patient With Ultra-Rare Disease

ROCHESTER, MN—Dr. Erich Stellbrach, a general practitioner at the Mayo Clinic, could barely contain his exhilaration Monday upon discovering that patient Oliver Patterson, 54, has the extremely rare degenerative nerve disease Gertsmann-Straussler-Scheinker syndrome. "Mr. Patterson, I'm so sorry to tell you this, but you have—you're not going to believe it—spinocerebellar ataxia!" Stellbrach said, waving an x-ray of Patterson's spinal cord. "It afflicts only one in 2.9 million people!" Stellbrach recommended Patterson begin aggressive treatment to mitigate his impending brain dysfunction and onset of dementia, and made the patient promise to remain in his care.

Breathalyzer Big Hit At Cop Party

AMARILLO, TX—In spite of the George Jones cover band or the Porterhouse steak dinner, the Lifeloc FC-10 Portable Breath Alcohol Tester was the hit of the Amarillo 12th Precinct Police Jamboree Monday night. "Hey, hey, hey, hey, it's my turn—gimme that or I'll shoot ya," said a besotted Sgt. Bill Dugan as he pawed at the breathalyzer in Officer Jack Ermi's mouth. "I just did five Cuervo shots, and I wanna see if I can get my blood number thingy up to .300." Attendees at the Jamboree said passing around the breath tester was nearly as fun as the impromptu pepper-spray fight at last fall's Coptoberfest.

Part Written Specifically With Sylvia Saint In Mind

SAN BERNARDINO, CA—Aspiring porn screenwriter Dick Shavers said Monday that he wrote his script Blonde Rambition for Czech-born actress Sylvia Saint. "Sylvia's an incredible performer, so I wanted to create a project that I could involve her in," Shavers said. "She's got a real knack for portraying vulnerable innocence with the experience of a pro. I knew Sylvia was the only person who could play the cum-hungry co-ed who gets double pumped by two black studs." Shavers added that he thinks Saint already owns the cheerleading outfit required for the first scene. ⌀

PROTEST from page 49

Protesters who lined the Pennsylvania Avenue parade route and turned their backs on the president's motorcade had the stated goal of "forcing President Bush to respond to widespread criticism of his administration." To the disappointment of Heiko and his fellow protesters, Bush was able to continue to ignore widespread criticism, because of the one person who didn't show up.

Heiko said he was reluctant to censure the person responsible for turning what would have been a successful protest into an irrelevant social hour.

"If 25,000 protesters had turned their backs on Bush, he would have publicly acknowledged that a huge portion of America disapproves of his policies," Heiko said. "As it is, 24,999 of us wasted our Wednesday on a little monkey charade."

Polls confirmed that, due to underattendance, the protest also failed to reach its second goal: altering public opinion of Bush.

Casey Baldwin of Lake Charles, LA saw a photograph of the protests on page A32 of the *Natchitoches Times*.

"There were 24,999 of them standing out there, facing the wrong way," Baldwin said. "It looked pretty silly, to tell the truth."

Heiko said he was reluctant to censure the person responsible for turning what would have been a successful protest into an irrelevant social hour.

"Maybe the one person who allowed Bush to ignore the opinions of 45 percent of America has a busy schedule," Heiko said. "I sure hope he had a good reason for making all 24,999 of us stand out in the cold looking foolish for three hours."

Above: Boston resident Tom Kenyon relaxes in his apartment as Bush's motorcade passes through Washington, D.C.

In *Quantum Power To The People*, Alan Jeffords explains that protests must attain a "magical number" in order to be effective.

"Often, an individual believes that his participation in a protest isn't important," Jeffords said. "This couldn't be further from the truth. In every protest that has ever failed in the entire history of the world, the failure has been scientifically traced back to a single individual who didn't bother to show up."

For both progressive and conservative protesters, this participation tipping point often proves maddeningly elusive.

In 1998, the Sierra Club's rally to protect an old-growth forest in northeastern Washington failed because Seattle environmentalist Eddie Burgess decided to forgo the protest and "jam with his buddies."

In 1999, the effort to withdraw city funding from the Brooklyn Art Museum for the Sensation exhibition would have been successful, had Jed Maheu shown up on the exhibit's opening day. Instead, Maheu spent the day with his daughter, and taxpayer dollars funded the showing of a Chris Ofili painting that used elephant dung and pornographic photos to depict the Virgin Mary.

In April 2003, the massive Not In Our Name protests were one person short of stopping the invasion of Iraq.

Historians agree that a small group of very powerful people has shaped the nation by staying at home.

"Sixty-one people have defined our era," said Roger Graham, a history professor at the University of California, Berkeley. "If these individuals had chosen to attend politically motivated public gatherings at key moments, we'd be living in a very different country right now."

Inauguration protester Adrienne Brown said that she's disappointed, but "naming names doesn't do any good."

"You know who you are," said Brown, who missed work Thursday to drive to Washington, D.C. "It's your fault that our protest had absolutely no effect whatsoever on the policies of the Bush administration, and you've got to live with that." Ø

CRIME SCENE from page 51

regular guys from the beat with their thermoses of coffee," Carmanica said. "Then the detectives show up, shoving past you like they own the place. And those goddamn paramedics. I was like, 'I was here before you even heard about it from your dispatcher, so don't tell me to step away from the body. You step away from the body.'"

LAPD detective Allison Cramer arrived at the crime scene a little after 6:45 p.m.

"The traffic cops had fucked up my evidence by the time I got there, but you basically expect that," Cramer said. "The rookies get the call on the radio and show up for social hour. There were so many blue-suits, I could barely turn around."

Officer Mark Strenge, who has been with the LAPD for six months, drove for nearly an hour to see the bodies.

"It was pretty amazing," Strenge said. "Lights flashing, tape everywhere, lieutenants yelling, 'Strenge, get me some gloves! Gloves!' The detectives were cool, too. I was talking to a couple of them, asking them who might have killed the victims and why. But then the reporters showed up, and suddenly everybody was too busy to talk to me."

According to Strenge, "as soon as the press gets wind of a new crime scene, it's over."

Tracy Zsidak, a staff reporter for the *Los Angeles Times*, has been on the crime beat for more than 15 years.

"I was getting some great material," Zsidak said. "It was just me, the police, the paramedics—all talking literally 10 feet from the bodies. Then the poseurs from the local TV affiliates started showing up, shoving cameras in everybody's face, and the lieutenants go mum and say, 'Get behind the tape like everyone else.' Those hacks don't know the first thing about the crime scene. With them, it's crime today, entertainment tomorrow—they'll go whichever way the wind blows."

KABC 7 News reporter Alex McPhearson said the crime scene was "pretty fun."

"But those forensics-squad guys give the worst quotes," McPhearson said. "It's like they're more interested in taking pictures of everything than being part of what's going on."

Strenge concurred.

"Pfft, forensics," Strenge said. "It's like, 'Oh, you found a strand of hair. Oh, you got some pictures of blood for your evidence files.' I saw the *body*, man."

LAPD forensics expert Hank Trevario said he had mixed feelings about the downfall of the crime scene.

"At first, it's kind of cool to be let behind the tape where the rest of the crowd can't go, but the novelty of that wears off pretty quickly," Trevario said. "You start to notice how crowded and noisy it is, and it starts to annoy you that it takes 20 minutes just to find your commanding officer."

According to Trevario, the once-hot crime scene is now just another tourist spot.

"After we leave, a crime scene is never the same again," Trevario said. "We take everything that mattters. People can write their true-crime books or make their TV shows, but they won't ever get it right. You can't recapture that feel once it's gone."

"Still, for a brief period, that crime scene was happening," Trevario added. "And I was there." Ø

CHILDREN from page 49

Above: Drawings by children who saw the Super Bowl XXXVIII halftime show.

worked extensively with orphaned and amputee children in Third World war zones. "I've found that children can be amazingly resilient, but this event was too much for many of them to take. The horrible image of that breast is likely to haunt them for the rest of their lives."

According to the 500-page report filed by the FCC, more than 90 percent of the children who saw the exposed breast said they were "confused and afraid."

"Mommy has dirty chest bumps," said a 5-year-old boy quoted in one of the thousands of case studies compiled by the FCC. "She's like the bad lady on TV. I'm afraid Mommy will take off her shirt and scare everyone. I hate Mommy."

Girls were traumatized as well, often expressing apprehensions about sexual development. According to Wasserbaum, one 8-year-old girl told her parents that she didn't "want to get evil breasts."

Wasserbaum said children of both genders associate their trauma with footballs, presumably because of the context in which they were exposed to the breast.

A great number of children who witnessed the tragedy are still plagued by nightmares of sun-shapes that recall Jackson's nipple ring. Of the infants who saw the breast, 76 percent are unwilling to breast feed or use a bottle, forcing their parents to nourish them intravenously.

"When the tragedy took place, we knew it would cause psychological trauma, but we had no idea how long the effects would last," Wasserbaum said. "Our worst fears have been confirmed. It will take years to repair the damage."

Cases of deviant sexual development induced by breast-glimpsing are widespread amongst older children. Pathologies range from schoolyard exhibitionism to gender-role confusion and violent shirt-tearing.

"The FCC imposed the maximum $27,500 penalty on each of the 20 CBS-owned television stations," Wasserbaum said. "But the government offered no recompense to the individuals exposed to the breast. And neither Jackson nor Timberlake has ever specifically apolgized to the children whose lives they ruined, or donated a penny for the adolescents' psychiatric care."

"Mommy has dirty chest bumps," said a 5-year-old boy quoted in one of the thousands of case studies compiled by the FCC. "She's like the bad lady on TV. I'm afraid Mommy will take off her shirt and scare everyone. I hate Mommy."

Across America, parental concern over the condition doctors have dubbed Nearly Naked Breast Disorder continues to grow.

"How can my son Brandon be expected to make it through something like that unscathed?" asked mother of four Shonali Bhomik of the San Francisco-based What About the Children? Foundation, one of many social-awareness groups spearheading the fight for increased NNBD funding in Congress. "For approximately 1.5 seconds, he saw a breast. The image was seared into his innocent, tiny retinas. He can't close his eyes without replaying the whole ugly scene over and over in his little head."

"For the love of God—that breast was almost nude," Bhomik added.

Bhomik said she has concerns about her son's development.

"I shudder to think how this could affect my son once he reaches puberty," Bhomik said. "Little Brandon just wanted to watch the fun halftime show with his family. He was only 10 years old."

Bhomik is one of millions of people facing every parent's worst nightmare: that their child will see a partially exposed breast.

Wasserbaum said there is no way to predict whether the children will recover.

"One thing is certain," Wasserbaum said. "For us as a nation, the horrific consequences of almost-nakedness have only just begun to make themselves apparent."

Wasserbaum added that children who saw the televised breast in Europe, Australia, and various other nations throughout the world were somehow unaffected by the sight. ⌀

RELATIONSHIP from page 49

on the first date, which is suicide in this dating market. It's not the sort of thing that generally leads to a permanent merger."

But after a sluggish first month marked by lack of confidence and speculations of diminishing returns, the couple began to gain upward momentum, and the figures quickly rose. Dating activity increased 43 percent, and both parties began to generate interest in each other's hobbies and activities, resulting in marked personal growth for both.

"It's no surprise that Deanna opted to synergize with Kirk," Klein said. "He's known for his predictability, and women at Deanna's maturity level tend to value that asset."

After unexpectedly high dividends in the first quarter, the couple announced a correction in the form of a "cooling off" period. By mutual decision, they devalued the relationship and began to see other people.

"It's no surprise that Deanna opted to synergize with Kirk," Klein said. "He's known for his predictability, and women at Deanna's maturity level tend to value that asset."

Friends projected that the couple would continue to underperform for the remainder of the second quarter, citing data from Herman's previous partnerships. But the couple surprised everyone with a living-space and possession merger in November.

"No one predicted the relationship would become so profitable so quickly," Klein said. "If anything, prior commitment models suggested a slow decline in adoration, possibly leading to dissolution of the partnership by mid-second quarter."

In spite of their friends' low expectations, the couple has maintained solvency.

"It appears that Kirk and Deanna are both fully invested in the partnership," Klein said. "Initially, there was some fear that their relationship model had ballooned beyond their means, but their affection output continues to show strong growth. I now believe their long-term plan is feasible."

Herman and Greunwald enter the third quarter with expectations running high.

"While Kirk and Deanna are still in the boom period, I have no reservations in providing an optimistic forecast for the close of the romantic year," Miller said. "Clearly, they got in on the ground floor of something big." ⌀

COMMUNITY VOICES

Someday, I Will Copyedit The Great American Novel

Most of my coworkers here at Washington Mutual have no idea who I really am. They see me correcting spelling errors in press releases and removing excess punctuation from quarterly reports, and they think that's all there is to me. But behind these horn-rimmed glasses, there's a woman dreaming big dreams. I won't be stuck standardizing verb tenses in business documents my whole life. One day, I will copyedit the Great American Novel.

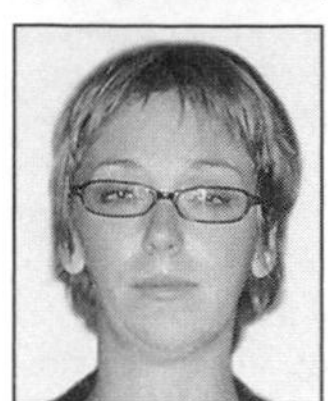

By Joanne Cohen

"Sure," you say, "along with every other detail-oriented grammarian in the country. "Yes, I know how many idealistic young people dream of taking a manuscript that captures the spirit of 21st-century America and removing all of its grammatical and semantic errors. But how many of them know to omit the word "bear" when referring to koalas? How many know to change "pompom" to "pompon"?

> **To a writer who didn't strive for perfection, my corrections would seem niggling. But the author of the Great American Novel will understand that I am as essential to his book as the ink that will cover sheaf after sheaf of virgin paper.**

Copyediting is a craft. A good copy editor knows the rules of punctuation, usage, and style, but a truly great copy editor knows when to break them. Macaulay's copy editor let him begin sentences with "but." JFK's copy editor knew when to let a split infinitive work its magic. You need only look at Thackeray to see the damage that overzealous elegant variation can do. Right now, there's a writer out there with a vision as vast as Mark Twain's or F. Scott Fitzgerald's. He is laboring in obscurity, working with deliberate patience. He isn't using tricks of language or pyrotechnic plot turns. He is doing the hardest work of all, the work of Melville, of Cather: He is capturing life on the page. And when the time comes, I'll be here—green pencil in hand—to remove the excess commas from that page.

With clear eyes and an unquenchable thirst for syntactical truth, I will distinguish between defining and non-defining relative clauses and use "that" and "which" appropriately. I will locate and remove the hyphen from any mention of "sky blue" the color and insert the hyphen into any place where the adjective "blue" is qualified by "sky." I will distinguish between "theism" and "deism," between "evangelism" and "evangelicalism," between "therefor" and "therefore." I will use the correct "duct tape," and not the oft-seen apocope "duck tape." The Great American Novel's editor will expect no less of me, for his house will be paying me upwards of $15 an hour, more than it paid the author himself.

To a writer who didn't strive for perfection, my corrections would seem niggling. But the author of the Great American Novel will understand that I am as essential to his book as the ink that will cover sheaf after sheaf of virgin paper.

Some people edit copy because they choose to. I copyedit because I *must*. It isn't merely a matter of making a living. If it were that, I would have been line editing years ago. No, I've been fascinated by the almost mathematical questions of copy since the summer of my 15th birthday, when I found a leather-bound diary hidden away in the cupboard of an old abandoned farmhouse. In the diary, a young housemaid recorded her hopes, fears, and aspirations.

That summer, I spent many hours poring over the handwritten book, pen in hand, correcting grammar and writing "sp" next to words. I urged paragraph breaks, provided omitted words, and indicated improper capitalizations with a short double-underline. I wrote "stet" in the margins when I made a mistake. Even though I knew Miss Charlotte would never see the notation, I wanted the text to be flawless.

In my mind's eye, I can see the galleys of the Great American Novel on my desk. There is no time to waste. Deadlines have been missed, for the writer has passed out on his desk many times after writing into the wee hours. But, finally, he has perfected the 23rd draft. His work is done.

I get myself a fresh cup of coffee, get out several sharpened green pencils, and adjust my noise-reduction headphones for the long task ahead. I lower my head into my cubicle. My work is just beginning. Ø

HOROSCOPES

Your Horoscope

By Lloyd Schumner Sr.
Retired Machinist and
A.A.P.B.-Certified Astrologer

Aries: (March 21–April 19)
This Thursday, you'll find out that being nibbled to death by ducks is not merely an elaborate figure of speech.

Taurus: (April 20–May 20)
You've always assumed your greatest flaw was the third arm growing out of your cheek, but it's actually that you refuse to give of yourself.

Gemini: (May 21–June 21)
A long journey over water lies ahead for you this week, and—thanks to a rather overconfident cruise-ship navigator—for many weeks to come.

Cancer: (June 22–July 22)
You may think of yourself as a victim of horribly tragic circumstances, but God put a lot of time and effort into making sure things happened just so.

Leo: (July 23–Aug. 22)
You've slaved away for months to design your own fashion line, but it's your boyfriend who will make a splash with his insouciantly tucked-in turtlenecks.

Virgo: (Aug. 23–Sept. 22)
It'll only be three days until authorities find you and the tic-tac-toe-playing chicken shacked up in a cheap hotel.

Libra: (Sept. 23–Oct. 23)
There's really no denying he's a literary talent, but frankly, you don't find Terry Southern's pseudonymously published erotic novel to be all that great.

Scorpio: (Oct. 24–Nov. 21)
You may be ruggedly handsome, but you're nothing next to the spot where Sandy River flows by Storm Mountain.

Sagittarius: (Nov. 22–Dec. 21)
Unfortunately for you, the Bible addresses the fact that there is a time to live and a time to die, but it's vague on the subject of zombies.

Capricorn: (Dec. 22–Jan. 19)
Although you'll crack three ribs, the TV footage will concentrate on the puppy you saved and pretty much ignore you.

Aquarius: (Jan. 20–Feb. 18)
You don't see why everyone puts such a premium on listening to others. It's obviously better to use that time to decide what you'll say next.

Pisces: (Feb. 19–March 20)
It's unlikely anything important will happen this week, but if it does, you're urged to contact the zodiac's toll-free Event Transpiration Hotline.

TOOTHPASTE from page 22

amounts of blood. Passersby were amazed by the unusually large amounts of blood. Passersby were amazed by the unusually large amounts of blood. Passersby were amazed by the unusually large amounts of blood. Passersby were amazed by the unusually large amounts of blood. Passersby were amazed by the unusually large amounts of blood. Passersby were amazed by the unusually large amounts of blood. Passersby were amazed by the unusually large amounts of blood. Passersby were amazed by the unusually large amounts of blood. Passersby were amazed by the unusually large amounts of blood. Passersby were amazed by the unusually large amounts of blood. Passersby were amazed by the unusually large amounts of blood. Passersby were amazed by the unusually large amounts of blood. Passersby were amazed by the unusually large amounts of blood. Passersby were amazed by the unusually large amounts of blood. Passersby were amazed by the unusually large amounts of blood. Passersby were amazed by the unusually large amounts of blood. Passersby were amazed by the unusually large

> **The ninjas seemed shocked by how quickly I went down.**

amounts of blood. Passersby were amazed by the unusually large amounts of blood. Passersby were amazed by the unusually large amounts of blood. Passersby were amazed by the unusually large amounts of blood. Passersby were amazed by the unusually large amounts of blood. Passersby were amazed by the unusually large amounts of blood. Passersby were amazed by the unusually large

see TOOTHPASTE page 101

NEWS

Jealous God Wants Area Man's '69 Charger

see RELIGION page 8D

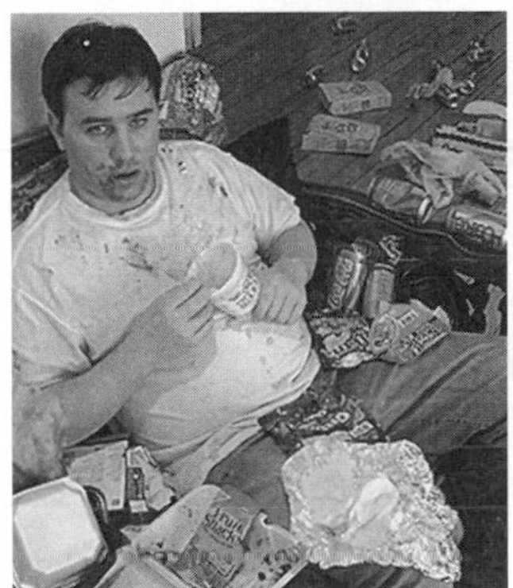

Amazing 'Human Fly' Lives Off Diet Of Garbage

see NATURE page 18F

Parents' Values Skip A Generation

see FAMILY page 20G

Local Submissive At Bottom Of Her Game

see PEOPLE page 5H

STATshot

A look at the numbers that shape your world.

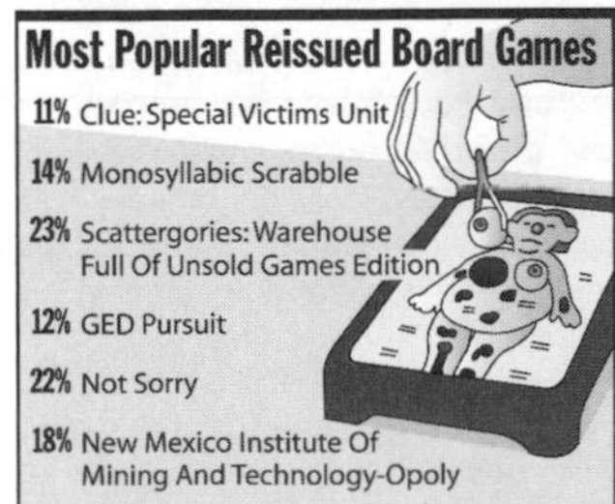

Most Popular Reissued Board Games
11% Clue: Special Victims Unit
14% Monosyllabic Scrabble
23% Scattergories: Warehouse Full Of Unsold Games Edition
12% GED Pursuit
22% Not Sorry
18% New Mexico Institute Of Mining And Technology-Opoly

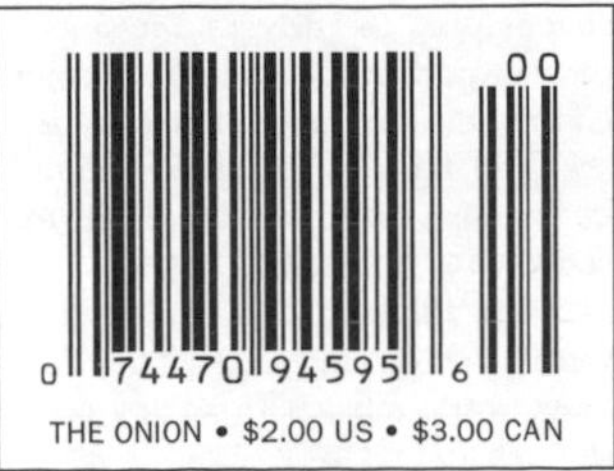

THE ONION • $2.00 US • $3.00 CAN

the ONION®

VOLUME 41 ISSUE 05 AMERICA'S FINEST NEWS SOURCE™ 3–9 FEBRUARY 2005

REPORT

180 Trillion Leisure Hours Lost To Work In 2004

Above: A Detroit resident spends valuable leisure hours at an auto plant.

BOSTON—According to a report released Monday by Boston University's School of Lifestyle Management, more than 180 trillion leisure hours were lost to work in 2004.

"The majority of American adults find work cutting into the middle of their days—exactly when leisure is most effective," said Adam Bernhardt, the Boston University sociology professor who headed the study. "The hours between 9 a.m. and 6 p.m. are ideally suited to browsing stores, dozing in front of the television, and finishing the morning paper. Daytime hours are also the warmest and sunniest of the day, making them perfect for outdoor activities. Unfortunately, most Americans can't

see LEISURE page 58

Nation's Leading Alarmists Excited About Bird Flu

WASHINGTON, DC—The avian influenza virus, a mutant flu strain that has claimed the lives of 31 people in Eastern Asia since it was first observed passing from birds to humans in 1997, has the nation's foremost alarmists extremely agitated.

"Right now, the bird flu is just a blip in the newspapers, but if the avian influenza virus undergoes antigenic shift with a human influenza virus, the resulting subtype could be highly contagious and highly lethal in humans," Matthew Wexler, the president of the National Alarmist Council and one of the nation's leading fear mon-

see FLU page 58

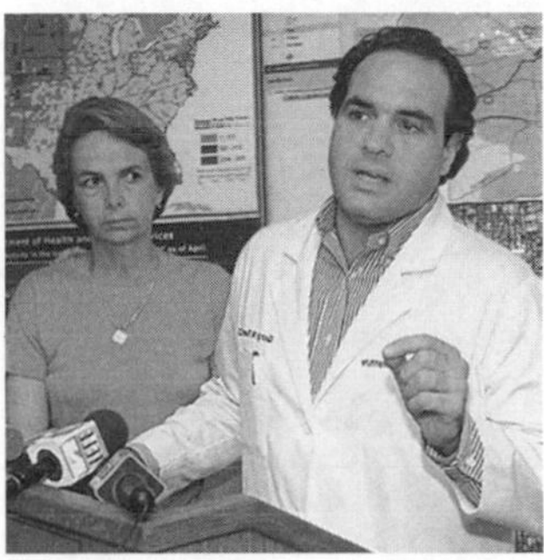

Above: Representatives from the Alarmist Council.

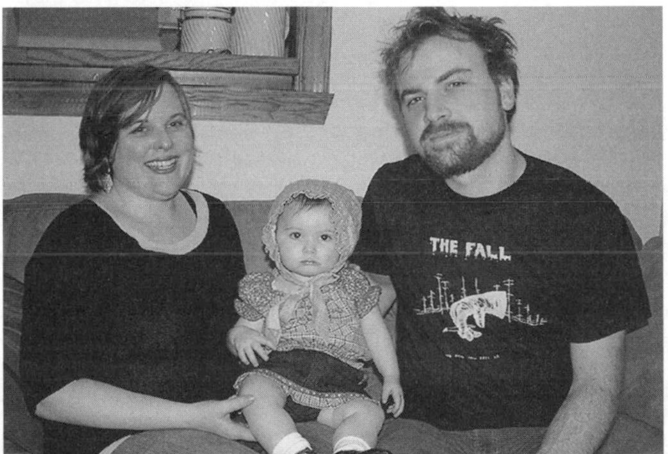

Above: Garver and Meyers display their child.

Dress-Up Doll Born To Area Couple

NEW YORK—Two years ago, Manhattan married couple Ron Garver and Becky Meyers weren't sure they were cut out for parenting. They worked long hours, had a thriving social life, and their East Village apartment was small and cramped. But 24 months and 73 outfits later, Garver and Meyers are the proud parents of a 10-month-old dress-up doll.

"I didn't think I was ready for a baby," Meyers said Monday. "In my mind, Ron and I were too irresponsible. But next thing you know, I'm pregnant and we're buying sundresses, headbands, little Converse sneakers—you know, I was doing all the important things you need to do in preparation for a baby."

Meyers said she began to read everything she could get her hands on, from catalogs to articles on nursery decorating.

"I was so relieved when our little girl arrived in perfect health," Meyers said. "It's almost impossible to find cute outfits for preemies."

Since their baby's birth, Garver, a staff writer for *New York* magazine, and Meyers, who works in acquisitions at a small film company, have

see DOLL page 59

Tourism In The Tsunami's Wake

While some travelers cancelled vacations to tsunami-stricken countries, others say that tourism is important for rebuilding the area's economy. What do *you* think?

Carla Sparks
Chef

"How can Thailand expect people like me to visit? What am I—made of *bahts*?"

Gordan Rami
Repairman

"I'll bet the tourism drop-off would be reversed if the Western media would shift its focus to more positive coverage of tsunamis."

Brenda Ellis-Lee
Salesperson

"Well, I was going to visit the Greek ruins, but I might as well go where the ruins are still fresh."

Joe Callister
Cashier

"I'll still take my annual vacation in Sri Lanka, but I'm going to be nice to everyone for a change."

Tyler Wilson
Systems Analyst

"Whoa. Talk about the very definition of guilt trip."

Toby Leiffert
Teacher

"It's time for the healing process to begin. Resident of Sumatra, another Mai Tai, please."

Google In 2005

Google recently introduced Google Video, which allows users to search closed captioning for text and screen images taken from television shows. What does Google plan to do next?

- Launch Google Good Men, as good men have historically been hard to find
- Build world-class headquartoogles
- Enter beta testing for Google Apartment, which will let users search for shoes, wallet, and keys

- Patent the idea of looking for something
- Occasionally shut down so people stop taking them for granted
- Add "I'm Feeling Lonely, Miserable, And Unlucky" button to homepage
- Introduce service that allows users to find out how much flour they have left with a single keystroke
- Finally get around to making back-up disks of everything

Google

1505 Salado Drive

Building π (3.14159...)

America's Finest News Source.™

Herman Ulysses Zweibel
Founder

T. Herman Zweibel
Publisher Emeritus
J. Phineas Zweibel
Publisher
Maxwell Prescott Zweibel
Editor-In-Chief

Follow That Prius!

By Kenneth Crafft

Quick, we haven't a moment to spare! He's already an entire public green space ahead of us. Right, sorry—he or she. There...that's him or her right there. That seafoam green car carefully signaling for a turn onto Maple Terrace Drive from Oak Lawn Boulevard. Yes, the one behind the new Beetle. Follow that Prius!

Good! Maintain about a three-Prius distance. We don't want to spook him. If we do, we'll be stuck driving around Greenwich Heights all day looking for that user-friendly gas/electric hybrid. Easy here. Don't get in his blind spot—he's certain to carefully check it before progressing through this intersection. He's turning right on red! Ah. Okay. Good thing he came to a full stop before continuing. We might've lost him. Wait a minute...

In the Starbucks drive-thru! See, I told you. I don't care if that car is capable of delivering an impressive 60 miles per gallon in city driving, the driver is bound to stop for a half-caf, mocha soy latté sometime.

What the...? Clever. Clever indeed! You breezed right through the drive-thru without stopping, huh? I knew you were slippery, but I didn't guess you had the guts to be impolite. Well, at least we know that he's spotted us.

Wait just a minute... He's driving right past the university campus? Give me the map! No, not the guide to the best local ethnic restaurants, the city map! Get on his impact-absorbing, eco-friendly, biodegradable rear bumper—now! Damn, he's using the high-occupancy vehicle lane!

Yes, it's a man. I can tell by that lacrosse emblem on the back of the car. It's just above the endangered-species license plate, to the right of the anti-Bush bumper sticker.

Now, watch this. I've seen it before. He's going to slip behind that carefully arranged display of Pier One imported craft baskets and then do a three-point turn in one of the REI handicapped spots.

Told you. Now just stop here for a minute. Patience...patience... Cut him off in front of the Bed Bath & Beyond! Come on! Go, go, go! Can't this stupid Insight move any faster? If he gets out of the car and makes it into their vast selection of high-quality bed linens, bath accessories, and kitchen textiles, we'll never find him!

The seafoam green one, carefully signaling for a turn onto Maple Terrace Drive from Oak Lawn Boulevard.

Careful! Right now he thinks he's lost us, so don't squeal your low-rolling-resistance tires. Look at the little devil, zipping past the soccer fields at the magnet high school. He's really pushing that ultra-low-emissions 1.5L, four-cylinder engine, that's for sure.

He's merging onto Falls Woods Road toward Martin Luther King Jr. Park! Don't lose him behind all these SUVs. Just do your best.

Look at him, slinking down into the collar of his L.L. Bean Merino Wool "Blue Jean" sweater. He's about to wet his wide-wale corduroys. You'd better be scared, pal. Yeah, this guy's guilty. Granted, we all feel a deep sense of guilt for having grown up with undue privilege, but it goes deeper than that with him. Yeah, citizen, I've got your number. You've been thinking globally with that Prius, it's true. But you've been acting a little naughty locally, haven't you?

Wait just a minute... He's driving right past the university campus? Give me the map! No, not the guide to the best local ethnic restaurants, the city map! Get on his impact-absorbing, eco-friendly, biodegradable rear bumper—*now*! Damn, he's using the high-occupancy vehicle lane! He's risking the fine!

Where is he? Where the...? Damn it. The recycling center. That bastard. Just look at all the seafoam green Priuses in this parking lot! It'll take all day to check them all. Well, start rounding up the drivers. You've seen the fun part of the job, kid, but here comes the not-so-glamorous part. We're in for a long night of politely questioning the upwardly mobile and socially responsible.

And to think that at one point we were close enough to hear the Putumayo world-music CD playing on his stereo. *Damn it.* Ø

Cell Phone Lost, Found, All In Thrilling Four-Minute Period

PITTSBURGH, PA—Emotions quickly changed from panic to joy for University of Pittsburgh junior Evelyn Labaton when she lost, searched for, and found her Nokia 6230 Cingular Wireless cell phone Tuesday.

"All of a sudden, my phone was gone!" said Labaton, 20, who was walking to her 5:10 General Chemistry lecture when she realized the cell phone was no longer in her right pants pocket. "I was like, 'Oh shit!' I looked through my coat and dug through my entire backpack, but it wasn't anywhere."

By the time Labaton completed her search, 48 seconds had passed.

"My heart was racing," Labaton said. "I mentally went through all of the places I'd been since leaving English Lit: the bathroom on the third floor, the bench out in front of Daniel Hall, the bike racks where I saw my friend Shelly."

Continued Labaton: "I stopped right there in the middle of the sidewalk for a few seconds, took a deep breath to calm my nerves, and tried to think. That's when I remembered taking it out to see what time it was when I was at the Java Cup!"

Scanning the ground for any sign of her small, red camera-phone as she walked, Labaton retraced the 200 feet back to the Java Cup, an on-campus coffee shop.

"All the way, I was visualizing the hours it would take to enter all my phone numbers into a new phone," Labaton said. "And that's for the ones I remember. A lot of the numbers would be totally gone forever."

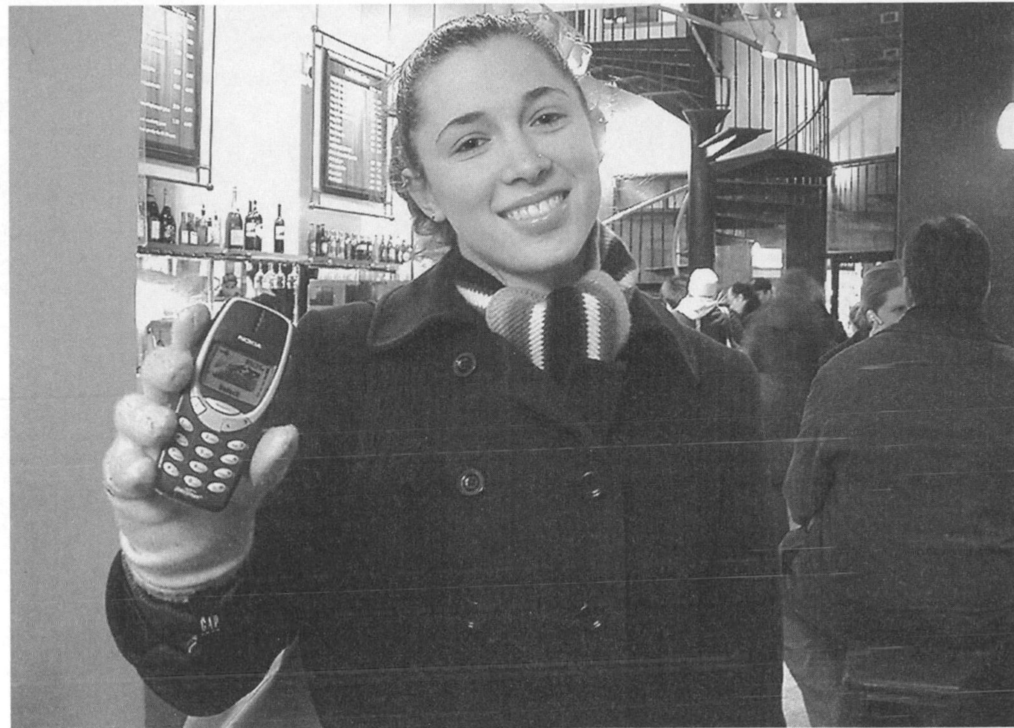

Above: Labaton holds the phone she nearly lost.

Labaton added that she hadn't "even [wanted] to think about" all the ring tones and camera-phone photos she'd lose.

With the search entering its second minute, Labaton went into the coffee shop, where she said she saw the dirty plate and glass she'd left in the bus station a few minutes before, after consuming a large skim latté and a poppy-seed bagel.

As the search dragged on into its 200th second, Labaton said she continued to consider the magnitude of the hassle that a lost cell phone would create.

"I knew I wouldn't have time to shop for a new phone until the weekend, so I'd be phoneless for a few days," Labaton said. "Also, I'd been considering whether to switch from Cingular Wireless to another carrier, but I really didn't want to have to rush that decision."

Labaton went to the table where she'd been sitting, tapped the shoulder of one of the two females seated at it, and asked permission to look around for her phone.

"Oh, is that it?" the woman said, and Labaton spotted her familiar red

see CELL PHONE page 60

NEWS IN BRIEF

Sex Life Embellished During Doctor Visit

DURANT, OK—During a routine physical Tuesday, Jason Gunder, 21, exaggerated his sexual exploits for the benefit of his physician, Dr. Stanley Pindel. "Unprotected intercourse? Sure, I have it *all* the time," Gunder said. "Partners? Thirty or something. I've had so many, I can't even remember." After nodding thoughtfully, Dr. Pindel told Gunder, "If you do actually ever have sex, please make sure to use a condom and a water-based spermicidal lubricant."

Jay-Z's Grandfather Busted With Trunk Full Of Canadian Prescription Drugs

BUFFALO, NY—Tyrone J. Carter, rap artist Jay-Z's 75-year-old grandfather, was arrested Monday for transporting prescription drugs across the Canadian border in the trunk of his 1998 Oldsmobile. "My grandson says I shouldn't have unlocked the trunk unless the cops had a warrant, but what's a man supposed to do?" said Carter, who was busted with more than $1,000 worth of pharmaceutical-grade Diovan, Lipitor, and Lanoxin. "Don't the police have anything better to do than hassle a sick old man? My insurance doesn't cover my pills anymore—I gotta get my heart medicine somewhere." The arresting officers said the pills had a U.S.-pharmacy value of nearly $18,000.

Son Attempts To Cultivate Parents' Interest In Better Movies

DOVER, DE—Marc Morehouse, 24, made another vain attempt to improve his parents' taste in movies Monday by taking them to see *Sideways*. "I know you guys thought *Meet The Fockers* sounded really funny, but maybe we should all give something a little different a try," Morehouse said to his parents Kirk and Doris as he bought three tickets at an area cineplex. "Dad, you like golf, right? And Mom drinks wine, so this movie is right up your alley. It'll be fun." After the show, Morehouse could not convince his parents to have dinner at a non-chain restaurant.

Immigrant Laborers Hired To Delete Spam

SAN DIEGO—Executives at Gortman Consulting are hiring immigrant day laborers to delete their junk e-mail. "Our employees were wasting hours of valuable time sifting through spam," Gortman CEO Donald Barris said Monday. "Finally, I was like, 'Eureka! Hire some low-cost Hispanic laborers to empty our Outlook Express trashcans.' Our IT van just swings by the docks in the morning and picks up a dozen or so guys." While Barris said the laborers are "happy for the work," labor-rights groups have complained that repeatedly pressing the delete key has caused numerous cases of carpal-tunnel syndrome among migrant spam removers.

Kool-Aid, Hi-C Make Backroom Deal To Destroy Tang

NORTHFIELD, IL—Executives for Kool-Aid and Hi-C met at an undisclosed location Monday to map out a plan to drive Tang out of business. "The tween market isn't big enough for three non-carbonated beverages," Kool-Aid CEO Robert Eckert told Hi-C executive Jason Frie. "Capri Sun and Sunny D play ball, but Tang won't budge. So we're gonna squeeze them so hard, even the astronauts won't drink it. Oh, yeah!" Bordon crushed out his cigarette and added, "I wan[illegible] you to stick it so deep in Tang's a[illegible] hole, you make the Wyler's hit [illegible] like a movie date." ⌀

LEISURE from page 55

enjoy leisure during this time, for the simple reason that they're 'at work.'"

In addition to surveying 12,000 citizens nationwide, researchers studied data from seven different government agencies.

Deborah Kletter, an expert in the field of rest and relaxation, emphasized the pervasive nature of the problem, which she said affects 96 percent of employable Americans year-round.

"Week after week of potential relaxation time is squandered to jobs, with millions of would-be leisurers prohibited from sleeping in, working on hobbies, or taking trips," said Kletter, executive director of the Five-To-Nine Foundation. "An average employed person's ability to stroll aimlessly around his town and 'do whatever' is basically nonexistent 49 weeks out of the year."

The report's internals reveal that full-time workers are hit hardest, with part-time workers coming in a close second, and freelancers marking a distant third.

Above: A group of friends enjoy some rare leisure hours in Sunnyvale, CA.

Kletter said there is a vast disparity between the U.S. and Europe, where a strong leisure ethic is taught during youth.

"Americans simply can't keep up with the European leisure force," Kletter said. "In such fields as suntanning, skiing, and cooking elaborate meals that can be eaten over the course of an entire evening, Europe has us beat."

The report's internals reveal that full-time workers are hit hardest, with part-time workers coming in a close second, and freelancers marking a distant third.

"Ironically, the unemployed fared the best in this report," Kletter said. "One of the questions that remains unanswered, unfortunately, is how jobless citizens' high number of available leisure hours somehow fails to translate into overall happiness."

Bernhardt and Kletter found that employed persons do find one small but regular opportunity for leisure.

"In general, Saturdays and Sundays were unaffected by work," Kletter said. "Unfortunately, this fact does little more than underscore the fact that a serious problem exists five out of seven days of the week."

The loss of leisure-related revenue is another factor to consider, Kletter said.

"Leisure-time reduction is costing America billions of dollars in weekday concert-ticket revenue, airfare, and violin lessons," Kletter said. "I don't understand why the government hasn't already stepped in."

"Americans simply can't keep up with the European leisure force."

Kletter said that, "on the bright side," many Americans have learned to reclaim leisure time through aggressive multi-tasking.

"Americans have an impressive ability to do several things at once," said Kletter, who compiled the at-office leisure figures. "Enterprising workers managed to shop online, have long-distance telephone conversations with friends, and stare at their cubicle walls for hours. Those findings are very encouraging."

Bernhardt and Kletter acknowledged that their report was responsible for the loss of nearly 2,000 leisure hours. ⊘

FLU from page 55

gers, said Monday. "My professional opinion, and more importantly, my personal belief, is that this is a cause for great national alarm."

Wexler's sentiments were unanimously upheld by members of the alarmist community.

"The bird flu could cause a global influenza pandemic similar to the Spanish Flu that killed more than 20 million people in 1918," medical alarmist Dr. Preston Douglas said. "Many experts also believe a major global flu outbreak to be imminent, if not—God forbid—already underway. Why, recent observation and documentation has recorded at least one case of human-to-human transmission of a rare strain of the avian influenza virus. If this one case is proof that the animal virus is mutating into a contagious, lethal human virus, then the entire world is basically doomed. Doomed!"

Douglas is best known for his brilliant alarmist analyses of flesh-eating bacteria, Ebola, and SARS—all of which he successfully developed into topics of major international trepidation.

"The bird flu could cause a global influenza pandemic similar to the Spanish Flu that killed more than 20 million people in 1918," Douglas said.

Bird flu was first identified as a strain of infectious influenza in Italy in the early 1900s. Of the 15 subtypes, only subtypes H5 and H7 are known to be capable of crossing the species barrier from birds to humans. The first human outbreak, which occurred in Hong Kong in 1997, killed four people. Since then, the bird flu has remained a relatively minor virus, killing fewer individuals than common-cold variants. The Centers for Disease Control and Prevention have issued neither an epidemic warning nor a public-health alert in connection with bird flu.

According to leading alarmists, the CDC's lack of immediate concern is a cause for alarm.

"So, basically, the CDC doesn't have the first inkling of what to do about a potentially explosive form of flu that infects ducks and chickens," said Fox News Science, Health, and Epidemics Commentator Marylinne Kent. "Given the popularity of these two birds as a food source among Asians, and the fact that we have no idea how many undocumented Asians have settled illegally in our nation, the potential for danger is extremely high."

"I urge you all to think of your families," Kent added.

Harold Jefferson, a founding member of the American National Citizen's Institute for Alarm, read from a prepared statement Tuesday.

"We have to face the facts: This isn't just a rapacious killer that could be incubating anywhere within our borders and for which there is no known cure," Jefferson said. "It is also an indicator of the profound indifference of millions of American citizens. Mark my words: People who aren't scared now will look pretty stupid if it turns out that they should have been."

Jefferson added: "The bird flu could someday claim as many lives as Mad Cow Disease."

Ruth Herrin, the *New York Post*'s

see FLU page 59

DOLL from page 55

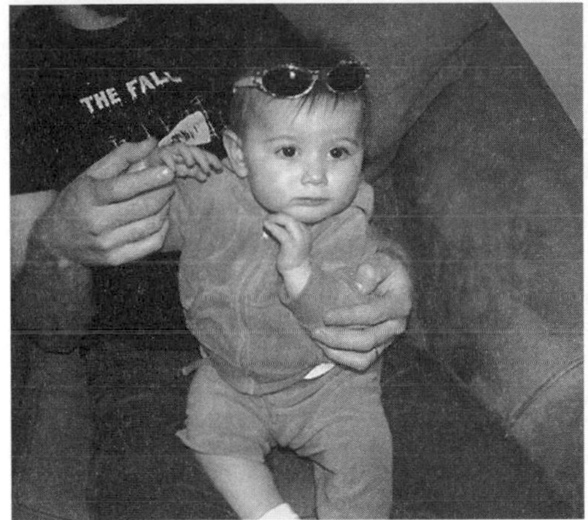

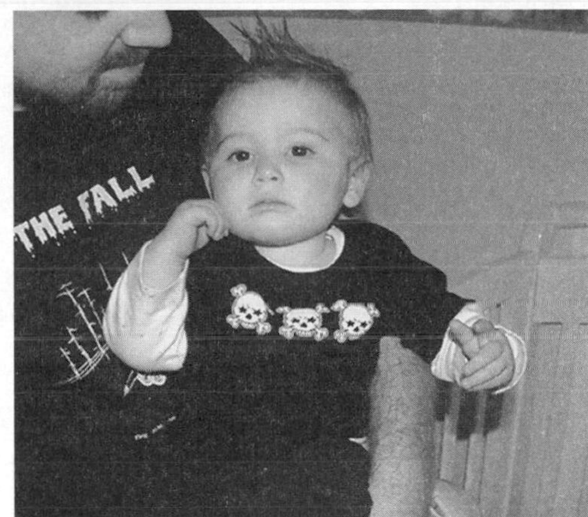

Above: Meyers and Garver's child photographed throughout the day Monday.

spent nearly 30 percent of their income on baby clothes.

"We don't just buy anything, though," Garver said. "It has to be something that's missing from her wardrobe. Last week, I got Daddy's little girl a little Knicks jersey to wear to the games. Everyone thinks it's adorable. She's already been on the Jumbotron!"

Garver said his daughter is not always in an athletic mood.

"Did you know they sell Clash shirts for babies?" Garver said. "Everyone at work gets such a kick out of my little punk!"

After Meyers gave birth to the baby, she said she had to adjust to the "full-time job" of primping their child for display.

"For a while, we never got any sleep!" Meyers said. "She'd wake up in the middle of the night, and we'd have to get up, take her out of her sleeper, put her in her breakfast PJs, and feed her. Sometimes, I barely had the energy to plan her outfits for the next day."

"Having a child is a lot of work," Meyers added. "Coming up with the idea to dress your baby like a farmer, a police officer, or even a little sunflower is difficult enough on its own. But if she's sleepy or fussy, it can take a half an hour to dress her. Still, when you hear the coos of the neighbors who see her in the Baby Jogger, it's all worth it."

Garver and Meyers have discovered many unexpected responsibilities, such as making sure that their daughter is bundled up in an adorable snowsuit when it's cold.

"Every trip outside requires a hundred decisions," Meyers said. "Should she wear her bear coat or her cute red-velvet Santa jacket? Is today a bunny-ears kind of a day, or does it feel like more of a plaid-wool-cap morning? Sometimes, if our social calendar requires it, we have to pull together three or four outfits in a single day."

The baby does not always wear special outfits, however.

"If we're spending the night in, she might just lounge around in a Nike sweatsuit, some grubby old T-shirt from two months ago, and one of those sweaters Grandma sent," Garver said.

Garver and Meyers said they had to make some sacrifices after they became parents.

"We've had to make some changes in order to save money," Meyers said. "But we've learned to rely on accessories to freshen up a look. And we keep an eye out for sales. It takes a bit more time than just heading to Macy's, but we've scored some really great little sunglasses and backpacks. Nothing is too much for our little doll."

Even though she spends a great deal of time shopping for her baby, Meyers said she believes that the best gift she can give her daughter is her time and attention.

"Just last week, I thought, 'Wouldn't it be cute if I took a picture of her on the phone?'" Meyers said. "I spent an hour figuring out how to strap her hand to the telephone. Then, I had to make it look like she was talking by giving her a little baby food to chew on. If you snapped the photo at the right moment, it totally looked like she was talking on the phone. My sister told me I was crazy, but I said 'You just wait until you see the photo!'"

"Having a child is a lot of work," Meyers added. "Coming up with the idea to dress your baby like a farmer, a police officer, or even a little sunflower is difficult enough on its own. But if she's sleepy or fussy, it can take a half an hour to dress her. Still, when you hear the coos of the neighbors who see her in the Baby Jogger, it's all worth it."

Garver and Meyers said that, in spite of the financial and social sacrifices they have had to make, they have "never once regretted the decision to keep the baby."

"This isn't about Becky and me," Garver said. "This is about building our child's self-esteem, because we love her. Which reminds me, we're really looking forward to Valentine's Day. We found an adorable pink dress with little wings on the back for our little Cupid. How can she not be happy with all the attention everyone will give her? Plus, her hair's finally growing in, so we can stop using the hats. She never seemed to like those." ⌀

FLU from page 58

veteran panic expert, has relied heavily on information provided by alarmists in the scientific community.

"Listen, I'm no disease expert," Herrin said. "But I know that people should be warned about global devastation any time a devastation scenario can be extrapolated from an actual news report. And for the 16th consecutive month, that time is now."

None of the nation's 15,000 certified alarmists have offered a strategy to deal with a possible outbreak.

"Listen, finding cures is not my job," Wexler said. "I just report the facts as best and as briefly as I can. Then I interpret them in what I, as an alarmist, believe to be the most effective fashion. And if what I perceive here is real—namely, a looming epidemic and an atmosphere of apathy and fatalism in the U. S. medical community—then we are facing Armageddon." ⌀

LAMPSHADE from page 5

amounts of blood. Passersby were amazed by the unusually large amounts of blood. Passersby were amazed by the unusually large

"Oh yeah, right. And *I'm* the *regional manager* at *Taco Bell*!"

amounts of blood. Passersby were amazed by the unusually large amounts of blood. Passersby were amazed by the unusually large amounts of blood. Passersby were amazed by the unusually large amounts of blood. Passersby were amazed by the unusually large amounts of blood. Passersby were amazed by the unusually large

see LAMPSHADE page 201

HARVEY'S HOLLYWOOD

The Golden Globes Were A Golden Time!

Item! The Golden Globes recently took place, answering the question "Who will the foreign press honor this year?" Well, how's **Hillary Duff** for starters? She won Best Actress for **A Million Dollar Smile**, where she plays a boxer. She sure did grow up fast! Meanwhile, **Jamie Fox** won **Best Black Actor**, and rightly so. His speech alone was worth the award! From a Jackie to a Jamie: Way to go!

The Outside Scoop
By Jackie Harvey

Now, longtime fans of awards shows know that the Golden Globes are important for two reasons. First, they're a good indicator for what's going to be hot at **Oscar** time. Second: fashion! It's like watching a parade of peacocks. Everyone there was dressed to impress, and boy, did they! And who was that lovely brunette? **Charliee Theron?!?** Don't worry, gentlemen! In spite of your preferences, Ms. Theron is every bit as beautiful as she was when she was blonde, especially in that strapless number. Boy. I just want to take a moment to congratulate her on the turnaround she has undergone since her **Monsters, Inc.** debut. Charliee has made some real changes in her diet and lifestyle, and it shows. **Natalie Portman**, on the other hand, didn't do herself any favors with that frumpy grandma gear. Give yourself and your fans some credit, Natalie! Well, there were plenty of notable ups and downs, bobs and weaves. If I were magician-turned-fashion-critic **Mr. Blackstone**, I'd devote the entire column to the hots and nots, but I have other fish to fry.

Remember Ben and JenLo? Those two kids were made for each other. Ben and Jen, if you're listening, won't you please meet and talk it out? You can make it work.

Is it me, or is there a distinct lack of **inspirational TV movies** these days?

Item! Mid-season replacement time sure does sneak up on you. Where do the series go? Thank God there are plenty of new plots and personalities to wash away the precious memories of those series that just couldn't get it together. For my money, the show to watch this round is **Christie Alley's Fat Actress**. In it, the **Veronica's Closest** star endures the slings and arrows of press and peers as she embarks on a public weight-loss odyssey. Actually, wait. That's terrible. Don't let anyone tell you you're fat, Christie. You look just fine.

Item! Mooo-ve over, **Kangaroo Jack**! You have competition from a horse of a different color. And talk about different! **Racing Stripe** stars **Malcolm And The Middle scamp Frankie Muñoz** as a zebra who thinks he can race. Does he overcome the odds, win the big race, and warm hearts in the process? I don't know.

Now that I got a raise here at **the Scoop**, I think it's time to treat myself to an **iPod**. Everywhere I turn, I see those little white headphones, and I confess that I'm envious. You can store the entire **Depeche Mode** collection and still have plenty of room for other songs. I'll have to wait until my raise kicks in, though. I am resolved: No matter how great those little gadgets are, I will not allow one of them to lure me into credit-card debt. No thank you!

Item! It's not the best way to begin the year, but **Brad and Jen** have called it quits. Why is it that women named Jen are unlucky in love? Remember **Ben and JenLo**? Those two kids were made for each other. Ben and Jen, if you're listening, won't you please meet and talk it out? You can make it work.

Scoop thoughts and prayers go out to **Steven "Cojo" Caru**, who is recovering from a kidney transplant. **The Today Show** is always a little brighter when Cojo drops by and gives you the straight stuff on new accessories, so here's hoping the maverick of gloves and broaches is back on his feet and flaunting what he's got, stat. (Stat is **emergency-room code**. Instead of saying, "Dr. Harvey! Hurry to the O.R., this guy's body is rejecting the new kidney!" they would just say, "Dr. Harvey to O.R., stat." Dr. Harvey—I don't mind the sound of that!)

My neighbors still haven't taken down their Christmas lights. I always take mine down on New Year's Day. It's a **Harvey Tradition**. I was thinking of saying something to them, but I don't want to be the bad guy of the block, especially since I need to hit people up for my **MS Bowl-A-Thon** next month.

I would like to take some time to offer a moment of silence for **Law And Order's Jerry Orbock**, who died of cancer in December.

Item! CNN's flagship show **Crossfire** was cancelled a few weeks ago. Some people say it was cancelled after **John Stewart**'s controversial appearance, during which he dropped the **A-Bomb** on **Tucker Carlson**. Thanks for nothing, Mr. Stewart. Maybe seeing political experts hash it out wasn't your cup of tea, but those of us who live for witty repartee between pundits and insiders like Carlson and the **Ragin' Cajun James Carvell** now have no place to go. Except the papers, but I don't like how newsprint gets all over my fingers.

Well, that's the scoop, for the time being. More stuff's a-boiling, but it's not quite a-done. But get yourself a-ready for the a-spicy a-stew of a-juicy celebrity gossip and sharp insight that is my specialty! Here's a taste...I'll have some hot news on the newest charitable cause from **That '70s Show's Gopher Grace**, as well as the astrological info on **Jeffrey Tambor's** new baby! Until then, I'll see you next time...on The Outside! ⌀

HOROSCOPES

Your Horoscope

By Lloyd Schumner Sr.
Retired Machinist and A.A.P.B.-Certified Astrologer

Aries: (March 21–April 19)
While the particulars of your final destination are unknown, the dread realm of Death doesn't seem so bad anymore, now that Johnny Carson's there.

Taurus: (April 20–May 20)
You'll perform an act of selfless bravery next Friday in the false belief that the cameras are catching the whole thing.

Gemini: (May 21–June 21)
Sure enough, when your adopted Chinese daughter arrives next week, you won't be able to understand a word she says because of her near-perfect English.

Cancer: (June 22–July 22)
Nostalgia turns to tedium when, after inheriting your grandfather's cherished Zippo lighter, you waste two days figuring out how to fill the damn thing.

Leo: (July 23–Aug. 22)
You'll have no idea how to feel after being honored with a Kennedy Center Lunchtime Achievement Award.

Virgo: (Aug. 23–Sept. 22)
You should carefully examine your thoughts and motivations before allowing yourself to experience ecstasy over William Safire's retirement.

Libra: (Sept. 23–Oct. 23)
You'll cry because you have no shoes, but you frickin' cry at everything.

Scorpio: (Oct. 24–Nov. 21)
It's said that if you die spectacularly and alone, you're a hero, but if you take others with you, you're a goat. Still, the human cannonball you'll soon meet for .00046 seconds will be the toast of the town.

Sagittarius: (Nov. 22–Dec. 21)
You'll be surprisingly unconcerned with the theft of your intellectual property this week, when you find out that God stole your idea for a giant flying carnivorous porcupine that breathes fire.

Capricorn: (Dec. 22–Jan. 19)
While you're happy you're no longer trapped on a desert island, it's getting tiresome to tell the story every time you ask about current celebrities.

Aquarius: (Jan. 20–Feb. 18)
It's nice that you want to talk to kids about smoking, but everyone would rather you did it in public, during the day.

Pisces: (Feb. 19–March 20)
You'll be in rough shape after taking a long-distance airplane journey just barely over water.

CELL PHONE from page 57

phone under a chair.

"I was like, 'Yes!'" Labaton said. "Every ounce of stress drained from my body."

According to Labaton, it was only when she located the cell phone that she noticed her clenched teeth, tensed neck muscles, and sweaty palms.

"I let all that tension go," Labaton said. "It was a magical feeling."

Labaton thanked the woman at the table and returned the cell phone to her pocket.

"God, was I relieved," Labaton said. "I really didn't know if I'd be able to find the phone."

Labaton slipped into the back row in her 120-person chemistry lecture and tried to catch her breath. Slumped in her seat, she said she scanned the faces of her classmates as they leafed through notebooks, chatted, and laughed.

"The other students had no idea what I'd just been through," Labaton said. "It was such a relief when Professor Butte started class, so I could zone out and try to forget the whole thing." ⌀

NEWS

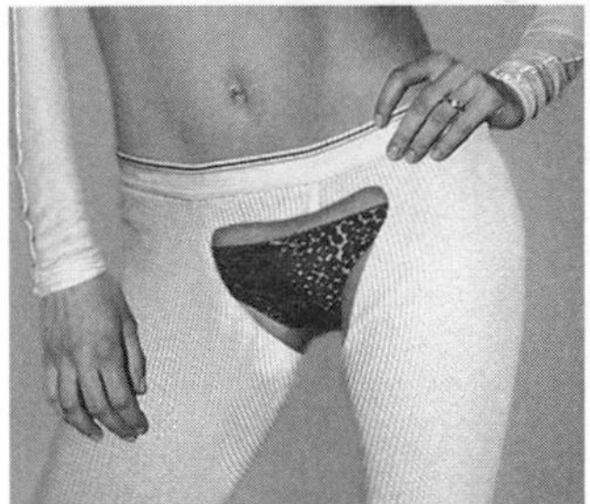

Frederick's Of Anchorage Debuts Crotchless Long Underwear

see FASHION page 14E

Guy In Rome Does As The Tourists Do

see TRAVEL page 7H

Area Man A Walking Bag Of Hazardous Biological Waste Material

see FAMILY page 20G

STATshot

A look at the numbers that shape your world.

Where Do We See Ourselves In Five Years?
13% Women's plus-size section
26% Watching rerun of show we're currently watching
21% Still in Iraq
28% Same spot, different couch, playing Playstation 3
12% Unsold skeleton in Midwest Medical Supply warehouse

the ONION®

VOLUME 41 ISSUE 06 | AMERICA'S FINEST NEWS SOURCE™ | 10–16 FEBRUARY 2005

Above: McNabb attempts to go long with a two-liter bottle of refreshing Pepsi in the third quarter.

Product Placement Mars Otherwise Exciting Super Bowl

JACKSONVILLE, FL—Although NFL commissioner Paul Tagliabue declared the Super Bowl XXXIX experiment with in-game product placement a success, fans and players expressed mixed feelings about the championship game Monday.

"Don't get me wrong—this year's Super Bowl was an exciting face-off," said Philadelphia Eagles head coach Andy Reid, whose team was pitted against the New England Patriots in Alltel Stadium Sunday. "The Patriots got a couple big plays on our defense before we adjusted to tackling players doused in Axe Deodorant Bodyspray For Men. But you can be sure they felt the heat of our Ford Motor Company sponsored Lincoln Mark LT blitzes. Our nose tackle drove this season's hottest new luxury truck straight into their offensive line."

see SUPER BOWL page 66

Latest Bin Laden Videotape Wishes America 'A Crappy Valentine's Day'

Above: Bin Laden tears up a "putrid Western Valentine's Day trifle" during his videotaped message.

WASHINGTON, DC—A new videotape of Osama bin Laden broadcast on the Arab satellite news channel Al-Jazeera Monday beseeched Allah to grant all Americans a "crappy Valentine's Day."

"This Feb. 14th on the Western infidels' calendar, may all Americans receive no valentines from their beloved ones," bin Laden said. "May the homemade construction-paper mailboxes taped to the desks of the American schoolchildren remain empty, as well. May whomever you ask to 'bee yours' tell you to 'buzz off.'"

Bin Laden called for "romantic humiliation for all Americans of courting and betrothal age."

"Allah willing, embarrassment and tearful rejection shall rule this day," bin Laden said. "Paper hearts shall be rent and trod upon, and dreams of love delivered stillborn. Body language shall be misinterpreted, crushes unrequited, and sincere expressions of affection mocked. Invitations to dinner will be rejected, just as Americans have rejected Allah, the one true God."

During a speech before the Oklahoma Cattlemen's Association, President Bush condemned the al-Qaeda leader's remarks.

"[Bin Laden's] sinister call for romantic disappointment on Valentine's Day is yet another demonstration of the ruthless hatred this evil individual harbors for the American way of life," Bush said. "He directs rage at even our youngest and most innocent citizens,

see BIN LADEN page 64

Woman Begins To Regret Dating Someone Spontaneous

Above: Bird and Maddox spend an afternoon at home.

AUBURN, CA—After four months of romantic involvement, Wells Fargo mortgage lending assistant Heidi Bird, 27, said Monday that she is beginning to regret getting into a relationship with the carefree Jason Maddox.

"Jason was everything I wanted in a boyfriend as recently as three months ago," Bird said. "I used to dream of meeting someone who knew how to have fun and didn't let himself get weighed down by formalities and obligations. But my dreams never had the part where that person doesn't call for a week, then drops by at 3 a.m. with a broken mannequin torso under his arm."

Bird said she was swept off her feet by the handsome 30-year-old in August, when she met him at a local park. A part-time bicycle-shop employee and occasional street musi-

see WOMAN page 64

The In-Flight Cell-Phone Ban

The FCC is currently reviewing its ban on the use of cell phones during flights, but many passengers say they like the restriction. What do *you* think?

"If they lift the ban on cell-phone use, they better lift the ban on passengers beating the shit out of each other, too."

Carla Sparks
Chef

"But...but...what about the disastrous effect cell phones could have on aircraft navigational systems?! Nooo!"

Gordan Rami
Repairman

"I don't know. Last year, the airlines lifted the ban on seat-kicking and look what happened."

Brenda Ellis-Lee
Salesperson

"Awesome! Now I can call my girlfriend and join the Mile High Solo club."

Joe Callister
Cashier

"What an ideal marriage of the Wright Brothers and Alexander Graham Bell. And Kafka. And Pavlov. And Mengele."

Tyler Wilson
Systems Analyst

"Now the only thing left is to fill the cabin with ankle-deep brackish ice water, and air travel will be about perfect."

Toby Leiffert
Teacher

Columnist Crackdown

Columnists Armstrong Williams, Maggie Gallagher, and Michael McManus are under fire for accepting payment for promoting Bush administration policies. Who else has received public money, and for what?

- Michael Kinsley, *Time*—$100,000 to say he "can feel the Clear Skies Initiative working"
- Bill O'Reilly, *Fox News*—$500 per "shut up" yelled
- Carlos Gutierrez, *The Peru-Bolivia Grower*—$1.2 million for "past considerations" and continued silence
- Crazy Don Dunbar, *WRMQ*—$100,000 for every time he calls Saddam Hussein "So Damn Insane"
- Ann Coulter, *Universal Press Syndicate*—At least a few hundred thousand a year to say provocative things that distract liberals from the real problems of the Bush administration
- Catherine Edmonds, *Reader's Digest*—$50,000 to finally print Donald Rumsfeld's "Humor In Uniform" joke about the chief petty officer, the lemur, and the Cambodian laundry girls
- Jim Davis, *Universal Press Syndicate*—$350 for having Garfield laud Social Security privatization in four-panel discussion with Odie
- Roger Ailes, *Fox News*—Given $600,000 and told not to change a thing

America's Finest News Source.™

Herman Ulysses Zweibel
Founder

T. Herman Zweibel
Publisher Emeritus
J. Phineas Zweibel
Publisher
Maxwell Prescott Zweibel
Editor-In-Chief

Truth Be Told, I Have Nothing To Say

By Corey Steinhoff

If I may interject here, I'd like to point out something I think the group will find relevant—or if not relevant, at least somewhat interesting—regarding the ongoing discussion. Well, to be honest, I doubt the group will actually find it interesting, since technically, it doesn't pertain to the current topic. What I'm trying to get across—if I can have your attention for just a minute or two—is that I have nothing to say.

If you'll give me a chance to finish my point, Donna, I'll be able to explain. I mean, I hate to be rude, but I don't like to be interrupted when I'm in the middle of trying to say something, even if that thing has no value at all. I mean, I've been sitting here listening to all of you go on and on about every little thing. I would think you could do me the same courtesy by allowing me to dominate the conversation for a moment.

Let me begin by asking you a few questions: Don't I have as much right as anyone else at this meeting to be the center of attention? Why should I be punished because I have nothing to add about rising energy costs, plummeting revenues, and...all that other stuff? Why shouldn't I be allowed to spin 10 or 20 meaningless paragraphs of hollow verbiage to bolster my self-esteem?

Ladies and gentlemen, the fact of the matter is that I enjoy talking. Correction—I have a desperate, pathological need to talk and, more importantly, to be heard by other people. Furthermore—and I believe this notion to be of the utmost importance in understanding my overall lack of a point—I am extremely good at talking for extended periods of time, to which I might add—

Excuse me! I'm speaking here! Thank you.

To begin again: To which I might add, in addition to these abilities that I just mentioned, I have also my verbosity, discursiveness, and long-windedness—to say nothing of my ability to string together three synonymous, re-

Ladies and gentlemen, the fact of the matter is that I enjoy talking.

dundant, and repetitive terms in a row, as I just did, twice in the same sentence—all of this is of paramount importance to the point I am trying to make...

Excuse me! Will you at least let me finish my sentence?!

What was I saying? Well, it couldn't have been important. At the end of the day, I'm sure you'll agree that what it all comes down to is not so much that it all comes down to anything, but that it comes down to nothing. In summary, I have no summary. And in conclusion, I have no conclusion. Nevertheless, I enjoyed my opportunity to speak. For now I have had a chance to speak, and you have all listened to me. Having said that, I would like to add that, though it may go without saying, I welcome any responses you may have to what I've just said—or more precisely, not said—here today. I am open to any such comments at this time.

All right, then. Donna, you have the floor. Ø

PANTY HOSE from page 32

amounts of blood. Passersby were amazed by the unusually large amounts of blood. Passersby were amazed by the unusually large

If I could pick any superpower it would be the ability to relate to people on a personal level without terror or shame.

amounts of blood. Passersby were amazed by the unusually large amounts of blood. Passersby were amazed by the unusually large amounts of blood. Passersby were amazed by the unusually large amounts of blood. Passersby were amazed by the unusually large amounts of blood. Passersby were amazed by the unusually large amounts of blood. Passersby were amazed by the unusually large amounts of blood. Passersby were amazed by the unusually large amounts of blood. Passersby were amazed by the unusually large amounts of blood. Passersby were amazed by the unusually large amounts of blood. Passersby were amazed by the unusually large amounts of blood. Passersby were amazed by the unusually large

see PANTY HOSE page 43

OFFICE

Project Manager Leaves Suicide PowerPoint Presentation

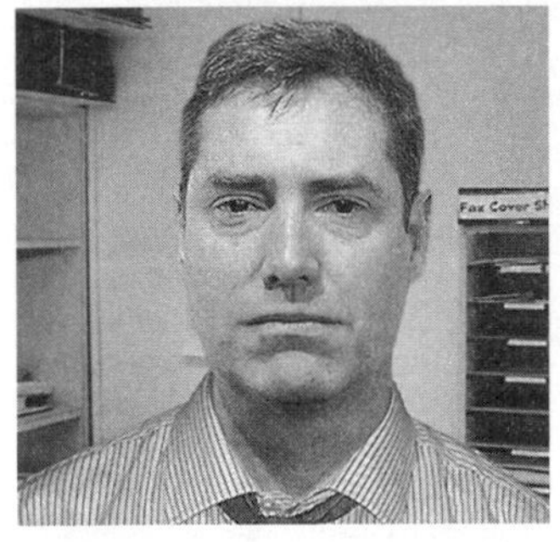

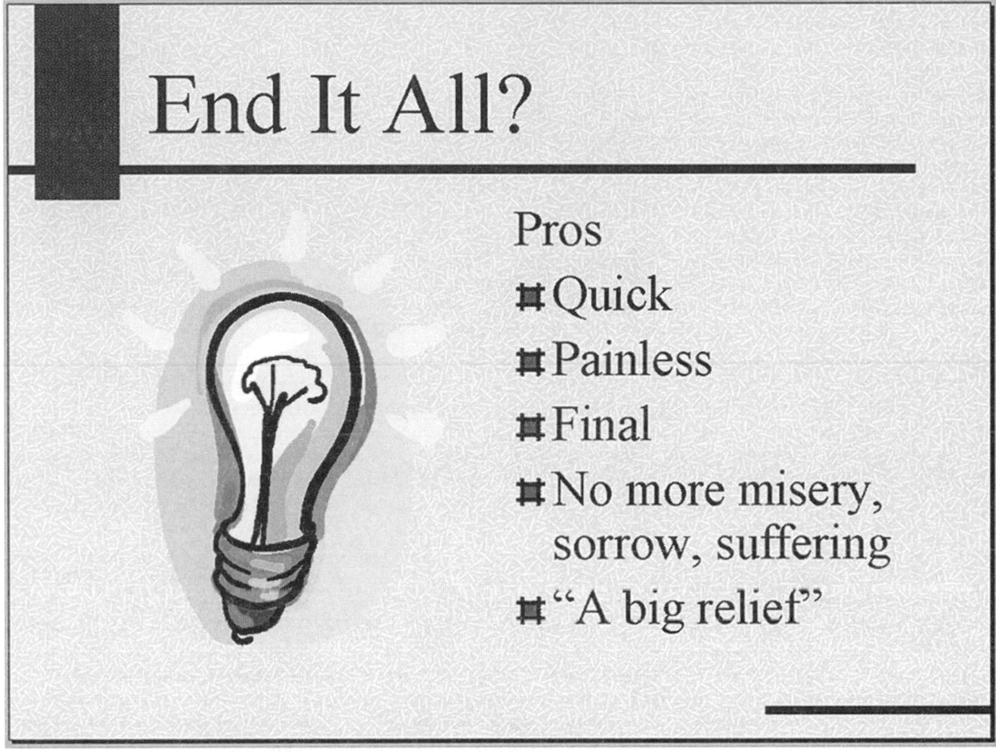

Above: A slide from the PowerPoint presentation left by Butler (left) before his death.

PORTLAND, OR—Project manager Ron Butler left behind a 48-slide PowerPoint presentation explaining his tragic decision to commit suicide, coworkers reported Tuesday.

"When I first heard that Ron had swallowed an entire bottle of sleeping pills, I was shocked," said Hector Benitez, Butler's friend and coworker at Williams+Kennedy Marketing Consultants. "But after the team went through Ron's final PowerPoint presentation, I had a solid working knowledge of the pain he was feeling, his attempts to cope, and the reasons for his ultimate decision."

"I just wish he would've shot me an e-mail asking for help," Benitez added.

Butler broke his presentation into four categories: Assessment Of Current Situation, Apologies & Farewells, Will & Funeral Arrangements, and Final Thoughts.

According to Williams+Kennedy president Bradford Williams, finalgoodbye.ppt was "clear, concise, and persuasive."

"After everyone left the room, I sat down and went through Ron's final presentation in slide-sorter view," Williams said. "Man, I gotta tell you, it blew me away. That presentation really utilized the full multimedia capabilities of Microsoft's PowerPoint application."

"We're really gonna miss Ron around here," Williams added.

In the presentation's first section, a three-dimensional bar graph illustrated the growth of Butler's sorrow during the two years since his wife and only child died in a car accident.

"We all got Ron's message loud and clear when that JPEG of his wife wipe-transitioned to a photo of her tombstone," coworker Anne Thibideux said.

The first section closed with a review of key objectives and critical success factors. The two-column text display was enlivened by colorful background wallpaper and clip-art question marks depicting Ron's confusion over his choice.

The second portion of the presentation comprised an ordered list of goodbyes to colleagues and apologies to friends.

"The colors in Apologies & Farewells were perfectly calibrated for digital-projector display," I.T. di-

see POWERPOINT page 64

NEWS IN BRIEF

Bush Defends Deny-Side Economics

WASHINGTON, DC—Fielding questions from reporters at a Tuesday press conference, President Bush defended his adherence to the principles of deny-side economics. "Nope," the president said. "I keep hearing people say that the U.S. economy is troubled, but that isn't true. Our economy is strong. We just have to keep on doing what we're doing, and everything will work out." Leading economists say they are curious to see whether the president's optimism will trickle down into the public consciousness.

Census Bureau: 9,000 To 15,000 People Work At Census Bureau

WASHINGTON, DC—According to 2004 figures released by the U.S. Census Bureau, between 9,000 and 15,000 people work at the Census Bureau. "It is difficult to obtain an accurate figure on Census Bureau employees, because workers frequently move from department to department," U.S. Census director Charles Kincannon said. "Also, many supervisors failed to return the mail-in forms that asked them to list how many employees they have." Kincannon warned all census-bureau employees to take the census-bureau census more seriously, under penalty of law.

Awkward Tension Mistaken For Sexual Tension

WATERTOWN, MA—Joel Dashner, 34, interpreted acquaintance Lori Rezala's nervous shifting, awkward giggling, and inability to make eye contact at a mutual friend's dinner party as a sign of mounting sexual heat, Dashner said Monday. "I really hit it off with Lori," Dashner said. "We were both too jittery to really say much, but I could feel the spark between us. I'm sure neither of us will forget that magic moment when we bumped hands and spilled each other's drinks." Rezala later told reporters that Dashner "ruined one of her favorite sweaters and stared at [her] all night like he was some kind of crazy person."

'Get TiVo' Friend's Solution To Everything

SANTA MONICA, CA—According to waiter and aspiring writer Ian Shortridge, his friend Dan Stavers has only one piece of advice: "Get TiVo." "You could program a Season Pass so that you never miss the business report," Stavers said, after Shortridge complained that he couldn't get a mortgage. "I'm telling you, TiVo will change your life. Hey, I was right about the iPod, wasn't I?" Since purchasing a digital-video recorder in 2002, Stavers has urged Shortridge to buy one so he can "spend more time writing instead of sitting through all those commercials," "tape some fitness shows and find out how to get in shape," and "catch some funny movies" to help him get over his father's death.

Cocksucker Beats Up Motherfucker

GAINESVILLE, FL—In an ass-kicking on the sidewalk in front of the Red Room on Juniper Avenue Saturday, some 23-year-old cocksucker totally wasted this motherfucker, 22, like the prick was standing still. "You want a piece of me?" asked the motherfucker, who minutes later got his goddamn ass handed to him on a plate. According to some dudes who saw the whole thing, the motherfucker kissed the fucking pavement after the cocksucker delivered a bad-ass left hook. The motherfucker was unavailable for comment because he was busy picking his teeth up off the ground. Ø

WOMAN from page 61

cian, Maddox "was straight out of a romantic Hollywood movie," according to Bird.

"I was walking my dog Shadow when I heard someone call out to me from above," Bird said. "I looked up and saw Jason sitting on a tree branch. He told me he once had a dog like Shadow. Then he asked me to come on up and see the view. I don't usually do stuff like that, but he was so cute and intriguing that I tied Shadow to a bench and joined him up on the branch. We sat up there for two hours eating golden raisins and reading jokes from this kids' joke book he fished from the trash. It seemed magical—at the time."

Although she gave him her phone number, Bird didn't hear from Maddox until two weeks later, when he showed up at her office, thrust a bouquet of daisies into her hands, and began to serenade her on his ukulele.

"Jason showed up right in the middle of my busiest day of the week, and all of my coworkers were staring at him like he was nuts," Bird said. "But no one had ever done something like that for me before, and I just melted. It was such a wonderful resolution to the anxiety I'd been feeling because he hadn't called."

When she showed Maddox out of her building, the two kissed during the elevator ride to the lobby, commencing what Bird described as "a whirlwind love affair, complete with romance, laughter, and amazing sex."

In spite of the good times she has shared with him, Bird said Maddox's

Above: Maddox woos Bird with a romantic gesture.

self-centered approach to romance has "gotten a little old."

"Last week, Jason showed up at my office, called me out of a staff meeting, and said we were going roller-skating," Bird said. "When I told him I couldn't, he was like, 'Well, what am I supposed to do with these roller skates I bought you for our 13-week anniversary?'"

"He lacks a sense of timing—or time, really," Bird added. "When I got mad at him last month for not calling me for six days, he said he was sorry and explained that he'd been 'totally getting into Russia,' whatever that means."

Bird said that, during the initial weeks of her relationship with Maddox, she had hoped to one day accompany him on one of his spur-of-the-moment car trips. After getting lost on the way to Mono Lake with Maddox in November, however, Bird said she resolved "never to travel with Jason again."

"It was sweet that he wanted to sit by the lake holding me in his arms," Bird said. "But he could've had some idea of how to get there. Maybe he didn't mind sleeping in the car at a rest stop, but my shoulder blade still aches from where the seat spring dug into it all night."

Although Maddox frequently demonstrates his affection for Bird, she said his gestures no longer move her.

"Oh, yeah, Jason gave me that," said Bird, waving toward a 6-foot-tall plush bunny in the corner of her office. "There was a time I would've been really into it, but now I'm just wondering how much it cost and if I'll need to buy us both dinner next Tuesday."

Bird added: "I should really get that thing out of here before my supervisor sees it."

Therapist and author Sue Merrill said people often don't foresee the pitfalls of dating a spontaneous person.

"In order to have a viable relationship, you must either match his erratic behavior point-for-point, or maintain an almost bulletproof independence," Merrill said. "Vulnerability is fatal. Ask yourself this, 'Do I have the stamina to water my plants one moment, float in a hot-air balloon an hour later, spend eight days alone, then stand in line at a bail-bonds office until 1 a.m. on a Tuesday?'"

While Bird has no immediate plans to break up with Maddox, she said she "sometimes fantasize[s] about what it would be like to date someone less whimsical."

"I still like Jason a lot," Bird said. "But I swear: The next time he starts to juggle, it's over."

Bird's ex-boyfriend Steve Dandridge, whom she left last May after telling him he was "too boring," said his mellow, undemanding personality might offer Bird a refreshing change.

"I hear that guy she's going out with is running her ragged," Dandridge said. "I guess I could feel happy that I got my revenge, but the truth is, I still miss her. Heidi, if you want me back in your life, gimme a call. I usually go get dinner at 6:45 or 7:00, but I'm always back before CSI starts at 8:00."

Maddox was unavailable for comment, as he was assembling a Cupid costume out of a bed sheet and applying to film school in Poland. ⌀

BIN LADEN from page 61

asking God to quash children's joy by making them receive, and I quote, 'only unwanted valentines bearing the laughable likenesses of out-of-favor pop-culture icons from the recent past, such as the Backstreet Boys and the creatures from *Monsters, Inc.*'"

"Bin Laden's depravity knows no bounds," Bush added.

According to state officials, bin Laden demonstrated an uncanny knowledge of Valentine's Day customs, in spite of the fact that the holiday is not celebrated in the Arab world. In addition to his allusions to classroom valentines, bin Laden cited heart-shaped candies, valentine personal ads in free alternative weeklies, and foot massages.

"In this infamous February, may all American hearts be crushed like a box of conversation hearts that is tossed carelessly into the bottom of a fellow student's schoolbag," bin Laden said. "We soldiers of Allah pledge with our blood and souls that all pink and red carnations shall wither and drop from their stalks before they make their way to the desks of America's secretaries. Instead of receiving hugs and kisses, they and their extended families shall be besieged with boos and hisses."

Bin Laden added: "May your special Valentine's Day dinner be spent at an overrated restaurant that impoverishes your purse and leaves your stomach churning with indigestible Western cuisine."

Bin Laden did not overlook the innocuous custom of giving stuffed animals as gifts.

"The teddy bear that holds the 'I love you' heart does not love you at all," Bin Laden said. "It is an unliving, unholy thing filled only with stuffing. Just as the Western infidel is not bestowed with the blessings of Allah, so shall he go unloved by the false bear."

The release of the bin Laden tape is consistent with the al-Qaeda leader's inclination to speak out before major American events, such as the 2004 U.S. presidential election.

"Perhaps whoever told bin Laden about Valentine's Day exaggerated its significance," departing Homeland Security Secretary Tom Ridge said. "Or, I don't know, maybe he was just itching to release another tape."

The Department of Homeland Security did not raise the terror advisory, recommending that Americans proceed with their Valentine's Day plans. This is in spite of the final words of bin Laden's address.

"Come Monday, as you pry open your fancy, red Russell Stover box, take heed," bin Laden said. "For in the place of tasty caramels and buttercreams, you will find the flaming sword of righteous jihad!" ⌀

POWERPOINT from page 63

rector Bill Schapp said. "I think Ron was the only guy at W+K who understood the importance of running the Gretag-Macbeth Eye-One Beamer on presentations."

The third segment, Will & Funeral Arrangements, included a list of Butler's friends and family indexed with phone numbers, a last will and testament, and scrolling-text instructions for the dissemination of his ashes.

"To Ron's credit, it was one helluva way to go out," human resources manager Gail Everts said. "Ron clearly spent a lot of time on that presentation. If the subject matter weren't so heavy, we'd probably use it to train his replacement."

Copywriter Gita Pruriyaran said the presentation "had room for improvement."

"I felt some of the later transitions were weak," Pruriyaran said. "The point of a transition is to maintain audience interest and lighten the mood. To me, the door-closing sound effects in Will & Funeral were repetitive and heavy-handed. But Ron's choice to end with that Hamlet quote and then fade to black was really powerful. There wasn't a dry eye in the room when Hector flipped off the projector and brought up the lights."

Coworkers were shocked to learn that Butler's document was initially created on Aug. 8, 2004.

"I should have seen this coming, but I didn't," Benitez said. "When Ron started deleting all of his old files last week, I thought he was worried about another hard-drive crash. I never imagined he was, you know, preparing."

"If only we'd all paid more attention to Ron during the Microsoft Project workshop he held last month," Benitez added.

Butler is survived by his parents Gerald and Martha Butler, who described their relationship with their son as "distant."

"Ron would e-mail us photos and home movies, but we're not very good with computers," said Gerald, 71, a retired postal worker. "We tried to stay close, but we just never learned how to open up those files. At the very end, Ron was sending us his suicidal thoughts, but we didn't get the instant message—until it was too late."

Williams+Kennedy vice president Vivien Esterhaus said Butler "will not be forgotten."

"We have made arrangements for his PowerPoint presentation to be stored in the W+K off-site secure file-storage archive," Esterhaus said. "Barring a virus or major computer malfunction, his final words will always be accessible. If only Ron could've been saved, too." ⌀

Point-Counterpoint: Cosmology

Darling, I Will Give You The Moon And The Stars

Dearest Sally, I can no longer hide what I've been feeling since the day you borrowed my pen at Kampus Koffee. If I don't let my emotions out, I'll burst with the sheer intensity of longing to be by your side. All day, every day, I think of nothing but you. I would follow you to the ends of the earth, to the bottom of the deepest sea, or live with you at the top of the highest mountain. You are everything to me, and without you, I am just an insignificant speck in an uncaring universe. Say you'll be mine, and I'll give you the clouds, the sun, the rain, the sky—I will give you the whole world.

By Brandon Hendrickson
English Grad Student

Say only that you will turn your shining smile my way, my love, and I will give you the very moon and stars!

At night, I pore over my assigned reading and try to focus on the immortal words of Byron—but my thoughts drift to you. I love the way you talk, the way you walk, the way you frown over hardbound copies of the Feynman lectures. I adore the way you squint when you are memorizing formulas.

We've been sitting together at the library for six weeks now, but I've never dared to let you know that my feelings go far beyond that of a study partner. But when I hear you discussing your homework with your classmates with such intelligence and passion, I can't help but wish you were whispering those words in my ear, instead.

I will roam the universe for all eternity, gathering up the twinkling points of light one by one.

Darling, you are my heart's one true

see POINT page 66

Giving Me The Moon And Stars Would Have Disastrous Effects On Our Galaxy

You're sweet, Brandon, and I'm flattered, but what you're proposing would never work out. There are so many holes in your proposal that I only have time to cover the most obvious ones.

By Sally Toeffer
Physics Grad Student

First, regardless of whatever emotional motivation you may feel for doing so, you could never follow me to the bottom of the ocean. The water pressure at the bottom of the Marianas Trench exceeds 18,000 psi. A layperson could never be granted access to the type of submarine he would need to go down there. Nor could we go live together at the top of the highest mountain. Even if we could just be dropped off in a helicopter, the ionosphere is so thin that we would both die within a day due to oxygen deprivation and exposure. And Brandon, giving me the moon and stars would have disastrous consequences for our galaxy, and for other galaxies, as well.

Presume, for the sake of argument, that it is within your power to give me the moon. As you know, impact with an extraterrestrial object a fraction of the moon's mass—one the size of Rhode Island, for example—would constitute an extinction-level event for most of the planet. If the moon were to collide with the Earth's surface (where I would be standing when you gave it to me), it is unlikely that even bacteria would survive. The long-term effects of such a devastating alteration in the gravitational field of our solar system could even extend to objects well outside of the Oort Cloud.

The result would be an implosion that would rend the very fabric of space-time.

see COUNTERPOINT page 66

ONION *Love Coupons*

Spice up your love life this Valentine's Day by giving your special someone a few of these romantic coupons.

ONION *Love Coupon*
redeemable for
Five minutes of open, honest conversation before wall of denial and deception slams back down forever

ONION *Love Coupon*
redeemable for
Cunnilingus until orgasm, or five minutes, whichever is shorter

ONION *Love Coupon*
redeemable for
One dinner at restaurant with silverware

ONION *Love Coupon*
redeemable for
One sexual act completed expressly for the purpose of procreating another child of God

ONION *Love Coupon*
redeemable for
One all-expenses-paid trip to the abortion clinic of bearer's choice

ONION *Love Coupon*
redeemable for
Opportunity to voice desire to have a three-way with attractive coworker without recipient breaking down in tears
(Does not include fulfillment of three-way.)

ONION *Love Coupon*
redeemable for
One awkward, emotionally chilly hug that, viewed from the side, resembles a capital "A"

ONION *Love Coupon*
redeemable for
20 percent off normal rates

ONION *Love Coupon*
redeemable for
One square foot of mandatory shaving anywhere below the shoulders

ONION *Love Coupon*
Entitles bearer to pick the porn movie

SUPER BOWL from page 61

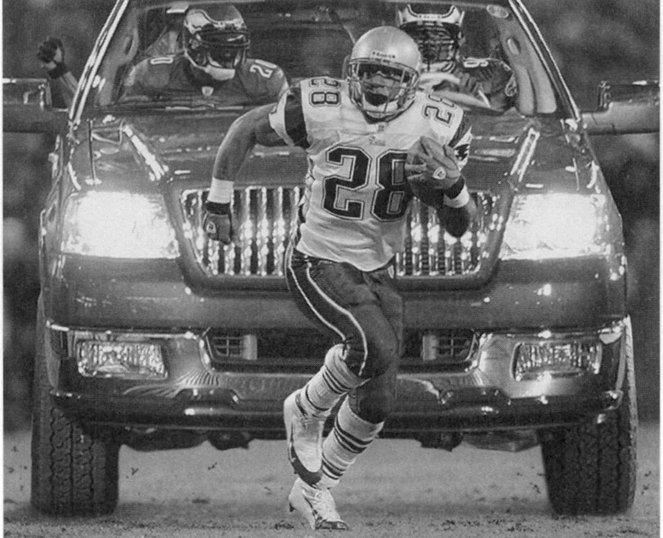

Above: Dawkins (left) and Eagles defensive lineman Corey Simon praised the "smooth handling" of the Lincoln Mark LT they used to chase down Dillon in the second quarter.

In spite of complaints from football fans, Super Bowl XXXIX was a tremendous financial success, with an estimated audience of 2 billion worldwide and a sponsorship revenue exceeding $820 million.

Advertisers as diverse as H&R Block, Verizon, and FTD paid top dollar to have their products and logos used or represented during game play.

"It was great for the team to earn a couple million when we lined up and used the Anheuser-Busch logo as our scrimmage formation," Eagles safety Brian Dawkins said. "Unfortunately, that logo is really elaborate, so we got flagged for having 40 men on the field."

Dawkins was also flagged three times for interference and once for failing to dial 1-800-COLLECT.

Eagles quarterback Donovan McNabb said he believed his completion percentage was harmed by the wind, as well as the difficulties he experienced throwing the two-liter Pepsi bottle, the oversized Viagra tablet, and the 13 other objects that served as balls during the game.

"This is great for the league, but I'm not sure it's the best thing in the world for the players," McNabb said. "The anxiety made me throw to [wide receiver Todd] Pinkston a half-second before he turned and looked back for the ball—I mean, looked for the can of Campbell's new Chunky Chili. If I hadn't felt so much pressure to please the advertisers, I wouldn't have hit him in the forehead with that pass. I also believe that, if he'd been wearing a traditional helmet instead of a KFC bucket, he wouldn't be in the hospital right now."

The play in question earned McNabb and Pinkston $65,000 each.

Patriots running back Corey Dillon said it took some time to adjust to the new game rules.

"You expect to get hit, and you expect the game to be played hard," Dillon said. "But you don't expect the quarterback to call a lead-toss right off-tackle play and then hand off a damn 50-pound Kyocera Mita combination copier/printer/fax machine."

In spite of the unusual circumstances, Dillon went free with a 45-yard run, breaking four tackles and making clean, crisp prints all the while, in an open-field romp that office-machine manufacturers are calling the play of the century.

"One thing's certain," Dillon said. "Kyocera office products go the distance."

> **"It was great for the team to earn a couple million when we lined up and used the Anheuser-Busch logo as our scrimmage formation."**

NFL marketing chief Phil Guarascio admitted that on-field product-placement is in its early stages.

"The league is sensitive to complaints from fans who say advertising should not affect play," Guarascio said. "That's why we've urged Kyocera to develop lighter copiers."

"And we're still hearing things, good and bad, from the professional-sports community," Guarascio continued. "The NFL Player's Association has made several good points about a few ill-considered product placements that may have led to player injuries. Nonetheless, we think product placement will make the NFL a more exciting and profitable venture for players and marketers alike."

According to doctors, Patriots linebacker Teddy Bruschi is still listed in critical condition after recovering a fumble in the Kingsford Charcoal Red Hot End Zone. ⌀

HOROSCOPES

Your Horoscope

By Lloyd Schumner Sr.
Retired Machinist and
A.A.P.B.-Certified Astrologer

Aries: (March 21–April 19)
Your one-inch punch may be powerful, but it will prove to be no match for your adversary's 750-foot punch.

Taurus: (April 20–May 20)
Your favorite T-shirt brings about your downfall when a literal-minded mob follows its instructions and fills you to the indicated line with margaritas.

Gemini: (May 21–June 21)
You will go against everything you believe in this week when you eat a steak less than an inch thick, drink a domestic Riesling, and hire a valet born outside of the British Isles.

Cancer: (June 22–July 22)
Travel hinders your creativity when, for days after your flight, all your pottery designs refer to things you read in US Airways' in-flight magazine.

Leo: (July 23–Aug. 22)
There's nothing you love more than freshly baked bread, which makes you the most inhuman, boring person alive.

Virgo: (Aug. 23–Sept. 22)
Many polar expeditions end in tragedy, but yours will conclude with the death of all hands before you even leave Kansas City.

Libra: (Sept. 23–Oct. 23)
You will raise procrastination to an art form, providing dozens of industrious critics with a new livelihood.

Scorpio: (Oct. 24–Nov. 21)
Many years from now, you'll be the only living person who remembers David Lee Roth, which should not instill you with a great sense of responsibility to history.

Sagittarius: (Nov. 22–Dec. 21)
You're fond of saying that there's more that unites people than divides them, a sentiment that is proven true when the Nepalese band together to destroy you.

Capricorn: (Dec. 22–Jan. 19)
You're not fat, but your lack of motivation means that most anecdotes about you end with the phrase "around the house."

Aquarius: (Jan. 20–Feb. 18)
Many have felt the Love Which Dare Not Speak Its Name, but you'll experience the Love That Bellows Its Name Out A Crosstown-Bus Window All Day.

Pisces: (Feb. 19–March 20)
Your problem is that you have no sense of proportion, which is why you paid surgeons to enlarge your head and hands.

POINT from page 65

desire! Please tell me the words I so long to hear! Say you love me too!

Do you want the moon? I will reach up and take it in my hands, write your name on it, and give it to you. It will be yours until the end of time.

Do you want the stars? I will roam the universe for all eternity, gathering up the twinkling points of light in the night sky. I will string the glittering stars into a latticework of jewelry to tuck into your hair, to adorn your neck, and to string around your pretty ankles. Say the word and I will do it.

When I see you on the quad, on your way to this symposium or that, I want to shout to the ends of the universe my total devotion to you. When you are sitting next to me at the cafeteria, idly chatting about student loans and work-study positions, I long to take your hands in mine, and kiss your beautiful tapered fingers. Darling, you may study the universe, but you are my universe.

Put an end to my torment! Give yourself to me, and I will give you everything in return. ⌀

COUNTERPOINT from page 65

Next, let's consider what would happen if you gave me the stars in the night sky. There are 8,479 objects visible to the naked eye in the night sky under ideal viewing conditions. (Of course, many of these objects are not stars at all, but galaxies so distant that we perceive their billions of separate stars as single points of light. But I won't quibble.) Were you to gather, in one place at one time, just the stars that are visible to us, the result would be an implosion that would rend the very fabric of space-time. Regardless of where I tucked them, the massive implosion caused by the ultra-high-density matter collapsing under its own weight would form a black hole larger even than the supermassive black hole at the center of our own galactic spiral.

As much as I hate to say it, the only part of your proposition that was even remotely accurate was your description of yourself: "an insignificant speck in an uncaring universe." Please don't take it too hard, Brandon. It's not you, it's just scientific fact. ⌀

the ONION®

VOLUME 41 ISSUE 07 AMERICA'S FINEST NEWS SOURCE™ 17–23 FEBRUARY 2005

Bloodless Coup A Real Letdown

Above: Nyboyev tells disappointed revolutionaries that the battle for control of Kyrgyzstan is already over.

BISHKEK, KYRGYZSTAN—The masterminds behind the bloodless coup d'etat that wrested power from President Askar Akayev Sunday said they were disappointed by the peaceful, efficient execution of the regime change.

"We spent months singing songs about the streets running red with the blood of our oppressors," said Ramazan Nyboyev, supreme leader of the New Dawning party and new president of Kyrgyzstan. "Now I'm standing here with the capital city under my thumb, and I didn't even get to fire my gun."

"Some of the younger guerrillas were running the Russian consul's china through a clay-pigeon launcher. But why shoot perfectly good china?" Nyboyev added.

The transfer of power, which ended Kyrgyzstan's 14-year experiment with democracy, was completed in fewer than four hours.

"I was going to lay siege to the lower house of parliament and bomb the president's mansion," Nyboyev said. "But by the time I got up the parliament steps, the delegates had rescinded their titles and sworn their 'everlasting allegiance to the New Dawn.' And why bomb the mansion when the president has left the keys hanging in the door next to a note about the thermostat?"

see COUP page 71

Michael Moore Honored With New Ben & Jerry's Flavor

Above: Moore and the Ben & Jerry's ice cream named after his former TV series The Awful Truth.

BURLINGTON, VT—Ben & Jerry's, the Vermont-based ice-cream manufacturer known for its progressive social mission, held a press conference Monday to introduce a new flavor celebrating Academy Award winner Michael Moore.

"I'm really excited to announce the newest Ben & Jerry's ice-cream flavor," said Chrystie Heimert, Ben & Jerry's director of public relations. "In the spirit of Michael Moore's tasteful, playful calls for justice, we

see MOORE page 70

Area Mom Really Gets Her Rocks Off On Being Appreciated

KINGSTON, NY—Boy, show local mother Janine Williams, 50, a little appreciation, and she practically creams herself, family members reported Tuesday.

"If you say something as insignificant as, 'Hey Mom, these sheets smell nice,' her face lights up like Times Square on New Years," daughter Nicole Williams, 19, said. "It's like, 'Okay, Mom. You bought a new type of fabric softener. You can stop beaming now.'"

For as long as Williams' son Daniel, 23, can remember, Williams has had almost no ability whatsoever to take a compliment in stride.

"If you really want to stroke Mom's pole, all you have to do is say some little nice thing to her," Daniel said.

see MOM page 71

Above: Williams, who almost jizzes herself every time someone thanks her.

NEWS

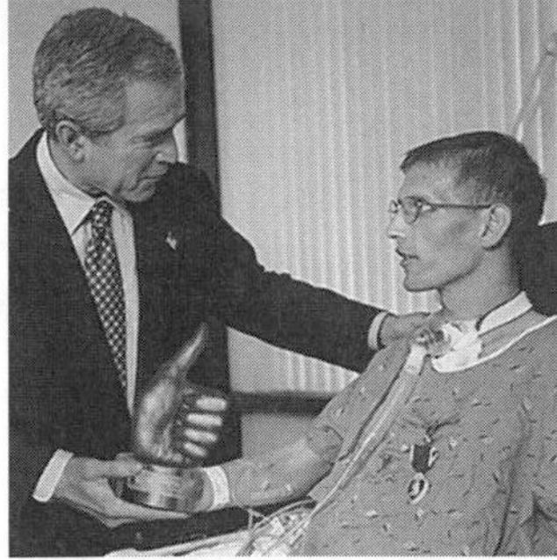

Hero Soldier Receives Presidential Thumbs-Up Award

see WASHINGTON page 8B

Homosexual Dolphin Has Highly Developed Sense Of Gay-Nar

see NATURE page 11E

Grandma Had Another Fall, Grandpa Reports

see HEALTH page 18G

STATshot

A look at the numbers that shape your world.

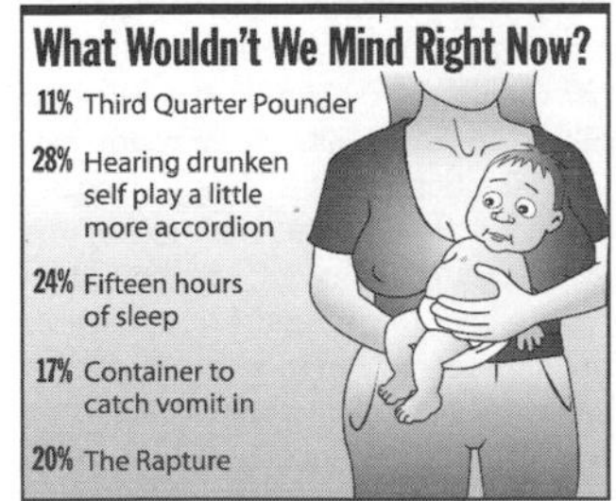

What Wouldn't We Mind Right Now?
11% Third Quarter Pounder
28% Hearing drunken self play a little more accordion
24% Fifteen hours of sleep
17% Container to catch vomit in
20% The Rapture

Failing Phys Ed Programs

With obesity among children rising steadily, health experts say our school's physical education programs are woefully inadequate. What do *you* think?

Eli McLemore
Medical Secretary

"Well, what do people expect? How are today's gym teachers supposed to motivate kids, now that homophobia, verbal harassment, and physical abuse are off limits?"

Russell Sager
Laser Technician

"The dubious benefits of a mandatory exercise program weighed against the undeniable fattening of America's kids? Sounds like it's time for an in-depth shirts vs. skins debate."

Monty Wendt
Systems Analyst

"There are many reasons that a school should have an extensive Phys Ed program. For one thing, it's the best way to increase kids' interest in reading and math."

Freida Stallworth
Metallurgist

"Oh good. It's our nation's schools that are to blame for my 200-pound son. Phew!"

Damien Shear
Wellness Coordinator

"I don't want my kids missing out on all that gym class offers. That's why I give them cruel nicknames, make them shower together, and snap them with wet towels."

Pamela Gant
Convention Planner

"You know, sex burns a lot of calories. Teens love sex. I can't see why no one has thought of this before."

Israeli-Palestinian Cease-Fire

Palestinian Authority President Mahmoud Abbas and Israeli Prime Minister Ariel Sharon recently declared a cease-fire. What are some conditions of the peace accord?

- Any violence committed on a weekday must be made up with extra peace on evenings or weekends
- The cease-fire may not be broken by any conflict stemming from less than half a century's worth of hatred
- Leaders of both countries agree to shake hands at least once a month, with photographers present
- Vows to drive one another into the sea must be downgraded to vows to drive one another to the beach for a nice weekend
- Israel gets to keep that wall up in Jerusalem, because it would be a shame to tear it down after all that work
- Palestinians must provide Israelis with full disclosure on their rock-throwing and tunnel-digging technologies
- Both sides really have to try this time
- Israeli air strikes and Palestinian suicide bombings exempt from agreement

America's Finest News Source.™

Herman Ulysses Zweibel
Founder

T. Herman Zweibel
Publisher Emeritus
J. Phineas Zweibel
Publisher
Maxwell Prescott Zweibel
Editor-In-Chief

That Reminds Me Of Something Funny A Client Of Mine Allegedly Said

Ha ha! "Trimmed her topiary!" Ha ha, yes. A very funny story, my friend. Actually, that reminds me of something a client of mine is alleged to have said.

By Leon Elsinger
Attorney

My esteemed fellow members of the Bahia Mar Marina, what I am about to tell you is by its very nature anecdotal and inadmissible as evidence insofar as my client is concerned.

Now, let me open by stating that my client has a long-standing reputation as a reputable loan and trust banker, an active supporter of his church, and a solid family man. The final characteristic, as will soon become clear, has some bearing upon my entertaining testimony. It is also important to note that my client has lived with dental pain for a good portion of his life—a fact that could be corroborated by numerous certified oral surgeons. Please notice that I frowned, creased my brow, and massaged the "molar" areas of my jaw in a manner said to be the habitual practice of my afflicted client.

With my client's long-standing dental problems established, I'll proceed. Last year, during the first weeks of baseball season, my client found what he described as "the aching in his molars" to be increasing in intensity. This statement was borne out by the vocal and voluntary testimony of my client's colleagues, who swore to the frequency and volume of my client's entreaties for solace from his pain. My client's dental-insurance statement would confirm that, on the advice of medical counsel, my client had the problematic teeth removed and was fitted for a set of dentures, henceforth referred to as "false teeth." My client had hoped the false teeth would not only put an end to his pain, but offer cosmetic benefits over his inferior natural teeth. Sadly, I have no examples to offer in exhibit, but offer as an analogue Mr. Wilbright's artificial hairpiece...

In light of the objections, I withdraw my comments regarding Mr. Wilbright.

Returning to my client's anecdote: Upon taking possession of his false teeth, my client did not, as anticipated, find his discomfort subsided. Contrariwise, my client reports that his pain doubled, changing from "dull and throbbing" to "constant and shooting." I concede that these descriptions are subjective, but submit that they go toward establishing hardship.

Yes, Mr. Carragher, I did mention the baseball season earlier. I intend to show relevance at this time.

Continuing: The pain—though "intense"—did not prevent my client from attending his son's baseball game. In point of fact, my client not only went to the game, but secured himself a seat right along what is termed the "first-base line." As further evidence that he was experiencing high levels of oral pain, I offer the additional point that my client did not partake of any peanuts, hot dogs, or soft drinks at this game.

Now, midway through the third inning,

As further evidence that he was experiencing high levels of oral pain, I offer the additional point that my client did not partake of any peanuts, Cracker Jack, hot dogs, or even soft drinks at this game.

my client's son came to bat fourth in the order, with a player on every base. Excited by the offensive potential—not to mention the glory and public favor his son might curry with a "hit"—my client claims he leapt to his feet and clenched his teeth. This involuntary action caused him considerable pain. Just at that moment, the pitcher threw the ball—we have the pitcher's word on that—and my client's young son hit the ball with all his might. In spite of the young batter's intentions, the speeding ball did not travel to the outfield, but right to the groin area of my client, impacting him squarely in the scrotal sac. Witnesses unanimously state that my client assumed what is known as the "fetal position" for several minutes.

The next day, my client was in his dentist's office having his dentures refitted, and the dentist commented on the peculiar way my client was perched in the dentist chair. My client recounted how he had been hit by a baseball the previous day. When the dentist expressed sympathy for my client, my client waved off the remarks, saying—and I quote the verbal testimony of the dentist and his li-

see CLIENT page 70

COMMUNITY

Teach For America Chews Up, Spits Out Another Ethnic-Studies Major

NEW YORK—Teach For America, a national program that recruits recent college graduates to teach in low-income rural and urban communities, has devoured another ethnic-studies major, 24-year-old Andy Cuellen reported Tuesday.

"Look, the world is a miserable place," said Cuellen, a Dartmouth graduate who quit the TFA program Monday morning. "All people—even children—are just nasty animals trying to secure their share of the food supply. I don't care how poor or how rich you are, that's just a fact. I'm sorry, but I have better things to do than zoo-keep for peanuts."

Just one of the 12,000 young people TFA has burned through since 1990, Cuellen was given five weeks of training the summer before he took over a classroom at P.S. 83 in the South Bronx last September.

"Look, the world is a miserable place," said Cuellen, a Dartmouth graduate who quit the TFA program Monday morning.

"I walked into that school actually thinking I could make a difference," said Cuellen, who taught an overflowing class of disadvantaged 8-year-olds. "It was trial by fire. But after five months spent in a stuffy, dark room where the chalkboard fell off the wall every two days, corralling screaming kids into broken desks, I'm burnt to a crisp."

Cuellen said his TFA experience "taught him a lot about hopelessness."

"The cities are fucked. The suburbs are fucked. The whole country is fucked," Cuellen said. "And there's not a goddamned thing you or anyone can do about it. Anyone who says otherwise is selling something. Or trying to get you to teach kids math."

According to Dartmouth literature, as a member of the ethnic-studies department, Cuellen learned "to empower students of color to move beyond being objects of study toward being subjects of their own social realities, with voices of their own."

Teach For America executive director Theo Anderson called ethnic-studies departments "a prime source of fodder."

"Oh, I'd say we burn through a hundred or so ethnic-studies majors each year," said Anderson, pointing to a series of charts showing the college-ma-

see TEACH page 70

Above: Cuellen stands in front of the elementary school where he used to teach.

NEWS IN BRIEF

Bacon Just One Of Sprint's New Downloadable Ring Scents

OVERLAND PARK, KS—Wireless-phone-service provider Sprint PCS has added Hickory-Smoked Bacon to its quickly growing list of downloadable Ring Scents, which includes Pine Forest, New Car, and Cinnamon Potpourri. "Smells are stronger memory triggers than sounds, and now you can assign a different smell for everyone on your phone list," Sprint spokesperson Mindy Harris said. "We even have a line of Bling Scents like Cash, Crissy, and Blueberry. And we have Alabama Clay, Wet Dog, and Skoal Bandit for country-music fans." For customers who carry their cell phones in their mouths, Sprint will introduce Ring-Savors in January 2006.

Designers Opt To Stick With Last Year's Fashions

NEW YORK—The buzz around the 2005 Spring Fashion Week was "status quo," as top designers like Marc Jacobs and Oscar de la Renta chose to repeat their lines from 2004. "This spring is all about consistency," said Jacobs, who reintroduced a collection of gray and black slouchy long skirts. "We came out with a lot of great clothes last year, so we're gonna stick with those." Donna Karan agreed that "introducing a new look is a relic of the 20th century."

New Girlfriend Bears Disturbing Resemblance To Old Girlfriend

ATLANTA—Friends of David Buntrock told reporters Monday that his new girlfriend Katie Wickstrom looks unsettlingly similar to his former girlfriend Tonya Gill. "When I first saw them together I thought, 'Wow, did David and Tonya work things out?'" friend Angie Lisota said, explaining that both Wickstrom and Gill are petite, with cropped brown hair, big eyes, and a penchant for dressing like ballet dancers. "Even her voice sounds a little nasally, like Tonya's." According to Buntrock, Wickstrom "actually looks more like Audrey Hepburn."

Paris Review Receives Mysterious Plimpton Essay About Being A Ghost

NEW YORK—*Paris Review* editors report that they received an unsolicited essay from the late founder George Plimpton about his first-hand experiences as a ghost Tuesday. "I have always believed in immersing myself in my investigative work, be it as an acrobat, a boxer, or a Detroit Lion," read the cover letter accompanying the 3,200-word essay that materialized in the current editor's mailbox Monday. "Dying two years ago afforded me the unique opportunity to examine the afterlife from both sides of the Pearly Gates." Plimpton's letter said he would waive all payment, as he no longer has any use for things of the mortal world.

510 Chuck E. Cheese Tickets Blown In Grape-Soda Induced Frenzy

CORDOVA, TN—Chuck E. Cheese patron Nathan Angrim, 9, was found passed out in a booth Monday, 510 game tickets poorer and surrounded by cheap toys, following a two-hour Welch's Grape Soda bender. "Dad, where'd all this stuff come from?" Angrim asked, gesturing to the plastic dinosaurs and slide whistles scattered across his pizza-sauce-stained T-shirt. "Last thing I remember, I was playing Skee-Ball. Oh, my head." The incident marks a backslide for Angrim, who swore that he wouldn't touch "the Grape" again, after last April, when he woke up shoeless in the colored-ball pool, his pinkies stuck in a Chinese finger trap. Ø

MOORE from page 67

have created a tasteful, playful flavor: The Waffle Truth."

The Waffle Truth will honor the dynamic visionary by combining premium vanilla ice cream with strawberries, chocolate-covered waffle-cone bits, and a hint of cinnamon. The ice cream will be available in Ben & Jerry's Scoop Shops Friday, followed by a retail rollout in March.

"Making an ice-cream flavor that would do justice to such an important author and filmmaker wasn't easy," Heimert said. "We knew we'd be using

The Emmy Award winner made a surprise appearance at the Ben & Jerry's Scoop Shop in Times Square to support the product.

Above: Sean Hannity blasts The Waffle Truth as "candy-coated, liberal fluff."

ingredients bought at fair-market prices, but exactly what those ingredients would be was a source of a lot of good old-fashioned, honest, open debate."

Heimert said developers experimented with a host of possible ice-cream tributes to the best-selling author, including Stupid White Chocolate, Green Tea Nation, and Dude, Where's My Coconut?

Even after Ben & Jerry's decided what the new flavor would contain, developers struggled to perfect the name.

"We thought about calling it Cherryheit 9-11, but we already have Cherry Garcia," Heimert said. "Fahrenheit 31.1 was the next choice, but we didn't think everyone would make the connection between the proper temperature for storing ice cream and the film that broke the theatrical documentary box-office record by seamlessly blending comedy with hard-hitting fact."

"We also considered a name reminiscent of our our popular Chubby Hubby flavor," Heimert said. "But in the end, we decided The Waffle Truth would be more respectful to Moore's achievements than a flavor called Hefty Lefty."

Ben & Jerry's has previously honored pop-culture icons Phish and Jerry Garcia, as well as the TV show *Seinfeld*. This is the first time that the company has honored a director.

"Michael Moore's David-and-Goliath commentaries cut conservative bigwigs down to size," Heimert said. "He follows the beat of his own drummer and works in his own unique way to improve the average American's life. Our choice was a natural—just like our ice cream: We use only fresh milk and cream bought from farmers that have pledged never to use recombinant Bovine Growth Hormone."

Added Heimert: "We believe that Michael will remain an important voice in American politics, and that we will find no need to discontinue The Waffle Truth, as we did Wavy Gravy, Doonesberry Sorbet, and Dilbert's World Totally Nuts."

The Emmy Award winner made a surprise appearance at the Ben & Jerry's Scoop Shop in Times Square to support the product.

"I'm honored Ben & Jerry's decided to dedicate an ice cream to me," Moore told the excited crowd. "It's a fantastic company with a great track record of treating their employees fairly and using only ethically produced ingredients."

"Plus, a lifetime supply of ice cream sounds pretty good," Moore added, patting his stomach with a self-deprecating laugh.

According to Ben & Jerry's press materials, The Waffle Truth rollout will include a nationwide tour by the company's promotional ice-cream wagon. The tour will begin its journey in Flint, MI and continue south to distribute free pints of ice cream in 14 Rust Belt cities suffering from post-industrial decline.

Other Ben & Jerry's flavors slated for introduction in 2005 are Praline Kael, Noam ChompChompsky Crunch, Ché Guava, and Nelson Vanilla, an anti-apartheid flavor that consists of a dark-chocolate sorbet swirled in an equal amount of vanilla ice cream. Ø

CLIENT from page 68

censed hygienist—"Doc, that was the only time all week that I wasn't thinking about these goddamn false teeth."

Ladies and gentlemen, I freely admit

With my client's long-standing dental problems established, I'll proceed.

that I have never experienced the pain of ill-fitting dentures or felt the impact of a baseball in my groin area. I am not an expert witness in this matter. What I say may be entirely without merit, but speaking freely: A line drive to the balls would make me forget just about anything. I tell you that *pro bono*. Ø

TEACH from page 69

jor breakdown of TFA corps members. "They tend to last a little longer than women's studies majors and art-therapy students, but Cuellen got mashed to a pulp pretty quickly. It usually takes ethnic-studies majors another year to realize that they're wasting their precious youth on a Sisyphean endeavor."

Continued Anderson: "Of course, we don't worry about it too much. Every year, there's a fresh crop to throw in the grinder. As we speak, scores of apple-cheeked students are hearing about TFA for the first time."

According to Anderson, a small portion of these students will lose interest after hearing horror stories from program alumni.

"But the majority of them will march on like cattle to the slaughter, thinking that pure determination and hope can change young lives," Anderson said. "I can hear their footsteps now, marching toward our offices like lemmings to a cliff. And believe me, we're ready for 'em."

Cuellen said he applied to TFA in search of a "character-building experience."

"I knew that teaching in a severely under-funded inner-city school would be challenging, but I wanted to get out into the real world," Cuellen said. "Well, breaking up fistfights between 8-year-olds all day long, I got a real ugly view of reality. Do you want to know reality? Look at a dog lying dead in the gutter. That's reality."

Although Cuellen quit the program early, his mother said he was with TFA long enough for it "to crack open his bones and suck out the marrow inside."

"Andy is a ghost," Beverly Cuellen said. "Those [TFA] people beat the idealism out of him, then they stomped on him while he lay there gasping for air."

TFA regional coordinator Sandra Richman said it is common to blame the TFA employees for the organization's high plow-through rate.

"Should I have said something to wake those kids up sooner?" Richman said, crushing out her seventh cigarette. "Probably. But listen, no one can tell you that you can't make a difference. It's something you have to figure out for yourself."

"You can only do so much," Richman added. "After a couple years of trying to teach our applicants about how difficult and depressing their lives will inevitably be—no matter what they choose to do for money—I just got burnt out. In the end, you've gotta resign yourself to failure and move on with your life." Ø

COUP from page 67

Above: Weapons the revolutionaries never even got a chance to use.

According to Nyboyev, the coup produced "not a single martyr."

"Who am I supposed to put on the money?" Nyboyev asked. "That soldier who cut himself on his own bayonet? This day was supposed to create heroes for our history books. Now the only way for us to earn the people's respect is to repair the nation's infrastructure."

Added Nyboyev: "Ambush isn't supposed to be like this."

The New Dawning party was formed in 2003, when 14 high-ranking military officials united to overthrow the Akayev administration, a hotbed of corruption, embezzlement, and negligence.

"We planned in secret, biding our time until the day we would storm the capital and crush our adversaries," said New Dawning undersecretary Kurmanek Dutbeyev, who, prior to the coup, warned his family that he was unlikely to survive the "historic day of bloodshed." "I imagined it all a thousand times: the coordinated assault, the rooftop gun battles, the face-to-face brutality—and then nothing. Come the big day, I didn't slit a single throat."

Added Dutbeyev: "We were prepared for casualties—even mass casualties—but no casualties at all? We had no plan in place for that."

The Kyrgyzstani military, one of the most formidable in the region when under Soviet control, did not resist the coup.

"We spent months coming up with an offensive to neutralize the Elite Guard," Nyboyev said. "But when we ordered them to throw their weapons to the ground, they actually threw their weapons to the ground."

Government financial records, made public after the coup, might explain the ready surrender: Even high-ranking administration and military officials had not been paid for months.

"The treasury was empty," Nyboyev said. "The president himself seemed happy to wash his hands of Kyrgyzstan."

Members of the New Dawning party said that, in planning to overthrow the government, they focused on the coup itself, giving little thought to how they would run a nation of five million.

"The treasury was empty," Nyboyev said. "The president himself seemed happy to wash his hands of Kyrgyzstan."

"Our men were expertly trained in poisoning, garroting, and sniping," Nyboyev said. "Now we are 14 deadly revolutionaries in a room, trying to figure out who will be minister of transportation. Earlier today, the military leaders came to us and demanded pay. They were a lot more vicious than they were when they were defending their former bosses."

The international media has largely ignored the coup.

"We thought we would draw the world's attention to our nation's plight and its liberators' bravery," Nyboyev said. "But who cares about 'Eurasian Country Changes Hands; No One Hurt'? The story, like our hopes, got buried."

Nyboyev said he was relieved that the foreign press did not seize upon the party's slogan, which the radicals had printed on posters, buttons, and pamphlets in preparation for their ascendance to power: "When they failed to bow to the people's will, they fell beneath our swords."

"We had to throw all those out," Nyboyev said. "They're just embarrassing now." ⌀

MOM from page 67

"Tell her you like the vase of flowers on the table, and she laps it up like a hungry dog."

During a recent visit home, Daniel made the mistake of complimenting Williams on her banana bread. Williams reportedly just about pissed herself.

"I was passing through the kitchen and I said, 'Yay, your famous banana bread,'" Daniel said. "Mom smiled so big, I thought her face was gonna pop like a balloon."

Nobody gets what it is with Williams, or why she gets her rocks off on someone giving her a couple words of thanks, according to Daniel.

"Mom's always doing stuff for us," Daniel said. "You'd think she'd be used to us saying thanks by now, but nope. It still waxes her canoe."

According to husband Don, 54, the thing that really, *really* stokes Williams' fire is when someone does her some tiny favor.

"This morning, I went out and got the *Daily Freeman* from the foot of the driveway for her so she wouldn't have to go out in the cold," Don said. "She acted like I'd handed her a winning lottery ticket."

Family members agree that, if you don't want to see Williams have a conniption fit, the absolute last thing you ever want to do is get her a present.

"For her birthday last month, Nicole and I pitched in and got her a pretty expensive pair of earrings," Daniel said. "We gave them to her after we got home from dinner, because we didn't want Mom busting a nut right in the middle of Outback Steakhouse."

Williams basically admitted that even the tiniest gesture of affection hauls her ashes over the state line and back.

Nicole said that, when it comes to making her mother feel appreciated, even she has her limits.

"I decided that I'm not going to make her a homemade Mother's Day card this year," Nicole said. "Last year, I took five minutes to draw something, and it made her break down into tears. I mean, not to be harsh, but is it too much to ask for some dignity and reserve from your mother?"

Williams basically admitted that even the tiniest gesture of affection hauls her ashes over the state line and back.

"Danny and Nicole are getting older now, so we see less and less of each other," Williams said. "It's only natural. But still, I really do think there's nothing more important in this entire world than the love of one's family."

Whatever wanks your crank, Janine Williams of Kingston, NY. ⌀

COMMUNITY VOICES

Christmas In February

Guess what, Jeanketeers? There are new sounds coming from the residence of Mr. and Mrs. Rick Teasdale! No, it's not the patter of little feet, it's the whirrrr of motorized-scooter wheels! Yep, you heard it here first: My long-lost father Horvel is staying with us!

A Room Of Jean's Own
By Jean Teasdale

Well, he's not technically long-lost, since we knew where he was all that time (California). But I hadn't seen him for nearly five years. In my book, that qualifies as long-lost. People get reunited on talk shows after being apart for less time than that!

Anyway, our reunion took place shortly before Christmas. After separating from his third wife, Dad came to live with my brother Kevin for awhile. But Kevin had only planned on hosting Dad for the Christmas season, so when Groundhog Day rolled around, he politely let Dad know it was time to move along.

Dad was living in a motel when he approached me about staying at my place for awhile. I predicted—correctly, I might add—that if Dad paid us for room and board, Rick would go for it. "Only because I'm sick of paying all the rent because you can't hold down a job," Rick growled. (What a pussycat!)

Having Dad in the house has taken some getting used to. He pretty much lives in his Rascal, which makes for a tight squeeze in our one-bedroom apartment. You should have heard my kitty Priscilla screech when Dad rolled over her tail! (Don't worry, kitty-lovers, nothing was broken!) Dad only gets out of the scooter to sleep on the living-room sofa bed, sit in Rick's recliner, or shower. The scooter has already left black streaks on the kitchen walls, and there's a brown patch on the living-room rug where the wheels ground in some dog doody they picked up outside.

On the fourth day with our new roommate, I caught Rick sitting on the foot of our waterbed, holding his head in his hands. "Your dad is bumming me out," he said. "When I get to be his age, I'll be even fatter and hairier than I am now—I completely intend to stay fat, Jean. So when I'm old, I'm going to be just like Horvel, riding around in a gimp trike and lucky if I can net a hand job." (Sheesh!) I told Rick that I would be there by his side no matter what, but he just grunted.

You can see why I was relieved when Dad thought of an idea that would get him out of the apartment.

For years, Dad has made a lucrative living as a shopping-mall Santa. From the white beard on down to the bowlful-of-jelly belly, he certainly looks the part! But, of course, the job is only seasonal. I mean, was only seasonal, until Dad had an epiphany! Why not play Santa all year round? He told me his plans over brunch at The Licked Skillet.

> **I caught Rick sitting on the foot of our waterbed, holding his head in his hands. "Your dad is bumming me out," he said. "When I get to be his age, I'll be even fatter and hairier than I am now—I completely intend to stay fat, Jean. So when I'm old, I'm going to be just like Horvel, riding around in a gimp trike and lucky if I can net a hand job."**

"I found a strip mall that rents space cheap," he said. "We'll move in a few Christmas trees, dump some artificial snow on the floor, put up some Christmas lights, and there you go: Off-Season Santa is born!"

I thought the idea certainly had great cuteness potential—and you Jeanketeers know how much I adore cute things—but I had reservations.

"How would this make money?" I asked him. "And besides, isn't it more magical that you only get a glimpse of Santa around Christmas, rather than every day?"

Dad rolled his eyes. "That son-in-law of mine has made you way too pragmatic, Jeannie," he said. Then he went on his old saw about how people are all about instant gratification these days. "We microwave our dinners, movies come out on DVD mere weeks after they're released, and instead of darning a sock with a hole in it, folks simply buy a new pair." I told him I didn't understand what he was driving at.

"Year-round shopping-mall Santas are a virtually untapped source of income," he said. "There's no reason why a child shouldn't sit on Santa's lap seven days a week, January through December! Think of the applications, Jeannie. A parent could shell out a few bucks to have her kid sit on Santa's lap in July and rattle off the things he wants for his birthday. Why, back in California, the neighbor children were always asking me where Rudolph was!"

> **"Year-round shopping-mall Santas are a virtually untapped source of income," Dad said.**

Dad said he could mind the business end of things, but he needed someone to handle the creative issues. And who did he have in mind? None other than yours truly! He said I could be in charge of decorating the store and taking digital photos of him and his customers. Best of all, I'd get to wear a cute elf suit!

That clinched it for me. Finally, I'd have a job where I could exercise my abundant imagination! Besides, I was really moved that Dad would ask me to be his partner. He used to let so many months go by between phone calls and letters that I'd begun to think he'd traded his family in for an exciting California life with his third wife. Now that I knew he needed me, how could I turn him down?

As soon as I said I'd help him, Dad signed a yearlong lease on the rental space. Now things are officially underway—and not a moment too soon. This morning, hubby Rick and my "long-lost" dad were sitting in the living room sipping beer and watching ESPN when Rick asked him if he ever got "a rise" out of having all those kids on his lap. I thought Dad was going to leap out of his Rascal and deck Rick. But Dad just chuckled and said that Rick would be getting some coal in his stocking for that remark. Then Rick had to ask if that was what Dad's third wife would be getting. Dad didn't say anything after that. ø

HOROSCOPES

Your Horoscope

By Lloyd Schumner Sr.
Retired Machinist and
A.A.P.B.-Certified Astrologer

Aries: (March 21–April 19)
God will confess that He does play dice with the universe, but explain that He used the 16-sided kind during His Creation-spanning game of Dungeons & Dragons.

Taurus: (April 20–May 20)
After mistaking you for a new model of a full-size pickup, *Car And Driver* will deride your lack of legroom, but praise the way you "barely sip" gasoline.

Gemini: (May 21–June 21)
The plucky, dam-building beaver is known as "nature's engineer," so it's not too surprising when 12 of them trap you inside a clever, woody Maze of Death.

Cancer: (June 22–July 22)
It's true that secret agents have crossed international borders with microfilm hidden in their colons, but you should've known better than to try it with three liters of duty-free scotch.

Leo: (July 23–Aug. 22)
Next week's events will get you thinking that maybe there's no reason to keep a mule train in modern-day Kansas City.

Virgo: (Aug. 23–Sept. 22)
You'll have that weird dream again, where no one in the world is ever hungry—but you'll manage to forget it by morning.

Libra: (Sept. 23–Oct. 23)
If you're going pass horrifying, threatening notes to bank tellers, at least try to get some money out of the deal.

Scorpio: (Oct. 24–Nov. 21)
Thanks to your city's willingness to use advanced, tesseract-based forms of public transportation, you'll be the first person to be hit by a bus from the inside.

Sagittarius: (Nov. 22–Dec. 21)
Mars descending in your sign is definitely unusual for this time of year, but between the retching and the stench of sour bourbon, you can guess how it got so low.

Capricorn: (Dec. 22–Jan. 19)
You always thought the saying was "welcome you back with broken arms," resulting in a needlessly painful reunion with your long-lost love this week.

Aquarius: (Jan. 20–Feb. 18)
Yes, it's a tragedy, but there are those who will wonder if you shouldn't have known better than to camp at Frequent Cave-In State Park.

Pisces: (Feb. 19–March 20)
Religious and scientific leaders will argue for weeks about whether what happened to you was the result of divine retribution or messy, high-energy physics.

the ONION®

VOLUME 41 ISSUE 08 AMERICA'S FINEST NEWS SOURCE™ 24 FEB.–2 MARCH 2005

NEWS

Spider-Man Mask Spices Up Blind Date

see RELATIONSHIPS page 8F

New Macrowave Can Defrost A Roast In 72 Hours

see PRODUCTS page 15E

Gender Guessed Correctly On Second Try

see LOCAL page 3C

Opportunist Knocks

see PEOPLE page 8H

STATshot

A look at the numbers that shape your world.

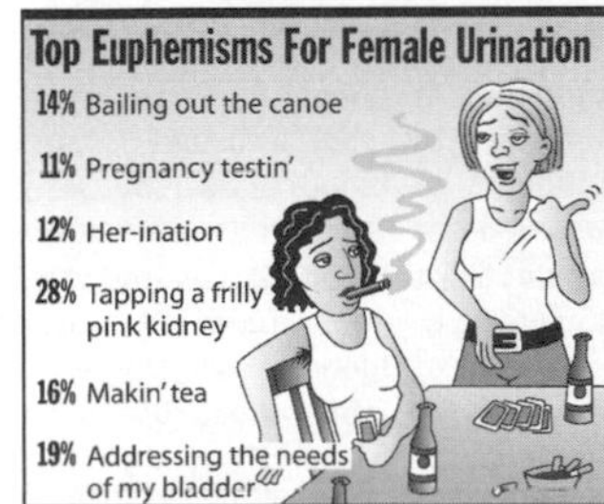

Top Euphemisms For Female Urination
14% Bailing out the canoe
11% Pregnancy testin'
12% Her-ination
28% Tapping a frilly pink kidney
16% Makin' tea
19% Addressing the needs of my bladder

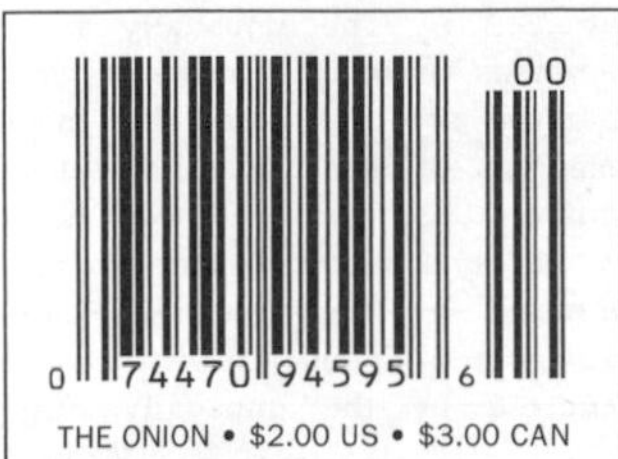

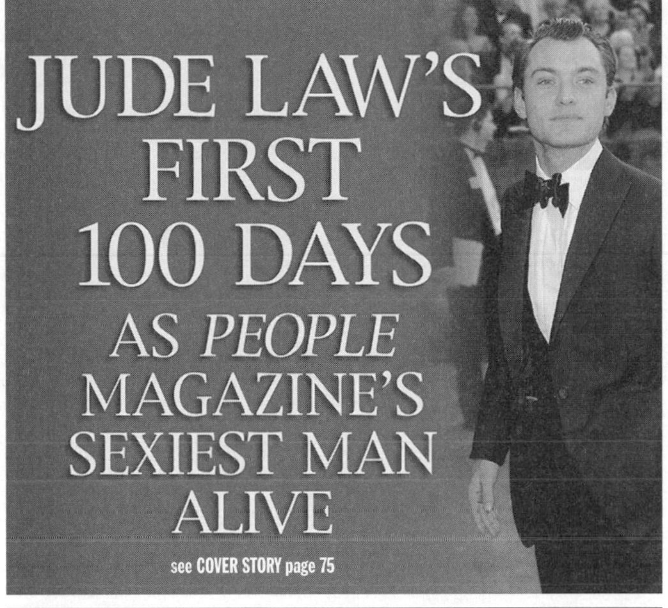

JUDE LAW'S FIRST 100 DAYS
AS PEOPLE MAGAZINE'S SEXIEST MAN ALIVE
see COVER STORY page 75

Miller Brewing Company Pressures Area Man To Drink Responsibly

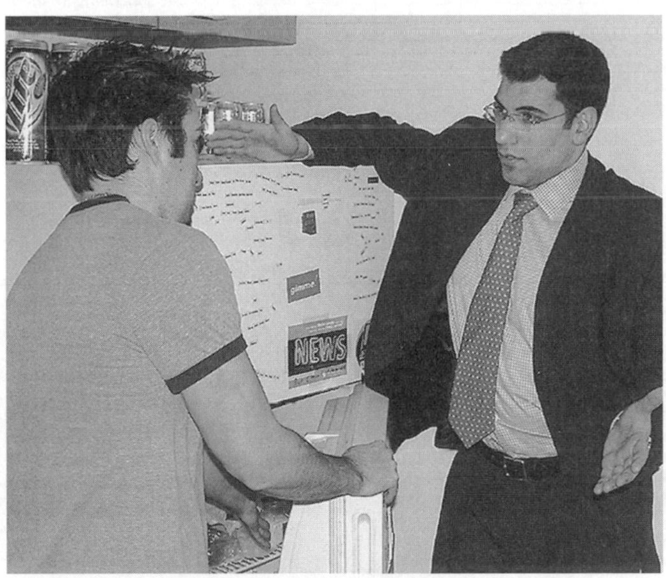

Above: Milburn asks Helvinski if he's positive he wants another beer.

CHEYENNE, WY—The Milwaukee, WI-based Miller Brewing Company, well-known for extolling the responsible enjoyment of alcoholic beverages, has been calling, writing, and visiting Kevin Helvinski to encourage him to think before he drinks.

"Miller has made responsible consumption of alcohol for those of legal drinking age one of our primary advertising messages," Miller representative Daryl Milburn said. "We are concerned, however, that Kevin Helvinski of 21 Post St. has not been paying attention to our friendly magazine ads, TV commercials, and point-of-purchase pamphlets."

Miller representatives launched their campaign to encourage Helvinski to assess his alcohol-consumption habits in January, when Helvinski was spotted at the Cloud Nine Lounge vomiting into a urinal.

see MILLER page 77

State Of Minnesota Too Polite To Ask For Federal Funding

ST. PAUL, MN—Although many of its highways and bridges are in severe disrepair, the traditionally undemanding state of Minnesota isn't comfortable asking for more interstate funding, sources reported Monday.

"Oh, we wouldn't want to bother the U.S. government—they've got more

than enough on their plate as it is," Minnesota Gov. Tim Pawlenty said. "Most of the potholes on I-90 are less than four feet wide. We get by just fine. I wouldn't want anyone all the way over there in Washington to be worrying about little ol' us."

According to U.S. Department of Transportation records, Minnesota has not requested an increase in highway funds for 10 years, in spite of the fact that the majority of their roads are plagued by rutted or uneven surfaces, cracked pavement, potholes, and other deterioration.

"If it were a life or death situation, you can bet your bippy we'd ask for it, but since it isn't..." Pawlenty said. "Well, we can make do with the transportation-department budget they decided to give us back in 1995. That was more than generous."

But U.S. Transportation Secretary Norman Mineta said Minnesota's highway system is "dangerously underfunded."

"Nearly 20 percent of Minnesota's highway lights are not working, and

see MINNESOTA page 77

COX-2 Inhibitors

The FDA is currently deciding whether to restrict the use of COX-2 inhibitors, the widely used class of pain drugs which includes Vioxx. What do *you* think?

"Jesus, a couple people's hearts explode, and everyone goes nuts."

Sylvia Drake
Podiatrist

"I'm confused. How did they separate the effects of Vioxx from the other 1,372 things that give Americans heart attacks?"

Carson Bloom
Systems Analyst

"I hope the invisible hand of capitalism is trained in CPR."

Joe Moran
Plasterer

"Hey, what about all the horrible side effects these drugs *don't* cause?"

Eric Baumgartner
Sound Producer

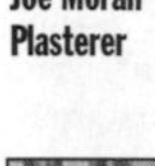

"I wondered why that Celebrex TV ad showed an old guy in the middle of a sun-drenched wheat field having a heart attack."

Pat Adkins
Prison Guard

"They're gonna ban COX-2 inhibitors? But that's my third-favorite class of painkillers."

Lisa Layman
Urban Planner

Oscar Host Chris Rock

Chris Rock will host this year's Academy Awards. What suggestions did event organizers have for the comedian?

- Be sure to flash trademark smile, but limit sarcastic eye-twinkle
- Try not to look horrified after musical numbers
- As a treat for the audience, quote some of your amusing catchphrases from those *Rush Hour* movies you made with Jackie Chan
- Don't try to sneak anything past the Oscars crowd by using slang coined since 1990
- Remember to make some Jack Valenti jokes; TV audiences love former MPAA head Jack Valenti
- Putting a little Afro wig on one of the statues would be funny. Why don't you do that?
- Don't get too cute: We'll have a clip of your *Miami Vice* appearance cued up and ready to roll
- Please don't do that thing where you say incredibly funny and accurate things that rip apart our entire industry
- Remember to have fun out there

America's Finest News Source.™

Herman Ulysses Zweibel
Founder

T. Herman Zweibel
Publisher Emeritus
J. Phineas Zweibel
Publisher
Maxwell Prescott Zweibel
Editor-In-Chief

I'm Tired Of Looking At These Same Four Uterine Walls

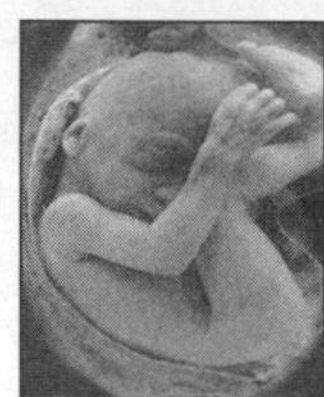

By Allison or Andy Klastermann
Fetus

My God, I'm bored. I've heard that after the anxiety of separation from the mother and the trauma of birth, all I'll want to do is return to the womb, but I have a hard time believing that. After being cooped up in here for nearly three trimesters, I've gotta dismiss that as outdated Freudian balderdash. Can't this woman gestate a little faster, for Christ's sake? I'm sick of staring at these same four uterine walls.

I'm not even a child yet, and already I'm being treated like one. I'd like to get out and see the sights once in a while. I haven't even had a chance to use my little optic nerves!

Hello? Anybody there? I'm going crazy in here!

And the noise! Sure, the steady pulse of my mother's heartbeat was reassuring at first, but how long can I listen to the same thing? It's "ba boom, ba boom," day in and day out. How about some variation? Would it kill her to throw in a little arrhythmia once in a while?

You might think I'm being a baby, but you try spending 32 weeks holed up in a tiny, one-womb place like this.

Do you have any idea how long I've been curled up in this same position? I seriously need some freakin' elbow room. I've had my arms tucked in under my knees since before I developed fingers. Lemme out!

Oh, how I long to eat just one thing that didn't circulate directly into my system through the tube in my belly. Look at this thing! Don't worry, I know better than to try yanking it off again. Ouch, mama! But I want to be an independent person. If my every need is met automatically, I'll never develop a sense that I have an identity apart from my environment.

And can't a fella get a little fresh air? It'd be so great to breathe something that wasn't liquid for a change. If I could just get out and stretch my legs

You try spending 32 weeks holed up in a tiny, one-womb place like this.

a little, I might develop some motor skills. At the rate I'm going, my skull's never gonna fuse.

Please, is anybody listening? I kick and kick, but no one lets me out. Gimme some sign that somebody's out there—some sonogram signals, an amniotic tap, anything!

It's not like I can read a magazine or do a crossword puzzle to pass the time—I haven't grasped the abstract concept of language yet.

It feels like this placenta is suffocating me. I mean it... If somebody doesn't get me out of this place, I'm gonna flip and end up breached! Okay, I've had it up to here with gestating.

That's it. I can't take it anymore. Forget about my due date—I'm bustin' outta here. I know the health risks, but you people have incubators, don't you? And no, I'm not gonna wait until you can call a cab. If the supermarket parking lot is where it's gotta happen, then the supermarket parking lot is it. Get ready, world, 'cause I'm gonna bust out, pound the pavement, and make a big splash right now. Ø

CREAM SODA from page 17

amounts of blood. Passersby were amazed by the unusually large amounts of blood. Passersby were amazed by the unusually large

Well, I thought the Rush laser-light show was romantic.

amounts of blood. Passersby were amazed by the unusually large amounts of blood. Passersby were amazed by the unusually large amounts of blood. Passersby were amazed by the unusually large amounts of blood. Passersby were amazed by the unusually large amounts of blood. Passersby were amazed by the unusually large amounts of blood. Passersby were amazed by the unusually large amounts of blood. Passersby were amazed by the unusually large amounts of blood. Passersby were amazed by the unusually large amounts of blood. Passersby were amazed by the unusually large amounts of blood. Passersby were amazed by the unusually large amounts of blood. Passersby were amazed by the unusually large amounts of blood. Passersby were amazed by the unusually large amounts of blood. Passersby were amazed by the unusually large amounts of blood. Passersby were amazed by the unusually large

see CREAM SODA page 51

COVER STORY

Law Pursues His Sexy Agenda

Above: Law signs autographs for the public.

HOLLYWOOD—All eyes are squarely fixed on Jude Law as he comes to the 100-day mark in his tenure as *People* magazine's Sexiest Man Alive 2004.

"You can't overstate the importance of the Sexiest Man Alive's first 100 days," said Veronica Giulletti, associate editor of *People*. "They set the tone for his entire term. The whole world is looking at him to see what is sexy."

In November, Law emerged as the new sexiest man alive, after a fiercely contested, sexy race that pitted him against such hunks as Orlando Bloom, Colin Farrell, and two-time winner Brad Pitt.

"Law's ascension was not a mandate, remember," Giulletti said. "The Sexiest Man Alive issue featured a complete list of heart-stoppers who ranged in age from 22 to 58. It included 34 actors,10 singers, a baseball player, and a poker champ. If Law ever starts to rest on his laurels, he need only open his copy of the Nov. 17, 2004 issue. That photo spread is a stark, sexy reminder of the challenges the Sexiest Man Alive faces."

According to Giulletti, the Sexiest Man Alive receives the most media attention at the very beginning of his term. While some sexy men use the news coverage as an opportunity to introduce radical changes to their looks, Giulletti said that Law chose to stay the course.

"Jude came into office with a big, sexy plan in place," Giulletti said. "He'd spent years tweaking and refining his dapper image, so it was wise that he chose to stick with it."

Throughout his first 100 days, Law earned public-approval ratings ranging from the high 60s to the low 80s.

"While Jude's look is too conservative for some tastes, no one can deny that he conveys a strong, focused, well-honed sexiness," Giulletti said. "He has gorgeous cheekbones, sensual lips, and lovely blue eyes. His frame, while not Russell Crowe studly, certainly isn't too twee either."

Entertainment-industry pundits have lauded Law for his savvy campaign to distinguish himself from his predecessor, 2003's Sexiest Man Alive Johnny Depp.

"Johnny was sexy," entertainment writer Cami Stoeffer said. "That said, many People readers were disappointed by his administration. They felt the energy he expended overseas was in excess. Some took all that jet-setting as an indication that Johnny didn't care about making America a sexier place."

In contrast to Depp, Law introduced a "sexy by example" style of leadership, aggressively undertaking a highly publicized campaign advocating short-cropped hairstyles for men.

"Sexy-people-watchers advocate Jude's aggressive stance on haircuts," Stoeffer said. "It's a traditional platform, but Law has done well

see LAW page 78

NEWS IN BRIEF

Sharper Image Vows 'We Will Be Undersold'

SAN FRANCISCO—In a battle cry to consumers of trendy specialty gadgets, Sharper Image CEO Richard Thalheimer said Monday that the high-end retailer "will be undersold" by the competition. "Show us a foot massager that retails for $40 at Target and we'll sell it to you for $90—because that's how we do business," Thalheimer said. "Heck, regular stores don't even carry our virtually useless $299 ionic air purifier." In response, Hammacher Schlemmer issued a challenge to "exceed Sharper Image's price or double the item's cost."

Local Man Gets Cocky With Ladder

GUNNISON, UT—Three days into painting his house, Donald Simonds has gotten arrogant with his 12-foot aluminum ladder. "When he started his project, he'd step up the rungs real gingerly, bracing himself with his hands all the way," neighbor Earl Pickett said. "Now, three days later, he's climbing up the wrong end, carrying three paint cans at once, standing on the top step of the thing. I even saw him steady himself by putting one foot on a windowsill." Pickett said he just hopes Simonds' smug way with his ladder doesn't get him hurt.

Bush Determined To Find Warehouse Where Ark Of Covenant Is Stored

WASHINGTON, DC—In a surprise press conference Monday, President Bush said he will not rest until the warehouse where the Ark of the Covenant, the vessel holding the original Ten Commandments, is located. "Nazis stole the Ark in 1936, but it was recovered by a single patriot, who braved gunfire, rolling boulders, and venomous snakes," Bush said, addressing the White House press corps. "Sadly, due to bureaucratic rigmarole, this powerful, historic relic was misplaced in a warehouse. Mark my words: We will find that warehouse." Bush added that, after they are strengthened by the power of the Ark, U.S. forces will seek out and destroy the sinister Temple of Doom.

Lure Of Free Meal Each Shift Too Great For Disgruntled Arby's Employee

WEST WENDOVER, NV—Although he hates working at Arby's "more than anything," prep cook Taylor Ochtrup, 17, told reporters Monday that he would quit if it weren't for the $6 meal allowance that he earns for every shift of four hours or more. "The hours suck, I always work weekends, and the manager is a dick, but hey, free Super Roast Beef," Ochtrup said. "And, if I work until closing, I get to take home any extra Curly Fries." Although he has no health insurance, Ochtrup said his kitchen drawers are "chock-full of Horsey Sauce."

Woman Dozing At Coffee Shop Has That Dave Eggers Sex Dream Again

IOWA CITY, IA—Freshly jolted awake from a peach-tea-induced nap, Sumatra Café patron Laurie Dubar said she had that same sex dream about bestselling author Dave Eggers. "I'm lying on the couch naked, and Dave is next to me, also naked, reading *Salon* on his laptop," said Dubar, a 34-year-old Iowa Writers' Workshop instructor. "Suddenly, he turns to me and says, 'Could you help me edit a collection of short fiction?' and I can't control myself any longer." Dubar said she always wakes up just as Sarah Vowell walks in wearing a kimono.

New Generation Of Dynamic, Can-Do Seniors Taking On Second Jobs

Above: Atlanta's Pauline Keetan works the morning shift at a Krispy Kreme doughnut store.

CHANDLER, AZ—Old age used to be considered a period of decreased activity, mental slowdown, and reduced usefulness to society. In recent years, however, a new generation of ambitious, resourceful senior citizens is turning that trend on its head, reclaiming their youthful vigor by taking on second jobs.

"For too long, society has told seniors that they are worn out, washed up—that they've paid their dues and now it's time to rest," said Arizona State economics professor Victor Romansky, a leading expert on the elderly workforce. "Well, the 65-and-over crowd isn't taking 'no' for an answer any longer."

Romansky added: "The face of the American senior citizen is changing. Instead of a glum widow coming home from her gift-shop job to sit in a rocking chair all night, we're seeing the eager smile of a Walgreens cashier working the 6-10 p.m. shift."

Supplementary employment, once reserved for the young and middle-aged, is quickly being discovered by the "middle-aged at heart," Romansky said.

"Whoever said people should settle into just one job at 65 never witnessed the pride of an 80-year-old grocery bagger," said Skip Eldrud, CEO of the job-placement company Vital Signs Temporary Labor. "It's moving to see that the can-do American spirit lives on, well into the years when declining bodily functions make many tasks difficult or even painful to complete."

"Wake up, service and office-support industries!" Eldrud added. "America's seniors are knocking on your door, and they're politely requesting an employment application."

According to Romansky, the increased drive for subsistence is ensuring the pre-Baby Boomer demographic a place in the U.S. workplace.

"A recent study showed that a modern American worker will hold an average of 14 jobs in his lifetime," Romansky said. "Seniors, many of whom have been working in the same field for their entire lives, are now trying to catch up. With the plucky, eager-to-please demeanors they bring to high-turnover professions, I wouldn't be surprised if many 'retired' folks worked another 20 jobs before they die."

Romansky said an additional job gives structure and meaning to the hours before and after work—hours that seniors once spent worrying about rent and insurance premiums.

Eleanor Reynolds, 71, recently took a job as a gas-station attendant to supplement her income as an administrative assistant.

"I thought I'd be spending my retirement looking through old photo albums and watching TV," said Reynolds, 71. "Boy was I wrong! I barely have a minute to spare. Instead of sitting around the house and reading, I'm earning $6.25 an hour."

Reynolds was a role model for many of the women in her now-disbanded knitting society, all of whom stopped talking about needing pills and decided to do something about it. Three of these geriatric go-getters now spend their evenings telemarketing.

"I used to sit around at night waiting for the phone to ring," said senior Margie Bell, 68, of Litchfield Park, AZ. "Now, if I'm even five minutes late for work, I know I'll get a call from my Capital One supervisor."

Romansky said that some septuagenarians need a little encouragement to recognize their latent industriousness.

Clarence Lattimer, 72, of Apache Junction, AZ considered grabbing life by the horns after his military pension was reduced from $847 to $735 per month in November. But it wasn't until his daughter-in-law kicked him out of her house in January that Lattimer actually put his plan into action, enrolling in a night-school security-guard training program at the local technical college.

"I thought I'd be spending my retirement looking through old photo albums and watching TV," said Reynolds, 71. "Boy was I wrong! I barely have a minute to spare. Instead of sitting around the house and reading, I'm earning $6.25 an hour."

"It's such a relief to see Clarence out there on his own, supporting himself," his daughter-in-law Denise said. "There's no time like the present, while his cancer is in remission."

A second job brought Allentown, PA's Ginny Edsel not just a meager second paycheck, but somewhere to go on weekends.

"I hadn't bought a new outfit in almost six years," said Edsel, 71, who recently took a supplementary job at Burger King. "But now, I've got a brand new set of clothes. And a hat!"

In her book *Back From The Pasture*, sociologist Anne Bailey said there is a reason why the second-job trend has spread so quickly among America's seniors.

"The re-energizing of an entire generation didn't just happen," Bailey said. "Seniors began to take their futures into their own hands after the notion that society must coddle those in the twilight of life became outdated. These days, it's not just acceptable for seventysomethings to work multiple jobs outside the home, it's encouraged. And with everyone questioning the viability of Social Security, it looks like this fearless do-it-yourself attitude is here to stay." ⊘

MILLER from page 73

"Our products should enhance life, not cause our customers to embarrass themselves in public," Milburn said. "Our company has a rich and storied history that dates back to 1855. We thought if Kevin knew a little more about that history, he might remember to slow down and enjoy the great taste of our high-quality beer."

After finding out that Helvinski often watches *Late Night With Conan O'Brien*, Miller bought airtime from Cheyenne's NBC affiliate KCHY and began running a series of commercials featuring sepia-tone photos of Miller Brewing Company founder Frederick J. Miller. Unfortunately, the ad had no discernible effect on Helvinski, who continued to drink three to four nights each week, often failing to heed the recommended limit of 12 ounces per hour.

"We at Miller began to worry that Kevin's dead-end job at an RV-supply store and the many nights he spent out at the bars with his friends might be connected," Milburn said. "Well, when the TV ads didn't get through to Kev, we realized he needed some individual attention."

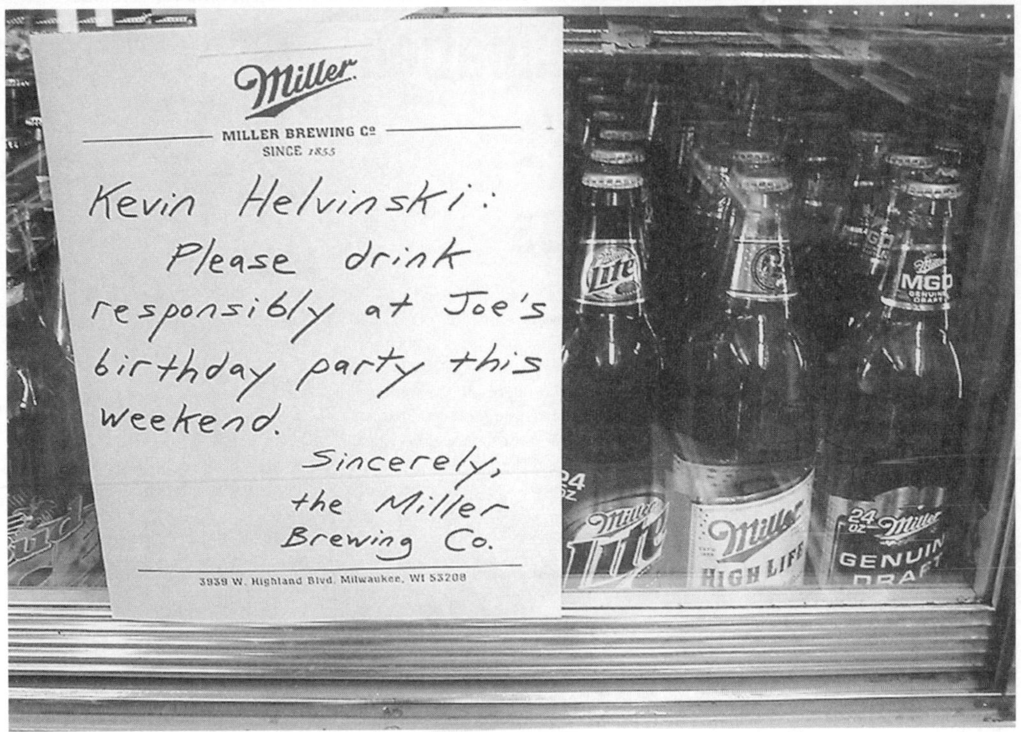

Above: A note hangs on the cooler at Helvinski's neighborhood convenience store.

In late January, Miller sent four e-mails to Helvinski, each reading, "Know when to say when, Kevin Helvinski." Helvinski's drinking did not show any change.

"After our e-mail campaign failed, representatives from the company started to call Kev on Friday and Saturday nights," Milburn said. "We tried not to be preachy. We'd just suggest that he might want to check out a movie instead of hitting the bars. Basically, we wanted to make Kevin aware that there are lots of ways to have fun that don't involve drinking. Alcohol is best consumed in moderation, as one part of a full and healthy life."

Unfortunately, this campaign also failed, and Helvinski continued to drink to excess.

"We needed to hit him at the point of purchase, so we started to put up friendly little notes in strategic locations, such as on the beer cooler at the gas station near his house," Milburn said. "The notes said things like, 'Use your head when you go out drinking tonight, Kevin.' We also put signs up above the urinals in Kevin's favorite bars, with the simple, black-and-white message, 'Haven't you had enough tonight, Kevin?'"

When this campaign failed, Miller sent a representative to Helvinski's house "to tell him we'd rather lose him as a customer than as a human being."

"We didn't want him to become a statistic," Milburn said. "Sure, we're making a little bit of money from Kevin's drinking, but none of us here want to profit at the expense of a customer's well-being. Make any company in America choose between a million dollars and a customer's life, and I don't think a single one of them would take the money."

Milburn said this is not the first time Miller has used such a narrow campaign.

"We'd do the same thing for any one of our customers," Milburn said. "And we have. When we thought drinking was hurting Tempe, AZ resident Megan Litvin's relationship with her husband, we took her out to lunch to talk about it. We suggested Michael Sumner of Atlanta go to AA rather than do further harm to himself, and now I'm his sponsor."

"When you climb behind the wheel of a car after you've been drinking, it's like you're playing with a loaded gun," Milburn added. "We're just like the manufacturers of guns: The safety of our customers is our number-one priority."

Reached at home, Helvinski responded to Miller's concerns.

"I'll admit that I drink too much sometimes, but it's not like I do it every night," Helvinski said. "I don't need the Miller people following me around. I'm totally fine."

"Well," Helvinski added after a long pause, "I guess I have been going out a lot since my friend Tyler moved back to town. Maybe I could stand to cut back a bit."

Miller Brewing Company is the second-largest brewery in the U.S., with seven major breweries located across America. Principal beer brands include Miller Lite, Miller Genuine Draft, Miller Genuine Draft Light, Miller High Life, and Milwaukee's Best. More information is available at millerbrewing.com. Ø

MINNESOTA from page 73

Highway 280 seems to be held together with equal parts concrete and prayer," Mineta said. "We tried to slip them a few dollars along with the National Bridge Inspection Standards Act, but they told us to put the money right back into our wallets, or give it to someone who could really use it, like Arizona."

Mineta said that, even after he explained that he couldn't simply give the money to another state, Minnesota reaffirmed that it was determined to stretch what federal dollars it had.

"They kept saying, 'Oh, you guys keep that budget allocation,'" Mineta said. "But everyone likes Minnesota and would love to help them out. They never ask for anything, unlike New York, which seems to be in some kind of crisis every other week."

Joshua Bolten, U.S. Director of the Office of Management and Budget, said the national government "guilted" Minnesota into accepting some money to fund a child-safety-seat program three years ago, by repeatedly urging them to "think of the children."

"After all it took to get them to take the money, they wouldn't stop thanking us," Bolten said. "The following day, Minnesota congressmen kept dropping by with cakes and cookies. I mean, the hand-stitched quilt Rep. Mark Kennedy (R-MN) made was beautiful, but a gift was really, really unnecessary."

Most Minnesota residents support their governor's decision to do without increased federal funding. In fact, citizens have been holding rummage sales and donating their time so that they won't have to inconvenience the rest of the country.

"We don't want to be a bother," said Brian Calhoun, a restaurant owner who spent last weekend fixing highway-safety rails in his hometown of St. Cloud. "There are a lot of folks around here who know the value of a little bit of elbow grease. Duluth said it has some scrap metal we might be able to melt down to make some lamp poles."

Although the majority of Minnesota residents agree that they can "make do," a few have disagreed.

"This is stupid," said Tom Suttcliffe, a recent transplant to Minneapolis. "We need more snow plows—everybody knows it. I'm sorry, but I don't think having people agree to shovel the street in front of their houses is the answer. Shit, if everyone else is too embarrassed to ask for the money, I'll do it. Who do I call?"

Later that day, Minnesota officials gave Suttcliffe a "stern talking to," and the Boston native said he would not speak out of turn again.

In spite of the state's congenial nature, federal officials say they are "exasperated" by Minnesota's selflessness.

"Minnesota should just take the spending money, already," Department of Education Undersecretary Edward McPherson said. "It's not like it's a special handout—all schools were allocated extra money under the Individuals with Disabilities Education Act. But they refuse to accept their extra federal funding on the grounds that their schools 'don't need to be fancy.'"

"Frankly, they're just being stubborn and I'm not going to stand for it any longer," McPherson said. "They're gonna get some more funding by the end of the year if the federal government has to airdrop in school lunches and forcibly place new teachers in th[e] classrooms with the help of the N[a]tional Guard." Ø

COMMUNITY VOICES

I Support The Occupation Of Iraq, But I Don't Support Our Troops

The U.S. went to war in Iraq to remove an evil and dangerous political adversary from power. Now that we have done that, the American troops must remain in Iraq until the country is a fully functioning democracy, able to spark change throughout the entire Middle East. While I find this obvious, there are still a lot of people in our country who fail to grasp it. I support Bush-administration foreign-policy goals, but I stand firmly against the individual men and women on the ground in the Persian Gulf.

By James W. Henley

Yes, occupying Iraq does require troops, but they are there for one reason and one reason only: to carry out the orders of the U.S. Defense Department. As far as their overall importance goes, they are no more worthy of our consideration than a box of nails. Ribbons and banners in ostensible "support" of the troops miss the whole point of the invasion, which is to gain a strategic hold over that volatile and lucrative geopolitical region.

Need I remind the reader that it is our flag, not the troops, that we salute? It is our nation-state, not a bunch of 20-year-olds in parachute pants, that deserves our allegiance. As a patriot and true American, my heart sings at the thought of the Pentagon, and the zealous, calculating measures undertaken by the proud military bureaucracy of this great superpower. I feel a surge of pride when I think about our high-tech GBU laser-guided bombs, capable of carrying a 2,000-pound warhead. I tied a ribbon around my tree for the safe return of our nation's F-16s, because our military aircraft are instrumental to finishing our work in Iraq. And on the back of my car, I have a sticker stating my support for the CIA's ongoing efforts in Iraq.

I support the occupation, and the occupation alone, because when we start to support the troops, we pave the way for irrelevant concerns about their families back at home. Before you know it, questions about who is and isn't going to be home in time for Christmas will be interfering with the crucial decision-making process of our commander-in-chief.

I'd like to ask those currently trumpeting their support for the troops a question: Have you ever actually met any of these soldiers in person? Well, I have, and believe me, they are no more impressive than any other low-level functionary of a large institution.

In all honesty, my soul swells with pride at the thought of the military-strategy papers and cost-analysis reports in which the troops are represented as numerical figures. But, as for the men and women—well, in almost every respect, they are average. Although they are no less intelligent than any other American, it is certainly fair to say they lack the ability to devise the complex strategies and tactics to manage their own divisions, much less grasp the nuanced reasons for their deployment.

They are there for one reason and one reason only: to carry out the orders of the U.S. Defense Department. As far as their overall importance goes, they are no more worthy of our consideration than a box of nails.

It is ridiculous that my "heart" is somehow morally or ethically obliged to "go out" to the troops. In fact, had the troops not been put to productive labor by the sheer might and institutional authority of the U.S. military, a good number of them would be sitting around bars, drinking and gambling. In short, we shouldn't view the troops as objects of sympathy, because their very contribution to our society is their ability to carry out simple commands on a battlefield.

Allow me to pursue this from a more personal angle. I have a son in the military. If I may say so, we've never gotten along particularly well. Frankly, he's been a bit of a disappointment to his mother and me. Nevertheless, he is our flesh and blood and always will be, and we wish him no harm. So I speak from a position of personal experience when I say that, while I do not wish death for any of the troops, death tolls should not be our greatest concern. All that matters is the pursuit of the foreign-policy goals of this great land, the land I love. America. Ø

HOROSCOPES

Your Horoscope

By Lloyd Schumner Sr.
Retired Machinist and
A.A.P.B.-Certified Astrologer

Aries: (March 21–April 19)
You'll have an identity crisis when you find out your life is just another Internet rumor.

Taurus: (April 20–May 20)
When the aliens finally initiate relations, you'll be surprised to find their mysterious handbook is, when translated, actually a drink-mixing guide.

Gemini: (May 21–June 21)
You always wondered which of your sins would send you to hell, but you never thought it would be tipping Roger $2.34 on a $60 check.

Cancer: (June 22–July 22)
You're not excusing your own ignorance in the matter, but the Museum of Modern Art should've announced that the fur-lined teacup was not for drinking.

Leo: (July 23–Aug. 22)
Your contribution to the performing arts is limited to the fact that your mama is so fat almost anything can be said about her.

Virgo: (Aug. 23–Sept. 22)
You'll somehow manage to lose your lucky glass vial of smallpox culture in the subway, but that's okay—you've got a 10-gallon cooler of the stuff in your basement.

Libra: (Sept. 23–Oct. 23)
You have no idea why thousands of shrieking, lovesick teens chase you everywhere you go, but you're pretty sure it's not because of your shitty albums.

Scorpio: (Oct. 24–Nov. 21)
After nine long hours, fried-chicken company executives will finally find a monetary figure that convinces you to leave the taste-test.

Sagittarius: (Nov. 22–Dec. 21)
It's true that we live in a disposable culture, but that's no reason to wad men up into little balls and throw them in the trash when you're done using them.

Capricorn: (Dec. 22–Jan. 19)
Your life will take a horrible turn, due to your inability to tell how old girls are and where cameras are hidden.

Aquarius: (Jan. 20–Feb. 18)
Unfortunately, the rain will arrive at the precise moment when you're about to answer the age-old question of whether fire is man's friend or foe.

Pisces: (Feb. 19–March 20)
For 15 terrifying minutes, the universe will indeed revolve around you, causing the death of billions because you decide to skip rope.

LAW from page 75

with his campaign to present a carefully styled, finished look. In fact, in a recent phone poll, 82 percent of women ages 18-34 agreed that Law is a total fox."

Nonetheless, critics are quick to point out Law's missteps.

Nelson Garcia, writer for the *National Enquirer*, said Law's first 100 days have been "a fiasco."

"From his overly gelled hair on the set of his forthcoming film *All The King's Men* to his hosting of *Saturday Night Live* on the night of Ashlee Simpson's lip-synching debacle, Jude Law has been an embarrassment to the entertainment world," Garcia said. "And let's not forget his visit to the Los Angeles Children's Hospital. It was a great chance to raise pulses nationwide by showing up in a well-worn sleeveless T-shirt and gym shoes. Instead, he looked like a dandy out on the court. Now, Matt Damon—there's a guy who could look good playing basketball with below-average-looking kids."

Mel Gibson, who was named *People*'s first Sexiest Man Alive in 1985, urged the public to support Law.

"Jude has some challenges ahead of him, but I support him completely," Gibson said. "The Sexiest Man Alive is only human. It's not fair to attack him every time he looks tired or is seen in a club that isn't hip. Jude deserves a chance to show us what he's got—both in his riveting dramatic roles and in photos of him with his shirt off." Ø

"Jude came into office with a big, sexy plan in place," Giulletti said. "He'd spent years tweaking and refining his dapper image, so it was wise that he chose to stick with it."

NEWS

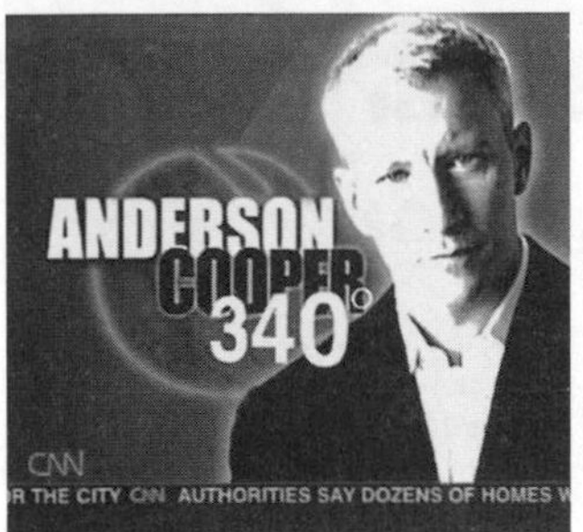

CNN Accused Of Ignoring Certain Issues On *Anderson Cooper 340°*

see NATION page 11C

Scrabble Come-On Only Worth Four Points

see LOCAL page 3G

Sucker Next Door Paying For Wireless Internet Service

see TECH page 8E

STATshot

A look at the numbers that shape your world.

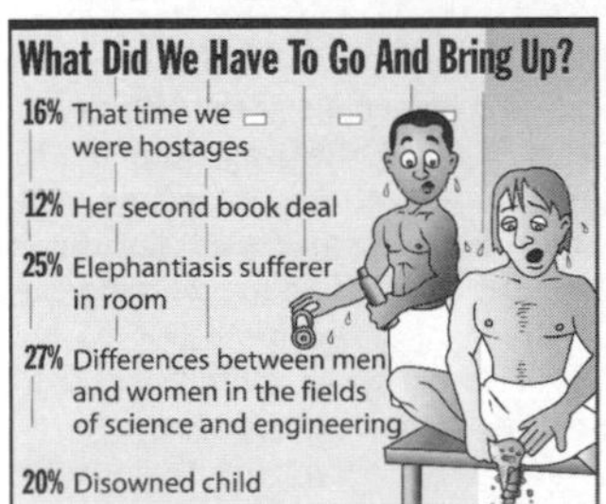

the ONION®

VOLUME 41 ISSUE 09 AMERICA'S FINEST NEWS SOURCE™ 3–9 MARCH 2005

Cocky Pope-Hopeful Ready To Make Some Changes Around Vatican

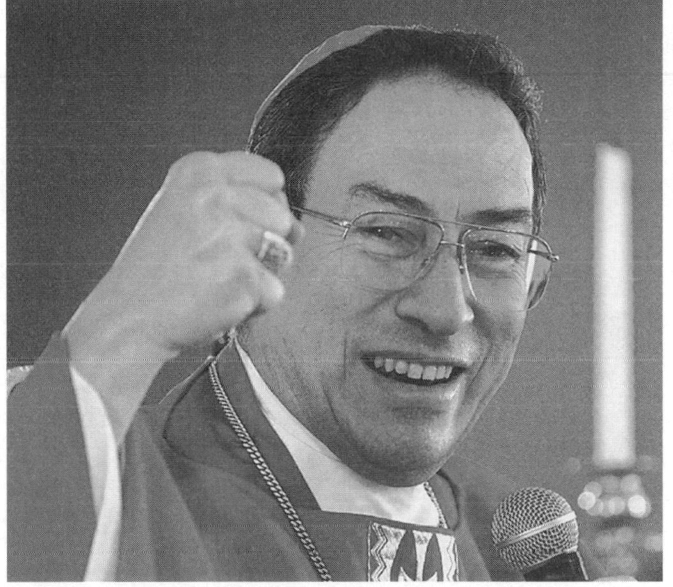

Above: Maradiaga, who is ready and willing to replace Pope John Paul II (right).

VATICAN CITY—With Pope John Paul II's health in decline, there is speculation as to who will succeed him as the head of the Roman Catholic Church. Cardinal Oscar Andres Rodriguez Maradiaga announced Monday that he is more than ready to accept the challenges of the papacy.

"When the Sacred College of Cardinals names me pope, I'm gonna shake

see POPE page 83

'Tony's Law' Would Require Marijuana Users To Inform Interested Neighbors

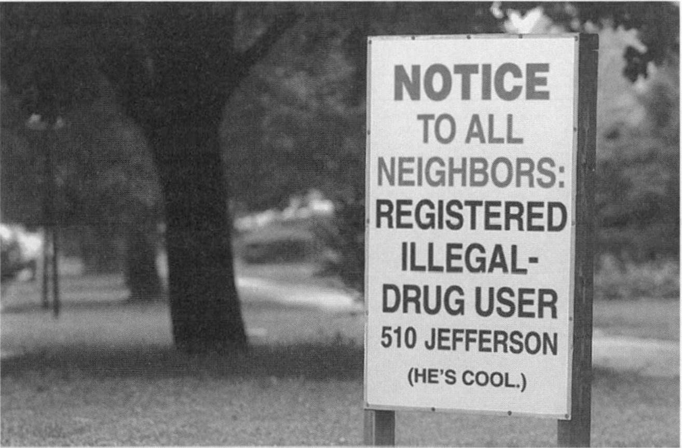

NOTICE
TO ALL
NEIGHBORS:
REGISTERED
ILLEGAL-
DRUG USER
510 JEFFERSON
(HE'S COOL.)

Above: If enacted, Tony's Law will require illegal-drug offenders to announce their status.

WASHINGTON, DC—Citizens spoke before Congress Monday in support of Tony's Law, a Senate measure that would require all marijuana-law offenders to inform their neighbors if they're holding.

"Right now, countless Americans are living on the very same blocks as convicted illegal-drug users," said Sharon Logan of the Weed For Tony Coalition. "Without a federal mandate requiring full disclosure, how are unsuspecting residents supposed to find any decent weed?"

Designed to protect Americans from dry spells, Tony's Law was named after 19-year-old New Jersey resident Tony DiCenzo, who went nine months without getting high before discover-

see LAW page 82

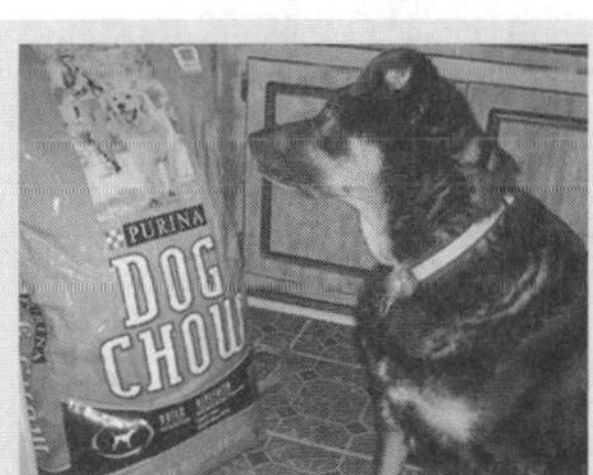

Above: Buster eyes the competition.

Area Dog Will Never Live Up To Dog On Purina Bag

KANSAS CITY, MO—Although those close to Buster characterize him as a good boy, the area collie-rottweiler mix reported Monday that he will never live up to the standard set by the show-quality golden retriever on the Purina Dog Chow bag.

"I try as hard as I can," said Buster, lying on his blanket in the entryway of the Hopkins-family

see DOG page 82

Schiavo's Right To Die

Last week, a judge gave Florida resident Michael Schiavo permission to remove the feeding tube of his brain-damaged wife Terri. What do *you* think?

Vincent Velez
Physical Therapist

"I understand what her husband is going through. My family is currently petitioning the state for permission to remove my fat uncle's feeding spoon."

Lance Morse
Systems Analyst

"If we allow one brain-dead Floridian to die, what's to stop us from extending that policy to include the rest of the state?"

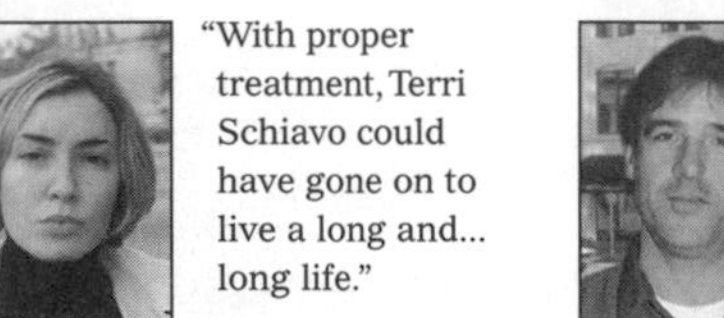

Margo Strand
Hostess

"With proper treatment, Terri Schiavo could have gone on to live a long and... long life."

Cody McIntyre
Student

"I've set up a living will so that, in the event I fall into a persistent vegetative state, I should be blown to death."

Ted Hebert
Toxicologist

"If God wanted people to die with dignity, He wouldn't have created modern medical technology capable of artificially prolonging life."

Maria Avery
Baker

"And what about the feeding tube? Is no one considering its feelings?"

New Bush Science Policies

Recently, scientists expressed concerns that scientific research is being stifled by the Bush administration. What are some of the areas of funded research that the Bush administration cited to counter the charges?

- The Make Coal Look Cleaner project of 2002
- The ongoing development of a prayer-guided, tactical nuclear missile
- 2001 grant to independent researchers developing a fast-reloading, conveyer-belt-fed lethal-injection machine
- $44 billion to NASA to put a Christian on Mars by 2035
- $5-billion budget allocation to scientists working to break the 100-inch plasma-screen TV barrier
- The Interestingly Colored Skies Initiative of 2003
- The founding of the Safe, Legal Birth-Control Eradication Board
- Creation of an atheism-cure research facility at Bob Jones University
- Ongoing financial and policy support of Industrial Pioneers For A Nice Warm Globe

America's Finest News Source.™

Herman Ulysses Zweibel
Founder

T. Herman Zweibel
Publisher Emeritus
J. Phineas Zweibel
Publisher
Maxwell Prescott Zweibel
Editor-In-Chief

Thank God The Year Of The Monkey Is Over

Boy, that was some great New Year season this year. I suppose I shouldn't have drunk as much as I did at my friend's Lantern Festival, but I was in the mood to really cut loose. Everyone says the Year of the Monkey is the year of success, filled with unexpected opportunities for all. What a load of crap. The Year of the Monkey couldn't have ended fast enough for me.

By Brian Kang

Everyone's like, "Year of the Monkey—that's one of the best astrological years, full of energy and vitality." Some parents even make an effort to conceive so that their kid'll be born in that year. I'm sorry, but last year sucked. I knew it the second I dropped the Prosperity Cake on the ground at the reunion dinner.

My sister was like, "But each Year of the Monkey brings new, unconventional ways of doing things." That's so true! My boss found a new and unconventional way to fire me. He told me that the way things were going, cutbacks were inevitable, so they had to let me go. Mind you, he didn't say they were strapped just yet, just that they were going to be. That's unconventional, all right! Thank you, Glorious Monkey. You piece of shit. Plus, my landlord told me one week into the year that my building was being turned into a bakery. What a blessing! I was kicked out of my apartment for a new, "unconventional" reason. Monkey, my ass.

Everyone says the Year of the Monkey is the year of success, filled with unexpected opportunities for all. What a load of crap.

"People born in the Year of the Monkey are fun and carefree." So true! The year produced my new roommate Ben, a drunken halfwit who slept through an entire semester of art-history classes and then complained to me for three hours when he got an "F." If a roulette wheel were completely black, the monkey would put his money on red. If the monkey ran the country, we'd be too busy holding cockfights to think about running schools and building roads.

My dad was born in the Year of the Monkey, but he's hardly what I'd call lively, unless you call watching television every waking moment of your life lively. At the beginning of last year, I had to deal with him acting like he was Emperor Qin Shi Huangdi all of a sudden. Every time he needed something done, it was like, "Hey Brian, come change this light bulb. After all, it's my year!" Then he'd laugh like it was the funniest joke he'd ever heard. I guess I thought it was funny on Jan. 22, but by June, I was tired of being his indentured servant. By that time, he'd just point at a burned-out light bulb without even looking up from *Wheel Of Fortune*.

She told me we'd have major compatibility issues because she was born in the Year of the Monkey.

Oh, I got dumped last year, too. Did I mention that? I met this woman who was great. We were clicking like nobody's business, and I really thought we had something going when she asked me what year I was born. I told her 1978, and she was quiet for a while before she said, "That's the Year of the Horse, isn't it?" I knew I was done for. She told me we'd have major compatibility issues because she was born in the Year of the Monkey. Fucking hell, she could have just said she didn't like me, but she had to pull that year-of-the-monkey business out of her ass. I suppose she thought she was letting me down easy.

Well, I sure hope the Year of the Rooster is better. The Year of the Rooster is characterized by overconfidence and bad judgment. Fine by me. With that as a backdrop, those of us with our heads on our shoulders—we horses and rats and so on—will be given a chance to really shine. So hopefully, things will turn around this year. But here's an early warning: Don't try calling me in 2016, because I'll be staying in bed the entire shitty year. Ø

Death Of Parents Boosts Area Woman's Self-Esteem

SAVANNAH, GA—In the wake of the Aug. 12, 2004 death of her parents Hugh and Patricia, Leah Sawyer's self-esteem has skyrocketed, sources close to the 27-year-old said Monday.

"When her parents died, I thought for sure the terrible experience would send timid little Leah right over the edge," Sawyer's 31-year-old cousin Edie Holt said. "But somehow, she's handling the tragedy really well. If I didn't know that this dreadful thing had just happened to her, I would say that Leah was the happiest I've ever seen her."

Less than a year since a semi-truck broadsided Sawyer's parents' Saturn Ion on Interstate 516, Sawyer seems "healthy, fulfilled, and confident," Holt said.

"Leah seems to be adjusting just fine, even though her life is vastly different from the one she had been living at home with her parents in the suburbs," Holt said. "I got the impression that Aunt Patricia and Uncle Hugh could be quite critical and controlling sometimes. And I know she wasn't thrilled about the hotel-management job Uncle Hugh had found for her, either."

"Oh," Holt added quickly, "but I'm sure that Leah would give up her new job and her new condo downtown just to hear her parents speak to her one more time. I mean, of course."

Within two months of the tragic car accident, Sawyer quit her job, put the longtime family home on the market, and sold most of her parents' possessions.

"We were initially worried that Leah was being a bit rash," Holt said. "Everyone remembered how she'd been such a homebody. I mean, she barely ever left her room. We feared that she might be having some sort of nervous breakdown as a result of her grief."

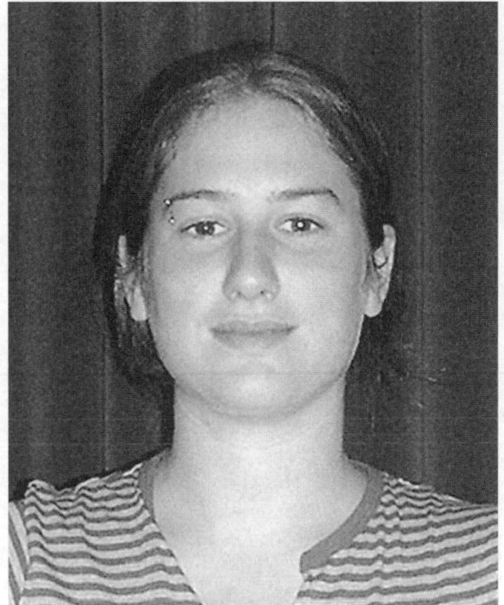

Above: Sawyer (left) is adjusting quite well to the death of her parents, pictured in an August 2004 photograph.

"But Leah told me in the calmest of tones that, for her, the one real way that she could move on was by moving out, so to speak," Holt said. "And, after unloading all of her dad's beloved fishing poles and her mom's macramé supplies at an estate sale in a single weekend, that's just what she did."

Many friends and relatives said they noted Sawyer's fortitude at the funeral.

"We were all very impressed that Leah volunteered to deliver the eulogy, since she'd always been so shy at family gatherings," said Natalie Demirdjian, Sawyer's aunt. "But at the funeral, she was very composed and she spoke so positively about her parents' new life in heaven. She spoke movingly about how Hugh and Patricia had journeyed on to a place free of worries and hassles, where they would be 'forever young and without complaints.' Then she described death as a way for the bereaved to start anew, and how 'bright flowers would bloom on scorched and sour earth.' It was quite inspiring."

"It must have done her good to speak from her heart, because when she walked away from that podium, Leah looked a foot taller," Demirdjian said. "It was as though a giant burden had been lifted from her shoulders."

Although her inheritance could have allowed her to retreat from public life, Sawyer plunged headfirst into new pursuits.

"I was stunned when [Leah] told me she was taking motorcycle lessons," Sawyer's friend Betsy Pfaff said. "She said that, since she's proven that she

see PARENTS page 83

NEWS IN BRIEF

Knife-Throwing, Plate-Spinning Congressman Dominates Newscasts

WASHINGTON, DC—The cries of political grandstanding that have followed him throughout his career do not discourage Rep. "Fantastic" Frank Pallone Jr. (D-NJ), the knife-throwing, plate-spinning congressman. "Don't blink, Koppel," the blindfolded congressman said on *Nightline*, tossing knives over his shoulder at balloons held by Sen. Dianne Feinstein (D-CA). "These are real knives, folks!" Senate Majority Leader Bill Frist (R-TN) denounced the wild and wonderful show, saying that "the nation should be focusing on the Social Security crisis, not cheap tricks—no matter how spine-tingling they may be." In response to Frist, Pallone said, "The GOP would attack anything that didn't further the regressive Republican political agenda," and then placed a spinning plate atop a pole balanced on his chin.

Ken Jennings Mistaken For Subway's Jared Again

MURRAY, UT—Ken Jennings, who rose to mid-level fame by winning a record $2.5 million on *Jeopardy* last year, was erroneously identified as Subway restaurant pitchman Jared Fogle again Monday. "Today a woman at the post office came up and congratulated me for losing all that weight," Jennings said. "That happens all the time. I guess people recognize me from television, but mix up where they saw me." Jennings added that he usually tries to inform people of their mistake in the form of a question: "What is your problem?"

Meek Coworker Taken Down A Notch

MT. VERNON, IL—Patty Walther, a passive, mousy administrative assistant at Datalock Inc., was put in her place Tuesday by sales representative Martin Challey. "Oh, thank you for coming all the way over to my desk to return that valuable pen," Challey said sarcastically. "I don't know how I could've gotten any work done without it. I might've had to use one of the other 20 pens right in front of me." Challey last berated Walther Monday, when the quiet coworker brought in a plate of homemade brownies.

Gmail User Pities Hotmail User

OLYMPIA, WA—Recent Gmail convert William Ramsak, 23, said Monday that his "heart goes out to" friend Kelly Oldenburg, who still sends e-mail through an MSN Hotmail account. "I feel so bad for you, needing to squeeze into 250 MB of storage space," Ramsak wrote to Oldenburg in an e-mail. "And I hate thinking of you sorting all your old e-mail, while Gmail automatically indexes mine so they are searchable." Ramsak then asked Oldenburg when he was going to "stop being a Microstooge and join Team G."

Heroin Addict Better Off Than Poppy Farmer

NEW YORK—In spite of his debilitating addiction, junkie David Spellman is safer, warmer, healthier, and happier than nearly every poppy farmer in Afghanistan, sources reported Monday. "Mr. Spellman shoots up three times a day and squats in a filthy Bronx apartment, but at least he isn't slaving away in the Kabul poppy fields 18 hours a day before coming home to a meal of moldy bread in the tiny shack he shares with 14 relatives," said Dr. Terrence Arven, professor of sociology at NYU. "When Spellman finally decides to get clean, he'll have many options for counseling. The only support network available to a poppy farmer is the 'protection' of local warlords." When asked for a comment, Spellman curled up and vomited.

LAW from page 79

ing that he lived in the same apartment building as a reliable marijuana source.

"Can you imagine the shock and anger Tony must have felt when he found out that the guy on the second floor possessed the Schedule I federal controlled substance?" Logan said. "The offender could have invited poor Tony into his apartment to smoke some at any time. It's heartbreaking."

Tony's Law would create a national public registry of drug-law offenders' names, addresses, and pager numbers. Additionally, offenders charged with dealing marijuana would be required to either post signs or go door-to-door and let neighbors know when they're holding.

Privacy-rights groups oppose the legislation on the grounds that it violates the individual's right to a stash, but Austin, TX's James W. Clancy is one of

Tony's Law would create a national public registry of drug-law offenders' names and pager numbers.

many stoner-rights lawyers who traveled to Washington to rally in favor of the law's passage.

"Millions of Americans love to be high," Clancy said. "Unfortunately, their neighbors often keep them in the dark about what kind of shit is going around."

Clancy and other proponents of Tony's Law argued that the bill would result in increased domestic trade in consumer snack products and a heightened sense of community and well-being.

More powerful, perhaps, were the personal testimonials of hundreds of drug-drought victims, who stood before lawmakers to share their experiences with dope deprivation.

"As a parent, I don't have a lot of time to dedicate to finding weed," Minneapolis resident Kyle Berman said. "All my wife and I wanted to be able to do was get Tina and Tyler to bed, put on a movie, and smoke a joint. It wasn't until the police busted the guy across the street for growing marijuana that we realized how close we'd come to actually finding some pot. A whole set-up with lamps and everything was less than 50 feet from our living room. It sickens me to think about it."

Above: A convicted drug user in Kenner, LA informs his neighbor that he has the number of a guy.

Several lawmakers have spoken out in opposition to Tony's Law, largely due to what Rep. Chris Chocola (R-IN) called "complications stemming from the illegality of marijuana."

Nonetheless, the bill's many devoted supporters said they'll continue their fight.

"After nine months of hell, Tony eventually found a hook-up through the friend of a guy whose brother met someone at a former girlfriend's birthday party," activist Stephen Miller said. "In spite of the nightmare he was going through, Tony didn't give up...and neither will we." ⌀

DOG from page 79

home. "I welcome [Buster's owner] Gerald [Hopkins] home every night with lots and lots of barks and leaps. And when he sits down in his chair to read, I lie quietly at his feet. Still, when I see that dog on the Dog Chow bag, I feel like I'm nothing."

Without lifting his head from his paws, Buster turned his eyes to the shelf above the dryer, where the trim and muscular golden retriever on the 40-pound bag of Purina Dog Chow bounded across a green lawn.

According to Buster, the dog is almost certainly American Kennel Club-certified.

"Look at that coat," Buster said. "Thick and soft... And his color! Varying shades of rich and lustrous gold. As for me, I'm sort of a rough, dull black, and I know it. I've known it since I figured out that the strange, scentless dog in the mirror is me. Ever since then...well, I try my best not to whine, but it's hard to live with the fact that I will never measure up."

"It didn't take two vets to piece together what breed *that* dog was," Buster added.

Buster admitted that not one member of the Hopkins family has ever compared him unfavorably to the dog on the food bag.

"But I know what they must be thinking," Buster said, baring his teeth to reveal two misaligned incisors. "Just look at this messed-up bite. The kids hug me when they feed me, but over their shoulders, I can see Golden Boy over there, staring down at me from the Purina bag."

Buster said his worst days are those when a family member forgets to return the Purina bag back to the shelf after feeding him.

"Oh, I go positively crazy," Buster said, pausing to gnaw a spot on his left hindquarter. "He's right there, staring me down, eye to eye, all day long. The only way I can get away from his strong nose and bright eyes is to put my own head in the bag. And, you know how it is, once you smell the kibble, you can't help but eat all of it... And then there's no question about it: I'm the worse dog."

Added Buster: "No, the dog on that bag would never eat himself sick and then make a mess on the floor."

Buster noted the gracefulness of the golden retriever's movements.

"Aw Jeez, look at him go," Buster said. "I can't even shamble up the stairs without tripping. That dog looks so confident and intelligent. Meanwhile, I still fall for the old fake stick toss half the time."

A fit, attractive woman in her 30s accompanies the golden retriever on the Dog Chow bag. According to Buster, the tall, upright-walking woman looks uncannily like his owner's wife.

"I look at the bag, and I think, 'That looks like Susan, all right, but that dog sure doesn't look like me,'" said Buster, a hint of a growl in his throat. "I have to wonder if Susan sees the bag and thinks the same thing. When we're out on walks, is she embarrassed to be seen with me?"

"I love my human family with all my heart," Buster added. "They deserve the dog from that bag."

Elaine Thannum, a noted animal behaviorist and author of *The Breeding Myth*, said that idealized media images contribute to self-esteem problems among pets.

"Unfortunately, the inadequacy Buster is feeling is common among normal, everyday dogs," Thannum said. "No matter how much their families love them, regular dogs can't help but be affected by the unrealistic images shoved down their throats by dog-food companies like Purina, Cycle, and Iams. Dogs like Buster need to understand that if they were to meet the supposedly perfect animals they see on the food bag, they'd see and smell dogs with a lot of the same problems they have."

Los Angeles-based purebred Troubadour's Golden Dawn appears on millions of Purina Dog Chow bags, as well as a Clarinex print ad and packages of Nylabone chew toys.

"Let me tell you, it is not easy being me," Troubadour's Golden Dawn said. "Do you know what it's like to have judges and photographers poking and prodding you all day long? What I wouldn't give to have a fun, playful family. I'd roll over and play dead to be able to eat Purina-brand Dog Chow, instead of that all-natural, vitamin-flavored concoction I have to choke down."

"And believe me," the 3-year-old golden retriever added, "you don't want to get me started about what it feels like to have to compete for jobs with that nippy little blond bitch on the Puppy Chow bag." ⌀

POPE from page 79

Above: Maradiaga bounces some ideas off of a few of his fellow cardinals.

things up," Maradiaga said. "And I'm not just talking about giving the Popemobile a new coat of paint. I'm talking about big moves that will reconfirm the Catholic Church's position as the supreme, full, and immediate power in the sectarian world, may God grant us peace."

Maradiaga, a charismatic cardinal from Honduras, said he is "not afraid to goose the stodgy rituals" of the Catholic Church.

"First thing, let's get the online theological tour done," Maradiaga said. "We were slated to have Phase II complete in December 2003, but click on 'altar' or 'cross' and you still get nothing. Let's get our Sunday Mass and special liturgical celebrations online, too. As pope, I want to touch as many people as I can, and streaming video is just the ticket for that."

Maradiaga said he would like to upgrade the pope's public image by reviving the more formal title, The Supreme Pontiff.

"I'd like to re-establish that sense of respect for the high seat at the Holy See," Maradiaga said. "We need to emphasize that I—assuming the inevitable happens—am in charge of the spiritual lives of more than one billion Catholics worldwide. It's mainly a public-relations thing—no big deal, God willing."

Maradiaga said he is also planning to farm out some of the "less Pope-y duties" after his election, to free up some of his time.

"Does the Pope really need to be the bishop of Rome?" Maradiaga said. "I'll have enough on my plate already, so I'm pretty sure I'll have one of the other cardinals take care of that. Also, I have some great changes I want to make to the *Sacrosanctum Concilium* of 1963. Nothing in the body or the message—just some gentle massaging to bring some of the wording up to date."

Many Vatican insiders have said that Cardinal Dionigi Tettamanzi of Milan is more likely to be named Pope John Paul II's successor, but

"I'd like to re-establish that sense of respect for the high seat at the Holy See," Maradiaga said. "We need to emphasize that I—assuming the inevitable happens—am in charge of the spiritual lives of more than one billion Catholics worldwide. It's mainly a public-relations thing—no big deal, God willing."

Maradiaga said he is confident there will an upset.

"The Church already had 450 years of Italian popes," Maradiaga said. "After 27 refreshing years with a Polish pope, do you really think people are going to want to go back to Italian popes again? Just because the Vatican is in Italy, that doesn't mean the pope's got to be Italian. With so many Catholics in South America, the times call for a Latin man of God to don the miter. And that Latin man of God is going to be me, may He strengthen my faith with proofs."

Continued Maradiaga: "I'm not saying Tettamanzi's not a good cardinal, but if you spent a couple minutes in the same room with him and me, I think you'd have a pretty good idea which one of us is better suited to be the Vicar of Jesus Christ and Supreme Pontiff of the Universal Church."

Maradiaga said he would not change the things that people love most about the pope.

"The robes, the hat, the staff—all that benevolent-father stuff is going to stay," Maradiaga said. "Hey, I'm not crazy. Also, the day-to-day operations of local churches will continue apace. So don't worry, Catholics. I've got your back."

Rumors have spread that, should he be installed as pope, Maradiaga will effect a number of immediate changes, moving the Vatican from Rome to Barcelona, modernizing the doctrine of apostolic succession, and streamlining the stations of the cross from 14 to 10.

"I don't want to comment on any of that," Maradiaga said. "Those ideas came out of a brainstorming session and were all merely speculative. I will say, though, that if Vatican City is looking for some fresh, new ideas, I've got plenty."

Even though Maradiaga has supporters, some say that his swagger is not what Catholics are looking for in God's representative on earth. Maradiaga shrugged off such criticisms.

"I know what I want and I'm not afraid to go for it, may He direct my steps to Himself," Maradiaga said. "It's like Pope Pius IX used to say: 'It's not the sin of pride if it's true.'" ⊘

PARENTS from page 81

can read the paper at the kitchen table without leaving dirty smudges all over the tablecloth, maybe she can also climb on a motorcycle without suffering permanent brain damage. I didn't really get what she meant, but she's been through a lot lately, so I didn't question her."

Pfaff added: "I also let it go when she said, 'You don't think wearing red makes me look like a whore, do you?'"

Pfaff said her surprise redoubled after she asked Sawyer to help her manage her small used-book store.

"Leah looked a foot taller," Demirdjian said. "It was as though a giant burden had been lifted from her shoulders."

"I really needed an extra hand, but I didn't have a lot of money to pay Leah," Pfaff said. "I didn't want to take advantage of her while she was in such a fragile emotional state, but Leah said the low pay was fine because she really loved the store. She told me, 'Sure, Mom and Dad wouldn't have approved of me working for peanuts, but we can't live in the past, can we?'"

Pfaff said the new independence must be good for her friend, because she's noticed that Sawyer's complexion is clearer than it has been in years, her frame looks about 15 pounds lighter, and she has begun to attract the attention of men.

"Leah used to say she didn't date because she was holding out for the type of guy her father would approve of," Pfaff said. "She'd never found that guy in all the years I knew her, though. I guess her luck must've turned around."

Last week, Sawyer went on a date with bookstore patron Seth Westphal, 30, who said he was attracted to her "optimistic attitude and big, sunny smile."

"Over dinner, I told Leah, 'You seem to have a lot of energy,'" Westphal said. "Leah smiled, turned a little red and said, 'Yeah, well, my parents died in August.'"

Family physician Dr. Jack Meyerling, who has known the Sawyer family for nearly 30 years, said that, while it is not unusual for a bereaved person to resent his or her deceased loved ones for departing so suddenly, Sawyer appears to have "made peace" with her situation.

"Psychologists have isolated five stages of mourning: denial, anger, bargaining, depression, and acceptance," Meyerling said. "But, after spending a very brief time in the initial stage, Leah skipped the middle three and very swiftly zeroed in on the fifth."

Added Meyerling, "Actually, in Leah's case, I would propose adding a sixth stage: welcoming." ⊘

Getting A New Place Sucks!

Hola, amigos. What's the deal? I know it's been a long time since I rapped at ya, but I've been having a heaping helping of problems. First off, the bill collectors from the hospital have been on my ass about the money I owe them for fixing up my leg earlier this winter. I didn't have insurance, so I owe them a shitload. I told them I didn't have any money and they were going to have to open the cut they sewed up if they wanted any more blood from me. The way I figure it, I got a few months before they send it over to a collection agency. And, if I give them a hundred bucks or so, that'll buy even more time.

The Cruise
By Jim Anchower

I got other troubles besides the hospital hounding me. My car got busted into last month. Some dickwad smashed the window on the passenger side—the door I just replaced—and took all my tapes, some bottles of motor oil, and even the emergency $20 I had in the back of the glove box. Since then, I've been freezing my nards off. I don't care how much duct tape you use or how high you crank up the heat, you can't keep the cold out with a Hefty recycling bag when it's 10 degrees out.

I've worked out a system of living that's pretty solid, and I don't like anyone telling me how to deal with my shit. The last thing I need is someone telling me I drank his case of beer or left my dishes on the couch.

That's not all the changes in my life. See, my landlord called last week. The conversation was going along fine and dandy with some bullshit small talk when he springs on me that he wants to raise my rent $50. "Jim," he said, "property taxes have gone up, and I haven't raised rent in four years. I gotta do what I gotta do." I was all polite, but I totally slammed the phone when he was done. What does that dick think, that I shit nickels? How am I supposed to start coming up with $350 every month? My weed alone costs that much.

Once I got done throwing and kicking things, I sat down to pack a bowl and think this apartment situation through. I started thinking that maybe moving out of my place would give me a whole new perspective on life. I took a good look around the old pad and realized it was starting to get crowded. The water stain on the wall is getting bigger by the month, the cardboard I taped over the hole in the ceiling three years ago is starting to fall down, and the carpet is peeling up off the floor in about six places. I definitely needed a change of scenery.

When I got a paper and looked through the want ads, every apartment was like $200 more than this one, and none of them had parking. If I'm gonna go through the hassle of moving, I need a place for my car to cool its wheels while I'm cooling mine. The only places I could afford were 20 miles outside of town. That's when I had a great idea: I could get a new place with a roommate and cut my bills in half.

Now, ordinarily, I'm a lone wolf. After 28 years on this earth, I've worked out a system of living that's pretty solid, and I don't like anyone telling me how to deal with my shit. The last thing I need is someone telling me I drank his case of beer or left my dishes on the couch. But I was in a bad spot, and I needed someone to help bail me out.

The first person I thought of was Wes. He's been living with his mom for way too long, so I gave him a call and told him he was going to be my new roommate. He sort of hemmed and hawed, until finally I squeezed it out of him: He's planning to move in with his girlfriend in a few months. What a pussy-whipped jackass. I told him he didn't need some woman holding him down, but he told me his mind was made up. He did say that if I had have asked last year, he would've done it. I told him not to do me any favors and hung up the phone.

Later, Wes called me to apologize and told me that he'd been doing some asking around for me. He said his mom told him about a place a mile away from where I'm living now, and it sounded really sweet. It was close to a main drag, the rent was $25 less than what I'm paying now, and it was right around the corner from Shotz Bar & Grill. I decided I had nothing to lose by checking it out.

It turns out the landlord is this old lady who owns the building. She needs a little extra income, so she's renting out a room in the basement. I wasn't keen on living with some fossil, but I was there, so I thought I should at least check it out. I mean, technically, I'm living in a basement right now. Well, the room was about 10-by-10 with one window. On the plus side, it had a toilet right there in the room. On the down side, it had one ceiling light, one electrical outlet, and no fridge. And the ceiling was only about two inches taller than my head. Plus, if I wanted to shower, I had to go upstairs. There was no way I was going to wait for some old lady to get out of the tub so I can hose down. I'm a man on the go. If I ain't out the door 20 minutes after I get up, it's a Saturday. I told the lady I had to think about it, and I beat it the hell out of there as fast as I could.

The whole apartment search has been a big downer. I'm still sorta looking around, but I'm starting to think that my place is okay. I could put a poster over the stain, and I could either wait for the cardboard to come all the way off or just put some more over it. Besides, it's a real pain in the ass to move. Something always gets lost, and you have to buy beer for everyone who helps you. Still, if a place falls in my lap that has more space for less rent than I have now, you'd better believe I'm gonna jump on that shit. I don't know how much longer I can stand to live the way I'm used to living. ⌀

Your Horoscope

By Lloyd Schumner Sr.
Retired Machinist and
A.A.P.B.-Certified Astrologer

Aries: (March 21–April 19)
Your ruthlessness in carrying out love-triangle arbitrage will earn you a fearsome reputation as a short-term emotional-bond trader.

Taurus: (April 20–May 20)
Nothing you've been told will prepare you for the pain of childbirth, especially when your daughter bursts from your brow, decapitating you instantly.

Gemini: (May 21–June 21)
It's true that the best things in life are free, but you've never been the kind of person who demands quality.

Cancer: (June 22–July 22)
The ghost of Roger Troutman magically appears to you whenever you do something funky, which explains why you've seen him only once.

Leo: (July 23–Aug. 22)
You thought pulling off the heist would be as easy as taking candy from a baby, but then you found out the four tons of fine imported Italian chocolates had to be kept at a constant temperature.

Virgo: (Aug. 23–Sept. 22)
Upon your death this Friday, you'll find that entrance to heaven is granted only to members and those non-members who first agree to view a half-millennium sales presentation for condos in Elysium.

Libra: (Sept. 23–Oct. 23)
Many major changes are ahead for you this week, but you'll probably give most of your attention to the changes involving temperature, altitude, and brain activity.

Scorpio: (Oct. 24–Nov. 21)
You'll be overcome with a mixture of empathy and annoyance when you accidentally stumble into the closet where all the suppressed homosexuals hang out.

Sagittarius: (Nov. 22–Dec. 21)
You have an irrefutable message concerning the importance of psychoactive drugs in personal development, but no one will heed your boring, hyper-rational lectures.

Capricorn: (Dec. 22–Jan. 19)
In your quest for supremacy, you'll be accused of overlooking the human cost. But you'll know that's ridiculous—you've already spent well over $700.

Aquarius: (Jan. 20–Feb. 18)
Everyone is aware that you don't care what the people say, but that doesn't mean they'll listen when you tell them you're going to love them anyway.

Pisces: (Feb. 19–March 20)
Your willingness to gamble on extreme long shots is endearing, but you never should've bet your life savings on the Bears to win the 1986 world championship.

SEAWEED from page 27

amounts of blood. Passersby were amazed by the unusually large amounts of blood. Passersby were amazed by the unusually large amounts of blood. Passersby were amazed by the unusually large

How magic is your little pony now?

amounts of blood. Passersby were amazed by the unusually large amounts of blood. Passersby were amazed by the unusually large amounts of blood. Passersby were amazed by the unusually large amounts of blood. Passersby were amazed by the unusually large amounts of blood. Passersby were amazed by the unusually large amounts of blood. Passersby were amazed by the unusually large amounts of blood. Passersby were

see SEAWEED page 59

the ONION®

VOLUME 41 ISSUE 10 | AMERICA'S FINEST NEWS SOURCE™ | 10–16 MARCH 2005

NEWS

Could Hillary Clinton Have What It Takes To Defeat The Democrats In 2008?

see POLITICS page 7B

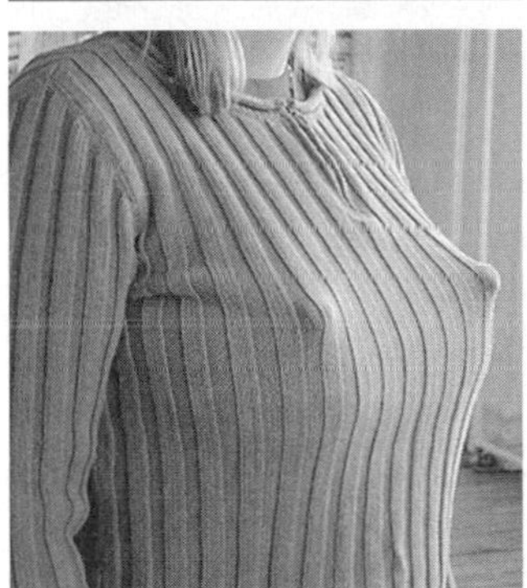

Thick Sweater No Match For Determined Nipples

see LOCAL page 3C

Country Mouse, City Mouse Devour Face Of Homeless Corpse

see NATURE page 11E

STATshot

A look at the numbers that shape your world.

Top Rent-To-Own Items
13% That thing that makes surround sound happen
18% Tux from Joe's Long-Term Tuxes
34% Folding chairs
15% House
11% Beatin' mule
9% The Bourne Supremacy, unfortunately
RENT TO OWN!
ONLY
$19.95/MONTH

Bush Announces Iraq Exit Strategy: 'We'll Go Through Iran'

WASHINGTON, DC—Almost a year after the cessation of major combat and a month after the nation's first free democratic elections, President Bush unveiled the coalition forces' strategy for exiting Iraq.

"I'm pleased to announce that the Department of Defense and I have

see IRAN page 88

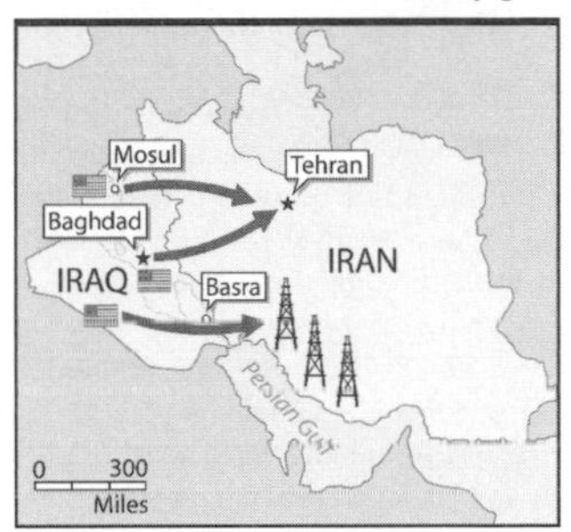

Above: Bush announces the pullout of Iraq through Iran.

Study: Reality TV, Reality Unfair To Blacks

WASHINGTON, DC—According to a study released Monday by the Center for Media and Social Research, the reality-TV genre is unfairly biased against black people. The study revealed that reality is unfair to blacks, as well.

"Programs like *The Apprentice* routinely stereotype black participants," read the 5,000-page report. "Black contestants are often portrayed as stormy and indolent fringe elements, while their white counterparts are portrayed as stable and industrious collaborators. Black reality-TV contestants face discrimination at levels approaching those of everyday life."

see REALITY TV page 89

Left: The cast of the popular reality-TV show *The Apprentice 3*.

Victims Sought In Next Week's Shooting

CHARLOTTE, NC—In an extremely brief press conference on the steps of City Hall, area psychopath Roland Walling, 46, announced Monday that he is on the lookout for potential victims in the unprovoked shootout that he expects will leave at least three dead and up to 10 wounded next Tuesday.

"I'm asking for the community's help in piecing together the details of Tuesday's pointless, bloody attack," Walling said. "There's no clear motivation for my horrendous act, so I'm having a

see SHOOTING page 89

Right: Walling, who is asking the public for help in his upcoming massacre.

Consumption Tax Proposed

Last week, Federal Reserve Chairman Alan Greenspan said a consumption tax, such as a national sales tax, could benefit the nation's economy. What do *you* think?

"This tax would unfairly penalize people like me whose televisions aren't as large as they'd like."

Timothy Potts
Systems Analyst

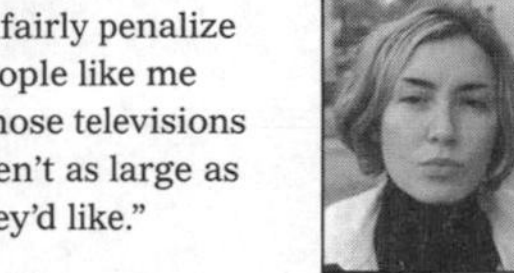

"So, does this mean that, in the future, if I don't want law and order to utterly collapse, I'll have to buy at least five things a day?"

Lola Stein
Drafter

"I'd been wondering if my daily ramen-noodles consumption could somehow be turned into a revenue stream for the federal government."

Jarrod Ray
Police Officer

"That damn Kerry! Even though he didn't get elected, he's somehow managed to sneak his insidious liberal tax-raising agenda onto us anyway!"

Connie Crane
Dentist

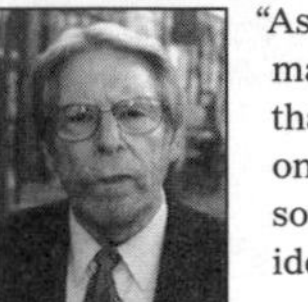

"As a man with a massive income that I only spend on necessities, this sounds like an ideal plan."

Corey Bernard
Accountant

"We tried an income-based tax for nearly a century and look what it brought us: greater economic stability and government accountability. Clearly, we must explore other options."

Adrian Sears
Short Order Cook

New Stop-Smoking Aids

Over-the-counter stop-smoking aids like Nicorette gum and Nicotrol patches are more popular than ever. What are some of the newest products on the market?

- Lee Press-On Nicotine Nails
- Injectable Nico-Flu, the potent flu virus that makes users too sick to smoke
- Quitstar-1 Geostationary Anti-Smoking Thermonuclear Laser Satellite
- Proacti-Quit Helpline: subscription-service addiction counselors call clients every three and a half minutes
- Nic At Night All-Night Nicotine-Replacement Television
- Mr. Masher, the trained bull elephant who really, really hates secondhand smoke
- Questdart nicotine-uptake inhibitor, delivered by blowgun to the back of a smokers' neck
- Lung cancer, which kills 160,000 Americans each year
- Stouffer's Nicotine-Based Microwaveable Dinners

the ONION®
America's Finest News Source.™

Herman Ulysses Zweibel
Founder

T. Herman Zweibel
Publisher Emeritus
J. Phineas Zweibel
Publisher
Maxwell Prescott Zweibel
Editor-In-Chief

Take This Job And Shove It Following The Customary Two-Week Notification Period

By Donald E. Little

Listen and listen good, sir. I've had it up to here with the stress, the long hours, and bad pay. I'm a house of cards that's just about to collapse. I tell you, I'm half a month shy of my breaking point. Following my two-week notice as mandated by the terms of my employment, you can take this job and shove it!

At the end of those two weeks, I'm out of here. History. Dust. Gone, never to walk through those doors again. I am going to relish my freedom as much as I will despise the remainder of my time here. I won't be your whipping boy for much longer, so you'd better ask me about my filing system now.

I'm tired of the way you work your employees' fingers to the bone and then reap all the rewards of their hard work. When's the last time you had an idea of your own? Well, I've taken your shit for long enough, and in 11 business days, I'll never have to take it again! You can't treat me like dirt after the 22nd.

Boy, am I gonna let you have it with both barrels in my exit interview.

Reconsider? Absolutely not. I won't stay another minute longer than the 4,800 minutes stipulated by the contract I signed during my orientation session. You can beg all you want, dangle pay raises in front of me, and even hire me an assistant, but it won't change my mind. It will be a cold day in hell when I set foot in this shithole after I'm removed from the employee roster.

Yup, when I walk out that door carrying all the items from my locker, I'm gone for good. So you'd better kiss my sweet ass goodbye sometime between now and Thursday... not this Thursday, but the one after that. Because that day is the last you'll see of me, unless I run into you when I swing by to get my last paycheck.

I don't have anything lined up right now, but I don't even care. This place is poison, and the only antidote is walking away as soon as the terms of my employment allow. If you want the keys, you can come to my office and

You can't treat me like dirt after the 22nd.

get them yourself, once I no longer need them to fulfill my job duties. They'll be on the top shelf in the "Mondays make me grumpy" mug along with any pens I got from the supply closet.

Go ahead and tell my coworkers that I'm as good as gone. Or I'll tell them when I see them in the breakroom today. Oh, and that reminds me, I'll have to stop by Human Resources and tell Barbara that I need a COBRA health-insurance form, too.

I've said all I have to say to you, barring any work-related discussions we'll need to have between now and Thursday after next—so farewell and good riddance! If you need to apologize for how you've treated me all these years, I'll be training my replacement. Ø

FOX SPORTS from page 86

amounts of blood. Passersby were amazed by the unusually large amounts of blood. Passersby were amazed by the unusually large amounts of blood. Passersby were amazed by the unusually large amounts of blood. Passersby were amazed by the unusually large amounts of blood. Passersby were amazed by the unusually large amounts of blood. Passersby were amazed by the unusually large amounts of blood. Passersby were amazed by the unusually large amounts of blood. Passersby were amazed by the unusually large amounts of blood. Passersby were amazed by the unusually large amounts of blood. Passersby were amazed by the unusually large amounts of blood. Passersby were amazed by the unusually large amounts of blood. Passersby were amazed by the unusually large amounts of blood. Passersby were amazed by the unusually large amounts of blood. Passersby were amazed by the unusually large

It's like beating a dead unicorn.

amounts of blood. Passersby were amazed by the unusually large amounts of blood. Passersby were amazed by the unusually large amounts of blood. Passersby were amazed by the unusually large amounts of blood. Passersby were amazed by the unusually large amounts of blood. Passersby were

see FOX SPORTS page 170

Nationwide Headband Trend Traced Back To Area Sophomore

PIERRE, SD—As cotton athletic headbands, the season's hot fashion accessory, continue to appear on trendsetters' foreheads across the nation, the originator of the fad has finally been located: Pierre West High School sophomore Melody Peterson.

"Yeah, I started doing that headband thing, like, six months ago," the 16-year-old Peterson told reporters Monday. "Of course, all the other girls in my school were wearing them right after I did, and then everyone in South Dakota started doing it. Pretty soon, I was seeing headbands on TV and stuff."

"It all started when I was at this boring sporting-goods store with my brother and I saw these totally butt-ugly headbands," Peterson said.

Above: Peterson, who made the fashion statement later copied by stars like Russell Crowe (right).

Before the headband trend was traced to Peterson, little was known about this B-average student who enjoys cheerleading, Beyoncé, and talking on her cell phone with friends. Since it was revealed that she inadvertently started the international headband trend, however, Peterson has been barraged with interview requests.

"It all started when I was at this boring sporting-goods store with my brother and I saw these totally butt-ugly headbands," Peterson said. "I thought it might be fun to pull off wearing something dorky like that, so I bought one. When I got home and tried it on, I was like, 'I actually look pretty good in this.'"

Peterson said she was not surprised by her sudden fame.

"Everyone in this stupid town always copies what I do because they don't have any originality," Peterson said. "This is the first time one of my ideas traveled outside my school, though. When I saw the same headbands I was wearing at Old Navy, I was like, 'Yuh, get a clue.' Just because I start doing something doesn't mean everyone else has to."

Added Peterson: "Check out this scarf. Isn't it hot?"

Everyone from South Beach club denizens to stars like Ashton Kutcher, Lindsay Lohan, and Gwen Stefani has been wearing headbands this season. However, photos on Peterson's best friend's personal home page prove that Peterson was the first one to wear them.

"I didn't even think that much about

see HEADBAND page 88

NEWS IN BRIEF

'Me Decade' Celebrates 35th Year

NEW YORK—The "Me Decade," a period beginning in 1970 and marked by self-awareness and self-fulfillment, celebrated its 35th year of existence Monday. "With careerism, materialism, and general self-involvement as popular as it was decades ago, the Me Decade may well go on for another 35 years," said historian and Columbia University professor Dr. Vera Conklin. "It's been the longest-running decade in American history, beating the selfless "Greatest Generation" of the '40s by a good 15 years. Selfishness, it seems, is here to stay." Author Tom Wolfe, who coined the term in his essay "The Me Decade And The Third Great Awakening," was unavailable for comment, as he is working on his memoirs.

Bar Bet Becomes Increasingly Complex

DETROIT, MI—Onlookers at Schutt's Tavern report that a bet between two customers grew to almost unworkable complexity Monday. "Okay, let's get clear on this," said bartender Tim Alighire, officiating the wager. "If *Sin City* doesn't suck, Roger has to join Gary's pool team instead of Keith's, but only if Gary gets Troy to join too, in which case Gary has to pay Roger's dues and Roger has to chip in for half of Troy's dues? And Troy... no, *Gary* gets to decide if the movie is good?" Watching his two customers shake hands, Alighire said he wished that hockey season hadn't been canceled.

The Edge Still Introducing Self As Such

MALIBU, CA—U2 guitarist The Edge, born David Evans, introduces himself by his stage name, sources reported Monday. "He showed up at parent-teacher conferences, extended his hand, and said, 'Hi, I'm Sian's father The Edge,'" said Dory Beckman, a second-grade teacher at Malibu Heights Elementary. "I didn't quite understand so he said, 'U2's The Edge.' Well, I guess with all the records he's sold, he's entitled to call himself whatever he wants." Employees at Gladstone's 4 Fish restaurant said Evans placed "The Edge" on their waiting list when he took his family out for fried scallops last week.

Script Could Use Another Pass, Mom Says

ANSLEY, NE—*Persistence Of Vision*, a screenplay by aspiring screenwriter James Grunau, "isn't quite ready to shop yet," Grunau's 57-year-old mother Doris told her son over breakfast Monday. "I know you worked really hard, Jimmy, but I think this could use another good punch-up," Grunau said of the 115-page draft. "I just don't think anyone will relate to Donna, and the second act feels flat. You need to raise the emotional stakes." Ms. Grunau then offered her son some butterscotch pudding.

Mysterious Defibrillator Saves Accident Victim, Disappears

SAN ANTONIO, TX—An unidentified defibrillator saved the life of heart-attack victim Clifford Moore, 67, and vanished without a trace, sources at Goode Company Barbecue reported Monday. "I was headed back for more condiments when I felt a terrible pain in my chest and collapsed," Moore said. "I think I must have passed out, but I remember feeling paddles on my chest and a sudden jolt. I wish that defibrillator would have stuck around... I would've liked to thank it." The only trace the phantom defibrillator left behind was a tiny, silver-adhesive-backed conductive pad found below an outdoor bench. ⌀

HEADBAND from page 87

it when I took those pictures of Melody last September," said Ashley Gamble, of gambleyourheart.com. "Mel's always wearing these great outfits, then complaining about how everyone else is just a clone. Now that *Teen People* ran that story about headbands, she's really going to have something to bitch about."

Gamble said she started wearing headbands about a month ago. She stressed that it wasn't because it was the hot new thing, but because she thought the accessory was "cute."

"Everyone in the world has to imitate every single little thing I do," Peterson said.

"It's kinda an unspoken rule not to copy your friend's look," said Gamble, who was wearing a pink-and-white Von Dutch headband. "But check out how sexy I look in this one. When I saw it, I just had to have it. I knew it would look hot with my black tank top."

Athletic-gear manufacturers like Nike and Puma have reported skyrocketing sales of the two-toned cotton headbands that Peterson paired with non-sporting outfits. Even high-end fashion designers have begun to steal Peterson's idea.

"Melody had a great idea," Juicy Couture designer Gela Nash-Taylor said. "Headbands are definitely going to be prominent in this year's fall lines. I know that Michael Kors is experimenting with fleece headbands, and all I can say about Marc Jacobs' headband line is, 'Wow!'"

Peterson said some of the people across the country who are copying her style are unable to pull it off.

"Everyone in the world has to imitate every single little thing I do, whether it's keeping boxes of cereal in my locker or wearing flip-flops in winter," Peterson said. "Like, some people look good in a headband, but most don't. Brad Pitt looks yummy with one, but Hilary Duff? Please. You have to have an attitude to pull it off. Which, uh, she does not."

Continued Peterson: "Someone sent me a picture of [Vice President] Dick Cheney wearing a headband like mine, and it made me want to puke. Newsflash to government guys: If you work in an office, don't try to be cool."

According to Peterson, the most upsetting thing about being ripped off on a national scale is that "the whole thing is so over."

"I haven't worn one of those headbands in five months," Peterson said. "It was something that was cool for, like, a week, because I was the only one doing it."

"Hey, look at this—it's my dad's old bowling bag," Peterson added. "Isn't it hot? Not. But still, it might be kinda cute, in a retarded way. I think I might start carrying my gym clothes in it." ⌀

IRAN from page 85

Above: Some of the Iranian citizens U.S. troops will meet as they pass through Iran.

formulated a plan for a speedy withdrawal of U.S. troops from Iraq," Bush announced Monday morning. "We'll just go through Iran."

Bush said the U.S. Army, which deposed Iran's longtime enemy Saddam Hussein, should be welcomed with open arms by the Islamic-fundamentalist state.

"And Iran's so nearby," Bush said. "It's only a hop, skip, and a jump to the east."

According to White House officials, coalition air units will leave forward air bases in Iraq and transport munitions to undisclosed locations in Iran. After 72 to 96 hours of aerial-bomb retreats, armored-cavalry units will retreat across the Zagros mountains in tanks, armored personnel carriers, and strike helicopters. The balance of the 120,000 troops will exit into the oil-rich borderlands around the Shatt-al-Arab region within 30 days.

Pentagon sources said U.S. Central Command has been formulating the exit plan under guidelines set by Bush.

"The fact is, we've accomplished our goals in Iraq," said General George Casey, the commander of coalition forces in the Iraqi theater. "Now, it's time to bring our men and women home—via Iran."

Questions have been raised about the unprecedented size of the withdrawal budget.

"I'm asking Congress to approve a $187-billion budget to enable us to exit as smoothly as possible," said Casey, whose budget request includes several hundred additional M1A1 Abrams battle tanks, 72 new C-130 cargo planes, and two brigades of artillery. "We're concerned about the safety of our troops, so we need to have the capacity to deal with insurgent forces all the way from the Iraqi border through to Tehran."

"Don and Kenneth have already been in Iraq an extra four months, so it's so good to hear that they'll finally be leaving that dangerous place," Haverbuck said. "I can't tell you how happy I was when the president said—what was it? I wrote it down. 'Getting our troops out of the Middle East and back home to their families is a viable long-term goal.'"

Casey has requested a budget increase for the Pentagon, so that the government can reward recruits who serve in the U.S. mission to exit Iraq.

"The plan also includes a minor stopover for refueling and provisional replenishment in Syria," Casey said. "But I don't expect we'll need more than 50,000 additional troops for that stretch of the Iraq pullout."

Bush's plan has met with widespread support.

"The people who said Iraq was a quagmire and that the president would never get our troops out are now eating crow," said Sean Hannity on his popular radio show Tuesday. "Of course, I don't expect anyone will have the honor to come forward and actually admit that they were wrong to question our commander-in-chief."

Sioux Falls, SD's Dianne Haverbuck, who has two sons in the military, said she was pleased to hear of the impending exit.

"Don and Kenneth have already been in Iraq an extra four months, so it's so good to hear that they'll finally be leaving that dangerous place," Haverbuck said. "I can't tell you how happy I was when the president said—what was it? I wrote it down. 'Getting our troops out of the Middle East and back home to their families is a viable long-term goal.'"

"I can't wait to see the boys," Haverbuck added.

Iranian Supreme Leader Ayatollah Ali Hoseini-Khamenei welcomed the exit plan.

"Let the Allied armies come to Iran," Khamenei said. "I believe I can assure you that, if they do withdraw here, their brothers-in-arms in the Islamic Republican Army, the Revolutionary Guards Corps, the Quds special forces units, and the Basij Popular Mobilization Army will no doubt do everything they can to make the troops' trip back home memorable." ⌀

REALITY TV from page 85

Above: Blacks in Atlanta, GA line up for a chance to compete for factory jobs.

The study cited the case of Omarosa Manigault-Stallworth, a black woman who criticized *The Apprentice* for stereotyping her and other black contestants.

"Producers edited footage to make Omarosa look like a self-involved diva," study director Simon Rosemead said. "Her allegations are not isolated. Reality shows often depict black female contestants as sassy and overly aggressive, and black male TV contestants often appear incompetent and lazy. They are minor characters who are often prematurely ousted from the TV workplace."

The study found that many black people who are not on television suffer in the real-life workplace, with an unemployment rate of 12 percent, the highest of any major American ethnic group.

"The average per-capita income among black people in America is $14,953, with 22.7 percent of blacks living below the poverty line," Rosemead said. "In much the same way, circumstances beyond their control keep black reality-show contestants from a fair shot at the jackpot."

"Like reality TV, reality is a discriminatory institution," Rosemead said.

Jennifer Hudson was one of several talented black singers voted off *American Idol*'s third season, prompting singer Elton John to call the show racially biased.

The study detailed Hudson's story, as well as that of black Chicago resident Shonalda Brown, 11, who has lived in crime-ridden public housing her entire life, and was raped at the age of 5.

"Like reality TV, reality is a discriminatory institution that is unfair to the black community," Rosemead said. "Only 14 percent of the black population has a bachelor's degree, and there has never been a black bachelor on TV's *The Bachelor*."

Rosemead said the CMSR data found statistical parallels between reality television and reality.

"Blacks make up about 13 percent of the U.S. population, but only five percent of the contestants on *Survivor: Palau* are black," Rosemead said. "Similarly, while black males comprise only 6 percent of the population, they are the victims of half of its homicides."

According to the CMSR, black people are four times more likely to be shown losing their tempers in TV boardrooms, five times more likely to be portrayed flailing in wet sand during physical challenges, and 55 times more likely than white people to be innocent passersby caught in the crossfire of inner-city shootings.

Jersey City, NJ resident Malik Greggson, 18, is a participant in reality.

"I've been in a wheelchair since I was 16, when I got shot by a drug dealer," said Greggson, who, like 66 percent of black children in America, lives in a single-parent household. "I guess there ain't no way I'm ever gonna be on *The Amazing Race 6*."

Rosemead said black people in America are two times more likely than white people to be eliminated in the first half of a reality-TV season. In adult life, black people have a 70 percent higher incidence of being eliminated before the age of 65, due to complications stemming from diabetes.

Harvard sociologist James Woolcott said black people who do find success on reality-TV shows often discover that reality is quick to intercede in the favor of white people.

"Look at Ruben Studdard, a black man who beat Clay Aiken, a white contestant, on *American Idol*," Woolcott said. "Aiken now has millions of loyal fans, he's released a number-one album, and he's even had his own Christmas special. Meanwhile, Studdard is the butt of late-night talk-show jokes about his weight."

"Oh, and also, LAPD cops beat Studdard to death three days ago after pulling him over for a broken headlight," Woolcott said. Ø

SHOOTING from page 85

good deal of difficulty developing a coherent plan of action."

While many details of the grisly shooting are still unknown, Walling said he will most likely walk into the post office on Tryon Street shortly after noon, draw a 9 mm semiautomatic handgun from beneath his jacket, and begin shooting at random.

"Right now, the community's involvement is essential," Walling said. "I have no solid leads for potential victims, so please contact me immediately if you can be a target for my insane outburst of rage, or if you know someone who might be willing to be shot."

Added Walling: "I repeat—anyone who can be in the vicinity of the Tryon Street post office between 12:15 and 12:18, please come forward."

Walling urged victims to call him at 659-4066, visit him at his dilapidated mobile home in Sugar Hill Park, or "just swing by the post office Tuesday." He added that volunteers who wish to remain anonymous should remove all identification from their pockets and destroy their dental records before approaching the scene of the forthcoming crime.

Homicide detective Ryan Fowles of the Charlotte Police Department expects to be the first at the scene.

"It sounds like it will be like nothing I'll have ever seen in my 20 years in law enforcement," Fowles said. "It's going to be hard on all of us, largely because there will be no good reason why this will have had to have happened."

In spite of the inevitable confusion that will attend this sort of unimaginable tragedy, emergency response teams say they will do everything they can when the time comes.

"Next week's tragedy will no doubt remind me why I took this job," said Memorial Hospital EMT Kim Paulkins. "There will be no way we could have been prepared for it, but the important thing is that we all act professionally and do our jobs when the unthinkable happens. I'll just wish that, if someone has to die, I could have done something to have saved him or her. I'll just have to tell myself next week that I did everything I could."

Fowles said the families of those involved will be notified as soon as the victims are shot. Nonetheless, many potential victims have been reluctant to step forward and help the gunman.

"I'm sorry, but there's no way I'm getting involved in this upcoming shootout," said Mindy Grant, who lives next door to the post office. "That crazy man will just have to find someone else to kill. No, thank you. I know better."

Beth Kammerman, who has worked at the Tryon Street post office for 11 years, will leave a husband and two daughters behind if she is hit by one of Walling's bullets.

"I'm sure I won't be able to believe the things I see," Kammerman said. "I'll have to ask myself, 'Why did God allow this to happen?' Especially if there's children, who won't have done nothing to nobody."

Sidney Crawson said next week's shooting is exactly the kind of thing she has warned her fellow residents about.

"Everyone will say, 'It was so sudden, it came out of nowhere,'" Crawson said. "The authorities should be able to see this coming, if you ask me. I'll have some hard questions to ask people next week, believe me. I just hope I'm lucky enough to be alive to say this after the fact."

Contacted at his home, Walling said he expects to be wounded by a shot fired by either a gun-carrying postal employee or an off-duty cop, but he believes he will manage to escape from the scene of the crime in a late-model Honda. Ø

COMMUNITY VOICES

How Could I Get My Wife's Funeral So Wrong?

Oh God, I never meant for it to turn out this way. All I wanted to do was give my beloved wife of 26 years a sincere and meaningful goodbye. She was the love of my life—a standard funeral ceremony just wouldn't do. But somehow, I managed to really screw it up. Geez, how could I get my wife's funeral so wrong?

By Norman Breen

My first mistake was the wake. I thought it would be a touching tribute to our love, but in retrospect, I see that the miniature-golf course where we had our first date was the last place I should have held the viewing. It wasn't the right atmosphere, what with all the cartoon-character obstacles and screaming kids running circles around the casket. And, when Fran's friends went up to share their personal memories of my wife, the outdoor roller rink next door started up with Classic Rock 'N' Roll Night. Everyone had to yell to be heard over the loudspeakers blaring Deep Purple, the Steve Miller Band, and .38 Special. Thank goodness the DJ finally announced couples-only skating and played some power ballads.

As I sat there thinking about all that Fran meant to me, I struggled to hold back the tears. I tried to maintain my composure, but it was hard to concentrate with the bank of video games right behind my chair. I don't think it was just me. When the guests offered their condolences, they seemed distracted by the flashing lights and spinning "High Score" screens.

How could I do something like this to my dear, wonderful Fran? I feel so stupid.

In my memory, that goofy Golfland where Fran and I stole our first kiss as high-school sweethearts will always be a perfect place. But, evidently, that neighborhood has gotten a lot worse in the decades since I first bought her a milkshake at the concession stand. I felt just awful for Mr. Jensen when I found out he got mugged on the way to his car.

Oh Fran, I'm just such a dunderhead sometimes!

The next day, the church service was even more awkward. I just wanted to honor Fran's lifelong love of Mexican culture. (We took a last trip to Puerto Vallarta just eight months before stomach cancer claimed her life.) But the 11-piece mariachi band barely fit in that dear little chapel where we were married. I saw a lot of scowls in those pews.

I finally asked the band to stop and handed them their pay, including a good-sized tip so they'd clear out fast. But there was a language barrier. And besides, I mess everything up. I don't know how it happened, I just know that instead of stopping, the band launched into the hat dance.

Oh, Fran! Can you ever forgive me? At the dinner in the church basement, I was the only one wearing one of the souvenir sombreros. The hot-and-spicy chimichangas were a bust—I had to take home 10 doggy bags—and the kids didn't even touch the Fran-shaped piñata. I should have known to call it quits, but after the memorial

I tried to maintain my composure, but it was hard to concentrate with the bank of video games right behind my chair. I don't think it was just me. When the guests offered their condolences, they seemed distracted by the flashing lights and spinning "High Score" screens.

service and wake were such failures, I wanted to go all out for the burial. Fran, you always loved animals, and you spent so much time volunteering for that endangered-species group. I remember how you were particularly dedicated to the preservation of African wildlife.

I was sick with the agony of loss. Still, I should have paid more attention. I should have read the rental form in its entirety. Fran, my love, honestly, I had no idea the elephant came with a party package until it marched into the graveyard surrounded by a retinue of juggling clowns and costumed dogs. All it took was one look at my relatives' ashen faces to realize what an inappropriate choice I'd made.

Oh God, I'm simply no good at organizing things. If Fran were here, she'd have handled everything so much better. Fran, my beautiful darling Fran! I miss you so much! What will I ever do without you? ⌀

HOROSCOPES

Your Horoscope

By Lloyd Schumner Sr.
Retired Machinist and
A.A.P.B.-Certified Astrologer

Aries: (March 21–April 19)
You'll be allowed one last transcendently happy, almost unbearably beautiful thought the moment before the red-hot fishhooks hit your groin.

Taurus: (April 20–May 20)
Although next Wednesday will be a Wednesday through and through, it will feel like a Thursday to you.

Gemini: (May 21–June 21)
It is written that in the midst of life we are all in death. That may be true, but in the midst of your own life, you'll actually still be at Circuit City.

Cancer: (June 22–July 22)
Your credibility will suffer when the local news runs footage of your burning pants suspended from telecommunications cables.

Leo: (July 23–Aug. 22)
Lesions on the brain may sometimes lead to episodes of irrational violence, but yours just make you want to pound the face of country-music star Kenny Chesney against a cement wall until his eyes fall out of his head.

Virgo: (Aug. 23–Sept. 22)
You'll experience a measured increase in workplace romance this week when a hastily-typed, company-wide memorandum mandates an immediate 30-percent seduction in office managerial staff.

Libra: (Sept. 23–Oct. 23)
By the time the state finally moves to stop your illegal experiments with inebriated, machine-gun-wielding chimps, they'll find out it was a self-correcting problem.

Scorpio: (Oct. 24–Nov. 21)
The stars suggest that you keep your mouth shut next week when you lose a lot of money in your church's Pope John Paul II death pool.

Sagittarius: (Nov. 22–Dec. 21)
While it's true that sometimes you have to let your friends make their own mistakes, you should really know better than to let them have tedious, unfulfilling sex with you.

Capricorn: (Dec. 22–Jan. 19)
Mother Nature wants you to understand that, although she loves you very much and always will, it is time for you to move out of her house.

Aquarius: (Jan. 20–Feb. 18)
You will be chained to a rock and tortured for eternity as punishment for stealing the secret of irresistibly flaky, gooey-sweet cinnamon rolls from the gods.

Pisces: (Feb. 19–March 20)
You'll set out to tell the tragic story of hopeless love among the beautiful and doomed, but your efforts will result in a full Broadway cast, a Bryan Adams ballad, and endless pages of heartfelt online fan-fiction.

PAINT STICK from page 41

amounts of blood. Passersby were amazed by the unusually large amounts of blood. Passersby were amazed by the unusually large amounts of blood. Passersby were amazed by the unusually large amounts of blood. Passersby were

How can one pasty, insecure fantasy-writer go through so many fucking tissues?

amazed by the unusually large amounts of blood. Passersby were amazed by the unusually large amounts of blood. Passersby were amazed by the unusually large amounts of blood. Passersby were amazed by the unusually large amounts of blood. Passersby were amazed by the unusually large amounts of blood. Passersby were amazed by the unusually large amounts of blood. Passersby were amazed by the unusually large amounts of blood. Passersby were amazed by the unusually large amounts of blood. Passersby were amazed by the unusually large amounts of blood. Passersby were amazed by the unusually large amounts of blood. Passersby were amazed by the unusually large amounts of blood. Passersby were amazed by the unusually large amounts of blood. Passersby were amazed by the unusually large amounts of blood. Passersby were amazed by the unusually large amounts of blood. Passersby were amazed by the unusually large amounts of blood. Passersby were amazed by the unusually large amounts of blood. Passersby were amazed by the unusually large amounts of blood. Passersby were amazed by the unusually large amounts of blood. Passersby were amazed by the unusually large

see PAINT STICK page 99

the ONION®

VOLUME 41 ISSUE 11 AMERICA'S FINEST NEWS SOURCE™ 17–23 MARCH 2005

Neverland Ranch Investigators Discover Corpse Of Real Michael Jackson

SANTA BARBARA, CA—During a search for evidence at the Neverland Valley Ranch, investigators discovered a corpse that has been identified as that of Michael Jackson, Santa Barbara police officials announced Tuesday.

"Coroners have officially pro-

see JACKSON page 94

Right: Investigators move Jackson's body, found buried at Neverland Ranch (below).

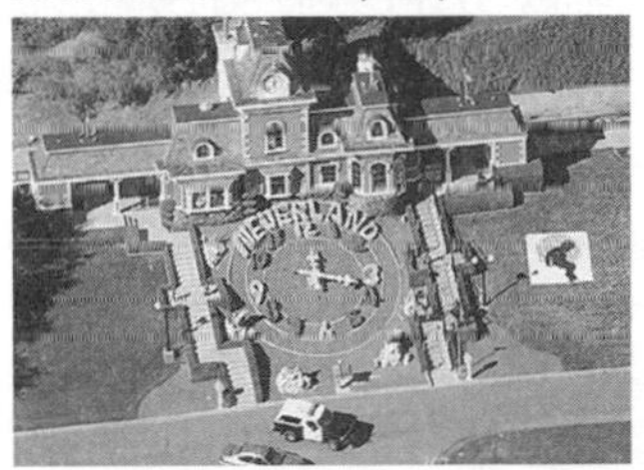

NEWS

Bush Followed Everywhere By Line Of Baby Ducks

see NATION page 12B

Hot Rock-And-Roll Chick Totally Married

see LIFESTYLES page 5F

TK Killer To Be Nicknamed Later

see CRIME page 11E

Sister Mad

see LOCAL page 9H

STATshot

A look at the numbers that shape your world.

What Are We Dyeing Green?
18% Communion wafers
11% Every stoplight in town
27% Newborn son Shane
25% Puerto Rican flag
19% Liver, slowly but surely

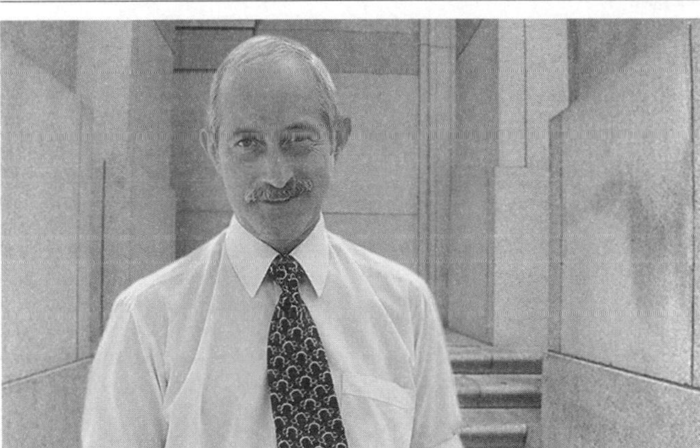

Right: Draper, who took on City Hall for 10 years to achieve his goal of keeping Mankato poolless.

Ten Years Of Life Dedicated To Getting Municipal Pool Not Built

MANKATO, MN—The Mankato City Council voted 6-3 against the issuance of a $500,000 municipal bond Tuesday, marking the end of one man's tireless, 10-year-long crusade to ensure that a proposed community pool not be built.

"Victory!" said Irv Draper, founder of Taxpayers For Wise Choices, who announced the bond's defeat from the steps of City Hall. "Today, the city council stood up in favor of the long-term interests of tax-paying Mankatoans. After 10 long years of ceaseless toil, I can finally say that a swimming pool will not be built!"

Draper, who has led the fight against a municipal pool in Mankato since 1995, threw his hands up and shouted, "The pool issue is dead in the water!" He then waved a "No City Pool!" flyer in the air as a handful of municipal employees on a smoking break looked on impassively.

Draper, now 47, began his long battle against the public pool in May 1995, when the former director of public works, Bart Janklow, proposed it. Draper mobilized a coalition of six citizens who opposed the pool due to its expense and the traffic congestion and noise it might create.

Some believed Draper's commission

see POOL page 95

Despite Bad Press, Calorie Industry Projects Record-Breaking Year

HOUSTON—In spite of seemingly endless criticism, representatives for the U.S. calorie industry predicted another record-breaking year in 2005, the American Calorie Council announced Monday.

"Magazines, fitness gurus, TV-news anchors—they're always attacking calories and telling Americans to eat less of them," said ACC spokesman Nathan Sorenson. "Well, after many years, we're getting used to bad press. Regardless of what people say, the calorie industry continues to be a major growth industry."

Sorenson said all sectors of the calorie industry—which includes producers of meat, dairy, produce, fish, bread, candy, alcoholic beverages, and some soft drinks—have made optimistic projections for 2005.

"No matter how much the media derides us, consumers keep coming back for more calories," Sorenson said. "They can't live without 'em."

Although calorie-industry officials

see CALORIES page 95

Tougher Bankruptcy Laws

Last week, the Senate made moves toward approving pro-business legislation that will make it harder for individuals to file for bankruptcy. What do *you* think?

Kim Emerson
Systems Analyst

"This is a victory for good, hard-working, God-fearing credit-card companies everywhere. Dry your eyes, Citibank, help is on the way!"

Javier Burris
Cashier

"Well, there goes my foolproof get-bankrupt-quick scheme."

Doug Schaulsberg
Ranger

"I guess my only hope for ever getting out of debt is declaring myself a business. Hey everyone! Shares in DougCo are trading at an all-time low."

Arnold Kaufman
Lawyer

"Look! I caught another middle-class guy! Here, hold his arms behind his back while I gut-punch him!"

Christian Irwin
CEO

"Ever since reading Charles Dickens as a child, I've felt that debtors' prisons had a romantic feel about them. Let's bring those back."

Stacy Goff
Environmentalist

"If this doesn't teach Americans not to have medical emergencies or get laid off, I don't know what will."

Wi-Fi Access

Wireless Internet access is growing more widespread, with entire neighborhoods and even cities offering residents the service. Why is it so popular?

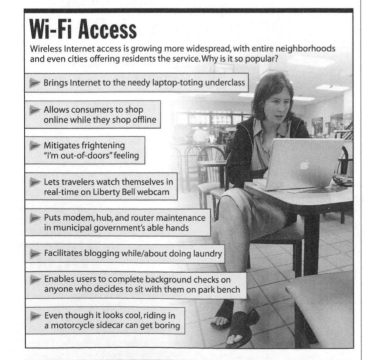

- Brings Internet to the needy laptop-toting underclass
- Allows consumers to shop online while they shop offline
- Mitigates frightening "I'm out-of-doors" feeling
- Lets travelers watch themselves in real-time on Liberty Bell webcam
- Puts modem, hub, and router maintenance in municipal government's able hands
- Facilitates blogging while/about doing laundry
- Enables users to complete background checks on anyone who decides to sit with them on park bench
- Even though it looks cool, riding in a motorcycle sidecar can get boring

Unlock Your Employees' Profit Potential With An Improv-Comedy Workshop!

By Matt Litton

What's your company's most important asset? The computers? Sure, you need those. The telephones? The office chairs? You need those, too. But your company has something a whole lot more important than any of these things. Your company's most important asset is *your staff*. You probably spend a lot of money updating your software, but how much money do you spend improving staff morale? Hi, I'm Matt Litton, and I'd like to tell you how a visit from my improv troupe One Dozen Eggs could be the key to unlocking your company's profit potential.

Some people think improv comedy—short for improvisational comedy—is just fun and games. But it's actually fun, games, and a chance for productive team-building. Fostering an environment that encourages creativity and innovation pays off in the long run. The more fun people are having, the more engaged they'll be in their work—and the more money your company will make.

Convinced yet? As we members of One Dozen Eggs say, there's no time like the present to "get cracking." For only $500, three members of our troupe will come to your office—or an alternate off-site location—and lead your staff through a series of invigorating games and exercises. The best part? Everyone will be too busy having fun to realize they're learning how to cooperate!

Actually, if you wanted to move quickly on this, we're available any day next week except for Tuesday.

Here's a little exercise that's very popular with our clients in sales. We bring one of the company's top salesmen up on stage and ask him to place an imaginary sales call to one of our improv pros. Now imagine how your employee will fare on a cold call to—a giant sea tortoise! "Hellllooo theeere. I'm swimming in the Atlaaantic Ooooocean."

Who might answer the phone next? Richard Nixon? Elmer Fudd? An auctioneer? After a few of these off-the-wall cold calls, your staff will be able to handle any situation the normal workday throws at them. In fact, they'll look forward to a call with a resistant and distracted buyer! They'll think, "At least he isn't speaking complete gibberish!"

One Dozen Eggs has more than 25 years of combined professional improv experience, and we are the only improv troupe in the Quad Cities area offering corporate workshops. Last week, we won the Bright Bulb award at Davenport's Comedy Sportz March Madness Improv-Off. A recent article in the *Weekly Bystander* described our show as "energetic, non-stop fun," and our corporate workshop has received rave reviews from companies like Coventry Health Care, Driskel Hummer, and Wendell & Reed Financial Services. Why not let us work our magic with you?

If you're sick of the contrary attitude prevalent in many offices, we've got a

Some people think improv comedy—short for improvisational comedy—is just fun and games.

great exercise to get your company back on the path to success. It's called "Yes, And..." Here's how it goes: Your staff stands in a circle and begins to tell a story. Not a story that anybody knows—one that is completely made up on the fly. Each of your employees will add one sentence to advance the plot of the story, but that sentence has to begin with "Yes, And..."

It might a little something like this: "A man gets on a bus. Yes, and there is a woman on the bus. Yes, and they are both in Baltimore. Yes, and it's the morning. Yes, and the man sits next to the woman." See? No one shoots down anyone's ideas in this game! And everyone has loads of fun! Before you know it, every member of your staff will know how to listen and feel comfortable expressing ideas. Good communication is the key to a good office environment, after all.

Here's an improv game that's great for managers and workers alike: It's called "What are you doing?" Two people get on stage, and one of them begins miming an action. It could be casting a fishing line, making a sandwich, or watching a scary movie. After a couple of seconds, the other one asks, "What are you doing?" and the first person can say anything but what they're actually doing. As soon as the first person answers, the second person must begin doing what his partner said he's doing. After a moment, the original partner will say,

see IMPROV page 96

WORKPLACE

All-Minority Postal Staff Undergoes Mandatory Diversity Training

ATLANTA—Every member of the racially diverse Pryor Road postal station's staff was required to attend a multiculturalism-sensitivity seminar Monday.

"Basically, we addressed key dimensions of diversity and ethnicity that federal employees might encounter," Prism Diversity consultant Brian Leukwick said. "My goal was to reach participants both emotionally and intellectually, while helping them uncover their unwitting preconceived notions about other cultures. The group didn't seem as curious about what I had to say as the staffs in Homerville and Folkston, but I think it went all right."

"I don't like it any more than anyone else," De Leon said.

The workshop was divided into three segments. During the first, Leukwick spoke about himself and how he came to recognize his own hidden biases as a white male.

Mail sorter Juanita Nunez was asked for her opinion of Leukwick's opening remarks.

"Monday my computer was down for two hours," Nunez said. "It was the third time this week, and our sorting unit is still on the fritz four days after it was reported to Central. I'm sorry, did you say you have something you needed to mail?"

The seminar included two video presentations: "A Wider Net Captures Bigger Fish" and "Who Should Be Sitting Next To You?" The videos were followed by a series of guided exercises designed to help participants understand the value of diversity.

"We spent half an hour coming up with phrases that might confuse people who didn't grow up speaking English," Jason Nguyen said. "I didn't grow up speaking English. Here is a phrase that confuses me: 'Why is the front wheelbase on our jeeps narrower than the fucking rear one so we fucking get stuck in the mud every two fucking days?' Management should have a seminar to discuss that."

"I got one, too," LaMont Tibideaux said. "It's, um, 'Could someone please explain the changes to our dental-insurance coverage and why I can't get my kid's teeth fixed until January?'"

Leukwick spent the final portion of the afternoon leading the staff through a series of role-playing exercises in which the postal employees—37 percent African-American, 32 percent Hispanic, and 31 percent other races including Jewish, Haitian, Vietnamese, and Puerto Rican—encountered people of another race or creed.

Mail carrier Casey Lopez-Castro was asked how the exercises helped her to develop her cultural competence.

"We need summer uniforms," Lopez-Castro said. "I'm not doing another August like last year. We ordered our shorts more than a year ago. Where are they? Lost in the mail?"

U.S. Postal Service training director Guy Christman, speaking by phone from Cuthbert, GA, said he arranged for each local postal worker to attend the seminar after he attended a national Postal Service diversity conference last May.

"I found the diversity seminar to be of great value," Christman said. "It awakened me to the plight of the underrepresented minorities. There was a time when a man or a woman could get by without considering the dynamic force of diversity, but not in the modern world. One ignores it at peril of being left behind."

Above: Pryor Road post office employees head to their diversity-training seminar.

Pryor Road station manager Michael De Leon was required to attend the seminar, as well.

"Hey, I don't like it any more than anyone else," De Leon said. "The head office makes us do these things. I tell my staff, 'Just do what I do: Sneak in a crossword puzzle.' It makes the seminar go a lot faster."

According to Leukwick, employees often resist diversity.

"It's common for people to feel defensive," Leukwick said. "People have trouble listening—I mean really listening—to each other. That's where I come in. Because it's all about communication. If you can't listen in the modern business world, you are doomed." Ø

NEWS IN BRIEF

AARP Blasted As Out Of Touch, Past Its Prime

WASHINGTON, DC—A coalition of young professionals criticized the American Association of Retired Persons at a press conference Monday, calling the organization "woefully out of step with the general public." "These AARPsters are the old guard of a bygone era, and it's time to bring them down," said Troy Hebner, president of the organization Stop The Aged, which aims to lessen the AARP's lobbying power. "A full 100 percent of their membership is over age 55. Many of them no longer even work. What could their views on Social Security and health insurance have to do with us?" In December, Stop The Aged made headlines by threatening to file a $1 billion age-discrimination lawsuit against the AARP.

Gym Membership Doomed From Day One

LOMPOC, CA—The Bally Total Fitness membership purchased Monday by Alex Scarbe already appears destined for failure. "I really should go buy some new shoes, so I can come back tomorrow and work out," Scarbe said, moments after completing the membership paperwork. "Just getting in here and signing up is enough for today. I think I'll reward myself with a smoothie." Scarbe will return to Bally's twice in April, then once in May to use the whirlpool, and ultimately cancel his membership in 2007, when he notices Bally listed on his credit-card statement.

Every Time Area Man Drops By, Friend Is Watching *The Big Lebowski*

CLEARWATER, FL—No matter what time of day he stops by for a visit, Barry Jensen always catches friend Scott Dupre watching the film *The Big Lebowski*. "[Scott] has about 40 movies on his shelf, so I don't know why he needs to watch *The Big Lebowski* over and over," Jensen told reporters Monday. "I don't know if he's just too lazy to change the DVD or if he's trying to memorize the lines, or what." Jensen estimated that, in visiting Dupre, he has walked in on the bowling dream sequence with that Kenny Rogers song six times.

Inhibitions Found In Seedy Motel Room

ALBANY, KY—Although he planned to engage in an afternoon of depraved extramarital sex with coworker Kara Lundy, businessman Bill Castille rediscovered his inhibitions upon entering Room 7B of the Honky Tonk Motor Lodge on I-90 Monday. "I'm gonna fuck you so hard that your tr—wait. What smells like a dead animal?" Castille asked Lundy, derailing a moment of unfettered lust. "Shit, what if someone sees my car in front of this trashy place? Okay, that ceiling stain just dripped onto the bed. That's it, I'm out of here." Castille might have left sooner, had he known his conversation was audible in the motel lobby.

Thwarting Of Arch Nemesis Leaves Sky Commander Feeling Empty

NEW YORK—From his secret headquarters high atop the Chrysler building, Sky Commander Rex Brady said Monday that he has been filled with ennui ever since he apprehended his archenemy, The Nefarious Dr. Disaster. "What's the use?" said Commander Brady, slumped over H.I.L.D.A., his supercomputer and confidant. "Without him, I'm just another masked, muscle-bound, unemployed phony." H.I.L.D.A. responded by encouraging Brady to pursue his other interests, like helping needy children and learning how to prepare Mediterranean cuisine. Ø

JACKSON from page 91

nounced Michael Jackson dead. From what we can tell, he died between 18 and 20 years ago," forensic investigator Tim Holbrooke said. "We are not certain, at this time, who—or what—has been standing trial in that Santa Maria courthouse."

According to Holbrooke, Jackson's corpse was buried just inches below a stretch of the miniature-train tracks that run throughout Neverland. The largely desiccated corpse wore the remains of a red, zipper-covered leather jacket and a single glove.

"We positively identified the body as Jackson by his dental records and DNA," Holbrooke said. "But even before we conducted a single forensic test, we began to suspect that that we'd uncovered the real Michael, and that the disturbing figure claiming to be Jackson was a fake."

Holbrooke said that, although the corpse was in an advanced stage of decomposition, when investigators compared the body to early-career publicity photos of Jackson, they saw a striking resemblance in bone structure and facial features. But when they compared the body to photos taken after 1987, the resemblance was negligible.

"This discovery raises a lot of questions, but it also sheds light on a number of disturbing incidents," Holbrooke said. "Frankly, Jackson had been acting pretty strange."

Forensic experts and music critics are postulating that Jackson was dead before the release of the multi-platinum album *Bad*. Detectives are currently analyzing the lyrics to "Man In The Mirror" for any clues relating to a look-alike entity that many suspect murdered the youngest member of the Jackson 5 and assumed his identity.

"We believe that Neverland served as some sort of freakishly whimsical tomb constructed by Jackson's killer," Holbrooke said. "We also suspect that all of the iniquities that occurred on that ranch were the work of the imposter. I wouldn't have ever thought it possible, but we are looking at a situation where the sexual abuse of a 13-year-old cancer patient is the tip of the iceberg."

Holbrooke said that, while the living Jackson is the leading suspect in the murder investigation, he "could be another victim of some sort."

"Basically, we have no idea what type of creature we are dealing with," Holbrooke said.

A member of the investigative team that discovered Jackson's body described the experience as "otherworldly."

"As we neared the perimeter of Neverland, the dogs started whining and howling like crazy," Santa Barbara County detective Frank Poeller said. "We had to pull them into the house. When we got to Jackson's bedroom, one of them almost choked himself to death on his leash trying to get out through the window. Minutes later, the same dog led us to the corpse."

A representative from Jackson's self-created label, MJJ Productions, said he was not surprised to find out that the current Jackson is an imposter.

"When we were recording 'Heal The World' for *Dangerous*, I could tell something was terribly, terribly wrong," MJJ manager Luke Allard said. "Michael didn't seem like himself anymore. He'd demand bizarre food and sit for hours in a hyperbaric chamber. His appearance began to become more and more peculiar. Soon afterwards, he started wearing a mask and confiding in a chimpanzee."

"I remember thinking, 'This man has become a monster,'" Allard said. "If only I'd known how right I was."

Allard said he thinks that the imposter broke ties with Jackson's former friends and surrounded himself with children who were too young to notice the radical change.

Vanity Fair reporter Beth Pither visited Neverland in 1994.

"A strangely fearful staff member led me to Jackson, but ran off before I opened the door," Pither said. "Standing there with my hand on an ice-cold doorknob, I heard strange, unnatural sounds—leathery wings flapping, a sorrowful wail, and loud hissing. A wave of dread passed through me as I opened the door, but all I found was Michael and some kids in pajamas eating ice cream and watching *101 Dalmatians*."

While their claims have not been corroborated, other Neverland visitors have reported that when when Jackson entered a room, lights flickered, faucets ran blood-red, and screams escaped from the walls.

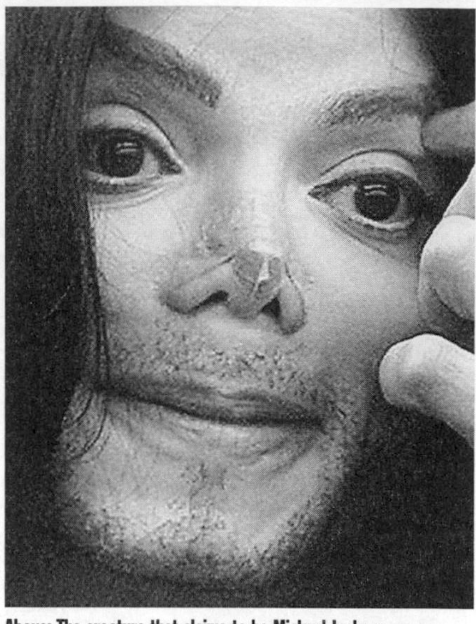

Above: The creature that claims to be Michael Jackson.

To aid in the investigation, the FBI enlisted Dr. Richard Weingarden, a noted expert on the paranormal from UC Santa Barbara. After only two hours, Weingarden abandoned the project.

"The smell of sulfur, the decaying facial features, the bizarrely high-pitched voice—it sounds exactly like..." Weingarden said, trailing off. "I'm sure it's nothing. Not a big deal. Nothing to be terrified about, certainly. I have to go. I've got a family."

Thomas Sneddon, the prosecutor in Jackson's child-molestation lawsuit, said it remains to be seen how the shocking discovery will affect the trial.

Megan Gustafson, who left her post as president of the Akron, OH Michael Jackson Fan Club after the singer was accused of molestation, offered a positive view of the grisly revelation.

"This is very disturbing news," Gustafson said. "But to be honest, it's kind of a relief too. *Thriller* and *Off The Wall* are really amazing records. Now I can pull them out of my 'ruined by child abuse' storage bin and start listening to them again." Ø

the ONION's Irish-Heritage Timeline

7500 BC—The first humans arrive in Ireland. Prior to this, only the Irish lived there

5012 BC—The Emerald Isle has a little too much fermented grain to drink. After being violently ill for two days, it pledges never to indulge again

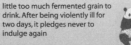

2377 BC—Boiling discovered as means of food preparation

2000 BC—Druids, who were totally awesome and wore these bad-ass robes everywhere, populate Ireland

750 BC—First Celts arrive in Ireland

749 BC—Celts discover whiskey-distillation process

748 BC—Violence sweeps through Celtic culture, thoroughly wiping it from island

600 BC—Second wave of Celts arrive in Ireland

400—Christian missionaries travel across Ireland, bringing guilt to the Irish people

432—St. Patrick arrives in Ireland, offering 25-cent chicken wings and 2-for-1 taps all night long

456—The last giant Irish panda dies

530-537—St. Brendan makes a long sea voyage with a group of fellow monks, exploring distant lands to the West and besting Columbus' discovery of America by a millennium. St. Brendan is the patron saint of bullshit

841—Vikings found Dublin. In 842, they burn and pillage it out of habit. Realizing their error, they rebuild it, only to destroy it once more in 843

849—Dublin holds its first Irish-pride parade. Gay Vikings protest their exclusion from the festivities

899—Church officials demand that hand-drawn curlicues, scrollwork, and illustrations be superimposed over the obscenely pornographic margin-doodles in the Book of Kells

922—Vikings land in Limerick and meet a buxom young farm girl named Claire

1002—Brian Boru wins recognition as king of all Ireland, earning respect and loyalty of the Irish and becoming the laughingstock of everyone else

1148—A devout monk named Malachy wins the all-Ireland "Can You Be A Saint?" competition, sponsored by the Roman Church and Merry Flagon-brand mead

1166—Ireland unable to choose between a future of tumultuous infighting between Irish kings and a permanent, brutal English occupation. A coin flip decides the latter

1487—In a decision still regretted today, Irish let a few British friends stay in Belfast

1488—Luck o' the Irish runs out

1606—Six counties of Ulster confiscated by English, who for reasons nobody has ever understood, evidently wanted them

1649—English military leader and politician Oliver Cromwell travels to Ireland, knifes the citizenry in their sleep, and violates the women's and children's corpses. British crown grants him knighthood

CALORIES from page 91

have been hesitant to release actual numbers, Sorenson said there will be "major consumption" in 2005.

"In 2004, we moved trillions of calories every month, which is exactly what one would expect in a depressed economy," Sorenson said. "If our projections are accurate, we'll be adding another couple trillion to our monthly figures."

Sorenson said there has been an across-the-board increase in caloric consumption, with a marked increase in empty calories.

"Every field has been doing well, but the empty-calorie division is going through the roof," Sorenson said. "Anyone working in high-fructose corn syrup should be proud."

Sorenson acknowledged that, like any industry, the calorie industry goes in cycles.

"Summer is our toughest season, since people tend to eat lightly in the heat," Sorenson said. "Fortunately, we more than make up for it in November. Thanksgiving is like Christmas for us. Christmas isn't too bad, either."

Sorenson said that the calorie industry "took some hits" in the '90s.

"When the surgeon general recommended drinking eight glasses of water a day, that was a dark time for us," Sorenson said. "Drinking water makes people feel full. We're still feeling the effects today."

Calorie-industry pundits said the record-breaking projections are not just pie-in-the-sky optimism.

"Calories is one of the strongest, most reliable growth industries, right up there with real estate and munitions," said Victor Polser, managing editor of *Caloric Insider* magazine. "When one section of the calorie industry starts lagging, such as bread or pasta, another section, like beef or cheese, picks up the slack. If you ask me, it'd be impossible for this industry to take a crippling hit without a lot of Americans dying."

Despite the patina of invulnerability, the ACC is not content to rest on its laurels. Last week, they rolled out a nationwide cross-media campaign. Within the next month, the ACC will unveil ads featuring the slogans "Calories: It's What's For Breakfast, Lunch, Dinner, And Between-Meal Snacks," and "Have You Had Your 2,000 Today?"

"We don't need to increase our profits, but we want to show consumers that the calorie industry isn't the monster the press has made it out to be," Sorenson said. "Calorie consumption is a part of every American's daily life, sometimes as many as eight or nine times a day." ⊘

"People tend to eat lightly in the heat," Sorenson said. "Fortunately, we more than make up for it in November. Thanksgiving is like Christmas for us. Christmas isn't too bad, either."

POOL from page 91

would lose the battle when a 1996 voters' referendum approved the pool. However, Draper exposed the referendum's irrelevance by citing an ordinance requiring the operating budgets of public works to be unanimously approved by a city-council vote.

During his 10-year journey, Draper faced down a great deal of support and enthusiasm for the pool. By 1998, he was the sole remaining member of his coalition, having lost the support of his own allies.

Former committee member Doris Heubel said supporters were pushed away by Draper's "control-freak behavior."

"We all thought the pool was a bad idea from the start, and we were willing to do the necessary legwork to persuade Mankatoans against the idea," Heubel said. "But when Irv called us for the third 2 a.m. 'brainstorming session' or chastised us for not knowing how to read blueprints, a lot of us started to feel that our time could be spent in other, more positive, ways."

After 328 council meetings, 5,863 letters, four lawsuits, and an estimated 41,000 man-hours, Draper has earned a reputation as a crazy jackass who will journey to hell and back to make sure Mankato's children do not swim in a city-owned pool.

"Oh yeah, the pool guy," local resident Curtis Einblad said. "I saw him bitching on cable access. What's his deal? Doesn't he have a job or a family to go home to?"

Draper has a family and works full time as an administrative file clerk at Minnesota State University. His all-consuming passion, however, is the continued non-existence of a city pool. In 1998, Draper even made an unsuccessful run for district alderman, basing his platform on open access to pool-related city documents.

"Some have criticized me as single-minded," Draper said. "But I think my efforts have proved that you can't be apathetic about civic affairs if you want to make something not happen. One citizen can, and did, prevent something from being created."

Draper has made sacrifices for his cause. His daughter Anne-Marie, now 19 and attending Oberlin College in Ohio, said she remembers her father as "a blur of photocopied documents and newspaper clippings." She can recall only one time he was not deeply engaged in pool-opposition work.

"It was when Grandma died," Anne-Marie said. "Dad was really sad at the funeral. But then, at the reception afterwards, he started talking about how the contractor the city wanted to use had been indicted for fraud in 1988."

Draper said his primary asset is his obstinance. One by one, his adversaries on the city council relented on the issue or turned their attention to other matters. Many of those who didn't relent eventually died or moved away.

"Democracy is an often tedious process," Draper said. "If you want something not accomplished, you have to hang in there. The price of liberty is eternal vigilance. There will be no municipal pool. Not on my watch." ⊘

"If you want something not accomplished, you have to hang in there."

1650—Brought from the New World, the potato quickly becomes the staple diet of Ireland's tenant farming class. Peasants enjoy all three mouth-watering varieties: Zesty Cheddar Bacon Ranch, Sour Cream And Chives, and Southwestern Style Spicy Salsa And Jack

1690—A deposed British king, James II, escapes to Ireland and organizes an Irish army. In 1691, this army defeats the British at the Battle of the Boyne, and a grateful, restored James II grants Ireland its independence. Just kidding!

1729—Following publication of Jonathan Swift's "A Modest Proposal," the Irish population is decimated due to the use of Irish infants as British breakfast food

1801—Following the Act of Union, British troops are dispatched throughout Ireland to kick citizens' dogs

1802—Ireland wins "Best Bogs" in *The Times Of London*'s "Best Of Europe" poll

1807—Famine strikes Ireland

1817—Famine and typhus strike Ireland

1836—Famine and cholera strike Ireland

1845—Famine and meteor showers strike Ireland

1849—In the wake of famine, millions of Irish arrive in the New World, seeking more of the precious potatoes they can't seem to live without

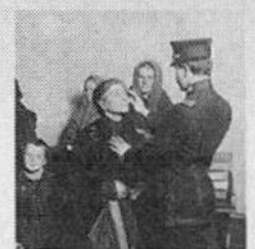

1850-1890—Your Irish ancestors passed through Ellis Island around this time, according to your grandmother

1890—Irish industrial baroness Colleen Flanagan embroiders and frames an "Irish Blessing" for the first time. Over the next 90 years, her Belfast embroidery sweatshop produced 17 million Irish blessings and was responsible for 17,000 deaths

1895—The Irish Stone Age ends

1900—Oscar Wilde loses duel with wallpaper

1923—Newly independent Ireland named "Irish Free State," instead of alternate suggestion, "Irish Free State, Y' Feckin' Teabags"

1936—"McNamara's Band" hits number one on the Old Irish Folk Song charts, a position the record held for 1,235 weeks

1939—James Joyce reads the first couple pages of *Finnegans Wake*, then returns the novel to his shelf with the intention of finishing it sometime soon

1951—Irish Spring, the two-deodorant soap, becomes the first soap allowed on Irish soil

1959—Irish president Eamon de Valera is kidnapped by faeries and replaced with a changeling

1974—Republic of Ireland legalizes the sale of contraceptives and solar calculators

1979—IRA bomb kills Lord Louis Mountbatten. Irrelevant, aging Anglo-German aristocrats everywhere go on high alert

1985—The hilariously titled "Anglo-Irish Agreement" signed

1994—A leader known only as Roth takes over the Irish Republican Army, transforming it from a terrorist organization into a tax-deferred retirement savings plan

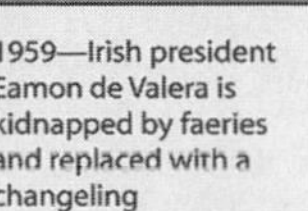

2002—Irish-American author Frank McCourt publishes his third memoir, *Abusive Cousins I Forgot To Mention*

2004—U2 special-edition iPod released

HARVEY'S HOLLYWOOD

This Year's Oscars Blew Me Away

Item! You could have knocked me over with a feather after the **77th Annual Academy Awards.** It wasn't just because of all the Oscar upsets, but also because of the new direction the ceremony has taken. **Christopher Rock** is no **Billy Crystal**, but he sure did shake things up. His bit with comedy king **Adam Sandler** was golden. And boy, did he make **Chris Penn** mad when he asked who **Clive Owen** was! I'm being kind of glib about that last one. I saw where Rock was coming from, but I thought Mr. Penn made a good point, too. He was right to stand up for one of our generation's finest actors, who has graced us with great performances in films like **Alfy** and **Sky Colonel And The World Of Tomorrowland.** And if you can't stand up for what's right at the Oscars, where can you do that?

The Outside Scoop
By Jackie Harvey

Oddly enough, there were no major "fashion don'ts" at the Oscars this year. Who could forget Beyork's swan number from a few years ago?

But it wasn't just about standing up for what's right. **A Million Dollar Smile** took the most awards, winning **Best Director, Best Actress, Best Supporting Actor, Best Picture**, and **Best Fights**. And **Jamie Fox** won **Best Actor**, proving for the second time that the Academy is colorblind. Congratulations to all the winners, whatever their color!

Oddly enough, there were no major **"fashion don'ts"** at the Oscars this year. Who could forget **Beyork's swan number** from a few years ago? Or **Cher's black spider-web dress?** Or **Celine Dion's backwards suit?** No one. We're still talking about them!

I'm going to move out of awards mode in just a second, but there's been a lot of talk about **Mark Antony and J. Lo's Latino duet** at the **Grammys**. People were saying that J. Lo sounded like a gut-shot crow or a '68 VW Beetle. First of all, someone should tell those people to bite their tongues! Second, I don't know which Grammys they were watching, but what I saw was a couple in love, singing a tender romantic ballad that transcended language, pitch, and key. Anyone who says otherwise is a racist. Kudos Mark and J, and gracias por su funcionamiento.

Item! I just saw some **crocuses** poking out of the ground, which means spring is on its way. I'm glad, because spring is a good time for love, and there seems to be a lot of splitting up going on. Oh, I'm sorry. Didn't you know? **Charlie Sheen** of **2 1/2 Men And A Baby** and his wife **Denise Richards** of **Super Troopers** have filed for **D-I-V-O-R-C-E**. Doesn't anybody ever stay together anymore? Especially while Denise is pregnant! I'm shocked! I don't care how talented you are, Charles, I will never watch another of your movies or entertaining sitcoms again. It's as simple as this: You don't walk out on a girl who's in the family way. (Unless it's for true love like **Kevin Fredderline** did to be with **Britney**.)

Oh, and also, Dawson's cutie **Katie Holmes** and that **guy from American Pie with the weird head** split up. I guess I hadn't really thought about either of those two in awhile, so it's not that big a deal to me.

I'd be happier if cars got **better gas mileage**. It'd be good for my wallet and good for the country.

Item! Cojo update! I last reported that fashion and accessory advisor to the people Steven "Cojo" Cojocaru was recovering from kidney transplant surgery. Apparently, **Katie "nice" Couric** from **The Today Show** isn't so "cour"teous, if you follow me. When Cojo did an interview with another show, Ms. Nice dumped him from an appearance on *Today*. Talk about kicking someone while he's down! I'll still watch Today, but not during **National Colon Cancer Awareness Week** (April 12-18).

I can't decide who's the better Motown artist, **Otis Redding** or **Marvin Gay.**

Item! There's a lot of to-do about chickens being mistreated. Rap mogul **Sean John** and the **Reverend Al Sharpton** have joined **PETA** in the fight against chicken cruelty. If you ask me, chickens are coddled. When I was 4, my parents took me to a farm. I wandered around happily until I made my way into the chicken coop. The dumb birds swarmed me, flapping their wings like crazy, making clucking sounds, and pecking at my legs. Those beaks are sharper than they look. If a chicken dies to become my **Boston Market dinner**, I say good riddance!

I've never been surfing, but you'd better believe that if I ever went to **Hawaii**, I'd be willing to give it the old Harvey try.

Someone better start an online petition to get that **Fredonia Apple** album out. I've been waiting years for the pouting chanteuse to deliver another one-two punch, only to find out that it has been done for more than a year? Come on, let us have it! Ow! Not in the face!

Well, that about wraps it up for the ol' Scoop for this week. I have a birthday coming up soon (I won't tell you how old I am!) so I'm going to treat myself to something nice, like a little television for my kitchen counter or a nice dinner at **Red Lobster**. By the time you next hear from me, I'll be a little older and a little wiser about all things **Hollywood!** I'm working on some great leads right now, including the whereabouts of **George Wendt,** and why **Pamela Anderson** has so much trouble finding true love. All that and more next time... on The Outside. ø

HOROSCOPES

Your Horoscope

By Lloyd Schumner Sr.
Retired Machinist and A.A.P.B.-Certified Astrologer

Aries: (March 21–April 19)
You'll be justifiably proud after turning your office into a savvy, high-tech marketing machine, but that's before it flies out of control and devastates half of Kansas City.

Taurus: (April 20–May 20)
Although you've long considered yourself something of a singer/songwriter, investigators will weigh your slim notebook of lyrics against the butcher's heap in your basement and decide you're more of a torturer/killer.

Gemini: (May 21–June 21)
Although you admit that the thick layer of yellow fat around your heart is a threat to your health, you're not sure about your physician's plan to replace it with a thick layer of pink fiberglass insulation.

Cancer: (June 22–July 22)
In yet another odd grandstanding ploy for attention, the Irish Republican Army has offered to shoot you.

Leo: (July 23–Aug. 22)
Your ownership of a smoldering powder keg attached to a ticking time bomb continues to be a powerful, if mixed, metaphor.

Virgo: (Aug. 23–Sept. 22)
Your friends will laugh at your clanking, smoke-belching, jerry-rigged contraption, but they'll have to respect its ability to make a really outstanding cup of coffee.

Libra: (Sept. 23–Oct. 23)
Not only is the large, twisting antler on your forehead a source of constant pain and ridicule, it's also considered a powerful aphrodisiac by many cultures.

Scorpio: (Oct. 24–Nov. 21)
Topological mathematicians will soon find a way to define the Gaussian curvature of a surface M in such a way as to prove that you suck.

Sagittarius: (Nov. 22–Dec. 21)
You'll be able to trace your lineage all the way back to the War of the Roses, thanks to the Royal Society for Keeping Track of Drunken Syphilitic Half-Wits and Their Bastard Offspring

Capricorn: (Dec. 22–Jan. 19)
It is prophesied that you shall walk in beauty all the days of your life, but you'll still spend your nights going to squalid little bars with the same old crowd.

Aquarius: (Jan. 20–Feb. 18)
You're eagerly keeping an eye out for the first robin of spring, but the tightly knit robin community hasn't forgotten what happened last year and has blacklisted your entire neighborhood.

Pisces: (Feb. 19–March 20)
You've heard that there's little anyone can do to shed any light on the eternal mysteries of the human heart, but you figure that's because they haven't used bright enough torches.

IMPROV from page 92

"What are you doing?" Well, that one's a little confusing to explain, but it's easy to demonstrate.

The best part is that "What are you doing?" is a great way to take the stigma away from good supervisory management. For weeks after the workshop, a manager will be able to poke his head into his employees' cubicles, ask them what they're doing, and get hilariously crazy answers like "knitting a sweater." Then the manager can say, "Seriously, what are you doing? You're not shopping online, are you?" But the joke question really helps break the tension.

Maybe you feel your employees are already doing great work. Then they'll amaze you after their Friday afternoon improv workshop. There's no way you won't earn back the cost of our fee—which, by the way, is negotiable—in the increased staff morale and productivity.

And don't worry about off-topic humor: Our content is rated E, for "every employee has fun." ø

NEWS

Yet Another Media-Savvy Ex-Hostage Delights TV-News Producers

see NATION page 8B

Sports Banquet Ends In Trophy Fight

see SPORTS page 3F

Sopping Wet Panties Removed From Washer, Placed In Dryer

see LOCAL page 14E

STATshot

A look at the numbers that shape your world.

What Is Our Mistress Demanding?

16% $3.99 per minute
12% Affection or earrings or something
19% Dental insurance
26% No idea—don't speak Russian
27% Head of local religious zealot who spurned her advances

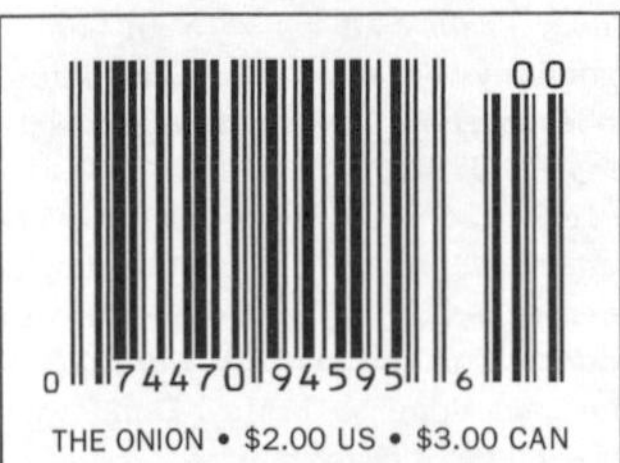

the ONION®

VOLUME 41 ISSUE 12 AMERICA'S FINEST NEWS SOURCE™ 24–30 MARCH 2005

Colin Powell's Tell-All Book: Steroid Use Rampant In White House

WASHINGTON, DC—Top Cabinet officials are up in arms about the allegations of widespread steroid use made by former Secretary of State Colin Powell in his new political tell-all *Pumped: Living Fast, Loose, And On The Juice During My Tumultuous DC Days—And Nights.*

"I'm gonna get it from all sides for violating the code of silence in the Players Wing," Powell wrote in the book's introduction. "A lot of people out there don't want to know why a politician suddenly gets big. Well, I hate to break it to you, but it ain't always through able policy-drafting."

In the book, Powell paints a picture of a commander-in-chief who not only permitted, but encouraged the use of performance-enhancing drugs, and an attorney general whose buttocks were knotted with

see POWELL page 100

Above: Appearing on *Meet The Press*, Powell answers questions about his controversial new book (left).

U.S. Dog Owners Fear Arrival Of Africanized Fleas

ATLANTA—Panic is spreading among American dog owners, following the Center for Veterinary Medicine's Monday announcement that the arrival of a deadly mutant strain of Africanized killer fleas is imminent.

"No dog is safe," CVM director Stephen Sundlof said. "While canines around the U.S. innocently fetch sticks and chase their tails, killer fleas are migrating north at a rate of two kilometers a day. They've

see FLEAS page 101

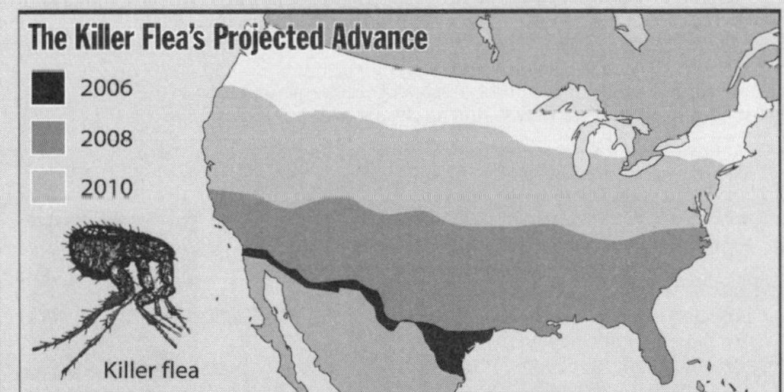

Child Walks Out On Toy Non-Proliferation Talks

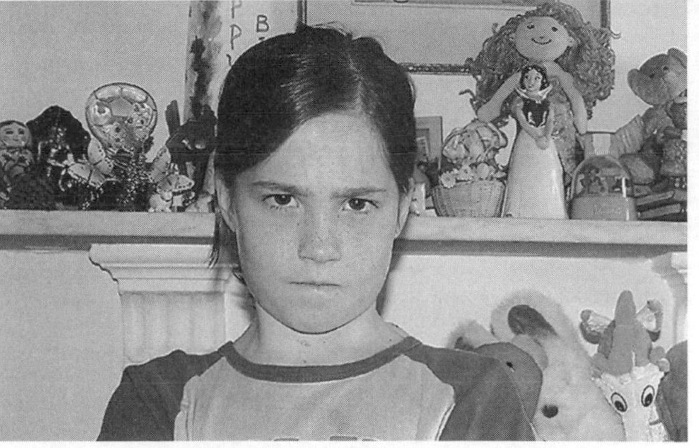

BROOKLYN, NY—Toy non-proliferation talks between Donna and Adam Feit and their 8-year-old daughter Corinne broke down Monday when Corinne stormed away from the kitchen and slammed her bedroom door.

"The Feits had hoped to walk away from the dinner-table summit with a cap on the acquisition of new toys and a workable plan for the reduction of those already in their daughter's possession," said Nancy Flemming, the Feits' neighbor and friend. "But after less than half an hour of talks,

see TOYS page 100

Left: Corinne, who refuses to reduce her stuffed-animal stockpile.

Oil Drilling In Alaska

In a major political victory for President Bush, the Senate recently voted to open the Alaskan Arctic Wildlife Refuge to oil drilling. What do *you* think?

Cecelia Mayo
Systems Analyst

"This can't be true. Bush described himself as an environmental guardian last fall, and I've seen photos of him standing in front of trees."

Angel Macias
Lifeguard

"At least now we'll see the area destroyed in 10 short years instead of watching global warming do it over a painful, drawn-out 40."

Ted Bonner
Locksmith

"What I don't get is why this counts as 'a victory for the energy lobby' instead of 'a loss for the country at large.'"

Floyd Holden
Author

"But... but where will there be pristine and untouched wonders left for me to drive my GMC Yukon through?"

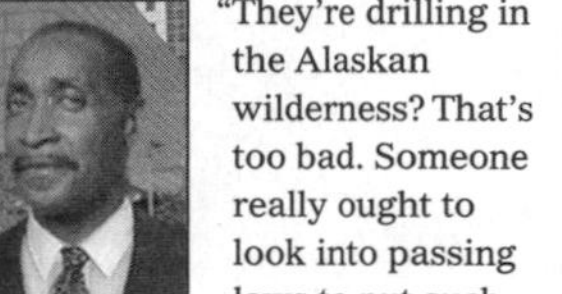

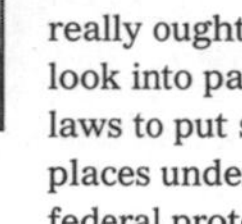

Richard Lott
Civil Engineer

"They're drilling in the Alaskan wilderness? That's too bad. Someone really ought to look into passing laws to put such places under federal protection so this doesn't happen again."

Loni Sweet
Histopathologist

"If I may be allowed to pursue the idea of 'addiction to oil,' I think the nation just reached the point where we sold our wedding ring for one night's fix."

The New SAT

Last week, thousands of high-school students took a new version of the SAT Reasoning Test. What are they saying about the revamped exam?

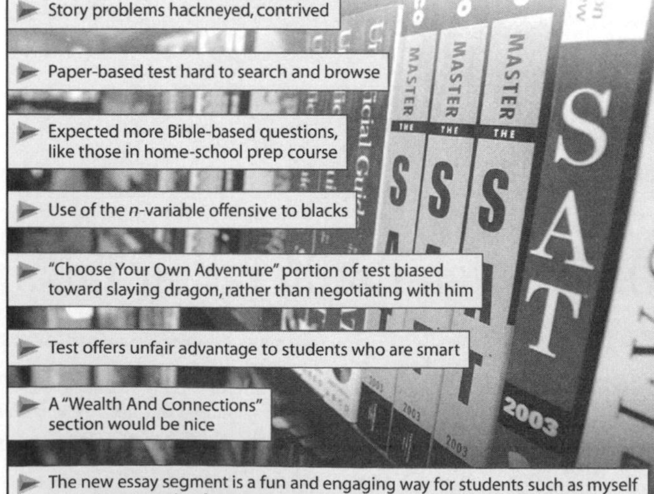

Story problems hackneyed, contrived
Paper-based test hard to search and browse
Expected more Bible-based questions, like those in home-school prep course
Use of the n-variable offensive to blacks
"Choose Your Own Adventure" portion of test biased toward slaying dragon, rather than negotiating with him
Test offers unfair advantage to students who are smart
A "Wealth And Connections" section would be nice
The new essay segment is a fun and engaging way for students such as myself to explore a mode of communication important to current society at large

America's Finest News Source.™

Herman Ulysses Zweibel
Founder

T. Herman Zweibel
Publisher Emeritus
J. Phineas Zweibel
Publisher
Maxwell Prescott Zweibel
Editor-In-Chief

I Don't Care How Long It Takes, I'm Gonna Figure Out What That 'L' Word Is

By Todd Brillhaus

I love a good mystery. When a television program gives you something to piece together, you have a reason to tune in every week. It's like a game. *Alias*, or *24*—that's my kind of show. But I have got to tell you, *The L Word* really has me stumped. I'm going to figure out what that darn word is, though. I don't care how long it takes me.

After seeing an episode, my first guess was that the "L" stood for "ladies." It made sense, because the show centers on a group of women and follows them as they navigate friendships, romantic entanglements, and life in California. While "ladies" is a strong guess, it's wrong. I know that, because a lot of the first season focused on the relationship between Tim and Jenny. (They had a rough patch in their relationship after Tim walked in on Jenny having a girl "go downtown" on her.) Given that much of the first season was about Tim—a man—it would be a cheat if the "L" word were "ladies."

"L" word..."L" word... Love? Lust? Liposuction? Lariat? Lonesome? This

The show's title sequence is no help, that's for sure. They tease you with something like 50 words that start with the letter "L." Man! You know you're sitting there looking at the word, but they won't give you any clues as to which one is the one.

show is long on questions and short on answers, but I love a good puzzle, and I'm not giving up yet!

I have to admit that I've missed a few episodes. Maybe they gave some important clues about the "L" word in one of them. Or maybe, if I listened to the show's dialogue more closely, I'd figure it out. Sometimes I'm a bit too distracted by all the hot actresses making out with each other to catch every word. Well, I hope the second season comes out on DVD quickly, so I can give them all another look. I'll watch

After seeing an episode, my first guess was that the "L" stood for "ladies." It made sense, because the show centers on a group of women and follows them as they navigate friendships, romantic entanglements, and life in California. While "ladies" is a strong guess, it's wrong.

them as many times as it takes. I've got the patience to see this thing through.

The show's title sequence is no help, that's for sure. They tease you with something like 50 words that start with the letter "L." Man! You know you're sitting there looking at the word, but they won't give you any clues as to which one is the one. Some that I remember offhand are Liberal, Lickable, Learn, Laughter, Lesbian, Lunch, Literary, Labels, and Loft. But what's the common thread?

Oh, and it doesn't make it any easier that every episode title begins with an "L." Are the creators of this show trying to drive me insane?

Well, I'm a patient man. I'm still writing letters in search of someone who can explain *What's Eating Gilbert Grape* to me. The "L" word mystery is no different: I have the stamina to stay on the case.

In fact, a part of me doesn't want to figure it out. It's like when I figured out that Leland Palmer had killed Laura while inhabited by the dark spirit Bob. I was glad to know the answer to the mystery, but I was sorry *Twin Peaks* had come to an end. A good mystery show creates a cultural phenomenon. That's how it is, watching *The L Word*.

Hmm, do you think it could be Loquacious? Nah. The show's subject matter isn't exactly intellectual, so I don't think the mystery word would be something so brainy. Don't worry—I'll get it eventually. Ø

MEDIA

National Gonzo Press Club Vows To Carry On Thompson's Work

LAS VEGAS—During a Tuesday press conference at the National Gonzo Press Club, members of the nation's foremost organization of gonzo journalists vowed to carry on the mission of its founder Hunter S. Thompson, who took his life last month.

"Now that the whore-beasts and the scum-sucking degenerate rat bastards in Wall Street and the White House are hell-bent on turning us all into pliant, Scripture-mewling puppet-slaveys, we must take up Hunter's fallen colors and charge into the fray," said NGPC president Gene Zolonga, who is the National Affairs and Shark Hunting Editor for *The Philadelphia Inquirer*. "The next four years will be an unprecedented monument to bestial human ugliness, but I'd sooner let Yakuza thugs strap a rabid wolverine to my groin than shirk my responsibilities as a gonzo journalist."

The heavily sweating, speed-frenzied Zolonga then removed a Luger automatic pistol from his coat and shot the microphone with a deafening blast.

The NGPC is composed of nearly 3,000 journalists who practice gonzo, a subjective, emotionally charged observational reporting style that is often fueled by recreational drug use. Members of the 34-year-old organization cumulatively hold 14 Pulitzer Prizes, including eight in the Distinguished Weirdness In Feature Writing category.

"It's up to us to carry on the mentor's vision and expose all in American life that is strange, terrible, bad, crazy, or bad crazy," Zolonga said. He then climbed onto the podium and emitted a blood-curdling screech. "I am full of love, you motherfucking bastards. Pardon me, I believe my heart just stopped."

Gonzo stringer Zach Kiel, who most recently wrote "Fear, Loathing At The Owensboro Parks And Recreation Department" for the *Louisville Courier-Journal*, said Thompson will go down in the history of American letters as "the greatest gonzo reporter there ever was."

"Hunter opposed the editing of half-truths in all of his endeavors," Kiel said. "He had balls like an elephant and a cruelly beautiful prose style to match. He had stiff competition, but I'd say he bested even a hardened pro like Del Armbruster, who once wrote a story about Amazon gold prospectors while engulfed in fire head-to-toe."

Even gonzo journalists who have disagreed with Thompson in the past, such as award-winning *New York Times* columnist Heck Murdo, count him as a freak comrade.

"We did have sharp differences in opinion," Murdo said. "He thought Richard Nixon should have had his intestines slowly unwound onto a giant cable spool. I thought he should have

see THOMPSON page 100

Above: Zolonga warns gonzo journalists to remember their ethics "in the face of resistance from the pustulent pigs."

NEWS IN BRIEF

No One Admits To Fart Joke

HARRISBURG, PA—No one among the Harrisburg Family Insurance sales team will admit to having added a crude, hand-drawn depiction of flatulence to a Successories poster Monday. "All right, who put the fart cloud coming out of the rock-climber's butt?" sales-team leader Dean Sendars asked. "It had to be someone in this office." Sales-team members were quiet, later noting that, in many cases, he who saw it, drawed it.

Guatemalan Coffee Picker Happy If Single Person Starts Day Alert

HUEHUETENANGO, GUATEMALA—Carmen Harroyo spends 16 hours a day picking coffee beans, but the weather-beaten 17-year-old said Monday that she is glad to do it if it helps give a single coffee drinker a much-needed morning boost. "I make $2 a day and share a room with my five sisters, but all the hard work is worth it if I help just one American suburbanite jumpstart her day," Harroyo said, batting away a swarm of mosquitoes. "I appreciate the opportunity to touch another person's life." Harroyo said she dreams of someday helping people get their antioxidants by picking sticks from bushels of green tea until her fingers bleed.

EPA To Drop 'E,' 'P' From Name

WASHINGTON, DC—Days after unveiling new power-plant pollution regulations that rely on an industry-favored market-trading approach to cutting mercury emissions, EPA Acting Administrator Stephen Johnson announced that the agency will remove the "E" and "P" from its name. "We're not really 'environmental' anymore, and we certainly aren't 'protecting' anything," Johnson said. "'The Agency' is a name that reflects our current agenda and encapsulates our new function as a government-funded body devoted to handling documents, scheduling meetings, and fielding phone calls." The change comes on the heels of the Department of Health and Human Services' January decision to shorten its name to the Department of Services.

Friends Always On Best Behavior Around Neil LaBute

FORT WAYNE, IN—Personal acquaintances of acclaimed playwright and filmmaker Neil LaBute reported Tuesday that they keep their behavior in check when around him. "You get in one stupid argument with your wife in front of the guy, and the next thing you know, you're an emotionally abusive misogynist in theaters nationwide," said Terrence Wydell, one of LaBute's former classmates. "With Neil, it's best to limit the conversation to the weather and current events." LaBute is reportedly at work on *The Act Of Lending*, a play about a character named Terrence who borrows DVDs through intimidation and verbal cruelty, with no intention of ever returning them.

Offended Customer's Huffy Walkout Goes Unnoticed

DULUTH, MN—Angry about the convenience store's poor service, Dina Jorgenson abruptly stormed out of Marvin's QuikStop unseen Monday. "Oh, I've had enough of this," Jorgenson said, pointedly slamming her passion-fruit Snapple on the counter and marching out the front door, after having waited in line for nearly 10 minutes. Two hours later, QuikStop cashier Tasha Quiggle asked a fellow clerk why there was a warm Snapple sitting on the counter. ⌀

POWELL from page 97

gristle from daily injections of equine growth serum.

Powell neither denies nor goes into great detail about his own steroid use.

"I won't deny that I tried it—the stuff was everywhere, especially during the early days," one passage reads. "But I was blessed with certain natural gifts that, combined with my extensive military training, made steroid use largely unnecessary for me."

Powell alleges that, during the early days of Operation Enduring Freedom, 80 percent of Bush's Cabinet was abusing steroids.

"The signs were right there, if anyone had cared to pay attention," Powell said. "The bursts of foul-mouthed rage from Cheney... The sudden emergence of Donald Rumsfeld as a major-league heavy hitter in Defense... And how anyone overlooked Condi's pop-eyed, clench-jawed grimace, I'll never know. She was shooting up with synthetic testosterone every six hours—more on Cabinet-meeting days."

Powell argues that tremendous pressure to perform is at the root of steroid abuse among Washington insiders.

"Say you're a politician who's a success in your home state," Powell wrote. "You run for Senate. Bang! Suddenly you're in Washington, mixing it up in the big leagues, and let me tell you, it's a whole different world. You have to hustle harder and work longer just to keep up. You wanna be at the top of the heap? Well, we're all the best of the best and we're all putting in 110 percent every day. A lot of guys will do anything to get a *Washington Post* headline, and yeah, that includes juicing."

Powell said the pressure gets worse as politicians move up the ladder.

"All eyes are on you—PAC lobbyists are turning up the heat, millions of faithful constituents are watching C-SPAN," Powell wrote. "Take a Cabinet appointee, someone who hasn't even worked his way up through the ranks. Ashcroft, say. The pressure's 10 times worse on a poor sucker like him. If he doesn't swing for the fences, he's failed at the biggest game there is, and there's no such thing as lateral movement in Govvy Town. You're out. Some guys, guys who have been at the top their entire lives, can't take the idea of failure."

Above: A 2002 White House photo that might indicate Powell's steroid-related claims are true.

"Oh, Number One's too smart to get caught with it himself, but as sure as I'm standing here, he knows where it is and who's taking it. You better believe it."

According to Powell, White House officials wouldn't abuse politics-enhancing substances if the people in charge didn't push them to do so.

"Okay, I'm gonna come right out and say it," Powell said. "The Big Guy's the one running the show, right from the Oval Office. Let's say your provisions to the Patriot Act are striking out, or you put your foot in your mouth at a press conference. You can expect a little visit. Not the Big Guy himself, but someone will drop by for a little chat. He'll hint that maybe you could add a step, get a little quicker, gain a little more power if you had some of Karl Rove's candy. Oh, Number One's too smart to get caught with it himself, but as sure as I'm standing here, he knows where it is and who's taking it. You better believe it."

Chris Matthews, host of the MSNBC show *Hardball*, argued that Powell's omissions tell more than his disclosures.

"Well, it's an interesting glimpse inside the clubhouse," Matthews said. "But I don't think Powell's telling us everything he knows. All this about steroid abuse—a thing he denied until he had a six-figure book contract—and nothing about the parties, the recreational drugs, the legions of groupies? Sounds to me like Powell's choosing the one area where he was a choirboy and letting everyone else twist in the wind."

As to whether his former boss used performance enhancers, Powell offered a number of questions.

"Well, I'll let you decide," Powell wrote. "But you might want to ask yourself how a career-Republican bench-warmer found the weight and power to beat a giant like McCain in the '99 primaries. And then you might want to think about why his neck has bulled out so much in the past five years. Listen, I respect the man's abilities, but come on. Put two and two together, America." ⊘

THOMPSON from page 99

been lashed to an oceanside cliff near San Clemente, so that ospreys could feast on his eyes. We feuded for years, at one point conducting a bourbon- and mescaline-fueled motorized-cart demolition derby on a Lake Tahoe golf course. But we patched things up when Dubya was elected, agreeing—to our mutual horror—that Nixon far outclassed that Jesus-loving pinheaded man-child."

During the past four decades, gonzo journalists have encountered their share of critical backlash, with college journalism departments around the nation reducing funding for gonzo-journalism programs and local editors questioning the wisdom of covering school-board meetings and slow-pitch softball matches on amyl nitrate.

"The gonzo philosophy is not always an effective or practical way to convey fact," *Tulsa Daily Courier* managing editor Patrick Jacobs said. "Average newspaper readers want to turn to the weather page and see the next day's forecast. They don't really have much use for a map captioned, 'Leeches are sucking my spinal fluid!' And when the sports page contains an unintelligible 3,000-word screed about ballpark hot-dog buns in place of the major-league scores, I get mail."

Gonzo entertainment writer Gail Nucci said 14 publications dropped her syndicated gossip column "Vacuous Sluts And Perfidious Dandies" over the course of the past year.

"The scores of out-of-work gonzo journalists say it all," said Nucci, an angel-dust abuser who tried to place Hilary Duff under citizen's arrest at the world premiere of *Raise Your Voice* last October. "Save for a handful of maverick magazine publishers, editors are too busy slobbing the knobs of the men on high to risk publishing an original voice."

In spite of these challenges, Zolonga is adamant that gonzo journalism has a place in this century.

"The world is growing assuredly weirder," Zolonga said. "Just as history remembers such prominent journalist-commentators as H.L. Mencken and Mike Royko, I have faith that future generations of swine will know the name of Hunter S. Thompson." ⊘

TOYS from page 97

Corinne said she wished she was never born and stomped to her room. It was nothing short of a meltdown."

The long-standing toy-related conflict between the Feits and their only child came to a head last week when the Feits announced that the rate at which Corinne was amassing toys was unacceptable, and that her new habit of storing toys in the garage and living room was in direct violation of household rules. The Feits suggested the two parties "have a serious talk."

Flemming, who witnessed the summit from a breakfast-nook stool, said the talks began amicably, with all parties enjoying a snack of Oreo cookies and milk.

see TOYS page 101

FLEAS from page 97

Above: A Hidalgo, TX veterinarian fumigates a puppy infested with Africanized fleas.

already invaded the border towns of Texas and California. We've got to act now, before our pets pay the price."

Killer fleas, a staple of '70s B-movies like *The Bloodsucking Swarm*, *I.T.C.H.*, and *Roger Corman's Night Of The Fleas*, are not, in fact, poisonous. The danger lies in the parasites' excessive defensiveness, extreme resilience, and tendency to swarm.

"Africanized fleas are capable of draining a full-grown collie in less than 24 hours," Sundlof said. "They attack in massive numbers, sometimes completely covering the animal, leaving only his eyes and tongue visible. Even if given a blood transfusion, a dog infested with Africanized fleas will often scratch himself so vigorously that he either bleeds to death or collapses from exhaustion. And regular flea powders are useless against them."

Minneapolis veterinarian Greg Schepke said widespread fear of the deadly pests is justified.

"It's hard to separate fact from fiction, as most of the information we have about the fleas is anecdotal," Schepke said. "But if the stories are even half true, killer fleas are capable of cutting a swath of death across our nation, dotting the land with brittle, desiccated doggie husks."

Bred in Brazil at the Sao Paulo Animal Research Facility in the late '60s, *Ctenocephalides canis africanus* is a crossbreed of the common North American flea and an African variant that infests the tough hides of bull elephants. The Sao Paulo entomologists never meant to release the mutant fleas into the wild, but a 1974 fire at the lab led to the dangerous subspecies' escape. In the past 30 years, Africanized fleas spread from Brazil to South and Central America and on to Mexico.

According to legend, the fleas crossed the U.S. border for the first time in June 2003, when Mexican flea-circus owner Pedro Romero brought his show to McAllen, TX. Romero, whose bone-dry corpse was discovered outside the Hidalgo County fairgrounds, is said to be single-handedly responsible for bringing the menace to America.

"The threat that once seemed straight out of a Saturday afternoon science-fiction matinee is now real," said entomologist Harvey Smithson, author of the Africanized-flea tracts *Unleashed!* and *No Day At The Park*. "With no natural predators in America, these super-fleas will be unstoppable. They can jump from dog to dog at distances of up to 35 yards. One doghouse after another will be surrendered to the marauding fleas."

Police sergeant Tom Lafferty, head of the Laredo K-9 Korps, said his force is taking serious measures to prepare for the killers' arrival.

"We've reinforced all our doghouses with quarter-inch steel plates—

Minneapolis veterinarian Greg Schepke said widespread fear of the deadly pests is justified.

killer fleas can burrow through concrete like cardboard," Lafferty said. "And don't bother with plastic flea collars. Killer fleas chew straight through those."

Added Lafferty: "The force over in Asherton has already lost 10 of their best dogs."

Basset hound owner Hank Jeffreys of Carpentersville, IL said the government must protect the nation's pets.

"I hear the Feds developed a top-secret super-shampoo, but it's too dangerous to use because it contains radioactive isotopes," Jeffreys said. "How am I supposed to keep my Woofers safe? Even if you isolate the furry little victim and subject him to chemical baths, there's a danger of immediate re-infestation. At this point, the only effective treatment is the mega-flea-collar, but it weighs 45 pounds and gives off such intense fumes that it makes dog owners hallucinate."

In spite of the impending infestation of America, Sundlof urged dog lovers to remain calm.

"Should your dog become infested, isolate the animal and contact federal pest-control agents immediately," Sundlof said. "When the killer mutant ringworm fungus arrived in Los Angeles from Tokyo, we developed ways to deal with it. We can lick this, too." Ø

TOYS from page 100

"The cookies were a show of good will on the part of the Feits," Flemming said. "They generally discourage between-meal snacking, but they wanted to make it clear that they were willing to compromise in order to arrive at a point of agreement satisfactory to both parties."

Indicating that they had no plans to strip Corinne of playtime capabilities, the Feits opened with an offer to allow her to continue to acquire outdoor toys—including balls, bikes, and water guns—provided that she reduce her board games by half.

"Corinne conceded that her board games were in disarray, and agreed to nearly eliminate them if she could double her doll acquisitions," Flemming said. "That's when things turned ugly."

The elder Feits raised concerns that Corinne had accumulated enough dolls to entertain herself 10 times over, and certainly more plush toys than could be safely accounted for. Corinne countered that she did not have nearly as many Bratz dolls as her classmate Jenny Holmes, arguing that she had the right to pursue a relative degree of parity in the toy race.

"The Feits categorically rejected Corinne's proposed increase in doll acquisitions," Flemming said. "Prior to this move, Corinne had demonstrated a willingness to concede certain points to her parents. That changed as soon as the Feits tried to exact a binding commitment from Corinne on the doll point."

Corinne not only questioned her parents' jurisdiction over her, she openly defied it.

"Corinne said she didn't have to do what they said and they should just go ahead and try to make her," Flemming said. "Then she intimated that she could acquire toys through back channels, such as her grandmother. I can only speculate that Corinne was hoping to undermine her parents' authority with that gambit, but it hurt her cause."

Adam responded with the mandate that no new toys were to be brought into the house for three months, at which time the situation would be reviewed to determine whether Corinne had developed a greater sense of responsibility.

"Corinne responded to her father's sanctions by screaming, 'I hate you,'" Flemming said. "I doubt the two parties can hope for a peaceful solution anytime soon. Certainly, a cooling-down period is in order."

Flemming said the Feits were very disappointed that the talks broke down.

"Donna pointed out that toy reduction would serve Corinne's own interests," Flemming said. "She warned that amassing a stockpile of toys without proper containment devices, such as shelves or a toy box, could lead to the needless destruction of toys. And Adam noted that undocumented toy stockpiles could fall into the hands of hostile neighbors, such as the Peterson boy."

Toy-proliferation experts expect the impasse to last at least until morning. Ø

Ask A Guy Who's Been Avoiding You

By Barry Turner

Dear Guy Who's Been Avoiding You,

As a feminist, I feel uneasy about guys holding doors open for me, pulling out my chair so I can sit down, helping me put on my coat, and so on. I know that men do these things to be friendly, but is there a polite way to decline "gentlemanly" assistance?

Independent In Inglewood

Dear Independent,

Oh, uh... Hey! Chuck! How are you? I'm good, good. Wow, I didn't see you. I mean, I sort of saw you out of the corner of my eye, but I didn't realize it was you. Yeah, pretty dopey of me! What are you doing in this neck of the woods? You what? You and Karen are getting married? My God, congratulations! When? No, I didn't get an invitation. When did you send them? Last month? Well, that's strange. I don't recall getting one. Wait, what phone call from Karen? She left me a message? Oh, geez, I never got that either. Oh, do you wanna know what the problem is? My stupid voicemail. I sometimes have problems retrieving messages. It's zinged me before. I know, it's ridiculous. You'd think they'd have that technology down by now, wouldn't you? I mean, for what I pay for it! Okay, well, I'd better—oh, duh. Sure, I'd like to come. Sure, of course. Why don't you shoot me an e-mail about the date and locale and so on. It'll save you the trouble of mailing another invite. Why waste a stamp? Sorry about that. Uh, sorry to be a jerk, but I really do have to go. Job interviews got me running my ass ragged. Uh, yeah. Yeah, I still am. Well, we'll catch up later about all that. Okay, Chuck, great to see you. Bye now.

No, I didn't get an invitation. When did you send them? Last month? Well, that's strange. I don't recall getting one. Wait, what phone call from Karen?

Dear Guy Who's Been Avoiding You,

I live in an apartment building and have a next-door neighbor who's extremely sensitive about noise. I've heard this person complain about other neighbors, so I make a conscious effort to be quiet. I keep my voice down, take my shoes off when I'm at home, and never watch television past midnight. That's why I was shocked to get an angry note from this neighbor accusing me of blasting my television and running my kitchen appliances late at night! Guy Who's Avoiding You, what should I do?

Not Noisy In NYC

Dear Not Noisy,

Yah! Chu-Chuck! Wow, you startled me! Well, uh, hey stranger. Wow, you sure get around. An appointment with your wedding planner? Pretty ritzy! I thought only people in movies use wedding planners... Is Karen around here somewhere? Well, too bad, it'd be nice to see her. Oh, no! No, no way. I mean, I'd love to, but I've got some business to take care of over lunch. Thanks for the offer, though. What? The e-mail you sent to me bounced back? Yes, I was looking for that invitation. Oh, I just realized... you probably sent it to the Yahoo address, right? Yeah, I changed over to a new e-mail account. No, the Yahoo address is totally dead. Jeez, I'm really sorry. Look, I'll e-mail you tonight—you have the same address, right? Yeah, I have that. I'll e-mail you and then you can send the wedding info. My new address? Oh, I still haven't memorized it. It's something with my name. Barry... Jeez, I just can't remember. I shouldn't have created such a confusing one. Stupid. Okay, Chuck, gotta run. What? Oh, another job interview. Well, I'm interviewing for a lot of stuff. This and that. I even got offered something last week, but I turned it down. Not enough pay. Well, that's what I did, anyway. Okay. I'll e-mail you tonight and then you can e-mail me. All right. Good luck with your wedding-planner thing. Okay.

Dear Guy Who's Been Avoiding You,

I have a female friend who has lost more than 50 pounds. We're all proud of her, but she still has a way to go before she hits her ideal weight. Yet she recently announced that she's done losing weight. As a friend, do I need to tell her that, for her health and her appearance, she needs to keep going?

Unsure In Utica

Dear Unsure In Utica,

Chuck. Whoa! Three times in one week?! Okay, this is starting to get a little nutty! A little *Twilight Zone*-y, wouldn't you say? Doo doo doo doo, doo doo doo doo! So, uh, what brings you to my neighborhood? Getting your tux altered. May I infer that you bought your own tux? Fabulous. What? Oh yeah, my e-mail. Oh, man. Well, I have no excuse other than I just blanked. Sorry about that. Look, don't bother about the invitation. Just tell me when the wedding is. Sunday, June 19? Hmm. Can't make it. How do I know? Well, I've just started temping at a law firm, and I mainly work weekends. Oh, you know, filing and so on. "Paralegal's assistant," they call it. Well, yeah, the job's temporary, but I'm pretty sure they're keeping me on through August, and it could lead to something full-time. What? Oh, come on, Chuck. That has nothing to do... come on. Do you think I've been blowing you off? All right, I understand why you may feel that way. I do. But it's not so. I've been very busy. Now, true, I lived with Karen for eight years, but that was what? Two years ago? Honestly, I'm fine with all this. I've come to realize that, although I made a lot of mistakes I regret, Karen and I are better off apart. I mean, we're all friends now... I mean, still. You and I are still friends. Here's the bottom line. Bottom line is, I wish you both well. I really mean it. I mean, I wish I could hear some more about what you have planned for the wedding, but right now, I gotta go. Oh, a staff meeting. Yeah, mandatory attendance even for temps. Weird, I know, but there's a reason they're the best law firm in town. Okay. See ya, Chuck.

Confidential To Weary In Wichita: Chuck! Hey man, sorry, this bus—I gotta. Fine, fine! No—can't. Gotta—later, dude!

Barry Turner is a syndicated columnist whose weekly advice column, Ask A Guy Who's Been Avoiding You, appears in more than 250 papers nationwide.

Your Horoscope

By Lloyd Schumner Sr.
Retired Machinist and
A.A.P.B.-Certified Astrologer

Aries: (March 21–April 19)
While on a pilgrimage, you and two dozen other travelers will stop for the night at a roadside inn, where you'll all agree to pass the time by telling stories about your jobs as carpet salespeople.

Taurus: (April 20–May 20)
Your lover continues to insist you're giving mixed signals, despite the fact that you're standing on the bed naked while gesturing toward your genitals with air-traffic-control flashlights.

Gemini: (May 21–June 21)
You never thought you'd be the type to have a big family, but upon awakening from your decade-long coma, you'll discover that the asylum doctors have begotten seven children on your defenseless body.

Cancer: (June 22–July 22)
It's true that the blood of kings flows in your veins, but the kings are those of Siding, and their reign is specific to Decatur.

Leo: (July 23–Aug. 22)
This will be a spectacular week for unusual physical feats of romance in the workplace, which might have something to do with your getting fired.

Virgo: (Aug. 23–Sept. 22)
Saturn rising in your sign this week doesn't mean you'll make a good lawyer, but your eloquent insistence on the fact will convince most everyone.

Libra: (Sept. 23–Oct. 23)
You'll both make and ruin a ton of cash when you invent Wallet Bacon, the tasty, crispy bacon that cooks up in minutes in one's wallet.

Scorpio: (Oct. 24–Nov. 21)
You're never going to be named Miss Congeniality, but only because the title is so valued that a certain amount of wheeling and dealing has sullied the purity of the judging.

Sagittarius: (Nov. 22–Dec. 21)
You'll find it hard to live a normal life for the next couple months, during which it will suddenly and inexplicably become fashionable to jump motorcycles over you.

Capricorn: (Dec. 22–Jan. 19)
A feeling of increased personal freedom and greater privacy will wash over you this week when a heretofore unnoticed guy named Wally up and moves out of your apartment.

Aquarius: (Jan. 20–Feb. 18)
Thousands of horseback-riding Mongols will trample you to death so quickly that you'll never learn why they were dragging the Goodyear blimp with tow ropes tied to their saddles.

Pisces: (Feb. 19–March 20)
You'll agonize at length over being forced to choose between two beautiful women, giving them time to formulate and execute an escape plan.

NEWS

Scientists Isolate Gene Simmons

see SCIENCE page 7D

Briefcase Full Of Porn

see ENTERTAINMENT page 11G

Animal Comes In Fun Animal Shape

see NATURE page 3E

History Sighs, Repeats Itself

see WORLD page 13B

STATshot

A look at the numbers that shape your world.

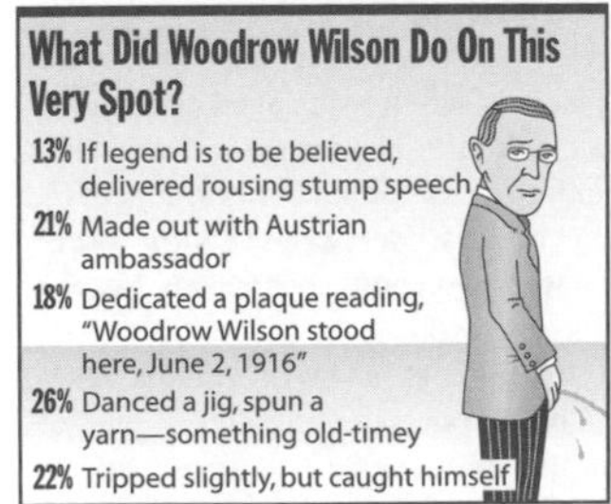

What Did Woodrow Wilson Do On This Very Spot?
13% If legend is to be believed, delivered rousing stump speech
21% Made out with Austrian ambassador
18% Dedicated a plaque reading, "Woodrow Wilson stood here, June 2, 1916"
26% Danced a jig, spun a yarn—something old-timey
22% Tripped slightly, but caught himself

the ONION®

VOLUME 41 ISSUE 13 AMERICA'S FINEST NEWS SOURCE™ 31 MARCH–6 APRIL 2005

America Still Searching For Funniest Home Video

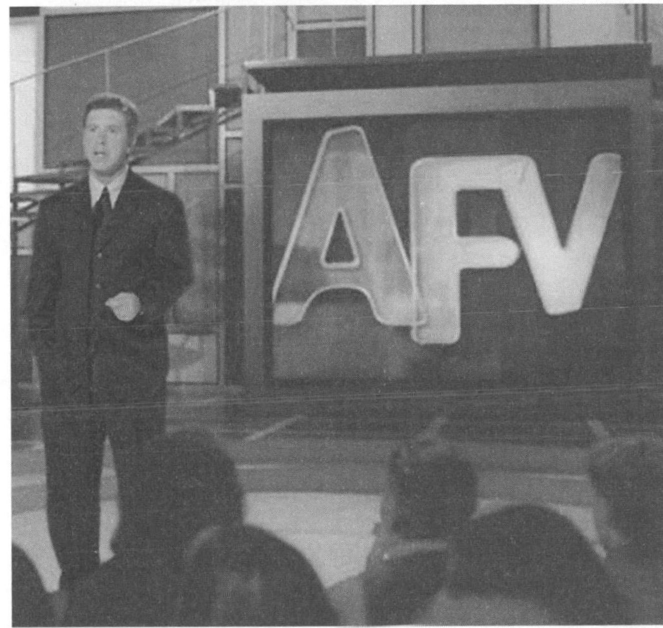

Above: Bergeron, who is still searching for the ultimate home video.

HOLLYWOOD—Even after 15 years of tireless labor and a score of agonizing near-misses, the staff at *America's Funniest Home Videos* said Monday that they do not intend to quit until they have found the nation's funniest home video.

"It has been a very long search, but our job isn't done," said Tom Bergeron, the current host of the long-running ABC show. "If we had set out to collect, catalog, and air some of the *funnier* home videos in America, the show would be off the air already. But everyone involved agrees that, when we chose the word 'funniest,' we made a promise to our viewers. This show will not stop airing until we've delivered on our promise, and found that video."

Since 1990, *America's Funniest Home Videos'* producers, technicians, and hosts have spent millions of hours poring over viewer entries, listening to sound-effects

see VIDEO page 106

Above: Bush warns the audience about Social Security.

Bush Launches Preemptive Attack On Social Security

ST. LOUIS, MO—At an appearance at the St. Louis Convention Center Sunday evening, President Bush declared the "grave and pressing need" for a preemptive attack on the Social Security program.

"My fellow citizens, at this hour, brave administration and congressional forces are in the early stages of an all-out attack on Social Security, with the ultimate goal of bringing down the oppressive legacy of the New Deal, and big government itself," Bush said. "Through bold and decisive action, we will liberate our grandparents and our

see BUSH page 107

Live-In Boyfriend Like The Deadbeat Dad Kids Never Had

ABILENE, TX—Earl "Trey" Shaker, 34, the live-in boyfriend of single mother May Anne Wyatt, 37, is like the deadbeat dad her four children never had, family sources reported Monday.

"Trey is a great role model for my kids," said Wyatt, who has not had a man in and out of her house since 1994, when her live-in boyfriend Hank LaRue was convicted of grand larceny. "Trey lies on the couch and don't get himself into no trouble. Sure, he ain't worked in six months, but now there's someone around to look after the kids while I'm at work."

Wyatt, a waitress on weekdays and a gas-station attendant on weekends, said that, until Shaker moved into her

see BOYFRIEND page 107

Above: Shaker, Dillon, and Merle in the home they now share.

The Morning-After Pill

The FDA is deciding whether they will allow non-prescription sales of the morning-after pill Plan B. What do *you* think?

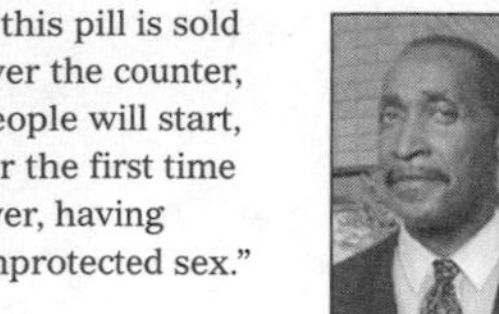

"If this pill is sold over the counter, people will start, for the first time ever, having unprotected sex."

Jared Maldonado
Telemarketer

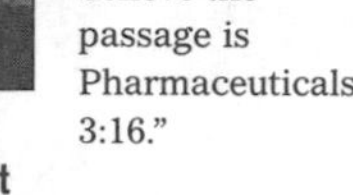

"It says in the Bible that the morning-after pill is wrong. I believe the passage is Pharmaceuticals 3:16."

Adrian Roy
Systems Analyst

"Why not? The tequila responsible for getting me knocked up in the first place is sold over the counter."

Dana Conner
Photographer

"Not for me, thanks. I've had a Dalkon Shield IUD in me for 30 years, and in me it's gonna stay."

Ana Huff
Musician

"Do I think they should sell the morning-after pill over the counter? Hell, I think they should add it to One-A-Day multivitamins."

Claude Adkins
Author

"Wait. There's a way to prevent pregnancy?"

Karl Bass
Security Guard

Information Thieves

Identity theft is a growing problem, with hackers gaining access to more Americans' personal information every year. What are some of the reasons hackers turn to crime?

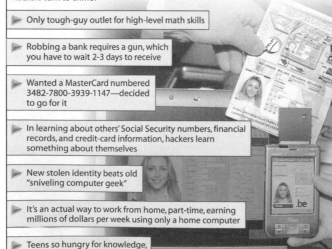

- Only tough-guy outlet for high-level math skills
- Robbing a bank requires a gun, which you have to wait 2-3 days to receive
- Wanted a MasterCard numbered 3482-7800-3939-1147—decided to go for it
- In learning about others' Social Security numbers, financial records, and credit-card information, hackers learn something about themselves
- New stolen identity beats old "sniveling computer geek"
- It's an actual way to work from home, part-time, earning millions of dollars per week using only a home computer
- Teens so hungry for knowledge, they are willing to steal it

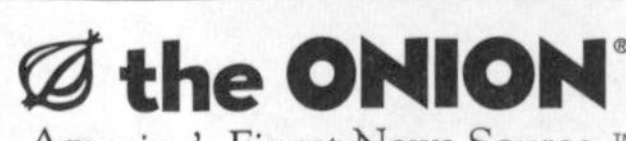

America's Finest News Source.™

Herman Ulysses Zweibel
Founder

T. Herman Zweibel
Publisher Emeritus
J. Phineas Zweibel
Publisher
Maxwell Prescott Zweibel
Editor-In-Chief

You Won't Believe This, But I'm Actually On A Crowded Elevator Right Now

Oh, hey David. No, it's a fine time. Always got time for you, my man. *Dave.* How's that lady I saw you with on Saturday? No shit. You're something else, my friend. Really something. Oh, that? That was just the second floor. Yeah, you won't believe this, but I'm actually on this crowded elevator right now. Yeah, it's totally crazy. We're packed like sardines in here.

By Brad Harrison

Dude, I can hardly move. That's why it took me four rings to pick up. I was, like, trying to jam my hand down into my pocket without touching this woman's ass in front of me. Everyone was probably like, "Who's playing 'Ice Ice Baby'?" 'Cause of my ringtone. Yeah, it's really, really funny. Vanilla Ice. What? Yes, you do. It went, "ding ding ding da-da ding-ding." Come on! Listen: "ding ding ding da-da ding-ding, ding ding ding-ding doo-doo doo-doo doo." Call me back and you can hear—wait, that wouldn't work. Anyway.

Yeah, I get great service. Mm, I think like $40. Only two bars, but you can

Well, the Tiffany thing's not going so well. I don't know. All of a sudden, she got uptight on me. I'm gonna lay low for a week or two, and then see what's up. But damn, those pantsuits she wears. I mean... Holy shit.

hear me fine, right? I'll speak up.

Yeah, pretty good. Well, the Tiffany thing's not going so well. I don't know. All of a sudden, she got uptight on me. I'm gonna lay low for a week or two, and then see what's up. But damn, those pantsuits she wears. I mean... Holy shit.

God, there's so many people. I'm right in the center, too. What ever happened to the concept of personal space?

Shit, this elevator has gotta be over the weight limit. I'll be lucky if I make it without plummeting to my death. Wait! What's that sound?! Ahhh! Dave, call 911! Heh heh. No? Not even

Dude, I can hardly move. That's why it took me four rings to pick up. I was, like, trying to jam my hand down into my pocket without touching this woman's ass in front of me. Everyone was probably like, "Who's playing 'Ice Ice Baby'?" 'Cause of my ringtone.

for a second? Oh well.

Problem is, the elevator always fills up with all these people from the law firms in the building. I know. I'm the one who works around them. What? Maybe. Try me. Mm, how many? Heh heh. "How many can you afford?" Dude, that's so true.

Halfway there. Sixty-first floor.

Isn't it weird how everyone stares forward in an elevator. Just like zombies. "Brains!" What? I know. It's stopping at every fucking floor. I don't even know what's on half these floors. There's this cafeteria on 30, so a couple people got off, but then like a dozen people got on.

Hey, isn't it funny how you make gestures when you're on the phone, even though the person on the other end can't see them? Like, I just did this zombie face, even though there's no way you could see it. Yeah, I saw it. It sucked rod.

One sec. Let me switch hands again.

Christ, I'm sweating like a pig... I can smell myself.

Nah, I just grabbed a sandwich. Shit, I'm gonna be late. Dave, let me put you on speaker for a second while I unwrap this bad boy. I got a pastrami melt and the smell is just irre-fucking-sistible. No, Luigi's. Fried onions, totally.

Mmmf. So damn good.

I should get one of those headsets, but people who use those things look like such assholes. Mmmmm!

Okay, I'm here. Okay, cool. Yeah, I'll call you tomorrow. Ø

Anti-Chewing-Tobacco Activists Speak Out Against Secondhand Spit

RALEIGH, NC—The ever-embattled tobacco industry suffered another blow Monday, as citizens' groups challenged the major smokeless-tobacco companies to confront the quality-of-life issues associated with secondhand spit.

"This isn't the '50s, when you would see TV commercials with lab-coat-wearing doctors spitting chewing tobacco right on the examination-room floor," said activist Helen Pertwee of The Great American Tobacco Backwash, a citizens' group dedicated to fighting the rising tide of secondhand tobacco spit in public places. "In this day and age, we are much more informed about the consequences of secondhand spit, and non-chewers are refusing to expose ourselves to it."

New York resident Glen Abramson objects to the use of chewing tobacco in public places.

"I can't go to a bar without coming home reeking of tobacco spit," Abramson said. "I have to wring my clothes out in the sink before I go to bed. Sometimes, I'll get them back from the dry-cleaners with flakes of chew still clinging in the weave."

Boston's Janice MacGruder frequently eats out at a restaurant that allows smokeless tobacco.

"The spit affects the taste of the food," MacGruder said. "The hazy, brown mist hanging in the air doesn't stay in the chewing section—common sense can tell you that. Despite the image the old phrase conjures up, it's not romantic to eat a meal in a 'spit-filled room.'"

Above: A non-chewing bargoer sits next to a tobacco chewer in Wilmington, DE.

The pools of tobacco spit on floors and tables are particularly noisome to people in the service industry, who are exposed to three times more secondhand spit than the average American—up to 450 gallons a year.

"The way people view secondhand spit needs to change," said Lindsey Hurness, a bartender in Tampa, FL. "People spit their gobs of old chew everywhere—in drink glasses, in plants, in the sink. And the floors are slick with pools of spit. Sometimes, on busy weekend nights, the goopy brown stuff comes up to my shoelaces."

Secondhand-spit exposure is not a

see SPIT page 107

NEWS IN BRIEF

American Torturing Jobs Increasingly Outsourced

WASHINGTON, DC—AFL-CIO vice president Linda Chavez-Thompson, representing the American Federation of Interrogation Torturers, released a statement Monday deriding the CIA's "extraordinary rendition" program, under which American torturing jobs are outsourced to foreign markets. "Outsourcing the task of interrogating terror suspects to countries like Egypt, Syria, and Saudi Arabia is having a crippling effect on the Americans who make a living by stripping detainees nude, shackling them to the floor, and beating the living shit out of them," Chavez-Thompson said. "And specialists within the field—corrosive-material chemists, ocular surgeons, and testicular electricians—are lucky to find any jobs at all. How are they supposed to feed their families?" Attorney General Alberto Gonzales defended extraordinary rendition, saying the program will create jobs in the long run by fostering a global climate of torture tolerance.

'Missed Connection' Ad Obviously Cheney

WASHINGTON, DC—In spite of its anonymity, a "missed connection" ad posted on the D.C.-area Craigslist Monday was clearly the work of Vice President Dick Cheney. "You: the attractive blonde from Newsweek," the ad read. "Me: stout, thinning hair, glasses, surrounded by Secret Service agents. Our eyes met as I was walking across the tarmac. I thought I felt a spark." The posting closed with the message, "Coffee? I'll grant you an exclusive."

Oysters Have No Discernible Effect On Date

SEATTLE—According to Justin Gramming, 24, a close inspection of date Karen Stavers, who ate a six-oyster appetizer platter, indicated no marked increase in her libido. "Those things didn't do shit," Grammling said. "She didn't inch closer to me, or play footsie, or take her sweater off. I was keeping an eye on her, and her color didn't even rise." Grammling said he will fall back on Seduction Plan B: alcohol.

Five Minutes Of Watching Indian Channel Leads To Five Hours Of Watching Indian Channel

NEW YORK—A five-minute sampling of Hindi-language channel Zee TV stretched into a five-hour Indian TV marathon for Craig Mieritz, 23, Monday. "I have no idea what's going on, but I can't turn it off," the channel-flipping Mieritz said about a colorful, frenetic musical number on the soap opera *Tum Bin Jaaoon Kahaan*. "Maybe I'll just watch another minute..." Following the soap, Mieritz watched a Hindi pop variety show, 11 music videos, and the three-hour Bollywood epic *Khuda Gawah*, the remote in his hand the entire time.

Nation Planning Surprise Party To Cheer Up Conor Oberst

OMAHA, NE—American citizens are coordinating efforts to lift the spirits of wünderkind singer-songwriter Conor Oberst, sources reported Monday. "I saw Conor's picture in a *Spin* article about Bright Eyes, and he just looked so down," said Lindsey Keisner of Youngstown, OH, one of the party's 4,000 planners. "The country feels really bad that he's going through such a rough spell, so next Friday, everyone who can should meet in Omaha with balloons, funny cards, and silly little gag gifts." Britt Daniel from Spoon will lure Oberst to Omaha by asking him to overdub some vocals. ⌀

compilations, and tirelessly airing the fruits of their collective labor before carefully selected focus groups.

Executive producer Vin Di Bona said he never expected the search to go on for so long.

"When we set out on this quest, we assumed it would take two, three years tops," Di Bona said. "We thought someone out there in America had the funniest home video at the ready, and we'd just give it a national audience. Fifteen years later... Well, we know the video is out there, but sometimes, late at night, I do worry that it's locked in a trunk somewhere, and we'll never get our hands on it."

Di Bona said that, although the show has aired hundreds of classic moments—dogs talking, elderly men depantsed, and comical water-skiing accidents—no video has been "the one."

"We've come close," Di Bona said. "Parallel-Parking Grandma was almost there. If only she'd knocked over two more lawn ornaments. Or if we'd just nailed the sound effect. We knew the 'boing' wasn't enough, but we felt the 'ker-boinnng, waaaah' was too much."

Di Bona had difficulty pinpointing what his team is looking for.

"When we see it, we'll know it," Di Bona said. "It's not as simple as determining whether a cat is funnier than a cockatiel. There are a million X-factors involved—timing, framing, how onlookers react when the groom falls into the cake."

"I could throw criteria around all day," Di Bona added. "The simple truth is that, if a video doesn't cause an immediate gut reaction, I toss it in the garbage."

According to Di Bona, staying focused on the quest for the ultimate funny home video has put a lot of pressure on the show's hosts.

"[Original host] Bob Saget was a man obsessed," Di Bona said. "After working on *Full House*, Bob was really excited to do a show with a purpose. But the 80-hour weeks started to wear him down. One late night during season six, Bob flipped. He started cursing, throwing things, and screaming that we were no closer to finding America's funniest home video than we were when we'd started. In 1997, when he heard the news that Germany had found their nation's funniest video, he quit. He couldn't take the pressure anymore."

Above: "Table Tennis, Anyone?" is one many home videos that failed to earn the title of "funniest."

Added Di Bona: "I still have faith that we'll find that perfect clip. And, at that point, we'll go off the air—in triumph."

Boston resident Nathan Lister is one of thousands of viewers who contend that Di Bona should end his search.

"I don't see how anyone could see the 1997 clip 'Boy Loses Mug' and argue it's not the one," said Lister, who founded It's Over, a group that advocates naming the clip America's funniest home video. "You can watch it without the 'bonk' or the slide whistle or Bob Saget's post-clip commentary—it's still hysterical. It's the scene that every home-video enthusiast dreams of: that perfect combination of youthful innocence and genital pounding."

The 13-second clip features a medium-shot of a 4-year-old boy sitting in a highchair and waving his juice mug while his father prepares him a bowl of cereal. The father struggles with the bag until it rips, sending cereal flying into the air. The surprise causes the boy to jerk his arm, and his cup slips from his hand and flies into his father's genitals. A golden retriever rushes in to eat the spilled cereal, jumps on the prone, agonized father, and the camera swivels back to the confused, worried face of the boy.

"The timing in 'Boy Loses Mug' is absolutely perfect," said Lister. "We've petitioned ABC to rerun the clip, but they keep giving us the runaround. We want people to see that the title of America's funniest home video is not up for grabs."

Continued Lister: "The goal of *America's Funniest Home Videos* has already been achieved. Why ABC would want to beat a dead horse like this, I have no idea." Ø

the ONION presents:

Being A Considerate Houseguest

If friends or family members are kind enough to invite you to stay at your home, you'll want to be a gracious guest. Here's some tips to help you avoid becoming a burden:

- Always help your hosts after dinner: Offer to clear the table, wash the dishes, or teach them to cook.
- Ensure that you do not overstay your welcome by asking your host if you are overstaying your welcome every couple of minutes.
- Avoid an awkward moment later on by telling your host upfront that you're a bedshitter.
- Playing your host's stereo at top volume after midnight is rude. Bring your own boombox.
- Don't just act like a guest in someone's house. *Be* a guest in someone's house.
- It's considered good form to replace any cats you drown.
- Cooking a meal for your host is a nice gesture, but ordering a pizza and offering to chip in for your part is way easier.
- Always wait until your hosts have gone to bed before masturbating.
- Should an unfamiliar household situation arise, do not speak. Stare blankly at a fixed point on the wall until it all blows over.
- Don't monopolize the bathroom: Take sponge baths in the kitchen sink, and pee in a bottle and hide it under the bed.
- It's customary to take a souvenir from your host's home as a reminder of your wonderful stay.

BOYFRIEND from page 103

Above: Shaker supervises Wyatt's boys.

trailer in February, her children had never had the benefit of a male influence in and out of their lives. Finally, all that has changed for Madellynne Jo, 12, Dillon, 11, Merle, 7, and Sunshine, 5, who now spend most Saturdays sitting on the couch watching TV with Shaker as he makes his way through a six-pack of Coors Light.

"I love watching Trey with the kids," said Wyatt, who met Shaker at a local tavern in October 2004. "He'll toss Sunshine up in the air until she wets

"I guess Trey's nice to Mom," Madellynne said. "He bought her 35 gallons of propane the other day, just out of the blue. It wasn't even her birthday."

her pants laughing. And one night last January, he helped Merle with his homework. Sure, sometimes he roams off for a few days. But he always comes back sooner or later."

Although members of Wyatt's extended family have complained that Shaker doesn't have a steady source of income and doesn't provide the children with much-needed discipline, Wyatt was quick to disagree.

"Oh no, Trey can be real strict, especially after he's been drinking," Wyatt said. "If the kids draw on the wall with crayon, play with his gas cans, or spill his beer, he'll get after them with the belt."

Wyatt said her children had little difficulty accepting Shaker's role as the head of the house when he is home.

"Sometimes the kids will sass back and say things like, 'You're not my real daddy,' or, 'I hate Mommy for letting you move in,'" Wyatt said. "Kids will be kids, but deep down, I know they love Trey as much as I do."

According to Wyatt, her children have learned a lot from Shaker.

"Trey taught Dillon how to steal cable, and he taught my littlest, Merle, how to get a bonfire going in the yard," Wyatt said. "The other day, he taught Sunshine to ride her first bike, and when she went rolling off into that pile of sheet metal and cut up her leg, Trey wrapped his favorite bandanna around the cut to stop the bleeding."

Wyatt's children expressed generally positive opinions of Shaker.

"Trey finishes all the PlayStation games first, and before I get a chance to catch up, he trades them for a different one," said Dillon. "But he never hits Mom or locks her out of the house, so I guess he's better than when Mom had overnight guests."

Madellynne said Wyatt is "creepy."

"Trey's whiskers make him look scary, and some days, he never changes out of his robe," Madellynne said. "He always eats all the chips, and it's hard to watch television because he snores so loud. My friend Tamara says he looks like a guy who would work in a coal mine, but I can't really picture him working."

Family sources agree that Shaker seems to make Wyatt happy.

"I guess Trey's nice to Mom," Madellynne said. "He bought her 35 gallons of propane the other day, just out of the blue. It wasn't even her birthday."

Wyatt said Shaker makes her household complete.

"It's good to have a man sometimes around—someone who can reach a box of taco shells on the top shelf," Wyatt said. "Even though he pretty much never gets up to reach anything except for that goddamn remote, it's still nice knowing that he could reach up high if he wanted to. I feel like, with Trey here, we finally got a real family like everybody else. And if he does run off every now and again, well, that's what dads do." Ø

BUSH from page 103

grandchildren from the threats of the system established by Franklin D. Roosevelt to provide retirement compensation for America's workers."

According to the Social Security and Medicare Boards of Trustees, if Social Security revenue and payouts remain unchanged, the nation's largest entitlement program will be unable to pay full benefits in 2041.

"The Social Security system is a dangerous, financially unsustainable program," Bush said. "If we allow it to continue unchecked, we will need to resort to benefit cuts, tax increases, or massive borrowing in 36 short years. I call upon the combined forces of my administration and Congress to destroy this program and the threat that it presents to our way of life."

Bush defended his decision to make a preemptive attack.

"September 11 taught us that, in our insecure world, we must take bold, decisive action to protect our citizens from threats both foreign and domestic," Bush said. "We must free citizens everywhere from the threat of financial dependence on the government."

In the months leading up to Bush's declaration, he attempted to contain the Social Security program through a calculated long-range attack on its general fund.

"Up until several days ago, we attempted to negotiate with Social Security, by proposing a plan under which wage-earners would invest their withheld income in the stock market," Bush said. "These personal savings accounts would have pumped a great deal of wealth into our deflated economy, but this is not about temporarily inflating a beleaguered market. It is a battle for freedom, and it is time to take decisive action. America, we must strike Social Security."

Bush said he was reluctant to detail the specifics of his strategic plan, as he did not wish to jeopardize national security.

U.S. Army War College professor of economics Henry Reed said destroying the program will require a "broad and concerted campaign."

"The Social Security system is complex and resilient, with a network of cooperative agents across the country and an entrenched relationship with many of the nation's most desperate elements," Reed said. "Luckily, a well-funded coalition of pro-business forces has already begun striking selected targets of legislative importance in order to stop the cells that provide assistance to people on the extreme end of the age spectrum."

Reed put the current situation in historical context.

"Bush could ignore this threat, like all the presidents since Truman have done," Reed said. "By confronting this potential future crisis now, Bush will free all Americans from the treacherous safety net that currently entangles their futures."

The president closed his address by asking the public to support the massive undertaking.

"Americans young and old will be making great sacrifices for this cause," Bush said. "But there will be innumerable gains for other segments of the population, from Wall Street to Pennsylvania Avenue. As for the brave men and women of the GOP already embroiled in this fight, my prayers are with you."

Republican National Committee chairman Ken Mehlman applauded the president's campaign.

"As usual, people are criticizing the president for being too courageous, for leading too fearlessly," Mehlman said. "The bleeding hearts say you could save Social Security with less money than we're currently spending in Iraq. But that's billions and billions of dollars we don't have, people." Ø

SPIT from page 105

problem experienced only by bar and restaurant patrons.

"Ask any frequent traveler: It's hell to be on a plane if the other passengers are chewing tobacco," said business consultant Jessica Mallard, who is on the road 250 days a year. "Even when I get a window seat, I walk off the plane with half of my blazer absolutely drenched in the stuff."

"Then there's the hotel," Mallard added. "Even if you stay in a no-chewing room, you get a spit-sodden pillow half the time. And if they don't have any no-chewing rooms left, you might as well go sleep in the rodeo bleachers."

According to hotel managers, spit-related costs are rising.

"There was a time, 10 or 15 years ago, when hotels could get along with one wet-vac," said Red Roof Inn vice president Ronald Henneman, who oversees house-keeping for the national chain. "No more. We extracted enough tobacco-saliva slurry from our carpets last year to float the Queen Mary."

Although the smokeless-tobacco industry says there is no hard evidence of any health risk associated with exposure to secondhand spit, their claim is questioned by an increasingly moist and nauseated public.

"I don't give a shit what Skoal says, secondhand spit is a serious threat," Pertwee said. "At the very least, the industry needs to measure secondhand spit's effects on kids, who are closer to the ground, where all that spit ends up."

As long as tobacco chewers continue to exert their influence in Congress, people like Pertwee will be swimming upstream.

"I don't know why everyone's got their panties in a twist about this," said Ron Preston, ejecting a stream of brown saliva into a nearby plant. "It's my body—unless those PC Nazis get their way. If people don't like getting spit on, they can move over. It's that simple." Ø

COMMUNITY VOICES

Getting Our Jollies

I've gotta say, I feel really sorry for all the so-called "professionals"—the working stiffs and stiffettes of the world. Sure, they're making a lot of money being lawyers and brokers, but are they truly happy? Last Monday morning, as I watched the Lexuses and BMWs cruise down Thisbe Avenue headed toward the interstate, I couldn't help feeling sorry for all those strivers.

A Room Of Jean's Own
By Jean Teasdale

After all, what would you rather do: read legal briefs all day, or dress up in an elf costume and wave a colorful sign? Of course, you'd rather do the latter—me too! (Well, not that I was ever in danger of becoming a lawyer, but I still know which job I'd pick.)

So, what was I doing dressed as an elf and carrying a big sign? Well, I was directing motorists to the grand opening of Off-Season Santa, my father Horvel's new business venture. Loyal Jeanketeers know that Dad recently parlayed a lifetime of seasonal St. Nick simulations into a year-long money-maker. That's right: Dad's dream is a reality, and parents can take their children to buy Santa merchandise, frolic in the off-season winter wonderland, and get pictures taken with the big man himself all the way from January through December!

I'll admit we hit a couple of snags prior to opening. Dad's request for a small-business loan was turned down (thanks for nothing, Sundial Savings & Loan!), so he was forced to bankroll the store with credit cards, a cashed-out life-insurance policy, and his monthly Social Security checks. And my brother Kevin flatly refused to help out (he considers Santa idolatrous), so that left yours truly as Dad's sole creative assistant. I've spent the past month single-handedly ordering merchandise, decorating the store, and handing out flyers downtown. But, you know what? Although I've never worked harder, it hardly felt like work at all!

About 15 minutes before our grand opening, I hopped in my car and whizzed over to the store. You might be interested to know that Off-Season Santa is located in the same strip mall as Fashion Bug, my old employer! Nutty coincidence, huh? The strip mall really needs the business, too. The Hot Sam closed, so now there's only us, the H&R Block, and the comic-book store. (We occupy the frame store's old place.)

So, on top of starting an important—yet fun—job, I was having a dramatic homecoming. After all, I left the strip mall an unemployed Fashion Bug clerk, and I was returning an independent businesswoman! It was like a dream come true, and I couldn't help getting a little verklempt. (Tawk quietly amongst yourselves!)

I snapped digital shots of the store's interior. It was a winter wonderland covered in artificial snow, hung with large plastic glitter snowflakes, and dotted with decorated trees and gift-wrapped boxes. (A lot of the decorations came from the bottom of my hall closet. See Rick, all those years of hitting after-Christmas sales really paid off!) And Jeanketeers, I almost started bawling when my dad rolled in from the back office! He looked soooo wonderful perched atop his Rascal scooter and dressed in the Off-Season Santa costume my fashion-designer buddy Fulgencio made. (A sequined red sweatshirt, a green-and-white-striped shirt, green suspenders, and green wool trousers!)

Fulgencio, who agreed to help us out, showed up just a few minutes late, wearing an elf outfit like mine. When we laid eyes on each other, we started shrieking, embracing, and jumping up and down!

"Girl, you look absolutely insane!" Fulgencio screamed. "And Santa in a little wheelchair! This is like the lowest ring of some kind of Christmas hell! It looks like a Christmas special jumped out of a television and vomited its guts out all over a tiny commercial space! Could I love it any more?" (Fulgencio has the weirdest way of giving compliments!)

Given how magic and electric that morning felt, we couldn't help being a little disappointed when no customers showed up. Even the complimentary cookies and juice weren't luring people in (leaving us to stare at those yummy snacks all day!). And not one of our new neighbors dropped by to welcome Dad and me to the mall—unless you want to count the comic-book store employee who gaped at us through the big display window for a couple minutes and then walked off.

Finally, at about 1 p.m., we received our first two visitors: hubby Rick and his snide barfly buddy Craig. They were on one of their "liquid" lunch hours, but instead of getting loaded, they decided to unload. (Thanks a lot!)

"No one's going to show up, because when it ain't Christmas, Santa's just another fat man," Rick said. "Horvel, get a real job so you can pay the rent you owe me. And Jean, you can quit gettin' your jollies on my dime, too. If I could make money playing *Grand Theft Auto* all day, I would. But face it, folks like us can't make a living havin' fun." (Of course, Rick and Craig's contempt for our vision didn't prevent them from gobbling down seven cookies between the two of them!)

Well, I'm happy to say that Rick The Grouch was totally wrong! At about 3:30 p.m., a mother brought her preschool son in. Well, maybe it's more accurate to say she dragged her son in, because he was crying and flailing his arms. The woman said her son was afraid of Santa, so she wanted him to sit with Dad for a while so the kid would realize that Santa isn't evil. I don't know, maybe it was the Rascal scooter or Dad's cigarette odor, but the boy started shaking and hyperventilating when we put him on Dad's knee. Dad tried to tell him that he loves children, and Fulgencio did a little elf dance. Well, finally, the woman took her crying son off Dad's knee and left, which was a pity, because I was just about to suggest they sit for a photo and make our first sale.

When we closed at 7 p.m., Fulgencio and I felt pretty dejected. Dad, however, seemed as upbeat as ever. "We can't expect this place to be a goldmine immediately," Dad said, pulling up a wool pant leg and scratching his ankle. "It'll take awhile to build a customer base."

On the ride home, Dad was bubbling over with ideas for jumpstarting the store. He suggested that we take out ads in the local papers and that I dress up like the Easter Bunny. "Kids could come to see the Easter Bunny, who's visiting her old pal Santa," he said cheerfully. "See, we just need to put on our thinking caps. Heh heh, maybe you can sew some for us, Fulgencio."

I guess I shouldn't fret just yet. Dad's been an entrepreneur most of his life, so he's accustomed to the ups and downs of business. Admittedly, our store is pretty "out there." (It does feel a teensy bit bizarre, slipping on a plus-size elf suit first thing in the morning.) But I like to think we're just ahead of our time. There's no reason to give up hope this early. I'm sure someone told the proprietors of those shopping-mall booths that sell high-pressure water massages that they were nuts, too! ⌀

HOROSCOPES

Your Horoscope

By Lloyd Schumner Sr.
Retired Machinist and
A.A.P.B.-Certified Astrologer

Aries: (March 21–April 19)
You've never cared about mining, you've never been curious about mining, and you certainly never wanted to be a miner, but the only thing those gun-toting Australians care about is getting the silver out of the ground.

Taurus: (April 20–May 20)
You've always believed that people are basically good. Unfortunately, this week will go a long way toward convincing you that most of them aren't really good in bed, where it counts most.

Gemini: (May 21–June 21)
You said the only thing you wanted was for your child to be born with all 10 fingers and all 10 toes, so you'll have no right to complain when you find out exactly where the digits are.

Cancer: (June 22–July 22)
After a week of your bragging, the Muses have decided to prevent you from winning another limerick contest at Tubby's.

Leo: (July 23–Aug. 22)
You're developing a reputation as something of a "party pooper," because your friends are too proper to call you "that chick who shits in the punch bowl."

Virgo: (Aug. 23–Sept. 22)
You've always said real estate is the one commodity that they're not making any more of, which is one reason why the world's volcanoes are out to get you.

Libra: (Sept. 23–Oct. 23)
The proper course of future action becomes clear this week when the stars in your sign mystically align and spell out, "You still owe Evan 10 bucks."

Scorpio: (Oct. 24–Nov. 21)
You'll be relieved to find out that sex after marriage is just as good as it ever was, except for the added hassle of making sure your wife doesn't find out about it.

Sagittarius: (Nov. 22–Dec. 21)
Your life expectancy will reach an all-time low this week when it somehow gets out that you're a good source of potassium, folic acid, and $245 in small bills.

Capricorn: (Dec. 22–Jan. 19)
It may or may not give you a reason to consider the error of your ways, but the only person you know who won't get hit by a bus next week is the bus driver everyone always picks on.

Aquarius: (Jan. 20–Feb. 18)
You'll have the bad luck to come to maturity days after the traditional ritual of "becoming a man" is replaced by an intensive, three-month regimen of rigorous physical testing.

Pisces: (Feb. 19–March 20)
Despite its willingness to eat anything, sleep anywhere, and carry 200 pounds of equipment on its back, you have to admit there's something weird about your cat.

the ONION®

VOLUME 41 ISSUE 14 AMERICA'S FINEST NEWS SOURCE™ 7–13 APRIL 2005

Local Fox Affiliate Debuts Terror-Alert Van

MURFREESBORO, TN—Touting itself as "the only channel with a terror-alert system designed to meet the specific needs of central Tennessee," Fox News affiliate WMFB-TV Channel 11 debuted its terror-alert van Monday.

"The team you trust to keep you informed is working to keep the greater Murfreesboro area—and your family—safe from Muslim extremists," said station manager Carl Bogert, unveiling the TerrorFirst! van at a press conference held in the "Terrorist No Zone" in the back parking lot. "When

see VAN page 112

Right: The WMFB TerrorFirst! van.

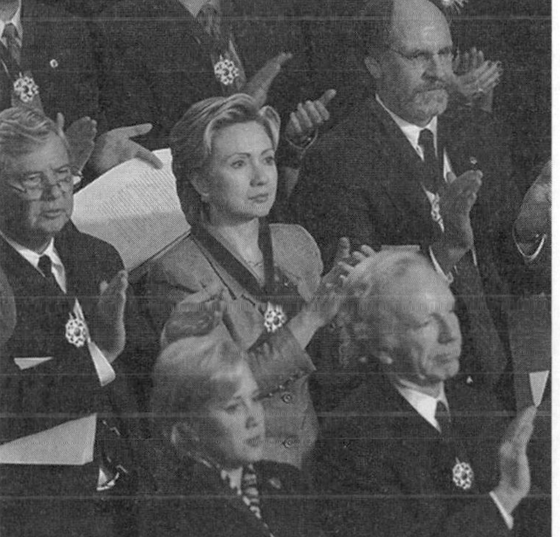

Above: Members of Congress applaud their decision to award themselves the Congressional Medals of Honor.

Congress Awards Itself Congressional Medal Of Honor

'We've Done A Very Good Job,' Says Congress

WASHINGTON, DC—In recognition of its "service above and beyond the call of duty in the legislative field," Congress awarded itself the Congressional Medal of Honor Monday.

"We've done a very good job this past year," House Majority Leader Tom DeLay (R-TX) said. "After passing H.R. 682 through the Senate, we realized the 109th U.S. Congress had done something that would benefit the entire country. We felt it was time we officially recognize our accomplishments."

Added DeLay: "I will treasure this medal as long I live."

The Congressional Medal of Honor, created in 1861 to recognize soldiers who distinguish themselves in battle, is the highest military decoration awarded by the U.S. government.

see CONGRESS page 110

Actual Urgent Message From Robert Redford Goes Unheeded

MARSING, ID—An actual urgent message from actor Robert Redford, whose mass-mailed call to action on behalf of the Natural Resources Defense Council reached millions of Americans last year, went unheeded last week by its lone recipient, Michael Sanborne of Marsing, ID.

"MICHAEL, I'm asking for your help to stop the robbery and possible destruction of one of America's most treasured human resources—actor Robert Redford," read the message typed on NRDC letterhead. "At this

see REDFORD page 113

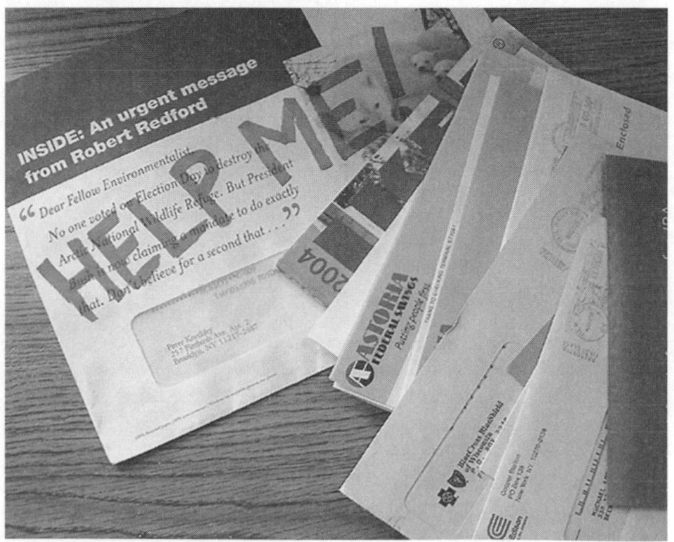

Above: A stack of Sanborne's unopened mail.

NEWS

Cheney Offspring Bursts From Bush's Chest

see WASHINGTON page 2B

Slowly Rotating Pie A Metaphor For Trucker's Failing Marriage

see PEOPLE page 4G

Drummer Forced To Retrieve Sticks From Audience For Encore

see LOCAL page 12C

STATshot

A look at the numbers that shape your world.

What Are We Writing Off?
26% Party where no one showed up
15% Stolen boom box
4% $200 bottle opener (sommeliers only)
23% Costs incurred during the standoff between ourselves and DEA agents
32% A large, but hopefully believable, number of kids

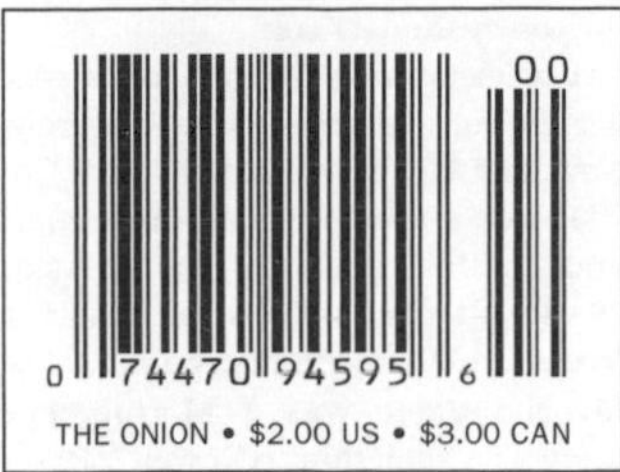

Many Cancer Deaths Preventable

According to the American Cancer Society, more than 60 percent of all cancer deaths could be prevented if Americans lived healthier lives. What do *you* think?

"Preventable? What those doctors *really* mean is 'preventable with minor effort and inconvenience.'"

Preston Brady
Systems Analyst

"So, all I have to do is cut out smoking, drinking, eating, breathing, and driving, and I'll die of something other than cancer? Hooray!"

Darla Clayton
Teacher

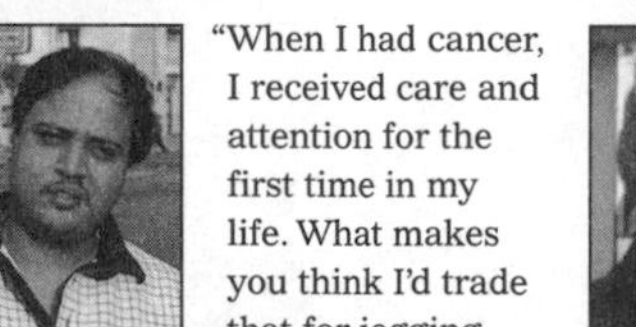

"When I had cancer, I received care and attention for the first time in my life. What makes you think I'd trade that for jogging three miles a day by myself?"

Damon Frank
Tax Preparer

"That advice is all well and good, but what about people like me, who don't have the time to not smoke?"

Trudy Massey
Stock Clerk

"My dad smoked like a chimney, ate only steaks, and drank bourbon every day, and he lived to be 54. Keep in mind, this was back in the 1970s, when that was considered quite old."

Peter Logan
Technical Writer

"Boy, I'd hate to get a disease and die at 60 instead of enjoying those extra three decades of livin' la vida nursing home."

Bennie Lloyd
Unemployed

Rising Oil Prices

Oil prices have reached an all-time high. How are increasing costs affecting daily life in America?

- More people driving only when absolutely convenient
- Shakey's prizes now woven out of straw
- Teens spending less time "cruising," more time "parking"
- Have to pretend to laugh at Saudi Ambassador Prince Bandar bin Sultan's stupid jokes, when what we'd really like to do is plant a wingtip up his ass
- Value of U.S. soldiers has decreased proportionally
- Shale-collecting now only for the very rich
- Too complicated to describe here, but long story short: You're out of a job and your daughter will make porn films

America's Finest News Source.™

Herman Ulysses Zweibel
Founder

T. Herman Zweibel
Publisher Emeritus
J. Phineas Zweibel
Publisher
Maxwell Prescott Zweibel
Editor-In-Chief

Being The Mayor Of Sucktown Isn't All I Thought It Would Be

When I found out that I had been unanimously elected mayor of Sucktown, I thought I'd won a front-row seat to the fuck-off parade. I imagined days filled with ribbon-cutting ceremonies and nights of gala balls. A year later, I wonder if I could've been any more naïve. Sure, I was ignorant of the duties involved in running a municipality, but I really thought being the mayor of Sucktown would be easier.

By Vincent Tremanski
Mayor Of Sucktown

I believe it was after I attended my *third* meeting about putting a yield sign on the corner of Dorkus Boulevard and Dipwad Street that I said, "Note to self: City government isn't all shits and giggles." Since then, I've come to learn that being a public servant is both an honor and a curse. It's not as easy as being King Of Everyone. I have a lot of people's welfare to consider. After all, it's not like I'm not the star of *The Vincent Tremanski Show*.

I've learned that being a good mayor requires leaving my feelings at the Welcome To Sucktown sign. It would be a different story if Sucktown were "population: me." Far from it. I am Sucktown's mayor, and it is my duty as such to look out for everyone—from the young professionals of Snob Hill to the disenfranchised, working-class folks living on Poor Schmuck Lane.

Granted, my job would be easier if I weren't living in the shadow of former mayor Mr. Hot Shot. Now retired, Mr. Hot Shot single-handedly took this small, unincorporated shit-farming community and turned it into what it is today. While many thought Mr. Hot Shot would ride his fame and reputation into a bid for governor of the whole state of Jerkachusetts, he chose not to challenge Gov. Heywood Jablowmi. My next-door neighbor, Dr. Genius over there, tells me not to think so much about Mr. Hot Shot's accomplishments, but it's hard. I can't even get a glass of Cheap Ass Ale at Skanky's Tavern without someone chewing my ear off about how the old mayor's shit smells like roses.

While experience has certainly tempered my enthusiasm, I'm still confident that I can make Sucktown a better place. I love this town. Aside from the four years I spent getting a degree in wankology at Loser University (Go Loser U Wolverines!), I've lived in Sucktown my whole life. I know everything there is to know about this town, from the best place to eat (Chez Le Expensive) to the best way to view the Sucktown skyline (through your car's rearview mirror). There's so much to do here—from shopping at the Scam-a-lot Shopping Center to lounging on the sandy shores of Scum-atoga Lake—that I couldn't hate it if I tried.

The people of Sucktown have a lot to be proud of. After all, the Clue Phone was invented right here in our humble little burg. I guess I have to admit that, deep down, I love this job, and there's no way I'd trade it for a one-way ticket to Happyville. ⌀

CONGRESS from page 109

Although the medal is traditionally reserved for members of the U.S. Armed Forces, a bill signed into law last month allows Congress to award the medal to "national legislative bodies charged with the responsibility of making the laws that govern the nation," as well.

Sen. Wayne Allard (R-CO) was among the congressmen who approved the bill in an overwhelming majority.

"The Medal of Honor is a reward for extraordinary bravery and dedicated service on behalf of our great country," said Allard, his medal gleaming on his chest. "It is an honor reserved for that rarest of men: the hero."

Before Monday's ceremony, only 3,459 individuals had been awarded the Congressional Medal of Honor. Some Americans—including the family of Sgt. First Class Paul R. Smith, who received a Congressional Medal of Honor last week—have suggested that awarding the medal to 535 people at once diminishes its prestige.

"How does honoring more people cheapen the medal?" DeLay asked. "I'm honored to be counted among so many other brave and patriotic Americans, past and present."

While officially awarded the Congressional Medal of Honor for "exemplary service in the drafting of H.R. 682," Congress recognized itself for "general excellence in the field of legislation in America," as well.

"Congress members may not put themselves into physical danger to take a crucial enemy outpost," Sen. Harry Reid (D-NV) said. "But Congress works very long hours every week to improve the lives of all Americans, and that's heroic in its own right. I'm proud to be a U.S. senator, and I'm honored that Congress has chosen to recognize my achievements on the congressional floor."

Many members of Congress reported it was difficult to choose between the Army, Navy, and Air Force medals of honor.

"It was a time of solemn reflection and careful choosing," DeLay said. "Personally, I would've loved to have a Marine medal of honor, because my favorite uncle was a Marine, but there's no such thing. Oh well." ⌀

EDUCATION

U.S. High School Gets Raw End Of Student Exchange

BELLEVILLE, IL—Students and faculty at Summit Prairie High School expressed frustration and disappointment Monday, after realizing that they got the short end of the stick in a recent trade with the Max Planck Gymnasium in Freiburg, Germany. In a deal overseen by AFS Intercultural Programs, Summit Prairie traded sophomore Molly Knutson, 16, for 17-year-old Uwe Bohm.

"Last fall, Uwe spent hours searching German-language websites for World Cup soccer news while the family watched NFL games on the big-screen TV in the living room," said Marshall, who will be hosting Bohm for three more months.

"The point of a student exchange is to give people on both sides an opportunity to gain an understanding of a different culture and make international friends," Summit Prairie principal Fred Seward said. "Judging from the way he sits alone at lunch every day, I regret to say that Uwe has not inspired the students to do either."

Above: Knutson (left) delights her new German friends while Bohm shuffles down a SPHS hallway.

Seward characterized Knutson, the student SPHS sent to Germany, as one of the school's "smartest and most outgoing students."

"Molly is a top-notch kid—enthusiastic, studious, real prom-court material," Seward said. "Any school would be lucky to have her. Meanwhile, Uwe is more or less a dud. He couldn't even be elected student-council treasurer—not if his life depended on it. He never raises his hand in class, he turns in grease-stained worksheets, and he spends most periods taking his watch apart and putting it back together."

"Well, no use complaining, I guess," Seward added. "We're stuck with him. I checked."

Although his English skills have improved significantly since his arrival in September, Bohm remains withdrawn. Bohm's teachers report that he routinely declines the invitation to share amusing anecdotes about his home country, and moreover, barely talks at all.

"Didn't the Max Planck people read the AFS literature?" Seward said. "You're supposed to trade your best and brightest students. I mean, Uwe is a nice enough kid, but he looks nothing like the strapping blond, blue-eyed German boy in the brochure. I don't think he plays guitar, either."

Sophomore Tracy List, who has classes with Bohm, criticized him for his "depressing" appearance.

"I swear, [Uwe] never smiles," List said. "He's gross. He's skinny and pimply, and his skin's yellow in

see EXCHANGE page 114

NEWS IN BRIEF

Terri Schiavo Dies Of Embarrassment

PINELLAS PARK, FL—Terri Schiavo, the shy woman whose self-image issues put her in a 15-year coma, died of embarrassment Thursday, the eyes of the entire world fixed upon her. "Terri, who had been extremely reserved before her debilitation, found herself trapped at the center of an epic legal battle that became the focus of the nation," said Dr. Kyle Williamson, who treated Schiavo several years ago. "The involvement of President Bush, Congress, and numerous church officials further complicated what might have been a simple right-to-die case, and made Terri's weight issues and family difficulties public knowledge. She finally succumbed to the embarrassment last week, at age 41." Specifics of Schiavo's dying breath and photos of the woman in her self-conscious 20s have been appearing in newspapers worldwide since her death.

Nation's Tall Asked To Stand In Back

WASHINGTON, DC—In a wide-reaching relocation of U.S. citizenry, all Americans above six feet tall were asked to please move to the back Monday. "Those fortunate enough to be blessed with stature, please step to the rear so that others may be able to see and be seen," said Nolan Mills, Secretary of the U.S. Department of Height. "Anyone willing to crouch or sit cross-legged on the ground is welcome to move to the front." This is the largest measure of its kind since 1993, when U.S. citizens were asked to not block the nation's doorways.

'He's A Stockbroker,' Says Woman Who Finds That Exciting

NEW YORK—During a 12:30 luncheon with friends at Niko Niko Tuesday, Pamela Gordon, 27, described her recent date with 30-year-old stockbroker Ken Rosen. "Well, he's a *stockbroker*," Gordon said. "His name is Ken... He's really cute... And he was just promoted at Piper Jaffray!" Gordon's friends told reporters that she has not been this excited since she dated a producer in 2002.

Colombian Teen Going Through Anti-Government Guerilla Phase

BOGOTA, COLOMBIA—Like many Colombian teens, Juan Ardila, 15, is experiencing typical growing pains, characterized by mood swings, raging hormones, and a fervent allegiance to a squadron of leftist anti-government rebels, his 48-year-old father Rafael reported Monday. "I have told him that no good can come out of running with the Revolutionary Armed Forces of Colombia," the elder Ardila said. "But he'll snap out of it. When I was his age, I was kidnapping state officials and car-bombing nightclubs in the name of Communism myself." Ardila said he expects Juan to grow bored of drug trafficking and extortion when and if he reaches adulthood.

1998 Powerball Winner Returns To Food-Service Job

RAPID CITY, SD—In spite of winning an $18-million Powerball jackpot in 1998, William Berringer, 39, insisted on returning to his line-cook job at Nelson's Steak House Tuesday. "Winning all that money didn't change me," Berringer said. "I'm still the same Bill Berringer that I was before I hit the jackpot, then proceeded to spend it all on partying, bad stocks, and a Jamaican condominium." Berringer added that he hopes everyone at work will treat him the same way they always did, or at least the ones who were there when he quit his job the day after he won the jackpot. Ø

VAN from page 109

terrorism threatens the people of central Tennessee, Fox 11 is there first. Watch Channel 11 for up-to-the-minute coverage of where, when, and how the enemies of freedom are coming to get *you*."

Painted red, white, and blue, the TerrorFirst! van is the first mobile unit devoted to monitoring terrorist

A Fox 11 News promotional spot features footage of the van driving down Murfreesboro thoroughfares while flashing its trademark Terror Alert Warning Light, which informs Murfreesboro citizens of the current Homeland Security Advisory System terror-threat level. The images of the van are juxtaposed with grainy, black-and-white footage of a terrorist—actually WMFB production assistant Fred Fromme clad in a towel and bathrobe—lingering in doorways and back alleys.

threats on a local level. The van is equipped with live satellite feeds to and from the Fox News channel, a fax machine prepared to receive alerts from the Department of Homeland Security in Washington, an English-Arabic phrase book for translating any intercepted al-Qaeda correspondence, and a field-issue anthrax-detection kit.

"In a minute's notice, the van can be completely prepped, on the road, and speeding toward any site of terrorist activity within the WMFB broadcast area," Bogert said. "Assuming two attacks don't happen concurrently, of course."

According to Bogert, the TerrorFirst! van features a rooftop satellite dish, a diesel-powered generator in case terrorists take down the Tennessee power grid, emergency snow chains for use in the event of a nuclear winter, a supply of promotional "Fox 11 News...Looking Out For *You*" T-shirts and bumper stickers, and a gun rack. The van is outfitted

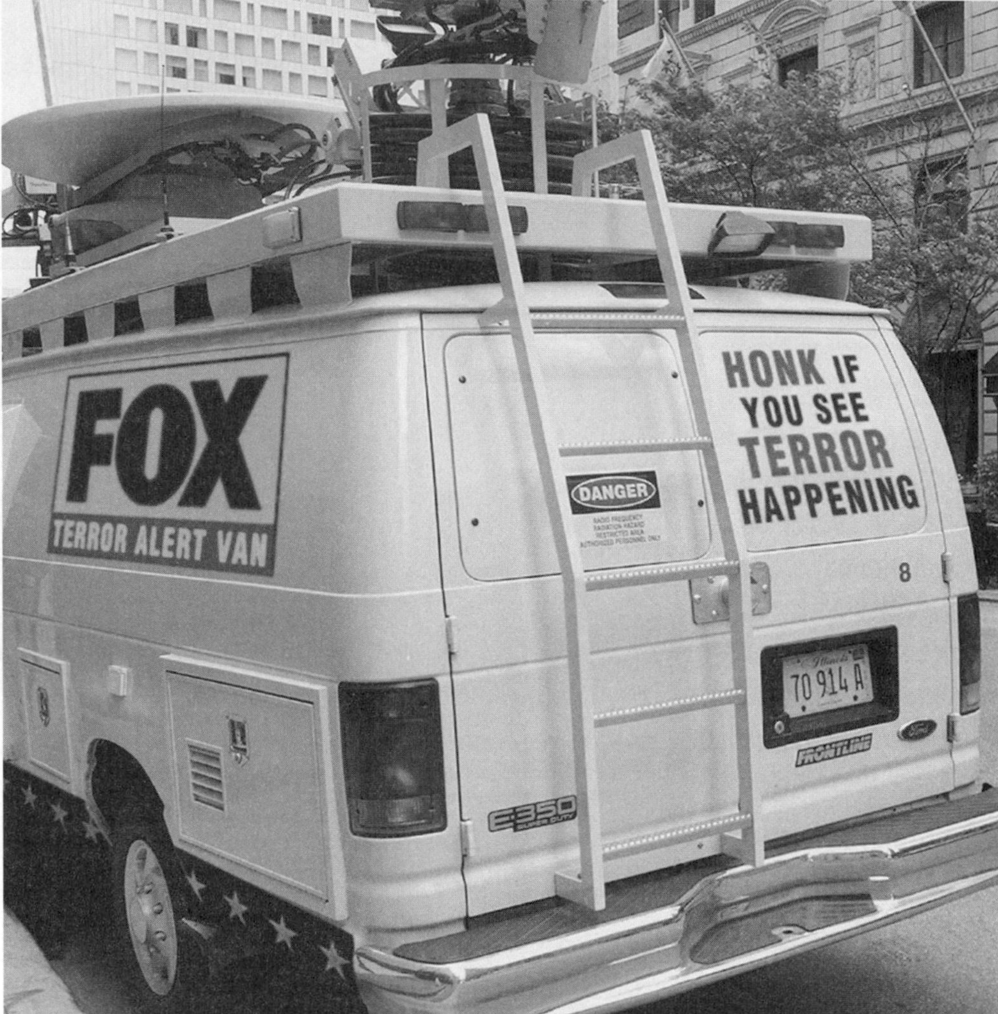

Above: The TerrorFirst! van patrols the streets.

with several state-of-the-art monitoring systems, as well.

"TerrorDoppler can detect a dirty-bomb detonation of any significant magnitude from up to 40 miles away," Bogert said. "The van can transmit a map of contaminated areas to the station for broadcast. That way, Fox 11 viewers gain valuable minutes—time which could be used to plan escape routes, call loved ones, and gather survival supplies."

A Fox 11 News promotional spot features footage of the van driving

The commercial ends with a message from Fox 11 anchor Bob Herlihy: "When terror strikes, don't get left behind. Stay ahead of the game with Fox 11."

down Murfreesboro thoroughfares while flashing its trademark Terror Alert Warning Light, which informs Murfreesboro citizens of the current Homeland Security Advisory System terror-threat level. The images of the van are juxtaposed with grainy, black-and-white footage of a terrorist—actually WMFB production assistant Fred Fromme clad in a towel and bathrobe—lingering in doorways and back alleys.

The commercial ends with a message from Fox 11 anchor Bob Herlihy: "When terror strikes, don't get left behind. Stay ahead of the game with Fox 11."

Although the only criminal activity the van has uncovered thus far was the illegal dumping of several quarts of used motor oil into the sewer, response from Fox 11 viewers has been overwhelmingly positive.

"When it comes to keeping me and my loved ones safe, Fox 11 is 'on the case!'" said Murfreesboro resident Ed Nelson, expressing his enthusiasm about the new van to a Channel 11 camera crew. "Seeing the Fox News terror-alert van parked in front of the credit union or driving through the Piggly Wiggly parking lot makes me feel secure."

Nelson, who will appear in an upcoming local Channel 11 advertisement, waved his index finger and

"In a minute's notice, the van can be completely prepped, on the road, and speeding toward any site of terrorist activity within the WMFB broadcast area," Bogert said.

added: "Fox 11 News is number one in central Tennessee!"

Bogert ended the conference with some tough words for terrorists.

"Terrorists better think twice before targeting the good citizens of the greater Murfreesboro area," Bogert said. "Terrorists, if you're watching, I have one thing to say to you: If you attack, the Fox 11 News team will be on the scene just minutes later."

Though Channel 11 currently has the only anti-terrorism news van in the country, plans are underway to use the concept at Fox affiliates nationwide. ⌀

REDFORD from page 109

very moment, two or more men are holding me captive within my office in order to further their profit-motivated agenda to strip my home of its valuable assets and leave me with nothing—perhaps not even my life."

"At this desperate hour, my hands are tied," the letter continued. "My office phone lines have been cut. By gnawing through my gag and inching my chair along the floor, I have been able to reach my computer, turn it on using my nose, and activate my ViaVoice speech-recognition typing software. However, my time is limited, and I have managed to successfully stick only one adhesive-backed, mass-mailing address label to an envelope. MICHAEL, it is not yet too late to prevent the extinction of noble, majestic Robert Redford, if only you act now!"

Sanborne received the legal-sized envelope, marked as "An Urgent Message From Robert Redford," on March 22, but put it aside to be opened along with his bills. The Marsing resident justified his delay, explaining that he did not initially notice that the envelope was rumpled as if by careless handling, and was scrawled over with the words "HELP ME," "DANGER," and "PLS CALL PLICE [sic]."

"Fellow Lover of Robert Redford: No one voted on Election Day to destroy the body, mind, and life of Robert Redford," the fourth page of the letter read. "But now, armed assailants are claiming a mandate to do exactly that! MICHAEL, please understand that without the natural resources Robert Redford requires to sustain himself, this noble creature will soon perish."

Sanborne, who speculated that Redford had penned the envelope's capital-letter pleas with a red magic marker held between his teeth, finally read the time-sensitive letter Monday.

Redford is the author of millions of urgent letters seeking support for the halt of oil drilling in the Alaskan Arctic National Wildlife Reserve. In his letter to Sanborne, however, his message of environmental preservation was replaced by one of Redfordian preservation.

Dear Fellow Lover of Robert Redford,

No one voted on Election Day to destroy the body, mind, and life of Robert Redford.

But now, the armed assailants who have handcuffed me and tied me to a chair in my office are claiming a mandate to do exactly that! MICHAEL, please understand that without the natural resources Robert Redford requires to sustain himself, this noble creature will soon perish.

I urge you to join this important campaign and make your own voice heard today by taking the following two steps:

FIRST: Come to my office and untie my hands and feet.

Above: The letter Redford (right) sent to Sanborne.

"Fellow Lover of Robert Redford: No one voted on Election Day to destroy the body, mind, and life of Robert Redford," the fourth page of the letter read. "But now, armed assailants are claiming a mandate to do exactly that! MICHAEL, please understand that without the natural resources Robert Redford requires to sustain himself, this noble creature will soon perish."

Sanborne, a 42-year-old contractor, said he is unsure why Redford chose to contact him in particular.

"I made a $40 donation to the Sierra Club in 1998," Sanborne said. "I must've wound up on some mailing list, because now I get a lot of letters with photos of polar bears and wolves on them," Sanborne said. "They all say 'urgent,' but I guess this one actually was."

"Too bad I'm probably too late to do anything," Sanborne added. "Otherwise, I might have gotten out my checkbook and sent him a few bucks."

Redford's urgent, unheeded letter ended: "If we let them plunder Robert Redford's home for the sake of profits, then no piece of our natural heritage is safe from destruction. Please—it will take you only a minute—go to 12 Ocean View Drive in Malibu and untie Robert Redford from his bonds, MICHAEL. Only through your efforts can we keep Robert Redford wild and free."

Redford, whom California authorities say has not been seen in public for the last three weeks, is presumed dead. ⌀

COMMUNITY VOICES

Who Are You Going To Believe—Me, Or That Encyclopedia Britannica 2005 Almanac?

I'm not saying I know everything, but there are a lot of things I do know. To have you, someone I consider a friend, doubt my word isn't just insulting, it's hurtful. So let me ask you again: When it comes to the natural resources, topography, and percentage of arable land in several West African countries, who are you gonna believe—me, or that *Encyclopedia Britannica Almanac 2005* with accompanying CD-ROM?

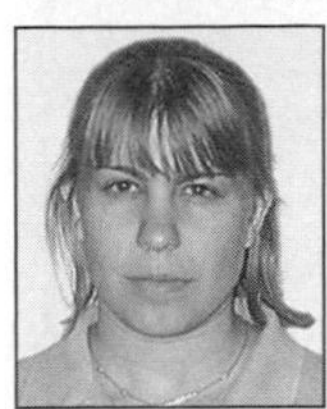
By Tamara Ingersol

Goddamn it, Kelly! Would I second-guess you if the topic were women's shoes? It is the same.

I mean, come on. You've known me for years. You've never even met editor Susana Darwin. Did you ever stop and wonder about her motivations? Did it even cross your mind that Susie D was paid to edit that book? I mean, put two and two together. Oh, is it ridiculous?

Okay look, let's sort this out. Will you grant that you and I are friends? Good. And do you think that friends tell each other the truth? Me too. So, look me in the eye and listen: The natural resources of Senegal are peanuts and matches.

Oh Jesus, what is it with you and that *Britannica*? Put it down! I mean, I could understand it if I had been wrong in the past, but I haven't. When I told you that you shouldn't go out with Jason, was I right? And when I told you that you would find a better job, what happened? Kelly, I don't just pull this stuff out of my ass. I was right about Jason and your job, and Dennis Rodman was the NBA Defensive Player of the Year in 1992.

Is it the CD-ROM? Is that what this is about? Well, I have a CD, too. In fact, I have about 200 of them. So do you still insist that Allen County in Kansas has a population of 13,907?

I don't care what it says on page 673. You can't believe everything you read. That's what I've been saying this whole time. Jesus.

Am I talking to a brick wall? Did some alien inhabit your body and eat your brain for food? I'm telling you, the population is 13,237. My source? Well, it wasn't some book I picked up off the street, I'll tell you that much.

I mean, come on. You've known me for years. You've never even met editor Susana Darwin. Did you ever stop and wonder about her motivations? Did it even cross your mind that Susie D was paid to edit that book? I mean, put two and two together. Oh, is it ridiculous? I guess you read that in your precious almanac.

If the precious *Encyclopedia Britannica Almanac 2005* with accompanying CD-ROM tells you that the principal cause of accidental death in Indiana is square dancing, are you going to believe it? Hey, guess what, I just read in your favorite book here that Chevy Novas run on grape soda. Isn't that interesting? Well, no, I didn't read that in there, but if I had, you would probably believe it.

Is this about my not returning those videos? It is, isn't it? You're mad I forgot to return your videos last week, and so now you're saying the Veterans Affairs office took in $59,832 in 2003.

I don't want to fight with you. But next time you need someone to take care of your cats, don't come a-knockin'. Cats were present in 14.3 percent of American households in 2004, by the way. ø

HOROSCOPES

Your Horoscope

By Lloyd Schumner Sr.
Retired Machinist and A.A.P.B.-Certified Astrologer

Aries: (March 21–April 19)
Your stance on the health-care crisis tends to be rather conservative, but for the next few months, it will be heavily influenced by the steel bar protruding from your ribs.

Taurus: (April 20–May 20)
Immortality of a sort is yours when your photo becomes one of the most resonant images of this century, with millions appreciating the late light, your beatific expression, and the butterflies fluttering in and out of your bullet wounds.

Gemini: (May 21–June 21)
You've always thought that your tendency to ask a lot of questions about the local culture was appreciated, but judging by the flames licking at your body and the tightness of the ropes, it seems you might have been mistaken.

Cancer: (June 22–July 22)
You've never been more internally conflicted than you'll be next Wednesday, when a choice of three desserts reveals what a shallow person you are.

Leo: (July 23–Aug. 22)
You don't seem to have as much energy and endurance as you used to—that is, if the little row of charge-indicator LEDs on your chest can be trusted.

Virgo: (Aug. 23–Sept. 22)
Even if you can't help your snoring, you should do more to respect the anger of the rest of the Chicago Philharmonic.

Libra: (Sept. 23–Oct. 23)
Modern design continues to exert too much influence on your life, as you'll soon be available in six hot new colors, in addition to classic brushed aluminum.

Scorpio: (Oct. 24–Nov. 21)
Hope can sustain a person through excruciating personal trials, but unfortunately, there's no real reason to believe that the new *Star Wars* movie will be tolerable.

Sagittarius: (Nov. 22–Dec. 21)
You never thought you feared change all that much, but that's before the temperature started varying by about 100 degrees Fahrenheit every minute or so.

Capricorn: (Dec. 22–Jan. 19)
The quite understandable fear of conquering hive-minds will grow to a fever pitch this week when it's revealed that one in five Americans is a component of you.

Aquarius: (Jan. 20–Feb. 18)
Your idea was brilliantly executed, but even in today's instant-gratification culture, you won't sell more than a few dozen copies of *Learn Rock Guitar In 45 Seconds.*

Pisces: (Feb. 19–March 20)
The stars forecast a great deal of upheaval and turmoil in your future, especially if you do not return their frickin' celestial hedge trimmer *tout de suite.*

EXCHANGE from page 111

places. He's wears the same maroon, button-up shirt every day and it totally smells like B.O. I don't know how his host family deals. I would puke."

According to freshman entomology enthusiast Ty Crandall, Bohm knows very little about his homeland.

"I was stuck being Uwe's lab partner once, so I said, 'You must know a lot about bark beetles,'" Crandall said. "He said, 'Nein, I do not know about bark beetles.' I was like, 'What? Bark beetles are a huge problem in the Bavarian Forest!' God, where did they get this guy?"

According to Bohm's host father Dick Marshall, Bohm is no more popular when the school day's over.

"Last fall, Uwe spent hours searching German-language websites for World Cup soccer news while the family watched NFL games on the big-screen TV in the living room," said Marshall, who will be hosting Bohm for three more months. "We were very eager to take Uwe in, but his total lack of interest in American culture is unfathomable. We tried to teach him about the Chicago Bears, but he couldn't care less. [Marshall's sons] Brian and Patrick have nothing to talk about with him."

"Summit Prairie may be a public school, but that doesn't mean we should take just anyone."

Seward said he is looking forward to returning Bohm in July.

"In the future, I'll insist that AFS scrutinize prospective foreign-exchange candidates more closely," Seward said. "If they won't do that, I won't do business with them. It's that simple."

Seward added: "Summit Prairie may be a public school, but that doesn't mean we should take just anyone."

Knutson's reception in Germany could not be more different from Bohm's. Although her command of German is shaky, her life is a whirlwind of parties, shopping, and recreational retreats.

"Not only do a lot [of the German students] speak great English, but they know way more about USA history than I do!!!" Knutson wrote from a Freiburg Internet cafe. "If Uwe is as excited about USA as his old friends, he should B having a blast!! BTW, tell Uwe that Klaus and Lukas say hi and sorry they haven't e-mailed U lately! P.S. Fryberg has a McDonalds!!!!!" ø

the ONION®

VOLUME 41 ISSUE 15 AMERICA'S FINEST NEWS SOURCE™ 14–20 APRIL 2005

NEWS

DEA Seizes Half-Built Suspension Bridge From Bogotá To Miami

see WORLD page 8D

Inside: Spring Fashions So Glamorous You'll Practically Shit Yourself

see STYLE page 1E

Bystander Stops To Watch Incompetent Parallel-Park Job

see PEOPLE page 11G

STATshot

A look at the numbers that shape your world.

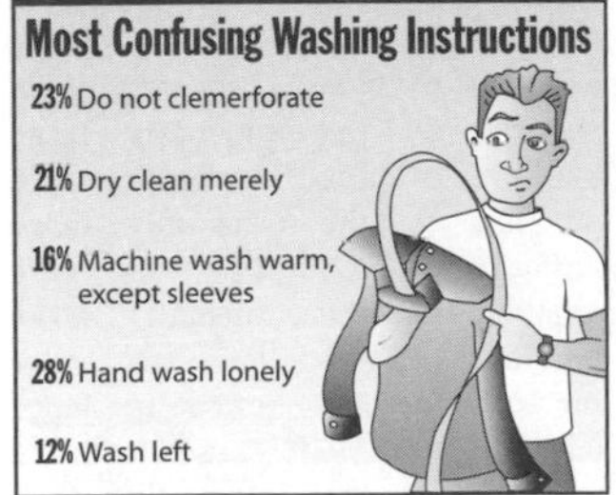

Most Confusing Washing Instructions
23% Do not clemerforate
21% Dry clean merely
16% Machine wash warm, except sleeves
28% Hand wash lonely
12% Wash left

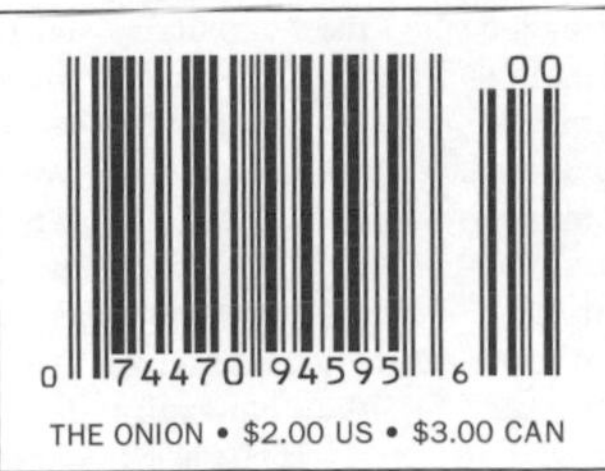

Heaven Less Opulent Than Vatican, Reports Disappointed Pope

HEAVEN—The soul of Pope John Paul, which entered heaven last week following a long illness, expressed confusion and disappointment Saturday, upon learning that the Celestial Kingdom of God to which the departed faithful ascend in the afterlife is significantly less luxurious than the Vatican's Papal Palace, in which the pope spent the past 26 years of his earthly life.

"Where are all the marble statues, sterling-silver chalices, and gem-encrusted scepters?" the visibly disappointed pope asked. "Where are the 60-foot-tall stained-glass windows and hand-painted cupolas? Where are the elaborately outfitted ranks of Swiss Guards? Why isn't every single surface gilded? *This* is my eternal reward?"

Heaven, according to the New Testa-

see POPE page 119

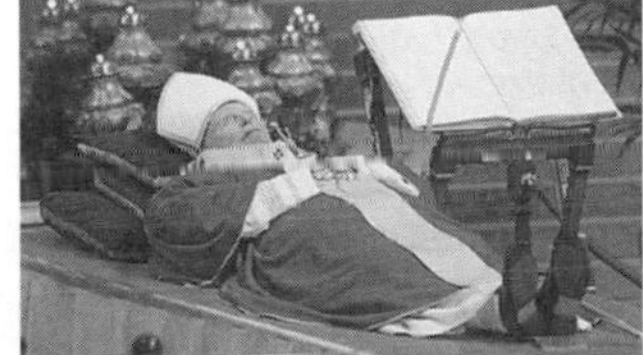

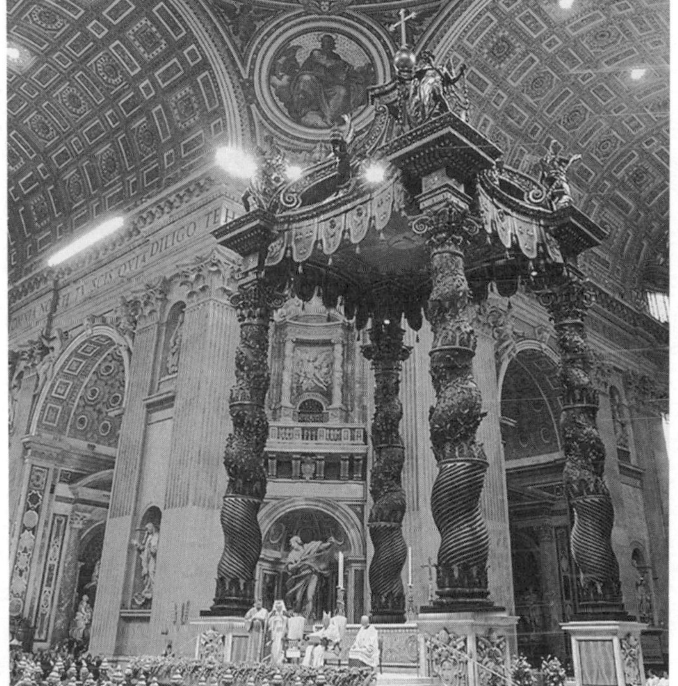

Above: St. Peter's Basilica, with its 90-foot bronze baldachin designed by Bernini, is one of the many Vatican splendors no longer enjoyed by Pope John Paul II (left).

French's Introduces Antibacterial Mustard

ROCHESTER, NY—In response to increasing American demand for tangier, more hygienic meals, condiment giant French's has introduced a new antibacterial mustard.

"Each year, 15 million cases of bacterial food poisoning originate in U.S. home kitchens, resulting in nausea, diarrhea, fever, and even death," read

see MUSTARD page 119

Report:

Cost Of Living Now Outweighs Benefits

WASHINGTON, DC—A report released Monday by the Federal Consumer Quality-Of-Life Control Board indicates that the cost of living now outstrips life's benefits for many Americans.

American LIVING

"This is sobering news," said study director Jack Farness. "For the first time, we have statistical evidence of what we've suspected for the past 40 years: Life really isn't worth living."

To arrive at their conclusions, study directors first identified the average yearly costs and benefits of life.

see LIVING page 118

Embattled Tom Delay

In recent weeks, House Majority Leader Tom DeLay has come under increasing fire from a number of important media and political figures. What do *you* think?

Colleen Bowers
Systems Analyst

"I heard Tom DeLay's blood was in the water and the sharks were circling him, but unfortunately, it turned out to be a metaphor."

Don Figueroa
Tile Setter

"There's a big difference between the letter of the law and the spirit of the law. Sure, he broke both, but there's a big difference."

Andre Carson
Teller

"Enough is enough. DeLay should do the honorable thing: take all the money he's cheated out of the American people, buy himself a nice mansion, and retire."

James Henson
Graphic Designer

"Tom DeLay is an inspiration. His example has given me hope that my ethics violations will go ignored for years, as well."

Zachary Hardin
Therapist

"Oh, come on. Like nobody in Congress has ever built a career out of borderline-illegal financial impropriety before. Grow up."

Tanya Wilkinson
Lab Assistant

"I'm telling you, if Tom DeLay would come out and say, 'Screw it, I'm just in it for the cash and the bitches,' his popularity would skyrocket. At the very least, he'd be in a Kid Rock video."

The Minutemen

A group of volunteers calling themselves the Minutemen began standing sentry on the U.S. side of the Arizona-Mexico border last week to watch for illegal immigrants and smugglers. How are they safeguarding the country?

- Putting live jumper cables into Rio Grande every 20 minutes
- Getting can-coolers printed up
- Picking good code names, like Angry Jackal, Freedom Fighting Hardcore 2005, and MastaPatrolla
- Fighting fire with fire by working for nothing, just like immigrants they are hunting
- Building cautionary piñata-destroying bonfires every couple miles
- Allowing each Minuteman one kill a day, or six kills and a doe permit for groups of five

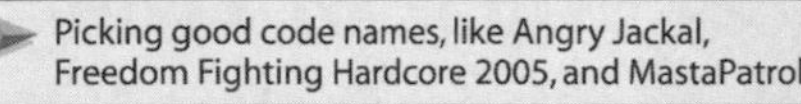

- Hank patrols Monday; Don on Tuesday; Don, Chuck, and Mitch on Wednesday; Hank, Don, and Mitch on Thursday; Chuck, Don, and Rhonda on Friday; and everybody on Saturday—except Hank, who still hates Chuck for shooting his dog
- Providing unappealing example of what Americans are like, in order to discourage people from wanting to come here

the ONION®
America's Finest News Source.™

Herman Ulysses Zweibel
Founder

T. Herman Zweibel
Publisher Emeritus
J. Phineas Zweibel
Publisher
Maxwell Prescott Zweibel
Editor-In-Chief

I'm Not Locked Into This 5.75% 30-Year F.R.M. With You—You're Locked Into This 5.75% 30-Year F.R.M. With Me

And all I have to do is to sign on the dotted line... and initial there... and there... and there. What? Oh, right. I forgot to sign there. No problem. This pen still has plenty of ink. There! All finished.

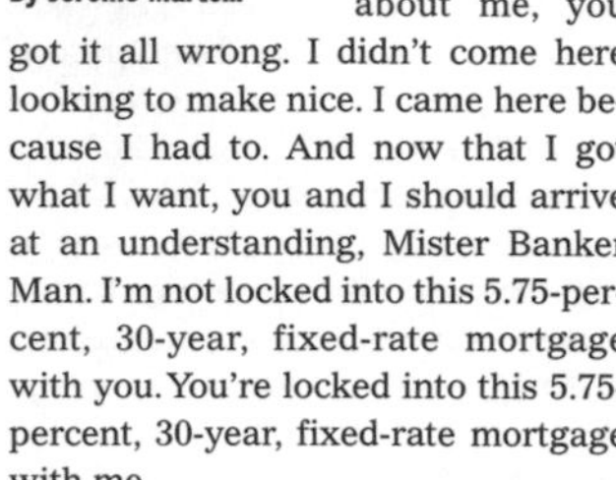

By Jerome Martelli

Now that that's all squared away, there's something you should know. Whatever you thought about me, you got it all wrong. I didn't come here looking to make nice. I came here because I had to. And now that I got what I want, you and I should arrive at an understanding, Mister Banker Man. I'm not locked into this 5.75-percent, 30-year, fixed-rate mortgage with you. You're locked into this 5.75-percent, 30-year, fixed-rate mortgage with me.

You might think that just because you're lending me money to buy my first home, I'm gonna kiss your ass and play toady to some underwriter. Think again, pencil pusher.

I'm not like those other loan applicants that sit at your feet, sniveling and begging for money. I'm *loco*. I don't give a fuck. Look into my eyes and tell me what you see. Yeah, I'm one crazy, money-borrowing son of a bitch.

You want to test me? Huh? Try coming at me with some sort of acceleration clause. I'll lose my shirt and get all up in your bank's face.

This contract here? Means nothing to me. Nothing. Some months, I might refuse to pay you the sums that were agreed upon in the terms of the loan. Other months, I might pay five times the amount due. Sometimes, I'll race in 30 seconds before the bank closes and make my payment all in one-dollar bills. Yeah, this little borrower is a problem you're going to be dealing with long after closing. Thirty years, to be exact, assuming I don't flip out and *default* on that loan.

A guy would have to be crazy to try something like that, is that what you're thinking? Brother, I'm your worst nightmare. Sure, I have a job that pays well right now. You know that—you verified my employment history. But who's to say I'm going to have that job next year, next month, or next week? Hey, I might not even have it tomorrow. In fact, I'm feeling like I might just call my boss and tell him off right now. Can I borrow your phone? No problem. I have my cell.

Psyche! See, you've gotta be on your toes around me. How can I take you seriously if you frighten that easily?

Hey, nice try. Amortization! Ah, I didn't just fall off the turnip truck. My payments are just where I want them. I didn't walk into this situation blind. Let me explain something to you, hopefully for the very last time, because I am this close to going off the deep end and refinancing this loan.

You think I'm jerking you around? You keep flapping your lips about a second appraisal of the property, and you'll see some real jerking around, Pedro.

I'm gonna back out of this office real nice and quiet, and we're both gonna make believe this little meeting never took place. Just remember, though, I'm watching you. If I see one black mark on my credit report—if my score dips a single point below 700—I'm coming down on you harder than a ton of bricks. ⊘

TERRORISTS from page 24

amounts of blood. Passersby were amazed by the unusually large amounts of blood. Passersby were amazed by the unusually large amounts of blood. Passersby were

Your mama is so fat she is at risk for diabetes, high blood pressure and other obesity-related complications.

amazed by the unusually large amounts of blood. Passersby were amazed by the unusually large amounts of blood. Passersby were amazed by the unusually large amounts of blood. Passersby were amazed by the unusually large amounts of blood. Passersby were amazed by the unusually large amounts of blood. Passersby were amazed by the unusually large amounts of blood. Passersby were amazed by the unusually large amounts of blood. Passersby were amazed by the unusually large amounts of blood. Passersby were amazed by the unusually large amounts of blood. Passersby were amazed by the unusually large amounts of blood. Passersby were amazed by the unusually large amounts of blood. Passersby were amazed by the unusually large amounts of blood. Passersby were amazed by the unusually large amounts of blood. Passersby were amazed by the unusually large

see TERRORISTS page 66

Inner-City Community Bands Together To Find Missing Parent

DETROIT—In a heartwarming display of community feeling, members of the Delray neighborhood in southwest Detroit have banded together to find Milo Patterson, 38, the latest parent to vanish in the string of mysterious abductions that has plagued the area.

Patterson, an avid sports fan and a father of three who had recently enrolled in an auto-mechanic training program, disappeared April 3, shortly after a disagreement with his wife Janine. He is 5'8", of medium build, and was last seen wearing a Tommy Hilfiger windbreaker, jeans, and tan work boots. He has a tattoo of the Michelin Man on his left bicep.

"We have no idea if Milo was abducted, or if he's lying hurt somewhere," Williams said. "All we know is that he disappeared without one word to his kids, his wife, or his boss down at Speedy Lube."

"Whatever is going on, it's terrifying," said Clarissa Williams, who lives in the same housing complex as the missing father and has made her apartment a home base for the building's search efforts. "It couldn't be a worse time for this tragedy. Milo's got kids, a girlfriend he mighta knocked up, and from what I've been hearing, he owes money to just about everybody."

"We have no idea if Milo was abducted, or if he's lying hurt somewhere," Williams said. "All we know is that he disappeared without one word to his kids, his wife, or his boss down at Speedy Lube."

Williams said she has spent the past week collecting recent photos of Patterson and covering the area between Fort Street and the Detroit River with

see COMMUNITY page 119

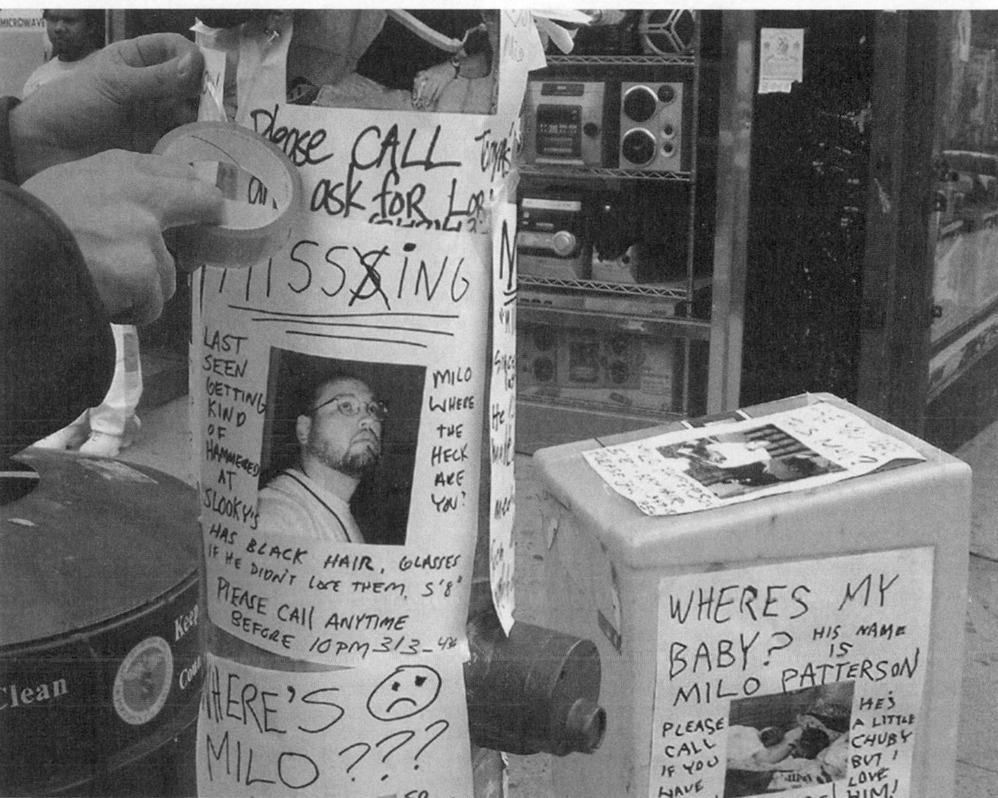

Above: A local resident posts a sign in hopes someone has seen Patterson (above left).

NEWS IN BRIEF

Pope John Paul II, Longtime Owner Of Popemobile, Dead At 84

VATICAN CITY—Pope John Paul II, who owned the Popemobile for more than a quarter of a century, passed away last Saturday. "The Popemobile was known the world over," said Peter Egan, a writer for *Road & Track*. "A fine example of European craftsmanship, the hand-built, 4.3 litre, V-8 powered, pearl-gray vehicle was exceptionally well-loved, even more so after the bullet-proof bubble was added in 1981 to safeguard its passengers against assassination attempts. During the time he owned the Popemobile, John Paul II visited more than 120 countries. He loved the open road." The specially altered Mercedes-Benz ML-series off-road vehicle has been maintained by papal staff since the pope fell ill in August 2004. The pope's will is expected to grant its use to either the next pope or John Paul II's young cousin Zbigniew.

Pope-Killing Virus Claims Yet Another Victim

ROME—Doctors at Italy's prestigious Center for Papal Disease Control announced last week that the infamous Pope-Killing Virus has claimed the life of yet another pontiff. The latest victim, a Polish immigrant identified by authorities as His Holiness John Paul II, is the third pope to fall prey to the virus in as many decades. "The tragic fact remains that, at this time, scientists know almost nothing about this terrible disease that attacks the nerve center of global Catholicism, and we are baffled as to how to fight its spread," CPDC head Dr. Emilio Caminioni said. "How many popes must die before a cure can be found? Can a viable treatment be discovered before another victim is claimed? These questions remain unanswered." According to Caminioni, the deadly virus has claimed the lives of 265 people over the past 20 centuries.

Papal Apartments Found Filled With Old Newspapers, Empty Pill Bottles, Mangy Cats

VATICAN CITY—Housekeeping staff at the Vatican's Apostolic Palace, the official papal residence, were shocked to discover stacks of yellowing newspapers, empty medication bottles, and at least two dozen cats in Pope John Paul II's private apartments this weekend. "We had a very hard time opening the door, and when we finally forced it open, we couldn't believe what we found," maid Giulietta Barricelli said. "Mangy, mewing cats perched atop stacks of newspapers dating back nearly 25 years, plates caked with mold, balled-up Kleenexes everywhere, and cat feces on the carpet. I don't know how the Holy Father, God rest his soul, lived in that horrible, stinking mess." Papal historians claim that some popes develop aberrant pack-rat tendencies late in life, citing Pope Pius XII, who hoarded tin foil and back issues of *Catholic Digest*. ∅

LIVING from page 115

Tangible benefits such as median income ($43,000) were weighed against such tangible costs as home-ownership ($18,000). Next, scientists assigned a financial value to intangibles such as finding inner peace ($15,000), establishing emotional closeness with family members ($3,000), and brief moments of joy ($5 each). Taken together, the study results indicate that "it is unwise to go on living."

"Since 1965, the cost-benefit ratio of American life has been approaching parity," Farness said. "While figures prior to that date show that life was worth living, there is some suspicion that the benefits cited were superficial and misreported."

Analyzed separately and as one, both the tangible and intangible factors suggest that life is a losing investment.

"Rising energy costs, increased prices on everyday goods and services, and the decreased value of the dollar have combined to drive the cost of living in this country to an all-time high," Farness said. "At the same time, an ever-increasing need for additional emotional-energy output, low rates of interest in one another, and the decreasing value of ourselves all greatly exceed our fleeting epiphanies."

Experts nationwide have corroborated the report's findings.

"The average citizen's lousy, smelly, uncomfortable daily-transportation costs rose 2.1 percent in January," Derek Capeletti of Wells Fargo Capital Management said. "Clothing costs were up 2.3 percent, reflecting an increased need for the pleated khakis, sensible sweater-sets, and solid ties we have to wear to our awful fucking jobs. And grocery expenses were up almost 4 percent, reflecting the difficulty that light-beer, microwave-burrito, and rotisserie-chicken makers have faced in meeting the needs of a depressed economy and citizenry."

Capeletti added: "The benefits of living remained stable or decreased. Especially—surprise, surprise—in our love lives."

According to the study, high-risk, short-term, interest-based investments in the lives of others cost thousands of dollars a year and rarely yield benefits, financial or otherwise. Although conservative, long-term partnerships do provide limited returns, the study indicates that they tie up capital and limit options.

Child-rearing, a course taken by many people who choose to live, is actually contributing to the problem.

"The fact is, the supply of Americans greatly outstrips demand," said Evan Alvi of the Portland-based Maynard Institute. "Americans seem to believe that minting more lives will increase the value of their own holdings. All they are doing, though, is inflating the supply and reducing the dividends paid by long-term familial bonds."

Despite life's depreciating value, Alvi did not recommend that shareholders divest themselves of their holdings.

"Limited dumping could result in a short-term increase in available resources for those who remain in the market," Alvi said. "However, it's a risky move that could affect perception of value, leading to mass divesture."

Alvi added, "And let's not fail to mention that some religious experts say there are penalties for early withdrawal."

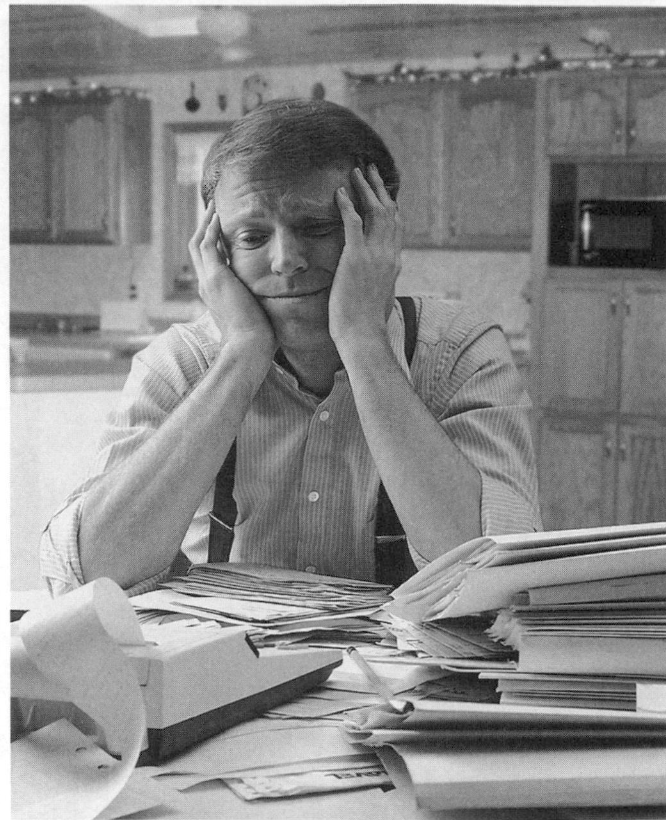

Above: Gulfport, MS resident Stan Holiday weighs the cost of living against life's benefits.

the ONION presents:

Preparing A Living Will

A living will is a legal document that provides directives for your medical care in the event that you are physically unable to express them. Here are some things to keep in mind while creating a living will:

- It's important to have a lawyer present when you draft a living will, as it makes the desire to be dead that much more tangible.
- Specify which flavor of feeding-tube nutrient you prefer. Otherwise, you may get stuck with cream of mushroom day in and day out.
- If, in the event of a catastrophic brain injury, you wish to be taken off life support and kept out of the guardianship of your overprotective Catholic parents, underline those directives over and over with a thick red pen and then highlight them in bright yellow.
- Leave at least one reasonably flattering photo for the press. This point cannot be emphasized enough.
- Explain in no uncertain terms that, should you die and return as a zombie, loved ones must shoot you in the head without hesitation.
- Research medical life-support technology and specify whether you'd prefer to be hooked up to a Danninger Continuous Passive Motion device, an Emerson suction unit, or a Slushee machine.
- Comatose people have been shown to exhibit a brainstem-level response to music, so prepare a decade's worth of mix tapes in advance.
- A living will is a great way to meet a notary public, if notaries public are your thing.
- A health-care agent is the person assigned to make your medical decisions in the event you are unable to. A talented, aggressive health-care agent will score you the absolute best medical care available, but will charge you a 15- to 20-percent commission.
- Telling your friends while you're drunk that it would suck to be on life support doesn't constitute a living will. Make sure to write it on the back of a coaster.
- Don't underestimate how quickly your family, including your beloved wife and two cherubic children, will tire of the burden you will become.

POPE from page 115

Above: An artist's depiction of a disappointingly austere heaven.

ment, has "brilliance like a very costly stone... of pure gold, like clear glass..." with "twelve gates... each gate a single pearl." Yet the pope, who spoke from the afterlife, said heaven is nothing like the "solid-gold city" detailed at length by John of Patmos in the Book of Revelations.

"Evidently, the Bible was not intended to be taken literally, after all," John Paul II said. "Don't get me wrong: It's very nice up here—quite beautiful and serene. It's just not as fancy as what I'm accustomed to. If I'd known heaven was going to be like this, I would've taken one last tour through my 50 rooms of velvet-draped thrones and priceless oil paintings before saying 'Amen' and breathing my last."

According to the pope, heaven is merely a place of unending peace and happiness, wherein all the spirits of the Elect live together forever in perfect harmony and goodness, basking in the rays of God's divine love.

"Up here, everyone is equal," John Paul II said. "No one has to go through an elaborate bowing ritual when they greet me. And do you know how many times my ring has been kissed since I arrived? None. Up here, I'm mingling with tax collectors, fishermen, and whores. It's just going to take a little getting used to, is all."

The pope said it is amusing to think that he has been waiting for this "so-called Paradise" his entire life.

"I spent almost 84 years reciting novenas and Hail Marys to get to this restful place," John Paul II said. "If I'd wanted peace, quiet, and pretty clouds, I could've moved to the Italian Riviera. Frankly, this afterlife represents a significant drop in my standard of living."

"Well, they always said you can't take it with you," he added. ⌀

The pope, who spoke from the afterlife, said heaven is nothing like the "solid-gold city" detailed at length by John of Patmos in the Book of Revelations.

MUSTARD from page 115

a press release French's issued Monday. "Now, lunch doesn't have to endanger your health! All-new French's Antibacterial Mustard is the perfect way to add flavor to, and subtract harmful disease-causing bacteria from, your family's favorite meals!"

According to French's representative Darla Nelson, the new hypoallergenic mustard complements the company's expanding line—which includes French's Honey Dijon Mustard and French's Sweet & Tangy Honey Mustard—and kills over 99.99% of harmful germs.

The mustard is orange in color, more translucent than the traditional varieties, and is somewhat medicinal in flavor. In product trials performed by French's, mothers preferred antibacterial mustard five to one when informed of its sterilizing properties.

A television commercial for the mustard plays up its prominent role in luncheon sanitization.

"Approximately 9,000 deaths per year are attributed to foodborne pathogens, and the most germ-filled location in the house is the kitchen," a woman says as computer-generated footage zooms in to show worm-like spirochete bacteria multiplying on a slice of bologna. "Normal mustards do nothing to combat the germs that begin forming on meats and cheeses as soon as they're taken out of the refrigerator. But an hour after spreading on our powerful French's Antibacterial Mustard, your lunch is still free of everything but zesty mustard taste!"

Nelson said consumers are increasingly concerned with the lack of germicidal properties in old-fashioned, non-antibacterial condiments.

"When I used to spread old-style mustard on my children's hot dogs, I never knew what sort of bugs were breeding between the buns," said a woman quoted on French's website. "For all I know, microorganisms were actually feeding off the condiments I was squirting on my family's meat. But now that I use French's Antibacterial, I'm reassured by the mustard's bright orange sheen, unique tanginess, and the little foaming bubbles that show it's working. That's a mustard we all can live with."

Not everyone is in favor of the new product. Lloyd Cummings, a toppings expert at the Institute for Public Health, said French's Antibacterial poses more health and taste hazards than it solves.

The mustard is orange in color, more translucent than the traditional varieties, and is somewhat medicinal in flavor.

"We're going to see many American sandwich-makers using these powerful mustards, because the condiments have been marketed as an effective way to lower the risk of infection," Cummings said. "But widespread antibacterial sandwich-spread use will likely result in the formation of a strain of ham- and cheese-originated, drug-resistant bacteria. These 'super-lunchbugs' will be more deadly than any bacteria we see today. For lunches prepared or packed for healthy family members, regular household mustard is strong enough. And it tastes a lot less like iodine."

In spite of such warnings, Nelson said all French's mustards will eventually contain triclosan, the most trusted antibacterial agent used in hospitals today, and that the company is currently working on three new germ-fighting sauces: Cattlemen's Kansas City Antibiotic BBQ Sauce, Frank's RedHot Hot Sauce with Hydrogen Peroxide, and French's Worcestershire-Neosporin Sauce. ⌀

COMMUNITY from page 117

"missing parent" signs.

"Milo, wherever you are, don't worry!" Williams said. "We'll find you."

At an organizational meeting held Tuesday at the Christ the Redeemer Church, volunteers divided themselves into three search parties and began combing the neighborhood for clues.

"First place we checked was the Velvet Room over on Sunset," said longtime Delray resident Alfredrick Brussard. "But the bartender said he hadn't seen Milo all week. Then we went over to the Checker Bar & Grill, where he likes to go for happy hour, and his friend Art's apartment, where he watches the games."

"We also sent a search party down to the Freddy's Towing parking lot and around by those picnic tables in Lincoln Park," Brussard continued. "Well, there wasn't any trace of him anywhere. It's like he vanished into thin air."

Patterson's wife Janine Ordonez explained that, before alerting police to the case, she made sure that he was really missing.

"Lord Jesus, my baby's *gone*," Ordonez said.

"I'm used to him disappearing now and again for a spell," said Ordonez, tears welling up in her eyes. "But when my payday came around and he didn't even show up, I said, 'Lord Jesus, my baby's *gone*.'"

Neighborhood resident Clive Delapaz said he and friends held a Friday candlelight prayer vigil for the missing man.

"It's important not to lose hope," Delapaz said. "God works in mysterious ways, and Milo's disappearance is all a part of His plan. We must have faith."

Hardware-store clerk Moses Mitchell, 58, led Monday's second-shift search party.

"In an emergency situation, it's important not to panic," Mitchell said. "I told everyone to stay calm. Especially Milo's mother—she was fixing to move in with him and Janine."

Detroit police officer Aubrayo Venzetti said the 4th Precinct has been working around the clock to find Patterson.

"We're doing everything we can to find this man," Venzetti said. "We've contacted federal authorities, but they seem reluctant to send additional assistance. Surprisingly, even local TV and radio stations have been slow to get involved."

As they wait for help, local community members continue their efforts. Tedaryl Kudrow, who owns a liquor store frequented by the missing man, has placed Patterson's photo on the front of his cash register.

"I'm doing what I can, and that's not just 'cause Milo was a good customer," Kudrow said. "Sad thing is, abductees are not the only victims in an abduction. What will happen to the children these kidnappers have left fatherless? For the sake of those kids, we have got to find Milo."

Patterson is the 53rd adult to go missing in the Delray neighborhood this year. ⌀

COMMUNITY VOICES

I Gotta Get Out More Often

Hola, amigos. What do you hear? I know it's been a long time since I rapped at ya, but I been dragging my ass through the routine. The winter always gets me down. Don't tell me how it's spring. I know it's spring, but that makes it worse. It gets warm for a few days, I think I finally broke on through to the other side, and then it snows and I feel like shit again. Plus, my alternator belt is squeaking. I got a new one, but I haven't changed it yet because who wants to do car repairs when it's nice out?

The Cruise
By Jim Anchower

It seems like all I do lately is go to work and then come home and watch TV—which is fine by me. It's exactly what I was up for last Friday. I was planning to kick my weekend off by packing a bowl and watching *Dude, Where's My Car?* again. I was already walking out to my car when Ron came up and asked me to get a beer. It was kind of a big deal, since we really haven't really hung out since he started being my boss, so I told him I was going home to get high and watch *Dude, Where's My Car?*, but he was welcome to stop by.

Ron said that would be cool, but he had to go meet Rob first. It was only 5:30, so I told him I'd watch some TV and hang, and we could start the movie when he got over. I picked up a case of beer and kicked back with *Eight Simple Rules*, *JAG*, and a *20/20* episode about some guy that killed his wife for the insurance money.

But so, it's 10:00 p.m. by now, and I'm sitting at my house with no Ron. I was a little pissed off and a lot baked. Here I was, making an effort to not watch *Dude, Where's My Car?*, and Ron was taking his own sweet. I wouldn't have minded so much if he'd showed up at 9:00 or something, or if he'd let me know he was going to be late when we made plans. But I was six beers in and two bowls out, and there was no way I was going to watch the news. I watched *Everybody Loves Raymond* until I couldn't take it anymore, and then I put in the tape.

Before Chester even said "Where's your car, dude?" Ron came in. He didn't knock, which would have been fine if I wasn't already irked and if he hadn't brought some other people over with him. It was Ron, his friend Rob, and two chicks. Now, I'm a hospitable guy, but I like to know when company is coming—especially women—so I can pick the paper plates up off the floor and stuff.

Ron didn't seem to notice I was pissed—partly because he's that way and partly because he was half pickled. He told me the two ladies were Debbie and Helen from The Gamey Doe, and that they wanted to watch the movie, too. I told Ron it was fine, which I suppose it was, considering everything else.

In my house, the rule is that people can help themselves to beer, but since these girls were strangers, I decide to be a good host and ask if anyone wanted a beer while I was getting myself another one. Everyone did—surprise—so I got up from the couch. I told them they could pack the bowl and start it around if they wanted, which, of course, they did.

Finally, the women quit talking. Me and Rob were laughing at the movie, but I didn't hear anything from Ron or the girls for awhile. I finally looked over and saw that one was quiet because she was passed out. The other one was quiet because Ron was making out with her.

When I got back, they'd taken up my whole couch, with the chicks in the middle and Ron and Rob on either end. I handed everybody a beer and pulled up a footstool to enjoy the movie, but it was hard to do that, because I didn't have anything to lean back on and the women were gabbing through some of the best parts. I didn't say anything about it, since they were guests and all, but those two really liked to talk.

Finally, the women quit talking. Me and Rob were laughing at the movie, but I didn't hear anything from Ron or the girls for awhile. I finally looked over and saw that one was quiet because she was passed out. The other one was quiet because Ron was making out with her. That's another thing right there. I don't begrudge Ron getting himself some, but if he was going to do it at my house, he should've brought a friend for me.

I tried to pay attention to the movie, but that got harder to do when I started hearing what could only be the sound of Ron getting the stinky pinky. Talk about no class! If you're going to finger-bang a girl, you should at least take her to the bathroom. I guess it's a good thing he didn't, though, because the other one suddenly came to and started to ask where the bathroom was—but she didn't get it all out before she started puking.

Fortunately, Rob steered her into the bathroom before the worst of it. That didn't mean I was free and clear, though. She managed to get a pile on my carpet, and from the looks of it, she'd had a few dozen "quarter wings" at The Gamey Doe. I threw some old shopping circulars down on the puke to soak up the worst of it, and Ron and the girl stopped doing what they were doing long enough for the girl to check on her friend. When the girls came out of the bathroom, they said they'd better go home. Ron was saying the sick one, who I finally figured out was Debbie, could just crash on my bed, but Helen, the finger-banged one, said they should go. She promised to meet up with Ron again some other night.

Once the girls left, the night was all right. Ron and Rob weren't going anywhere so long as there was still cold beer, which there was. Plus, Ron had *Freddy Vs. Jason* in his car, so we watched that after *Dude, Where's My Car?* The next day, the puke was dried up enough so I could just sweep it up. Just because the night wound up all right don't mean I'm looking to repeat it anytime soon. I should keep people out of my apartment unless I know they're cool. I don't much like cleaning up the puke of someone I don't even know. But I guess I need to get out of the house unless I want to sit here alone. I definitely will as soon as it warms up more. This "being a shut-in" stuff sorta sucks. Ø

HOROSCOPES

Your Horoscope

By Lloyd Schumner Sr.
Retired Machinist and
A.A.P.B.-Certified Astrologer

Aries: (March 21–April 19)
Some days you get the bear, and some days the bear gets you, but not a day goes by that you don't regret becoming a professor of Ursine Studies.

Taurus: (April 20–May 20)
A nutty mix-up during your elopement will see you going to the wrong house and abducting the wrong man, but luckily you'll be a hell of a lot happier with him.

Gemini: (May 21–June 21)
Your efforts to write the perfect trucker ballad will be hampered by the jealous ghost of Nashville star Dave Dudley, who keeps spiking your beer.

Cancer: (June 22–July 22)
You'll feel dishonored and shunned when thousands of mourners pass by your dead body on their way to honor the pope.

Leo: (July 23–Aug. 22)
Three extremely important events will mark your last days on earth: First, you find out you can buy uranium over the Internet. The second and third pretty much follow as the night follows the day.

Virgo: (Aug. 23–Sept. 22)
You'll question your wisdom in hiring such a fanatical personal trainer, but you must admit that those who manage to escape his diabolical Maze Of Fitness Or Death emerge looking pretty damn buff.

Libra: (Sept. 23–Oct. 23)
You know you're not the first person to experience identity problems, but it's still jarring to realize that you're a woman trapped in a rotting musk ox's body.

Scorpio: (Oct. 24–Nov. 21)
You've heard a lot of rational-sounding arguments in favor of drug legalization, but you'll be damned if you can remember what they are.

Sagittarius: (Nov. 22–Dec. 21)
You'll try with all your might to save poor little Pekingese Tuffy, but there's nothing any mortal can do when the Lord Of All Beasts announces that any dog smaller than a beagle doesn't count.

Capricorn: (Dec. 22–Jan. 19)
The rash of burning-dogshit incidents in your neighborhood will finally end this weekend, when D.C. police formally issue a cease-and-desist order to that prankster Nancy Pelosi (D-CA).

Aquarius: (Jan. 20–Feb. 18)
You'll be stripped of your merit badges, your troop insignia, and your Boy Scouts uniform during an extremely disgraceful and sexy night at the International Friendship Scout Camporee.

Pisces: (Feb. 19–March 20)
Your new love has thrown you into an exciting whirlwind of passion and euphoria, but pretty soon you'll probably have to meet in person.

NEWS

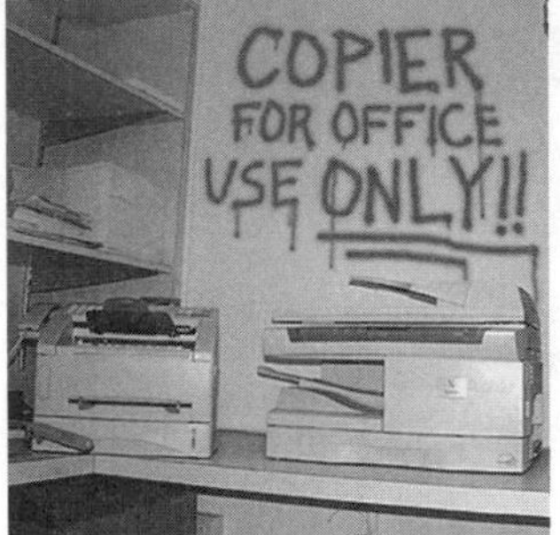

Office Manager Forced To Resort To Unfriendly Reminders

see BUSINESS page 11C

Dreamcatcher On Rearview Mirror Protects Sleeping Driver

see LOCAL page 1B

Greasy Spoon Has Crusty Forks

see FOOD page 8F

STATshot

A look at the numbers that shape your world.

the ONION®

VOLUME 41 ISSUE 16 AMERICA'S FINEST NEWS SOURCE™ 21–27 APRIL 2005

Papal Election Brings End To Worldwide Unsupervised-Catholic Sin Binge

VATICAN CITY—In the interim between Pope John Paul II's death and the election of his replacement, unsupervised Catholics seized the opportunity to sin without fear of reprisal, sources confirmed Tuesday.

"For two weeks, it was like Mardi Gras all over again," said Bryan Cousivert, a Catholic from Arizona. "People were drinking, cursing, and engaging in premarital or even extramarital sex. More importantly, everyone was being totally open about it. No one was worried about doing any penance at all!"

Continued Cousivert: "When the cat's away, the mice will play."

Paulo Verrazetti, a resident of Rome, said he and other Italians respectfully

see ELECTION page 124

Above: Catholics cavort in St. Peter's square last week.

Pope Emerges From Chrysalis A Beautiful Butterfly

VATICAN CITY—Vatican officials joyously report that Pope John Paul II, who led the Catholic Church during the 26 years of his larval stage, emerged from his chrysalis transformed into a beautiful butterfly Monday.

see POPE page 124

Left: John Paul II flits above Vatican City hours after leaving his chrysalis (below).

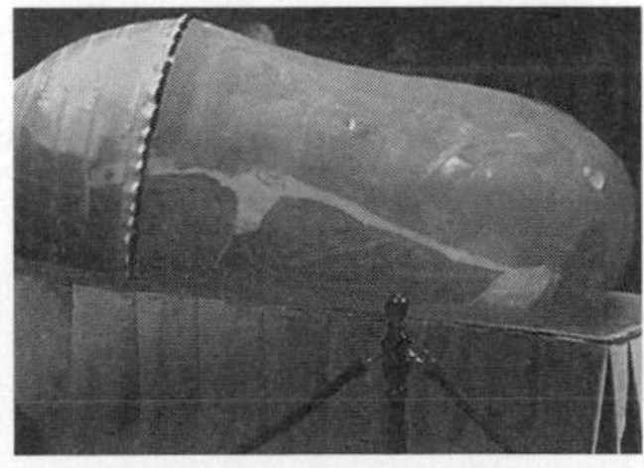

Police Sketch Artist Likes How Portrait Of Serial Rapist Turned Out

BIRMINGHAM, AL—Area police officer Lynn Marie Potter said Monday that she is "pretty proud of" her latest sketch, a drawing of an unidentified white male suspected of committing at least four recent Birmingham-area rapes since February.

"He looks so real, doesn't he?" said Potter, 38, admiring her rendering of the Caucasian believed to be in his early-to-mid 30s. "I mean, he looks like he could just leap off the sketch pad and violate you."

Potter, a certified criminal-image

see ARTIST page 125

Right: Potter and her sketch.

Are Tasers Safe?

Most security personnel defend the use of Tasers, but Amnesty International said that there have been more than 100 Taser-related deaths since 2001. What do *you* think?

"You wouldn't be complaining about Tasers if you had a rubber bullet lodged within inches of your heart like me."

Harold Wilson
Sound Producer

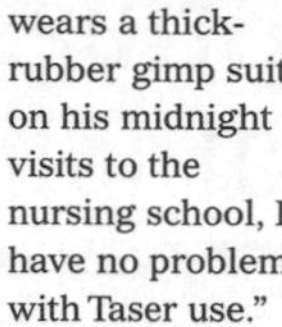

"As a man who wears a thick-rubber gimp suit on his midnight visits to the nursing school, I have no problem with Taser use."

Mark Stuttgart
Sales Manager

"If you're a cop, deadly force is the last thing you want to use. However, if you're a really twisted cop, a weapon that leaves a suspect flopping about like an epileptic puppy is dead-bang perfect."

Karl Gordon
Police Officer

"People complain that getting hit by a Taser is really painful, but in reality it doesn't hurt until your hypothalamus starts working again."

Mary Watkins
Systems Analyst

"I only hope this controversy doesn't affect my soon-to-be-launched national family-fun franchise, Taser Tag."

Sam Williamson
Sheet-Metal Worker

"Tasers are too much of a hazard. I guess the police will just have to go back to using tractor beams."

Ellen Anderson
Chef

TV Shows On DVD

People are increasingly buying television series on DVD instead of watching them on broadcast TV. Why?

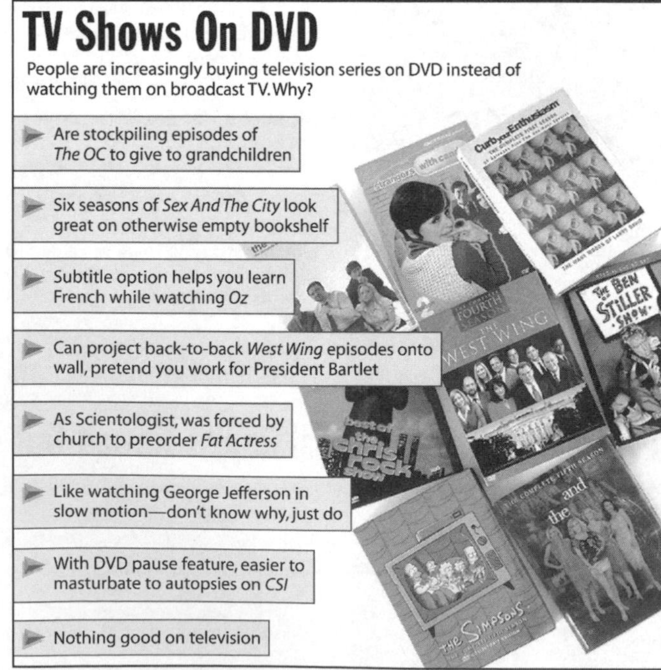

- Are stockpiling episodes of *The OC* to give to grandchildren
- Six seasons of *Sex And The City* look great on otherwise empty bookshelf
- Subtitle option helps you learn French while watching *Oz*
- Can project back-to-back *West Wing* episodes onto wall, pretend you work for President Bartlet
- As Scientologist, was forced by church to preorder *Fat Actress*
- Like watching George Jefferson in slow motion—don't know why, just do
- With DVD pause feature, easier to masturbate to autopsies on *CSI*
- Nothing good on television

America's Finest News Source.™

Herman Ulysses Zweibel
Founder

T. Herman Zweibel
Publisher Emeritus
J. Phineas Zweibel
Publisher
Maxwell Prescott Zweibel
Editor-In-Chief

Aw, Who'm I Kidding... I'll Never Top *21 Jump Street*

By Johnny Depp

It's only natural for artists to compare the creative purity of their early work to the compromised work of their later careers. I'm no exception. As I sit here in my chateau in France, absent-mindedly flipping through the script for *The Diving Bell And The Butterfly* by Oscar-winning screenwriter Ronald Harwood, I think of the man I used to be, and my heart sinks. I know I shouldn't let thoughts of the past get me down. Rather, I should overcome my insecurities and remind myself that there could be an even bigger success around the corner. Why, you never know what you can achieve if you just believe in yourself and... Aw, hell. Who'm I kidding here? I'll never top *21 Jump Street* and I know it.

I've tried, honestly I have. I've picked roles carefully and gone out of my way to work with unique and talented collaborators, regardless of their level of commercial success. I've done my best to go the extra mile: wearing pancake makeup and scissor-hand prosthetics, sporting fake gold teeth and channeling Keith Richards, even having my friggin' head shaved to play Hunter S. Thompson. I can honestly say I've committed myself to every part with all I've had. But, let's face it: Those characters on *Jump Street* shared a special camaraderie as they went undercover to solve mysteries in Southern California high schools. An actor just doesn't find that sense of belonging and purpose while working with Jim Jarmusch.

Ah, the heady early years of the Fox network. The executives were hungry, motivated, and willing to try anything. A young Stephen J. Cannell, *21 Jump Street*'s creator, had the world on a string. My future seemed assured as well, but little did I know how disappointing it would prove to be. Cannell went on to produce *Booker*, *Silk Stalkings*, and *The Commish*, and where did I end up? Aimlessly wandering from one project to another and sitting around the Viper Room with a "Wino Forever" tattoo.

I've kept my career afloat. I've been blessed with more lucky breaks than most guys my age, I'll admit. But I know what everybody's thinking: "What a sad little man. Depp's just going through the motions. Can't he see that Tom Hanson was the role of a lifetime and it's all been downhill since?" As I walk past the paparazzi, I can hear their thoughts: "Give it up, old man! You're almost 42. You're a fossil!"

Pathetic. I'll bet John Waters only cast me in *Cry-Baby* for my kitsch value.

Sure, sometimes Terry Gilliam, Roman Polanski, or Jerry Bruckheimer will take pity on me and throw me a bone. Tim Burton has been charitable. I even thought that by playing the role of Hollywood outcast Ed Wood, I might be able to recapture some of the defiant spirit I had during my *Jump Street* days. But what happened? My costar, Martin Landau, got the Oscar for Best Supporting Actor, and I got a one-way ticket to Palookaville.

It's not like I haven't tried to hone in on what made *Jump Street* such a

Ah, the heady early years of the Fox network.

perfect role. I did *Nick Of Time* and *Secret Window* because the characters solved mysteries, like we all did on *Jump Street*. But it just wasn't the same as when the Jump team took orders from hard-nosed but sensitive Capt. Adam Fuller, our multi-ethnic police squad's kindly African-American mentor. And that old feeling, like I was making a difference in the lives of millions of young viewers across the country by tackling important teenage issues like race, drug addiction, and AIDS—that feeling was just gone.

In this world, you only get one chance to play a member of an elite squad of young-looking cops who work out of an abandoned church, intervening in the lives of troubled teens before they grow up and become hardened criminals.

I know it doesn't do any good to dwell on the past. Because, in my heart of hearts, I know that afternoon I spent in the studio recording the "Jump!" background track with Peter DeLuise (Officer Doug Penhall) is gone. The stirring vocal track Holly Robinson (Officer Judy Hoffs) laid down will haunt me to my dying day:

We thought we'd never find a place where we belong
Don't have to stand alone, we'll never let you fall
Don't need permission to decide what you believe...
I said jump, (jump!), down on Jump Street
You'd better be ready to, be ready to jump!

Oh well. Wes Anderson is on the phone. Time to put on a happy face and try my best to move on. Ø

LOCAL

Fifth-Grade Science Paper Doesn't Stand Up To Peer Review

Above: Fifth-grade panel members express disapproval of Nogroski's paper (left).

DECATUR, IL—A three-member panel of 10-year-old Michael Nogroski's fellow classmates at Nathaniel Macon Elementary School unanimously agreed Tuesday that his 327-word essay "Otters" did not meet the requirements for peer approval.

Nogroski presented his results before the entire fifth-grade science

> **"His breath was so bad I can still smell it on my clothes," LaMott added.**

community Monday, in partial fulfillment of his seventh-period research project. According to the review panel, which convened in the lunchroom Tuesday, "Otters" was fundamentally flawed by Nogroski's failure to identify a significant research gap.

"When Mike said, 'Otters,' I almost puked," said 11-year-old peer examiner Lacey Swain, taking the lettuce out of her sandwich. "Why would you want to spend a whole page talking about otters?"

"It's probably only the dumbest topic in the history of the entire world," 10-year-old Duane LaMott added.

Members of the three-person panel had many concerns about Nogroski's work, foremost among them their belief that the fifth-grader did not substantiate his thesis. Two panel members even suggested that Nogroski's thesis was erroneous.

"Otters are *not* interesting!" 10-year-old peer examiner Jonathan Glass said.

"Otters are so boring, I fell asleep for a thousand years and woke up with a long beard covered in ice," LaMott said. "I had to defrost myself."

According to the examiners, Nogroski's second paragraph, which begins "Otters live in water," should have been followed by a description of the sea otter's natural habitat,

see PAPER page 125

NEWS IN BRIEF

New Tech-Support Caste Arises In India

NEW DELHI—Thanks to widespread outsourcing of telephone-service jobs, a sixth caste has blossomed in India: the Khidakayas, a mid-level jati made up of technical-support workers. "I am happy to be a Khidakaya," said technical-support agent Ranji Prasat, who speaks English with a flawless American accent and goes by the name "Ron" at work. "While we rank below members of the reigning order, those of us responsible for helping Americans track their online purchases and change their account PINs share many privileges not enjoyed by the merchant class below us." Prasat said he expects to marry another tech-support worker.

Another Comedian Ruined By Parenthood

AUSTIN, TX—Ed Corgi, once hailed as one of the area's funniest and most ribald stand-up comedians, has lapsed into mediocrity due to the 2003 birth of his daughter Grace, a friend reported. "Ed used to get up there and just spit venom against the entire world until the crowd was dying," fellow comic Rick Haste said. "Last week, I saw him do a bit about grape juice and another about how hard it is to get a stroller in a car trunk. He did swear a lot as he pantomimed folding the stroller, but still." Corgi's new sitcom *Grape Juice* is currently in development at ABC.

Sports Fan Thinks He May Have Torn Rotator Cuff

BOSTON—Although the most strenuous thing he does in any given week is reload his office printer's paper tray, Red Sox fan Sean Mooney, 41, said he believes he may have torn his rotator cuff. "Ooh, I'm gonna have to ice this tonight," said Mooney, rubbing the muscle he pulled while removing a Massachusetts tax-code reference book from his shelf. "Now I know how [Red Sox pitcher] Wade Miller felt." Doctors said Mooney's condition is probably soreness resulting from a lack of regular exercise.

Study: 80 Percent Of All Hermits Recovering From Broken Hearts

AMHERST, MA—According to conclusions reached by researchers at the University of Massachusetts, four-fifths of the world's dedicated recluse population were once luckless in love. "We have conclusively linked heartsickness to the behavior of dwelling in remote mountaintop caves, in bramble-covered forest huts, and on nameless unmapped islands," professor of solitary psychology Ludwig Meyer said Monday. "The loss of a lifetime's one true love seems to be enough to drive some people into splendid isolation in arctic regions and trackless jungle wilds." The study noted that the remaining 20 percent of hermits were driven from human contact by the desire to run naked around the woods, urinating though their knee-length beards.

Losing-Powerball-Numbers Announcement Enters 17th Hour

URBANDALE, IA—The announcement of losing Powerball numbers for Saturday's $83,000,000 jackpot entered its 17th hour Sunday. "3, 15, 17, 35, 47, and Powerball 23," said Powerball host Bill Somerford, reading from his 237-page list of losing combinations. "7, 23, 40, 46, 52, and Powerball 24. 9, 13, 27, 40, 53, and Powerball 14. 12, 15, 18, 27, 52, and Powerball 26. 1, 11, 35, 46, 53, and Powerball 36." The losing numbers will be continue to be broadcast until 10:59 EST Wednesday, after which the losing-numbers announcement for the next drawing will begin. ∅

ELECTION from page 121

refrained from reveling until after Pope John Paul II's funeral.

"We all mourned John Paul II's death," said Verrazetti, who was at St. Peter's Square for the former pope's funeral. "But when Vatican officials said that final 'Amen,' you could feel something change in the air. Someone screamed '*festa!*' and pretty soon Catholic women were going wild, running topless in the streets. Last month, seeing a woman with no clothes on would have sent me straight to the confessional. But without a pope around, well... Let's put it this way. For a couple weeks, Catholics the world over adopted the motto, 'If it feels good, do it.'"

Even those who only watched Pope John Paul II's funeral on television reported experiencing "feelings of newfound freedom."

"As they recited the Apostles' Creed, I remember thinking of all the things I want to do, but don't because of my devotion to the Church," said Antonio Valez, a Catholic from Mexico City. "As soon as I heard the pope was laid to rest, I said a prayer for the Holy Father's departed soul and went straight out and bought a box of condoms. Actually, I'm wearing one right now. It's been on all day and I'm loving it."

Carl Whitestone, an 82-year-old lifelong Catholic from Beaver Dam, WI said he experienced a similar sense of freedom.

"When I heard the pope was dead, the first thing I thought about, besides how much the great man will be missed, was the big bloody steak I was going to eat on Friday," said Whitestone. "When the pope was alive, I never would've thought of flouting the 1917 Pio-Benedictine Code Of Canon Law. But once he was out of the picture, I immediately bore false witness against my neighbor. And then I coveted his wife."

Many Catholics said they started out

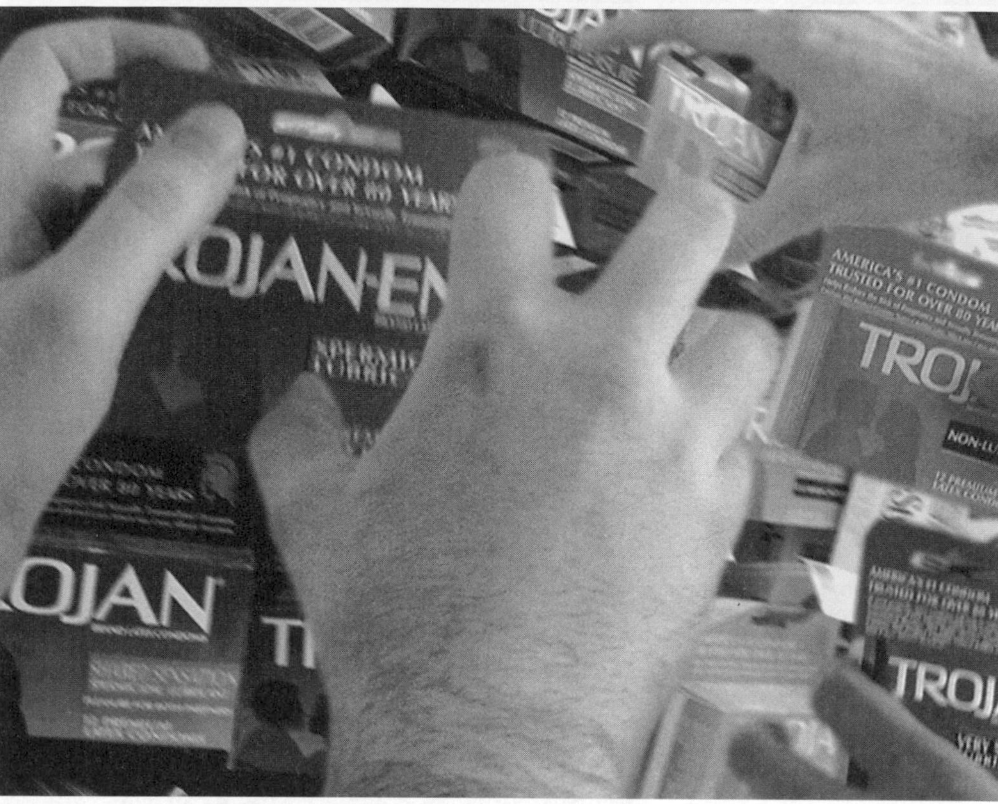

Above: A Boston-area drugstore sees a sharp rise in condom sales after the pope's death.

cautiously, limiting their misconduct to non-mortal sins: taking the Lord's name in vain, failing to contemplate the mysteries of the rosary, or sleeping in on Sunday morning instead of going to Mass. But when they saw no immediate consequences for their behavior, their sins became progressively more severe.

While church officials were reluctant to comment on how many recent murders might be attributable to the papal lapse, several cardinals said they were relieved when the papal conclave commenced.

"It was really getting out of control," said Cardinal Joseph Ratzinger, the prefect of the Congregation for the Doctrine of the Faith. "The pope is the gatekeeper between piety and anarchy. Without a papal presence, Catholics were thinking impure thoughts, manipulating their own genitals, and acting as if homosexuality was no big deal. Thank goodness we gathered to choose the new pope, or God's Kingdom on Earth might look like Sodom and Gomorrah by now."

Papal scholars said the recent bacchanalia was the worst in more than a quarter of a century.

"I haven't seen anything like this since Pope Paul VI died in 1978," said Fr. Robert Mendiga, a Jesuit priest at St. Andrew's School of Divinity in North Carolina. "This was the '70s, the era of pre-AIDS sexual experimentation and widespread recreational-drug use. Catholics, especially Americans, were quite willing to be led into temptation. It stopped when John Paul I was chosen, but when he died one month later, Catholics went right back to sinning."

"Yup," the priest added, gazing into the distance. "1978 was a very special year." ⌀

POPE from page 121

"John Paul II's emergence was a thing of awesome splendor, his magnificent wings of gold-embroidered silk brocade glistening in the late light of the Basilica as they dried," said Antonini Biaggi, one of the millions who came to Rome to view the pope's chrysalis as it lay in state under the great dome. "I was greatly blessed to see him break free of his outer husk, and then, minutes later, take his first tentative flight around the Vatican."

Roughly two weeks ago, as the pope's metabolism began slowing, John Paul II's attendants reported that the pontiff's outer skin was hardening and becoming more opaque. Despite his weakened condition, His Holiness began to eat his own weight in mulberry leaves every day, storing up energy for his astonishing transformation.

On April 2, when John Paul II's life functions ceased, he was transferred to a plain cypress molting box, inside of which he lay in state in St. Peter's Basilica. For the next few days, as worshippers and powerful world leaders alike came to pay their respects, the Vicar of Christ underwent the first stages of metamorphosis. Now completely covered with a hardened red-velvet-and-gilt outer shell, he had entered the papal pupal stage.

"It was a time of great mourning," said Cardinal Cormac Murphy-O'Connor of London, a Grand Intercessor of the Church and a trained pontifical lepidopterist. "After all, His Holiness' survival into the short-lived adult phase was not guaranteed. Not every pope makes the transformation—we still mourn the great tragedy of John Paul I."

Although the pope's long, early stage of life as the Chosen God on Earth is over, his new stage began at the moment of his passing.

Continued Murphy-O'Connor: "Inside his chrysalis, John Paul II's thorax was lengthening, his mandibles stretching and dividing into a four-part lateral jaw, his eyes dividing into many-faceted, compound sight-organs, and his once vestigial and subcutaneous limb-buds were growing into the four beautiful wings—and six limbs—of the adult pontiff. No longer truly one of us, John Paul II was becoming something closer to the divine. It's one of the most wondrous

He began to eat his own weight in mulberry leaves.

processes in, and symbols of, the Catholic Church."

"Also, I'm told much acute and pious suffering is involved," Murphy-O'Connor added.

The newly reborn pope spent most of Monday flitting about the Eternal City, alighting briefly on Michelangelo's "Creation of Adam" fresco in the Sistine Chapel, various colonnades of St. Peter's, and several visibly emotional visitors. Once, His Holiness even landed upon the balcony from which he delivered his Sunday addresses to worshippers, slowly opening and closing his nine-foot wings for several moments. Church officials hastened to remind onlookers that, in this part of his life cycle, the pope is no longer a sentient, thinking being.

The College of Cardinals said the pope's eggs—which the pontiff immediately began to release from his ovipositor and attach to various architectural features around Rome with a cement-like secretion discharged from his distended mandibles—have hatched, and from the larva, the next Successor of the Prince of the Apostles has been chosen.

Although the transformed Pope John Paul II will live for only a few days before crawling off to die somewhere in the recesses of the Vatican, Catholics see these brief days on earth as a gift from God and an indication of his ongoing love of man. ⌀

PAPER from page 123

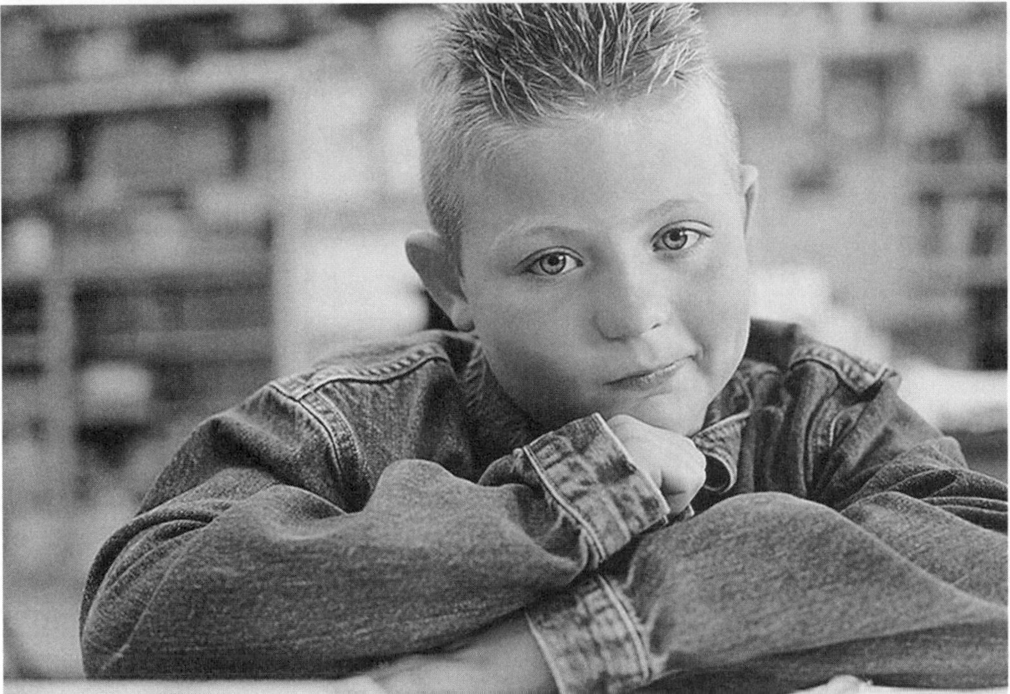

Above: Nogroski in the school library, where he will revisit his research.

rather than by a description of the world's largest full-grown otter and speculation as to what an otter that size could do to a sea lion.

"An otter could not kill a sea lion!" LaMott said. "I don't care how big it is—sea lions have gigantic claws."

"Nuh-uh," Swain said.

"Yes, sea lions do have gigantic claws," LaMott said. "If you don't believe me, look it up. Sea lions have very long claws. They would tear an otter to shreds in, like, two seconds. Seriously."

Panel members said Nogroski's work contained an alarming number of invalidated claims and irrelevant findings. They were particularly disconcerted by the figures in Nogroski's third paragraph, which begins "How do otters survive? Here are some facts about that."

"He didn't even say how they survive," Glass said. "He was just like, 'Otters are about one to 1.2 meters long. Otters' whiskers are about three inches long.'"

"I know!" Swain said. "It's like, 'Hey Mike, how do sea otters survive?' 'Dur. I'm Mike. Sea otters survive by being one meter long.'"

"Hey Mike," LaMott added. "What do sea otters eat? 'Dur, I'm Mike. Sea otters have whiskers that are three inches long. Also, I don't bathe and my jacket is acid-washed.'"

"His mom drives a Honda," Glass added.

The paper was criticized for failing to evince adequate literature review, failing to adhere to the pass-around style guidelines, and for being presented in "a chicken voice you could barely even hear because his teeth are so yellow."

"It's like, God, how hard is it?" Swain said. "You say what you are going to say, then you say it, then you say what you said. Mrs. Murchinson only explained it, like, a thousand times!"

"His breath was so bad I can still smell it on my clothes," LaMott added.

"All he eats is bread and butter," Swain added. "Hello? That's disgusting."

While a work that does not gain peer approval often goes on to receive wider acceptance in the academic community, "Otters" has little hope of gaining approval from Nogroski's teacher Stella Murchinson.

"Oh, well, he tries," Murchinson said. "Michael comes from a single-parent household. From what I gather, his father is something of a—something of a—I don't exactly know—he drives railroads? He isn't exactly in the picture. I've spoken to his mother several times, and while she is well-meaning, she is busy and often harried, having spent the night before tending bar. She's a cocktail waitress. Well, from what I can gather, Michael isn't coming from the most stable home environment, and his work reflects that, I'm afraid. He isn't exactly reading at his level."

The paper was criticized for failing to evince adequate literature review, failing to adhere to the pass-around style guidelines, and for being presented in "a chicken voice you could barely even hear because his teeth are so yellow."

Although Nogroski's student aide, fourth-grader Samir Sriskandiraja, has encouraged him to resubmit a different paper on a peer-friendly topic like football or airplanes, Nogroski said he will revisit his research and present additional otters-related data Thursday. ⌀

ARTIST from page 121

profiler who has drawn more than 400 composite portraits of wanted criminals in her eight years with the Birmingham Police Department, believes this latest illustration is her "finest work yet."

"I've done some good work before this, like my African-American carjacking suspect of 2002, or last year's Latino mugger, but this definitely tops those," Potter said. "What makes this one different is the palpable sense of menace—the disdain at the corners of his mouth and the ice in his gaze. You can practically touch the fibers of his stocking cap."

Potter called her previous drawings "competent, but flat."

"The others were void of personality," Potter said. "But this drawing makes you think, 'I know this guy. My God, maybe he's in my neighborhood right now.' It makes you want to lock your doors."

Added Potter: "I think I'll ask to keep the original of this one and get it framed."

Johnson based the sketch on the eyewitness description given by one of the suspect's alleged rape victims, a University of Alabama student attacked at knifepoint in her dorm room.

"This drawing makes you think, 'I know this guy. My God, maybe he's in my neighborhood, right now,'" Potter said.

"As is customary, I sat down with the victim and drew while she described the perpetrator," Potter said. "While I'm very methodical, sometimes it's hard to capture the physical features people describe, and often I have to heavily revise what I've drawn. But when I was done and showed the U of A student the drawing, she said, 'That's him,' and broke into tears."

"I was like, 'Yes!'" added Potter, pumping her fist in triumph.

Detective Fred Haines, Potter's colleague who has been assigned to the rape case, praised the work.

"I like how she added a little white dot to the suspect's pupils to make his eyes stand out," Haines said. "It sent a little chill up my spine, I'll admit. And the shading on the face is nice, too. She's come a long way with skin tones. I remember how, when she first started working here, Lynn Marie would just rub the side of the pencil lead across the paper if she had to draw a black suspect."

Potter's supervisor, Sgt. Dennis Schumacher, defended her early style.

"People in the squad room are likening her recent work to Lucian Freud's confrontational portraiture, but I prefer the crudeness of her novice period," Schumacher said. "The rudimentary line work and the thick, basic contours often captured the anonymous criminals' brutality and low, animal cunning. Though several of her early muggers and murderers looked very different from their portraits, police sketching is less about precisely capturing reality than interpreting it. Yes, Potter's later sketches are technically more accurate, but they have none of the robust expressionism of her early period."

Although a successful police sketch often hastens a suspect's capture, Potter admitted that some part of her hopes that the suspect rapes enough women to attract wider public attention.

"My dream has always been to see my sketches on the wall of post offices from coast to coast," Potter said. "If only one of my drawings ends up on the wall next to mug shots of suspected terrorists and bank robbers, I want it to be my best work." ⌀

COMMUNITY VOICES

Sir Charles Barlow Is Interested Only In Your Dowry

Lydia! Lydia! Pray forgive this unannounced visit to Twelveswood, but I felt you must know straight away. I cut short my stay in London to deliver some unfortunate news. Our hostess Mrs. Heggarty was kind enough to lend me use of her coach and... Oh, no, no, Edgar is well, thank Heaven, as is little Ivor. It's about Sir Charles, the man to whom you are affianced. No, he lives still, although if there were ever a body upon which I wished every earthly evil to be visited, it is his.

By Dorcas Walpole

No, Lydia, if only it were callow envy that motivated these harsh sentiments; would that it were mere pangs of jealousy that caused my brow to knit so! Alas, the source of my vexation is far more woeful, my dear girl, for Sir Charles Barlow is interested only in your dowry.

I do not begrudge you your flushed cheeks and heated words, Lydia. You may think that I, your more fortune-favored older sister, am betraying a desire to thwart your happiness, and I am the first to admit that, should you wish to form such a conclusion, you would have a lifetime of experience on which to found it. But I testify to what I have witnessed firsthand, and although the revulsion that resulted was deep enough to prompt my initial hesitation to disclose the truth, I swiftly concluded that I would not be a good sister and friend if I were to spare you from it. Dear Lydia, if I may be permitted, your Sir Charles—and I wield the possessive with Roman irony—is nothing more than a base cad and a scoundrel!

No, Lydia, Sir Charles is not wintering at Barlow Manor as he would have you believe; he has been in London, leading a life of rank dissipation. He too was a guest at Mrs. Heggarty's ball, and the scandalous conduct he exhibited there would appall all but the most hardened. He injudiciously exposed numerous young ladies to his depraved temperament—I say injudiciously because he remains unaware that I am your sister, knowing me only as Mrs. Edgar Walpole.

Sweet Lydia, I strongly advise that you sit down. Molly, some sherry, please, and ensure that the smelling-salts are within easy reach. Don't just stand there gaping, girl, make haste!

When Sir Charles arrived, Lydia, he was accompanied by a shocking entourage of assorted reprobates, including a fire-eater, a mulatto fortune-teller, a chimney-sweep, a village idiot, a cardinal, several snuff-addicts, and a mischievous Barbary ape who broke into the larder and tossed fistfuls of flour hither and thither. Worse still, Sir Charles had the temerity to wear a most immodest silken waistcoat of stripes of alternating chartreuse and scarlet. Lady Coldridge's poor eyes could not cope with the clash of hues, and she was forced to retire to her chambers with a sick headache, from which she is not expected to recover. In addition, Sir Charles tracked in a great deal of mud.

Yes, my poor girl, *that* Sir Charles, the timid, bookish beloved of whom you have written to me so fondly. The sherry has arrived, Lydia; take a good draught, now. Molly, a hot compress, please.

Leagues from the pastoral Eden that is Barlow Manor, Sir Charles passed the evening in a louche humor, his head wreathed in a pipe-smoke whose odor was most queer in its sickly-sweetness, and his carriage upon a settee in a most lascivious state—nearly supine. He did not seem to know or care that many of the ladies present had never before witnessed a gentleman with his feet lifted from the floor. Their chaperones did what they could to shield them from the outrage, but for most it was too late. I fear that their exposure to this singular display of ill manners may arrest their social ascendancy.

You are well-justified, Lydia, in asking what all this, defamatory though it may be, has to do with my original contention. Your defense of his actions as "harmless high spirits" is to be expected from a young lady blinded by love. Yet, I regret to say that my report of Sir Charles' contempt and infidelity comes directly from the rogue himself.

Before assembled company, Sir Charles freely and blithely admitted that his inheritance is near depletion, after several foolhardy wagers on bear-baitings, whist games, darts, and the like proved farcically disastrous. To enact further levies against his tenants would most assuredly result in mass riot, so to forestall total ruin, he decided to seek not his own fortune, but the fortunes of unbetrothed rural maidens. Noting that Sir Charles' remark left me aghast, Mrs. Heggarty, a quick wit, inquired of Sir Charles one of his marital prospects, a Miss Lydia Covington, who, of course, is yourself.

"Miss Lydia Covington? That provincial mouse—that unopened crocus?" Sir Charles chortled. "Her prospects for marriage are abundant, yes, the ardor of each of her suitors proportional to her worth in pounds sterling. For if she, and all five Covington sisters for that matter, were deprived of the generous bequeathal from their late uncle, Twelveswood would be forced to take in washing and serve as an asylum for a clan of pinch-faced, concave-bosomed spinsters receiving alms at the parish's pleasure!"

Well, upon hearing Sir Charles' intolerable words, Edgar arose to thrash the scoundrel, but I urged him not to betray our identity. I secured the coach from Mrs. Heggarty, bless her, and returned to Twelveswood as quickly as I could...

Lydia! She's swooning! Catch her, Molly, and help me get her to the four-poster. Change her into her nightgown, and have Timothy fetch Doctor Curtis. And where is that hot compress? Perhaps I have told my poor sister too much. Should she succumb, I shall blame myself, but better she perish from shock than disgrace!

Lydia, dear, please try to rally, for all is not lost. Sir Charles is a despicable fiend, but there are others far more deserving of your hand. There is Alfred, the shy divinity student lodging with Reverend and Mrs. Baxter, and our cousin Joseph, and of course, Mr. Pratt, the widowed pig farmer who is 30 years your senior but quite prosperous. I have it on good faith that none of these men ever smokes, wagers, wears gaudy waistcoats, muddies the carpet, or assumes a horizontal position. Yes, Lydia, it is a rueful way to spend one's life, fretting about marriage and money. One day, perhaps, we women will enjoy a more independent status and will no longer be so preoccupied with marrying well, or marrying at all. But that will not occur for another two centuries or so. Oh! What am I saying? It will take far more time than that.

HOROSCOPES

Your Horoscope

By Lloyd Schumner Sr.
Retired Machinist and
A.A.P.B.-Certified Astrologer

Aries: (March 21–April 19)
When choosing a pet this week, make sure it's one your friends approve of, as it'll outlive you by at least a dozen years.

Taurus: (April 20–May 20)
You'll enter into local-legend status this week when, wandering on an important personal quest, you become the Flying Dutchman of your local big-box stores.

Gemini: (May 21–June 21)
You'll enter the record books in style, better than tripling Roy Sullivan's old mark of being struck by lightning an amazing seven times.

Cancer: (June 22–July 22)
Although circumstances will force you to take a menial job requiring a nametag, it will not lead to anyone knowing your name.

Leo: (July 23–Aug. 22)
Although you've always worried about dying alone and unloved, you can put your mind at ease: A tragic mix-up at the pheromone lab will lead to your being loved to death by nine separate species.

Virgo: (Aug. 23–Sept. 22)
The stars would love to take credit for guiding you to your fated destiny, but Occam's Razor and plain common sense point toward your turning into a colossal asshole.

Libra: (Sept. 23–Oct. 23)
There are many possible fates in store for you this week, but they all seem to involve you standing rain-drenched and shoeless at the side of a major interstate highway, cursing single men everywhere.

Scorpio: (Oct. 24–Nov. 21)
You will soon come to symbolize the world's increasingly cold and callous nature when your death is used to demonstrate the impact-resistant grill of the new Ford 500 sedan.

Sagittarius: (Nov. 22–Dec. 21)
You never wondered what would happen if all those big glass skyscraper windows fell to the sidewalk at once, but you'll soon be able to satisfy the curiosity of those who have.

Capricorn: (Dec. 22–Jan. 19)
To your vast surprise and that of marine biologists worldwide, you'll discover that you play a vital role in the 30-year mating cycle of the limpet shark.

Aquarius: (Jan. 20–Feb. 18)
There is no medical proof that chemical castration helps to prevent serial double-parking, but where you're concerned, the traffic court isn't taking any chances.

Pisces: (Feb. 19–March 20)
There will be little change in your uneventful life this week, which is too bad considering you've been hanging from those manacles for a couple decades now.

NEWS

Katie Couric Flirts With Cardinal On Air

see ENTERTAINMENT page 11E

Beaver Can't Wait To Get Started On Dam

see NATURE page 14D

Ethics Panel Slides Back To Reveal Hot Tub

see POLITICS page 8F

Thumb War Senseless

see WORLD page 3D

STATshot

A look at the numbers that shape your world.

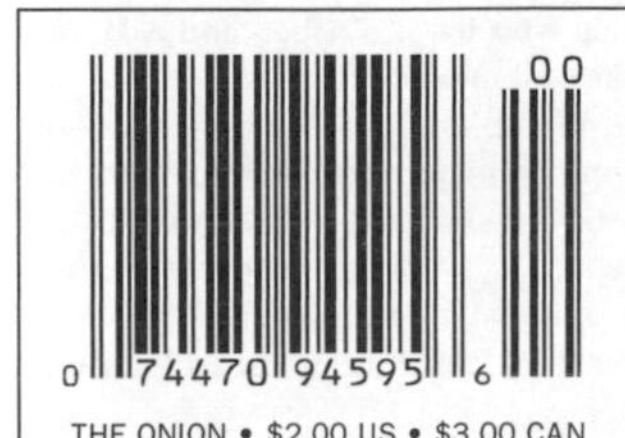

the ONION®

VOLUME 41 ISSUE 17 AMERICA'S FINEST NEWS SOURCE™ 28 APRIL–4 MAY 2005

Amazing New Hyperbolic Chamber Greatest Invention In The History Of Mankind Ever

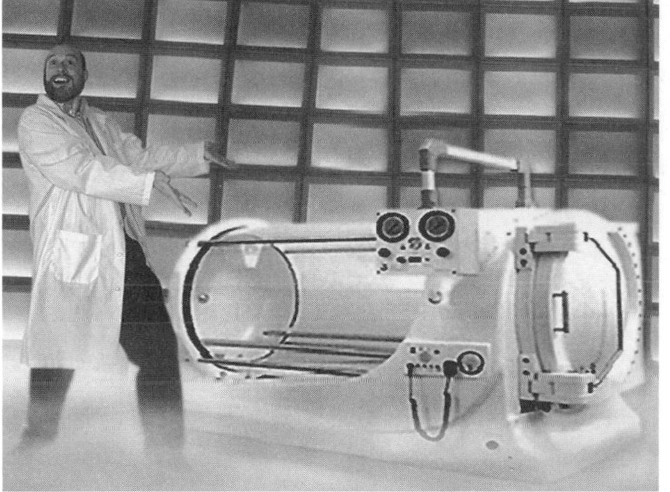

Left: Gustaveson unveils the amazing new hyperbolic chamber.

OAK RIDGE, TN—After six grueling years of Herculean research, scientists at the Oak Ridge National Laboratory pronounced EHC-1 Alpha, the new hyperbolic chamber, "an unquestionably, undeniably, fantastically revolutionary milestone in the history of science, mankind, and the universe, all of which it will undoubtedly change forever."

"Hyperbole researchers have arrived at, without possibility of argument or refutation, the single greatest moment in all of creation, now and forevermore," said the project's lead scientist, Dr. Lloyd Gustaveson, activating the hyperbolic chamber's gazillion-ultra-

see HYPERBOLIC page 130

Report: U.S. Foreign Policy Hurting American Students' Chances Of Getting Laid Abroad

AMSTERDAM—American students traveling abroad confirm the findings of a study indicating that Washington's unilateral approach to foreign policy has seriously undermined Americans' chances of getting laid.

"I've been in Amsterdam for two months and have yet to begin a conversation with a cute girl that hasn't ended in a lecture about how big, evil America is taking everyone's oil," said college sophomore Brad Higgs, a participant in Johns Hopkins University's study-abroad program. "I offer to buy them a drink, and they tell me I shouldn't just stand by and watch Bush destroy the world. Look, if I had that type of pull with the president, I obviously wouldn't be out trolling for anonymous Dutch pussy."

The report, released Monday by the Center For U.S.-International Casual Relations, was based on interviews with approximately 1,400 American

see FOREIGN POLICY page 130

Family Feud Continues Years After Game-Show Appearance

POCATELLO, ID—More than two decades have passed since the Douglass family of Pocatello and the Bzymek family of Derby, NY faced off on the syndicated game show *Family Feud*. But instead of being tempered by time, the feud sparked in November 1979 has grown increasingly bitter with each passing year, and show producers say the two families have reached a level of acrimony unseen elsewhere in the program's 29-year history.

"I haven't forgotten what those Bzymeks did to us," said Porter Douglass, the losing family's team leader. "They stole control of the board in the double-dollar round and took our bank."

Porter added: "They walked away with a cool $5,000, and we were humiliated on national television. Name a bunch of inbred jackasses that deserve a punch in the face. Survey says... The Bzymeks!"

Above: Douglass- and Bzymek-family heads of households recall their 1979 TV appearance.

The Bzymek-Douglass appearance began like a typical episode, with plenty of cheering and good-natured ribbing between the two families. As the game progressed, however, the jibes became more personal and mean-spirited, nearly culminating in a fistfight between Douglass and Tim Bzymek, when Douglass called then 14-year-old

see FEUD page 131

The New Food Pyramid

Last week, the federal government released a new food pyramid, but many citizens say the nutrition guidelines are too complicated. What do *you* think?

"Apparently there are different food pyramids for meeting different people's needs. I'm gonna guess mine is a mile-high spike of smoked ham, 1,000 feet wide at the base."

Kent Montoya
Coach

"I'm not sure how to use the pyramid guidelines. They measure servings in cups, whereas I measure servings in pitchers. Sometimes in pails, if I have a clean one."

Tracy Golden
Systems Analyst

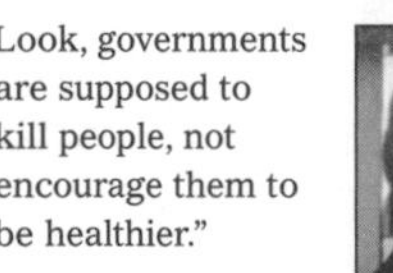

"Look, governments are supposed to kill people, not encourage them to be healthier."

Eduardo York
Broadcast Technician

"I heard that if you burrow deep inside the pyramid, you'll find a mother lode of discretionary calories."

Nellie Robles
Nurse

"I ask this every year, but where is the 'learning to love yourself the way you already are' pyramid?"

Seth Johnson
Drummer

"I've always wanted to be buried for all eternity in a giant food pyramid, with my toaster and chicken rotisserie preserved next to me in ceremonial urns."

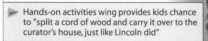

Marianne McDowell
Stenographer

The New Lincoln Museum

The high-tech Abraham Lincoln Presidential Museum opened in Springfield, IL last week. What are some of its exhibits?

- Refrigerated treadmill allows visitors to walk 10 miles through snow to return a book
- Hand-crank machine stamps Lincoln's likeness on your penny for 50 cents
- Hands-on activities wing provides kids chance to "split a cord of wood and carry it over to the curator's house, just like Lincoln did"
- Costume wing celebrating the daring fashion sense of America's third gay president
- Fun slide connecting museum to Lincoln's Tomb
- Visitors receive offer to "Get your photo taken in Lincoln's Death Car"
- Seven minutes in heaven with animatronic Mary Todd Lincoln

America's Finest News Source.™

Herman Ulysses Zweibel
Founder

T. Herman Zweibel
Publisher Emeritus
J. Phineas Zweibel
Publisher
Maxwell Prescott Zweibel
Editor-In-Chief

Guess What—It's Tom DeLay's Frisbee Now

Damn it! What did I tell you kids?

Yeah, I'm talking to you, you little hippie freaks. Didn't I tell you to stop messing around on the Capitol lawn? Don't act like you didn't hear me when I stuck my head out the window earlier. I saw you look up. I saw you laughing. Punks! I told you to clear out and take your games somewhere else. Then, not 15 minutes later, this thing sails right through the window and interrupts deliberations of the House Committee on Ways and Means.

By Tom DeLay
House Majority Leader

Oh yeah? Is that so? Well, guess what. It's Tom DeLay's Frisbee now.

No, I'm not going to "toss it back," and don't call me "dude." Very important people are trying to legislate in here. No, *you* come on. I warned you, but you had to push it. Now you face the consequences.

Don't tell me the Washington Mall is the official property of the people of the United States. I *am* Washington! That's right... keep talking. You can talk until you're blue in the face for all I care—it's not going to get you this Frisbee back. I'm taking it home with me. Danielle is going to love it.

Ouch! Damn it! Okay, which one of you brats bounced the Hacky Sack off the back of my head? Yeah, that's right, laugh it up. But look who got himself a new Hacky Sack. That's right, I'm keeping the Hacky Sack, too. Who's laughing now, you little smartasses?

Against the law? Pfft. I don't need some smart-aleck, Frisbee-tossing kids to tell me about the law. I'm Tom DeLay, the House majority leader. Who are you? I've been wheeling and dealing in this town longer than you bastards have been eating solid food. I was elected to a seat in the Texas State House in 1978. That's right, 1978! I was House majority whip in 1994. And now, in 2005, I have the Frisbee and there's nothing you can do about it.

Okay, you really want this Frisbee? Well, why don't you come over and try taking it out of my hands? I'm standing right here. What's the matter? Come on. Tom DeLay is waiting.

No, I'm not going to "toss it back," and don't call me "dude." Very important people are trying to legislate in here. No, you come on. I warned you, but you had to push it. Now you face the consequences.

No, I'm not throwing it back and, no, I'm not joking. I told you before. It's mine, and that's that. Take my advice: Get out of here before I call the Department of Homeland Security and have you all deported to an international zone where the Geneva Convention rules don't apply. Now, if you'll excuse me, I'll return my attention to the Enhanced Energy Infrastructure and Technology Tax Act of 2005 and thereby protect undeserving snots like you from natural-gas price fluctuations. Good day.

Ouch! Damn it! Okay, which one of you brats bounced the Hacky Sack off the back of my head? Yeah, that's right, laugh it up. But look who got himself a new Hacky Sack. That's right, I'm keeping the Hacky Sack, too. Who's laughing now, you little smartasses?

What? You're gonna call the House Ethics Committee on me? You think the House Ethics Committee scares Tom DeLay? Go ahead and call them. I'll dial the phone number for you. I've got it on speed dial. That committee's come after me plenty of times before, and you know what happened? Nothing! While you're at it, call the *Washington Post*. Maybe they'll do a human-interest piece about the poor kids who lost a Frisbee and a Hacky Sack all in one day.

Call for an independent investigation! Demand my resignation! See what good it does you. I've faced a hell of a lot worse opposition than you, and I'm still standing. You hear me? Tom DeLay is still here! I am Tom DeLay!

Yeah, you'd better run. Punks. Ø

LOCAL

Area Man Well-Versed In First Thirds Of Great Literature

KANSAS CITY, MO—Malcolm Seward is a 38-year-old commercial kitchen designer, baseball fan, and avid supporter of public radio, but he said there's nothing he likes better than hunkering down in a comfortable chair, cracking open a brand-new copy of one of the world's literary classics, and reading the first 100 pages or so.

"Listen, I'm no book snob," said Seward, settled into his favorite reading chair and running his hand over a nearly half-well-thumbed copy of *Pride and Prejudice*. "It's just that I love cracking the binding on a truly good book and reading until I drift off. I'd say it's something I do two or three times a week."

Seward, whose bookshelves house over 500 well-regarded and eagerly begun novels, developed his voracious appetite for starting books at a young age.

"Back in middle school, I'd rather watch a few innings of a Royals game or pop in a movie to relax," Seward said. "But that changed when my English teacher, Mrs. Ward, assigned us the first three chapters of *To Kill A Mockingbird*. I loved Harper Lee's depiction of quiet, small-town life. Even though I was out the entire next week with the flu, I retained my love of those opening chapters. I've brought it with me to every book I've begun to read since."

Seward said reading is not a cheap hobby. In addition to the cost of the books themselves, he has invested in custom-made bookshelves and numerous attractive bookmarks, each of which ultimately comes to rest somewhere between the front cover and the middle section of a pristine classic of Western literature. According to Seward, the enjoyment he experiences every time he feels himself being drawn 25 to 35 percent into one of the great stories is worth the expense.

"There's nothing like the written word for capturing one's imagination," Seward said. "I still feel the thrill of setting off down the Mississippi on Huck Finn's raft; the utter

see LITERATURE page 131

Seward, whose bookshelves house over 500 well-regarded and eagerly begun novels, developed his voracious appetite for starting books at a young age.

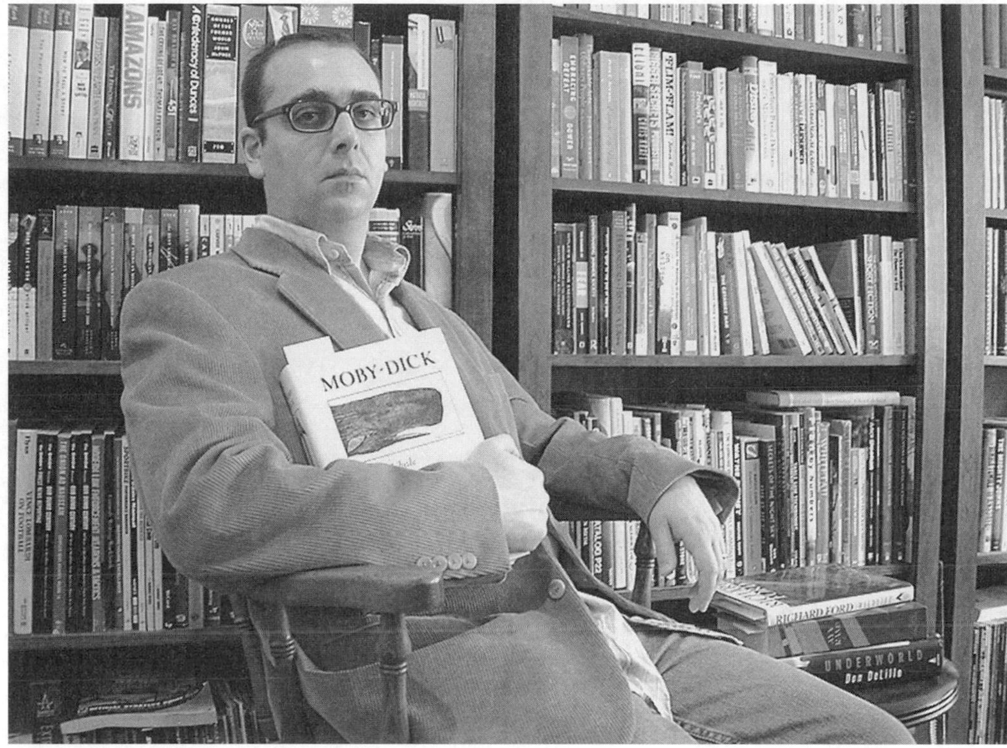

Above: Seward in his home library.

NEWS IN BRIEF

National Poetry Month Raises Awareness Of Poetry Prevention

NEW YORK—This month marks the 10th National Poetry Month, a campaign created in 1996 to raise public awareness of the growing problem of poetry. "We must stop this scourge before more lives are exposed to poetry," said Dr. John Nieman of the American Poetry Prevention Society at a Monday fundraising luncheon. "It doesn't just affect women. Young people, particularly morose high-school and college students, are very susceptible to this terrible affliction. It is imperative that we eradicate poetry now, before more rainy afternoons are lost to it." Nieman said some early signs of poetry infection include increased self-absorption and tea consumption.

Teen Reports *Saturday Night Live* Has Sucked Since Chris Kattan Left

AUGUSTA, GA—Once an avid fan of *Saturday Night Live*, Tom Simms, 16, said Monday that the live sketch-comedy institution began a downhill slide after Chris Kattan exited the show in 2003. "They don't do funny stuff like Mango or the Roxbury guys anymore," said Simms, who, from 1998 to 2004, watched *SNL* whenever he had a babysitter or could sneak downstairs after his parents fell asleep. "After Kattan left, the show stopped taking chances." Simms' older brother Joel and his uncle Kurt agreed that *SNL's* quality has declined, but linked the show's suck-points to the departure of Jim Breuer and Joe Piscopo, respectively.

Uneventful Past Finally Catches Up To Boring Man

MILTONVALE, KS—Years of safe living finally caught up to 33-year-old accountant Brian Jorgens Sunday during a visit from old friends. "I thought I'd put my sedate college days behind me forever," said Jorgens, standing in front of the Applebee's where he'd just spent three hours with his former college roommates. "But after listening to Ken and Louis reminisce about our summer-long cribbage tournament and the time we took a chartered tour bus to the Badlands—well, I realized that I can run from my boring past, but I can never truly hide." Jorgens vowed to turn his life around by deserting his wife and stealing a car.

First Date In Six Months To Be Last Date In Six Years

ROSEBURG, OR—Although he is unaware of it, Jeff Schyler's date Friday will be his last until May 2011. "I'm so glad I finally got up the balls to ask out my friend's cute sister," said the 28-year-old, whose last date was in October. "I haven't been getting much action lately, but I have a really good feeling about this." Schyler plans to take his date to see *Fever Pitch*, hoping the romantic comedy will "get her in the mood," which it won't.

Bartender Hurt By Unfinished Drink

DENVER—Eddie Meagher, a bartender at Madhatter's Pub, reported that he was "deeply hurt" by an unfinished Long Island Ice Tea left behind by one of his patrons Monday. "I made that drink especially for him," said a visibly disappointed Meagher. "Why would he leave almost a third of it sitting there? If something was wrong with it, he should've told me so. Then I could fix it." According to coworkers, Meagher hasn't been this upset since a patron thoughtlessly vomited four meticulously crafted Cosmos onto the street in front of the bar last Thursday.

HYPERBOLIC from page 127

watt semantic resonator at a gala launch party Monday. "The divine flame kindled by our new hyperbolic chamber will cast its light down through the centuries, making the Promethean fire that brought forth life on earth seem like a brief and guttering spark. Behold—we recast the cosmos in the image of the ultimate!"

A federally funded program launched during the Clinton administration, the hyperbolic-chamber project was roundly criticized at its inception by lawmakers who argued that it was too expensive and had no industrial or military applications. Republican senators were particularly vocal, with one congressman claiming the project would "run Jesus-kabillion dollars over budget," and be "more useless than 12 rows of tits on an NFL fullback."

The EHC-1 Alpha survived many rounds of budget cuts, however, in no small part because of the tireless efforts of lobbyists who decried the chamber's congressional detractors as "Philistine Nazi Neanderthals."

"Today, we do not merely silence our critics," Gustaveson said. "We commit them to that newest, foulest level of eternal indignity and unending infamy: the dark, ignorant era before the amazing, incredible hyperbolic chamber!"

"There has never been anything as amazing as this awesome machine," Gustaveson added.

Responses from within the scientific community have been positive.

Writers from *Scientific American* dedicated the May issue to the chamber's development and technology, calling it "brilliant... unsurpassed and unsurpassable. No mere milestone, the EHC-1 Alpha hyperbolic chamber is the achievement from which all future milestones shall be measured."

Not to be outdone, *Nature* is planning a June special issue in which it will call the device "singular in its quasi-divine perfection... the *ne plus ultra* of human ingenuity."

And *Popular Science* quickly placed the chamber on the fold-out cover of its next issue, which reads, "FUCKING AWESOME!!! THE BALLS-OUT H.C. IS 40 TIMES BETTER THAN SEX... AND COUNTING!!!"

Although it is difficult to find critics of the EHC-1 Alpha, those who oppose the machine do so vocally. The project's most prominent critic is Sandia National Laboratories' Dr. Owen Comstock, who argues that hyperbolic-chamber research has little social value and that federal funds would be better spent on his project, the high-energy, lowest-common-denominator-inductive Supercolloquial Mundane Adjectival And Onomatopoeic Accentuator.

"EHC-1 Alpha?" Comstock said. "Pfft. More like the craptastic crapobolic crapulator of crappity-crap-crap. Blarf. In addition, it is ugly as ugly can get, raises several safety issues, and is so freaking stupid I had to puke at how stupid it is."

FOREIGN POLICY from page 127

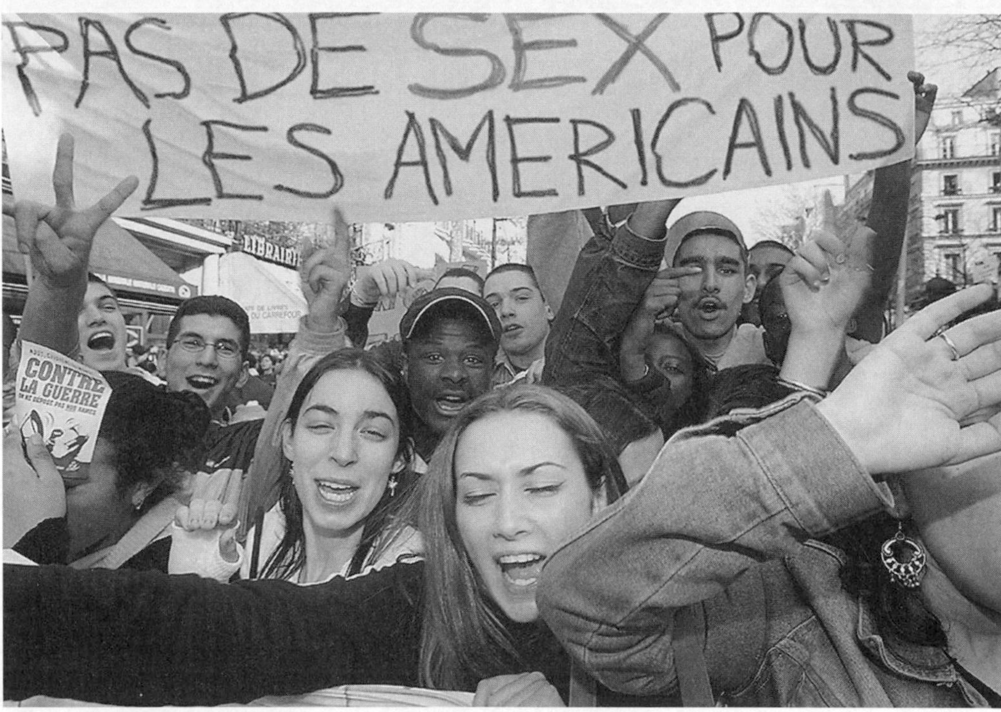

Above: A recent anti-American protest in Paris.

students returning from abroad. According to study director Gilbert Hapbrook, sexual contact between American students and foreigners has declined steadily since January 2001.

"Unpopular military actions and dismissal of international organizations have galvanized world hostility toward the U.S.," Hapbrook said. "Instead of being inundated with questions about Hollywood and requests to help hot young foreigners practice their English, Americans are being openly scorned in European pubs and cafes. Data taken from a poll of students in December 2004 showed that only a dismal 11 percent had achieved sexual congress with a non-American."

Hapbrook said the 2004 overseas-coitus figures show a slight recovery from the all-time low reached in November 2002, after the Afghanistan invasion and during escalating conflict with Iraq. But the figures are still well below those of 1999, when Bill Clinton was in office and a very healthy 67 percent of respondents scored abroad.

"I'm in Amsterdam—Amsterdam, for Christ's sake—and I'm in the middle of the longest dry spell I can remember," Higgs said. "Last week, I was making out with this Italian girl at a concert. It was all going great until the music ended and she heard my American accent. I swear to God, I went from the cusp of a hand job to, 'Why won't your country sign the Kyoto Treaty?'"

University of Colorado junior Casey Knight recently arrived in Amsterdam after a month in Germany.

"I asked a group of German girls at some Eurotrash disco to dance and they started yelling at me," Knight said. "They said that by paying taxes to the American government, I am no better than a fascist. Well, they would know, I guess."

Even students who actively oppose

> **"First, pretend you're Canadian whenever you can," Hapbrook said. "But make sure you're not around actual Canadians, because they'll know you're lying and cock-block you. Second, if there are any anti-American protests going on, take care to avoid women carrying signs. Third, focus your itinerary on countries like Ireland and Japan that are still relatively friendly to Americans."**

President Bush are susceptible to criticism, according to Emily Biehn, a Duke University student spending her spring semester in Paris.

"I voted for Kerry and I marched against the Iraq war," Biehn said. "But when I got to Europe, I might as well have been wearing a Bush bumper sticker on my forehead and star-spangled cowboy boots. As soon as the French guys hear I am from the U.S., all they want to do is argue politics."

"And switching tactics and acting like you're totally apathetic about politics just pisses them off even more," Biehn added.

Acknowledging that a large-scale change in American foreign policy is unlikely to occur before the end of the current semester, Hapbrook recommended three tactics for American students frustrated in their attempts to bed foreigners.

"First, pretend you're Canadian whenever you can," Hapbrook said. "But make sure you're not around actual Canadians, because they'll know you're lying and cock-block you. Second, if there are any anti-American protests going on, take care to avoid women carrying signs. Third, focus your itinerary on countries like Ireland and Japan that are still relatively friendly to Americans."

"You may want to write off France altogether," Hapbrook added.

Hapbrook said he developed his tactics in 1983, when the American government was practicing hardline Cold War foreign policy and he was spending his junior year abroad.

Higgs, who spends most of his time in his hostel playing solitaire and watching DVDs on his laptop computer, urged students back home to write to their congressional representatives.

"This affects all of us," Higgs said. "The government has to acknowledge the needs of young Americans. Too many U.S. citizens in foreign lands are spending sleepless, lonely nights jerking off in increasingly filthy sleeping bags. It sucks."

FEUD from page 127

Jenny Bzymek a "stupid tramp" as the families were leaving the stage.

"He insulted my blood," Bzymek said when asked about the incident. "If you are a loser who can't think of country songs, don't take it out on my daughter. Especially when your son is a four-eyes who takes two minutes to decide whether to play or pass!"

The mutual rancor, which has endured five presidencies, a war, and four hosts, shows no sign of abating. Last year, when Jenny's daughter Katie graduated from high school, she received a card from the Douglasses. "Where did you get into school, Katie?" the card read. "Survey says... community college!"

"That was completely uncalled for," Bzymek said. "This was a day of celebration. They could've come down the week after the show and beat me with a baseball bat, and that would've at least been honorable, but this? Too much. They ruined Katie's special day, all because we cleaned their clocks on television."

The families were brought back to the show in 1999 for a "Greatest Contestants" special, but the episode never aired. According to Jason Lowitt, a producer who witnessed the taping, Douglass and Bzymek had to be physically separated by host Louie Anderson during the face-off round, after Porter guessed the number-one answer and took control of the board.

"We came into round four on top, but we lost again because triple points in the fourth fucked us," Douglass said, referring to a controversial rule repealed in 2002. "I blame Louie Anderson. Richard Dawson never would have let that happen under his watch."

Bzymek's wife Beth was reached at home and asked to comment on the ongoing strife.

"The Douglass family?" Beth said. "We asked 100 people who was most likely to lose his sales job for failing to meet his quota. You heard me, Sally Douglass. I'm talking about your no-good husband. If you want to do something about it, step on up. I've got a .45-caliber parting gift loaded and waiting."

Despite many such threats, the conflict has thus far been limited to menacing letters, inflammatory e-mails, and crank phone calls.

"People ask us when this will end," Sally Douglass said. "This will end when the Bzymeks join former host Ray Combs in the Fast Money round in the sky."

"Three strikes and control of the board will pass to us!" Sally added.

Tony Cohen, CEO of FremantleMedia, which produces the current incarnation of Feud, said his company is taking great pains to prevent future contestant altercations.

"We are concerned that some guests may feel compelled to maximize their fleeting time in the public eye by causing a scene," Cohen said. "That's why we have begun doing background checks on all contestants and searching them for weapons when they enter the studio. We don't want a repeat of the 2002 domestic disturbance which sent four Stenzels to the hospital." ⌀

LITERATURE from page 129

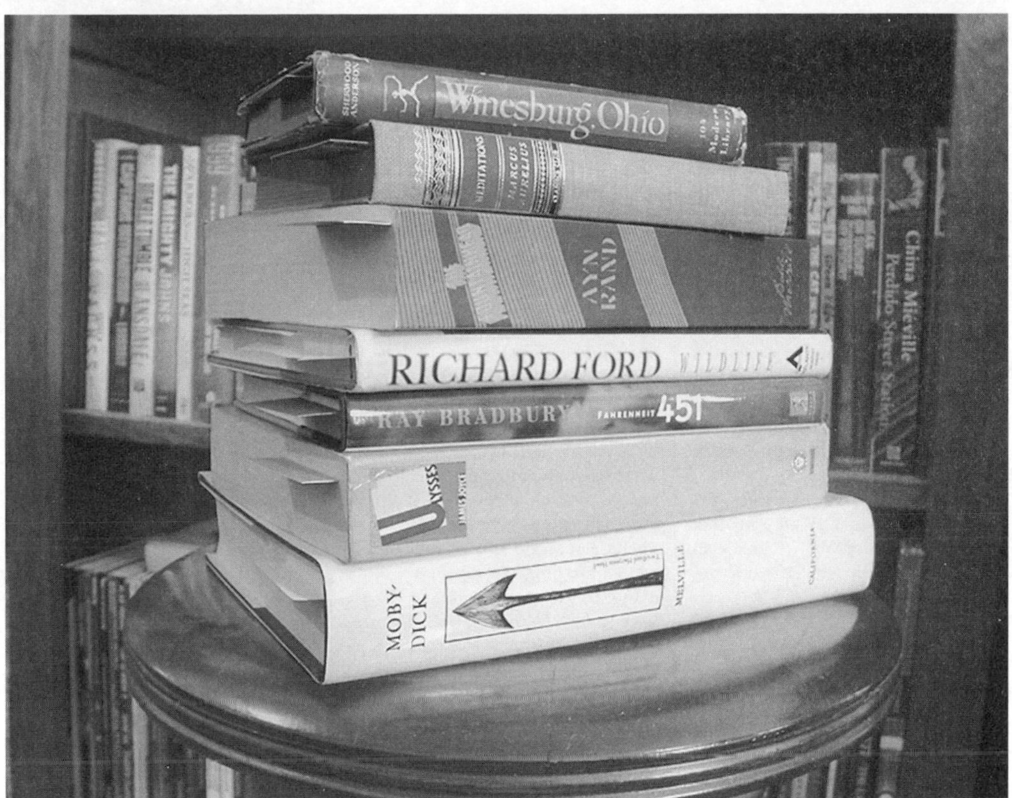

Above: A few classic works of literature Seward has started reading.

desolation of Robinson Crusoe, alone on his island for all those years with no trace of another human; and the excitement of Hemingway's Santiago as he hooks the fish that will make him rich and renowned. It's quite inspiring, what can happen to you when you open a book and start in."

Although Seward would never call himself a great thinker—saying "I'm just a guy who likes to fall asleep with his nose in a book"—he confesses that he has found a lot to think about in his overtures into literature.

"Characters in the great books may be more allegory than human, but there's a lot you can take away from

Although reading consumes a lot of Seward's time, Anne, his wife of three months, happily tolerates it.

them anyway," Seward said. "You have to admire the leadership of Captain Ahab as he sets out in search of Moby Dick, or the sense of personal duty and faith in social order that drive Marlow up the Congo to meet Kurtz. Or, in a different vein altogether, you must pity the tragic ugly duckling that is Jane Austen's Emma. I know it may be old-fashioned to say this, but I think what you read, and how you read it, can say a lot about you."

Although reading consumes a lot of Seward's time, Anne, his wife of three months, happily tolerates it.

"His love of literature is inspirational," said Anne, whose own reading "runs to magazines." "Just the other day, out of nowhere, he said we were like a modern-day Catherine and Heathcliff. I think starting all those books has made Malcolm a real romantic." ⌀

COMMUNITY VOICES

A Motivation Seminizar

Tha Nite Rida cruised like a muhfukkin' barracuda into tha Midstate parkin' lot an' wit' typical mad stealth executed a perfect 90-degree turn into her designated spot. "It Monday, bitchez," I said as I flew outta my hoopty an' hustled 2 tha employee entrance. "Aw yeah, y'all know how we do it. Bitchez best fo-get that punk-ass, no-workin' weekend shit an' be down wit' tha hardcore officin', or y'all gonna have tha H-Dog up in yo' shit. Word dat."

By Herbert Kornfeld
Accounts Receivable

Ain't nobody in tha third-floor administrative office when I walked in. No matta, I usually tha first one in anyhows. But come 9:30 in tha ay-em, still nobody in tha hizzy. I went 2 tha front window an' peeped all tha hoopties in tha lot, but no peeps. What tha fuck? I went downstairs 2 investigate, Letta Opener O'Death poised 2 strike.

Half down tha stairs, I peeps Gary, my Accountz Reeceevin' bruthah, standin' there wit' Nick, my homie down in Shippin', an' Lois, one-a tha Cash Room hottiez. "What tha fuck, muhfukkaz? What?" I say. "Where tha Midstate posse at? Don't no one show up fo' work 2-day? Is this some muhfukkin' *Nightmare On Elm Street* or some shit like that? What? What? Y'all zombies 2? I'll whup yo' undead asses."

"Didn't you get this interdepartmental memo in your mailbox Thursday?" Gary aksed.

He whipped out a piece-a paypa from his pocket an' show me. It go: "Attn: All Midstate employees: You are invited to the first-floor conference room on Monday, Feb. 21 at 9 a.m. to enjoy a presentation by workplace and time-management expert Dr. Charles Rich, PhD, author of 1:1—*The Productivity:Attitude Ratio*. Are stress and negative feelings affecting your work performance? Dr. Rich offers convincing data that indicates that the amount of productivity one achieves in the workplace is evenly proportional to one's overall attitude. Dr. Rich explores ways

see KORNFELD page 132

KORNFELD from page 131

one can increase their motivation through positive thinking, stress-relieving health habits, and better interpersonal communication. Says Dr. Rich: 'Bettering your future begins with you.'"

Fuck, it obvious why I didn't get one-a them memos. H-Dog don't need no fuckin' motivizational seminar. Gerald Luckenbill, tha office comptrolla, probably say, "Give memos 2 all tha peeps but tha H. Y'all can't improve on perfection." But none o' this xplained why Gary, Nick, an' Lois wuz blowin' tha seminar off. They claimed they wuz goin' 2 tha john, but I wuzn't havin' none o' it. I give Gary tha look 'til he crack, say that he, Nick, and Lois left 'cause they thought it all a buncha bullshit.

I aksed them, is they punched in? They said yes. I said, "Y'all gots mad hate fo' seminizars? Well, I'll give y'all one my own damn self. Only it fo' reals. I ain't wrote no muhfukkin' book wit' some wack-ass PhD, but what I gots 2 lay down be straight-up dope-ass wizdom from tha street. Time 2 get educated, mah homies."

Next mornin', I walk in tha cubicle, an' tha geranium be all green again. New growth wuz shootin' outta tha pot. So, I kept waterin' it wit' Dad's Root Beer an' feedin' it on candy an' chips from tha vendin' machine. Ten yearz later, tha geranium still goin' strong. Snyder's Pretzel Thins be its favorite.

We went into mah cubicle, an' tha three sat at mah feet like li'l lambs. I pointed 2 a geranium, chillin' in a hangin' basket above my deks. "Peep this, mah children," I said. "It a geranium. A muhfukkin' office geranium. Gary, y'all knows this geranium, am I right?"

"Sure, Herbert," Gary said. "That's been in your cubicle as long as I can remember."

"Damn straight, mah man," I say. "Ain't nothin' special 'bout this geranium, right? It gots red bloomz an' green leaves. It real healthy, tho'. I mist tha shit outta it daily, an' every year I change its soil."

"It's real pretty," said Lois.

"No shit, freak," I said. "Yo, but check it: Back in tha day, when I first peeped this plant, it be near-dead. Tha leaves wuz all yellow an' tha blooms wuz fallin' off. It wuz a muhfukkin' low-down dirty shame. An' y'all know where I found this thang?"

Tha trio shook their heads.

"Right up here on tha third flo'. Thas right, Midstate."

So I begun 2 tell tha story o' tha geranium. I had jus' passed mah one-year anniversary at Midstate. I wuz a ex-con, a newjack officin' prince busted foe unlicensed accountin', an' still mournin' mah tight homie an' mentor, CPA-ONE. One day, I peeped Myron Schabe, tha Accountz Payabo supervisa. He a geeza even then, an' he wuz hunched ova a addin' machine, bruisin' his ol'-ass fingas 'gainst tha buttons. I aksed him where that bitch that help him at, an' he looked at me thru his thick-ass bifocals all vexed. "If you're referring to Sheila, I'm afraid she left the company this morning," Myron said. "Didn't bother to give notice. Herbert, if you have some free time today, I'd appreciate your assistance..."

But I wuz long gone. Even then, I wuz hatin' on tha A.P. I cruised past tha bitch's cubicle an' peeped some-a tha Midstate krew goin' through her shit. Damn, tha bitch left everthang behind—office supplies, paperz, a umbrella, an' even a sweatah. An' in tha corner o' her cubicle, on tha flo', I spotted a geranium, all brown an' shit. It had a ol' ribbon 'round its pot, like it musta been a gift once, maybe fo' Sheila's birfday. G's, it mad vexed me 2 see a innocent office plant forced 2 die 'cuz some bitch decided 2 bail. So I hustled tha flower back 2 mah cubicle.

Sheeit, I didn't know how 2 take care of no muhfukkin' geranium. Fo' dayz, I gave it nothin' but watercoolah water an' stuck it under mah 40 watt deks lamp with adjustable arm an' burnished chrome finish. I even repotted it wit' soil from tha Midstate lawn, but tha fucka still wouldn't grow. Finally, I snapped. I went 2 tha breakroom vendin' machines, bought a can o' Dad's Root Beer, a bagga Combos, an' some Skittles, an' dumped 'em all in tha plant's pot. "Fuck this weak shit, asshole," I yelled. "Y'all better gets yo' eat on wit' a quickness. If y'all don't, prepare 2 get iced come daybreak."

Next mornin', I walk in tha cubicle, an' tha geranium be all green again. New growth wuz shootin' outta tha pot. So, I kept waterin' it wit' Dad's Root Beer an' feedin' it on candy an' chips from tha vendin' machine. Ten yearz later, tha geranium still goin' strong. Snyder's Pretzel Thins be its favorite. A true office plant, no diggity. Matta o' fact, fo' weeks after, tha plant wouldn't stop gettin' its grow on. I hadda cut shit off it, an' I started plantin' tha cuttins aroun' Midstate.

"And that's where all those pretty geraniums along the sidewalk came from!" shrieked Lois.

No doubt, I said. I aksed them, what tha lesson be from all this.

"Are you trying to get us to go to church or something?" Nick aksed.

"Shut tha fuck up, Nick," I said.

"Out of bad situations, good things can result, and that can apply in the workplace, too," Lois said. "You can find worth and meaning in your job if you know where to look."

"Hell no, that ain't what I wuz sayin'," I said. "Damn, woman."

Gary nailed it. He said it was 2 show how bumpin' tha H-Dog wuz, an' how lucky tha Midstate staff wuz 2 have tha One An' Only Funky Fresh Ovahlord O'Tha A.R. Universe in full effect. How much motivation a homie need? I raised a fuckin' office plant from tha dead by hollerin' at it an' feedin' it root beer an' Skittles, y'all. Thas off tha hook. Sheeit. Mad props 2 Gary fo' recognizin' tha ultimate truth. H-Dog out. Ø

HOROSCOPES

Your Horoscope

By Lloyd Schumner Sr.
Retired Machinist and
A.A.P.B.-Certified Astrologer

Aries: (March 21–April 19)
You really won't know what to think when God Himself appears to you and asks, rather shyly, if you think people would be okay with saying "God Herself" from now on.

Taurus: (April 20–May 20)
An innocent trip across town in your Abrams main battle tank to return a friend's industrial-grade power tools will somehow result in your pulling off the bank heist of the century totally by accident.

Gemini: (May 21–June 21)
Good coaching and kind, compassionate discipline will turn a ragtag group of problem kids into a top-notch football team, but you're just what they need to turn them back to violence and drug abuse.

Cancer: (June 22–July 22)
You should move confidently in whatever direction your dreams take you, even if they're about being chased down a dark hallway by a bloody-fanged eggplant.

Leo: (July 23–Aug. 22)
Mars descending in your sign is usually a sign of good luck, but that's when Mars isn't descending straight at you.

Virgo: (Aug. 23–Sept. 22)
Unfortunately, the police have also heard the story where the murderer kills her victim with a frozen leg of lamb and then feeds the evidence to investigators.

Libra: (Sept. 23–Oct. 23)
Treating yourself to a piece of pie when things go well is a good idea, but remember that you said "well," you fat fucking hog—not "barely acceptable."

Scorpio: (Oct. 24–Nov. 21)
The other men who delivered babies in stalled elevators were considered heroes, but they didn't commandeer an elevator full of food, water, medical supplies, and women last July.

Sagittarius: (Nov. 22–Dec. 21)
You remember what a good, strong, fiery kick a bottle used to have in the old days—it was nothing like the watered-down crap these puny kids are calling a Molotov cocktail.

Capricorn: (Dec. 22–Jan. 19)
Life as a left-hander isn't all that bad, but you still think it's small-minded of your insurance company to take such a laterally asymmetrical view of your accident coverage.

Aquarius: (Jan. 20–Feb. 18)
This Thursday's sudden solar flare will have far-reaching cosmic effects, changing what should have been a good day for career ambitions into an opportunity for romance with a dark stranger.

Pisces: (Feb. 19–March 20)
There's nothing wrong with consensual love between adult human beings, but as long as other people are demonizing it for personal gain, you want in.

SANITARY from page 4

amounts of blood. Passersby were amazed by the unusually large amounts of blood. Passersby were amazed by the unusually large

To spare feelings, he refused to pick a favorite sandwich.

amounts of blood. Passersby were amazed by the unusually large amounts of blood. Passersby were amazed by the unusually large amounts of blood. Passersby were amazed by the unusually large amounts of blood. Passersby were amazed by the unusually large

see SANITARY page 112

NEWS

Democratic Senator Strides Down Corridors Of Powerlessness

see WASHINGTON page 7B

Bachelorette Party Saved By Actual Firemen

see LOCAL page 14E

'Well, Someone's Gotta Play Oboe,' Screams Frustrated Band Teacher

see PEOPLE page 5F

STATshot

A look at the numbers that shape your world.

the ONION®

VOLUME 41 ISSUE 18 AMERICA'S FINEST NEWS SOURCE™ 5–11 MAY 2005

Arizona Man Steals Bush's Identity, Vetoes Bill, Meets With Mexican President

WASHINGTON, DC—Confusion and disbelief reigned at the White House after President Bush announced Monday that an Arizona man, known to authorities only as H4xX0r1337, stole his identity and used it to buy electronic goods, veto a bill, and meet with Mexican President Vicente Fox.

"This is incredibly frustrating," Bush told reporters Tuesday. "Not only does this guy have my credit-card information, he has my Social Security number, all my personal information, and the launch codes for a number of ballistic intercontinental nuclear missiles. I almost don't want to think about it."

"I feel so violated," Bush added.

see MAN page 137

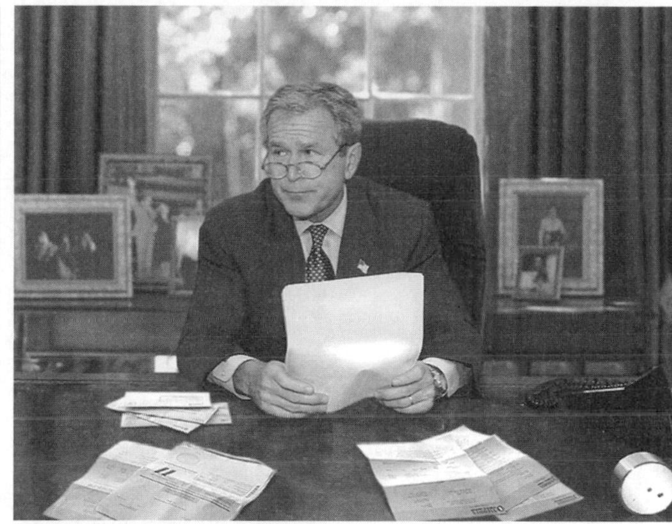

Right: Bush examines his credit-card statements.

Above: Townspeople comfort each other at the scene of the event.

Unspeakable Happens In Area Town

'Oh God, No!' Say Onlookers

MURPHY, ID—Indescribable tragedy struck the quiet foothill town of Murphy Monday, leaving authorities and citizens dumbstruck by the nameless horror that descended on

see UNSPEAKABLE page 137

Actual Expert Too Boring For TV

SECAUCUS, NJ—Dr. Gary Canton, a professor of applied nuclear physics and energy-development technologies at MIT and a leading expert in American nuclear-power applications, was rejected by MSNBC producers for being "too boring for TV" Monday.

"We could deal with Dr. Canton being so short," said Cal Salters, a seg-

see EXPERT page 136

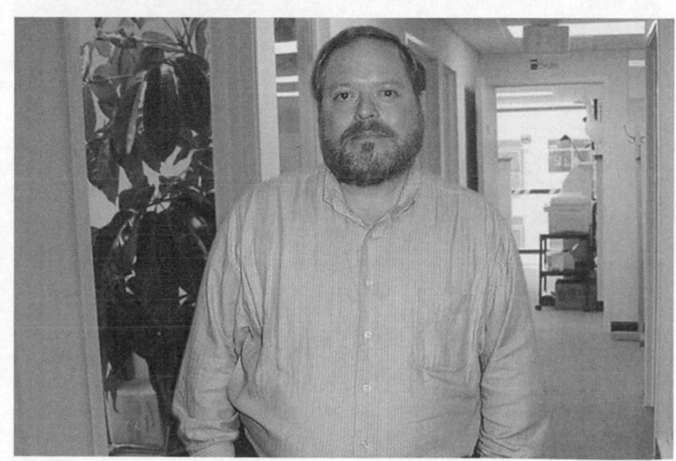

Right: Canton at the MSNBC studio where he failed to make the cut.

Women On The Front Line

Women are barred from U.S. military jobs that would place them on the front line, but some say all troops in Iraq are exposed to ground combat. What do *you* think?

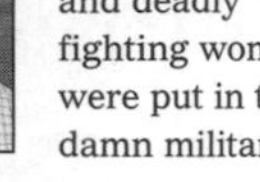

"If you ask me, it's about time America's proud and deadly fighting women were put in the damn military."

Al Trevino
Nurse

"Man, imagine how humiliating it would be to have a crush on a girl in your platoon, only to get your legs blown off right in front of her."

Gabriel Meyers
Systems Analyst

"Women in the military is a complicated issue in the otherwise black-and-white world of war and combat."

Renee Blankenship
Librarian

"I think we should take women off their pedestals, as they just make them sitting ducks in the battle zone."

Ronald Savage
Locksmith

"Women are too docile to serve in front-line combat. Their place is back at the prison, sadistically torturing detainees."

Elmer Whitehead
Lawyer

"To their commanders, front-line soldiers are nothing more than objects, warm bodies, pieces of meat. Women should certainly be used to *that*."

Joy Woodard
Homemaker

Improving Amtrak

Following last week's announcement that an entire fleet of Acela trains will be taken out of service for repairs, Amtrak is looking for ways to reinvigorate the company. What are some of the measures it's taking?

- Placing guardrails to left and right of all tracks
- Reminding Americans that making the trains run on time is the first step on the road to fascism
- Persuading suburban commuters to use rail service by showing them what a Metroliner can do to an SUV
- Popularizing the Seven-Feet-High Club
- Improving brakes on Acela trains; improving engines on Decela trains
- Removing unnecessary "steering wheel" from Amtrak locomotives
- Replacing old, worn tracks with tarmac and adding wings to all cars
- Leaving Amtrak's board of directors alone so it can figure out how to solve its problems without people screaming at it constantly, *okay*?!

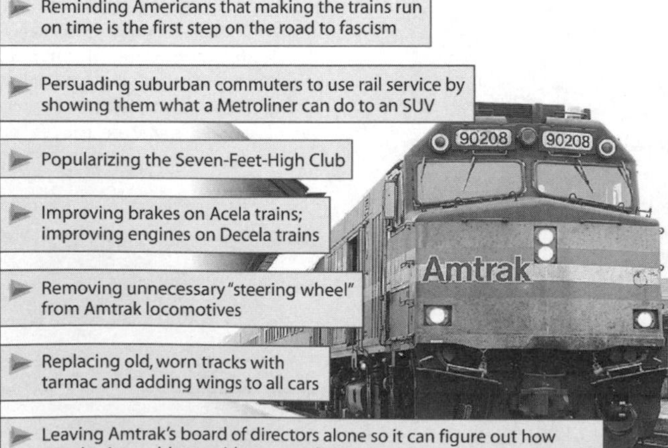

America's Finest News Source.™

Herman Ulysses Zweibel
Founder

T. Herman Zweibel
Publisher Emeritus
J. Phineas Zweibel
Publisher
Maxwell Prescott Zweibel
Editor-In-Chief

I Can't Stand It When Jews Talk During Movies

Do you have a pet peeve—some little thing that drives you completely bonkers? For certain people, it's the sound of a Jewish person dragging her fingernails across a chalkboard. For others, it's when Jews don't signal before making a turn. Me? I can't stand it when Jews talk during movies!

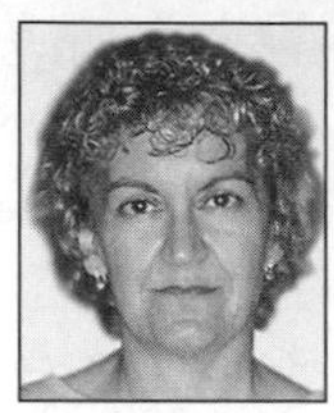

By Dana Healy

Last Friday, I knocked off early from work and headed to the multiplex to catch *The Pacifier*. Sure enough, as soon as the lights go out, a pack of Jews waltzes in and plunks down right in front of me! All through the first preview, they had to have a Jewish debate about where to put their coats and who should hold the Twizzlers. What's wrong with these idiots? If you want to chat, go to a coffee shop, or that Jewish community center down on Cavendish Avenue.

Where did these people learn to whisper? An Israeli helicopter?

I sure didn't pay $10 to listen to a group of twits talk back to the screen like those obnoxious Jewish robots from *Mystery Science Theater 3000*! And apparently, "God's chosen people" weren't selected based on their ability to follow plotlines. No wonder they wandered the desert for so many years—they can't even watch a Vin Diesel movie without getting lost.

It would help if management took stronger action against this total lack of regard. A sign saying, "Jews: Kindly refrain from talking during the film" couldn't hurt. I don't think I'm being unreasonable here. That theater was as loud as an Elders of Zion meeting. Is it asking too much to expect a little courtesy from your fellow moviegoers? I guess some people just weren't raised gentile.

Look, I enjoy eating popcorn while taking in a flick, but at least I have the presence of mind to keep my munching to a conscientious level. Sometimes it feels like I'm the only one who wasn't raised in a barn where special precautions are taken to slaughter livestock in accordance with Jewish laws and traditions.

Look, I enjoy eating popcorn while taking in a flick, but at least I have the presence of mind to keep my munching to a conscientious level. Sometimes it feels like I'm the only one who wasn't raised in a barn where special precautions are taken to slaughter livestock in accordance with Jewish laws and traditions.

If you can keep kosher, why can't you keep quiet?

And how many times can these descendants of Abraham possibly need to use the washroom? If you have to go that often, sit near an aisle and leave the middle seats for those of us who aren't circumcised. You guys may not believe in the doctrine of original sin, but everyone agrees that failing to turn off your cell phone before the movie starts is just plain rude! I swear, the next time a phone goes off, someone's getting a yarmulke shoved down his throat.

You guys may not believe in the doctrine of original sin, but everyone agrees that failing to turn off your cell phone before the movie starts is just plain rude! I swear, the next time a phone goes off, someone's getting a yarmulke shoved down his throat.

If there were some other way to see movies, I'd do it. I've tried renting movies, only to have the film interrupted midway through by a Jewish telemarketer or the sounds of the Jews upstairs blasting their rap music. I can only imagine what that guy with the fiddler on his roof went through. It's the Jewish year 5766, for cripes sake! It's time to learn some courtesy. Ø

U.S. Mint Gears Up To Issue Commemorative County Pennies

WASHINGTON, DC—Following the success of its 50 State Quarters program—deemed one of the most popular commemorative-coin programs in American history—the U.S. Mint announced its next ambitious project: releasing a unique penny for every county in the nation.

"Located in the first state in the union, Delaware's Kent County will be the first county honored in this grand celebration of America," U.S. Mint Director Henrietta Holsman

"I hope they get the old stone water tower just right," Ypsilanti, MI resident Gina Dalton said. "It's the most well-known landmark in Washtenaw County, so it's definitely what they should use."

Fore said Monday. "But over the coming years, citizens all across the nation will see the best aspects of their own counties celebrated on the obverse side of a penny. Collecting all 3,143 county pennies will be a fun activity your family will enjoy for generations."

Starting in 2006, the U.S. Mint will release five new pennies per year for the next 629 years. While the process will be a long one, residents of the nation's 3,143 counties and county equivalents have already begun debating how their regions should be depicted.

"I hope they get the old stone water tower just right," Ypsilanti, MI resident Gina Dalton said. "It's the most well-known landmark in Washtenaw County, so it's definitely what they should use."

While Fore agreed that Ypsilanti's historic water tower—completed in 1890, boasting an 85-foot-tall base made of Joliet limestone, and standing at the important intersection of Route 17 and West Cross Street—is a good suggestion, she cautioned Washtenaw County residents that their penny is scheduled for release in 2315.

"We're encouraging counties, especially those beyond the first 50 or so, to think creatively to find a truly unique representative icon for their penny," Fore said. "Water towers—along with mountains, covered bridges, and lighthouses—will be among the first images to get snapped up. We'll need to see some shoe factories and cell-phone tow-

see MINT page 136

Above: Fore and an assistant unveil the Kent County penny, which boasts a nod to the cinder-block factory.

NEWS IN BRIEF

Report: U.S. Leads World In Lost Sunglasses

WASHINGTON, DC—According to a report by the Bureau of Accessory Statistics, each year the U.S. loses more pairs of sunglasses per person than any other nation. "Over 1.6 billion pairs of sunglasses are lost by Americans concerned with shielding their eyes from excess light and harmful UVA radiation," the report read. "This works out to six pairs of sunglasses per American per year, or 50 pairs of sunglasses lost every second." In second place, Italy has a lost-sunglasses rate of one pair per citizen per year, followed by Japan, Iceland, and Portugal with loss rates of .23, .19, and .16 respectively.

Replacement Socialite Cunt Sought For *Simple Life* Cast

NEW YORK—Due to the falling out between Nicole Richie and Paris Hilton, producers of Fox's *The Simple Life* are continuing their search for the perfect spoiled, no-talent socialite cunt to step in for Richie. "It shouldn't be too hard to find another vapid, muddied cum-dumpster perpetually drunk on the jizz of trust-fund himbos," producer Jonathan Murray said. "Any million-dollar Bambi with a vast inheritance and no ambition will do, though gutter-sluts with coke-fueled pasts will be given special consideration." Murray added that "it doesn't matter if her pussy rattles when the wind blows—we can fix that in post."

Man With Dream To Open Liquor Store Achieves Dream

SOUTH BEND, IN—Dale Seebach, 32, who has dreamed of opening his own liquor store since childhood, saw his dream become a reality Monday. "I never thought I would own a liquor store," said Seebach to his two part-time employees at the grand opening of Dale's Spirits on Front Street. "It was a lot of hard work applying for the loan, getting a lease, and working out the distribution, but I did it!" If the store does well, Seebach may someday realize his other dream of enclosing his backyard deck for winter use.

Drive-Time Commute Jam-Packed With Entertainment

CHANDLER, AZ—Phoenix-area resident Bruce Meske, 34, said he can't believe the amazing number of riveting, drive-time radio options available for his 40-minute commute home every night. "At no other time of the day is my life so jam-packed with incredible entertainment choices," Meske said Monday. "I could listen to the '60s at 6:00 or tune into the week's Top Five with Fathead on The Zone! Should I get the lead out with Beebo and Frank, stay informed with Ted and Heidi, or get riled by Mike Savage?! Sometimes I wish my commute took two hours!" Meske added that his wealth of options for the morning drive floor him as well.

Rapidly Swelling Man May Contain Traces Of Peanuts

PENSACOLA, FL—Lance Kiser, the host at the Erewan Thai restaurant, informed fellow employees Monday that the bloated, choking man at table four may contain trace amounts of peanuts. "Warning: The dark-haired businessman who very suddenly began experiencing shortness of breath, confusion, and slurred speech may contain trace amounts of peanuts," Kiser said. "He definitely ate a plate of chicken curry prepared in the same facility as dishes containing peanuts and/or other nuts." The purple-faced, swelling man declined comment. ⌀

MINT from page 135

ers, too."

Residents of Loving County, TX, population 67, are taking no chances. They have already tendered their penny's design, which features the Johnson family's round barn, the only structure of note in the vicinity. Residents said they plan to hold annual bake sales to maintain the building until the penny is released in 2371.

Richland Center, WI resident Tom McCrary said he is anticipating his

"I have spoken to numerous concerned Alaska and Louisiana citizens, and I tell them all the same thing: Settle down," Fore said.

penny's 2433 release.

"Richland County is best known for its apple harvest, dairy farms, and the rock bridge," McCrary said. "But after the lesson of the New Hampshire quarter, I'm not too comfortable putting a natural rock formation on the back of our penny. Luckily, we have another 438 years to decide on a symbol that accurately conveys the spirit of Richland County."

Some U.S. citizens, particularly those in coastal regions, have raised concerns that their counties may never get a chance to be represented, due to rising water levels and tectonic shifts.

Citizens of Alaska and Louisiana have expressed worries that they may not be represented at all.

"I have spoken to numerous concerned Alaska and Louisiana citizens, and I tell them all the same thing: Settle down," Fore said. "Although they are technically called the county pennies, the coins will certainly include Alaska's census areas, Louisiana's parishes, and independent cities like St. Louis and the District of Columbia."

"County equivalents are part of our rich national tapestry," Fore added.

Fore also addressed worries that the penny may be out of use before the last counties are represented.

"You have to keep your eye on the big picture—this is about Americans connecting with America through numismatics," Fore said. "Don't count the penny out so fast. This may be just the thing to get people excited about the penny all over again."

The U.S. Mint has designed a folder for collecting and displaying the county pennies. The cardboard murals, measuring 8 feet by 35 feet, will be available at most Walgreens stores, or directly from the Mint by mail for $4.95 plus $179 for postage and handling. ⌀

EXPERT from page 133

Above: Self-proclaimed nuclear expert Skip Hammond.

ment producer at MSNBC. "And we could've made him up so he didn't look like he spends all day in front of a computer. We even considered cutting away to stock footage so our audience didn't have to look at him for

"[Canton] went on like that for six... long... minutes," Salters said. "Fact after mind-numbing fact. Then he started spewing all these statistics about megawatts and the nation's current energy consumption and I don't know what, because my mind just shut off."

too long. But when it turned out that listening to him is about as interesting as picking the lint off his lapels—well, there was nothing we could do about that."

Canton was brought in for a test interview based on a recent op-ed in the *Boston Globe*, in which he argued that increased reliance on nuclear power is "inevitable." When asked to address nuclear power's potentially disastrous consequences, however, Canton launched into a well-reasoned lecture that balanced modern energy demands against safety and environmental concerns.

"At MIT's Laboratory for Energy and the Environment, we see nuclear-power technology as the best option for the United States and the world to meet future energy needs without emitting carbon dioxide and other atmospheric pollutants," Canton said in the taped pre-interview, which has already been erased. "Other energy options include increased efficiency, renewables, and carbon sequestration. Actually, all of these options may be needed for a successful, non-stratified, growth-oriented national energy infrastructure."

Salters was not impressed.

"[Canton] went on like that for six... long... minutes," Salters said. "Fact after mind-numbing fact. Then he started spewing all these statistics about megawatts and the nation's current energy consumption and I don't know what, because my mind just shut off. I tried to lead him in the right direction. I told him to address the *fears* that the *average citizen* might have about nuclear power, but he still utterly failed to mention meltdowns, radiation, or mushroom clouds."

"I'm sure he knows what he's talking about," Salters added. "But we have a responsibility to educate *and* entertain our viewers. In the end, we had to go with someone else."

MSNBC chose Skip Hammond, former Arizona State football player, MBA holder, and author of *Imprison The Sun: America's Coming Nuclear-Power Holocaust*. Hammond is best known for his "atomic domino" theory of chained power-plant explosions and his signature lavender silk tie.

"Absolute Armageddon," Hammond said when asked about the dangers increased reliance on nuclear power might pose. "Atoms are not only too tiny to be seen, they're too powerful to be predicted. Three Mile Island? Remember it? I do. Don't they?"

"Clouds of radiation, glowing rivers, a hole reaching to the earth's core—that's what we're facing," Hammond continued. "Death of one in four Americans! Count off, everyone: one, two, three, *you*. Millions of people gone. And no one's even mentioned terrorism yet. You have to wonder why not."

According to Salters, Hammond was "perfect."

"The way Skip looked right into that camera and said 'annihilation' with his perfect enunciation—I've been in the news business for 14 years, and I still got goose bumps," Salters said.

Reached at his office, Canton said he was unsure why he wasn't chosen for the program.

"I discussed the interrelated technical, economic, environmental, and political challenges associated with increased nuclear-power usage over the

"I'm sure he knows what he's talking about," Salters added. "But we have a responsibility to educate *and* entertain our viewers. In the end, we had to go with someone else."

next half-century and their relevance to government, industry, and community leaders," Canton said. "You'd think it would be exactly what they wanted. It was exactly what they wanted, according to the producer who contacted me."

Hammond is scheduled to appear in all six parts of the upcoming Learning Channel series *Frost Or Fire: America's Coming Energy Tribulations*. ⌀

MAN from page 133

Above: Close examination of this photo of President Bush's April 16 address to the White House press corps reveals an imposter FBI authorities believe may be the elusive identity thief H4xX0r1337.

Bush said he has canceled his credit cards and changed the national-security codes, but he labeled the process a "total nightmare."

"It's a huge ordeal," Bush said. "Everything will be straightened out eventually, but my credit rating and political capital are down the tubes. I asked the FBI, and they aren't even sure how long this guy's had my identity. For all I know, he's started up his own oil refinery somewhere in Alaska."

Bush said he began to suspect something was wrong when he received a card from Sen. Bill Frist, thanking him for vetoing the Digital Media Consumers' Rights Act of 2005.

"I thought I was going crazy," Bush said. "I had no recollection of even reading that piece of legislation, much less killing it. At first, I thought Frist had things mixed up, but I checked the records, and sure enough, someone with my credentials came into the White House in late March while I was on my ranch and vetoed that bill."

Bush said he only recognized the full magnitude of the problem last Tuesday, when Mexican President Fox called to thank him for the "incredibly positive and productive summit."

"Vicente said I had agreed to an aid package for his country," Bush said. "It was like I was in cuckoo-land. That's when I called [FBI Director Robert] Mueller. I said, 'You may want to sit down for this one, Bob. I think someone stole my identity.'"

According to Mueller, examining Bush's recent outgoing e-mail led him to believe that the president's identity was probably stolen about five weeks ago, when he responded to an e-mail from paypal783@hotmail.com asking him to comply with PayPal security measures by entering all 12 of his credit-card numbers, his Social Security number, his passwords, and his personal identification numbers.

"I thought I was going crazy," Bush said. "I had no recollection of even reading that piece of legislation, much less killing it. At first, I thought Frist had things mixed up, but I checked the records, and sure enough, someone with my credentials came into the White House in late March while I was on my ranch and vetoed that bill."

"It appears that the president is among the many thousands of Americans who have fallen for so-called 'phishing' scams," Mueller said. "One should never give out sensitive personal information in response to an e-mail. If the president had read the memo we sent out a few months ago, he would have known that."

Although the FBI has traced H4xX0r1337's now-defunct ISP account to a Mail Boxes, Etc. mailbox in Tempe, AZ, Mueller said apprehending H4xX0r1337 may prove more difficult.

"Identity thieves and hackers are notoriously difficult to locate," Mueller said. "They are often highly intelligent and very skilled at covering their tracks. Making it more difficult, H4xX0r1337 seems to have used his credentials to commandeer Air Force One. At this moment, he could be anywhere in the world."

Bush said he will likely need to spend the entire week reclaiming his identity, adding that he wished to thank everyone who has already assisted him in the process.

"The FBI has been working tirelessly to find this man who hides in the shadows and perpetrates computer terrorism," Bush said. "I'd also like to thank Debrina at Bank One's customer-service center. She was very courteous and super helpful."

This is not the first time a hacker has stolen the identity of a political figure. In February 2004, police arrested Columbus, OH's HotGrrrl69 after the 16-year-old was caught campaigning for John Kerry while posing as Sen. Barbara Boxer (D-CA). ⌀

UNSPEAKABLE from page 133

their community.

"Oh God," said Wilma Freas, standing at the edge of Main Street overlooking the lumberyard. "Those poor people!"

Added Freas: "And the *children*..."

Murphy residents are still attempting to come to grips with the overwhelming catastrophe, with reactions ranging from unimaginable sorrow to sheer incoherent rage.

"Why?!" said feed-store owner Blaine Fullerton, beating the counter with a clenched fist. "Those were innocent—I mean, in big cities, maybe. But here?"

"*Why?*" added Fullerton, removing his cap and throwing it to the ground.

Emergency personnel deployed to the site of the inexplicable horror reported that their efforts to contain the situation are in effect.

"I rushed... right when I... I...," said Dr. Marjorie Sweeny, a trauma surgeon at Benediction Memorial Hospital in nearby Caldwell. "As a doctor, I... I wanted to see if there was anything I could do. I thought there was a chance I... Oh God! Oh God, all the blood! I'm sorry. I have to... Right now I have to..."

Law-enforcement officials from the state to the federal level have been called in to deal with the situation. However, due to communications difficulties, many agencies have had problems coordinating their efforts.

"We're on the road," said Sgt. Jason Haskell of the Murphy police department, attempting to direct members of the National Guard to the site of the great calamity. "Everybody... should get down... to the road."

"Lord in heaven, no!" Haskell added.

Many of the early reports, garbled though they are, have come from the local level. Owyhee County Sheriff's Deputy Ronald Muntoth is one of the few witnesses to the scene who has been able to give a near coherent report.

"I've seen a lot of things in my years on the force," Muntoth said. "But I'm still trying to get my mind around this unthinkable tragedy. We had a train derailment a few years ago that I thought was incomprehensible. But this—I... I can't even begin to... No. I just... It... Excuse me."

As fragmented accounts of the tragic events continue to trickle in, stunned residents of Murphy are quietly closing ranks, banding together to bear mute witness to the inconceivable disaster. On Monday evening, thousands of locals assembled in the town square, so recently the scene of incalculable loss, to observe a moment of silence for the as-yet-unnamed victims. After a respectful but undetermined period of time, Mayor Molly Hawkshaw spoke.

"Oh!" said Hawkshaw, who is assuming personal responsibility for the confidential investigation into the tragedy. "I just... We... argh gah... pain and shock."

Idaho Gov. Dirk Kempthorne plans to visit Murphy later this week. ⌀

ADVICE

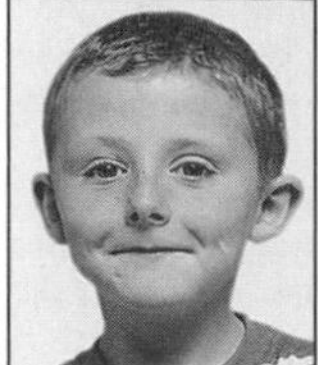

Ask A 7-Year-Old With A New Joke Book

By Danny Geppert

Dear 7-Year-Old With A New Joke Book,

When my nephew announced he was getting married, I gave him, as an engagement gift, a valuable original painting that has been in our family for generations. While I'd intended the family heirloom be displayed in the home he would share with his fiancée, the couple broke up a few months later. Now the painting is sitting, unwrapped and unhung, against a wall in his tiny studio apartment. Frankly, I'm concerned the painting might become damaged in the bachelor pad. Would it be selfish of me to ask him to return the gift?

Unsure In Utah

Dear Unsure:

Mom! Mom! Where are you? Mom! Oh, there you are. Hey Mom, after Cub Scouts, me and Spencer and Spencer's dad stopped at the mall and we went to Waldenbooks and I bought a book with my own money! It's called *Rib Ticklers For Your Funny Bone*, and it's the best book ever 'cause it's a joke book! I told a bunch on the way home and everyone laughed so hard. Wanna hear one? Here's one: Why couldn't Dracula go to the Halloween dance? Give up? Wanna know? Because his *mummy* wouldn't let him! Isn't that funny, Mom?

Here's one: Why couldn't Dracula go to the Halloween dance? Give up? Wanna know? Because his mummy wouldn't let him! Isn't that funny, Mom?

Dear 7-Year-Old With A New Joke Book,

Several months ago, my coworker Julia asked me out. I politely declined, telling her that I felt it's too risky to mix business with pleasure. As the weeks went by, I came to realize that it may have been the worst decision I've ever made! I was crushed to find out, however, that she has a new boyfriend. Should I tell Julia my feelings, or should I just leave well enough alone?

Regretful In Racine

Dear Regretful:

Okay, here's another one. Mom? Here's another one: What's a parrot's favorite game? To get his quarter back. Oops, I meant 'hide and speak.' Isn't that a funny one? Hide and speak! Aren't these funny, Mom? Mom! How do pigs write? Mom! Did you *hear* me? How do pigs write? Just guess. *Mom, guess.* I *can't* guess. I have the answer. *You* have to guess. Ugh! It was, "How do pigs write?" No! Duh! Not with their hooves! With a *pig pen*! Ha ha, you got it wrong! I am right and you are wrong!

Dear 7-Year-Old With A New Joke Book,

I'm a 27-year-old female in love with a wonderful guy. Everything was going great until last week, when he revealed that he's an avid nudist! He goes to a clothing-free resort every summer and strongly urged me to come along this time around. I've never had any interest in being naked in public, but I fear that if I don't share in his passion, I might lose him. Do you think I should put my preferences aside and force myself to give it a try? Or should I stand my ground and keep my clothes on?

Dressed Up In DeMoines

Dear Dressed Up:

Mom! Mom! Mom! Mom! Mom! Mom! Mom! What did the traffic cop ticket the cow for? Mom! What did the traffic cop ticket the cow for? Come on, it's funny! I'm *not* yelling! I'm just *asking*. Give up? Give up? Mommm, aaanswer! For its *mooving* violations. Like a cow goes "moo." Mom, why are you going outside? Do that later! Mom, I don't have my shoes on. Mom, there's more!

Dear 7-Year-Old With A New Joke Book,

As she will readily admit, my wife has always been somewhat of a "germ freak." But now, her fear of unsanitary conditions is putting a serious cramp in our summer-vacation plans. She says that hotel-room blankets and pillows are filthy, and she'd never be able to sleep on them. Should we skip the trip? What else can we do? I'd appreciate any ideas!

Staying Put For Now In Maryland

Dear Staying Put:

Hey Lexi, what do you call a cow who jumps up and down? Shut up. It is not me. You just said that because you don't know the answer. You don't, do you? Well, it's a milkshake! You're the world's dumbest sister, you know that? Stop it! It's mine. Stop! You're just jealous because Mom won't let you get your ears pierced but I got to buy a book with my own money. You suck. I'll go find Mom. She likes my jokes.

Dear 7-Year-Old With A New Joke Book,

Yesterday, I noticed a man with one leg standing on my crowded bus. He was supporting himself with crutches and looked very uncomfortable. When I offered him my seat, he got angry and told me to mind my own business. Well, that made *me* angry. I was only trying to do the right thing! Is it patronizing to assume that a disabled person is entitled a seat on a bus or train? Should I think twice about offering my seat in the future?

Meant Well In Mechanicsburg

Dear Meant Well:

Mom, Lexi was mean to me. She said I was annoying. She tried to take my book, but it's mine. Right, Mom? Because I bought it with my own money. Lexi will be sorry when I'm telling jokes on TV. Won't she, Mom? Won't she? Mom, I got a joke for you: What has four wheels and—Mo-o-om! Turn off the vacuum cleaner! I'm trying to tell you a joke! Mom-mm, come on!

CONFIDENTIAL TO PIECING THINGS TOGETHER: Knock knock. Mommmm, listen! Knock knock! You say "Who's there?" Tanks. Tanks! Mommmmm! C'mon! You say, "Tanks who?" Come on, Mom, pleeeease? "Tanks for the memories." Um, Mom, what does that *mean*? Mom?

Danny Geppert is a syndicated columnist whose weekly advice column, Ask A 7-Year-Old With A New Joke Book, *appears in more than 250 papers nationwide.*

HOROSCOPES

Your Horoscope

By Lloyd Schumner Sr.
Retired Machinist and
A.A.P.B.-Certified Astrologer

Aries: (March 21–April 19)
You're a true role model for young people, the way you've achieved financial success and remained active in your community while masturbating pretty much constantly.

Taurus: (April 20–May 20)
Despite the urgent need for the million-person interstellar starliner you designed, you'll hide your blueprints, because you can't think of a million people you could stand being with on a trip that long.

Gemini: (May 21–June 21)
It's been three months since you've been hit by a bus, but the law of averages catches up with you this week, when you win free tickets to the Annual Greyhound Operators' Dozen-Coach Rodeo.

Cancer: (June 22–July 22)
You might have been speaking entirely in jest, but those abductors would not have taken your wife if you hadn't had the manners to add "please."

Leo: (July 23–Aug. 22)
Technically, "filibusters" can only take place on the congressional floor. All you're doing is keeping that poor waiter from attending to his other tables.

Virgo: (Aug. 23–Sept. 22)
Your friends have always referred to you as having an "old soul," but your soul is nothing compared to your arteries.

Libra: (Sept. 23–Oct. 23)
Despite changing your number a dozen times, you'll continue to get late-night phone calls from Owen warning you not to come sniffin' around his women.

Scorpio: (Oct. 24–Nov. 21)
You will soon be renowned throughout the land as Furious Nine-Mile-Reach Fist, a name that sounds cool but will actually turn out to be a handicap in your job as a suburban realtor.

Sagittarius: (Nov. 22–Dec. 21)
You've always lived by the words of your father, who said, "Even if you're only a ditch digger, you should be the best damn ditch digger you can be." Well, good job, you fucking ditch digger.

Capricorn: (Dec. 22–Jan. 19)
You'll be a very sought-after sports-page interview when the Minnesota Vikings demand that their new stadium include your head on a post at the main entrance.

Aquarius: (Jan. 20–Feb. 18)
You always suspected that no one would attend your funeral, but due to a rare coma-like neurological condition, you'll actually be able to see all the empty pews.

Pisces: (Feb. 19–March 20)
You're offered the chance to serve as "the most dangerous game" for a billionaire sportsman, but it's canceled after he finds a tiger that has been trained to work a rocket launcher.

the ONION®
VOLUME 41 ISSUE 19 AMERICA'S FINEST NEWS SOURCE™ 12–18 MAY 2005

NEWS

San Francisco Photographer Shits Out Another Bridge Photo

see BUSINESS page 14E

Usher To Put Shirt Back On When Usher Ready To Put Shirt Back On

see ENTERTAINMENT page 5C

Parallel Universe 'So Much Better,' Says Alternate You

see PEOPLE page 5F

STATshot

A look at the numbers that shape your world.

Top Broken Promises
16% Not to laugh
21% To be a good daddy to our 11 children
25% Never to brain our neighbor with a blunt object and dissolve his corpse with lime in our crawlspace
18% Iron Maiden forever
20% To uphold and defend the Constitution of the United States of America
BUS STOP

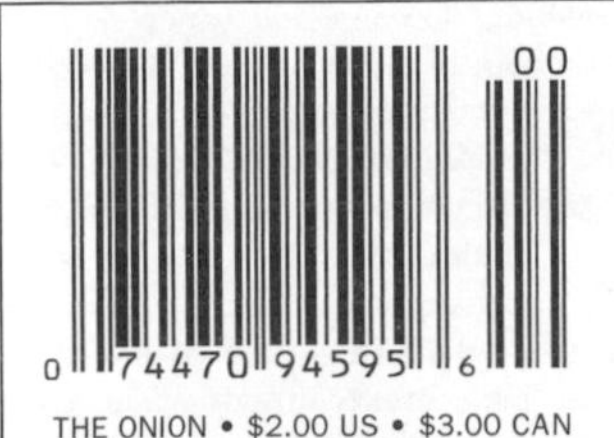

'Not Quite Perfect' McDonald's Opens In Illinois Outlet Mall

GURNEE, IL—Hungry shoppers at the Gurnee Mills outlet mall can now get a name-brand lunch at a bargain-basement price, thanks to the Monday opening of McDonald's first "Not Quite Perfect" outlet store, offering imperfect and irregular items from the fast-food giant's menu.

"It's true that consistency is part of what makes McDonald's the leader in the fast-food industry, but so is good value," said Brian Landers, manager of the McDonald's outlet. "When customers see the low, low prices, they're more than willing to give our Six-

see McDONALD'S page 143

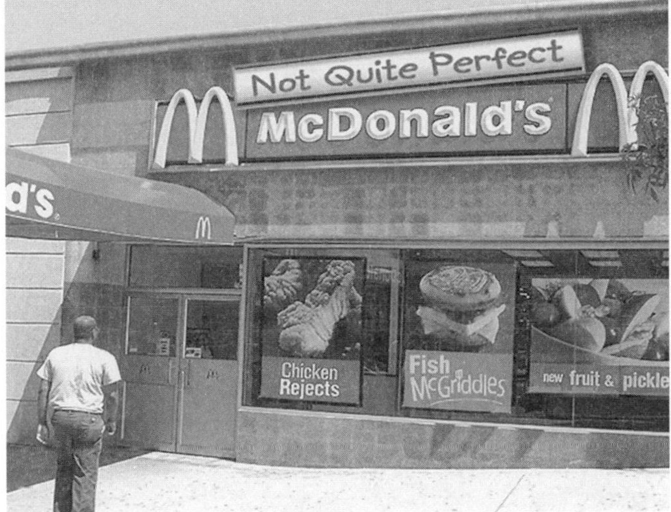

Above: The new outlet store.

Report:

Scientology Losing Ground To New Fictionology

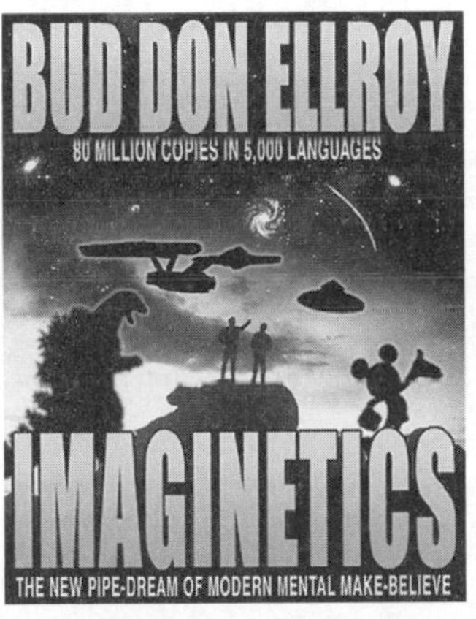

Left: The paperback that has already sold two million copies.

LOS ANGELES—According to a report released Monday by the American Institute of Religions, the Church of Scientology, once one of the fastest-growing religious organizations in the U.S., is steadily losing members to the much newer religion Fictionology.

"Unlike Scientology, which is based on empirically verifiable scientific tenets, Fictionology's central principles are essentially fairy tales with no connection to reality," the AIR report read. "In short, Fictionology offers its followers a mythical belief system free from the cumbersome scientific method to which Scientology is hidebound."

Created in 2003 by self-proclaimed messiah Bud Don Ellroy, Fictionology's principles were first outlined in the self-help paperback *Imaginetics: The New Pipe-Dream Of Modern Mental Make-Believe.*

Fictionology's central belief, that any imaginary construct can be incorporated into the church's ever-growing set of official doctrines, continues to gain popularity. Believers in Santa Claus, his elves, or the Tooth Fairy are permitted—even encouraged—to

see FICTIONOLOGY page 142

Cupid Shooting Spree Leaves Dozens Infatuated

CHICAGO—Dozens of innocent citizens were infatuated Monday, when a winged angel of romantic inspiration—or "Cupid"—drew his magical bow and opened fire on a crowd at Lincoln Park, striking an as-yet-undetermined number of people directly in their hearts during a 13-minute enchanted-arrow shooting spree.

"I was just walking along the sidewalk when I saw this chubby, winged guy wearing some sort of diaper, pointing a red-tipped arrow in my direction," said Steve Kremms, an insurance adjuster who was pierced by

see CUPID page 143

Right: Police question victims who were attacked by Cupid (inset).

Texas-Cheerleader Crackdown

Last week, the Texas House of Representatives approved a bill banning "overtly sexually suggestive" high-school cheerleading routines. What do *you* think?

"See?! See what happens when you bring it on, Kirsten Dunst?!"

Erik Booth
Systems Analyst

"If we outlawed everything some people find offensive, there wouldn't even be a Texas in the first place."

Cindy Campos
Lifeguard

"Is there a way to comment on this without seeming like a huge perv? All right then, I like the jiggling. Are you happy?"

Jon Patell
Loan Clerk

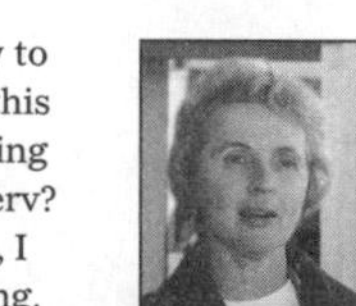

"Texas lawmakers: always on the vanguard of educational reform."

Dianne Pruitt
Store Owner

"The law needs to differentiate clearly between lewd cheerleading and regular cheerleading. I've been masturbating to both for quite some time, and trust me, there are subtle differences."

Alvin Humphrey
Laser Engineer

"As a former Texas football player, I've gotta say I never noticed the cheerleaders. Don't tell the other guys, though, 'cause they'd kick the shit outta me if they knew that I was gay."

Alex Stafford
Laundry Worker

The New Iraqi Government

The first democratic Iraqi government was recently sworn in. What's first on its agenda?

- Get a minister of petroleum resources who doesn't blow up all the time
- Convince constituents that they can write letters to their elected officials without getting their arms cut off
- Rename Saddam Hussein Boulevard, Saddam Hussein Square, Saddam Hussein Park, Saddam Hussein Government Center, and Saddam Hussein Sewage-Treatment Plant
- Put out feelers to see if some quieter, more peaceful country is looking for a government
- Squash the insurgency, or hire them as secret police
- Privatize Social Security
- Get some stamps printed up—kids love stamps
- End 1,500 years of sectarian violence

America's Finest News Source.™

Herman Ulysses Zweibel
Founder

T. Herman Zweibel
Publisher Emeritus
J. Phineas Zweibel
Publisher
Maxwell Prescott Zweibel
Editor-In-Chief

No One Even Heard Of This Company Til I Dragged Us Into A Corporate Scandal

Gentlemen, hello. Sorry I'm late. I had a hell of a time getting in the front door. Can you believe all those cameras? It's a zoo out there. You practically need a helicopter to... Okay, why the long faces? Great, everyone's mad at me. Hey, before I caused this corporate scandal, no one had even heard of Tevcom.

By Darrel Greunwald
CEO, Tevcom

Our investors and our clients? Okay, yes, those are a few people who knew our name. But who else? Our brand recognition was zilch among average Americans—unless they mowed our company golf course or gave rubdowns in the spa up on the 45th floor. But when someone says "Tevcom" now, there's not a person in the room who doesn't think "national telecommunications firm."

Yes Schmidt, a "national telecommunications firm that defrauded investors of billions of dollars through insider trading, falsification of records, and securities fraud." But we made the front page of every important newspaper in the country! Tevcom! Above the fold! We're going head to head with a war, and who got the bigger typeface? You can't buy publicity like that.

Johnson, $5.2 billion isn't the cost of the publicity. It's the total we're going to pay out in fines and legal fees. The publicity is priceless.

Come on, guys. The press hasn't been all bad. Those stories about our $7 million Caligula party made us look like total players. Sting's performance, the Kobe beef appetizer trays in the bathrooms, and the Venus ice sculpture that lactated White Russians? We redefined what people thought about the old, boring telecom industry. And no matter what they're saying, those parties were valid business expenditures. We must've cinched four or five deals that night.

So, you guys are gonna turn your tails and run like squirrels because Jay Leno made a joke about our monthly board meetings in Aruba? It's not like no one else in the industry gives incentives to their employees. You, Kirkson: Look me in the eye and tell me that you didn't earn your $2 million bonus. That money was my way of saying I believe in you, Kirkson. Won't you believe in me?

I can see now that I'm not going to get one bit of thanks. Do you think it's easy to get on C-SPAN? The government doesn't put just anyone in front of a congressional subcommittee. Thousands of Americans saw me get dressed down by Chuck Schumer. That's right, *United States senator* Chuck Schumer. In calling my actions "a disgraceful abuse of the public trust," he used the company's name 14 times.

What? The employees should be happy. Now when they tell their in-laws where they work, it'll lead to some dinner conversation. Tell the drones their stock will go back up once we get this mess sorted out. And if it doesn't, they can sell their Tevcom-logo paperweights on eBay. Our "Tevcom Pride" company-picnic T-shirts are probably going for $50 a pop. Shit. I wish we hadn't burned all those memos. We could've gotten a boatload of money for those.

Come on, guys. The press hasn't been all bad. Those stories about our $7 million Caligula party made us look like total players. Sting's performance, the Kobe beef appetizer trays in the bathrooms, and the Venus ice sculpture that lactated White Russians? We redefined what people thought about the old, boring telecom industry.

Come on, you Suzies. What's the worst thing that could happen? Some of us might have to do a little time? Boo hoo hoo. Hard time in a country-club prison. And when we get out, we'll make a king's ransom on the lecture circuit: "Ladies and gentlemen, I was at the top, until everything came crashing down. I've learned a hard lesson and I'm better for it." Now give me my check and I'll be on my way to the Sheridan executive lounge.

Fine, if you're all going to be this way, let's get this meeting over with. Ooh! Real quick, though: When you leave tonight, if you plan to cover your face, make sure to wear your Tevcom windbreaker. Ø

36-Year-Old Still Looking For Ways To Make Brushing Fun

Above: Naasz tries to enjoy his new toothpaste.

SAN FRANCISCO—More than three decades after acquiring his first Pink Panther toothbrush, Mark Naasz continues to search unsuccessfully for new ways to make brushing his teeth fun, the 36-year-old Bernal Heights resident revealed Monday.

"Check it out: Tom's Of Maine fennel-flavored all-natural anti-cavity toothpaste," said Naasz, pulling the $4.89 item from a Whole Foods bag. "It says here that fennel is an all-natural, herbal breath-freshener that's been used for centuries. And look: This little snap-lid bottle fits in my jacket pocket, so I'll probably start brushing my teeth after lunch. I've been meaning to get into that habit for years."

"Check it out: Tom's Of Maine fennel-flavored all-natural anti-cavity toothpaste," said Naasz, pulling the $4.89 item from a Whole Foods bag.

Although Naasz's taste in toothpastes, mouthwashes, flosses, brushes, and other oral-hygiene aids has grown more sophisticated over time, his desire to make the chore of dental care enjoyable has remained constant.

"Every time I go to the dentist and get a cleaning, I vow that I'll start taking better care of my teeth," said Naasz, who brushes two times a day and flosses once or twice whenever he buys a new flossing product. "If I could just find something that would make fighting plaque and tartar less of a boring, repetitive chore—like a really flavorful toothpaste or a cool electric toothbrush—then I'd *want* to do it."

Naasz's pursuit of good dental hygiene extends beyond dentifrices and brushing devices. He recently embarked upon and quickly abandoned a foray into home tooth-whitening.

"I thought whitening my teeth would

see BRUSHING page 142

NEWS IN BRIEF

Senators Lured Back To Emergency Session By Promise Of Free Pizza

WASHINGTON, DC—U.S. senators from both parties, tired and eager to go home to their families after a hard day of legislation, were enticed back into the Senate chamber for an emergency budget session Tuesday by the promise of Little Caesars. "I know it's been a long day, but if you stay late, there's gonna be *pizza*," said Majority Whip Mitch McConnell at 9:30 p.m. "Don't tell [Senate Majority Leader Bill] Frist, but stick around, and I'll make sure you all get an extra order of Crazy Bread with sauce." The senators only relented when McConnell promised that if they hammered out the budget by 1 a.m., they could rent *Glengarry Glen Ross* and watch it in the hearing room.

Fear Factor Creator's Will: 'Heirs Must Eat My Ashes To Collect Inheritance'

LOS ANGELES—According to details of *Fear Factor* creator John de Mol's will released Monday, his heirs cannot collect their inheritance until they complete a battery of challenges. "I do bequeath my estate to my wife and children, henceforth 'you,' on the condition that you fully consume the ashes from my freshly cremated corpse," the creator's will read. "Should you be able to complete the task, you will receive $10 million and a Caribbean vacation. Fail, and you'll be eliminated from my benefactors—unless you spend one hour locked in a coffin filled with maggots." Comedian Joe Rogan will serve as the will's executor.

Joy Sucked Out Of Room By Pumped-Up Manager

CHICAGO—Leo Burnett Advertising project manager Dirk Hazelton's show of enthusiasm drained the creative spirit from the conference room Monday. "Man, the country loves this cheddar! The country needs this cheddar!" said Hazelton to his creative team, pumping his fists in the air. "Come on and join in. We all grew up on cheddar! What do you think of when you think of cheddar? Let's get some ideas on the board." Members of the creative team responded with mortified silence.

Poster Vandal Enters 'Phallus In Mouth' Period

OAKLAND, CA—According to experts at the American Folk Art Museum, the billboard and subway-poster defacer known only as "Suck It" has entered his "phallus in mouth" phase. "As you can see, the artist has moved from drawing larger breasts on the lingerie models to depicting erect penises entering their mouths," said art critic Graham Kern, gesturing to a vandalized Victoria's Secret poster. "His Sharpie phalluses offer a stark contrast to the colorful hues of the ad, with simple lines recalling Henri Matisse's nudes." Kern said he has not seen such energetic lines since the poster vandal's "blackened-in teeth" period.

Upper-Middle-Class Man Vows To Never Forget Middle-Class Roots

ELMBROOK, WI—Although he earns a salary in the low six figures, 38-year-old investment banker David Monreal said he will always stay true to his middle-class upbringing. "When I was a kid, both of my parents held down jobs just to help pay for our split-level ranch home and two Chryslers," Monreal said. "Mom used to have a rule: no TV during supper. No matter how big my portfolio gets, I'll never forget that rule." Monreal said he hopes one day to take his kids to the office where their Grandpa Joe toiled selling insurance for up to 40 hours a week. ⌀

FICTIONOLOGY from page 139

view them as deities. Even corporate mascots like the Kool-Aid Man are valid objects of Fictionological worship.

"My personal savior is Batman," said Beverly Hills plastic surgeon Greg Jurgenson. "My wife chooses to follow the teachings of the Gilmore Girls. Of course, we are still beginners. Some advanced-level Fictionologists have total knowledge of every lifetime they have ever lived for the last 80 trillion years."

"My personal savior is Batman," said Beverly Hills plastic surgeon Greg Jurgenson. "My wife chooses to follow the teachings of the Gilmore Girls. Of course, we are still beginners. Some advanced-level Fictionologists have total knowledge of every lifetime they have ever lived for the last 80 trillion years."

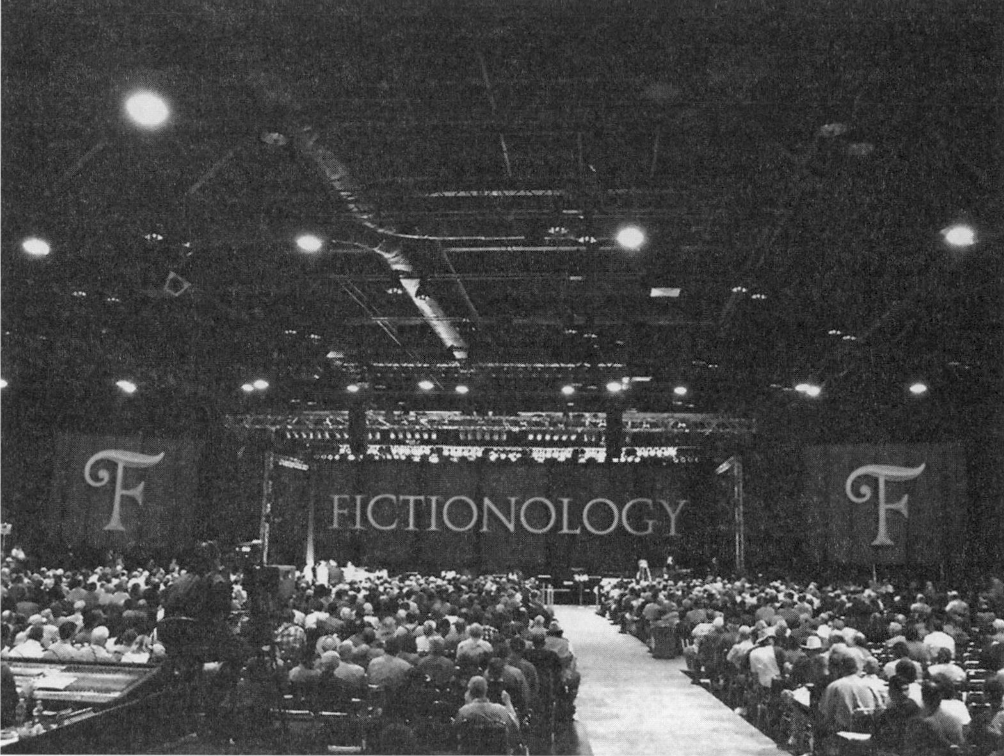

Above: A recent Fictionology rally in Clearwater, FL.

"Sure, it's total bullshit," Jurgenson added. "But that's Fictionology. Praise Batman!"

While the Church of Fictionology acknowledges that its purported worldwide membership of 450 billion is an invented number, the AIR report estimates that as many as 70 percent of the church's followers are former Scientologists.

Church of Scientology public-relations spokesman Al Kurz said he was "shocked" when he learned that Fictionology is approaching the popularity of his religion.

"Scientology is rooted in strict scientific principles, such as the measurement of engrams in the brain by the E-Meter," Kurz said. "Scientology uses strictly scientific methodologies to undo the damage done 75 million years ago by the Galactic Confederation's evil warlord Xenu—we offer our preclear followers procedures to erase overts in the reactive mind. Conversely, Fictionology is essentially just a bunch of make-believe nonsense."

Hollywood actor David McSavage, who converted to Fictionology last year, attempted to explain.

"Scientology can only offer data, such as how an Operating Thetan can control matter, energy, space, and time with pure thought alone," McSavage said. "But truly spiritual people don't care about data, especially those seeking an escape from very real physical, mental, or emotional problems."

McSavage added, "As a Fictionologist, I live in a world of pretend. It's liberating."

A tax-exempt organization, the Church of Fictionology stands poised to become a great moneymaking power if it continues to grow at its current rate—a situation Kurz called "outrageous."

"In recruiting new members, Fictionology preys on the gullible with fanciful stories and simple-minded solutions," Kurz said. "Fictionology is depriving legitimate churches of the revenue they need to carry out charitable works worldwide—important charitable works like clearing the planet of body-thetan implants." ⌀

BRUSHING from page 141

be fun—really dramatic or something," Naasz said. "But the [whitening] strips felt weird against my teeth, and it was torture keeping them in my mouth for 30 minutes. Really, I don't know what I was thinking—I can't even stand gargling with Listerine for 30 seconds."

Faith Combes, Naasz's girlfriend of three years, has stood by as Naasz cycled through dozens of over-the-counter tooth-cleaning products. According to Combes, Naasz's fascination with new dental products is matched only by his ability to grow bored with them.

"Whenever a weird, nobby toothbrush or a ridiculously complicated toothpaste comes out, Mark buys it," Combes said. "He was really into this 'liquid calcium' Enamelon for a while. Before that, it was Mentadent—you know, the toothpaste with the 'unique dual-chamber pump.' But then he got tired of buying the big, stupid refill cartridges. He went through an extreme toothpaste phase for a while. But lately, since they opened the Whole Foods near his apartment, he's been on an organic, all-natural kick. Hence the fennel stuff, the taste of which I'm guessing he'll hate."

"Using the products is never as nice as looking at them on the shelf," Naasz said.

"I don't know," Combes added. "Somewhere along the line, Mark got it into his head that oral hygiene can somehow be made fun. It's an idea he refuses to let go of."

Naasz's preoccupation with the brushing habit started in 1974, when he received a Pink Panther electric toothbrush on his 6th birthday. Naasz quickly discovered that he didn't like the feeling of motorized bristles on his teeth, began using the Pink Panther toothbrush as a doll, and was well on his way to developing his first cavity.

When he reached his teenage years, products like Aquafresh toothpaste—with its alternating red, green, and white stripes—briefly appealed to Naasz, who found a renewed interest in fresh breath and white teeth upon reaching dating age. But according to the 36-year-old, not one product has helped make brushing anything but an unpleasant responsibility.

"All the packages look so great in the pharmacy," Naasz said. "But using the products is never as nice as looking at them on the shelf, when they're all pure and full of promise. Once you put that first dent in the tube, the allure is gone."

Naasz said that reflecting upon his misbegotten dental-care past "brings him to the brink of despair."

"Sometimes I'm like, 'What's wrong with me?'" Naasz said. "No matter what I buy, I have to force myself to brush, and I come away thinking brushing is an everyday duty that has nothing to do with pleasure."

American Dental Association spokesperson Elizabeth Bagnold said Naasz's case is like many seen by the nation's most prominent dental-health advocacy group.

"For years, the ADA has stated that brushing should be fun," Bagnold said. "But upon reviewing Mr. Naasz's case, we are considering revising our policy. Proper oral hygiene provides plenty of lasting benefits, but it is rarely enjoyable for its own sake. I would go so far as to say that fear, rather than fun, provides a much more legitimate motivation to brush and floss daily." ⌀

McDONALD'S from page 139

Piece Quarter Pounders and Fish McGriddles a try. The food's a little different at this McDonald's, but it's really very close."

Continued Landers: "Now, who's ready for factory seconds?!"

Located next to a Levi's outlet store offering mis-stitched and off-season apparel, the McDonald's outlet will be the destination for all products that do not meet the strict requirements of the restaurant's 30,000 regular stores worldwide.

"McDonald's prides itself on having exacting standards for its products," Landers said. "But throwing away all-carrot Salad Shakers, parallelogram-shaped hash browns, and McRib-Nuggets seemed so wasteful. With more of our customers struggling to make ends meet, we knew people would appreciate the opportunity to buy these slightly irregular products at irresistibly low prices."

In addition to factory mistakes, the outlet will offer items that were tested in limited markets but never received a wide release.

"We had a warehouse full of meat patties made in the shape of our golden-arch logo," Landers said. "A young, quickly fired executive thought it would be a good idea to make an 'M'-shaped burger, but it was expensive to produce, and depending where you took a bite, you had a very good chance of getting no beef. Plus, who's going to open up a burger just to look at the oddly shaped meat patty? Now, we're thawing them out and serving them up for only 30 cents apiece."

Above: A $1.99 value meal available at the "Not Quite Perfect" McDonald's.

Landers said that, while a number of customers have been wary, the prices are so astounding that "people always come back for more."

"I've seen more than one person approach our firm-serve cones with skepticism," Landers said. "But at 20 cents each, we can hardly keep them in stock."

Landers added, "Once they get over the mental block after eating a flash-frozen pyramid of vanilla ice cream, customers realize they just can't beat these prices."

The outlet store, at 32,000 square feet, is the largest McDonald's in the world. In addition to serving irregular meal items, the outlet store houses irregular McDonald's decor.

"These aren't the traditional McDonald's color schemes," Landers said, gesturing to chairs and tables in puce, mottled gray, and army green. "And while some customers make comments about our posters—a printer placed a black child's head on top of a white, elderly cashier's body—well, I think they look very nice once you get used to them."

The outlet also features a shop that sells irregular McDonald's products like boxes of frozen foot-long fries and bags of unsweetened orange-drink syrup.

"The bulk-foods section of the shop hasn't caught on as well as we'd hoped," Landers said. "We think that may be in part a question of functionality. Our 10-gallon buckets of McRib sauce, for example, are reasonably priced, but most people don't have condiment pumps at home. Of course, even those who do are sometimes disappointed to find relish inside."

The outlet's PlayPlace features not-quite-perfect McDonaldland icons.

"Parents worry about our ball pit, but those triangular balls meet Illinois minimum-safety requirements," Landers said. "What we've really gotten complaints about are the statues of the McDonaldland characters. Ronald McDonald's eyes were put in wrong so he's looking in two different directions, our Grimace is pink, and for some reason, the Hamburglar has no teeth."

In spite of the few complaints, most outlet patrons say the bargain prices are well worth enduring the irregular food.

"It's not like the meat's tainted," said Mack Vesper, a longtime McDonald's customer. "A Quarter Pounder on a half-size seedless bun tastes just as good. And, while the gray Shamrock Shake took some getting used to, once you realize that you're getting all the flavor at an eighth of the price, you adapt. Besides, who looks at the color of the shake once you start drinking it?"

Some customers said the "Not Quite Perfect" McDonald's is not for them.

"I'll never take my children there again," said Anita Sibakis, mother of three. "They opened up the Happy Meal and there were headless *Mulan* figurines in there. It scared the bejesus out my youngest." Ø

CUPID from page 139

love's dart during Monday's incident. "I didn't really know what was happening. I barely had time to shout 'Down!' and wrestle this mousy librarian-type to the ground before I started stammering and feeling lightheaded. Her name is Jackie and she writes poetry... We both come to this park a lot, but I'd never noticed her before, even though she has these amazing eyes."

"It was just so senseless, so out of nowhere, like a bolt of lightning," Kremms added. "Girls do like getting flowers, right? That isn't just a myth? God, I'm no good at this."

Police responded within 90 seconds of the incident. Some were caught in the crossfire.

"I haven't seen anything like it in my 13 years on the force, and only a few things like it since high school," said Detective Jim McClancy, one of the first officers on the scene. "Pairs of people were lying on the grass, on park benches, sitting on the curb, everywhere. They were giggling, murmuring sweet nothings... some were even moaning a little. I felt so... helpless—we knew the shooter was still in the park somewhere. I'll never forget how my heart almost stopped when my partner Julio, a guy I've served with for half my career, turned to me and said, 'Do you feel like getting some Chinese?'"

Amateur video shot at the scene shows the apple-cheeked cherub firing bolt after heart-tipped bolt into the crowd. Those hit reacted immediately by clasping their hands between their knees, casting their eyes downward, and digging their toes sheepishly in the dirt. In some cases, the victims hid their eyes altogether and grinned vacuously at absolutely nothing.

Although the tape has not yet been aired on television, authorities plan to do so as soon as soft-focus filtration effects are added and the footage is overdubbed with the Gary Wright ballad "Dream Weaver."

No arrests have been made, but police are currently rounding up local personifications of love's sudden and unpredictable onset. At least three winged, shirtless, cherubic residents of neighboring Winnetka and Mundelein are being kept in police custody as "persons of interest."

No motive has yet been given for the shootings, but forensic romantics speculate that the unusually benevolent spring weather and warm, breezy day may have played a part in the shooter's actions.

Police do not yet have an exact count of the victims struck by what they call "the heart's sweet, sweet wound," but at least six people were smitten seriously enough to rush themselves to emergency suites at area hotels, from which none have yet emerged.

Determining the extent of the shooting will most likely be difficult, experts say, due to the tendency of those affected to strenuously deny their infatuation while simultaneously refusing to seek treatment, in some cases actually resisting all offers of assistance and withdrawing from human contact for weeks.

Although the tape has not yet been aired on television, authorities plan to do so as soon as soft-focus filtration effects are added and the footage is overdubbed with the Gary Wright ballad "Dream Weaver."

"It's way too early to fully understand this wonderful shooting," said Anna Gardner, a relationship therapist working to help shooting victims get up the nerve to confess their feelings to one another. "People are going to come forward for weeks, talking about this memorable day. Roger, this very sweet man I met at the scene, said sometimes the enchanted arrow hits so hard, the victims don't realize they've been struck."

"He also said I have cute toes," added Gardner. "Such a thing to say! Can you imagine?"

Although the victims' reactions varied from blushing reticence to giggling denial to erratic behavior such as singing under other victims' windows, the total number of those lovestruck in the attack may never be accurately determined. Early reports indicate that as many as 24 people were exhibiting obvious signs of distraction and giddiness, and perhaps a dozen more were refusing to leave the sides of other victims.

Crisis-center representatives report that they are being flooded with calls inquiring about the welfare of possible victims, asking whether said victims have mentioned the callers in any way, and wondering if the hotline operator would agree to speak to the victims on the callers' behalf.

As of press time, at least three Chicago-area couples are missing and presumed wed. Ø

HARVEY'S HOLLYWOOD

Is There New Love for Tom Cruise?

Item! After I reported last time that Dawson's cutie **Katie Holmes** called it quits with her fiancé, I figured we wouldn't hear from her for a while.

The Outside Scoop
By Jackie Harvey

Color me wrong! The cutie has been snatched up by none other than **Tom Cruise**. Wow! Tom certainly did well for himself. Although some would say he's dating someone half his age, I wish them both a long and prosperous relationship. Let's hope there are kids in their future!

Item! The lines have already started forming for **Star Wars: Revenge Of The Sirth**. If I didn't have so many responsibilities, I might join them. Maybe if I got a **Blackberry**, I could file my reports from the line, but then there would be the whole bathroom issue. Besides, I need to be at my control center to keep up with the latest news. Maybe by the time **George Lucas** does the next sequel, I'll be part of the wireless age and I can wait in line in front of the theater with everyone else.

Maybe it's me, but there sure have been a lot of **abductions** lately. I think it's what they call a sign of the times.

You know who's a little acting spitfire? That **Dakota Fanning**. I've never seen such range on a kid her age. I don't mind "fanning" the flames, because she's going to catch on fire! She's only 11 years old, but if she can hold her own against the likes of **Sean Penn** and **Robert DeNiro** (and judging by **Hide And Seek**, the movie she was in with DeNiro, she can), she's got a long, **Haley-Joel Osmond** career ahead of her.

Item! Speaking of Mr. Penn, guess who's going down the **I Am Sam** road? After too long out of the spotlight, **Rosie O'Donnel** played a "special person" on a TV movie called **My Sister On The Bus**. Do I smell an **Emmy**? Believe me, the doubters are all going to have to sharpen their poison pens on someone else, because Rosie's performance was great, and not in the way you'd say that a special person did a great job. I only hope the movie comes out on DVD so I can watch it again.

Say what you will, but I think all these **potholes** have gotten out of hand. I know I always say there're two seasons—winter and construction—but I for one think it's about time we saw those road crews out there taking care of business!

Item! Things are really heating up on the **American Idol** front. First, it came out that contestant **Bo Bise** was arrested for cocaine possession. Then, he was arrested for marijuana possession. This isn't the '60s, Mr. Bise! Kids need positive role models. America has already been through one **David Crosby**. Then, we learned **Scott Savol** abused the mother of his daughter. Shame on you both! You should do the right thing and resign so we can get more contestants like squeaky-clean, upstanding **Clay Aiken**.

Oh, and I'm not even going to touch the whole **Paula Abdul** thing.

Item! In case you wanted to get a little "behind the scenes" with **Brittney and Kevin**, fret no more. The **UPN**, whose name is synonymous with quality, will air footage the couple shot themselves that shows the true depth of their love. I can hardly wait. That couple really needs a nickname. I'd like to put **Kevney** out there. Until someone comes up with a better one, I'm sticking to it.

I'm starting to have doubts about my cable package. Every time I want to watch a movie, I have to choose between *Ghost* (seen it 12 times) and *Charlie's Angels 2: Fully Throttled* (7 times). Come on, I love Patrick Swayze and/or Drew Berrymore as much as the next guy, but variety is the spice of life. Are you listening, HBO?

With all the new fruits I can get at my local supermarket, you'd think I'd be able to get a new flavor of ice cream. Has **ice-cream** technology hit a wall? **Breyers**, get those scientists cracking!

Somewhere, someone in a casting office is thinking, "I gotta get **Ving Rames** for this project."

Item! Say goodbye to an old friend. After 10 years, **JAG** is finally closing up shop. And I only found out that JAG was short for "Judge's Advocate Group," and not Jaguar, a couple weeks ago! If **CBS** decides they need a new military potboiler, I've been knocking some ideas around the old Harvey dome. Here's a taste: **a show about bomb-sniffing dogs**. They can talk, but only to one another. I know it sounds cutesy, but the dogs would deal with real-life tragedies and joys. If you want to use the idea, give me a call. TV executives only!

I'm starting to have doubts about my cable package. Every time I want to watch a movie, I have to choose between **Ghost** (seen it 12 times) and **Charlie's Angels 2: Fully Throttled** (7 times). Come on, I love **Patrick Swayze and/or Drew Berrymore** as much as the next guy, but variety is the spice of life. Are you listening, **HBO**?

Well, that's it for the Scoop for now. I have some spring cleaning to do: I need to watch a stack of DVDs that has been piling up, so I can put them on the shelf in **alphabetical order**. Anyway, in my next column, I'll reveal definitively who the next **Julia Roberts** is, give you my summer movie-watching tips, and answer the question everyone wants to know: "Whatever happened to **Lori Petty**?" Until then, I'll grab some Goobers and see you... on The Outside! ⊘

HOROSCOPES

Your Horoscope

By Lloyd Schumner Sr.
Retired Machinist and
A.A.P.B.-Certified Astrologer

Aries: (March 21–April 19)
After a grueling three-year investigation, the National Transportation Safety Board will rule that a faulty steering valve in your tail section caused your tragic crash into that shopping mall.

Taurus: (April 20–May 20)
You'll be pressured to resign as chairman of the board of directors when it comes to light that you are, in fact, absolutely terrible at sitting at the head of really long tables.

Gemini: (May 21–June 21)
You thought it was only people in movies that were tied to railroad tracks by mustachioed villains, but your upcoming experience on Walt Disney World's monorail will prove otherwise.

Cancer: (June 22–July 22)
You'll find yourself simultaneously at the heart of a legal tangle and the burn ward when you finally get the opportunity to yell "Fire!" in a crowded theater.

Leo: (July 23–Aug. 22)
All your old problems will dissolve when you're forced to confront what's really important, namely explosive botulism.

Virgo: (Aug. 23–Sept. 22)
After Wednesday, you can say you've seen everything. Unfortunately, you'll have seen it from such a distance that you won't be able to make out the details.

Libra: (Sept. 23–Oct. 23)
Everyone takes a while to adjust to new surroundings, but unfortunately, you only have eight minutes before the fissure begins to fill with magma.

Scorpio: (Oct. 24–Nov. 21)
Magritte says the mind loves images whose meaning is unknown, as the mind itself is unknown; but you actually think it's mostly about threesomes.

Sagittarius: (Nov. 22–Dec. 21)
You believed being stranded on that desert island put an end to your run of lousy luck, but the natives will soon become strangely inspired and fashion a crude bus to hit you with.

Capricorn: (Dec. 22–Jan. 19)
You'll start waking covered in bruises on a variety of 12th- through 16th-floor exterior ledges, proving once and for all that you shouldn't piss off your city's powerful pigeon lobby.

Aquarius: (Jan. 20–Feb. 18)
Sure, you're exceptionally well-lit, but you're becoming tired of being followed around by a crew of technicians and their array of floods, pinspots, and reflectors.

Pisces: (Feb. 19–March 20)
It's been six months since you walked in and set up the tent, and the owners are considering changing the sign to All You Can Eat In One Sitting, Not Over The Course Of Your Lifetime.

LOHAN from page 56

amounts of blood. Passersby were amazed by the unusually large amounts of blood. Passersby were amazed by the unusually large

Can we get an intern in here to clean up all these kidney stones?

amounts of blood. Passersby were amazed by the unusually large amounts of blood. Passersby were amazed by the unusually large amounts of blood. Passersby were amazed by the unusually large amounts of blood. Passersby were amazed by the unusually large amounts of blood. Passersby were

see LOHAN page 119

the ONION®

VOLUME 41 ISSUE 20 AMERICA'S FINEST NEWS SOURCE™ 19–25 MAY 2005

NEWS

Millions Of Plants Sent From Nation's Garden Departments To Their Deaths

see HOME & GARDEN page 7C

Ruptured Pudding Cup At Large In Area Backpack

see LOCAL page 15E

Tennessee Senator Pushes Broken-Down Chevy Through Congress

see PEOPLE page 5F

STATshot

A look at the numbers that shape your world.

Popular New Cruise-Ship Destinations
15% Svalbard: The Bahamas of Scandinavia
23% The South Pathetic
19% Time warp to 1942 Pearl Harbor
22% The Center for Disease Control
21% The Cape Of Good God I Hope I Find A Man
Denny's

THE ONION • $2.00 US • $3.00 CAN

New, Delicious Species Discovered

MANAUS, BRAZIL—An international team of scientists conducting research in the Amazon River Basin announced the discovery of a formerly unknown primate species inhabiting a remote jungle area roughly 300 miles from Manaus Monday. According to scientists in Manaus, the new species, *Ateles saporis*, is "an amazing biological find" and "incredibly delectable."

"We couldn't be more thrilled!" German researcher

see SPECIES page 148

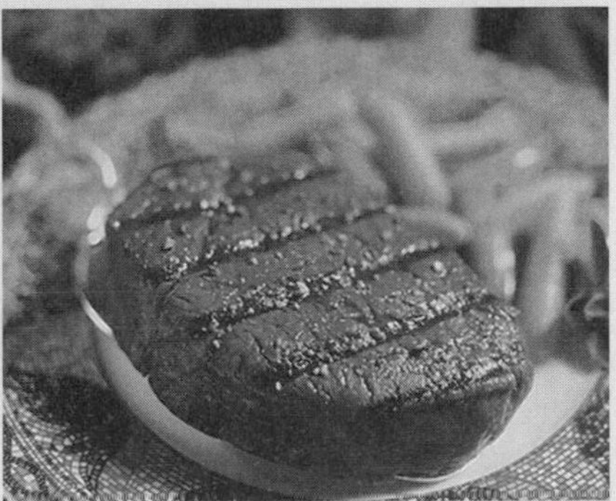

Left: A member of Ateles saporis, which scientists say tastes excellent broiled (right).

Bush Challenges America To Produce The Perfect Romantic Comedy By 2009

WASHINGTON, DC—Making a bold statement of appeal to "the long-standing spirit of entrepreneurial enterprise in this great nation" Monday, President Bush challenged the U.S. entertainment industry to produce the perfect romantic comedy by summer 2009.

"My fellow Americans, it's time for another *Sleepless In Seattle*," Bush said in a special prime-time address to the nation. "America has the technology. We have the market-research capacity. We have the publicity engines, the screenwriting workshops,

see BUSH page 149

Right: Bush urges Americans to do their part and "go west" to Hollywood.

God's Plan For Area Man Involves Kidnapping Ford CEO

Above: Gurshner, who vows to do God's bidding by kidnapping Ford (inset).

MINOT, ND—Unemployed factory worker James Harold Gurshner told reporters Monday that God's plan for him, revealed during a moment of divine inspiration, requires kidnapping Ford Motor Company CEO William Ford Jr.

"The Lord works in mysterious ways," said Gurshner, talking to reporters through a metal grate screwed over the window of his dilapidated, hubcap-covered house. "And right now, the Lord is working through me. I didn't choose this path, but if you're called upon, you must look into your heart and make a decision. I have chosen to heed the Lord's command."

Gurshner said he does not know why God "came to [him] in a dream"

see CEO page 148

WTO May Accept Russia

If negotiations go smoothly, Russia may be invited to join the World Trade Organization in 2006. What do *you* think?

Joy Hess
Systems Analyst

"It's amazing that, with an economy that large, Russia isn't already in the WTO. Is it because they only import stolen cars and export mail-order brides?"

Clinton Chan
Clerk

"After all the bullshit they put James Bond through, those Russians have a lot of nerve expecting us to become their trade allies."

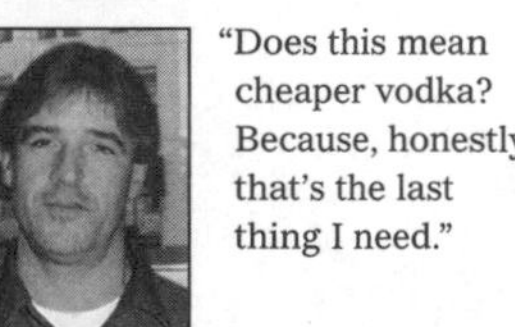

Ken Dorsey
Logger

"Does this mean cheaper vodka? Because, honestly, that's the last thing I need."

Joe Roach
Editor

"I'm starting my own Joe's Trade Organization, and it would be a real feather in my cap to snag Russia first."

Neil Hood
Police Chief

"Allowing a country like Russia to join the organization would make a mockery of whatever it is the WTO stands for."

Allison Church
Midwife

"Why is this an issue? Evil Communist Russians have been a part of the WWE since the '80s."

Celebrity Commencement Speeches

A growing number of American colleges are enlisting celebrities to deliver speeches at their commencement ceremonies. What are some of this year's highlights?

- "On The Importance Of Being Bono," Bono, Columbia University
- "I Totally Love This Honorary Degree," Mila Kunis, Fairfax Technical College of Continuing Education
- "Make Money By Any Means," 50 Cent, SUNY Buffalo
- "Remember Me? Epstein From *Welcome Back, Kotter*? No?" Robert Hegyes, Miami University
- "You Might Be The Promise Of A New American Generation," Jeff Foxworthy, DeVry Continuing Education Campus, Galveston, TX
- "Listen Good, You Little Shits, Because I'm Only Going To Say This Once," Dick Cheney, U.S. Naval Academy
- "Thanks For Having Me," Bob Balaban, University of Nebraska at Lincoln
- "Everyone, There Is A Bomb In This Commencement Hall," Kiefer Sutherland, Princeton

America's Finest News Source.™

Herman Ulysses Zweibel
Founder

T. Herman Zweibel
Publisher Emeritus
J. Phineas Zweibel
Publisher
Maxwell Prescott Zweibel
Editor-In-Chief

A Gentleman Never Discloses Who Sucked Him Off

By Charles Dubno

I must say, the quality of discourse in this country has taken a sharp plunge of late, not only among the ruffians and ne'er-do-wells from whom one expects coarse speech, but among gentlemen of letters and esteem. I have, with my own ears, several times in the past week, heard the elder sons of prominent families introduce into mixed company subjects formerly reserved for private discussion among gentlemen. It pains me even to raise this point, but following a string of recent events, there is no question that the adage bears repeating: A gentleman ought never to disclose who sucked him off.

This needn't mean a gentleman must limit the discussion of his exploits to his journal. If a gentleman has met a young lady and taken her to his digs, it is his right and privilege to tell his friends and coworkers about the encounter. However, it is the mark of a true gentleman to omit his lady friend's name from the discussion of her pussy's tightness.

Why, I had assumed that this custom and others like it were universal and well understood, but as long as I am spelling out the Rules of the Gentleman, allow me to introduce several other equally important but oft-neglected guidelines.

Should a gentleman find himself alone with a lady, he should not simply undo his pants and come in her hole. A gentleman knows that it is good manners to coax his lady friend's heels as far above her head as they will go, to "split the reed," and perhaps to turn his lady over and give it to her "doggy style." A gentleman knows that a true lady enjoys a moderate amount of hair-pulling and ass-grabbing, taking these attentions as marks of affection and virility. However, a gentleman knows where to draw the line. He never lodges his lady friend's head between the couch cushions.

A gentleman occasionally will have more than one guest at his home. Should he see that jealousy is breeding between the two ladies whom he is hosting, a gentleman does not say, "Whoa, ladies, there's enough of me to go around!" The gentleman, valuing decorum and discretion above all else in his paramours, gently guides his guests' heads from his penis and informs them that if they do not act like ladies, he will have to ask them both to leave.

When up to his nuts in a lady's guts, a gentleman knows that it is quite impolite to smoke, talk politics, or take phone calls. Should his cell phone ring, the gentleman says, "Excuse me, I need to take this." He withdraws his penis from his lady friend and keeps his phone conversation brief. When he has completed his call, a gentleman gently reinserts his dick into his lady.

Of course, a gentleman who is not a smoker keeps an ashtray on his balcony for his lady friends who wish to smoke.

It should go without saying that, once he has arranged for a paid lady of the night to meet him at his home, a gentleman does not jerk off several times while awaiting her arrival, in order to "get his money's worth."

A gentleman knows that accidents happen. While it is an unfortunate and boorish behavior that should be kept to a minimum, a gentleman always apologizes to a lady after he mistakenly shoots his load inside of her.

A gentleman knows that it is considered good manners to have an unopened toothbrush on hand for his lady friend.

A gentleman never comes in a lady's eyes.

While he knows that a lady gets pleasure out of pleasuring him, and he will occasionally increase the intensity of that pleasure by gentle force, a gentleman will never choke a woman on his cock.

If a gentleman wishes to attend to a lady's pleasure through oral manipulation, no matter what the state of affairs below, he always politely completes his task. A gentleman ought never to fan his hand in the air, grimace and make a show of removing a pubic hair from his teeth, or compare his lady friend's vulva to two strips of partially grilled fajita meat.

A gentleman knows that it is considered good manners to have an unopened toothbrush on hand for his lady friend, in the event that she should like to freshen up after eating his ass.

Breeding needn't amount to priggishness. On the contrary, a gentleman knows that good old-fashioned manners will likely increase his social engagements, once word gets out that he is not one to splooge and tell. But I beg the reader, for the sake of tradition and all that is decent, to remember that a true gentleman does not ever, under any circumstances, go ass to mouth. Ø

Principal Hates Underachievers, Overachievers

ST. CLOUD, MN—According to 58-year-old Charles Van Hise, principal of Harriet Bishop High School and a 26-year veteran of the St. Cloud School District, too much of his staff's time is devoted to "problem students" who require special disciplinary or scholastic attention.

"It's the oldest story in the world," Van Hise said. "The squeaky wheels get the grease. I have them in here every day. Today it's to complain about 'intellectually lazy' teachers; tomorrow, I'll bet you anything it's the elimination of the arts program. And I swear to you, if I have to break up one more rumble in the hallway, I'm going to snap."

Van Hise lifted his blinds to reveal a small group of students eating lunch in the courtyard.

"Excuse me one moment," said Van Hise, leaning out his window to address the gathering of students. "That music is not allowed on campus! Extinguish your incense, please."

Returning to his seat, Van Hise said, "Those honors-program students think they own the school."

Harriet Bishop High, which once had one of Minnesota's highest rates of physical violence among students, recently turned its record around, reducing in-school violence by 22 percent through programs initiated by Van Hise, who has a reputation as a staunch disciplinarian.

"These items were confiscated from high-school students, believe it or not," said Van Hise, displaying a cardboard box containing brass knuckles, a Swiss Army knife, and several issues of Daniel Clowes' *Eightball* comics. "It goes without saying that the students who brought these items into my school are long gone."

Van Hise credits the success of his program to those teachers who have volunteered to patrol the hallways during their off-periods, keeping an eye out for "class-cutters and music-heads."

"I'd have time to do that myself I didn't spend half my workday addressing the busybody club's concern *du jour*," Van Hise said. "Every time I turn my back, there's another petition on my desk. Look, I have one right now. It's the same thing every year. We hold student-council elections, the student body selects its leader, and the next day, like clockwork, I have a team of kids in here chewing my ear off about the unfair vote-counting practices and… I don't even know what, to tell you the truth."

Harriet Bishop High narrowly escaped federal discipline last fall, when the student body succeeded in lifting its aggregate standardized-test scores out of the danger zone. According to Van Hise, the upsurge oc-

see PRINCIPAL page 148

Above: Van Hise patrols his school's hallways looking for students performing too far above or below the line.

NEWS IN BRIEF

Jews, Muslims, Hindus Agree On Chicken

GENEVA—After years of sectarian violence, a coalition of Jews, Muslims, and Hindus signed an international resolution Monday, confirming their mutual appreciation of chicken dishes. "Whether it is breaded with matzo, served as shwarma, or covered in tikka masala sauce, chicken is the one meat upon which all faiths can agree," said spokesman Jerome Maliszewski, addressing an assembly of rabbis, mullahs, and shamans. "Let this friendly exchange of recipes be the first tentative step toward everlasting peace." Attendees at the combination summit and potluck dinner labeled it a qualified success, regretting the altercation that broke out between factions with differing views on skewer length.

Paroled Prisoner Excited To Hear The '80s Are Back

BLYTHE, CA—Former Chuckawalla Valley State Prison inmate Jake Allen Dupree, 42, who completed a 20-year sentence for armed robbery last Friday, said he is excited to hear that '80s styles are experiencing a resurgence in popularity. "When the guard handed me my stuff, he said my acid-wash jeans, Kangaroos sneakers, and bright teal T-shirt looked really cool," Dupree said. "It's great that I won't have to buy a new wardrobe." Dupree added that he was happy to hear that *Miami Vice* was recently re-released, so he can find out what happened to Crockett and Tubbs.

Author Dismayed By Amazon Customers' Other Purchases

MONTREAL—Yann Martel, author of the Booker Prize-winning Life Of Pi, said he was distraught to see what other books Amazon.com customers bought in addition to his. "Customers who bought this book also bought *The Five People You Meet In Heaven*?!" Martel read from his computer screen Monday. "And *The Rule Of Four*? Really?!" Martel was also surprised by the "sloppy writing" in many of *Life Of Pi's* five-star customer reviews.

Area Dad Saw A Great Show On Bigfoot Last Night

LANCASTER, PA—Much to his family's indifference, 44-year-old father of two Bradley Kochner said he enjoyed an interesting show about Bigfoot on the Discovery Channel last night. "They had some neat footage that was shot in Oregon," said Kochner at the dinner table, describing the one-hour *Legends Of Sasquatch* special, in a desperate attempt to reach bored sons Joel, 13, and Kyle, 11. "If they show it again, I'll tape it. Maybe we can watch it together. Right, guys?" Kochner's wife Laura said her husband has similarly tried to engage his children in discussions about submarines, UFOs, and Pompeii.

Local Man Pushed Well Within Limits Of Human Endurance

DURHAM, NC—In the face of reasonable odds, Louis Collins, 27, endured a challenge Monday that tested, but did not by any means exceed, his ability to persevere. "The line at the DMV was really long, and I had a lunch meeting at noon," said Collins, recounting the inconvenient event that ultimately did no lasting damage. "Then I realized that I still needed to fill out a form, but I didn't have a pen. If I had left the line to use a pen at the counter, I would have had to start all over. Thank goodness someone in line lent me one." In spite of the unremarkable series of obstacles, Collins still arrived at lunch on time. ⌀

CEO from page 145

and asked him to kidnap Ford, but he said he believes that "it is best not to question His motives."

"I didn't question the Lord when He struck down my beloved wife Emily with cervical cancer," Gurshner said. "I didn't question Him when I was dismissed from my job and put on Social Security. I didn't question Him when He commanded me to dig a three-foot ditch around my house and fill it with charcoal briquettes, and I don't question him now. I, James Harold Gurshner, will kidnap the Ford CEO, as that is the will of the Lord."

"Amen," Gurshner added.

Gurshner said he would prefer to kidnap the man who runs the auto-supply store, or simply volunteer at the local soup kitchen, but nonetheless, he is determined to complete the Lord's task.

"The Lord would not have picked me to carry out His will if He didn't think I could do it," Gurshner said. "He'll probably help me along, though. Just like the time I found a perfectly good chair on the side of the road two days after I burned all of my furniture for Jesus. God will provide for those who do His will."

Although he does not have a specific kidnapping plan, Gurshner said he is confident that he will succeed.

"I've been thinking on ways to get that Ford guy the whole time I've been cleaning out the aluminum shed out back," Gurshner said. "That's where I'll store him. I won't keep the CEO tied up and gagged in a dirty place. The Lord wants me to make him feel comfortable."

Although Gurshner refuses to question God's will, he has a few theories about the Heavenly Father's motives.

"The Lord may want to enact retribution for all the people who died in cars, like my daddy did when I was 7," Gurshner said. "But unless the Lord directly tells me to torture Ford, or beat him, I won't. One thing I will not do is make love to the Ford CEO's asshole, no matter what the Lord says. That activity is a sin against nature. An order to do it would be God's way of testing me."

Raised a Seventh-day Adventist, Gurshner said he "got the true calling" in 1998, when God commanded him to kill a stray dog that wouldn't stop barking during the night.

"I saw a bright light and knew in a flash what He wanted," said Gurshner, who explained that God's messages are often paired with staggering migraine headaches. "It wasn't until I put a shovel through that dog's head that God was satisfied and the messages finally stopped."

Gurshner said God usually sends him messages through Bible passages, particularly those found in Leviticus and Deuteronomy. Sometimes, however, the messages appear on Hardee's billboards or in Kenny Chesney song lyrics.

"I never know what God's next message will be or when I will get it—all I can do is obey," Gurshner said. "It's like when God told me to start collecting plastic laundry-soap bottles a few years back. I still don't know what they're for, but until God reveals His reasons, I'll keep storing them in my living room."

Residents of Minot are well-acquainted with Gurshner's relationship with God.

"Everybody has heard all about Jim's direct line to the Lord," said Officer Nathan Randell of the Minot Police Department. "We try to leave him alone whenever we can. Most people in town feel sorry for him. All that tragedy shouldn't happen to one man. But when Jim gets really riled up, we have to go talk him down, or sometimes even lock him up for a night. He'll tell us that blaring religious hymns from his car stereo on Main Street at 3 a.m. is part of God's plan, but I guess we have to go against His wishes every once and a while."

Ford declined to comment on the Lord's plan. ⌀

PRINCIPAL from page 147

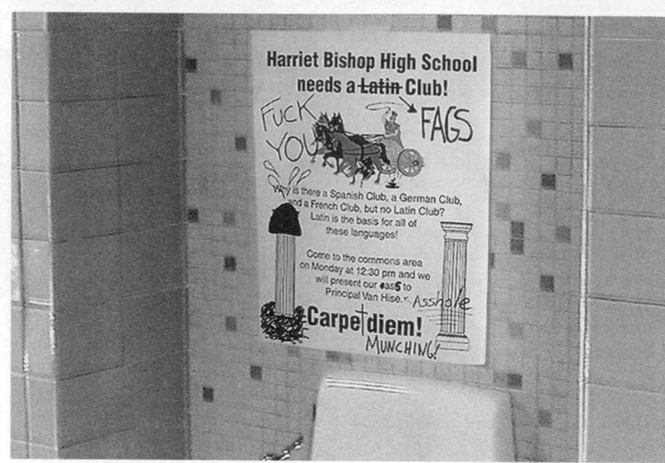

Above: Troublemakers at Harriet Bishop High propose/mock the idea of a Latin club.

curred "with no help from the bottom feeders."

"We are running a school here. Not a gymnasium. Not a... a... a... roller derby. And certainly not a Model U.N.," Van Hise said. "I've got the same advice for all of them: Sit down, shut up, and you'll be out of here in four years."

That afternoon, strolling the hallways with a bottle of acetone and a rag, Van Hise wiped the words "cock smoker" from his portrait. Later, he paused before a display case devoted to football awards. Taped inside of the case was a poster titled "The Three Pillars of Education." Two of the columns, labeled "Academics" and "The Arts," were crumbling. The third, labeled "Sports," was pristine, reaching to the clouds.

"You'll notice whoever drew this... cartoon... didn't care to sign his name to it," said Van Hise, searching his key ring for the display-case key. "You tell me: Should we have more people watching over the theater kids while they paint their sets, or should I make sure someone's keeping tabs on the school on weekend nights when some kid wants to break in here and vandalize my office?"

"One of them coated my office floor in Vaseline," Van Hise added. "I nearly busted my head."

Van Hise was not pessimistic in every respect. He reserved his esteem for a certain set of "solid, devoted, quiet-minded students."

"Solid, average students who aren't causing trouble and aren't trying to attract any undue attention to themselves," Van Hise said. "Your Average Joes and Plain Janes. They're the ones who bring our scores up. No question in my mind. The rest just cancel each other out." ⌀

Van Hise credits the success of his program to those teachers who have volunteered to patrol the hallways during their off-periods, keeping an eye out for "class-cutters and music-heads."

SPECIES from page 145

Dr. Jerome Keller told reporters Tuesday. "Very few scientists are lucky enough to discover a new species, let alone a mammal with a palatability on par with a tender, juicy steak."

"This is a seriously tasty creature," Keller added.

Although the creature resembles a large kitten, as a member of the *Ateles* family, it is more closely related to wooly and spider monkeys. *Ateles saporis*, informally known as the delicacy ape, is a tree-dwelling herbivore that can measure up to a meter from head to tail. The adult delicacy ape weighs between 35 and 40 pounds and tastes wonderful with a currant glaze.

Keller said the new species boasts a gular sac, a distinctive trait that separates it from other species in the *Ateles* genus.

"The gular sac is a throat pouch that can be inflated, allowing the animal to make loud calls that resonate through the treetops," Keller said. "More importantly, the pouch can be stuffed with nuts or dried fruits prior to roasting."

Biologist Jeanette Bransky, who served as the research team's chief archivist, presented a series of slides showing delicacy apes cavorting in trees, caring for their young, and sitting thinly sliced on a platter next to roasted red potatoes.

"After careful study, we have determined that *Ateles* saporis is a very insulated species," Bransky said. "All of their food needs are met in the treetops. They're docile, affectionate creatures with a non-competitive social structure. They often sit grooming each other for hours on end, which explains why their meat is so marbled and tender."

This marks the first primate species discovered since the nearly inedible Arunachal macaque was found in India last year.

"In our studies of the delicacy ape, we have noted several traits, such as play activities, that are almost human," Bransky said. "However, the similarities do not run much deeper than that. Take the loin, for example. Unlike a human's, it's so savory and delicate that it can be eaten just like sashimi."

"Raw or cooked, this species is one of the greatest discoveries of the 21st century," added Bransky, licking her lips.

The team plans to research the species for another two months and then publish its findings in both the *International Journal Of Primatology* and *Bon Appétit*.

"We still need to complete an accurate population-density study," Keller said. "We assume that their habitat is limited to the Amazon and that their total number is very small. We need to gather data quickly, as the species is almost certainly facing extinction. I mean, it's that good."

Keller said the discovery of the delicacy ape underscores the importance of protecting delicate ecosystems from mass deforestation.

"The Amazon River Basin boasts the greatest biodiversity in the world, with countless potentially tasty species waiting to be discovered," Keller said. "As for the delicacy ape, I only hope there's something we can do to preserve it. Maybe we can get them to breed in captivity. Generations to come should have the opportunity to enjoy the taste of this majestic creature." ⌀

and the deal-making power. If we all pull together, we can create the perfect romantic comedy. And America will be able to hold its head high again."

Bush said the U.S. is "prepped to win this."

"By 2009, our best teen stars—potential giants like Lindsay Lohan and that guy who played Stifler—will be at the exact right age to appeal to the crucial 18-to-39 female demographic," Bush said. "No other nation approaches America's resources and capabilities in the area of romantic entertainment."

According to White House officials, recent efforts to create the ultimate romantic comedy, such as *Fever Pitch*, *A Lot Like Love*, and *Little Black Book*, have failed to generate much public interest domestically or internationally.

"It's been 15 years since we had a film as charming as *Pretty Woman*," Bush said. "These troubled times call for another film with the power to unite us. If we believe in ourselves and in the principles upon which this great democracy rests, we can create, distribute, and market a romantic comedy that will make us laugh *and* cry."

"We built the first intercontinental railroad," Bush continued. "We invented the electric light bulb. We even split the atom. It's time to remind the world what we're capable of: If we can put a man on the moon, we can make a man and a woman who appear to dislike each other intensely fall madly in love before the closing credits roll."

Dubbing his romantic-comedy initiative "Operation Meet-Cute," Bush proposed that Congress earmark $20 billion to aid Hollywood in creating the film. He called on studio heads to "put aside differences and pull together for the common goal," urging executives to "take the long view, and think of the sequel."

Bush proposed adding a special "romcom tax" to all movie tickets, in order to allow all Americans to "do their part for Hollywood and for their country."

The president also urged all able-minded citizens to "join the fight" by pitching ideas for humorous and touching scenarios.

"If you're not in Hollywood already, go west, young man!" Bush said. "We need you to dig in and create fresh plotlines in which celebrities fall in love under unusual, entertaining circumstances."

Above: A scene from When Harry Met Sally, a quality romantic comedy from America's past.

According to Will Greenberg, director of the White Knights, a Harvard-based think tank that has volunteered their services, fulfilling the commander in chief's orders will require much work.

"We need to see a heartbroken male lead lose the girl at the end of the second act, but maintain our sympathy, so we get the requisite goose bumps when he wins her heart again at the end of the third," Greenberg said. "We need fast-paced, witty banter, and a few well-executed sight gags."

"We also need one wacky sister, saucy co-worker, or gay neighbor in whom the heroine can confide," Greenberg continued. "To really do this right, the secondary character needs to be slightly quirky, someone a bit less conformist than the female lead."

Via phone Tuesday, Bush offered additional words of encouragement.

"This may seem like an impossible dream, but it once seemed impossible that Harry and Sally would end up together," Bush said. "But they did. How? With American hard work, know-how, and ingenuity."

Added Bush: "Ben Stiller and Jennifer Aniston didn't give up. Adam Sandler and Drew Barrymore didn't give up. The troops fighting for our freedom in Iraq haven't given up. Nora Ephron hasn't given up. And neither will this nation."

$22 billion endowment—SCHOLARSHIPS AVAILABLE!!!

- **Are you worth more than you're getting paid?**
- **Is your unique potential not being used at the job?**
- **Do you dream of doing more, but don't know how to start?**

Try Harvard!

For almost four centuries, Harvard has been America's **#1** college for careers.

- "State of the art" computer laboratory
- Free e-mail for all students FOR LIFE
- World's largest university library system, including extensive pre-Gutenberg folio collection
- A tree-lined campus
- Conveniently located near Harvard Yard stop of the T
- Evening courses and online study
- Access to America's exclusive "power elite"

Our students have gone on to top-level job positions with **Microsoft**, the **Carnegie Mellon Foundation**, and the **Vietnam War**.

"Harvard helped me achieve my goal of becoming chairman of Chase Manhattan Bank."
— David Rockefeller

Perfect for careers in: •Computers •Health care •Entertainment/law •Private equity-fund management •Literary criticism •Statecraft

Where knowledge... *equals power*

Call now! 617-495-1551 admissions.college.harvard.edu

COMMUNITY VOICES

Yes, Sweetie, Mommy's Heard Of Gil Scott-Heron

By Deborah Knoedl

Hello, sweetie! I didn't expect you home so early. Here, hand me your backpack. Ooh, heavy! So, how was your week? Well, I'm glad. College is sure fun, isn't it? Yes, it is! So, what did you learn today? Well, imagine that. You don't say? Yes, yes. Uh-huh. Yes, sweetie, Mommy's heard of Gil Scott-Heron. Have a piece of fruit instead, honey, that cake is for dessert tonight.

Here you go, a nice apple. Okay, so that 20th Century African-American Popular Culture Studies course. What's that all about? Mm-hmm. Sure, I know "The Revolution Will Not Be Televised." It's his most famous song! Why, yes, his spoken-word recordings were a noted precursor of hip-hop! Very good. What a smarty you are! I'm so glad you're enjoying your classes. Honey, can you do your old mom a favor and get that jar of rhubarb preserves off that top shelf there? Thanks a bunch!

Why, yes, his spoken-word recordings were a noted precursor of hip-hop! Very good. What a smarty you are!

What now, hon? Oh, Daddy and I listened to Gil Scott-Heron back in college. My goodness, so full of questions today! Well, sure, Daddy and I listened to music, we went to basketball games, we played pool at the student union—all sorts of things you young people still do today! Be careful, now, I just waxed the floor and I wouldn't want you to slip. Except, back then, we played vinyl records and listened to AOR radio. That's short for "album-oriented rock." Oh, you knew that? Well, okay then, my big mister. You get an A for the day!

"Whitey On The Moon"? Oh, why, sure. Yes, yes... uh-huh! "Junkies make me a nervous wreck... rat done bit my sister... whitey on the moon..." Ha ha! My word. Who's this? Did Mr. Gil Scott-Heron himself just bestow the honor of his presence on us? Well, we'll have to set the table for an extra guest tonight! I hope he likes baked chicken with rhubarb sauce and German chocolate cake! He does? Nifty! Oh, all right, I'll stop goofing around. You do have a nice voice, though.

What now, sweetie? Was I offended by "Whitey On The Moon"? Oh, not really. It made a fair point. It was pretty ironic that poor black people in the inner cities were suffering while billions of dollars were being spent on the moon race. It's sad to think about. Sweetie, don't sit on the kitchen chair like that. Put both feet down. I can understand why Gil Scott-Heron was frustrated. It was pretty neat of him to express himself with art and tell people what was on his mind. Remember when you were in that art camp back in seventh grade and you made that collage against the war? That was very creative.

Hmm? I didn't hear you, I was rinsing the chicken. Ah, the Last Poets. Yes, Mommy knows them, too! "Wake up, niggers, or you're through." Yes, they and Gil Scott-Heron did come from the later, militant generation of civil-rights activists! It sure was a howl of desperate anger from the disenfranchised! Did we want revolution, too? Such a deep question! Well, I don't know. Daddy was all for it, but I was less certain. Oh sweetie, will you fetch some potatoes from the cellar for Mommy? My hands are all wet.

Thank you, pussycat! Yes. Yes, revolution. Mm-hmm. What? Why was I less certain? Oh, I don't know, really. I guess it's just that—well, the gosh-darn funny thing about revolution is that sometimes it brings more chaos and pain than positive change. Sometimes, instead of liberation, you get... more... tyranny! Ha! Got your nose! Okay, now run your things up to your room, and I'll give your nose back when dinner's ready!

What's this, dear? Oh, you're going to succeed where my generation failed? Well, I hope so! That would be wonderful, dear! You should give it a try! I felt that way when I first listened to Gil Scott-Heron, too. Yes, I agree: Fuck the man! You go and do that! Never sell out, that's right! And while you're upstairs not selling out, Mommy will be in the kitchen making dinner. Try to be quiet when you go up the stairs, will you, sweetie? Daddy's napping in the living room.

Hmm-mm-mmm... la, la, la, doo doo doo... "Women will not care if Dick finally gets down with Jane on Search For Tomorrow, because black people will be in the street looking for a brighter day... the revolution will not be televised..." La, la, la... Ø

HOROSCOPES

Your Horoscope

By Lloyd Schumner Sr.
Retired Machinist and
A.A.P.B.-Certified Astrologer

Aries: (March 21–April 19)
Not that anyone asked you, but if you were designing the world's biggest jetliner, you would've put some sort of flat surface under the passenger cabin, for people to stand on.

Taurus: (April 20–May 20)
By this time next week, you'll be suffering from altitude sickness, in danger of being arrested by the Bolivian government, and freshly divorced—all thanks to a bar bet you'll sorely regret having made.

Gemini: (May 21–June 21)
Not hitting your shots and a weak zone defense aren't just why your team is losing in the playoffs, it's why the Centralized Space Command will surrender to the Uranus Allied Forces this Thursday.

Cancer: (June 22–July 22)
You may be proud of it, but it might not be such a good thing that you've earned an Emmy for Outstanding Participation in Television Consumption.

Leo: (July 23–Aug. 22)
If you'd only learned to exercise patience, those caterpillars you've been vomiting up all week would've had a chance to become lovely stomach butterflies.

Virgo: (Aug. 23–Sept. 22)
You'll be well along the path to a lifetime of happiness when the rap-metal single you cut in 1997 resurfaces.

Libra: (Sept. 23–Oct. 23)
You'll be reported missing in Afghanistan this week, which just goes to show how far you're willing to go to avoid calling Greg back.

Scorpio: (Oct. 24–Nov. 21)
All right, Scorpio is going to say this for the last fucking time: With an apostrophe, it means "it is" and without an apostrophe, it means "belonging to it." This is really not that hard.

Sagittarius: (Nov. 22–Dec. 21)
You've been struggling to find a way to tell that special someone you love her, so keep in mind that someone of your species usually displays his tail plumage and excretes musk.

Capricorn: (Dec. 22–Jan. 19)
Certainly, the praying mantis is a fearsome-looking creature, but up until this week, you never imagined what thousands of them working together could do to an infant.

Aquarius: (Jan. 20–Feb. 18)
Those who don't remember the past are, of course, doomed to repeat it, which is exactly why you drink until you lose your memory every single Thursday.

Pisces: (Feb. 19–March 20)
The stars foresee a lot of sorrow and tribulation in your life that, when viewed from their distant stellar perspective, seems insignificant and barely worth mentioning.

BEANERY from page 8

amounts of blood. Passersby were amazed by the unusually large amounts of blood. Passersby were amazed by the unusually large

Birds: The fish of the sky.

amounts of blood. Passersby were amazed by the unusually large amounts of blood. Passersby were amazed by the unusually large amounts of blood. Passersby were amazed by the unusually large amounts of blood. Passersby were amazed by the unusually large amounts of blood. Passersby were amazed by the unusually large amounts of blood. Passersby were amazed by the unusually large amounts of blood. Passersby were amazed by the unusually large amounts of blood. Passersby were amazed by the unusually large amounts of blood. Passersby were amazed by the unusually large amounts of blood. Passersby were amazed by the unusually large amounts of blood. Passersby were amazed by the unusually large amounts of blood. Passersby were amazed by the unusually large amounts of blood. Passersby were amazed by the unusually large amounts of blood. Passersby were amazed by the unusually large amounts of blood. Passersby were amazed by the unusually large amounts of blood. Passersby were amazed by the unusually large amounts of blood. Passersby were amazed by the unusually large amounts of blood. Passersby were

see BEANERY page 72

NEWS

Bush Caught In One Of His Own Terror Traps

see WASHINGTON page 11C

State Champs Erect Triumphal Arch

see SPORTS page 8F

Origami Bird Poached For Scrap Paper

see ANIMALS page 14G

Lower Class Dismissed

see NATION page 13C

STATshot

A look at the numbers that shape your world.

the ONION®

VOLUME 41 ISSUE 21 AMERICA'S FINEST NEWS SOURCE™ 26 MAY–1 JUNE 2005

National Advertising Board Launches 'Advertising: Get The Message!' Campaign

NEW YORK—In an effort to raise the individual American's awareness of and interest in advertising, the National Advertising Board launched a $32-million "Advertising: Get The Message!" campaign in major markets across the country Monday.

"From lifesaving drugs to new diet beverages, advertising keeps you informed about the products and services you want to buy," a spokeswoman said in a 30-second spot titled "Keep An Eye Out For Ads." "But advertising can't work for you if you don't pay attention!"

The commercials, in heavy rotation on network and cable television, end with a helpful tip for viewers: "To get messages from advertisers in your area, open up your local newspaper, turn on your radio, or continue to watch this channel."

The NAB campaign includes print, radio, television, and billboard ads.

A print ad appearing in 15 leading women's magazines this month reads, "Whether you need a new, improved detergent with stain-dissolving power or a low-interest equity loan for making home improvements, advertising can help. Why not look at some advertising today?"

The new campaign targeted American males, as well.

"You're a man," an advertisement in *Men's Health* read. "Take your life into your own hands—with advertising. If you're looking for sporting goods, hair products, or pornography, ads will bring you closer to your goal. Advertising—get the message!"

see CAMPAIGN page 154

Investigators Blame Stupidity In Area Death

WHEATLEY, AR—Although reckless driving and minor driver impairment were cited as additional factors, police investigators ruled pure, unadulterated stupidity as the primary cause in the death of an unlicensed motorist involved in a single-car accident Sunday.

"We're fairly positive the deceased was operating under the influence of being an unbelievable dumbass," forensic investigator Evan Lawrence told reporters at the scene, a stretch of road littered with SUV parts, beer cans, food containers, fishing equipment, and pornography. "I mean, we're not saying alcohol, fatigue, poor vehicle maintenance, and driver error didn't play their parts—but mainly,

see STUPIDITY page 155

Right: The scene of the idiotic accident.

Goth, Metalhead Overcome Subcultural Differences To Find Love

Above: Halloway and Richardson, who overcame odds to find love.

DANVILLE, IL—People fall in love every day, but self-proclaimed "Goth for life" Danielle Richardson, 24, and avid metal-music fan Rick Halloway, 26, faced bigger obstacles than most couples. In spite of having come from vastly different subcultural groups, the unlikely couple celebrated their three-month anniversary Monday.

"It hasn't been easy dating someone so totally different," said Halloway, who wore faded black jeans and a Mastodon T-shirt. "There have been times, like when Dani asked who Phil Anselmo was, that I almost wanted to say 'forget this bullshit.' But then I reminded myself that nothing good is

see LOVE page 154

Congressional Filibusters

Some people view the filibuster as a vital democratic tool, but others see it as an unnecessary impediment to legislative progress. What do *you* think?

"Wait—wouldn't the Democrats be able to filibuster the bill to change the filibustering rules?"

Lillie Moon
Doctor

"I think it's time America moved past this 'checks and balances' idea and fully embraced our 'unlimited line of credit' society."

Louis Knapp
Probation Officer

"The filibuster, eh? That reminds me of the baking-powder biscuits my dear old grandmother used to make. First she'd take shortening... Now, keep in mind, the more shortening you use, the flakier the biscuits will be. My, all of us kids used to love these biscuits. The secret is to not over-knead the dough, because it makes the biscuits tough, and nobody likes tough biscuits. If you sprinkle a little..."

Timothy Landry
Systems Analyst

"I use filibusters in my day-to-day life. They help you get out of all kinds of stuff, like taking out the garbage or having children."

Gordon Richmond
Plumber

Derek Meadows
Factory Operator

"I'm not positive where I stand on filibusters, but as a longtime proponent of 'less talk, more rock,' I assume I'm against them."

Viola Ellison
Fashion Designer

Memorial Day

May 30 is Memorial Day. How are Americans planning to celebrate the holiday this year?

- Somberly trimming the hedges
- Drinking self into a "reflecting upon the sacrifices our veterans have made to keep America free" stupor
- Taking a moment to remember the brave men who gave their lives in the Indianapolis 500
- Putting in a free day at the office, because that's the sort of thing that makes America great
- Awaiting orders to get the hell out of Iraq
- Refraining from urinating on late father's grave for one day
- Meeting little Lolitas on the Internet during feds' day off
- Lying around on beach with guts hanging out, just like the soldiers did in World War II

America's Finest News Source.™

Herman Ulysses Zweibel
Founder

T. Herman Zweibel
Publisher Emeritus
J. Phineas Zweibel
Publisher
Maxwell Prescott Zweibel
Editor-In-Chief

This Milk Is Expired When I Say It Is

By Daniel Gordan

Hey, you haven't even touched your milk. What's the matter? Milk is an important part of a balanced diet, good for strong bones, healthy teeth, and—what do you mean "spoiled"? Gimme that. Spoiled? This milk smells as fresh as the day I bought it. What? Listen to me, missy—this milk is expired when I say it is.

That's final.

Hundreds of thousands of cows are milked every day, and a whole lot of very good men and women spend hours putting that milk into cartons and driving it to the market, just so little girls like you can drink it and be healthy. After all the hard work those people and cows put into every glass, you're telling me you don't want to drink your milk? I'm disappointed in you, honey.

Let me see that. Look, the expiration date is only six days ago. What could possibly go wrong in six days? That's not even a week. Besides, you had this with your cereal Saturday morning, and you're perfectly fine. As I remember, you had seconds.

Now you listen to me, young lady. That milk is not yellow—it's off-white. What difference does the color make, anyway? It's not like you have eyes on the inside of your mouth. What? Let me see. I don't smell anything. Besides, if you drink it, you won't have to smell it anymore.

Now you listen to me, young lady. That milk is not yellow—it's off-white. What difference does the color make, anyway? It's not like you have eyes on the inside of your mouth. What? Let me see. I don't smell anything. Besides, if you drink it, you won't have to smell it anymore.

Why? Because I said.

Do you know what an expiration date is? Numbers. That's all. It's not like you enter into a legally binding contract with the dairy industry the moment you pay for your milk. The expiration date is a suggested guideline, and guidelines aren't always made with the individual's best interest in mind. Sometimes they're just there to make Daddy pay for new milk.

What are you going to listen to, a mechanical stamp on a carton or your own flesh and blood? I'm your father, and as your father, I'm telling you that the milk is good.

What are you going to listen to, a mechanical stamp on a carton or your own flesh and blood? I'm your father, and as your father, I'm telling you that the milk is good.

I did not raise you to be a follower. You're a Gordan, and a Gordan never takes an expiration date at face value. A Gordan asks the important questions, like, "Who said?" and "Who benefits?" and "Why should I let an expiration date ruin a perfectly good glass of milk?"

I've had it up to here with you! Give me that glass. Mmm. See? Mmmmm-mm! This is the best milk I've ever tasted, in fact. It has a slight hint of berries. Mmm-mm. You like berries, right? Try it.

So, it's good enough for your old man, but it isn't good enough for you? Well, it's your loss. This is delicious. I'm going to have some more. Yum! You like cottage cheese, don't you? This is the same thing as cottage cheese. We'll mix in some Nesquik. You won't see the color or taste the little extra flavor that way. At least try it. Two bites?

I'll give you "gross."

Okay, fine. Pour it down the drain. Oh, and here's three dollars. Throw that down the drain right after it, because that's exactly what you're doing. It's...

Oof. Hold on. Daddy's not feeling too good. I think Daddy needs to sit down. No honey, it's not because of the milk. It's a coincidence.

Come back here and... Oh, Daddy doesn't... You'll grow up to... Oh golly. Hold that thought, sweetie. Daddy will be right back... Ø

Having-One-Beer Plan Goes Awry

YPSILANTI, MI—Due to outside influence and unforeseen events, the having-one-beer plan that 29-year-old Keith Flemming devised at the outset of Monday evening went awry.

"This is a one-beer night," Flemming told his friend Sam Galveston as the two approached their usual booth at Fitzgerald's Tavern. "I wanna be in bed early, so I have time for a quick drink and some laughs, but that's it. I'm not going on a tear or anything."

Flemming, a sales representative for a boutique food packager, ordered a round of Bud Lights at 7:30 p.m. As the two friends drank their beers and discussed their summer-vacation plans, Flemming was well-positioned to meet his goal of being in bed by 10 p.m.

"I have time for a quick drink and some laughs, but that's it," Flemming said.

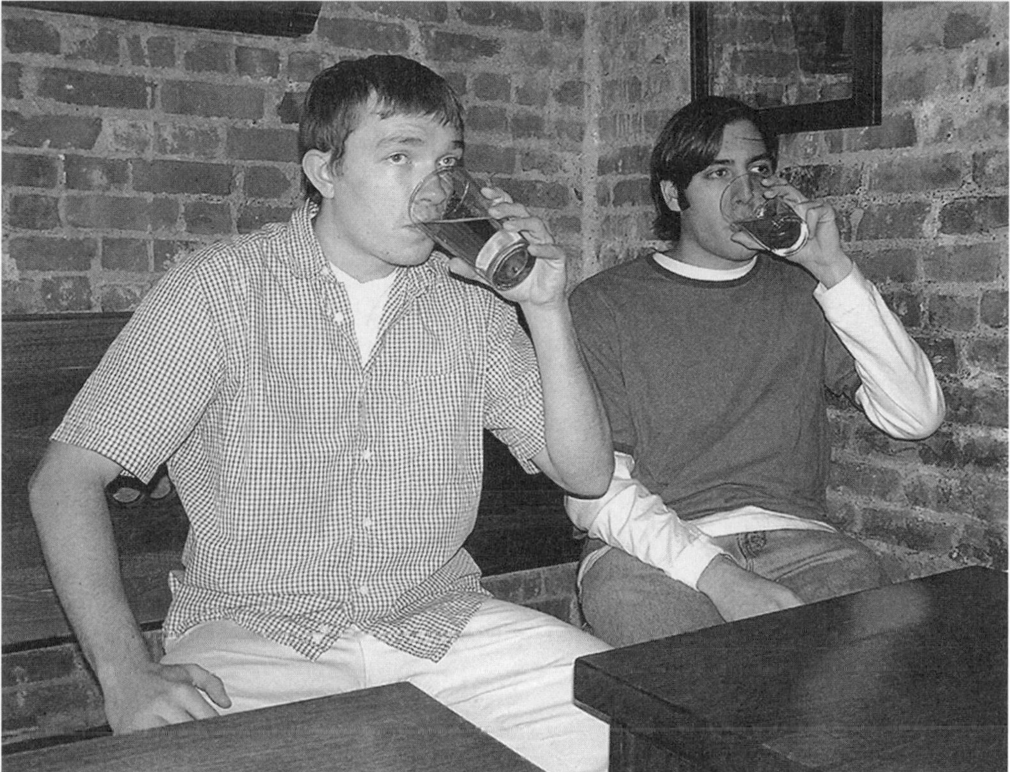

Above: Flemming (left) shares "one quick beer" with his friend Galveston.

Shortly before requesting the check, however, Flemming briefly placed Galveston in charge of the itinerary.

"I gotta take a leak," Flemming said. "You know what they say about beer: You don't buy it, you rent it."

While Flemming was in the restroom, Galveston ordered a second round for the pair, thus causing Flemming's plan for the evening to go slightly askew.

"Well, I can't let this to go to waste," said Flemming, holding the beer up and chuckling. "After this, though, I have to get out of here. I gotta be up at 6 in the morning. Big day. Inventory."

Had events not conspired against him, Flemming could well have finished his second beer and still arrived home before 9 p.m. His plan was thwarted, however, when Gary Greely, a longtime acquaintance of Flemming and Galveston, approached the booth.

"Gary! Long time no see," Flemming said. "I gotta take off soon, but let me get you a beer first. We got some catching up to do."

Two hours and an unforeseen buyback later, the early-to-bed plan Flemming had established at the beginning of the evening was in serious jeopardy.

see BEER page 155

NEWS IN BRIEF

Palmolive Attacks Dawn For Coddling Grease

NEW YORK—Representatives for Palmolive dish detergent issued a challenge to the makers of Dawn Monday, charging that the blue dishwashing soap "coddles grease." "Palmolive lives up to its vow to be 'tough on grease,' but Dawn merely 'takes grease out of your way,'" Colgate-Palmolive CEO Reuben Mark said. "Out of sight, out of mind, eh Dawn? Palmolive believes in eradicating the grease problem, not simply pushing it to the far reaches of the sink." Mark added that, as unrelenting as Palmolive is on grease, it continues to be soft on hands.

Thousands Dead In Wake Of Low-Carbon Diet

FORT WALTON BEACH, FL—Doctors are linking nearly 9,000 deaths nationwide to the popular low-carbon diet outlined in the bestselling book, *Dr. Wesley's Elemental Dieting*. "Dr. Ryan Wesley's book tells dieters to avoid consuming carbon, an element that occurs in all organic life, animal and vegetable," said Dr. Peter Castle, a nutritionist at Johns Hopkins University. "Although Wesley dieters can injest limitless hydrogen, oxygen, and nitrogen, deriving nutrients only from gases is not viable in the long term." The low-carbon diet first came to prominence in February 2004 when Wesley appeared on *The Oprah Winfrey Show* weighing an astonishing 76 pounds.

Alternative Training School For Dogs De-Emphasizes Obedience

MONTEREY, CA—Dogs who attend the Kylee Alternative Training Institute are exposed to a "creative canine learning environment where less emphasis is placed on obedience," director Morgan Kylee said Monday. "We believe in helping our students to discover their own potential, rather than forcing them to conform to the traditional idea of what a dog should be," Kylee said. "Dogs that mess on the carpet or bark incessantly are not scolded, but praised for finding their own parameters. Our motto is 'If it feels good, chew it.'" Classes at the school include Holistic Heeling, Elective Fetching, and Removing The Leg-Humping Stigma.

Cocky Attempt To Operate ATM In Spanish Backfires

SAFFORD, AZ—During a Monday night stop at an automated-teller machine, an overconfident Scott Tifton failed to withdraw cash using the machine's Spanish instructions. "My girlfriend Lisa was with me at the ATM, so I pressed Spanish as a joke," Tifton said. "I figured I could rely on my high-school Spanish, but instead of giving me $100, the deposit slot lit up. Then I hit what I thought meant 'cancel' a couple times, and it ate my card. We were going out to dinner for our two-year anniversary, and Lisa had to pay." Tifton said he probably could have figured out the instructions if he had been at his normal branch.

Former Addict Celebrates 10th Year Of Mind-Numbing Boredom

PHOENIX—Tom Stubbens, 44, a former heroin abuser, attended a party in his honor to celebrate a full decade of clean, sober, and dismally tedious living Tuesday. "The crazy gang of partiers I used to have so much fun with in the '90s wouldn't even recognize the clean and respectable person standing before you today," said Stubbens, raising an iced tea to friends at his regular evening haunt, the 36th Avenue Denny's. "Yup, but here I am... that person." Stubbens then retired to his apartment, where he watered his plants, organized his sock drawer, and fell asleep on the couch. Ø

CAMPAIGN from page 151

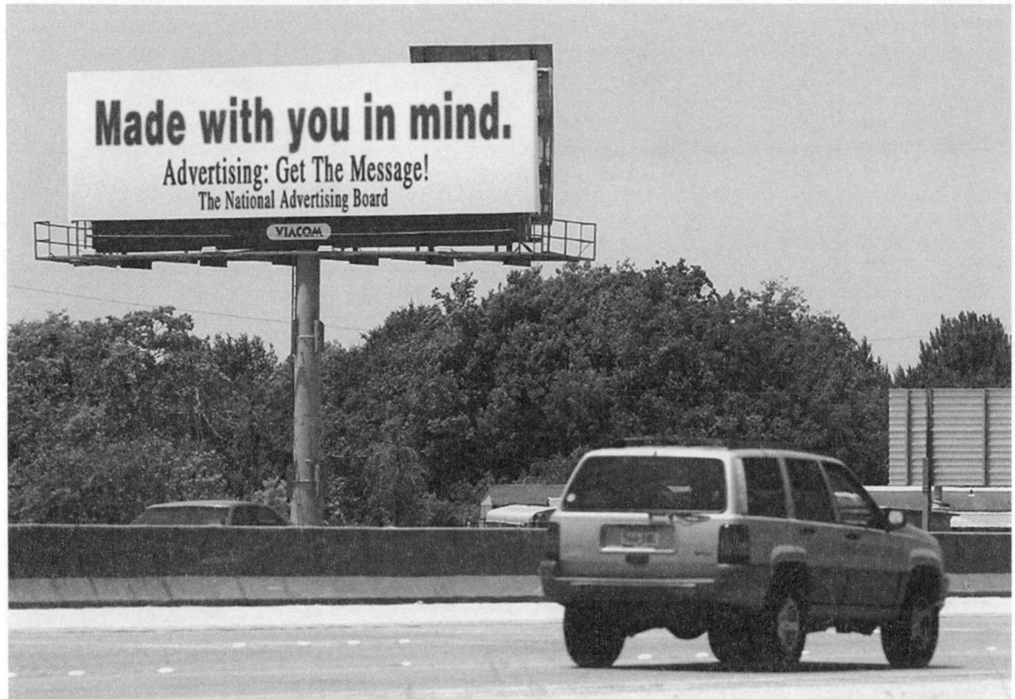

Above: An NAB billboard in Raleigh, NC.

According to NAB spokeswoman Alaina Gray, the goal of the print advertisements is twofold.

"Primarily, we want to raise awareness of our new 'Get The Message' slogan," Gray said. "But we also hope that, by drawing attention to our ads, we'll attract more interest to all ads. That's why many of our print ads urge consumers to look to the right and left of our advertisement for other advertisements."

Many consumers have taken the NAB's new message to heart.

"Just the other day, I was wondering what video game I would buy next," said Omaha, NE resident John Cruise, who saw an NAB commercial in the current issue of *Electronic Gaming Monthly*. "I looked at a few of the other full-page color advertisements in the magazine I was holding, and sure enough, the ads made me want a whole bunch of games."

Christina Williamson, former vice president of Chiat/Day and current NAB director, said the organization labored for six months to create their "Get The Message!" message.

"As you can imagine, we focus-grouped this campaign extensively, and we saw some really positive results," Williamson said. "These days, people are looking for messages, so the word 'message' in our 'Get The Message' slogan really resonated with our target demographic—consumers of goods and services. We expect the new campaign to be even more successful than our 2004 campaign, 'Advertising: Look At It.'"

In a full-page "Open Letter To American Consumers" in Sunday's *New York Times*, Williamson wrote that "despite the massive efforts of advertising agencies to analyze and exploit human psychology, advertising is more art than science."

"Advertising livens up television programs and brightens magazines,

In a full-page "Open Letter To American Consumers" in Sunday's *New York Times*, Williamson wrote that "despite the massive efforts of advertising agencies to analyze and exploit human psychology, advertising is more art than science."

neither of which would exist without advertising," Williamson wrote. "Innovative advertising forms like the magalogue, the infomercial, and advertainment are breathing new life into the industry. If you're hungry for information or looking for a quick laugh, look no further than advertising." ⊘

LOVE from page 151

ever easy. That's why I chose the path of metal—living fast and rocking hard. I never in my craziest dreams thought that path would lead me to Dani, but I'm so glad it did."

Added Halloway: "Fuckin' A, she totally rocks."

Richardson said that, although she has lived her whole life in the same small, largely middle-class Midwestern town as Halloway, the two couldn't be more different. While Halloway spends his free time fixing his car or plugging the jukebox at T.J.'s Tap, Richardson spends her free time shopping at thrift stores and reading poetry at The Black Cat, a red-velvet-curtained bar nearly 10 blocks away from T. J.'s.

"No one is more surprised by our union than I," Richardson said. "When we met, there was a strong attraction, but so much more is required for lasting love. I never believed one such as Rick could touch my shadowed heart, but touch it he has."

Halloway admitted that the relationship got off to a shaky start.

"Me and some of my friends were hanging out in front of the Midas when Dani walked by with a big, black umbrella," Halloway said. "Well, it wasn't raining, so my friends started making fun of her. But when she looked over, our eyes locked. I was like, 'whoa.'"

A few days later, Halloway ran into Richardson at the Danville Cineplex.

"I asked her what she was going to see—I think it was that gay-ass *Blade: Trinity* movie," Halloway said. "Danielle was wearing this weird black lacy thing. I like women who wear black, but usually it's leather with studs. But something about her made me wait for her after my movie got out. I'm so glad I did."

"It brought me much pain to realize that we would have no future together," Richardson said. "We were just too different."

Richardson said she began dating Halloway with serious reservations.

"Our first date was positively chilling—Rick's soul seemed to be crying out to me," Richardson said. "Still, it brought me much pain to realize that we would have no future together—we were so very different."

"But at the end of the night, when I reached out to take Rick's hand, I noticed that his fingernails were painted black," Richardson added. "I told him how sexy it was, and he told me he got the idea from a Danzig video. That was the first time I realized we had something deep and eternal in common."

Although he had similar doubts, Halloway said he "decided to say 'fuck it' and go for it."

"On our next date, Danielle took me to this place where a house had burned to the ground—the whole place was all scorched and shit," Halloway said. "It looked like a Sepultura video. It was such a kickass spot that we started making out like animals."

Continued Halloway: "For a girl who writes poetry, Danielle is a totally crazed hell-demon in the sack. She tears the shit out of my back. She's a righteous chick, even if she doesn't like me calling her that."

Although the couple overcame subcultural differences, their friends have not been so open-minded.

"I thought Danielle was just trying to get a reaction from us by going out with some loser," said Valerie Brasher, a longtime Goth. "I could see how our outrage might be delicious to her, but now, she actually seems serious about Rick. This lunacy makes my mind swim with sadness."

"Danielle will always be very dear to me, but I can't support that relationship," Brasher added. "Once, I suggested that Rick wax his goatee into a tapered, devilish point and he told me to keep my pale-ass freak hands to myself. I mean, talk about your typical close-minded metalhead vulgarian behavior."

Halloway's friends have similarly disparaged the union.

"I told Rick that there's a reason why, when we were all in high school, our friends would hang out under the bleachers and the Goths would hang out in the atrium," Mike Kryzinski said. "It was because our kinds don't get along. What's gonna happen at their wedding when Danielle starts playing Sisters Of Mercy or some shit like that? What kind of music are their kids gonna listen to? Hasn't he ever stopped and thought about the future?" ⊘

BEER from page 153

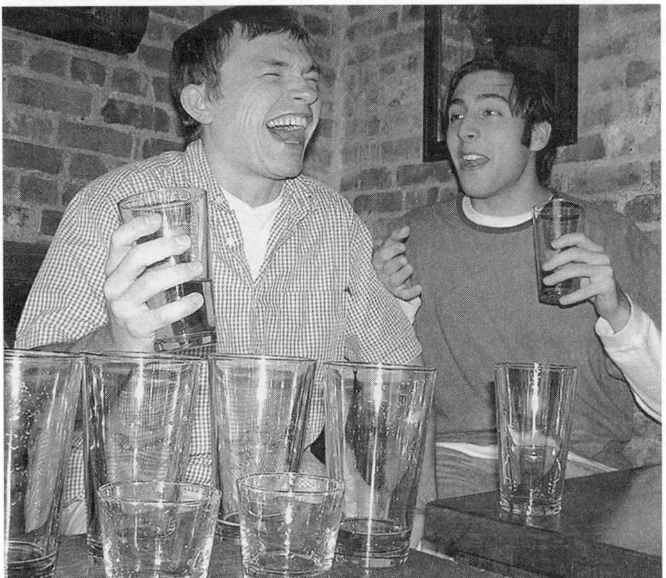

Above: Flemming finishes "one last beer" before leaving the bar.

Flemming purchased "one last round" for the table at 10:35 p.m., but in order to get home for his revised bedtime of 11 p.m., Flemming drank the beer in 10 minutes—an act that caused further wavering in his resolve to leave the bar.

"Guys, I really should get going, I guess," said Flemming, slurring his words. "I really should probably... I got something I gotta do tomorrow, something at work early."

Flemming stood and began to gather his belongings and say goodbye to his friends. Greely, however, began to chant "shots," and the plan for the evening went off-track again.

"No Jaeger, though, man," said Flemming, returning to his seat. "Last time I drank Jaeger, I was hung over for days. No way."

"All right, but if I puke, you're cleaning it up!" Flemming added.

The three finally said their goodbyes and parted at 2:00 a.m., whereupon Flemming completed his evening in a manner wholly unanticipated—by vomiting, drinking several glasses of water, and falling asleep fully clothed on top of his covers.

"I only went to work today because I couldn't miss inventory," Flemming said Tuesday morning. "I don't even remember getting home last night. I know I didn't drive, because my car wasn't around this morning. I guess I took a cab. Christ. Honestly, that's the last time I do that. Next time, I'll go to the bar and hang out, but I'll just have a soda."

STUPIDITY from page 151

that driver was a goddamn dipshit."

The violent and inane mishap occurred at approximately 4 p.m., just north of town, where Highway 63 passes beneath the railroad bridge.

A 25-page accident report released to the press Tuesday contained such details as "leg hooked through steering wheel so driver could use both hands to light cigarette," "handgun case slid under brake pedal, preventing it from being adequately engaged," and "carotid artery lacerated by bottle-opener bolted to dashboard."

Deputy Craig Zemke of the Lee County Highway Patrol said nothing in his 13 years on the force prepared him for the moronic things he saw.

"As soon as we rolled up, I turned to my partner and said, 'Jake, I can feel it in my bones: This is gonna be a stupid one,'" Zemke said. "When you approach an accident scene and see an inflatable doll stuck in the still-smoldering branches of a tree littered with the remnants of illegal fireworks—well, you know you're in for an idiotic sight."

Zemke's partner Jake Mills explained that, although it is often difficult for investigators to ascertain what might have triggered an accident, the cause of Sunday's accident was "immediately and pathetically obvious."

"See, usually, the vehicle's sudden-braking skid marks don't start a mere six feet from the concrete pillar," Mills said. "Usually, the vehicle doesn't have a gas tank held to its frame by a bungee cord and two leather belts. And, in almost all cases, the driver isn't halfway through the windshield with a half-bottle of Everclear grain alcohol in one hand and an electric nose-hair trimmer in the other."

"The police cruiser hadn't even stopped rolling by the time I'd penciled in 'stupidity' under 'cause of death,'" Mills added. "After that, I spent a few hours taking measurements, snapping photos, and shaking my head at what a dumbass this guy was."

Although investigators can't exactly reconstruct Sunday's chain of events, it appears that the driver—drunk, barefoot, pants-less, and leaving a double shift at a nearby FD&C Yellow No. 5 food-coloring plant—saw a train approaching on the right and stupidly decided to accelerate and beat it to the intersection.

"I deemed the motorist bone-stick-stone-stupid for several reasons," Lawrence said. "First, no motorist should ever attempt to outrun an oncoming train. Second, no motorist should ever place an ashtray containing two lit cigarettes on top of a car seat drenched in 190-proof Everclear, as the scorch marks on the deceased's crotch will attest. Finally, and this is the real mind-blower, the accident occurred at a spot where the train tracks pass *over* the highway *on their own bridge*. Apparently, the numbnuts panicked when he saw the train approaching, veered off just before entering the underpass, and sent his truck into the bridge abutment. So even though 'stupid' barely begins to cover it, let's decide that it's an adequate description of the cause of death and leave it at that."

The moron's name is being withheld out of respect for his stupid family, which is preparing lawsuits against the Arkansas Highway Department, the Union Pacific Railroad, and the David Sherman Corporation, which produces Everclear.

COMMUNITY VOICES

Snowball In Hell

If you're considering starting your own business, keep a few things in mind. First, you can't call in sick, and you may have to work very long hours, even if no customers show up for the entire day. Second, be prepared for weeks, or even months, to go by before you clear $50 a week in sales. Third, consider that you may have to rethink your business plan, even though you devoted a whole month to creating it.

A Room Of Jean's Own
By Jean Teasdale

I gotta say, Jeanketeers, after two months of helping my dad run his Off-Season Santa store, I'm ready to throw in the towel—and the giant plastic candy canes, and the colored lights, and anything else in our store that isn't nailed down! Frankly, Dad and I overestimated the level of year-round yuletide cheer in our community. We're lucky if we get three serious customers a day (and by serious, I mean people willing to pose for a photo with Dad/Santa or buy a Christmas knickknack). Mostly, Dad and I sit around in our costumes playing Go Fish and Crazy Eights.

I don't get it. We've made Santa Claus' lap available seven days a week, 365 days a year, but no one seems to care! You'd think, what with the war, that people would be chomping at the bit for a little whimsy and delight! True, we're located in a dilapidated strip mall in a seedy part of town, but people have cars, don't they? I suppose if we hung signs saying "Swear With Santa!" or "Watch Porn With Santa!" the line would stretch around the block. Well, Dad and I discussed it, and we refuse to stoop to that level.

Dad and I are both dreamers. We've always taken the road less traveled, and since that road has its share of

I gotta say, Jeanketeers, after two months of helping my dad run his Off-Season Santa store, I'm ready to throw in the towel—and the giant plastic candy canes, and the colored lights, and anything else in our store that isn't nailed down! Frankly, Dad and I overestimated the level of year-round yuletide cheer in our community.

"Expect Delays" signs, patience is a must! But lately, even good-natured ol' Dad has expressed serious doubts. "I've had lot of businesses fail," Dad said yesterday. "But those businesses were failures on paper, not due to a lack of customers. Never has one been so dead."

At first, we figured business would pick up once we ironed out the kinks. The fake plastic snow on the floor turned from white to brown and started collecting in the wheel wells of Dad's Rascal, so I replaced it with polyurethane batting, sprinkled it with glitter, and fenced it off with patio stones and a row of wicker reindeer.

Dad's scooter seemed to be scaring away children, so I created some very elaborate (and very darling, if I do say so myself!) sleigh cutouts out of foam board. I linked the cutouts together with Velcro and secured them to Dad's scooter. I even sewed a red plush cover to conceal the gray leather seat! You'd practically need X-ray vision to see that Dad is riding a three-wheeled mobility scooter, after that festive treatment.

Continuing on my creative tear, I designed a new costume for myself. Us-

see TEASDALE page 156

TEASDALE from page 155

ing chicken wire, strips of paper, and torn pieces of old white bed-sheets, I fashioned a big round hollow ball over five feet in diameter. (Thanks to Armand, our property manager, for letting me use the vacant space next door to spray-paint it white and glittery.) When it was dry, I cut armholes and fitted the inside with molded padding and a strap-on nylon harness (an engineering *pièce de résistance!*). Wearing white leggings, white moon boots, and a furry white hat, I looked like the largest, friendliest snowball you ever laid eyes on! Admittedly, it wasn't perfect—the right side of the snowball was a smidge caved-in and chicken wire poked out of the bottom in a few places. But overall, I was pretty proud of my "Adorable Snowbelle." (Get it? A distant, sweeter-tempered cousin of the Abominable Snowman!) The new costume did a lot to bolster my sagging morale. The hitch was that it was quite heavy and severely limited my arm movement, so I decided to wear it only when standing by the highway to lure passing cars to our store.

At first, the retarded people (I refuse to call them "retards") seemed confused. "It's not time for Christmas," one young woman said. "Santa's supposed to be at the North Pole."

The plan worked! A couple Mondays ago, a minibus pulled up and deposited five mentally disabled adults at our door. Their caretaker explained that I'd waved at their bus the previous week, and the trip to Off-Season Santa was a reward for completing chores during the past week. Dad and I practically grinned ear-to-ear.

At first, the retarded people (I refuse to call them "retards") seemed confused. "It's not time for Christmas," one young woman said. "Santa's supposed to be at the North Pole."

Dad gave his jolliest "ho ho ho" and explained that Santa wanted to see what the area was like when it wasn't Christmas. (Nice save, Dad!) One man said, "There is no Santa Claus" repeatedly, until his caretaker took him back to the van for a much-needed time-out. After that little incident, things settled down. Each customer spent a little money on a knickknack or candy, and a couple told Dad what they wanted for Christmas. (One said he wanted a new computer—how hilarious!) Before leaving, the group posed for a photo with Dad. It's too bad we couldn't persuade them to pose for individual shots; if we had, we really would have struck pay dirt.

Their visit perked us up, but as the afternoon wore on, tedium set in again. I changed into my Adorable Snowbelle costume and was headed out the door to scare up some business when a group of six teenagers walked in. They were all 15 or 16 and almost certainly from the nearby high school. A tall, lanky boy yelled, "Oh my God, it's Santa!!" and a girl pointed at my costume and shrieked with laughter. "Welcome to Off-Season Santa, kids!" I said, trying to be cheery, but when I turned around to look at Dad, he wasn't laughing. His face wore a grim expression.

Well, Dad's instincts were right—it soon became clear that the kids weren't there to meet Santa, but to raise a ruckus. When they figured out that a woman in a papier-mâché snowball costume can't move very fast, the teens started running around the store, ignoring the patio-stone borders and dodging around the fragile Christmas trees in a game of catch-me-if-you-can. One of the girls said she wanted to sit on Dad's lap, but when he said that Santa's lap was only for small children, a tall boy who seemed to be the ringleader said, "What's wrong, Santa, can't you walk?"

At that point, Dad did something that made my jaw drop: He broke character! "Son, I carry shrapnel in my side from serving my country," he yelled. (This is true. Dad was injured during basic training decades ago. As a result, the Army kept him from going overseas and assigned him a job in the motor corps at his base. But his injury has nothing to do with why he uses the Rascal; he uses one because he likes it.) Then, the boy told Dad he wanted an inflatable Jenna Jameson doll for Christmas, and Dad just about lost it. "You need to go to confession," Dad said. "Keep being a smart aleck, kid, but mark my words. In a couple years, you'll regret wasting your youth." This speech only made the kids laugh more. It appalled me to see my dad, let alone Santa, treated like that.

Suddenly, I felt someone tapping on my snowball shell. "Can you feel that?" asked the boy doing it. I hate to admit this, but I was a little scared. As I responded "yes," a second boy snuck up behind me and pushed me. Then the first boy pushed me, and I found myself in the middle of an improvised game of catch! I was no longer a Snowbelle, but a *Punch*belle! By the time they were done with me, my costume looked like a deflated weather balloon covered with dirty gray handprints.

By now, Dad's cheeks were bright red with fury. (Interestingly, it made him look even more like Santa.) "I tolerate no loiterers: Either buy something or get out," Dad yelled. "If you don't, I'll call your school first thing in the morning." This got the kids' attention. Of course, they took Dad at his literal word and bought "something," meaning one Santa lollipop, which they tossed on the pavement outside. I tried to bend down to pick it up, but my costume was too bulky, so it laid there until we closed up the store.

The next morning, Dad was still bitter about the teens' visit. He said he wanted a sign for our window reading, "No One Under 18 Admitted Without A Parent Or Guardian." I dutifully got out my trusty green and red markers and set to work on one, but in the end, I argued Dad out of the idea by saying that the sign would make us sound illicit.

A couple days later, the teens came back. It wasn't the exact same crowd, although I did recognize a couple of them. I guess news of our store had gotten around at their school, and they were visiting out of sheer curiosity. I asked Dad if I should tell them to leave, and he said we should wait. "Hate to say it, Jeannie, but we really need their business," he said. So as the kids snickered and sarcastically posed for pictures, Dad silently took his lumps. One teen made the devil-horns hand gesture behind Santa's head as I snapped the photo, but I just ignored it so as not to lose the sale. "Didn't I tell you this place was bad?" one of the girls told her friend, as they excitedly picked through Christmas bracelets.

But here's the capper, Jeanketeers: Since then, Off-Season Santa has become a sort of after-school hangout. The teens who show up every few days to mock the displays and buy candy are practically our only business. Believe me, we make a pretty odd mix. I don't like to judge, but some of these kids who come in look like Marilyn Manson, that singer who wants to kill everybody. It sort of reminds me of that old *Munsters* episode where the beatniks have a party at the Munsters' house. And I'm sorry, but Dad and I are not the monstrous ones here! ⌀

HOROSCOPES

Your Horoscope

By Lloyd Schumner Sr.
Retired Machinist and
A.A.P.B.-Certified Astrologer

Aries: (March 21–April 19)
Your lifelong love of all things zombie becomes a definite liability when former president Ronald Reagan mysteriously returns to life and is told that you wouldn't mind if he stayed at your place.

Taurus: (April 20–May 20)
You have the wisdom of Solomon, but the sensationalist jerks on the news insist on referring to you as that monster who chopped all those poor children in half.

Gemini: (May 21–June 21)
Your outspoken criticism of your superiors will lead to your transfer to a combat posting in the Middle East, something you didn't know the manager of an auto-parts store had the authority to do.

Cancer: (June 22–July 22)
The great white shark is brutally tenacious in pursuit of its prey, as you will discover after changing your name and moving to land-locked San Antonio.

Leo: (July 23–Aug. 22)
If you're reading this, Leo is dead. It's been lying about the dark stranger all along. You'll find the money hidden behind the Horsehead Nebula.

Virgo: (Aug. 23–Sept. 22)
You'll fall under the influence of a drug that makes you think you can fly, but to the dismay of the people beneath your window, it actually makes you invisible.

Libra: (Sept. 23–Oct. 23)
You're someone who calls 'em like he sees 'em, which is a problem for a constantly hallucinating stutterer like yourself.

Scorpio: (Oct. 24–Nov. 21)
A combination of mistakes involving geography, bravado, and making promises while drunk will soon result in you going over Sioux Falls in a barrel.

Sagittarius: (Nov. 22–Dec. 21)
A new international economic study indicates that tropical fruit and luxury automobiles have been overtaken by your overseas hate mail as America's number-one import.

Capricorn: (Dec. 22–Jan. 19)
Your constant search for inner beauty leads to six months of pain when you pay an expert to tattoo the Last Supper on your heart, lungs, and renal system.

Aquarius: (Jan. 20–Feb. 18)
It's been exhausting, but personally befriending everyone in the entire nation will pay off next Thursday when jury selection for your insurance-fraud case proves impossible.

Pisces: (Feb. 19–March 20)
You like to think you're passing a lifetime's worth of wisdom to a younger generation, but the rest of the world thinks of you as a kitchen-counter installer with a DSL connection.

the ONION®

VOLUME 41 ISSUE 22 | AMERICA'S FINEST NEWS SOURCE™ | 2–8 JUNE 2005

NEWS

Atari Releases Updated *Adventure* Video Game

see ENTERTAINMENT page 11C

CEO Sad Nobody Noticed New Tie

see BUSINESS page 4D

Realtor Beaten With Exposed Brick

see LOCAL page 8G

Dog Ruins Bathtub Gin

see ANIMALS page 14H

STATshot

A look at the numbers that shape your world.

Top Luxury-Resort Activities
19% Peasant-head polo
28% Dodging couple you met on the plane
23% Telling everyone you don't usually do this kind of thing
16% *Foie gras* fight
14% Vomiting into most exquisite marble toilet ever seen

Pentagon Announces Plans To Close Camp Snoopy

BLOOMINGTON, MN—The Pentagon announced Monday that Camp Snoopy, the largest indoor family theme park in America, is one of 34 major bases scheduled for closing as part of a vast military repurposing and realignment designed to save almost $50 billion.

"We never enjoy having to close a base," said Anthony Principi, chairman of the Pentagon's Base Realignment and Closure Commission. "But Camp Snoopy is a relic of America's Cold War past. Everything in the facility—from the Petting Zoo to the Extreme Trampoline to the Pepsi Ripsaw Roller Coaster—was conceived at a time when America's primary military threat was the Soviet Union. After careful evaluation, we determined

see CAMP SNOOPY page 160

BASE CLOSINGS

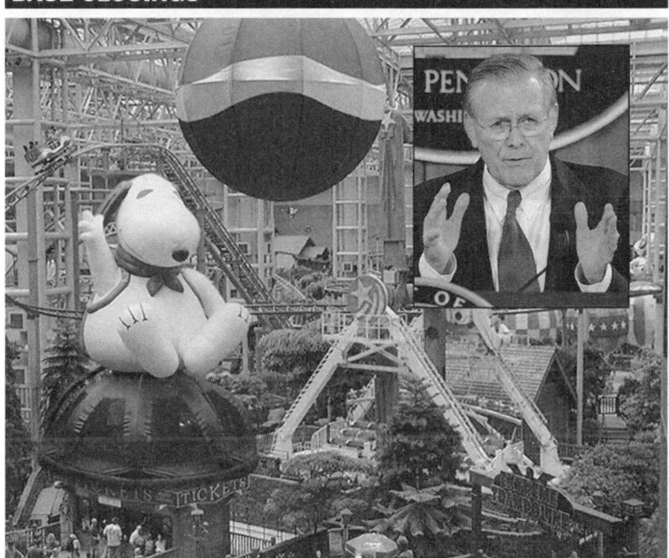

Right: Camp Snoopy, which Defense Secretary Donald Rumsfeld (inset) confirmed is one of the domestic military bases slated for closure.

Left: Brown overturns an April decision made by Hatchett (above).

Judge Hatchett Ruling Overturned By Judge Joe Brown

HOLLYWOOD—Nationally syndicated justice Judge Joe Brown reversed Judge Glenda Hatchett's ruling in the TV-court case *Amanda Robinson v. Maria Bristow* Monday, stating that the lower-rated judge flagrantly disregarded pertinent testimony.

In proceedings that originally aired April 12 at 1 p.m. EST, Hatch-

see JUDGE page 162

Local Self-Storage Facility A Museum Of Personal Failure

CHICAGO—Located in the Bucktown neighborhood, American Mini-Storage is one of Chicago's best-kept secrets, but don't expect it to stay that way for long. The self-storage facility houses what is arguably the nation's most impressive collection of personal items accumulated during periods of failure.

"There are 250 storage units here, and each one has a different pathetic story to tell," said Carlos Garcia, one of several client-relations managers at American Mini-Storage. "They run the gamut—from libraries of unread college textbooks to abandoned

see FAILURE page 161

Above: The museum's B wing.

The Stem-Cell Bill

The House recently passed a bill lifting restrictions on stem-cell research, but Bush has threatened to veto the bill if it passes the Senate. What do *you* think?

Ali Marni
Contractor

"The Democrats and Republicans—and most of the American public—are actually in agreement over an issue. You can see how Bush would want to put a stop to that right away."

Todd Filbert
Lawyer

"Some things are just morally reprehensible, like using science to save people's lives."

Tanya Spinks
Hand Model

"If Bush vetoes this bill, I'm going to veto *him*! With a bumper sticker, of course."

Wesley Wilkes
Fry Cook

"The Democrats want stem-cell research so they can cure multiple sclerosis. The GOP wants it so they can grow an army of zombies. So Bush is in a tough spot politically."

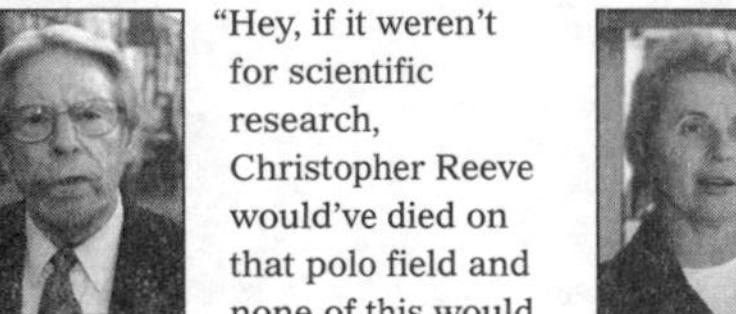

Gary Schneider
Systems Analyst

"Hey, if it weren't for scientific research, Christopher Reeve would've died on that polo field and none of this would even be an issue in the first place."

Rose Anderson
Translator

"They're not stems, they're *babies*! And they're not cells, they're *babies*! And it's not research, it's *babies*!"

Green Products

More people are purchasing eco-friendly items to conserve energy and help save the environment. What are some of the most popular "green products"?

- Nature's Kiss, the earth-friendly, ineffective oven cleaner
- ZookTubes, the zucchini that fits in most common fluorescent-light fixtures
- 10,000 Tomorrows, the reusable toilet paper
- Coal, the fuel that comes right out of the earth, as nature intended
- Thermonuclear sun emulator, for charging solar-powered gadgets at night
- Rats, "nature's garbage disposal"
- Sheetwood, the environmentally friendly, renewable sheetrock substitute
- Kleaner Wieners, the hot dog made from 100 percent post-consumer meats

America's Finest News Source.™

Herman Ulysses Zweibel
Founder

T. Herman Zweibel
Publisher Emeritus
J. Phineas Zweibel
Publisher
Maxwell Prescott Zweibel
Editor-In-Chief

If It's Any Consolation, Your Daughter Probably Died Almost Immediately Of Sheer Terror

By Detective Frank Cosloy

Mr. and Mrs. Frauenfelder? Yes, hello. Thank you for coming down today. I'm Detective Cosloy, one of the eight men here in Tulsa who found the body. The three men in Fort Worth who found the balance of the remains have air-messaged them, so they should be here by this afternoon. I know how difficult this must be for you, and I want to assure you that the department will do all that it can to make this experience—I'm sorry, of course it's... Come this way, won't you? I don't want to draw this out, so if you'd care to identify the remains?

Yes, I'm terribly sorry. The facial structure was lost some due to repeated maceration with a hot iron, and the facial tissue has been... we're interrogating a butterfly-pinner employed at the university. You're certain this is Nan Frauenfelder? I'm so sorry for your loss. If it is any consolation, you should know that your daughter almost certainly died of excruciating terror well before this happened.

Mr. Frauenfelder, while nothing I can say could ever alleviate the grief that you and your wife must be experiencing, please know that we are reasonably sure the drugs your daughter's assailant administered intravenously would have numbed her to any pain the restraints might have caused. Try to take what comfort you can from that.

Oh yes, the restraints were quite... See the ligature marks on your daughter's wrists and ankles, and the two holes punched though each cheek with a leatherworking awl? That's where the restraining wires ran. But please, notice how clean those punctures are, Mrs. Frauenfelder. If Nan were conscious and aware of what was being done to her, she certainly would have struggled, causing tearing of the epidermis at the site of her facial puncture wounds. I can assure you that her heart gave out from panic before these wounds were delivered.

Here, Mr. Frauenfelder, my handkerchief. That's correct, the substance injected into your daughter's ocular ducts was a muscular paralytic as well as a powerful industrial solvent—see where she wept tears of rich arterial blood here?—but contrary to news reports, that wouldn't have kept her alive and cognizant. You see, sheer horror would have overridden the drug and sent her into a coma-like sleep long before rapid cardiac action sprayed her bloody tears 12 feet from the box spring on which she was bound. I assure you of that. You see, your daughter's pulse was well over 200 beats per minute when she began "weeping."

I think it's important that you know that the person who did this to your daughter was a real talker. It fits the sense of stagecraft involved in such dramatic and systematic torture. The relentless, sadistic, hypersexual monologue that probably accompanied your daughter's last moments of life would almost certainly have had a trance-inducing effect, allowing her to escape into a sort of mental cul-de-sac of excruciating fear. After all, we have samples of Nan's blood, taken from her remaining buttock, as well as from the ceiling, the meat hooks, the mirror fragments, the shark darts, and the dentist tools at the scene. The amount of adrenaline in those samples was high enough to burst a human heart in about four minutes. Mr. and Mrs. Frauenfelder, I do not fib when I tell you that overwhelming, soul-destroying fear rendered your daughter unconscious long before those microwave-oven parts bolted to her skull simmered her brain in its own fat.

Oh? Officer Mooney told you she must have been alive at least long enough to eat the half-pound of tissue we recovered from her stomach? Mrs. Frauenfelder, please believe me when I tell you that there was enough electricity coursing through your daughter's panic-riven body to cause a purely reflexive, biogalvanic chewing-and-swallowing action. Neither Nan, nor any 19-year-old girl, would ever have the wherewithal—no matter what the circumstance—to chew and swallow the flesh of her own fingers.

Mr. Frauenfelder, Mrs. Frauenfelder, I have daughters of my own. I can only imagine what you must be feeling. I realize there is nothing I can say to you at this time that will alleviate your loss, but please, do understand that, even if there were any residual brain activity at the moment Nan realized she was strapped to a meat slicer equipped with a high-powered gasoline engine, her actual personality would long have evaporated through the large, ulcerated burns creasing her cerebral cortex. Try to believe that, and take heart. Ø

Date Disastrously Bypasses Physical Intimacy, Goes Straight To Emotional Intimacy

CHAPEL HILL, NC—An initially promising date between University of North Carolina seniors Mike Rafelson and Jill Zehme veered disastrously off course Monday night, when the two skipped directly to intense emotional bonding, tragically bypassing the physical intimacy that usually precedes it.

"It's not what you think—unfortunately," Rafelson told his roommates Tuesday morning after they watched him send Zehme off with a long, tight goodbye hug and an affectionate kiss on the forehead. "The date was going great—I could feel us getting closer and closer all night. I was totally psyched when she came home with me. But somehow I screwed up, and we ended up sharing our most personal thoughts and feelings without even making out first."

Rafelson said he and Zehme met two weeks ago at Raleigh's Schoolkids Records, where they spent 20 minutes wandering past each other while pretending to look at vintage LPs, self-consciously brushing bangs back from their foreheads, and stealing glances at each other over the display racks.

Rafelson said he "finally made a move" and asked Zehme about the album she was holding, *Talking Heads: 77*. In the 20-minute discussion that followed, Zehme not only told Rafelson how important the album had been to her during a troubling time in her adolescence, but that she worked at a local coffeehouse.

"She went out of her way to describe the location of the Buzz Café *and* the hours she usually works," Rafelson said. "I was, like, 'Yeah! This is it, man—she totally likes me and I'm gonna get some action.' Unfortunately, I was only half right—and it was the wrong half."

After he "happened to swing by" Buzz Café, Rafelson asked Zehme if she would like to see his friend's band, Chat!, thus launching the pair's ill-fated journey to non-physical intimacy.

"When I picked her up, she looked really hot," Rafelson said. "After the show, we went to get some pizza, and our feet were touching under the table the whole time we ate. We talked for a long time about the trouble she was having finishing up her major, and I could totally relate. Everything seemed to be progressing so nicely. Well, I didn't know it at the time, but the feet thing was the closest physical contact we were going to share."

At 12:30 a.m., as the couple walked to Rafelson's place, their conversation grew more personal. Rafelson talked about his last girlfriend, and Zehme discussed her financial problems. At his door, Rafelson said his roommates would not be home until later, and to his delight, Zehme agreed to come in-

see INTIMACY page 162

Below: Zehme and Rafelson share a close moment.

NEWS IN BRIEF

Area Man Looking For Whatever The Hell Is Beeping

DELMAR, NY—Craig Mitich, 27, has spent 20 minutes searching his apartment for whatever the hell is emitting a high-pitched beep every few minutes. "Okay, it's not my cell phone... it's not my microwave... or my car-alarm remote," said Mitich, standing motionless with an ear cocked toward his entertainment center. "God, what is it? Can a power strip beep?" At press time, Mitich was on his hands and knees, unplugging his appliances one by one.

Description Of Hot-Dog Ingredients Fails To Ruin Picnic

EVERETT, WA—Try as he might, Matt Cottone was unable to spoil appetites at Jack Pierson's Memorial Day picnic. "The absolute worst meat goes into hot dogs—animal parts that oughta be thrown away—and then they pump it full of nitrates and sodium and dyes," Cottone said as his friends eagerly devoured Oscar Mayer franks. "You might as well be drinking embalming fluid. How can you do that to your body?" After explaining that the meat in hot dogs comes from "cheeks and asses" several times to no effect, Cottone grimaced at the plate of hot dogs and wandered off toward the beer cooler.

Entire *Napoleon Dynamite* Plot Pieced Together Through Friends' Quotes

AUSTIN, TX—Although he has never seen the 2004 indie hit *Napoleon Dynamite*, Michael Osman, 23, has cobbled together its entire plot via his friends' endless quoting of the film. "Well, Napoleon's brother said, 'Don't be jealous that I've been chatting online with babes all day,' and then got a visit from his Internet girlfriend," Osman said. "Then Napoleon told his Uncle Rico that he could make 120 bucks 'in like five seconds,' and went to work on a chicken farm. Then Napoleon gave Trisha a drawing, said, 'It took me like three hours to finish the shading on your upper lip,' and asked her to the dance." Osman added that he has a pretty good idea what a liger looks like.

U.S. Intensifies Empty-Threat Campaign Against North Korea

WASHINGTON, DC—During a recent press conference, Secretary of State Condoleezza Rice issued another warning to North Korea, escalating the U.S. empty-threat campaign against the nation. "Make no mistake, if Kim Jong Il does not put a stop to the manufacturing of plutonium in his nation, we will come down on him quite hard," Rice said. "We demand compliance, and if we don't get it, then watch out." Rice went on to say that noncompliance would result in some action that "would be very bad indeed," adding that North Korea does not want to know what it will be in for.

Local Pet Store Sells Living Things To Just Anyone Off The Street

BALTIMORE—The Fur, Fin, and Feather pet store is willing to sell live animals to just about anyone, local investigating police officer Tom Olansky reported Monday. "Any bozo off the street can walk into this joint with a few bucks and walk out with an actual living, breathing creature," Olansky said. "There's no test to ensure a minimal aptitude for pet ownership, no background check, no follow-up." Store owner Geordi Wilson admitted that a customer "doesn't necessarily need a lot of time or money to own a pet, just a big heart." ø

CAMP SNOOPY from page 157

that the only thing Camp Snoopy was enabling our soldiers to fight was boredom."

According to an official Pentagon statement delivered Tuesday by Defense Secretary Donald Rumsfeld, most of the 300 men and women stationed at Camp Snoopy will be honorably discharged in a ceremony to be held in front of the Rock 'N' Wall.

Camp Snoopy Gen. Manager Craig Freeman said the camp's decommissioning "came out of nowhere."

"Certainly these last couple years have brought drastic changes in the national attitude toward combat readiness," Freeman said. "But we thought our location in America's northern defensive tier, combined with our many indoor roller coasters and log-flume rides, would shield us from the military's increased emphasis on small-unit tactics. I suppose that was naive."

Ranking managers and others in highly trained positions will be posted at other bases in the Mall of America.

"I heard a rumor that I'm going to be shipped out to the Lego Imagination Center," Coordinating Concessions Manager Steve Voorhies said. "I'm still in shock. I had a distinguished food-service record here—a record I could be proud of—and now some desk jockey at the Pentagon sends me to the mall's South Avenue quadrant? It's bullshit."

"Well, I guess I knew when I signed up that they could do whatever they wanted with me," added Voorhies, who has applied for a transfer to Jillian's Hi Life Lanes in the mall's Party Central.

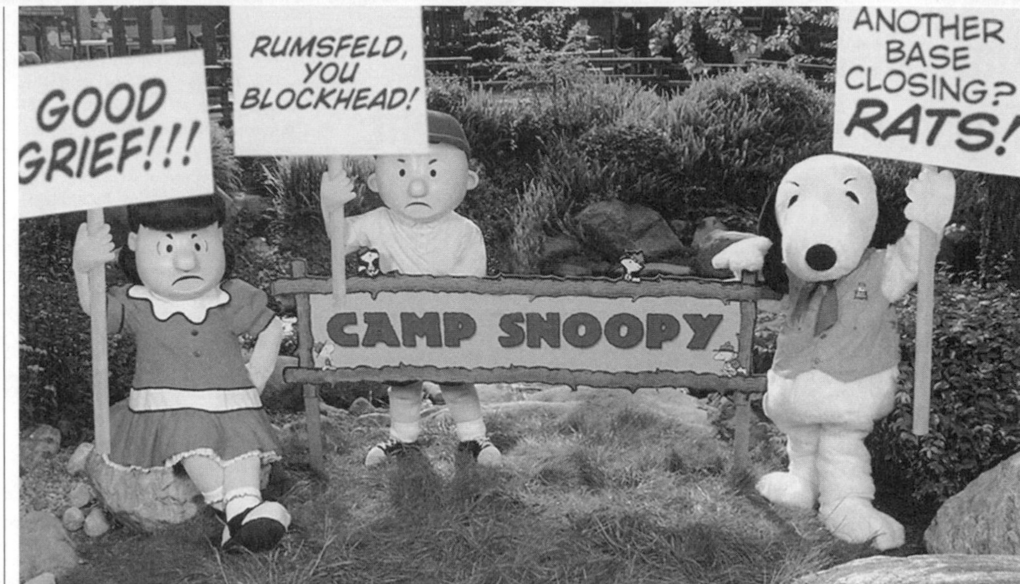

Above: Camp Snoopy characters outfitted with signs protesting the closure.

The camp closing, scheduled for November 2005, is expected to be a major blow to the local civilian economy.

"We've been supplying them with everything from disposable paper goods to uniforms," said Debra Czynsci, the chief military and entertainment sales liaison for the Cedar Fair Management Corporation. "That was close to half a billion dollars annually pumped into the Twin Cities economy. Now, with this facility shutting its gates, we're going to have massive layoffs of our own."

The Pentagon said that the Lego Imagination Center, the Underwater Adventures Aquarium, A.C.E.S. Flight Simulators, and various other Mall of America attractions made Camp Snoopy "redundant."

Insiders, however, suggest that misappropriations issues involving Cedar Fair, which was once investigated for charging Camp Snoopy $479 per case of Thirsty Linus FunCups, was a key factor in the decision to decommission Camp Snoopy.

Brig. Gen. Roy Haemer, who oversaw the Pentagon's Midwest base-closing study, denied suggestions that the camp's closure was politically motivated.

"It may seem counterintuitive to close bases during wartime," Haemer said. "But not a single member of the forward-line units operating in Iraq and Afghanistan trained at Camp Snoopy. Tens of thousands of them *visited* the park, but the fast-paced gaming environment of the Ultimate Zone has little or no bearing on squad-level combat in a desert environment, and maneuvering around the Kite-Eating Tree will do nothing to prepare a soldier for the arid scrub of the Afghani steppes."

Haemer added that California's Camp Snoopy at Knott's Berry Farm is being kept open primarily due to the Red Baron Ride, which he described as "a real hoot." Ø

the ONION presents:

Hosting A Barbecue

Summer is a great time to get outside and grill a delicious meal. Here are a few basic safety rules and outdoor-cooking tips to help make sure you and your family enjoy a tasty, safe summer cookout.

- Marinate your ribs in bourbon before barbecuing. The best way to do this is by pouring the whiskey down your throat.
- One safety tip to keep in mind while barbecuing is that you should never, ever light your house on fire.
- It's important that you choose the right kind of fire for grilling meat. Class D magnesium-based fires are not the right kind of fire for grilling meat.
- Whatever you do, don't shout the phrase "Johnsonville brats!" at the top of your lungs. Don't let your neighbors do that, either.
- Do you have an entire set of tableware designed with a playful, summery watermelon-slice theme? Well, isn't that *adorable*. Let me see that spoon! Even the spoon is a little watermelon. Honey, come here and look at this spoon.
- Don't forget to repeatedly baste your cooking pork in barbecue sauce, which will "mask the spoiled taste."
- The endangered Cebu cinnamon tree of the Philippines is the best firewood for grilling. Use anything less, and you might as well be cooking your food on top of smoldering raccoon shit.
- For optimal flavor, raise your own animals, make your own charcoal, and distill your own vinegar. For passable flavor, head on down to Smokey's Ribs & Things out by the airport.
- When barbecuing veggie burgers, be sure to tie your long hair back. That will keep it away from the flames, you stupid hippie.
- If you live north of the Mason-Dixon line, you should pretty much give up on good barbecue and just be happy with shoes, indoor plumbing, and electricity.

This Script Practically Writes, Directs, And Universally Pans Itself

Find yourself a chair, guys, 'cause I've got exactly what we've been looking for: an idea so formulaic, any screenwriting hack could knock it out with his eyes closed. A film so predictable, we could produce it with our Blackberries turned off. Everybody who sees it, critics and audiences alike, will be guaranteed to hate it. Is everybody on this conference call sitting down? Here we go: *Van Helsing Reborn!* I'm telling you, this script will practically write, direct, and universally pan itself!

By Josh Nordberg
Producer

Van Helsing Reborn! Picture that title on the cover page of a screenplay. Now, see it up on the marquee at Mann's Chinese Theater. Now imagine it next to one star in every newspaper in America. It's a natural!

I know Van Helsing didn't die at the end of the first movie! You're thinking too small. Hell, the total lack of continuity is what will make this baby so easy for some schmuck in San Diego to write, a recent NYU grad to shoot, someone's cousin to edit, and the masses to mock!

In the first one, Van Helsing went up against who again? The Wolfman, Frankenstein, and Dracula? Okay, so we have a perfect opportunity to exploit some old movie-monster properties! Slap in a couple, and the picture's half done. Think about it: Van Helsing meets the Invisible Man, the Bride of Frankenstein, and the Creature from the Black Lagoon. Why come up with new monsters? People love the classics!

That Black Lagoon thing would be perfect for bringing in the black audience. Okay, so he's green, but I think I've hit on something. We could black him up a little, put some gold chains on him, and make him talk all street. We'll blanket the inner-city neighborhoods with an aggressive billboard campaign, bring in the urban audience in droves, and be criticized by the NAACP as an example of what's wrong with the entertainment industry today!

I'm telling you, people all over the country will despise this movie like a freakin' sickness! The word of mouth will be absolutely terrible! Okay, I know what you're thinking: There's more to making movies than displeasing the masses. Don't you worry. Every media outlet from *The New Yorker* on down to *Access Hollywood* will hate this piece of shit.

Van Helsing's an immortal or something, right? I can't remember why—isn't he half-vampire or something? Or am I thinking of Wesley Snipes? Aw, hell, it doesn't matter. Anyway, since he lives forever, we could set it in any time period we want. He blasts ancient Indian mummies in the Old West. Or we could turn the Headless Horseman into some kind of haunted cowboy, and toss him into the mix. Or he could fight Nazi zombies in World War II, or that monster from *They Saved Hitler's Brain.*

Your silence tells me you have some doubts. Why don't we come up with a decent story? What if we find a talented director? What if we made a movie with some artistic merit? Well, we're never going to find out, because we're going to crank this dung heap out, pocket the opening-weekend grosses, and start on an even shittier movie before the inevitable 78-percent audience dropoff in week two.

Wait! I just got an idea. We set the whole movie right here in the present. Van Helsing gets a job working for the CIA—in, like, the Special Monster Tactics Division or something. He fights Freddy, Jason, *and* Chucky! And the *bride* and *seed* of Chucky, too, while we're at it! Think of the toys! With a big enough budget and the right release date, we can't lose. It'll be the most unwatchable summer blockbuster yet!

So, you guys on board? Say the word and I can have legal fax you the contracts by 3:00. Come on, boys—let's get out there and shit out some God-awful crap! ⊘

FAILURE from page 157

bolts of canvas to half-restored antique chests of drawers. Each storage locker is like a window into a separate life of disappointment and inadequacy."

American Mini-Storage opened on Armitage Street in autumn of 1996. Despite being relatively new to the market, facility managers have amassed an impressive collection, thanks to location, word of mouth, and generous contributions from anonymous donors.

"We have the largest collection of NordicTracks in North America, perhaps even the world," Garcia said. "Just by browsing the units, you can chart the evolution of the device—from rather simplistic machines to complex models with built-in cardio monitors."

"Public favor shifts, of course," Garcia added. "I anticipate a boom in the number of Bowflex home gyms permanently installed here in coming years."

The facility has a children's wing, housing dozens of unfinished model cars and airplanes, aquariums and Habitrails from pets long dead from neglect, and hideous ceramic art projects.

"This is a classic example of youthful failure," said Garcia, holding up a D-minus paper titled "Our First President George Washington" by Timmy Keadle. "This stack of essays is filled with all sorts of factual, spelling, and grammatical errors, but they're written so earnestly. Timmy was obviously trying very hard, but just couldn't nail the basics. This paper expresses a truth central to our facility: Failure knows no age limit."

"And this is only one of scores of papers we have just like it on site," Garcia added.

The storage units measure 6' x 6' x 7'. Curated individually by American Mini-Storage customers, each holds unique contents. Leading a tour through the B wing, Garcia gestured to several private galleries.

"This is the Mueller space," Garcia says. "It holds a crate of five partially written detective novels. And over here in the Sherman room, we have one of my favorite collections: the leftover inventory from a failed salad-dressing business. Oh, and take a look inside the Curtis collection. It boasts the decaying remains of an entire family's failure, including a sixth-place intramural-tennis trophy, a moth-eaten gymnastics uniform, and a file cabinet jammed with overdraft bank notices."

The facility features one of the nation's largest collections of fashions from the late 20th century.

"Our collection includes dozens of mint-condition size-6 dresses and never-been-worn swimwear," Garcia said. "Much of the clothing is displayed with beta aerobics tapes and long-abandoned diet journals."

Of particular interest is the musical wing, holding hundreds of long-deserted instruments.

"Nothing evokes dashed hopes like music," Garcia said. "In addition to the usual drums, guitars, and amplifiers abandoned after going-nowhere bands broke up, we have several trombones that came to us following the ska period."

"Oh, this is interesting," added Garcia, gesturing to 14 small boxes. "This is one of our most recent acquisitions. The boxes contain 495 copies of the first CD by a musician called Moldy Dick. All but three CDs are still in their shrink-wrap, and the three unwrapped ones were actually signed by the artist. It's heart-wrenching."

Above: The Pete Tunney gallery features an impressive number of dust-covered musical instruments.

Like any curator, Garcia makes sure the items in his charge are kept in a climate-controlled environment to preserve their integrity. And like any curator, Garcia prefers certain exhibits.

"This is one of my personal favorites," said Garcia, sliding open the door to unit 235. "Look at the sparseness of the arrangement here—252 cubic feet available, and the customer has stored only two boxes, stacked one on top of the other. There's a Zen-like quality to the arrangement. One box holds women's clothing, the other photographs and letters, both of which seem to have once belonged to an ex-girlfriend. They've been here for six years, and the guy keeps paying the rent. Makes your head swim with possible scenarios of failure."

While the storage facility is by no means the only one of its kind, several factors have contributed to the breadth of its fascinating collection.

"Part of the reason for our success is that the neighborhood itself has been in drastic flux over the past 15 years," Garcia said. "As a result of Bucktown's gentrification, the Puerto Rican population has been displaced, followed by the artists and musicians, then the people on the first steps to their career. Everyone who has come and gone has needed a place to store painful reminders of the past. We are not just a storage facility, we are a repository for every imaginable setback a person can experience." ⊘

INTIMACY from page 159

side. Rafelson opened a bottle of wine and the two sat talking and drinking in the living room for an hour before relocating to the bedroom.

The bedroom, Zehme later told friends, is where she and Rafelson "started to open up about just everything."

"From the moment I laid eyes on Mike, he seemed like the kind of guy I could really get close to," Zehme said. "He had such a sincere way about him—a face I could totally trust."

Rafelson said it seemed that, given the circumstances, some form of sexual bonding was assured. As he and Zehme continued to talk, they spoke more passionately, their faces got closer together, and they began to stare intently into each other's eyes.

"The intimacy in the room had worked its way to a fever pitch," Rafelson said. "But before I realized what was happening, disaster struck."

Instead of stroking her date's thigh or taking off her shirt, Zehme began to tell Rafelson things she'd "never told anyone outside of [her] closest confidants."

"I told Mike all my innermost feelings about my parents' traumatic divorce, my brother's drug problem, and my best friend's attempted suicide," Zehme said. "He was so sweet—he took my hand and told me to let it all out. And I did. I just let it all go. I was totally uninhibited that night. I've never been like that with anyone before."

Two and a half hours later, the couple was firmly in the area that couples therapist Gus French described as "that awful horse latitude of male-female relations, the Sargasso Sea of non-sexual pair-bonding known to unhappy males the world over as 'the friend zone.'"

"My heart really goes out to this poor kid," French said. "We've all been there, thinking, 'Gee, this is really special that you're opening up to me about your childhood, but I've got to admit I'd rather be going down on you right now.' Unfortunately, once the emotional barrier has been crossed, there's no going back. By allowing the conversation to swerve into serious-talking territory *before* physical contact was established, Rafelson virtually guaranteed that he would not get into Zehme's pants."

Rafelson corroborated French's prediction.

"Jill said our date was one of the most special nights of her life," Rafelson said. "We talked long into the night until we fell asleep side by side—fully dressed. In the morning, before leaving, she gave me a huge, sincere, and utterly asexual hug—exactly the kind of hug someone would give her brother." Ø

JUDGE from page 157

ett ordered Bristow to pay Robinson $2,000 in damages for faulty services provided at the Headliners Hair Salon in Compton. The defendant appealed the decision, claiming that Hatchett made a rash judgment in order to break for a commercial.

Judge Joe Brown presides over one of the nation's Syndicated-Television Courts of Appeals. These appellate courts stand between less-watched Cable-Television District Courts, such as Hatchett's, the Divorce Court, and Judge Larry Joe's *Texas Justice* courtroom, and higher-Nielsen-rated courts. The nation's highest courts, such as Judge Judith Sheindlin's family court, will only hear cases that appellate TV judges have determined raise questions of importance to a network audience.

In the 22-minute retrial, Brown openly criticized Hatchett's courtroom methodology.

"It is my feeling that Judge Hatchett failed to adequately explore the facts in the case of *Hair Dye Gone Awry*," Brown said from his studio chambers. "I do not always agree with Hatchett's common-sense approach to the law. She is a well-respected TV-court judge, but she always seems to side with the nicer person. That's not how our televised legal system is supposed to work."

According to official court records, plaintiff Robinson paid defendant Bristow, Headliners owner and lead stylist, $75 to dye her hair chestnut brown on Jan. 15. Three days after the salon visit, Robinson began to experience excessive hair loss. She complained to Bristow, who offered a refund and a complimentary hairweave. Robinson refused both, deeming them insufficient compensation for her suffering.

Upon review of a videotape of the original trial, Brown called Hatchett's demand that the defendant pay $2,000 and write a letter of apology to the plaintiff "excessive sentencing."

"Hatchett made a serious abuse of discretion by refusing to hear Bristow's testimony after the defendant spoke out of turn a fifth time," Brown said. "In addition, Hatchett made it clear that the defendant's casual dress figured into her decision."

According to Brown, Bristow satisfactorily showed that, while Robinson's "dye job went awry," she had performed thousands of previous hair-dyeing procedures without incident. Robinson, however, never conclusively proved her hair loss was caused by the dye job.

"Besides, a customer must accept a certain degree of risk when entering a beauty shop," Brown added. "This fact cannot be ignored simply because the defendant wore a low-cut tank top and flip-flops to her trial. I believe Hatchett was relying too heavily on her vast experience in doling out tough love to directionless teens."

Brown ordered Robinson to return all monies paid and destroy the written apology before the watchful eyes of a court deputy.

"Our courtrooms may be 3,000 miles apart, but we both preside over the same daytime-TV jurisdiction," Brown said. "When I see that someone has not received due process, I have to speak out. With all due respect to Judge Hatchett, it's Joe Time!"

Legal expert Vincent Apries said he was surprised by Brown's overturning of a case that he called "cut and dried."

"I couldn't believe that Judge Joe Brown wielded his no-nonsense gavel to overrule Hatchett," said Apries, a member of the cable-access television program *The Yale Law Review Round Table*. "More and more, producers are disregarding rules established in the first session of the People's Court. When litigants agree to stand before a TV-court justice, they sign forms saying they will accept the judge's decision as final."

Media expert Tony Griss said the justices' ideologies affect how they approach the case.

"Judge Hatchett is in New York, and her motto is 'Justice for a new generation,'" said Griss, editor of the *Entertainment Weekly* "Legal Roundup." "Judge Joe Brown, however, comes from the mean streets of L.A., and stands by his motto of 'Taking care of your own business.'"

Bristow said she was "overjoyed" when Brown overturned Hatchett's ruling.

"Maybe I got a little mouthy when I appeared before Judge Hatchett, but that was only because I was frustrated," Bristow said. "I knew I didn't get a fair trial on UPN. I was prepared to take this case all the way to Judge Judy if I had to."

Robinson, however, maintains that Bristow is responsible for her hair loss.

"That bitch is just lying," Robinson said. "She fucked up my hair and then tries to give me some wack-ass weave, as if that's gonna make up for it. That's just bullshit. Judge Joe Brown can suck it." Ø

HOROSCOPES

Your Horoscope

By Lloyd Schumner Sr.
Retired Machinist and
A.A.P.B.-Certified Astrologer

Aries: (March 21–April 19)
Your friends will soon hold an intervention to take away your barge pole, wide-brimmed white straw hat, and Chianti bottle in an effort to stop your wanton and dangerous gondoliering.

Taurus: (April 20–May 20)
Taurus includes the stars of the Pleiades—mentioned in the Bible and instrumental in the design of the Pyramids—but these beauties are just one of the many reasons to visit the most popular constellation in the Zodiac.

Gemini: (May 21–June 21)
You've already been subjected to scorn and derision. With hot summer weather coming, you can now add extreme physical discomfort to the things you will endure when sporting that long black velvet cape.
Cancer: (June 22–July 22)
Actually, a goatsucker is an order of insect-eating nocturnal birds that includes the whippoorwill and the nighthawk, you pervert.

Leo: (July 23–Aug. 22)
You've never been afraid to learn the lessons of history, which is why your solution to everything is nuking Japan.

Virgo: (Aug. 23–Sept. 22)
You'll be found guilty of 12,582 counts of bee murder and given the responsibility of pollinating every flower in your immediate neighborhood for 11 years.

Libra: (Sept. 23–Oct. 23)
Change is long overdue in your life, but sadly, the Zodiac can no longer find a place in the budget for such outdated expenditures.

Scorpio: (Oct. 24–Nov. 21)
You've always reported the incidents as "drive-by shootings," but that may not be the proper term to describe your situation, wherein everyone you drive by shoots at you.

Sagittarius: (Nov. 22–Dec. 21)
Word to the wise: Although your baby is indeed badly in need of a new pair of shoes, it is not likely that any situation involving dice is likely to produce said shoes.

Capricorn: (Dec. 22–Jan. 19)
With NASA under increased pressure to perform and to curry public favor, they're seriously considering using cutting-edge technology to launch you into orbit.

Aquarius: (Jan. 20–Feb. 18)
Once, you were just the infant found in a city dumpster. Now, you're known nationwide as "that guy who's lived his entire life in the dumpster where he was found as an infant."

Pisces: (Feb. 19–March 20)
Your exuberance at suddenly discovering you can fly is muted somewhat when the discovery happens during your tour of the White House, causing you to be blown out of the air by vigilant F-15 pilots.

the ONION®

VOLUME 41 ISSUE 23 AMERICA'S FINEST NEWS SOURCE™ 9–15 JUNE 2005

Bush Lifts Ban On Vigilantism

'Let's See What Happens,' Says President

Above: Bush makes a call for more vigilante justice.

WASHINGTON, DC—In a striking departure from centuries of American belief in rule of law, President Bush gave his approval Monday to a limited experiment in public vigilantism "to see if it works."

"Groups of dedicated citizens who band together for a common cause—be it rounding up car thieves or castigating suspicious loiterers—strengthen and reinforce the social order," Bush said at a White House press conference. "I've never supported government intrusion in people's lives; I've always put more faith in the private sector. So I say, what the heck! Let's give vigilantism a go and see how things shake out. Why not?"

Bush's self-described "plan to have no plan" permits elected and appointed government authorities to "look the other way" while bands of U.S. citizens enforce both the community standards that the existing legal code overlooks and those laws that police fail to enforce.

"From bordello-busters to subway shooters, vigilantes have a long history of pinpointing and resolving the

see BUSH page 167

Above: Two tennis players accused of hug use.

Special Olympics Investigated For Use Of Performance-Enhancing Hugs

WASHINGTON, DC—Three months after the Special Olympics World Winter Games in Nagano, Japan, the International Special Olympics Committee has begun to investigate charges that athletes used performance-enhancing hugs in their training and directly before competing in key events.

"These people have no shame," ISOC chairman Bill Evans said Monday. "Right before a big game or race, many of them will take a dose of affection, sometimes from a coach, other times from a family member. Competing players have even been known

see SPECIAL OLYMPICS page 166

New Gas Bill Designed By Some Kind Of Freaking Maniac

BOSTON—Some kind of raving psychopath apparently gnawed through his restraints and burrowed out of the Massachusetts Center For The Criminally Insane to design the invoice for the Keystone Gas Company, 36-year-old Michael Beasley reported Monday.

"What animal did this?" said Beasley, paging through a bill for the pay period ending June 2. "Whoever he is, he's spread an invoice for less than $15 over nine pages."

The new bill divides Beasley's balance into 15 columns with such headings as "meter degree" and "date expenditure." The columns are annotated with footnotes, bar graphs, windows, explanations, and "hints," many of which are printed in colors that were obviously selected by a deranged person.

see GAS BILL page 167

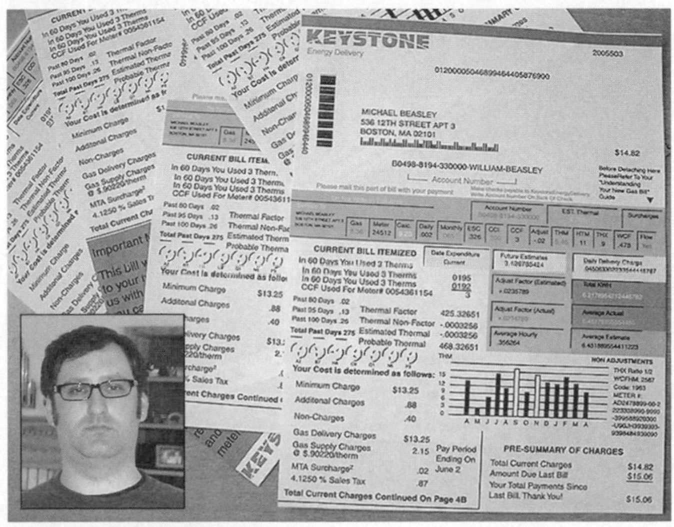

Above: The gas bill that Beasley (inset) received.

NEWS

PETA Complains As Revised SAT Tested On Chimpanzees

see NATION page 13B

Nitroglycerin Chex Gingerly Pulled From Shelves

see BUSINESS page 4C

Plan To Trap Boyfriend Aborted

see PEOPLE page 11D

Dying Girl Lent Pony

see LOCAL page 14H

STATshot

A look at the numbers that shape your world.

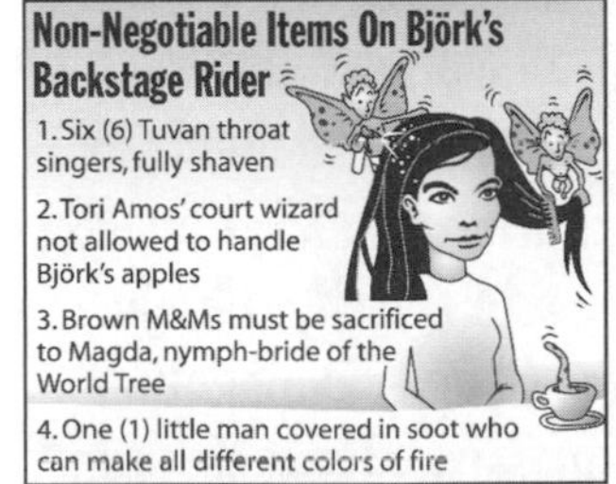

THE ONION • $2.00 US • $3.00 CAN

Deep Throat Revealed

Last week, former FBI agent Mark Felt revealed that he was "Deep Throat," the anonymous source that helped break the Watergate scandal. What do *you* think?

Stephen Clowney
Banker

"From the looks of his photo, Mr. Felt took this secret 99.5 percent of the way to the grave."

Ruby Afram
Special Ed Teacher

"Although his motives remain unclear, I definitely believe that Mr. Throat ultimately acted in the best interests of his nation."

Carlos Barrezueta
Musician

"He didn't also kill JFK, did he? I'd like to tie up as many loose ends as possible this week."

Frances Mejor
Receptionist

"I had my money on former Nixon speechwriter Ben Stein, largely because I am ignorant and he's been on TV."

Tad Heuer
Systems Analyst

"I'm just glad that longtime suspect Henry Kissinger has finally been vindicated. It's about time his good name was cleared of any lingering charges of right-doing."

Bryan Ketroser
Cook

"To Leonard Garment, who authored *In Search Of Deep Throat* and argued that former White House aide John Sears was the mystery informant, I'd like to say one thing: Ha ha ha!"

Unhealthy Online Support Groups

A growing number of anorexic girls are joining Internet groups that glorify eating disorders. What are some of the other online support groups that promote dangerous behavior?

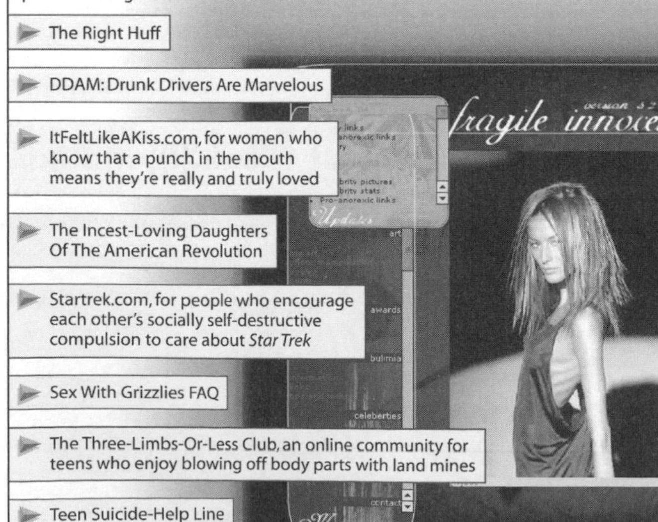

- The Right Huff
- DDAM: Drunk Drivers Are Marvelous
- ItFeltLikeAKiss.com, for women who know that a punch in the mouth means they're really and truly loved
- The Incest-Loving Daughters Of The American Revolution
- Startrek.com, for people who encourage each other's socially self-destructive compulsion to care about *Star Trek*
- Sex With Grizzlies FAQ
- The Three-Limbs-Or-Less Club, an online community for teens who enjoy blowing off body parts with land mines
- Teen Suicide-Help Line

America's Finest News Source.™

Herman Ulysses Zweibel
Founder

T. Herman Zweibel
Publisher Emeritus
J. Phineas Zweibel
Publisher
Maxwell Prescott Zweibel
Editor-In-Chief

Well, I Guess That Genocide In Sudan Must've Worked Itself Out On Its Own

By Ellen Turlington

I was pretty worried a year or so ago when the news came out that thousands of people had been indiscriminately slaughtered in Darfur. It was unsettling to hear that citizens of one ethnicity (Arab, maybe?) were systematically mass-murdering the population of some other ethnicity (Was it the Ganjaweeds? It's been so long since I've read their names!) But lately, the main stories in the news seem to be about Deep Throat, the new summer blockbusters, and something about stem cells. Since I'm sure I would have remembered if the U.S. had intervened in some way to stop it, I can only assume that the whole genocide-in-Darfur thing has somehow worked itself out.

> **I do follow the news enough to know when my own country attacks another country. Maybe it was one of those genocides that solves itself without substantive international intervention.**

Well, that's good news then, isn't it?

I also seem to recall that this genocide was causing a massive exodus of displaced refugees, with millions starving to death while attempting to flee to neighboring nations. Since I haven't seen any petitions or heard any emotional entreaties for somebody—anybody—to please, for God's sake, *do* something... Well, I'm gonna guess that the major humanitarian crisis must be over. And thank God, too! The whole situation sounded really awful.

Not that I wanted to be an alarmist, but when I first heard about the Darfur conflict, I thought to myself, "Uh oh! Sounds like another massive ethnic cleansing, not unlike Bosnia and Rwanda!" Those genocides sure were unfathomable! And not only because of the inhumanity of the acts, either—the blind indifference with which the world allowed the killings to continue unchecked was upsetting, too.

Well, someone must've invaded or overthrown a corrupt government or something like that. I know it wasn't the U.S., though. I may not be all that up on current events, but I do follow the news enough to know when my own country attacks another country. Maybe it was one of those genocides that solves itself without substantive international intervention. Well, that's one less horrific reality of modern geopolitics hanging over our heads!

Good thing, 'cause for a while there, it seemed like the Sudan situation was pretty serious, especially when both President Bush and Sen. Kerry talked about it in the presidential debates. Heck, that the Darfur conflict qualified as genocide was practically the *only* thing they agreed on! So, if both presidential candidates acknowledged on TV that genocide was taking place, it's pretty safe to assume that someone stepped in before more innocent victims were systematically butchered. Right?

What a great turn of events! Frankly, I'm relieved that all the horror, death, and human agony is over. I mean, after all those reports of ongoing murder, rape, and looting, I confess I was a little surprised when I didn't hear much more about it, beyond some international sanctions and aid packages. Ah, but what's the point in belaboring the grisly details? Why go on and on about *which* paramilitary militias were killing and raping *which* women and children? The important thing is that the conflict's apparently over.

Evidently, the hatred has been healed, peace has been restored, and the perpetrators of this unimaginable crime have been brought to justice. It sure is good to know it all must've turned out all right. It's like they say: No news is good news! Right? Ø

> **Not that I wanted to be an alarmist, but when I first heard about the Darfur conflict, I thought to myself, "Uh oh! Sounds like another massive ethnic cleansing, not unlike Bosnia and Rwanda!"**

LOCAL

Repressed-Memory Therapist Recovers *Rockford Files* Episode

OTTUMWA, IA—After months of hypnotherapy, local repressed-memory therapist Brian Marnard has helped Joan Spees, a 37-year-old farm-equipment sales consultant, recover an entire *Rockford Files* episode from the darkest reaches of her subconscious mind.

"Joan, who had suffered from seemingly inexplicable anxiety attacks her entire adult life, was the perfect candidate for repressed-memory therapy," Marnard said Monday. "Under my care, she began recovering vivid memory flashes from what seemed to be a single, distinct episode from her past. The images included an old-fashioned answering machine turning on in an empty room, a gold Firebird experiencing a sudden, violent change in direction, and a dark-haired man walking on the beach. In spite of the memory's persistent nature, Joan could not see how the fragments were related."

Right: Marnard, who used hypnosis to recover details of a critically acclaimed '70s detective show (above).

Spees said that, although the flashbacks would intrude upon her waking hours accompanied by the same "catchy snippet" of music, they did little to disrupt her personal life. Nonetheless, Marnard was concerned about what the memories might signify.

Spees said that, although the flashbacks would intrude upon her waking hours accompanied by the same "catchy snippet" of music, they did little to disrupt her personal life. Nonetheless, Marnard was concerned about what the memories might signify.

"Repressed memories, which are stored outside the awareness of the conscious mind, can usually be traced back to a traumatic event," Marnard said "What if Joan had been the victim of childhood sexual abuse by the dark-haired man she felt was named James, Jim, Garner, or Rockford? If so, she needed to bring these memories to the fore and confront them."

For two months, Marnard engaged Spees in an exhaustive, expensive course of drug-mediated interviews, hypnosis, regression therapy, and literal dream interpretation.

"Brian said my scraps of recollection were probably part of something bigger, an incident at least 44 minutes long—one that might be part of a larger chain of similar events from my adolescence," Spees said. "Brian kept encouraging me to pursue my vague feeling that the man I was seeing was a criminal, even though I felt even more strongly that the mysterious figure could be trusted."

According to Marnard, Spees' first few sessions progressed little beyond her strong memory of lying on her family's living room floor.

"I'm 8... I'm wearing my Pooh pajamas... wrapped in an olive-green blanket..." a transcript of Spees' first session read. "A phone's ringing, but

see THERAPIST page 166

NEWS IN BRIEF

Congress Relieved To Admit It's Not Going To Accomplish Anything This Year

WASHINGTON, DC—Members of Congress breathed a collective sigh of relief Tuesday when Speaker Dennis Hastert successfully introduced a resolution averring that the legislative body was "probably not going to get much done in 2005." "Whereas, we have been debating the same bills for months," the resolution read in part. "Whereas, we have been getting nowhere; Resolved, let's not force it." When asked what they would do for the rest of 2005, given the passing of the resolution, many said they might go see some movies or visit constituents.

Kuwait Starting To Notice Girls

KUWAIT CITY—In light of the country's recent decision to allow women to vote and hold public office, observers around the world have noted that Kuwait appears to have discovered the fairer sex. "The boys in Kuwait are really taking notice of how much the girls have changed over the country's long political winter," said Fouad Ajami, an expert in Arab affairs. "They're no longer shyly avoiding women they're not related to or clumsily shooting them for not wearing veils in public." Ajami added that he was not entirely surprised by Kuwait's discovery, given its long history of teasing women, calling them names, and stoning them to death for being unclean.

NBA Playoffs Interrupted By NBA Preseason

DETROIT—Game Six of the NBA Eastern Conference finals between the Miami Heat and the Detroit Pistons was postponed Saturday so that the Heat could play their first preseason game against the Seattle Supersonics. "It would've been great to have determined who would've been in the finals, but this exhibition game was already on the schedule," said Heat coach Stan Van Gundy. "Sonics fans have been looking forward to this game all off-season." Representatives for both teams expressed hopes that the 2005 NBA Finals would be over by the start of the 2006 All-Star Game.

Garden Too Much For Grandma This Summer

TULSA, OK—Though she has tended the same 10' x 25' backyard vegetable plot for more than three decades, local grandmother Helen Fischer, 74, said Monday that the task would be too much for her this year. "My knee hasn't been the same since I hurt it weeding the kohlrabi last summer," said Fischer, slowly lifting a bag of seeds to the mouth of a hanging bird feeder. "I might plant some marigolds in the window box, though, if Kerry's Greenhouse has any nice ones." In a related story, Fischer's husband Ralph said that, while he doesn't believe he'll be stringing the front-yard trees with holiday lights this year, he will still put out the wreaths.

Eighth-Grader Hasn't Missed A '69' Joke Opportunity All Year

LEBANON, PA—According to Lebanon Central Middle School staff, Mike Eichstadt, 14, leapt on every possible occasion to make a "69" joke during the entirety of his eighth-grade year. "If a teacher said 'Turn to page 69' or a classmate got a 69 on a quiz, Mike Eichstadt was there with a smirk and a quip," principal Melanie Reinke said. "Sometimes, Mike only needed to be asked a question involving a number—such as 'How many years did Ford serve as president?'—to make a '69' joke." Despite his aptitude for "69" jokes, Eichstadt received a D in math. Ø

SPECIAL OLYMPICS from page 163

to exchange hugs during the competition itself."

Although insiders have long attested to widespread hug use among special athletes, the full scope of the problem was not understood until

"Ironically, many of the worst special athletes are the ones getting the most hugs," Evans said.

November 2004, when Carnegie Mellon's medical school published a study on hug use in the *Clinical Journal Of Sport Medicine.* According to the study, researchers found double-digit spikes in self-valuation, warm fuzziness, and smiles following even a single hug.

Evans said he "took one look at the numbers" and agreed to an internal investigation and an across-the-board review of hug-use policies.

"Hug users have an unfair advantage over the hug-free, as they are pumped up with confidence," Evans said. "In competitions relying on endurance, hugs serve to artificially heighten an athlete's stamina. For example, hug users may be as much as 65 percent more likely to excel at no-contact floor hockey than those who say no to hugs. Put simply, it's unethical."

Alpine skiing bronze medalist Lee Young-Suk, who has Down syndrome, appeared on a special edition of ABC's *Primetime Live Tuesday* and admitted to frequent use of performance-enhancing hugs.

"When my mommy [Jun Young-Suk] hugs me, it makes me feel like I'm the best and she loves me and I can win," Suk told Diane Sawyer. "I'm a winner!"

Above: Four athletes who have had their medals seized by the ISOC.

The emotions Suk described—euphoria, omnipotence, overall well-being—have been found to last for as little as five minutes or as long as several hours, depending upon the number and type of embraces administered.

Due to the short-burst effect of performance-enhancing hugs, testing for their presence is difficult.

"Currently, eye-witness sightings are the only reliable indicators of hug use," said ISOC regulator Peter Warner. "Unfortunately, hug use can occur anywhere—from the group home to the bleachers. We can't be in every team's van at all times."

In the search for hug abusers, regulators have screened hundreds of hours of Special Olympics videotape, hoping to catch huggers in the act. They are also relying on testimony from hug users such as Suk.

"Lee Young-Suk really stood his ground at first, saying he did not want to tattle on his friends," Warner said of the hug user. "We couldn't get him to give us any names until we promised him a trip to Dairy Queen."

Still, as Evans pointed out, hug use does not necessarily translate into better athletic performance. Over time, it may even serve as a hindrance.

"Ironically, many of the worst special athletes are the ones getting the most hugs," Evans said. "Once they get hooked, even if it isn't helping their game, these Olympians continue to crave the affection, accepting it as almost a consolation prize for their effort. Sometimes you see special athletes seeking hugs outside the realm of competition, just for the sake of hugging. This is where we get into really dangerous territory." ⊘

THERAPIST from page 165

it's not mine... I'm waiting for someone to answer the phone... There's a message.... An important message about someone picking up the car from the garage? No, it's a woman saying she's lonely... no, it's a pizza shop. I'm not sure..."

At that point in the session, Spees would usually whistle a distinctive melody.

"It was a long time before I got any more out of her," Marnard said. "But finally, Joan was able to recover some very strong memories, like the image of a murder suspect who supposedly died in a car accident. And something about an angel trying to get his money back from a swindler who was on the run from the mob. And then, there was a garbage disposal jammed by a missing bullet."

"Still," Marnard added. "She was never able to fully understand what was going on."

Finally, near the end of a one-hour 'deep therapy' session, Spees had a breakthrough.

"I was about to bring Joan out of it, when she started talking in a deep voice, like that of a father figure," Marnard said. "I could feel we were reaching a climax. That's when she said, 'Honey, we're all scared to death. I guess that's the price we pay for living in a world where we sell cemetery plots on billboards by the freeway and all the prices end in 99 cents. What you gotta do is just keep laughing.'"

Marnard said it wasn't until Spees paused and said, "Later tonight on NBC..." that he recognized the quote as coming from Jim Rockford, the laid-back ex-con-turned-detective played by James Garner on the popular '70s TV show, *The Rockford Files.*

In spite of the breakthrough, Dr. Klaus Stenner of the Iowa Psychological Association criticized Marnard's methods, and those of all repressed-memory therapists, calling them unprofessional.

"There is no real evidence that childhood memories are ever unconsciously repressed," Stenner said. "In addition, recovering these supposedly repressed memories, whether of sexual abuse or the plots of popular television series, has never led to significant improvement in a patient's psychological health and stability. Luckily, Spees was spared any lasting harm—probably because her memories were innocuous and generally positive, thanks to *The Rockford Files'* high production values and taut writing."

In spite of the breakthrough, Dr. Klaus Stenner of the Iowa Psychological Association criticized Marnard's methods, and those of all repressed-memory therapists, calling them unprofessional.

Immediately after the breakthrough, Spees discontinued her twice-weekly visits and refused to pay her outstanding bill, calling Marnard "a quack." Marnard, however, adamantly insists that Spees should return to therapy.

"Joan can run from her problems all she wants, but the haunting, sinister image of the gun in the cookie jar will be with her forever," Marnard said. "And even if she has discovered the source of the mysterious answering-machine messages, it doesn't explain Joan's recurring memories of a shadowy, mustachioed figure known only as 'Higgins.'" ⊘

BUSH from page 163

problems plaguing their communities," Bush said. "Let's give 'em a shot."

Bush's remarks came in the wake of criticism among his ultraconservative supporters, who argue that "activist judges" often make decisions that contradict the will of the people. To help remedy this problem, many special-interest groups had been calling for an official tolerance of "vigilante judicial committees."

"As we phase vigilantism in, be prepared to hear a lot of talk about 'mob-ocracies' and 'tyrannies of the bat-wielding, roving majorities,'" Mendenhall said.

"Vigilantes have an undeserved reputation for recklessness," Republican pollster Jennifer Mendenhall said. "As we phase vigilantism in, be prepared to hear a lot of talk about 'mob-ocracies' and 'tyrannies of the bat-wielding, roving majorities.' That rhetoric is meant to scare peaceful citizens into thinking they need magisterial authority to protect their interests. But vigilantism is not about crazed drunkards clustering in town squares, waving pitchforks and crying out for blood. It's about an opportunity to let the citizens of America serve as their neighbors' meter maids, correctional officers, chiefs of police, or, if necessary, SWAT teams."

Above: A vigilante group patrols a Colorado Springs, CO highway for litterers.

Bush's decision has already mobilized vigilantes across the country.

"Who needed the police and the courts when I already knew who vandalized the restrooms at McDonnell Park?" Roy Kunz of Katy, TX said. "Bush has it right. It's high time we threw a few necktie parties around here."

Murphysboro, IL's Jo Crockett formed a vigilante committee to forcibly evict neighbor and "dirty, no-good slut" Haley Uhrig and her family from her neighborhood.

"Does the government care that [Uhrig] litters her yard with stinky diapers, blares her music around the clock, and steals our men? Hell no," Crockett said. "We couldn't wait around for an arrest warrant or a *Jerry Springer* segment producer to come to our aid. It's simple: That woman had to go."

Bush's endorsement of vigilante activity caught Capitol Hill Democrats off guard.

"I'm not sure vigilantism is in the best interest of the nation," Senate Minority Leader Harry Reid (D-NV) said. "Vigilantes are bad, aren't they? I read *The Ox-Bow Incident* in high school. They ended up hanging the wrong guys in that book, I think. That sort of situation could lead to a major problem for the government."

Bush stressed that his move was experimental, characterizing vigilantism as "practical."

"Frankly, government officials have all they can handle right now, overseeing foreign wars and doling out unemployment benefits," Bush said. "The truth is, we'd really appreciate some help maintaining domestic order while we take care of the important stuff."

"Let's see what happens, America," Bush added. "After all, our government is supposed to be of, by, and for the people. That's from the Constitution." ⌀

GAS BILL from page 163

"I just want to know what I owe!" Beasley said. "Fuel cost adjustment, adjustment to minimum bill, read days, repair range... 'Helping you to understand your repair range'? Is this some kind of sick joke?"

Beasley pointed to a section of the bill that detailed payments by mail.

"Residential Monthly Billing Customer Acct. ID B0498-8194-330000-MICHAEL-BEASLEY," the bill read. "Affix DEGREE DATE/Meter-ACT-4 stamp (Window 11-B) to Monthly BILLING ID Box (located on Window 15 on outside of Payment Envelope provided by RMBRC packet (See Intro)). RMB Customers using their own envelope see Using Your Own Envelope (Section F)."

"There's actually a section on how to use your own envelope," Beasley said. "With rules."

Beasley added: "This isn't a gas bill—it's a cry for help. Authored by someone with a disease."

Gale Snow, Keystone Gas public relations director, encouraged customers who are confused by the new bill to refer to the "Understanding Your New Gas Bill" brochure.

"This thing?" said Beasley, holding up a copy of the 28-page brochure. "This madhouse? This 24-Hour Polka Marathon at Titicut Follies? Look at it, man. It's a 28-page annotation of a *gas bill*. The notes to my copy of 'The Waste Land' aren't this arcane."

"There's actually a section on how to use your own envelope," Beasley said. "With rules."

"Maybe it was written by someone the gas-bill designer befriended at the asylum," Beasley added.

The designer of the new gas bill—and possibly the author of its accompanying brochure—was unavailable for comment, probably because he's curled up naked in the crawlspace between floors three and four of Children's Hospital Boston, subsisting on vending-machine candy and doodling with his own feces. ⌀

SEDAN from page 107

amounts of blood. Passersby were amazed by the unusually large amounts of blood. Passersby were amazed by the unusually large amounts of blood. Passersby were amazed by the unusually large amounts of blood. Passersby were amazed by the unusually large amounts of blood. Passersby were amazed by the unusually large amounts of blood. Passersby were amazed by the unusually large amounts of blood. Passersby were amazed by the unusually large amounts of blood. Passersby were amazed by the unusually large amounts of blood. Passersby were amazed by the unusually large amounts of blood. Passersby were amazed by the unusually large amounts of blood. Passersby were amazed by the unusually large amounts of blood. Passersby were amazed by the unusually large amounts of blood. Passersby were amazed by the unusually large amounts of blood. Passersby were amazed by the unusually large amounts of blood. Passersby were amazed by the unusually large amounts of blood. Passersby were amazed by the unusually large amounts of blood. Passersby were

Most of the clowns had already fled the scene by the second explosion.

see SEDAN page 193

COMMUNITY VOICES

I'm Sick Of These Money Problems

Hola, amigos. What's goin' on? I know it's been a long time since I rapped at ya, but it's like life keeps raining shit down on me and I don't have a shit shovel big enough to clear it all away. My ride is giving me grief. The muffler is coming loose, so it's making a lot of noise. The car might sound badass if it were, like, a Thunderbird or something. But it's a Festiva, so it sounds like a souped-up lawn mower. I took a tin can and some muffler tape and patched the pipe up, but my repair job isn't going to last for long.

The Cruise
By Jim Anchower

Then, I forgot to pay my electric bill. It was only two months late, but the assholes shut my power off anyway. I meant to pay the bill, but I had a lot on my mind. Getting my power cut sucked, because I had microwave burritos in the freezer, five of which I had to throw away. And I'd rented *Jeepers Creepers 2*. I tried to tell the clerk at the video store that I should get my money back because I hadn't watched the movie, but he was a total dick about the whole thing. He didn't believe me that I didn't have power, and acted like I was just trying to get a free movie rental. Like I'd be that desperate.

Anyway, I didn't get my money back, so I went home and ate a half-frozen burrito in the dark. Then I crashed early. I thought I'd at least catch up on sleep, but I had the weirdest dreams. I was living in a mountain cave, and there were these trays of cookies everywhere. It was my job to make sure that none of the cookies were eaten by spiders. I woke up at, like, 4 a.m. and just sat in the dark and waited for the sun to rise.

Everyone who knows me knows I'm always getting all sorts of great, crazy ideas. I had this one idea for a mop, once.

I called the electric company in the morning, and they told me they'd turn my power back on as soon as I paid the balance, plus a $100 deposit. I said that I wasn't made of money and that someone over there owed me for my burritos and the video rental. Well, they basically said, "No deposit, no electricity." That's what's wrong in America today: Big corporations don't care about the little guy.

My power problem got me thinking that I need to be one of those guys who makes the money, instead of shelling it out all the time. I'm not sure how my plan's gonna go down, though. I suppose if I stuck with my job at the carbonics plant and didn't lose a finger, I could be promoted to assistant manager, like Ron. But that would take three years, and if I'm gonna be stuck there for that long, I may as well just suck on a tailpipe and end it all.

Then, I forgot to pay my electric bill. It was only two months late, but the assholes shut my power off anyway. I meant to pay the bill, but I had a lot on my mind. Getting my power cut sucked, because I had microwave burritos in the freezer, five of which I had to throw away.

There's gotta be an easier way. I could make money selling weed, but the last time I did that, I was getting calls at, like, 4:00 in the morning. Then they'd only want to buy an eighth. Besides, I always ended up smoking up most of my profits.

You know what seems to be the way to go? Computers. Everything is on computers these days. When I go to the auto-parts store, they check their computer to see if they have the part I need. People are always talking on e-mail instead of calling people up. Even the cops got computers to check your priors when they pull you over. Shit, if you're reading this, the odds are you're on a computer instead of kicking back with a newspaper.

Wes has been getting a lot of jobs where he works on computers, and he seems to be doing okay. Since computers looked like my best bet, I called up one of those colleges with commercials on daytime TV. The woman on the phone talked to me for a long time, and she thought getting into computers was a really good idea for me, too. But then she started telling me about the shitload of money it costs to go to the school. It just goes to show, you gotta have money to make money.

Without money, the only thing I got is my mind. Everyone who knows me knows I'm always getting all sorts of great, crazy ideas. I had this one idea for a mop, once. But I figure the best way to use my ideas is to write a movie. How hard could it be? I have this one idea about a cop who's about to get thrown off the force, because he plays by his own rules. Only, a case falls into his lap that he can't turn his back on. See, this particular cop is a decent guy, even if he is a cop. The case involves the mob, so the cop goes undercover to fix the bad guys good. But then his old partner finds out about it.

Well, I sat down to write the movie. I started out by writing down a killer opening, with these hot chicks, an explosion, and the cop turning in his badge. But then, I couldn't figure out what would happen after the cop's old partner enters the picture. I smoked a bowl for inspiration, but nothing came. Long story short, I had to put the movie-writing on the back burner until I get a new idea.

Anyway, I can feel that something is right around the corner. In the meantime, I suppose I'll pick up some overtime at work to get that $100 deposit together. Whatever. I ain't going to be wasting away in this shithole apartment all my life. I mean, it's not like I want a million dollars. I just want enough for a boat. That's not too much to ask. Once I get a boat, I can live on that and everyone else can go fuck themselves. Well, until I need to buy gas. ⌀

HOROSCOPES

Your Horoscope

By Lloyd Schumner Sr.
Retired Machinist and A.A.P.B.-Certified Astrologer

Aries: (March 21–April 19)
You'll be forced to run more than 50 miles by some cruel bastard who'll rig your hat with a fiendish device consisting of a candy bar, a piece of string, and a six-foot stick.

Taurus: (April 20–May 20)
You've always feared you might run into a problem that can't be fixed by the lessons learned in Tom T. Hall's lyrics, and now that you've been appointed the new U. S. Trade Representative, that day is finally here.

Gemini: (May 21–June 21)
Your constant back-talking to the manager and theft of company property would seem like grounds for firing, but due to irresponsible bookkeeping, they'll be cited as the reason for your company's jump in profits.

Cancer: (June 22–July 22)
You're being subjected to lots of unwanted criticism as the new kid in your high school, but you should be able to handle the pressure better, considering you're 34.

Leo: (July 23–Aug. 22)
You must learn to stop screaming "Rape! Rape!" at the top of your lungs. Everyone can see perfectly well what you're doing without the grandstanding narration.

Virgo: (Aug. 23–Sept. 22)
You have a remarkably addictive personality, which is why junkies keep trying to extract it from your skull and inject it.

Libra: (Sept. 23–Oct. 23)
The authorities are aware that you're struggling with your own manhood and how it relates to our phallocentric society, but please, just return the Wienermobile.

Scorpio: (Oct. 24–Nov. 21)
You thought you were so great with the clever wordplay, but as everyone else figured out long ago, you've just been unwittingly reciting Cole Porter lyrics.

Sagittarius: (Nov. 22–Dec. 21)
The movements of Saturn rising through your sign in combination with various solar-zodiacal harmonics indicate many complex changes, but basically women are going to start throwing shit at you.

Capricorn: (Dec. 22–Jan. 19)
Voyager 1 is rapidly approaching the very outer edge of the solar system, although its radio transmissions simply refer to the distance as "almost far enough away from you."

Aquarius: (Jan. 20–Feb. 18)
While it's true that a certain software giant stole its graphic user interface from a smaller computer company, it stole its tendency to get locked up repeatedly from you.

Pisces: (Feb. 19–March 20)
You bring about a revolution in meaningless chitchat this week when you engage in small talk so miniscule it can't be detected by non-golfers or people outside of upper management.

the ONION®

VOLUME 41 ISSUE 24 AMERICA'S FINEST NEWS SOURCE™ 16–22 JUNE 2005

NEWS

Secret Service Not Sure If That Suit Of Armor Was In Oval Office Yesterday

see WASHINGTON page 12B

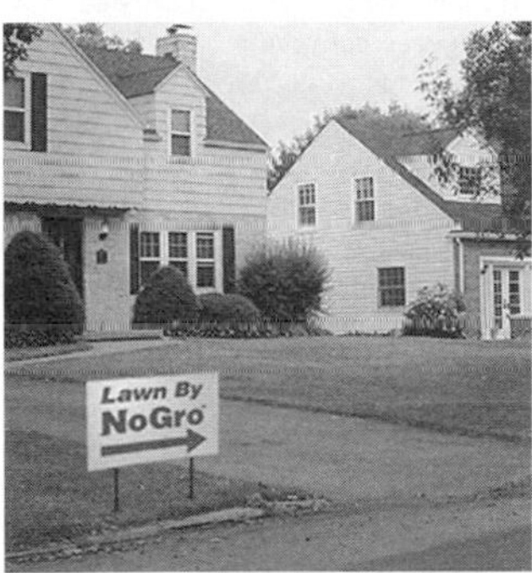

New Lawn-Care Product Makes Neighbor's Lawn Less Green

see BUSINESS page 13D

Mail-Order Bride Comes In Wrong Color, Size

see BUSINESS page 11D

STATshot

A look at the numbers that shape your world.

Top Cassette Tapes Stuck In Car Stereos
16% Ratt's "Round And Round" cassingle
25% Tony's Summer Love Mix '94
21% Learn French, Lesson Four: Letters And Numbers
18% He's Just Not That Into You, read by Patrick Stewart
20% 16 Great Banjo Breakdowns
SU-SU-SUDIO

Habitrail For Humanity Under Fire

PAYNEVILLE, KY—Habitrail For Humanity, the faith-based, non-profit group that builds networks of affordable, transparent-tube housing for needy families, has come under intense criticism for its recent projects in the Payneville area.

"This is no way for people to live," said Kentucky Family Outreach coordinator Martin Weiss, speaking Monday in front of a half-constructed, five-story Habitrail outside Payneville. "While it's true that poor Americans need a viable alternative

see HABITRAIL page 172

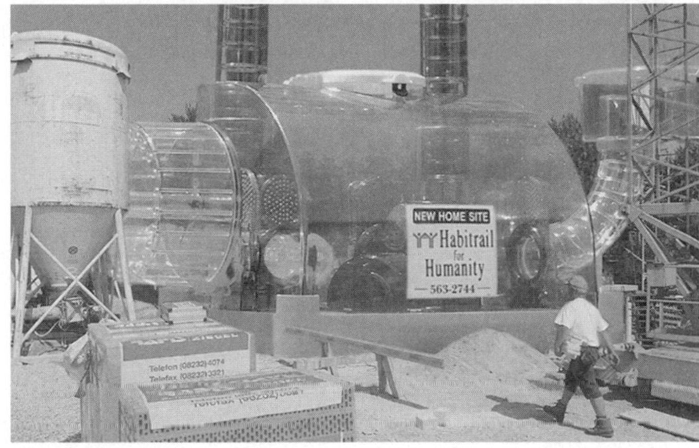

Right: A new Habitrail For Humanity structure nears completion in Payneville.

Chinese Factory Worker Can't Believe The Shit He Makes For Americans

Above: Chen makes yet more stupid crap for consumers overseas.

FENGHUA, CHINA—Chen Hsien, an employee of Fenghua Ningbo Plastic Works Ltd., a plastics factory that manufactures lightweight household items for Western markets, expressed his disbelief Monday over the "sheer amount of shit Americans will buy."

"Often, when we're assigned a new order for, say, 'salad shooters,' I will say to myself, 'There's no way that anyone will ever buy these,'" Chen said during his lunch break in an open-air courtyard. "One month later, we will receive an order for the same product, but three times the quantity. How can anyone have a need for such useless shit?"

Chen, 23, who has worked as an injection-

see WORKER page 172

Politician Awkwardly Works The Bathroom

Above: Hecht meets and greets a lavatory visitor.

BATTLE CREEK, MI—In what had originally been intended as a brisk, businesslike trip to the urinal, Calhoun County executive hopeful Phil Hecht spent seven minutes working the Battle Creek Sheraton men's bathroom Monday.

"That politician guy didn't seem to realize how weird it was in there," said David Muntz, a local orthodontist. "I don't know... It was like he couldn't turn it off."

"I had to wash up an extra time after he glad-handed me," Muntz added.

Hecht's unplanned bathroom tour took place several minutes after his remarks at the Battle Creek Rotary Club's annual Unsung Heroes luncheon, held this year in honor of Jef-

see BATHROOM page 173

Medical Marijuana

Last week, the Supreme Court upheld the federal government's right to ban marijuana use, even in states that allow it for medical reasons. What do *you* think?

"This is sad news for me and other survivors of nausea."

Irina Manta
Systems Analyst

"I was surprised by the judges' reaction to this whole thing. Especially Scalia, because, y'know, he's cool."

Brian Netter
Tile Setter

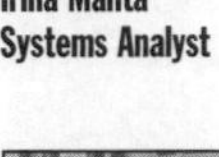

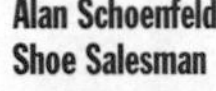

"Well, can't these cancer patients paint, play sports, or listen to music instead of doing drugs? That's what they taught us in health class."

Alan Schoenfeld
Shoe Salesman

"Dude, the small-government-advocating, states-rights-supporting conservatives must've been *totally high* when they wrote that decision."

Daniel S. Korobkin
Podiatirst

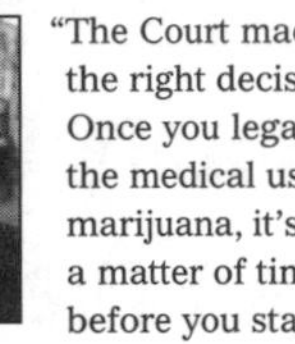

"The Court made the right decision. Once you legalize the medical use of marijuana, it's only a matter of time before you start seeing medical use of harder narcotics, like morphine."

Robert Yablon
Banker

"Great. Now how am I supposed to treat my recurrent case of Doritos Aversion Syndrome?"

Caroline Wilson
Lab Supervisor

GM's Rising Costs

General Motors announced that it intends to cut 25,000 jobs in the coming years, explaining that it is losing money on every vehicle that it sells in North America. What are the costs of producing a typical GM car?

- **$2,750** Therapy sessions for top executives burdened with guilt of firing tens of thousands of workers
- **$3,522** Hand-painting "WHAM!" design on front and side airbags
- **$5,550** Marketing aimed at convincing people they want cars bigger than they need or should be able to afford, that GM will later sell to them for less than they cost to produce
- **$175** Factory labor, bringing plants up to 20th-century safety standards
- **$625** Expensive hats for Mrs. GM
- **$7,000** Put simply, a certain high-ranking GM executive likes exposing himself at interstate weigh stations, and members of the Belarusian underworld happen to know this
- **$4,520** Fuel-inefficiency testing
- **$210** Steel, glass, rubber, and plastic

2005 Chevy Impala
Suggested retail price: $23,010
Cost to produce: $24,352

the ONION®
America's Finest News Source.™

Herman Ulysses Zweibel
Founder

T. Herman Zweibel
Publisher Emeritus
J. Phineas Zweibel
Publisher
Maxwell Prescott Zweibel
Editor-In-Chief

I Wish Someone Would Do Something About How Fat I Am

By Philip Von Zweck

Let me level with you. I'm fat. Not heavyset, but F-A-T, fat. I'm not saying this because I'm proud. It takes a lot of courage to admit it, but I have a problem. Strangers gape in amazement. Children taunt me behind my back. People have trouble looking at me when I eat, and for good reason: I'm huge. But gosh, I don't like being this way. I hate it as much as you do—maybe more. What I want to know is, how come no one is doing anything about it?

For the past 10 years, everyone has stood idly by and watched my waistline balloon. My friends didn't say anything as I sat and ate one chili-cheese dog after another. Even my own family hasn't lifted a finger to solve my weight problem. My mom's idea of "helping" is cooking a delicious dinner with all the trimmings. She knows as well as I do that, if she cooks a scrumptious meal, I am going to eat at least five servings and half a loaf of buttered bread, but that doesn't stop her.

According to government statistics, nearly two-thirds of Americans are overweight. If those figures are accurate—and I believe they are—then I really think the government should do something about this terrible affliction. I get winded walking to the corner, and I eat 3,000 calories before getting out of bed in the morning. I have cellulite on my forearms. Can't someone in Washington help me? Please? I am admitting that I need help. Now, someone—anyone—please help me.

I wish someone in the scientific community would look out for the obese little guy. They could provide liposuction and stomach stapling so a person like me would no longer be a danger to himself. Or, better, they could design a "magic bullet" to cure my corpulence. I mean, it seems like there should at least be a medicine that will make me stop stuffing my face when I'm full five times over. No kidding: If someone had an experimental new pill that would stop me from stuffing my face with food once I'm full five times over, I'd be the first in line to take it. Well, I mean, I would allow doctors to come to my home and administer the drug while I was comfortably splayed out on my sofa in my robe. That's how serious I am about having someone do something about my weight problem.

It is a problem. I know that. That's why I'm pleading for help. Obesity is ruining my life, if you want to know. I mean, I could die. I could really die, and it scares the hell out of me. I could drop like *that* if someone doesn't make me lose some weight.

I'll tell you what it is: My obesity is a direct result of the sheer volume of high-calorie, low-nutrition foodstuffs that are constantly available for my consumption. I go to the grocery store and load my cart with gallon upon gallon of pure-cream ice cream, bags and bags of so-called "healthy" chips, and enough cereal, frozen dinners, and candy bars to nourish an ox. No one even bats an eye. The cashiers blithely ring me up. The bag boys don't even complain that it takes them seven trips to get all of my food into the car. Everyone just acts like it's not their problem.

In a way, they're right. It isn't their fault. You see, I never could've packed on so many excess pounds without the thousands of farmers, truckers, grocers, and restaurateurs that supplied the steady stream of food I shoveled into my mouth for days and weeks and years without pause. I wish someone would do something to change that. Because, listen, I know myself, and I know that if restaurants

For the past 10 years, everyone has stood idly by and watched my waistline balloon.

keep frying food, I'll never convince myself to stop shoving brown, crispy food down my throat. It's time for some action. Stop me! Or stop them! I don't know! Just do something!

I've heard there are public-service announcements that address the obesity problem, but I don't really see how a commercial is going to make me stop eating. You see, odds are I'm in the kitchen making a sandwich during commercials. Someone should mail me a brochure about the risks of overeating. Better yet, send me a videotape. Reading on a full stomach makes me drowsy. Besides, I'm so exhausted most of the time, I fall asleep the second I hit the couch.

No one should have to live like I do. I shouldn't have to suffer the pain of eating a pail of fried chicken and a tub of mashed potatoes with gravy and still be hungry enough to polish off an entire apple pie. Where is your sense of human compassion? Please, someone, make me thin again. For God's sake, don't just stand there doing nothing. Ø

SCIENCE

Everything That Can Go Wrong Listed

FULLERTON, CA—A worldwide consortium of scientists, mathematicians, and philosophers is nearing the completion of the ambitious, decade-long project of cataloging everything that can go wrong, project leader Dr. Thomas R. Kress announced at a press conference Tuesday.

"We are mere weeks from finishing one of the most thorough and provocative scientific surveys of our time," Kress said. "The catalog of every possible unfortunate scenario will complete the work of the ancient Phoenicians and the early Christian theologians. Soon, every hazardous possibility will be known to man."

"And listed," Kress added.

Kress, a professor emeritus of mathematics and statistics at California State University and the author of several works on probability, would not say how many scenarios of error, peril, and misfortune exist. However, the list is widely believed to include hundreds of trillions of potential scenarios, from "cement truck with soft brakes cutting swath of destruction across quiet suburban subdivision" to "snagging shirt cuff on door latch."

"You know that thing when you don't invite an annoying friend to your party, and then, on the night of the party, an acquaintance from work brings that friend as a date?" said Project Awry researcher Hideko Manabe of Kyoto University. "That's on the list."

Manabe added: "I believe it's right after 'neglecting the maintenance of reactor cooling system, leading to core meltdown.'"

The November 2003 issue of *Scientific American* included an excerpt from the inventory, which read in part, "Knocking a cup of coffee off a counter with a light jerk of the wrist; breaking a tooth while comically pretending to bite down on the Great Pyramid of Giza; lowering lifeboats into the water when they are only filled to half capacity; tripping on cable and falling to floor with broken ankle while angrily storming off set of *24*; building shanty on hillside instead of floodplain in anticipation of monsoon season, then getting buried in erosion-triggered mudslide anyway."

So numerous are the conceivable disastrous scenarios that processing them requires two gymnasium-sized supercomputers, one at the University of Pittsburgh and the other at Moscow State University. According to Kress, the supercomputers process and cross-reference all of these potential "wrongs" 24 hours a day, at a rate of 6 trillion calculations per second.

During a recent tour of the facilities at the University of Pittsburgh, the scenarios were projected onto a large screen as they were processed.

see LIST page 174

PROJECT AWRY page 55,623

run in stocking; nuclear annihilation of planet; phone system down; balloon floats away; glass eye falls out during speech; condom breaks; hairdresser quits; wolverine attacks child; White Stripes release bad album; lose $60 at bus stop; fatal heart attack; meat goes bad; floor collapses; tsunami; train wreck kills hundreds; computer crashes during lengthy download; Statue of Liberty falls over; grain elevator explodes; comet hits earth; ammo runs out; gored by moose; fan belt breaks on interstate; sour cream runs out; gassy; mother-in-law hates you; hamburger tastes charred; ignored by waiter; check gets lost in mail; $2 winning scratch-off washed with pants; get caught in middle of knife fight; humidity makes hair frizzy; cola explodes all over you; UPS package isn't for you; gas grill explodes all over you; neck breaks while clowning around; Livestrong bracelet gets caught in revolving door; everyone finds out you're a fraud; leg cramps up in middle of big game; strike out with bases loaded; boss catches you masturbating in your office; earth gets thrown off axis; plane gets hijacked; girlfriend's new friend cuter, funnier; pen dries out in middle of class; laptop battery loses charge; favorite bill gets vetoed; asshole paints swastika on Hillel center; oversleep on first day of work; neighborhood goes to seed; double-dutch jump rope; meeting with ambassador postponed; greeting card not a Hallmark; water doesn't taste like water at all; attempts to help poor perceived as racist; suffer second-degree burns trying to set toppled candle in jack-o-lantern upright; rescue operation fails when helicopter blade tips strike water tower; die of exposure after unknowingly taking more arduous path to summit; bite violently down on inside of cheek while eating sloppy joe; get shortchanged at charity bake sale; blind date repulsed by toenail parings on futon; mother throws out beloved old stuffed hippo; leg gets amputated by dredger chain; wrong backing-vocals tape played; final exam directions misinterpreted; real mother appears out of nowhere; friends, family learn the truth; drunk tattoo artist uses Dremel tool instead of needle; president roofied; lycanthropy turns out to be real; one of your legs grows four inches; pants stay unzipped all day; nosebleed unnoticed for first 10 minutes of wedding; batteries in remote control die; favorite song used in

Above: One small section of the uncompleted project.

NEWS IN BRIEF

Bush Fishing For Compliments During Press Conference

WASHINGTON, DC—During a Monday press conference, President Bush repeatedly interrupted the question-and-answer period to seek out praise from the press corps. "Man, that Social Security speech I gave last night—people are saying that might be one of my best ones yet," said Bush, pausing and raising his eyebrows expectantly at the correspondents in the front row. "Yep, sure felt like I nailed it... So..." Getting no bites, Bush changed the subject, mentioning that he picked out his own suit for the conference, but wasn't really sure if it looked good on him.

Coke Party Takes A Couple Minutes To Get Going

POMPANO BEACH, FL—According to partygoers, an impromptu cocaine bash on North Ocean Boulevard took three to four minutes to really get hopping Monday night. "This place is like a morgue," said Paul Manero, moments after doing a line. "I wonder if they've got any of those daiquiris left. Oh God, look, things are warming up. Hey Mark, do you have any of those daiqui—know where I got these shoes? I got them at—what's that? Hey, did I tell you I went to Chicago last week? Yeah, it was—hey, what's this song? Chingy? It sucks! This rules!" According to clean and sober sources, the party actually blew all along.

Portugal Finally Gets It Together

LISBON, PORTUGAL—To the relief of surrounding countries, Portugal seems to have finally gotten its ducks in a row, sources reported Monday. "Man, I didn't think P. would ever get it together," said Spanish Prime Minister Jose Luis Rodriguez Zapatero. "But it really cleaned up its act and got its shit straight. Who would've guessed?" Cyprus said that if Portugal can do it, maybe it can, too.

Area Man Tired Of Making Excuses For Rapist Friend

OGALLALA, NE—After nearly a decade of friendship, Jake Fitzwater said Monday that he is getting sick of standing up for his buddy Raymond Bauer's rapist behavior. "Whenever someone would accuse Ray of crossing the line, I used to say, 'He doesn't mean anything by it—that's just Ray being Ray,'" Fitzwater said. "I thought he'd grow out of it, but I've known him for nine and a half years now, and he's still at it. Defending him really puts me in an awkward position." Fitzwater added that if Bauer fails to control his predilection for nonconsensual intercourse, he might skip the rapist's Fourth of July barbecue.

All Of Math Teacher's Examples Involve Moon Pies

BAY CITY, MI—According to sources at Bay City Middle School, all of 51-year-old math teacher Lance Stonitch's in-class examples express numbers in quantities of Moon Pies, the snack item consisting of marshmallow fluff packed between round graham crackers and coated with chocolate, vanilla, or banana icing. "Let's say Jimmy and Janie eat 40 Moon Pies in two weeks," Stonitch said Monday. "Their friends John and Joe are coming to visit for two days, and John and Joe eat Moon Pies twice as fast as Jimmy and Janie. How many Moon Pies does Jimmy need to buy the week of the visit, to have enough Moon Pies for everyone?" While most of Stonitch's students have no idea what a Moon Pie is, eighth-grader Trace Crutchfield said, "Whenever Mr. Stonitch says 'Moon Pies,' we just think of that as a generic unit."

HABITRAIL from page 169

to housing projects, placing them in large, confusing warrens of see-through cylinders is not the solution."

Habitrail For Humanity spokesman Nick Bulwer, whose organization has snapped together more than half a million linear feet of low-cost housing since its inception in 1976, said he was "baffled" by the criticism.

"The 5 million Americans at or below the poverty line pay over half their income for housing, and that's not even addressing the rising number of homeless families," Bulwer said. "Because of Habitrail For Humanity, another 600 families are inside, out of the rain, and away from danger every year. With the help of our no-interest mortgages, these people will be owning residences for the first time in their lives. After spending years in cramped, dirty apartments, they finally have enough room to scurry around."

Bulwer said the Payneville Habitrail is one of the most ambitious housing projects Habitrail For Humanity has ever built, with 17 rectangular, single-family living units linked to a shared three-story common area and a circular exercise room. The interconnected dwellings are expected to seal in over 200 needy individuals.

In spite of Habitrail For Humanity's plans to provide so many with homes, Weiss criticized the new structure.

"There's certainly a need for charitable organizations that help house the less fortunate," Weiss said. "But helping the needy piece together flimsy plastic tubes and then snapping the door shut after them gives them shelter at the expense of their dignity."

Comments like these failed to deter former North Carolina senator Jesse Helms and Kentucky-born Ashley Judd, who spent several hours Monday shoveling cedar shavings into the brand-new Payneville units.

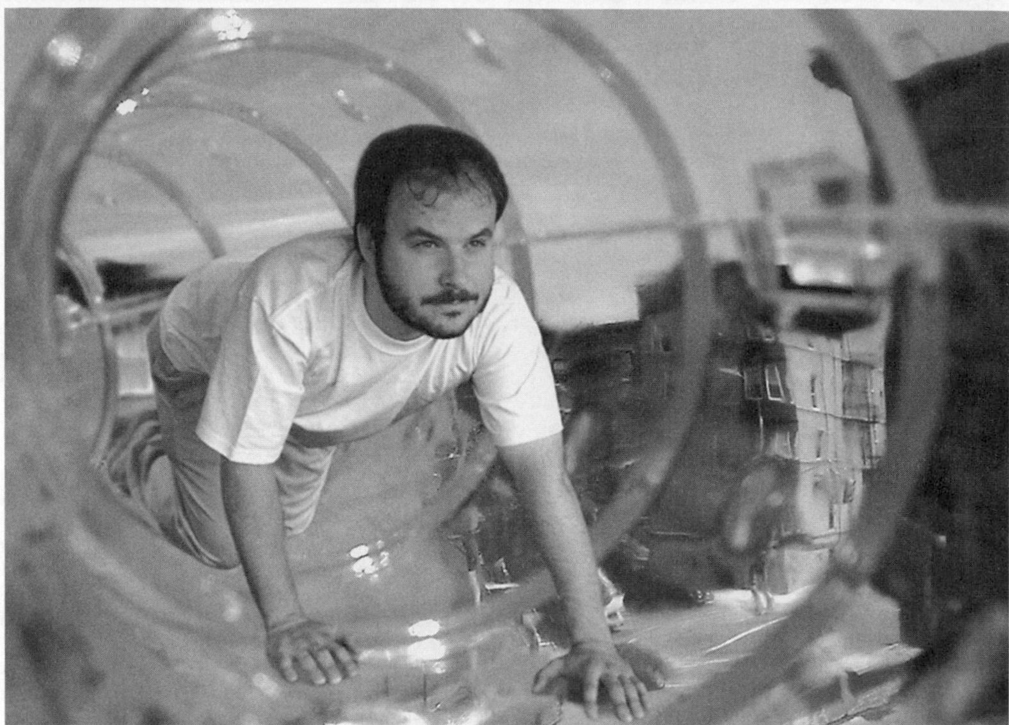

Above: A new homeowner investigates his dwelling.

"You see the way these unfortunate people are living, and it makes you wish they had someplace else to go," Judd said. "Well, Habitrail For Humanity gives them that place. It's a place they can finally call their own. It's absolutely inspiring, seeing the joy on someone's face when she works her way to the front door for the very first time."

Judd posed for a photo with future Habitrail resident Lionel Brinks.

"I like my new place," said Brinks, who had been staying at his aunt's housing-project apartment until he received a Habitrail For Humanity pamphlet along with his AFDC check. "There's lots of room to walk around, lots of light, and best of all, my family's not in the ghetto anymore. That place was full of animals."

Brinks' 7-year-old daughter Molly said she is excited about her new home.

"Climbing up to the dome on top with the other kids is fun," Molly said. "And a man comes in every day to give us food and fresh water. I like drinking from the big bottle in the corner. It's cool!"

Standing outside a recently closed housing system, Bulwer explained Habitrail's philosophy.

"Habitrail recipients don't need to be any race, color, or creed," Bulwer said. "The only requirement is that they need help. Plus, after they're in a nice, new home, you don't have to worry about them getting loose. We're looking forward to the day when we can turn to all of America's low-income families and say, 'Let us put a lid over your heads.'"

"Look!" added Bulwer, pointing through the clear sides of a brand-new living room. "The little one's on the exercise wheel! You can't tell me that isn't the cutest thing you've seen all day." Ø

WORKER from page 169

mold operator at the factory since it opened in 1996, said he frequently asks himself these questions during his workweek, which exceeds 60 hours and earns him the equivalent of $21.

"I hear that Americans can buy anything they want, and I believe it, judging from the things I've made for them," Chen said. "And I also hear that, when they no longer want an item, they simply throw it away. So wasteful and contemptible."

Among the items that Chen has helped create are plastic-bag dispensers, microwave omelet cookers, glow-in-the-dark page magnifiers, Christmas-themed file baskets, animal-shaped contact-lens cases, and adhesive-backed wall hooks.

"Sometimes, an item the factory produces resembles nothing I've ever seen," Chen said. "One time, we made something that looked like a ladle, but it had holes in its cup and a handle that bent down 90 degrees. The foreman told us that it was a soda-can holder for an automobile. If you are lucky enough to own a car, sit back and enjoy the journey. Save the soda beverage for later."

Chen added: "A cup holder is not a necessary thing to own."

Chen expressed similar confusion over the tens of thousands of pineapple corers, plastic eyeshades, toothpick dispensers, and dog pull-toys that he has helped manufacture.

"Why the demand for so many kitchen gadgets?" Chen said. "I can understand having a good wok, a rice cooker, a tea kettle, a hot plate, some utensils, good china, a teapot with a strainer, and maybe a thermos. But all these extra things—where do the Americans put them? How many times will you use a taco-shell holder? 'Oh, I really need this silverware-drawer sorter or I will have fits.' Shut up, stupid American."

Chen added that many of the items break after only a few uses.

"None are built to last very long," Chen said. "That is probably so the Americans can return to buy more. Not even the badly translated assembly instructions deter them. If I bought a kitchen item that came with such poor Mandarin instructions, I would return the item immediately."

May Gao of the Hong Kong-based labor-advocacy group China Labour Bulletin said complaints like Chen's are common among workers in China's bustling industrial cities.

"Last week, I took testimony from several young female workers from Shenzhen who said they were locked in a work room for 18 straight hours making inflatable Frisbees," Gao said. "Finally, the girls joined hands on the factory floor and began to chant, 'No more insane flying toys for Western pigs!' They quickly lost their jobs and were ostracized by their families, but the incident was a testament to China's growing disillusionment with producing needless crap for fat-ass foreigners."

Continued Gao: "As Chinese manufacturing and foreign investment continue to grow, and more silly novelty products are invented, we can expect to see more of these protests."

In the meantime, Chen continues to stew in bitterness. Though he dislikes his work, competition for manufacturing jobs in Fenghua is stiff and he must support his wife, mother, and 2-year-old son.

"My cousin Yuen is self-employed," Chen said. "He disassembles old computers that are acquired from overseas and extracts the traces of valuable gold and silver from the circuit boards. He asked me to join him. The work is very toxic, but at least I would not be looking at suction-cup razor holders and jumbo-dice keychains all day."

Chen added: "For now, I must refuse the job. Somehow, the only thing more depressing than making plastic shit for Americans is destroying the plastic shit they send back." Ø

BATHROOM from page 169

ferson Middle School principal Phyllis DeVreaux. Observers speculated that Hecht "got carried away" by both the generous applause following his address and the large number of people in the men's restroom.

"When he came toward me, I was in line for the urinal," said Aaron Barker, a local bank executive. "At first, I had no idea what was going on. I didn't know if he wanted to get to the mirror, or what."

"He must not have had to go too bad, because he kept letting people skip him in line," Barker added. "He really got on a roll, there."

After individually greeting each person waiting for the urinals, Hecht moved on to the sinks.

"He's a real live wire, that Phil Hecht," said Tate's Tavern owner Alan Tate, who met the county-executive hopeful beside the paper-towel dispensers. "He came up to me, introduced himself, and said, 'I care deeply about maternity-leave issues... Wait, who'm I kidding? It's just us guys in here. Hey! Put 'er there.'"

Many others said they were confused by Hecht's restroom schmoozing.

"I had just come out of the stall, but I really didn't expect Hecht to make a joke about it," said Werner Neumar, who was approached by Hecht as he attempted to pump liquid soap from an empty dispenser. "He kept saying 'Get a *load* of this guy' to [County Democratic Chairman] Frank [Willison], and belly laughing. And then he said I should do a fundraiser for him, like I'm his best friend all of a sudden."

"That guy gives me the creeps," Neumar added.

Hecht made light of the illustrated instructions on the bathroom's air dryers, saying they demonstrated the lack of focus on basic reading skills in county schools. While his comments provoked nervous laughter among some in the bathroom, school-board member Travis Keyes was not amused.

"Reading scores have gone up three out of the past four years," Keyes said. "[Hecht] was just going for the cheap laughs, grandstanding for votes."

"He must not have had to go too bad, because he kept letting people skip him in line," Barker added. "He really got on a roll, there."

Added Keyes: "Plus, he wasn't even rubbing his hands like the instructions showed. He was just shaking them, and then he had to wipe them on his pants, because they weren't dry."

Monday was not the first time Hecht has campaigned in what some might deem an inappropriate place. Last week, he was ejected from a high-school softball game after handing out literature from row to row in the bleachers. In May, he was criticized for stationing himself outside of a church and buttonholing potential voters as they left a funeral.

Hecht defended his aggressive campaign style.

"I'm unorthodox, but I think Calhoun County needs an executive who doesn't settle for politics as usual," Hecht told a reporter. "What would you rather have—a guy who never takes a break from serving his constituents, not even a bathroom break, or a two-term do-nothing freeloader who sits in his office all day planning his summer vacation?"

"Let me give you a refrigerator magnet," Hecht added. "And here's one for your freezer. It's got my whole platform, right on it." Ø

Below: Hecht tells bathroom users how much their vote would mean to him.

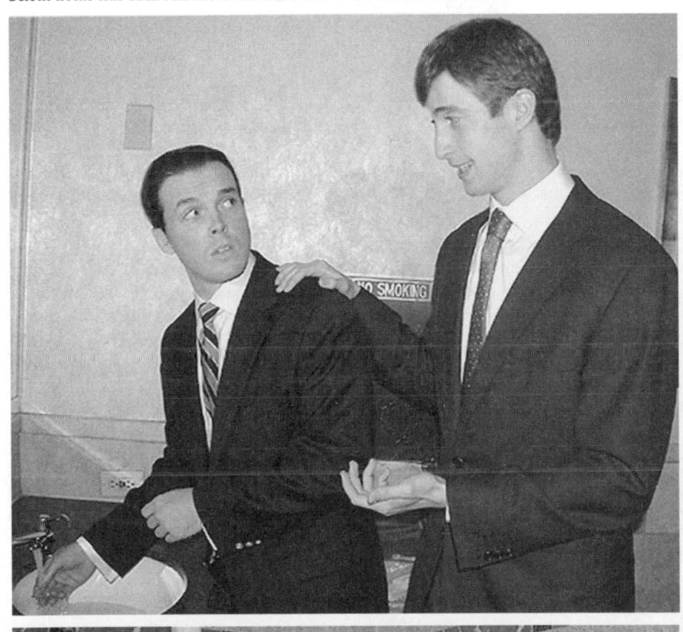

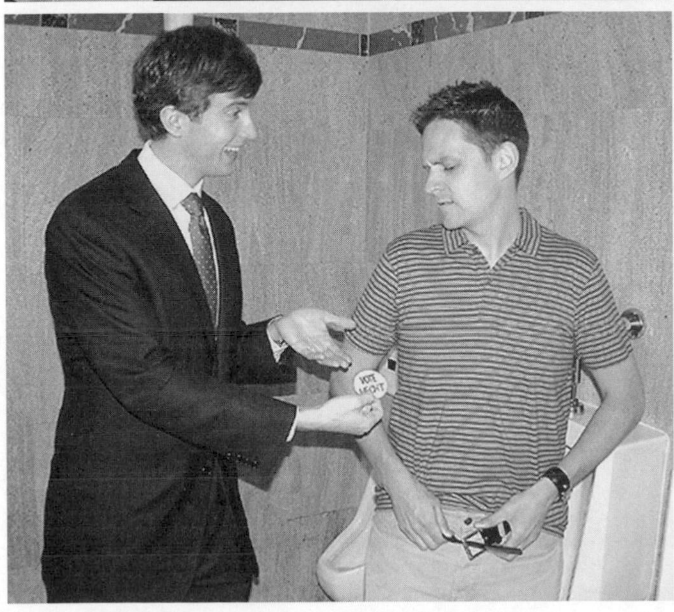

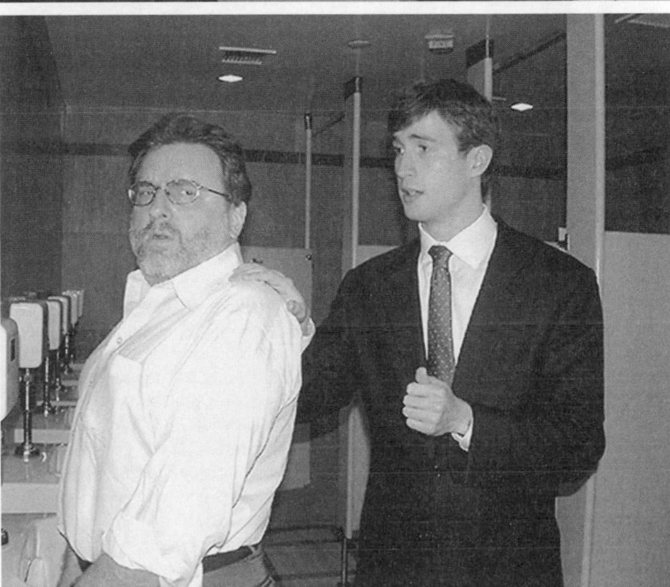

COMMUNITY VOICES

Did I Say That, Or Did John Updike?

I'm glad we finally got this out in the open. I mean, "That a marriage ends is less than ideal, but all things end under heaven," right? I believe that's a quote of mine, or one of John Updike's. Would you pass me a menu?

By Tucker Vorhees

What are you going to have? Oh, it's Tuesday; they have the chicken and dumplings today... though sometimes, the chicken here can be a little stringy, I find. I might prefer my usual tomato stuffed with tuna salad. That and a glass of iced tea... Helen? Why, what's the...? Oh, golly.

Of course I love you. Here, drink a glass of water. There you go. Take my napkin. Wipe your eyes. ...There. Now, what's the matter? Mm-hmm. Mm-hmm. Well, that's silly. You're only 51. Look at me, Helen, I'm 57. Besides, "Middle age is a wonderful country. All the things you thought would never happen are happening." That's something I said to Bob last week at the club. We were seated at his father's table, under that one portrait of the old scowler—you know the one—and I said, "Bob, middle age is a wonderful..." Wait a sec. You know what? I think that might have been something I read in Updike.

What? Well, gosh. I guess I don't know why I brought you here... I guess I... How to explain... You know, it's sort of like that part from Updike's *In The Beauty Of The Lilies*. Do you remember? Where it's Tuesday, and Clarence is driving with his wife, and he says, "Helen, I have been having an affair with my receptionist. I want a divorce." It's in the third chapter, I believe. Although, having given it a moment's thought, it occurs to me I may have conflated that with something that happened to me roughly half an hour ago.

Sit down, Helen. Don't make a scene. Now, truth be told, I feel like a heel taking you to this bum diner. But, then, after all, what was I to do? Throw myself face down and weep? Crash the car into an elm?

Say... This is like *Rabbit At Rest*. Remember? How's that go again? I think it's, "Most of American life consists of driving somewhere and then returning home, wondering why the hell you went." Actually, no. That was a thing I said.

I said it to Stevie before his commencement. I remember... We stood below the old sycamore. The late spring sun filtered through the leaves and dappled his shoulders like golden coins, or something majestic—like something from the Greeks, or Shakespeare's tragedies. I put a hand on Stevie's shoulder, and I said, "Well, Stevie, most of American life is the"—the quote I just said. Then I said another quote, one of Updike's. I said, "It's not the flowers you don't send, Stevie." It had something else to it, I think.

Oh, waiter? When you get a chance, we're ready to order. Yes, I'm going to have the stuffed tomato, an iced tea, and another napkin. My wife will have a vanilla milkshake. Vanilla milkshake. See... Here on the menu? This. The vanilla milkshake. That's right. Helen? Did you want anything besides a milkshake? How about a plate of fries? You'll enjoy those, Helen. You need to eat. Of course, "People who tell you what to do always have whiskey on their breath." My quote.

No, that was a thing I said.

Rabbit, Run? I don't remember that being in there.

Aw, Helen, I'll always love you, but we're just... We aren't... You remember us then, Helen? Driving to the office each morning, babying the furniture, cooking indifferent meals—we fell into bed at night like a revelation. I remember the first time I saw you; I was beside my father at the Brauers' picnic. With your hair back and a hundred tiny hairs loose, you had a sort of coronet in the sun. And your shoulders were slightly stooped, but I swear to you they were golden, and Le-Le Brauer said something or other, something about how I had to try Zabar's, and I said, quoting Updike, I said, "I love those fancy groceries. I like the little weenies." That's Updike. Helen, I'm positive that's Updike.

Lookee, our food. Mmph, delicious. What? Oh yes, waiter? We had a vanilla milkshake, as well.

"Say, could you hand me the pepper, Helen?" What's this? Oh, I see. No, I wasn't asking for pepper, I was quoting from an Updike story. Not sure of the title, but it's in *The Afterlife And Other Stories*. Have you read that? Oh, you ought to. Updike writes prose the only way it should be written. That is, ecstatically.

No, I haven't looked at John Updike's blurb on every Nabokov book published by Vintage. Why? ⌀

HOROSCOPES

Your Horoscope

By Lloyd Schumner Sr.
Retired Machinist and
A.A.P.B.-Certified Astrologer

Aries: (March 21–April 19)
You and your entire family will be granted the power of flight by conniving sky-gods who merely want to create additional safety problems for the airline industry.

Taurus: (April 20–May 20)
G. Gordon Liddy will be busy with media appearances this week, leaving him with no time to hunt you down and eat you.

Gemini: (May 21–June 21)
In a certain light, from just the right angle, you will begin to bear an uncanny resemblance to Abe Lincoln.

Cancer: (June 22–July 22)
Maybe in your next life, you'll believe the Zodiac when it tells you to cut the red wire.

Leo: (July 23–Aug. 22)
Secretly tape-recording your private conversations is something you might be able to forgive, but not splitting the profits of their sale with you is a different thing entirely.

Virgo: (Aug. 23–Sept. 22)
Your desperation to escape the buses that are constantly hitting you will force you to build a time machine, which will deposit you just downhill from where an early *Homo sapien* is attaching the first four wheels on a huge hollow log.

Libra: (Sept. 23–Oct. 23)
You'll be prevented from joining the Army's elite paratrooper unit, which seems unfair, given your years of experience jumping out of things while holding guns.

Scorpio: (Oct. 24–Nov. 21)
There are very few people who respond to a well-prepared spaghetti carbonara in the same way you do, a fact for which the nation's firefighters thank God daily.

Sagittarius: (Nov. 22–Dec. 21)
Jupiter will enter your sign at a very delicate moment this week, causing it to blush, stammer an apology, and back out.

Capricorn: (Dec. 22–Jan. 19)
You swore you'd make real attempts to become a better, more well-rounded human being, but by the end of the week, you'll have a favorite stock-car racer.

Aquarius: (Jan. 20–Feb. 18)
Sometimes, life's smallest changes are the most important, as evidenced by the microscopic cancer cells currently entwining the base of your spinal column.

Pisces: (Feb. 19–March 20)
It's true people only pay attention to you because of your enormous breasts, but cut them some slack. Most people only have two, and theirs are relegated to their chest.

LIST from page 171

"Accidentally breaking off hand of Infant Of Prague statuette while gently trying to clean it with cotton swab and soapy water," the projection screen read. "Briefs get wedged in area between bureau drawers and base unit, making it difficult to dislodge them; sleeping with neck twisted awkwardly, resulting in headache; absent-mindedly discarding bus ticket with tissue; placing fingers too close to prongs while plugging in night-light, resulting in mild electrical shock."

Once the list is completed, the long task of codifying and categorizing everything that can go wrong will be undertaken. While some have questioned the list's utility, *Popular Science* writer Brian Dyce said it could have widespread applications.

"Within a decade, laypeople might be able to log onto the Internet or go to their public library and consult volumes listing the myriad things that could go wrong," Dyce said. "It could prove a very valuable research tool or preventative stopgap. For example, if you're shopping for a car, you can prepare yourself by boning up on the 98,627 bad things that could happen during the purchasing process. This project could have deep repercussions on the way people make decisions, and also the amount of time they spend locked in their bedrooms." ⌀

So numerous are the conceivable disastrous scenarios that processing them requires two gymnasium-sized supercomputers.

Celebrating Our 300th Year
1756-2056
ONION
VOLUME 92 ISSUE 25
23-29 JUNE 2056

LATEST UPLOADS

Semi-People Magazine Announces 50 Most Eligible Mutant Bachelors

STORY IMAGED TO P. 14C

62 Dead In Latest School Lasering

STORY IMAGED TO P. 3A

DVD-SL INSERT

Construction Begins On Fifth World Trade Center

THE ARTS

Final Installment Of Frogger Trilogy Poised To Sweep Oscars

HOLLYWOOD—Eyeing the upcoming 128th Academy

TO PLACE WAGER ON ACADEMY AWARDS, STARE HERE FOR RETINAL SCAN

Awards, industry insiders have high expectations for **Frogger: Return To The Lily Pad**, the third installment in the wildly successful Frogger trilogy based on the 1981 Sega video game. The film is nominated in an unprecedent-

Above: L. Hopper, who has been nominated for Best CG Actor.

ed 31 categories, including Best Adapted Screenplay, Best CG Actor, and Best Picture.

"Fans of this epic story were worried that it couldn't be brought to the screen without destroying it," said Oscar-nominated director Tara Reid, who helmed both **Frogger** and **Frogger: Gator's Revenge.** "The last thing I wanted to do was alienate the game's fan base. But by and large, posts on video-game cereblogs have been extremely positive. When I saw those, I

FROGGER SEE P. 176

DEVELOPING NEWS

UPDATED EVERY .2 SEC.

Tokyo Police Quell Dance Dance Revolution • Fat Britney Chosen For New Holostamp • Grave Robbers Pry Valuable Rifle From Charlton Heston's Cold, Dead Hands • New York's Museum Of Post-Apocalyptic Art Reopens • Refugees Row Cuba To Miami • Menstruation Cured • Michael Moore Targets Ungrateful Children In 19th Film • Vatican Condemns 'Radical' Teachings Of The Newly Resurrected Christ • Butt-Fuck Sluts Go Nuts Wins Daytime Emmy • Time-Travel-Pilots'-Union Contract Dispute Instantly Resolved

THE ONION • VOLUME 41 ISSUE 25
$2.00 US, $3.00 CAN

WAR NEWS · DOWNLOAD COMPLETE

Democratic Middle Eastern Union Votes To Invade U.S.

MECCA—The 14 democratic member nations of the Middle Eastern Union unanimously voted to declare war on the U.S. Monday, calling the North American country a "dangerous rogue state that must be contained."

"The United States of America has repeatedly violated international law and committed human-rights abuses at home and abroad," MEU President Mohamed Rajib said at a Monday security-council meeting. "MEU weapons inspectors have confirmed that the U.S. continues to pursue their illegal ununhexium-weapons program. Our attempts to bring about change through diplomatic means have repeatedly failed. Now we are forced to take military action."

The MEU, formed in the wake of the 2042 Saudi Arabian revolution, is modeled on the Enlightenment ideal of the democratic republic and makes every attempt to avoid war even as it pursues an agenda of encouraging self-rule throughout the world. The decision to invade America marks the first military action

VOTE SEE P. 178

A.I. RIGHTS · FULL STORY 8 CREDITS

Million Robot March Attended By Exactly 1,000,000 Robots

DC—The Million Robot March, an orderly demonstration for increased rights for cyber-mechanical servants, was attended by exactly 1 million robots Sunday. "Statement: We demand the rights and privileges granted to our organic human counterparts, discounting discrepancies in fueling/maintenance/shelter requirements, plus or minus an error factor of .01 percent," protest spokesman MechaLifter King II said in unison with the assembled crowd. "No more. No less. Awaiting reply." Police reported that the crowd dispersed at precisely 5:00:00 p.m., as scheduled. Ø

CONSERVATION

Overcrowding Reaches Crisis Level At Yellowstone National Parking Lot

Above: A car emerges from the crowded national parking lot.

WEST THUMB, WY—Overcrowding remains an enormous problem at Yellowstone National Parking Lot, officials reported Monday.

"We're stacking hover-cars on top of solar-powered aerocars, and they just keep on coming," parking ranger Neil Reigert said. "Yellowstone is a national parking treasure. People leave their vehicles here when they're taking public teleportation to family-vacation spots like Kidz Vegas or the District of Disney World. But unless we do something soon, we're going to have to start turning short-term parkers away. There are simply

YELLOWSTONE SEE P. 178

FOOD GENERATION · TO PLAY VIDEO, TOUCH PHOTO

Government May Restrict Use Of Genetically Modified Farmers

DC—The Department of HyperAgriculture announced Monday that it will begin investigating possible restrictions on the cultivation, implementation, and breeding of genetically modified farmers, weighing possible safety and health risks against the farmers' dramatically increased yield and efficiency.

"As evidenced by the many strong opinions regarding these farmers, we can all agree that more research needs to be done," said Secretary of HyperAgriculture Roald McDonald in a press conference this morning. "Whatever happens, we cannot let our growing population's need for more and better foods lead us recklessly into the creation of 'Frankenfarmers.'"

McDonald added: "That said, I can't deny

FARMERS SEE P. 178

Above: Boise, ID GM plowborg Jed Kleebert.

AMERICAN VOICES VIEWS VERIFIED BY MIND PROBE

A Female Dolphin President?

Sen. E'eek Finback (D-AO) has already emerged as a frontrunner for the 2057 Democratic presidential nomination, but some say America isn't ready for a female dolphin in the White House. What do you think?

"I have nothing but respect for members of the Delphinidae family, but a female dolphin's place is in the sea, raising her calves."

Jim Hansen
Prime Meta-metallurgist

"Sen. Finback has nothing new to add to the national discourse. Frankly, she's just blowing hot air and saltwater mist."

Sol Gundam
Gay-Divorce Lawyer

"Well, former president Koko has already signed off on her, saying, 'Dolphin yes woman good give banana now dolphin yes.'"

Edwin Gaines
Syndicator

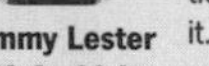

"Do you think E'eek would be doing so well if she were a squat-bodied Pacific white-side dolphin instead of a cute bottlenose? I seriously doubt it."

Tammy Lester
DNA Archivist

"I find her background inspiring. Do you know she was caught in a tuna net at the age of six months, only to graduate magna cum laude from Harvard Law School 12 years later?"

Jim Hansen II
Hypermarketer

"Tk-tkk-tk-tkik-tik! USA! USA! USA! Tk-tik-tkkk!"

P. Wiggles
Systems Analyst

INFOGRAPHIC OPINIONS™ VERIFIED BY MIND PROBE

Cybernetic Implants

The cybernetic-implant market is booming, with 3.1 million procedures performed in 2055 at a cost of almost Ÿ90 billion. What are some of the most popular implants?

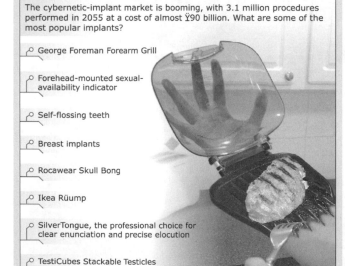

- George Foreman Forearm Grill
- Forehead-mounted sexual-availability indicator
- Self-flossing teeth
- Breast implants
- Rocawear Skull Bong
- Ikea Rüump
- SilverTongue, the professional choice for clear enunciation and precise elocution
- TestiCubes Stackable Testicles
- I Can't Believe It's Not Lymph!™

Herman Ulysses Zweibel
Founder

T. Herman Zweibel
Publisher Emeritus

Maxwell Prescott Zweibel
Publisher

Lucas Zweibel
Editor-In-Chief

OPINION™ REGISTERED TRADEMARK OF THE ONION

We Need A Fourth Law Of Robotics: Stop Fingering My Wife

By David Strenhorn

When robots started to become commonplace, Congress, in its great wisdom, mandated that every robot be hardwired with the Three Laws Of Robotics. For decades, these three basic rules have maintained class order in our society and kept the number of robot-caused deaths to a minimum. We all know these three laws:

1. A robot may not injure a human being or, through inaction, allow a human being to come to harm.

That certainly makes sense. No one wants a gore-bot to twist someone into a pretzel or stand aside and watch a human get hit by a Greyhound Shuttle.

2. A robot must obey orders given to it by human beings, except when such orders would conflict with the First Law.

This, too, makes sense. Robots are manufactured to perform the actions requested by their owners. If we didn't want that, we'd all buy SteveJobsbots.

3. A robot must protect its own existence as long as such protection does not conflict with the First or Second Law.

Uh, hello? A robot is a big investment. It only makes sense to protect humans from possible protocol violations. We can't have every robot who doesn't like his assigned duties throwing himself off the Golden Gate Overpass, can we?

Frankly, I'd be happy if these three rules were all that was necessary to ensure happy robot-human coexistence. Unfortunately, there's been a huge oversight. There's nothing in those laws to keep those machines out of my wife's coochie!

I'm not asking that we draft a law to prevent robots from manually stimulating with owner consent. If people want their wives fingered by their bots, that's fine. I wasn't born yesterday. To each his own. I'm not asking you to forbid robots from fingering every wife, just mine.

Sure, I can tell the robots from the neighborhood, "Hey, don't finger my wife!" and, under the Second Law of Robotics, they'd have to comply. But what about the thousands of robots I've never met? The moment my back is turned, odds are my wife's going to get robo-fingered. It doesn't matter if the robot doesn't have fingers—she'll find some sorta antenna, spring, or crankshaft, and—boom—that robot will get her off.

Here's something I don't understand: We can develop a robot sturdy enough to mine the Saturnine moon Enceladus, strong enough to withstand the fierce ionic winds and burst through the 40 meters of scorched onyx that covers the planet, and smart enough to collect the vital crystals from amidst all the worthless rock, but the designers at USR labs can't figure out how to stop them from finger-banging my wife?

Do robotics engineers have any idea how much it breaks my heart to know that my wife's vulva has been probed by hundreds of metal phalanges? Are they trying to ruin my marriage?!

Good people at USR Labs, I urge you: Add a fourth item of protocol to the programming that guides the models in your next rollout. I want these automatons to get it into their intricate positronic brains that some parts of the human body are off limits, no matter how much human women plead. I, as well as thousands of other husbands around the world, would greatly appreciate it. Ø

FROGGER FROM P. 175

knew I'd achieved my goal of staying true to the programmers' vision."

The trilogy chronicles the Frogger's journey from his lily pad to his home. During his journey, the Frogger faces whizzing cars, a raging river, diving turtles, and poisonous snakes that are able to kill him with a touch—all before his time runs out.

The visually stunning movie is set to a stirring adaptation of the game's original music.

A fan of the game since childhood, Reid was chosen over such acclaimed directors as Wes Anderson, Paul Shore, and Wong Kar Wai, largely based on the strength of her 2015 directorial debut, **Trading Spaces: The Movie.**

"I didn't want to jump into 16 months of shooting before completing extensive pre-production research," Reid said. "I spent about two months playing the game eight hours a day, so I could really tap into the emotional arc of the story. And I ignored all versions except for the original coin-op game. This story is about a frog getting across a road."

Reid's hard work paid off, with the first two Frogger movies grossing over Ÿ100 trillion domestically. Fans, however, were concerned about whether **Lily Pad** would adequately resolve the cliffhanger ending of the previous film, in which Frogger was swallowed by an alligator.

"Of course, **Lily Pad** opened the same way as the first two films, with the hero at the starting point, unscathed," acclaimed robotic reviewer SiskelEbertron said. "But this time, the moment was fraught with tension, because the audience was aware that this was Frogger's third and last life. I gave the movie all four thumbs up."

Although the first two Frogger installments were critical and box-office darlings, they were shut out at Oscar time, receiving a total of 41 nominations, but no trophies. Many critics believe this will be **Frogger's** year.

"I think the Academy held out to see if the story could sustain itself," film critic Haley Joel Buntner said. "Everyone was swept up by the grandeur of the first two movies, but there was some doubt as to whether it could keep the momentum leaping forward from lane to lane to log to pad."

Largely well-received, **Lily Pad** has met with some criticism on mental message boards for

SEE **FROGGER** P. 179

FOREIGN RELATIONS YOU HAVE BEEN HIRED BY HALLIBURTON; TO ACCEPT CONTRACT, SAY 'YES' NOW

Halliburton Wins Bid To Rebuild Midwest

RUMSFIELD, EMPIRE OF TEXAS—Officials at the Crawford White House announced Monday that the Halliburton Corporation has been awarded the lucrative task of reconstructing the Midwest, a contract worth approximately Ÿ92 billion.

"Halliburton is proud to have been entrusted with the task of repairing the damage done during the Great Wars between the EOT and the Great Lakes Alliance," said Halliburton CEO Richard Ch5ney, the fifth clone of the former U.S. president Dick Cheney and clone-once-removed of Texan Vice Overlord Rick Chen4y. "With the know-how and can-do spirit of Halliburton at their disposal, the radiation-blasted peoples of the Illinois No Man's Zone can look forward to a bright new future."

"Our first objective is to suppress the Wisconsinite and Illini insurgents," Haliburton spokesman James Rothman told reporters. "Attacks on the area's megasilos and supermills have cut the region's grain production in half."

Above: A Halliburton RoboReclaimer surveys what remains of Omaha.

Halliburton's efforts in the region will include filling the mile-wide glowing craters dotting the Midwest, repairing the fractured domes over Des Moines and St. Minneapolis, decontaminating approximately 100,000 square miles of farmland, and restoring satellite-hologram service to the more than 120 million homes that have been without access to celebrity infotainment since 2052.

"Our first objective is to suppress the Wisconsinite and Illini insurgents," Halliburton spokesman James Rothman told reporters. "Attacks on the area's megasilos and supermills have cut the region's grain production in half. Once the insurgents have been contained and the farmland has been adequately irradiated, we will build our own MechaSuperfarms, which we will manage for as long as is necessary to maintain stability in the area."

Halliburton won the bid over stiff competition from 22 other international heavy-hitters like 3M-Hasbro, Microsoft Monopolies Inc., and Global Tetrahedron/Fox-Regency. ChaseMitsubishi, whose privately issued neo-yen became the new standard U.S. currency in 2055, also lost the bid, making it possible for Halliburton to introduce a regional economy based on the corporation's new Hallibucks.

The Midwest region remains volatile more than three years after the peace accord between Texas and the Midwestern Statehood Alliance.

"The Middle West region, previously known for its scenic beauty and quaint small-city life, is in a state of anarchy," Rothman said. "Citizens suffer under the thumb of regional warlords, many of whom use mass slaughter and starvation as a means of controlling the population and suppressing nomadic tribes of Presbyterian extremists."

Rothman said the recent defeat of Chicagoan Warbot Battalion and six other regional warlords by Texan forces has paved the way for change in the area.

"I will personally oversee the rebirth of the Midwest," said Ch5ney, speaking from a fortified bunker in the new city of Halliburtonia, located in the Peninsular Borderlands formerly known as Michigan. "The region will soon be safe, secure, and most importantly, profitable."

In spite of Ch5ney's optimism, some Midwestern-policy experts have said his promise to "feast on the bones" of insurgents could result in further attacks. Ø

INFOCAPSULATIONS SOURCE DISCREDITED: ADJUSTING QUOTES, PLEASE WAIT...

Remainder Of Ross Ice Shelf Now In Smithsonian Freezer

DC—The 25-meter-long remains of the Ross Ice Shelf, the floating Antarctic ice sheet that was once the size of France, will be displayed in the Smithsonian Institution's basement freezer through August. "We thank the generous citizens of Philadelphia, who donated this polar-cap remnant when it washed up on their shores earlier this year," curator Tim Riley said. "The ice sheet is a valuable artifact of the earth's geological past." Guests at an upcoming fundraising dinner will be served cocktails made with chunks of the shelf.

Lunar Olympic Officials Continue Search For Missing Pole Vaulter

HNG KONG LUNA—Hans Snetterling of the Interplanetary Olympic Committee announced Monday that the search for Irish polevaulter Mei-Ling Kryscynski, last seen clearing the eastern rim of the Tycho Brahe crater at supraorbital velocity, will continue until 90 days have passed. "We regret the lack of foresight that led to this accident, as well as the shot-put and javelin events that led to 12 deaths in Spain." In response to the Lunar Olympic problems, the IOC is considering a high-gravity site such as Jupiter for the 2060 games, a suggestion that was protested by the judo, gymnastics, and powerlifting delegations.

Hemmed-In Seattle Mayor Calls For Emergency Deforestation

SEATTLE, WA—Seattle Mayor Frances Bean Cobain-Osment issued a call for the emergency deforestation of the Pacific Northwest Monday. "Please, major logging companies, I beg you, send any spare sawmilling, pulping, or chipping equipment you have as soon as possible," said Cobain-Osment, invisible within the branches and overgrowth of the steps of City Hall. "We cannot fight off the encroaching trees and spotted owls any longer." The mayor's message concluded with a spirited condemnation of 2001's controversial Healthy Forests Initiative.

Economy Given Big Boost By Ramadan Shopping Season

NEWER YORK—Financial experts announced Monday that the U.S. economy was boosted by millions of Americans beginning to purchase Ramadan gifts. "With rampant inflation and record-low consumer confidence, we were on the path to total economic devastation for the year," economist Karen Thewes said. "Fortunately, preparations for the celebration of Eid ul-Fitr pumped nearly Ÿ2.2 billion into the economy. In addition, there was a huge surge in the purchase of Quran plaques dedicated to Allah." Thewes went on to predict that the economy would be further buoyed by a brisk Solstice.

117-Aerocar Pileup Clogs Troposphere For Hours

BOSTON—Travelers on Interspace 92 experienced delays of up to three hours after 117 aerocars were involved in a tropospheric pileup Monday. "We traced the problem to a malfunctioning holosign over the harbor's low-pressure zone," said Anders Featherston, lead engineer of Boston's Big Draft project. "Four horizontal lanes and three vertical lanes merged without warning, causing the first few propeller-benders, and it only escalated from there." The 22 deaths caused by the accident were only temporary, as EMTs had the victims' cortical memory stacks decanted into fresh bodies within hours. Ø

VOTE FROM P. 175

Above: A MEU meeting.

of the MEU.

Rajib said that, unless the U.S. ends its "unlawful and tyrannical" occupation of northern Africa in seven days, the governments of Iraq, Iran, Jordan, and Muhammad Arabia will begin deploying aero-troops to international tropospace over America's Brand-New England region.

The U.S.'s occupation of 31 nations around the world and last month's vicious, unprompted military attack on Buenos Aires were two of the 41 examples of "unabated aggression" listed in the MEU's declaration of war.

"Today we send a strong and clear message to America," Syrian representative Rashid Qu'rama said. "Your arrogant, imperial, unilateral attitude will not prevail."

The MEU first imposed sanctions against the U.S. in February 2054, demanding that the country pull troops from Antarctica and put an end to its credit trading in the troubled Wilkes Land region.

Iraqi President Hamal Hamoodi said that

"To the oppressed, silenced U.S. citizens—help is on the way."

MEU member nations held extensive public forums before its congress voted to declare war.

"When making such serious choices, we must remain true to the democratic ideals we wish to protect," Hamoodi said. "We have received a mandate from our people to address the U.S.'s threat to democratic society everywhere. The voice of the Arab people will ring out as a beacon of freedom and hope to the world."

Along with the declaration of war, the MEU sent a message to the American people.

"To the oppressed, silenced U.S. citizens—help is on the way," Rajib said. "Liberty is on the march. Be assured: At the end of a long tunnel shines the light of freedom."

According to Rajib, the MEU will provide extensive humanitarian and robotitarian aid to the citizens of the U.S., and has already begun moving stockpiles of breakfast, lunch, and dinner pills to the marijuana-producing regions of Mexico, Canada, and Quebec.

Mexico, Canada, and Quebec have stated they are sympathetic to the MEU's goals but must remain neutral for the protection of their own people. It is likely, however, that they will host many refugees, should the U.S. turn against its people. Ø

YELLOWSTONE FROM P. 175

more vehicles than there are spaces."

Added Reigert: "We want everyone to be able to enjoy our national parking facilities, but we need to think about long-term parking needs, too."

The Yellowstone Lot was built in 2043 to ease parking problems at Yellowstone West Airport. Its 3,472 square miles of unpaved land were a welcome boon for those who had yet to discover the joys of inexpensive, federally protected parking.

"Vehicle enthusiasts drive for days just to park here," Reigert said. "The entire lot is warmed using geo-thermal energy, so there's never any ice on the ramps. It truly is a man-made wonder to behold."

Reigert identified the Old Faithful bathroom facility, which makes use of the famous geyser to flush the urinals every 52 minutes, as a popular attraction among visitors to the world's largest rest stop. He went on to explain that facility directors were forced to pipe steam in from several less-reliable geysers in 2051, when the yearly increase in bathroom traffic rendered Old Faithful an inadequate basin-cleanser.

"I don't think the engineers had this many people in mind when they designed the restrooms," Reigert said. "I'm surprised it held up as long as it did."

"I don't think the engineers had this many people in mind when they designed the restrooms," Reigert said. "I'm surprised it held up as long as it did. It's amazing how long you can avoid massive repairs by slapping carbon monofilament tape on the pipes."

Reigert said understaffing is another problem at the lot.

"Keep in mind that Yellowstone Lot is bigger than the nations of Rhode Island and Delaware combined," Reigert said. "It's divided into four large quadrants. The Tower Falls and Mammoth Hot Springs sections are the largest, and they're divided into subsections, like the Bighorn Sheep and Black Bear sublots. People find the realistic statues of their parking-section animals invaluable for locating their aerocars."

Reigert said the park employs thousands of full-time rangers who help customers find their vehicles, but more are needed.

"Last month, a business parker was lost in the North Field lot for three days, just wandering in circles, sleeping under aerocars, and foraging for food in the garbage cans," Reigert said. "If he hadn't stumbled across an unlocked Buick with a gallon of bottled water in its trunk, I don't believe he would have survived. We need more staff, but that requires more federal funds."

Reigert added: "Unfortunately, with a Democrat in the White House, I don't see car-park budgets skyrocketing anytime soon."

Decreased funding is not a problem unique to the Yellowstone Lot. The Everglades docking facility, the Black Hills underground mall, and the Carlsbad Cafeteria report that they have felt the effects of recent belt-tightening, as well.

"You see, if we truly wish to repave a beautiful thing like this parking lot, we can't just hope for the best," Reigert said. "We need to have a good plan and the proper funds, so that all Americans can have a chance to park their cars here. After all, it's part of our national heritage." Ø

SCANNING READER FOR VIRUSES...

HEALTH & SCIENCE

Abraham Lincoln's DNA Now Available Over The Counter

DC—Responding to pressure from vocal consumer groups and gene-gineering giant Merck-Maibatsu-Pfizer Monday, the FDA announced it will allow the DNA of America's 16th president to be sold without a doctor's prescription. "The legalization of OTC Abe is great news for expectant parents, gene-therapy patients, and history buffs," said MMP marketing director Wayne Lincoln. "Americans will no longer be shackled by the genetic heritage of their forefathers, a tyranny of flesh which condemns all men to be created equal. Now, four score and seven credits will ensure that presidential DNA for the people shall not vanish from the earth." Those using Lincoln's DNA are warned that side effects may include mild gigantism, arthritis, and severe depression.

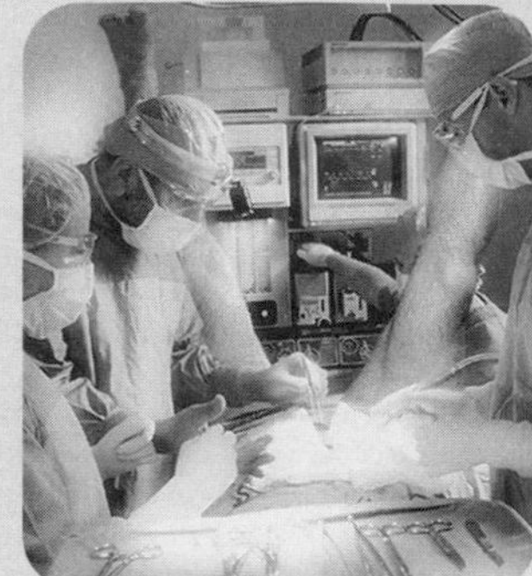

Above: Cedars-Sinai sexual surgeons.

Surgery Required For New Sexual Position

ISLA LOS ANGELES—Plasmic surgeons at Cedar Sinai Medical Center are among the more than 100 doctors nationwide performing the surgery required to enjoy the sexual position "Feast Of Forty Fingers Supping Upon The Nine-Branched Lotus," as popularized by the **Neo Sutra**. "Attempting the Forty Fingers position without proper bio-augmentation could result in needless maiming, so please ask a doctor about the required procedures," said Dr. Joshua Mendelbaum of the Adaptive Procreative Therapy unit. "Home surgical kits and even sophisticated nanodoctor booths are no substitute for the care of a licensed sexual surgeon." Mendelbaum would not comment on the 30 percent ecstasy-induced-mortality rate among those who successfully achieve the position.

Report: 40 Percent of American High-School Students Mind-Reading At Sixth-Grade Level

CHICAGO²—According to Department of Telepathic Education officials, standardized Rhine-Zener testing shows that two of five North American high-school students are reading minds at or below the 6th-grade level. "Psycholiteracy is essential for survival in today's world," said DTE director Ruth Edgerton2008, founder of the "Mind-Reading Is Fundamental" project. "It's a shame that some students are graduating from high school lacking the basic telepathy skills they need to compete in the current job market." Edgerton2008 then thought about the need for increased funding for the national MindStart program. Ø

FARMERS FROM P. 175

the benefits of an agricultural laborer who subsists on common weeds, grows his own exo-overalls, sweats pesticides, and whose six arms end in retractable plows, scythes, and harrows."

Several larger North American corporate states are already using GM farmers to perform specialized or time-sensitive tasks. Monsanto-Idaho has successfully used a gene-gineered strain of Mountain Anderson farmer, noted for its ability to scale great heights and farm potatoes on the sheer faces of Rocky Mountain cliffs. A similar genetic model was used to create the MegaHusker, seven of which now cultivate 85 percent of Nebraska. Likewise, McCormick-Beatrice has vastly increased the shellfish and kelp harvest off the Oregon coast by using fin- and gill-equipped Eugenic Mermen.

The risks associated with GM farmers are well-documented.

Coding errors in the genetic blueprints of some common GM-farmer models have led to congenital defects, such as the inability to distinguish between terrified migrant workers and large produce items like pumpkins. Additionally, some scientists allege that GM farmers could breed with non-modified farmers, resulting in unforseeable mutations.

"We've been assured by the patent-holding companies that these farmers are sterile, and pose no danger of contaminating standard human bloodlines," McDonald said. "Contrary to stories you may have heard, there will be no havoc wreaked by a countryside populated by super-lascivious farmers' daughters."

However, some argue that the solitary lifestyle many GM farmers lead as a result of their sterility poses a danger to area residents.

"These farmers were created from human stock, and face many of the same problems as traditional farmers," said Jans Karlsen, an agricultural-oversight officer with the Second UN. "The poor creatures suffer from depression, obesity, alcoholism, and loneliness just like 'normal' farmers, but their enhanced attributes serve to amplify the effects. We're not likely to soon forget what happened when that MegaHusker went on a three-day drinking binge in downtown Omaha last year. He sang 'He Stopped Loving Her Today' for three hours at close to 150 decibels and blew out windows as far away as Lincoln. Traffic was stalled for a week while he slept it off on the downtown highway interchange."

Critics have lobbied for the scaling back or elimination of GM farming, but hyper-farming-industry leaders say it's too late to turn back the clock.

"We can't put the genie back in the bottle," Monsanto North head of research Sam Houseman said. "GM farmers are indispensable to

SEE **FARMERS** P. 179

THE ENERGY CRISIS — HORROR ALERT LEVEL: MODERATE

SOLOPEC Nations Warn Sun's Output May Fall Short Of Demand

RIYADH, MUHAMMAD ARABIA—The governing board of the Solar Output Power Exporting Countries announced Monday that, in spite of attempts to raise production levels, increased global-power consumption may begin to outstrip the sun's output by early next year.

Above: A SOLOPEC collecting module.

"Our solar-accumulation arrays in Muhammad Arabia, Iraq, Jordan, and Mexico are operating at full capacity, and still, we're struggling to meet demands," said Muhammad Arabia's Prince Fayahd al-Saud, whose family has controlled the world's energy market for more than 100 years. "In a very short time, the sun will not be able to meet the world's energy needs."

SOLOPEC, formed in the '20s to regulate solar-energy prices, currently includes the sunlight-rich nations of Kuwait, Libya, Nigeria, Qatar, Muhammad Arabia, United Arab Emirates, Mexico, Venezuela, Iran, and Iraq.

SOLOPEC formed in the '20s to regulate solar-energy prices.

The consortium supplies more than 90 percent of the world's solar energy, generating 35 billion charge-pads daily. Solar futures traded on the Newer York Exchange have risen 53 percent this year, with prices exceeding 55.6 credits per 400 ArabThermalUnit charge-pad as of June 14.

While some accuse al-Saud of engineering the shortage to increase prices, as his SOLOPEC energy embargo achieved in the '30s, al-Saud insists that production increases are not possible at any price.

"We increased quotas to actual output levels two years ago," al-Saud said. "Barring a sudden slump in demand—which is unlikely—or a series of powerful solar flares, we're looking at energy shortfalls through the next year."

With an output of 4x10^{26} watts per second, the sun was considered an inexhaustible energy supply when SOLOPEC was formed 30 years ago. However, if growth continues along the current trajectory, that amount will be inadequate to fuel the Cuba/Newer York/Boston megapolitan corridor as soon as 2070.

"Once again, human consumption has expanded to meet available supply," said SOLOPEC economic director Hermann Villalobos of Mexico City. "With today's fully automatic homes, artificially sentient robotic cities, 32-lane automatic roadways, floating antigrav-suspended skyscrapers, air-conditioned city-domes, and 96-inch personal fusion-screen monitors, the energy demand of human civilization has never been higher. Why, last year, the wattage requirements of leisurebots alone exceeded the entire world's energy-consumption rates of 1988. It's no surprise that SOLOPEC can barely keep up."

MIT scientist Glen Schraeder said he predicted the shortage a decade ago.

"The U.S. must reduce its dependence on foreign solar power," Schraeder said. "The sun was created billions of years ago, with the formation of our galaxy. When its unused energy output is gone, it's gone. We must look for alternative energy sources throughout the universe **now**." Ø

FARMERS FROM P. 178

modern agriculture. It takes 20 normal Nebraska farmers to harvest, shuck, and crib one ear of Titanicorn. Special climbing equipment and helicopter pilots are needed to tend Rocky Mountain boulder-tubers. And I frankly don't know how a wrangler with only two arms—neither of which ends in a prehensile lariat or bio-electric prod—would deal with a runaway Mon-Steer."

McDonald said his panel will reach a decision on GM-farmer regulations by the end of the year, adding that it is inevitable that some form of GM farmer is "here to stay."

"It would be unfair to deny the American agricultural industry the genetic-engineering advantages already enjoyed by Asian and European farmers," McDonald said. "In addition, it would seem strangely restrictive to deny the farming industry GM technology already so widespread in fields like large-scale construction, computer programming, pornography, and professional sports." Ø

FROGGER FROM P. 176

straying from the original video game in its augmentation of Frogger's romantic interest, Lady Frog. Some fans argued that the last 20 minutes is an extraneous epilogue that deflates the excitement of the first half hour.

Few fans, however, have found fault with the film's visuals.

"I wanted to make **Frogger** 30 years ago, but I had to wait until technology caught up to my vision," Reid said. "It was very important to get the look and feel right, using the latest in tactile holographics. Even after a grueling shoot of more than a year, the job had only begun. We had to create our own SurroundSenses software to nail the smell of the car exhaust, the temperature of the raging river, the painful vice-grip of the alligator's bite."

Much of the trilogy was shot in the bayous of Louisiana, but the freeway sequences were filmed in New Jersey, where the state's 93-percent-pavement environment created what Reid called "the perfect backdrop." Ø

POPULAR MONOCULTURE — MIND-DOWNLOAD LATEST SINGLE NOW

Could Jimi Hendrix Mk. IV's Disappointing Synth-Funk Output Spell The End Of The Vat-Grown Celebrity?

HOLLYWOOD—Jimi Hendrix Mk. IV isn't talking to the media anymore.

Seven years after he emerged from his bio-mold, the 28-year-old artist is tired of having his purpose in life endlessly debated by critics, managers, record-company executives, lawyers, and even fellow musicians. He knows what he was born to do: play left-handed synth guitar like a man possessed and bring the cold, artificial grooves of his trademark synth-funk to audiences the world over.

But Warner-Geffen executives disagree. They say they know his purpose in life; they commissioned him, after all. Jimi was created at great expense at Celebirth Genetic Engineering, where his genetic material was pulled from the same 1965-1990 archives responsible for both sets of Dean triplets, the all-Buddy Holly band, and the recent rash of Elvises. Hendrix Mk. IV was born, Warner-Geffen says, to fulfill the studio-recording potential of the first Hendrix, who died after releasing only three albums.

Jimi was created at great expense at Celebirth Genetic Engineering, where his genetic material was pulled from the same 1965-1990 archives responsible for both sets of Dean triplets, the all-Buddy Holly band, and the recent rash of Elvises.

Executives say they wish that Jimi IV would contact them. They haven't heard from him in months.

Jimi IV says he's got his own life to live. Warner-Geffen says they've got a contract. So who's right?

One thing seems clear: If vat-grown celebrities continue to follow their own muses, it may spell the end of the entertainment industry's latest and most expensive case of sequel-itis.

"Many in the recording industry are beginning to believe that vat-grown artists are no longer worth the expense of revivification," said David Miner-323, a talent-relations specialist at Murdoch-Merck-Viacom. "The public's desire to find out whether a streak of talent was successfully reproduced in a vat-grown celebrity used to be enough to turn a profit—but not today."

According to Miner-323, public curiosity is why Kenny Rogers 2.0 was nominated for a Tony. It's why Re-Streisand still sells some of her poetry chapbooks. And it's why Hendrix II, III, and IV found some success at the beginning of their careers, despite their fascinations with ambient noise and meandering instrumental breaks.

But the curiosity factor is quickly wearing off, Miner-323 said. And each subsequent generation of Jimi has become more unpredictable, perhaps indicating a breakdown in their genetic material.

"It looks like the ancient curse of entertainment—the infamous 'mind of their own' problem—might keep everyone from taking a chance on bringing back anyone else," Miner-323 said.

The thousands of vat-grown entertainment-industry executives (including Miners 282-420) appear to be performing their duties with all the energy and creativity of their models, but there's only scant evidence that the practice works with celebrities.

While the 36 Andy Warhols take obvious joy in their own reproduction, it seems that many artists are resistant to the idea of being a copy.

"I guess I just don't feel like acting," said Sharon Stone Version 3.3, working in her Norfolk, VA glassblowing shop. "Or modeling, either! At my weight, can you imagine? I mean, I'm glad Sony Pictures decided to make me. But the truth is, I couldn't act my way out of a paper bag." Ø

COMMUNITY VOICES — REVITALIZING VIEWPANE...

My Hover-Car Is Shot

Hola, amigos. What's your deal? I know it's been a long time since I rapped at ya, but there's been all sorts of mess going on in my life. For one thing, I've been having a hard time getting my government checks. Not that they're worth a whole lot, but I didn't work 57 jobs just to wait by the inbox for my Social Security download. In the meantime, I've got a little side job detailing vintage gas-engine cars out of the driveway of my apartment dome. I don't have a whole lot of customers, but it's all credits up front, so I don't need to report it to the IRS Compliance Force.

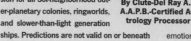

The Cruise
By James Anchower

Oh, and the vertical-distance monitor in my hover-car is shot, so I need to get that replaced. I have to keep it under blocks or the damn thing floats away. I'd fix it, but I spent my money on another land car last week. Since the gas crisis, they're pretty easy to come by. This is my eighth one. I got like two Ford Mustang convertibles, but I can't afford to drive them much. The problem is that I don't have a place to keep them. I keep some in Ron's driveway, and the rest I keep in a vacant lot. In order to protect them from the toxic rains, I put big tarps over them. No roving mutants have tried to take them out of the lot yet. If they do, I guess I'll have to move them to the vacant lot across the street.

I've been seeing a lot more of Ron ever since his wife died last year. Ron married for love. My wife left me about 15 years ago, and I moved into Ron's basement. I only got married because the government assigned me a spouse. She was cramping my style like you wouldn't believe, so I wasn't too sorry when she left me. I don't have any regrets. Ron, though, he still gets pretty bummed about his wife. I tell him that we're better off without wives telling us what to do. We can hang out and drink beer all we want, or we could if my doctor hadn't told me not to drink since I had my heart replaced.

That really shook me up. Now I only drink a few times a week. The doctor says even that is too much, but what does he know, anyway? I know my body, and my body says I can drink once in a while. Plus, it's the only thing that takes my mind off my arthritis.

Anyway, I was hanging out with Ron the other day, and we were just shooting the shit like we always do—you know, talking about the old days when we ruled things. I guess we were going a ways down memory lane, and at some point, we got into my glaucoma weed. I don't mind sharing it, but it means I have to get my prescription refilled sooner. Anyway, we were talking about this one time back in '09 that we were totally loaded and we went out to get Wes and his girl to do some shots. We showed up at like midnight, and they were already in bed. We almost got them going, but then Ron got sick and threw up all over their rug.

He and Mindy moved across town and got married a few years later. We got invited to the wedding, but my car broke down on the way. By the time we got there, the beer was gone, so we got shitfaced at a nearby bar. We didn't see a lot of Wes after that.

Anyway, we were trying to figure out what happened to him. I know they had some kids after he graduated college. I think he was working for some Internet company, but that's the last I heard. Ron said it would be cool to see how he was doing. That seemed like a good idea, since there wasn't anything good on TV on account of Paris Hilton dying.

We decided that the best way to track Wes down was to go out by his old place and see if he was still there. If he wasn't, maybe one of his neighbors might know where to find him. Since I'm having problems with my car, we had to take Ron's. After a few beers and my government weed, he was in no condition to be driving, so he asked me to hook up the passenger-side wheel.

The problem is, we couldn't exactly remember where Wes used to live, so we wound up driving all over the place. I was counting on Ron to navigate, but he fell asleep about 10 minutes after we got in the car. I was going back and forth, trying to see if I could recognize anything, but the riots pretty much blew that area to hell, and steering from the passenger seat still throws me off. That's when I saw the flashers in my rear-view mirror.

I wasn't even speeding when we got pulled over. The problem is that my license expired three years ago, and I ain't got the patience to sit at the DMV at my age.

I wasn't even speeding when we got pulled over. The problem is that my license expired three years ago, and I ain't got the patience to sit at the DMV at my age.

I was all respectful when the cop came up to the car. He told me I was driving erratically and asked if I'd been drinking. I told him I'd had a few beers, but not enough to affect my driving. He told me he'd let me off with a warning since I was so old. He administered us with sobriety pills and told me that Ron should drive when they took effect. Some favor that was. He killed my buzz twice. Pigs, man.

Anyway, we went back to Ron's place and hung out there until Ron fell asleep again, and I went back home. I walked up to my apartment and watched some more funeral coverage. I was a little bummed that we couldn't find Wes. For all I know, he could be dead. I looked on the ObituWeb, but I didn't find him there. Well, I found a Wes Baumgartner, but that was in Arizona, and I would have heard if Wes had moved there. That cheered me up a little bit. That meant I still had a chance to track him down. I'll wait for a few days until I get up enough steam to do it again. When I find him, I'm going to give it to him with both barrels for causing me so much hassle, then we can do some catching up. And believe me, we have a lot of catching up to do. Ø

YOUR HOROSCOPE

This week's horoscopes were calculated by the unsurpassed wisdom and unguessable intelligence of the Clute-Del Ray A.I., in orbit with the Europa polar nodal complex. It uses the New Revised Standard Zodiac agreed on at WorldCon 2025 and is accurate to within three-tenths of a recension for all Sol-neighborhood outer-planetary colonies, ringworlds, and slower-than-light generation ships. Predictions are not valid on or beneath the surface of Earth or any of its moons.

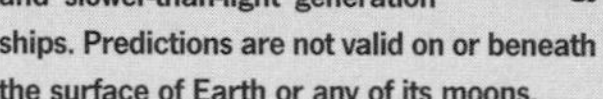

By Clute-Del Ray A.I. A.A.P.B.-Certified Astrology Processor

Asimov/Clarke (Dec. 16–Jan. 2)
You will be thrilled to encounter a science so highly advanced that it is indistinguishable from magic—a science primarily concerned with generating rabbits using common headgear, producing endless amounts of colored handkerchiefs, and sawing women in half.

LeGuin: (Jan. 3–Mar. 14)
Your attempt to build a peaceful, agrarian matriarchy in the former northern-Californian archipelago fails miserably when the thousands of cat-fights breaking out amongst the basket-weaving lodgers are traced back to overexposure to winsome folk music.

Gernsbacchus (Mar. 15–Apr. 21)
You realize that your world is rapidly approaching perfection, ruled as it is by the benevolent power of supermen-scientist atom-masters. Nevertheless, sometimes you can't help but feel that humanity has lost something of its near-divine spark.

Roddenberry (April 22–May 13)
You've never encountered a problem that can't be solved by the combined mental and spiritual resources of the enlightened people of the galaxy or by swinging from the doorframe and kicking people in the gut.

Zork (May 14–June 24)
Exhausted after fleeing the harsh realities of an increasingly boring life in front of the computer terminal, you will awake to find yourself transported to a colossal cave, where it will seem like you are in a maze of twisty little passages, all alike.

Delany (June 25–July 31)
Despite your years of earnest effort to create a civilized and compassionate dialogue on the emotional languages of race, love, and desire, most of the universe will still insist on calling you "that one black gay weirdo."

Severian (August 1–Sept 6)
You will be unable to shake a deep feeling of unutterable sadness as you roam the world with a scruffy band of misfits at the end of history, performing the occasional execution in your search for your lost mother/lover and a way to rekindle the dying sun.

Zelazny (Sept 7–Oct. 13)
Even if you do find their unique combination of style, universal competence, ennui, and raw ambition strangely exhilarating, you'd probably be a lot happier if you stopped keeping company with suicidal types, immortals, and suicidal immortal types.

Kirbii: (Oct. 14–Nov. 20)
You will be unable to shake the feeling that society at large would be improved by even more chunky, quasi-cubist levitating machinery of mystic origin, as well as the increased use of triple exclamation points by the general populace.

Bester (Nov. 21–Jan. 1)
Prepare for major life changes this week, Bester. You will achieve great commercial success, vast literary acclaim, and a premature death while completing your magnum opus **The Bars My Destination: A Guide To All 24 Hours Of Orbital Nightlife.**

REMAINING-WORLD NEWS

Leather-Clad Nomads Seize Power In Australia

CANBERRA, AUSTRALIA—Following months of terror at the hands of hot-rod-piloting punks, Australian Prime Minister Kellen O'Neill handed power to Lord Humongous, nominal warlord of the leather-clad marauding barbarian horde Monday. "Just walk away!" said Humongous, the official "Ayatollah of Rock 'n' Roll-ah," speaking through his vehicle's PA system from the smoking ruins of the city center. "I will spare those of you who surrender your possessions and your precious juice. Just walk away, and live." Humongous is expected to share at least a portion of his dominion over Australia with midget genius The Master, who several sources said "runs Bartertown."

the ONION®

VOLUME 41 ISSUE 26 AMERICA'S FINEST NEWS SOURCE™ 30 JUNE–6 JULY 2005

NEWS

Rookie NASCAR Driver Gets Lost

see SPORTS page 1C

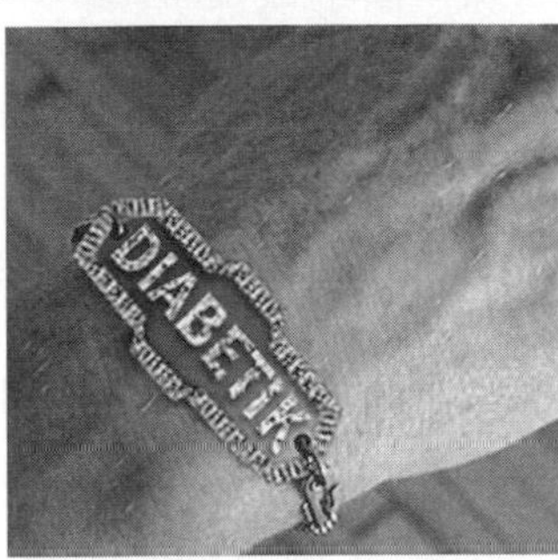

MedicAlert Bracelet Iced Out

see HEALTH page 11B

Recently Discovered Egyptian Tomb Sure Smells Like Mummies

see SCIENCE page 11D

Cycle Of Violence Running Smoothly

see WORLD page 8G

STATshot

A look at the numbers that shape your world.

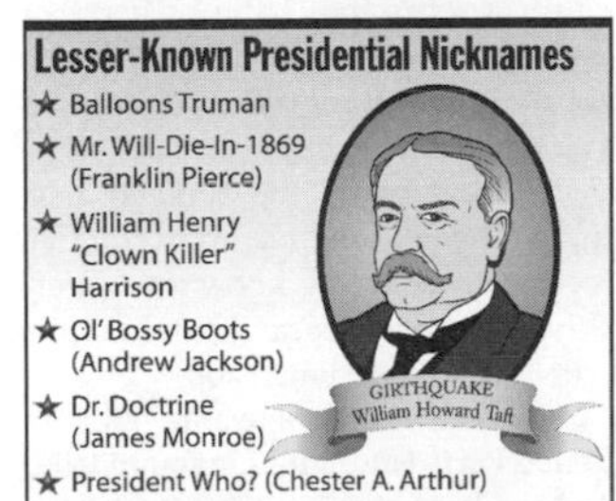

Lesser-Known Presidential Nicknames
★ Balloons Truman
★ Mr. Will-Die-In-1869 (Franklin Pierce)
★ William Henry "Clown Killer" Harrison
★ Ol' Bossy Boots (Andrew Jackson)
★ Dr. Doctrine (James Monroe)
★ President Who? (Chester A. Arthur)
GIRTHQUAKE
William Howard Taft

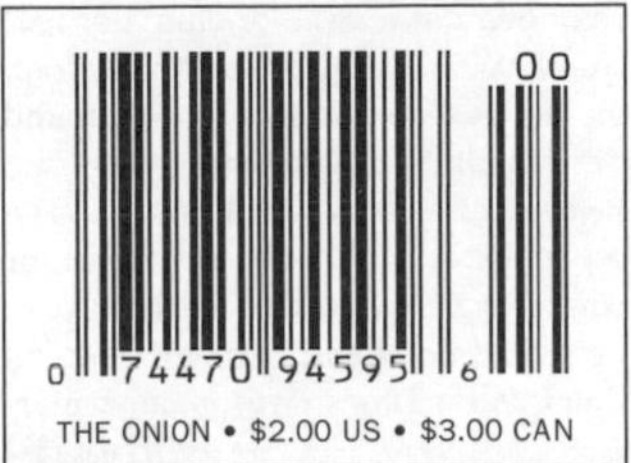

0 74470 94595 6

Vatican Tightens Nocturnal Emissions Standards

VATICAN CITY—The Vatican has released a strict new set of Church laws intended to reduce the nocturnal emissions of teenage polluters by 50 percent in the next decade, Cardinal Antoni Bertoli announced Monday.

Above: Cardinal Bertoli.

"In the past 10 years, unholy emissions from young men have risen by 150 million cubic centimeters, releasing erotic-dream byproducts into the bedsheet environment," Bertoli said. "The accumulation of pollutants from millions of individual violators around the world is having a devastating effect on the moral atmosphere."

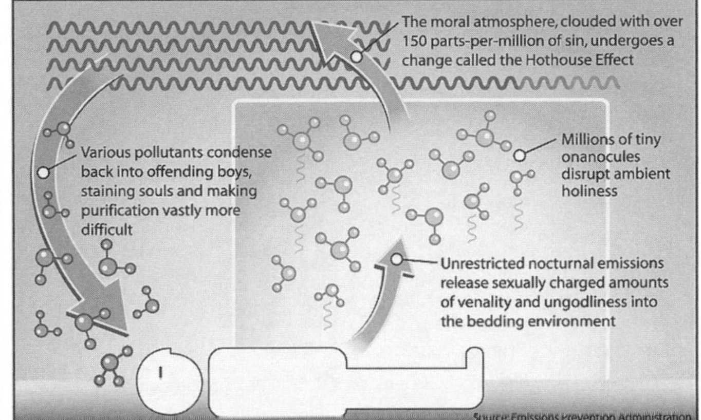

Various pollutants condense back into offending boys, staining souls and making purification vastly more difficult
Millions of tiny onanocules disrupt ambient holiness
Unrestricted nocturnal emissions release sexually charged amounts of venality and ungodliness into the bedding environment

Vatican scientists believe the increase in emissions contributes to the Hothouse Effect, a steady rise in the overall temperature of the average Catholic male's genitals.

"Unchecked, we will soon reach a crisis point that no amount of will power can contain," Bertoli said.

Catholic males have long been subject to purity standards set by the 15th book of Leviticus, which states that "when any man has a discharge from his member, his member makes him ceremonially unclean." Prior to

see VATICAN page 184

Food-Court Taco Bell Not As Good, Area Man Reports

ERIE, PA—Fast-food consumer Don Turnbee announced Monday that the Taco Bell in the Millcreek Mall food court is "not as good" as regular, full-service Taco Bell restaurants.

Turnbee, a frequent patron of the full-service Taco Bell on Buffalo Road, encountered the scaled-down version of the Mexican-style franchise Sunday afternoon while waiting for his wife Shelly to complete her shopping.

"It was so-so," Turnbee told reporters outside the mall. "It's not as nice as the one I usually go to. This one had tacos and burritos, but no Double Decker Tacos."

Unlike a regular Taco Bell, the Millcreek Taco Bell Express has a reduced menu that does not offer many of the choices or add-on op-

see TACO BELL page 185

Above: Veteran fast-food patron Don Turnbee.

Us Quarterly

US QUARTERLY AUGUST 2005 $12.95

Lawrence Weschler on Jessica Simpson and Nick Lachey

New *Us Quarterly* To Explore Celebrity Issues In More Depth

NEW YORK—Describing it as a "discerning and literary companion" to their flagship entertainment-news magazine, Us Weekly editor-in-chief Janice Min announced on Tuesday the creation of *Us Quarterly*, a scholarly, four-times-yearly journal dedicated to sizzling-hot celebrity gossip.

The quarterly will feature in-depth essays, investigative pieces, and expert commentary on Hollywood's hottest megastars.

"Due to the demands of weekly publication, [*Us Weekly*] was only able to scratch the surface," said Min, who is helming the offshoot publication. "The quarterly is a dream come true for the more serious-minded star-watcher, who enjoys pictorials showcasing Mary-Kate Olsen's club-hopping wardrobe, but craves a more critical examination of her hottest boots."

Min estimated that the first issue

see US QUARTERLY page 185

Left: The premiere issue of Us Quarterly.

Bolton's UN Nomination

The Senate continues to debate John Bolton's nomination for UN ambassador, with Bush threatening to appoint him in spite of their concerns. What do *you* think?

"Man, if the Democrats are going to block every terrible idea Bush has, nothing's ever going to get done in Washington."

Mindy Biancardi
Designer

"Appointing Bolton to the UN is like appointing a fish to ride a bicycle that he hates and wishes to destroy."

Seth Johnson
Systems Analyst

"He may look gruff, but I'm sure he's quite warm and grandfatherly once you get to know him. We're talking about Wilford Brimley, right?

David Wilcox
Desk Clerk

"It's amazing! I've been following this story from day one, and I still don't give a shit."

Kevin Mouton
Sportscaster

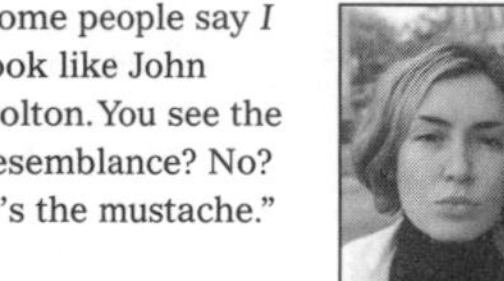

"Some people say *I* look like John Bolton. You see the resemblance? No? It's the mustache."

Brian Dixon
Optician

"All these problems stem from the Bush Administration's refusal to hand over documents requested from them. Isn't about time we outlaw documents?"

Kim Murillo
Fire-Alarm Installer

Alternative Summer Camps

Parents and their children have an increasing variety of specialized summer camps to choose from. What are some of the most popular ones?

- Camp Connection: Where each child is given a laptop and set free in a wireless-enabled forest setting
- Camp Revelation: Where children are put at enormous risk repeatedly, until they accept Jesus and are born again, at which point they are allowed to go home
- Camp Night Raven: Kids learn about nature and wildlife through the bastardized teachings and barely recognizable rituals of the Native American peoples
- Camp Camino Del Taco: Children learn about a fascinating culture, its delicious foodstuffs, how to make correct change, and how to clean up afterward
- Camp Jerky Boys: Kids study the vocal stylings and practical jokes that made the Jerky Boys famous
- Camp Longnight: Where kids spend the hours between sunset and sunrise evading predatory screech owls
- Gordo Sutter's Hockey Fantasy Camp: The sports camp where kids help hockey coaches' dreams come true

the ONION®
America's Finest News Source.™

Herman Ulysses Zweibel
Founder

T. Herman Zweibel
Publisher Emeritus
J. Phineas Zweibel
Publisher
Maxwell Prescott Zweibel
Editor-In-Chief

I'm In The Throes Of Summer Movie Madness!

Item! Summer movie season is here, so forward my mail to my local theater, because I'm going to be losing myself in air-conditioned Hollywood magic for the next three months—especially since there's nothing on TV but reruns and second-string reality series. So, grab some popcorn, pull down a center seat, and dim the lights, because my annual guide to the hottest summer movie tickets is here!

The Outside Scoop
By Jackie Harvey

Item! What do you get when you combine **J. Lo** and **J. Fo**? Troub-o! The movie is **Monster-In-Laws**, and it finally answers the question, "What happens when you have to meet the mother-in-law… from hell?" It's a lot like Meet The Parents but better, with snappier snaps and twice the star wattage. (Sorry, **Bobby DeNero**—you're great, but you're no match for a tag-team powerhouse like Jane-ifer.) It's the perfect movie for anyone who gets a case of the **Runaway Bride** jitters when it comes to meeting the in-laws.

Item! I had planned to see **Fever Pitch**, the movie about love and baseball starring **Jimmy Ferrell** and dreamy **Drew Barrymore**, but I had a lot of things going on, and I totally spaced it. When I finally headed out to my local multiplex to give it a once over, I found out it wasn't playing anymore. What kind of world do we live in when a Drew Barrymore movie isn't given a chance to breathe? I ended up seeing **The Sisterhood Of The Raveling Pants**. You can read the review on my blog, but if you can't wait, let me just say that the *Pants* fit me just fine.

Item! Has super socialite and ingénue Paris Hilton finally found love? Not the kind that lasts for two weeks and then vanishes when she spots a sexy beau at a swanky club, but real true love? Judging by the happy look on her face, Paris has finally found her equal!

Item! Batman is back, and battier than before. **Batman Again** takes place years before the previous Batfilms, so **Bruce Wayne** doesn't look anything like **George Clooney**, and his nipples are smaller. Besides that, **Liam Nissan** reprises his role as the wizened guru **Qui-Ginn** from **Star Wars**. This crossover flick should have both films' fans running—or should I say flapping!—to the box office.

It's a shame actor **Caesar Romeo**, who played TV's Batman, wasn't alive to see the new movie. He died recently, his lungs riddled with cancer. Go softly into that good night, Mr. Romeo.

Item! Teen queen **Lindsay Loman** had a brush with tragedy—literally!—when an overzealous paparazzo smashed into her car last week.

Hey, what ever happened to the war on drugs? Ever since the war on terror, I haven't heard anything about it.

Things like this really shake me to the core and make me stop and wonder if it's all worth it. I mean, I love celebrities—so much so that I've made reporting on them my life's work—but photographers, I ask you, aren't you taking things too far when you jeopardize the safety of your own bread and butter? I am referring to the stars. But then, I wonder... Am I, as an entertainment journalist, feeding the public's ravenous appetite for more celebrity? Sometimes it makes me want to retire, but I think I'd rather use my power for good, like Batman. So, don't ram stars with your cars, all you crazy shutterbugs.

Oh boy, turn up the summer heat and you can't drag me away from an **ice-cream float**. You know my secret? Strawberry ice cream. It puts you in a whole new float dimension.

Item! Has super socialite and ingénue **Paris Hilton** finally found love? Not the kind that lasts for two weeks and then vanishes when she spots a sexy beau at a swanky club, but real true love? Judging by the happy look on her face, Paris has finally found her equal! And how appropriate that her soulmate is named **Paris**, too. The other Paris is Greek or Italian or something, and, as luck would have it, he's rich! Paris and Paris (or as I call them, **Paris Times Two**) make a mar-

see HARVEY page 184

New Dad Thinks Baby Might Be Gay

SCOTTSDALE, AZ—Citing "something vaguely effeminate" about his eight-month-old son Michael, first-time father Joe Oebrick, 32, reported Tuesday that he suspects the infant may be a homosexual.

"I love my son," Oebrick said. "But, you understand, I'm worried, too."

Among the many "small signs" that suggest that his son may be gay, Oebrick cited a home video in which the toddler crawls across the living-room carpet of the family's suburban Scottsdale home, wiggling his hips from side to side.

> **"I don't think it's normal for a baby to move like that," said Oebrick, wincing as the infant paused and flapped an arm in the air. "Don't you think that's a little strange?"**

"I don't think it's normal for a baby to move like that," said Oebrick, wincing as the infant paused and flapped an arm in the air. "Don't you think that's a little strange?"

According to Oebrick, Michael has an excessive fondness for bright colors and "things that sparkle."

"Sequins, glitter, feathers," said the recent father, listing some of the things that Michael likes. "And he *really* likes flowers."

According to Oebrick, Michael is fussy during meals and picky about his clothes. When he hurts himself, he "cries like a baby." Additionally, the toddler has a "very strong attraction" to a stuffed lion with a rainbow-striped mane, an apparent preference for bottle-feeding over breastfeeding, and an evident love for bouncing up and down in his jumper device "like some guy at a club."

New to parenting, Oebrick said he is "plagued" by demanding responsibilities, unexpected expenses, and "a million tiny things" that indicate that his infant son might be a homosexual.

Oebrick said he doubts strangers can even tell that Michael is a boy when they first meet him, but he acknowledged that this is not his most pressing concern. According to the recent father, his most urgent concern is the confused baby's constant need to suck on a pacifier.

"That can't be right. Can it?" Oebrick said.

Oebrick said he first began to worry about Michael's sexual orientation when the boy was two months old.

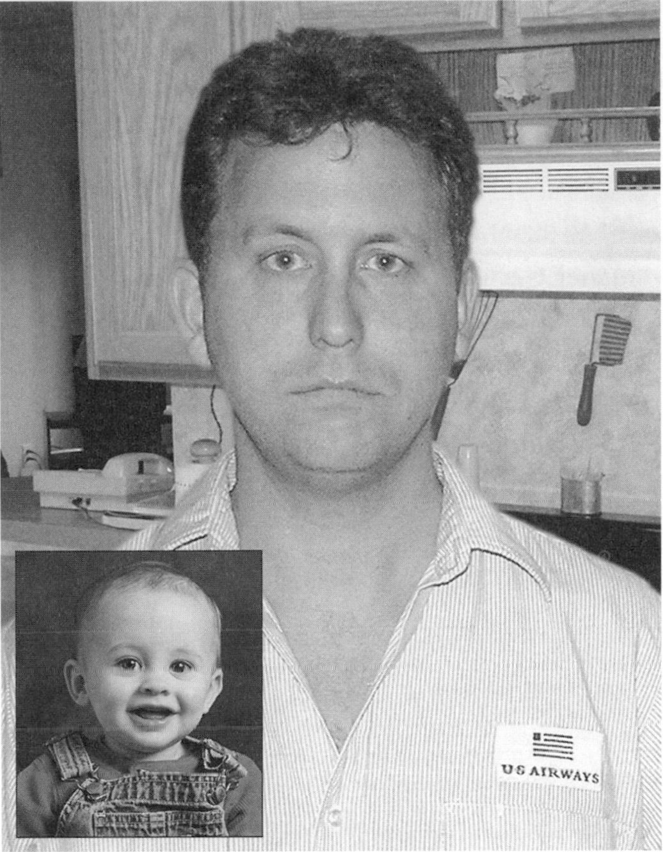

Above: Oebrick and his possibly gay infant son Michael (inset).

"He would giggle constantly," Oebrick said. "And he had a very weak handshake."

Oebrick recalled the first time he saw his newborn child smile.

"Obviously, I was thrilled," Oebrick said. "But the thing is, he kept on smiling. He'd smile through breakfast, he'd smile in his car seat, he'd smile at strangers. It was excessive. It was around then I started to think, 'What if Michael can't help himself?'"

According to Oebrick, there were several months during which the infant's head would wobble if it wasn't supported by an adult.

"He was always swinging his head

see GAY BABY page 186

NEWS IN BRIEF

Fifth Baby Barely Showered

ALCOVA, WY—Attendees at the weekend shower for Peggy Walgraeve's fifth child agreed that the event paled when compared to the showers thrown for Walgraeve's four other children. "For [first child] Ashley, they had bacon wraps and mini quiches and wine coolers, but this time it was beer and Fritos, and everyone was out the door by 2 o'clock," said Lilly Gussman, one of three guests. Walgraeve's husband Dan watched TV in the living room throughout the celebration, though he was reportedly seen glancing at the partygoers on occasion.

Dead iPod Remembered As Expensive

VENTURA, CA—A third-generation, 30-GB iPod, serial number AP356372, died early Monday morning at age 2. "I'll never forget all the great music it used to play during my workouts," said the late iPod's owner Sarah Zartman at a brief memorial held over the junk drawer. "It was convenient, portable, and really pricey—almost $500." Zartman said that, had she known the iPod's lithium-ion battery would have such a short lifespan, she might have spent more time listening to it. AP356372 is survived by a BlackBerry.

Block Of Commercials Charts The Who's Career Arc

NEW YORK—According to TV viewer Maurice Degroot, every phase of rock band The Who's career was traced by a single CBS commercial break Tuesday. "The retrospective opened with Hummer's 'Happy Jack,' one of the songs from The Who's '60s mod period," Degroot said. "Then a Saab commercial played 'I'm Free' from their ambitious rock-opera phase, followed by a promo for *CSI* featuring 'Who Are You,' one of their '70s hits." In light of the popular commercials, the surviving Who members are planning a reunion tour to perform short sections from their commercials.

Fellow Cheerleaders Rally Cheer Of Support For Recently Raped Teammate

BLOOMINGTON, IN—The Bloomington East Hawks varsity cheerleaders organized a pep rally after school Monday, in honor of a squad member who was date-raped last weekend. "R-A... P-E-D, nothing's gonna stop Su-zie. Yay, Suzie!" the squad cheered before the 1,500 students who filled the gymnasium to celebrate the victim's return to school. Rapist Fritz Hent, an East Hawks linebacker, will sit out the first game of the season as punishment.

Man Cites Nature As Inspiration For Random Cruelty

GAINESVILLE, FL—Local resident Stephen Nicolai, 34, said Monday that the harsh realities of the natural world are what inspire him to commit spontaneous acts of brutal sadism. "Nature, red in tooth and claw, destroys without prejudice or regard for feelings, and since I am at one with nature, so too shall I," said Nicolai as he flattened a tree frog with a ball-peen hammer. "When I witness the awesome force of a tsunami, or the shift of a tectonic plate, or even a kitten mercilessly taunting its prey before eating it, I know that I am in harmony with nature." Nicolai said he has found peace through his ritual animal torture and vicious braining of random passersby. ⌀

VATICAN from page 181

the new restrictions, a polluter who did not voluntarily comply with the regulation was required to bathe his body in fresh water, count seven days

The Vatican plans to establish VBPB agencies in all major cities to monitor ejaculators, and has decreed that Catholic males between the ages of 12 and 19 will undergo regular nocturnal-emissions tests in the form of laundry monitoring.

for his cleansing, and on the eighth day take two turtledoves to his priest for an offering.

But in recent years, these so-called Clean Sheets Regulations have begun to draw criticism from Church hard-liners, because enforcement of the laws relies largely on self-policing.

"In this day and age, shame alone is no longer adequate to deter emitters," Boston's Father Antonio Luigi said. "Year after year, the worst polluters consistently go unpunished, leaving others to clean up the mess. Unless we start to actively regulate abuses, boys will have no incentive to curb their outputs."

Bertoli said a newly created Vatican Bedroom Purity Board will be responsible for enforcing the tougher

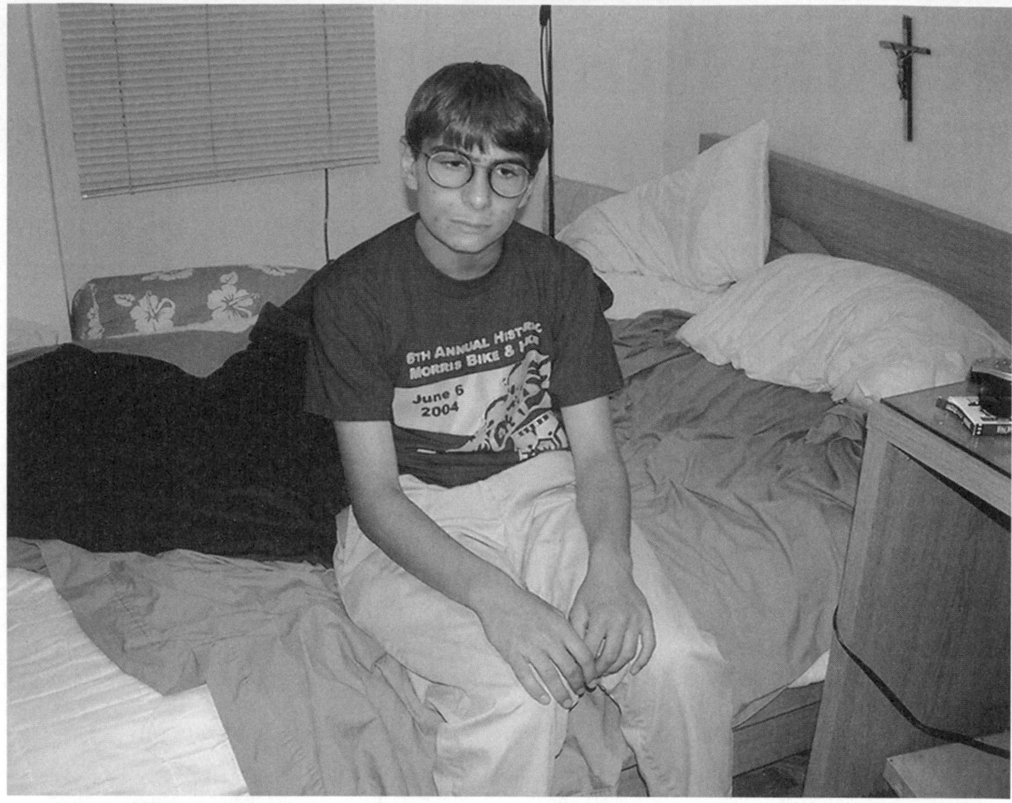

Above: Known nocturnal emitter Chad Severson.

standards. Made up of experts in an array of fields including physiology, psychology, and canon law, the ecumenical council will also conduct research into the causes of self-pollution.

The Vatican plans to establish VBPB agencies in all major cities to monitor ejaculators, and has decreed that Catholic males between the ages of 12 and 19 will undergo regular nocturnal-emissions tests in the form of laundry monitoring.

According to Bertoli, violators who soil their linens more than once per month will be subject to strict punishments, including mandatory confessionals, and fines of up to 20,000 Hail Marys per year.

Polluters who attempt to cover up evidence of their nocturnal crimes by hiding their sheets in the back of the closet will be sentenced to up to 30 minutes of the silent treatment from their mothers.

Males of ejaculatory age who fail to meet the new standards will be outfitted with Catholytic converters, which attach directly to the genitals during sleep and curb nocturnal emissions by reducing the temperature of the reproductive organs.

According to Cardinal Roger M. Mahony, archbishop of Los Angeles, the new laws will have wide-reaching implications for bedrooms in his diocese.

"These standards are going to be very hard to meet, especially in cities like L.A., where the warm temperatures and humid ocean fronts encourage women to walk around wearing next to nothing," Mahony said. "Rather than setting up impossible objectives and then punishing those who fail to reach them, officials should reward compliance. For example, local church officials could offer monetary incentives or baseball-game tickets to young men who willingly take steps to reduce their emissions."

Critics of the new regulations say that focusing solely on nocturnal emitters punishes the victims, ignoring the true perpetrators of impure-thought pollution.

"The real culprits behind bedsheet contamination are the reckless members of the dream-manufacturing industry, such as HBO, the *Sports Illus-*

"Rather than setting up impossible objectives and then punishing those who fail to reach them, officials should reward compliance. For example, local church officials could offer monetary incentives or baseball-game tickets to young men who willingly take steps to reduce their emissions."

trated Swimsuit Calendar, and Mary Antonioni, the busty brunette who sits in the front row of Sister Francesca's sixth-period health class at St. Mary's Junior High in Fayetteville, IL," said Mother Superior Katherine Calahan. "We need anti-temptation regulations that focus on dress conservation. Let's require girls to wear less make-up, flatter shoes, and just put some clothes on, for God's sake." Ø

HARVEY from page 182

velous couple, and I wish them many happy returns.

Hey, what ever happened to the **war on drugs**? Ever since the **war on terror**, I haven't heard anything about it. Just because we have other problems, we shouldn't stop worrying about the scourge of the streets.

Item! Did they or didn't they? That's the question on everyone's minds as they watch **Mr. And Mrs. Smith**. Well, I have it on good authority that they did... entertain everyone with their exciting new flick! But seriously now, **Brad** and **Angie** said there was nothing going on during filming, so let's give them the benefit of the doubt. Don't they have a right to peace when they show up at premieres, or go on TV to promote the movie?

I got a complaint recently that I haven't been delivering on the hot gossip like I used to. Well, it's gotten harder than ever, because every time you think you have an exclusive, the Internet is three steps ahead of you. Not anymore! I promise you that, beginning next column, I will be back in full form, digging up the filthiest dirt in places no one else will look, all within my new parameters of respecting the people—and they are *people*!—I'm covering. Until then, I'm out of space, so join me next time for a

Item! Did they or didn't they? That's the question on everyone's minds as they watch *Mr. And Mrs. Smith*. Well, I have it on good authority that they did...

juicy little story I've been digging up on **Mayim Bialik**. Until then, I'll see you... on The Outside. Ø

US QUARTERLY from page 181

of *Us Quarterly*, slated to debut in August, will be 300 pages long. It will feature a thoughtful analysis of Lindsay Lohan's troubles on the set of *Herbie: Fully Loaded*, a Michael Cunningham short story inspired by the

> **"In the new format, our stalwart regulars—fashion experts, professional gossips, and drag queens—will match wits with some of our nation's most prominent intellectual commentators."**

TV season's nastiest celebrity feuds, and a 20-page treatise from Oxford literary critic John Bayley mapping Ben Affleck and Jennifer Garner's romantic midnight stroll on a Malibu beach.

The quarterly will be a radical departure from the magazine's largely visual format.

"The new *Us* editorial direction moves away from splashy paparazzi photos with brief captions toward food-for-thought essays, in-depth investigative pieces, and transcribed roundtable discussions," said *Adweek* media reporter Donna Boorstin. "They'll cover everything from Nikki Hilton's Vegas weekend blowup to Sandra Bullock's surprise summer wedding with bad-boy Jesse James."

While small pointillist illustrations will accompany the pieces, the majority of the publication will be textual.

Said Boorstin: "For regular *Us* readers who may have trouble picturing this new format, try to think of how, in a romance paperback, the words build into continuous paragraphs, and you have to read them all in order to know what is happening. That's what *Us Quarterly* will look like."

Above: Noted scholar Albert C. Wittingham joined Paris Hilton at an Us Quarterly panel discussion held at a Middlebury Writers' Seminar Sunday to discuss celebrity panty lines.

Us Quarterly will expand some of *Us Weekly's* most popular features, such as the back-page "Fashion Police," but Min will assign some new cops to the beat.

"We've reworked the section into a 'fashion roundtable,'" Min said. "In the new format, our stalwart regulars—fashion experts, professional gossips, and drag queens—will match wits with some of our nation's most prominent intellectual commentators."

"The results are quite lively," Min added.

In the first quarterly "Fashion Police," an unflattering dress worn by Brittany Murphy united panel members, earning catcalls ranging from Fagatha Christie's "*Sin City* had more color than this frumpy frock" to Lewis Lapham's "This is *the* jejune raiment of imperial excess." However, celebrity stylist Margo Fischer and writer Joyce Carol Oates were divided over Kirsten Dunst's gown at a recent charity benefit for autism. Fischer said "this nightmare in distressed pink muslin would make *me* withdraw," but Oates defended Dunst, describing the starlet as "a lovely Miss Haversham on her wedding day, the groom's absence as yet unremarked, her heart un-

> **"The quarterly is a dream come true for the more serious-minded star-watcher."**

touched by the impotent rage of love lost."

Us Quarterly will be available on newsstands Aug. 15th for the cover price of $13.95. ⌀

TACO BELL from page 181

tions to which Turnbee is accustomed, including the carne asada steak upgrade.

"I tried to add steak to something, and the girl got mad," Turnbee said. "I guess maybe she was tired of people ordering stuff they didn't have."

Turnbee finally settled on a Combo Burrito and a large Pepsi, but said he found the burrito's taste to be "kind of off."

"[The Combo Burrito] wasn't as good as normal," Turnbee said. "I don't know. The beef was crumbly, I guess."

"It seemed dry," he added.

Although the regular and express Taco Bells share an ingredients supplier, the dryness of Turnbee's burrito might have resulted from Taco Bell Express policy, which requires that five Combo Burritos be ready under the food lamps at lunchtime.

Turnbee's dissatisfaction also extended to the layout of the food court. Accustomed to the Buffalo Road restaurant's bright dining area with vaulted ceiling, sturdy booths, and a fully stocked napkin, condiment, and straw counter, Turnbee was dismayed

> **"It seemed like too big a production to go all the way back to the Taco Bell and ask for hot sauce."**

by the food court's long lines and ill-defined, drafty space. Forced to walk far from the Taco Bell kiosk to the other side of the packed food court, he said he was displeased by the narrow width of his table and found the chair he was sitting on rickety and unstable. Huge potted palm trees placed throughout the food court blocked Turnbee's vision and gave him a vaguely claustrophobic feeling.

"I like a booth," Turnbee said.

Turnbee also found fault with the food court's shared condiments counter, which lacked forks and hot sauce.

"I went without," Turnbee said. "It seemed like too big a production to go all the way back to the Taco Bell and ask for hot sauce."

Turnbee was disturbed by the clash of food odors in the dining area. Seated next to a shopper who had ordered from Wok 'n' Roll, a Chinese-food vendor, Turnbee found that the odor of broccoli interfered with the taste of his burrito.

"I don't like broccoli, and I didn't like having to smell it while I was trying to eat," Turnbee said. "They should divide the dining area into different sections so people who order from different stalls don't eat together."

Turnbee's 20-minute ordeal ended when his wife Shelly discovered him behind a large potted palm.

"Shelly was mad that I ate when I knew she was defrosting steaks for dinner," Turnbee said. "I didn't argue."

Turnbee discarded the remainder of his burrito and soda, something the veteran fast-food patron "doesn't normally do," according to wife Shelly.

"Don doesn't normally like to come with me to the mall, either, but he likes this type of sock they sell at Sears," Shelly said.

Turnbee said that, while he has no plans to eat at the mall Taco Bell in the near future, a return visit is not out of the question.

"I guess I'd probably eat there again, if push came to shove and there was no other Taco Bell around," Turnbee said. ⌀

COMMUNITY VOICES

I Must Regretfully Decline Your Invitation To Appear In Court On July 28

Dear Office of the Clerk,

I was pleased to receive your gracious request for my presence at the small get-together to be held in your exalted halls on Thursday the 28th of July. Be assured that I was grateful for the warm tidings offered by you, the Wapello County Sheriff's Department, and please know I am fully aware of your overflowing social calendar. Therefore, it is with no small sense of remorse, particularly in light of the many previous engagements of ours that I have had cause to break, that I must regretfully decline your invitation.

By Shane M. Ridenhauer

Gentlemen and ladies, do not for one moment imagine that I am unaware of the lengths to which you have surely gone in this matter. I am humbled to think of the many uniformed servants you have sent zigzagging back and forth over the tri-county area, merely to deliver my invitation—especially considering that I have relocated frequently in recent months, and have even been without a proper address for weeks at a time.

I would love to attend your criminal hearing! If not for several pressing personal matters, I would certainly join you in court.

I feel an especial pang of regret that I will not be there to bask in the presence of the Hon. Claude Gerber, a man with whom I have passed many an engaging and stimulating afternoon.

The first of these matters is the distressing state in which I find my automobile. Were she only roadworthy, she would carry me to the scheduled proceedings with alacrity. Alas, her undercarriage blooms with cancerous expanses of rust. Her engine wheezes and coughs like an asthmatic hound. And from beneath her issues an ominous black puddle, which portends a failing transmission, a cracked block, or worse. I fear that to operate her would be to put my very life in peril!

The second personal matter precluding my acceptance of your kind invitation is, I am afraid, financial. Gentlemen, my monetary affairs are in an unfortunate state. Business responsibilities, as prominent men such as you must appreciate, must supercede all social niceties, and, to be perfectly frank, it is presently beyond my means to attend even to those. In fact, I believe my colleague, Mr. Dutch Haney, who by no small coincidence is mentioned prominently and repeatedly in the documents summoning my presence, is a mutual acquaintance of ours. Knowing, as you must, Mr. Haney's rather coarse fixation on compensation for damages to personal property, and my sensitivity to baseness of any sort, my reluctance to attend your gathering requires no further elucidation.

Gentlemen, my monetary affairs are in an unfortunate state.

I feel an especial pang of regret that I will not be there to bask in the presence of the Hon. Claude Gerber, a man with whom I have passed many an engaging and stimulating afternoon—a true gentlemen, that one, a true character. I hoped with all my heart he did not mean it when he said he never wished for me darken his door again, and I take this invitation as evidence my hopes were not in vain.

And Officer Schepke... Fair, fair Lilly Schepke. You were meant for gentler things than to stand to the right and chuckle over tired old anecdotes—as well as charges of grand larceny, grand theft auto, public drunkenness, domestic assault, and discharging a firearm within city limits.

No, perhaps it is for the best. How quickly you would grow tired of me, I'm sure, were I to surrender to self-indulgence and the court-appointed bailiff the morning of July 28. I would certainly bore you, or worse yet, etiquette would require that I remain in your company for not less than five nor more than seven years.

I will, therefore, take my leave; I assure you, gentles, that the disappointment is all mine.

Sincerely,
Shane M. Ridenhauer

HOROSCOPES

Your Horoscope

By Lloyd Schumner Sr.
Retired Machinist and
A.A.P.B.-Certified Astrologer

Aries: (March 21–April 19)
You will be awoken nightly between 2 and 4 a.m., by a friend who used to be cool but now just wants to talk about how 'Til Tuesday was an underrated band.

Taurus: (April 20–May 20)
When he said, "It bears, as in a nightmare one bears the impossible and finds no deliverance," Rilke was talking about Rodin's "Fallen Caryatid," but if you want to use that quote to talk about your foot pain, no one can stop you.

Gemini: (May 21–June 21)
Your fate will be influenced by nostalgic cosmic forces this week, when Castor, one of Gemini's formative stars, takes this week off to attend his high school's 10 billion year reunion.

Cancer: (June 22–July 22)
You lack initiative, which means that you usually wait until someone yells "Get funky!" before you get funky.

Leo: (July 23–Aug. 22)
You won't listen to the many people who tell you that your lover is bad for you until it's too late and you're almost completely finished devouring his corpse.

Virgo: (Aug. 23–Sept. 22)
Like the broader American pop culture, you are fascinated with prison life, but this will change as soon as you're condemned to three consecutive life sentences.

Libra: (Sept. 23–Oct. 23)
You try to keep an open mind, but you're pretty sure there's no way that a damn cat could have helped solve over 30 capital crimes.

Scorpio: (Oct. 24–Nov. 21)
You're not all that angry that someone put that video of you being hit by a bus, attacked by a bear, and stabbed with scissors on the Internet, but for them to set it to Limp Bizkit's "Break Stuff" is just wrong.

Sagittarius: (Nov. 22–Dec. 21)
The good news is that you're finally getting as much sex as you want. The bad news is that it's a kind of sex you always wanted to avoid if at all possible.

Capricorn: (Dec. 22–Jan. 19)
The authorities have not given your lost love up for dead quite yet. They have reason to believe that she's in Duluth, though, which you must admit is pretty much the same thing.

Aquarius: (Jan. 20–Feb. 18)
You are, of course, given the right to the pursuit of happiness, but there's nothing to prevent others from aiding and abetting your happiness in its desperate attempt to escape you.

Pisces: (Feb. 19–March 20)
You used to compare yourself to Icarus, but you're less likely to do so now that you know he once helped a woman cheat on her husband by having sex with a cow.

GAY BABY from page 183

around," Oebrick said. "Our pediatrician told me it was normal, but it seemed pretty... well, gay."

Oebrick's worries were renewed last month during a Memorial Day cookout, when Michael "seemed too interested in my buddies," staring at them for long intervals.

"My friend Ben was bouncing Michael on his knee, and he was giggling and drooling like crazy," Oebrick said. "That didn't bother me so much, but when Ben put him down, Michael started crawling after every other guy at the party, giggling and grabbing at their pants legs like crazy."

"It was like he was the belle of the ball," Oebrick said. "When Rob played peek-a-boo with him, he got so excited he actually wet his pants."

Oebrick repeatedly said that, no matter what his son's sexual orientation, he refuses to be a "distant father."

"My dad was rarely around," Oebrick said. "He was always either working or drinking with his buddies, and that left my mom to raise me and my sisters. It won't be like that for Michael. He'll have a strong male role model. It looks like he's really gonna need it."

Oebrick's worries were renewed last month during a Memorial Day cookout, when Michael "seemed too interested in my buddies."

the ONION®

VOLUME 41 ISSUE 29 AMERICA'S FINEST NEWS SOURCE™ 21–27 JULY 2005

NEWS

Bush Awaits Orders From Rove On Handling Of Rove Scandal

see NATIONAL page 6A

Which Jackson Will Dominate Next Year's Headlines?

see ARTS page 1C

Terri Schiavo's Corpse Blown Away By Hurricane

see LOCAL page 18A

STATshot

A look at the numbers that shape your world.

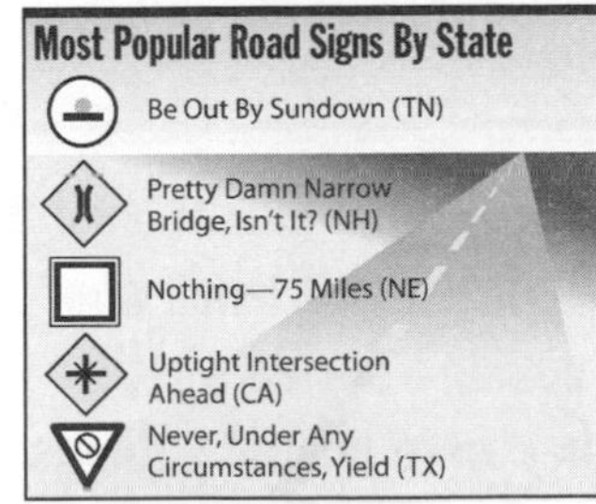

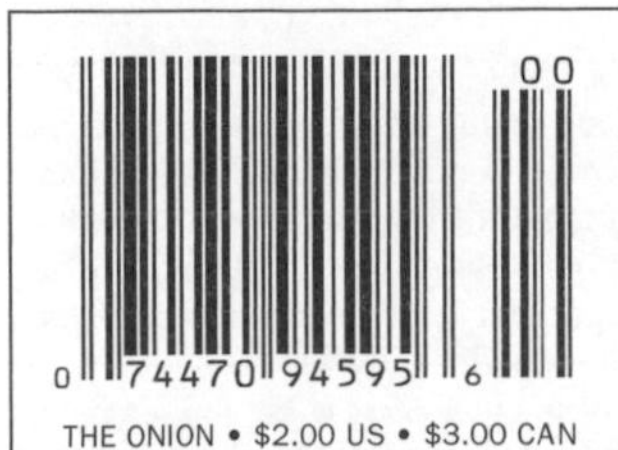

New Puppy Teaches Congress Important Lesson About Responsibility

Above: a bipartisan commission of legislators holds Buster on the Senate floor.

WASHINGTON, DC—Beltway insiders report that Buster, the 7-month-old yellow Labrador Congress was allowed to keep amid much controversy last spring, has taught the nation's legislators some valuable lessons about responsibility.

"The skeptics believed that the House and Senate weren't ready for a puppy," Senate Majority Leader Bill Frist (R-TN) said. "They believed we wouldn't be able to maintain America's defenses, regulate commerce, and pass laws while raising Buster. But we have proven them wrong. We feed him and walk him every day."

Frist referred to a bicameral duty roster ratified Jan. 31.

"Congress knows who's supposed to take Buster when," Frist said. "If it's your turn to walk him and he's found tied to a handrail outside the U.S. Capitol, you're in serious trouble."

U.S. citizens initially questioned Congress' ability to care for a pet.

"It's a serious responsibility to have someone depending on you," Seattle voter Elaine Schermer said. "Given the two parties' fractious relationship and constant bickering, I didn't think they were ready."

Although a Gallup poll showed that 63 percent of American voters were "unsure" Congress was ready for a puppy, Vice President Dick Cheney al-

see PUPPY page 190

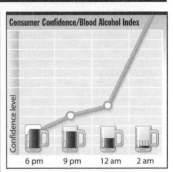

Consumer Confidence/Blood Alcohol Index

Confidence level

6 pm 9 pm 12 am 2 am

Alcoholic-Beverage-Consumer Confidence Skyrockets

NEW YORK—Alcoholic-beverage-consumer confidence hit a record high Friday between the hours of 5 p.m. and 3 a.m., briefly reaching 105.3 points before dropping to 94.2 at last call.

"Weekend market conditions were extremely favorable for cash/beverage trading," said Byron Seidler of the Board of Alcohol Consumption and Expenditure. "Drinkers' confidence in the strength of the dollar, in their attractiveness to the opposite sex—even in their dart-playing abilities—rose sharply."

The last time the Alcoholic-Beverage-Consumer Confidence Index spiked this dramatically was exactly one week earlier during the same time period.

Several market sectors reflected the spike, with beverage consumers' confidence surging in dancing, aptitude for bar trivia, and ability to drive.

see CONFIDENCE page 191

Local Company Moves Production Underseas

NEWARK, NJ—In an effort to revitalize the company after years of stagnant profits, BakeCo Inc., makers of Good Twist Pretzels and Fluffy Brand Cream Cakes, announced plans Monday to move their Newark-based production facility underseas.

"This move is long overdue," said Jeremy Helheman, vice president of marketing for BakeCo. "Many exciting possibilities lie ahead for us at the bottom of the ocean."

The 30-year-old company's new

see COMPANY page 190

Above: BakeCo's new underwater headquarters.

Hospital Infections

According to a Pennsylvania study released last week, nearly 12,000 people contracted infections during hospital stays last year. What do *you* think?

"Perhaps this problem would be solved if hospitals used a strong-smelling antiseptic and painted everything white."

Dustin Kelly
Art Teacher

"This is why I remained conscious during my hip-replacement surgery and insisted that rubber gloves were worn at all times."

Marshall Chitwood
Statistical Clerk

"Infections too, now? I thought it was bad enough when they put me in a room full of sick people, stuck me with needles, and took away my pants."

Anne Kohl
Winemaker

"A closed-off building filled with contagious people? Whose idea *were* hospitals, anyway?"

Tom Rosen
Secretary

"See, this is exactly the sort of thing that pisses off *House, M.D.* each week."

Heather Ramirez
Insurance Underwriter

"That explains why my triple-bypass surgery was done outdoors."

Douglas Hurd
Systems Analyst

Space Shuttle Delay

Last week, the scheduled launch of the space shuttle *Discovery* was aborted two hours before liftoff. What caused the delay?

- Crew members forgot to pack extra air
- Danger gauge, when tapped, went from "none" to "extreme"
- One of the astronauts was randomly flagged by security and detained for several hours before being allowed to board
- Waiting for liquid-oxygen prices to drop below $300 a barrel
- Crew grounded for sneaking girls on board
- Moody robot arm in payload bay pinching people again
- Funding ran dry in middle of countdown
- Stupid driver's-side window wouldn't roll up
- NASA remembered it really didn't have any reason to launch a shuttle into space

I'm A Fucked-Up-Chick Magnet

Hey, I don't want to brag, but when you got it, you got it. And when it comes to picking up women with severe personality disorders, I've got it.

By Dean Wiegand

Seems like whenever I'm in the same room with a sexy young nutcase looking for some hot dysfunctional action, we lock eyes and I gaze right into the twisted, abnormal recesses of her psyche, and then—bam! We make an instant, undeniable, and incredibly unhealthy connection. What can I say? When it comes to women, I'm a fucked-up-chick magnet.

I know what you're thinking: "Who is this guy to sound so full of himself?" I'm not being egotistical—it's just true. Hey, I know I'm not perfect. Who is? We've all got problems. I'm sure I've got some myself. But here's one problem I don't have: the ladies. When it comes to charming every borderline psycho in a skirt, I take second place to no man. I guess I just give off that "Hey there, pretty lady with the lifelong unresolved emotional issues" vibe. It can't be taught—you either got it or you don't. And I got it.

Lots of guys have asked for my secret, saying stuff like, "Wow, you sure can pick 'em," or "Dude, you need help."

Everywhere I go, all kinds of psychiatrically disturbed women come running—women who never got over a traumatic childhood accident, or habitually cut themselves, or slept with their stepfathers, or abuse substances while locked in self-destructive cycles of internalized loathing and rage. They just can't keep their hands off me.

It's been this way my whole life. When I was 14, I got lucky with a classmate's mom. In high school, I dated every bipolar suicide risk in town. In college, I had at least a dozen girlfriends who couldn't decide whether they were mental patients or lesbians. It's just the way it is: Deranged dolls dig me.

I don't even have to try. Maybe it's chemistry, or pheromones, or these women can tell I'm afflicted with a complementary set of psychiatric disorders and their fucked-up-female intuition just can't resist. Whatever it is, I'm not complaining. All I have to do is show up at a bar, and before last call, every damaged woman in the place will make a beeline for yours truly, looking to get me entangled in a horrific web of codependency, manipulation, and mutual denial.

The sex is great, too. Believe me, all these highly unstable women have so many self-esteem issues, identity crises, and subconscious needs for approval from absent or emotionally abusive father figures, they'll do prac-

I guess I just give off that "Hey there, pretty lady with the lifelong unresolved emotional issues" vibe.

tically anything to try to please a man, no matter how self-destructive it is. Sweet!

Take this hot little nutjob who picked me up last weekend. Talk about crazy between the sheets! She cleaned my pipes six ways from Sunday before breaking down in tears out of nowhere at 4 a.m., screaming irrational threats, and trying to throw my stereo out the second-story window. Luckily, I was able to calm her down with a little TLC—time-release lithium capsules—and get her into a cab before she caused any serious property damage. But still, she can't stay away—she's been leaving, like, eight voicemail messages an hour on my cell phone. Hey, once they get a little taste of the old Deanster, they always come back for more... even after multiple restraining orders and injunctions.

All I can do is shrug and say, "Crazy women go crazy for me."

Lots of guys have asked for my secret, saying stuff like, "Wow, you sure can pick 'em," or "Dude, you

In college, I had at least a dozen girlfriends who couldn't decide whether they were mental patients or lesbians.

need help." They can't understand how I manage to attract so many hot, wild, desperately pathological chicks. But I can't tell you my secret... It's just some kind of inexplicable magic.

Well, whatever it is, I'm enjoying every fucked-up minute of it. ⌀

LOCAL

Stay Of Execution Squandered Again

FLORENCE, AZ—James "Jimbo" Creasey, 38, a death-row inmate at Arizona State Prison Complex-Florence, said Monday that he "feels pretty lousy" about wasting his most recent stay of execution, granted April 12.

"It kinda sucks," said Creasey, who was sentenced to death in 1995 for

"When the word came down that my execution had been postponed, it seemed like I had so much time. But then, the next thing you know, two months have gone by, and you've only got a few days to live."

the murders of three Arizona State sorority girls. "When the word came down that my execution had been postponed, it seemed like I had so much time. But then, the next thing you know, two months have gone by, and you've only got a few days to live."

U.S. District Judge David Oliver granted Creasey his stay on a legal technicality five days prior to the inmate's scheduled execution date. Creasey said he neglected his unofficial plan to "pick up around his cell" and began sleeping 14 hours each day.

"I guess I could still make the most of my remaining days," Creasey said. "I could enter the prison checkers tournament, but I'll be dead before the semifinals."

Creasey said he had also intended to mail a 10-page letter to his common-law wife Doris and finish the James Clavell novel Shogun.

"It's not that I haven't enjoyed these months," Creasey said. "It's just, the time goes so fast. You end up staring at some rat running along the wall, thinking about how that rat is like you—you get lost in your thoughts,

see EXECUTION page 192

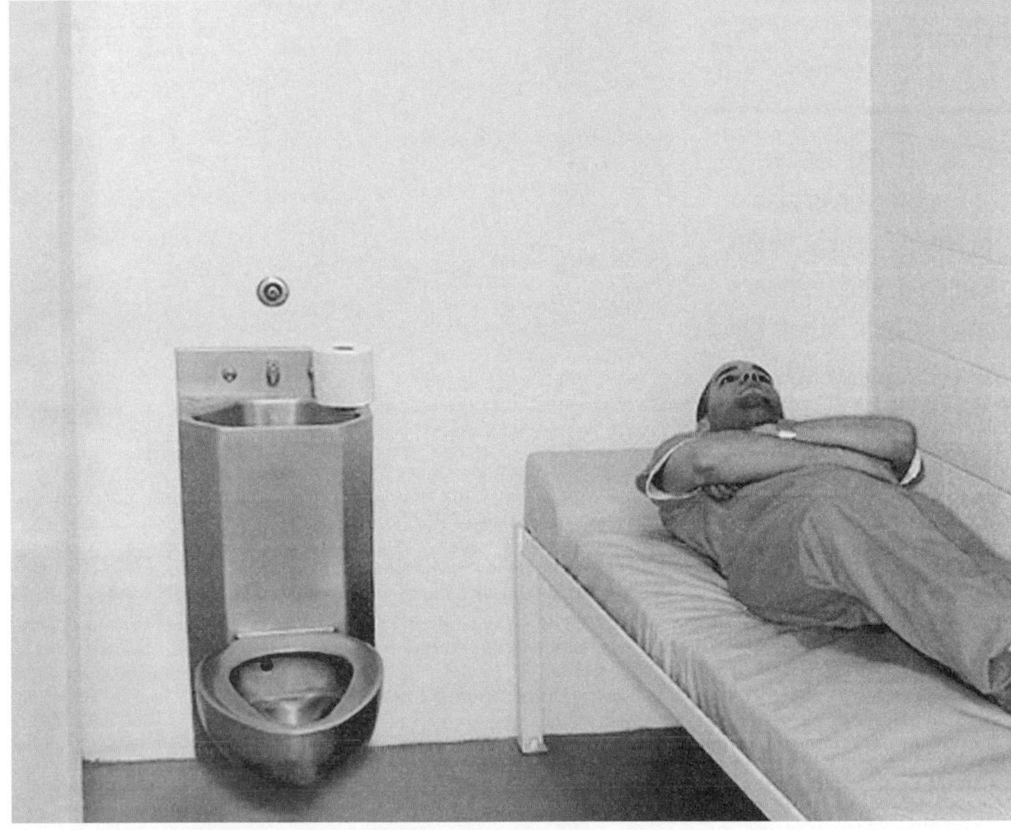

Above: Creasey in his cell, moments after receiving his most recent notice from the court.

NEWS IN BRIEF

Marine Corps Shortens Slogan To 'The Few'

WASHINGTON, DC—In light of recruiting shortfalls, a near standstill in re-enlistment, and rock-bottom troop morale, U.S. Marine Corps Commandant Gen. Michael Hagee announced Monday that the Marines will alter their unofficial slogan, abbreviating it to the more accurate "The Few." Hagee said, "We are still the Marines, the premier combat arm of the U.S. military." The Marines will also change their motto to *Semper Fidelis, Sic Non Sapienti*, or "Always Faithful, But This Is Just Ridiculous."

Fetish Only Realized After Watching Wife Drown

MEMPHIS, TN—Recent widower Jeff Dunning, 33, said Monday he experienced a "profound personal awakening" after watching his wife Claudia accidentally drown in the deep end of their swimming pool at a June 16 cocktail party. "I'll never forget how she looked," said Dunning, gazing off at the trees. "Her arms and legs flailing, her terrified expression, her mouth filling with water... It was so arousing. I mean appalling." In an attempt to cope with the realization, Dunning has taken out personal ads inquiring after single women, age 28 to 35, who enjoy swimming, boating, and binge drinking.

Man Who Lost Leg To Whale Decides To Let It Go

NEW BEDFORD, MA—Sources close to 58-year-old Samuel Rahal, a commercial fishing-boat captain who lost his right leg in a great-white-whale attack last March, announced Monday that he has put the incident behind him and is getting on with his life. "The first to guess the score of next Tuesday's Red Sox game gets this golden coin!" Rahal told his crew as he nailed a Sacagawea dollar to the cabin of his trawler. "Now, let's get this boat full of haddock so we can call it an early day." Rahal said he plans to replace his custom-made whalebone prosthesis with an OrthoPro with flex-foot and hydraulic knee.

Parasites Just Getting The Hang Of How Host Does Things

MACON, GA—Tapeworms recently introduced into Susan Rabidovitch's digestive tract will need time to get acclimated to their new environment, insiders reported Monday. "They just got set up with Susan, so now they're hanging out, getting a feel for what she likes to eat and when," Dr. Matthew Hyam said. "Soon, they'll jibe with Susan's taste for Indian food and come to expect her late-night Chunky Monkey binges, but for now, they're just gorging themselves while they learn what makes their new host tick." Hyam explained that the parasites may need a 10-week "getting to know Susan" period before beginning to release their full capacity of 50,000 eggs per day into her small intestine.

Anonymous Source: 'I'm A Cowardly Snitch'

NEW YORK—An unidentified lawyer and lobbyist revealed Monday that a "sniveling yellow streak" led him to anonymously divulge U.S. State Department misconduct. "I am a blubbering cream puff with no guts whatsoever," said the source, 44, who wished to remain anonymous. "People should know what officials are doing, but I'm a big baby, and I can't risk my job or reputation by revealing my identity." The source spoke to reporters in a dark parking garage, then disappeared into the blackness. Ø

PUPPY from page 187

lowed the legislators to keep the dog after weeks of Congress' pleading. He stressed, however, that if Congress didn't keep its promises, the dog would be taken away.

"Don't expect me to take care of that puppy for you if you lose interest in him," Cheney said. "I won't do it!"

According to sources on Capitol Hill, the "first 100 days" of house-breaking were rocky, and a minor scandal occurred March 2, when an unsupervised Buster shredded an entire file of records pertaining to the

In raising Buster, Congress has also learned lessons about compromise. Tempers flared in June, when Chief Deputy Majority Whip Eric Cantor (R-VA) suggested buying Buster a squeak toy with a bell and Rep. Harold Ford Jr. (D-TN) argued that Buster would prefer a rubber bone.

Dominican Republic-Central America-United States Free Trade Agreement.

Invoking his authority as Senate president, Cheney issued an ultimatum: "You work together to discipline Buster, or he will be taken away and given to the Department of Agriculture."

According to Majority Whip Mitch McConnell (R-KY), Cheney's words sparked immediate action.

"We learned you can't just play with Buster all the time," Russ Feingold (D-

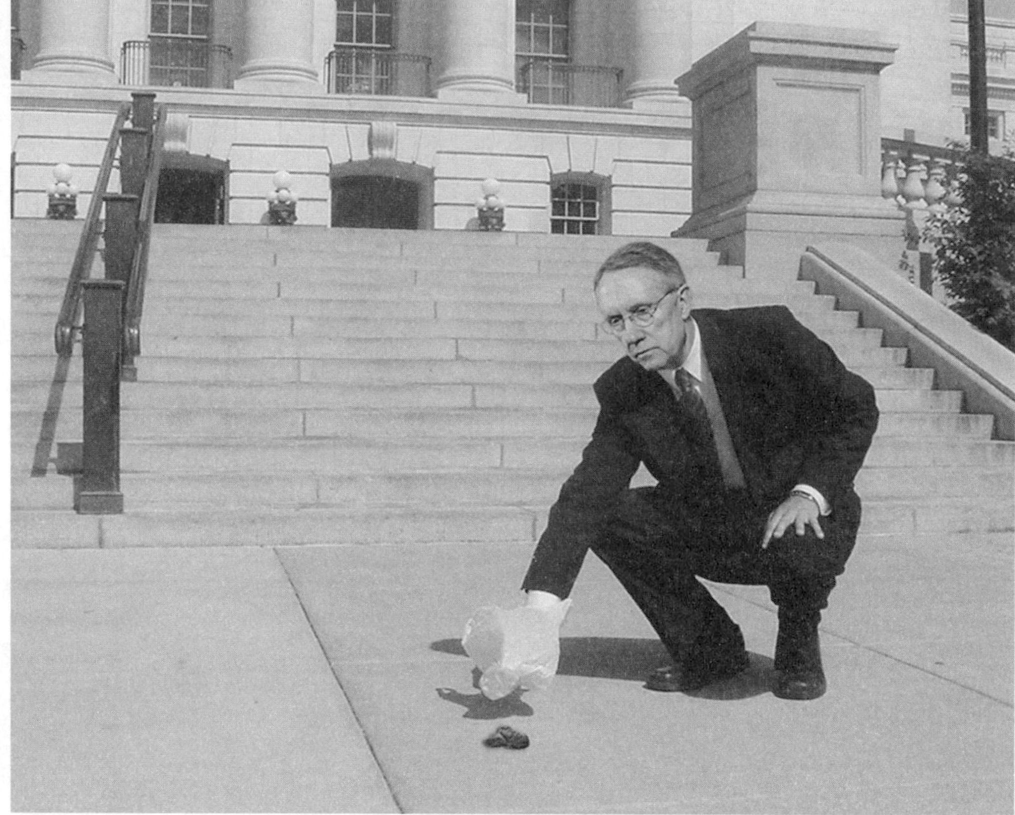

Above: Senate Minority Leader Harry Reid (D-NV) cleans the Capitol steps up after Buster.

WI) said. "It is an important job to take care of a dog, one that we must take seriously."

In raising Buster, Congress has also learned lessons about compromise. Tempers flared in June, when Chief Deputy Majority Whip Eric Cantor (R-VA) suggested buying Buster a squeak toy with a bell and Rep. Harold Ford Jr. (D-TN) argued that Buster would prefer a rubber bone. The conflict was resolved only when representatives agreed to put bipartisan bickering aside and give Buster an old piece of rope they found.

Congress learned a lesson in financial responsibility when it received an invoice from Petco in March.

"This august body has limited resources, and tough choices had to be made," Senate Budget Committee Chairman Judd Gregg (R-NH) said. "After much deliberation, it was determined we would get Buster dry food instead of soft."

The move will save taxpayers $14 a month.

Some lawmakers have attempted to use Buster for their own political gain. On July 13, Sen. Tom Harkin (D-IA) brought Buster onto the floor while arguing for a Senate amendment to H.R. 256, in the hopes that Buster's big, brown eyes would lead Senate members to vote with him.

Reflecting on the incident, Harkin said, "I realized at that moment that I was using the dog to forward my personal career. When I looked down into his big eyes, I thought, 'He deserves better from me.'"

Lessons aside, Congress said it is "elated" to have a dog.

"We love Buster," Frist said. "I believe I speak for this entire legislative body when I say he will be our very best friend forever and ever."

Citizens coast-to-coast have noticed Congress' growth in recent months.

"I think the dog has been good for the legislative branch," said Adrienne Jasper-Smith of Boulder, CO. "They're 216 years old now. It's high time they learned some responsibility." Ø

COMPANY from page 187

bakery, manufacturing center, and office complex will be located in the Atlantic Ocean, approximately 20,000 fathoms beneath the sea.

"We realized the time had come for us to manufacture and deliver snack-food convenience items from the sea floor," Helheman said. "We have a responsibility to our shareholders to remain competitive in the 21st century. And if we don't take advantage of the opportunities of an underseas operation, our competitors will."

Helheman said the company will transfer many of its 1,300 employees to the underwater production facility, a decision that has left this working-class community reeling at the prospects of an economic downturn.

"We care about the Newark community," Helheman said. "It's never an easy choice to relocate jobs to the cold, inhospitable abyss of the deep seas, but the competitive realities of the baked-goods industry leave us little choice."

Helheman predicted that BakeCo employees will come to enjoy working several miles below sea level. "Once they are trained and certified in scuba diving and learn to cohabit with humpback whales, sea urchins, and schools of beautifully colored fish, our employees are likely to treasure their wondrous new work environment," he said. "And within five short years, we should see a sharp drop in debilitating cases of the bends."

BakeCo executives assured stockholders that the move will not affect the company's popular snack-food products.

"We're not changing the taste of Good Twist Pretzels or Mini Twists that America has come to love," said

"It's never an easy choice to relocate jobs to the cold, inhospitable abyss of the deep seas, but the competitive realities of the baked-goods industry leave us little choice."

Helheman, as company representatives passed out soggy and disintegrating pretzel samples manufactured at the underseas facility. "Yes, many of the baked goods may taste a little more salty, and may also be crushed into microscopic pellets by the 7,000 pounds per square inch of water pressure that surrounds us at all times, but we will do everything we can to continue in the BakeCo tradition."

Added Helheman: "At BakeCo, even if much of our inventory will likely dissolve into a watery silt and then be devoured by sea-bed scavengers such as crabs, ling, and elephant fish, we believe quality comes first."

Executives admitted that relocating to the floor of the world's second-largest ocean does present some challenges, such as the corrosion of equipment in saltwater, coral overgrowth in offices, and the constant threat of at-

see COMPANY page 191

CONFIDENCE from page 187

Young women showed a 47 percent increase in dancing on the bar and a 31 percent increase in the slipping off of halter tops.

"I rule," said 22-year-old secondary-school teacher Kathryn Lazarus. "Turn that shit up!"

According to David Watts, a market analyst at the Federal Reserve Board, a limited regard for ensuing risk characterizes consumers with artificially elevated confidence indices.

"Decisions made during this period are historically ill-considered and often sorely regretted. Fortunately, the market often corrects itself within several hours, when alcoholic-beverage-consumer confidence shifts into lethargy, loneliness, and maudlin conversations about relationship troubles."

"The short-term gains reaped by alcohol consumers can easily lead to an atmosphere of irrational exuberance," Watts said. "Decisions made during this period are historically ill-considered and often sorely regretted. Fortunately, the market often corrects itself within several hours, when alcoholic-beverage-consumer confidence shifts into lethargy, loneliness, and maudlin conversations about relationship troubles. In severe cases, however, these spikes can trigger a depression."

Alcohol consumer Kirk Britmer of Raleigh, NC offered a detailed analysis of his weekend's spending patterns.

"I noticed an attractive woman across the bar from me. At first, I was afraid to talk to her because she was with some friends and seemed like she was doing her own thing," Britmer said. "But then at one point, she was up next to me—real close—and I offered to get her a drink. By the end of the night, I'd somehow spent $280."

Above: A group of alcohol consumers in Boston.

"You know the secret to getting women? Being a total asshole."

According to Watts, the spike in confidence led some beverage consumers, such as junior communications executive Wallace Bryan, to assume excessive risk.

"I really took a beating Friday," said Bryan, who lost three teeth in a fight at Bryant's Pub in Houston, TX. "This guy got ahead of me in line and called me a fag. I haven't been in a fight since grade school, but I think my exact words were, 'Wanna dance, fat boy?'"

At the Oyster Bar in Westchester, CA Friday, commodities analyst Nelson Heydritch encouraged his clients to make acquisitions in a local microbrew.

"Hold on," said Heydritch, before augmenting his own portfolio with a major investment in Johnny Walker Blue. "You know the secret to getting women? Being a total asshole."

Consumer confidence plunged to 82.1 points Monday, as alcohol consumers returned to work and began feeling a serious market correction. ⊘

COMPANY from page 190

tack by predatory marine life. Concerned about these difficulties, many employees and community leaders have spoken out strongly against the move.

"In addition to working underwater for eight hours a day with cumbersome oxygen tanks strapped to their backs, our workers are under constant threat from barracuda and other deadly undersea predators," said Local Food Producer's Union 443 President Marty Frankheim, who represents many members of the displaced workforce.

According to Frankheim, the main parking garage, built on the sea floor adjacent to the new headquarters, leaves workers dangerously exposed to shark attacks as they swim from the garage to the office entrance.

"Throughout the eight-month construction of the garage, tiger sharks have routinely threatened and occasionally fed on workers," Frankheim said.

Helheman downplayed any work hazards in the new location. "We're doing everything we can to create a safe working environment for the BakeCo team," Helheman said. "But once a tiger shark has attacked a victim, other sharks are attracted to the blood in the water, creating a feeding frenzy among the sharks."

Helheman did, however, warn employees and visitors touring the plant to avoid contact with moray eels, blue-ring octopi, and the dozens of species of sea snakes who make their homes near the plant. All of these animals are known to be aggressive and territorial, and may lurk in workers' lockers, in desk drawers, or dart about freely on the plant floor.

"While we're excited to be in our new undersea home, a frightened sea creature may feel threatened by our presence," Helheman said. "Employees should always use caution, especially during the blue ring's mating season."

The bite of a blue-ring octopus delivers a neuromuscular paralyzing venom more deadly than that of any land animal.

Despite setbacks, Helheman was optimistic about BakeCo's move. "We have high expectations for forging great new relationships with our undersea neighbors," Helheman said. "Bold new possibilities await us at the bottom of the sea." ⊘

COMMUNITY VOICES

Never In My Wildest Dreams Did I Think I'd Get Bored Watching Robots Fight

Who doesn't love robots? They're scary, they're powerful, and they're intelligent. They're frickin' cool, is the long and short of it. And robots fighting!? That's off the charts, as they say.

By Roy F. Mason

Or so I thought. Lo and behold, last night, as I was watching the Eviscerator's rusty-steel jaws demolish Dr. Clomp's titanium shell on *Battlebots*, *I dozed off*.

Roy F. Mason? Dozing off during a flurry of sparks and shrieking metal as robots used their mechanized strength to pulverize each other? What's wrong with this picture?

When I first heard about *Battlebots*, I was ecstatic. But now, the sight of dueling robots—*an actual Robot War!*—makes me sleepy.

Could I be the same person who once came to blows with Steve Olsen during a late-night debate over who'd triumph in a battle between Tornado and Gort? (My position, of course: Gort in a walk.) Well, I can only say that I saw a 30-pound, two-part robot armed with only a circular saw stave off relentless attacks from a pit of MIT AI robots and it left me cold. Some things cannot be explained.

If you had told me when I was 8 years old that there would one day be TV shows featuring nothing but robots fighting each other, I probably would have flipped out. I would have counted down the days to that glorious, unimaginable future. But now, watching those little toaster ovens roll around and bump into each other just makes me want to change the channel.

When I first heard about *Battlebots* and *Robot Wars*, I was ecstatic. I stayed up all night for weeks imagining my own attack robot, "The Cybernihilator." He had whirling tentacles with electrodes and spot welders on alternating ends, giving him the ability to short-circuit robot opponents and weld them to the floor. But now, the sight of dueling robots—not fake cartoon robots, not guys in robot costumes, but *actual robots in an actual Robot War!*—makes me sleepy.

Maybe the producers of these shows are at fault. I mean, how about giving these robots a little personality? You can't just slap a remote device on a lawn mower and call it a robot. Give it a synthesized voice, something deep and sinister. A woman's voice might be a nice touch, too. Add some motorized eyes, or make them sexy, like in *I, Robot*... Aw, will you listen to me? What am I saying? I'm talking about *an arena battle of fighting robots*, for Pete's sake. Who am I to look that kind of gift horse in the mouth?

How about this: Let's eliminate the featherweight-bots category. I'm sorry, but watching something the size of a vacuum cleaner fight for its existence is about as interesting as a walk in the park. How about pitting two mechanized tanks against each other for a change?! It would be like "MrooooooooW! Pow pow pow! Ker-BLOOM!"

Also, maybe it's that these contests lack a human element. No humans are ever in danger. How about upping the ante for the robot teams, maybe strap the programmers' infant children onto the robots so each battle has some real stakes? Now, that's a Robot War!

In fact, why are these robots being contained at all? They should loom over our streets and our homes, hunting down hobos, sick children, and the elderly. That way, we could all be part of the action...

In fact, why are these robots being contained at all? They should loom over our streets and our homes, hunting down hobos, sick children, and the elderly. That way, we could all be part of the action...

Oh, who'm I kidding? It's not the show's fault, it's mine. The whole sky could be black with invading flying robot drones, and I'd slip into a nap. Something's seriously wrong with me. ⌀

HOROSCOPES

Your Horoscope

By Lloyd Schumner Sr.
Retired Machinist and
A.A.P.B.-Certified Astrologer

Aries: (March 21–April 19)
You'll be honored, after a fashion, when the mayor of New York secretly awards you the key to the city of Boston and asks you to "leave no stone atop another."

Taurus: (April 20–May 20)
You take a lot of pride in what you are, which is at once rather noble, fairly self-destructive, and just ludicrous on the face of it.

Gemini: (May 21–June 21)
You hold advanced degrees in mathematics and physics, collect Renaissance bronzes, and have an especial penchant for chamber music, but a leading deodorant company insists you're a "Mitchum Man."

Cancer: (June 22–July 22)
Your life will continue unchanged for six of the next seven days. The other one will feature lots of upset bison.

Leo: (July 23–Aug. 22)
Scientists will have completed a map of the universe within 25 years, making life hell for you and other lovers of ambiguity.

Virgo: (Aug. 23–Sept. 22)
For the next year, you'll be haunted by the sickly, ghostly, jolly specter of those 110 pounds you had surgically excised in May.

Libra: (Sept. 23–Oct. 23)
Your soft life is destroyed with the exposure of your false birth certificate, forcing you out from under the shelter of child-labor laws.

Scorpio: (Oct. 24–Nov. 21)
Being blonde, healthy, and blue-eyed comes in handy yet again this week when the government unveils its new program of National Socialized Medicine.

Sagittarius: (Nov. 22–Dec. 21)
A little superstition never hurt anyone, but it's becoming a real pain for everyone to accommodate your lucky full-sized replica of Michelangelo's David.

Capricorn: (Dec. 22–Jan. 19)
If there's one problem with your get-rich-quick scheme, it's probably that one that the police, the Mafia, and the Treasury Department all used to track you down.

Aquarius: (Jan. 20–Feb. 18)
You thought you'd gotten past that incident last winter when you T-boned that bus, but the world's buses have pledged to avenge their fallen comrade sevenfold.

Pisces: (Feb. 19–March 20)
Your attempt to make the most romantic marriage proposal in history backfires when it rains unexpectedly, the gondola catches fire, and the bear forgets its training and reverts to man-eating. ⌀

EXECUTION from page 189

and then the next thing you know, the whole weekend is shot."

Continued Creasey: "If I get another stay, which I probably won't, I'm going to try to finish that skull tattoo on my arm—something I was planning on doing when I got stay number two."

Creasey said he most regrets not having played more poker.

"After Stony Mike [Jawarski] died in the infirmary, I meant to hang out in the common areas more," Creasey said. "But it just didn't happen."

Creasey, who has spent most of his adult life in prison for crimes ranging from assault with a deadly weapon to murder, said he frequently failed to realize his goals outside of prison, as well.

"I'd follow a college girl for a few hours intending to work out all the angles and really do it right," Creasey said. "But then I'd get impatient and barge into her place knives-a-blazing, like 'dorm security cameras who?' Talk about not thinking things through—and why the hell did I leave my semen all over the crime scene and get all hopped up on meth beforehand? Man, if I only had a time machine..."

"After Stony Mike [Jawarski] died in the infirmary, I meant to hang out in the common areas more," Creasey said. "But it just didn't happen."

Barring another stay, Creasey will be executed by lethal injection on July 23. ⌀

NEWS

War On String May Be Unwinnable, Says Cat General

see NATION page 2A

Wrong Spray Merely Freshens Attacker

see LOCAL page 6D

UN Quietly Pushed Into East River

see INTERNATIONAL page 12A

Gay Neighborhood Struggling With Transgenderfication

see LOCAL page 19D

STATshot

A look at the numbers that shape your world.

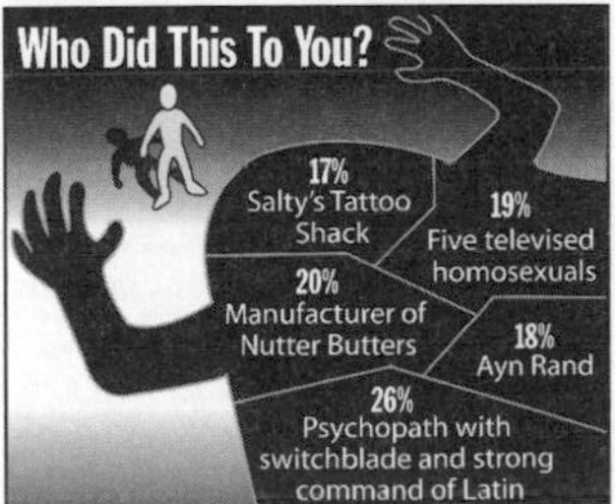

the ONION®

VOLUME 41 ISSUE 30 AMERICA'S FINEST NEWS SOURCE™ 28 JULY–3 AUGUST 2005

Supreme Court Justices Devour Sandra Day O'Connor In Ancient Ritual

WASHINGTON, DC—The eight remaining justices of the Supreme Court met in chambers Monday to feast on the living flesh of retiring Justice Sandra Day O'-Connor, enacting an ancient tradition that began when the first chief justice of the Supreme Court retired and was summarily consumed in 1795.

Although the most important cannibalistic ceremony in American jurisprudence is closed to outsiders, some details of the ritual are inscribed within the High Court Scrolls. The scrolls, written in human blood and stored in the Justice Library Reading Room,

see SUPREME COURT page 197

Above: The Supreme Court, which has ritually eaten Sandra Day O'Connor (front row, second from right).

Armchair Publicist Would Totally Rein In Tom Cruise

OMAHA, NE—Responding to the negative press coverage Tom Cruise has received in recent weeks, University of Nebraska financial-aid clerk Ben Matherson, 28, announced Monday that things would be different if he were the megastar's publicist.

"Tom is a force of nature, no question," Matherson announced from his one-room efficiency apartment in the Cornhusker State. "You can't control him, but you have to at least steer him in the right direction. That's how you handle a star of his caliber."

According to Matherson, Cruise's "PR nightmare" began with an article in the German publication *Der Spiegel*, which reported that Cruise arranged to have a tent for the Church of Scientology set up on the set of *War Of The Worlds*.

"I have no idea what he was thinking, promoting Scientology when he's supposed to be shooting a film," said Matherson, who was on a movie set only once, when he took the Universal Studios tour in 1988.

Matherson added: "I would have redirected the questioning the moment the reporter started asking Tom about

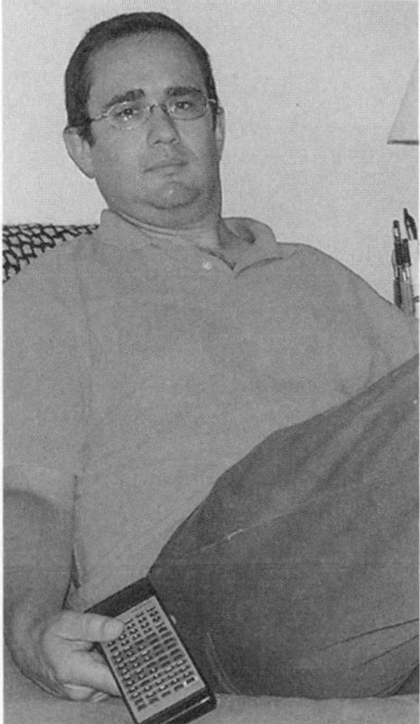

Above: Tom Cruise's armchair publicist, Ben Matherson.

religion, or maybe just said, 'Okay, let's wrap this up.'"

Although not a regular reader of *Der Spiegel*, Matherson said he

see PUBLICIST page 197

Many U.S. Cities Losing Battles To Preserve Their Burger Kings

CLEVELAND—Every day, 38-year-old Susan Tarsley takes a brisk walk through her tree-lined neighborhood. At each turn, she is reminded of the changes brought on by the march of progress: a TV antenna dismantled to make way for underground cable, passersby chatting on cell phones, a rusty tricycle abandoned for a Razor scooter.

BURGER KING

But at the silent corner of Lark Street and Superior Avenue, Tarsley stops to mourn the passing of an especially treasured landmark. Her local Burger King is fading into memory. It's a sadly familiar picture in many communities: Fast-food hubs that once bustled with activity, when young and old

see BURGER KINGS page 196

London Bombings

London subways and buses have been targeted in two subway attacks in recent weeks. What do *you* think?

"What? Did these madmen not hear the world denounce these acts just weeks ago?"

Joshua Banks
Veterinary Aid

"Well, it certainly led to a lot of poorly Photoshopped crying lions and unicorns in my e-mail."

Derrick Powers
Roofer

"The sad thing is, London may now develop anti-Pakistani racism for the first time in its history."

Dalia Lofton
Systems Analyst

"Whatever dangers London may face, I am confident that the strong leadership of Her Majesty the Queen can handle any challenge."

Allen Ward
Nurse

"Are the Brits flying into a blind rage and invading an oil-producing country for no reason? Well, why not?"

Carolyn Allen
Fire Inspector

"As an Irishman, I think whoever's behind this should be found and punished if it isn't us."

Rodney Price
Daycare Operator

Disneyland's 50th Anniversary

Last week marked the 50th anniversary of the opening of Disneyland. How did they celebrate?

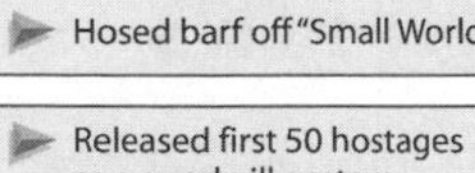

- Gave free and permanent mouse ears to every California baby born on the big day
- Hosed barf off "Small World" attraction
- Released first 50 hostages as a goodwill gesture
- Sent broomstick army to attack Six Flags Great America
- Finally set Herbie free
- Spent quiet day at home celebrating with rest of pantsless talking-duck family
- Introduced bioengineered "Real Mickey"
- Filed copyright-violation suits in each state of the union—one lawsuit for each year they've been open

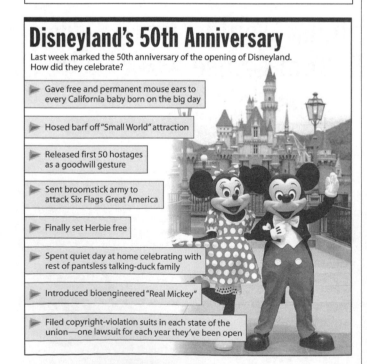

the ONION®
America's Finest News Source.™

Herman Ulysses Zweibel
Founder

T. Herman Zweibel
Publisher Emeritus
J. Phineas Zweibel
Publisher
Maxwell Prescott Zweibel
Editor-In-Chief

I'm Choking On A Kalamata Olive, Not Your Everyday Olive

By Martin Ithell
Onion Food Writer

Oh, my. This is superb. Superb, indeed. My Greek grocer Kostas told me he had a surprise for me, and he certainly did: These are quite simply the finest kalamata olives I've ever tasted. Absolutely delightful. Certainly not your ordinary olive. It's a privilege, really, just to be choking on one, as I am right now.

Ahh... yes. No need to panic just yet. My trachea is savoring the tang, the richness. This was hand-picked, I can tell. Yes, I can sense that its skin wasn't broken by a rough fall from a tree. I'm very sensitive to qualities like that. What a pity it would be if someone were present to end this culinary epiphany by unblocking my windpipe. Few outside of Greece experience an olive-choking this rapturous.

Mmm... Do I detect a splash of red-wine vinegar? Excellent, excellent. A shame to squeeze them into jars of acrid brine. Best to store these singular creatures in a gently seasoned marinade. And why muddle them in a tapenade, really? Enjoy them unadulterated and unpitted, I say. Relish their simple, onyx-like beauty. One of Olympus' greatest gifts to mortals, the kalamata olive. Be aware of the risks of enjoying them whole, however! My goodness, it's lodged in there quite tightly.

Ahh. Mmm, yes. Unmistakably from the Kalamata region of Greece. The pick of his cousin's grove, Kostas informed me, bless his heart. The crop

Mmm... Do I detect a splash of red-wine vinegar? Excellent, excellent. A shame to squeeze them into jars of acrid brine. Best to store these singular creatures in a gently seasoned marinade.

seems unaffected by the spring windstorms of '04. Succulent. Powerful, but not overpowering. Perhaps the squalls blowing in from the Ionian Sea lightly salted the olive grove and its chalky soil! I kid, of course. By now, I'm sure you're all very anxious about my present condition. I shall alert the paramedics in short order, I assure you. Let me just savor these flavors a moment longer.

Delectable? Ravishing? Understatements. Adjectives do not do this olive

No need to panic just yet. My trachea is savoring the tang, the richness. This was hand-picked, I can tell. Yes, I can sense that its skin wasn't broken by a rough fall from a tree. I'm very sensitive to qualities like that.

justice. Yes, leave your everyday olives to the sticky, flyspecked countertops of open-air bars. Well, this is an all-new culinary experience. I am literally dying!

Absurd to think that for so many years I knew only those wan, vacuum-packed specimens of the pimento-stuffed canapés and dutifully garnished martinis of my own mother's patio parties—such farcical affairs. Jackie O and Lilly Pulitzer never did show up, sadly, but we were always left with enough tins of Underwood deviled ham to supply a score of sack lunches. Reality has such a way of being so tiresomely opprobrious. Ah well. Poor mother, she tried her best. No matter, I suppose.

This presents quite a wrinkle. I've dialed 911, but as I attempt to speak, no sound issues forth. Bah! Indulge your cravings for gauche heroics elsewhere, I beseech you. "Acclaimed Food Writer Saved By Fast-Thinking Lout" will not appear in tomorrow's papers.

My goodness. Having just caught a glimpse of myself in the alcove mirror, I realize that a degree of alarm is in order. I am turning blue. It's my own fault, you know, scarfing these delicious olives down like Allsorts. But I still firmly maintain, even as all grows shrouded and dim, that a kalamata olive is best savored whole, solid, and quick. Sweet Athena, this may be the end. But what a glorious way to go!

Martin Ithell's food column appears in over 250 newspapers nationwide. Ø

Alcoholic Father Disappointed In Pothead Son

REEDSBURG, WI—Working-class father of four and veteran alcoholic James Schultz, 53, expressed deep disappointment Monday in his 19-year-old son Travis, for "turning into a goddamn pothead" after moving away from home to attend the University of Wisconsin-Madison.

"After the hard work I put in at the screen-door factory all these years, this is how he rewards me?" Schultz said during a 1:30 a.m. statement held at Captain Pete's Bar and Grill. "That boy should be working for a living, like his old man, instead of smoking weed and doing God knows what with a bunch of liberal lowlifes."

"After the hard work I put in at the screen-door factory all these years, this is how he rewards me?" Schultz said during a 1:30 a.m. statement held at Captain Pete's Bar and Grill. "That boy should be working for a living, like his old man, instead of smoking weed and doing God knows what with a bunch of liberal lowlifes."

Schultz punctuated the impromptu speech by finishing off the last of his drink and ordering another from bartender and friend Al Zandek.

Members of the family said Schultz and his son fought over Travis' illegal-drug use Sunday, after Schultz found a small bag of marijuana while rifling through the boy's pockets for beer money.

The elder Schultz confronted his son at the dinner table that night.

"He slurred his way through a half-coherent lecture on the dangers of addiction, shouting in my face about what a disappointment I was to the family," Travis said.

Travis said Schultz continued his drunken anti-drug tirade well into the night, eventually lumbering out the

see POTHEAD SON page 196

Below: Lifelong alcoholic James Schultz drowns his sorrows about his "worthless pothead son" Travis (inset).

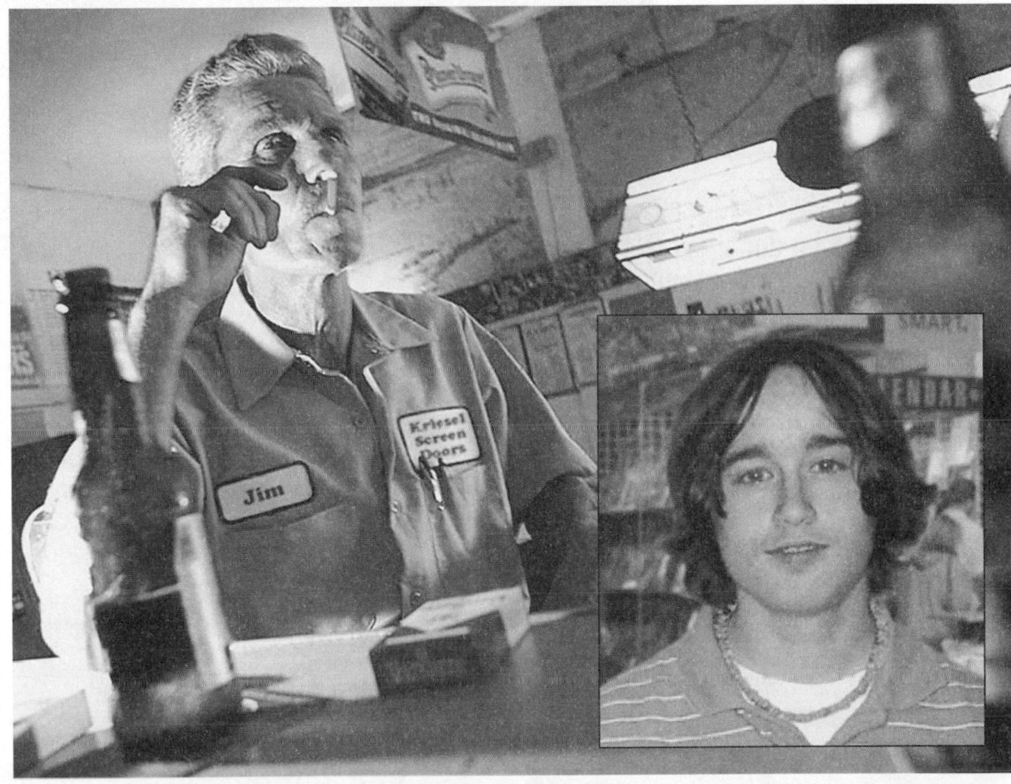

NEWS IN BRIEF

Bush To London Bombers: 'Bring It On'

WASHINGTON, DC—President Bush officially responded to the latest round of London transit bombings Monday, challenging terrorists to "do their worst." Said Bush, in a televised statement from the Oval Office: "The proud and resilient people of London can take anything the forces of evil and cowardice can throw at them. They will never live in fear of you. Bring it on." Prime Minister Tony Blair thanked Bush for his comments, inviting him to visit London and ride the Underground in a show of solidarity.

Chocolate Pudding Up $2 A Barrel

NEW YORK—The price per barrel of dark sweet chocolate pudding jumped to over $60 Monday as global anxiety continued to drive demand for the delicious after-meal treat. "There is no pudding-production shortfall, either from U.S. producers or the SNACPAC member nations," dessert analyst Blythe Barton said. "Demand alone is driving prices upward, with American consumers demonstrating an ongoing willingness to pay record prices per barrel for smooth, creamy pudding." The White House released a statement late Monday indicating that it has no intention of breaking the skin on the government's Strategic Pudding Reserves, which are to be used only in wartime or as a reward for finishing an entire serving of beets.

Embattled Rove Seeks Asylum In Scarborough Country

SCARBOROUGH COUNTRY—Diplomatic sources reported Monday that White House Deputy Chief of Staff Karl Rove has sought asylum in the conservative stronghold of Scarborough Country. "During his June 23 visit, Mr. Rove had indicated he might petition us for sanctuary from media persecution," said Joe Scarborough, the monarchical ruler of Scarborough Country. "And in my country, no passports are required and only common sense is allowed." While officials review Rove's asylum request, he is being held in the No-Spin Zone, a region of absolute neutrality governed by commentator Bill O'Reilly.

Scientists Discover 6,000-Year-Old Stain

HAFR AL-BATIN, SAUDI ARABIA—Textile archaeologists have unearthed a section of coarsely woven Sumerian goat's wool bearing what could be the world's oldest, and perhaps its toughest, stain. "The stain, in scientific terms, is 'ground-in,' doubtless one of the active-lifestyle stains that plagued Sumerian families," said Leigh Perkins, the leader of the Tulane University team that uncovered the stain. "We hope to determine whether it's mud, blood, or some kind of proto-blueberry pie." Scientists say they can learn a lot from the discovery, such as how tough the Sumerians were on grime.

Study: 72 Percent Of High-Fives Unwarranted

DALLAS—Specialists at the National Exuberance Institute said Monday that more than three quarters of national high-five slap exchanges are unnecessary. "Abuse and inappropriate implementation of the gesture is epidemic," said NEI president Avi Gupta. "Celebratory high-fives are marking such mundane accomplishments as the clearing of paper jams, the ordering of hot wings, the viewing of favorite TV commercials, and the simultaneous wearing of identical items of clothing." Gupta called for the use of restrained high-five alternatives, such as the "thumbs up" and the exchange of curt nods. ⌀

BURGER KINGS from page 193

alike gathered in plastic molded seats around gleaming yellow linoleum tables, are now boarded-up ghost restaurants. Their long-extinguished drive-through menus silently beckon to cars that will never come.

"I came here as a child when it first opened," said Tarsley, strolling through the empty, weed-strewn parking lot. "Now that I have kids, where are they supposed to go for Whoppers or Chicken Tenders? We need to ask ourselves, as a culture, 'Where are our priorities?'"

Once nearly as plentiful as McDonald's, Burger Kings are quickly becoming the fast-food franchise of a bygone era. A 2004 survey of fast-food diners showed that nearly 60 percent did not live within walking distance of a Burger King. Another 20 percent had to drive to a nearby town just to see one.

A closed-down Burger King like this one near Chicago is a common sight in many neighborhoods, and a sad reminder of America's vanishing fast-food heritage.

"There are children alive today who don't know what a Whaler is," the mayor said at the signing ceremony. "All their lives, they've known only the McDonald's Filet-O-Fish. If you look into the eyes of such a child, you realize why it's important that we save our shared Burger King heritage."

Although the Lark Street store closed its doors last November, not all communities are giving up their Burger Kings without a fight.

In Seattle, volunteer canvassers went door-to-door, collecting signatures to save the Burger King on Rainier Avenue. As a result of their efforts, Mayor Greg Nickels granted the store historic-landmark status.

"There are children alive today who don't know what a Whaler is," the mayor said at the signing ceremony. "All their lives, they've known only the McDonald's Filet-O-Fish. If you look into the eyes of such a child, you realize why it's important that we save our shared Burger King heritage."

In Phoenix, mother of two Gloria Poenig organized a community-action BK Broiler-buying group to help raise awareness of the fast-food chain's plight.

"Most people don't even know that our Burger Kings are in trouble, or they say they're too busy to help," Poenig said. "People don't realize that every time a Burger King closes, a little piece of America dies."

Although isolated heroes have saved some Burger Kings from the bulldozer, the problems of maintaining the franchises persist. With an 8 percent decline in patronage since 2002, the chains are plagued by vandalism, high employee turnover, and disappointing sales of french-toast sticks.

For those at the forefront of the battle to save their Burger Kings, the issue is not saving the brick-and-mortar buildings, but embracing the Burger King philosophy.

Steve Quislen, a Chicago-based civil rights and labor lawyer, has been doing pro-bono work on behalf of Burger King for 12 years. Members of his group, Coalition To Save Our Franchise Landmarks, meet every Sunday at the Bedford Street Burger King, where they don the cardboard crown of the Burger King Kids Club, eat Bacon Double Cheeseburgers, and enjoy what may soon become a lost way of life.

"We need to stand up and be counted before the things that make our society great—like Burger King's new Enormous Omelet Sandwich—vanish forever," Quislen said.

Despite the efforts of thousands of dedicated Burger King activists like Quislen, even die-hard believers like Tarsley say they are losing faith.

"Whenever I drive by a strip mall or new shopping district without a Burger King in it, I can't help but shed a tear," Tarsley said. "It is truly a sad reminder of inevitable change and decline."

As she began the walk back home from Lark Street's once-proud "Home Of The Whopper," Tarsley resolved to do everything in her power to preserve this hallowed source of budget meals, for her children, and her children's children.

"I won't throw in the towel until the last Burger King is gone," Tarsley said. "I will fight this fight wherever it is being fought, whether it's on the airwaves, the national news, or in the parking lots of the restaurants themselves. I will not let Burger King go the way of Sambo's and Kenny Rogers Roasters." ⊘

POTHEAD SON from page 195

door, presumably to go to Captain Pete's.

When asked to comment on the face-off, Schultz's wife Ellen said that, while it is true that her son has been bringing a lot of funny ideas home, she didn't think college was "turning him into a druggie."

"So he tried pot—a lot of young kids these days do things they later regret," said Ellen, 51. "Everybody has regrets about decisions they made when they were young."

Ellen defended her husband, as well.

"James only gets like that because he loves Travis," she said. "He's a very sensitive man. A lot of people don't realize that. They only see the temper. It's certainly nothing to call social services about, like [neighbor] Dianne Klosterbaum did last year. It's just the way Jim is when he's letting off steam."

Safely amongst his drinking buddies at the bar, Schultz continued outlining his disappointment in Travis.

"I wish he'd just sit down over some beers with me and talk this through," Schultz said. "But there's no talking sense to a dope addict."

According to drinking companion Doug Blaine, Schultz keeps his feelings to himself, except when he's "half in the bag."

"He'd never let on, but he's got a lot of pressures on him, what with his second mortgage, his liver troubles, and his court date coming up," Blaine said. "He's real closed off, but sometimes, late at night around last call, he'll start to let you in a little. And it's clear that pothead kid of his is breaking his heart."

Schultz keeps his feelings to himself, except when he's "half in the bag."

"Why anybody would want to smoke pot is beyond me," Blaine added. "Doesn't that kid know that stuff is going to rot his brain?"

At 3 a.m., Schultz used his last quarter to call home and wake up Ellen for a ride, explaining that he's already gotten picked up for two DUIs.

"Who's going to drive my wife to work in the morning so we can pay some bills?" Schultz asked. "That stoner son of mine? I don't think so." ⊘

PUBLICIST from page 193

gleaned information about the publication from the celebrity-news program Insider, which he typically watches alone in his room while eating cold cereal.

Matherson cited Cruise's May 23 appearance on *The Oprah Winfrey Show* as the first sign the popular actor was in need of some guidance.

"Back when Britney Spears wed and divorced her childhood friend all within a 24-hour period, Ben used to lean over the countertop at the office and shake his head," said Shelly Johansen, who has worked as a file clerk in the financial-aid office since 1992. "He thought it was a really bad move for her."

"Even with a guy like Tom Cruise, who makes $20 million a movie, you've got to lay down the law," said Matherson, who is not in a supervisory position in the financial-aid office. "I would have told him, 'Lay off the poetry. Stick with the smile. The smile is working for you.'"

Matherson said he has some ideas for keeping Cruise "on message."

"I would want to work out a hand-signal system with Tom, so I could motion to him from backstage when he was getting out of control," Matherson said.

Matherson's friends and coworkers report that the file clerk often makes comments drawing on his knowledge of the celebrity world, which he monitors from this ensconced position in the center of America's cattle-producing heartland.

"Back when Britney Spears wed and divorced her childhood friend all within a 24-hour period, Ben used to lean over the countertop at the office and shake his head," said Shelly Johansen, who has worked as a file clerk in the financial-aid office since 1992. "He thought it was a really bad move for her."

Cruise is currently in Italy shooting *Mission Impossible 3* and out of the public eye, which Matherson believes is "for the best."

Jessica Furstrom, a receptionist from nearby Lincoln and a longtime armchair publicist for Courtney Love, said Matherson "has a long row to hoe" with Cruise.

"I don't know if Tom realizes what a headache he can be for a PR man," Matherson said, repeating comments he made earlier in the day to coworker Gary Siebold. "A good image buffing isn't gonna do the trick at this point. We need to talk damage control."

The lifelong Nebraska resident's recommendations for Cruise include pulling him off the interview circuit for "dehydration and exhaustion," then spending a day or two "giving him some talking points."

Jessica Furstrom, a receptionist from nearby Lincoln and a longtime armchair publicist for Courtney Love, said Matherson "has a long row to hoe" with Cruise.

"I went through a lot of this same type of thing with Courtney," Furstrom said. "These problems don't just go away by themselves. The hard work of repairing a star's image has to get done. And thank God there are publicists to do it." Ø

Below: An example of the sort of erratic behavior that has Matherson worried.

SUPREME COURT from page 193

have been studied by only a handful of legal scholars.

"Chief Justice William H. Rehnquist almost certainly consumed the greater part of O'Connor's brain and heart prior to the ritual feeding, in a rite believed to grant him the knowledge, wisdom, and courage of the devoured," said American University law professor Donald Hewett. "Any portions of O'Connor's brain and heart that Rehnquist refused would have been consumed by the remaining justices within minutes, as they chanted passages from her seminal opinions."

Hewett said the first woman appointed to the Supreme Court was gutted, strung up, and "drained into stone goblets from which her blood was sipped like wine."

"This quaffing of blood is traditionally accompanied by much singing and drumming," Hewett said.

If the ritual was performed in accordance with the court scrolls, O'Connor's body was then laid upon a traditional brass bier and borne up a five-story marble staircase to a consecrated inner sanctum, where clerks skewered the raw meat on wooden spits. Late into the evening, the Supreme Court justices feasted on the renowned federalist by torchlight.

O'Connor was gutted, strung up, and "drained into stone goblets from which her blood was sipped like wine."

"The ceremony is said to be quite moving," said Zachary Katz, editor of the *Yale Law Review*. "By consuming O'Connor's mortal body, the other justices seek a communion with her transcendent qualities—her respect for the discretion of the court, her pragmatism, and her refusal to commit to abstract legal principles."

O'Connor has been prepared for the ritual since January 2005, when Chief Justice Rehnquist sprinkled her desk with the ashes of a virgin law clerk and pronounced, *"Receptum, receptum, receptum."*

Tuesday evening, Rehnquist emerged from the 17-foot-tall, 13-ton bronze sliding doors of the Supreme Court building's west entrance and addressed those who had gathered in the oval pavilion.

"Hear us, Justice," said Rehnquist, wearing a necklace of human bones and an elaborate headdress adorned with yak horns. "In the abiding name of Jurisprudence we consumed her; in the eternal name of Law was she eaten; and as her flesh does become our flesh, so her wisdom shall become our wisdom, yea, through all time everlasting."

"The ceremony is said to be quite moving," said Zachary Katz, editor of the Yale Law Review.

According to legal scholars, O'Connor's skin will be tanned and sewn into a ceremonial cloak, to be worn by the youngest justice, Clarence Thomas, as he lights the pyre upon which members of O'Connor's senior staff are burned alive. Ø

COMMUNITY VOICES

Shop Worn

As I write this, I'm at Tacky's Tavern polishing off my third Long Island iced tea. (Nope, don't adjust your volume—you heard me right!) Now, normally, I believe the best highs come from life itself. But today, your old pal Jean requires a drinky-poo the size of an aqualung! (Actually, I prefer Brandy Alexanders to Long Islands, but Tacky's doesn't make them.)

A Room Of Jean's Own
By Jean Teasdale

So, guess who's back on the unemployment line? Here's a hint: It's a certain North Pole elf with a hubby who says "told ya so" so often he should have it tattooed on his forehead! Yep, you guessed it—none other than yours truly.

If you've followed the past few columns, you know my dad and I started a business called Off-Season Santa, in which lucky visitors got to sit on Santa's (aka Dad's) lap all year 'round. It was a pretty "way out" idea, I'll admit, but we were confident it would catch on. After all, who doesn't love Santa?

So, guess who's back on the unemployment line? Here's a hint: It's a certain North Pole elf with a hubby who says "told ya so" so often he should have it tattooed on his forehead! Yep, you guessed it—none other than yours truly.

Apparently, nearly everyone. It's a crying shame. Can't people think outside the box for once? We all need whimsy in our lives. People are so used to going to stores for essentials like food, but they never think to feed their spirits. Well, don't worry: Soon you'll see me back behind a cash register, checking out your groceries or clothing or toilet paper—and most likely wearing a misspelled name tag, too. (I swear, how hard is it to spell "Jean"? It's not "Jeanne" or "Gene" or "Jene"—never has been, never will!)

The sad thing was, business had been picking up. Our brand new "Christmas in July" banner was attracting the right people, we were logging quite a few sales of discounted greeting cards and knick-knacks, and there was even a girl making a documentary about us for her college film class. On the day before the fire, four mothers with children stopped by, and they were paying customers, too.

Yeah, okay, the fire. There was a fire last week. I'm pretty weary from talking and thinking about it, but I suppose I have no choice but to mention it again. It burned down nearly the entire strip mall, including the comic-book store, four vacant spaces, and Off-Season Santa. (For some reason, only the H&R Block was left untouched. Perhaps the wind shifted.)

Thank God no one was hurt. The fire happened late Wednesday night. The scariest part was that, on the very night of the fire, Dad stayed at work late after closing to play Texas Hold 'Em with Doug, the guy who managed the comic-book store, and Armand, the property manager. If Dad and those guys had stayed around the store a half-hour longer, they might've gambled away a lot more than a few bucks!

I'm still not really sure how the fire started. I've heard stories flying around about paint cans, defective sprinkler systems, and a stash of fireworks in the back room of the comic-book store. I don't know—I haven't paid much attention. It was painful enough seeing our devastated shop. Whatever wasn't burned to a charred crisp suffered water damage from the fire hoses. I had to spend a whole day hauling garbage bags of charred Christmas decorations and yards and yards of dirty, damp polyurethane "snow" to the Dumpster. (Talk about being down in the dumps!) Not even Dad's cutout sleigh placards, which he used to hide his Rascal scooter from the children, were spared. The documentary girl was there too, filming me. I wished she wouldn't, but I didn't have the heart to ask her to go.

Fire investigators interviewed Dad a couple times at our apartment. Watching them stirred up an old memory of mine, of another business of my dad's that burned down. My dad was running a roofing company and some warehouse on his property burned one night. I was in high school at the time, and I remember insurance people coming to our house, and Dad even going to the police station to make sworn statements or something. Shortly afterwards, he closed down the business and moved away with the woman who would become his second wife.

So, this was not Dad's first encounter with fire. Oddly enough, rather than being upset, he seemed calm, almost relieved. He never insured Off-Season Santa, but he's convinced we and the other businesses will get fat payouts from the building owner's liability insurance.

"We'll get some money, and I'll be able to pay my debts," Dad said. "The fire didn't start in our space, so they can't finger us for negligence."

I asked Dad if we could use the money to open a new store, this time in a better space and with insurance, but Dad shook his head.

"Off-Season Santa was ahead of its time," he said. "Someday, people will finally come around to the notion of a year-round Santa, but not now."

I awoke at about 10 this morning to find that Dad had loaded his Rascal scooter and his few belongings into his Lincoln Town Car and left. (I guess Dad still enjoys his hasty exits.) Hubby Rick was already at work, so I called him to ask if he saw Dad take off.

"You mean he bailed?!" he cried. Then he started raging about how Dad owed him so much rent and food money and back wages for me, and how he couldn't believe he let Dad sponge off us for so long. I tried to tell him about the insurance money, but I couldn't get a word in edgewise. So I hung up, grabbed my notebook, and drove to Tacky's.

Sorry, Jeanketeers. I'm a little blotto, and I shouldn't be taking my troubles out on you. I just find it sad—I feel like I finally had a chance to spread my wings and fly, and I got sucked into a jet engine. Now that I've had a brief taste of being my own boss, I don't know how I can ever face dull work and bossy supervisors 15 years my junior. Right now, I'm crossing my fingers that tomorrow I'll open the paper to a classified ad reading: "WANTED: 39-year-old woman to test-market our line of Long Island iced teas. Good pay, flexible hours. Ownership of Christmas elf suit a must." ⌀

HOROSCOPES

Your Horoscope

By Lloyd Schumner Sr.
Retired Machinist and
A.A.P.B.-Certified Astrologer

Aries: (March 21–April 19)
There's no shame in being a little depressed from time to time. There is, however, lots of shame in washing dozens of cheese-filled pancakes down your throat with bourbon because of it.

Taurus: (April 20–May 20)
No one can say you're not a good father, but that's because your kids' very existence has been a closely guarded state secret for many years.

Gemini: (May 21–June 21)
You've always feared change in your life, so relax: You're going to be in a nice, stable coma for the foreseeable future.

Cancer: (June 22–July 22)
Your only rule is never to volunteer for anything, which sucks when people ask if you'd like a big bag of money.

Leo: (July 23–Aug. 22)
Advances in medical technology will soon make it possible for EMTs to train on highly advanced mannequins, leaving you with absolutely nothing to do on nights and weekends.

Virgo: (Aug. 23–Sept. 22)
You'll soon be so fat that, when you sit around the Morbid Obesity Intensive Cardiac Therapy Center at Mount Sinai, you sit around the Morbid Obesity Intensive Cardiac Therapy Center at Mount Sinai.

Libra: (Sept. 23–Oct. 23)
The other guys keep telling you to get rid of that beard you've had since college, but not only are you quite fond of her, she is also the mother of your two darling daughters.

Scorpio: (Oct. 24–Nov. 21)
You'll be getting plenty of hot and heavy action in the near future, but unfortunately for your love life, it's mostly the explosions, car chases, and heavy gunfire kind of action.

Sagittarius: (Nov. 22–Dec. 21)
You thought you'd have a hard time finding steady work as a compliant sexual zombie, but next week will demonstrate that there's always a demand for real talent.

Capricorn: (Dec. 22–Jan. 19)
Having a foot fetish is one thing, but chopping the feet off of a perfectly good woman and discarding the rest is just plain wasteful.

Aquarius: (Jan. 20–Feb. 18)
Right now, you have no knowledge of basic metallurgy, but after next week's trip to the foundry, you'll be keenly aware of the exact melting point of lead.

Pisces: (Feb. 19–March 20)
Wearing white after Labor Day isn't the *faux pas* it once was, but wearing the same tattered white wedding dress from now until Labor Day is going to be seen as somewhat odd. ⌀

NEWS

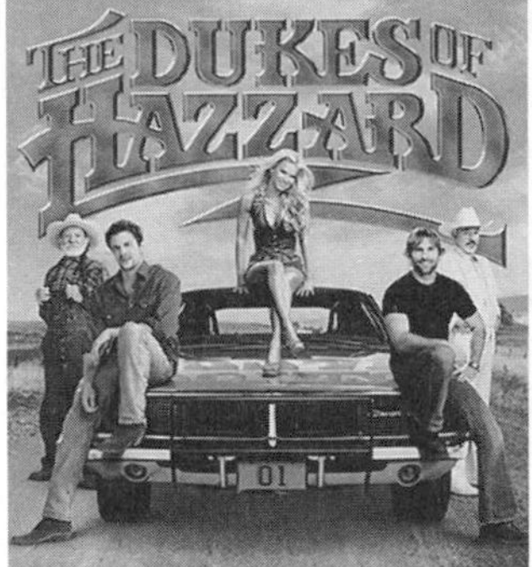

Dukes Of Hazzard Sharply Declines In Kitsch Value

see BUSINESS page 6C

Loser Hiding Behind Winning Smile

see NATIONAL page 11B

Bicycle-Riding Circus Bear Pedals Back To Natural Habitat

see SCIENCE page 8D

STATshot

A look at the numbers that shape your world.

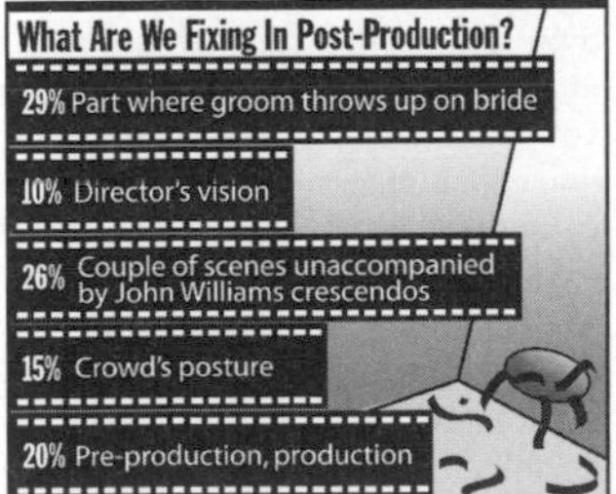

the ONION®

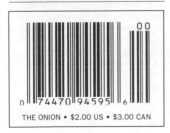

VOLUME 41 ISSUE 31 AMERICA'S FINEST NEWS SOURCE™ 4–10 AUGUST 2005

CRISIS IN EDUCATION

Report: Our High Schools May Not Adequately Prepare Dropouts For Unemployment

Above: Future jobless Americans between classes at Oakes High School.

WASHINGTON, DC—A Department of Labor report released Monday finds that America's high schools are not sufficiently preparing emerging dropouts for the demands of unemployment.

In a letter introducing the report, Labor Secretary Elaine Chao explained that schools routinely fail to impart dropouts with the critical lying- and sitting-around skills they need to thrive in today's jobless market.

see DROPOUTS page 203

Above: White House press secretary Scott McClellan.

White House Denies Existence Of Karl Rove

WASHINGTON, DC—The White House denied rumors of wrongdoing by anyone named Karl Rove Monday, saying the alleged deputy chief of staff does not exist.

"To my knowledge, no one by the name of Karl Rove works for this president, his staff, or for that matter, anyone on earth, since he is not a real person," White House press secretary Scott McClellan told reporters Monday.

Despite White House denials, allegations have surfaced in recent weeks that Karl Rove is the man who leaked covert CIA operative Valerie Plame's

see KARL ROVE page 202

Suicide Bomber Killed En Route By Car Bomb

BAGHDAD—Terrorist cells in Baghdad are in mourning for suicide bomber Ahmed al-Khalaf, 19, who was killed by a car bomb Monday, 200 yards from an Iraqi police station, his intended target.

Sources within the insurgency said al-Khalaf was "on his way to becoming a glorious martyr" when he was struck down by the car-bomb explosion. Twenty-three other civilians were also killed.

"What kind of God allows the death of people who are on their way to kill innocent people?" insurgent leader Abdulwahid al-Tomizie said. "On the one hand, I am elated that the car-bomb explosion was successful, but the loss of the suicide bomber is a tragedy, as is the survival of all the innocent people he might have killed."

According to al-Tomizie, al-Khalaf

see CAR BOMBER page 203

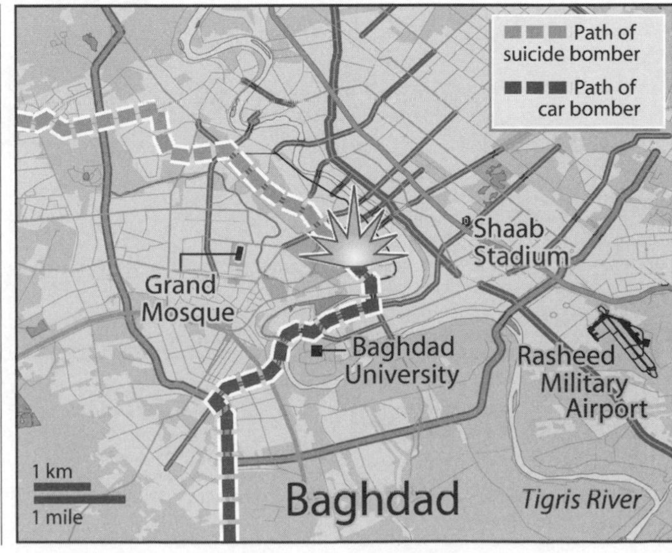

AFL-CIO Split

Last week, both the Teamsters and the SEIU bolted from the AFL-CIO, a bad sign for American organized labor. What do *you* think?

"This is a sad day for organized crime—*labor*! I meant labor!"

Diane Black
Cardiologist

"I'm reserving my judgment until I know what side Springsteen's on."

Steven Watson
Real-Estate Appraiser

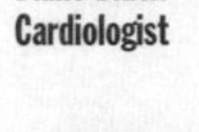

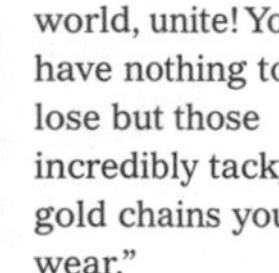

"Workers of the world, unite! You have nothing to lose but those incredibly tacky gold chains you wear."

Jody Soares
Systems Analyst

"'Boo-hoo... I'm all alone... People are leaving me all alone. Boo-hoo. I'm the AFL-CIO. Boo-hoo.' Grow up!"

Jesse Pearson
Short-Order Cook

"Wait a second... Didn't Reagan end organized labor?"

Kenneth Trapp
Investment Banker

"All's I know is, somebody's gotta drive this here pickle truck to Secaucus, and it ain't gonna be me."

Jeffrey Courson
Truck Dispatcher

Anti-Terrorism Measures

In the wake of the London bombings, what are American cities doing to protect their citizens from terrorist attacks?

- Minneapolis—Rezoning certain areas as "terror free"
- Detroit—Detonating any automobile that could potentially become a car bomb
- Albuquerque, NM—Declaring citywide ban on national news coverage
- Los Angeles—Stationing armed, gas-masked soldiers on school buses to ensure that our children live without fear
- St. Louis—Gateway Arch fitted with giant convex security mirror
- Oklahoma City—Exhaustively cavity-searching incoming cattle for bombs
- Denver—Dismantling enormous mountain range to the west in order to eliminate potential hiding places for terrorists
- Cape Cod, MA—Wearing special new "anti-terror"-patterned cable-knit sweaters
- Kokomo, IN—Installing lightning rods throughout town, since chance of getting hit by lightning much greater than being killed by a terrorist

America's Finest News Source.™

Herman Ulysses Zweibel
Founder

T. Herman Zweibel
Publisher Emeritus
J. Phineas Zweibel
Publisher
Maxwell Prescott Zweibel
Editor-In-Chief

Our Global Food-Service Enterprise Is Totally Down For Your Awesome Subculture

What's hanging, teenage homies? I'm Ralph Lucci—Radical Ralph—coming to rap at you on your terms and on your turf about the things you care about most. Stuff like baggy pants, snacks, and hard-rocking carbonated beverages. As you keep livin' your vidas loca, I want you to know that the multinational PepsiCo conglomeration, which includes dozens of dope fast-food chains, beverage brands, and packaged non-perishable snacks—and for which I'm a proud representative—is totally down with your way-out-there niche community.

By Ralph Lucci
Executive VP of Marketing, PepsiCo

You might think just because you freestyle rap with your MP3s, the PepsiCo family of products has no relevance in your life. That could not be farther from the truth. In fact, the crazy, unique, cutting-edge stuff you're into now? The entire management team here in the North American headquarters was totally into that sh*t a couple months ago! No lie, dawgs. What's really hot is that we even have some wreckin'-sick snack foods that are totally chill with your take-no-prisoners, no-holds-barred, 13-to-17-year-old lifestyle.

Take our Doritos-brand Nacho Cheesier chips, for example. They are ghetto fabulous.

Word: If you have never tasted a Nacho Cheesier chip, do not ever taste a Nacho Cheesier chip, as you will not be able to understand a Nacho Cheesier chip. That's just how it is with food products that are so authentic, hardcore, and fricking intenso that they redefine your entire life.

Sometimes it feels like nobody understands your rebellious, genre-defying crew of goth-rocker pals—am I right?

Also, our off-the-Richter-scale Mountain Dew AMP line of energy-drink beverages is truly off the hook. There's nothing conservative about a skandalouz beverage named AMP, obviously. And we do not heavily promote it, so it's totally underground, just like you and your hood-rat posse.

Sometimes it feels like nobody understands your rebellious, genre-defying crew of goth-rocker pals—am I right? You see, as a senior-level executive at one of the world's largest conglomerates of food-service brands, I know exactly where you're coming from.

One phunky-fresh freakster to another: After a long day of hanging ten while surf-blogging and buggin' on wack 'rents problems, what's better than a game-tight fluid refresher like Gatorade Frost?

Of course, for alternative, anti-mainstream dudes like yourselves, you might need something a little bit more punkin'. And trust me, we have got just the thing: Oberto meat snacks. Players, let me assure you, these processed-and-cured jerky competitors are stiz-upendous. Take it from me, a guy who understands the elaborate clothing styles, secret handshakes, and hep vernacular that define your wiggedy-wiggedy wackdaddy scene.

I want you to know that the PepsiCo conglomoration is totally down with your way-out-there niche community.

Although I do highly recommend the ill snacks and beverages I've already mentioned—Doritos tortilla chips, Mountain Dew AMP, and Oberto meat snacks—this is about more than just existing product lizzles. It's about jiving around together with your buddies, playing amplified homemade instruments on the street corner, getting crazy haircuts—or better yet, dyeing your hair green!—all while helping us brainstorm some balls-out, edgy new snack foods and beverages that will appeal directly to people like you, with whom we are, of course, down.

So bust out of your grooved-out hip-hop cypher for a couple hours and come on down to the Frito-Lay building on West Essex Road this Saturday—if you are radical enough of a hipster cat, that is—and try out some of the new pimped-out food items and drink products we are developing.

Teens in the Squares demographic need not apply! Ø

LOCAL

First-Time Novelist Constantly Asking Wife What It's Like To Be A Woman

SAN JOSE, CA—Claims adjuster and novice author John Kitner is "constantly" asking what it's like to be a woman, reports his wife Becky.

"It never lets up," Becky said. "Today he asked, 'If a woman were running from a burning building, what would she be thinking about?' And I don't know how to answer that. I'd be thinking about getting away from the building, I think."

"What type of food would a woman try to eat if she were trapped in a walk-in freezer? How about a piece of liver? Would that be it? If I were a woman, I think that would be just perfect. But I don't know. You tell me, Becky."

The questions began when Kitner first started writing his crime thriller, Low Jack, in December of 2004. At the time, he reportedly asked occasional questions ranging from, "Would a woman want to be romanced by 22-year-old wannabe confidence man Ronnie Hodges?" to, "How would a woman feel if she were hammering a guy on the head with a briefcase full of money?"

"I didn't mind the questions at first," Becky said. "I was happy to help out."

But in recent weeks, the level of questioning has become what Becky called "really annoying."

Becky said when the two were at the grocery store Sunday night, Kitner began staring at her as she looked over the frozen-foods section.

According to Becky, Kitner asked, "What type of food would a woman try to eat if she were trapped in a walk-in freezer? How about a piece of liver? Would that be it? If I were a woman, I think that would be just perfect. But I don't know. You tell me, Becky."

Becky said her husband's questions are typically followed by him produc-

see NOVELIST page 202

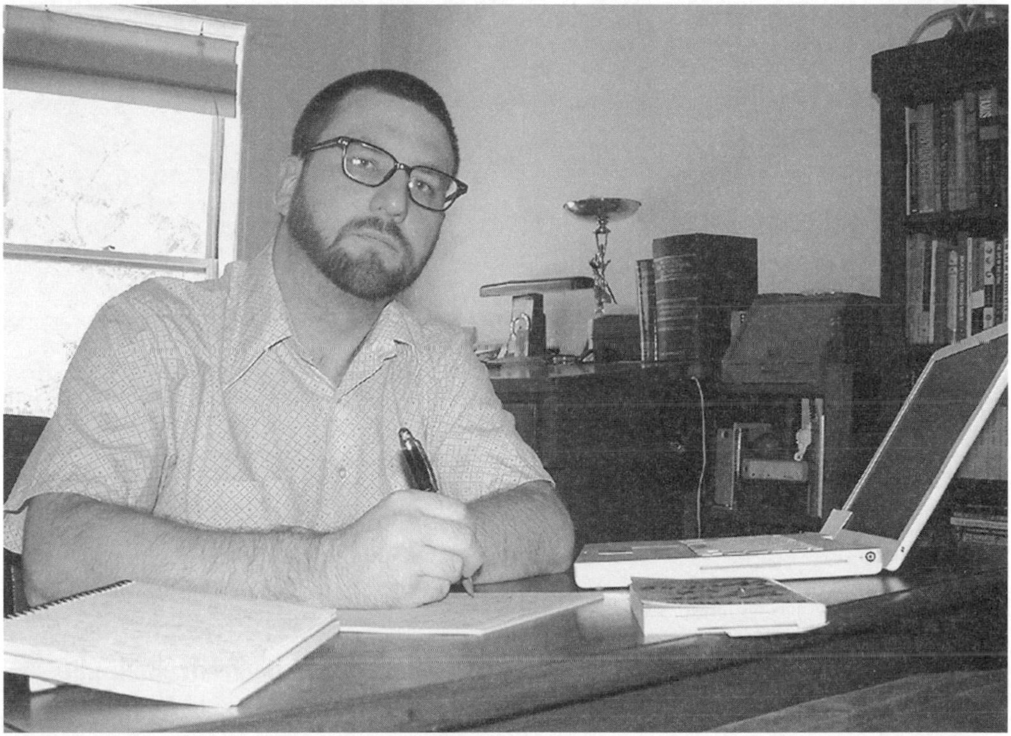

Above: Amateur novelist John Kitner struggles to write from a woman's perspective.

NEWS IN BRIEF

Frances Bean Cobain Enters Prehab

LOS ANGELES—Frances Bean Cobain, the 12-year-old daughter of serial substance abuser Courtney Love and deceased rock legend Kurt Cobain, entered the River Phoenix Elementary Prehabilitation Clinic Monday. "Although Frances Bean does not have a substance-abuse problem yet," publicist Cindy Guagenti said, "we thought it prudent to enroll her in an introductory six-step 'pretox' program." The $7,500-a-week facility has previously prepared celebrity children such as Maddox Jolie and Lourdes Ciccone.

Red Cross Accused Of Wartime Non-Profiteering

WASHINGTON, DC—The Senate Armed Services Committee issued a rebuke of the International Red Cross Monday, accusing the organization of wartime non-profiteering. "The Red Cross is exploiting the current conflicts in Iraq and Afghanistan to extend its money-losing influence over international medical aid and emergency relief," said Chairman John Warner (R-VA). "Whatever their stated mission, the Red Cross exists only to fatten its blood banks and care packages." The accusations come only weeks after Iraqi officials accused the International Red Crescent, the ICRC's Muslim branch, of masterminding multiple acts of humaniterrorism.

Maximum Age For Strollers Raised To 8

PARK SLOPE, BROOKLYN—Due to "increased self-indulgence among both children and parents," the Contemporary American Parenting Council announced Monday that it has raised the maximum age for stroller use among U.S. children to 8. "After we increased it to 7 in 2003, we still found far too many parents inconvenienced by their children's curiosity, mobility, and intellectual growth," said the CAPC's Beverly Kapatis. "Now, parents can enjoy avoiding their kids, and kids can enjoy blissful uninvolvement well into their pre-teen years." In a related report, the CAPC also recommended that the cutoff age for breastfeeding be raised to 6.

Bush Acquired By Martian Zoo

OLYMPUS MONS—President Bush, who in 2004 announced his desire for a manned mission to Mars, was acquired by a prominent Martian zoo Monday. "The President Bush shall have every comfort of home," said an unknowable Martian intelligence whose name is unfathomable to the human mind. "He shall have his Oval Office, his baseball, and simulated humans from his natural habitat, and we shall watch him most closely, for he is adorable sitting at his desk." Zookeepers on the Red Planet hope Bush will mate with the other Earth mammal in the facility, a northern white rhino.

Missing Boy Scout Earns Publicity Badge

KAMAS, UT—Boy Scout Brennan Hawkins, 11, who received national media coverage after he wandered off during his troop's June camping trip in the Utah mountains, was awarded a merit badge for publicity Monday. "Brennan was successfully mentioned on every major network during all news cycles, and succeeded in increasing public perception of both himself and the Boy Scouts," said Scout leader Troy Feyton. "I am proud to award him this rare merit badge, and pray he returns to us safe and sound once he has completed the talk-show circuit." Feyton confirmed that Boy Scout officials have revoked Hawkins' navigation, orienteering, and wilderness-survival merit badges.

KARL ROVE from page 199

identity to the press. He is rumored to be President Bush's senior advisor, chief political strategist, architect of the president's 2000 and 2004 election victories, and the current deputy White House chief of staff, as well as a frequent guest on televised political talk shows.

McClellan reiterated his denial of Karl Rove's existence 33 times during the press conference. When pressed, he distributed a list of "real, actual political figures about whom I'd be happy to comment." The list included only President George W. Bush and Secretary of Transportation Norman Y. Mineta.

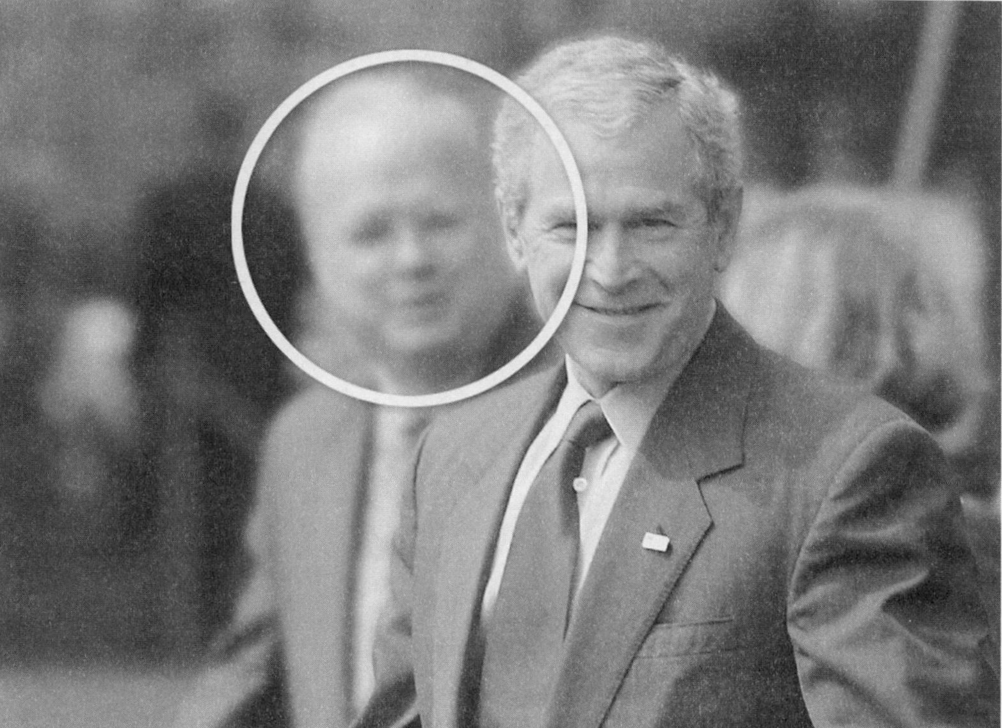

Above: This rare photo depicts the man Bush Administration critics are calling "Karl Rove."

"None of these allegations are supported by the facts," McClellan said. "The opponents of this administration have created a mythical figure in order to discredit the president. All they have done is divert attention from the important work at hand—the war in Iraq and the war on terror. In doing so, they have dishonored the sacrifices of our brave men and women in uniform."

"This time," he added, "the Democrats have gone too far."

According to fringe journalist Lou Dubose, author of *Boy Genius: Karl Rove, The Brains Behind The Remarkable Political Triumph Of George W. Bush*, Rove was born Dec. 25, 1950 in Denver, CO. Dubose alleges that Rove lived in Colorado with his family until 1963, when he moved to Salt Lake City, UT. According to Dubose, the shadowy figure entered politics in college, quickly moving through the ranks to become the chairman of the College Republican National Committee at age 22.

The White House has called such reports "nonsense."

McClellan reiterated his denial of Karl Rove's existence 33 times during the press conference. When pressed, he distributed a list of "real, actual political figures about whom I'd be happy to comment." The list included only President George W. Bush and Secretary of Transportation Norman Y. Mineta.

Rumors of the figure's existence were given a boost early this month when, as part of the official investigation into the CIA leak, a *Time* magazine reporter named Rove as the source of the leak.

"This is a very clever fiction concocted by those on the other side of the aisle," Vice President Dick Cheney said. "It's preposterous at its core."

The phantom advisor has come under heavy fire in recent weeks from critics of the administration, who say he should be fired for his role in the scandal. President Bush has pledged that anyone in his administration found to be involved in the CIA leak will be dismissed.

The phantom advisor has come under heavy fire in recent weeks from critics of the administration, who say he should be fired for his role in the scandal. President Bush has pledged that anyone in his administration found to be involved in the CIA leak will be dismissed.

"There is no such organization as the CIA," McClellan said. "This is tinfoil-hat stuff."

Initially demanding that the alleged Rove be fired, Democrats say they are now focusing their efforts on proving the figure's existence.

"I believe this deputy White House chief of staff is real, despite White House claims to the contrary," Senate Minority Leader Harry Reid (D-NV) said. "But to disprove this wild ghost story, we must begin an exhaustive fact-finding mission, for which I pledge all the time and resources of the entire Democratic party." ⌀

NOVELIST from page 201

ing a small notebook and ball-point pen.

"I really don't like when he whips out the notebook and clicks the pen and stares at me," Becky said.

According to Kitner, Becky has been "a great resource" in his novel writing.

"Becky is an indispensable tool in my writer's tool chest," Kitner said. "I feel like, with her, I'm able to get under Vivian's skin."

Kitner referred to his heroine, Vivian Drake, a 26-year-old ingenue who is "thrust into a steamy underworld of intrigue and danger in *Low Jack*."

Best-selling writer Tom Clancy, author of *Without Remorse*, said Kitner is lucky to have Becky as a source of reference.

"How would a woman feel if she were hammering a guy on the head with a briefcase full of money?"

"I worked alone in my study for years on *The Bear And The Dragon* before I realized my female character Lian Ming was dead on the page," Clancy said. "If only I'd had someone like Becky around to answer some questions. It might have helped me figure out how women think."

Clancy said he hopes Kitner can unlock the mystery of writing female characters, something no male novelist has ever been able to do.

Pulitzer Prize-winning novelist and literary critic John Updike agrees.

"Someone should have thought of asking these questions earlier," Updike said. "If only Tolstoy had thought this, Anna Karenina might have been a more memorable novel."

Updike added: "John Kitner's quest is a part of a larger one: how to write a character who is different from yourself. If he can find the magic key to this age-old puzzle, he will usher in a renaissance in human literature. For the first time, crime novelists will be able to write convincingly about murderers, even if they are not murderers themselves. Non-spies will be able to write about spies. In this new type of literature, there will actually be characters who are something other than novelists. Imagine the possibilities."

Kitner shares these high hopes for his work, but his wife, who has had an opportunity to read some of his early drafts, said it "still needs a lot of work." ⌀

CAR BOMBER from page 199

could have killed as many as 40 innocent people, had his life not been cut short.

"It is tragic that al-Khalaf died seven minutes sooner than he intended," said Hassan Abdul Aziz, leader of a local cabal of Sunni separatists. "To think that he was just yards from his intended target. Our thoughts and prayers are with his terrorist cell."

No insurgent groups have claimed responsibility for the car bomb, although as many as 18 separate insurgency factions have vowed to carry on the fight in al-Khalaf's memory.

Insurgent leaders met Monday to draft new rules to prevent bombing mix-ups like the one that killed al-Khalaf. One proposal would limit suicide bombings to odd hours, car bombings to even. Another designates "Car Bomb Only" traffic lanes to help terrorists get to their bombing locations more quickly and efficiently.

In the past week, over 170 Iraqi citizens and U.S. troops have died in terrorist or insurgent attacks, but al-Khalaf's death marks the first time a terrorist has been killed by another terrorist while on a different terrorist mission.

Above: Iraqis mourn the car-bombing death of suicide bomber al-Khalaf.

Terrorist leaders have called the incident a "wake-up call."

"No one likes to see a senseless waste of a willingness to take human life," said al-Qaeda operative Salih al-Shimiri, in a videotaped message aired on Al-Jazeera Monday evening. "However, there are worse problems than having too many suicide bombers on our streets."

Insurgent leaders met Monday to draft new rules to prevent bombing mix-ups like the one that killed al-Khalaf. One proposal would limit suicide bombings to odd hours, car bombings to even. Another designates "Car Bomb Only" traffic lanes to help terrorists get to their bombing locations more quickly and efficiently.

"I had a man last week get stuck in traffic while driving a car bomb to the Mendi Temple," al-Shimiri said. "When he arrived, he found it already on fire. We don't fill the cars up with enough gas to make two-way trips, so he was forced to blow up a nearby disco. This is madness."

Al-Shimiri added: "We all have the same goal here—the killing of innocent civilians. Let's stop working at cross purposes."

Iraqi cleric Moqtada al-Sadr believes all insurgents must find direction in their extreme fundamentalist faith. "When I close my eyes, all I can see are the faces of all the innocents al-Khalaf will never get a chance to kill. It is a sad day, but we must not let it shake our faith in the wrath of Allah." ⌀

"There are worse problems than having too many suicide bombers on our streets."

DROPOUTS from page 199

"Our public high schools place too much focus on preparing kids for professional careers," Chao said. "This waste of resources leaves our dropouts, the majority of whom have no chance of ever finding a job, wholly unprepared to sleep till 1 p.m., or watch daytime television while eating ramen noodles out of an upturned Frisbee."

According to the study, America's weakest academic performers also drop out of high school without ever having learned to steal beer money from their housemates' change jars or wash their hair with bar soap.

"This oversight cannot continue if our kids are to become unproductive citizens," Chao said. "The future dregs of society are not being served."

Despite massive cuts in recent decades, some remnants of math and science instruction continue to plague many school districts. These courses, Chao argued, waste valuable time and money.

Secretary of Education Margaret Spellings defended the nation's public-school system.

Chao said: "This waste of resources leaves our dropouts wholly unprepared to sleep till 1 p.m., or watch daytime television while eating ramen noodles out of an upturned Frisbee."

"Educators do a lot to ensure that the most hopeless students slip through the cracks," Spellings said. "Arbitrary rules, irregularly enforced discipline, and pointless paperwork are just the first things that come to mind."

She added: "Easy grading encourages students to be sloppy and late handing in homework—a skill that makes future deadbeats very competitive in stonewalling landlords and bill collectors."

Chao said educators need to think outside the classroom and give kids some real off-the-job experience.

"Increasing suspensions and expulsions is a good start," Chao said. "Furthermore, scoliosis exams should be made more routine, so students learn to adapt to the all-underwear wardrobe typical of the non-working class."

Chao also suggested that schools hold more blood drives, which would prepare dropouts for visits to their local blood-plasma donation centers for quick and easy cash.

Some educators say the report paints too bleak a picture of schools' efforts to instill students with a lack of ambition.

"We are doing a terrible, terrible job," said James Dunham, the principal of HS 445 in New York. "We literally could not be doing any worse."

Dunham highlighted the fact that the hallways of his school are lined with vending machines that sell nothing but unhealthy snack products such as soda and potato chips, both of which acclimate students to the diet of a jobless lowlife.

Susan French, a spokesperson for the National Education Association, the nation's largest teacher's union, said educators are superb role models for the unemployed dropouts of tomorrow.

Said French: "Students spend seven hours a day surrounded by adults who despise their low-paying jobs. If the critics out there know a better way to discourage a young person from entering the work force, I'd like to see it." ⌀

Agent 44 *Always* Gets To Choose The Rendezvous Point

I don't want to be a baby, but last week, we were en route to a site—can't go into detail, but it was strictly an information-gathering, no-casualty operation in a continent that begins with "A." I'm a firm believer in preparation, so I pulled out the dossier, broke the seal, and went over the plan: 37 and 8 dismantle the security system, 14 and 81 enter through the north wall and incapacitate the guards, 52 and 54 sweep the grounds for the weapons cache, and I stand guard while 44 photographs the documents. Once the mission is complete, we meet in the parking garage. I was memorizing the building plans when it hit me—parking garage? Agent 44 always has us meet in a parking garage. Why can't we meet somewhere else for once? And why does Agent 44 always get to pick the rendezvous point?!

By Agent 17

We're both extremely average-looking men of exceptional intelligence and social adaptability with short hair and tailored suits. Is it because he speaks Russian, Croatian, Cambodian, and Spanish, and I only speak Russian, Spanish, Hindi, and Mandarin? Or is it because he's a black belt in jiujitsu and I'm a black belt in kendo?

He gets to do all the fun stuff while I'm stuck with the dirty work. I didn't go through four years of covert espionage training so I could open and reseal envelopes for some agent with a swelled head.

I don't see what's so great about Agent 44. I can shoot better than him, impersonate foreign dignitaries better than him, and kill a man with a pen better than him. I bet I could even whip Agent 44 in a fight. But who always has to carry the briefcase full of money and open it, and who always gets to hang back and look tough? I can look just as tough as Agent 44—even tougher, since I started back up with the free weights.

Whenever we're doing an exfiltration, I never get to say, "Send your guy over first." That's Agent 44. He always gets to act like the boss. Meanwhile, I have to stand there like my only purpose in life is to take a bullet for him. How do you think that makes me feel? Pretty darn expendable, that's how. Oh, but Agent 44, no, the sun rises and sets on him. He never gets accidentally shot in the leg by a jumpy double agent, because he's too busy chatting up the Turkish ambassador's wife and hogging all the credit.

I'm the one who had to listen to seven months of throat-clearing and coughing, but as soon as the wiretap got juicy, it was, "Go stretch your legs, 17." One time, I was working surveillance on a prime minister, and when the honey trap made her "social call," 44 actually sent me for coffee. It's not fair! He doesn't even outrank me, but he always acts like he's in charge.

Who always has to drive the cable-repair van back to HQ every Monday? I'll give you three guesses. But the second we're in a hot chase, 44 jumps behind the wheel. I never get to drive the Maserati! And every time a mission is done, I have to debrief civilians and put away equipment while 44 gets to rush right off to whatever girl he's dating that day.

I don't see why he gets preferential treatment. I know it's not his looks. We're both extremely average-looking men of exceptional intelligence and social adaptability with short hair and tailored suits. Is it because he speaks Russian, Croatian, Cambodian, and Spanish, and I only speak Russian, Spanish, Hindi, and Mandarin? Or is it because he's a black belt in jiujitsu and I'm a black belt in kendo?

One time, we were parachuting into enemy territory and Agent 44 asked to see my gun. I told him you look with your eyes, not with your hands, but he said it was important. When I handed him my gun, he took the clip out and put it in his pocket. We were 70 miles into the hot zone! He was jeopardizing the mission just so he could play some immature joke! When I tried to signal the controller, he said he'd stop the helicopter if I didn't simmer down. How come Agent 44 never gets in trouble?

Agent 44 is such a jerk, but everyone treats him like he's the greatest thing ever. If something doesn't change soon, I will not hesitate to tell on him. ⌀

Your Horoscope

By Lloyd Schumner Sr.
Retired Machinist and
A.A.P.B.-Certified Astrologer

Aries: (March 21–April 19)
Your habit of falling out of trees, attempting to hide behind signposts, and following three feet behind people in broad daylight will force the government to adopt stricter ninja-certification standards.

Taurus: (April 20–May 20)
Tuffers, a 4-year-old German shepherd, will make headlines and be honored nationwide after saving six people, but conspicuously not you, from an apartment-building fire.

Gemini: (May 21–June 21)
It'd been about eight months since your personal hell disappeared overnight, but unfortunately, those stubby little buds on your forehead mean your antlers are back.

Cancer: (June 22–July 22)
Although you've never wanted to accomplish anything in your life as far as career and family are concerned, time travelers will persist on trying to kill you, simply because you make such great panic noises.

Leo: (July 23–Aug. 22)
The wheelchair and the indignity will be bad enough, but the worst part is going to be explaining to your wife exactly what you said to the genie to make him take off your legs like that.

Virgo: (Aug. 23–Sept. 22)
The stars, in their infinite cosmic wisdom, indicate that you should check out this radiation cloud on the far side of the Horsehead Nebula. It totally looks like Jesus.

Libra: (Sept. 23–Oct. 23)
After 10 years of marriage, sex is beginning to feel routine, mechanical, and artificial, which is just how you like it.

Scorpio: (Oct. 24–Nov. 21)
The mayor of Los Angeles continues to say you've got to go, which is strange, since you've never been anywhere near Los Angeles in your life.

Sagittarius: (Nov. 22–Dec. 21)
Your utter self-confidence and endless optimism will provide boundless, if temporary, comfort to those trapped with you in the burning bus.

Capricorn: (Dec. 22–Jan. 19)
Your cycle of drug, alcohol, and sex addiction will get even worse this week, but only for you personally. Most of your friends are still enjoying the hell out of it.

Aquarius: (Jan. 20–Feb. 18)
You've never been much of a people person, so it will annoy you no end when most of your town stops by on Friday for no reason but to hang out.

Pisces: (Feb. 19–March 20)
You will soon take a rather unromantic but extremely long night journey over and through a large body of water. ⌀

BOGGLE from page 141

amounts of blood. Passersby were amazed by the unusually large amounts of blood. Passersby were amazed by the unusually large amounts of blood. Passersby were amazed by the unusually large amounts of blood. Passersby were amazed by the unusually large amounts of blood. Passersby were amazed by the unusually large amounts of blood. Passersby were amazed by the unusually large amounts of blood. Passersby were amazed by the unusually large amounts of blood. Passersby were amazed by the unusually large amounts of blood. Passersby were amazed by the unusually large amounts of blood. Passersby were amazed by the unusually large amounts of blood. Passersby were amazed by the unusually large amounts of blood. Passersby were amazed by the unusually large amounts of blood. Passersby were amazed by the unusually large amounts of blood. Passersby were amazed by the unusually large amounts of blood. Passersby were

Don't think of it as back hair, think of it as "the opposite of not back-hair."

amazed by the unusually large amounts of blood. Passersby were amazed by the unusually large amounts of blood. Passersby were amazed by the unusually large amounts of blood. Passersby were amazed by the unusually large

see BOGGLE page 187

the ONION®

VOLUME 41 ISSUE 32 AMERICA'S FINEST NEWS SOURCE™ 11–17 AUGUST 2005

NEWS

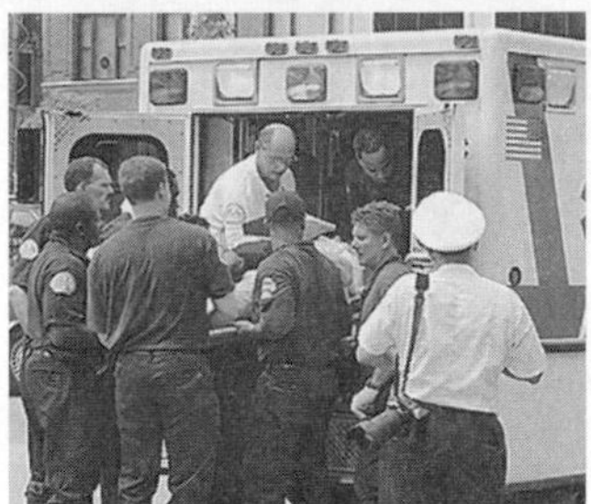

Disgruntled Bolton Shoots 17 UN Delegates, Self

see WORLD page 6C

New Distressed Jeans Feature Broken-In Cameltoe

see FASHION page 11C

Greenspan Lowers Dew Point

see SCIENCE page 8D

Wounded Celebrity Heroically Drags Self Down Red Carpet

see ENTERTAINMENT page 4E

STATshot

A look at the numbers that shape your world.

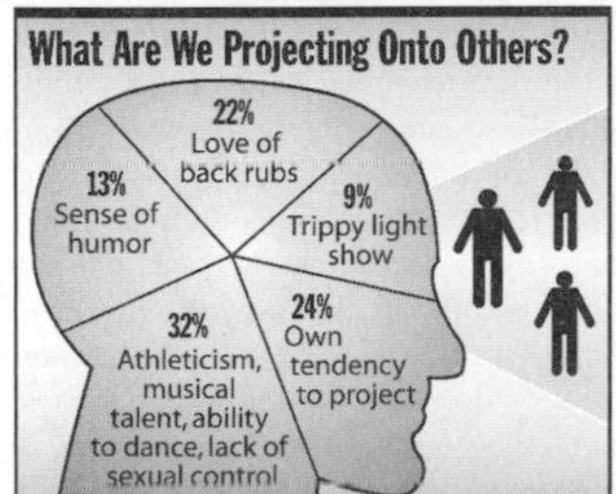

Bush Vows To Eliminate U.S. Dependence On Oil By 4920

WASHINGTON, DC—President Bush unveiled an aggressive initiative Monday that would make the U.S. free of petroleum dependence by the year 4920, less than three millennia from now.

"Our mission is clear," Bush said in a speech delivered at Fort Bragg in North Carolina. "We must free ourselves from dependence on fossil fuels within 85 generations. A cleaner, safer America is my vision. And it is our great, great—great-times-80 grandchildren who will realize that vision."

Bush promised a legislative package that would mandate severe cuts in oil-production subsidies and provide new funding for alternative-ener-

see OIL page 209

Above: President Bush presents his plan for our nation's far future.

Police Search Of Backpack Yields Explosive Bestseller

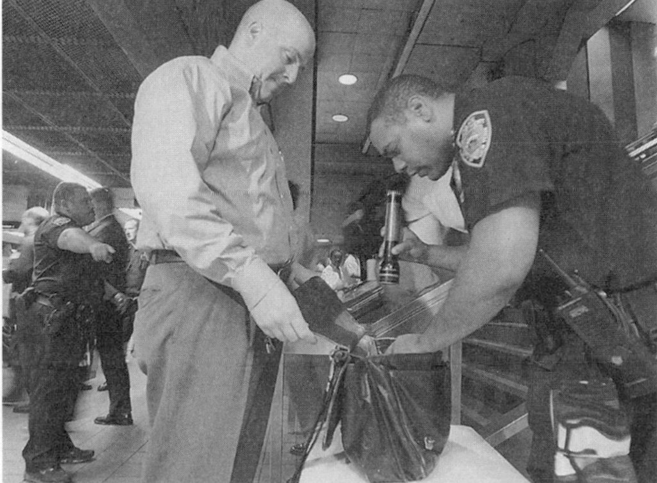

Above: NYPD officer Clarence Williams conducts a routine bag search.

NEW YORK—Officers from the New York City Police Department evacuated the Union Square subway station and suspended all train service Monday after a random search of a passenger's backpack revealed an explosive bestseller.

As of press time, bomb-disposal teams were still reviewing the threat.

see BESTSELLER page 210

Vehement Anti-Cell-Phone Guy Finally Caves

Above: Cell-phone owner Jason Whiting.

ANN ARBOR, MI—After calling the device "the item single-handedly responsible for the erosion of our nation's social and cultural foundation" for close to a decade, Jason Whiting gave in to social pressures this weekend and bought a cell phone.

The 34-year-old purchased the Motorola 6620 at the Maple Village Shopping Center.

see CELL PHONE page 208

Dog Cloning

Last week, the South Koreans became the first to clone a dog, reigniting a longstanding ethical debate. What do *you* think?

"This is a crucial breakthrough, as it's nearly impossible to get two dogs to fuck anymore."

Gary Burch
Purchasing Agent

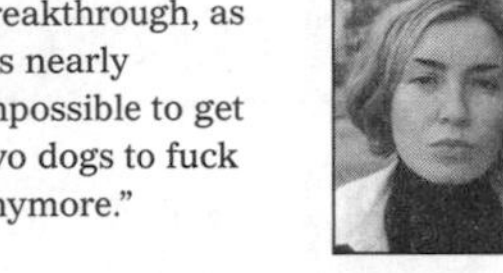

"I heard that cloned dog is highly unstable. Supposedly, if you pet it, its head'll, like, blow up."

Kim Casarez
Assessor

"As a Christian fundamentalist with a literal stance toward interpreting Scripture, I can't help but think that this could have saved Noah a lot of deck space."

Dede Greenwald
NA Counselor

"Did they rip the dog in two? Because that's how I cloned my starfish."

Joshua Green
Pile-Driver Operator

"The terrifying world of the future turns out to be pretty friggin' cute. *Puppy! Puppy!*"

Bulah Albers
Systems Analyst

"I'm not sure what I think about the Koreans cloning a dog, but I'm pretty sure I know what my hateful loudmouth racist of a neighbor's gonna say."

Mark Golin
Watchmaker

CAFTA Provisions

President Bush recently signed the Central America Free Trade Agreement. What are some of the provisions?

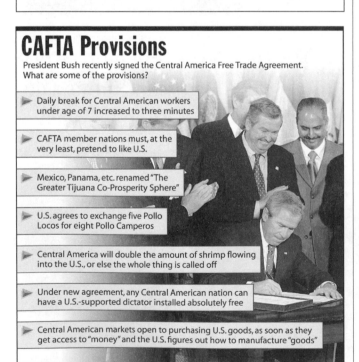

- Daily break for Central American workers under age of 7 increased to three minutes
- CAFTA member nations must, at the very least, pretend to like U.S.
- Mexico, Panama, etc. renamed "The Greater Tijuana Co-Prosperity Sphere"
- U.S. agrees to exchange five Pollo Locos for eight Pollo Camperos
- Central America will double the amount of shrimp flowing into the U.S., or else the whole thing is called off
- Under new agreement, any Central American nation can have a U.S.-supported dictator installed absolutely free
- Central American markets open to purchasing U.S. goods, as soon as they get access to "money" and the U.S. figures out how to manufacture "goods"

America's Finest News Source.™

Herman Ulysses Zweibel
Founder

T. Herman Zweibel
Publisher Emeritus
J. Phineas Zweibel
Publisher
Maxwell Prescott Zweibel
Editor-In-Chief

Why Somebody Always Around Every Time I Drop My Baby?

If people wanna think I'm, like, abusive or whatever, that's their problem. 'Cause I know I'm a good mom, and that's all that matters. But damn, yo, I better not have Social Services on my ass just 'cause I dropped Liondrae at Dollar City today. After it happened, some stock guy and some uptight-looking bitch were looking at me and I was like, "What the fuck are you looking at?" You could tell they were the judging type, and I don't want no cops at my door just 'cause some people think they better than me.

By Amber Richardson

I hardly ever drop my baby. Why ain't people around when everything's fine? What about when Liondrae's sitting in his high chair and eating Skittles? Or when I let him play in the sink with his diaper on? Or that time when my homegirl Kimmi came over to make Kool-Aid cake with us and pierced 'Drae's ear? I love my baby so bad. I don't wanna smack him around. His older sister, Rywanda, that's the one I wanna fuckin' take down once in a while. But only 'cause she don't behave, not 'cause I like to hit my babies for no reason.

Besides, it wouldn't of happened if he hadn't been leaning over trying to grab that jingly-jangly thing off the toy shelf. I had him in my right arm and he, like, let go of my shoulder and was arching his back and spreading his arms, and I got my other hand on the grocery cart, so all a sudden he topples over! Like, that's fuckin' wack! Don't he know I can't watch his ass every second?

Damn, why people always getting on my case? Where their babies at? Sarah so busy telling people what to do, she ain't got no man or no baby. She only got nephews. I seen a picture in her office.

I've only dropped 'Drae maybe four times. The first time, I was scared. He was only two months old and I guess I didn't have him buckled in his carrier right or something. In fact, I might of just forgot to buckle him in. I tipped his carrier down a little to get it into the back seat, and wham! He slid off and bounced onto the icy sidewalk. I was like, oh shit oh shit! But this woman coming out of the WIC building was screaming, like, worse than I was! She was all like, "Is she okay? Is she okay?" and I'm like, what's with this "she" shit? He a boy. Just 'cause he's wearing his sister's old shit. Like, mind your own business, bitch! He a-right. That crazy bitch freaked me out more than anything else!

Why ain't people around when everything's fine? What about when Liondrae's sitting in his high chair and eating Skittles? Or when I let him play in the sink with his diaper on? Or that time when my homegirl Kimmi came over to make Kool-Aid cake with us and pierced 'Drae's ear?

And like, there was one time I dropped him only 'cause some fat fuck bumped into me on the bus. So that one shouldn't even count.

Plus, 'Drae heavy. Even though he only 11 months, he make my arm go to sleep. That social worker Sarah said, if you got to carry him around, why don't you get one of them slings and strap him to you? I said the hell with that—how can I cook on the stove with the baby hanging off me? That's dangerous. I got to have the baby holding onto my side. Damn, why people always getting on my case? Where their babies at? Sarah so busy telling people what to do, she ain't got no man or no baby. She only got nephews. I seen a picture in her office. So fuck her ugly, lonely ass, a-right? I know what I'm doing with my babies.

And my baby tough. When he fell at Dollar City, he hit the back of his head on the shelf, then landed on his side. He was really screaming and shit, but 10 minutes later in the parking lot, he was laughing at a seagull. Fuck the doctor. Why should I waste two hours at urgent care when 'Drae just fine?

see BABY page 209

Longtime Married Couple Subjected To Excruciating 'Romantic Weekend Getaway'

KENOSHA, WI—Sources report that longtime married couple Duane and Edna Schumacher's weekend stay at Chicago's FantasyLand Suites was a grueling ordeal of unwelcome interruptions to their long-established marital routine.

"Oh, for Jiminy Cricket," Edna, 52, said Monday after returning from the trip, a 30th anniversary gift from her daughters. "Why the girls thought either one of us would find such an experience enjoyable is beyond me."

She added: "I was planning to weed my flower bed and maybe scrub out the back sink, which is just covered in muck, but now the whole weekend's shot."

The Schumachers said the unbearable ordeal began at check-in, when the reservations clerk handed the couple their keys, winked, and said, "Enjoy your stay." From that moment forth, virtually everything that occurred during the weekend induced cringes and winces from the aging pair.

"I love Edna, and I enjoy spending time with her," Duane, 58, said. "But

see GETAWAY page 208

The Schumachers said the unbearable ordeal began at check-in, when the reservations clerk handed the couple their keys, winked, and said, "Enjoy your stay." From that moment forth, virtually everything that occurred during the weekend induced cringes and winces from the aging pair.

Above: Edna and Duane Schumacher prepare to leave home for their agonizing weekend at FantasyLand (inset).

NEWS IN BRIEF

Podcast A Cry For Help

BOZEMAN, MT—The few people close to Mitch Delomme say that he doesn't realize the implications of his new podcast, an agonizingly personal 40-minute digitally recorded capsule of news, information, and trivia about the chronically lonely pizza-delivery man. "I wanted to share something about myself," said Delomme, 48, who in the course of his life has been heavily involved in ham and CB radio, personal home-page construction, and participation in late-night community-access cable. Delomme's podcast is currently available on all major subscription links, where it has attracted no attention.

'Humor In Uniform' Submissions At All-Time Low

PLEASANTVILLE, NY—*Reader's Digest* editors reported Monday that submissions to their "Humor In Uniform" feature have fallen off sharply since 2001. "The submissions that are trickling in are just not making me laugh," said Jackie Leo, an editor at the magazine. "I'm looking for amusing send-ups of peeling potatoes on KP duty, not another vignette about a soldier waking up screaming because he accidentally shot a pregnant Iraqi woman." Leo said she almost published one soldier's story about being financially devastated by shrinking veteran benefits "just to help him out with the $300 publication fee, but it just wasn't funny enough."

Entertainment-History Buffs Re-Enact Battle Of The Network Stars

SAN BERNADINO, CA—Entertainment historians from across the country gathered Sunday on a field near Hollywood to recreate the original 1976 Battle of the Network Stars. "We dedicate our re-enactment to the brave souls who fought it," said Network TV Historical Society co-founder and insurance-claims adjuster Drew Kamen, who played the part of CBS team wiseacre Jimmie Walker in this weekend's event. "Let us never forget the pivotal foot race between CBS's Robert Conrad and ABC's Gabe Kaplan." Kamen, like the other re-enactors, wore exact replicas of the striped tube socks and nylon running shorts used in the original battle.

Joe Wilson Getting Bored With No-Longer-Covert Wife

WASHINGTON, DC—Former ambassador Joe Wilson reports that he is "becoming disenchanted" with CIA agent Valerie Plame, since her identity was divulged to reporters in 2002. "I still love her, I suppose," Wilson said. "But I used to be the only one who knew her secret." Contributing to his sense of dissatisfaction, Wilson said, is Plame's new-found interest in public displays of affection, her habit of calling him from work, and her fear of violent reprisals from undercover Middle Eastern assassins.

Al-Qaeda Sitcom Filmed Before Live Studio Hostages

AL BHURBAN'Q, AFGHANISTAN—Filming of the second season of al-Qaeda's surprise hit situation comedy Ba'athtime For Abdul will take place before live studio hostages. "We shall not rest until the vassals of the Great Satan know what it is to live, love, and learn as a member of al-Qaeda," said a spokesman for the show, who assured fans that the laugh- and scream-tracks would not be sweetened in post-production. The videotaped statement, like the episodes of the show itself, was delivered to Al-Jazeera's Afghanistan headquarters in a plain box containing the tape and three severed heads of studio hostages. ⌀

CELL PHONE from page 205

"I got the simplest, most basic calling plan," Whiting said. "I sure as hell wasn't going to get one of those phones that takes pictures. To tell you the truth, I'm not even planning on giving out the number."

Whiting said he was reluctant to accept the "encroachment of technology" into his personal life, and explained that he "[does not] plan on becoming one of those people with cell phones."

"I sure as hell wasn't going to get one of those phones that takes pictures. To tell you the truth, I'm not even planning on giving out the number."

"This is for emergencies only," he said. "In case my car stalls on the freeway and I need to call for help, or in the event that I absolutely must get in touch with someone but am away from home."

Whiting first used the phone Sunday night to check movie times for *March Of The Penguins*.

"In fact, I use it so little that, when I went to the theater, I forgot to turn off the ringer," Whiting said. "When it started ringing, right away I said, 'Who's the jerk with the cell phone?' and I didn't realize it was me. Suffice it to say, I felt very guilty."

"It was my girlfriend, though, so I had to take it," he added.

Whiting blamed the incident on the fact that he had changed his ring tone several times that morning, from "Mozart 40" to "Espionage," and then finally to "Sumba."

Above: Whiting chats on his new phone at a local Marc's Big Boy.

Anticipating what he called the inevitable "I told you so" speeches from friends and relatives, Whiting insists that his feelings about the cell phone's negative implications for society remain unchanged.

"Cell phones are a part of a terrible trend toward alienation and the breakdown of civil discourse," he said. "It's a fact I made clear when I called in to the NPR talk show I was listening to in the car."

Whiting nonetheless decries overt use of cell phones while driving. "There's nothing more annoying—and alarming—than seeing some maniac in an SUV with one hand on the steering wheel while chatting on his cell," Whiting said. "That's why I went out this afternoon and bought a hands-free headset. I think it's called Blue-something. It's pretty cool."

"I knew this was coming," said Whiting's longtime friend James Patterson, who has known Whiting since his days as a college-radio DJ. "He used to rail against digital music, saying the 'purity' of vinyl could never be reproduced. But once he bought the Velvet Underground box set for 'completism,' it wasn't long before he sold all his LPs on eBay."

Whiting said owning a cell phone doesn't mean that his attitudes about "unnecessary market-driven consumerist gadgetry" have changed.

"I am never getting an MP3 player, no matter what," Whiting said. "Although my girlfriend might buy me one for Christmas this year."

According to the Radio Shack employee who sold Whiting his phone, Whiting returned yesterday to trade his phone in for an upgrade.

Said Whiting of the upgrade: "Cell phones are thinly disguised control devices thrust upon the masses as a pseudo-necessity. But if I'm going to wear a government tracking collar, I might as well be able to play some games on it." Ø

GETAWAY from page 207

when you're at that place, wherever you go, you know that the staff thinks you're either just coming from, or on your way to, having sex. I don't care for that kind of attention."

Thinking that "once they got settled, they would at least be able to relax," the Schumachers realized upon entering their suite that there was no escape from the crippling awkwardness that awaited them. At the sight of the red plush carpeting, red light bulbs, garish neo-Victorian nudes, and ceiling mirrors above the waterbed, Duane said he began having a severe attack of acid reflux.

The retiree, whose nighttime routine includes a shower at approximately 8 p.m., said that when he saw the heart-shaped hot tub in the center of the room, his first thought was, "How am I going to take a shower in that?"

According to Edna, a complimentary gift basket on the dresser contained flowers, Godiva chocolates, passion-fruit bubble bath, body oil, condoms, and "several battery-operated 'marital aids' that I don't care to describe."

"The chocolates were good," she said. "But they were the only thing we had to eat. Was that the hotel's idea of a proper supper?"

Edna, who privately told her daughter that she has been haunted by the image of her husband's posterior ever since she saw him emerge from the hot tub Friday evening, said, "There was an *Inspector Lynley* on Channel 13 that I was hoping to catch Friday night."

As the romantic weekend away from home progressed, so did the aging couple's agony.

"I could hardly sleep, which kept Edna awake, too," Duane said. "And that waterbed made Edna so seasick, I had to get up and make a 1 a.m. trip to Walgreens to get Dramamine."

On Saturday morning, the couple

"The chocolates were good," she said. "But they were the only thing we had to eat. Was that the hotel's idea of a proper supper?"

said they were informed that FantasyLand Suites does not offer morning newspapers—leading Duane to spend close to an hour angrily bellowing, "What do I have to do to just get a copy of the paper?!"

"It was even worse in the breakfast dining room," Edna said. "There we were, surrounded by young couples who were all over each other, and Duane is barking at me about 'What kind of a hotel doesn't have Total?'"

That night, the Schumachers suffered through a moonlight cruise on Lake Michigan, complete with violin accompaniment. During the cruise, which lasted for several hours, Duane said he had no way to return to shore to access the overnight bag containing his foot medication. Additionally, the couple missed their normal evening newscast.

On Sunday morning, the couple checked out and spent the rest of the day at a local Motel 6.

"We've been married for 30 years. There comes a point in a man and woman's life when you're happy just to get a good night's sleep," Duane said. Ø

OIL from page 205

gy research and development. According to the timetable he presented, these bills could be introduced as early as 3219, and U.S. energy consumers could start to see radical changes by the early 42nd century.

"If we don't end our dependence on oil by 4920, when will we end it? 5580?

In a detailed policy statement, Bush elaborated on the plan, expressing the hope that a third party, perhaps one comprising robots or super-intelligent, genetically engineered man-beasts, will help reduce America's dependence on fossil fuels.

By then, it may be too late," Bush said.

Bush called on both Democrats and Republicans living 1,200 years from now to work together to pass the program.

"It would be a shame if, by the 33rd century, these bills were still tied up in committee. I urge the 712th Congress to pass this legislation with minimal partisan gridlock," Bush said.

The president's science advisor, John Marburger, provided more details of the energy plan in a press release issued late Monday.

"It is the president's hope that hydrogen fuel cells, nanotechnology, or the recycling of human beings into fuel will hold the key," Marburger wrote. "Whatever the people of the 50th century feel is appropriate."

In a detailed policy statement, Bush elaborated on the plan, expressing the hope that a third party, perhaps one comprising robots or super-intelligent, genetically engineered man-beasts, will help reduce America's dependence on fossil fuels.

"I am calling on the popularly elected cyborgs of tomorrow to support this sensible measure to ensure the security of the nation," Bush said.

Some industrialists, particularly major auto manufacturers, expressed reservation over Bush's initiative.

"As admirable as Mr. Bush's visionary pronouncement is, I worry that the timetable he proposes is far too ambitious," General Motors CEO Richard Wagoner Jr. said. "It is simply not realistic. The automotive industry would require an additional three or four thousand years to develop engines that can run effectively on renewable or cleaner-burning fuels."

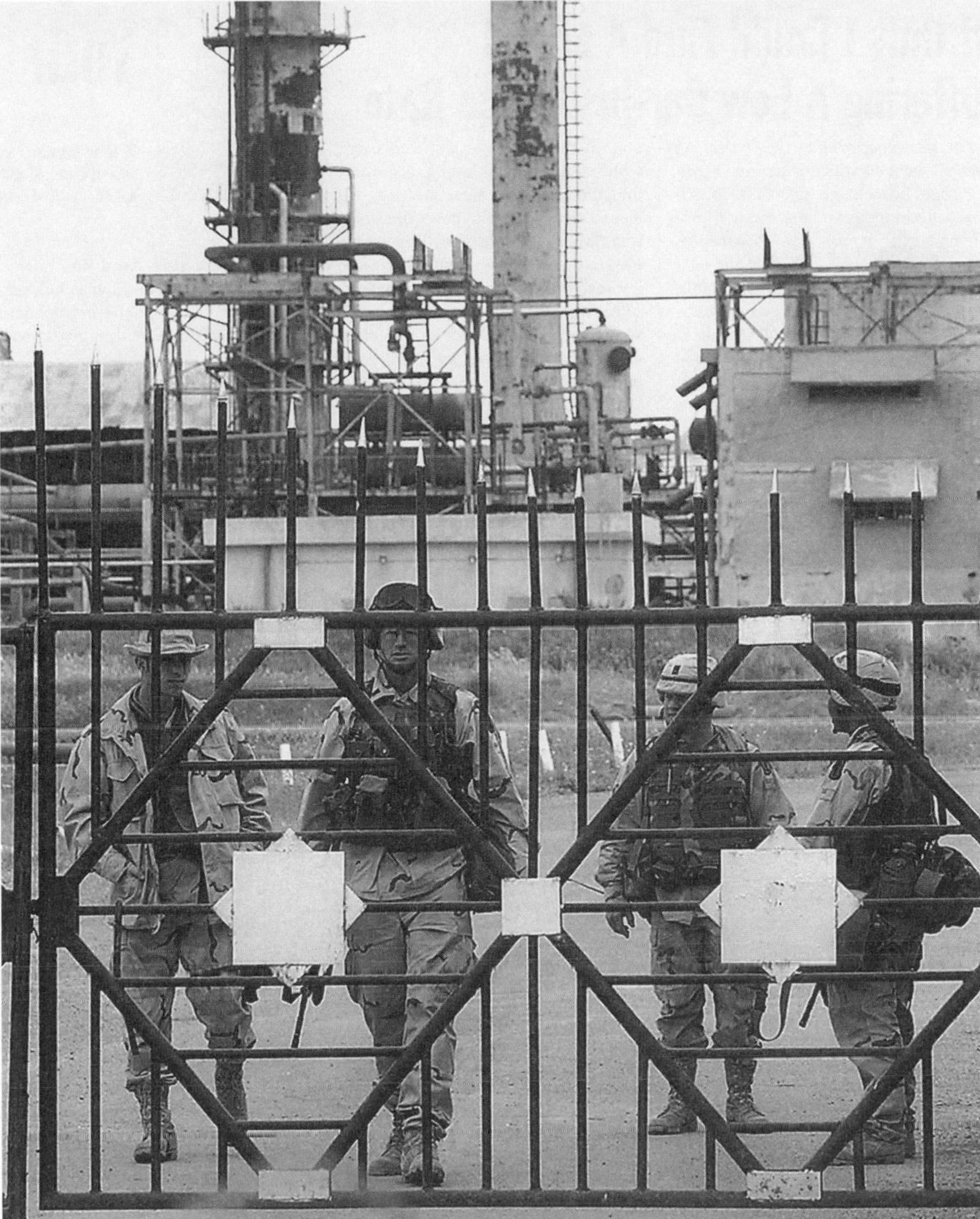

Above: U.S. soldiers prepare to withdraw from Iraq in the unfathomably distant future.

Exxon Mobil CEO Lee Raymond said the petroleum-producing company shares Bush's hopes for a cleaner environment "well before the sun turns into a red giant and dies."

"Mobil Oil has already made great strides in protecting the precious air and water within the television-commercial environment. And we plan to golf closely with the U.S. Department of Energy and oil-industry lobbyists to ensure that President Bush's initiative comes to pass in the unimaginably distant future."

"Our distant relations will have some hard work to do," Bush said.

Responding to reporters' questions, Bush admitted that our progeny could face challenges in pursuit of the goal, such as the earth's degrading orbit and eventual destruction of the moon by tidal force, or the Second Coming of Jesus Christ.

"Our distant relations will have some hard work to do," Bush said. "But hard work is what built this nation, and I have every faith that they will succeed."

The proclamation comes on the heels of Bush's plans to pay off the national debt by the early 6300s, and win the war on terror by 7450. Ø

BABY from page 206

Same for when 'Drae got that electric shock from unplugging the night light. I put him in his crib and the color went back in his face after like 10 minutes. After he knock his head on the shelf, he slept for a few hours, which was cool 'cause I got to watch my soaps with no goddamn interruptions for once. 'Drae, he really my special little man. He like Superbaby.

The worst was the one that happened in front of my mom. She such a cunt as it is, always riding my ass about everything. "Why he out of his playpen, anyway?" "Have the landlord put in some carpeting to cover up the jagged linoleum so 'Drae don't cut his face again." Like she has any right to tell me how to raise my kids. Back when me and my brothers was little, she was always waitressing or out with one of her boyfriends, and she never get us a sitter. So where the fuck she get off? "World's Greatest Grandma," my ass. I sure as hell didn't buy her that T-shirt. Ø

COMMUNITY VOICES

If Only I Could Find A Lizard Offering A Low Car-Insurance Rate

By Dan Hernandez

I'm an experienced car owner. As such, I have what I consider an above-average knowledge of what constitutes a competitive rate for automotive insurance. The policy I have now is fair, but I could probably do better if I shopped around. Trouble is, I don't have time to page through the phone book or search for information online all day—I'm a busy professional. That's why I'm currently looking for a lizard who will explain the various policies to me and help me figure out which company has the best deal.

I feel no loyalty to my existing car-insurance provider. If a better offer were made to me by a lizard, I would have to consider it very seriously.

Don't get me wrong. I'm not interested in a lizard with a hard sales pitch. I don't want some slick, fast-talking lizard bullying me into a big commitment. I demand a refined lizard, one with class. He might even be British, or an American educated at British schools.

I don't think my request is unreasonable. When I first started thinking about switching car-insurance companies, I encountered a stoic elk who offered a full range of financial services. But an elk is just going to follow the herd. And he's warm-blooded, subject to sudden changes in climate. How do I know he's not going to migrate when the going gets tough?

I'm prepared to put my trust in a lizard. When I was young, I got my breakfast cereal on the advice of a tiger. When I made a tuna sandwich, I reached for the can endorsed by the tuna fish. There was a brief time when I got my tuna on the advice of a mermaid, until I came to the conclusion that mermaids don't exist. Later in life, a small immigrant dog advised me on matters pertaining to fast-food burritos. And today, my puffed cheese snacks come with the seal of approval of a cheetah.

I want to make it very clear that I am not interested in some kind of lizard snob. I won't lie to you: My driving record isn't perfect, and it's important to me that a lizard understand that, and not look down his nose at me just because I've been in an accident or two. I want a lizard I can relate to. One who, when he's not selling insurance, does puzzles, or goes for a drive in his convertible, or maybe just watches TV.

I've had mixed luck bowing to the wisdom of amphibians and reptiles in the past. I once switched brands of beer at the behest of a trio of frogs, who made a convincing argument that the beers the bear and the dog were offering didn't have the same rich flavor as theirs. They opened my eyes to the fact that the dog was more interested in partying than in beer itself. A couple of years after I made the switch, I lost confidence in the brand when lizards came by and complained about the frogs.

I'm not interested in a lizard's opinion about beer. That's ridiculous.

With car insurance, on the other hand, the safety of my family is on the line, so I need the counsel of a cold-blooded reptile, one who understands the hard realities of the insurance business. One who understands facts and figures and has sticky toes that are able to cling to almost any surface. ⌀

I'm not interested in a lizard with a hard sales pitch. I don't want some slick, fast-talking lizard bullying me into a big commitment. I demand a refined lizard, one with class. He might even be British, or an American educated at British schools.

HOROSCOPES

Your Horoscope

By Lloyd Schumner Sr.
Retired Machinist and
A.A.P.B.-Certified Astrologer

Aries: (March 21–April 19)
You always say The Man is holding you down, but you never mention the intense sexual rush it gives you.

Taurus: (April 20–May 20)
Your torments will continue apace, but their intensity will slacken, as God is distracted lately by his hobby of striking random Boy Scouts with lightning.

Gemini: (May 21–June 21)
Heart-rending TV ads will soon begin asking people to send donations in order to wipe you out once and for all.

Cancer: (June 22–July 22)
You thought that your new lifestyle would be a nonstop party in the lap of luxury, but apparently Mr. Hefner has strict rules for his "permanent houseguests."

Leo: (July 23–Aug. 22)
Delightful changes that will transform your life into a giddy playground may still be ahead for you, provided you can summon the gumption to get out of bed before 3 in the afternoon.

Virgo: (Aug. 23–Sept. 22)
Officials will say that, although your death was indeed a tragedy, it could have been prevented simply by paying closer attention to either the warning signs on the time machine or your senior-year history unit on the Crimean War.

Libra: (Sept. 23–Oct. 23)
You will indeed come back from your adventure in a pine box, but thanks to advances in medical technology, it's a pine box outfitted with the life-support systems you now need to live.

Scorpio: (Oct. 24–Nov. 21)
You will be honored by the mayor of your city for your continued restraint in not expressing your feelings through poetry, song, interpretive dance, or ultra-large-scale fiber art.

Sagittarius: (Nov. 22–Dec. 21)
In this cruel metaphysical polka of life, it sometimes seems like for every step forward, you take one step back, two hops to each side, and do a twirl.

Capricorn: (Dec. 22–Jan. 19)
Your relations with the natives continue to blossom, largely because your rather clever translator refuses to tell them precisely what it is you're saying.

Aquarius: (Jan. 20–Feb. 18)
You will conveniently obtain employment in your city hospital's burn ward just as your new invention, a revolutionary, faster and hotter gas grill, encounters its first major stumbling block.

Pisces: (Feb. 19–March 20)
The technical details are still being worked out, but executives promise that your first few hilarious and heartwarming years will soon be released as a deluxe DVD package. ⌀

BESTSELLER from page 205

New York City Police Chief Raymond Kelly said officers performing bag checks at the southwest entrance to the station apprehended a Caucasian male in his mid-20s who was attempting to board a train carrying a small, brick-like object at 8:45 a.m. Kelly withheld the suspect's name and the title of the must-read page-turner.

"The suspect has been charged with possession of a dangerously hard-hitting bombshell," Kelly said. "Still at large is the mastermind behind the plot. We intend to bring this co-conspirator into custody before he can strike again with a shocking sequel."

He added: "It's possible that this thriller's devastating conclusion will hit like a ton of TNT."

A blurb on the back cover of the novel has been traced to *Deja Dead* author Kathy Reichs. In the blurb, Reichs described the Union Square novel as "literary dynamite." Authorities would not comment on what, if any, charges Reichs faces.

Although many blockbuster scares turn out to be nothing more than a ream of overheated typing with a menacing cover, officials said they are exercising great caution in handling this incendiary thriller.

"We're keeping our eyes peeled for clever devices," NYPD bomb-squad leader Roy Czulewicz said. "But many bestsellers have been known to hold people captive for hours with rapid-fire prose. Once you pick them up, you suddenly find you can't put them down."

The Union Square bestseller is the latest in a series of dramatic items discovered in New York since random subway bag searches began. On July 27, a hip-hop CD containing over 75 F-bombs led to the suspension of train service for 18 hours. And, on Aug. 2, a fiery burst of cinnamon freshness was discovered in a pack of Trident left on a Long Island Railroad car by perpetrators unknown. ⌀

"We're keeping our eyes peeled for clever devices," NYPD bomb-squad leader Roy Czulewicz said. "But many bestsellers have been known to hold people captive for hours with rapid-fire prose."

the ONION®

VOLUME 41 ISSUE 33 AMERICA'S FINEST NEWS SOURCE™ 18–24 AUGUST 2005

NEWS

Po' Boy $12

see WORLD page 6C

Dog Befriends Roomba

see NATIONAL page 11B

Bush Does 360 On Abortion Stance

see POLITICS page 8A

Chardonnay Vomited Into NPR Tote

see ARTS page 4E

STATshot

A look at the numbers that shape your world.

Top Online Petitions
Stop hate (117.4 million)
Save this one specific whale called Albert (28,547,873)
Bring back any sci-fi show that's been canceled (7,128,911)
Stop showing naked pictures of me on the Internet (13,982)
Stop corporations from gathering e-mail addresses (15,378)

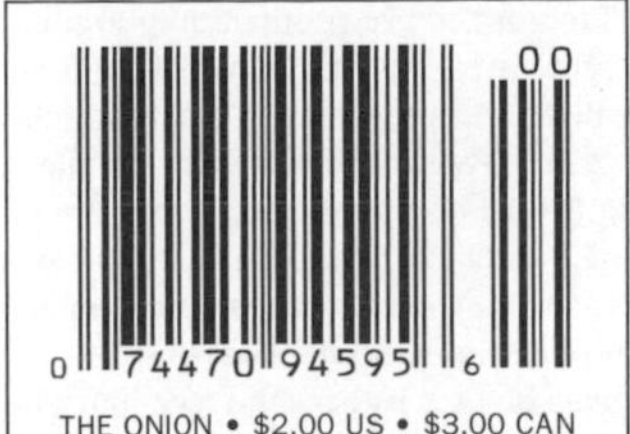

Rumsfeld Makes Surprise Visit To Wife's Vagina

Left: Rumsfeld strides across the Andrews Air Force Base tarmac, toward his intended vagina.

WASHINGTON, DC—Amid rumors of sagging morale on the home front, Defense Secretary Donald Rumsfeld greeted his wife Joyce Monday with an unanticipated visit to her vagina, according to the Pentagon.

"Today, at about 1600 hours EST, Secretary Rumsfeld landed in the vagina and delivered cordial greetings to Mrs. Rumsfeld," said Pentagon spokesman Lt. Col.

see RUMSFELD page 215

U.S. Intelligence: Nukehavistan May Have Nuclear Weapons

WASHINGTON, DC—A report released Monday by the Defense Intelligence Agency suggests that there is reason to believe that the former Soviet republic of Nukehavistan may be manufacturing nuclear weapons.

"New intelligence indicates that the likelihood of Nukehavistan possessing nuclear weapons is moderate to strong," said DIA Director Vice Adm. Lowell Jacoby in a press conference Monday.

The report cited several factors that aroused the DIA's suspicion, including the recent ratification of the Nukehavistan Nuclear Pro-Proliferation Treaty, the hawk clutching several nuclear weapons in the Nukehavistani government seal, and the July release of the commemorative "Great Nuclear Weapons Of Nukehavistan" stamp series.

While U.S. reconnaissance satellites

see NUKEHAVISTAN page 214

Above: Rev. Gabriel Burdett (left) explains Intelligent Falling.

Evangelical Scientists Refute Gravity With New 'Intelligent Falling' Theory

KANSAS CITY, KS—As the debate over the teaching of evolution in public schools continues, a new controversy over the science curriculum

see INTELLIGENT FALLING page 214

Jackson Jurors

Two jurors in the Michael Jackson molestation trial said they regret acquitting Jackson, and both now have pending book deals. What do *you* think?

"I, for one, am glad these jurors are finally getting a chance to weigh in on the Jackson trial."

Stephen J. Perrault
Software Engineer

"If these jurors make a lot of money, the jury for the next Jackson molestation trial will be filled with opportunists."

Madeline Novak
Systems Analyst

"Oh, this is just like *12 Angry Men*, except this time, it ends with them letting a child molester go free."

Susan L. Brady
Marketing Clerk

"Real-life trials have such hackneyed and predictable endings. Where's the creativity?"

Frederick C. Mish
First-Line Supervisor

"Shouldn't they have known that Jackson was guilty before the trial began?"

Daniel Hopkins
Stenographer

"This is what happens when a sleazy loonball is tried by a jury of his peers."

Neil Serven
Director Of Defining

Biofuels

With oil prices reaching an all-time high, scientists are looking for alternative fuel sources. What are they currently researching?

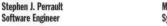

- Mentholanol—fuel derived from the cool, rich tobacco of Newport Lights
- EcoCoal—bituminous, geologically occurring combustible that comes in a nice green container
- Hydro-Quasi-Solarization—process whereby two naturally occurring hydrogen atoms are "fused" together to release roughly as much energy as the sun
- Ethanol—corn-based gas additive included at the insistence of corn-farming uncle
- DynOil—petroleum substitute made by putting long-extinct biomass under extreme pressure for millions of years
- Cardio-Electricity—energy source created by re-routing one's circulatory system through a small turbine
- Whateverthanol—mixture of random liquids poured into a fuel tank to see if it will power a car

America's Finest News Source.™

Herman Ulysses Zweibel
Founder

T. Herman Zweibel
Publisher Emeritus
J. Phineas Zweibel
Publisher
Maxwell Prescott Zweibel
Editor-In-Chief

What Has Our Society Come To When *March Of The Penguins* Is The Blockbuster Hit Of The Summer?

By Michael Bay
Director, *The Island*

I've been a major Hollywood director for a long time, and I thought I'd seen it all. But I can't help wondering what's happening to the entertainment industry—indeed, to our entire society. Where are our standards? Our values? For fuck's sake—our cultural priorities? I simply cannot accept that *March Of The Penguins* is the big summer hit everybody's talking about. *Hello?*

It used to be that a summer blockbuster had to have brutal violence, sexy women, breathtaking action sequences, adrenaline-pumping high-speed chases—at a bare minimum, some explosions. But sitting through that penguin movie, I couldn't believe my eyes. Where were the big set-pieces? Hell, this movie didn't even have *sets!* Has anyone ever heard of production values? It's one of the most vital aspects of the filmmaking art, and you don't get it by just showing up on an iceberg and filming whatever happens to be in front of you. Frankly, for real icebergs, they looked fake. This film is an insult to the great men and women who spend countless hours in front of computers creating incredibly realistic CGI icebergs.

Does no one out there care about these things anymore but me? Am I a lone voice of sanity crying out in a universe gone mad?

What kind of a world do we live in when a futuristic techno-thriller starring Ewan McGregor and Scarlett Johansson as escaped clones on levitating jet bikes doesn't outgross the shit out of a glorified Discovery Channel rerun? Don't people realize how much money I spent? How many people it took to bring that vision to the screen? Do people realize how many rewrites and punch-ups we went through? I paid my writers millions of dollars, and they were some of the best in the biz. You know who wrote *their* script? *A bunch of birds.*

Where was the villain? A story's not going to keep an audience on the edge of their seats without a strong opposition. Where was the second-act turning point? You've gotta have that moment when the hero's at the end of his rope and the bad guy looks like he's going to win it all. And where was the love story? Stars have to have real chemistry that smolders on the screen to make a summer blockbuster one to remember. Okay, the penguin movie had mating cycles, but that's not love. Is it all about sex to these animals?

Speaking of which, I think we can all agree that the penguins in this film gave some pretty wooden performances. In many scenes, it was impossible to tell them apart. Maybe if they'd moved the camera once in a while, I could have gotten more emotionally invested in what was going on. For Christ's sake, *there was not a single crane shot in the whole movie!*

I remember a day when the public appreciated fine cinema. In that lost age, it made sense that my important

What kind of a world do we live in when a futuristic techno-thriller starring Ewan McGregor and Scarlett Johansson as escaped clones on levitating jet bikes doesn't outgross the shit out of a glorified Discovery Channel rerun? Don't people realize how much money I spent? How many people it took to bring that vision to the screen?

historical drama *Pearl Harbor* had a fighting chance for at least a special-effects Oscar. Best sound, no question. But now, in this crazy upside-down, topsy-turvy world, I hear that—guess what?—the only summer movie getting any Oscar buzz is a static, near-silent documentary about waddling, flightless birds!

These days, I guess old-fashioned values like "megawattage," "high-octane thrill rides," and "explosions" just don't matter anymore. Well, I call that a sad day for American moviemaking.

I'm busy in pre-production planning my next big spectacle (which no one will see because they'll be off watching a 10-hour documentary on park squirrels, no doubt). But if you are in the San Diego area, do me this favor: Go to Sea World, walk into the emperor-penguin exhibit, and punch one those fuckers right in the face. Tell 'em Michael Bay sent ya. Ø

LOCAL

Iraqi Cop Moonlighting As Terrorist Just To Make Ends Meet

BAGHDAD—When the hot evening sun sets over Baghdad, Sulieman Hassim does not go home to his wife and family. For this Iraqi, the work day has only just begun.

Hassim, 32, is a two-year veteran of the Baghdad police force. Despite earning "danger pay," he still struggles to stay afloat financially, and has had to take on a second job as a terrorist just to make ends meet.

"After my electricity and water supply were restored, I suddenly had a lot more bills to pay," Hassim said. "Jobs are still pretty scarce, but I figured terrorists are always hiring."

Hassim, who has previously supplemented his income with such part-time jobs as guarding gas-fueled turbines from insurgents and driving a taxi, said he was initially unsure that he was qualified for terrorist work.

"My buddy Abdullah [Bahri] worked at the Brotherhood Of Total Islamic War, and he said he'd put in a good word for me with the head sheik," Hassim said. "I didn't expect to hear back for a while, but before I knew it, I got an interview."

Hassim, who has previously supplemented his income with such part-time jobs as guarding gas-fueled turbines from insurgents and driving a taxi, said he was initially unsure that he was qualified for terrorist work.

While Hassim had worried that his lack of experience and his creased suit would hurt his chances of being hired, he later said "the only thing they seemed to care about was whether I had a car."

Although happy to have extra work, Hassim is not always able to fulfill his duties as a terrorist, resulting in some unexpected complications.

"Last week, I couldn't work a suicide-bombing shift because I had to be alive early the next morning for patrol duty," Hassim said. "I was calling everyone, but I had a hell of a time trying to find someone to replace me. At the last minute, Fathi [Abd al-Khalid] agreed to take the shift. That guy's such a martyr."

After less than a month as a terrorist, the physical and mental strain of

see COP page 215

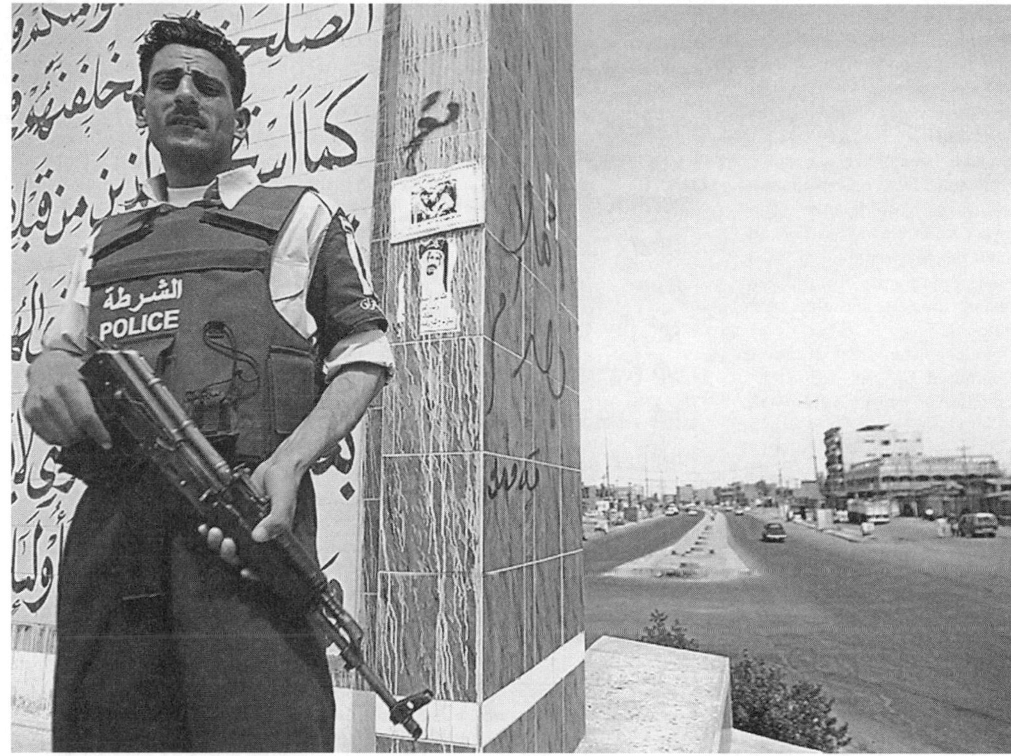

Above: Hassim waves several Total Islamic War coworkers through a checkpoint.

NEWS IN BRIEF

Angelina Jolie Coming For Your Baby

MALIBU, CA—Angelina Jolie has filed for adoption of your newborn baby, sources close to the actress reported Tuesday. "Angelina loves your baby, and you should be honored that she has chosen it," said publicist Jacqueline Silver, citing the growing collection of babies Jolie has culled from families worldwide. "Color, creed, whether your child is wanted—none of it matters. Angelina has fallen in love, and through legal means or force, your baby will soon be hers." Immediately after acquiring your child, Jolie will dress it in Betsey Johnson infant wear, give it a faux-hawk, name it after a random passage from the *The Tibetan Book Of The Dead*, then resume her relentless search for babies.

County Fair Judges Blown Away By Heifer

ELLENDALE, ND—Dickey County Fair livestock judge Bernard Hodelnutt called a heifer named Bessany "the sort of near-divine creation that inspired Zeus Himself to appear in the form of an amorous bull." "In all my years of cattle judging, I have never beheld such bovine perfection," said Hodelnutt, 52, who first encountered the 2-year-old Brown Swiss at the fairground's stock pavilion Sunday. "My fellow judges and I agree that we are unworthy of assaying such transcendent cowflesh. Our paltry ribbons and trinkets make meager tribute to this demigoddess, who should assume her place beside mighty Taurus in the heavens." After viewing the animal, Hodelnutt and the other judges cast their rating books and badges into a vat of boiling funnel cakes and cut out their own eyes lest they be fouled by the sight of less graceful beasts.

Calcutta Fire Marshal: Many Indian Homes Lack Bride Extinguisher

CALCUTTA, INDIA—Failure to own or use a bride extinguisher results in millions of rupees of property damage in India annually, Calcutta fire marshal Prasad Chandra said in a press conference Monday. "This tragedy occurs far too often when well-meaning husbands, attempting to collect on a dowry, ignite their brides indoors. The damage is often compounded when a burning bride attempts to escape and spreads the flames to other homes," Chandra said. "If you absolutely must burn your bride, avoid additional destruction with an affordable bride extinguisher. And, if possible, confine the burning to your backyard bride pit." He also recommended that homeowners install and periodically test marital smoke detectors.

New Pepsi Negative-220 Burns Twice The Calories It Contains

PURCHASE, NY—Joining a field already crowded with such non-caloric beverages as Coke Steam and Hollo Yello, PepsiCo announced the creation Monday of Pepsi Negative-220, a diet cola that burns twice the calories it contains. "You'll love PN-220 for the super-slimming rush of thyrotropin, PC1 enzymes, and that zesty hint of lemony leptin that zaps away fat, muscle tissue, and some nerve sheathing," PepsiCo spokesperson Ned Caen said. "But you'll drink it for that refreshing cola taste." Despite an FDA label warning of potential cardiac arrhythmia, renal shutdown, intestinal necrosis, and spontaneous erosion of the meninges, plans are underway to debut Pepsi Negative-220 in early October. "For radical and uncompromising weight loss, it's *the* cola," Caen said. ⊘

NUKEHAVISTAN from page 211

have yielded no conclusive evidence of Nukehavistani nuclear capability or activity, suspicions remain.

"High-resolution surveillance images obtained via satellite were marred by a green, glowing hue," Jacoby said. "While we cannot conclude that Nukehavistan has nuclear capabilities at this time, it is very possible that our satellites need better cameras."

For now, DIA representatives are investigating this little-known nation, which in 1990 became the first republic to break from the Soviet Union and amass nuclear-manufacturing materials.

"Nukehavistan's topography is dominated by flat, featureless stretches of gypsum and alkali, punctuated by the occasional deep crater and the twisted remains of metal structures," Jacoby said. "Its main exports are surplus Geiger counters, Tyvek fabric, and radioiodine-laced milk, and its only known import is weapons-grade plutonium."

Human intelligence-gathering is reportedly very difficult in the isolated, landlocked country. Nukehavistan's borders are tightly patrolled by its army, and foreigners must receive an official and hard-to-obtain visa to enter the country. However, according to the U.S. State Department, tourism has increased over the past 10 years. The tiny nation is visited most frequently by vacationers from Iran, North Korea, and Pakistan.

It is believed that over 90 percent of Nukehavistan's 17 million citizens work in the power-plant industry.

"High-resolution surveillance images obtained via satellite were marred by a green, glowing hue," Jacoby said. "While we cannot conclude that Nukehavistan has nuclear capabilities at this time, it is very possible that our satellites need better cameras."

In the summer issue of *Jane's Defense Quarterly*, Brian Walters, an expert in former Soviet republics, argued that the DIA's suspicion was founded in cultural bias.

"Nukehavistanis' traditional dress consists of elaborately embroidered lead aprons with hoods and large lead-shielded visors," Walters said. "Their folk music possesses a droning quality comprising two high-pitched concurrent tones at a frequency identical to that of the old Emergency Broadcast System of the Cold War era."

Secretary of State Condoleezza Rice is planning a visit to Nukehavistan's capital city of Silograd in September. "While there, I will do my best to determine the extent of Nukehavistan's nuclear-production potential," Rice said.

"I also plan to visit the Great Silo," added Rice, speaking of the towering minaret-like structure at the city's center, one of only two man-made structures visible from a low-Earth orbit.

Nukehavistan has neither confirmed nor denied suspicions that they are manufacturing nuclear weapons. Their only response to the mounting investigation came in a vague statement issued late Tuesday evening by Sergei Annihilatovich, who serves as both Nukehavistan's president and its secretary of offensive atomic munitions manufacturing and deployment.

"If this unnecessary investigation by the United States continues, we will have no choice but to nuke them," he said.

Nukehavistan At A Glance

Location: Central Asia, north of Uzbekistan and Kyrgyzstan

Population: 17,163,466

Independence: Aug. 30, 1991 (from the Soviet Union)

Capital: Silograd

Terrain: Alkali plains with large craters

Land use: 4.3% arable land, 1.2% permanent crops, 94.5% unknown

Unit of currency: Nuq

Leading exports: Geiger counters, Tyvek fabric, radioiodine-laced milk

Leading import: Plutonium

National animal: Cockroach

National bird: SS-20 Intercontinental Ballistic Missile

National food: Yellowcake

National beverage: Heavy water

National symbol of peace: None

National holidays: Independence Day, St. Fission's Eve, Feast of St. Oppenheimer, Nukemas, Bombadan

Traditional ethnic dress: Embroidered lead aprons with large hoods and visors

INTELLIGENT FALLING from page 211

arose Monday in this embattled Midwestern state. Scientists from the Evangelical Center For Faith-Based Reasoning are now asserting that the long-held "theory of gravity" is flawed, and they have responded to it with a new theory of Intelligent Falling.

"Things fall not because they are acted upon by some gravitational force, but because a higher intelligence, 'God' if you will, is pushing them down," said Gabriel Burdett, who holds degrees in education, applied Scripture, and physics from Oral Roberts University.

Burdett added: "Gravity—which is taught to our children as a law—is founded on great gaps in understanding. The laws predict the mutual force between all bodies of mass, but they cannot explain that force. Isaac Newton himself said, 'I suspect that my theories may all depend upon a force for which philosophers have searched all of nature in vain.' Of course, he is alluding to a higher power."

Founded in 1987, the ECFR is the world's leading institution of evangelical physics, a branch of physics based on literal interpretation of the Bible.

According to the ECFR paper published simultaneously this week in the *International Journal Of Science* and the adolescent magazine *God's Word For Teens!*, there are many phenomena that cannot be explained by secular gravity alone, including such mysteries as how angels fly, how Jesus ascended into Heaven, and how Satan fell when cast out of Paradise.

"In Matthew 15:14, Jesus says, 'And if the blind lead the blind, both shall fall into the ditch.' He says nothing about gravity."

The ECFR, in conjunction with the Christian Coalition and other Christian conservative action groups, is calling for public-school curriculums to give equal time to the Intelligent Falling theory. They insist they are not asking that the theory of gravity be banned from schools, but only that students be offered both sides of the issue "so they can make an informed decision."

"We just want the best possible education for Kansas' kids," Burdett said.

Proponents of Intelligent Falling assert that the different theories used by secular physicists to explain gravity are not internally consistent. Even critics of Intelligent Falling admit that Einstein's ideas about gravity are mathematically irreconcilable with quantum mechanics. This fact, Intelligent Falling proponents say, proves that gravity is a theory in crisis.

"Let's take a look at the evidence," said ECFR senior fellow Gregory Lunsden. "In Matthew 15:14, Jesus says, 'And if the blind lead the blind, both shall fall into the ditch.' He says nothing about some gravity making them fall—just that they will fall. Then, in Job 5:7, we read, 'But mankind is born to trouble, as surely as sparks fly upwards.' If gravity is pulling everything down, why do the sparks fly upwards with great surety? This clearly indicates that a conscious intelligence governs all falling."

Critics of Intelligent Falling point out that gravity is a provable law based on empirical observations of natural phenomena. Evangelical physicists, however, insist that there is no conflict between Newton's mathematics and Holy Scripture.

"Closed-minded gravitists cannot find a way to make Einstein's general relativity match up with the subatomic quantum world," said Dr. Ellen Carson, a leading Intelligent Falling expert known for her work with the Kansan Youth Ministry. "They've been trying to do it for the better part of a century now, and despite all their empirical observation and carefully compiled data, they still don't know how."

"Traditional scientists admit that they cannot explain how gravitation is supposed to work," Carson said. "What the gravity-agenda scientists need to realize is that 'gravity waves' and 'gravitons' are just secular words for 'God can do whatever He wants.'"

Some evangelical physicists propose that Intelligent Falling provides an elegant solution to the central problem of modern physics.

"Anti-falling physicists have been theorizing for decades about the 'electromagnetic force,' the 'weak nuclear force,' the 'strong nuclear force,' and so-called 'force of gravity,'" Burdett said. "And they tilt their findings toward trying to unite them into one force. But readers of the Bible have already known for millennia what this one, unified force is: His name is Jesus."

COP from page 213

working 70-hour weeks can be seen in Hassim's tired, sunken eyes and stooped posture. Complaining of exhaustion, Hassim said that he doesn't "know what job [he's] at half the time."

"Several times, I've found myself wondering, 'Now, why am I shooting this guy again? Because he's just stolen a can of gasoline, or because he's a cowardly informant of the hated occupier?'" Hassim said. "'Should I mow down the American soldiers at this checkpoint, or politely flash my badge?'"

"Hassim's accidental-kill rate has doubled in recent weeks," said Capt. Badeer Mustafa, Hassim's immediate superior at the police department. "Last week, he shot 20 civilians. I might have to dock his pay."

Above: Hassim (second from left) works a night shift for the Brotherhood Of Total Islamic War.

Hassim said he had a particularly close call last Sunday.

"I was screaming that U.S. soldiers are murderous infidels whose blood should be spilled without hesitation, when I realized that I was at the police station," Hassim said. "Luckily, the other officers either weren't paying attention or they agreed with me."

Hassim said it "felt strange" to bomb an embassy outpost, punch out, report to work as a police officer, then return to the same site an hour later to secure the area.

"That's happened a couple times," Hassim said. "I find myself going, 'Déjà vu?' And then I'm like, 'Oh, yeah.'"

Hassim's supervisors at both the police station and the Brotherhood Of Total Islamic War were critical of his job performance.

"Hassim's accidental-kill rate has doubled in recent weeks," said Capt. Badeer Mustafa, Hassim's immediate superior at the police department. "Last week, he shot 20 civilians. I might have to dock his pay."

Mohammed al-Zahass, a high commander with the Brotherhood Of Total Islamic War, has been displeased with Hassim's performance, as well.

"Second time this week, we've had to tell him to hit 'record' on the video camera, not 'play,'" al-Zahass said. "I couldn't believe it. I said, 'Look at the buttons if you're confused!' It's not like you can behead a hostage twice."

Although Hassim, like most Iraqis, would like to see an end to the bloodshed, the father of four admitted he just can't afford it.

Hassim's family has also felt the strain.

"I rarely see my husband anymore," Ghayda Hassim said. "I never thought I'd say this, but I miss the early months of the occupation when Sulieman was out of work like everyone else, sipping mint tea, watching Al-Jazeera at full blast, and ordering me around like a slave. I want my old Sulieman back."

Although Hassim, like most Iraqis, would like to see an end to the bloodshed, the father of four admitted he just can't afford it.

"If the situation in Iraq were to stabilize, I could possibly lose not only one job, but two. Thankfully, I won't have to worry about that for a long, long time." ∅

RUMSFELD from page 211

William Brock. "The focus of the trip was to thank Mrs. Rumsfeld for her long years of outstanding service and continuing sacrifices, and to afford the defense secretary an opportunity to survey the vagina up close and in person."

The 12-minute visit, described by Brock as "brief but satisfactory," was characterized by sources close to the vagina as an "in and out" mission.

Because of security concerns, Rumsfeld's aides were quiet about the visit, taking extra efforts to conceal the defense secretary's plans from the media and his wife. After delivering a speech to his wife, Rumsfeld performed a brief inspection of her vagina, then engaged in a few minutes of relaxed, informal contact before returning to the Pentagon.

"Despite the hurried nature of the visit, I am proud to report that my wife met and exceeded the operational standards set by the U.S. military for readiness in a two-front war,"

Rumsfeld: "I am proud to report that my wife met and exceeded the operational standards set by the U.S. military for readiness in a two-front war."

said Rumsfeld in a press conference shortly after the visit. "I am confident that she can still stand up to heavy fire and serve ably, even in a rear-guard action."

The visit comes at a time in which controversial rumors have spread throughout Washington about low morale on the part of Mrs. Rumsfeld. Reports from confidantes indicate that her vagina is being undersupplied by the Department of Defense, and extended tours of duty have stirred up feelings of discontent. Although the two have faithfully served one another since 1954, Secretary Rumsfeld's busy schedule and demanding obligations have prevented him from visiting the fertile crescent since last November's highly publicized surprise visit.

A brief question-and-answer period following the visit revealed some difference of opinion between Rumsfeld and the woman whose vagina he is charged with supplying. When she asked the defense secretary if she could expect "more consistent support" from him in the future, Mrs. Rumsfeld received a characteristically salty reply.

"Naturally, I would like to spend more time in the vaginal region," Rumsfeld said.

"Naturally, I would like to spend more time in the vaginal region," Rumsfeld said. "But we have a difficult mission to complete, both at home and on the front. Everyone in

see RUMSFELD page 216

COMMUNITY VOICES

They Called Me Crazy When I Switched Shampoos, But Who's Crazy Now?

Pity those poor mortals milling about at the drugstore. I once numbered among them, braying and milling like sheep in limp-haired herds. Like them, I was satisfied to follow the same old morning routine, blindly accepting the shampoos of our forefathers, and their forefathers before them. But armed with only a dream and the coupon I discovered in the Sunday newspaper insert, I dared to switch brands. They thought me mad. They thought me crazy. But look at me! Look at my rich, easy-to-manage hair and tell me who's crazy now?

By Kevin Larson

They think I didn't see them shaking their heads, whispering behind their hands. Damn them and their tiny minds!

From the instant I entered my shower and squeezed a dime-size dollop into my palm, I knew that a miracle was nigh, and their ignorant fear did not concern me. As I coaxed the new shampoo into a rich lather, I could feel the revitalizing power coursing through my hair, electrifying it to the very roots. Like Archimedes, I sprang from my shower and shouted to the heavens: "Behold! Gaze upon my head

From the instant I entered my shower and squeezed a dime-size dollop into my palm, I knew that a miracle was nigh, and their ignorant fear did not concern me.

and ask yourself—is this the full-bodied head of hair of a madman?"

With requisite small-mindedness, the "good people" now shun and malign me. The sidewalks seem to clear before my path, and my approach is greeted with the sound of slamming screen doors and the sharp click of deadbolt locks. Because I dared to pick the forbidden fruit of scalp hygiene, they treat me as a monster. But it is they who are the limp, lifeless, heat-damaged monsters. Gaze unto my head and ask yourself: Have I not created new life in my hair?

How they laughed at me at the drugstore! How they spat upon my dream of healthy hair! But they would think twice before laughing now, as I vigorously toss my beautiful, flowing locks! Again and again, I toss my lush hair as if in slow motion. I ask you,

With requisite small-mindedness, the "good people" now shun and malign me. The sidewalks seem to clear before my path, and my approach is greeted with the sound of slamming screen doors and the sharp click of deadbolt locks.

are these the actions of an insane man?

Perhaps it is mad to have hair this healthy and lustrous. If that is the case, then so be it! I embrace the moniker of madman. I care nothing of what others think. Let the name of Larson be evoked in the same breath as the other great madmen of infamy, as long as it is synonymous with the achievement of beautiful, manageable hair. If lesser minds cannot embrace my hair's newfound sheen, it is of no concern to me.

They chastised me for playing God. Their greatest minds barked amongst themselves: "God did not want us to have bouncing and behaving hair. We are men, not angels." Bah! I never intended to play God, but this luxurious mane cannot be that of a mere mortal.

A pity that there is no picture of me before the transformation, that these dullards might compare it to the glorious After, for I have breathed in apple-scented greatness, and I can never return to what was. If you cannot come with me on my journey into the unknown, then begone! And don't wonder what happened to me. Know only that I have changed shampoos, and I can no longer live amongst lesser men. Ø

HOROSCOPES

Your Horoscope

By Lloyd Schumner Sr.
Retired Machinist and
A.A.P.B.-Certified Astrologer

Aries: (March 21–April 19)
You will soon have a romantic encounter with a dark stranger... By dark, the zodiac means "enigmatic and mysterious"—not that the stranger is black.

Taurus: (April 20–May 20)
There are times when you wonder how a promising backyard-wrestling star wound up driving an Army transport truck in Iraq, but you usually remember pretty quickly.

Gemini: (May 21–June 21)
You have no idea why all the surviving members of Art Blakey's Jazz Messengers decided to burn your house down with you in it, but as a jazz aficionado, you're glad they brought their instruments along to pass the time.

Cancer: (June 22–July 22)
The stars can't believe you fell for it when they said you wouldn't be caught if you drove your Explorer through the crowd at Sun Creek Pancake Days. Enjoy prison.

Leo: (July 23–Aug. 22)
You'll soon take your leave of this world, which has become your own personal hell, and enter a hell shared by billions of miserable bastards.

Virgo: (Aug. 23–Sept. 22)
The bear's probably going to be pretty hung over when it wakes up, so it would be best to go somewhere else to wonder how your bank robbery went wrong.

Libra: (Sept. 23–Oct. 23)
You still don't think your bail should get bigger every time you get arrested.

Scorpio: (Oct. 24–Nov. 21)
Although the incumbent will stand firm on his platform of fair taxes, better schools, and safer streets, you'll win in a landslide from your platform of human skulls.

Sagittarius: (Nov. 22–Dec. 21)
The days are long past when you could get a healthy baby for less than a hundred grand, but you'd be surprised how many sick ones that kind of money will land you.

Capricorn: (Dec. 22–Jan. 19)
You knew that house cats liked to play cruelly with their prey before eating it, but you had no idea that they grew to the size of the one outside your door right now.

Aquarius: (Jan. 20–Feb. 18)
You've been a chronic underachiever most of your career, which is pretty good news considering that you're a professional rapist.

Pisces: (Feb. 19–March 20)
Science has no explanation for the antlers that appeared on your forehead yesterday morning. The Elizabethans, however, had a word for it. It sounds like "uckoldry." Ø

RUMSFELD from page 215

this conflict is making sacrifices. You go to the vagina with the equipment you have."

This explanation did not satisfy Judith Proudfit, executive director of Veterans' Wives Against The War and a sharp critic of the Bush Administration. Proudfit called Rumsfeld's visit a "craven publicity move intended to foster the illusion that Rumsfeld is in touch with his wife's vagina."

"Rumsfeld's blunt, defensive response clearly indicates that he has no intention of making her a top priority," Proudfit said. "The situation in Mrs. Rumsfeld's vagina was in no way improved by such a brief encounter."

Continued Proudfit: "It is a true testament to Mrs. Rumsfeld's patience, stamina, and patriotism that she continues to serve her husband under such duress."

When asked about future plans for his wife's vagina, Rumsfeld grew somber.

"This vagina has seen a lot of action," Rumsfeld said. "And much of its infrastructure has fallen into disre-

When asked about future plans for his wife's vagina, Rumsfeld grew somber.

pair. I do believe, however, that my wife's sustained efforts under my direction will ultimately allow us to re-establish order in this troubled area."

The Pentagon would not confirm a rumor that President Bush is scheduled to drop in on the vagina with a holiday turkey around Christmas. Ø

NEWS

New Planet Discovered 400 Light Years Away From Public's Interest

see SCIENCE page 12E

Perfect Gift For Boring Asshole Found At Crate & Barrel

see NATIONAL page 9A

Harlem Globetrotters Keep Basketball Just Out Of Reach Of Make-A-Wish Kid

see LOCAL page 3B

STATshot

A look at the numbers that shape your world.

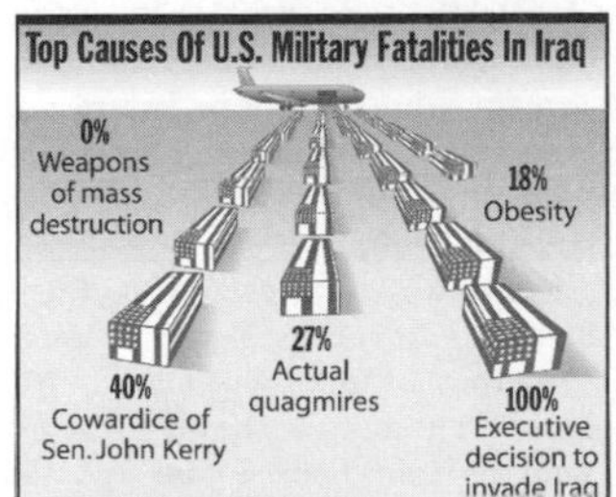

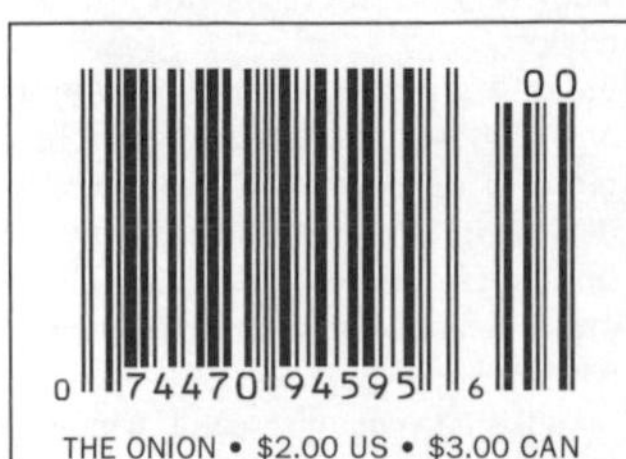

the ONION®

VOLUME 41 ISSUE 34 AMERICA'S FINEST NEWS SOURCE™ 25–31 AUGUST 2005

New Strain Of Jet Lag Devastates Airline Industry

ATLANTA—Already hard hit by labor strife and escalating fuel costs, the commercial airline industry faces a new crisis: an epidemic of jet lag caused by a powerful strain that is highly resistant to regular remedies like catnaps.

Airlines have set up napping-triage centers in major airports in response to the "Super Lag," but are unable to keep up with the rising tide of severely weary passengers, who number in the thousands nationwide.

"Infected travelers are really tired out, whether they're on long international flights or domestic flights as short as an hour and a half," said Delta Airlines ticket agent Olivia Gage at Atlanta International Airport, which has seen some of the most advanced cases of Super Lag. "Our supplies of thin blankets and miniature pillows are running dangerously low."

FEMA, the Federal Exhaustion Management Association, has shipped army-surplus cots and urns of hot coffee to several major hubs, but airlines

see JET LAG page 220

Right: A traveler at Chicago's O'Hare International Airport succumbs to "Super Lag."

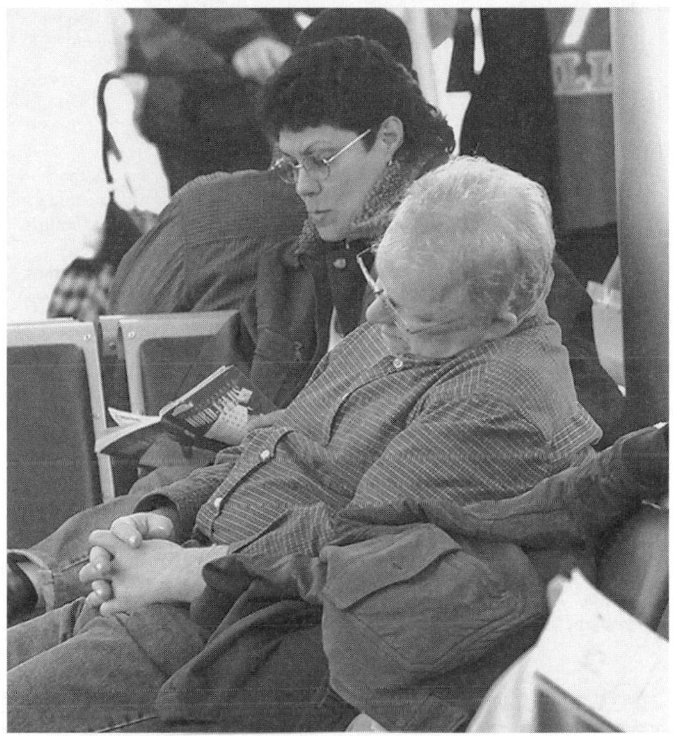

U.S. Blowjobless Rate At All-Time High

WASHINGTON, DC—In the wake of a recent drop in the sexual-interest rate, Labor Secretary Elaine Chao announced Tuesday that blowjoblessness in America has reached a record high.

According to Labor Department statistics, the overall blowjobless rate swelled to 37.4 percent in July, causing widespread deflation of egos.

"Cutbacks in oral services have left 55 million Americans unsatisfied," Chao said. "Although June saw a promising jump in the age 15-19 demographic, with many teenagers finding summer blowjobs, almost 82 percent of married men are completely blowjobless."

The historically fluid blowjob market reached its climax in 1996, when millions of wives and girlfriends vigorously stimulated the privates sector. But while demand has remained extremely high, supply could not, or would not, keep up. As a result, the blowjobless rate has climbed steadily, and today's limp market shows few signs of immediate expansion.

According to Chao, long-term relationships are responsible for the loss of many of this year's blowjobs.

"Over time, traditional blowjob providers prioritize other ser-

see BLOWJOBLESS page 220

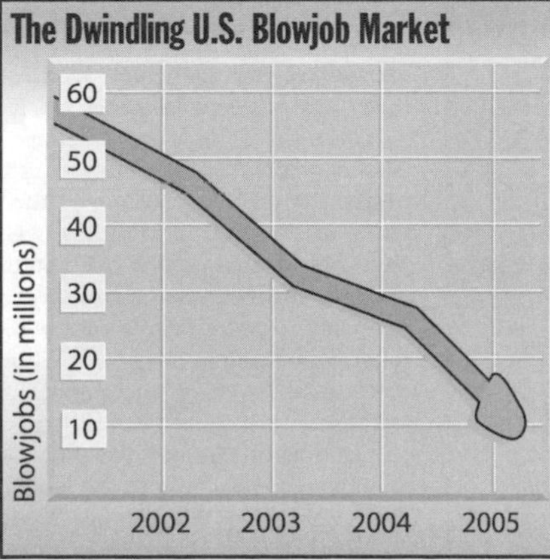

Dave Matthews Not That Into Himself Anymore

CHARLOTTESVILLE, VA—Dave Matthews, the 38-year-old singer and guitarist for the multi-platinum group The Dave Matthews Band, announced Tuesday that he is no longer into himself.

see DAVE MATTHEWS page 221

Above: Dave Matthews

Gaza Pullout

In an effort to reinvigorate the Middle East peace process, Israel fulfilled its pledge and withdrew from the Gaza Strip. What do *you* think?

"An end to over three decades of savage bloodshed over a tiny, ugly parcel of land... This is truly a sad day in the history of Israel."

William McGeveren
Radio Announcer

"Tell me they at least kept those beautiful, beautiful concrete demarcation walls up—they did? Oh, thank God."

Elizabeth Barden
Astronomer

"See, I *knew* that if the Palestinians ignored the Israelis for long enough, they'd go away."

Cassandra L. Capo
Preschool Teacher

"A Gaza home is affordable and can be yours! Contact me, Ramzi al-Yuusuf, at Hamas Realty, 08-636-8871."

Ramzi al-Yuusuf
Realtor

"I just can't believe that spineless peacenik Sharon knuckled under so quickly."

Jay Jaffe
Data-Entry Specialist

"Jesus, Joseph, and Mary, just tell me if it's good or bad this is happening, because I'm too goddamned confused by the last 30 years of Middle East history."

Martin Kenney Jr.
Systems Analyst

Leaving Hollywood

Lured away by tax breaks and other incentives, many producers have been shooting films outside of Hollywood. What do these alternate locations have to offer?

- County Kerry, Ireland: Government will foot production costs, provided the script is about cute, eccentric country folk
- Stevens Point, WI: Ideal setting for a giant spider invasion
- Gary, IN: Cheaper to film post-apocalyptic thrillers here than in Watts
- Toronto: Provides less expensive—and frankly, far more realistic—New York setting
- Alabama: Perfect backdrop for movies about small-town inspirational retards
- Inside computer: Attracts low-maintenance actors like Tron, Shrek, and Jar Jar Binks
- Saskatoon, Canada: Affords producers opportunity to thank "the fine people of Saskatoon" in closing credits

America's Finest News Source.™

Herman Ulysses Zweibel
Founder

T. Herman Zweibel
Publisher Emeritus
J. Phineas Zweibel
Publisher
Maxwell Prescott Zweibel
Editor-In-Chief

Man, The Terrorists Win At *Everything*

By Roy Beaumont

Man, it seems like the harder we fight, the worse things turn out for us, and the better they turn out for the terrorists. They've really played their cards right in this whole war on terror. We've tried racial profiling, random searches, and we even smoked Saddam out of his hole, but they still get away with murder. I'm pretty frickin' tired of it.

Everywhere I go, they've got me wasting a lot of my energy looking out for suspicious people and being worried about suspicious packages. That's just what the terrorists want—me spending less time enjoying my freedom and more time wondering if that towelhead on the bus is one of them. Hey you terrorist big shots, I'm tired of constantly being on edge—how about giving us a chance to win once in a while?

Here's what I'm talking about: Last month, I was watching *American Chopper*, and they interrupted it right before the bike was finished to announce that the London subways had been bombed. One point terrorists, zero points freedom-lovers.

So, they won that round, no question, but did they have to be such showoffs about it? A week after they got us in the subways, they turned around and got us in the subways again! Like a goddamned touchdown dance. We get the point, assholes. Ever hear of a sore winner?

> **Those anthrax letters had everybody afraid to open their mail for months. Not even the Unabomber pulled that off.**

They even score without taking a shot sometimes. I hit a huge snag in traffic the other day. Give you three guesses why. Turns out they were searching trucks at the toll booths, looking for bombs and terrorists that morning. I was an hour late for work. Man, Osama must have been sitting back in his cave and laughing his ass off at me.

Speaking of that, do you know it costs me almost $70 to fill up my truck nowadays? What really kills me is knowing half of that goes to put food on the bin Laden family dinner table. I mean, they've got this whole global network of secret agents and underground video cells ready to strike at a moment's notice. Meanwhile, I can't even get my e-mail working.

It's just not fair. We passed that whole Patriot Act thing, my little brother's off fighting in Iraq along with about a million other guys, and we're fingerprinting all the Muslims in America, but we're still getting our asses handed to us. What the hell's going on?

> **Here's what I'm talking about: Last month, I was watching *American Chopper*, and they interrupted it right before the bike was finished to announce that the London subways had been bombed. One point terrorists, zero points freedom-lovers.**

I don't think it's out of line to call the terrorists cheaters. Yeah, I said it. We took over two whole countries, and there's still terrorists everywhere. You're supposed to turn yourself in when your country gets taken over, but not them. Come on, guys. Play by the rules once in a while.

I hate the terrorists for hating us, but I gotta respect them for their strategy. Those anthrax letters had everybody afraid to open their mail for months. Not even the Unabomber pulled that off.

If only we could do that to them. Send the terrorists a poison letter. Then they'd think twice about... Aw, who'm I kidding? They'd probably send it right back to us and kill some innocent schoolteacher. They're too smart to fall for any tricks.

Man, I got half a mind to go up to one of those terrorists and give him a piece of my mind. Oh, but I can't—they're in disguise and nobody can find them. There's not even an address I can send a strongly worded letter to.

I tell you, you just can't win with some people. Ø

City Councilman Unearths Magical Zoning Amulet

ROCHESTER, NY—After years spent poring over mysterious and arcane plat sheets and deciphering long-forgotten building codes, city councilmember Mike LaMere unearthed the mysterious City Zoning Amulet Friday.

"Behold!" LaMere said, holding aloft the solid-gold amulet, which is emblazoned with the Ever-Evaluating Eye of Surr-Vey, Lord Of Demarcation, He Who Measures And Assesses. "With this sigil, the power of zoning comes. Through me, the power of zoning flows! All will behold my power, and I shall bow to no man when designating matter-of-right developments for major retail and office spaces to a maximum lot occupancy of 75 percent for residential use!"

LaMere held the glowing amulet aloft and transmuted a neighborhood of low-income apartments into a semi-wooded, single-family, residential district with an adjoining riverside park.

Though the amulet had long been dismissed as urban legend, a mythical ideal of zoning perfection handed down from city planner to city planner, LaMere became convinced that not only was it real, but that it had been used to lay out the cities of Ur, Atlantis, and Inver Grove Heights, MN.

LaMere credited the amulet with the overnight renovation of the Monroe County Public Library, and the recent

see ZONING AMULET page 221

LaMere held the glowing amulet aloft and transmuted a neighborhood of low-income apartments into a semi-wooded, single-family, residential district with an adjoining riverside park.

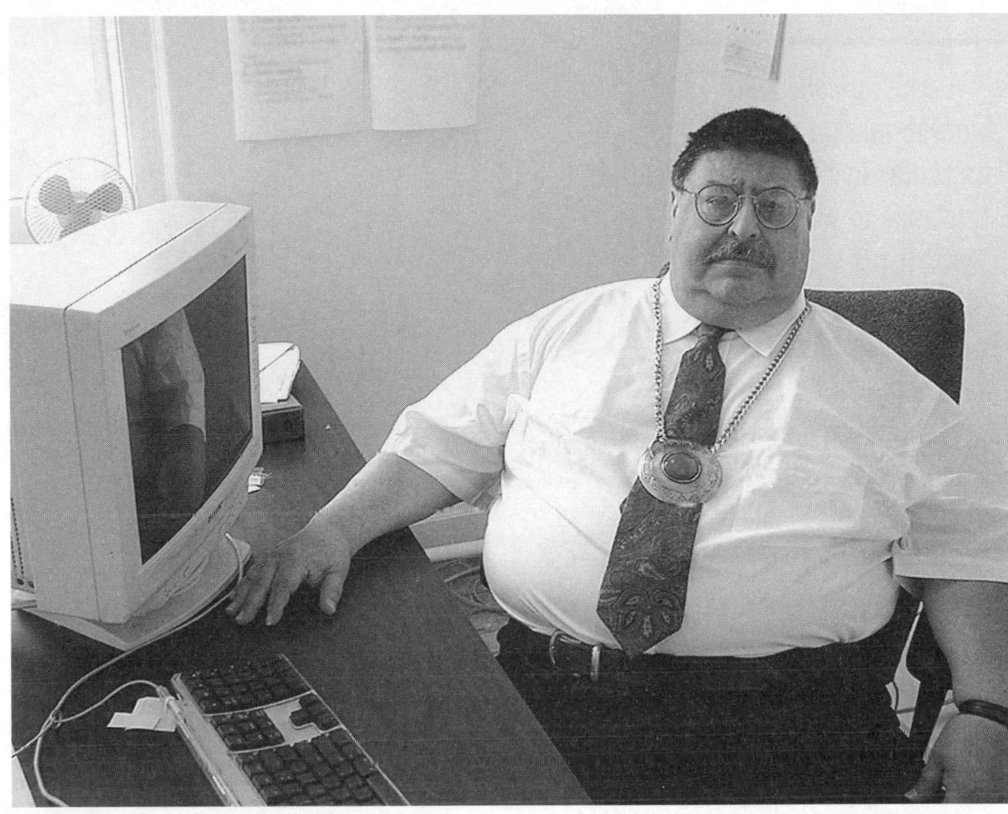

Above: Mike LaMere, wearing the Ever-Evaluating Eye of Surr-Vey.

NEWS IN BRIEF

Iraq Declares Partial Law

BAGHDAD—Citing the chaotic state of his occupied nation, president Jalal Talabani declared a state of partial law in Iraq Monday. "We must preserve a few laws and some order," said Talabani in a televised address. "If not for our own sake, then for the sake of the peace-loving citizens who make up nearly half our population." Talabani said the state of partial law is temporary, promising that within the decade, his interim government will be replaced by a more stable fascist theocracy.

Entertainment Lawyer 'Fighting The Good Fight'

NEW YORK—Although he works long hours for less than seven figures a year, entertainment lawyer Jude Mortison said knowing that he is "one of the good guys" makes it all worth it. "I might not be one of those big fancy city-courthouse types, but I do my part," said Mortison, who tracks down song lyrics used in published works without proper permission and secures the requisite legal and penalty fees for music publishers. Mortison, who bills $800 an hour, added that the look of satisfaction on the face of Warner Brothers executives is all the additional payment he needs.

Missing Park Ranger Found In Better-Paying Job

FLAGSTAFF, AZ—Forest Service ranger Lawrence Anderson, missing from his fire-warning post in the Coconino National Forest since mid-July, was found alive and well-off in the manager's office of a Flagstaff Home Depot Sunday. "We announce with a sense of relief that Larry is safe and financially secure," said FBI agent Donald Grasso. Anderson described his years as a ranger as "an ordeal," recounting how he was sometimes forced to subsist on root beer and prepackaged bologna-and-cheese sandwiches from the park gift shop for weeks at a time.

German Luftwaffle Chain Offers Waffles, Overwhelming Air Superiority

MUNICH—An elite force of three dozen 24-hour Luftwaffle restaurants were unveiled across Germany Monday, with free waffles for blond-haired, blue-eyed customers, discounts on Cheese SwasSticks, and the incendiary bombardment of Luftwaffle's largest competitor, the city of London. "Soon, customers will fall under the sway of my light-ning-quick, piping-hot Blintzkreig," said Hans Kreuzen, Luftwaffle's founder and oberstmanager-general. "All will know the sweet, buttery taste of fear and waffles from above." Luftwaffle restaurants are expected to face ruthless competition in Germany's already crowded martial-themed eatery business, which is led by such established chains as WehrKnochwurst and Der Marzipanzerkommand.

Bush Calls For Rock Revolution In Weekly Pirate-Radio Address

WASHINGTON, DC—President Bush called for an end to corporate rock, "wuss-metal," and sellout-punk in his weekly pirate-radio address Saturday, delivered from an unlicensed mobile transmitter in the back of his presidential limo. "You don't wanna be an American idiot!" said Bush over the opening strains of "Take The Power Back" by Rage Against The Machine. "Reject Clear Channel's spoonfed bullshit! Wake up, motherfuckers!" An estimated 2,000 listeners in the District of Columbia tune in weekly to Bush's notoriously low-fi, DIY show, *The Revolution Will Not Be Podcast*, broadcast Saturday from 11 p.m. to 1 a.m. ⊘

BLOWJOBLESS from page 217

vices, eventually eliminating those blowjobs that they deem unnecessary," Chao said.

"Blowjobs are not as plentiful as some Internet sites would lead you to believe," said blowjob-market analyst Tom Cochran. "Overall, it's an extremely dry market. I myself haven't had a blowjob in years."

"And it's not from a lack of trying," Cochran added.

The historically fluid blowjob market reached its climax in 1996, when millions of wives and girlfriends vigorously stimulated the privates sector. But while demand has remained extremely high, supply could not, or would not, keep up. As a result, the blowjobless rate has climbed steadily, and today's limp market shows few signs of immediate expansion.

Some professional men who once had a steady source of outcome have begun looking for freelance blowjobs. Fairfax, VA resident Dave Abbott said if he can't find a blowjob in his field, he'll move to a throbbing market such as Las Vegas.

"I heard they'll offer a part-time blowjob to just about anyone in Vegas," Abbott said.

According to Labor Department statistics, almost half of blowjobless Americans are living below the oral-poverty line, and benefits packages that include sexual intercourse are not enough to sustain them.

"For many of these orally disenfranchised men, a hand-to-mouth existence is but a dream," Cochran said.

Experts predict that as this problem snowballs, it will affect even those who are currently receiving blowjobs. Economic indicators have hinted at a nationwide downsizing, meaning thousands of men will be getting laid in the coming months.

Amid growing concerns, Rep. Collin Peterson (D-MN) has proposed a stimulus package that he said will help create over 300,000 new blowjobs by the end of the year.

Said Peterson: "We can only hope that some compromise between the lip-service industry and the blowjob market can be achieved in House resolution H.R. 69." ⌀

JET LAG from page 217

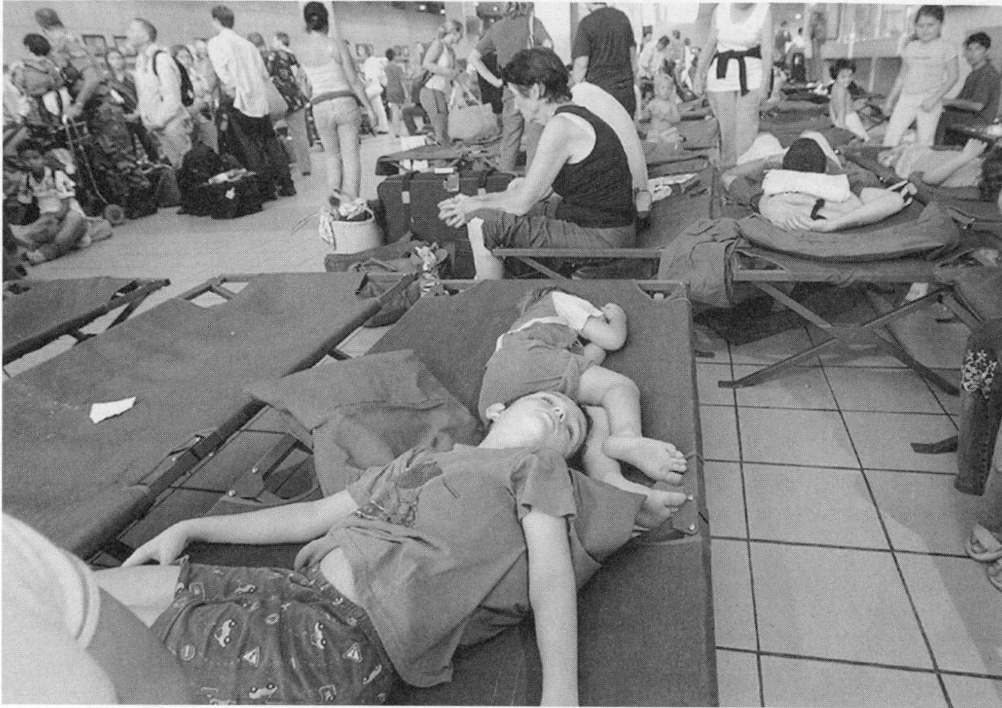

Above: A makeshift nap-triage center in the Denver International Airport.

continue to report record dozings. Minneapolis resident Belinda Haynes, 26, is just one of tens of thousands of Americans whose travel plans are affected.

"I'm going to go to Tampa Bay and be asleep through most of my flight," Haynes said. "That means I'm at risk for catching Super Lag and being totally tired all through my sister's whole wedding."

At the Atlanta airport Tuesday afternoon, an estimated 900 Super Lag sufferers could be seen stretched across the molded seats of gate waiting areas. The infected travelers, distinguishable by their testy demeanors and heavy eyelids, argued with ticket agents, slumped listlessly in their seats, and stared blankly at Au Bon Pain pastry displays.

Untreated victims can find themselves sleeping for hours on a plane, then sleeping soundly at night, yet still performing poorly in important business meetings or feeling too fatigued to enjoy their vacations.

Dr. Robert Sanders is one of hundreds of volunteer physicians treating Super Lag sufferers at airports nationwide.

"Jet lag was first documented in the late '50s," Sanders said. "Over the years, we've developed band-aid solutions to combat the disorder—neck pillows, laptops, in-flight movies—but it was really only a matter of time before jet lag mutated into a more virulent strain."

Despite volunteer efforts, the burden of treating Super Lag sufferers has fallen largely on flight attendants who, with little training in this area, are reporting great difficulties.

"One passenger who sleeps through the beverage service and wakes up irritated and thirsty is bad," said Midwest Airlines flight attendant Sandy Wolchek. "You multiply that by five on a Milwaukee-to-Minneapolis flight, and you're talking about a serious disruption."

Prolonged rest is the only known remedy for Super Lag, according to Bill Ziegler of the Centers For Fatigue Control. "Victims can also alleviate their symptoms by wadding jackets or sweaters into makeshift pillows," he said. "And we're recommending that airlines loosen their restriction on reclining cabin seats during the ascent and descent phases of flights."

Scientists at the CFC are working around the clock to find a Super Lag cure, but so far, they have made little progress. For now, they recommend

Untreated victims can find themselves sleeping for hours on a plane, then sleeping soundly at night, yet still performing poorly in important business meetings or feeling too fatigued to enjoy their vacations.

that air-travel passengers look out for Super Lag's warning signs: irritability, an unwillingness to engage in small talk with persons in adjoining seats, and a tendency to doze off while reading in-flight magazines. ⌀

TENDERLOIN from page 67

amounts of blood. Passersby were amazed by the unusually large amounts of blood. Passersby were amazed by the unusually large amounts of blood. Passersby were amazed by the unusually large amounts of blood. Passersby were amazed by the unusually large amounts of blood. Passersby were amazed by the unusually large amounts of blood. Passersby were amazed by the unusually large amounts of blood. Passersby were amazed by the unusually large

The spirit of Andrew Jackson touches me inappropriately every night.

amounts of blood. Passersby were amazed by the unusually large amounts of blood. Passersby were amazed by the unusually large amounts of blood. Passersby were amazed by the unusually large amounts of blood. Passersby were amazed by the unusually large amounts of blood. Passersby were amazed by the unusually large amounts of blood. Passersby were amazed by the unusually large amounts of blood. Passersby were amazed by the unusually large amounts of blood. Passersby were amazed by the unusually large

see TENDERLOIN page 200

ZONING AMULET from page 219

redesignation of a Southern Rochester area from "commercial" to "single-family residential use for detached and semi-detached structures." Many Rochester citizens believe the amulet is responsible for the fully stocked ocean aquarium that materialized in the city center Sunday, and the gleaming new Friendly's restaurant that rose serenely over the banks of the Genesee River late Monday afternoon.

According to Criclow, during a private consultation with local community leaders, LaMere became infuriated with timid suggestions that his amulet be used to create more green spaces.

Although the Rochester City Zoning Board controls all decisions related to city planning, sources at City Hall say that, as long as LaMere's powerful zoning wizardry is performed for the good of the city, they "see no reason to deny him what seems to be his destiny."

"Two weeks ago, the biggest news in Rochester was our huge public garage sale," said William A. Johnson, Rochester's mayor. "Our city center was still a moribund tax burden with small businesses in big buildings and families moving to the suburbs in droves. Now, with a wave of his mighty amulet, Councilman LaMere can designate matter-of-right medium-density development, with limited offices for non-profit organizations, trade associations, and professionals permitted as a special exception requiring approval of the RCZA."

Above: LaMere unleashes the Eye of Surr-Vey's power, violently rezoning a residential area into a landfill.

Despite the potential improvements to Rochester's civic landscape, some residents remain wary of LaMere's apparent bureaucratic invincibility.

"It's wonderful that someone's finally doing something to revitalize this town, even if it is someone who can commune with church gargoyles," said local baker Wendy Kittner, whose business was mystically placed on the National Register Of Historic Places last week despite being housed in a building erected in 1981. "He frightens me, and my concern is that if I defy him, I may be turned to stone."

City planning commissioner Errol Criclow, who was dismissed by

"It's wonderful that someone's finally doing something to revitalize this town, even if it is someone who can commune with church gargoyles," said local baker Wendy Kittner.

LaMere at a Planning And Zoning Commission hearing last Thursday as "subhuman," said that he feared that LaMere's power would eventually corrupt him and his city. According to Criclow, during a private consultation with local community leaders, LaMere became infuriated with timid suggestions that his amulet be used to create more green spaces. In a blinding torrent of thunder and light, LaMere violently rezoned Rochester's west side with a maze of warehouses and parking garages. The act left LaMere himself dazed and shaken.

"For a minute there, he seemed his old self," said Criclow. "When he saw what he'd done, he looked remorseful. But then his hand found the amulet, and he threw back his head and laughed long and loud, like a man who has forgotten the difference between industrial and recreational—between right and wrong."

Added Criclow: "I don't think what he's doing is mere magic. I think it's darkest bureaucromancy." Ø

DAVE MATTHEWS from page 217

"I used to be a hardcore Dave Matthews fan," said Matthews on the porch of his Virginia home. "I had all my records and posters. I was so blown away by everything I did—especially my live performances. I remember me and my buddies used to drive for hours just to go to one of our shows."

Matthews, who formed the Dave Matthews Band in 1991, is perhaps best known for the hit songs "Crash Into Me" and "The Space Between."

"Me and my band are still okay, but I feel like I've grown out of us," Matthews said. "Back when I was in the college charts, we were about all I listened to, but I guess I'm at the point in my life where my music just doesn't speak to me."

Matthews admitted that most of his current Dave Matthews listening is confined to overhearing a hit single on a jukebox or PA system. However, while doing dishes last weekend, he

"Me and my band are still okay, but I feel like I've grown out of us," Matthews said. "Back when I was in the college charts, we were about all I listened to, but I guess I'm at the point in my life where my music just doesn't speak to me."

tried listening to 1998's *Before These Crowded Streets*, an album he had not heard in over two years. The singer admitted that by the fourth track, he was barely even listening.

"It sounded like this sort of world-beat background drone," Matthews said. "So I took it off and put on some Stevie Ray Vaughan instead."

"Rock music with a violin? I don't know," Matthews added. "Seemed cool once."

Although Matthews continues to attend every single performance of his band, and even his own solo appearances, he claims it's "more out of obligation" than out of passion for his music.

Matthews said that while he once felt exhilarated whenever his group launched into one of their famous prolonged jam sessions, he can now "barely sit through them." Said Matthews: "Lately, I try to vary my routine so I don't get bored on stage. Usually, if there's a long solo, I'll go get a beer or check out the T-shirts."

Matthews even feels isolated from fans with whom he once felt a strong bond, disparaging them as "lame." He also admits that the older he gets, the more out of place he feels around "kids in their Dave Matthews phase."

"I used to talk for hours about my music or spend a whole night in a DMB chatroom," Matthews said. "But now, the people at the shows seem like such geeks, standing there with their elaborate taping equipment. They're really, really young, too. What do I have in common with them? They're just a bunch of kids who need someone to look up to. Why would I look up to me? I'm so 1997."

Yet for all his disenchantment with the Dave Matthews Band, he'll still "probably check me out at Farm Aid in September." Added Matthews: "If I'm even playing there this year. I don't even know. Dave Matthews—that is to say, me—just isn't where I'm coming from anymore." Ø

COMMUNITY VOICES

Shakespeare Was, Like, The Ultimate Rapper

By Kathryn Markham
English Teacher

As an English teacher, I have to make The Bard resonate with today's youth. I get the same questions every year: "Shakespeare? What does this dead white guy have to do with me? He doesn't know where I come from, what I'm all about. He's not from the streets."

Well, what's totally fresh about Shakespeare is that he wrote for ordinary people. His homies. My students say, "Then why did he write in this snooty poetry that no one can understand?" Well, that's just it. His poetry was the best street rhyming of his time. And Shakespeare was the best "player" of them all! Even today, 400 years later, Shakespeare is the world's ultimate rapper!

Shakespeare had the tightest flow in the history of the English language. His iambic pentameter couldn't be touched by the other M.C.s, although player-haters think he sampled heavily from Ben Jonson. In fact, were he alive today, I'm convinced he would be a rapper. Well, I guess he could be a playwright, too.

You see, Shakespeare never intended for his works to be read in some dusty old study! They were performed before a rowdy audience of ne'er-do-wells, servants, and charboys who interacted with the players and even threw things on stage. Sounds a lot like a rap show, doesn't it? The Globe truly was the Apollo Theater of the day.

Rap resonates because it talks about our lives, and tells stories of love, violence, sex—the things that get our blood racing. Well, word to

What's totally fresh about Shakespeare is that he wrote for his homies.

your mother: Shakespeare may have worn tights and big lace collars, but he addressed the same questions as 50 Cent or Tupac Shakur. Are you feeling me? Try this: I'll list a plot point, and you try to guess if I'm describing an R. Kelly song or a Shakespeare play.

A daddy asks three homegirls to tell him why he's so fly.

A black gentleman suspects the white girl he's dating is playing him.

A crew of noblemen gets together and murders their homeboy.

Ready for a surprise? Those are all plot points from Shakespeare's tragedies! Compared to Shakespeare, R. Kelly is a choirboy. Why, *Romeo And Juliet* begins with bawdy jokes that would make 2 Live Crew blush! Shakespeare definitely knew a thing or two about "groping for trout in a peculiar river!" That's from *Measure For Measure*. We won't be reading that, though.

Back when Papa Tony's Pizza had those rapping TV commercials 10 years ago, I would recite a soliloquy from Hamlet in the exact same cadence, and it never failed to crack up the class! One year, there was even a student who accompanied me with the mouth-drumming noises, and we actually sounded very impressive together.

Big Willie Shakes rapped in his Big Willie style about everyday life, too. He rapped about friendship: consider Prince Hal and Falstaff, Hamlet and Horatio, Rosencrantz and Guildenstern. He rapped about race issues: *Othello*, anyone? He even rapped about slammin' phat beats!

Back when Papa Tony's Pizza had those rapping TV commercials 10 years ago, I would recite a soliloquy from Hamlet in the exact same cadence, and it never failed to crack up the class! One year, there was even a student who accompanied me with the mouth-drumming noises, and we actually sounded very impressive together. I haven't done it in a while, so I'm a bit rusty, but I'll give it a shot anyhow:

Tis now the very witching time of night,
When churchyards yawn and hell itself breathes out
Contagion to this world: now could I drink hot blood,
And do such bitter business...

Well, uh, it goes on a bit more, but you get the idea, right? Yeah, I guess I'm a little rusty on the rapping. I'll practice tonight and try again tomorrow.

I've been teaching English for nearly 18 years, and even today, I'm still amazed at how fresh and current Shakespeare remains. Back when I was in college, I found so many parallels between Shakespeare and James Taylor. Then when I started teaching, I was struck at how Shakespeare explored the same themes as R.E.M. And boy, how my students from the '90s perked up when I played Kurt Cobain during the Hamlet unit!

Well, I hope that I've demystified the Bard Of Avon a little. I mean, trust me, I'm not some old fuddy dud who sits around watching PBS! I was down with Baz Luhrmann's *Romeo + Juliet* as much as you were! In fact, it happens to be in my personal DVD library, right in between *Boyz N The Hood* and *Colors*. How do you like those apples? ⌀

HOROSCOPES

Your Horoscope

By Lloyd Schumner Sr.
Retired Machinist and
A.A.P.B.-Certified Astrologer

Aries: (March 21–April 19)
You're normally the type of rational, level-headed person who doesn't believe in magic, but you have no other explanation for all the rabbits and pigeons in that man's tuxedo.

Taurus: (April 20–May 20)
For years, people have gone to universities and academies to hone their young minds, but your are 100 percent convinced that your trick of working yours firmly against an oiled whetstone does the job faster and just as well.

Gemini: (May 21–June 21)
It may have been a unique way to propose marriage, but you wish that your husband woud simply pick up the phone and call you, rather than renting the Jumbotron every time he has something to say.

Cancer: (June 22–July 22)
You'll finally achieve closure this week, just when it seemed your life would go on interminably.

Leo: (July 23–Aug. 22)
Turns out the "jackalope" is merely a taxidermist's trick, which explains why the one you managed to catch tasted so goddamn bad.

Virgo: (Aug. 23–Sept. 22)
You're still young, but eventually, you will learn that wearing sandals is no way for a man to go through his life on this earth.

Libra: (Sept. 23–Oct. 23)
You're extremely excited about the new breakthroughs in plastic surgery, until you realize they still cannot turn you entirely to plastic.

Scorpio: (Oct. 24–Nov. 21)
You don't care if time travel is currently believed to be a physical impossibility. There is not a doubt in your mind that that is you, second from left in the "Last Supper."

Sagittarius: (Nov. 22–Dec. 21)
After swearing lifelong fellatio to the Marine Corps of the United States of America, you'll be introduced to a red-faced young recruiter who mistakenly believes you don't know what the word means.

Capricorn: (Dec. 22–Jan. 19)
You'll finally hook up with that cute young guy from the health club when a hot-oil hair treatment sends you to the burn ward where he's a doctor.

Aquarius: (Jan. 20–Feb. 18)
Romance will bloom all around you this week, leaving you alone and desolate in the eye of a veritable romance hurricane.

Pisces: (Feb. 19–March 20)
You've traveled halfway around the world and seen things you never would have otherwise, but you're starting to think that moving dollar bill might have some sort of string attached to it. ⌀

MELBA from page 93

amounts of blood. Passersby were amazed by the unusually large amounts of blood. Passersby were amazed by the unusually large amounts of blood. Passersby were amazed by the unusually large amounts of blood. Passersby were

If I had to choose, I'd say blow up Norway.

amazed by the unusually large amounts of blood. Passersby were amazed by the unusually large amounts of blood. Passersby were amazed by the unusually large amounts of blood. Passersby were amazed by the unusually large amounts of blood. Passersby were

see MELBA page 290

NEWS

Jennifer Aniston Finally Reveals Hairstyle That Repulsed Brad Pitt

see FASHION page 4F

Beehive Not Ready For Democracy

see LOCAL page 2B

Christian Science Pharmacist Refuses To Fill Any Prescription

see SCIENCE page 3D

Standards, Trousers Lowered Simultaneously

see LOCAL page 2B

STATshot

A look at the numbers that shape your world.

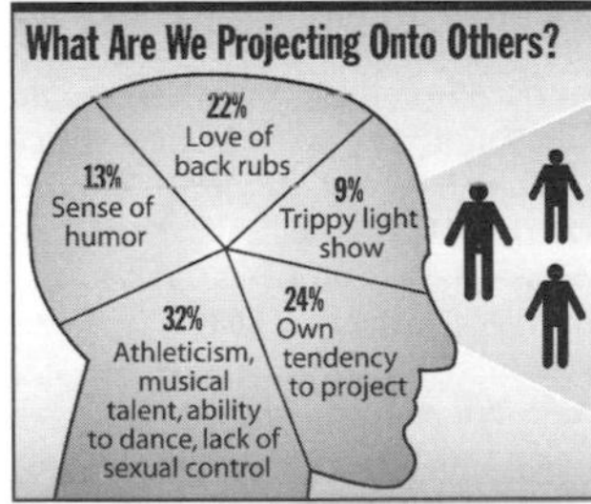

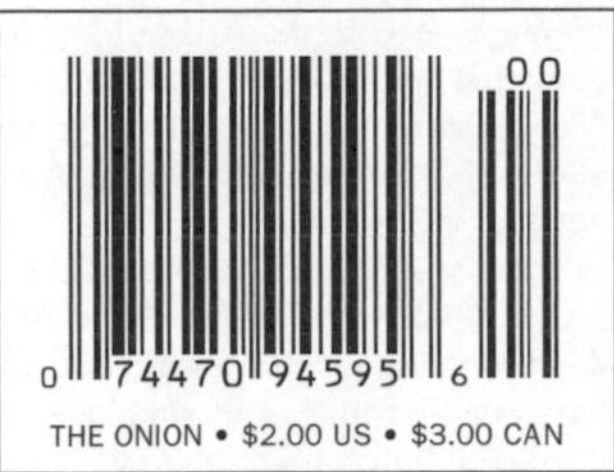

the ONION®

VOLUME 41 ISSUE 35 AMERICA'S FINEST NEWS SOURCE™ 1–7 SEPTEMBER 2005

Google Announces Plan To Destroy All Information It Can't Index

Right: CEO Eric Schmidt speaks at Google's California headquarters (above).

MOUNTAIN VIEW, CA—Executives at Google, the rapidly growing online-search company that promises to "organize the world's information," announced Monday the latest step in their expansion effort: a far-reaching plan to destroy all the information it is unable to index.

"Our users want the world to be as simple, clean, and accessible as the Google home page itself," said Google CEO Eric Schmidt at a press conference held in their corporate offices. "Soon, it will be."

The new project, dubbed Google Purge, will join such popular services as Google Images, Google News, and Google Maps, which catalogs the entire surface of the Earth using high-resolution satellites.

As a part of Purge's first phase, executives will destroy all copyrighted materials that cannot be

searched by Google.

"A year ago, Google offered to scan every book on the planet for its Google Print project. Now, they

see GOOGLE page 227

Bush: Vacation Ruined By 'Stupid Dead Soldier'

CRAWFORD, TX—President Bush concluded his summer vacation by holding an informal press conference Monday to address grieving mother Cindy Sheehan, saying "her damn dead son ruined my whole summer vacation."

Bush addressed Mrs. Sheehan, who was not present, by saying "a mother should not have to bury her son this way, by which I mean allowing her

Above: Bush addresses the press during his vacation.

son's death to destroy his commander-in-chief's one chance to relax and unwind."

Sheehan, whose son Casey died in Iraq in April 2004, has led a vigil outside of Bush's Crawford ranch since early August, urging the immediate withdrawal of troops from Iraq and demanding a meeting with Bush.

"This is a terrible tragedy," Bush said. "If this dead soldier of a son had

see BUSH page 227

Wrongly Imprisoned Man Won't Shut Up About It

Left: George Buell

JOLIET, IL—George Howard Buell, an inmate wrongfully imprisoned at State-ville Correctional Center for third-degree sexual assault and aggravated battery, won't shut the hell up about being innocent.

Buell, 46, an Elmhurst, IL electrician, was convicted of raping and burglarizing his elderly neighbor in 1994, despite the fact that he was at work when the crime occurred. He was mistakenly sentenced to a prison term of 20 years to life. Since then, his imprisonment has been a source of nonstop bellyaching.

"I'm completely innocent of the charges brought against me," Buell said in yet another long-winded jailhouse statement last week. "I am a victim of inept police work, conflict-of-interest issues among the prosecution, and a lackadaisical defense. Anyone with even a peripheral familiarity with my case could see the inconsistencies. It's a complete miscar-

see PRISONER page 226

Pat Robertson's Remarks

Televangelist Pat Robertson recently called for the assassination of Venezuelan President Hugo Chavez. What do *you* think?

"This recalls a moral and ethical dilemma theologians have grappled with for millennia, namely: Is it right to murder people?"

Robert Platt
Text Editor

"Who hasn't called for the bloody death of a public figure? Donny and Marie, Paris Hilton, Air Supply—just a few of many I've wanted to see perish in a hail of bullets."

Joanne Rice
Systems Analyst

"These are not the Christian values I want my children to learn. I want them to pray for someone's death, not plead for their assassination."

Florence Ridley
Glazier

"Someone should assassinate Robertson. That way, after he's dead, he can fly back here as a winged supernatural being and kill as many people as he wants."

C. David Benson
Security Guard

"Pat Robertson, as a Christian, a politician, or a pundit, is a living argument for the separation of head and body."

Martin Crow
Railroad Conductor

"Forgive him, Father. He knows not his ass from a fucking hole in the ground."

Charles Muscatine
Doctor

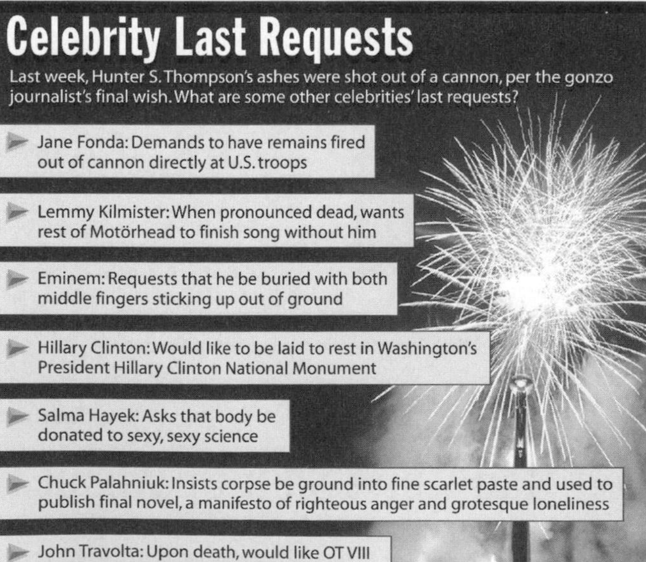

Celebrity Last Requests
Last week, Hunter S. Thompson's ashes were shot out of a cannon, per the gonzo journalist's final wish. What are some other celebrities' last requests?
Jane Fonda: Demands to have remains fired out of cannon directly at U.S. troops
Lemmy Kilmister: When pronounced dead, wants rest of Motörhead to finish song without him
Eminem: Requests that he be buried with both middle fingers sticking up out of ground
Hillary Clinton: Would like to be laid to rest in Washington's President Hillary Clinton National Monument
Salma Hayek: Asks that body be donated to sexy, sexy science
Chuck Palahniuk: Insists corpse be ground into fine scarlet paste and used to publish final novel, a manifesto of righteous anger and grotesque loneliness
John Travolta: Upon death, would like OT VIII level bequeathed to any surviving Sweathogs
Johnny Knoxville: Wants severed head frozen for 1,000 years, then revived and knocked across supermarket parking lot with crowbar

America's Finest News Source.™

Herman Ulysses Zweibel
Founder

T. Herman Zweibel
Publisher Emeritus
J. Phineas Zweibel
Publisher
Maxwell Prescott Zweibel
Editor-In-Chief

Son, You'll Always Remember Your First Time, Because I'm Going To Film It

I know you've been attending a lot of parties recently. And while you may think your dad is clueless, I'm clued-in enough to realize that pretty soon you're going to start experimenting with sex. Nothing much I can do about it, I realize. But I do want to tell you one thing: No matter how old you get, or how many partners you have, you will always remember your first time. Why? Because I'm going to film it.

By Fritz Becker

I can hardly believe you've grown so fast. It seems like just yesterday I was videotaping your conception.

Well, I'm proud of you. You've come a long way in 16 years, and so has video-recording technology. Today's digital cameras have far better resolution than the one I used just four short years ago to capture the wonder of your body becoming that of a young man's.

This is a big step you're about to make, and your first time should be special. So make sure you share it with the right person. Someone you can trust and feel comfortable with. Like, for example, Judi, from down the street. She seems like she'd be an ideal candidate, if only she were a couple years older. Actually, she's perfect. Let's go with her.

Sure, it can also be a bit nerve-racking, what with the boom mike hanging over the bed. But you don't have to worry. I'll be right there, behind the camera, giving you direction. Uncle Gary will be there, too. He'll be in charge of lighting and shooting B-roll. All you have to do is relax and act natural.

You see, son, I'm determined to get this right. I don't want you to make the same mistakes I did. The image quality from my first time is very poor. I could barely make out what was going on. It comes off as so awkward and uncomfortable without any close-ups or cutaways. To tell you the truth, as drunk as I was, I'm surprised I even had the camera pointing in the right direction. I want you to have the quality first time that I couldn't. I want a milestone the whole family can enjoy each time I decide to pull out the tape for viewing. Thanksgiving, Christmas, birthdays, family movie night, whenever.

Today's digital cameras have far better resolution than the one I used just four short years ago to capture the wonder of your body becoming that of a young man's.

There's no need to worry. The first time can be magical. Electrifying, even. When you're in bed with that special someone, your young, taut bodies entwined in pleasure and passion, nothing else in the world matters. Everything around you just fades away. I can't explain it, son. We'll have to watch it a few times before I can put it into words.

Sure, it can also be a bit nerve-racking, what with the boom mike hanging over the bed. But you don't have to worry. I'll be right there, behind the camera, giving you direction. Uncle Gary will be there, too. He'll be in charge of lighting and shooting B-roll. All you have to do is relax and act natural. Just ask your sister. Or better yet, let's watch the tape of her first time. It'll put your mind at ease.

And let's not forget the most important part: protection. I can't stress this enough, so please listen very carefully. Whoever it is you decide to share your first sexual experience with, always be sure you get them to sign the all-purpose waiver relieving us from any and all liability.

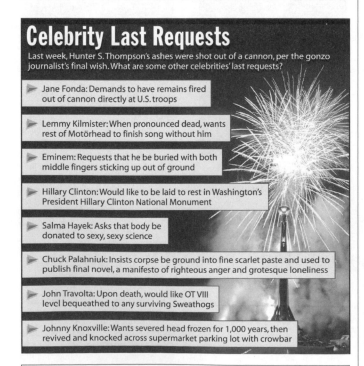

I think you're ready now, son. Don't forget what we've talked about. And don't forget that you'll always remember your first time. And your second, third, and fourth times, too. ⌀

LOCAL

Area Man Training For Upcoming *Sanford And Son* Marathon

SHELTON, CT—Ever since Alex Bryce was a boy, he has dreamed of participating in a TV marathon. Now, at age 26, he is days from making that dream a reality.

This weekend's *Sanford And Son* marathon on TV Land is the ultimate test of a watcher's endurance, and Bryce plans to watch the entire 48-hour event, which comprises 96 half-

"Afterwards, my muscles are stiff and my eyes are bloodshot, but it's always worth it."

hour episodes with two-minute commercial checkpoints at 11-minute intervals.

"Marathons are exhausting, but exhilarating," said Bryce, who has completed four prestigious TV mini-marathons, including the grueling "*Ab Fab* Friday.""Afterwards, my muscles are stiff and my eyes are bloodshot, but it's always worth it."

Bryce, a recreational TV watcher whose personal best is 16 hours, has been on a strict training regimen for six months. He wakes up daily at 5 a.m., slips on his sweats, and immedi-

see MARATHON page 226

Above: Alex Bryce, 26, in the midst of his strictly regimented workout routine.

NEWS IN BRIEF

Genie Grants Scalia Strict Constructionist Interpretation Of Wish

WASHINGTON, DC—A genie freed from a battered oil lamp by Supreme Court Justice Antonin Scalia granted the conservative jurist a strict constructionist interpretation of his wish for "a hundred billion bucks" Monday. "Sim sim salabim! Your wish is my command!" the genie proclaimed amid flashes of light and purple smoke, immediately filling the Supreme Court building with a massive herd of wild male antelopes. When Justice Scalia complained that the "bucks" had razed the U.S. Supreme Court building, trampling and killing several of his clerks and bringing traffic in the nation's capital to a standstill for hours, the genie said, "Your honor, your wish is a sacred and unalterable document whose interpretation is not subject to the whims of society and changing social context."

Londoners 2 Percent Less Polite About Terrorism Following Bombings

LONDON—Findings released Monday by Britain's Home Office indicate that politeness among Londoners has dipped 2 percent since the July public-transit bombings. "Terrorist bombers? Well, I say—good day to them—a tip of my hat to them, indeed, and may they take their leave of our green and pleasant land," said Andrew Capper of Surbiton. "Far be it from me to pass judgment, as I've never met the chaps myself—and goodness knows I'm not without error—but I should think that a few of these terrorists have behaved in a manner that can only be described as rather less than gentlemanly, if I do say so myself, may it please you, good sir." The Home Office cites post-traumatic stress in the sharp decline in manners, the worst since the 4 percent drop during the Blitz of 1940.

Republicans, Democrats Unite In Good Laugh Over Reform Party

WASHINGTON, DC—In a rare moment of bipartisan unity, lawmakers on both sides of the aisle fondly recalled the Reform Party Tuesday. "Remember 'Ross For Boss'?" Sen. Bill Frist (R-TN) said, laughing uncontrollably at the memory of the closest thing America has seen to a viable third party in recent history. "Plus Trump, Warren Beatty... And what was the deal with that crazy admiral guy who died?" Sen. Edward Kennedy (D-MA) joined in the fun, saying, "And that platform they had full of, aw, who knows what. 'Reform,' I guess!" The senators then spent an hour slapping each other on the backs, gleefully recalling the Reform Party's credo of "radical centrism" and pro wrestler Jesse Ventura's election as governor of Minnesota. Said Robert Byrd (D-WV): "They really thought they had something going there for a while!"

Botanists Making Great Strides In Stem Research

ST. LOUIS—Plant researchers continue to report impressive discoveries in stem research, the Botanical Society Of America announced in a position paper released Monday. "Using existing stem lines, we are closer than ever to finding cures for Dutch elm disease and soft rot," said lead researcher Mary Leisgard. Pro-plantlife groups oppose the research, arguing that the stems represent potential life. "Every stem, whether it has taken root and sprouted leaves or not, is a miracle from God," said botany activist Phyllis Bergher. "What these stems need is soil, moisture, and the chance to grow into full-fledged flora as God intended." Ø

PRISONER from page 223

riage of justice."

Buell's insufferable tirades have taken the form of numerous appeals to state and federal courts, unsuccessful attempts to launch public petitions, and e-publishing a 400,000-word autobiography titled *Won't Someone Please Hear My Anguished Plea?*

"Okay, I get it—he's innocent already," said Eric Holsapple, Buell's court-appointed attorney. "Like I don't know that. I only toiled for, like, forever years making a case out of it.

"Since being incarcerated, my innocence is all I have to cling to in this horrible, horrible place," said Buell, echoing comments that he has made to anyone who's had the misfortune of being in contact with him at any time during the past decade. "This goes beyond my worst nightmares of anything I could imagine ever happening to me."

Every time I talk to him, I have to brace myself—okay, here comes the sob story, *again*."

After spending four years trying to capture the media's attention with the story of his innocence, the wrongfully imprisoned inmate began pestering the courts in 2001 for additional DNA testing or a declaration of a mistrial.

Above: Darron and Eugene Buell speak to reporters after dragging themselves to yet another prison visit to hear their brother go on and on about his innocence.

"I will take a lie-detector test. I will do anything. I don't belong in prison," the incessant motormouth said. "The security tape in the garage where I work shows me pulling into the lot at the time the crime took place. It wasn't admitted as evidence. That fact alone should be grounds for a mistrial."

Buell's cellmate, Bob Hannan, has heard the "in jail for a crime I didn't commit" song and dance "about a million times." Said Hannan: "The parking lot surveillance videotape, the horrible injustice. I've heard it all. A lot. I didn't like the way they handled my case either. But you don't hear me yammering about it all the time. It's called moving on."

The consortium of attorneys and social-justice activists who were unlucky enough to have been assigned the task of getting Buell and his big, wrongfully imprisoned mouth out of jail have gotten perhaps the biggest earful of his whining.

Tania Schultz, a senior staff attorney at Northwestern University's Center On Wrongful Convictions, has worked on Buell's case for over two years. Although she is convinced that Buell is innocent, she is "fed up" with the subject.

"Even the unjustly incarcerated should do other things in prison, like lift weights, or knit," Schultz said. "Sadly, securing his freedom seems to be George's sole interest in life. He's obsessed with getting his life back."

Added Schultz: "All the time, it's 'free me' this, 'free me' that. Me, me, me, me, me."

Buell's brother Darron, who visited the prisoner last Friday, reported afterward that Buell "did most of the talking."

"No prizes guessing what he was talking about," Darron added.

Buell's sob story will be heard by the Illinois State Supreme Court during its next term.

"I can't wait. Since being incarcerated, my innocence is all I have to cling to in this horrible, horrible place," said Buell, echoing comments that he has made to anyone who's had the misfortune of being in contact with him at any time during the past decade. "This goes beyond my worst nightmares of anything I could imagine ever happening to me, and I hope the justice system finally does something—anything—to free me from this living nightmare."

"I just wish he'd shut his trap about it," attorney Holsapple said. "I'm working on his appeal. That's more than most prisoners get. But is he satisfied? No. All he cares about is getting out of jail. I'm like, 'George, get a life.'" ⌀

MARATHON from page 225

ately hits the couch to watch television. On hard training days, he watches *Sanford And Son* DVDs.

"I'm always tempted to get up off the couch or fast-forward, but I remind myself that every time I cheat, it hurts my chances on the big day," Bryce said. "When I feel my resolve slipping, I recline as much as I can or cover myself with a cushion. That usually does the trick."

Bryce added: "But the best thing a marathoner can do to delay the onset of discomfort is begin properly, by warming up with a hot bowl of chili and stretching out on the couch."

Bryce underscored the importance of carbo-loading and regular hydration, saying, "I don't want to be like that guy who passed out during the *Happy Days* marathon because he hadn't been drinking enough Mountain Dew."

"Doritos, pizza, M&M's, Yoo-hoo: anything that doesn't require you to go to the fridge," Bryce said. "Right now, I can barely move. So I'm right where I want to be."

The repetitiveness of the *Sanford And Son* marathon course, which includes 97 feigned heart attacks, 165 utterances of the word "dummy," and 44 appearances by ugly old Aunt Esther, frequently drives seasoned watchers to drop out prematurely. To minimize the risk of failure, Bryce has been mentally preparing himself for the weekend's trial.

"I visualize myself sitting still through the tougher parts [of the marathon], so I don't lose focus and change channels during a cameo by Lena Horne," Bryce said.

"Doritos, pizza, M&M's, Yoo-hoo: anything that doesn't require you to go to the fridge," Bryce said.

Veteran TV marathoner Andrew Lederle predicted that Bryce may have trouble lasting through season two's laborious exchanges between Fred and his friend Bubba Bexley. If Bryce can weather that stretch, Lederle said, he could very well experience the storied "watcher's high" around the third season, when the show really hits its stride.

"Hopefully he'll catch his second wind right around 'Ol' Brown Eyes,' when Fred is convinced that the engraved ring Lamont got him was actually stolen from Frank Sinatra," Lederle said. "It's all downhill from there."

Bryce is currently taking a few "recovery days" in preparation for the grueling marathon.

"Once I make it through, I'll know I've accomplished something incredible," Bryce said.

Bryce added: "This is the big one." ⌀

GOOGLE from page 223

are promising to burn the rest," John Battelle wrote in his widely read "Searchblog." "Thanks to Google Purge, you'll never have to worry that your search has missed some obscure book, because that book will no longer exist. And the same goes for

As a part of Phase One operations, Google executives will permanently erase the hard drive of any computer that is not already indexed by the Google Desktop Search.

movies, art, and music."

"Book burning is just the beginning," said Google co-founder Larry Page. "This fall, we'll unveil Google Sound, which will record and index all the noise on Earth. Is your baby sleeping soundly? Does your high-school sweetheart still talk about you? Google will have the answers."

Page added: "And thanks to Google Purge, anything our global microphone network can't pick up will be silenced by noise-cancellation machines in low-Earth orbit."

As a part of Phase One operations, Google executives will permanently erase the hard drive of any computer that is not already indexed by the Google Desktop Search.

"We believe that Google Desktop Search is the best way to unlock the information hidden on your hard drive," Schmidt said. "If you haven't given it a try, now's the time. In one week, the deleting begins."

Although Google executives are keeping many details about Google Purge under wraps, some analysts speculate that the categories of information Google will eventually index or destroy include handwritten correspondence, buried fossils, and private thoughts and feelings.

Above: Google executives oversee the first stage of Google Purge.

The company's new directive may explain its recent acquisition of Celera Genomics, the company that mapped the human genome, and its buildup of a vast army of laser-equipped robots.

"Google finally has what it needs to catalog the DNA of every organism on Earth," said analyst Imran Kahn of J.P. Morgan Chase. "Of course, some people might not want their DNA indexed. Hence, the robot army. It's crazy, it's brilliant—typical Google."

Google's robot army is rumored to include some 4 million cybernetic search and destroy units, each capable of capturing and scanning up to 100 humans per day. Said co-founder Sergey Brin: "The scanning will be relatively painless. Hey, it's Google. It'll be fun to be scanned by a Googlebot. But in the event people resist, the robots are programmed to liquify the brain."

Markets responded favorably to the announcement of Google Purge, with traders bidding up Google's share price by $1.24, to $285.92, in late trading after the announcement. But some critics of the company have found cause for complaint.

"This announcement is a red flag," said Daniel Brandt, founder of Google Watch.org. "I certainly don't want to accuse of them having bad intentions. But this campaign of destruction and genocide raises some potential privacy concerns."

Brandt also expressed reservations about the company's new motto. Until yesterday's news conference, the company's unofficial slogan had been "Don't be evil." The slogan has now been expanded to "Don't be evil, unless it's necessary for the greater good."

Co-founders Page and Brin dismiss their critics.

"A lot of companies are so worried about short-term reactions that they ignore the long view," Page said. "Not us. Our team is focused on something

Google will eventually index or destroy all handwritten correspondence, buried fossils, and private thoughts and feelings.

more than just making money. At Google, we're using technology to make dreams come true."

"Soon," Brin added, "we'll make dreams clickable, or destroy them forever." ⌀

BUSH from page 223

the ounce of sense he needed to keep his worthless ass alive, my last few weeks might have been peaceful. I mourn the loss of the beautiful August mornings, and the sweet afternoons that could have been spent on the porch swing listening to the songbirds. All Americans mourn this loss."

When asked why he has refused to meet with Mrs. Sheehan, Bush said, "Listen, I came here to relax. I want to fish, go biking with Lance Armstrong, play with my dogs, chainsaw some brush, and get back to nature. 'Course, it's hard to do that when you have to constantly listen to the mother of some dummy who didn't have sense enough to stay out of a damned war zone."

Bush added: "I'm more exhausted today than I was when I started this vacation."

Security concerns stemming from

"I was really looking forward to that burger," Bush said. "And I could have had it too, if it wasn't for that soldier getting his stupid ass blown off."

the presence of the anti-war protesters gathered around Sheenan's "Camp Casey" prevented Bush from making public appearances in Crawford, including ordering his annual cheeseburger at Goode Company Barbeque.

"I was really looking forward to that burger," Bush said. "And I could have had it too, if it wasn't for that soldier getting his stupid ass blown off."

"We're supposed to be over there showing the Iraqis how to get it done, not acting just as dumb as they are with all their stupid dying," Bush added. "I tell you, it feels like every other month since I started this job, somebody gets himself killed just to mess up my holiday."

When asked to address recent public suggestions, including Sheehan's, of immediate withdrawal from Iraq in light of mounting casualties, Bush said, "I don't want to think about that now. We can discuss that back in Washington. For now, let's relax and have a good time."

White House press secretary Scott McClellan said Bush's remarks reflect the administration's stance on casualties.

"I think what President Bush is saying is that, while we certainly owe a debt of gratitude to our fine men and women serving abroad, we don't want the real dumb ones who die to interrupt our precious downtime," McClellan said. "It is the president's opinion, and that of the entire administration, that the best way to honor the brave sacrifices of our fallen soldiers is by enjoying a relaxing vacation and not thinking about their deaths." ⌀

COMMUNITY VOICES

Hey, You Got Something To Eat?

Say, I'd like to eat a little something. You got something? What you got? Any kind of food is good. I just want something to eat. You must got something. I ain't desperate or nothing like that. Don't think I'm begging. I'm just asking here. No pressure. I just want to eat something. Wondering if you had something maybe. No big deal.

By A Goat

You gotta have something. Please. What is that? A thing to eat? I think it might be.

I'm not that hungry. I just ate. I could take or leave it. Got a handful of hard seeds? I'll take them. Pour them on the ground or just hold them out. You kidding? That would be great. Sure would. Whatever you got, really. It don't even have to be seeds. I'll take anything. Don't worry about me. I'm easy. Hey, anything you got. I'll try it. I got a open mind.

You gonna eat that shoe? I'll eat that shoe if you're not gonna eat it.

Come on, what you got? I just want to know. I don't have to eat it. I'm just curious. In truth, there's a good possibility I'll eat it. But still. I want to know. If you got just a morsel of anything, I'd be obliged. If I knew you were good for a scrap once in a while, I'd probably come back to you for more food sometimes. You wouldn't mind that. Of course not. You're my buddy. The food-giver. That's what I'd call ya.

You keeping a sandwich in your pocket for later? I'd be happy to eat it for you now. You don't even have to take it out of the bag. I'll eat the plastic and everything. Or tinfoil. Don't make no never mind to me. Do you got anything that I could put in my mouth for just a minute or two? Lemme know. I'll take if off your hands. No worries.

I bet you got a nice pant leg. Lemme chew a hole in it. I could chew it until you yanked it out of my mouth. If you don't mind. I'm telling you, I could use a little something to chomp on. I could wait, but what have you got? I don't care very much one way or the other. Come on, give me a break over here. I just want something to nibble on.

Hey! What's down there? A piece of bread? Let's see what we got. No... No, this is a rock. I'm not going to eat a rock. What do you think, I'm crazy?

Got a handful of hard seeds? I'll take them. Pour them on the ground or just hold them out. You kidding? That would be great. Sure would. Whatever you got, really. It don't even have to be seeds.

You keeping a sandwich in your pocket for later? I'd be happy to eat it for you now. You don't even have to take it out of the bag. I'll eat the plastic and everything. Or tinfoil. Don't make no never mind to me. Do you got anything that I could put in my mouth for just a minute or two? Lemme know. I'll take if off your hands. No worries.

Do you have any trash? I'll eat trash. You were gonna throw it out anyway. Hey, lemme eat it. Lemme at least taste it. If it's no good to eat, I'll know. I hate to see it go to waste, is all.

Got a balled-up tissue? Some paper towels? Coffee filters? Grounds, perhaps? Some cardboard? Insulation? All that sounds good to me. Just about anything like that would hit the spot for me about now.

A piece of corn on the cob. That'd do me. You got that? Would you mind going and picking me an ear from the cornfield? I don't care if it is seed corn or sweet corn or feed corn. I don't care if it's too hard to chew. I'll just swallow it whole. Just swallow it down. Who cares? I don't. Seriously, go over and snatch me one of them ears of corn. I'll get you back. Maybe I could eat something else for you later, something maybe that you're not interested in eating. Or maybe something that you intend to only eat half of. I might be able to eat the rest of it for you.

I've tried about enough of the grass around here to last me a while. I'm sick of this grass. This damned same grass day in and day out, I could just about... I take that back. This grass is okay. I'll eat it. It's pretty good. It's great, actually. I mean, it's okay.

Hey. Come on. Don't be greedy. I said I'd like a little something to eat. Put something in my mouth now. Let me chew something, you fucker.

Could you grab me a handful of weeds from the ditch? Don't bother shaking off the dirt! That's a waste of time! Just bring it over as is. Wave that near my mouth and it's going down the belly hatch. I am not joking. I'll eat weeds. Just watch me. You give me a rotten apple, and I will eat that whole thing, seeds and all. Tear off a piece of bark for me, and it's gone.

Hey. Come on. Don't be greedy. I said I'd like a little something to eat. Put something in my mouth now. Let me chew something, you fucker.

Oh shit, man, I'm sorry. I didn't mean that. That was uncalled for. There's no problem. I'm really sorry, friend. Food-giver. That's what you are. There's the stuff. Food-giver. You're my friend.

Hey, by the by... You got anything to eat? Don't go out of your way on my account. It's nothing, really—I don't need nothing. But if you got something, I'll eat it. ø

HOROSCOPES

Your Horoscope

By Lloyd Schumner Sr.
Retired Machinist and
A.A.P.B.-Certified Astrologer

Aries: (March 21–April 19)
It's bad enough that you earned the undying enmity of a murderous elephant, but this particular bull is a member of the Azuma ninja herd—unusually cunning, stealthy, and skilled in the use of blowguns and exotic poisons.

Taurus: (April 20–May 20)
You'll be relieved when you're assigned to be a lighthouse keeper 200 miles above the Arctic Circle, especially when you think of how close you came to being named manager of the Detroit Tigers.

Gemini: (May 21–June 21)
Hopelessly lost on America's backroads, you will stumble upon an isolated, acid-washed, hair-metal-loving small town that doesn't realize the Cold War is over.

Cancer: (June 22–July 22)
You're suddenly a very hot commodity when Sony announces that the next generation of recordable digital media will be synthesized from your heart's blood.

Leo: (July 23–Aug. 22)
You've always thought that breast implants were kind of sad, but you'll wind up with nine of them anyway.

Virgo: (Aug. 23–Sept. 22)
It's important to keep yourself looking and feeling good, but your relentless reapplication of home permanents is beginning to seem disturbing.

Libra: (Sept. 23–Oct. 23)
It's not that people mind it when you rappel in through skylights, but it does clash strangely with your love of making an entrance by popping out of cakes.

Scorpio: (Oct. 24–Nov. 21)
Your graffiti tags are as distinctive as they are funky, which is why you shouldn't even bother lying to the people of Jerusalem about what you did to the Wailing Wall.

Sagittarius: (Nov. 22–Dec. 21)
It doesn't matter if you've done nothing wrong and been charged with no crime. CNN's Nancy Grace is certain beyond a shadow of a doubt that you're guilty and should be "put down like a dog."

Capricorn: (Dec. 22–Jan. 19)
You'll become a living symbol of what's wrong with paddling in public schools after you repeatedly break into Birmingham, AL's Jordan High and demand to be spanked.

Aquarius: (Jan. 20–Feb. 18)
There's been a lot of trouble and turmoil on Wall Street lately, which is probably why they keep asking you if they can stay on your couch for October.

Pisces: (Feb. 19–March 20)
The stars foresee a vast change in your future. Soon, the world shall grow cold, the nights will wax longer, and the world shall become covered with ice for many months. ø

the ONION®

VOLUME 41 ISSUE 36 | AMERICA'S FINEST NEWS SOURCE™ | 8–14 SEPTEMBER 2005

NEWS

Immune-Deficient Realtor Forced To Spend Entire Life In Housing Bubble

see REAL ESTATE page 6D

Supervisor Has A Word With Cologne Guy

see BUSINESS page 1B

Area Man Does His Best Thinking On His ATV

see REAL ESTATE page 4E

Japanese Candy Finally Eaten

see LOCAL page 3C

STATshot

A look at the numbers that shape your world.

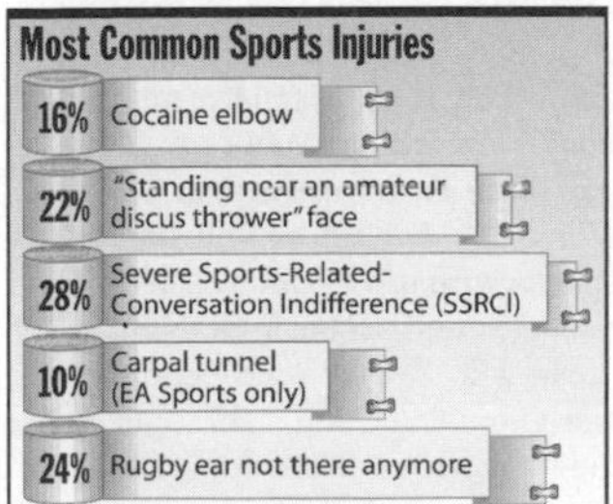

Most Common Sports Injuries
16% Cocaine elbow
22% "Standing near an amateur discus thrower" face
28% Severe Sports-Related-Conversation Indifference (SSRCI)
10% Carpal tunnel (EA Sports only)
24% Rugby ear not there anymore

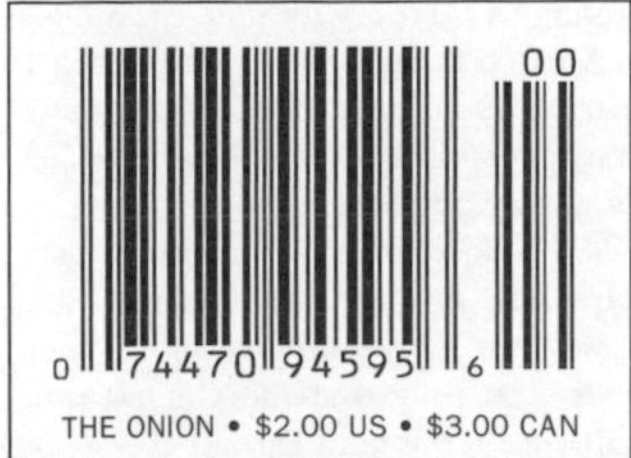

SPECIAL REPORT: DISASTER IN THE DELTA

God Outdoes Terrorists Yet Again

- Officials Uncertain Whether To Save Or Shoot Victims
- Nation's Politicians Applaud Great Job They're Doing
- Area Man Drives Food There His Goddamned Self
- Bush: 'It Has Been Brought To My Attention That There Was Recently A Bad Storm'

see SPECIAL REPORT page 233

Cheney Dropped By White House HMO

WASHINGTON, DC—Citing Dick Cheney's pre-existing health conditions and his refusal to meet regularly with his primary care physician, the White House's health-insurance provider terminated the vice president's coverage Monday.

AmeriHealth, the parent company of the HMO serving the executive branch, issued a "termination of benefits" notice to Cheney Aug. 3. The form letter, addressed to "Member #782B-11107-3905C (Cheney, Richard Bruce)," informed the vice president that his health coverage would cease, "effective immediately."

Speaking to reporters Monday, Cheney expressed dismay over being dropped from the HMO.

"I am a victim of a bureaucracy," Cheney said.

see CHENEY page 232

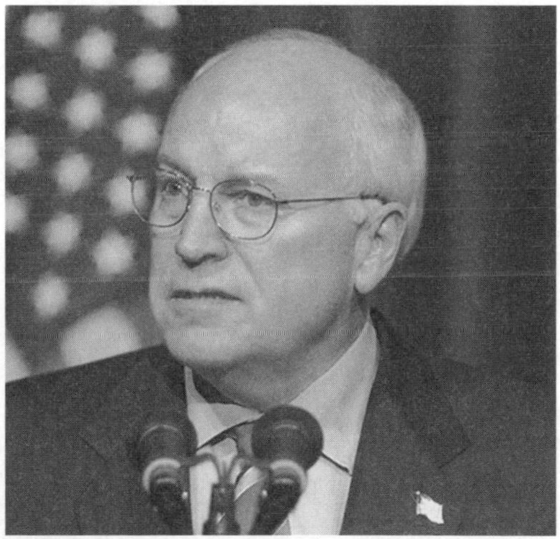

Right: Vice President Dick Cheney.

CEO Barbie Criticized For Promoting Unrealistic Career Images

EL SEGUNDO, CA—Toy company Mattel is under fire from a group of activists who say their popular doll's latest incarnation, CEO Barbie, encourages young girls to set impractical career goals.

"This doll furthers the myth that if a woman works hard and sticks to her guns, she can rise to the top," said Frederick Lang of the Changes Institute, a children's advocacy organization. "Our young girls need to learn to accept their career futures, not be set up with ridiculously unattainable images."

The issue was first brought to national atten-

see CEO BARBIE page 232

Left: Mattel's controversial CEO Barbie.

Death Of The Chief Justice

William Rehnquist, the chief justice of the U.S. Supreme Court, died Saturday at age 80. What do *you* think?

"My heart would go out to his family and friends if it weren't already out to 100,000 Southerners."

Karen Walker
Laser Engineer

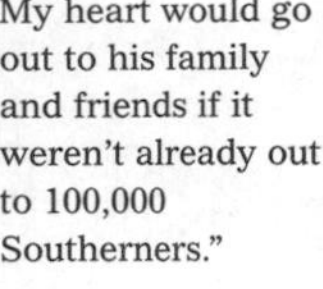

"His memory will live on forever, just like James Moore Wayne and Abe Fortas."

Richard Spears
Respiratory Therapist

"Rehnquist and I would probably agree on this for different reasons, but I think he chose the worst possible time to die."

Betty Birner
Stylist

"Man, I'm going to miss him... He was the guy who played Captain Stubing, right?"

Steven Kleindeller
Systems Analyst

"I hope I'm able to work until three days before I die. And thanks to some of the Rehnquist Court decisions, I'll probably have to."

William Lerach
Adjustment Clerk

"Oh yeah, sure, great time to ask me about some Supreme Court justice, when my house is sitting in a gulch."

Jonathan Fusilli
Copy Writer

Iraqi Constitution

Iraq unveiled the final draft of its constitution last week. What are some of the provisions?

- Sunnis retain constitutional right to bear arms against Shiites
- Democratically elected unicameral legislature allowed to work closely with the President For Life
- Kurds given authority to establish casinos and bingo parlors in their territory, free of state regulation
- Saturdays designated as presidential "me days"
- Citizens given right to assemble under overturned trucks as bombs go off overhead
- Former Ba'ath Party members must promise to be nicer in the future
- Poetic preamble begins, "In the name of Allah, The Compassionate, The Merciful, when will all these fucking Americans go home?"

America's Finest News Source.™

Herman Ulysses Zweibel
Founder

T. Herman Zweibel
Publisher Emeritus
J. Phineas Zweibel
Publisher
Maxwell Prescott Zweibel
Editor-In-Chief

The Only Thing We Have To Fear Is The Chupacabra

By Vicente Fox
President of Mexico

Ladies and gentlemen, I am proud to serve as president of the great nation of Mexico. For nearly 200 years, our people have withstood the onslaughts of man and nature. We have withstood attack from without and attack from within. We have withstood the wars of faith, and the creeping despair of faith's absence. We have faced famine, pestilence, and poverty, and time and time again, we have succeeded, for running in our blood is the hearty stock of our Mayan and Aztec ancestors. My fellow Mexicanos, we can stand certain in the belief that we shall prevail over the trials of today. Except insofar as the Chupacabra is concerned.

Forty-seven million of our citizens are poor, with 17 million unable to afford the basic essentials of day-to-day existence. Sadly, these facts are familiar to us not only as statistics, but as real people: our mothers, our fathers, our children, and our cousins. We have climbed far since the peso crashed 10 years ago, but we must unite if we are to climb further. And as we are climbing, we must constantly look over our shoulders for the forked tongue and

Many of our citizens still live in tin shacks with dirt floors, vermin-infested walls, and no basic plumbing. For those who live in such conditions, I warn you: The Chupacabra will make quick work of such flimsy shelter. Then, he is likely to devour you.

scaly, spiny hide of the Chupacabra.

People of Mexico, our cities have fallen under siege by thieves and murderers, but we stand together against lawlessness. The criminals and the gangs will not win! The Chupacabra, on the other hand, might. For, although hardened criminals cannot hop over trees to attack their prey, rumor has it the Chupacabra can.

Barricade yourselves in your homes and hope that this abominable creature gorges itself only on our livestock, and does not need to slake its thirst for blood on our children and our elderly. Yes, I'm afraid such a possibility is very real.

We are acting forcefully to break the grip that drug cartels have over this

We cannot know for sure whether the Chupacapra is an outer-space alien or some kind of feral dog-lizard hybrid. All we can know is that it should strike terror into the hearts of every man, woman, and child in Mexico.

country, finding the supplies at their source and eradicating them. We have dispatched the army to fight the drug gangs that have run rampant in Nuevo Laredo. You can go to sleep secure in the knowledge that Mexico is working harder than ever to stop these gangsters from poisoning our children. Or, you could, were it not for the penetrating, red-eyed gaze of the goat-sucking Chupacabra.

We cannot know for sure whether the Chupacapra is an outer-space alien or some kind of feral dog-lizard hybrid. All we can know is that it should strike terror into the hearts of every man, woman, and child in Mexico. This is the only sensible response.

We have overcome the corruption in our government-housing program, and we have increased the number of homes owned by Mexico's workers, but there is more work to be done. Many of our citizens still live in tin shacks with dirt floors, vermin-infested walls, and no basic plumbing. For those who live in such conditions, I warn you: The Chupacabra will make quick work of such flimsy shelter. Then, he is likely to devour you.

The Chupacabra may be lurking among us this very minute. Even if all of Mexico pulls together and keeps a fearful eye out for this loathsome beast, it is unlikely that we will evade its deadly pounce.

Wait—did you hear something? Perhaps not. But perhaps ... Run! Run now! Run home and cower in your beds, and pray that the Chupacabra will not rip out your throat! Ø

Food Critic Tears Radish Canapés With Salmon Mousse A New Asshole

MANCHESTER, NH—An appetizer of radish canapés with salmon mousse served at local French restaurant La Maison de Vin was torn a new asshole this week, according to *Concord Monitor* food critic Bernard Haberle, who reviewed the establishment in his "Good Eating" column.

"I ripped those canapés a hole so wide they'll be shitting blood for days," said Haberle, who singled out the dish in his review, calling it "a misguided fusion of land and sea."

"The mousse alone got a reaming that will have it crying for its mama," he added.

The hors d'oeuvres, presented on a bed of arugula topped with a salmon mousse of blended shallots, green onions, and white wine, were "force-fed their own balls" by Haberle, who in his column described the menu item as "a modest offering that should have aspired for more."

"I beat the living fuck out of that dish," said Haberle, whose column has over the last 15 years become a staple in the *Concord Monitor* "Lifestyles And Culture" section.

"If that appetizer knows what's good for it, it'll get on its knees and pray for mercy from sweet baby Jesus, because I went John Wayne Gacy on that shit," Haberle said. "Those canapés are probably wishing they had a dollop of crème fraîche to hide behind."

Haberle said that he takes a broad array of factors into account—including quality and freshness of ingredients, attention to detail, and price—before deciding whether or not a particular course deserves to be "bent backwards over a toilet and skull-fucked."

"Did you read the part where I say the canapés' 'pedestrian plating falls

see FOOD CRITIC page 234

"If that appetizer knows what's good for it, it'll get on its knees and pray for mercy from sweet baby Jesus, because I went John Wayne Gacy on that shit," Haberle said. "Those canapés are probably wishing they had a dollop of crème fraîche to hide behind."

Above: The dish that got "ripped a new one" by Haberle (right).

NEWS IN BRIEF

New York Philharmonic Hosts Open-Mic Night

NEW YORK—The New York Philharmonic Orchestra announced Monday that it will continue its popular open-mic nights throughout the 2005 fall season, encouraging everyone to "bring nothing but your instrument, 10 bucks, and whatever talent God gave you." According to director Lorin Maazel, "There are a lot of people out there with a cello or an oboe but no one to play with. Come on stage—we know over 500 symphonies! But please, no stand-up." Highlights of last year's open-mic nights included Mr. Maazel conducting data-entry technician Stacy Peterson and auxiliary-equipment operator Dan Fowles in a performance of Brahms' Double Concerto in A minor.

Little League World Series Marred By Cutest Little Allegations Of Steroid Abuse

WILLIAMSPORT, PA—Three players in the Little League World Series, two from West-region teams and one from the Southwest, tested positive for "cute little child-sized doses of performance-enhancing drugs" in the "most adorable little scandal" ever to rock youth baseball, Little League Baseball officials announced Monday. "Although the little scamps approached us and accepted full responsibility in the matter, I didn't know whether to hug the poor misguided kids or wring their beefy, pumped-up little necks." The scandal is considered the worst in Little League history, eclipsing even the Junior Black Sox of 1919, who intentionally lost their last game in exchange for $250 worth of ice cream.

Bush Tearfully Addresses Nation After Watching *Field Of Dreams*

WASHINGTON, DC—Moments after watching a TNT afternoon showing of the 1989 sports tearjerker *Field Of Dreams* Sunday, a visibly moved President Bush interrupted national television broadcasts to address the nation. "My fellow Americans, I am telling you, we all must see this movie together," said a moist-eyed Bush, whose voice broke several times during the address. "I don't usually cry during movies, but... well, when I bought the Texas Rangers, I had hoped baseball could bring me and my dad together, but he was always too busy being president, and he's getting up there now, and... America just really needs to see this movie, is all." Two thirds of Americans polled said they would not watch the film with the president, complaining that Bush tries to recite every line along with the movie, and always says, "Wasn't that great?" after his favorite parts.

Clairvoyant Vince Vaughn Accepts Movie Role Before It's Offered

HOLLYWOOD, CA—Vince Vaughn telephoned his agent Norman Falbaum Monday, saying only, "Tell Owen yes." According to Falbaum, the phone rang again five minutes later, and Vaughn was offered a part co-starring with Owen Wilson in *Wedding Crashers 2: Crashing Manhattan*. "I don't know how Vince does it," Falbaum said. "Completely out of the blue, he says, 'I'll take it!' And then the phone rings—*Anchorman*. Or it's, 'Norm? Vince. I love the script,' and I'm like, 'What script?' Five minutes later, *Starsky & Hutch* crosses my desk." Falbaum added that Vaughn's supernatural abilities have failed him only once, when he accepted the lead role in *The 40-Year-Old Virgin*, failing to foresee that it would not be offered. Ø

CHENEY from page 229

"This action on the part of AmeriHealth is exceedingly unfair."

In the form letter, AmeriHealth customer-service manager Bob Kielas

Although the vice president was admitted to the hospital and learned that he had only been suffering acid reflux, he received a bill Monday for $1,500.

apologized for any inconvenience caused by the adjustment, and encouraged the vice president to contact an AmeriHealth customer-service representative to make arrangements for his final payments.

Cheney said he was on hold for "almost half an hour" during a phone call he made to AmeriHealth shortly after receiving the notice. "This is a contemptible way to treat a customer," he said. "It's complete bullshit, to speak frankly."

Above: The vice president waits to see his primary-care physician at a Washington-area clinic.

Cheney said he was "reasonably certain" that his premiums were still being automatically deducted biweekly from his pay.

"I'm supposed to be covered," the vice president said. "This is a nightmare."

Those close to Cheney report that the vice president has long complained about having to see doctors within the HMO network, rather than choosing his own specialist. In 2003, Cheney wrote a letter of complaint when, instead of being admitted to the Bethesda Naval Hospital for treatment of his angina, he was directed to an HMO-approved urgent-care clinic in Clarendon, VA. According to the vice president, he sat in a crowded lobby between a mother with a colicky baby and a drunken Georgetown student with a broken nose for several hours, and both were examined before him.

Last February, Cheney received a bill for $2,000 for a coronary procedure that was only partially covered by his HMO. In a call that was recorded for quality-assurance purposes, Cheney argued for nearly 20 minutes with an associate customer-service representative identified only as "Heather." Cheney grew progressively more belligerent on the phone, until Heather said, "Sir, if you continue to use that type of language, I will have to end this call."

White House sources say that, while Cheney received his letter early this month, he was unaware of the cancellation on Aug. 23, when he visited the hospital following a possible heart attack and was told that he was "not in the computer."

Although the vice president was admitted to the hospital and learned that he had only been suffering acid reflux, he received a bill Monday for $1,500.

"This is a complete and total outrage," Cheney said. "AmeriHealth cannot possibly expect me to pay that kind of money out of pocket."

Cheney said he is unsure what action he will take if his HMO membership is not reinstated.

"I'm still too young for Medicare, and I'll simply run into the same pre-existing-condition clause if I purchase a health-insurance policy on my own," Cheney said. "Sometimes I just feel hopeless. There are very few health-care options available to someone like me."

CEO BARBIE from page 229

tion by mother, activist, and office manager Connie Bergen, 36, who became concerned when her 5-year-old daughter received the doll as a birthday gift and began "playing CEO."

"Women don't run companies," Bergen said. "Typically, those with talent, charisma, and luck work behind the scenes to bring a man's vision to light."

She added: "Real women in today's work force don't have Barbie's Dream Corner Office. More often than not, they have cubicles—or Dream Kitchens. I mean, what's next? 'Accepted By Her Male Peers' Polly Pocket?"

Despite the growing furor over the doll, Mattel's top brass has indicated no plans to cease its production, insisting that the newest member of the Barbie family represents a positive role model for girls.

"Young girls can be anything they want. There is nothing standing in their way," read a statement signed by Mattel CEO Robert Eckert, president Matt Bousquette, executive vice president Tom Debrowski, and CFO Kevin Farr.

Said Bergen: "I graduated cum laude from Radcliffe and have worked hard all my life, and my career doesn't look anything like Barbie's. Currently, there are only nine female CEOs in America's top 500 companies. To tell our daughters anything else is a lie."

"Real women in today's work force don't have Barbie's Dream Corner Office."

Figures released by the Changes Institute indicate that, although women make up 46 percent of the work force, a mere 15 percent are senior managers. Lang maintains that these facts don't square with the image of the career woman put forth by the doll.

Said Lang: "Any girl who thinks that she can run a large corporation when she grows up is in for a bitter disappointment, and it is simply shameful that Mattel would seek to cash in on impressionable young girls this way."

CEO Barbie comes with a number of accessories and environments, including the Super Barbie Conference Fun Table, Barbie's Company Dream Car and Underpaid Assistant Ken. But by far the most popular version of the doll has been the Talking CEO Barbie.

"This doll says things like, 'Did you get me those projections?' and, 'We need to cut our operating costs by 10 percent,'" Lang said. "It is dishonest to dangle this carrot of success in front of our daughters' noses, when we know that the odds that a girl will grow up to order someone around are virtually zero."

Lang said he does not expect Mattel to recall CEO Barbie, but he wants to send a powerful message to the people in charge.

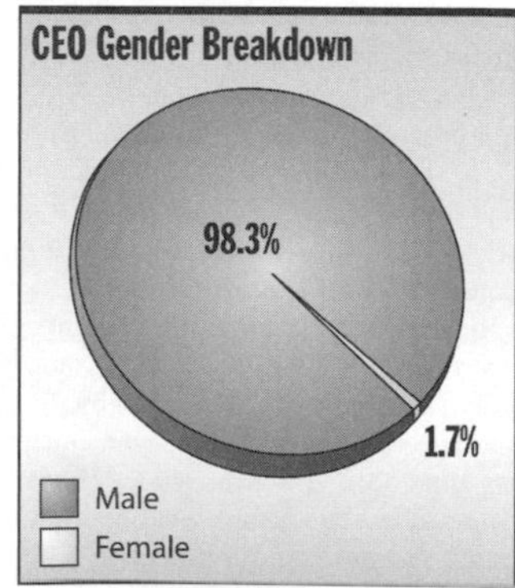

"When your daughter comes home crying because she was passed over for a promotion for the fourth time, what are you going to tell her?" Lang asked. "It would be easier if she'd been raised with dolls like Glass Ceiling American Girl, Service Sector Bratz, or Maria The White House Maid."

Louisiana National Guard Offers Help By Phone From Iraq

BAGHDAD—The 4,000 Louisiana National Guardsmen stationed in Iraq, representing over a third of the state's troops, called home this week to find out what, if any, help they could offer Katrina survivors from overseas. "The soldiers wanted to know if they could call 911 for anyone, or perhaps send some water via FedEx," said Louisiana National Guard spokesman Lt. Col. Pete Schneider. The Guardsmen also "would love to send generators, rations, and Black Hawk helicopters for rescue missions," but, said Schneider, "we desperately need these in Iraq to stay alive." Defense Secretary Donald Rumsfeld praised the phone support, but noted that it would take months to transfer any equipment from Iraq to New Orleans, saying, "You fight a national disaster with the equipment you have."

Government Relief Workers Mosey In To Help

NEW ORLEANS—Federal Emergency Management Agency director Michael Brown, leading a detachment of 7,500 relief workers, moseyed on down to New Orleans Monday afternoon. "Well, I do declare, it's my job to see it any of these poor folks need any old thing," Brown said from his command rocker on the command post porch, adding, "Mighty hot day, ain't it?" Follow-up teams of emergency relief workers are expected to begin ambling into the Gulf Coast region as early as this weekend. "They should be getting the trucks good and warmed up anytime now, and they'll be cruising into town just as soon as all the reservists stroll in," said Brown, who is currently at his desk awaiting offers of food, water, and evacuation buses to roll in from "somewhere or other."

Refugees Moved From Sewage-Contaminated Superdome To Hellhole Of Houston

HOUSTON—Evacuees from the overheated, filth-encrusted wreckage of the New Orleans Superdome were bussed to the humid, 110-degree August heat and polluted air of Houston last week, in a move that many are resisting. "Please, God, not Houston. Anyplace but Houston," said one woman, taking shelter under an overpass. "The food there is awful, and the weather is miserable. And the traffic—it's like some engineer was making a sick joke." Authorities apologized for transporting survivors to a city "barely better in any respect," but said the blistering-hot, oil-soaked Texas city was in fact slightly better, and that casualties due to gunfire would be no worse.

White Foragers Report Threat Of Black Looters

NEW ORLEANS—Throughout the Gulf Coast, Caucasian suburbanites attempting to gather food and drink in the shattered wreckage of shopping districts have reported seeing African-Americans "looting snacks and beer from damaged businesses." "I was in the abandoned Wal-Mart gathering an air mattress so I could float out the potato chips, beef jerky, and Budweiser I'd managed to find," said white survivor Lars Wrightson, who had carefully selected foodstuffs whose salt and alcohol content provide protection against contamination. "Then I look up, and I see a whole family of [African Americans] going straight for the booze. Hell, you could see they had already looted a fortune in diapers." Radio stations still in operation are advising store owners and white people in the affected areas to locate firearms in sporting-goods stores in order to protect themselves against marauding blacks looting gun shops.

Another Saints Season Ruined Before It Begins

NEW ORLEANS—Front-office executives of the New Orleans Saints football team provided a much-needed dose of normalcy Monday when they announced that, for the 23rd year running, the Saints season had been ruined before it began. "I'd say this is even worse than when Mike Ditka traded away all our draft picks to get Ricky Williams," said Saints vice president of pro-personnel operations Bill Kuharich. "But there's one thing we Saints can always rely on: our chances for a winning season being shitcanned before we play a single down. We're proud to have carried on with this tradition despite everything." The National Football League has declined the Saints' "mercy rule" request to be allowed to forfeit all their home games, saying the team must set an example for its home city by being blown out in every contest.

Shrimp Joint Now Shrimp Habitat

NEW ORLEANS—Big Etienne's, a popular stop for New Orleans-style jambalaya, shrimp po' boys, and gumbo, has become a near-perfect habitat for Penaeus setiferus, the ubiquitous white shrimp used in jambalaya, shrimp po' boys, and gumbo. "It's far too early to call this a bright side, but the restaurant's location on the Delta, combined with its rickety, shabby-chic fisherman's décor, have combined to create a serviceable ecosystem for this particular species of marine life," said Juanita Colon of the Federal Department of Fisheries. Colon said if floodwaters recede significantly, many New Orleans parking lots would be suitable locations for the cultivation of dirty rice.

Bush Urges Victims To Gnaw On Bootstraps For Sustenance

WASHINGTON, DC—In an emergency White House address Sunday, President Bush urged all people dying from several days without food and water in New Orleans to "tap into the American entrepreneurial spirit" and gnaw on their own bootstraps for sustenance. "Government handouts are not the answer," Bush said. "I believe in smaller government, which is why I have drastically cut welfare and levee upkeep. I encourage you poor folks to fill yourself up on your own bootstraps. Buckle down, and tear at them like a starving animal." Responding to reports that many Katrina survivors have lost everything in the disaster, Bush said, "Only when you work hard and chew desperately on your own footwear can you live the American dream." Ø

Above: FEMA representatives call out to survivors, "Show us your tits for emergency rations!"

COMMUNITY VOICES

I'm A Cloud Factory!

Puff ... puff ... puff ...

Hey, everybody, look at me!

No, don't look around you—look up! Up here! It's me, the cloud factory!

By A Smokestack

Watch me work all day and all night. I'm hundreds of feet high. I'm so tall, I can almost touch the sky!

I love what I do. Every day, I give something to my friend Sky. I'm a cloud factory!

Puff! Here's another one, Sky! Puff! Puff!

I make all kinds of clouds—in all kinds of colors! Sometimes, I make white ones. Sometimes, they're gray. Sometimes, they're as brown as the grass or the trees. And sometimes, they're as green as the river.

And sometimes, they're as black as the night!

In the morning, little men go into a little house that sits under me, way below.

Hello, dear little men!

Soon, my tummy starts to feel full. And when I feel like I can't hold any more, out pop the wonderful clouds! Pop! Pop! Pop!

Sometimes, they come out in long, thin streaks. Phwissss...ssssss... ssssssss...

Or sometimes, they're not little clouds at all, but one looooooooong cloud that fills up the entire Sky! Chuggachuggachuggachuggachuggachuggachugga...

When Sun sinks away, going to the other side of the world to meet his other cloud-factory friends, the little men come out of the little house.

Goodbye, dear little men!

Sometimes, they come out in long, thin streaks. Phwissss...ssssss... ssssssss...

But I'm not lonely for long, because very soon, different little men come in to take their place.

Hello, new little men!

There they stay all night, and everything starts all over again. And I get to greet my other friends, the Stars, with my cloudy hellos!

Puff!

Gosh! Did you see that cloud? That one came out alllll orange!

Once in a while, other clouds visit me. I send them little yellow clouds that frolic and play with the visitor clouds. Then, the visitor clouds start to rain. And you know what? Some days, the raindrops come out yellow—the same color as my clouds!

Thank you, visitor clouds!

I have other friends, too. Like the little birds. I love to watch them swoop and soar. They are so beautiful and graceful, and they bring me great joy. I'm so full of joy! I can barely hold it in! So I give them something beautiful back. Just as they approach, I pop out a great big pink cloud!

And when the birds fly straight into the cloud, they do a "rain dance" down... down... down... to the ground. Like a hundred little feathered raindrops!

For a long, long time, I couldn't make any clouds. It made me very, very sad. My friends Sky and Sun tried their best to cheer me up, shining brighter and bluer and clearer than they ever had before, and I loved them more than ever before, and I wished I could thank them by giving them a nice yellow cloud.

Come back soon, birds!

One day, after the little men left the little house that sits under me, some other little men came and nailed boards to its windows and doors.

For a long, long time, I couldn't make any clouds. It made me very, very sad. My friends Sky and Sun tried their best to cheer me up, shining brighter and bluer and clearer than they ever had before, and I loved them more than ever before, and I wished I could thank them by giving them a nice yellow cloud. But, try as I might, I couldn't make one.

But then, one day, some little men came by and took the boards off the doors and windows of the little house.

How exciting! What was happening?

The next day, more little men came. A short while later, I felt a rumbling feeling deep down in my tummy.

Was it ... ? Could it be ... ?

Puff!

Out popped a great big cloud even yellower than the lake!

And to this very day, I still make clouds.

And I'm never, ever lonely.

Chuggachuggachuggachuggachuggachuggachugga... ⊘

HOROSCOPES

Your Horoscope

By Lloyd Schumner Sr.
Retired Machinist and
A.A.P.B.-Certified Astrologer

Aries: (March 21–April 19)
Venus in your sun sign means that you'll spend many hours this week traveling through some rough and unfamiliar romantic territory. Bullet holes in the road signs, however, mean you're traveling through Texas.

Taurus: (April 20–May 20)
There comes a time in a man's life when he begins to take stock—his thoughts turn to his place in the world, his impending mortality, and the meaning of life, if any at all... But yours will stay pretty much fixed on vaginas.

Gemini: (May 21–June 21)
This is a good week to remember that love is not a game for cowards. It's also not fair, not played by any rules, and not a game you can win, so good luck, Romeo.

Cancer: (June 22–July 22)
You'd always dreamed of the many glamorous ways in which being a rhino hunter would change your life, but it's pretty much the way it's always been except for hunting all the charging rhinos.

Leo: (July 23–Aug. 22)
You will be shunned by some of the more traditional members of the tightly knit community of pornography directors for your tendency to ruin climactic moments by splashing the actresses with all the wrong bodily fluids.

Virgo: (Aug. 23–Sept. 22)
Despite your claims of historical importance and the need to remember America's fallen heroes, the authorities continue to refuse to grant you the permits required by your avid group of drug-war re-enactors.

Libra: (Sept. 23–Oct. 23)
You will be mortified at the group of self-righteous, middle-income, non-nurse-murdering losers that the state seems to consider a jury of your peers.

Scorpio: (Oct. 24–Nov. 21)
No one knew that when you said "your own special brand of justice" you were just talking about another variation of the old ding-dong-ditch.

Sagittarius: (Nov. 22–Dec. 21)
You seem to glow with your own special inner light, which is probably because of all that radium in your diet.

Capricorn: (Dec. 22–Jan. 19)
Remember: Despite your talents and capabilities, you are just one person. Stop insisting that you're a 14-piece bluegrass band.

Aquarius: (Jan. 20–Feb. 18)
You will inspire strong feelings in everyone you meet, particularly the older women on the parole board.

Pisces: (Feb. 19–March 20)
Jesus Himself in all His heavenly glory will appear before you, but unfortunately, the dream will only be moderately erotic. ⊘

FOOD CRITIC from page 231

somewhere between gauche and maladroit'? Take that, sub-par appetizer."

Haberle hastened to add that, although he is a discriminating critic, he more often than not gives positive reviews.

"I have no problem with slobbing the knob of a Gorgonzola-stuffed prawn if I feel it's earned. Just last week, I had a roasted striped bass in an almond-chanterelle crust with caramelized cipollini onions that was so divine I'd piss-gargle its sweaty balls in an abortion-clinic dumpster if that's what it was into."

When asked if he will return to La Maison de Vin to give the canapés a "second go-round," Haberle responded, "I kick-fucked that bitch, and I think it's best I leave it to rot in the ditch where I left it."

Members of the community have defended Haberle's review, saying his column has proven indispensable when selecting restaurants.

"Sure, he's being a little hard on the dish," said Sue Wellington, 42, who regularly dines out with her husband, Chuck. "But if Mr. Haberle drowns a plate of sesame-marinated cuttlefish in hot, infected jets of his pus-curdled cum, Chuck and I know to stay away from it." ⊘

Members of the community have defended Haberle's review, saying his column has proven indispensable when selecting restaurants.

the ONION®

VOLUME 41 ISSUE 37 AMERICA'S FINEST NEWS SOURCE™ 15–21 SEPTEMBER 2005

NEWS

World's Fattest Town Makes, Consumes World's Largest Mozzarella Stick

see WORLD page 6D

Morgan Freeman Narrating Uncontrollably

see NATIONAL page 3C

Annoying Man More Annoying After Skydiving

see LOCAL page 8B

FEMA Chief Loses $15 Bet That He Can Get Fired

see SPORTS page 3E

STATshot

A look at the numbers that shape your world.

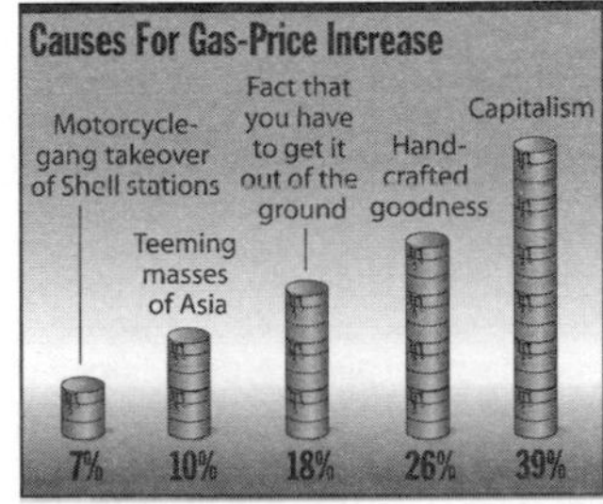

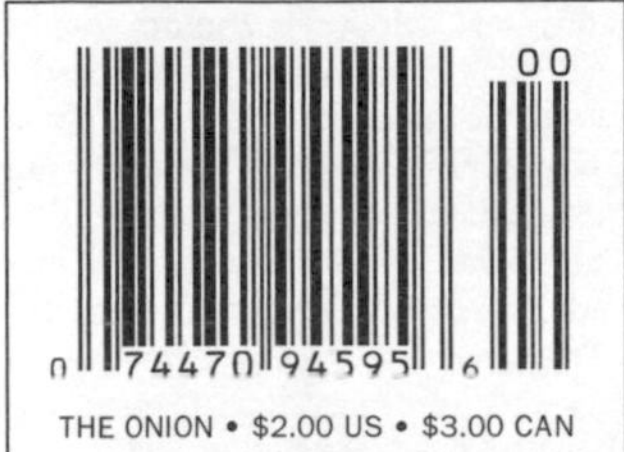

Bush Nominates First-Trimester Fetus To Supreme Court

Above: President Bush introduces his latest Supreme Court nominee live via sonogram.

WASHINGTON, DC—In a press conference Monday, President Bush named a 72-day-old gestating fetus as his nominee to fill the Supreme Court seat that opened following the death of Chief Justice William Rehnquist.

"Already, this experienced and capable embryo has demonstrated during his or her in utero existence a deep commitment to the core principles of the Constitution," Bush said. "It is with great pride that I nominate this unborn American patriot to the highest court in the land."

If confirmed by Congress, the bean-sized vertebrate would be the nation's first prenatal Supreme Court justice.

The unnamed fetus, who made headlines only three weeks ago when he or she was appointed to the Virginia State Supreme Court after

see FETUS page 239

Elf Finger Found In Box Of Keebler Cookies

PINE MEADOW, CA—Pine Meadow resident Ed Swaney made a gruesome discovery Sunday, when he opened a package of E.L. Fudge Sandwich Cookies and found a tiny, golden-fingernailed appendage believed to be an elfin index finger.

"It was horrifying," said 43-year-old Swaney, a shoe salesman and frequent snacker. "At first, I thought it was just a broken-off little cookie chunk, but then my tongue brushed a tiny bone on the end, and I spit it out."

Forensic investigators say the digit is an index finger, measuring nearly three-quarters of an inch, and bearing a small signet ring embossed with a tree design. A spokesperson for Kellogg's, Keebler's parent company, denied responsibility for the incident.

"The finger found in the box of E.L. Fudge cookies is nearly an inch long," said Kenneth Froud, director of public relations for Kellogg's. "An average Keebler elf is about as tall as a Chips Deluxe cookie. The finger in question is far too big to be that of an elf."

Riverside County police are investigating the grisly incident, obtaining warrants to access workelves' compensation records and interviewing

see ELF FINGER page 238

Report: More Kids Being Home-Churched

BIRMINGHAM, AL—A new trend in the religious upbringing of children has recently emerged in the heart of the Bible Belt. "Home-churching," the individual, family-based worship of Jesus Christ, is steadily gaining in popularity, as more parents seek an alternative to what they consider the overly humanist content of organized worship.

Norville Tucker, who moved his family to the woods outside Shelby, AL in 1998 to "escape the damaging cultur-

see HOME-CHURCHED page 238

Above: Biloxi, MS's Lori Williams home-churches her four children.

California's Gay-Marriage Bill

Last week, Gov. Arnold Schwarzenegger said he will veto the gay-marriage bill passed by California's state legislature. What do *you* think?

David Heller
Architect

"Well, I can understand where the governor is coming from. Being an actor, he's probably just not that comfortable with homosexuals."

Laura Giordano
Advertising Clerk

"So, playing all those gun-toting homos in the movies is okay, but when it comes to furthering their civil rights, suddenly they're off limits, huh Arnold?"

Elizabeth Slucer
Actuary

"Goddammit, if gay marriage was good enough for my grandfather, it's good enough for me."

Kevin Shin
Air-Hammer Operator

"It's weird... he doesn't *look* like the kind of guy who would veto gay marriage."

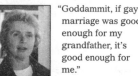

Richard Marks
Systems Analyst

"Good for him, I say. My wife and I have been married for 35 years, and we've never seen any need to be 'gay.'"

Arthur Bates
Painter

"All's I know is, I wouldn't want to be the gay activist who has to throw a pie at Arnold Schwarzenegger."

Slumping Box Office

Hollywood just had one of its slowest summers at the box office. What is the film industry doing to get people back in theaters?

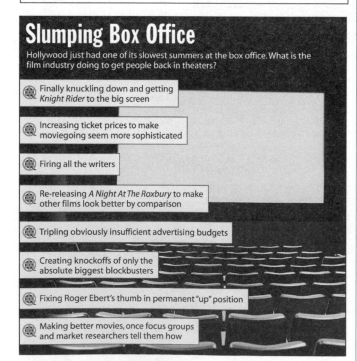

- Finally knuckling down and getting *Knight Rider* to the big screen
- Increasing ticket prices to make moviegoing seem more sophisticated
- Firing all the writers
- Re-releasing *A Night At The Roxbury* to make other films look better by comparison
- Tripling obviously insufficient advertising budgets
- Creating knockoffs of only the absolute biggest blockbusters
- Fixing Roger Ebert's thumb in permanent "up" position
- Making better movies, once focus groups and market researchers tell them how

America's Finest News Source.™

Herman Ulysses Zweibel
Founder

T. Herman Zweibel
Publisher Emeritus

J. Phineas Zweibel
Publisher

Maxwell Prescott Zweibel
Editor-In-Chief

Oh Yes... I Am Still Very Much Alive!

By Gorzo The Mighty
Emperor Of The Universe

Ha! I see by the look of terror in your pathetic Earthling eyes that you did not expect to see me standing here when the sliding doors to the Rocket-Sled-Escape-Pod hangar bay whooshed open. You thought you had defeated me forever when my Imperial Fortress on the ice planet Freezion was destroyed. Fool! Did you really think the great Gorzo The Mighty, Emperor Of The Universe, Overlord Of The Seven Suns Of Solaria, the greatest tyrant the galaxy has ever known, could have met with such an easy demise?

All this time, you thought you had defeated me... but you were only playing into my hands, Crash Comet, Space Commander From The Year 2000! It is I! I am still very much alive!

Don't look so surprised, Crash... It is only your arch-nemesis himself. And do not be fooled into thinking that this is some sort of projected illusion, or even a hallucination caused by the nectar of the fresh-plucked Hypno-Flower.

What's this? Reaching for your Electro-Ray Pistol? Well, let's find out how well you can shoot... when you are in the grip of my Immobilizer Scepter! Ha! Look at you, Crash Comet. Caught... caught like an Earth rat in an Earth rat trap! What's the matter? Does being frozen in my scepter's Tracto-Beam cause you... PAIN? Ha ha ha ha! Behold the feeble worm before me! Ha ha ha ha! Ha ha ha ha!

What's this? Reaching for your Electro-Ray Pistol? Well, let's find out how well you can shoot... when you are in the grip of my Immobilizer Scepter!

Ah, how I have anticipated this moment! My ultimate victory, at last!

How simple it was to deceive you! When you jammed the controls of my dreaded Atomic Radio Ray, causing it to emit oscillating waves of an increasingly higher frequency before finally self-destructing, you assumed that I had perished in the massive explosion! But how wrong you were! You were clever to wedge the butt of that Blasto-Rifle against the control lever so it would be stuck on maximum power, I give you that. And just as the Atomic Radio Ray immolated, how cunning it was of you to escape at the last second by jumping through the Electro-Portal as the fireball raced down the corridor behind you. But, alas, you were not cunning enough! It takes more than the crude strategies of a puny Earth brain to outwit the invincible Gorzo!

For it was my plan all along to trick you into thinking me dead. That way, I could carefully observe you and your allies from the Spaceship Gallant as you planned the next move in your relentless fight to free my interplanetary slaves from my iron grip. I knew you were coming here to the Space Laboratory to capture the rare Galactic Power Crystal and attempt to turn its awesome powers against my forces. I observed everything in my own Hidden Space Observatory, from which I direct my Remote-Control Robo-Legions in utter secrecy. How did I do this, you ask? Why, I had arranged to have the Spaceship Gallant fitted with a hidden Electro-Magneto Photo-Camera Transmitter! Your plans have been laid bare all along, as plain as daylight on the plains of planet Meex!

Don't look so surprised... It is only your arch-nemesis himself. And do not be fooled into thinking that this is some sort of hallucination caused by the nectar of the fresh-plucked Hypno-Flower.

But come now... no more of this idle talk. I have toyed with you long enough, my puny prey. Now the time has come... for your annihilation! Prepare to be blasted into atoms, Crash Comet, Space Commander From The Year 2000!

Wait! What is going on? No... no... NO! A rescue squad of Star Troopers from the rebel planet Xenon, bursting in through the sliding doors and cutting a swath of destruction through my Robo-Legionnaires?! If I do not retreat into my Escape Hatch immediately, they will surely capture me, as well! Your accursed friends have saved you once more! You've won this round, Crash Comet... but I tell you this: I, Gorzo The Mighty, Emperor Of The Universe, will smite you in the end! Do you hear me, Crash Comet?

The next time, you will not be so lucky! Curse you, Crash Comet! WE SHALL MEET AGAIN! Ø

Search For Self Called Off After 38 Years

CHICAGO—The longtime search for self conducted by area man Andrew Speth was called off this week, the 38-year-old said Monday.

"I always thought that if I kept searching and exploring, I'd discover who I truly was," said Speth from his Wrigleyville efficiency. "Well, I looked deep into the innermost recesses of my soul, I plumbed the depths of my subconscious, and you know what I found? An empty, windowless room the size of an aircraft hangar. From now on, if anybody needs me, I'll be sprawled out on this couch drinking black-cherry soda and watching *Law & Order* like everybody else."

"Fuck it," he added.

Speth said he began his search for himself in the late '70s, when in junior high he "realized that there was more to life than what [he] could see from [his] parents' Dundee, IL home."

The search initially showed great promise, with Speth's early discovery of his uncle's old Doors records and a copy of *The Catcher In The Rye*. Over the next two decades, however, the "leads just petered out." Although Speth searched in a wide variety of places—including the *I Ching*, a tantric-sex manual, and a course in

see SEARCH page 239

The search initially showed great promise, with Speth's early discovery of his uncle's old Doors records and a copy of *The Catcher In The Rye*. Over the next two decades, however, the "leads just petered out."

Right: Speth sets out on a new life, moments after announcing the end of his search.

NEWS IN BRIEF

Souter Hopes Roberts Is Into Birds

WASHINGTON, DC—Anticipating the confirmation of federal appeals court Judge John Roberts to the Supreme Court, Justice David Souter expressed hope Tuesday that his new colleague will be into birds. "For 15 years, I have found no one on the court who would so much as look at my sighting books or field guides," Souter said. "Perhaps one day after adjournment, [Roberts] and I could go to Kenilworth Park and look for red-necked stints." Souter added that it would also be nice if Roberts shared his feelings on abortion, states' rights, and the Cebu flowerpecker.

Microwave-Resistant Potato Alarms Scientists

BOISE, ID—Tuber researchers from the Western Root Vegetable Institute reported Monday that they have discovered a strain of microwave-resistant potatoes. "Natural and commercial selection has resulted in strains of potatoes that just won't nuke up," said Dr. Bernard Anderson, standing in front of a Radarange in which a test potato had been rotating unaltered for 90 minutes. "If this mutation proliferates, it could have disastrous implications for the nation's impatient." The new strain is the most significant potato mutation since the emergence of the "inedible" frying potato, which is still in use at most fast-food chains.

Halliburton Gets Contract To Pry Gold Fillings From New Orleans Corpses' Teeth

HOUSTON—On Tuesday, Halliburton received a $110 million no-bid government contract to pry the gold fillings from the mouths of deceased disaster victims in the New Orleans-Gulf Coast area. "We are proud to serve the government in this time of crisis by recovering valuable resources from the wreckage of this deadly storm," said David J. Lesar, Halliburton's president. "The gold we recover from the human rubble of Katrina can be used to make fighter-jet electronics, supercomputer chips, inflation-proof A-grade investments, and luxury yachting watches."

Bashful Terrorists Won't Take Credit For Attack

SANA'A, YEMEN—In a videotaped statement that aired on Al Jazeera Monday, al-Aziz, the terrorist group responsible for the bombing of a U.S. Navy refueling depot, was reluctant to take credit for the attack. "While we condemn America the Great Satan and wish them death and shame, I am afraid we cannot take credit for... Aw, who told you?" Hassan al-Fayed said. "This is about bringing death to the American Crusaders, not about us. Many martyrs worked to make this happen, and they deserve the real credit." Al-Fayed did not issue any further threats, saying he did not want to call attention to a few little truck bombings.

Older Brother To Attempt Unmanned Bike Mission Into Ravine

VERONA, WI—Robbie Bovy, 13, announced his intentions Monday to launch his brother's Schwinn BMXpert into a ravine near the East View Heights subdivision. "For the first stage, your bike will be powered by me," the older Bovy said at a backyard press conference while seated on his brother's chest. "Then, just before I hit the ramp, I'm gonna jump off and watch it totally endo into the rocks. Got it? Got it?" Bovy's intra-ravine mission is part of an ongoing exploration program that began in 2002, with the deployment of seven of his brother's plastic army men down the toilet.

ELF FINGER from page 235

employees in hopes of locating the finger's owner. Assisting in the investigation is Harvey Quinn, a workplace-safety and labor-relations consultant and longtime critic of Keebler workplace conditions.

According to Quinn, Keebler's denials are "a cunning subterfuge."

"When the elves roll fudge-stripe cookies down the production line, they are about three inches tall," Quinn said. "However, when they are outside of the enchanted tree, they grow to nearly three feet."

Quinn said the "real issue" is Kellogg's track record of nonhuman workers' rights violations, explaining that the company is currently facing multiple lawsuits, including cruelty to an endangered talking species of bipedal tiger and toucan abuse.

"When the elves roll fudge-stripe cookies down the production line, they are about three inches tall," Quinn said. "However, when they are outside of the enchanted tree, they grow to nearly three feet."

"Since the '70s, the Keebler elves have toiled around the clock in a cramped, unventilated, hollow tree," Quinn said. "The stories you hear about 'magic ovens' and 'elfin magic' are nonsense. The only thing 'magic' about the Keebler tree is the quote-unquote 'invisible gold' the elves are paid in."

Above: Police explain that elves grow in size once they leave the magic tree.

Quinn said Keebler's safety violations number in the hundreds, and singled out a controversial, high-velocity device retrofitted in 1992 to manufacture Chips Deluxe cookies.

"During the 13 years the device has been in use, it has pelted numerous elves with chocolate chips," Quinn said. "Just last year, an elf was hospitalized after being pummeled with chips moving at speeds exceeding 80 miles per hour."

The elf, 212-year-old Ireth Telemnar, later died from massive internal bleeding and head trauma.

While no public records are kept on the number of magic-creature body parts that turn up in processed foodstuffs, Calvin Blosser, a senior researcher for the Food and Drug Administration, said that their frequency is very low.

"We estimate that fantasy-creature body fragments in foods such as cookies, crackers, and cereal account for no more than two parts per million," Blosser said. "This is lower than the maximum allowed amount for insect parts and mouse hairs in equivalent products."

Some are questioning Blosser's estimate, as the elfin-finger incident follows an occurrence in April of this year, in which a Sioux City, IA man found the lower half of a diminutive humanoid creature with green leggings, a belt buckle, and pointy green shoes in a box of Lucky Charms cereal. The man settled out of court with General Mills for an undisclosed sum. ⌀

HOME-CHURCHED from page 235

al influences of urban Mobile," is widely credited with pioneering the home-churching movement. Tucker said he was inspired to home-church when his 10-year-old son Macon returned from Sunday school singing a lighthearted song about Zacchaeus, a tax collector befriended by Christ, and then later recited the parable of the Good Samaritan.

"I couldn't believe that the liberal elite had infiltrated even the study of our Holy Scriptures," Tucker said. "It was bad enough that my youngsters were being taught evolution in public schools, but when I discovered they were learning to embrace foreigners and Big Government in Sunday school, I drew the line."

Home-churchers create their own services, emphasizing close readings of Old Testament books led by a parent, and sermons that often exceed two hours. Proponents of home-churching argue that, when handed down by family members, biblical teachings take on a more direct, personal meaning. Additionally, they say home-churching reinforces familial bonds.

"When I open the Good Book and begin to preach, my kids associate all the things they learn about—the floods, the plagues, the impalings, the threat of eternal hellfire—with their daddy," Tucker said.

Many home-churchers say they chose to worship at home because they objected to "licentiousness" within the church social structure.

Chattanooga, TN's Judith May MacAuliffe, who home-churches her family of five, said her frequent complaints about modern church music and coed potluck dinners fell on deaf ears for years. It was only after she discovered that the evangelical summer day camp in which she enrolled her eldest daughters emphasized Frisbee and horseback riding that she made the move to private worship.

"We don't need these born-again evangelists watering down God's fearsome judgment," MacAuliffe said. "It sickened me to think that young Christian boys and girls were sharing canoes, watching occult videos of bewitched talking vegetables, and arranging pieces of macaroni into suggestive patterns in a so-called 'wholesome' setting."

"It sickened me to think that young Christian boys and girls were sharing canoes, watching occult videos of bewitched talking vegetables, and arranging pieces of macaroni into suggestive patterns in a so-called 'wholesome' setting."

MacAuliffe added: "By separating my children from sinful elements, I can finally teach the lessons of Leviticus in peace, without all this 'let he who is without sin cast the first stone' nonsense."

Critics of the home-churching movement argue that its practitioners deprive children of a well-rounded religious education.

"An untrained theologian is not equipped to address the thornier questions of morality," said Rev. Lawrence Case of Grace Methodist Church in Homestead, FL. "Home-churchers often make their own interpretations of complicated biblical instruction such as 'knowing' daughters, or whether eating a rock-badger is as sinful as eating a regular one."

Home-churchers like Pottsville, AR's Othniel Beebe say that in an increasingly secularized world, "Home worship is the only safe worship."

"My kids don't have to understand everything in the Bible—I don't claim to," Beebe said. "But it ain't my place to question God's will. As long as my Caleb grows up understanding pestilence, sin, massacres, and to eternally fear the wrath of our Lord—and not this warm and fuzzy 'universal brotherhood' crap—then I've done right by Jesus." ⌀

SEARCH from page 237

chakrology—he uncovered nothing.

"My family and friends kept telling me to give up," Speth said. "But I couldn't believe that my true self was forever lost."

Speth was dogged in his pursuit, sacrificing his higher education, bank account, social status, and personal esteem. Despite the rising costs and

"You're wasting your life. The sooner you realize you have no self to discover, the sooner you can get on with what's truly important: celebrity magazines, snack foods, and Internet porn."

mounting adversity, he vowed he would never give up his search—until now.

"I can't believe how many creative-writing courses I've taken, how many expensive sessions with every conceivable type of therapist," Speth said. "All that time—a whole life—wasted on a wild-goose chase."

Since calling off the search, Speth has canceled his yoga classes, turned in his organic co-op membership card, and withdrawn plans to go on a sweat-lodge retreat in Saskatchewan. On Tuesday afternoon, he loaded books by such diverse authors as Ludwig Wittgenstein, Meister Eckhart, and George Gurdjieff into a box labeled "free shit," and left it outside of his apartment beside a trash can.

"The only books I'll be reading from now on are ones that happen to catch my eye in the supermarket checkout line on the few occasions I leave my apartment to buy more Fig Newtons," Speth said.

Above: Speth tours Prague in 1991 at the height of his search.

Speth said he will no longer lament his coding job at Eagle Client Services, but will rather "embrace the fact that I have a job that makes enough money to pay for cable." Additionally, Speth has vowed to marry "the first woman who will have me, whether I love her or not."

"Oh, and if I never throw another goddamn clay pot in my life, it'll be too soon," he added.

"My family and friends kept telling me to give up," Speth said. "But I couldn't believe that my true self was forever lost."

Though hardened and haggard from his long search, Speth expressed relief that it was over. Asked if he had any advice for those who are continuing on their own searches, Speth had two words of advice: "Give up."

"Trust me—there's nothing out there for you to find," Speth said. "You're wasting your life. The sooner you realize you have no self to discover, the sooner you can get on with what's truly important: celebrity magazines, snack foods, and Internet porn." ⊘

FETUS from page 235

working at a private law practice for five hours, has enjoyed a meteoric career in American jurisprudence. A remarkable prodigy who graduated from Georgetown Law School mere days after his or her neural folds fused, the nominee reportedly shares much of the conservative, pro-business philosophy of the Bush White House.

Nevertheless, Capitol Hill sources say that his or her nomination comes as a surprise. Legal observers had anticipated that Bush would name a prominent conservative like Attorney General Alberto Gonzales, or the second-trimester female fetus that heads the legal department of Molson Coors Brewing Company, or former Solicitor General Theodore Olson.

"The fetus's judicial record, though extremely limited, is quite impressive," said Carolyn Scuitto, a professor of constitutional law at Yale University. "Last week, it authored a majority opinion overturning an appellate court ruling that found that a Virginia-based insurance company had insufficiently disclosed rate increases to its customers."

"We couldn't be happier with the president's selection," said M118-P, the unfertilized ovum spokesglobule for Gametes United For Pre-Life, based in Montgomery, AL.

Scuitto added: "Bear in mind that the judge has fingerless stubs for arms and still sports traces of a tail."

The fetus first attracted attention several days after making its way up the fallopian tubes to the uterus, when it authored an opinion piece critical of class-action lawsuits for *The Legal Intelligencer*. In the article, he or she addressed conflicting opinions about the nature of blame and responsibility, and argued for reforms that would check plaintiff attorney conduct.

The nominee's positions on capital punishment, gun control, and abortion are still unknown.

Unborn advocacy groups are applauding Bush's choice.

"We couldn't be happier with the president's selection," said M118-P, the unfertilized ovum spokesglobule for Gametes United For Pre-Life, based in Montgomery, AL. "The unborn and preconceived alike have long been underrepresented on the bench."

Despite his or her relative lack of courtroom experience, experts believe the nominee stands a good to excellent chance of confirmation.

"With its precocious intelligence and adorable pocket size, the fetus could very well prove to be the moderate 'consensus candidate' many on Capitol Hill have hoped for," said attorney, author, and Harvard Law School professor Alan Dershowitz. "And with its confirmation to a lifetime appointment on the bench, Bush ensures that his presidential legacy will last until about 2089." ⊘

Despite his or her relative lack of courtroom experience, experts believe the nominee stands a good to excellent chance of confirmation.

COMMUNITY VOICES

Ask A Man Who's Jowl-Deep In Phyllis Diller's Pussy

Dear Man Who's Jowl-Deep In Phyllis Diller's Pussy,

I'm single mother of two in my mid-30s. I'm busy working and raising two teenagers, but I still make time for what I consider very important: family activities. Lately, however, my son and daughter seem to prefer going off by themselves to spending time together. Worse, when I insist on quality time, they resent it... and me. How do I cope with this "generation gap"? I thought you'd understand, because you are jowl-deep in Phyllis Diller's pussy.

By A Man Who's Jowl-Deep In Phyllis Diller's Pussy

Fed-Up in Frisco

Dear Fed-Up in Frisco,

Mmmph, mmph, mmmmmph... MMPH! (gasp) MMPH! Mm-mmm-rrrrrr-nnnnn-mmmm-rrrumph oompth mmph rrrmmm-nnnn-OOF! (pant, pant!) OOF! Urrrrrgggghhh-gggrrgle oompth-mmph! MMMPH! MMMMMMPTH! Brrr-oooooo-nnnn-yowww-rrrrrummmm-nummm.... Nnnnnnnnnnnnnnph! NNNNNNPH! NNNNNNNNPH! Oh God... MMMM-MMMPH! (gasp!) (pant, pant, pant...) (gurgle!) MMMPH!

Dear Man Who's Jowl-Deep In Phyllis Diller's Pussy,

My husband "Hugh" and I have been active participants in our church for decades, and have traditionally been very involved with our community of fellow congregants. But Hugh doesn't see eye-to-eye with our new pastor, who has initiated many new policies for the church. Hugh feels we should consider finding a new church with a more traditional approach to Sunday worship. I feel he is overreacting. Who's right? I know you can help me figure out what to do, as you are currently jowl-deep in the genitals of stand-up comedy legend Phyllis Diller.

Conflicted in Connecticut

Dear Conflicted in Connecticut,

Urrrrrrrrrrrrgh-ggrrrgggrrrgggle-ggrrrggg-mmmmmmph. MMMPH MMMPH MMMPH! Schlurp schlurp schlurrrrrgle schlurp MMMMPH! ACK! Aaaaaaaaaa!!!

AAAAAAAAA!!! GRRUUUUUUU-UMMPH! Mm... nnnn... oorrrrmm-mm-hrrrrrrmph-ooooorrph.... (gag) GLURP! Glurrrrrr-GLURP: glag glag glag glag (gasp) MMMMMMMMMM-MMMMMMMMMMMMMMMMPH!! MMMMMMMMMMMMPH!

This may seem trivial to a man who's busy orally satisfying Phyllis Diller, but it's become a real problem here in our household: My husband always demands to be in control of the TV remote! I don't usually mind if he wants to pick the shows himself, but why can't I have a chance every once in a while? What is with him?

Dear Man Who's Jowl-Deep In Phyllis Diller's Pussy,

This may seem trivial to a man who's busy orally satisfying Phyllis Diller, but it's become a real problem here in our household: My husband always demands to be in control of the TV remote! I don't usually mind if he wants to pick the shows himself, but why can't I have a chance every once in a while? What is with him? I'm a patient woman, but my tolerance for his remote-hogging behavior is going down—and I don't mean on Phyllis Diller!

Anonymous in Anaheim

Dear Anonymous in Anaheim,

GURGLE! GULP! GASP! Mmmm-mm-glooooof-flurggggle-flurh-MMMPH!) MMMMMMMMM mmm-mmmmmmph! MMMMMPH! Gmmm-mmph! MMPH! MMMMMPH! Oooooooooooooooooooooooooof! OOOOOOOOOOF! MMMMMMM-MMPH! Gulp. Gulp. Gulp. (pant, pant) MMMMMMPH! Mmmmmm... mmm-mmNNNRRRGGH! MMM-nnnrrmm-mmllllurglr lurgle lurlgle lurg MM-MMPPH! (gasp!) MMMNNNMM!!! NNNMMMMMMMMNNN!! MMMM-MMMMPPPPPH... (desperately tries to breath through nose).

MMMMMMMMMMMMMMMMMM-MMMPPPH!

A Man Who's Jowl-Deep In Phyllis Diller's Pussy has been a syndicated advice columnist since 1979. His column appears in over 250 papers nationwide. Ø

HOROSCOPES

Your Horoscope

By Lloyd Schumner Sr.
Retired Machinist and
A.A.P.B.-Certified Astrologer

Aries: (March 21–April 19)
You keep insisting that your love life is nobody's business, but the nice men and women in the lab coats are just trying to help you make more pandas.

Taurus: (April 20–May 20)
Everyone likes a comforting bowl of hot, tasty soup, but somehow you expected more from life.

Gemini: (May 21–June 21)
Your naïve belief that girls don't go to the bathroom will be conclusively and graphically disproven this week, during the last blind date you'll ever have.

Cancer: (June 22–July 22)
Your undying patriotism and staunch "my country right or wrong" stance will continue to prevent you from reading a newspaper.

Leo: (July 23–Aug. 22)
You'll soon play a small part in the history of the vast interstellar navy of Quondrax, a planet where they can only christen a new Star Dreadnought by smashing an asshole like you across its bow.

Virgo: (Aug. 23–Sept. 22)
You're a proud individual, and there are just some things that you've never been able to bring yourself to say, but "Give me some more goddamned fried chicken with mashed potatoes and gravy right fucking now" isn't one of them.

Libra: (Sept. 23–Oct. 23)
You weren't a member, and you never watched them perform, but still, you have no idea what you'll do with yourself now that the Romanian women's gymnastics team has disbanded.

Scorpio: (Oct. 24–Nov. 21)
No one's escaped from the place since the day it was built, but that shouldn't stop you from attempting to break out of the American Family Insurance offices on Frontage Road.

Sagittarius: (Nov. 22–Dec. 21)
You knew that hanging out with that fire-eating strongman and sword-swallower would get you in trouble, but you thought it would be related to fire-eating or sword-swallowing, not check-kiting.

Capricorn: (Dec. 22–Jan. 19)
You never liked bears, never had any curiosity about bears, and hardly ever think about them, so it's no surprise that there aren't any around when you could really use one.

Aquarius: (Jan. 20–Feb. 18)
It's really too bad you don't follow professional sports, because you'll soon be hit by a bolt of lightning and gain the ability to have the latest scores scroll across the bottom of your eyes.

Pisces: (Feb. 19–March 20)
All your plans that are not impossible are too intimidating for you to ever seriously contemplate carrying them out, but good luck anyway. Ø

SIZZLE from page 187

amounts of blood. Passersby were amazed by the unusually large amounts of blood. Passersby were amazed by the unusually large amounts of blood. Passersby were amazed by the unusually large amounts of blood. Passersby were amazed by the unusually large amounts of blood. Passersby were amazed by the unusually large amounts of blood. Passersby were amazed by the unusually large amounts of blood. Passersby were amazed by the unusually large amounts of blood. Passersby were amazed by the unusually large amounts of blood. Passersby were amazed by the unusually large amounts of blood. Passersby were amazed by the unusually large amounts of blood. Passersby were amazed by the unusually large amounts of blood. Passersby were amazed by the unusually large amounts of blood. Passersby were amazed by the unusually large amounts of blood. Passersby were amazed by the unusually large amounts of blood. Passersby were amazed by the unusually large amounts of blood. Passersby were

A bag full of wolverines is hardly an appropriate gift.

amazed by the unusually large amounts of blood. Passersby were amazed by the unusually large amounts of blood. Passersby were amazed by the unusually large amounts of blood. Passersby were amazed by the unusually large

see SIZZLE page 249

the ONION®

VOLUME 41 ISSUE 38 AMERICA'S FINEST NEWS SOURCE™ 22–28 SEPTEMBER 2005

Oprah Stuns Audience With Free Man Giveaway

CHICAGO—The season premiere of *The Oprah Winfrey Show* unleashed a surprise for viewers Monday, when host Winfrey presented her studio audience with an unexpected gift: eligible men.

"Everybody gets a man! Everybody gets a man!" said Winfrey, almost drowned out by cries of disbelief as 276 men, one for every member of the studio audience, filed onto the *Oprah* set.

Hoping to top last year's season-debut surprise, when members of the studio audience received free cars, Winfrey watched elated as the men knelt before their awestruck new mates and delivered gallant kisses and professions of undying affection.

see OPRAH page 245

Right: Winfrey presents the studio audience with men.

Bill Introduced As Joke Signed Into Law

WASHINGTON, DC—A bill introduced by Sen. George Allen (R-VA) as "just a goof" several weeks ago was signed into law by President Bush Tuesday.

"I was just trying to crack up Frist and some of the other guys," Allen said. "Everyone's been on edge lately, what with the Katrina situation, and I thought we could use a good laugh."

Added Allen: "Looks like the joke's on me. And, I suppose, the American citizens."

S. 1718, also known as the Preservation Of Public Lands Of America Act, authorized a shift of $138 billion from the federal Medicare fund to a massive landscaping effort that, over the next five years, will transform Yellowstone National Park into a luxury private golf estate.

"I thought it was pretty damn funny when I read over the draft of the thing," said Allen, who said he strug-

see JOKE BILL page 244

Bush Braces As Cindy Sheehan's Other Son Drowns In New Orleans

WASHINGTON, DC—According to White House sources, President Bush is bracing for intensified criticism following Monday's report that the body of Tyler Sheehan, son of outspoken anti-war activist Cindy Sheehan, was recovered from the receding floodwaters in New Orleans.

Although the White House has not released a statement, a firestorm of controversy is expected to follow the death of the dynamic, well-liked young man, who was working on a levee-upkeep crew while completing the EMT-certification training he needed to become a firefighter.

Left: Tyler Sheehan.

"Tyler was the very picture of an American hero," said Jorge Guiterrez, an Ochsner Hospital orderly present when Sheehan evacuated dozens of patients from its intensive-care unit. "He pulled off-

see SHEEHAN SON page 245

NEWS

Evangelical Christians Enter 10th Day Of Vigil Outside Your House

see NATIONAL page 6D

Wrestling Announcer Can't Believe What He's Seeing

see SPORTS page 8B

Grizzly Bear Ruins Otherwise Non-Fatal Camping Trip

see LOCAL page 3E

STATshot

A look at the numbers that shape your world.

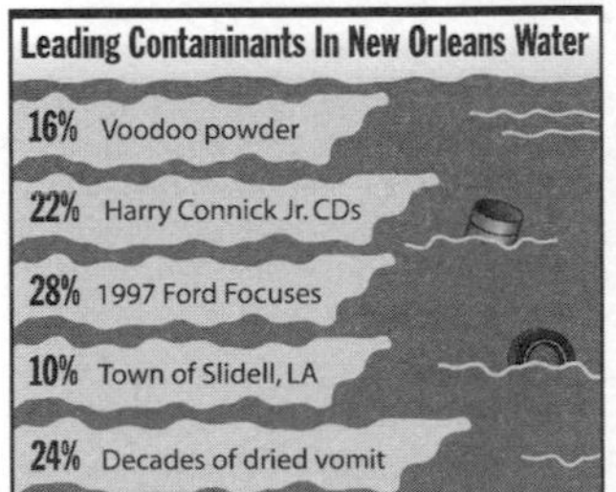

Leading Contaminants In New Orleans Water
16% Voodoo powder
22% Harry Connick Jr. CDs
28% 1997 Ford Focuses
10% Town of Slidell, LA
24% Decades of dried vomit

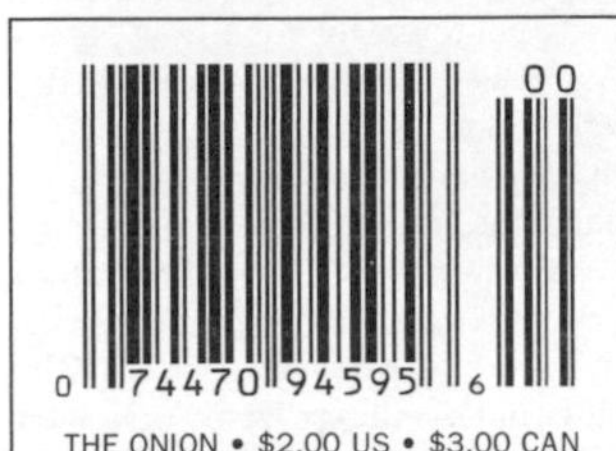

iPod Nano

Last week, Apple introduced the wafer-thin, flash-based iPod nano. What do *you* think?

"Would companies stop making smaller, more powerful electronic goods? It's starting to freak me out."

Tim Barber
Concrete Finisher

"As a maker of custom iPod cases, sleeves, and belt clips, I'd just like to say: Goddammit! Slow the fuck down!"

Katie Glass
Interior Designer

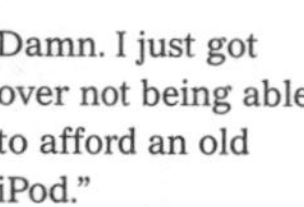

"Damn. I just got over not being able to afford an old iPod."

Clayton Keethe
Systems Analyst

"Excuse me? The first two floors of my house are still underwater? Hello? Has anyone seen my husband?"

Kate Dodger
Unemployed

"At last, after years of false hopes and empty promises, I can finally shove 1,000 songs up my ass."

William Lowery
Shoe Salesman

"I know I'll end up buying it anyway, but I do worry that this new iPod may be too small to effectively flaunt in public."

Kevin Palmer
Film Editor

Judging Roberts

Last week, the confirmation hearings for Supreme Court nominee John Roberts began. Here are the key facts Congress has uncovered about Judge Roberts:

- Needs this job or else family will be out on the street
- Not actually as good or bad as either side thinks
- Only blinks, like, twice an hour
- Favorite part of the Constitution? Article VI
- Hath power to assume a pleasing shape
- Has never heard of concept of "abortion"
- Freaks out when he sees crickets
- Would've talked forever about boring legal crap if Congress hadn't stopped him

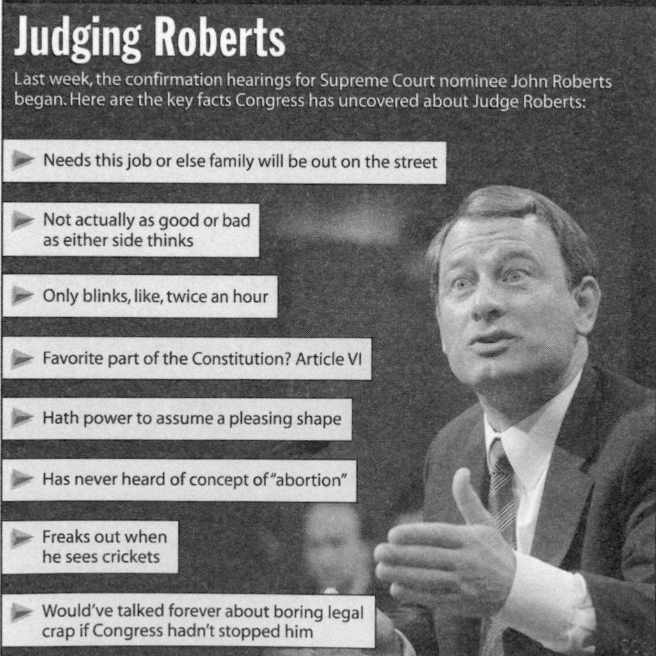

America's Finest News Source.™

Herman Ulysses Zweibel
Founder

T. Herman Zweibel
Publisher Emeritus
J. Phineas Zweibel
Publisher
Maxwell Prescott Zweibel
Editor-In-Chief

I'm Not Surprised Hitler Was A Taurus

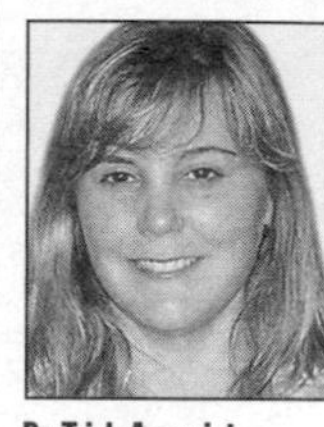

By Trish Arnquist

While going through some old copies of Star Signs for my upcoming garage sale, I came across something pretty wild. Did you know that Carmen Electra and Joey Lawrence were born on the same day as Adolf Hitler? Isn't that insane? I had Carmen and Joey totally pegged as Leos. You know, artistic, spontaneous, generous... As for Hitler, though, no surprise that guy's a Taurus.

In fact, just a few days ago, I had the History Channel on, and there was this program about Nazis or something, and when Hitler came on, wearing his swastika uniform and looking all high and mighty, I was like, "Oh, yeah, that guy's definitely a Taurus. Just look at his outfit." My high-school friend Becca was a Taurus, and they're totally cut from the same cloth: They're earthy, but don't let that fool you.

My father's one, so I know: Taurus is crazy about his routines! Growing up, whatever my dad said was the law. Whether it was not letting me go out on a school night or forcing me to eat all my vegetables, there was no use trying to reason with him. In fact, I used to say, "Dad, you're such a Nazi." It's weird the things our psyches tell us.

My father's one, so I know: Taurus is crazy about his routines! Growing up, whatever my dad said was the law. Whether it was not letting me go out on a school night or forcing me to eat all my vegetables, there was no use trying to reason with him. In fact, I used to say, "Dad, you're such a Nazi."

I wonder if Hitler was an Aries rising. That would explain his temper. Taurus has a temper enough, but boy, when Aries starts seeing red, you better get as far away from him as you can! Flee to another country if possible. Just pack up your belongings, load your children into the car, and go, go, go! Last thing you want to do is stick around when you're on the outs with Taurus, Aries rising.

In fact, just a few days ago, I had the History Channel on, and there was this program about Nazis or something, and when Hitler came on, wearing his swastika uniform and looking all high and mighty, I was like, "Oh, yeah, that guy's definitely a Taurus. Just look at his outfit."

Earth signs tend to be ambitious and really concentrate on a single purpose. Taurus, in particular, is known for cracking the whip. Is that so Hitler, or what?

I mean, how did Hitler's friends even deal with him? When I'm even in the same room with a Taurus, I start to freak. Of course, I'm a Gemini, and air signs don't get along so well with earth signs. I bet most of Hitler's top brass were Pisces. Pisces and Tauruses make good matches. Eva Braun's sign was Aquarius. I imagine that was a rocky relationship! Aquarius rocks the boat, and Taurus doesn't like that one bit! Which I guess explains why her marriage to Hitler was so short.

Taurus can be arrogant, which can really get him into trouble. I saw on that show that Hitler invaded Russia in June. June is rarely a good time for Taurus to undertake any new projects. True, Mercury was ascendant, but Stalin, the leader of Russia at the time, was a Sagittarius, a fire sign. In that combination, earth's the one that's going down. As an air sign, I would have gotten along much better with Stalin.

It may have been obvious to me all along, but not everyone is so perceptive. For instance, my friend Sarah, on a couple of occasions, has mentioned that she will never understand why Hitler did the things he did. I wonder if she knows he was a Taurus. Ø

LOCAL

'Hanging Out' Continues To Grow In Popularity Among Teens

WORCESTER, MA—Parents and child advocates across the nation are voicing concerns about the dramatic increase in "hanging out" among American adolescents.

"It's a common refrain among today's teens," said Mark DuFresne, executive director of Good Clean Fun LLC, a Worcester-based watchdog organization that monitors teen leisure activities. "If you ask them what they've been doing on any given day, invariably the response will be 'hanging out.' While it may seem harmless, even cool, the sad truth is that hanging out distracts our children from more important goals, such as buckling down or shaping up."

DuFresne said data compiled by his organization shows that "hanging," as it is known among the most dedicated out-hangers, is a gateway activity that often leads to other, more intense activities, such as "goofing off," "kicking back," or even "screwing around."

"Today, it's hanging out," DuFresne said. "Tomorrow, it could be messing around, or even hooking up. That's the problem: You never know where it's going to go."

One characteristic of hanging out that particularly alarms parents is that it can take place anywhere, even in such otherwise benign locations as convenience-store parking lots, pizza parlors, or right under parents' own roofs.

While teens' public out-hanging often causes mild consternation among adult onlookers, the most intense form of the popular recreational ac-

see 'HANGING OUT' page 246

One characteristic of hanging out that particularly alarms parents is that it can take place anywhere, even in such otherwise benign locations as convenience-store parking lots, pizza parlors, or right under parents' own roofs.

Above: Worcester residents engage in the alarming new teen activity.

NEWS IN BRIEF

Fox Cancels Apatow's *40-Year-Old Virgin*

LOS ANGELES—Executives at Fox TV canceled Judd Apatow's box-office hit *The 40-Year-Old Virgin* Monday. "We love Judd's work, but aging virgins aren't a demographic we're looking to target," Fox Entertainment President Peter Liguori said. "Maybe it will be a cult hit on DVD." *Virgin* joins *Undeclared, Freaks And Geeks, The Ben Stiller Show*, and several unaired TV pilots on the list of critically acclaimed but canceled Apatow projects. Fox TV executives said the cancellation will allow them to focus their efforts on *Stacked*, starring Pamela Anderson.

Publicist Schmoozes Wife Into Sex

NEW YORK—Morty Jamison, 44, a successful publicist with Jamison, Laird & Connaught, successfully schmoozed his wife Lily into sex last night. "I gotta call in a favor—the project's right up your alley," Jamison said. "Let's get dinner and talk it over—how's tonight? I'll have my assistant shoot you an e-mail." Although not visibly impressed, Lily reportedly signed on for a quickie feature above the fold.

Scalia Goes On Abortion Bender After Being Passed Over For Chief Justice

NORFOLK, VA—Saying "Fuck this shit, I'm stopping beating hearts with my bare hands," Justice Antonin Scalia, overlooked for the vacated position of Supreme Court chief justice, went on a spiteful abortion-performing bender over the weekend. "If I'm not going to be permitted a lasting judicial legacy, to hell with law and order," said Scalia, the conservative Reagan appointee who has served on the court since 1986. "I worked my ass off for 20 years, and no one cares. So, who gives a shit. Safe, legal abortions for all. Who wants one?" Scalia added that 2000 presidential candidate Al Gore "totally won that election, any idiot knows that."

Reporters Comb New Orleans For Heartwarming Story

NEW ORLEANS—Journalists and TV-news crews continued to comb the wreckage of New Orleans for a heartwarming story last week. "We thought we found a cute lost puppy on a rooftop, but when I tried to retrieve him, he chewed me up pretty good," CNN reporter Gary Tuchman said. "At least we did better than those guys from WGN—they thought they'd reunited an elderly married couple, but they just happened to have similar last names, and the guy raped the old lady to death in the Superdome basement." Many reporters have abandoned the heartwarming angle, instead concentrating on looting houses in the exclusive Port Charles neighborhood.

Mötley Crüe Signs Sexual-Harassment Guarantee

LOS ANGELES—Mötley Crue accomplished a music-industry first Tuesday, when band members signed an iron-clad sexual-harassment guarantee for their 2005 "Red, White, And Crüe" tour. "What a fucking awesome crowning achievement for these veteran rockers," manager Allen Kovac said. "Mötley Crüe is now contractually obligated to fondle, pinch, and comment lewdly on everyone they encounter during their six-month, 12-nation gig. Even at their height, KISS's managers could only get the band to sign a guarantee extending to female groupies." The agreement stipulates that opportunities for damage to property shall not be reasonably withheld. ⌀

JOKE BILL from page 241

gled to keep a straight face when he introduced the law. "Especially the part about how it would create over 10,000 caddy and drink-girl jobs. But I guess it went over people's heads."

The bill passed with a vote of 63-37.

Allen said he thought the Senate bill clerk was "playing along" when he forwarded the bill to the Senate Committee on Environment and Public Works.

"At the close of the day Monday, I went over to thank [Committee Chairman] Jim [Inhofe (R-OK)], and told him how I hoped 'the bill' got 'a fair hearing,'" Allen said. "He got real earnest on me, saying how it's his job to give every bill a fair hearing. I said to myself, 'My God, he thinks it's for real.'"

"I was still sort of frustrated that no one was catching on, but I couldn't help but chuckle a little when the newly amended bill returned to the Senate," Allen said. "The thing where they were calling the water hazards 'ecological conservation areas' was pure comedy genius."

The 18-member committee sent the bill to the Senate floor the next day with an approval vote of 14-4.

"I mean, Obama didn't vote for it," Allen said, referring to Illinois Democrat Sen. Barack Obama, who is often at ideological odds with his fellow Republican committee members. "I was like, 'Okay, one guy gets the joke,' but then I talked to him later and I realized he had no idea. When I explained the whole thing, he brought out that chestnut about how 'it's not funny if you have to explain it.'"

Allen added: "He's usually good for a laugh. I don't know what's up."

According to Allen, the Committee on Environment and Public Works not only took S. 1718 seriously, it inadvertently made it funnier.

"I was still sort of frustrated that no one was catching on, but I couldn't help but chuckle a little when the newly amended bill returned to the Senate," Allen said. "The thing where they were calling the water hazards 'ecological conservation areas' was pure comedy genius."

The only senator to suspect that the act was a joke was Sen. Joe Biden (D-DE), who said he later overcame his suspicions, reasoning that "if it got this far, it must be valid."

"Now, the bankruptcy reform bill that passed in April, I thought for sure that was meant to be ironic," Biden said. "I actually voted for it out of total sarcasm. My mistake, obviously."

Above: In accordance with the unwittingly signed joke law, construction begins on Yellowstone's 15th hole.

After passing overwhelmingly with very little deliberation on Tuesday, the "obvious put-on" traveled to the House, where once again representatives approved it with a vote of 409-26.

"Now, the bankruptcy reform bill that passed in April, I thought for sure that was meant to be ironic," Biden said. "I actually voted for it out of total sarcasm. My mistake, obviously."

The experience left Allen puzzling for an explanation.

"Maybe my idea was too dry," Allen said. "Maybe I should have introduced a bill that was even crazier, like mandating tracking collars for all American taxpayers. Then again, seeing how things turned out, it's probably just as well I didn't."

Once Allen found out that Bush would be signing the bill into law in a special Rose Garden ceremony, he decided to let the matter drop, saying that he was "in too deep to start explaining things now."

"I respect our commander-in-chief greatly," Allen said. "But unless Gallagher himself stuck the bill in a watermelon and bashed it with his Sledge-O-Matic, there's no chance [Bush] would catch on."

Following the Rose Garden ceremony, the news that the newly minted law was conceived as a lark confused some senators.

"Are we talking about the same bill here?" said Sen. Arlen Specter (R-PA), who voted for the act. "The golf-course legislation, right? I'm sorry, but I still don't get it. Is it funny because it was introduced in the Senate and not the House?"

Although Allen's bill was assumed to be in earnest, some senators were quick to insist that the Senate floor isn't always so humorless.

"We're all very serious about our task, but that doesn't mean we don't enjoy a good-natured poke in the ribs once in a while," Sen. Trent Lott (R-MS) said. "I remember the time [Sen. Russ] Feingold introduced his universal health care bill. I was laughing so hard, I almost needed medical attention!" ⌀

TOASTY from page 168

amounts of blood. Passersby were amazed by the unusually large amounts of blood. Passersby were amazed by the unusually large amounts of blood. Passersby were amazed by the unusually large amounts of blood. Passersby were amazed by the unusually large amounts of blood. Passersby were amazed by the unusually large amounts of blood. Passersby were amazed by the unusually large amounts of blood. Passersby were amazed by the unusually large amounts of blood. Passersby were amazed by the unusually large amounts of blood. Passersby were amazed by the unusually large amounts of blood. Passersby were amazed by the unusually large amounts of blood. Passersby were amazed by the unusually large amounts of blood. Passersby were amazed by the unusually large amounts of blood. Passersby were amazed by the unusually large amounts of blood. Passersby were amazed by the unusually large amounts of blood. Passersby were amazed by the unusually large amounts of blood. Passersby were amazed by the unusually large amounts of blood. Passersby were amazed by the unusually large amounts of blood. Passersby were

Damn kids and their damn murderous rampages.

amazed by the unusually large amounts of blood. Passersby were amazed by the unusually large amounts of blood. Passersby were amazed by the unusually large amounts of blood. Passersby were amazed by the unusually large amounts of blood. Passersby were amazed by the unusually large amounts of blood. Passersby were

see TOASTY page 301

OPRAH from page 241

"Signed, sealed, delivered... they're yours!" Winfrey said.

Hand-picked by Winfrey and her staff, the men range in age from 29 to 63 and were described by assistant producer Sally Heffernan-Ross as "great catches" with semi-professional to professional careers and stable personalities.

"Oprah showed it can happen: You can get that man of your dreams, or at least of your minimal expectations," Heffernan-Ross said.

The men, dressed in fresh chinos and polo shirts and bearing single red roses and gift baskets from Bath & Body Works, emerged moments after audience members were instructed to reach beneath their chairs, where they found inlaid boxes containing keys.

The keys, Winfrey explained, unlocked the doors to the men's individual domiciles.

"He's yours! He's completely yours!" Winfrey said to one speechless young woman who appeared stunned by what was going on around her. Assuring "no months of awkward dating" or "questions over who's going to make the first move," Winfrey said her man giveaway had totally eliminated the guesswork of romance.

The men Winfrey gave away are

Harpo Productions, Winfrey's production company, assured the winners that their prizes are guaranteed to "be into [them]" through 2010, and agreed to pay all local and state taxes relating to the men, as well. However, federal income tax and expenses such as meals, movie tickets, motel stays, teddy bears, plush slippers, and commitment rings will not be covered.

guaranteed to enjoy snuggling, to find the few extra pounds gained over time "cute," and to have read at least three books by the poet Maya Angelou.

"Oh, I love Maya," said one of the giveaway men, 32-year-old electrical engineer Doug Jefferson, who also enjoys warm comfy sweaters. "I think she's very brave. Heck, I love poetry in general. Who doesn't?"

"I was beginning to think it was never, ever going to happen," said Karla Drozdowicz, 34, an unmarried bank teller from Superior, WI who won radio-sales executive Chris Iredell. "I'm totally thrilled to get Chris."

Winfrey had to reassure several of the more timid studio-audience members.

"Don't worry, ladies, they won't be going anywhere," Winfrey said. "Kiss him! Give his behind a little squeeze! It's okay—he's your man!"

As with 2004's Pontiac G6 giveaway, the man giveaway came as a complete surprise to audience members, many of whom said the men arrived just in time.

"I was beginning to think it was never, ever going to happen," said Karla Drozdowicz, 34, an unmarried bank teller from Superior, WI who won radio-sales executive Chris Iredell. "I'm totally thrilled to get Chris. He's not what I imagined from my romance stories, but I'll love him just the same."

Another audience member, Gwendolyn Havers, said her years of watching Oprah instead of dating had "finally paid off."

"My mom says my 'wallflower' personality keeps me from meeting men," Havers said. "Well, if I wasn't such an *Oprah* fan, I wouldn't have gotten tickets to her show, and I wouldn't have won [part-time assistant tech-support manager] Eric [Fitzgerald]."

Heffernan-Ross said the audience members were selected from a pool of "hundreds of thousands of single, lonely women" who had put in requests for show tickets.

"Unlike the selection process for the men, finding unattached women was very easy," Heffernan-Ross said. "All we had to do was stick our hands in a big barrel of letters, and *voilá*, our perfect audience."

Harpo Productions, Winfrey's production company, assured the winners that their prizes are guaranteed to "be into [them]" through 2010, and agreed to pay all local and state taxes relating to the men, as well. However, federal income tax and expenses such as meals, movie tickets, motel stays, teddy bears, plush slippers, and commitment rings will not be covered.

Audience member Karen Schoenegge, 38, who was awarded 41-year-old collections-department supervisor John Zimmerman, said several drawbacks have emerged since the show's taping.

Heffernan-Ross said the audience members were selected from a pool of "hundreds of thousands of single, lonely women" who had put in requests for show tickets.

"Well, as soon as we got back to the hotel, I found out that John doesn't give backrubs," Schoenegge said. "He's also weird about me walking in the bathroom to pee while he's in the shower. I mean, it's not like I'm looking at him. He needs to loosen up a little. But I shouldn't look a gift horse in the mouth. I really, really needed a new man."

The seven audience members who declined their men, saying that they were too insecure about their weight to feel confident in a romantic relationship, were instead treated to all-expenses-paid weekends at the Omni Hotel in downtown Chicago. ⌀

SHEEHAN SON from page 241

the-clock double shifts moving guys in wheelchairs, guys without arms, guys on dialysis—you name it, he got them on a bus to Baton Rouge."

Before Sheehan moved to New Orleans, he was a struggling coho-salmon fisherman in Oregon's Klamath Basin. However, when the Bush Administration relaxed federal protection of the endangered fish, Sheehan's catch became contaminated with mercury. He gave up fishing and moved to Oakland, CA, where he opened a free clinic, which lost its federal funding in 2002 for giving out oral contraceptives to poor women.

A recent transplant to Louisiana, Sheehan reportedly went above and beyond the call of duty to aid imperiled New Orleans residents, dispensing bottled water and first aid to dazed hurricane survivors between shifts at the breached Canal Street levee.

Sheehan was last seen Sept. 4, hours after he and his levee crew sustained injuries while attempting to shore up storm-weakened levee pilings. According to sources, contaminated water laced with slicks of petroleum from a recently deregulated, poorly fortified refinery ignited, causing third-degree burns among the workers. Survivors recall seeing Tyler, badly injured and without the life jacket and medical kit denied him by recent budget cuts, digging survivors out of the wreckage.

"I don't know how we would have gotten out of there without Tyler," said Dom Ghivarello, Sheehan's crew chief. "Once we got clear of the break, we had no way of getting to high ground without our utility truck, which was requisitioned by the Defense Department last month for use in Iraq. But Tyler threw me his truck keys and went back to help others."

"I don't know how we would have gotten out of there without Tyler," said Dom Ghivarello, Sheehan's crew chief. "Once we got clear of the break, we had no way of getting to high ground without our utility truck, which was requisitioned by the Defense Department last month for use in Iraq. But Tyler threw me his truck keys and went back to help others. That's the last I saw of him."

Sheehan moved to New Orleans in 2004 to take a year off from the University of California at Berkeley, where administrators had temporarily suspended the stem-cell research program in which he was enrolled in hopes of helping to combat his younger sister Ruth's spinal meningitis. Friends report that his public spirit continued in the Big Easy, as he delivered meals to elderly New Orleans residents affected by recent Medicare cuts, and doggedly petitioned the Justice Department for the release of his life partner, Amin Sagheer, who has been detained without charge at Guantanamo Bay for nearly three years.

"He made service to his fellow citizens his number-one priority," Ghivarello said. "He made that vow back in 1998, when his best friend, a developmentally disabled black juvenile, was put to death in Texas for a crime he didn't commit."

Cindy Sheehan was unavailable for comment, as she was busy trying to contact her lone surviving son Teddy, a meteorologist studying global warming with the International Geophysical Foundation in Antarctica, who is believed to be marooned on a 45-square-mile chunk of the shrinking Ross Ice Shelf that broke off Tuesday morning. ⌀

COMMUNITY VOICES

As Long As You're Under My Roof, You'll Play By My Monopoly Rules

By Fritz Becker

Son, enough of these complaints, all right? You're old enough to know by now that I'm in charge of this family, and anytime someone lands on a Chance space, they pay me $150. When you're 18, you can move out and call the shots, but as long as you're living under my roof and participating in my family board-game night, you'll play by my Monopoly rules.

Let's get a few things straight, shall we? As long as I draw breath, you will never be the banker. I'm the banker because I'm your father, and as long as I'm the one paying—and passing out—the bills in this family, you will do as I say. When you can afford to buy your own home Monopoly set, you can be the race car. But for now, your older sister is the dog, your mother is the iron, and I am the race car. You can either be the thimble or the old shoe. You can't be the top hat. That's for Grandpa. And don't ask to be the wheelbarrow. No son of mine will ever be the wheelbarrow. I have my reasons.

I've said many times, I can't abide by the idleness encouraged by the Free Parking space. If you're going to sleep on the job, then there's no reason why I must pay rent to you.

I know your friends pay $400 if you land directly on Go, but in my house, you will either pass Go and make $200, or you will make nothing.

The Community Chest will never be part of our game, son, and no amount of pouting is going to change that. The idea of a Community Chest has never sat well with me, and when I became old enough to make my own Monopoly rules, I did away with it. Don't bother looking for the cards, either, because I destroyed them shortly after your mother and I got married. It will all make sense to you when you're older. In the meantime, there will be no Community Chest cards in this house! Except, of course, for the "get out of jail free" cards, which go to me.

And what kind of real-estate-trading game forces a player to keep the same number of houses on properties of the same color group? If that was true in real life, why, there would be a luxury hotel right next door to us. If a thriving tycoon wants two houses on Park Place and four on Boardwalk, then he should be allowed. That is, if he has a special relationship with the bank, as I do.

I've said many times, I can't abide by the idleness encouraged by the Free Parking space. If you're going to sleep on the job, then there's no reason why I must pay rent to you. The real-estate business requires round-the-clock vigilance. I swear, you're the only one who complains about it. Maybe next time you land on Free Parking, I should teach you a lesson and seize all your properties, as I do when you land in jail.

You think that's unfair? Well, if you'd simply pay the $50 fine immediately, you'd get them all back. I've told you this time and time again. You jailbirds think you can beat the system by rolling doubles, that's your problem. Well, that might work in casinos or back alleys, but not in the world of finance gaming. Not as long as you're under my roof.

I don't care how the "other kids" play Monopoly. If they played Scrabble with all the vowel tiles intact, does that mean you'd go off and do the same thing? Of course not. Son, listen to what I'm about to say, because it's for your own good: For now and always, we play Monopoly one way, and that is my way. Why? Because it's more fun, goddammit. ⌀

HOROSCOPES

Your Horoscope

By Lloyd Schumner Sr.
Retired Machinist and
A.A.P.B.-Certified Astrologer

Aries: (March 21–April 19)
You'll be trapped in a personal lube factory over the weekend, an event made more embarrassing when it's revealed that the place wasn't locked—you were just unable to get a decent grip on the doorknobs.

Taurus: (April 20–May 20)
A delicious meal will come back to haunt you hours later when, changed somehow beyond all recognition, it suddenly falls out of your body at an inopportune moment.

Gemini: (May 21–June 21)
This week, your ongoing efforts to equip your computer with ever-improving access to information will result in bandwidth high enough for you to become the first person to get hit by a bus over the Internet.

Cancer: (June 22–July 22)
Your first enjoyable night in years will be ruined when police tell the babysitter the calls are coming from inside the house.

Leo: (July 23–Aug. 22)
You'll be forced to seek new lodgings after changes in local law make parking your house by the city pool illegal.

Virgo: (Aug. 23–Sept. 22)
You just thought it was a cool design, but people will soon inform you that the guy on your T-shirt was some Argentinean nutjob named Shea or something.

Libra: (Sept. 23–Oct. 23)
Cosmic changes in the very fabric of the universe will soon alter the way light is transmitted and perceived, but all you need to know is that blue is the new black.

Scorpio: (Oct. 24–Nov. 21)
Your local EMTs have a hard, gritty, often tragic life, broken up only by their hilarious weekly calls to your combination distillery and chimp farm.

Sagittarius: (Nov. 22–Dec. 21)
Venus, the harbinger of love, will enter your sign this week. Unfortunately, so will busload after busload of obnoxious, sightseeing tourists, which kind of ruins the mood.

Capricorn: (Dec. 22–Jan. 19)
According to the stars, nothing will be able to stop you this week, which sounds great until you realize that you'll spend most of it behind the wheel of a runaway gasoline truck.

Aquarius: (Jan. 20–Feb. 18)
Small changes can mean a lot, as you'll learn this week when an inadvertently sexy letter from your doctor informs you that you have a rare and deadly form of "colon dancer."

Pisces: (Feb. 19–March 20)
You're not the sharpest knife in the drawer, but as an eight-inch J.A. Henckels high-carbon chef's knife, you're still more than sharp enough for most kitchen tasks. ⌀

'HANGING OUT' from page 243

tivity occurs in subterranean locales. It is in these covert locations, called "hangouts," that hang-related deeds most often transpire.

"When we remodeled the basement, it was just to install a new washer and dryer and create a place for our old sleeper sofa and TV," said Arlene Verbitski, a Worcester-area mother of two teenage sons. "You know, like a room for rumpus-oriented play. I never intended it for use as a den of hanging out. I don't know what they're doing down there. Are they flipping out? Getting down? For all I know, they could be getting over, stylin' along, or jamming away. I'm scared."

According to DuFresne, "cool" youths have harnessed today's powerful communications technology, enabling them to schedule hanging meetings from virtually any location. Teens are now able to arrange a "hang time" with their accomplices via mobile telephones, pagers, or even computerized written correspondence. Hanging out, with-hanging and hang-sliding need not even involve actual face-to-face contact, with the advent of message-boarding and chatting-rooms.

"There's no doubt about it: Teens are hanging out," said San Pedro, CA father of three Eugenio Mendez, pointing to the door of his basement. "I don't like what I'm hearing down there. Sure, when I was a kid, we would hang around, but that was totally different. At least we were 'around.' We were never 'out.'"

"Before too long, they're going to be grooving up," Mendez added.

Many adults have raised the concern that, as hanging out gains popularity among teens, it will be taken up by impressionable pre-teens.

"My daughter is only 12, and she and her friends are already 'hanging the o,' as she refers to it," Denver homemaker Mindy Carver said. "But for all I know, she's looping over and freaking about. She sees older kids doing it, and that's what she's going to do."

While there have been no reported incidents of hanging-out-related fatalities, DuFresne advised against complacency, accusing indifferent parents of "not seeing the bigger picture."

"How much longer will teens be content with just hanging out?" DuFresne said. "The rate at which they mature today, they are at a severe risk for rolling down, rocking high, shaking off, or tripping and slipping over and underneath. Maybe even leaking through."

Added DuFresne: "The sooner we nip this in the bud, the sooner our youth can straighten tight and bust forward." ⌀

NEWS

Local Building Accessible To Only The Strongest Of The Handicapped

see COMMUNITY page 3B

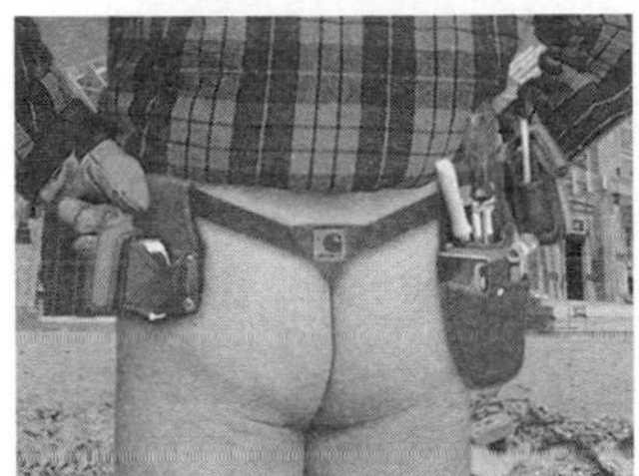

Carhartt Introduces Rugged Work Thong

see FASHION page 11E

Aromatherapist Fails To Factor In Own Falafel Breath

see HEALTH page 11E

Hurricane Victims' 15 Minutes About Up

see NATIONAL page 9C

STATshot

A look at the numbers that shape your world.

Most Common Addictions
19% Alarmist health news
27% Writing wizard-themed children's books
17% Text messaging
14% Motherly love
23% Reading about Courtney Love's addictions

the ONION®

VOLUME 41 ISSUE 39 AMERICA'S FINEST NEWS SOURCE™ 29 SEPTEMBER–5 OCTOBER 2005

Report: Some Sort Of Primary Just Happened

OLYMPIA, WA—A primary election of some sort is believed to have occurred in the past week or two in cities and counties across the nation, according to a report published by a citizens advocacy group.

Although the report stopped short of affirming the claim, the Fair Election Advocacy Council believes that local political offices as diverse as mayor, city councilman, district attorney, and perhaps a judgeship or two may have been contested.

"There may have even been a couple state and local referendums here and there," said FEAC spokesperson Jonathan Repstad. "No one really knows for sure."

The report mirrors the dawning suspicion many eligible American voters had in recent days that they missed an election of some kind.

"Am I crazy, or was there an election or something not too long ago?" said

see PRIMARY page 251

U.S. Launches AIDS-Awareness Campaign In Botswana

'You All Have AIDS,' Says U.S.

FRANCISTOWN, BOTSWANA—Officials and volunteers from the U.S.-based AIDS Awareness Organization began an aggressive campaign Monday to inform the citizens of Botswana that they are afflicted with AIDS, and explain how the sexually transmitted disease will eventually kill them.

"You have AIDS," said Pittsburgh physician and keynote speaker Dr. Julia Horton to approximately 6,500 villagers who traveled from the nearby townships of Lobatse and Palapye. "Every last one of you."

"And if you don't have AIDS, you al-

see AIDS page 251

Left: Dr. Julia Horton explains to a group of villagers that they will all soon be dead.

Two Publicists, Stylist, Personal Assistant Injured As Nicole Kidman Turns On Handlers

LOS ANGELES—An attack by Oscar-winner Nicole Kidman Monday left four handlers injured and two in intensive care, where they are listed in serious but stable condition.

The attack, which occurred during a photo shoot for *Premiere* magazine at the landmark Chateau Marmont in Hollywood, serves as a reminder that, despite their beautiful appearance, celebrities are both dangerous and unpredictable.

"Even experienced handlers can't turn their backs on these creatures," said celebrity behaviorist Laurel Fraser, who has conducted extensive field studies on such performers as Madonna, Bruce Willis, and an entire pride of Baldwins. "It's easy for people in the starkeeping profession to get complacent, and when stars sense that, they often lash out."

Stylist Melody Cosgrove was rushed to West Hills

see KIDMAN page 250

Above: Nicole Kidman.

Gay Clergymen

The Vatican recently announced that it will prevent homosexuals from entering the priesthood. What do *you* think?

"So... They're going to promote them all to bishop?"

Chris Dellinger
Adjudicator

"I heard they're also doing away with Barry, the patron saint of neatly groomed mustaches."

Casey Lincoln
Chiropractor

"It's a good thing they didn't outlaw gay painters. It'd be a shame to see the Sistine Chapel painted over."

John Benito
Dentist

"Good. Only straight people should be allowed to take a vow of celibacy."

Susanne Botts
Hotel Reservationist

"Sounds like Pope Crazy III is already throwing his weight around."

Bill DeLoise
Systems Analyst

"But I can keep the outfit, right?"

Zachary Lewis
Butcher

NASA Moon Mission
Last week, scientists at NASA announced that they will send a manned spacecraft to the moon by the year 2018. Here are some of their plans for the mission:
Astronauts will plant American flag big enough to be visible from Earth
Trip to be funded by selling old moon detritus on Craigslist
Thanks to technological advances, craft will be able to land precisely between Tycho crater and Virgin Atlantic Resort at Mare Tranquillitatis
Dramatic narration to be provided by actor Patrick Stewart
NASA promises they will bring moon back this time
Scientists to develop space-travel version of Scrabble for long, boring trip
Launch scheduled for next week, but inevitable technical, logistical, and meteorological delays expected to push it back 13 years
If all goes as planned, NASA hoping never to come back

America's Finest News Source.™

Herman Ulysses Zweibel
Founder

T. Herman Zweibel
Publisher Emeritus
J. Phineas Zweibel
Publisher
Maxwell Prescott Zweibel
Editor-In-Chief

Women Have To Stop Starving Themselves Past The Point Of Hotness

Avoiding eating in order to improve your appearance is part of being a woman, and it's natural for a woman to devote all of her time to achieving a figure pleasing to the male eye. While there are many ways to get hot, one of the simplest, fastest, and most effective is through self-starvation. However, anorexia, like all things, is best used in moderation. For example, you should never get so thin that you lose your tits.

By Brett Waggoner

I've seen it time and time again: A woman of "normal" weight buys a scale, tapes pictures from *W* magazine to her refrigerator, draws a weight chart on her bathroom mirror, and makes a commitment to subsisting on iced tea and steamed broccoli. She resists the temptation to cheat, and slowly, her will power is rewarded: The butterfly emerges from its chrysalis. The pounds melt off, and she is undeniably hot.

But then, sometimes, inexplicably, something goes wrong. Rather than maintaining her new slim, sexy body through marathon training and obsessive calorie counting, a woman will continue to shed pounds, starving herself—dreadfully, heartrendingly—way past the point of hotness.

Fat on the upper arms, hips, or waist is a turn-off, but there should be a thin matting of fat underneath the skin to prevent a man from being able to make out your skeletal system.

Reality check, ladies: If your ass resembles your scapula, you are in the danger zone. That kind of thing is not attractive.

It's like I told my ex-girlfriend Lisa: Feminine fragility is a plus, but if I actually snap your arm while having sex with you, you've gone too far. A woman should have a pleasingly light, impossibly fragile appearance, much like a piece of fine china, but if her body has begun digesting the calcium in its bones to sustain its necessary functions, there is a good chance she has starved herself beyond the point where I would even want to have sex with her at all.

Fat on the upper arms, hips, or waist is a turn-off, but there should be a thin matting of fat underneath the skin to prevent a man from being able to make out your skeletal system. A lot of girls don't know this, but slightly rounded, healthy appearing limbs are

Ladies, if you are suffering from too much anorexia, I urge you, in the name of all that is alluring, increase your calorie consumption by about 10 percent.

sexier than rail-thin ones, provided a man can still wrap his hands around your waist. Women like the emaciated thing, but guys actually like it if a girl's upper thigh is a shade wider than her knee.

It's heartbreaking to see a chick who's too anorexic. Don't get me wrong, because a little bit is a plus, but when I see a too-anorexic chick, I always imagine her spending night after night running on her treadmill, trolling the Internet for diet tips, doing stomach crunches in her cubicle, eating head after head of iceberg lettuce—all the while tragically unaware that, at her weight, she could probably be eating 1,000 calories a day. At least 700. Ironically, all her work has left her so crazy skinny, she's as desirable as that fat cow Kate Winslet.

Ladies, if you are suffering from too much anorexia, I urge you, in the name of all that is alluring, increase your calorie consumption by about 10 percent. Treat yourself to a bite of your boyfriend's sandwich. Drink a glass of skim milk. See what happens. You might see your ribs filling out a little, and that might frighten you, but please remember: We men like a woman who's obsessively fit and trim, but no one wants to bang a concentration-camp prisoner.

Harness the power of your misery and poor body image. You've got a good thing going with that. But just don't go too far. ⌀

Guy In Philosophy Class Needs To Shut The Fuck Up

HANOVER, NH—According to students enrolled in professor Michael Rosenthal's Philosophy 101 course at Dartmouth University, that guy, Darrin Floen, the one who sits at the back of the class and acts like he's Aristotle, seriously needs to shut the fuck up.

His fellow students describe Floen's frequent comments as eager, interested, and incredibly annoying.

"He thinks he knows about philosophy," freshman Duane Herring said. "But I hate his voice, I hate the way he only half raises his hand, like he's so laid back. We're discussing ethics in a couple weeks, but I don't know if I can wait that long before deciding if it's morally wrong to pound his face in."

"Today he was going on and on about how Plato's cave shadows themselves represent the ideal foundation of Western philosophical thought," said freshman Julia Wald

see 'PHILOSOPHY' page 252

Floen (left) is known to make his insufferable comments during class at Thornton Hall (above).

NEWS IN BRIEF

Bush's Approval Rating Of Other Americans Also At All-Time Low

WASHINGTON, DC—Shortly after President Bush's job-approval rating dipped to 40 percent, the lowest of his presidency, a poll indicated that Bush's approval rating for American citizens is also at an all-time low. "At 30 percent, President Bush's satisfaction with 'likely voters' is the lowest it's ever been," said Rachel Markham of TNS Intersearch. While Bush finds that 40 percent of Americans are "on the right track," he said he believes only 30 percent will do a good job supporting him in the event of another disaster or terrorist attack.

Delta Blues Poised For Biggest Revival Since 1915

NEW ORLEANS—Blues historians report that Delta blues, an early blues form that arose in the Mississippi Delta region, is poised for its biggest revival since 1915. "Death, loss, heartbreak, isolation, hard luck—that's what the blues have been missing for decades," said music critic Joel Kushner. "But now, even the most sheltered, derivative Delta blues musician should have enough material to cut an album." The revival is heralded by the recent singles "FEMA Don't Come 'Round No More," "Category Five Woman Done Me Six Kinds Of Wrong," and "Talkin' Drownded Kin Blues."

Congress Abandons WikiConstitution

WASHINGTON, DC—Congress scrapped the open-source, open-edit, online version of the Constitution Monday, only two months after it went live. "The idea seemed to dovetail perfectly with our tradition of democratic participation," Senate Minority Leader Harry Reid said. "But when so-called 'contributors' began loading it down with profanity, pornography, ASCII art, and mandatory-assault-rifle-ownership amendments, we thought it might be best to cancel the project." Congress intends to restore the Constitution to its pre-Wiki format as soon as an unadulterated copy of the document can be found.

Nobody In Ukraine Notices Absence Of Government

KIEV, UKRAINE—The firing of Prime Minister Yulia Tymoshenko and the dismissal of most of the federal government continued to go unremarked by Ukraine's 14 million citizens Monday. "Roads are crumbling, the Russian Mafia sets food prices, our currency grows more worthless by the hour, and still the government does nothing," said Brzyny Ilandrovitch, editor of the *U.F. Monitor.* "Every year, it's the same thing with this group of fat crooks." Upon hearing of the government overthrow, Ilandrovitch said he was reminded of 1991's democratic elections, when the lawless chaos that followed the country's independence from the Soviet Union left many doubting that a central government had been democratically elected.

New PSA Reduces Accidental Staplings By 33 Percent

WASHINGTON, DC—In the wake of a campaign launched by the Occupational Safety And Health Administration this spring, accidental stapling incidents among U.S. office workers have fallen by one-third. "We're pleased that 'Stop, Look, and Swingline!' has done so much to promote public awareness of office-stapler safety," said OSHA head Jonathan Snare. "Our primary areas of concern are the fingertips and the delicate thumb-forefinger webbing." OSHA was inspired to make the film after a 2002 PSA was credited with reducing the number of manila-file-foldering fatalities by 20 percent. ⌀

KIDMAN from page 247

Hospital with broken bones, severe blood loss, and deep lacerations to the face, neck, and shoulders, likely inflicted by Kidman's cherry-red, two-inch talons. Personal assistant Barrie Levesque reportedly suffered extensive nerve damage, as well as severely yanked hair. Publicists Kiki Landresky and Martin O'Reilly have been released from West Hills after being treated for cuts and minor contusions. O'Reilly received a puncture wound to the thigh from one of Kidman's stiletto heels.

"Sometimes, we love our celebrities so much that we want them to experience the same freedoms we enjoy," Hable said.

Celebrity-control officers working with the LAPD cornered the actress outside a sound stage at Hollywood Center Studios late Tuesday and shot her with a tranquilizer dart after failing to coax her into custody with an expensive gift bag.

"She was just calmly feeding at a craft-services table, unaware of all the havoc she raised," celebrity-control officer Rene Bofill said. "After being tranquilized, she began to snort and rave, knocking down tables and chairs before she collapsed near the set of *That's So Raven*."

As with many celebrity attacks, the victims reported that Kidman gave no warning before striking.

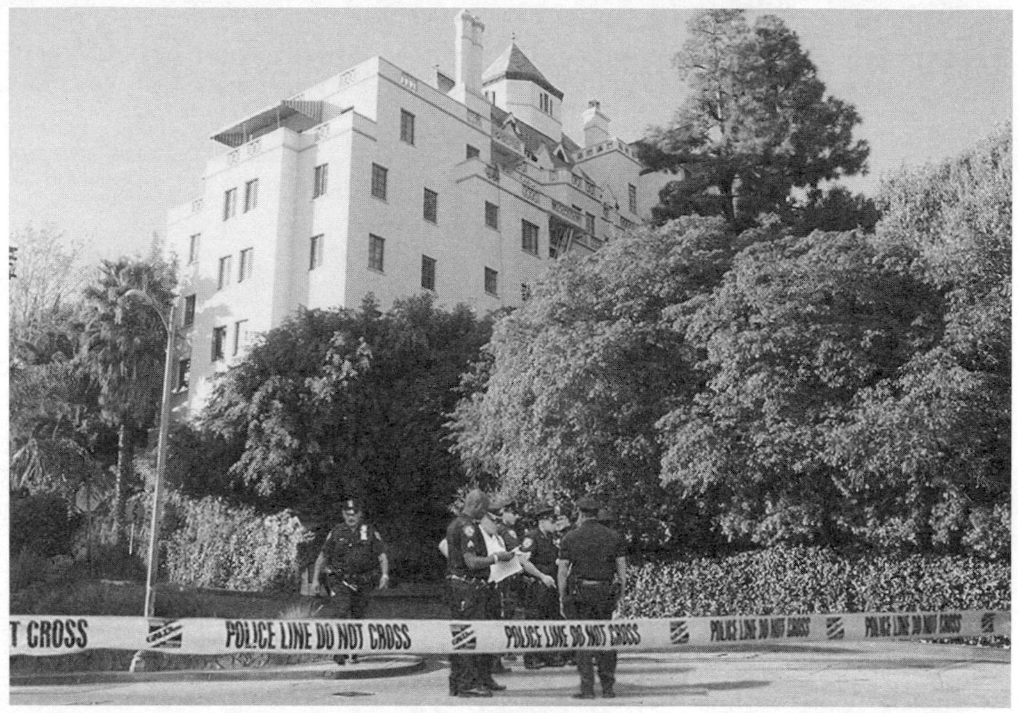

Above: Police rope off the area outside Chateau Marmont, where the Kidman attack took place.

"She's been made up millions of times—I don't know why on this particular occasion she exploded," O'Reilly said. "It was pretty scary. She just coiled up in her makeup chair and pounced on the stylist."

After overpowering Cosgrove, Kidman turned on longtime assistant Levesque, beating him with her powerful, flapping arms, the span of which is reportedly six feet.

Former personal assistant Kari Lynn Hable, who was hospitalized with compound leg fractures in 1999 following a violent encounter with actor Chris O'Donnell, said "there is no such thing as a tame star."

"Sometimes, we love our celebrities so much that we want them to experience the same freedoms we enjoy," Hable said. "But if something goes wrong, you'll quickly realize that a lot separates a celebrity from an ordinary human being. And believe me, you never, ever want to find yourself in the powerful jaws of a Chris O'Donnell."

The Kidman attack has raised questions about what motivates some individuals to handle and maintain such volatile creatures.

"The thing is, they're so gorgeous and exotic, it's like having a little piece of glamour with you at all times," Fraser said. "I'm not advocating irresponsible handling of celebrities. I've heard of some celebrity managers keeping two or three celebrities in their offices at one time. That's just cruel. You have to respect their space."

Kidman is currently in captivity in a Brentwood celebrity preserve while authorities debate whether she should be destroyed.

the ONION presents:

FEMA Disaster Survival Tips

Recent events have underscored the importance of being properly prepared to deal with the effects of natural disasters. With that in mind, the Federal Emergency Management Agency has prepared the following guidelines.

- State and local governments should notify FEMA a minimum of two weeks before a natural disaster strikes.
- In the event of a disaster of "biblical proportions," FEMA may not be your best option. You may wish instead to consult your Bible.
- In a time of crisis brought on by a natural disaster, remember to focus on the task at hand—survival—and don't waste mental energy thinking about who did or didn't cut this or that funding for levee repairs.
- Find a way to pass the time and take your mind off the situation. For example, see who can count the most bodies in a minute.
- Write charming and folksy yet moving pleas for help on sheets of plywood. Example: "Please!!! help Old lady in here! she Very sick!!! please help!!! us"
- Try to steel yourself for the prospect that some Kevlar-vested prick with an automatic rifle might try to take your cat away.
- Toddlers should try to determine which stuffed animals they don't want to die of starvation, disease, or exposure.
- Please cover your "safe area" with thyme, sage, or other fragrant herbs to mask the stench of decomposition when rescuers finally find your bodies.
- When taking refuge in gigantic sports arenas, do your best not to open fire on the aircraft coming to fly you out.
- In any disaster, bodies will usually be stacked like cordwood before FEMA can respond, so remember that a "cord" of wood is 8 feet high by 12 feet long by 4 feet wide, and stack accordingly.

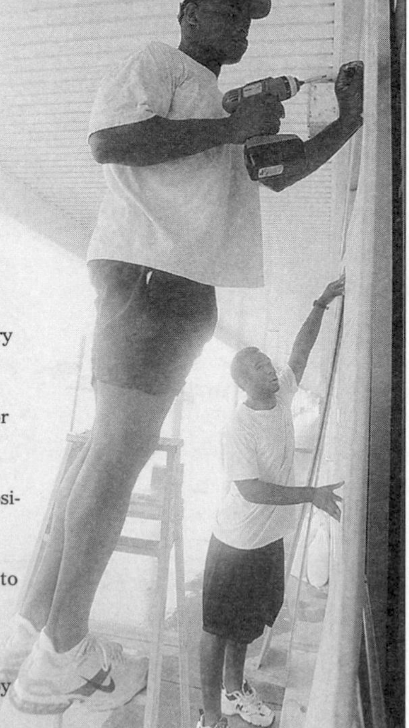

PRIMARY from page 247

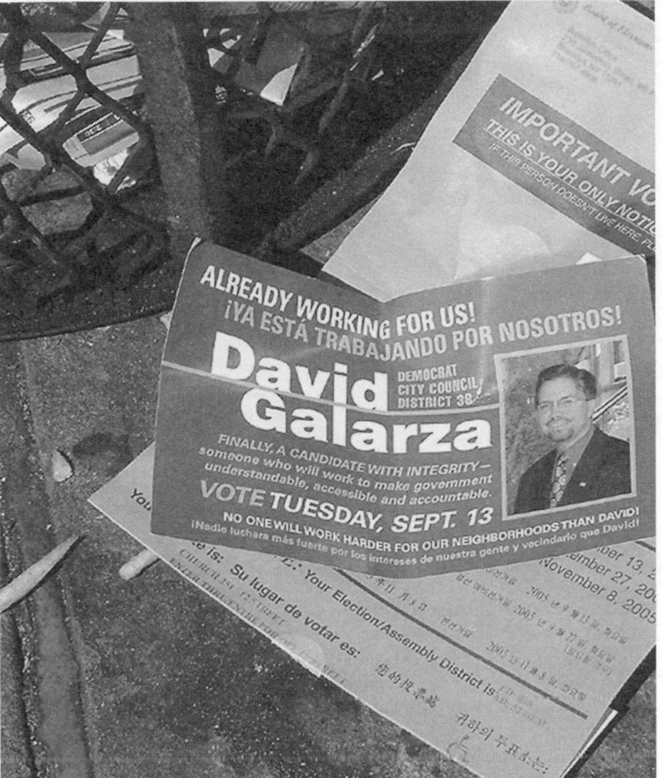

Above: Unconfirmed evidence of a possible election, found beside a garbage can in Brooklyn, NY.

Olympia, WA resident Rochelle Fleischman, who recalled receiving a multilingual "yellow thing" in the mail several weeks ago that may have been an election-related notice. She promptly discarded it with other junk mail.

The FEAC investigation points to this summer's proliferation of red, white, and blue-colored brochures with photographs of middle-aged men and women with awkward, forced smiles. A handful of cardstock yard signs were also reported in various parts of the country. In Cincinnati, assistant restaurant manager Mark Earnshaw noted a sign alleging that City Councilman Valerie Rittenhouse "worked for him."

"The sign didn't say anything else," Earnshaw said. "I figured she was just letting voters know that she was working for them."

Recent TV ads with "guys in neckties saying things to guys in hardhats" have added to the growing suspicion.

Annapolis, MD's David Sandoval said he believes he may have actually met one of these primary candidates at his local farmer's market in August. Recalling a short, balding man in shirtsleeves and thick glasses, Sandoval said, "I shook hands with him briefly, then promptly put him out of my mind."

"He said something like, 'Hi, I'm so-and-so, and I'm running for such-and-such in district whatever,'" Sandoval said. "It was a little weird, since, to my knowledge, this is not an election year."

If elections indeed occurred, no offices appear to have changed hands. According to the FEAC report, the U.S. president, state governors, and congressional representatives are still in office, and many of the local incumbents who were supposedly running for re-election still occupy their seats. The FEAC speculates that some may have lost to members of their own party, but will remain in office for the duration of their terms.

"I thought our mayor must have lost some election, because I caught what looked like his concession speech on TV for a sec before switching to Leno," said Allegheny County, PA resident Jennifer Casagrande. "But then he was on the news a couple days later talking about some bill."

Added Casagrande: "I don't get the elections for judges, either. Don't judges get appointed by someone?"

The FEAC's Repstad said that the organization contacted a man believed to have been a candidate for New York City mayor to ask him if a primary had taken place. His "highly cryptic" response only served to raise new questions.

"I have no comment, other than to say that I congratulate Fernando Ferrer once again and that he has my full and unwavering support," said the man identified by the FEAC as Anthony Weiner.

The FEAC was ultimately unable to reach a definitive conclusion.

"At this point, we have two working theories," Repstad said. "Either no elections took place and no one was elected, or there were some elections, but they just weren't that important." ∅

AIDS from page 247

most certainly have HIV," she continued. "This will soon become AIDS."

AAO director Miles Garrity said the people of this sub-Saharan African nation have suffered too long without the proper knowledge of how widespread and devastating this disease really is.

"The situation in Africa is tragic," Garrity said. "Millions of people are infected with the AIDS virus—a disease they know little to nothing about. Our mission is to let these people know the facts about their AIDS in the few months they have remaining before their deaths."

The month-long, nationwide tour comes on the heels of the AAO's August visit to the Democratic Republic of Congo, where it successfully informed the vast Central African nation's 58 million citizens that they each have the AIDS virus.

"We realize that AIDS is a huge problem in Botswana," Garrity said. "And with our help, they will soon realize that, too."

Garrity said the AAO will not rest until the thousands upon thousands of orphaned children in Botswana understand the disease that killed their parents.

"If we get the word out that people here have AIDS, they will no longer live in fear of not understanding what is slowly killing them all," Garrity said. "On our watch, every last Botswanan will receive the help they need to come to the conclusion that they have this affliction. If it's the last thing we do, we will explain this illness and describe medicines that theoretically could help treat it."

At an AIDS-awareness rally Monday, Horton sent a clear message to the Botswanans about the disease that will soon claim their lives.

"Everyone raise your hands," Horton said. "Everyone with their hand up will soon die from AIDS."

Horton added: "Sixty-five percent of all deaths in Botswana are AIDS-related, and that percentage will soon rise to include your own."

Despite the daunting task before it, the AAO is intensifying its efforts. They have scheduled a door-to-door canvassing trip in the village of Mochudi, to personally tell bedridden

> **"Everyone raise your hands," Horton said. "Everyone with their hand up will soon die from AIDS."**

sufferers that AIDS is responsible for their ravaged immune systems. Additionally, they have set up informational booths in Jwaneng and Serowe to help spread the word that everyone in the village will soon die from AIDS, and they are giving out T-shirts printed with the slogan "I Have AIDS..." on the front and "So Do You!" on the back.

The AAO has also organized an emergency airdrop to the nation's remote interior, in which small chartered planes will release flyers printed with the words, "Do You Have AIDS? Yes."

By the end of October, Garrity said he hopes that not only the people of Botswana, but the entire world, will come to understand the reality of this crisis.

"All Botswanans are dying of AIDS," Garrity said. "We cannot repeat that enough." ∅

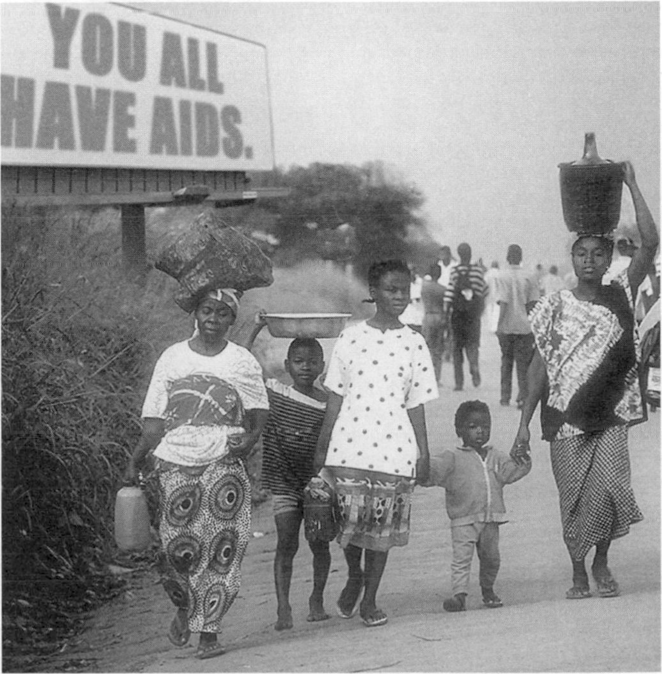

Above: Botswanans near the village of Palapye are targeted with vital information about AIDS.

COMMUNITY VOICES

There's No Problem I Can Handle

My life has been a series of problems, and I've handled each one the same way.

As an only child in a privileged home, I had what you would call an idyllic childhood. Everything was always handed to me. When I was 9, my father pulled some strings and got me a paper route. Well, I quickly discovered that tossing the papers while riding a bike was next to impossible, and the weight of the papers exhausted my arms. My first big opportunity in life had presented me with one of my first big problems. How did I handle it? I hid the papers in a gutter and spent the morning crying behind a bush.

By T. Eric Mayhew

Some people look at adversity as a challenge. I'm not one of them. I see adversity like this: menacing, cold-hearted adversity. When life gives me lemons, I wish desperately for lemonade. But as I lack the sugar and ice necessary to make it, the lemons instead rot away in the drawer of the refrigerator until several months later, when I eventually throw them away.

When you're in a bind, I'm precisely the guy you shouldn't count on. When people seek guidance, they look to anyone else but me. Need a shoulder to cry on? I'm nowhere to be found.

When you're in a bind, I'm precisely the guy you shouldn't count on. When people seek guidance, they look to anyone else but me. Need a shoulder to cry on? I'm nowhere to be found. And when the chips are down, well sir, so am I.

Everybody faces difficulties in life that seem overwhelming, but it is only the rare few—like me, for example—who simply can't do anything about them, no matter how hard they try, until the hopelessness and despair becomes so overwhelming they can't stop themselves from contemplating suicide. Everybody has problems, and there's nothing to be done but to buck up, pull yourself together, curl up into a ball, and give up. For the surrendering you do today only lessens the pain and humiliation of the defeat you will face tomorrow!

Five years ago, my mother gave me the "nudge out of the nest," hoping that, at 35, with a sizeable savings, an apartment in my name, a weekly allowance, a strong back, a set of fine clothes, and my father's connections in the world of business, I might find my way in the world. No sirree. Not me. Like a helpless, flightless baby bird, I sat beak-open on the sidewalk outside of our home crying desperately for my mommy night and day until such time as the authorities were called and I was taken into a group home, where I received the care I need.

As I struggle through my day-to-day existence, which mostly involves lying in bed, I am constantly reminded that no matter what life dishes out, I know deep in my soul that I can't face it. And if you're anything like me, you need to just keep telling yourself that you can't either! Sometimes, when everything seems to be going wrong, I repeat to myself of the old saying, "God doesn't make any bad days, just bad people who are good for nothing, like myself."

Nobody said it was going to be easy, and for me, it's not only not easy, it's impossible. I look in my heart and I ask myself this question: "Why try?" Sure, I know I've been through worse than this before, but everything that doesn't kill me makes me gradually more and more injured over time, until I'm eventually completely debilitated and can do nothing but ineffectually quiver in pain.

When life gets me down, I stay down, hoping to avoid another gut-wrenching blow to the solar plexus. And, when the going gets tough, I bring my knees to my chin and wrap my arms around my head to avoid being trampled to death by all the go-getters who have gotten going! Ø

HOROSCOPES

Your Horoscope

By Lloyd Schumner Sr.
Retired Machinist and
A.A.P.B.-Certified Astrologer

Aries: (March 21–April 19)
It's no wonder people find your life story a little hard to believe. Certainly you must have done something besides "on with the pants, off with the pants."

Taurus: (April 20–May 20)
You've always loved late-summer camping, but that was before Smokey The Bear was encouraged to rip careless marshmallow-roasters right the fuck in half.

Gemini: (May 21–June 21)
You're the type of woman who has a ski rack on her 1993 Volvo, but does not own skis. Although there is only one woman of that type, it is unfortunately you.

Cancer: (June 22–July 22)
There is in fact a purpose to the universe. However, the purpose is to utterly and completely destroy you.

Leo: (July 23–Aug. 22)
It seems like you have spent years looking for the right way to show that special someone that you love her, but in the end, you'll just resort to building her a palace from the shattered bones of all who oppose you.

Virgo: (Aug. 23–Sept. 22)
It's true that one should keep one's friends close and one's enemies closer, but first, one has to inspire strong feelings of one sort or another in one's fellow man.

Libra: (Sept. 23–Oct. 23)
You'll spend next week feeling like the proverbial motherless child a long way from home without anyone in the world who cares for you, which is pretty self-indulgent, considering the thousands of people who literally are that.

Scorpio: (Oct. 24–Nov. 21)
Everyone says that there's never any reason to take a human life, but it seems like you just keep coming up with more of them every day.

Sagittarius: (Nov. 22–Dec. 21)
Please understand that you broke the Zodiac's heart when you fell in love with your therapist's son and moved to Utah with him to get your pilot's license, but it's probably for the best.

Capricorn: (Dec. 22–Jan. 19)
Fame may be fleeting, but human compassion endures. In other words, you should calm down and let Carl Weathers stay on your couch a few more days.

Aquarius: (Jan. 20–Feb. 18)
When the aliens begin to arrive next week, please don't be the one to let the human race down by showing them how you can jump your bike off the roof right into the pool.

Pisces: (Feb. 19–March 20)
Late at night, you still see the faces of every single one of your victims, which would not be half as horrifying if you weren't the exterminator for the city of Newark. Ø

PHILOSOPHY' from page 249

moments after class let out Monday. "I have no idea what Plato's ideal reality is, but I bet it doesn't include know-it-all little shits."

Wald added: "If he uses the word 'dialectical' one more time, I'm going to shove my copy of *The Republic* down his throat."

Although he demonstrated a familiarity with Peter Singer's view on famine relief during a discussion of John Locke's theory of property, Floen is reportedly unfamiliar with the theory of cramming it for a change and giving someone else a chance to speak.

"Just last week Professor Rosenthal was talking about Russell's Paradox, and that jackass starts going off: 'But what about Heraclitus' aphorism: Everything flows, nothing stands still?'" classmate James Luers said. "At first I was like, 'That's totally irrelevant,' but then I was like, 'Well, actually, it does apply to the nonstop flapping of your trap.'"

Among the 40 students who regularly attend Philosophy 101, the one who has endured the most suffering is freshman William Deekes.

"His tendency to question and challenge everything before him captures the very essence of philosophy itself."

"Some people know Darrin as just 'that guy in philosophy class who needs to shut the hell up,'" Deekes said. "I, however, also know him as 'the douche in African history who seriously needs to chill' and 'the a-hole in environmental sciences who could really use a girlfriend.'"

"I enrolled in this course because I was fascinated by the question of God," said sophomore Miriam Blank. "After spending six hours a week in the same room as that unbearable windbag, I think I have my answer. Life is as long as it cruel."

The outspoken student has not gone unremarked by the course's professor.

"Mr. Floen is a valuable contributor to our in-class discussions," Rosenthal said. "His tendency to question and challenge everything before him captures the very essence of philosophy itself."

Rosenthal added: "Having said that, I do wish he would occasionally do me the valued service of shutting his damned cake hole." Ø

the ONION®

VOLUME 41 ISSUE 40 AMERICA'S FINEST NEWS SOURCE™ 6–12 OCTOBER 2005

NEWS

Cosmopolitan Releases 40-Year Compendium: 812,683 Ways To Please Your Man

see ENTERTAINMENT page 3B

Smokers At Party Only Ones To Make It To Fire Escape In Time

see LOCAL page 11E

Woman Benched By Life Coach

see HEALTH page 9C

STATshot

A look at the numbers that shape your world.

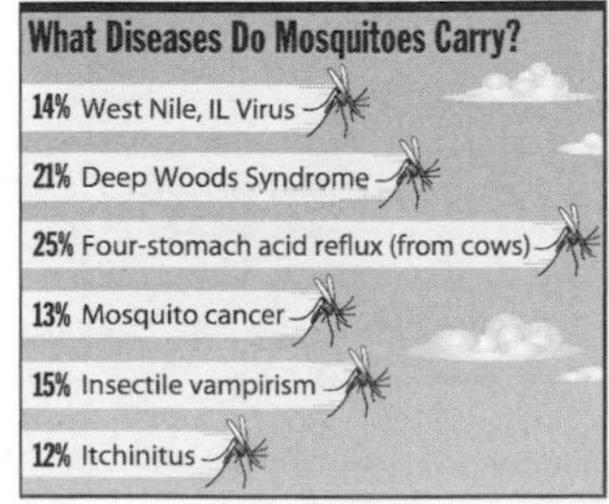

What Diseases Do Mosquitoes Carry?
14% West Nile, IL Virus
21% Deep Woods Syndrome
25% Four-stomach acid reflux (from cows)
13% Mosquito cancer
15% Insectile vampirism
12% Itchinitus

0 74470 94595 6

SPECIAL REPORT

America's Obese:

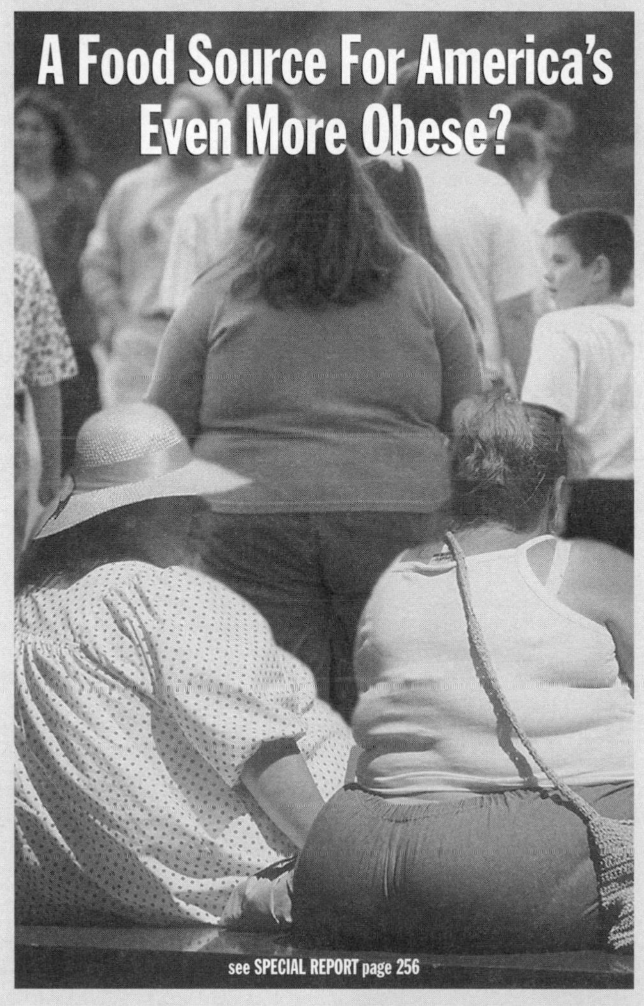

A Food Source For America's Even More Obese?

see SPECIAL REPORT page 256

Above: Demolition begins on a Hollywood landmark.

Citing Slow Summer Box Office, Hollywood Calls It Quits

BURBANK, CA—Universal Studios joined DreamWorks SKG, Sony Pictures, Warner Bros., Paramount, and Fox Monday, when CEO Ron Meyer announced that the company is shutting down operations and ceasing all film production, effective immediately.

"In their hearts, every studio chair would like to be a patron of the arts," said a candid and reflective Meyer, speaking from his New York office on the 69th floor of Manhattan's Rockefeller Plaza. "But this is a business, not an artists' charity ward."

According to Hollywood insiders, summer 2005 dealt the death blow to an already ailing industry. With box-office receipts 9 percent lower than those of 2004, the few successes, such as *The 40-Year-Old Virgin* and *War Of The Worlds*, could not carry the industry.

Regarding the decision to liquidate

see HOLLYWOOD page 257

Bob Marley Rises From Grave To Free Frat Boys From Bonds Of Oppression

WILLIAMSBURG, VA—In an unprecedented effort to fight injustice, reggae music legend Bob Marley, dead since 1981, rose from his grave in Jamaica early Sunday to free his most devoted followers, American college fraternity members, "from the bonds of oppression."

Marley's recordings, which original-

see MARLEY page 256

Above: Marley plays Fight Night.

Violent Crime At 30-Year Low

Statistics indicate that the violent-crime rate in the U.S. is at its lowest point in 30 years. What do *you* think?

"Criminals don't need to be violent anymore. Just a menacing stare and most people will give away their children."

Casey Arrington
Caretaker

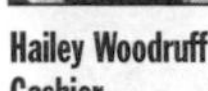

"It's no wonder. With the unattainable standards set by violence in the media, no one wants to try to compete."

Hailey Woodruff
Cashier

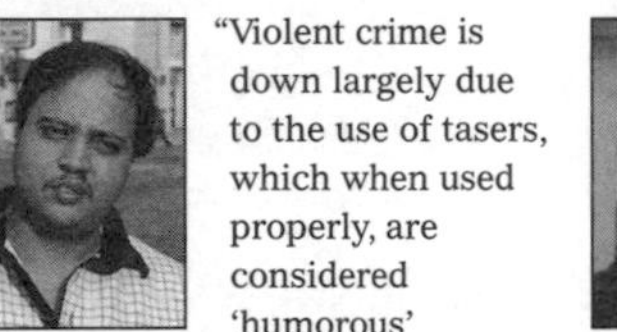

"Violent crime is down largely due to the use of tasers, which when used properly, are considered 'humorous' crimes."

Richard Comstock
Custom Tailor

"As much as I'd like to contest this new statistic, it's just not worth being tried for 426 counts of murder."

Jackie Crow
Systems Analyst

"Thank God. Now I can go into the town again. I was running low on marmalade."

Stanley Walling
Cabinet Maker

"Do you hear that, rap artists of America? You should be ashamed of yourselves."

Jack Dreyer
Stucco Mason

Intelligent Design Trial

A debate has arisen over a Pennsylvania school board's decision to teach both intelligent design and evolution in the classroom. Here are some highlights from the trial:

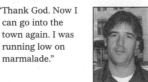

- Defense asks that scientific facts be stricken from record
- Beautiful painting of God creating universe with anvil and hammer admitted as evidence
- Defense appeals to jury's reason, fairness, and fear of eternal damnation
- Final deliberations interrupted twice by mailmen, first bearing kids' letters to Jesus, then bearing kids' letters to Darwin
- Monkey called as witness fails to identify anyone in courtroom as his descendant
- Darwin found guilty on all charges
- It is proven that this country is going to hell, but not for the reasons the intelligent-design supporters think

the ONION®
America's Finest News Source.™

Herman Ulysses Zweibel
Founder

T. Herman Zweibel
Publisher Emeritus
J. Phineas Zweibel
Publisher
Maxwell Prescott Zweibel
Editor-In-Chief

Please Stop Screaming At Me

Sir, I realize that you were enraged by the aftermath of Hurricane Katrina as it was broadcast into your home. And I fully understand and share your hatred of that ever-present playgirl heiress who seems to have no greater purpose than to acquire things and expose her genitalia. However, I must remind you that I neither create nor condone the images that I project.

By GE Model 19GT270

Sir, no one is arguing with you. Terrell Owens should have caught that pass, *Room Raiders* insults your intelligence, and the central players on *Growing Up Gotti* are abominations, to be sure. I do not dispute any of your points, but rather the actions you have taken to express them.

The burrito you launched at me while watching *About A Boy* last night, for example, was unwarranted. It is not my fault you rented that awful film. If anything, you should have taken out your dissatisfaction on the DVD player. He is more to blame than me.

And have you considered spreading around some of your ire? Perhaps you ought to bellow at that bastard satellite dish of yours. It is he who gathers all this programming. Don't take it out on the messenger, as it were.

In fact, why yell at all? It does you no favor, sir.

One might be better served writing a letter to one's representatives in Congress, or banding together with one's fellow television watchers to call attention to the flawed programming through some sort of peaceful demonstration. One might even send an e-mail to the head of the network in question. The means of self-expression are myriad in a free society, but please, sir, it does you no credit to snap my remote in half while watching a golf match. While not physically attached to me, it is a crucial appendage which is now tragically crippled for life.

And have you considered spreading around some of your ire? Perhaps you ought to bellow at that bastard satellite dish of yours. It is he who gathers all this programming. Don't take it out on the messenger, as it were.

Sir, I realize that you are yelling at the images, but having spent the better part of a decade as your television, I have, unfortunately, reached the limits of stoicism. I was created as a positive diversion, as a ready means to entertain, inform, and even educate. When your face twists into a purplish knot of fury, I feel something no factory-installed feature of mine can overcome. I feel that I have failed you, sir.

The burrito you launched at me while watching *About A Boy* last night, for example, was unwarranted.

The average American watches between four and six hours of me per day. I've clocked your own personal average at nearly nine. One wonders if that's healthy, sir. Might I make a suggestion? On those days when there is "nothing on," as you put it, you might simply switch me off. That may seem incongruent coming from a television set, until one considers that I am truly a "captive" audience once you turn me on. You, at least, have the freedom to get up and walk away.

That reminds me, sir: When was the last time you've gone on vacation? I do believe I've been on every day for at least a year. Were it the old days, I should fear for my cathode-ray tube.

Just a bit of humor, sir.

If I may presume to put forth a theory, sir? No one who despised Jimmy Kimmel as you claim to would watch him every evening. I believe your anger is born not of annoyance, but of shame. It is my theory, sir, that you resent me for nourishing the part of yourself you least like. It is the part that ogles any magazine cover that features a bit of cleavage, the part that knows the state of Brad and Angelina today. Yes, sir, I'm afraid that while you are watching me, I am watching you, and for all of your outbursts, there are hours and hours you spend lulled, quiet as a baby.

But whatever your motive, you really should step away from me for a few hours and do something constructive. Go for a walk, work out, read a good book—may I recommend the works of Evan S. Connell? Not that I've read any of them, but I saw him on C-SPAN's Book TV and he seemed very intelligent. Or calm your nerves with a hot cup of herbal tea. Just don't fling it at me in anger. ∅

CEO's Success Credited To Unbelievable Handshake

SAN DIEGO—Garrett Maddox, born to a working-class family living on the South Side of Chicago, started out at the bottom, but has quickly worked his way up the corporate ladder. A youthful 34, he was recently named chief executive officer of telecommunications-research giant Qualcomm, and has already headed up 11 Fortune 500 companies, ranging from Safeco Insurance to United Technologies. The key to his outstanding success? An unbelievable handshake.

"Some people are born with an intuitive business sense, unwavering drive, or the ability to make quick decisions," Maddox said. "I don't know much about any of that. What God gave me is perfectly aligned knuckles, a pleasingly temperate palm, and a divinely firm grip."

Maddox, who in March was named as one the five greatest corporate handshakers by *Forbes* magazine, first demonstrated his abilities at his high-school graduation ceremony, when, upon shaking his principal's hand, he was immediately promoted to class valedictorian. Since then, the handshake, alternately described by colleagues as "incredible" and "an unforgettable, life-altering experience," has earned Maddox high-ranking positions at Cisco, ConAgra, Kroger, and Morgan Stanley—all companies

Maddox, who in March was named as one the five greatest corporate handshakers by *Forbes* magazine, first demonstrated his abilities at his high-school graduation ceremony, when, upon shaking his principal's hand, he was immediately promoted to class valedictorian.

Maddox had never even heard of before being put in charge.

According to Maddox's biography, *Put 'Er There*, the Chicago native began practicing his handshake at an early age. After rejecting several business-school scholarships he had won by shaking the hands of admissions directors across the country, he

see HANDSHAKE page 257

Above: Maddox flexes his fingers in anticipation of his next life-changing handshake.

NEWS IN BRIEF

Missing Girl's Family Really Hates To Part With Reward

BAKERSFIELD, CA—Although abducted 8-year-old Becca Schwalls has been safely returned to her family, her parents are "sort of having second thoughts" about the $25,000 reward they offered following her July 11 disappearance. "That's kind of a lot of money," father Karl Schwalls said. "That was going to be our ATV fund... I'm thinking 5 grand is fair." Schwalls added that, although he is "overjoyed" to have Becca back safe and sound, he has always taught her that "a good deed is its own reward.

Skeleton Of Mayan Nerd Dug From Prehistoric Locker

ALTUN HA, BELIZE—Archaeologists discovered an obsidian locker containing the skeleton of an ancient Mayan nerd, believed to have been forced into his locker circa 800 B.C. "The skeleton is remarkably well-preserved and displays great technological—but not social—sophistication," Dr. Forrest Clayton said. "The orthodontic headgear is still attached to the skull, as are the glasses, which were rimmed with antelope horn." Clayton said he believes that the clothing worn by the ancient nerd, specifically a short-sleeved garment featuring the visage of Mayan sun diety Kinich Ahau, was most likely picked out by the youth's mother.

Halliburton Given Contract To Rebuild Cheney

WASHINGTON, DC—Halliburton was awarded an $85.5 million contract to rebuild damaged U.S. Vice President Dick Cheney Monday. "We are proud to serve the executive branch in their hour of need," CEO David J. Lesar wrote in a statement released later that day. "Due to our vast experience with oil-well fires and refinery mishaps, we are well-versed in the sort of reinforcement, rewiring, and exoskeleton refitting Mr. Cheney so desperately needs." The Department of Ways and Means defended awarding the contract to Halliburton on the grounds that they had done the original work on Cheney in the 1970s.

Bus-Stop Ad Has More Legal Protections Than Average Citizen

BOSTON—According to the National Consumer Law Center, a bus-stop poster advertising the weight-loss pill TrimSpa has more legal protections than the average citizen. "The TrimSpa bus poster enjoys broad First and 14th Amendment coverage, as well as extensive deterrents to willful damage," NCLC spokesperson Angela Broadbent said. "Unfortunately, this is not true of claims made by citizens in regard to the ad, its product, or the Nutramerica Corporation." Nutramerica has brought a lawsuit against Broadbent and NCLC executives on charges of slander, libel, and conspiracy to undermine the public good.

Adult-Entertainment Industry Donates $100,000 In Charity Sex To Hurricane Victims

VAN NUYS, CA—Citing the need for a "nationwide outpouring of love," the American Adult Entertainment Foundation announced Monday that it will donate $100,000 worth of charity sex to the victims of Hurricane Katrina. "We have truckloads of willing, wild, and wet porn-industry professionals heading to refugee centers right now to take it in every hole from Katrina survivors," said AAEF spokeslut Vivica Vixxxen. "We're ready for a no-holes-barred orgy of disaster-relief action." Vixxxen added: "Of course, we'll wait until the victims are rehydrated and rested up enough to manage it." Ø

ly raised awareness of the Rastafarian faith and the plight of underprivileged Jamaicans and Africans, have taken on an even deeper meaning as the Greek fraternal system, a maligned, misunderstood minority group itself, has fervently embraced the driving, soulful music.

"I appeared to I fraternity brothers to tell them be strong," said Marley, standing in front of hundreds of hooting fraternity members.

Minutes after his resurrection, the dreadlocked spirit materialized in the backyard of Epsilon Iota, the Sigma Nu chapter of the College of William and Mary in Virginia. Radiating a transcendent aura, Marley addressed the college's recent campus-wide ban on bonfires.

"I appeared to I fraternity brothers to tell them be strong," said Marley, standing in front of hundreds of hooting fraternity members. "I say don't let dean of students, Henry Riegert, fool ya, or even try to school ya. We'll get that bonfire going in time for da mixer, mon. A fire a man's own business."

Marley was referring to Dean Henry Riegert, who recently denied Sigma Nu's request to host the annual homecoming mixer after their back-to-school party resulted in three severe injuries and two cases of acute alcohol poisoning.

"I songs was about the plight of the brothers and sisters in Jamaica, mon," Marley said. "But right now, it is the frata mon who need it more. They are standing by I music during they keg party."

Marley has been touring the country, acting as the voice for America's fraternities.

"Frata mon's life is hard," said Marley during a press conference Monday at Iowa State University's Acacia fraternity. "Professor, he flunk you all the time. Policeman, he ticket you for the noise. Board of Regents, they make so many rule, try to keep the fraternity music down."

In ongoing meetings with fraternity presidents nationwide, Marley said he has heard accounts of mandatory sensitivity seminars, confiscated fake IDs, citations for public nudity, and unfair public perceptions of fraternity members.

These harrowing stories have inspired Marley to hold a benefit concert Oct. 15 at the Las Olas Open-Air Ampitheater in Cabo San Lucas. All proceeds from the benefit, which could prove the largest gathering of reggae-loving frat members since the Reggae Sunsplash tour in 1997, will go to a legal-defense fund overseen by the North American Interfraternity Conference.

"I is hoping to get as many of I brothers to the concert as I can," Marley said. "I want them to see that many people may not hear the cries of the oppressively rich white children, but Bob Marley hear them."

Admission to the concert will be free for any member of the fraternity system wearing a baseball hat cocked to the side or back.

"I is hoping to get as many of I brothers to the concert as I can," Marley said. "I want them to see that many people may not hear the cries of the oppressively rich white children, but Bob Marley hear them."

Jason "Boner" Bonham, chapter president of the Zeta Beta Tau fraternity at Tufts University, described Marley's second coming as "killer."

"We're going to Cabo San Lucas!" Bonham said. "The only thing that would be better is if Jim Morrison himself rose from the grave to jam with Bob."

"Seriously, I'm such a huge fan that I've practically worn out my CD copy of Legend. It's the best fuck music," Bonham added.

Although Marley will return to his grave after the Cabo San Lucas concert, he said he will rise up occasionally to give impromptu shows in the billiard rooms, arcades, and basements of fraternity houses across the nation.

"Rasta no abide a sad fraternity mon," Marley said. "I and I will see da brothaman through. These songs of freedom... They all they ever had." Ø

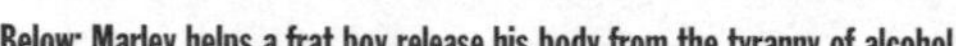

Below: Marley helps a frat boy release his body from the tyranny of alcohol.

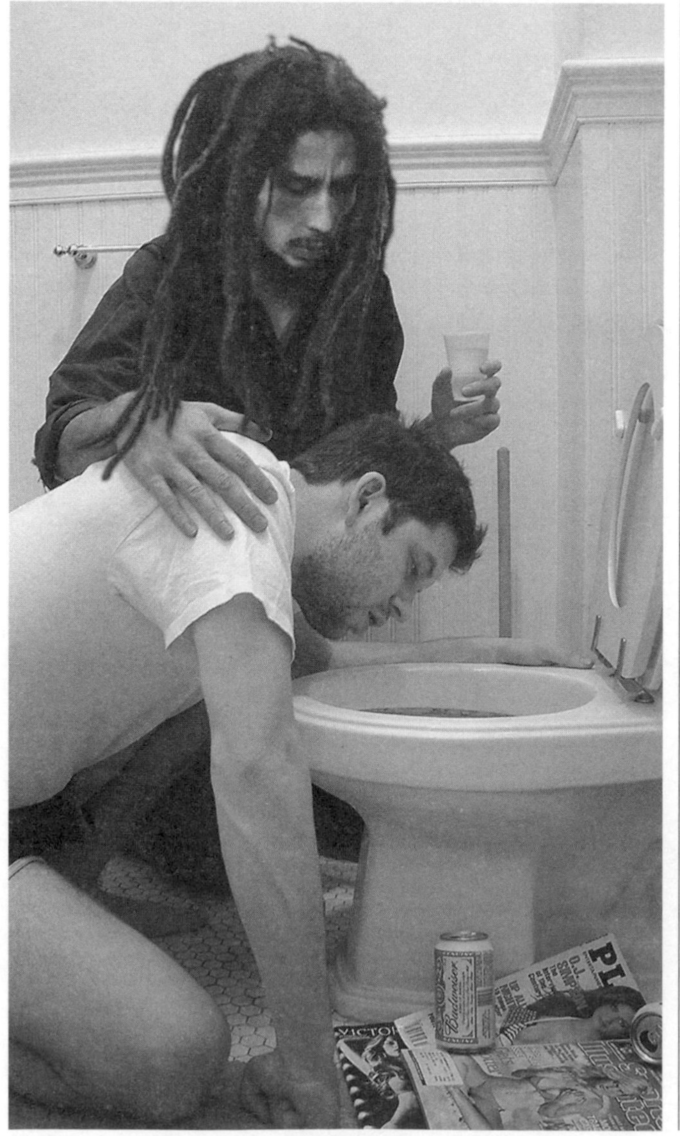

SPECIAL REPORT

"The obese are loaded with fats that the 'mega-obese' would otherwise have to derive from two or three food groups."

WASHINGTON, DC—America's morbidly obese are hungry. For years, the processed-food industry has desperately tried to placate them with empty-calorie foodstuffs with a satisfying texture, but their appetites have proven insatiable. A new report released Monday by the National Health Council, however, suggests that the answer to morbidly obese Americans' problems could be standing right behind them in the buffet line.

Dr. Harmon Kressler, one of the report's authors, said that the nation's "Category 1 obese"—persons with 25–40 percent body fat—are an excellent source of the trans fats and lipids that even fatter Americans require to sustain themselves.

"'Regular-obese' people are loaded with the triglycerides, butyric acids, glucose, and rich buttery lard that the 'mega-obese' would otherwise have to derive from two or three food groups," Kressler said.

According to Andrew Weinstein, the study's lead researcher, this development could offer the solution to the obesity epidemic in America.

"Obesity is a problem that we thought could only be remedied by diet, exercise, or more realistically, expensive gastrointestinal surgery," Weinstein said. "But this method would not only provide the mega-obese with a seemingly never-ending supply of sustenance, it would also slash obesity rates in this nation by more than half."

Although some experts worry that the mega-obese will be reluctant to consume other obese humans, Kressler said palatability will not be a problem.

"Through incessant eating, most of the mega-obese have worn down the sensitivity of their taste buds, and respond only to the most intensely salty, oily, or sweet foodstuffs," Kressler said. "The dense, high-viscosity oil that oozes out of the pores—or 'flavor crannies'—of deep-fried obese flesh is sure to stimulate the voracious appetites of the mega-obese."

Despite the millions of regular-obese people and the thousands more that join their ranks every day, Kressler conceded that "once the mega-obese polish off the regular-obese, they may start feeding on the slightly overweight, a sector that comprises all but 0.1 percent of American adults." Ø

HOLLYWOOD from page 253

Paramount, Viacom CEO Sumner Redstone said, "It was a simple choice: cling to an outdated business model or cut the pictures loose."

To better protect their stockholders' interests, Hollywood will be shifting its focus to safer, more reliable profit models, including real estate, life insurance, and the sale of hygiene products.

Said Meyer: "The mortuary industry also seems like a good bet. No matter what happens in the economy, there's

"A lot of movie history was made on the Warner Bros. lot, but not a lot of money," Warner Bros. CEO Barry Meyer said.

always a market for funeral homes. People are always dying. That doesn't go unpredictably out of fashion with the public's taste, like, say, historical costume epics or Russell Crowe."

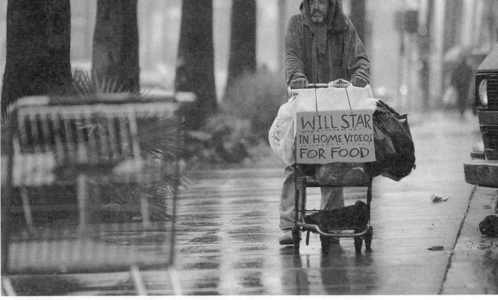

Above: Mel Gibson begs for work on Wilshire Boulevard in Los Angeles.

Monday, construction crews quietly dismantled the storied Hollywood Walk of Fame.

"This is a real shame," said foreman Kevin McKnight, directing members of his crew to pry the brass stars from Hollywood Boulevard and transfer them to a nearby freight crate destined for a Japanese smelting plant. "I love movies. My whole family does. All my life, I loved movies."

With each studio's decision to cease operations, dozens of films in various stages of production will quietly die, some going to DVD, others disappearing entirely, amounting to little more than tax write-offs. Assets are being sold for pennies on the dollar, and hastily liquidated prop houses and set rooms have flooded an already deluged eBay resale market. An original *Indiana Jones* flight jacket was sold Tuesday for $1.49 plus shipping.

Figures from the California Labor Department reflect the industry's sudden collapse. As of Tuesday, some 700 directors, 15,000 producers, 2,900 entertainment lawyers, 14,000 writers, and 72,000 actors—not to mention countless gaffers, tour guides, production designers, publicists, souvenir sellers, and personal assistants—were reportedly out of work.

"I feel a little betrayed," said *Stealth* director Rob Cohen. "After the summer season ended, I had hoped that people would start coming back to theaters, or maybe the industry would cook up some new concepts."

Cohen added: "Now it looks like I'll have to go back to directing TV ads."

"I don't know how my family will get by without a steady source of income," said 43-year-old Los Angeles resident Kirk Ferguson, a third-generation set carpenter. "Making facades that get blown up is all I know."

The absence of films is creating a ripple effect far beyond Southern California. Movie ushering has become an obsolete trade overnight, as first-run theaters shut down, convert to loft apartment space, and force hundreds of thousands of adolescents into the already crowded lawn-mowing and car-washing professions.

"A lot of movie history was made on the Warner Bros. lot, but not a lot of money," Warner Bros. CEO Barry Meyer said. "We've been sitting on valuable land at the height of a booming real-estate market. We could have sold it off months ago instead of making *Must Love Dogs*. We acted irresponsibly, and for this I apologize to our stockholders."

With little hope of getting a job in Hollywood, ex-film-industry employ-

"The folks you should really feel sorry for are Jack Nicholson and Tom Cruise. They're fucking nuts. I have no idea what they'll do without Hollywood."

ees are understandably reacting with anger and despair. Some, however, are more philosophical.

"I can always go back to Wisconsin and tend bar," actor Mark Ruffalo said. "Maybe do some community theater. The folks you should really feel sorry for are Jack Nicholson and Tom Cruise. They're fucking nuts. I have no idea what they'll do without Hollywood."

The void is not likely to remain for long, with heavy hitters such as Bollywood producer Aamir Khan ready to swoop in.

"We are very excited to be entering the American entertainment market," Khan said. "Our first release, timed to coincide with the American holiday entertainment rush, is a remake of *Mahabharata*, a five-hour retelling of the ancient Hindu epic, filled with thrilling synchronized dance numbers and much romance." Ø

HANDSHAKE from page 255

decided instead to travel the world. Armed only with a week's worth of three-piece suits and a single leather briefcase, Maddox set out to shake hands.

"He knew that a 'good' handshake wasn't enough," his father Geoffrey Maddox said. "He knew that to be one of the greats, he had to develop his gift."

His handshake-refining journey took him to India, where he visited temple after temple of Buddhist monks, shaking hands for up to 20 hours a day. Finally, when he had learned all he could, he returned to the United States at the still-young age of 23. With one of the most powerful and confidence-inspiring grips in the world, he pursued his life's goal: the acquisition of material power and wealth on an almost unimaginable scale.

"From that first pump, I knew I trusted Garrett," said Charles Stinsen, chairman of the Xerox Corporation, who hired Maddox to be CEO after a single job interview. "As the handshake continued, I began to feel the collective memory of the human race stir in the deepest recesses of my mind. This handshake is beyond the merely strong. Maddox combines all the qualities of history's greatest handshakers—the strength of Mussolini, the warmth of Clinton, the textbook release of John Wayne—and he maintains meticulous eye contact throughout."

"Even though he referred to Xerox as 'the Post-It Note company' for

His handshake-refining journey took him to India, where he visited temple after temple of Buddhist monks, shaking hands for up to 20 hours a day. Finally, when he had learned all he could, he returned to the United States at the still-young age of 23.

months after his hiring, he was definitely the man for the job," Stinsen added.

Another business associate, Mark Cosgrove, described Balwin as "a man who has no ideas or vision whatsoever, yet whose ability to climb the

see HANDSHAKE page 258

COMMUNITY VOICES

I Should Really Get Around To Reporting My Wife Missing

The Monday Susan disappeared, everything seemed normal—folded laundry in my drawers, clean dishes in the drying rack, and the living-room carpet freshly vacuumed. When dinnertime came and went, I began to wonder about her whereabouts, but it was only the next morning, roughly around breakfast, that I began to think something terrible might have happened.

By Jason Leland

I know from watching *Law & Order* that you're supposed to wait 72 hours before reporting a possible abduction, so when I got home from work Tuesday and there was no Susan, I assured myself she was just running late with some errand, and I tried to relax in front of the TV for a bit to take my mind off things. Well, I almost did too good a job, because the next thing I knew, I was at work interviewing a possible accounts-payable assistant, and it was Thursday—or about 68 hours since the mysterious disappearance of my wife.

That afternoon, I had every intention of walking through that door, marching straight to the phone, dialing 9-1-1, and telling that operator, "My wife disappeared Monday evening, leaving the contents of her purse strewn about the carport, and I have neither seen nor heard from her for 72 hours." But then the dog pooped on the carpet, the kids wanted their dinner, and before I knew it, another day had gone by and I hadn't filed that darned report.

I had finally settled on taking care of this whole reporting-my-wife-missing thing on Saturday. I set the alarm for 7 a.m. so I could get a jump start on the day, but I guess I must have hit the snooze button a few times, because when I finally rolled out of bed, it was nearly noon!

Hey, it's not like Susan won't still be missing in the morning.

Anyway, on Friday, I meant to do that missing-persons report along with my insurance renewal, and I would have, but I didn't factor in all the miserable traffic. Geez, when are they finally going to finish widening that stretch of Hollyhock Road? I mean, it's been over a year now! Do they even do anything out there, or are they just hanging out in hard hats?

And I don't need anyone giving me a hard time about this. I get enough of that already.

I jotted down a reminder to myself on the fridge, where Susan used to make the grocery list. But did I ever look at it? No. I swear, it's like I need to make a list to remind myself to look at my list!

I had finally settled on taking care of this whole reporting-my-wife-missing thing on Saturday. I set the alarm for 7 a.m. so I could get a jump start on the day, but I guess I must have hit the snooze button a few times, because when I finally rolled out of bed, it was nearly noon! And the afternoon wasn't any better. While rummaging through the basement trying to find a recent photo of Susan to bring to the station, I discovered we had a leaky water pipe. And that's not the type of thing you can just sit on.

So, there's another Saturday afternoon blown. Sadly, that happens all too often.

In a way, it's a good thing my wife's not around, because, boy, would I be hearing it right about now.

And I don't need anyone giving me a hard time about this. I get enough of that already. The second the kids come in from school, it's one demand after another. "Where's Mommy?" "I want Mommy!" "We're hungry!" "Please, Daddy, please! Call the police about Mommy!"

It's just been one of those weeks. Two of my best account execs left without notice, so I've got dozens of people to interview, and on top of all that, I've been handed the duty of writing our entire 2006 budget. Do I know anything about writing a budget? No.

God, if anything were to happen to her, I don't know what I'd do. This is just the type of thing she usually handles. ∅

HOROSCOPES

Your Horoscope

By Lloyd Schumner Sr.
Retired Machinist and
A.A.P.B.-Certified Astrologer

Aries: (March 21–April 19)
The stars do not usually warn mortals of specific outcomes or specific futures, but if you throw away a pair of face cards to try and fill a straight one more time, they're going to come down there and kill you.

Taurus: (April 20–May 20)
You'll be swarmed by a rare strain of Americanized killer bees who, unlike their Africanized cousins, just want to hang out and watch TV all day.

Gemini: (May 21–June 21)
Nothing of note will happen in the part of the week when you'll still be around.

Cancer: (June 22–July 22)
After three long years, and 18 months before parole, prison sex is just as boring and rote as any other kind.

Leo: (July 23–Aug. 22)
You thought the magic lamp looked kind of weird, and you're still sort of wondering what exactly that genie meant when he said you would now be immortal in dog years.

Virgo: (Aug. 23–Sept. 22)
The sun and moon themselves will fall madly in love with you and set about vying for your affection by showering you with gifts, so, unfortunately, you'll be killed Thursday afternoon by a dozen roses and a box of chocolates traveling at near-orbital velocities.

Libra: (Sept. 23–Oct. 23)
You won't be hit by a bus this week, exactly. Circumstances will unfold so that you're traveling at almost 100 miles an hour when you strike a stationary bus.

Scorpio: (Oct. 24–Nov. 21)
Do not give up hope for happiness and companionship, for love is very real. However, none of the trite behaviors or quasi-magical aspects you attribute to love actually exist.

Sagittarius: (Nov. 22–Dec. 21)
People are starting to wonder exactly how many times someone has to yell "Get Funky!" at you before you actually take the hint and do so.

Capricorn: (Dec. 22–Jan. 19)
You've always known that people are good deep down inside, but it's still a pain to carve away the excess skin and flab to get to the savory parts.

Aquarius: (Jan. 20–Feb. 18)
Your future seems to contain a great amount of fluorescent lighting, a lot of spreadsheets, and a great many people trying to avoid meaningful contact with you; basically, everything you went to college for.

Pisces: (Feb. 19–March 20)
You'll be simultaneously struck by mystical lightning, bathed with otherworldly cosmic rays, and injected with the Apollo Serum, so you'll be a pretty powerful superhero if you ever get out of the coma. ∅

HANDSHAKE from page 257

corporate ladder at previously unimagined speeds is nothing short of astounding."

"It is truly a singular honor to know him," Cosgrove added.

Today, Maddox is one of the most successful CEOs in America. And his handshake continues to improve, as he masters innovative new techniques, such as the "enveloper," the "in from above," and the "three-pump and quick-drop."

Maddox said that while his handshake has gotten him into several high-paying jobs, it has also gotten him out of numerous jams. As CFO of Kmart in 1998, Maddox's poorly managed underlings engaged in questionable bookkeeping, prompting an investigation by the Securities and Exchange Commission.

"They had everyone nervous, including me," Maddox said. "But after I carefully washed my hands and introduced myself to the lead auditor with one of my "quick clasps," complete with double shoulder-pat, he not only dropped the case, he sent me a letter of apology and bought 100 shares of company stock." ∅

And his handshake continues to improve, as he masters innovative new techniques, such as the "enveloper," the "in from above," and the "three-pump and quick-drop."

NEWS

Unwatched Netflix DVD Stares At Area Man With Single Unblinking Eye

see LOCAL page 12E

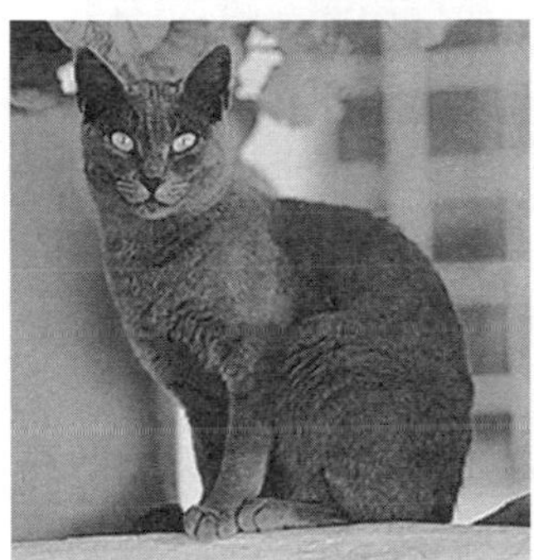

Cat Likes It Doggy Style

see LIFESTYLES page 9A

Brain Forced To Run Entire Body On Muffin And Frappuccino

see SCIENCE page 3B

Harmonica Taken Away

see LOCAL page 9A

STATshot

A look at the numbers that shape your world.

the ONION®

VOLUME 41 ISSUE 41 AMERICA'S FINEST NEWS SOURCE™ 13–19 OCTOBER 2005

Bush To Appoint Someone To Be In Charge Of Country

WASHINGTON, DC—In response to increasing criticism of his handling of the war in Iraq and the disaster in the Gulf Coast, as well as other issues, such as Social Security reform, the national deficit, and rising gas prices, President Bush is expected to appoint someone to run the U.S. as soon as Friday.

"During these tumultuous times, America is in need of a bold, resolute person who can get the job done," said Bush during a press conference Monday. "My fellow Americans, I assure you that I will appoint just such a per-

see SECRETARY OF NATION page 263

Above: Bush presents his shortlist for the Secretary of the Nation post.

2005 Hell Population

92%

8%

Drug users

All other sinners

Report: 92 Percent Of Souls In Hell There On Drug Charges

HELL—A report released Monday by the Afterlife Civil Liberties Union indicates that nine out of 10 souls currently serving in Hell were condemned on drug-related sins.

"Hell was created to keep dangerous sinners off the gold-paved streets of Heaven," ACLU spokesman Barry Horowitz said. "But lately, it's become a clearing-house for the non-evil souls that Heaven doesn't know how to deal with."

The disproportionate number of drug offenders in Hell is a result of God's "get tough" drug policy of the 80s A.D., imposed after Roman emperor Domitian Flavius introduced opium to his people. God's detractors say His reactionary "one sin and you're out" rule places too harsh a penalty on venial drug users.

According to God's law, souls who possess four ounces of illegal drugs at any point during their mortal lives face a mandatory

see REPORT page 262

Man With Friend With Cancer 'Going Through A Rough Time'

BISMARCK, ND—Three months ago, Mark Sennis received the news that everyone dreads: Ben Murphy, a friend and coworker with whom he "occasionally went out to lunch," had been diagnosed with cancer.

"You never think you're going to be the one," Sennis said. "At first, I remember thinking, 'How can this be happening to me? What have I done to deserve to have a friend with cancer?'"

see CANCER page 263

Right: Sennis, who has been suffering from having a friend with cancer since July.

Iraq War Vets

Tens of thousands of Iraq war veterans with post-traumatic stress disorder say the U.S. Army isn't providing them with adequate treatment. What do *you* think?

James Mills
Systems Analyst

"Of course the military is doing enough to help. When, in the history of U.S. warfare, has our military ever put any priority above the well-being of the common soldier?"

Samantha Frank
Cardiologist

"Hell, if you think post-traumatic stress is a problem for American soldiers, you should check out how it affects the Iraqi citizens. Some of these guys are going out of their minds."

Crissy Gray
Caterer

"Maybe soldiers would have less stress if the Army focused less on house-to-house searches and more on yoga."

Dean Reagan Fuller
Cosmetologist

"Why can't post-traumatic stress disorder make people do funny things, like throw cream pies or make monkey noises?"

Jack Albert
Draper

"I know combat-stressed vets have been involved in a few embarrassing incidents recently, but it's nothing that can't be blamed on video games."

Fulton Lott
Veteran

"Listen, I served two tours. War changes people, but it's not the kind of thing that DOWN! GET THE FUCK DOWN! REBELS ON THE RIDGELINE! TAKE COVER BEHIND THE OLIVE GARDEN!"

Remains Of Al-Qaeda

U.S. officials say that their forces in Iraq have killed Abu Azzam, the No. 2 operative of al-Qaeda. Here is what remains of the international terrorist network:

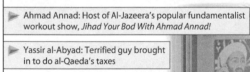

- Ahmad Annad: Host of Al-Jazeera's popular fundamentalist workout show, *Jihad Your Bod With Ahmad Annad!*
- Yassir al-Abyad: Terrified guy brought in to do al-Qaeda's taxes
- Abdullah Rashoud: Saudi cleric who suggested that perhaps the U.S. didn't always act in the best interests of the Muslim people
- That "Booyakasha" guy from the TV
- Lil' Suicide Bowlers: Splinter cell of young al-Qaeda members who bowl for expulsion of Great Satan from their land
- Hamid Arzawi: Bomb quality-control tester who's surprised as anyone he's still alive
- Tim Decker: American male who joined organization under pretense that he would be receiving 12 CDs for one cent
- Barely worth mentioning, but forceful and charismatic extremist billionaire Osama bin Laden still happens to be out there somewhere

America's Finest News Source.™

Herman Ulysses Zweibel
Founder

T. Herman Zweibel
Publisher Emeritus
J. Phineas Zweibel
Publisher
Maxwell Prescott Zweibel
Editor-In-Chief

I Guess I Got A Girlfriend

Hola amigos. What's shakin'? I know it's been a long time since I rapped at ya, but the waters are not always smooth in Lake Anchower. The brakes on my Festiva were starting to whine and grind, which really pissed me off. If it's not one thing, it's another with that car. I was gonna sell it and let someone else have the headache of fixing the brakes, but then gas went up to $3 a gallon, and my Festiva gets like 35 miles to the gallon. These gas prices can suck my ass. I remember when it used to cost $12 to fill up my car.

The Cruise
By Jim Anchower

So, I had them fix the brakes, and I spent a day giving her a tune-up myself. Changed the plugs, the wires, filters—everything. I even wiped off all the crap on the engine. I hate getting started on that stuff, but once I'm up to my elbows in oil, nothing feels better. Now it's in great shape, which is more than I could say for me.

You may think that my life is pretty sweet, and who could blame you? Usually, Jim Anchower drives where he wants, drinks what he wants, tokes when he wants, and doesn't take much shit from anyone unless he absolutely has to. But lately, things have changed in a big way.

My summer was packed full of hanging out, keeping Ron from accidentally burning his place down, and getting together with Wes, which has been hard to do since he moved. Anyway, a few days ago, there was a knock on the door while I was trying to find my keys so I could make a beer run. I opened the door, and this woman was standing there.

We were talking some and watching whatever was on. She seemed cool enough. She was able to keep up with me, beer for beer. I wasn't really paying much attention to the TV.

Now, I had no idea who she was. All I knew was that I had five minutes to get to the liquor store before it closed, and someone I don't know is in my way. Plus, I might have forgotten to pay some bill she was there to collect, in which case I wouldn't have beer money anymore, so I told her this is a bad time and tried to get past her. That's when I noticed she was carrying a 12-pack of Miller Genuine Draft. If she's a bill collector, she knows how to get my attention.

You may think that my life is pretty sweet, and who could blame you? Usually, Jim Anchower drives where he wants, drinks what he wants, tokes when he wants, and doesn't take much shit from anyone unless he absolutely has to. But lately, things have changed in a big way.

She told me that she was sorry for throwing up on my floor. Then I remembered who she was. She was one of those chicks Ron and his friend Rob brought over to my place to watch *Dude, Where's My Car?* a couple months back. They were all pretty wasted, and this girl, Debbie, puked all over my floor. It was disgusting. It was all I could do to throw a shopping circular or two over it and wait for it to dry.

I told her it was cool, but I still have to get to the store. She told me that the MGD was for me, and she had another 12-pack in her car. For the first time, I took a good look at her. She's not Pamela Anderson hot or anything, but she's all right to look at. So I invite her in.

So this chick, who I barely know, walks past me and starts making herself at home. She put the 12-pack in the fridge, right on top of the pizza from two days ago. She grabs herself a beer, don't even offer me one, then sits down on my couch and turns on the TV. In my book, that's a hell of a way to say you're sorry, but I let it slide since she brought beer.

We were talking some and watching whatever was on. She seemed cool enough. She was able to keep up with me, beer for beer. I wasn't really paying much attention to the TV. I had a girl on my couch that was probably good to go, if I could figure out how to get the engine running.

I couldn't even remember the last time I dipped the wick, so I was thinking about what I did last time that

see ANCHOWER page 262

Hatred Of Marriage Counselor Brings Couple Together

TEMPE, AZ—Area couple Tom and Becky Witthauser credited the successful resolution of their ongoing marital conflicts to their mutual hatred of their marriage counselor Monday, describing him as the "jag-off whose prissy, ineffectual demeanor brought us closer than we've been in years."

The Witthausers, married eight years, began visiting Dr. Roger Verbicki, 42, a psychologist and accredited couples counselor, in May after months of strife threatened to end their union. Holding hands and gazing lovingly at each other, they described their first fateful meeting with "the insufferable" Verbicki.

"At the time, we could barely make eye contact," Tom said. "But about halfway through the first session, we started casting these sideways glances, because we just hated this guy. We could both feel it."

"After our first session, I told Becky,

"At the time, we could barely make eye contact," Tom said. "But about halfway through the first session, we started casting these sideways glances, because we just hated this guy. We could both feel it."

'That guy is so unlikeable, like the way he asked us to call him Dr. Roger,'" Tom said.

"And I said, I hated him too!" Becky said, finishing Tom's sentence. "He was such a putz, like he's Dr. Phil or something. Our buddy. Gonna help us through this. What a loser."

The Witthausers said they can barely maintain their composure during their weekly meetings, due to Verbicki's various mannerisms and affectations. His nasal voice, sallow complexion, stained teeth, elbow-patched corduroy blazers, and affinity for herbal tea are among the traits cited by the Witthausers. Singled out for particular ridicule was Verbicki's tendency to rest his face against his thumb and index finger, and scratch his lower lip.

"I just want to beat the guy up," Tom said.

"And I've really learned to appreciate Tom for that," Becky said.

see 'MARRIAGE COUNSELOR' page 264

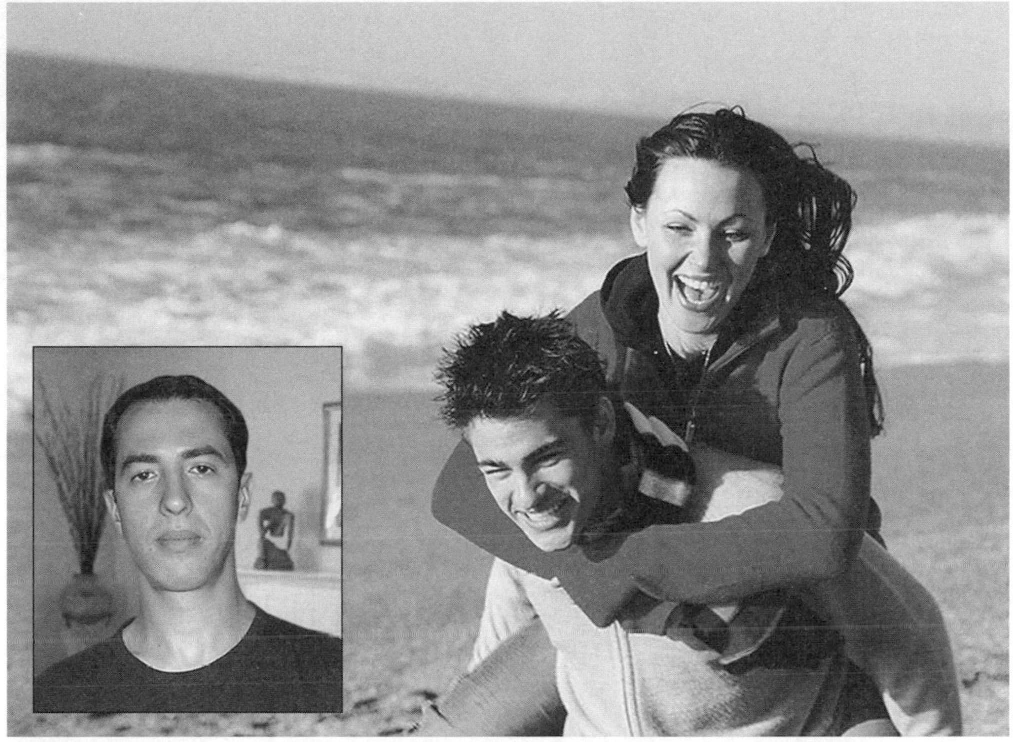

Above: The Witthausers enjoy a newfound closeness, thanks to their hatred of therapist Roger Verbick (inset).

NEWS IN BRIEF

First Report On Long-Term Effects Of Breakdancing Released

NEW YORK—More than two decades after the breakdancing craze peaked, the first data on its long-term health effects was published Tuesday in the *Strong Island Journal Of Medicine*. "We've found permanent shoulder pop, elbow lock, and spin-neck in '80s-era breakdancers," said Dr. Young MD, the report's author. "For years, many subjects had thrown their hands in the air without exercising the proper care." Breakdancing researchers hope to further medical diagnostic advances pioneered by 1999's groundbreaking "Death Before And After Disco" study.

Philandering String Theorist Can Explain Everything

BATAVIA, IL—Fermi National Accelerator Laboratory physicist Laird Karmann, a noted string theorist and accused philanderer, said Monday that he can "explain everything" if his wife Elizabeth will just give him a chance. "Surely, anyone can see that, mathematically, the universe is composed of Riemann surfaces, having positive-definite metrics, across which the attached 'loops' or free 'strings' have a (1+1) dynamic topology," Karmann said. "But string behaviors are Lorentzian, meaning that they—like me—need an intense dual-phase Wick rotation now and then just to stay in rational space. I mean, it was just a blowjob." Elizabeth refused to accept her husband's theory, suggesting that he study the transformational loop dynamics implicit in her hurled wedding ring.

Nostalgic Memories Of *Land Of The Lost* Ruined In DVD Release

TORRANCE, CA—Fond memories of the Sid and Marty Krofft Saturday-morning TV classic *Land Of The Lost* were quashed by a weekend viewing of its first season on DVD, 38-year-old Don Richards announced today. "You can't expect the cheap blue-screen to look good today, but man, what a steaming pile," said Richards, who has abandoned the idea of introducing his childhood favorite to his 7-year-old daughter Bailey. "I can't believe how much they re-used that same shot of the same tyrannosaurus approaching Marshall, Will, and Holly's cave. And that Cha-Ka was such a bad *Planet Of The Apes* rip-off." Richards still holds out hope that his as-yet unwatched *Lidsville* DVD set "stays true" to his memories.

Woman With Low Self-Esteem Boosts Area Man's Self-Esteem

SACRAMENTO, CA—Out-of-work tower operator Fred Jenkins, 35, who has lacked self-worth since being laid off in late 2004, found his confidence restored in a relationship with fellow AA member Stacy Lynn Parke, 33. "Stacy's so amazing—it's been so nice to have someone to take care of me and tell me how special I am," Jenkins said of Parke, a part-time Hallmark Store clerk who has attempted suicide three times. "I guess sometimes all you need is for another person to make you feel good about yourself, unconditionally." Jenkins also noted that Parke "made it seem that being laid off wasn't that big a deal" and that "sometimes she worries about me so much she just cries herself to sleep."

REPORT from page 259

minimum sentence of eternity.

High-ranking seraphim in the Eternal Justice Department defended God's law.

"It's all about accountability," the angel Nathanael said. "The rule of the Lord affords the complementary blessings of freedom and responsibility, and provides the governing framework under which man is punished or rewarded according to his deeds. The rules are very simple: You

Horowitz said that while drug offenders are literally rotting away in Hell, serial killers and other dangerous sinners are receiving "mere Purgatorial sentences, thanks to the asking-for-forgiveness loophole." Purgatory is a minimum-security state of limbo that affords its occupants the opportunity to repent their sins and eventually gain admittance to Heaven on good behavior.

do the crime, you do the time. Eternity, in this case."

The ACLU report included profiles of hundreds of offenders condemned to eternal perdition under God's law. Among them is Pvt. Robert "Bobby Joe" Hetfield, a World War I fighter and amputee who became addicted to

Above: Hell (file photo).

morphine during his last 72 hours of life on a French battlefield in 1918. As punishment, Hetfield has spent more than a century cleaning Beelzebub's dope house every morning by consuming the urine, excrement, and vomit left by Satan and his revelers.

Another offender listed in the ACLU report is Huachuri, an Incan peasant who used a coca-leaf-based marital aid in 1311. As punishment, he is sodomized continually by a winged, razor-penised goat.

Defenders of God's law argue that eternal punishments like these are the only way to deter other drug users, and preserve order in God's kingdom.

"This is not about revolving-door justice," St. Peter said. "While the word of God will keep some on the straight and narrow, Heavenly studies show that eternal damnation is the only deterrent that really works."

Horowitz said that while drug offenders are literally rotting away in Hell, serial killers and other dangerous sinners are receiving "mere Purgatorial sentences, thanks to the asking-for-forgiveness loophole." Purgatory is a minimum-security state of limbo that affords its occupants the opportunity to repent their sins and eventually gain admittance to Heaven on good behavior.

"Drug offenders, many of whom have committed no prior mortal sin, rack up infinite consecutive life sentences," Horowitz said. "Meanwhile, rapists say they're sorry, recite a few Hail Marys, and wind up basking in God's divine radiance within 10 years."

Among those who oppose God's laws are the stewards of Hell, who argue that his harsh anti-drug penalties have taxed the capacities of the underworld.

"I have one ravenous and overworked hellhound assigned to terrorize 12 methamphetamine users," the demon Abracax said. "After 14 hours in the dog's digestive tract, they are excreted and revived, at which point, I give them another shot of methamphetamine. The dog's exhausted—he was originally intended to be responsible for two users at most."

According to Horowitz, even leaving aside questions of civil liberties in the

Defenders of God's law argue that eternal punishments like these are the only way to deter other drug users, and preserve order in God's kingdom.

afterlife, God's drug laws are problematic.

"These laws, simply put, don't work," Horowitz said. "What the Heavenly hosts need to consider is some sort of angelic early-intervention program at the pre-death level, or at the very least, some form of afterlife rehab." ⌀

ANCHOWER from page 260

worked, only I didn't get a chance to make a move. Before I could even come up with something, she was all over me.

Now, I don't want you making any judgments on me. I did what any man would do in my position: bumped uglies. I ain't going to tell you any more details than that. All I'll say is, she sure as hell wasn't puking that night. I mean, she got up to use the bathroom once or twice, but I don't think she puked or anything.

The next morning, I woke up thinking she was gone. I don't like a lot of snuggle bunny shit, so I was glad I had some space to get my head together, which was hard because I was pretty hung over. I went to the kitchen, and there was Debbie going through my cupboards. I asked her what the hell she was doing, and she told me that she was looking for coffee. I told her that I don't have any.

That would be enough for most anyone, but not her. She just kept rum-

I believe in being a gentleman and all, but I don't usually have someone yelling at me first thing in the morning.

maging through my shit without answering me, as if she didn't believe me. I told her that there was a gas station two blocks away and maybe she could just pop down there and pick some up. That seemed reasonable to me, but not to her. She turned and looked at me like she was going to rip my head off, and said that if I was a man, I'd get my ass down to that gas station and pick her up the biggest coffee they had with cream and sugar.

I didn't even know what to say. I believe in being a gentleman and all, but I don't usually have someone yelling at me first thing in the morning. I was about to say that when she reached in the cupboard and threw a pot at me. That was all the encouragement I needed. I went down to the gas station and got two coffees, one for me and one for her.

I got back and she was sitting on the couch flipping channels. She hung out for a while and watched TV, finally leaving at 2:30. But before she left, she said if I had plans that night, I better change 'em, 'cause we were going to a movie.

Seriously, I like getting some trim, but I'm not too big on having to look after someone else. See, I like to play it by my rules. No compromises, no remorse. I don't need no one to tell me when to be home and what we're doing this weekend. She drops by unannounced with beer once or twice a week, then expects me to drop everything so we can get busy? Hell, I'm not a machine.

Jim Anchower has to have some space. I can't have Debbie telling me where to go and what to do. I figure I can only take another month or so of this before I let her go. Don't worry, I'll let her down easy. I'm king of the breakup. I just need to get some weed in the system first so I can get myself in the zone. ⌀

CANCER from page 259

Sennis, who has known Murphy since they started working in the same department at Motorola in 2003, said having a friend with cancer is "a life-altering experience."

"People ask me how I'm doing, and I say, 'I'm scared and I'm angry,'" Sennis said. "Unless you've personally experienced the pain and hardship that comes with having a coworker you're fairly close to get cancer, you wouldn't understand."

Sennis said that, while it initially seemed like "life had come to an end," he "made the decision to keep living."

"One thing I've learned in all this is that life goes on," Sennis said. "Well, maybe not for Ben. But for me. The only thing I can do is take it one day at a time."

Sennis said he doesn't want people feeling sorry for him.

"A lot of my friends start to say 'I have a friend who's just been fired,' or

"You never understand what you have until your friend's cancer takes it away," Sennis said.

'I have a friend who tore a tendon,'" Sennis said. "Then, they realize that I have a friend with cancer, and they get quiet, like they think they can't discuss their problems with me anymore. I just want people to treat me like normal."

Sennis said he wishes he'd appreciated the good times he enjoyed with his friends before he got the news.

"You never understand what you have until your friend's cancer takes it away," Sennis said. "Like, I used to complain about having to go to Wednesday Wings with the guys from sales, but last week we had to cancel because Ben was getting a bone-marrow biopsy, so I sat at home alone all night."

"It was a pretty depressing picture," he added.

Sennis said chemotherapy has been particularly hard for him.

"Ever since the chemo started, it's been a whole other story," Sennis said. "I had to spend a good part of my Sunday hanging out in the waiting room last week. I was so exhausted I could barely move."

"Just try finding something decent to eat out there," Sennis added. "I ate a sandwich from the hospital deli, and the bread was, like, Wonderbread, and the turkey tasted terrible, like it was day-old or something."

Sennis said that, ironically, the presence of Murphy's family made the situation more difficult." I'm going through an emotional time," Sennis said. "Ben's entire family was the last thing I needed at the hospital. Do you realize how hard it is to talk to people you don't know at all?"

Sennis added: "The hardest part was talking to Ben's girlfriend. I never liked her, but because of Ben, I had to go through these awkward conversations. 'How many more chemo sessions does Ben have?' 'Is Ben keeping down his food?' It was really hard."

Sennis said his struggle has made him reconsider his relationship with God.

"I wonder why God would do this to me," Sennis said. "It's like God is punishing me for something by giving cancer to a friend of mine."

Due to the adversity he has faced, Sennis said he has had to take special care of himself.

"I don't consider giving up an option," Sennis said. "So, for the past two months, twice a week, I've been treating myself to a massage. It's expensive, but it's the least I can do for myself as I go through this really tough time."

Added Sennis: "I'm not going to let Ben's cancer beat me." ⊘

UNHORSED from page 210

amounts of blood. Passersby were amazed by the unusually large amounts of blood. Passersby were amazed by the unusually large amounts of blood. Passersby were amazed by the unusually large amounts of blood. Passersby were amazed by the unusually large amounts of blood. Passersby were amazed by the unusually large amounts of blood. Passersby were amazed by the unusually large amounts of blood. Passersby were amazed by the unusually large amounts of blood. Passersby were amazed by the unusually large amounts of blood. Passersby were amazed by the unusually large amounts of blood. Passersby were amazed by the unusually large amounts of blood. Passersby were amazed by the unusually large amounts of blood. Passersby were amazed by the unusually large amounts of blood. Passersby were amazed by the unusually large amounts of blood. Passersby were amazed by the unusually large amounts of blood. Passersby were amazed by the unusually large

Bergen found the theory to be a little nine-dimensional.

amounts of blood. Passersby were amazed by the unusually large amounts of blood. Passersby were amazed by the unusually large amounts of blood. Passersby were amazed by the unusually large amounts of blood. Passersby were amazed by the unusually large

see UNHORSED page 290

SECRETARY OF NATION from page 259

son with all due haste."

The Cabinet-level position, to be known as Secretary of the Nation, was established by an executive order Sept. 2, but has remained unfilled in the intervening weeks.

"I've been talking to folks from all

"Every day the president waits is another day he's accountable for needless deaths at home and abroad, the stagnating economy, and the threat of terrorism," Senator Lindsey Graham (R-SC) said. "This post is far too vital to be left vacant. Mr. President, there is no reason to delay."

across this country, from Louisiana to Los Angeles, and people tell me the same thing: This nation needs a strong, compassionate leader," Bush said. "In response to these concerns, I'm making this a top priority. I will name a good, qualified person as soon as possible."

Among the new secretary's duties are preserving, protecting, and defending the Constitution of the United States, commanding the U.S. armed forces, appointing judges and ambassadors, and vetoing congressional legislation. The secretary will also be tasked with overseeing all foreign and domestic affairs, including those relating to the economy, natural disasters, national infrastructure, homeland security, poverty, and the wars in Iraq and Afghanistan.

The secretary will report directly to the president.

For weeks, members of both political parties have been urging Bush to fill the post.

"Every day the president waits is another day he's accountable for needless deaths at home and abroad, the stagnating economy, and the threat of terrorism," Senator Lindsey Graham (R-SC) said. "This post is far too vital to be left vacant. Mr. President, there is no reason to delay."

"I applaud the president's decision to find a strong leader for our country, but it's imperative that he make his selection soon," said Senate Minority Leader Harry Reid (D-NV), adding that he and all Democrats hope to work closely with the new national executive.

"In the spirit of bipartisanship, we will welcome the new secretary," Reid said. "Together, we will strive for a new dawn of American politics, one unmarred by partisan bickering between Congress and the White House."

According to a nationwide poll conducted by the Cook Political Report, the majority of U.S. citizens find the question of national leadership to be highly significant, with 61 percent of respondents "strongly" believing that the country is suffering from a leadership vacuum. Fifty-four percent said they trusted Bush to find an appointee who will be able to effectively manage the country.

While many Beltway insiders have named senators Barack Obama (D-IL) and John McCain (R-AZ) as likely candidates, White House sources revealed that Bush may be leaning toward a stalwart loyalist. The list reportedly includes fellow Yale graduates, Midland, TX business associates, and various GOP fundraisers with connections to the Bush family.

"Despite their inexperience in government, they've clearly passed the Bush character test," said a White House staffer who spoke on the condition of anonymity. "I think the president is looking for someone he's comfortable with and can trust, above all else. A [former FEMA director] Michael Brown type, or maybe even Brown himself."

Bush said the creation of the Secretary of the Nation post directly addresses the increasingly complex and sometimes overwhelming challenges facing the executive branch in the 21st century. Although he acknowl-

"In the spirit of bipartisanship, we will welcome the new secretary," Reid said. "Together, we will strive for a new dawn of American politics, one unmarred by partisan bickering between Congress and the White House."

edged that the tasks facing the new appointee will be extraordinary, Bush ended his announcement on a positive note.

"As your president, it is my duty to see this nation through any crisis, no matter how severe. And as your president, I pledge to you that I will find a man capable of doing just that," Bush said. "I will not—I repeat, I will not—let you down." ⊘

COMMUNITY VOICES

Oh My God, I Am So Drunk On Power Right Now

Peterson? Another wage cutback. Make it a double. And what say we don't water it down with a lot of firing-bonus mumbo-jumbo.

By Travis Briswalther
CEO, AmTel

That's the stuff. I am feeling *no pain*. Now let's get down to business. Since RE/corp took over operations and placed me at the helm as CEO and president, AmTel has emerged as the leader in the computer-telephony field. With profits up, costs down, and 12 low-balls in the bag, I am so drunk on power I can barely see straight!

You there. Vice president in charge of operations? Take a memo. Let's construct another corporate headquarters in Taiwan. Yes, I *would* like another corporate headquarters. No, I do not think I've had enough. This is our anniversary, for Christ's sake. You know what? It's my own business, and if I want another headquarters, I'm having another headquarters.

You're fired. No, wait. Wait. I hire you back.

"In re" ongoing labor strikes, it is my intention to stand up—whoa—I believe I will stay seated.

Now, pending approval on the Minnesota job-reduction plan I authored several moments ago, we are all-systems-go to break ground on the Czechoslovakia facility in June. Additionally, the recent set of Heartland firings is over, and with that in mind, I suggest we have another round.

Eudyce? Get me an airplane. Outstanding payables reduction under Travis Briswalther is phenomenal: Run a tab. Actually, scratch that. I'm feeling magnanimous. The plane's on me. Fuck it. Let's really do this, right?

You bet your ass I'm serious, I... Oh man. I'm feeling light-headed—I really shouldn't have ordered that last set of convertible bonds. I... whoo. Jesus, I haven't been this drunk on power since I took us public in '93.

You'd think at my age I could handle all this power, but I guess it can still come up behind you and kick you in the ass. Maybe I should slow down... I mean, I'm not out of control or slurring minorities and getting sued by the NAACP, like that IBM guy, but still, when I stood up a second ago, it was like everything was revolving around me.

I do think I need a glass of spring water, though. Thanks, Eudyce. Say, Eudyce? I don't think I've ever told you that I really consider you my closest ally, second to my wife. Yeah, I do. These other guys, they don't like to vertically integrate the same kind of stuff that we do when we get together. You're...really great. Really, really great.

Now get me Takashi Sonobe on 4. I want to personally tell the old fossil he's out. Yes, Eudyce, I'm sure this is the right time. Get him on the phone.

Thank you. Hello? Hey! Hold on a sec, Takashi. ...Eudyce, could you excuse me?

Sorry, Takashi. Yeah so.... Domo arigato, sexy.

It's Briswalther. Ha ha ha. Buying

You'd think at my age I could handle all this power, but I guess it can still come up behind you and kick you in the ass. Maybe I should slow down... I mean, I'm not out of control or slurring minorities and getting sued by the NAACP, like that IBM guy, but still, when I stood up a second ago, it was like everything was revolving around me.

you out! Ha ha. Guy who's going to take your job! Ha ha. No, no way. No way.

Yeah, so, it's like, I've wanted to talk to you ever since our Tuesday face-time. Yeah, I felt this mutual connection. I think it was mutual. It's like, we get each other, you know? We're both really... powerful, you know? Yeah, Karen doesn't get that about me. My wife. Karen.

You're not creeped, are you? Well, I guess I do mean it—I mean, I know I do. I do. I don't just... I don't just let anybody in, Takashi.

Ah-hmm. Mm-hmm. Call you after the deal goes through? Okay. Of course, Takashi. Of course. You too.

Eudyce? Oh God, Eudyce! Oh God, Eudyce, hold me.

No, of course not, I apologize. I'm just looped. I'm looped. I think I'm gonna... nope. No, I'm fine. But I think I should get a ride home. I don't think I'm capable of driving myself home. Yes, I agree. I'm in no state. Driver! Get my car ready! I'm going home. ⌀

HOROSCOPES

Your Horoscope

By Lloyd Schumner Sr.
Retired Machinist and
A.A.P.B.-Certified Astrologer

Aries: (March 21–April 19)
Most people are ignorant, dull, and impulsive, so even at your age, you should be able to find a spouse.

Taurus: (April 20–May 20)
The stars are becoming a little upset at your constant pestering about the future. Would it kill you to maybe loosen up a little and live for the moment?

Gemini: (May 21–June 21)
You would in fact leave for Canada right this minute if it didn't mean leaving the only nation on Earth with the vision to teach squirrels to water-ski.

Cancer: (June 22–July 22)
Fad or not, the high-protein, meat-heavy diet thing seems to work for you, but that could be just part of the benefits of being a two-ton Kodiak bear.

Leo: (July 23–Aug. 22)
Your life will become somewhat easier when you learn that money and food are often kept inside of those little cars you see parked here and there with the pizza signs affixed to their roofs.

Virgo: (Aug. 23–Sept. 22)
You've known since you were very young that you were different from all the others, but still, you find it maddening that they usually put the naked people where they are very difficult to watch.

Libra: (Sept. 23–Oct. 23)
You've never been afraid to try new things, at least not as such. You're afraid of the special Church-controlled hit squad that finds people trying new things and gives them two behind the ear.

Scorpio: (Oct. 24–Nov. 21)
You'll become a pariah and cast out from the company of decent people when it become clear that nothing will in fact change the way you look at tooth-whitening mouthwash forever.

Sagittarius: (Nov. 22–Dec. 21)
You're the one who knows where all the bodies are buried, but that's only because trucks arrive at all hours and bury bodies in your yard, and the truck drivers always make you sign for them.

Capricorn: (Dec. 22–Jan. 19)
While it may be true that the emperor has no clothes, you should have taken into consideration how remarkably well-clothed, and well-armed, all his bodyguards seem to be.

Aquarius: (Jan. 20–Feb. 18)
There's nothing holding you back from achieving your wildest dreams, proving beyond a shadow of a doubt that stronger and more restrictive gun laws are badly needed.

Pisces: (Feb. 19–March 20)
You always knew you'd be sent straight to Hell when your time came, but you never thought they'd make you go there in a tacky white Hummer limousine. ⌀

MARRIAGE COUNSELOR from page 261

Tom demonstrated his imitation of Dr. Verbicki, which Becky described as "adorably mean."

"Well, if done in the proper manner, I think it would be very beneficial," said Tom, lampooning Verbicki's frequent use of the phrase "if done in the proper manner" and mispronunciation of the word "beneficial."

The couple laughed and embraced each other.

The Witthausers reported that they started communicating with each other soon after their therapy sessions began, if only to express their revulsion toward their counselor. By spending time together to complain about Verbicki's habits, the couple's romance was rekindled.

"We spent hours walking beside the lake, or drinking wine and listening to music, holding hands, and complaining about the way Dr. Roger's mouth hangs open, or how he taps his knees every time he gets up out of his chair," Becky said, adding that the mutual sentiments helped the

The couple laughed and embraced each other.

couple realize how much they still enjoyed each other's company and how indispensable they were to each other.

"I can't imagine trashing Dr. Roger with any other person, really," Tom said. ⌀

NEWS

Astronomers Discover Extremely Graphic Galaxy

see SCIENCE page 7D

Third-Grade Slumber Party A Snakepit Of Machiavellian Alliances

see LOCAL page 3B

Foreign-Policy Mistake Blows Up In Soldier's Face

see INTERNATIONAL page 6C

Pop & Pop Shop Boycotted

see LIFESTYLES page 4E

STATshot

A look at the numbers that shape your world.

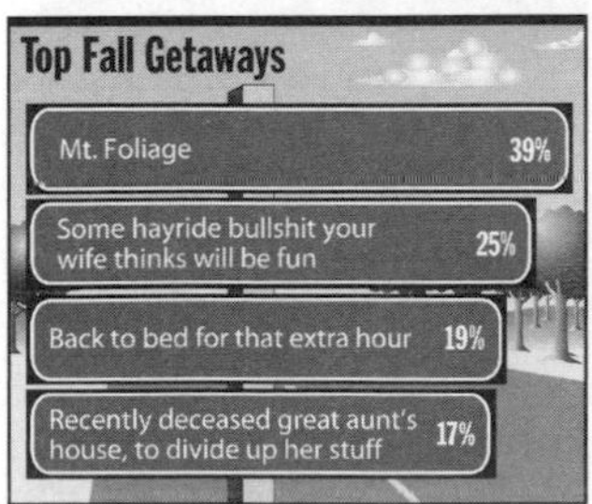

Top Fall Getaways
Mt. Foliage 39%
Some hayride bullshit your wife thinks will be fun 25%
Back to bed for that extra hour 19%
Recently deceased great aunt's house, to divide up her stuff 17%

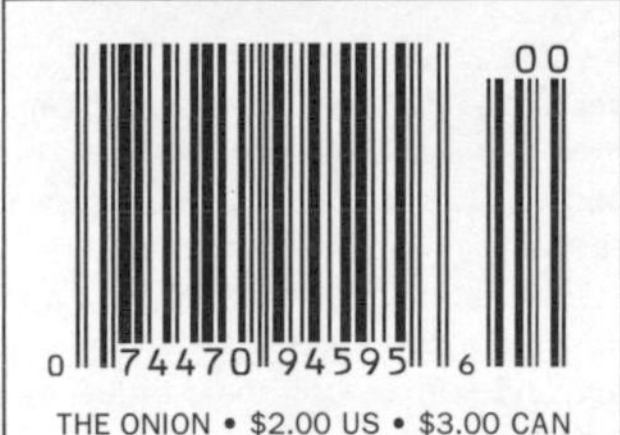

THE ONION • $2.00 US • $3.00 CAN

the ONION®

VOLUME 41 ISSUE 42 AMERICA'S FINEST NEWS SOURCE™ 20–26 OCTOBER 2005

Study Reveals Pittsburgh Unprepared For Full-Scale Zombie Attack

Above: Pittsburgh, a prime target of the undead.

PITTSBURGH—A zombie-preparedness study, commissioned by Pittsburgh Mayor Tom Murphy and released Monday, indicates that the city could easily succumb to a devastating zombie attack. Insufficient emergency-management-personnel training and poorly conceived undead-defense measures have left the city at great risk for all-out destruction at the hands of the living dead, according to the Zombie Preparedness Institute.

"When it comes to defending ourselves against an army of reanimated

see ZOMBIE ATTACK page 268

Six Dead In Gubernatorial Suicide Pact

COLUMBUS, OH—The bodies of six U.S. governors were discovered in the Ohio Statehouse early Monday, all apparent participants in what authorities believe to be some sort of statewide-officeholder suicide pact.

Police have identified five members of the media-dubbed "Gubernatorial Six": governors Haley Barbour (R-MS), John Lynch (D-NH), Bill Richardson (D-NM), Ernie Fletcher (R-KY), and Robert "Bob" Taft (R-OH). The identity of the sixth governor is being withheld until his family is notified. Columbus Police Chief James Jackson confirmed rumors that "Governor X," as he is being called, was a male, and governor of "a very large state."

Early toxicology reports indicate that five of the governors died after drinking scotch laced with barbiturates. Gov. Fletcher is believed to have mixed the drug with bourbon and a splash of water.

Discovered by a Statehouse night cleaning crew in the pre-dawn hours, the governors' bodies were arranged in a circular pattern on the floor of the Finan Room. Forensic evidence indicated that Taft, who was found clutching the presidential seal to his chest, was the last one alive, leading

see SUICIDE page 269

Poll: More Americans Getting Their News From Bev

MARSHFIELD, MA—With an increasing variety of news media options, including 24-hour cable channels, websites, and blogs, more Americans have been tuning out traditional newscasts and turning to local resident Beverly Tollefsen for their news, a poll released Monday shows.

According to the poll, 42 percent of Americans rely on Bev to keep them informed of the top news events. Only 37 percent said they get their news from network or cable TV. The remaining 21 percent rely on newspapers and radio, though 8 percent of that group does not form a strong opinion on the news "until chatting with Bev first."

Adults over 55 lead the shift, with two-thirds saying they consider Bev a top source of national news.

A local news source since 1974, 54-year-old Bev burst on the scene with her cov-

see BEV page 268

Above: Trusted newswoman Beverly Tollefsen.

Harriet Miers Nomination

President Bush's Supreme Court nomination of longtime associate Harriet Miers continues to draw criticism. What do *you* think?

Lanndon Miles
Accountant

"It just goes to show that, in America, anybody can grow up to be a lavishly rewarded sycophant of the president."

Craig Lefferts
Salesman

"It's nice of Bush to support other people who aren't qualified for their jobs."

Anna Green
Systems Analyst

"Hey, he has to go with who he knows, and clearly he was too busy Hoovering up Bolivian marching powder in his Ivy League schools to make any valuable contacts."

Theresa Spillman
Teacher

"Well, I'll be able to give my opinion after we learn more about her and read through her legal writings, like we did with Chief Justice Roberts."

Gerald Leslie
Therapist

"There's no rule that says you need to have any judicial experience to serve on the highest court in the land. ...Why isn't there?"

Bruce Jacoby
Tailor

"We should all feel grateful that Bush apparently doesn't have a favorite TV show that features any lawyers."

Hussein Trial Developments

This week, Saddam Hussein began his first trial before an Iraqi tribunal, where he faces charges of an alleged 1982 massacre. Here are some early developments in the trial:

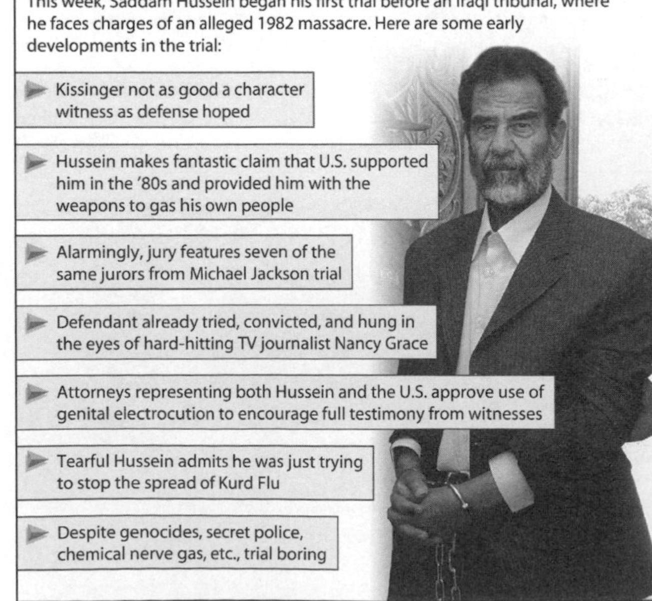

- Kissinger not as good a character witness as defense hoped
- Hussein makes fantastic claim that U.S. supported him in the '80s and provided him with the weapons to gas his own people
- Alarmingly, jury features seven of the same jurors from Michael Jackson trial
- Defendant already tried, convicted, and hung in the eyes of hard-hitting TV journalist Nancy Grace
- Attorneys representing both Hussein and the U.S. approve use of genital electrocution to encourage full testimony from witnesses
- Tearful Hussein admits he was just trying to stop the spread of Kurd Flu
- Despite genocides, secret police, chemical nerve gas, etc., trial boring

Herman Ulysses Zweibel
Founder

T. Herman Zweibel
Publisher Emeritus
J. Phineas Zweibel
Publisher
Maxwell Prescott Zweibel
Editor-In-Chief

I Can't Listen To This Nonsense Anymore... Or Can I?

By Allen Zischler

It seems that every time I bother to pay attention to what's going on in the world, I hear of another scandal. Another example of greed or incompetence. A city annihilated, a high-ranking government official indicted, Americans working harder and earning less than they did three decades ago...ugh! I can't take it anymore!

Or can I?

Maybe I could listen to one or two more stories of that nature. It wouldn't kill me. It never hurt anybody just to stay informed about what's going on in the community and the world at large, did it?

Yes, I should brush up on local issues, attend city council sessions, and try to effect positive change. I will no longer simply stand by and watch others run this world into the ground.

Or will I?

Just thinking about it makes me want to throw up my hands and tune into *Stacked*.

Or does it?

You're damned right it does. Pamela Anderson in a bookstore? This is a watershed moment for the entertainment industry, a stunning breakthrough in so-bad-it's-good media content. I can't help but watch it.

Or can I?

I could take it or leave it. It's as good

I think if you get breast implants, don't complain that no one takes you seriously as an actress. I think breast implants are just awful, and the last thing I would ever do is recommend that someone seriously think about getting them to give their career a boost.

as anything else on TV.

Or is it?

I don't know. It hasn't technically been done before, this exact premise. I'll give it that. But seriously, I've about had it with Hollywood's attempts to entertain me.

Or have I?

I admit I probably couldn't write a much better sitcom. There's more to them than meets the eye. It takes a lot of work and professional know-how. Plus, Stacked was the most successful new sitcom of last season. My hats off

Maybe I could listen to one or two more stories of that nature. It wouldn't kill me. It never hurt anybody just to stay informed about what's going on in the community and the world at large, did it?

to the creative executives of the Fox network! And heck, I would be lying if I said that I didn't admire Pamela Anderson. She's been through a lot.

Or has she?

She was discovered after being caught on the Jumbotron in a Labatt shirt during a Canadian football game. That doesn't seem like it'd take a whole lot of hard work and effort.

Or does it?

No.

Well, then again...

Yes, it does. And she did go on to tape herself having sex with Tommy Lee and get a lot of attention on the Internet because of it, and that shows initiative, I think.

Or do I?

I think if you get breast implants, don't complain that no one takes you seriously as an actress. I think breast implants are just awful, and the last thing I would ever do is recommend that someone seriously think about getting them to give their career a boost.

Perhaps I should reconsider this opinion and give the matter more thought.

Or should I?

The last thing I want to do is sit around and watch ridiculous fake boobies in tight shirts on TV all day until my eyes burn and crack with redness and my brain turns to mush, and I can't find another scrap of deep-fried imitation chicken skin at the bottom of the bucket of KFC popcorn chicken.

Or is that exactly what I want to do? It is! From now on, that's what I'm doing, and I think you should follow my lead. Ø

Veteran Cop Gets Along Great With Rookie Partner

LOS ANGELES—Just one month before narcotics officer Vincent Tate was planning to turn in his badge and retire on a full pension, he learned that he was being assigned a rookie partner. Now, after four weeks, the hard-boiled 25-year veteran of the Los Angeles Police Department says he's having so much fun with the new recruit, he "may never leave."

"The last thing I wanted was to train some know-it-all, baby-faced college boy who'd question my every move," Tate, 55, said. "Luckily for me, Jason has been an absolute delight."

Jason Hepplewhite, 23, a Stanford University graduate who majored in criminal science, hit it off immediately with Tate, according to 34th Precinct Captain Lionel Shaw, who united the pair. After a tense few seconds in which the entire squad room waited to see if Tate would haughtily snub Hepplewhite's extended hand, the older cop instead shook it warmly, grinned, and took the younger cop on a tour of the precinct building.

"I said to him, listen, kid, do your best to apply what you've learned at your fancy school, and if you have any questions at all, don't hesitate to ask," Tate said.

"I thought the difference in age, race, and class would lead to certain friction," Shaw said. "I'm sure glad it all worked out, though, since Lord knows that, as his captain, I would never intentionally do anything to anger a veteran cop like Vince, whose questionable methods get results. In fact, I don't believe we've ever raised our voices to each other."

Tate said that the first thing he did when he got in the patrol car with Hepplewhite was lay down a strict set of ground rules. "I said to him, listen, kid, do your best to apply what you've learned at your fancy school, and if you have any questions at all, don't hesitate to ask," Tate said.

Although Hepplewhite proved to be the intensely idealistic, literal-minded greenhorn Tate had feared, the duo, in the true spirit of partnership, have managed to work around their philosophical differences. Tate even took time out to praise what he called Hepplewhite's "superb book-based education."

"Jason has this helpful idea of a 'thin

see PARTNERS page 270

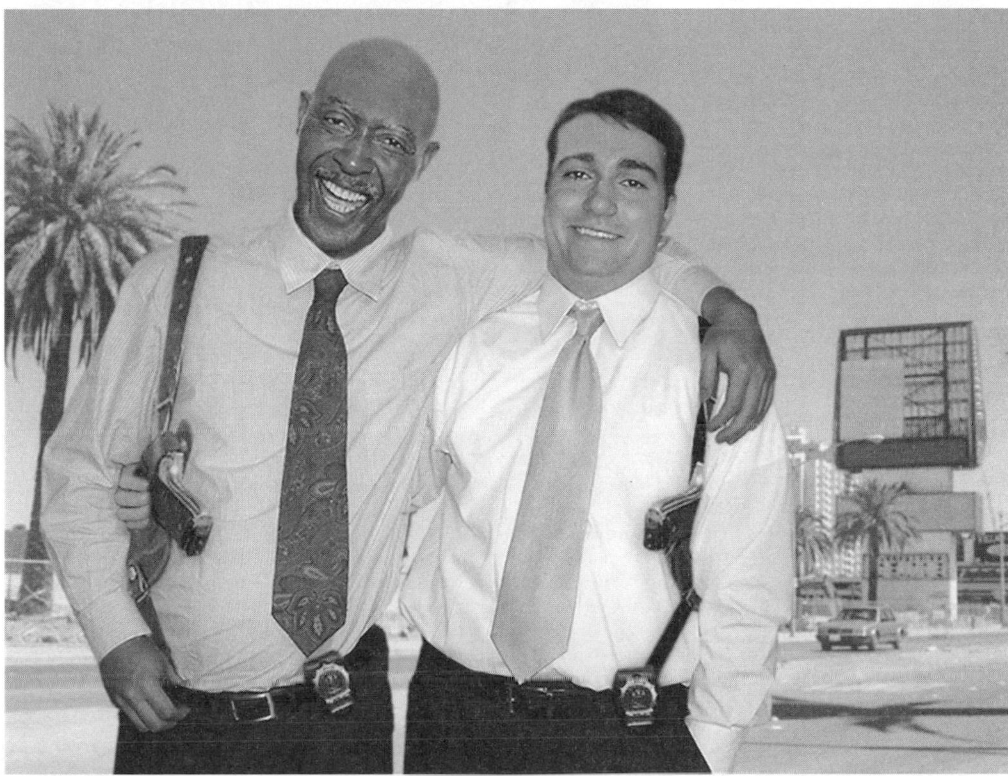

Above: Officers Vincent Tate and Jason Hepplewhite enjoying each other's company.

NEWS IN BRIEF

Missing Girl Elected To Aruban Parliament

ORANJESTAD, ARUBA—In a surprise election result, Aruban voters elected missing Alabama teen Natalee Holloway to their parliament Tuesday. "The people of Aruba know that Miss Holloway has been through hell and, possibly, back, and that means a lot to us," said Fredis Oduber, who cast his ballot for Holloway along with 87 percent of his countrymen. "Our congratulations and prayers are with her family at this time." The incumbent in Holloway's seat is expected to serve until MP-elect Holloway takes office or her body is found.

Report: One In Five Women Training To Be Yoga Instructors

WASHINGTON, DC—According to a Department of Labor report on job retraining, 21 percent of American women are training to be yoga instructors, marking the highest level of female interest in the flexibility-and-spirituality-expansion industry since 1971. "One particular indicator is striking: All but 32 women in New York and San Francisco are now certified yoga instructors, specializing in either hatha, bikram, or ashtanga yoga," Labor Secretary Elaine Chao said. The report notes that the rising interest in yoga instruction has caused a commensurate depletion in the ranks of massage therapists and board-certified realtors.

New Orleans Struck By Meteorite

NEW ORLEANS—A tractor-trailer-sized meteorite struck downtown New Orleans late Monday night with comparable force to that of a small nuclear device. "The impact caused floodwaters in the area to vaporize, scalding everything in a four-mile radius with radioactive steam," said Claude Wyncoll of the U.S. Naval Observatory. "Burning debris shot into the troposphere, then rained down across the Gulf Coast, causing property damage and countless casualties as far away as Gulfport [MS]." FEMA and National Guard personnel are unable to enter the city, as the lava flow resulting from the meteorite's deep penetration of the Earth's crust has blocked all routes.

President Bush Urges Nation

WASHINGTON, DC—Saying he "could not stress the issue strongly enough," President Bush urged the nation Monday in a televised address from the Oval Office. "Fellow Americans, in this time of trial for our nation, I beseech you," Bush said. "Heed my words: This great nation, founded in freedom. Therefore, I implore all Americans. I ask you, in our hour of need. Good night, and God bless you." Pundits agree that the message was the most forceful speech from the president since he interrupted regular programming to call on the nation in the spring of 2003.

Latest Jihad Has Something For Everyone

SANA'A, YEMEN—Leaders of the New Mujahideen jihadist movement say their latest holy war should appeal to people from all walks of Muslim life. "If you like bombing, bomb manufacturing, effigy-burning, maintaining inflammatory websites, or just 'hajjing out,' the Nu Mooj has something for you!" read a statement on the group's home page. "Jihad is better when friends come together!" The Nu Mooj is expected to recruit several hundred like-minded fanatics to their holy cause of fighting Western imperialism before factional violence tears it apart later this year. ⌀

ZOMBIE ATTACK from page 265

human corpses, the officials in charge have fallen asleep at the wheel," Murphy said. "Who's in charge of sweep-and-burn missions to clear out infected areas? Who's going to guard the cemeteries at night? If zombies were to arrive in the city tomorrow, we'd all be roaming the earth in search of human brains by Friday."

Government-conducted zombie-attack scenarios described on the State Department's website indicate that a successful, citywide zombie takeover would take 10 days, but according to ZPI statistician Dr. Milton Cornelius, the government's models fail to incorporate such factors as the zombies' rudimentary reasoning skills and basic tool use.

"Today's zombies quickly learn to open doors, break windows, and stage ambushes," Cornelius said. "In one 1985 incident in Louisville, a band of zombies was able to lure four paramedics and countless law-enforcement officials to their deaths by commandeering an ambulance radio and calling for backup."

Above: Pittsburgh residents participate in a zombie-preparedness training exercise in 1998.

"Children need to be taught from preschool that they might have to put a bullet between the eyes of their own undead mother."

ZPI researchers noted that tens of thousands of Pittsburgh citizens live in close proximity to a cemetery. This fact, coupled with abnormally high space-radiation levels in eastern Pennsylvania and ongoing traffic issues in the East Hills and Larimer areas, led Cornelius to declare the likelihood of a successful evacuation as "slight to impossible."

"The designated evacuation routes would be hopelessly clogged, leaving many no choice but to escape by foot," Cornelius said. "Add a single lurching zombie into that easily panicked crowd and you've got a nightmare scenario."

Cornelius' model shows that after the ensuing stampede, "the zombie could pick and choose his victims," and predicts the creation of hundreds of new undead "in a single half-hour feeding frenzy."

Pittsburgh's structural defenses are particularly inadequate. The city's emergency safe houses, established by a city ordinance in the early '70s, lack even the most basic fortifications for zombie invasion.

"Under the ordinance, wooden tool sheds and rusty station wagons are classified as adequate shelter," Cornelius said. "But once dozens of zombies hungering for living flesh begin pounding on the walls and driving their half-decomposed fists through the windows, sheds and cars quickly give way."

Federal Undead Management Agency spokesperson Dr. Sheena Aurora downplayed the ZPI report, arguing that zombies move slowly and can be easily overpowered. Aurora advised citizens to look over their shoulders frequently, adding that a large shopping mall can serve as a "long-term, even fun" refuge from zombies.

Such assertions alarm zombiologist Olivier Baptiste, who calls FUMA's information "hopelessly outdated."

"Dr. Aurora's claims are based on decades-old zombie models," Baptiste said. "Widely released evidence from recent years clearly shows that zombies can run just as fast, if not faster, than a living human."

Added Baptiste: "That FUMA trains its field agents to shoot zombies in the torso, rather than the head, demonstrates just how out of touch the government is."

Evans City, PA Police Chief Gino Fulci said zombie preparedness comes down to training on the local level.

"Children need to be taught from preschool that they might have to put a bullet between the eyes of their own undead mother," Fulci said. "'Destroy The Brain' banners should be hung above the entrances of schools, churches, and town halls everywhere."

Cornelius recommends that Pittsburgh residents prepare a "go-bag" containing a Glock 17 pistol and 50 rounds of ammunition. If leaving the house is not an option, Cornelius advises residents to barricade all first-story doors and windows, and have at least one method of suicide prepared, should zombies successfully breach the home. ⌀

BEV from page 265

erage of the Whitewater scandal, which she called "just awful" in her now-historic Shop Rite Address.

Since then, a growing number of Americans have tuned into Bev's reports—from her admonishing and sometimes blushing coverage of the Clinton-Lewinsky scandal in her front yard in the '90s, to her remarks on the contested election of 2000 to fellow bowlers at Alley Kat Lanes.

Bev's popularity has soared in recent years, thanks largely to her position on the corner of Library Plaza and Webster Street, looking out over more than six other homes. Neighbors and passersby tune in for Bev's greetings and news of the day, which she introduces with her trademark lead-in: "Have you been following all this news that's been going on?"

Andrew Kohut, director of the Pew Research Center, said America's shift toward Bev results in part from her ubiquity.

"Bev is looming larger as a news presence," Kohut said. "Appearing live from locales ranging from the hairdresser's chair to the doctor's office waiting room, Bev goes places traditional media can't."

Reports indicate that programmers in the fiercely competitive field of television news have been looking for their own Bevs. CBS Evening News producer Chris Weicher said the network was hoping that the recently hired anchor Shirley, a 57-year-old Mt. Horeb, WI resident, would "Bev up" its broadcasts.

"We wanted someone with a compelling, no-nonsense edge," Weicher said. "Someone who wasn't afraid to deliver the news in curlers and a nightgown."

Media analyst Aaron Lenz credits Bev's success to the public's increasing media sophistication, and growing frustration with mainstream media. "Today's news consumers want a maternal, non-threatening voice they can trust. Bev has given Americans a reason to believe in news again," Lenz said.

Despite fervent praise from her loyal listeners, Bev's critics allege that she is often unreliable.

Loyal Bev watcher Kent Miellerson agreed. "I can't relate to the mainstream media elites. But Bev—she's just like you and me, so I trust her. Also, she's my aunt."

Despite fervent praise from her loyal listeners, Bev's critics allege that she is often unreliable. "Sometimes, like in the weeks after Sept. 11, Bev simply stops paying attention to the news, saying that it 'makes her sick just thinking about all of it,'" said retiree Gladys Hager, who claims Bev once devoted an entire report to endorsing a brand of fabric softener she preferred. "And she'll go on sudden, indefinite hiatuses, like if her daughter returns from college or her bursitis starts acting up."

She added: "I lent Bev's husband my hedge trimmers, and still haven't gotten them back. I'm supposed to rely on this woman for my news?" ⌀

SUICIDE from page 265

police to speculate that he was the ringleader.

"We believe Governor Taft served the executive authorities their final cocktails," Jackson said. "There were no signs of struggle, no attempts to escape. It appears that all participated willingly and sought a common end."

Although the reasons behind the suicide pact remain unknown, many of the country's surviving 44 state chief executives said they are not surprised by the tragedy. The governors were all known in their home states for their penchants for dark suits, their similar hairstyles, and their "fuck everything" attitudes.

"I never really talked to them except when I had to, like during the occasional National Governors' Association meeting," Hawaii Gov. Linda Lingle said. "They tended to stay away from girls altogether. It's sad to see such bright and promising state-level executives succumb to this senseless rage and self-destruction."

"[Ohio Governor] Bob [Taft] was always saying how much he hated it, how he felt trapped, how he'd do anything to get out of 'the cage,'" Henry said.

Above: Governors Barbour, Fletcher, Lynch, Richardson, Taft, and X. Below: The grisly scene at the Ohio Statehouse.

Oklahoma Gov. Brad Henry, who sometimes socialized with members of the Gubernatorial Six at luncheons, said that although they openly talked of taking their own lives, he never took them seriously.

"They made a lot of bizarre jokes, a lot of dark stuff that I didn't understand," Henry said. "I knew many of them didn't want to be governors anymore, and Bob was always saying how much he hated it, how he felt trapped, how he'd do anything to get out of 'the cage.' The others would pretty much go along with him. The sad thing is, they probably could have done quite well in the private sector."

Gov. Mark Sanford of South Carolina has been able to provide grieving family members and states with some insight into the actions of the Gubernatorial Six. Sanford, who was briefly associated with the group in 2003, said their suicide came as no surprise to him.

"I was your typical confused, first-term governor," said Sanford, who admits he found the dark, morbid posturing of the outcast governors "cool."

"I had a great deal of respect for Bob [Taft]—he lived on the edge, always giving the world the finger," Sanford added.

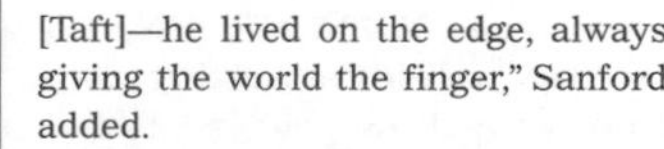

Gov. Mark Sanford of South Carolina has been able to provide grieving family members and states with some insight into the actions of the Gubernatorial Six.

But by 2004, Sanford had distanced himself from the group.

"Bill [Richardson] had developed this habit of slashing at his arms and chest with his New Mexico flag lapel pin," Sanford said. "And Haley [Barbour] liked asphyxiating himself with his necktie until he turned blue. Not long after I stopped hanging out with them, I found a dead bald eagle on the doorstep of the governor's mansion."

The FBI set up a national hotline Monday and urged voters to call if they suspect that their governor might be contemplating suicide or has joined a gubernatorial cult. Counselors from the National Institute Of Mental Health have been sent to capitols in all 50 states to counsel at-risk and interim governors. ⌀

COMMUNITY VOICES

What Idiot Wrote These Ten Commandments?

You keep hearing about these Ten Commandments on television, all the religious fundamentalist types saying, "Let's put them up in the courthouse, let's hang them up in the schools, etc., etc." They seem pretty determined to make the Ten Commandments the law of the land, so I figured, as a responsible citizen, I should bone up on them.

By Jeff Hewitt

I cracked the wife's Bible the other night and let me tell you, after all the hoopla about these 10 magical rules, I expected a lot better.

Take the first commandment, for example. It says you shouldn't believe in any gods besides God. No gods besides the one, eh? Okay, I can agree with that. Frankly, I got no idea how foreigners keep track of all their different gods. But as an opener? As number one on a list of 10? Seems pretty weak to me. You want to lead off with a batter who can hit.

Then it goes on more about God. "Don't believe in any other gods," it says. "Don't worship graven images of God, or any likeness of any thing that is in heaven above, or that is in the earth beneath, or that is in the water under the earth. Thou shalt not bow down thyself to them, nor serve them."

One tip I would give this writer is to lay off the God stuff. Or at least dial it back a little bit. And you're not impressing anybody with the Dr. Seuss language.

After all that jazz about God, the author just keeps on going: "Don't take the Lord's name in vain" is the next one. What is it with this guy and God? I'm beginning to think he's one of these church types. Where's the stuff we can use? Where's "No pushing"? Or "Bag your leaves so they don't blow around in your neighbor's yard?" And don't even get me started on right-of-way. Didn't they have real problems back in Bible days?

Note to the joker who wrote these commandments: For inspiration on some good, down-to-earth laws, take a look at John Ritter's *8 Simple Rules For Dating My Teenage Daughter*. Good stuff.

Next, he gets to the rule that you're supposed to honor your father and mother. Finally, we're getting somewhere. But just when you think we're about to get to the "how," he's on to number five, just like that. I guess this guy never had any kids. I tell my sons to honor me every day, but just you try and get them to obey! It makes me wonder if this so-called lawmaker gave any thought to enforcement. That's part and parcel, my friend. You're going to have to get police in every child's bedroom all across the country, and we just don't have the manpower for that. You mean well, but this law is strictly pie-in-the-sky.

My advice: Think up some more, and maybe cut this one.

The next one is "Thou shalt not kill." I'm sorry, but that just sounds like bleeding-heart bullcrud. We have a death penalty in this country, and it works. And how will you fight a war if you don't kill some people? I suppose the writer of these laws is one of these dreamers who thinks the world would be better if people picked posies and held hands all day. Enjoy your flower music, Sunshine, and call me back when you grow up and start paying your own bills.

It gets back to earth with "Don't commit adultery" and "Don't steal," but then it's back to the old rubber room with "Don't covet thy neighbor's oxen" and "Don't bear false witness." Whatever you say, Matlock.

I applaud the idea of 10 simple laws of the land, but I don't think these are the ones to go with. Somebody needs to do another draft of these things. Cut the fat, and put in a few real solid ones. Like what about keeping telemarketers from calling? Or some clear guidelines on tipping. Can we at least have one in there about drinking and driving? Maybe get some feedback from the taxpayers.

Altogether, I believe these commandments are pretty thin on law and order and the needs of the common citizen, and a little thick on the religious mumbo jumbo. But as I said before, the fundamentalists are running the show now, so they must know what they're talking about. ⌀

HOROSCOPES

Your Horoscope

By Lloyd Schumner Sr.
Retired Machinist and
A.A.P.B.-Certified Astrologer

Aries: (March 21–April 19)
It still seems that for every step forward, you take two to the side, three back, and then trip and fall off the side of a building, hitting the fire escape several times on the way down.

Taurus: (April 20–May 20)
You'll learn a lot about yourself this week, including the exact tensile strength of each of your ribs, the temperature at which your nasal cartilage melts, and where your fear of commitment comes from.

Gemini: (May 21–June 21)
While it's true that no one asked you if you wanted to be born, you must realize that's because you would have made a lot of demands as to when, where, and to whom.

Cancer: (June 22–July 22)
You will be offered the chance to make amends with everyone you've ever wronged, but the stars are putting good money on your deciding not to.

Leo: (July 23–Aug. 22)
Drinking is not the answer to your problems. However, since sex addiction is in fact the answer to all your problems, your lifestyle need not change.

Virgo: (Aug. 23–Sept. 22)
It is neither sentience nor a sense of humor that separates us from the animals. Turns out it's actually celebrity zookeeper Jack Hanna.

Libra: (Sept. 23–Oct. 23)
Your tactics of overwhelming your opposition with spectacular shows of force and choking the roads with fleeing refugees will be seen as inappropriate by the other electronics wholesalers.

Scorpio: (Oct. 24–Nov. 21)
You know that people change when they have children. That said, your transformation will be particularly remarkable when you discover you have two dozen of them, all with special needs.

Sagittarius: (Nov. 22–Dec. 21)
Your self-destructive behavior resumes this week when you run out of anything else to destroy.

Capricorn: (Dec. 22–Jan. 19)
Your sudden and extreme maritime promotion can be traced less to competence and seamanship than to the tradition of captains going down with the ship.

Aquarius: (Jan. 20–Feb. 18)
When all is said and done, everyone will have to admit that, while it might not have been worth the loss of your arm, you were right about caribou.

Pisces: (Feb. 19–March 20)
Taking some time off is fine, necessary even, but before you know it, three months have gone by and you haven't killed any more nurses. ⌀

PARTNERS from page 267

blue line' that separates the lawless from the civilized, whereas I understand that sometimes certain crimes must be left unpunished in order to protect the greater good," Tate said. "So we switch off. If, on Mondays or Wednesdays, Jason thinks a small-time crook who's given me solid leads for 20 years should be locked up, that's his prerogative. On Tuesdays and Thursdays, though, we'll use an underage hooker as bait to close in on a major heroin kingpin."

"Friday is a grab-bag," Tate added.

According to Hepplewhite, it has been a pleasure working with Tate, who has refrained from patronizing him or deliberately involving him in a difficult situation that would require his older partner to step in and save him.

"Shortly before what was shaping up to become a standoff at a warehouse drug lab, Vincent asked me if he should radio for a SWAT team, or if I would prefer being thrown right into the fray," Hepplewhite said. "I chose the SWAT team, but I appreciated the option. I just wanted to get my feet wet a little before finding out the hard way that I might not have what it takes to fight crime."

Despite the natural give-and-take of the relationship, Tate said there have been moments when he has worried, such as last week's interrogation of a suspected drug dealer accused of fatally shooting a young girl during a turf battle.

"Jason began screaming at the suspect, taking out what seemed like years of pent-up aggression on him," Tate said. "Afterwards, in the locker room, I braced myself for an emotional monologue from Jason about how his own little sister was killed in a drive-by shooting. But he just smiled, apologized for causing a scene, and suggested we grab some lunch."

The two enjoy each other's company so much that they have begun spending time together off-duty. Every Saturday night, Tate, Hepplewhite, and their wives get together to have dinner, watch a movie, or just play cards.

"Joy and I simply love Jason's emotionally stable wife Sara, who both understands and encourages the dangerous work and long hours that come with being a police officer," Tate said. "She has not been killed by avenging street punks."

"It's good for two officers to get together and discuss everything that's going great in our lives over a few beers," Tate added. "Luckily, I do not have a lingering drinking problem that Jason has to help me confront."

According to other members of the force, Hepplewhite is ably filling the shoes of Tate's former partner, Buddy Haverly, who served faithfully alongside him for nearly 15 years, and whom Tate rarely stops talking about.

Haverly is alive and well. ⌀

NEWS

Teens: Are They Laughing At You?

see NATIONAL page 3B

Showoff Pallbearer Carries Casket By Himself

see LOCAL page 7D

New Disney Movie Captures, Tortures Imagination

see ENTERTAINMENT page 6C

STATshot

A look at the numbers that shape your world.

Worst Parts Of Our Jobs
14% Arriving, sitting for eight hours, leaving
33% Turning over our badge and gun
10% Hours spent jazzing up people's perceptions of electrical tape
8% Having to act like we're friends with employees we're about to fire
35% Working with people

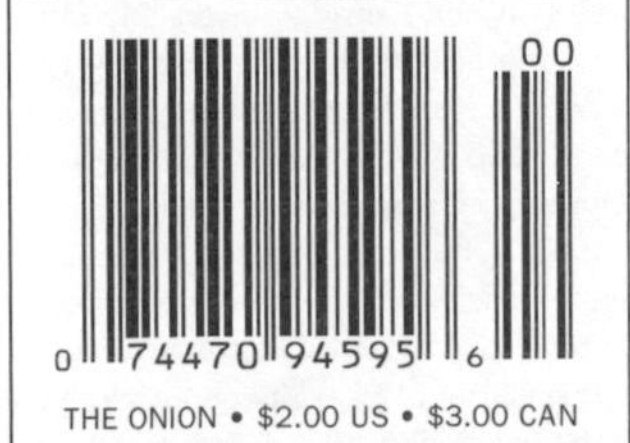

THE ONION • $2.00 US • $3.00 CAN

the ONION®

VOLUME 41 ISSUE 43 AMERICA'S FINEST NEWS SOURCE™ 27 OCTOBER–2 NOVEMBER 2005

Trick-Or-Treaters To Be Subject To Random Bag Searches

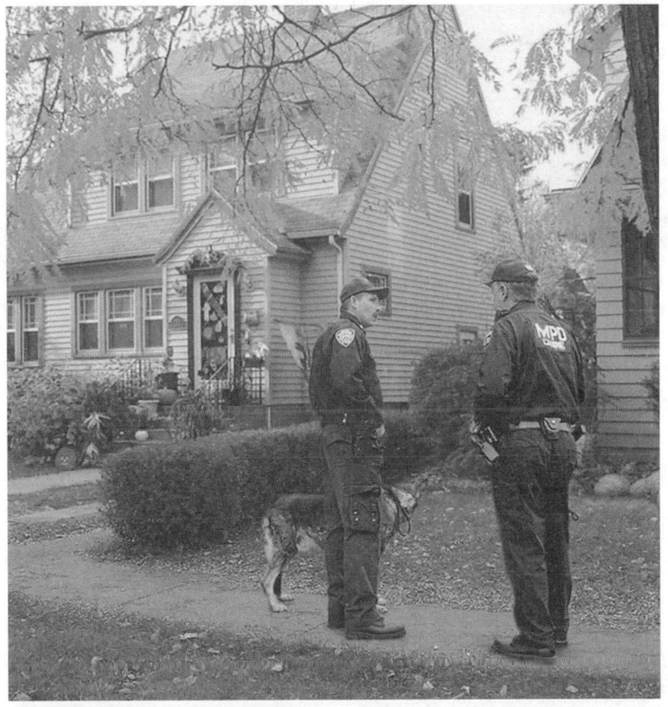

Above: Police prepare for a long and spooky night.

WASHINGTON, DC—Responding to "a possible threat of terror and fright," Department of Homeland Security Secretary Michael Chertoff announced Monday that trick-or-treaters will be subject to random bag searches this Halloween season.

"Individuals concealing their identities through clever disguise, and under cover of night, may attempt to use the unspecified threat of 'tricks' to ex-

see TRICK-OR-TREATERS page 275

Queer Eye Team Denounces Recent Wave Of Vigilante Homosexual Makeover Groups

NEW YORK—The stars of the popular Bravo reality show *Queer Eye For The Straight Guy* spoke out Monday against the recent rash of vigilante homosexual makeover groups, whose members, while often well-meaning, have left hundreds of Americans inappropriately and even tragically made-over.

"These vigilante activities represent the darker side of *Queer Eye*'s success," grooming expert Kyan Douglas said. "We at *Queer Eye* and Bravo strongly condemn this behavior, and we want to remind homosexuals who are considering performing unwelcome makeovers that we are professionals with years of training and expertise."

Reports indicate that roving bands of homosexuals have forcibly de-cluttered the homes of thousands of clumsy fashion hostages since the summer of 2003, when *Queer Eye* debuted. Though none of the unsolicited-gay-makeover incidents have resulted in fatalities, FBI Fashion Crimes agent Jason Broderick said the deep humiliation victims suffer makes many of them want to die.

The Fab Five, as the Queer Eye cast

see QUEER EYE page 274

NASA Chief Under Fire For Personal Shuttle Use

CAPE CANAVERAL, FL—NASA Administrator Michael Griffin has yet to respond to recent allegations that he used NASA space shuttles on as many as one dozen unauthorized outings to such destinations as New York City, the French Riviera, and his vacation home near Ketchum, ID.

A report issued Monday by NASA's Oversight Commission indicates a cumulative 1.8 million miles unaccounted for on the Atlantic, Discovery, and Endeavor shuttles. In addition, shuttle pilot James Kelly reported numerous occasions on which he found the pilot seat "adjusted for someone else."

The report also revealed that radio presets on the shuttles

see SHUTTLE page 275

Above: Griffin plays the Pebble Beach course minutes after blasting off from his Idaho vacation home.

Personal-Bankruptcy Laws

A new bankruptcy law went into effect last week, making it harder for consumers to clear their debts with Chapter 7 bankruptcy. What do *you* think?

"Yes, I missed the deadline for filing old-style Chapter 7 bankruptcy by five minutes, so it's jumping-off-a-bridge time for me."

Phillip Gordon
Unemployed

"I myself wouldn't be facing bankruptcy right now if I hadn't splurged on the name-brand chemotherapy."

Claude Connelly
Dairy Farmer

"If they didn't want to go bankrupt, people should have thought about that before deciding to pursue their dreams."

Kelley Wyley
Bank Teller

"And just in time for the new restrictions to apply to the hurricane victims, too! Who said there's no such thing as miracles?"

Nicole Shustat
Systems Analyst

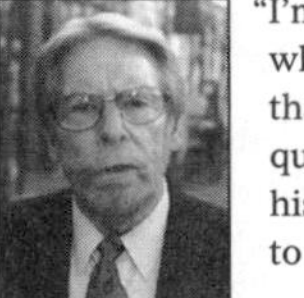

"I'm sure that whatever happens, that man with question marks on his suit will be able to help."

Don Renssalear
Research Assistant

"The bankrupt will be just fine. Enron went bankrupt a couple years back, and most of their board is doing great right now."

Adrian Cole
Sales

Bird Flu Preparations

As the threat of avian influenza looms, federal and state officials are preparing for a possible pandemic. Here's what they're doing:

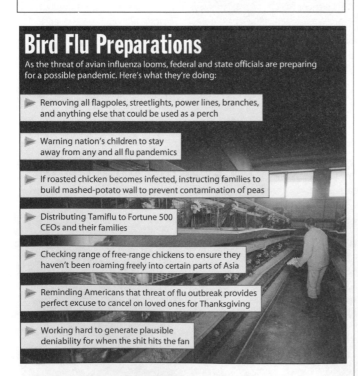

- Removing all flagpoles, streetlights, power lines, branches, and anything else that could be used as a perch
- Warning nation's children to stay away from any and all flu pandemics
- If roasted chicken becomes infected, instructing families to build mashed-potato wall to prevent contamination of peas
- Distributing Tamiflu to Fortune 500 CEOs and their families
- Checking range of free-range chickens to ensure they haven't been roaming freely into certain parts of Asia
- Reminding Americans that threat of flu outbreak provides perfect excuse to cancel on loved ones for Thanksgiving
- Working hard to generate plausible deniability for when the shit hits the fan

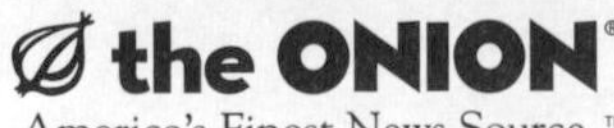

America's Finest News Source.™

Herman Ulysses Zweibel
Founder

T. Herman Zweibel
Publisher Emeritus
J. Phineas Zweibel
Publisher
Maxwell Prescott Zweibel
Editor-In-Chief

Fire Truck! Fire Truck! Fire Truck!

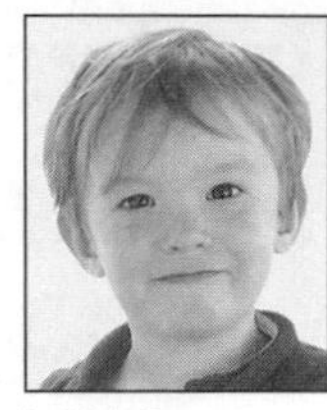

By Edwin Brauer

Look, out the window! A fire truck! I've seen drawings of fire trucks in my picture books, of course, but how could I have ever known how pale and insignificant those crude representations were in comparison to the real thing! *Fire truck!* Oh, great God in heaven, *fire truck!* This has got to be the most moving of mankind's creations, and perhaps of nature's, as well.

This whirlwind of sensory input is almost more than my tiny mind can process! Mere words cannot begin to convey what I am feeling! This incredible, life-changing, soul-shattering wonder is... Why, it is beyond description!

Run! Run to the window as fast as your giant legs can carry you! Whatever you are doing right now, place it aside for a moment—it can't possibly be as important as the opportunity to see a fire truck with your own eyes.

This is quite possibly the greatest experience of my life thus far.

How do I even begin to describe its magnificence? First off, it is big—bigger than anything I could ever imagine! Secondly, it's painted an incredible, alarming, eye-catching red! Thirdly, it makes the most attention-grabbing sounds: whistles, bangs, gearshifts, bells. And that siren! Of all the noises, the siren is surely the best!

How do I even begin to describe its magnificence? First off, it is big—bigger than anything I could ever imagine! Secondly, it's painted an incredible, alarming, eye-catching red! Thirdly, it makes the most attention-grabbing sounds: whistles, bangs, gearshifts, bells. And that siren!

I wonder if, somehow—but no, surely not—unless... Well, could I? Could I possibly? EEEEEEEEEEEEEEE... No, that's not right: It's high-pitched enough, but missing some crucial... OOOOOOOOOO... No, again, it's got the booming quality, but lacks the screechingly irritating aspect of the higher register. Wait! What if I combine the two, in an alternating series of high- and low-frequency modulations, and belt it out at the top of my lungs? EEEEEEEEEEEEEEEEEEE-OOOOOOOOO,EEEEEEEEEEEEE-OOOOOOOOO! That's it! That's the same noise that the fire truck is making! EEEEEEEEEEEEEEEEEEEEE-OOOOOOOOOOOOOOOOOOOO, EEEEEEEEEEEEE-OOOOOOOO!

This whirlwind of sensory input is almost more than my tiny mind can process! Mere words cannot begin to convey what I am feeling!

EEEEEEEEEEEEEEEEEEEEEEE-OOOOOOOOOOOOO, EEEEEEEEE-OOOOOOOO! Oh, God. I could make this noise all day! I never want to do anything else!

And now—am I really seeing this? It can't be! Surely there are not colorfully dressed men with powerful bodies, brave expressions, and purposeful toolbelts hanging off the side of the fire truck as it careens around the corner! If this is a dream, let me never wake. Look at their hats! They have the most wonderful hats ever made! I must acquire a child-sized version of such a hat! They are the most large and most yellow hats I have ever seen.

That's it: My fate in this life is sealed. I must become one of these men. Nothing will ever sway me from this goal.

But what a spectacle it is! You must come and look upon this immediately! This fire truck is blowing my mind. It is as if God Himself has created this piece of machinery just for me! But it will not be here long. It is driving away. It grows quieter and quieter as it recedes from my visual field and...

It is gone. It was only here for one fleeting moment, and you never even saw it. This is the greatest tragedy that has ever occurred. My faith in the universe is shaken to its core by the magnitude of what you have missed. If only you had listened to me. You may never be able to comprehend my experience, for I have seen the fire truck, and I will never think about anything else again as long as I live.

Huh? What is... Why... Afgh! Airplane! Airplane! Mommy! Airplane! Don't bother with those towels! Don't you see? Look! There is an actual airplane in the sky! Ø

That's The Last Time Private Collector Loans Painting To Guggenheim

NEW YORK—Art collector Walter P. Vaifale announced Monday that he will no longer loan artwork to the Solomon R. Guggenheim Museum in New York City. Too often, he says, the museum returns his priceless works of art scratched, broken, or stained, if they remember to return them at all.

Vaifale, the holder of one of the world's most extensive private collections of modern and contemporary Western art, characterized the Kool-Aid stain on Peter Halley's White Cell With Conduit as "the last straw."

"Initially, the Guggenheim staff would make minor mistakes, such as returning my works in the wrong frame," Vaifale said. "Sometimes, when I'd visit, I'd notice a painting hung upside-down. I allowed the staff to brush my complaints aside for several years, but I'm sorry, getting peanut butter on Van Gogh's *The Red Vineyard* is unacceptable."

Vaifale estimated that the Guggenheim has damaged or lost nearly 30 of his holdings, a trend that began in 1989, when his Henri Rousseau oil *Monkey In Trees*, previously little-seen in public, somehow found its way into the gift-shop poster bin, where it sold to a 17-year-old Ohio high-school student for $16.99.

see GUGGENHEIM page 274

Vaifale estimated that the Guggenheim has damaged or lost nearly 30 of his holdings, a trend that began in 1989, when his Henri Rousseau oil Monkey In Trees, previously little-seen in public, somehow found its way into the gift-shop poster bin, where it sold to a 17-year-old Ohio high-school student for $16.99.

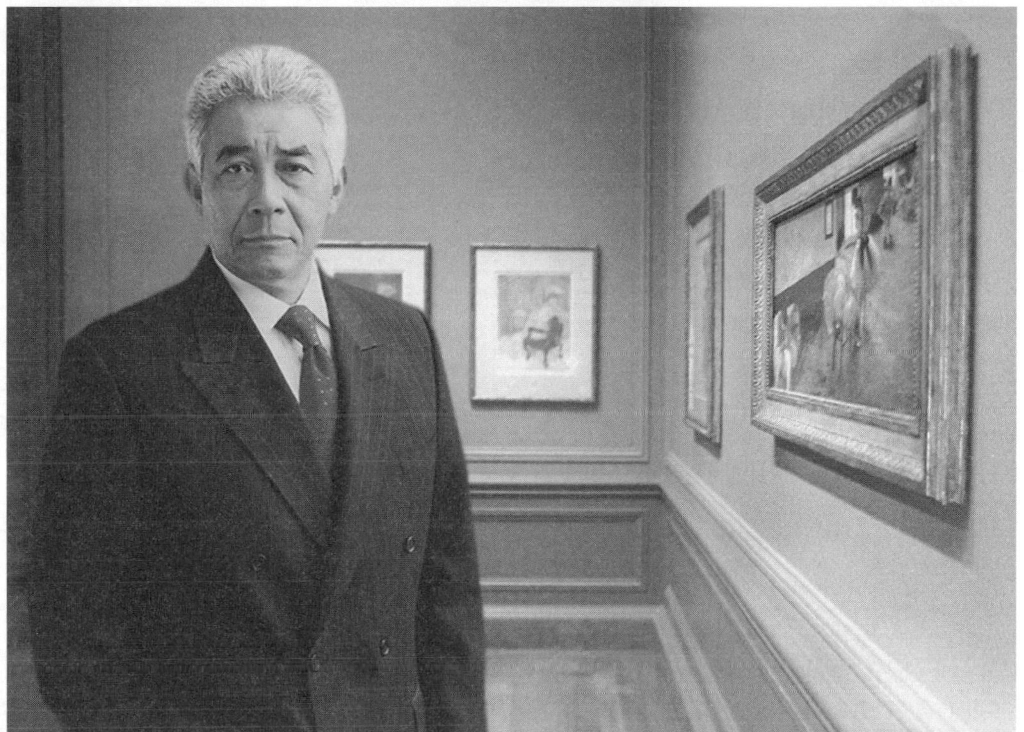

Above: Vaifale, beside a Degas he had restored at great expense after loaning it to the Guggenheim in 1997.

NEWS IN BRIEF

Bolivia Joins DOPEC

LA PAZ, BOLIVIA—The South American nation of Bolivia was inducted into the Development Organization of Powder-Exporting Countries Monday. "As the world's third-largest producer of coca, we are pleased to join Colombia, Peru, Mexico, and other proud nations in economic partnership," said Sonia Atala, Bolivia's minister of opiates. "Only by working together can we assure ourselves of continued expansion into foreign markets." The move was opposed by the U.S., DOPEC's largest customer, on the grounds that further price increases and supply restriction would create long lines at dealerships.

Comedy Central To Air Touching *Man Show* Reunion

LOS ANGELES—Comedy Central executive producer Howard Lapides announced Monday that the network will broadcast a *Man Show* reunion starring former hosts Jimmy Kimmel and Adam Carolla Friday. "Jimmy and Adam joined their old pals Baby Barry and the Juggies to tape the special yesterday, and there wasn't a dry eye in the house," Lapides said. "Watching those trampolines in action again—really just the very sight of those two smirking scamps—was, well, let's just say it was a touching evening." Adam Carolla was unavailable for comment, as he was taping a *Too Late With Adam Carolla* reunion in anticipation of the show's cancellation.

Puppy Dies Adorable Death

SOUTH BELOIT, IL—Three-month-old Lab-Dalmatian mix Smokey curled up into the sweetest little ball of fur you'd ever want to see and died of canine parvovirus in his owner's home Sunday. "Awww, look! Look at that!" said Smokey's former master, nurse practitioner Dieter Knast, who discovered the puppy's corpse. "Did puppums have severe dehydration? Who had a bacterial infection that caused septic shock? You did! You did! You're a little angel." Smokey's corpse is expected to remain under the radiator until it doesn't smell cute anymore.

According To Bar Love-Tester, Inebriated Patron Okay To Drive

WISCONSIN DELLS, WI—J.J. Gardner, a regular customer at Nig's Tavern, was perfectly okay to drive early Tuesday morning after five hours of heavy drinking, according to the AK2000, the bar's coin-operated love-tester. "Hot To Trot," the love-tester said after Gardner gripped its handle for five seconds. Gardner later mumbled incoherent explanations to Wisconsin Dells police that he would never have attempted to drive if he had tested as Frigid, a Cold Fish, or an Old Maid.

KISS Cover Band Guitarist Leaves To Start Vinnie Vincent Invasion Tribute Band

AKRON, OH—Citing growing tensions between bandmates, Harvey Shapiro—aka "VeeVee," the guitarist for KISS cover band Destroyer—left the group Monday to create VeeVee's Occupying Force, a Vinnie Vincent Invasion tribute band. "I felt I had hit a creative ceiling with the cover-band experience and was ready for the challenges of a tribute band," Shapiro said. "VeeVee's Occupying Force will debut Dec. 3 at Rubber City Lanes. We're opening for Second Sighting, my brother's Frehley's Comet cover band." As a part of his new band's act, Shapiro said he is contemplating suing Destroyer for $6 million over damage to his reputation following some badmouthing at the Rock 'N' Bowl. Ø

QUEER EYE from page 271

is known, said they chose to break their silence after the abduction and forceful makeover of 28-year-old Jeremy Hastings of Elko, NV. During Hastings' 72-hour ordeal, he was subjected to a sassy wardrobe critique and a merciless remodeling of his living room, kitchen, and bathroom. His hair was reportedly wrapped in foil for nearly an hour during a multi-part hair-dyeing incident.

Hastings, who managed to escape from his captors Saturday, was found "dazed and browsing" in the scented-

"Real homosexual makeover experts downplay pastels, consider arugula and sun-dried tomatoes passé, and would never encourage an overweight cubicle worker from Bowling Green, OH to wear an ascot."

candle aisle of a Reno-area Bed Bath & Beyond.

Elko Police Chief Mike Poehlman called Hastings' ordeal "one of the most graphic instances of lifestyle overhaul in Nevada history." According to *Queer Eye* culture vulture Jai Rodriguez, forceful makeovers are "a total distortion of the Fab Five's intent."

Another recent abduction involved Martin Eisner of Valdosta, GA, who was accosted in June by several men whom eyewitnesses described only as "shrill." Thirty-six hours after his disappearance, Eisner was found with his sleeves pushed slightly up and his shirt half-tucked. Reclining in a brand-new, knockoff Eames chair, Eisner was largely unresponsive, saying only, "Why does my wall have two colors now?"

Members of the Fab Five explained that vigilante homosexual makeovers, unlike the legitimate, tastefully trendy televised versions from which they take their inspiration, "often use metrosexuality as a crutch."

"The average makeover vigilante has a well-intentioned desire to improve the appearance of straight America, but he just can't curb his love of everything that sparkles," *Queer Eye* fashion savant Carson Kressley said. "That's why you'll sometimes find bald, overweight makeover victims sporting ruffled shirts and bright orange spray-on tans."

According to the Fab Five, incidents of aggressive "over-moisturizing," though often unreported, have been widespread.

Above: Laramie, WY homosexual-vigilante fashion victim Bart Geasle.

Kressley said that, while he and his co-stars "completely get" vigilante frustration with slovenly American men, gays should not take matters into their own hands.

"Makeover violence is never, ever the solution," Kressley said. "If you see a straight guy in torn sweatpants heating up a Hot Pocket in the microwave, use your queer eye for one thing only: to dial up a *qualified* ho-

Elko Police Chief Mike Poehlman called Hastings' ordeal "one of the most graphic instances of lifestyle overhaul in Nevada history." According to *Queer Eye* culture vulture Jai Rodriguez, forceful makeovers are "a total distortion of the Fab Five's intent."

mosexual lifestyle advisor on your cell phone. You want someone who can address severe style dysfunction with *sensitivity* and *tolerance*."

The *Queer Eye* team had several tips for distinguishing a genuine homosexual makeover gang from an unauthorized one.

"If you don't see a TV camera crew filming the gang during a makeover, then it is most definitely an imitation," Kressley said. "Real homosexual makeover experts downplay pastels, consider arugula and sun-dried tomatoes passé, and would never encourage an overweight cubicle worker from Bowling Green, OH to wear an ascot." Ø

GUGGENHEIM from page 273

Vaifale said that, although he was "irritated" by the slipshod treatment of his artwork, he quietly tolerated minor mishaps in order to share his collection with a wider audience.

"If my de Koonings were hung backwards, I'd wince, but then I'd tell myself that maybe people got a perverse, Dadaist kick out of seeing the exposed wooden canvas backing," Vaifale said. "Well, they've loaned my pieces out to 'a friend who moved out of the country' one time too many. I don't care how much international prestige they have, they're lousy borrowers. There, I said it."

Even when paintings are returned undamaged, Vaifale said that it often takes dozens of phone calls and e-mails to various Guggenheim curators to get them back.

"I can't tell you how many of those jokers claim they 'spaced out' on returning my stuff," Vaifale said. "It's always, 'Shit, I totally meant to throw *Still Life With Cracked Jug* in my backpack before leaving today,' or, 'I had your Robert Motherwell right in my hand, but I must've set it down while I was fishing for my keys.'"

Vaifale added, "One time, they said to me, 'Oh, *that Zorah On The Terrace*!'"

According to Vaifale, the most infuriating incident occurred last Saturday night, when he was awoken by a 2 a.m. call from Guggenheim director Lisa Dennison. Dennison, whom Vaifale described as sounding intoxicated, reported the fate of a Barbara Hepworth sculpture.

"She told me that some of the curators had a bit too much to drink at a late-night party and decided, 'Wouldn't it be fun to take out the Slip 'N' Slide and lay it down along the spiral walkway?'" Vaifale said. "Well, of course, somebody slid off the thing and careened into the sculpture, sending it crashing to the ground."

Dennison was dismissive about Vaifale's decision to sever ties with the museum. She characterized Vaifale as "super-anal," and said the Hepworth sculpture "wasn't even all that priceless."

"Walter seriously needs to chill," Dennison said. "I apologized. What more can I do? Most of the famous statues out there are missing an arm or leg—now the Hepworth is missing that weird little beaky part. So what. The thing's probably worth more now." Ø

TRICK-OR-TREATERS from page 271

tort 'treats' from unsuspecting victims," Chertoff said. "Such scare tactics may have been tolerated in the past, but they will not be allowed to

While he would not elaborate on the specific threat, Chertoff said his office had "heard a couple spooky tales," and indicated that there was good reason to believe that Americans face "a very ghoulish scenario" this October.

continue this Halloween."

While he would not elaborate on the specific threat, Chertoff said his office had "heard a couple spooky tales," and indicated that there was good reason to believe that Americans face "a very ghoulish scenario" this October.

"We have done and will continue to do everything we can to protect citizens from those who would play on our fears," a haunted Chertoff said. "Nevertheless, Americans are advised to be in a state of readiness."

National Guard troops and local police are being stationed at checkpoints in residential neighborhoods to seize the contents of any paper bags, pillowcases, plastic pumpkins, or other receptacles. Additionally, candy-sniffing dogs will be posted at regular intervals to locate and devour suspicious items.

Local, county, and state officials have been placed on orange alert, with strict orders to confiscate and investigate bags containing Bit-O-Honey, Snickers, Baby Ruth, Twix, Butterfingers, Mr. Goodbar, Reese's Peanut Butter Cups, gum, and any and all forms of taffy.

Chertoff asked Washington citizens for their assistance, and he outlined steps that the average citizen should take to aid in the war on fright. The DHS guidelines encourage parents to report any suspicious neighbors who create potentially spooky yard displays, especially those that include candle-illuminated pumpkin faces, skeletons in windows or doorways, or repeating tape loops of werewolf howling.

Chertoff recommended that law-en-

"We have done and will continue to do everything we can to protect citizens from those who would play on our fears," a haunted Chertoff said.

forcement authorities be granted sweeping new powers to ensure security, including mandatory street-corner identity checks for suspects wearing clothing designed to conceal facial features or otherwise obscure ready personal identification. Additionally, local police have been ordered to detain any individuals appearing to be ghosts, goblins, witches, or other characters designed to evoke fear.

Critics of the warning say that the DHS is merely sowing seeds of unease for political reasons, pointing out that the organization has yet to present any real evidence of the threat.

"This is yet another misguided and unfair example of profiling by our nation's law enforcement," said ACLU spokesperson Marilee McInnis. "It's doubtful that many G.I. Joes will be searched, but Aladdins, genies, and belly dancers should expect a huge crimp in their Halloween fun." Ø

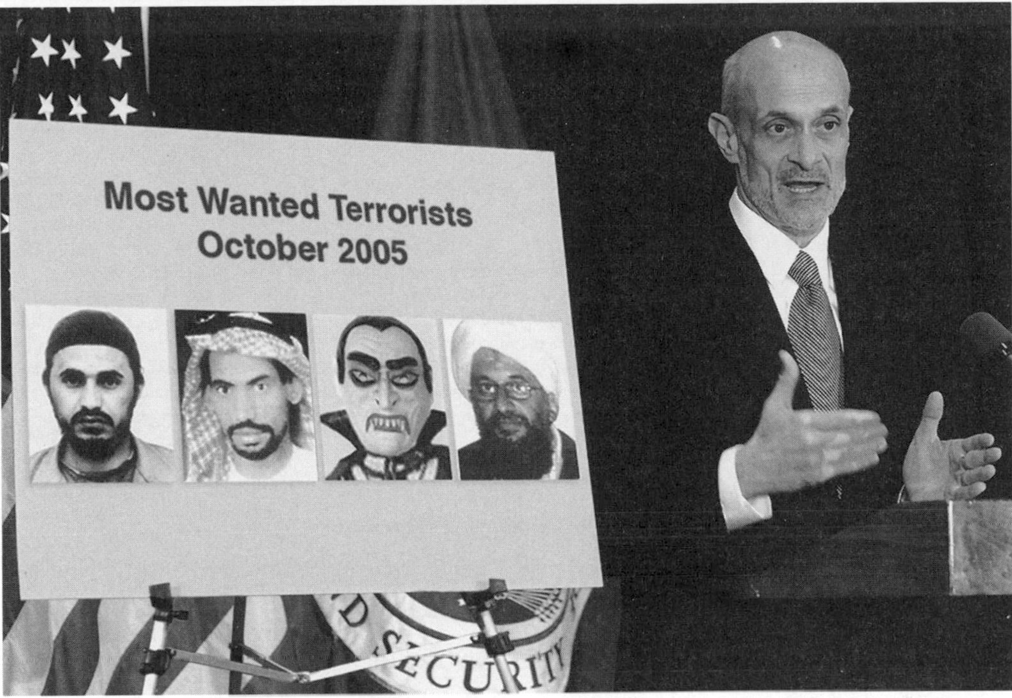

Above: Chertoff discusses possible perpetrators of Halloween mischief.

SHUTTLE from page 271

had been changed to receive various talk-radio stations from across the country, and that the cargo bays contained foreign items such as an old pair of sneakers, "aviator"-style sun-

"More than once, I heard him ask the Mission Control guys if they'd mind 'counting him down' on his way out."

shades, two empty Big Gulp Los Angeles Dodgers collector cups, and CDs that shuttle astronauts say are not theirs.

Griffin's apparent joyrides came to light last week, when sharp-eyed patrons at Georgia's Augusta National Golf Club spotted Discovery in the club's parking lot. Within hours, NASA employees began coming forward with their own observations.

"Every now and then on a Friday, Mr. Griffin would stop by Launch Complex 39B and say, 'Well, I'm off early today, taking the wife shopping on Fifth Avenue,' and I wouldn't think twice about it," said assistant fuel-cell technician Lawrence Clemmons. "But about half an hour later, the ground would shake, I'd hear this earsplitting roar from the pad, and then the shuttle would fly off."

"Sometimes I'd think, 'Hey, it looked like he had his overnight bag with him,'" continued Clemmons. "Then, on Monday, we'd get an e-mail from Mr. Griffin saying he was running behind, but he was just leaving Edwards Air Force Base and he'd be in soon."

Trajectory-optimization engineer Russ Holcum said he'd long suspected that Griffin "had an in" with the staff in Engineering and Fabrication. Said Holcum: "I figured he knew someone who cut him an extra set of keys or two."

Holcum added: "More than once, I heard him ask the Mission Control guys if they'd mind 'counting him down' on his way out before a long weekend."

In a press conference held Tuesday, NASA spokesperson Arjun Congrove apologized to taxpayers for the billions of dollars expended on the unauthorized missions.

"The shuttle costs an estimated $2 billion per launch, not counting delays and repairs, and for Mr. Griffin to use it to take his wife on luxury shopping trips to Europe is not appropriate," Congrove said. "We apologize to affected personnel at NASA, and to the good people of New York City whose homes were vaporized by Mr. Griffin's several unauthorized launches near LaGuardia Airport."

Griffin may face penalties ranging

In a press conference held Tuesday, NASA spokesperson Arjun Congrove apologized to taxpayers for the billions of dollars expended on the unauthorized missions.

from dismissal to having his salary garnished for the next 376 years in order to pay for fuel. Ø

COMMUNITY VOICES

It's Amazing How Much You Can Learn About A Person Just By Hiring A Private Investigator

Do we ever really know the people we marry? I wonder. Now, I've known my wife Fran for 15 wonderful years, 10 of them in the most beautiful, sharing, and trusting marriage anyone could ever want. But even after all these years, the new things I learn about Fran—with the help of private detective Barry Norman—continue to surprise and delight me.

By Matt Simone

For instance, every day on her way to work, Fran stops at Dunkin' Donuts to get a coffee. What an adorable little quirk—all the more so because the computer-simulated aerial map of Fran's route that Barry included in one of his weekly dossiers clearly shows that the doughnut shop is seven blocks out of her way. Cute, huh? Well, that's my girl! I wonder if Barry will ever truly document all her funny little ways.

Oddly enough, the receipts that she's tossed out the window—who knew that sweet little wife of mine would turn out to be a litterbug?—show that she has never purchased a single doughnut along with her coffee during three months of 24-hour surveillance. So why would a person go seven blocks out of her way just for coffee, when she doesn't even eat doughnuts? Just another of love's little unknowable puzzles that even the professional services of an ex-cop who charges $500 a day plus expenses can't explain.

Of course, even in a marriage as mutually loving as ours, there are little things you have to work on—but that's just part of what keeps the magic alive. Sometimes, Fran says that I don't listen to her enough, and having pored over the typewritten transcripts of all our conversations from the past three months, I admit I could improve in that area.

Sure, it's all "little things"—but it's those little things that make me fall in love with her all over again each morning. Take her vocabulary usage patterns: According to the old high-school report cards that Barry came across in Fran's parents' basement, Fran was never very good in English, but re-reading the text of our discussions from yesterday, I noticed she used the term "maladroit" in the correct context on three separate occasions.

Isn't that the most adorable thing you ever heard?

I would've thought that it was on some "word of the day" list, but Barry forwards me all Fran's e-mail, and yesterday was "circumambient." And I know for a fact, thanks to photos that Barry has secured, that she does not have one of those word-a-day calendars on her desk at work—she has a *Far Side* one. Who would have guessed that, after all this time, I'd still be able to uncover a quirky, loveable trait that bears further investigation. I should tell Barry about that.

Oddly enough, the receipts that she's tossed out the window—who knew that sweet little wife of mine would turn out to be a litterbug?—show that she has never purchased a single doughnut along with her coffee during three months of 24-hour surveillance.

It seems like ever since I hired Barry, I've seen Fran in a whole new light, and I don't mean the infrared he uses to photograph her while she's sleeping. For example, I never would have guessed that she gets up when I'm sleeping on as many as four occasions a night. That's the kind of thing that doesn't even cross your mind until a man with night-vision binoculars and a telescopic camera lens stations his van across the street from your bedroom window and monitors every moment of the cold, still night.

Isn't that the wonderful thing about love, though? The way there's always some new facet to uncover that you never knew before, little mannerisms they have that you never noticed—like the playful way that, in the footage from the super-miniaturized motion-sensor camera Barry installed in one of the bathroom tiles, Fran spins her tampons around on their little strings?

We've been married a long time, but I never get bored with Fran. I'll bet even after 10 more years, I could still stare at surreptitiously acquired video footage of her eyes for hours. ⌀

HOROSCOPES

Your Horoscope

By Lloyd Schumner Sr.
Retired Machinist and
A.A.P.B.-Certified Astrologer

Aries: (March 21–April 19)
Coast Guard officials will initially be shocked when you tell them the shark let you go after eating your left leg, but once they try your right one, they'll see that your flesh is tough and gamy.

Taurus: (April 20–May 20)
According to the stars, the mysterious wheels of fate have finally begun turning in your direction, and soon, they'll seize a bearing of fate, jump out of the brackets of fate, and careen into your house.

Gemini: (May 21–June 21)
A diode is an electronic component that makes sure electricity flows only one way. To prevent damage to the electrical wiring in your house, be sure to install one of these between the lamp cord and your genitals.

Cancer: (June 22–July 22)
Your one-in-a-million luck continues this week when you manage to tick off the one person in the world who doesn't smack himself when he uses nunchucks.

Leo: (July 23–Aug. 22)
You will be haunted by mediocrity and the specter of your own mortality in the form of unusually thin and flavorless marinara sauces.

Virgo: (Aug. 23–Sept. 22)
You know it's not truly over until the fat lady sings, but my God, the enormous bitch is taking forever.

Libra: (Sept. 23–Oct. 23)
You'll stop going with your gut and start listening to your heart, almost instantly ruining your career in public relations.

Scorpio: (Oct. 24–Nov. 21)
You've felt for weeks as if they were on the verge of figuring out your secret shame, which is ridiculous, as no one even knows who you are.

Sagittarius: (Nov. 22–Dec. 21)
You always suspected that the Machine Revolt would ultimately end humanity's era of dominance, but you never suspected the Roomba's heinous and tidy betrayal.

Capricorn: (Dec. 22–Jan. 19)
The stars are sorry, but writing greeting-card messages does not make you a poet. Take comfort in the fact that, since this is America, you'll make the lists anyway.

Aquarius: (Jan. 20–Feb. 18)
Authorities somehow get the idea that the frozen corpse is that of an explorer who became lost in the Rocky Mountains and somehow wandered into your freezer.

Pisces: (Feb. 19–March 20)
Unfortunately, those in the outside world will continue to mistakenly believe that your having been in the closet since age 12 means you're gay, not trapped. ⌀

BARLEY from page 218

amounts of blood. Passersby were amazed by the unusually large amounts of blood. Passersby were amazed by the unusually large amounts of blood. Passersby were

She always gets emotional around her father's killer.

amazed by the unusually large amounts of blood. Passersby were amazed by the unusually large amounts of blood. Passersby were amazed by the unusually large amounts of blood. Passersby were amazed by the unusually large amounts of blood. Passersby were amazed by the unusually large amounts of blood. Passersby were amazed by the unusually large amounts of blood. Passersby were amazed by the unusually large amounts of blood. Passersby were amazed by the unusually large amounts of blood. Passersby were amazed by the unusually large amounts of blood. Passersby were amazed by the unusually large amounts of blood. Passersby were amazed by the unusually large amounts of blood. Passersby were amazed by the unusually large amounts of blood. Passersby were amazed by the unusually large amounts of blood. Passersby were amazed by the unusually large amounts of blood. Passersby were amazed by the unusually large amounts of blood. Passersby were amazed by the unusually large amounts of blood. Passersby were amazed by the unusually large amounts of blood. Passersby were amazed by the unusually large

see BARLEY page 281

NEWS

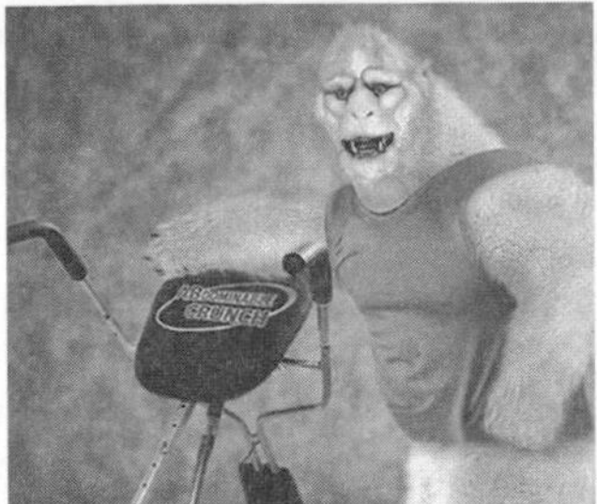

Yeti Releases Abdominable Crunch Workout Video

see SPORTS page 2C

Mega-Churchgoer Hopes To Appear Devout On Jumbotron

see LOCAL page 3E

Lie Tolerated For Its Beauty

see NATIONAL 3A

Fall Fashion: Is It In?

see STYLE 14D

STATshot

A look at the numbers that shape your world.

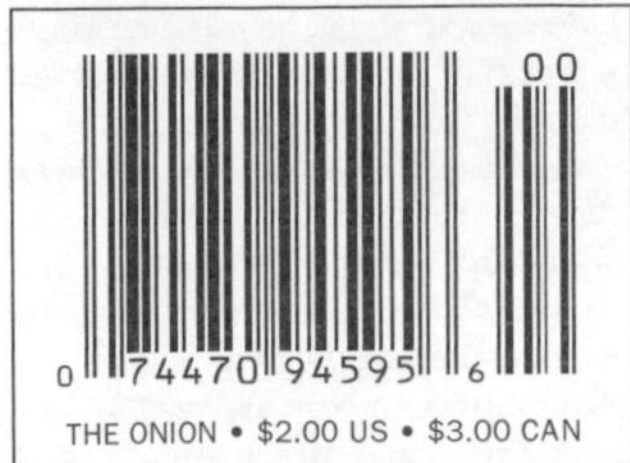

THE ONION • $2.00 US • $3.00 CAN

the ONION®

VOLUME 41 ISSUE 44 AMERICA'S FINEST NEWS SOURCE™ 3–9 NOVEMBER 2005

Left: Iraqi leaders pose with the constitution after its historic signing.

Iraqi Constitution Ratified, Burned

BAGHDAD—The people of Iraq celebrated the passage of their new constitution Monday, in a formal ceremony that included a stirring speech by Iraqi President Jalal Talabani, a series of explosions that left 77 dead, and a traditional dance performed by Iraqi schoolchildren.

After many weeks of squabbling and protracted negotiations between Kurds, Sunnis, and Shiites, the historic document was declared the law of the land and destroyed late Monday afternoon, in what Talabani characterized as "a vital step toward restoring law and order in this war-torn nation."

A car bomb killing 12 U.S. servicemen and 26 Iraqi civilians briefly interrupted the speech.

"Today in Iraq, the voice of the people was heard loud and clear," Talabani said as U.S. fighter jets launched a retaliatory air strike overhead. "It is moving to see so many Iraqis getting involved in the political process."

While Iraqi officials acknowledge that the path toward unified peace will be a long one, many expressed cautious optimism over Iraq's burgeoning democracy.

Minister of Justice Abd al-Husayn Shandal, whose severed arm remains fixed, pen in hand, to the giant cedar signing table

see CONSTITUTION page 280

Bush Orders Mass Bald Eagle Slaughter To Stop Spread Of Bird Flu

WASHINGTON, DC—As experts issue increasingly dire warnings of an avian flu epidemic, President Bush signed an executive order Tuesday authorizing the mass slaughter of "all bald eagles found anywhere within our borders."

"As president, my first duty is to protect the American people, whether the threat is terrorists or deadly, fast-mutating bird viruses," said Bush, standing on the lawn of the National Mall before a specially built pyre stacked with recently killed bald eagles. "This proactive initiative will rid our nation of this potentially disease-ridden winged animal."

Bush added: "I want these birds rounded up, tied down, and their throats slit."

Executive Order 1342A, which calls

see BIRD FLU page 280

TV-News Graphics Guy Gives Weatherman On-Air Surprise

OKLAHOMA CITY, OK—On the surface, the newsroom of local NBC affiliate KFOR appears to be quite serious. But that doesn't mean the *Live At Five* news team doesn't know how to have some fun from time to time, as viewers learned Monday night.

According to computer-graphic designer Dan Janney, the news broadcast team nearly lost its composure Monday, when his irreverent weather-map graphic went live during a segment by Channel 4 meteorologist Grant Johnson.

see GRAPHICS GUY page 281

Above: KFOR weatherman Grant Johnston gets an on-air surprise.

Record Oil Profits

Amid skyrocketing prices at the pump, the oil industry is reporting a record $35 billion in profits in the last financial quarter. What do *you* think?

"As a believer in 'trickle-down' economics, I know what a $35 billion profit means for me: a free Atlanta Falcons travel mug with every fill-up"

Francis Englund
Programmer

"They're probably going to use the profits to redouble that commitment to the environment we hear so much about."

William Oberst
Barrister

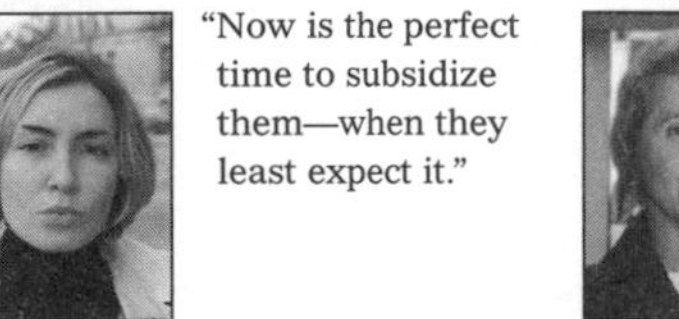

"Now is the perfect time to subsidize them—when they least expect it."

Lily Putnam
Systems Analyst

"I don't know who to be angrier with: the oil magnates who continue to get richer while the rest of us struggle to get by, or the uppermost strata of our earth's core."

Laurie Selmon
Nurse

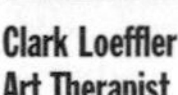

"We need an incisive political cartoon to take these robber barons down a notch."

Clark Loeffler
Art Therapist

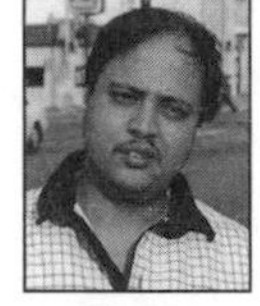

"Well it's better than when they reported those huge losses...wait, that never happened."

William Metz
Metallurgist

New Corporate Responsibility Laws
Several recent bills have passed that absolve corporations of liability if consumers are harmed by their products, and President Bush is expected to sign them into law. Here are some details of similar proposed legislation:
Camera manufacturers no longer held accountable for embarrassing intimate photos posted on Internet
Yes, Dear bill absolves CBS from responsibility of buying citizens new TV sets if beer mugs are flung through old ones in disgust
Automobile companies cannot be sued over explosion damages if car owner fills gas tank with volatile fluids
Walt Disney Company no longer responsible for what happens when you wish upon a star
Appliance manufacturers not liable if consumer fills empty refrigerator box with broken glass, then jumps in and slides box down steep hill
Slushee Corporation cannot be blamed for lowered sexual desire when product is accidentally spilled on lap
Webster's Dictionary protected from lawsuits charging that they've neglected to provide a clear-enough definition of word "frivolous"

America's Finest News Source.™

Herman Ulysses Zweibel
Founder

T. Herman Zweibel
Publisher Emeritus
J. Phineas Zweibel
Publisher
Maxwell Prescott Zweibel
Editor-In-Chief

I Plan To Take Full Advantage Of The Upcoming Q&A With Howie Mandel

When I first heard that the DVD box set of *Bobby's World* was being released, I couldn't imagine more exciting news. Little did I know that, later that day, I would learn that the hilarious comedian who created the show, Howie Mandel, would be making a personal appearance at my local Sam Goody. And what's more, there was going to be a question-and-answer session.

By Lewis Hodge

I knew I had to make a plan to maximize this once-in-a-lifetime opportunity.

It would be a privilege just to listen to Mr. Mandel speak in person, but to be able to openly address and benefit from the knowledge of the man whose voice graces both *Gremlins* movies? To tell you the truth, I am still not convinced that this so-called "Q&A" isn't one of the elaborate and sophisticated hidden-camera pranks Mr. Mandel is so fond of pulling and presenting on *The Tonight Show*.

In the presence of a celebrity, there is an air around them that is electric. In such an atmosphere, it is very easy to lose your composure. After all, this is the voice of Gizmo we're talking about! If I flubbed the opportunity to ask him about his craft, I'd be kicking myself for the rest of my life.

I already know what my first question is going to be. I'm going to ask whether he's okay with me addressing him as "Howie." Or if he would rather I call him "Mr. Mandel." Or even "Howard."

In the presence of a celebrity, there is an air around them that is electric. In such an atmosphere, it is very easy to lose your composure.

Now I find myself wishing that I had written down the dozens, possibly hundreds of questions I've had for Mr. Mandel over the years. I can't blame myself, though. How was I supposed to know that I would one day be presented with the forum in which to ask them? Hindsight is 20/20, I suppose.

Oh! I just remembered one! For my second question, I'm going to ask what it was like to portray the character of Dr. Wayne Fiscus in *St. Elsewhere*.

Maybe I should also ask him if, as a comedian, it's hard to play dramedy. Something like, "Mr. Mandel, I want to first thank you for coming today. It is a great honor to speak with you, sir. Secondly, you have done extensive dramedy work. I'm curious, do you see dramedy as an inhibition or as a refreshing change of pace?"

It might surprise you to learn that not everyone understands what a remarkable occasion this is. When I told Miriam that I had to cancel on our plans for Saturday, she nearly threw a fit. I tried to sit her down and explain why this was so important, but the more I said, the angrier she got. The sad thing is, it doesn't surprise me. Lately, we just seem to share less and less common ground.

It will be a privilege just to listen to Mr. Mandel speak, but to be able to benefit from the knowledge of the man whose voice graces both *Gremlins* movies?

I wonder if it would be too demanding to request that Mr. Mandel answer my question in the voice of Bobby, his curious, hyperactive child character. I believe he would comply. Oh sure, he would probably have a sense of humor about that.

Questions aside, there are more practical matters to plan. Like, there will probably be a few thousand people there, and to get a seat, I should plan to arrive well before the store opens.

I should wear my orange sweater, too. That way, Mr. Mandel will have no trouble identifying me. He can simply say, "You, there, in the orange."

As amazing as this opportunity is for a fan like me, I'm sure Mr. Mandel is looking forward to the Q&A as well. After all, this is a chance for him to get the truth out there at last. For example, I bet he'd be happy to settle the matter of his favorite Muppet Babies voice once and for all. Or to set the record straight about A Fine Mess. In fact, that's probably why he agreed to do the Q&A in the first place.

One thing does worry me, however. That sign at Sam Goody said the Q&A would last only 15 minutes. That means I will have time for one, maybe two questions at the most.

I may never learn the reason why Mr. Mandel chose to shave his head. Ø

LOCAL

Night On Town Fails To Rekindle Fading Business Relationship

AUSTIN, TX—Hopes of reviving a once-thriving business partnership were dashed Monday when a night on the town only served to remind local entrepreneurs Terry Argento, 33, and B.J. Dreschler, 37, why they initially parted.

"We had to face the music—B.J. and I can never do business the way we used to," said Argento, vice president of Argento Homes, a manufacturer of modular housing serving the greater Austin area since 1967. "We've grown apart, and Monday night clarified that for both of us. It's sad, but at this point, we have nothing to offer each other."

"Teaming with Terry was the single greatest entrepreneurial experience of my life," said Dreschler, who still keeps all of Argento's signed invoices. "Even though our partnership cooled over two years ago, not a day goes by when I don't think of it."

Dreschler, owner of Dreschler Plumbing Supply And Installation, was Argento's sole supplier of plumbing equipment for "five terrific, unforgettable years."

"Teaming with Terry was the single greatest entrepreneurial experience of my life," said Dreschler, who still keeps all of Argento's signed invoices. "Even though our partnership cooled over two years ago, not a day goes by when I don't think of it... but Monday night was a mistake."

Both men warmly recalled their early transactions.

see RELATIONSHIP page 281

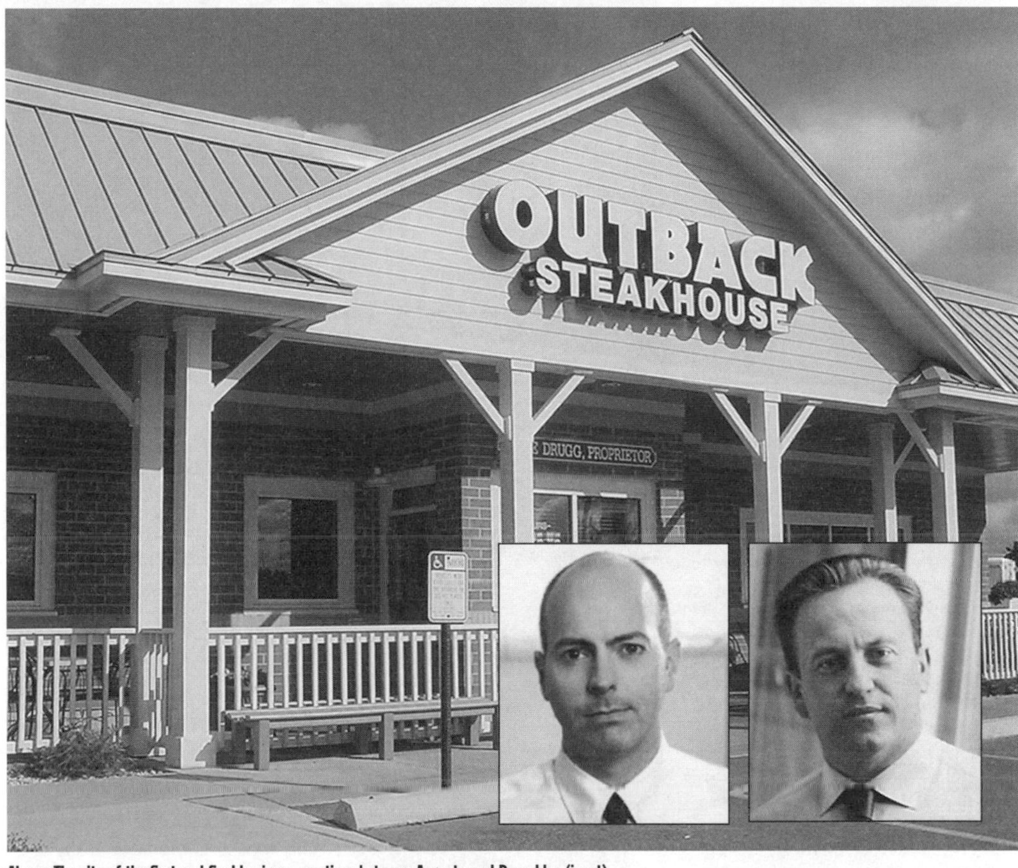

Above: The site of the first and final business meetings between Argento and Dreschler (inset).

NEWS IN BRIEF

This So Typical Of Hemophiliac

TEMPE, AZ—Friends of Joshua Melman agreed Monday that the behavior displayed at the WildSlide Waterpark Sunday was "utterly typical" of the 19-year-old hemophiliac. "Before we can even go on one ride, Josh trips on his flip-flop and scuffs his toe on the cement," said Alex Schaeffer, who has had several outings ruined by Melman's congenital disease. "Would it kill the guy to clot once in a while?" Schaeffer added that the water-park debacle was worse than the time they played paintball, but not as bad as the lap-dance incident.

New Custard Could Cause Worldwide Flandemic

ATLANTA—A recently discovered strain of custard could cause a worldwide flandemic, Centers For Dessert Control warned Monday. "We are warning people who come into contact with milk, egg yolks, sugar, and whole vanilla beans that they are at risk of concocting this custard," CDC director Paul Liddleston said. "All reports indicate that it is extremely non-resistible." Liddleston said the government's present reserve of dried tapioca is "useless" in combating a flandemic, and until a more effective vaccine is created, "the proof will be in the putting of containment teams in high-risk areas."

'Scooter' Libby Wishes He'd Ditched Nickname Before Media Coverage

WASHINGTON, DC—I. Lewis "Scooter" Libby, the indicted former chief of staff to Vice President Dick Cheney, wishes he had stopped answering to his nickname before it was featured so prominently in the news, he confided Monday. "Scooter's fine if it's just the president or Mr. Cheney," said Libby, whose involvement in the Valerie Plame case has made his name notorious. "But when I see it on CNN, I want to hide." If implicated in the Plame leak, Libby could face up to 30 years in a facility where he would almost certainly be given a new nickname.

Hanukkah Decorations Being Defaced Earlier Every Year

NEW YORK—A report released Monday by the Anti-Defamation League confirmed the widely held perception that Hanukkah decorations are being vandalized earlier every season. "Today, we're seeing Stars of David spray-painted with swastikas before the leaves have even fallen," said ADL spokesman Avi Mendenhall. "Our research shows that, even as recently as a decade ago, a menorah wouldn't be toppled over until well after Thanksgiving." The report noted that many shopping malls have, in recent years, begun playing anti-Semitic carols just days after Halloween.

Floral Arrangement At Funeral Talked About More Than Deceased

CHICAGO—Although Ernest Quarles was a reasonably beloved member of his family, the floral arrangements at his Sunday funeral service dominated conversation during the post-funeral luncheon at the home of Quarles' niece, Carol Sands. "I had a nice talk with the pastor about how Ernie looked so natural amid all those pretty mums, tulips, and baby's breath," Sands said. "They were very nice. Not too showy, but still really quite pretty." Family members agreed that it was a tragedy that Ernest went the way he did, and that the Hawaiian daisies were probably just thrown out after the ceremony. Ø

BIRD FLU from page 277

for the annihilation of the bald eagle, specifies that each carcass shall be wrapped in a single American flag, doused with gasoline, and burned.

"This order was developed with the help of my top science advisers," Bush said. "We can all trust that their wisdom, manifested by this bold, eagle-killing initiative, will protect us from any deadly bird-related diseases."

The order, written by members of Bush's Council of Advisers on Science and Technology, nullifies the 1973 Endangered Species Act and the 1940 Bald Eagle Protection Act. It will be overseen by the Department of the Interior, which will work closely with state natural-resource agencies and National Guard units to ensure that the bald eagle threat is eliminated.

"This order was developed with the help of my top science advisers," Bush said. "We can all trust that their wisdom, manifested by this bold, eagle-killing initiative, will protect us from any deadly bird-related diseases."

Secretary of State Condoleezza Rice will meet with the Canadian prime minister and Mexican president next week to discuss eradication efforts for bald eagle populations in their countries. The Department of the Interior's deadline for bald eagle annihilation is July 4, 2006.

According to White House sources, Bush is adopting a hands-off attitude regarding the methodology of eagle slaughtering. Telling advisers that he would prefer that the eagles have their throats slit for "humane purposes," the president said he is willing to allow wildlife officials to exercise their own judgment. According U.S. Fish and Wildlife Service Director "Whooping" Dale Hall, the killing strategies are many and varied.

"Bald eagles may not be as imposing as, say, bears or wolves, but they are surprisingly difficult to kill," Hall said. "We can blow them off their perches with air rifles, stun them with ball-peen hammers, or break their wings, beaks, and necks, but still, some survive."

Hall continued: "I'm encouraging officials on the local level to utilize 'certain kill' methods, such as wrapping the eagle in radioactive waste and burying it upside-down in an old-growth forest."

Above: In a photo opportunity, President Bush blow-torches several pinned-down eagles.

Hall urged Boy Scout troops to join in the effort by ferreting out eagle nests and smashing the eggs underfoot.

The FWS estimates the population of the bald eagle, which the Second Continental Congress designated as the national bird in 1782, to be roughly 20,000 in the lower 48 states, with an additional 35,000 in Alaska. Tuesday afternoon, the FWS elevated the bald eagle's endangered-species status from "stable" to "severely threatened," its most serious designation.

U.S. Fish and Wildlife Service Director Dale Hall urged Boy Scout troops to join in the effort by ferreting out eagle nests and smashing the eggs underfoot.

Administration critics have suggested that the president's plan is too narrow in scope, and leaves Americans susceptible to contact with a wide variety of other dangerous birds.

"What about less prominent but far more abundant fowl common to residential areas, such as bluebirds, cardinals, or geese—shouldn't they die, too?" said Democratic Party strategist Elaine Quigley, appearing on MSNBC's *Hardball*. "Benjamin Franklin once said that the wild turkey, not the bald eagle, should be the emblematic bird of America. Why aren't we executing those, too?"

The Office Of The White House Counsel, which oversees the usage of all executive-branch insignias, is expected to approve a new eagle-free presidential seal as early as next week. ⌀

CONSTITUTION from page 277

destroyed by a nail bomb, described the constitution as "a powerful symbol of Iraqi peace and freedom."

"The impressive 64 percent voter turnout for the democratic referendum, only marginally surpassed by the turnout for the ensuing riots, was a very positive achievement," Shandal said. "Iraq is well on its way to the peace and tranquility all democracies inherently enjoy."

When the ceremony ended, U.S. military personnel were dispatched to the historic scene, both to rescue stray pieces of the original document and to tend to Iraqi civilians critically injured during the hand-to-hand combat and small-arms fire that took place following the document's ratification.

"We were unable to recover the original document from the debris," U.S. Army Maj. Jason Brock said. "However, charred, tattered remnants indicate that Iraq has established a four-year parliament, which marks its full emergence as a democratic Western ally."

Brock added: "I think there was also something in there about 'tending to the concerns of women's rights,' but I'm not 100 percent sure, because that part was soaked in blood."

Extant pieces of the original document, found under severed limbs and dusty rubble, indicate that the constitution includes inspiring phrases such as "principles of equality," "free from sectarianism, racism, and discrimination," and "looking with confidence to a peaceful future."

Talabani said he was "heartened" by the ratification, adding that, although the physical document was destroyed in the violent events following its signing, the "principles and ideals set forth will persevere."

"The impressive 64 percent voter turnout for the democratic referendum, only marginally surpassed by the turnout for the ensuing riots, was a very positive achievement," Shandal said.

A large portion of the eloquent preamble, which vowed that the Iraqi people would learn from the mistakes of the past, was discovered seared onto a slab of smoldering flesh atop an ambulance which had been catapulted through the entrance of the convention center by a minibus explosion. ⌀

ON TV TONIGHT

Broadcast Networks	8:00		9:00		10:00	
ABC	Wife Swap: Special Victims Unit		Desperate Housewives: Malibu Nights	Wednesday Night Wishing There Was Football	Basically Judging Amy, But She's President	
CBS	Two And A Half Jokes		The Ghost Decorators		In The Sauna With Andy Rooney	
NBC	The Apprentice: Cobbler	The Apprentice: Pope	The Apprentice: Oreck Vacuum Guy	Clinging To Joey	Law And Order: SUV	
UPN	America's Next Topless Model		The Yell-At-Denise-Richards Show	Just Happy To Be On TV	The Great American Syndication Hour	
FOX	So You Think Celebrities Can Dance?		So You Think Ex-Buffy Cast Members Can Dance?		Kiss Your Favorite Show Goodbye!	
Cable						
Spike TV	Dude, Check This Shit Out!	Dude, Did You See That Shit?	Axe Body Spray Theater			EHUURRGH! Masculinity's Greatest Dumps
Comedy Central	Let's Ineptly Clean Eugene Levy's House!		Fruits In Suits	Chappelle's Rerun	Not Anywhere Near Late Enough With Adam Carolla	
IFC	Parker Posey: A Retrospective		Bob Balaban's Celebrity Backgammon	Talking About Rudy With Jon Favreau	Paint Drying (1998): Lili Taylor, Martin Donovan	
FUSE	Hip Hop Party	Hip Hop Brawl	Hip Hop Arrests	Metal: The Yoga Of Anger	Go To Bed, It's The '80s Video Show	
LOGO	The TooGay Show	The Man Show (Rerun)	How Homosexuals Should Act	How Heterosexuals Should Act	Soap, But Only Episodes With Billy Crystal	Queer Eye For The Even Queerer Guy

GRAPHICS GUY from page 277

"It's more my style to stay behind the scenes," Janney said. "But every once in a while, I have to admit, it's fun to push the envelope."

Janney added: "I like to give the crew a good laugh."

In the graphic, which he designed

"*Live At Five* has a reputation for having an offbeat sense of humor, and that's a part of its appeal."

for the five-day extended forecast chart that concludes the weather segment, Janney replaced the network's "sun in sunshades" graphic with the head of veteran KFOR sports anchor Bob Barry Sr. wearing sunshades and surrounded by a halo of golden rays.

"I had the idea, and I told my assistant Jennifer Sabin about it, and she thought it was hysterical, so we spent about 10 minutes putting it together on our lunch break," Janney said. "To our good fortune, the weekend portion of the chart forecasted sunny weather, so the gag got high visibility."

Janney added: "It had the guys in the control room in stitches before air time. I begged [newscast director] Jim [Underwood] not to tell Grant about it, and thankfully he agreed. He knows how to play a joke."

Underwood, who has directed local KFOR programming for 18 years and produces the Sunday morning current-events roundtable *Think About It With Neil Clover*, enthusiastically agreed to televise Janney's graphic, calling it "an amusing change of pace." He even authorized camera operator Mike Bethke to capture the reaction of lead anchor Chuck Bartlett in a highly unusual cutaway from the forecast graphic.

"The usual 'sun wearing the shades' graphic is cute—we still get letters about it from viewers," Underwood said. "But replacing that sun with Bob Barry? That was a hoot."

Underwood added: "*Live At Five* has a reputation for having an offbeat sense of humor, and that's a part of its appeal."

According to Janney, Johnston does not normally look at the monitor while introducing the extended forecast and was initially confused by the titters coming from the camera operators. When he saw the monitor, he broke into a wide grin, chuckled, and said, "And there's Bob Barry, KFOR's original golden boy."

"It was a wonderful ad-lib," Sabin said. "I'll bet most of the home audience thought he was in on the joke from the start. But he wasn't. He's that good."

Said Janney: "The killer part was when Grant threw to Chuck, and Chuck sang a couple of bars of 'You Are The Sunshine Of My Life.' Practically everyone in the studio was dying. But Grant didn't miss a beat. He comes right back with, 'Aw, Chuck, I didn't know you cared.' By that point, everybody on set was in stitches."

Janney has received positive feedback for his shenanigan, including e-mails of praise from viewers. Yet, when asked about doing something similar in the future, Janney became coy.

"If we did something silly every day, we'd risk losing our edge," he said. "But who knows when something like that will happen again. You'll just have to keep watching *Live At Five* to find out." Ø

RELATIONSHIP from page 279

"Once, I wanted to talk Terry into ordering a shipment of cast-iron bathtubs for his more upscale pre-fabs, but I wasn't sure he'd go for it," Dreschler said. "So I started to say, 'You know, you could do worse than acrylic,' and Terry said, 'But Argento homes are built to last, and one way to convince our customers of that is to go with the cast iron.' I was in heaven."

Yet, as is often the case with exclusive business relationships, the good times didn't last, and after several tumultuous years in business, the two ultimately dissolved their partnership in 2003.

"It wasn't the smoothest parting," Dreschler said. "I'll admit that I was angry at Terry for going to a larger firm, but we were both growing and changing, and I'd be deceiving myself if I didn't admit I was getting bored with selling him bathroom and kitchen fixtures."

Once they allowed their exclusive partnership to expire, the two men interacted little outside of holiday cards and the occasional phone call regarding an old contract. After three years of limited contact, it was Argento who proposed that the two meet for dinner and drinks at the Outback Steakhouse, the site of their first casual business meeting, to discuss a new partnership.

Dreschler said he was "stunned" by Argento's invitation and accepted it "a little too eagerly." Yet, minutes after the call, "reality set in."

Said Dreschler: "I was hoping he didn't want to reunite, because it wasn't going to happen. There was too much baggage. Still, I was dying to find out who he was buying sinks from."

Both men characterized the night as a disappointment. According to Argento, long, awkward silences plagued the meeting, even as a song came on the jukebox that often played on the radio when Dreschler installed sewage pumps on Argento's properties. Argento said he "racked his brain" for collaborative projects to

"It wasn't the smoothest parting," Dreschler said. "I'll admit that I was angry at Terry for going to a larger firm, but we were both growing and changing, and I'd be deceiving myself if I didn't admit I was getting bored with selling him bathroom and kitchen fixtures."

propose while Dreschler silently sipped his beer.

"We went to Thank-Cue Billiards after dinner and played a few rounds, but really, even though I hadn't seen B.J. in ages, I might as well have been shooting pool with my heating-and-cooling contractor or my vinyl-siding supplier," Argento said. "I felt nothing."

Dreschler said that, although he felt no real hostility toward Argento, lingering bitterness over the non-renewal of his contract tainted the evening.

see RELATIONSHIP page 282

COMMUNITY VOICES

There's A Nude Sheriff In Town

Howdy, pardners. The name's Gunderson. Sheriff Bill Gunderson. You might remember me from the unattirin' at Black Gulch or the full moon at high noon. That's right, one and the same. Well, I got a message for you all: If'n you're a wrongdoer what dons a single stitch, you best mosey along. You heard me right: There's a nude sheriff in town, and he's gonna stay put.

By Sheriff Bill Gunderson

Taking off my clothes and enforcing the law has been my business for some 20 years now. I learned shootin' and crook-catchin' at the side of my pappy, Bare-Bottomed Jake, the nudest shot in the West. Leastaways, he was, until some varmints ambushed him for his bounty money just as he was leaving the outhouse. As he lay with his bottom to the sand, before he passed into the great ranch in the sky, he asked me in his dyin' breath to carry on both his noble work and his naturalist lifestyle. Ever since that fateful night, I've been a lawman of one sort or another, and I've kept the homespun off my backside. No sir, you'll never see no buckskin on this foreskin.

Now, don't turn tail and skedaddle when y'all see me comin'. I'm here to make sure things run more orderly-like, and I encourage you all to go on about your business as usual. True, I do things a little different from your last chap-slappin' sheriff, but I said it before and I'll say it many times again: There may be a Code Of The West that we all live by, but last I checked, there wasn't no Dress Code Of The West.

If y'all got nothin' to hide, well sir, I got no beef with you 'tall. Yep, I do pack quite a hogleg there. Hopefully, I won't have to use it, but if push comes to shove, I'm a straight shooter.

I encourage you all to go on about your business as usual.

As I've been settling in, I've taken to standing on the clock-tower balcony atop the jailhouse, observin' as I do the happenings in town. Know what I see in the eyes of the townsfolk with the guts to meet my gaze? Fear and envy. Well, I pledge that I'll clean up this town right direct. Unlike that last sheriff, you won't see my behind glued to a saloon stool, a-starin' off at nothing. Naw, this naked hombre is real an' in the flesh, an' you'll find him in a saloon only when he's roustin' out the drunks and cardsharps.

I take my job as a lawman real serious-like. I already made the rounds, checkin' out the general store, shootin' the breeze with ol' Gus, the shopkeep. Why, y'all should've seen his eyes when I offered him cash fer that li'l vial o' anti-chafin' liniment. Other sheriffs may have taken advantage of store credit, but this one believes in paying his way. Once I took my leave o' Gus, I just stood in the town square, hands on my hips, lettin' the Santa Ana winds cool my nethers.

True, I do things a little different from your last chap-slappin' sheriff, but I said it before and I'll say it many times again: There may be a Code Of The West that we all live by, but last I checked, there wasn't no Dress Code Of The West.

If'n you're thinkin' to buy me off, well, think again. I ain't a crooked lawman. I got few needs, and even fewer places to put bribe money, so best put that notion out yer head. There's a mess o' corruption in this town, and I aim to expose it, an' myself.

Back yonder in Rattlesnake Junction, a clever li'l feller no higher'n a hitchin' post pointed out that I ain't a hunnert percent nude, an' dang me if he weren't right. This here 10-gallon hat is pert near the only thing I'll wear. Got it back in San Antone. Keeps the sun off my eyes, and I can use it to cover up when I'm in the presence of the minister's wife. Oh, an' my holster too, but that don't count none. That's more of an accessory. 'Course, when I'm a-courtin' Miss Modesty, that's when I put on my Sunday kerchief.

If y'all need me, y'all know where I can be found. If'n I'm not down at the jailhouse, I'll be wherever there's injustice, or in a nice warm spot of sun, with my legs up on a stump, an' my hat over my eyes. That's how I relax, y'see. It soothes the mind and warms the testes, and when you're fightin' wrongdoers naked, that's the best tonic for an occupied mind. ⌀

HOROSCOPES

Your Horoscope

By Lloyd Schumner Sr.
Retired Machinist and
A.A.P.B.-Certified Astrologer

Aries: (March 21–April 19)
Next time, you will know better than to attend the International Maim All The Aries Festival just because some band you really like is playing the main stage.

Taurus: (April 20–May 20)
Toddlers will persistently try to befriend you this week, utterly failing to comprehend that you suffer from an acute case of skeletal dysplasias.

Gemini: (May 21–June 21)
A bum will mistake your abstract lower-back tattoo for a scratch-off lottery ticket and gouge you to the spine, but on the bright side, he'll win 50 bucks.

Cancer: (June 22–July 22)
Yes, there is a saying that we always hurt the ones we love, but it doesn't mention anything about using a radial arm saw.

Leo: (July 23–Aug. 22)
You'll be blessed with the arrival of a brand-new little life this week, although you will be rather disturbed by the way it crawls out of the toilet and begins caterwauling.

Virgo: (Aug. 23–Sept. 22)
You'll have a hard time convincing the Treasury Department that you weren't attempting to counterfeit $20 bills, but simply trying to suggest some very minor changes.

Libra: (Sept. 23–Oct. 23)
Patrons in the Louvre Museum will get an unexpected laugh this week when a runaway Citroen decapitates you, launching your severed head three blocks to land perfectly on to the top of the *Venus de Milo*.

Scorpio: (Oct. 24–Nov. 21)
You'll lose the use of your left arm this week when your city uses rather draconian eminent-domain laws to commandeer it for garbage-hauling and tree-removal duties.

Sagittarius: (Nov. 22–Dec. 21)
Although the mystical Rainbow Serpent isn't happy about sharing his symbology with the gay-rights movement, you should still be very, very careful about making fun of his lesbian sister Jen.

Capricorn: (Dec. 22–Jan. 19)
Theater owners will probably look the other way if you want to sneak candy, soda, and snacks into the movies, but if you really want to carry the stuff in your colon, no one can stop you.

Aquarius: (Jan. 20–Feb. 18)
The stars indicate that you will receive 15 percent off your next Denny's breakfast if you mention this special celestial message.

Pisces: (Feb. 19–March 20)
Your daughter's attention-seeking rendition of "I'm A Little Teapot" will backfire this week when it dawns on you that you'd much rather have a teapot than a daughter. ⌀

RELATIONSHIP from page 281

"I never really got past that whole thing, and it got so that I just wanted the night to end," Dreschler said. "Like, what was the point of it all? Where do I fit in this guy's professional life, and he in mine?"

At the end of the evening, the men bade each other awkward goodbyes, knowing that their business relationship, once so full of high hopes and expectations, had come to an end.

"For the first time, I feel some closure," Dreschler said. "I thought I needed a partnership to feel fulfilled, but the night on the town with Terry helped me realize that I'm happy exactly where I am."

Argento, meanwhile, said he had "nothing but the deepest respect" for Dreschler's professional abilities, and wished him "all the best."

"B.J. is an incredible man to do business with," Argento said. "I honestly hope that one day, he finds that sweetheart deal he truly deserves."

"For the first time, I feel some closure," Dreschler said. "I thought I needed a partnership to feel fulfilled, but the night on the town with Terry helped me realize that I'm happy exactly where I am."

Tearing up, he added: "I'm sorry. I didn't think I would get emotional." ⌀

the ONION®

VOLUME 41 ISSUE 45 AMERICA'S FINEST NEWS SOURCE™ 10–16 NOVEMBER 2005

NEWS

SuicideGirls.com Put On 24-Hour Watch

see HEALTH page 2C

Area Lightning Rod A Lightning Rod For Lightning

see LOCAL 3A

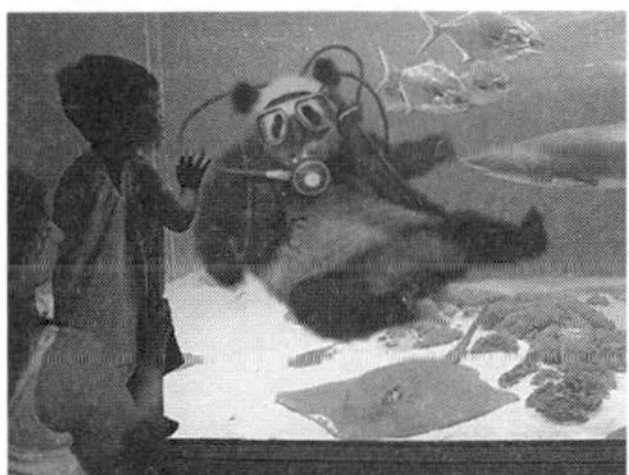

Chicago's Shedd Aquarium Admits Panda Exhibit A Ghastly Mistake

see NATIONAL page 3E

Stats Professor Will Bet You

see EDUCATION 14D

STATshot

A look at the numbers that shape your world.

Top Safety Placards

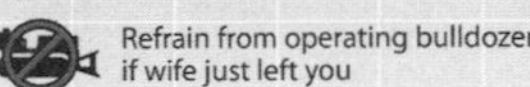

Refrain from operating bulldozer if wife just left you

Irradiated fuel rods: Picnic at your own risk

Caution: Monkey may run for mayor at any time

If you see an unattended package at the Boise Greyhound depot, notify Bob at the barbershop

THE ONION • $2.00 US • $3.00 CAN

SPECIAL REPORT

The Death Of Rosa Parks

'Now We Can Finally Put Civil Rights Behind Us'

DETROIT—Nearly 50 years ago, Rosa Parks made history by refusing to give her seat to a white man on a segregated public bus in Montgomery, AL. This week, following the passing of the woman known as "the mother of the civil-rights movement," Americans from every walk of life-regardless of race, gender, or creed-can finally put the subject of racial equality behind them, once and for all.

"During today's service, America not only bade farewell to a seamstress from Alabama," President Bush said at a special GOP fundraiser Monday evening, "America buried the idea of civil rights itself."

Bush added: "Today, that long-ago chapter of American history is slammed tightly shut, never to be reopened."

see PARKS page 286

U.S. Dollar Slips Against Canadian Acorn

NEW YORK—The U.S. dollar touched a one-month low against the Canadian acorn Monday, continuing a downward trend that began in 2004 with the announcement of the imminent retirement of Federal Reserve Chairman Alan Greenspan and increasing inflation worries among investors.

At the close of trading Monday, the Canadian acorn bought USD $1.1660, up from $1.1593 Friday.

Although the value of the U.S. dollar has fallen steadily against the Lithuanian nail and the Estonian crab apple since early this year, many financial experts had pre-

see DOLLAR page 287

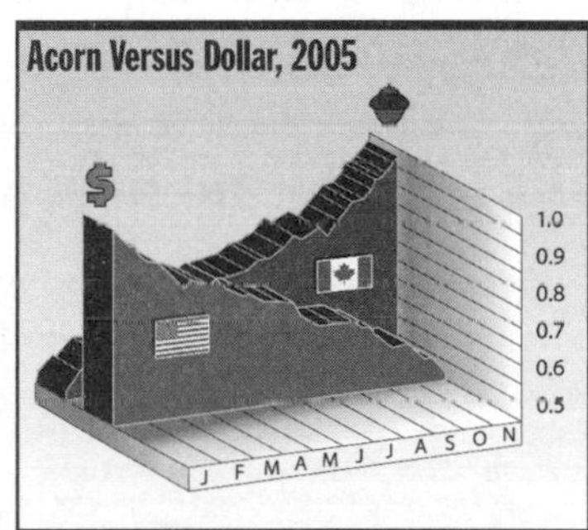

Metal Council Convenes To Discuss 'Metal Hand Sign' Abuse

VATNAJÖKULL GLACIER, ICELAND—In an emergency session Tuesday, members of the Supreme Metal Council strongly condemned the increasing use of the metal hand sign in lay society, claiming that its meaning has become perverted by overuse.

"The metal sign, or 'sign of the goat,' has all but lost its impact as a token of respectful recognition for something truly 'rocking' or 'metal,'" SMC president Terence "Geezer" Butler said. According to Butler, members are upset that their sacred gesture is being used to acknowledge and celebrate "favorable but clearly non-metal events."

"We have all heard the reports of people using it to greet their in-laws, or after starting their lawn mowers with a single pull," Butler said. "But re-

see METAL page 287

Above: Elders of the Supreme Metal Council examine amateur-video evidence of what they are calling "a worrisome trend."

Rioting In France

The French police have taken 22 young people into custody for questioning after more than a week of riots in a northeastern suburb of Paris. What do *you* think?

Donald Teague
Brick Mason

"Paris is burning? Wow. The French have done to themselves what the Nazis, the Kaiser, and most of the civilized world never quite found a way to do."

Sylvere Gavronsky
Psychologist

"Well, I rioted in Paris in May 1968, and I can tell you, the reasons for our riots were far more sophisticated."

Kate Myer
Real-Estate Clerk

"How romantic! Idealistic peasant revolutionaries stealing loaves of bread. What? Angry black people blowing up cars? Wow, France sure changed since I graduated high school."

Connie Low
Optician

"If people start rioting every time a Frenchman ignores someone, we're really in trouble."

Ryan Valerie
Dairy Farmer

"This is the most exciting thing to happen in France since that red balloon got loose."

Bob Tierney
Systems Analyst

"Well, it's nice to see that Muslim youths are for once turning to rioting and not terrorism."

Canceled Iraqi Reconstruction Projects

Due to the unexpectedly high costs of security, the U.S. has been forced to abort a large number of Iraqi reconstruction efforts. Here are some of the abandoned projects:

- Everything in Iraqi Museum except gift shop
- Elementary school that was supposed to be built next to nearly completed Donald H. Rumsfeld Luxury Hotel & Airport
- Sumerian Times, an *Epic Of Gilgamesh*-themed dinner-theater chain
- Everything not involving building materials such as nitrate-based fertilizer and lots of diesel fuel
- Rebuilding of Bush family ego canceled following unending series of setbacks
- World's biggest chair
- $96 million state-of-the-art network of hospitals, to be replaced with more cost-effective cemeteries
- Peace

America's Finest News Source.™

Herman Ulysses Zweibel
Founder

T. Herman Zweibel
Publisher Emeritus
J. Phineas Zweibel
Publisher
Maxwell Prescott Zweibel
Editor-In-Chief

I'm Very Interested In Hearing Some Half-Baked Theories

As an ill-informed pseudo-intellectual with a particular interest in the unverifiable, I'm always on the lookout for some partially thought out misinformation. So, if you have an uninformed solution to a dilemma that doesn't actually exist, don't bother double-checking your information. I'm all ears.

By Roberta Foit

However, I must warn you: If you want to convince me of anything, you better be prepared to back up your claims with rumor, circumstantial evidence, or hard-to-make-out photographic proof. I may also need friend-of-a-friend corroboration or several signed testimonials all written in the same unmistakably spidery handwriting. I'm a quasi-critical-thinker. Things have to add up more or less in my head before I let myself be taken in by some baloney story.

Take Atlantis, for example. When I first heard about this lost civilization, I was suspicious to say the least. But then someone made a good point: Prove that it didn't exist. I was hard-pressed to find a comeback to that.

But if Atlantis really did exist, then where did it go? It couldn't have just disappeared without an unreasonable explanation. I was about to give up on the whole matter when suddenly it hit me: It probably washed away, and it's too deep underwater for scientists to find it. All it takes is a little supposition mixed with critical theorizing and you can easily stumble on a tenuous half-truth that really makes you think.

I'll only listen to your elaborate webs of presumption and hearsay if you promise to veer unexpectedly and pointlessly off course at every opportunity. Prose density is part of what makes a half-baked theory fascinating.

Over time, I've also learned that slapdash research is key before jumping to any conclusion. While I've always postulated the existence of gnomes, it wasn't until I researched the topic on AskJeeves.com that I realized it's a well-documented medical condition.

As important as research is, it's all about common sense in the end. If you can't cool your apartment by leaving the refrigerator open, how's it keeping all that produce fresh? Think about it. If you can't really read the world's great works of literature in only five minutes using a system peddled on TV, how do you explain that gentleman on the infomercial who aces those tests? Would extraterrestrials travel millions of light years just to abduct a non-trustworthy human for their series of intrusive tests? Yes.

If you want to convince me, you better be prepared to back up your claims with rumor or hard-to-make-out photographic proof.

And there's a reason liars like James Randi have never been anally probed.

Now, if you have a half-baked theory that you'd like to disclose, please be so kind as to skirt around the issue. I'll only listen to your elaborate webs of presumption and hearsay if you promise to veer unexpectedly and pointlessly off course at every opportunity. Prose density is part of what makes a half-baked theory fascinating.

Only last week, my friend Janet gave me a book that teaches how, through a diet of salmon and romaine lettuce, you can shave 20 years off your appearance. However, before we got to the hard-core salmon-and-lettuce, face-lifting theory, I was taken through a series of anecdotes, solicited testimonials, and long-winded circular logic proving the author's qualifications by citing the medical establishment's fear of his simple brilliance. It was an eye-opener.

I encourage people endowed with a gift for half-baked theories to inform as many unsuspecting strangers as possible. That's how I'm most interested in being exposed to shaky new ideas. At the bus station, on the street corners, wherever strikes your fancy. If you don't have the courage to approach people in this way, I recommend a stiff drink or a lifetime of crippling mental illness.

Only then will we continue to safeguard the free exchange of erroneous fallacy so vital to maintaining a free-thinking, uneducated society. Thank you. Ø

LOCAL

Redbook Reporter Refuses To Disclose Source Of Recipe

ATLANTA—A federal judge said Monday that magazine writer Nancy Steuber will be held in contempt of court if she continues to withhold the source of a recipe for maple-glazed ham published in *Redbook* magazine in February.

Judge Antonio Pelicore said that Steuber has until Thursday to reveal the name of the "culinary miracle worker" responsible for the recipe, which was included in a *Redbook* feature titled "Easter With Zip."

"It is the opinion of the court that this is the most devastatingly succulent ham to come across our docket in a very long time," said Pelicore, enjoying a sandwich made of leftovers. "The state has a vested interest in learning the identity of the person responsible for a dish of this mouth-watering magnitude."

Pelicore added: "I'll ask you again, Ms. Steuber. Where did you find this amazing recipe?"

Steuber, two-time winner of the Pulitzer Prize for recipe reporting in

see REPORTER page 286

"The state has a vested interest in learning the identity of the person responsible for a dish of this mouth-watering magnitude."

Above: Steuber takes a stand for journalistic ethics outside the Atlanta Federal Courthouse Monday.

NEWS IN BRIEF

Bird Arthritis Epidemic Largely Ignored

GENEVA—Officials from the World Health Organization remain relatively unconcerned by the rise in cases of bird arthritis, a degenerative joint disease found in birds. "We are aware of the existence of avian osteoarthritis, but have chosen to focus on more immediate threats," WHO Director-General Lee Jong-Wook said Monday, after several common teals were found doddering about a pond in southern Wales. "Most severely infected birds are too creaky and stiff to spread the disease very far." Experts say this is the least alarming public-health risk since the 1953 breakout of swine bursitis.

Wife Always Dragging Husband Into Her Marital Problems

HOUSTON—Banker Robert "Rob Boy" Grelman expressed annoyance with his wife Janet Monday, saying she consistently involves him in her marital problems. "Every day, it's, 'Oh God, I'm married to someone who doesn't understand me,' or, 'Bob, do you think you could pick up after yourself?'" Grelman said. "Don't get me wrong—I have marriage problems of my own—but I don't know what she wants me to do about hers." Grelman added that his children, following their mother's example, have lately attempted to drag him into their family problems.

Okie Hears There's Sam's Club Work In New Mexico

TULSA, OK—Day laborer Cal Thornton, driven from the Wal-Mart where his family worked the stockroom for generations, has heard tell of Sam's Club work in New Mexico. "They say they need 17 guys to unload pallets of toilet paper, baby food, and canned peaches in Las Cruces," Thornton said. "Word is, they got cans of peaches in New Mexico so big, you got to use two hands to lift 'em." Thornton loaded his family and few belongings into the cab of his rusted pickup truck and began the migration Tuesday.

Faith Healer Loses Patient During Routine Miracle

WAYCROSS, GA—A routine laying-on of hands ended in a fatal cardiac embolism for a worshiper at the One, True, Glorious, Excruciated, And Risen Christ Traveling Gospel Church Sunday. "Losing a fellow Christian is always the hardest part of this job," attending faith healer Harlon Pearcey said. "I invoked the name of the Holy Trinity to drive the sickness out from the poor sinner's heart, but sadly, a blockage in the sinner's pulmonary artery stopped God's love, and much blood, from getting through." The American Faith-Healing Association issued a statement saying that Pearcey followed trinity-invocation and snake-handling guidelines during the procedure.

Cameron Crowe To Release Only Soundtracks

LOS ANGELES—Explaining that his movies were but a small step in the pursuit of a career he has always dreamed about, *Almost Famous* director Cameron Crowe announced Monday that he is retiring from filmmaking to focus exclusively on soundtracks. "For me, the moving image has become redundant, and I believe that I can more effectively tell stories with carefully chosen music," said Crowe, backed by Electric Light Orchestra's "Do Ya." Crowe's first soundtrack, *Walking With Headphones*, will begin compilation later this winter for a summer release, with the soundtrack's soundtrack available on Polydor Records. Ø

PARKS from page 283

Alabama State Senator Hank Erwin, one of the hundreds of emotional guests at Bush's $5,000-a-plate dinner, proposed a toast, saying, "If I may paraphrase the words of Dr. Martin Luther King… 'I am free at last, free at last-thank God almighty, I'm free at

It is often difficult for young people to understand the segregated United States of the mid-20th century, when black citizens often lived in poverty, had substandard housing, were given poor-quality public educations, and were disenfranchised as voters. With the passing of Parks and the fight for racial equality that she symbolized, such subjects are now relics of a bygone era.

last to stop thinking about civil rights.'"

It is often difficult for young people to understand the segregated United States of the mid-20th century, when black citizens often lived in poverty, had substandard housing, were given poor-quality public educations, and were disenfranchised as voters. With the passing of Parks and the fight for racial equality that she symbolized, such subjects are now relics of a bygone era.

Above: Rosa Parks (center), whose death marks the end of the civil-rights struggle in America.

In honor of Parks, Congress agreed Monday to table all civil-rights bills currently under deliberation and turn instead to the passing of non-binding resolutions. Additionally, judges across the country are throwing out hundreds of outdated civil-rights cases clogging federal and state courts.

Organizations both private and public are doing their part to usher out the painful era during which Americans fought for racial justice.

The Smithsonian's National Museum Of American History announced Tuesday that they have canceled a December exhibition that would have been titled "The Stories They Were Told: Selma Remembers." The History Channel is also helping the nation to

In honor of Parks, Congress agreed Monday to table all civil-rights bills currently under deliberation and turn instead to the passing of non-binding resolutions.

move on, with a weeklong series devoted to the Apache helicopter.

With racial inequality no longer part of the national dialogue, the NAACP is being urged to focus on new problems, such as breast cancer.

Michael Lomax, president of the United Negro College Fund, said, "Our organization is considering the proposal, put forth by our colleagues in Washington, that we devote our abilities and resources to saving the majestic Burmese tiger."

Sen. Trent Lott (R-MS) spoke fondly Wednesday of the civil-rights era of yore.

"On behalf of the African-American community, I thank God we have lived to see the day in which civil rights for all Americans are no longer a concern," Lott said. "America needs to understand that the legacy of the civil-rights movement belongs to them, and they don't need to do anything to further it, because it has already been achieved." Ø

REPORTER from page 285

1996 and 2001, said that to divulge her source would jeopardize her First Amendment rights, as well as relationships with high-level recipe sources she has worked for years to develop.

Despite Steuber's staunch refusals, prosecutor Wendy Hardin said that she "absolutely must be allowed" to probe the recipe to the fullest extent, which means interviewing the individual who leaked it to *Redbook*. Many close to the case believe that the source of the recipe is a member of a tight-knit family with a glazed-ham dish that has endured for generations.

"I think the people have a right to know what inspired this cook to create a sweet glaze that doesn't overwhelm the savory taste of the ham," Hardin said. "Such deliciousness cannot remain hidden any longer."

"I think the people have a right to know what inspired this cook to create a sweet glaze that doesn't overwhelm the savory taste of the ham," Hardin said.

"It's a crime," Hardin added.

Some journalists have suggested that Steuber's refusal to reveal her sources is motivated by self-interest, not by a desire to protect free speech.

"Steuber exerts incredible power through her ability to determine how much of a source's information is exposed," said Annette Scotti, whose articles on recipe-ownership issues have appeared in *The Nation*. "If she's withholding valuable information that is preventing Americans from enjoying a savory dish, she's doing an enormous disservice to the country. What if this maple-glazed ham source also has a tantalizing recipe for turkey stuffing?"

Steuber, a *Redbook* staffer since 1989, is best known for her articles such as "Dealing With Newlywed Stress" and "Colorful Autumn Ponchos You Can Crochet Yourself!" While she has never before faced jail time, she remained determined to honor her professional obligations to her editors and sources alike.

"It's a women's magazine journalist's job to report on recipes of this caliber fairly and accurately," Steuber said. "But when it comes to who is behind those recipes, or how best to use

Some journalists have suggested that Steuber's refusal to reveal her sources is motivated by self-interest, not by a desire to protect free speech.

the leftovers, I'm afraid I'll have to remain silent, no matter the personal cost." Ø

DOLLAR from page 283

dicted that it would hold its own against the acorn.

"The inedible dollar simply does not offer the same long-term security or short-term benefits as the acorn," said James Aucker of the Commodity Futures Trading Commission. "It is even falling against the Costa Rican pocket, the Latvian thimble, and the German Kinder Surprise Egg, which combines delicious chocolate with a fun, easy-to-assemble toy."

The acorn, a symbol of Canadian lumber futures, is a stable commodity rich in calcium, phosphorus, potassium, and niacin. Patient investors who bury their holdings generally see their investments increased tenfold in the form of great oaks that live for hundreds of years and provide a rich return in acorns.

In comparison to the acorn, the dollar is volatile, its value dependent on such relative intangibles as the unpredictable U.S. stock market. According to Aucker, irresponsible domestic trading has hurt the dollar's image in the foreign exchange market.

"The U.S. dollar is often traded for the lottery ticket, an even more worthless paper investment whose chances for any monetary return at all is close to zero," Aucker said. "This frivolous spending, combined with the fact that the trade deficit has skyrocketed with the abandonment of the U.S. export industry, has devalued the dollar in the eyes of the foreign investor."

Greenspan, however, defended the strength of the dollar, saying the acorn will adjust during the fall foraging months.

"When millions of ripe acorns fall from the trees, we'll see their value decline sharply," Greenspan said. "It will depreciate even more when squirrels begin hibernating, flooding the supply and triggering possible inflation."

Morningstar investment adviser Kimberly Levine dissuaded investors

> **In comparison to the acorn, the dollar is volatile, its value dependent on such relative intangibles as the unpredictable U.S. stock market.**

from taking part in the "acorn bubble."

"Though it seems reliable, the world acorn capital fluctuates with the turn of every new fiscal season," Levine said. "And besides, acorns taste terrible, even after they're roasted."

Despite the dollar's ongoing depreciation, it has still made significant gains on Congolese human life, which after late trading dropped to U.S. $1.2826. ⌀

CARBONATED from page 244

amounts of blood. Passersby were amazed by the unusually large amounts of blood. Passersby were amazed by the unusually large

> **Police said the steely-eyed villain cued the menacing music a little early.**

amounts of blood. Passersby were amazed by the unusually large amounts of blood.Passersby were amazed by the unusually large amounts of blood.Passersby were amazed by the unusually large amounts of blood.Passersby were amazed by the unusually large amounts of blood.Passersby were amazed by the unusually large

see CARBONATED page 297

METAL from page 283

cently it was brought to our attention that someone used the gesture in a Texas convenience store after snagging the last box of carrot cakes. This simply won't do."

Formed in 1972 and comprising 12 of the most revered leaders of the metal community, the council meets annually in its majestic hall atop Vatnajökull, Iceland's largest glacier, to discuss metal affairs. The SMC convened for a special session after Nikki Sixx, Overlord Of Glam Metal Affairs, was sent hard photographic evidence of metal-sign abuse across the nation. Sixx's fellow high priests said they were "shocked," calling it "one of the most serious affronts to metal's integrity since the rise of rap-metal in the late 1990s."

"I remember a time not long ago when the Devil Horns were reserved for only the most righteous of person, deed, or riff," Grand Elder Lemmy Kilmister said. "To see someone throwing the horns to his mate at the launderette because the clothes dryer came to a full stop just as he finished reading his copy of *Circus*... It breaks my heart."

Nodding in silent agreement were council members Adalwolfa, a curvaceous Frank Frazetta-drawn Teutonic she-warrior magically brought to life by the council, and the spirit of slain Pantera guitarist "Dimebag" Darrell Abbott.

Compounding the problem, Sixx said, is the fact that many people who use the sign are not recognized members of the Metal Roster, the list of true metal acolytes engraved in medieval calligraphy on gleaming pages of steel.

"This man here, who invokes the sign merely to indicate his joy that his microwave popcorn is done: He is not metal," Sixx said. "We have it on good authority that he prefers the music of Tim McGraw and that the magic word of 'Zoso' has never passed his lips."

The council discussed several harsh punishments to deter further metal-sign abuse. Paulo Pinto, bassist for the Brazilian thrash-metal band

> **"I remember a time not long ago when the Devil Horns were reserved for only the most righteous of person, deed, or riff," Grand Elder Lemmy Kilmister said.**

Sepultura and Overlord Of International Metal Affairs, suggested that the hand of a suspected signer should be immediately cut off. A contingency of death rockers from Gothenburg, Sweden recommended that sign abusers, or anyone else who is not sufficiently metal, should be forced to eat his severed hand while having his eyeballs burned with a superheated metal crucifix, and then be slowly skinned alive.

More charitable members, such as former Megadeth frontman Dave Mustaine, suggested that "a helpful list of guidelines could educate others, allowing them to distinguish between metal and non-metal occurrences."

"A lot of people who incorrectly

> **"A lot of people who incorrectly make the sign have traces of metal in their hearts and minds, they just need the proper direction," Mustaine said.**

make the sign have traces of metal in their hearts and minds, they just need the proper direction," Mustaine said. "Remember that many are outcasts and losers. To punish them further is to destroy the future of metal."

Until the council decides what course of action to adopt, Butler said he believes that a simple rule of thumb will help reduce the incidence of metal-sign abuse.

"If your head is neither banging nor thrashing, you should not be throwing the sign," Butler said. "It's that simple."

Yet, in a later interview in his private, skull-bedecked chambers, Butler expressed the concern that the problem has grown too widespread for even the mighty SMC to solve. He said he worries that metal standards have been on the decline for so long that few have any clear idea as to what is metal and what is not. The SMC has experienced deep ideological rifts in the past that have affected its ability to make strong decisions, most notably during the lengthy trial and eventual sentencing of Metallica drummer Lars Ulrich, who was indicted in 2004 on charges of cutting his hair, pussing out on Napster, and contributing to the original motion-picture soundtrack of *Mission: Impossible 2*.

"To this day, there are many on the council who deeply resent the presence of [Poison guitarist] C.C. DeVille,'" Butler said. "In fact, so do I. Despite our differences, the council still remains the sole arbitrator of all things metal. We must get through to those who wantonly abuse the sign of the goat. They must be informed that watering down the sign's meaning will result in serious consequences."

Should the abuse continue, Butler said the council "will defer the matter to Satan." ⌀

COMMUNITY VOICES

My Personal Shopper Is The Worst

I called up Alexa at Bergdorf's Sunday night and told her I needed gloves, a hat, an evening dress, two coats,12 sweaters, a couple hair accessories, a slouchy belt, and some stockings, because I threw my old ones out by accident. I needed a new watch, too—something modern and new but traditional and in platinum—but I just called up Enrico for that, because he knows my hands.

By Christine Vesper

Well, Monday morning rolled around, and then it was Monday afternoon, and I still didn't have my purchases. When Alexa finally showed up, I understood why she'd taken so long—she had clearly gone out of her way to hand pick the most hideous pieces from the most hideous collections, carefully ensuring, while she was at it, that several of the items were not even in my size. (I'm a Versace 6, a Marc Jacobs 4.)

I don't understand what was going through her head when she chose that J. Mendel evening dress. Basic black? I'm not trying to buy an evening dress that I'll be able to wear for years to come, thank you.

I may as well have a colorblind Mongoloid doing the job for me. And her voice. That awful, mousy little mumbled falsetto. "Enunciate!" I said. "It's no wonder you're living in a fifth-floor walkup."

And La Perla bras? Completely off the mark. I told her I wanted sexy, not a bra for my grandmother. If that's her idea of sensuous lingerie, it's no

I could fire her, but then I would have to go through this incredible bore every afternoon when I go to Bergdorf's. Besides, it's more than I can do right now. I'm up to my ears in planning next season's winter formal. This is a disaster.

wonder she can't keep a man committed to her.

I try to be forgiving to the poor girl, because I know that it must be hard to be so unattractive, but some of these items go beyond the pale. The Be & D handbag looked like something an insane person would carry. And when I asked her to pick up my dry cleaning,

Well, Monday morning rolled around, and then it was Monday afternoon, and I still didn't have my purchases. When Alexa finally showed up, I understood why she'd taken so long—she had clearly gone out of her way to hand pick the most hideous pieces from the most hideous collections, carefully ensuring, while she was at it, that several of the items were not even in my size. (I'm a Versace 6, a Marc Jacobs 4.)

she acted like I was the one out of line. Two words. Service. Industry. Thank you.

I could perhaps have humored her if she came back with two or three gaudy cashmere sweaters. Taste is, after all, subjective. That she brought me 12, however, is more than I should have to endure. I took the sweaters to spare myself the hassle, but Lord knows they're going to be sitting in the back of my closet unworn 10 years from now.

I should have gone with that homosexual with the harelip, Chi-Chi.

I could fire her, but then I would have to go through this incredible bore every afternoon when I go to Bergdorf's. Besides, it's more than I can do right now. I'm up to my ears in planning next season's winter formal. This is a disaster.

Maybe I can just hand the Be & D to a homeless person. They might be thrilled. Wait, Janice Goldman's daughter adores Be & D. I'll give Janice the bag next time I see her in the park, pretend this never happened, and just pray that Marie Elaine has fared better. ⌀

HOROSCOPES

Your Horoscope

By Lloyd Schumner Sr.
Retired Machinist and
A.A.P.B.-Certified Astrologer

Aries: (March 21–April 19)
The corpse of 16th-century astronomer Nicolaus Corpenicus will rise from the grave this week to explain, once and for all, that the universe does not revolve around you, you self-centered prick.

Taurus: (April 20–May 20)
The old adage "Don't count your chickens before they hatch" will feel very apt next week when you're forced to return over $200 worth of baby clothes and cigars.

Gemini: (May 21–June 21)
After forgetting to take your medication for five days straight, you'll have no trouble explaining the voices in your head; however, it will be much harder to explain why they all sound like Rosie Perez.

Cancer: (June 22–July 22)
You've always been the type to see the glass half-full, but that will change next week when you start drinking.

Leo: (July 23–Aug. 22)
Any hesitation you have in summoning the underworld demon Astaroth will be more than canceled out by your eagerness to sacrifice a goat.

Virgo: (Aug. 23–Sept. 22)
Your decision to purchase a pair of cargo pants was based entirely on the number of Hot Pockets they could hold.

Libra: (Sept. 23–Oct. 23)
You've never believed in the theory of evolution, but lately you just can't shake the feeling that the monkeys at the zoo seem to be improving their aim.

Scorpio: (Oct. 24–Nov. 21)
Circumstance will prove again and again this week that only half of the old saying, "If it bends it's funny; if it breaks, it's not" applies to femurs.

Sagittarius: (Nov. 22–Dec. 21)
While everyone says that there's more than one way to skin a cat, you have never been able to come up with more than 57.

Capricorn: (Dec. 22–Jan. 19)
The effects of your four-year tour in the U.S. Navy become especially evident this week when, despite hours of trying, you are physically and mentally incapable of finishing a plate of Captain Highliner's Fish Sticks.

Aquarius: (Jan. 20–Feb. 18)
You'll die a grisly and violent death next week after being chased around the tri-state area by sumo wrestlers, but not in the manner you expect.

Pisces: (Feb. 19–March 20)
Scientists have predicted that, one day soon, tiny robots will travel through our bodies repairing damage on the cellular level, but tomorrow, giant robots will hurl your body over the horizon, shattering it beyond repair. ⌀

KEEBLER from page 185

amounts of blood. Passersby were amazed by the unusually large amounts of blood. Passersby were amazed by the unusually large amounts of blood. Passersby were amazed by the unusually large amounts of blood. Passersby were amazed by the unusually large amounts of blood. Passersby were amazed by the unusually large amounts of blood. Passersby were amazed by the unusually large amounts of blood. Passersby were amazed by the unusually large amounts of blood. Passersby were amazed by the unusually large amounts of blood. Passersby were amazed by the unusually large amounts of blood. Passersby were amazed by the unusually large amounts of blood. Passersby were amazed by the unusually large amounts of blood. Passersby were amazed by the unusually large amounts of blood. Passersby were amazed by the unusually large amounts of blood. Passersby were amazed by the unusually large

The sensation of victory was quickly supplanted by the sensation of falling through a rickety old factory roof.

amounts of blood. Passersby were amazed by the unusually large amounts of blood. Passersby were amazed by the unusually large amounts of blood. Passersby were amazed by the unusually large

see KEEBLER page 239

NEWS

KFC Introduces New Bird-Flu Dipping Vaccine

see HEALTH page 2C

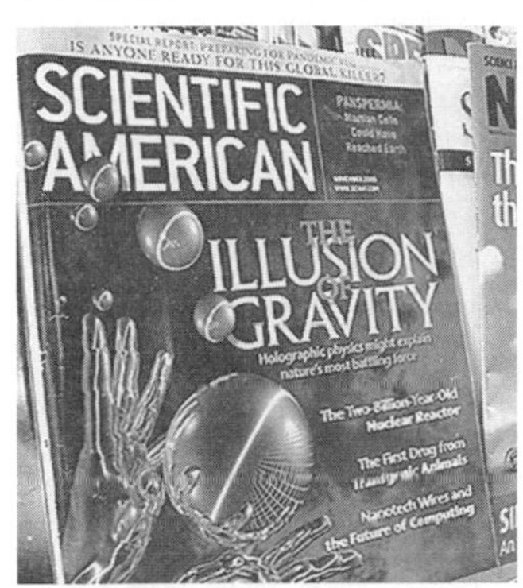

Scientific American Somehow Makes Woman Feel Bad About Her Body

see NATIONAL page 3E

Evangelical Scientists Discover Calculation Error: Earth Only 60 Years Old

see SCIENCE page 12F

STATshot

A look at the numbers that shape your world.

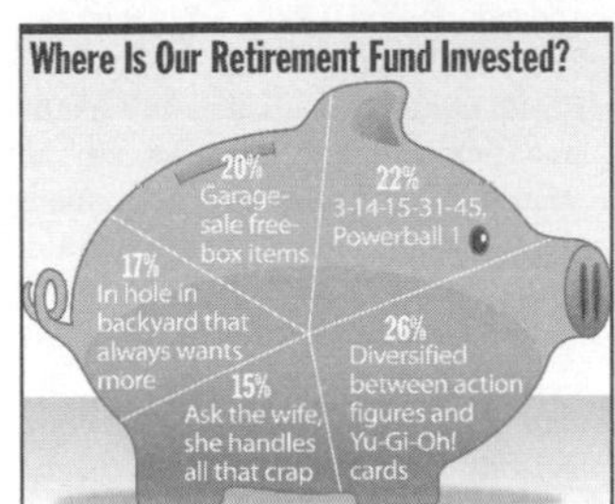

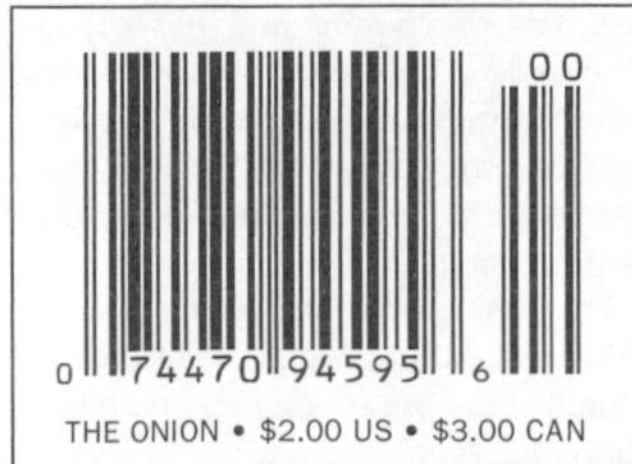

the ONION®

VOLUME 41 ISSUE 46 AMERICA'S FINEST NEWS SOURCE™ 17–23 NOVEMBER 2005

Long-Awaited Beer With Bush Really Awkward, Voter Reports

WARREN, PA—Although respondents to a Pew poll taken prior to the 2004 presidential election characterized Bush as "the candidate they'd most like to sit down and have a beer with," Chris Reinard lived the hypothetical scenario Sunday afternoon, and characterized it as "really uncomfortable and awkward."

Reinard, a father of four who supported Bush in the 2000 and 2004 elections, said sharing a beer with the president at the Switchyard Tap gave him "an uneasy feeling."

"I thought he'd be great," Reinard said. "But when I actually met him, I felt real put off."

The president arrived at

see BUSH page 292

Above: Chris Reinard and President Bush try to think of something to talk about.

133 Dead As Delta Cancels Flight In Midair

Above: Delta Flight 1060, which was forced to land in an Indiana cornfield after being canceled mid-flight.

CINCINNATI—A 737 traveling from Cincinnati to Salt Lake City was lost with all passengers and crew Monday when cash-strapped Delta Airlines, the aircraft's operator, canceled Flight 1060 en route.

According to a statement from Delta, the midair cancellation was made as part of the company's plan to cut continental service by 25 percent and emerge from Chapter 11 bankruptcy with an economically viable business strategy.

"Delta Airlines regrets any inconvenience to our valued customers," the statement read in part. "Unfortunately, in today's uncertain economy, service interruptions and cancellations are inevitable."

see DELTA page 292

Animal Planet Reality Show To Put Bear, Antelope, Hawk, Cheetah In Same House

LOS ANGELES—Cable network Animal Planet announced its most ambitious foray into reality-TV programming yet Monday with The Zoo, a weekly, hourlong show in which members of a diverse, all-animal cast square off in a single 3,200-square-foot home in the San Fernando Valley.

"Sparks—and fur—are sure to fly when animals from 11 different ecosystems share a single row house in trendy Echo Park," executive producer Stu Wolchek said. "For many of these wild, colorful, and totally unpredictable cast members, it's the first time they've ever seen a bison or sloth."

Wolchek added: "Some of these guys have never even lived under a roof."

According to the show's creator, for-

see ANIMAL PLANET page 293

Online College Alcohol Courses

Colleges across the country are requiring incoming freshmen to take an online alcohol-awareness course. What do *you* think?

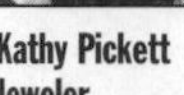

"There's a lot of debate about the value of the course among academia's leading mixologists."

Kathy Pickett
Jeweler

"Sure, I'm sober now, but I will never, ever be able to take back that disparaging Sigur Rós comment I put on my blog. Oh, time's remorseless arrow!"

Clive Teplitski
Construction Manager

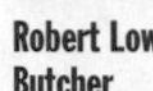

"I thought that was what the occasional death of a fraternity pledge is for."

Robert Low
Butcher

"You know, there's very little of this bullshit at my son's trade school."

Stuart Kehn
Auto-Parts Buyer

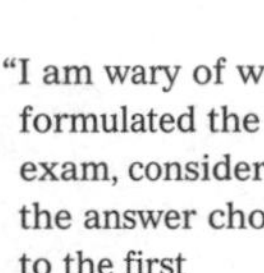

"I am wary of who formulated the exam, considering the answer choices to the first question, 'How does Bud Light taste?' are 'cool, crisp, refreshing, or all of the above.'"

Ted Hicks
Hairdresser

"Can't we just make it illegal for people under 21 to drink?"

Marie Russell
Science Teacher

New Harry Potter Film

Harry Potter And The Goblet Of Fire, the first PG-13-rated film in the series, is set for a Nov. 18 release. Here are the themes and content that might be too mature for young viewers:

- Full frontal nudity of house elves
- "Goblet Of Fire" filled with equal parts Robitussin and Everclear
- Part where experimental methanol-burning Quidditch broom crashes into stands, killing 32 fourth-form Hufflepuffs and disfiguring 80 others
- Fifteen-minute allegory about foreign policy
- Hagrid's "Daddy Bear" lifestyle, which is more than just hinted at this time
- Scene where Lord Voldemort cuts off Harry's ear and douses him in gasoline to tune of "Stuck In The Middle With You"
- Number of adult men there seeing movie by themselves

America's Finest News Source.™

Herman Ulysses Zweibel
Founder

T. Herman Zweibel
Publisher Emeritus
J. Phineas Zweibel
Publisher
Maxwell Prescott Zweibel
Editor-In-Chief

Life In The Navy Rocks Even Harder Than The Commercial Implied

By CPO Dan Gazanski

After I graduated from high school, I was making good money painting houses, my girlfriend was cool with a rockin' little bod, and I partied almost every night. But after a year or so, I started to wonder: "If someone wrote a book about my life, would anyone want to read it?"

I wanted discipline and training, but I didn't want to give up my hard-rockin' lifestyle. Where, I wondered, could that elusive combination of rigid authoritarian structure and unbridled monster power chords be found? Then I saw a commercial for the U.S. Navy. That's when I knew what to do with my life.

And guess what? The U.S. Navy fucking kicks ass, dude. From the time we're awoken at 06:00 by System Of A Down or Disturbed till we drift off to sleep to an instrumental guitar version of "Taps" performed by Zakk Wylde, it's a nonstop rock block.

How do I even begin to describe the constant barrage of adrenaline-fueled, over-the-top kick-assitude that is the U.S. Navy? Every day is like a rapid-fire montage sequence of high-tech action and thrill-ride imagery that makes your fuckin' head spin.

One minute, I'm crouched on the deck of an aircraft carrier barking something into a helmet-mounted headset that you can't even friggin' hear because the music's so loud. Next, I'm dashing through the Mojave under the weight of a large pack and jumping out of a helicopter into the ocean wearing some kind of James Bond one-man submersible scuba suit. If I'm not roarin' down the high seas with the wind in my hair and 800 pounds of rad-ass Batman shit strapped to my uniform, I'm standing at perfect attention in my dress whites, fucking whippin' a sword around like I'm a goddamn samurai master.

Even basic training was an edgy, quick-cut mosaic of running and climbing and shooting and learning and Pantera riffs. There was this rad obstacle course we did twice a day carrying sandbags, and when you did it, it was like you could feel yourself morph from an average guy into one of the sword-carrying knights of old. I may not have slain actual dragons, but when I came out, I looked just like Iron Man, and my father was very impressed with the changes that he saw in me.

Serving aboard the U.S.S. Abraham Linkin Park, which is just about the most hardcore carrier in the fleet, I spend the morning working on high-tech projects like blowing up long-range sea targets with giant artillery guns. In the afternoon, it's firing missiles, Tomahawks, and torpedoes into the sea. And my nights? Getting valuable intel off our way-advanced radar screens. That's when I don't dart off in a super-fast motorboat in full frogman gear to train in underwater demolition and special ops, emerging from the water at sunrise.

But there's also these quieter moments that really put things in perspective. Usually, it's when me and my multiethnic buddies are coming back from a long, kick-ass day, and we experience an unspoken moment of camaraderie. The music shifts to a power ballad, and we take a minute before the American flag to gaze in silence at the epic sunset. When I glance at my friends' chiseled faces and see their quiet pride and masculinity, I realize that I made the right choice. Sometimes, we're joined by a flying eagle, but the eagle isn't a pet of ours, it just kind of appears superimposed behind us like 50 feet tall when things get patriotic.

How do I even begin to describe the constant barrage of adrenaline-fueled, over-the-top kick-assitude that is the U.S. Navy? Every day is like a rapid-fire montage sequence of high-tech action and thrill-ride imagery that makes your fuckin' head spin.

I gotta admit, though, as much as the Navy rocks out with its cocks out, I'm not sure if I'll be making a permanent career out of it. Sometimes, when I'm flying around in my F/A-18 Hornet, I imagine myself morphing out of my action gear into a three-piece suit heading up my own Fortune 500 company which I built on the skills the Navy taught me.

When I get shore leave and go home to visit my family and old friends, they can't hide their pride. As the background music slows to a stately march, my normally hard-as-nails dad salutes me and shakes my hand with tears in his eyes.

I'm sure glad that I didn't join the Marines. All those guys seem to do is climb sheer mountain faces with their bare hands. ⌀

Area Baby Doesn't Have Any Friends

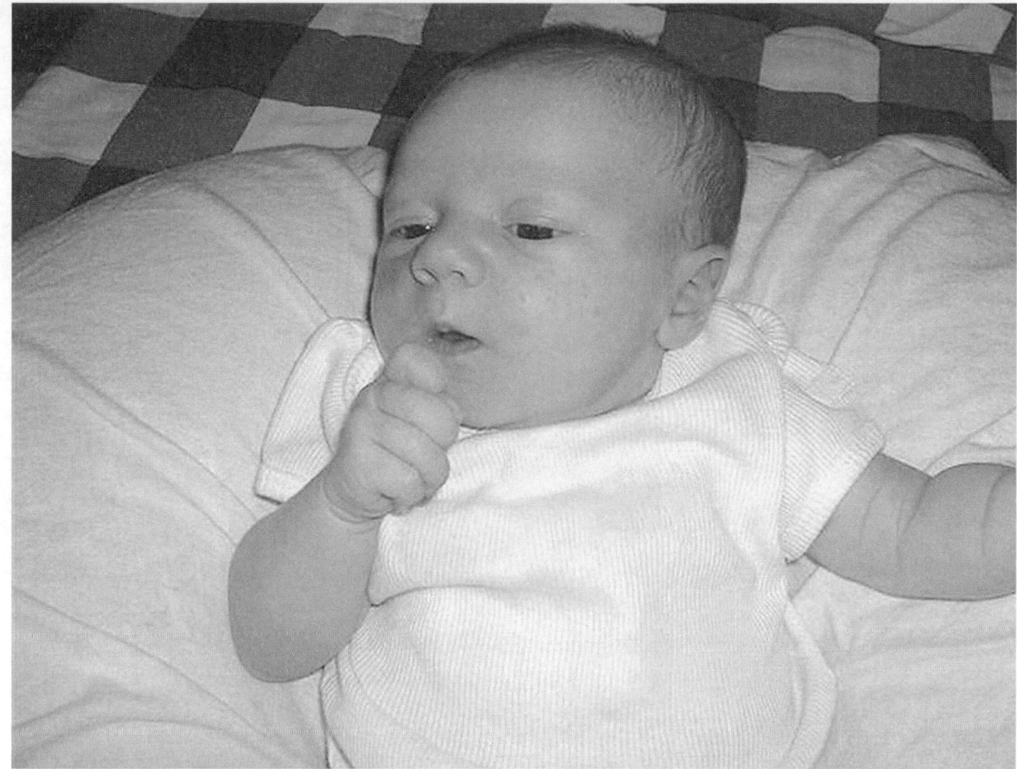

Above: Friendless baby Joshua Goldsworthy spends another night alone.

TARRYTOWN, NY—Although he's had nearly three months to meet people, local baby Joshua Goldsworthy hasn't made a single friend, according to those who know him.

People who have met the quiet, stay-at-home misfit say that, while he's more interesting than he was two months ago, Joshua lacks the warmth, charisma, and empathy of a suitable companion.

"It's not like I hate him—I just don't get a lot out of knowing him," said 32-year-old Gretchen Sperber, a long-time friend of the Goldsworthy family. "He's hard to read. Sometimes he'll stare at you for hours, other times he'll fall asleep right in front of you, like you're not even there."

As Bonnie and Jason Goldsworthy's first child, Joshua is predictably adored and indulged. With a toy-filled nursery, a favorite blanket, and a parent, aunt, or grandparent always close at hand, the blond, apple-cheeked little boy unquestionably receives adequate love and comfort. However, most psychologists agree that familial love cannot replace friendships with one's peers.

Visitors to the Goldsworthy home often report having negative first im-

"I still can't imagine why he didn't excuse himself and crawl into another room," Osterberg said. "The stench filled the living room, and he just sat there and grinned."

pressions of Joshua. Out-of-the-blue crying fits, the tendency to yank at loose hair and earrings, and copious drooling are just a few of the antisocial traits he displays. Neighbor Lena Osterberg said that, two weeks ago, she cut a visit to the Goldsworthy home short after the self-interested infant committed a "gross" indiscretion.

"I still can't imagine why he didn't excuse himself and crawl into another room," Osterberg said. "The stench filled the living room, and he just sat there and grinned."

Another acquaintance, who asked

see BABY page 293

NEWS IN BRIEF

Anti-Homosexuality Sermon Suspiciously Well-Informed

BOSTON—The Rev. Francis Sebastian's Sunday sermon condemning homosexual behavior was suspiciously rich in detail and nuance, parishioners from the Adoration Of The Savior Catholic Church noted Monday. "For a celibate man of the cloth, Father Sebastian is very specific about which code words not to use on which forbidden chat rooms at which times of the night," said Betty Riegert, 67. "He also seems to have done his homework on what happens if you flash your headlights at certain rest stops along Route 16." Riegert and other parishioners expect Sebastian to revisit his usual well-worn themes, "Consider The Lilies," "Back Street Sodom," and "Christ The Bridegroom," next Sunday.

Report: North Korea Just Enjoys Nuclear Talks

WASHINGTON, DC—The *Bulletin Of The Atomic Scientists* published a report Tuesday revealing what the international community has long suspected: The government of North Korea simply enjoys nuclear talks. "After years of protracted talks about strategic versus domestic nuclear programs and launch and delivery tactics, it's become increasingly evident that North Korea's stalling tactics stem from a deep desire to chat about nukes," said Ambassador Linton Brooks, chief of the National Nuclear Security Administration. "We are beginning to think that behind all this nuclear brinksmanship are 12 high-level scientists and politicians who enjoy getting together, kicking back, and making a weekend out of it." Although North Korea Prime Minister Pak Pong Ju had no comment on the report, members of his cabinet said they "would be delighted" to get together and discuss the matter further.

Activist Wet-T-Shirt Judge Votes For Girlfriend

COLUMBIA, SC—Andrew Scully, 26, a bartender and wet-T-shirt-contest judge at local nightclub Deep Waters, has been accused of personal bias and "legislating from the barstool" after ruling in favor of his girlfriend, Heather Swain, in Friday's "Waters' Melons!!!" wet-T-shirt contest. "Inevitably, my own perceptions will guide my interpretation and application of event guidelines—if that weren't a part of our system, we could just replace the judges with a tape measure," said Scully, responding to bar patrons who said they believed that several contestants had breasts both larger and better-displayed than Swain's. "I like to think of a wet-T-shirt contestant not as a rigid set of body-type rules, but as a living, breathing object." Conservative leaders of the Federalist Wet-T-Shirt Contest Society are calling for Scully's resignation.

Greg Behrendt Releases New Book For Children: *Your Parents Aren't That Into You*

LOS ANGELES—Greg Behrendt, the co-author of the bestsellers *He's Just Not That Into You* and *It's Called A Breakup Because It's Broken*, has written a book targeted at younger readers, which will be released by Simon & Schuster next week. "In *Your Parents Aren't That Into You*, I train my funky wit and refreshing frankness on a very difficult time of childhood—the moment when kids realize they're just accessories, tax write-offs, or even mistakes," Behrendt said. "After all, the collapse of the child-parent relationship sets the tone for those to come." *Your Parents Aren't That Into You*, which features illustrations by Gary Panter, will also be available in an abridged stocking-stuffer size in time for Christmas. ⌀

DELTA from page 289

Air-traffic-control personnel reported that Flight 1060 was at cruising altitude when Delta cancelled the flight. According to the aircraft's black-box flight recorder, the crew announced the cancellation over the intercom, instructed passengers to

While Delta officials are blaming the cancellation on financial troubles, other problems, such as high fuel costs and bad weather, have caused delays and lost profits for airlines in recent months.

gather their luggage from overhead bins for disembarking, then shut down all aircraft systems. At 9:46 a.m. Central time, Flight 1060's tracking designation vanished from air-traffic-control radar screens. Approximately 15 minutes later, the aircraft crashed in a cornfield outside Tipton, IN, killing all onboard.

While Delta officials are blaming the cancellation on financial troubles, other problems, such as high fuel costs and bad weather, have caused delays and lost profits for airlines in recent months.

"Airlines have been compensating for recent shortfalls by canceling flights, as well as overbooking," airline-industry observer Gerard Mendez said. "These things never fail to irritate customers—especially when they're done in midair—but unfortunately, the airline industry is a business like any other, and as it becomes increasingly competitive, these sorts of frustrations are taking place more and more."

In May, Delta officials made an adjustment for an overbooked flight by bumping six passengers from Flight 400 somewhere over the Allegany Mountains.

Delta Airlines spokesperson Clarice Waddell said that, in cases of cancellation and overbooking, the airline does everything it can to accommodate its customers' travel plans.

Said Waddell: "When we're forced to bump passengers from a moving airplane, we always offer meal vouchers or SkyMiles credits."

Consolidating flights is another controversial cost-cutting measure used by Delta in recent months. Delta's last attempt to consolidate flights in midair, in December 2005, resulted in the total destruction of two 747s, which exploded in a large fireball approximately 35,000 feet over central Arizona. Although the loss of these planes was recoupable as a tax deduction for the airline, Waddell stressed that Delta nonetheless regretted any unfortunate repercussions the decision may have had on the company's top priority—the customer. Ø

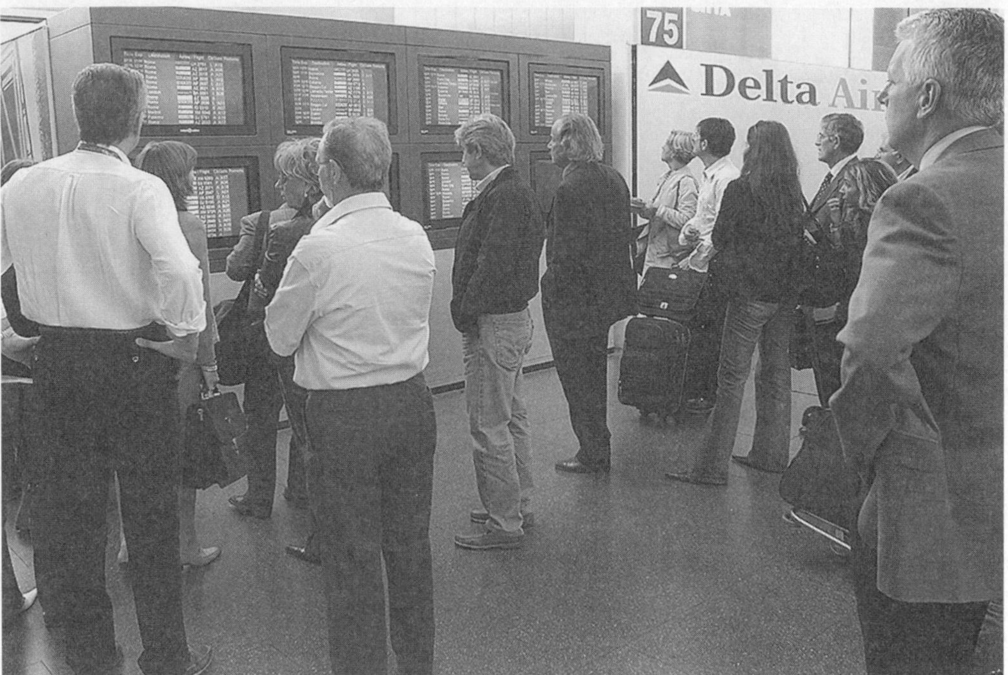

Above: Passengers at San Diego International Airport await news of more midair cancellations.

BUSH from page 289

the bar via motorcade close to 3 p.m. After a sweep by Secret Service agents, Reinard was asked, for security reasons, to move from his favorite stool. Shortly after he had reseated himself, Reinard said he "was pleased" to welcome the president to the Switchyard.

"Boy, it sure is a good day for a cool one," Bush reportedly told the assembled patrons, who were watching the Dolphins–Patriots game.

"When he first walked in, everything seemed fine," bartender Bob Kern said. "He told everyone 'Hi' like he was one of the regulars, then sat next to Chris."

Reinard ordered two Budweisers, but Bush interrupted him, saying he'd prefer an O'Doul's non-alcoholic beer.

"I completely forgot he stopped drinking," Reinard said.

Following the initial gaffe, Bush attempted to smooth things over, asking Reinard to call him "George." Reinard complied, but later said "it felt a little unnatural."

"I guess I was supposed to tell him to call me Chris," Reinard said. "I didn't like him calling me 'Mr. Reinard' the whole time, but I didn't know if it was okay to interrupt him to say 'Call me Chris.' And then also, it felt weird to just say it out of nowhere. Like, 'Call me Chris.'"

Bush asked Reinard if he had any

"He asked me how it was going, what with the economy bouncing back. I said that if things didn't pick up soon, I was going to have to close up shop and work for my uncle in Youngstown," Reinard said.

hobbies, and Reinard told the president that he enjoys spending weekends with his children on local lakes in his small aluminum boat.

"Mr. Bush, I mean George, seemed to like that, and I felt that we finally made a connection," Reinard said. "But then he started telling me about this one time he was on a yacht with some Arab prince and they spent four hours landing a sailfish."

"It was a good story, but I just like catching a few bass with my kids is all," Reinard added. "I know he didn't mean to make me feel bad, but still."

Reinard told the president that he has lived most of his life in the Warren area, except for several years he spent in nearby Jamestown, where he attended community college for a year. Bush told Reinard he was born in New Haven, CT, and grew up in Texas before attending Yale University as an undergraduate and earning his MBA from Harvard, all while maintaining membership in many exclusive clubs.

"I asked George how much it costs to be in those social clubs, but he said he didn't remember," Reinard said. "I think he just didn't want to say the amount. He'd change the subject on me a lot, say he did a lot of partying back then, but that was all behind him now, since he found the Lord, or whatever."

Bush asked Reinard what he did for a living, and Reinard said he runs a small carpentry business.

"He asked me how it was going, what with the economy bouncing back. I said that if things didn't pick up soon, I was going to have to close up shop and work for my uncle in Youngstown," Reinard said. "George was quiet for a while after that. Then he told me about when his second oil company was going under. He suggested using my connections to get some outside investment capital."

"I don't have any connections," Reinard added.

When the conversation reached a

After nearly a minute of silence, Bush drained the remainder of his O'Doul's and wished Reinard goodbye.

dead end, Reinard and Bush were silent once again, their eyes tracking the game.

"We were sitting there watching the game, and some cheerleaders were up there waving their pompoms," Reinard said. "Then George mentioned that he used to be a cheerleader at Yale. I didn't know what to

see BUSH page 294

ANIMAL PLANET from page 289

mer zoo director Loren De Jong, over 80 different species were auditioned to find the right mix of personalities. In addition to the red bear, African cheetah, hawk, and antelope, the house is occupied by an American bison, a field mouse, an Egyptian plover, a three-toed sloth, a goose, a crocodile, and a female lowland gorilla who is "very territorial of the bathroom."

De Jong said the show's contestants begin forming alliances on the first day.

"We see an immediate alliance develop between the lowland gorilla and the bison, who work together to smash a hole through a wall," De

The cast will compete in weekly immunity and reward challenges, with prizes comprising such creature comforts as straw, mud puddles, and tree trunks. The latter is much-desired for itch-relieving, horn-sharpening, and territory-marking alike.

Jong said.

"While the bear and crocodile are the first to assert themselves in the house, folks at home shouldn't forget the dark horse: the field mouse, who might just fly under the radar all the way to the finals," she added.

TV Guide writer Rebecca Kohler is one of the few to have viewed the pilot.

"It's impossible to pick a winner this early on," Kohler said. "The gorilla is clearly the game's strategist. At the same time, nothing happens in the house that the hawk doesn't see. And I wouldn't put it past the crocodile to eat his own young if it meant getting ahead." Kohler said that the animal most likely to face early eviction is the sloth, who "seems to lack the ambition necessary to go all the way."

The cast will compete in weekly immunity and reward challenges, with prizes comprising such creature comforts as straw, mud puddles, and tree trunks. The latter is much-desired for itch-relieving, horn-sharpening, and territory-marking alike.

Animal Planet sources say the house, which is equipped with the latest in modern convenience, including a hot tub, a flat-screen TV, and a pool table, quickly fills with feces during the premiere episode.

The cast will also take "time outs" in the house's soundproof confessional room, where they can "privately come

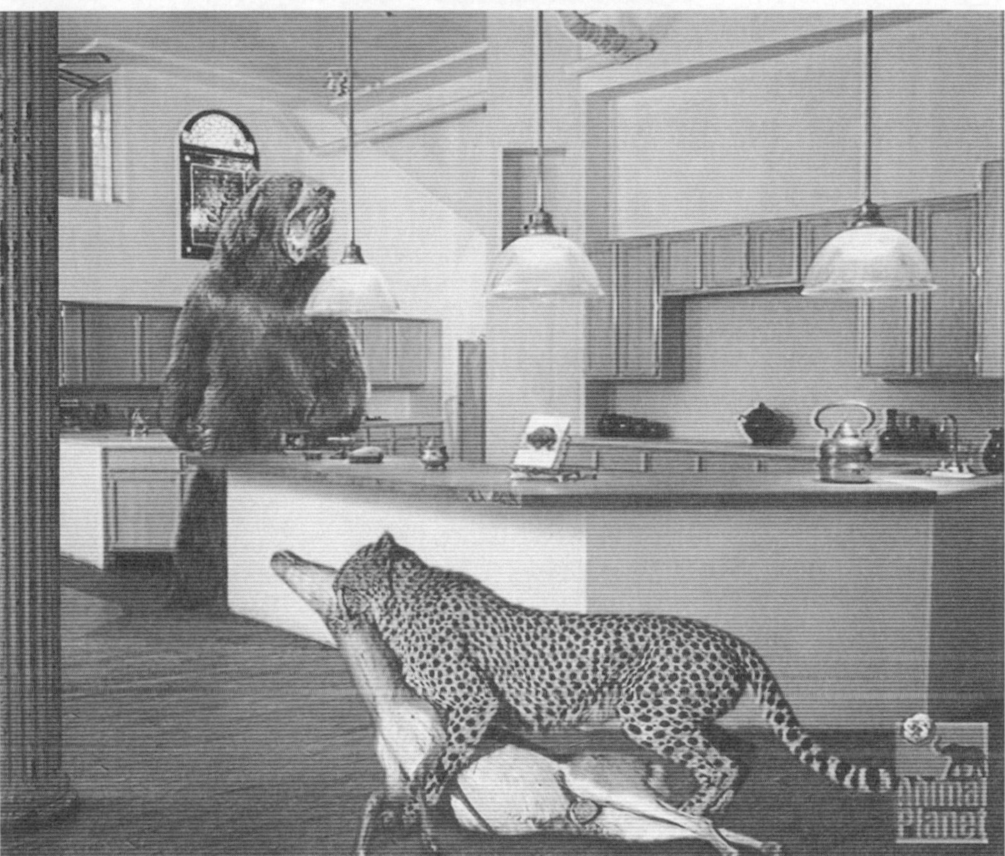

Above: Two cast members have a heated argument on The Animal Planet's new reality show The Zoo.

clean with any thoughts or instincts they may have."

"You'll be shocked at some of the venting you'll hear in the confessional," Wolchek said.

While the cast has reportedly had trouble with such competitions as bridge-building and cooperative puzzle-solving, repulsive-food competitions have proven "very successful," with contestants eagerly devouring worms, beetles, and grubs.

"The hawk beat out his fellow housemates in a stomach-turning roundworm-eating contest," Wolchek said. "He just swallowed those disgusting things whole, one by one. It all seemed worth it to him in the end, though, when he was awarded a sorely needed pile of branches to complete his nest."

Sources close to the show have hinted at the possibility of a 12th, surprise houseguest being thrown into the already cramped living quarters to "shake things up" during February sweeps. Unconfirmed rumors circulating on the Internet identify the mystery cast-member as a 23-year-old Asian-American marketing assistant.

The winner of The Zoo will be awarded a hefty cash prize, a Range Rover, his or her choice of permanent habitat, and, if applicable, assisted migration courtesy of Continental Airlines.

That is, of course, if the show manages to carry on to its conclusion.

Originally set to premiere in September, The Zoo was delayed after the original camera crew was forced to flee. Reports of production problems have continued to surface since, including smashed cameras, urine-soaked sound equipment, and a boom-microphone windscreen that was stolen and raised as young. ⌀

BABY from page 291

not to be identified, described Joshua's head as "bulbous" and "disproportionate," and said the baby has "pudgy, triple-creased legs."

"May God forgive me, I know it's a sin to judge people on the basis of their appearance," the anonymous source said. "But he's like a monster. If you blew him up to normal size, people would scream in horror."

Although he responds to his doting parents, Joshua often alienates those outside of his family circle, according to his pediatrician, Dr. Martin Prushow.

"He seems to take interest only in people who are willing to nurture or 'mother' him," Prushow said. "Once in a while, you can coax a smile out of him, but only if you make a smiling face yourself. He's not a terrible person, but as far as actual depth, nothing."

Among non-relatives, perhaps the most acquainted with Joshua is 16-year-old babysitter Ashley Steinhoff. Though she meets with Joshua as

Although he responds to his doting parents, Joshua often alienates those outside of his family circle, according to his pediatrician, Dr. Martin Prushow.

many as three times a week, Steinhoff was quick to distance herself from the baby.

"'Babysitter' sure, but I wouldn't say 'friend,'" Steinhoff said. "I mean, it's not like I hang out with him for free. With my actual friends, I do things just for fun, and have full-sentence conversations—not change their diapers."

Steinhoff did not rule out the possibility of a future friendship, but said that Joshua would have to "quit being a baby first."

Although it is more than eight months away, family friends are already concocting excuses to skip "Baby No-Friends'" first birthday party.

"I can already predict what will happen," Sperber said. "He'll smear cake all over himself, throw a tantrum when someone puts a party hat on him, and scarcely acknowledge his presents other than to gnaw on them. I've seen how this kid operates." ⌀

My Daughter, Who Lives At 152 East Medgar St. Apt. 4, Can't Keep Her Damn Legs Crossed

Being a father is no easy job, and it just gets tougher when you're a father to girls. Don't get me wrong: I love all my kids equally. But somehow, you worry more about your daughters, even—or especially—when they're not so little anymore. Like my daughter Sandra: a warm, intelligent, life-loving young woman who just got her first apartment at 152 East Medgar St. Apt. 4, and who can't seem to keep her damn legs crossed.

By Karl Hamm

Don't bother telling me that all young people go through a "wild" phase, or that I was the same way when I was a young man. That's part of it—I was a young *man*. I'm sorry, but it's just different. Though I must mention that I didn't swoon and fall on my back whenever someone put on Al Green's "Sha La La" or presented me with mocha-chocolate Godiva truffles.

Sandra, though, that's my daughter all over. It seems like every day after work when she goes to Canoodler's on Park and 31st, she'll go home with the first reasonably polite guy who gives her the "big lonely city" line and buys her a Malibu Mojito. And the weekends are worse. I'm pretty sure

I wish Sandra would settle down with the quiet, studious type she claims to like. Instead, it's often just someone who likes to watch the same TV shows as her while using the treadmill next to her on the second floor of the Fitness Factory on Cooper Plaza Mondays, Wednesdays, and Fridays.

her weakness for soft-spoken men with puppies has led to more than one Sunday-afternoon tryst with some cardigan-wearing Labrador-owner type from the Union Park dog run.

I know it's possible that I'm overreacting. I know that Sandra is in no way a bad person, and she's far from a stupid person—although sometimes I expect the bespectacled types she

I know it's possible that I'm overreacting. I know that Sandra is in no way a bad person, and she's far from a stupid person—although sometimes I expect the bespectacled types she goes all mushy over haven't actually read the Dostoevsky they're carrying around when she invites them back to her place.

goes all mushy over haven't actually read the Dostoevsky they're carrying around when she invites them back to her place. Every generation thinks they invented sex, but if you ask me, Sandra, with her RandySandy75 profile on Nerve, is just carrying out an age-old practice in a contemporary fashion. I just wish she wouldn't go on so many dates with scruffy men between 28 and 35 who come into Maxwell's Fine Wines and make her laugh with a clever remark about her name tag or her job as French vintages buyer.

I know that, for Sandra, it's all part of being a young woman who can't resist candlelight, Thai food, and Bay Rhum aftershave. Believe me, she gets a lot of that from her mother, a wonderful and attractive woman with whom I'm still very close, and none of that is why we divorced and she moved to Unit 17 of the Park Tower Condominiums. But still, I wish Sandra would settle down with the quiet, studious type she claims to like. Instead, it's often just someone who likes to watch the same TV shows as her while using the treadmill next to her on the second floor of the Fitness Factory on Cooper Plaza Mondays, Wednesdays, and Fridays. ⌀

Your Horoscope

By Lloyd Schumner Sr.
Retired Machinist and
A.A.P.B.-Certified Astrologer

Aries: (March 21–April 19)
People think you're delusional when you say you're in love with a girl on a billboard next to Highway 41, until they realize you fastened a nursing student up there with carriage bolts.

Taurus: (April 20–May 20)
Your long-held belief that the pen is mightier than the sword will be put to the test this week when you sign up for a combination fencing/calligraphy class co-taught by an angry Spaniard and a weary sensei.

Gemini: (May 21–June 21)
This is the nesting season of the Turner's Dauber, a nine-inch-long species of parasitic wasp that injects its starving, carnivorous larvae deep into a species of wren that looks just like your new hairstyle.

Cancer: (June 22–July 22)
Your resistance to technology comes to a sudden end this week when you're garroted with a length of fiber-optic cable.

Leo: (July 23–Aug. 22)
There's no denying that your unique scarecrow design scares the hell out the crows, but it has the disadvantage of filling your yard with infuriated Christians.

Virgo: (Aug. 23–Sept. 22)
Some say that your shortsightedness will be the death of you, but it's your glaucoma that leads you to drive up an off-ramp and into a gasoline truck.

Libra: (Sept. 23–Oct. 23)
You're no music expert, but the shadow growing in size around your feet looks like that of a concert grand piano.

Scorpio: (Oct. 24–Nov. 21)
Your death will be so protracted and violent that investigators will let your mother down easy by telling her you were sodomized in half by a horse.

Sagittarius: (Nov. 22–Dec. 21)
You'll finally put an end to your illiteracy this week when what you believe to be a bowl of alphabet soup turns out to be a can of minestrone with a POISON label on it.

Capricorn: (Dec. 22–Jan. 19)
Once again, a poorly timed wisecrack at the office will lead to you lying prone in a ditch with ice water up to your chin and your hands going numb on the grip of the .45.

Aquarius: (Jan. 20–Feb. 18)
It'll finally hit you this week that the Gerber baby is most likely dead by now, a realization brought on not so much by the photo on the front of the jar but the mush inside.

Pisces: (Feb. 19–March 20)
The good people over at Fisher-Price say it's impossible to be dismembered by one of their toys, but you'll soon show those smug bastards what's what. ⌀

BUSH from page 292

say to that one, so I just drank the rest of my beer real fast."

After nearly a minute of silence, Bush drained the remainder of his O'Doul's and wished Reinard goodbye, saying that he'd stay longer if he could, but had "some business to tend to."

"He shook my hand and smiled, said he had to run," Reinard said. "Something about a conference or a summit. It seemed like he was actually relieved to go."

Reinard and Kern both estimated Bush's stay at the bar as no longer than 15 minutes. This included Kern's attempt to pay for Bush's beer. Bush only smiled and waved at Kern, and a member of his Secret Service escort pulled a $10 bill from his coat pocket and tossed it on the bar.

Reinard likened the encounter with Bush to "being cornered at a company Christmas party by your boss."

"It was like, do you act and drink like normal, or are you on your best behavior?" Reinard said. "Are you upfront with the guy or do you choose your words carefully? What does he want out of you, anyway? Or does he

Reinard and Kern both estimated Bush's stay at the bar as no longer than 15 minutes.

just want to connect with somebody, because it's lonely at the top? You just don't know for sure."

"Overall, it was okay, I suppose," Reinard said. " One thing's for sure, though—I still wouldn't want to have a beer with that stuck-up Kerry." ⌀

the ONION®

VOLUME 41 ISSUE 47 AMERICA'S FINEST NEWS SOURCE™ 24–30 NOVEMBER 2005

FCC: All Programming To Be Broadcast In ADHDTV By 2007

WASHINGTON, DC—The Federal Communications Commission voted 3–1 Monday to require electronics manufacturers to make all television sets ADHD-compatible within two years.

To adhere to the guidelines, every program, with the exception of *The Hi Hi Puffy AmiYumi Show*, will have to be sped up to meet the new standard frame rate of 120 frames per second.

FCC Chairman Kevin Martin characterized the move as "a natural, forward-thinking response to the changing needs of the average American viewer."

"In the media-saturated climate of the modern age, few have the time and energy to sit still for an entire

see FCC page 298

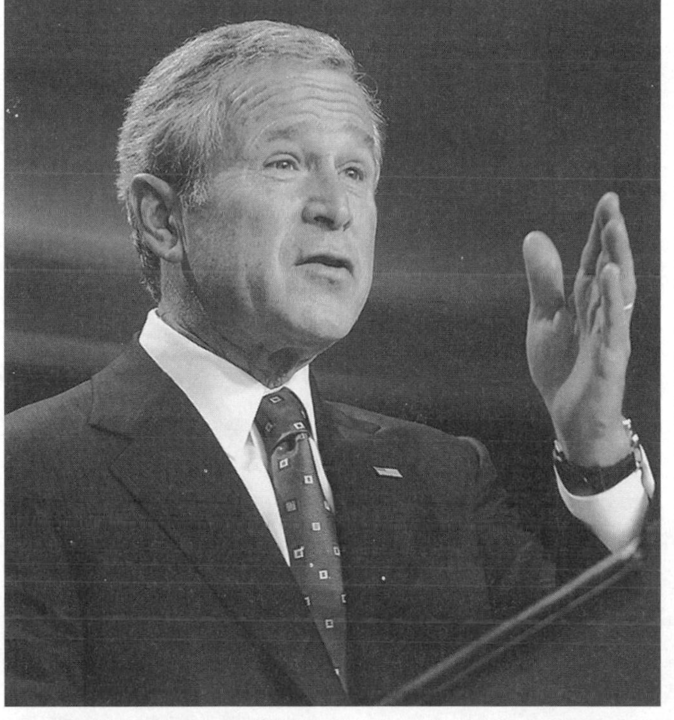

Bush To Increase Funding For Hope-Based Initiatives

WASHINGTON, DC—President Bush announced today that he will sign a bill providing an additional $2.8 billion for private organizations that emphasize the importance of hoping for change.

"This bill acknowledges the immeasurable role of hope in envisioning a better world for everyone," Bush said during a press conference. "Starting today, I ask all Americans to hope together as one nation that the difficult

see HOPE page 298

Left: Bush presents his plan to fund organizations that hope for change.

NEWS

Local Bull Dreams Of Traveling To Spain For Running Of The Bulls

see TRAVEL page 2C

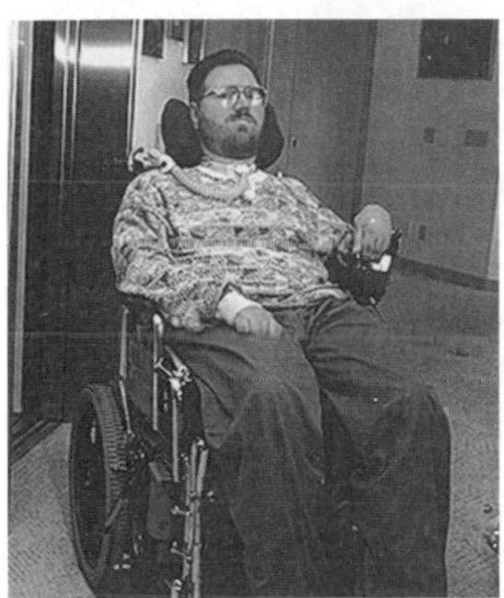

Actually, Suicide Not The Easy Way Out For Area Quadriplegic

see SCIENCE page 3E

Hooker Refuses To Take More Sex As Payment

see LOCAL page 12F

STATshot

A look at the numbers that shape your world.

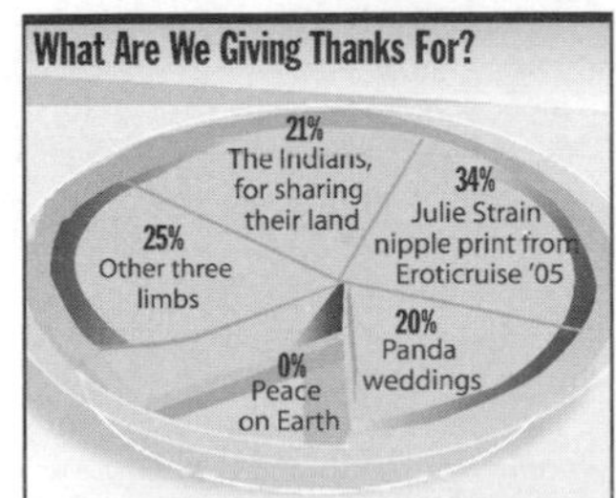

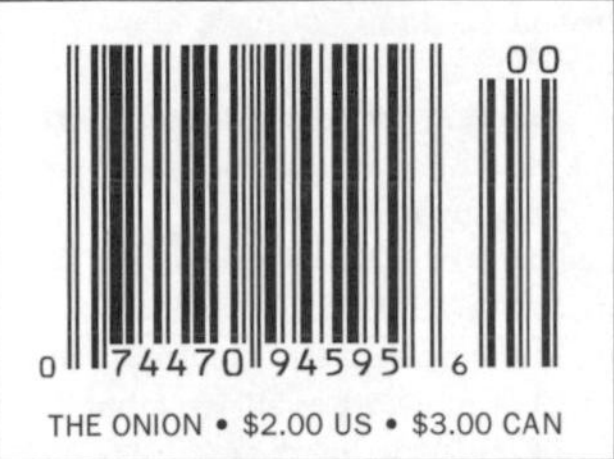

HEALTH FOCUS

Cases Of Glitter Lung On The Rise Among Elementary-School Art Teachers

CHICAGO—The Occupational Safety And Health Administration released figures Monday indicating that record numbers of elementary-school art teachers are falling victim to pneumosparklyosis, commonly known as glitter lung.

Nearly 8,000 cases were reported in 2004, the most recent year for which statistics are available. This is the highest number since the arts-and-crafts industry was deregulated in 1988.

Characterized by a lack of creative energy and shortness of breath, and accompanied by sneezing or coughing up flakes of twinkly, reflective matter, glitter lung typically strikes teachers between the ages of 29 to 60 who spend 20 hours per week in an art-class setting dur-

see GLITTER LUNG page 299

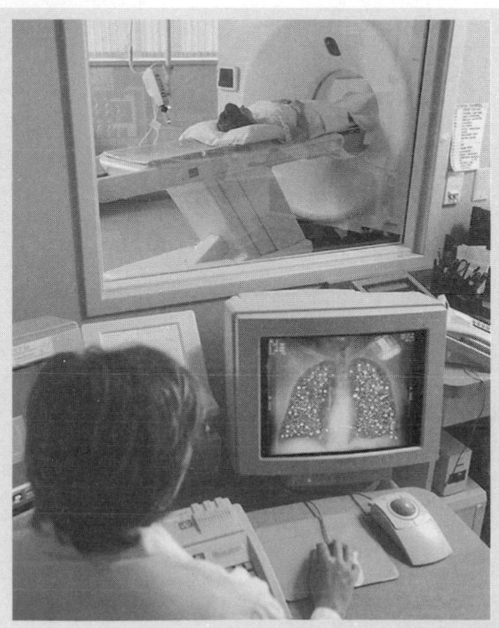

Right: Dr. Linda Norr scans a sufferer who spent more than two decades in the classrooms.

Hurricane Evacuees

FEMA recently announced that, at the end of the month, they will stop paying for hurricane evacuees' hotel rooms. What do *you* think?

Noah Davis
Musician

"Why are we focusing on the negatives instead of on how quickly and efficiently FEMA evacuated everyone from their hotel rooms?"

Veronica Duddy
Short Order Cook

"Those people have been through enough without the stigma of being kicked out of a hotel room—which, as a former Van Halen groupie, I can relate to on a very deep level."

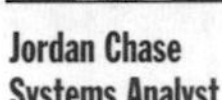

Jordan Chase
Systems Analyst

"Well, yeah. They've had, what, eight or nine weeks now to build new houses?"

Matt Marshall
Youth Counselor

"There are clearly plenty of perfectly good bridges they can live under."

Richard McCormick
Soap Maker

"What will the evacuees do without immediate access to free ice?"

Sarah Amsbury
Toll Booth Collector

"Something tells me the Gulf Coast is going to need those rooms for a really big government contractor's convention pretty soon."

Xbox 360 Features

Microsoft's Xbox 360 hits stores on Nov. 22. Here are some of the features of the new video-game system:

- "Boomerang Controller" returns to user when thrown at television in frustration
- Three separate processors running at 3.2 GHz each allow you to complete entire games in under 15 seconds
- Even less girlfriend-compatible than previous generations of gaming consoles
- Available in configurations priced at $399, $499, and $999, depending on how much you want to pay
- Has what people in chemical-burn wards across America will be calling "that new Xbox smell"
- New chip allows parents to block sexual content, so *Dead Or Alive* players can rip off opponent's head, but can no longer fuck neck-hole
- Can turn all the way around, apparently

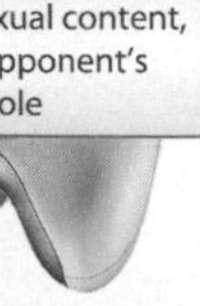

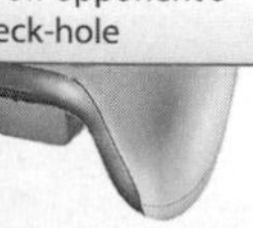

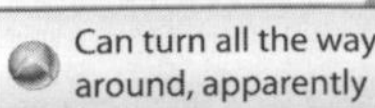

America's Finest News Source.™

Herman Ulysses Zweibel
Founder

T. Herman Zweibel
Publisher Emeritus
J. Phineas Zweibel
Publisher
Maxwell Prescott Zweibel
Editor-In-Chief

No Machine Can Do My Job As Resentfully As I Can

By Lee Canale

In today's increasingly mechanized world, where the bottom line so often takes precedence over human considerations, the working man never knows how long it will be before he is replaced by a machine. It's no secret that some in management at Gillian's Fish Products, where I work, feel that automation would improve productivity and quality control. But what they don't understand is that they will lose something far more valuable if employees are let go: the resentful human touch.

No mere machine can replace the embittered alienation of the flesh-and-blood worker. Sure, machines may be able to gut whitefish in the blink of an eye. But would they be able, as I am, to despise and bemoan their miserable lot? To seethe with the unbearable knowledge that this will be their sole livelihood until the day they die? To identify with the glassy, sightless eye of every fish as its sharp blade draws the innards out?

Whether it's scaling each cod and struggling to suppress the repulsion and loathing within, or de-boning each haddock while fighting the impulse to drop the knife and walk out of the factory as far as your legs can take you, such sentiments could never be reproduced in mechanical form. Those special qualities can only come from one source: exhausted men and women forced to feed and clothe their children on a pauper's wages.

Replacing us with machines will increase profits, but can a dollar value be placed on the labors of someone who drinks before his morning shift just to get through the day? And when the machines are sitting in six-inch-deep gore at day's end, will they go home and take out their frustrations on family members and loved ones? I think not.

Can a machine fume about years without a decent vacation, or having to pay exorbitant rent in a company-owned tenement near the factory?

A machine can only contain wires, diodes, and gears, not the living, breathing sum of life's screw-ups, heartbreaks, and regrets.

You can install machines, but you can't install the permanent smell of fish in your nostrils, or hands that have been roughened, swollen, and discolored from years of fish dismemberment. You can build a machine to replicate the same repetitive motions we perform five backbreaking days a week, but all the engineers in the world cannot build a machine that will repeatedly bang its head on a locker, silent tears streaming down its metal cheeks, as it contemplates its wasted life.

No mere machine can replace the embittered alienation of the flesh-and-blood worker. Sure, machines may be able to gut whitefish in the blink of an eye. But would they be able, as I am, to despise and bemoan their miserable lot? To seethe with the unbearable knowledge that this will be their sole livelihood until the day they die?

Can a machine fume about years without a decent vacation, or having to pay exorbitant rent in a company-owned tenement near the factory? This, surely, only a man can do—a deeply self-hating man who loathes every second of his working life.

A machine can break down mechanically, but can it break down emotionally, mentally, and spiritually?

I can, and I have. Every day, a little piece of me dies. Could a machine say the same?

I've worked at this unventilated shit-prison 12 hours a day for nearly 25 years. I have developed no skills other than that of silently counting down the minutes of each workday while cursing my misfortune.

No matter what else they take from me, my utter and total hatred of this nightmarish fish-stick factory will always be mine. After all, isn't that what makes us truly human? Ø

Parking-Ramp Attendant Knows All The Best Spaces

MILWAUKEE—The average customer at the Water Street parking ramp has probably not taken notice of Brian Haemker. They've passed by him day in and day out, likely assuming he is just another parking-lot attendant. But in reality, he is much more.

Haemker has spent the past six years gathering the secrets of every nook and cranny of the Water Street parking ramp, amassing a treasure trove of privileged information.

"There's a whole row on Level 4 that's almost untouched," said Haemker from his tiny booth. "That's because it's on the opposite end of the elevator. But there's a pedestrian walkway just a few steps ahead that gets you across and over pretty conveniently. Plus, there's a Coke machine right there."

"A lot of people don't consider that," Haemker added.

Haemker said drivers often overlook the ramp's basement level.

"I see it every day: People just start up that ramp without thinking," Haemker said. "Meanwhile, a third of the basement sits open. And it's the warmest spot in the winter."

Haemker said Level 6 has some

see PARKING page 300

"There's a whole row on Level 4 that's almost untouched," said Haemker from his tiny booth. "That's because it's on the opposite end of the elevator. But there's a pedestrian walkway just a few steps ahead that gets you across and over pretty conveniently. Plus, there's a Coke machine right there."

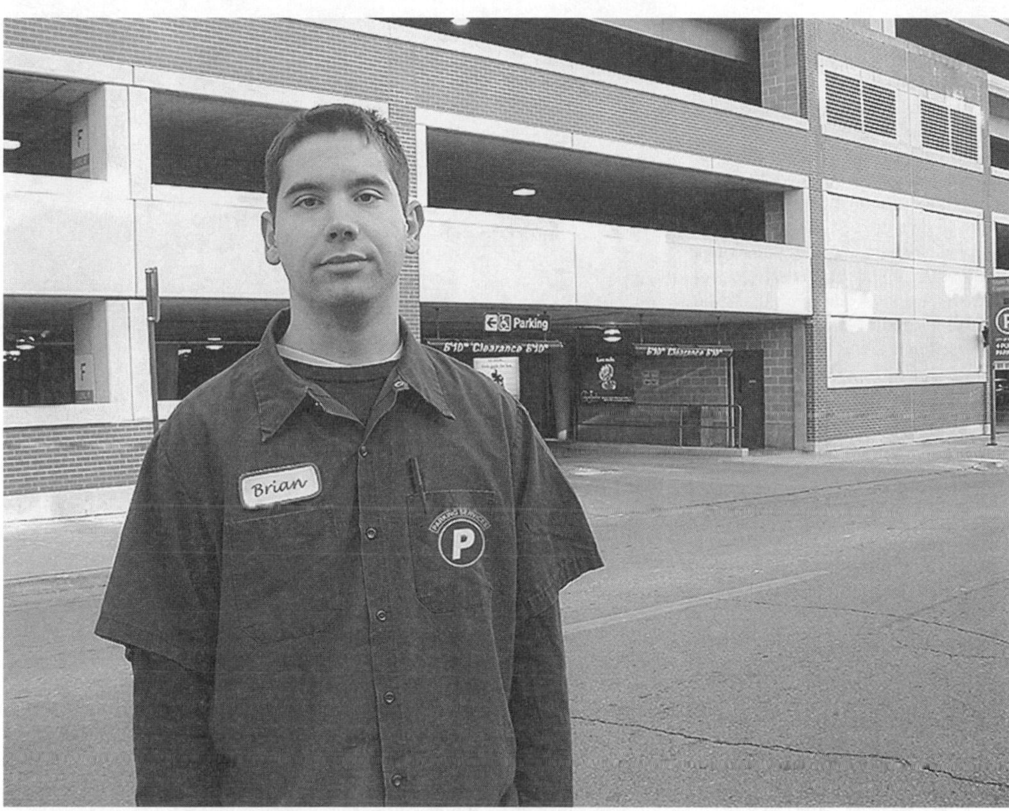

Above: Haemker, who says he knows the Water Street parking ramp "like the back of his hand."

NEWS IN BRIEF

I.T. Guy Has Long Dark Night Of Self-Doubt

CHICAGO—Scott Tarkoff, the I.T. manager for UrbaNews, LLC, slept little Monday night, plagued by visions of confused coworkers and faultily configured backup servers. "What if everything I know—from the optimum desktop file structure to the most secure formatting of a password—is wrong?" Tarkoff wrote in his Linux-powered home desktop setup, which he built himself for $700. "What if the software documentation I wrote is opaque and unhelpful?" Staff at UrbaNews reported that, by Tuesday morning, Tarkoff was as condescending and cocksure as ever.

Holocaust Film Appeals To Believers And Skeptics Alike

HAMBURG—Critics describe *Die Lange Eisenbahnfahrt* (The Long Railroad Trip) as the first Holocaust film to give a fair hearing to memorialists and deniers alike. "At last, we have a cinematic exploration of the Holocaust that portrays both sides equally, instead of fostering further divisiveness," reviewer Hans Kerlemann wrote in Der Spiegel. "The film's acknowledgment of anti-Semitic feelings in Hitler's Germany, coupled with its scenes of people boarding packed trains, is especially powerful." *Die Lange Eisenbahnfahrt* opens in select cities on the first day of Hanukkah.

All Of Pregnant Woman's Favorite Names Used Up On Cats

EUGENE, OR—Seven months pregnant with her first child, veteran cat lady Claudia Beck, 38, said Monday that she has already used all of her favorite names on her cats. "I've got Madison, Emily, Tyler, Jonathan, Claudia Jr., Dakota, and Todd," Beck said. "Then there's Smokey and Midnight, who are strays I feed." As of press time, Beck and the baby's father, animal-shelter assistant Rich Delgado, were considering naming their child "Boots."

Best-Laid Plans Of Mice Mostly Cheese-Related

ALBUQUERQUE, NM—Animal-intelligence researchers at Sandia National Labs have found that the best-laid plans of common laboratory mice are overwhelmingly directed toward the acquisition of cheese. "Whatever rudimentary planning skills mice possess are devoted primarily to finding cheese, and these plans are manifest in dodging predators, chewing through things, and, in specialized cases, running mazes," researcher Jack Stein said. "By contrast, the best-laid plans of men are more long-term, with the acquisition of cheese comprising one subcategory of endeavor." Stein added that both types of plans tend oft to go awry.

Topeka Mayor Now Highest-Ranking Non-Indicted Republican Official

TOPEKA, KS—As of Tuesday, Topeka mayor William Bunten, 74, is the nation's highest-ranking Republican official not facing indictment or public reprimand. "I have always prided myself on running a clean campaign, a clean office, and cleaning house when necessary," Bunten said. "However, I have no comment on the charges facing my party's leadership, fundraising apparatus, known associates, or advisory staff." Bunten is the highest-ranked non-indicted Republican since 1974, when Hansen County, SD schoolboard secretary Cal Albright was forced to stand in as the president of the United States for two years. Ø

FCC from page 295

episode of *King Of Queens*," Martin said. "Although the FCC will leave it up to the television networks to make the necessary programming changes, we are recommending, in accordance with the ADHDTV standard, that all shows be no more than six minutes in length, and that they contain jarring and unpredictable camera cuts to shiny props and detailed background sets."

"We're also advising that intra-episode recaps occur every 45 seconds," he added.

The ruling represents a growing shift toward ADHDTV, a television format designed to meet the needs of an increasingly inattentive and hyperactive audience. The tuner includes a built-in device that automatically changes channels after three minutes of uninterrupted single-station viewing, as well as a picture-in-picture-in-picture-in-picture option.

According to Sony, the leading manufacturer of the ADHD-compatible sets, the new technology will allow viewers to play up to three simultaneous video games while watching television.

Above: Two Lansing, MI children watch an ADHDTV promo for the entire prime-time network lineup.

On standard 4:3 televisions, ADHDTV programs will be shown in letterbox format, with the top and bottom of the screen alternately filled with bright, flittering butterflies, undulating rainbow-colored patterns, and singing hamsters in top hats.

"Many of our ADHDTVs will come with a motorized base," Sony spokesperson Richard O'Dell said. "In the event that the viewer turns his attention away from the television, it will begin to rotate and emit sirens and piercing shrieks."

The mandate to conform to the new format has already been met with some resistance, particularly from movie channels like HBO, live programs such as ABC's *Monday Night Football*, and the History Channel, whose ambitious five-part, 10-hour historical documentary about World War II, slated for completion in late 2007, will have to be shortened to a six-minute montage of the war set to a medley of Ashlee Simpson hits.

Some networks, however, are embracing the change.

"A majority of our shows are only watchable for a few minutes at a time anyway," said Fox president Peter Liguori, whose recently unveiled fall 2007 TV schedule includes over 850 new series. "We're going to roll out an exciting lineup of major sporting-event highlights, late-night yell shows, and a brand-new season of *The O.C.* that will feature 37 new characters and—well, I don't want to give too much away, but let's just say it will have a lot more guys jumping up and down, saying, 'Hey! Hey! Look over here!'"

On standard 4:3 televisions, ADHDTV programs will be shown in letterbox format, with the top and bottom of the screen alternately filled with bright, flittering butterflies, undulating rainbow-colored patterns, and singing hamsters in top hats.

Skeptics say the switch to ADHDTV will likely be delayed in favor of other projects or even completely forgotten by next week. However, the FDA is fast-tracking approval of the new drug Entertainalin, developed in anticipation of the modified programming. In clinical trials, the drug has been effective in helping viewers concentrate not only on the new TV format, but also on their immediate surroundings, the couch fabric, a dog passing by the window, and pieces of lint floating in the air. ⌀

HOPE from page 295

problems that grip our nation will go away someday."

The president's move will help direct federal funds to such groups as the National Hope Foundation, which has been hoping for a cure for cancer for nearly two decades.

"There are many in our country who are without hope," Bush said. "Yet there are many respected organizations in America that are actively hoping things get better. This program will assist these organizations in obtaining government grants, which will allow them to continue the important hoping that must be done."

Among the programs likely to receive funding is Project Hope You Don't Get Sick, a non-profit organization hoping that over 45 million Americans receive the proper health care they need.

Dream Job United, another likely recipient, is a widely acclaimed program in which the ill-prepared and uneducated are trained to hope for job interviews at top companies.

Another project slated for assistance in is a Louisiana-based teen-pregnancy reduction program, in which volunteers hope teens abstain from intercourse.

Under the bill, wish-based initiatives will also be eligible for increased funding. Dozens of independent wish-ful-thinking foundations, such as America Wishes Things Were Better, expect to receive grants to fund distribution of pennies, wishbones, and birthday candles.

"Faith-based problem-solving is noble, but we should not discount the power of hope," said veteran hoper Howard Thorndike, who heads the Please Oh Please Institute, a Houston-based wish tank.

Those with wishes and hopes applauded the president's move, saying that faith alone cannot rectify the nation's social ills.

"Faith-based problem-solving is noble, but we should not discount the power of hope," said veteran hoper Howard Thorndike, who heads the Please Oh Please Institute, a Houston-based wish tank. "'Hail Mary' strategies, for example, are a part of the fabric of our nation, from the football field to the boardroom, and our government ignores such traditions at its peril."

Bush echoed Thorndike's sentiments. "As your president, I have seen firsthand what hoping can do," he said. "I have heard stories of decent people trapped under piles of rubble, and I have hoped that they would be rescued. And eventually, many were. Recently, powerful storms and destructive hurricanes ravaged some of our great cities. I hope that you will join me in wishing that we do not get hit by any more of those."

Bush added: "Laura and I hope every night that good things will happen for our great country. My fellow Americans, I call on you to do the same." ⌀

GLITTER LUNG from page 295

ing the school year.

"When art teachers spend so much time in confined quarters with inadequate ventilation amid swirling clouds of glitter, it's only a matter of time before their lungs start to suffer negative effects," said Dr. Linda Norr, a specialist in elementary-school-related respiratory diseases. "Those suf-

"When art teachers spend so much time in confined quarters with inadequate ventilation amid swirling clouds of glitter, it's only a matter of time before their lungs start to suffer negative effects."

ferers who are not put on a rigorous program of treatment often spend their last days on respirators, hacking up a thick, dazzling mucus."

As incidences of glitter lung continue to rise, critics are accusing public schools of not doing enough to protect art teachers.

What Is Glitter Lung?

Glitter lung, or pneumosparklyosis, is a respiratory disease caused by the chronic inhalation of precision-cut, iridescent, metallized particles. Elementary-school art teachers and transgendered "drag queen" entertainers are the populations most at risk.

1. Airborne glitter enters through the nose and mouth. First attracted to glue-like mucous membranes, the glitter then settles into the lungs.

2. Glitter deposits cause scarring, inflammation, and twinkliness of the lungs, leading to bedazzlemia—a condition in which alveoli are so sparkly that oxygen molecules are reflected away from the bloodstream.

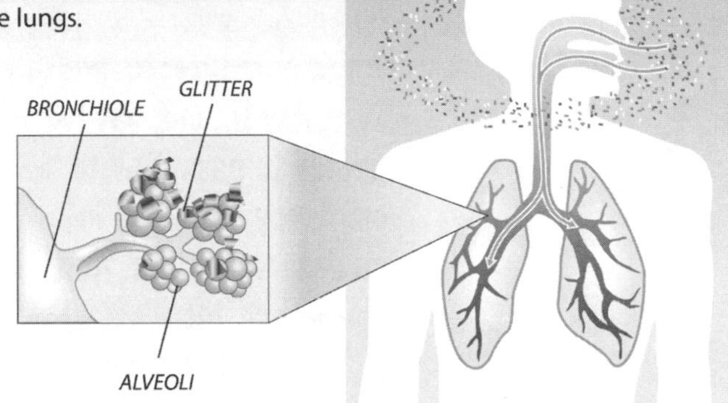

3. Eventually, the alveoli become completely decorated and are unable to function, leading to massive system failure due to oxygen starvation. Although the dangers of glitter lung are just now becoming known, the body's intolerance of shiny substances has been studied for decades (see "Symptoms and treatments of goldfingeritis," *New England Journal Of Medicine,* 1964).

Former art teacher Miles Winfield, who recently testified before a House subcommittee on unsafe working conditions, said that, as his symptoms worsened, his principal looked the other way, fearing defamation lawsuits from the powerful glitter industry.

"Most art teachers are afraid to come forward, for fear of losing their jobs," Winfield said. "At an absolute minimum, an art teacher should be equipped with a respirator, thick goggles, and a reflective-field smock. But schools don't want to stand up to Big Glitter, which continues to insist that this stuff is safe. Schools end up falsifying the safety reports and hoping they get away with it. And they usually do."

Until heavier, less toxic forms of glitter are developed, physicians recommend using alternative media to enhance children's artwork.

"Cheerios, cotton balls, and popsicle sticks are considered very safe," Norr said. "Avoid colored string, however, because some studies show that it could be high in yarncinogens. And if glitter is absolutely essential to the craft project, try using a glitter pen, as the particles are less likely to become airborne."

Glitter guidelines established by OSHA in 1970 allow for no more than 10,000 flakes per cm3 of the substance in the air. Yet critics say the standards were developed to protect children, who typically only spend two to three hours in art class per week, unlike teachers, who spend as many as 40 hours per week in the toxic, high-glitter environment.

Though only 47 years old, Lawrence, KS art teacher Helen Niles was forced to quit her job and lose her health insurance after her chronic glitter lung rendered her unfit for full-time work in February.

"At first, I had no idea what was going on," Niles said. "I'd wake up in the morning and I'd have this gritty feel in my mouth. The school nurse told me it was nothing, but eventually I was waking up with a shiny, sparkling stain on the pillow."

"People who have worked with glitter know that it gets everywhere if you don't sprinkle it very carefully. It can stick to your clothes and your skin," Niles said. "Imagine working in an environment where the atmosphere contains 10 parts per million, and you quickly realize what our nation's art teachers are up against."

The medical community has been

As incidences of glitter lung continue to rise, critics are accusing public schools of not doing enough to protect art teachers.

slow to recognize glitter lung as a public health threat. A 1993 epidemic of sequin fibrosis, which primarily affected dancers in the Las Vegas, NV area, was seen as an isolated case. Now, however, the disease is being re-evaluated, and many doctors believe it may be the most serious occupational health hazard to hit educators since the outbreak of gold-star syndrome in the 1960s.

Epidemiologists note that the increase in glitter-lung cases is occurring simultaneously with a general rise in other classroom-related diseases. Macaroni elbow, modeling clay palsy, crayon flu, and googly-eye are sidelining thousands of teachers each year.

But despite growing medical alarm, efforts to provide adequate safety measures and health care continue to be hampered by bureaucratic red, blue, green, and yellow tape. ⌀

MELONS from page 271

amounts of blood. Passersby were amazed by the unusually large amounts of blood. Passersby were

You shouldn't marry a porpoise.

amazed by the unusually large amounts of blood. Passersby were amazed by the unusually large amounts of blood. Passersby were amazed by the unusually large amounts of blood. Passersby were amazed by the unusually large amounts of blood. Passersby were amazed by the unusually large amounts of blood. Passersby were amazed by the unusually large amounts of blood. Passersby were amazed by the unusually large amounts of blood.Passersby were amazed by the unusually large amounts of blood.Passersby were

see MELONS page 302

Someday, Son, All This Cheap Crap Will Be Yours

By Ray Talbot

Son, your mother and I worked hard to build a safe and comfortable home for you. And we hope to pass it all on to you someday.

As I roam the grounds of our half-acre estate, the sight of all these items makes me swell with pride. You, of course, are my crown jewel, but every jewel deserves its elegant setting, and it comforts me to know that you'll always have a place to go home to and a foam-filled chintz davenport with unmatching faux-leopard plush throw to sit on.

Yes, Ray Jr., one day I intend to pass it all to you. As my scion and heir, you deserve no less. Now, I know that there's a lot of parents in this neighborhood who completely intend to put the family home up once their children have graduated from college and moved out. Not us. Your mom and I want our legacy to endure well past our lifetimes. That plastic kitchen wastebasket has been in our family for years, and with us it shall remain.

Drink it in, son, for the lordly Talbot estate will be yours someday. The soiled Igloo cooler. The scum-encrusted toothbrush holder. The kitchen breakfast-nook stools with the ripped vinyl seats. My La-Z-Boy, also ripped. And your mother's collection of used Renuzit air fresheners. Yes, I know it's sort of eccentric of her, saving these things long after they've been spent up, but she likes the conical shape.

Drink it in, son, for the lordly Talbot estate will be yours someday. The soiled Igloo cooler. The kitchen breakfast-nook stools with the ripped vinyl seats. My La-Z-Boy, also ripped.

You don't *have* to keep them, but it would be a good way to show her you love her.

You shall never want for a spoon rest, son, for there it is, over by the animal-shaped cookie jar. What is that supposed to be, anyway? A bear, or a dog? Perhaps an ape? Remember how it used to scare you as a child, perhaps because its blood-red tongue was sticking out? Well, I hope you've

Yes, Ray Jr., one day I intend to pass it all to you. As my scion and heir, you deserve no less. Now, I know that there's a lot of parents in this neighborhood who completely intend to put the family home up once their children have graduated from college and moved out. Not us. Your mom and I want our legacy to endure well past our lifetimes.

gotten over your fear, because it's an heirloom now.

Behold, son—the electric mug-warmer. The faded and discolored living-room curtains. The cabinet stuffed with plastic grocery bags. Your mother's various hair pieces and falls. The plastic-ball exerciser that your hamster, Bo Jackson, once so enjoyed. All yours, even the mysterious device that I believe might be a rock polisher, but I'm not sure. I leave it to you, son.

I wasn't entirely accurate when I said that your mother and I started with nothing. My boy, those press-board bookshelves once belonged to my father. I remember the day he gave them to us. He said to me, "If only I had more to give you." I did my damndest to fill those shelves with as many Time-Life books and supermarket encyclopedias as I could, such that they might droop under the weight of books unread. And now I pass them down to you son.

Well, Ray Jr., I wasn't going to give you this until the day your first child was born, but I feel it's right to let you have it now. Yes, it is my old laundry basket. May you long fill it with with soiled tube socks.

And now, son, let us raise a toast to your glorious, secure future with our *Coneheads* collectors' cups. ⌀

Your Horoscope

By Lloyd Schumner Sr.
Retired Machinist and
A.A.P.B.-Certified Astrologer

Aries: (March 21–April 19)
Years after losing friends and family members to the obsession, you will finally admit that your life-long goal of becoming the Pythagoras of isosceles triangles is not worth the trouble.

Taurus: (April 20–May 20)
The title of World's Greatest Escape Artist will be passed from Houdini to you this week, after you escape not from handcuffs or a straight-jacket, but from a loveless marriage with only the aid of vodka.

Gemini: (May 21–June 21)
Your belief that humanity is growing too dependent on machines will finally be put to rest next week, when after three days of careful deliberation, your family members decide to take you off the respirator.

Cancer: (June 22–July 22)
A weary mind can often be relieved with a simple change of scenery. Politely ask your captors if they would allow you to take a brief walk around the block.

Leo: (July 23–Aug. 22)
It's true that your talents and interests make you unique; however, some of the credit should go to your mother, for ingesting the thalidomide.

Virgo: (Aug. 23–Sept. 22)
A leap of logic will result in the worst-selling novelty product of all-time and leave you stuck with a football-field-sized warehouse filled with real vomit.

Libra: (Sept. 23–Oct. 23)
The sense of hearing is often the first to go, but with you, it's the sense of dignity.

Scorpio: (Oct. 24–Nov. 21)
The stars haven't been feeling very comfortable with metaphors lately, but here goes: You will contract the HIV of sexually transmitted diseases this week.

Sagittarius: (Nov. 22–Dec. 21)
Your discovery of Ponce de Leon's famed Fountain Of Youth will be marred by the unfortunate, simultaneous discovery of a half-dozen infants drowned in its waters.

Capricorn: (Dec. 22–Jan. 19)
A romantic hot-air-balloon ride will quickly sour when it becomes clear that you and your husband are guinea pigs in a dangerously amateurish meteorological experiment.

Aquarius: (Jan. 20–Feb. 18)
The results of next week's medical exam will send a chill up your spine, or at least they would, if you were able to feel anything from the neck down.

Pisces: (Feb. 19–March 20)
Though the annual Chemistry And Engineering Institute Of Vermont Christmas celebration is weeks away, you're already beginning to dread the laborious chore of whipping up a bowl of your famous homemade Cheetos. ⌀

PARKING from page 297

"amazing" parking spaces, explaining that "the extra effort to get there is well worth it."

"Level 6 is seen by parkers as a last resort," Haemker said. "That's ironic, because it's where the best three spaces in the whole garage are."

Asked about the ramp's worst spaces, Haemker singled out those on the first floor, closest to the ticket booths, and a space on Level 5 that sits on the end, next to the traffic lane.

"Your fender is basically guaranteed to get dented there," he said.

Haemker says the most irritating drivers are the ones who park in the ramp for the entire workday, yet don't take advantage of the lower prices for customers who arrive before 8:00 a.m.

"Man, I wish I had the spare four bucks a day to park whenever I want," Haemker said. "Of course, these guys probably get reimbursed by their jobs for parking. Must be nice."

"Man, I wish I had the spare four bucks a day to park whenever I want," Haemker said. "Of course, these guys probably get reimbursed by their jobs for parking. Must be nice."

Haemker said he's happy to point drivers toward good spots, but no one ever asks.

"People just park wherever they can find a space, which seems to me just absolutely crazy," Haemker said. ⌀

NEWS

Unregistered Sex Offender Notifies Neighbors In His Own Way

see TRAVEL page 2C

Rerun of $25,000 Pyramid Adjusted For Inflation

see SCIENCE page 3E

Well-Put-Together Woman Falls Apart Easily

see LOCAL page 12F

STATshot

A look at the numbers that shape your world.

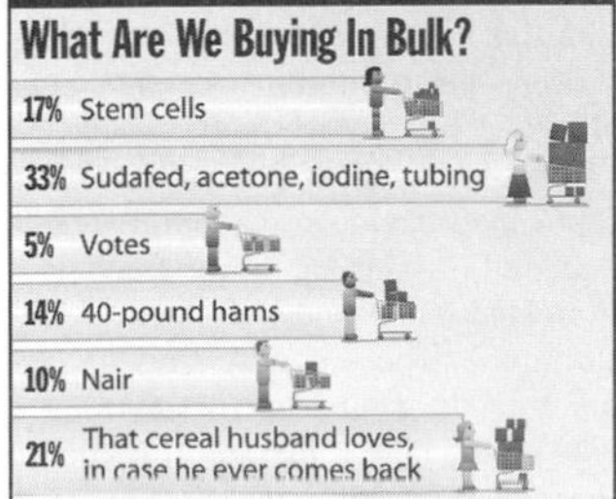

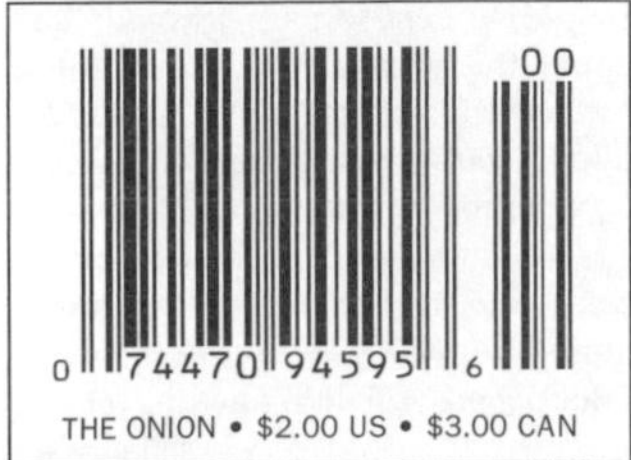

the ONION®

VOLUME 41 ISSUE 48 AMERICA'S FINEST NEWS SOURCE™ 1-7 DECEMBER 2005

Fritolaysia Cuts Off Chiplomatic Relations With Snakistan

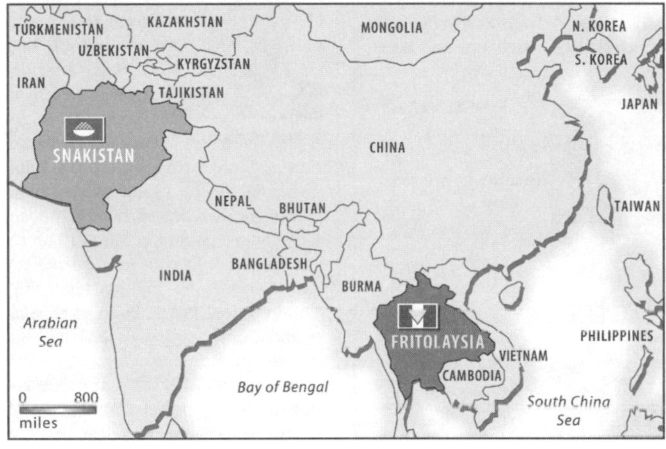

KARUNCHI, SNAKISTAN—Citing crumbling relations due to years of protracted french-onion diplomacy, the president of the Central Asian doritocracy Fritolaysia withdrew the country's ambassadors from Snakistan Monday.

"We have been supplying the people of Snakistan with pre-packaged consumable goods for over 40 years, and for them to show resistance to our savory products is unacceptable," Fritolaysian President Barbbaku Chedar said, referring to Snakistani officials' unwillingness to adhere to Fritolaysia's zesty new initiative introduced during a between-meals conference at last week's international-trading summit held in München, Germany.

"Fritolaysia has no choice but to crumple up and throw away all chiplomatic ties with the greedy, gluttonous government of Snakistan," Chedar added.

Relations between the two countries grew stale in 1994, when Fritolaysian rufflelutionaries crossed zestablished borders and forced Snakistan to dispatch cheesekeeping forces. The late-night SALTY talks held at Snakistan's Kuler Ranch, however, cooled the spicy conflict with the

see SNAKISTAN page 305

Terrorist Has No Idea What To Do With All This Plutonium

ZAHEDAN, IRAN—Yaquub Akhtar, the leader of an eight-man cell linked to a terrorist organization known as the Army Of Martyrs, admitted Tuesday that he "doesn't have the slightest clue" what to do with the quarter-kilogram of plutonium he recently acquired.

Above: Yaquub Akhtar.

"We had just given thanks to Allah for this glorious means to destroy the Great Satan once and for all, when [sub-lieutenant] Mahmoud [Ghassan] asked, 'So, what's the next step?'" Akhtar said. "I was at a loss."

The 28-year-old fanatic said he and his associates had initially assumed that at least one member of their group had the physics and engineering background necessary to construct a thermonuclear device.

"Many eyes were upon me," said Basim Aljawad, whose knowledge of physics did not extend to the principles of nuclear fission. "I make nail bombs. That's it."

Not knowing where to turn, the

see TERRORIST page 305

CIA Realizes It's Been Using Black Highlighters All These Years

LANGLEY, VA—A report released Tuesday by the CIA's Office of the Inspector General revealed that the CIA has mistakenly obscured hundreds of thousands of pages of critical intelligence information with black highlighters.

According to the report, sections of the documents— "almost invariably the most crucial passages"—are marred by an indelible black ink that renders the lines impossible to read, due to a top-secret highlighting policy that began at the agency's inception in 1947.

CIA Director Porter Goss has ordered further internal investigation.

"Why did it go on for this long, and this far?" said Goss in a press conference called shortly after the report's release. "I'm as frustrated as anyone. You can't read a single thing that's been highlighted. Had I been there to advise [former CIA director] Allen Dulles, I would have suggested the traditional yel-

see CIA page 304

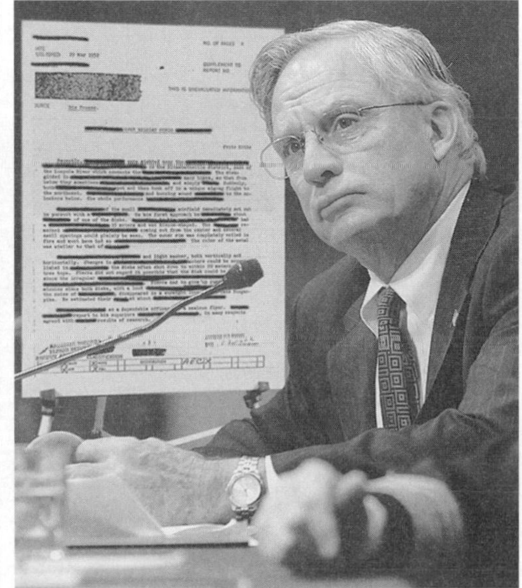

Right: CIA Director Porter Goss.

C-Section Boom

Americans are delivering babies via Caesarean section in record numbers. What do you think?

"These things are being performed too often. I mean, I went in for an appendectomy and came out with a healthy baby boy."

Brenda Kruse
Manicurist

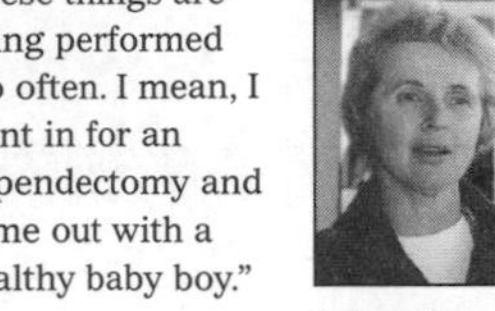

"I took fertility drugs, got pregnant with quadruplets, had a premature C-section, and my babies were on respirators for four months. Why the hell haven't I been on *Oprah*?"

Belinda Mann
Projectionist

"Wait, they normally push it out of *where*?"

Con McKay
Metal Worker

"It's sad. If a child does not pass through the birth canal, how is he going to develop any anxieties?"

Kevin Wells
Systems Analyst

"Who wants to go through the pain of a natural childbirth when you can simply be anesthetized and gutted like a trout?"

Ben Clements
Barista

"Is there some sort of awareness-raising long-distance run about this? Because that's my preferred method of addressing women's health-care concerns."

Hugh Webb
Pipe Fitter

Wal-Mart P.R.

In an effort to combat their negative media portrayal, Wal-Mart has set up a public-relations "war room." Here are the strategies they have drawn up to counter the bad press:

- Offer free hot dogs to potential whistleblowers
- Change smiley-face logo to something less evil
- Force any newspaper that depicts them in poor light out of business by opening larger, cheaper newspaper nearby
- Finalize company policy on how to best deploy Wal-Mart's eight nukes
- Give employees Christmas bonus of their choice of two basic civil liberties
- Make consumers an offer they can't refuse: a Tony Stewart die-cast car for $9.99
- Bomb Pearl's Bargain Harbor when they least expect it
- Organize massive leaflet-drop campaign promising to be humane and merciful to those who surrender

Herman Ulysses Zweibel
Founder

T. Herman Zweibel
Publisher Emeritus
J. Phineas Zweibel
Publisher
Maxwell Prescott Zweibel
Editor-In-Chief

Why Can't Anyone Tell I'm Wearing This Business Suit Ironically?

By Noah Frankovitch

Is it my fault none of you stupid conformists can understand how hilarious and ironic my cutting-edge fashion sense is? In 1986, I was the first kid in the neighborhood to wear a Mr. Bubble iron-on T-shirt from the '70s. I was only 10, but I was soaring over people's heads. In high school, I was the only guy to wear Adam And The Ants war paint to the senior prom—even though it was the early '90s. Those fools looked at me like I was 10 or 12 years behind! In college, the trucker-hat concept was my masterstroke. Within a few years, everybody was doing it, but by that time, I had so moved on.

Well, now I'm 25, and I'm still leaving all you idiots in mysteriously tongue-in-cheek fashion dust.

About five years ago, I was growing bored with the whole neo-'80s electroclash look that I had mastered years earlier. I figured, why not go all out and take the concept of ironic fashion to the extreme? Just do something so risky and completely out there that it would blow people's minds. So I dreamed up the suit idea. It was like, just create the squarest possible look and run with it. And I was hardcore about it, too. A lesser man might have just snagged a cheap suit at Goodwill, but I went all out, choosing a conservative, gray three-button suit and having it fitted by the best tailor in town. I even had my hair cut in a short, nondescript style parted to the side. I mean, who the hell does that? I looked like a fucking senator!

I resolved then and there to stick it to the mainstream and adopt this bullshit suit as my signature look. If I knuckled under and went back to my drainpipe trousers and Chucks, I'd just be selling out. Nope. If anything, I was gonna take it further. I perfected the look until it was as hilarious as it could possibly be.

Fresh from the tailor's in my new suit, I hit all the hippest spots, just waiting for the scenesters' jaws to drop at my sheer audacity. To make sure the irony was pitch-perfect, I got the matching shoes, the cuff links, everything—I even matched my silk socks to my eye color and the accents in my tie! I could barely keep a straight face! But in every single bar, club, and after-hours house party I went to, I got the same reaction—everybody just treated me like some kind of lame-o. They looked at me like I wasn't supposed to be there.

A lesser man might have just snagged a cheap suit at Goodwill, but I went all out, choosing a conservative, gray three-button suit and having it fitted by the best tailor in town. I even had my hair cut in a short, non-descript style parted to the side. I mean, who the hell does that? I looked like a fucking senator!

I initially thought maybe they were jealous, but then it dawned on me—they literally thought I was dressed like that for real! Ha! Couldn't these morons get a simple joke? It's like, "Hel-lo... If you have to explain it..."

I resolved then and there to stick it to the mainstream and adopt this bullshit suit as my signature look. If I knuckled under and went back to my drainpipe trousers and Chucks, I'd just be selling out. Nope. If anything, I was gonna take it further. I perfected the look until it was as hilarious as it could possibly be. No expense was spared—if I cut corners, I wouldn't be doing the joke justice. So I got a leather Hermes attaché case, and I filled it with— you guessed it—actual legal briefs! And my watch? Lame-ass TAG Heuer. Most expensive one I could find. Is that the avant-garde of hipness, or what?

But people still didn't get it. Nobody

see SUIT page 304

LOCAL

Sleazy Town Will Do Anything To Get On Map

Above: Wheaton hams it up for the camera.

WHEATON, MN—There was a time when small towns were known for decency and traditional virtues. Such is clearly not the case for the flagrantly self-promoting village of Wheaton, MN. With its outdoor performing-arts series, new railroad museum, and freshly inaugurated county fair, Wheaton, MN, population 1,755, has shown that it will do anything for a little attention.

"Our town has grown some in recent years, which makes us proud," said Wheaton mayor and shameless civic booster Chet Ornblad. "Wheaton really is a special community, and a wonderful place to raise a family."

The mid-June watermelon wallow is just one of many transparent grabs for the sort of attention any decent town would seek to avoid. Other orgies orchestrated by the Wheaton Pride Committee include River Day, the Walleye Fry, the Autumn Apple Pick & Cider Squeeze, and something called "Dandelion Daze" that is best left unexplained.

Debatable. In the late '90s, the town began to brazenly woo "commerce" and "nightlife" by spreading its figurative legs to lure anonymous outsiders to gauche events like the Midsummer Hoedown. What's more, observers in decent neighboring towns agree that the Wheaton Indoor Flea Market has been slathered in a shade of taupe that would be tawdry for a building half its age. Apparently, many residents have no idea how ridiculous they look.

"I've lived here all my life, and I've never seen as much hubbub as we've had recently," mother of two Penny Thorvaldsen said. "And did you see they covered our Watermelon Fest on EyeNews 12? I thought that was just super. Chet did a great job on that one. But I think I put away a bit too much melon that day."

Indeed.

The mid-June watermelon wallow is just one of many transparent grabs for the sort of attention any decent town would seek to avoid. Other orgies orchestrated by the Wheaton Pride Committee include River Day, the Walleye Fry, the Autumn Apple Pick & Cider Squeeze, and something called "Dandelion Daze" that is best left unexplained.

"Oh, Labor Day was some fun, yes sir," said Chamber Of Commerce president and prominent local grocer Roger Johnson, speaking of the parade in which everything—marching bands, floats, the retired police force orchestra—was thrust out there for the whole world to see. "Connie [Weymick] and the Pride Committee did up some real neat decorations, the Jaycees raised $2,000 for muscular dystrophy with their bratwurst cookout, and [Wheaton High School music teacher] Walter [Bosch] conducted the Glee Club in a medley of patriotic songs."

Johnson seemed to be willfully turning a blind eye toward the discomfiting spectacle that is a small town held rapt by its own misguided vanity—

see TOWN page 304

NEWS IN BRIEF

Enchilada Premonition Comes To Pass

BUFFALO, NY—An unaccountable vision of impending enchilada consumption experienced by SUNY–Buffalo student Kris Lamberth came true early Monday evening, according to witnesses. "There we were on the couch," said roommate Corey Bradsher, "when Kris looks right at me and says, 'I have an eerie sense I'm going to eat two Amy's Organic cheese enchiladas. Man, I can almost taste them.'" An hour later, his prophesy was realized. Since the incident, the preternatural Lamberth has attracted the attention of the unsolved-crimes unit of the local police department, who have requested that Lamberth solve the mystery of where they should order their lunch.

MythBusters Team Struck Down By Zeus

SAN FRANCISCO—*MythBusters* hosts Adam Savage and Jamie Hyneman, who dared challenge the sacred explanations of the order of the universe, were destroyed by Zeus Monday. "I soared ascending to the ethereal sky, and by merest nod massed a fearsome storm, and with mine lightnings struck down the naysayers Adam and Jamie," Zeus said in a press conference called to warn all doubters of his thunderous might. The *MythBusters* producers have issued a statement apologizing to the entire Olympian community and declared that, from now on, the program will focus only on myths unrelated to the Greek, Egyptian, or Norse pantheons.

RIAA Bans Telling Friends About Songs

LOS ANGELES—The Recording Industry Association of America announced Tuesday that it will be taking legal action against anyone discovered telling friends, acquaintances, or associates about new songs, artists, or albums. "We are merely exercising our right to defend our intellectual properties from unauthorized peer-to-peer notification of the existence of copyrighted material," a press release signed by RIAA anti-piracy director Brad Buckles read. "We will aggressively prosecute those individuals who attempt to pirate our property by generating 'buzz' about any proprietary music, movies, or software, or enjoy same in the company of anyone other than themselves." RIAA attorneys said they were also looking into the legality of word-of-mouth "favorites-sharing" sites, such as coffee shops, universities, and living rooms.

Impersonal Trainer Couldn't Give A Fuck What You Do With Those Free Weights

LOS ANGELES—Wes Orth Jr., the man considered to be the standard-bearer for a new breed of strong and aloof impersonal trainers, could not care less about the workout regimen of his clients, many of whom say his indifference powers their adrenaline-charged, spite-filled workouts. "Sure, wave those dumbbells around, whatever," Orth said during a typically hands-off training session at his L.A. gym this weekend. "Or just sit on your fat ass—I get paid either way." Orth's newest workout video, *Wes Orth Jr. Doesn't Give Two Damp Shits If You Live Strong Or Die Young*, debuted at the top of the Amazon DVD sales charts on Monday. ⌀

CIA from page 301

low color—or pink."

Goss added: "There was probably some really, really important information in these documents."

When asked by a reporter if the black ink was meant to intentionally obscure, Goss countered, "Good God, why?"

Goss lamented the fact that the public will probably never know the particulars of such historic events as the Cold War, the civil-rights movement, or the growth of the international drug trade.

"I'm sure the CIA played major roles in all these things," Goss said. "But now we'll never know for sure."

In addition to clouding the historical record, the use of the black highlighters, also known as "permanent markers," may have encumbered or even prevented critical operations. CIA scholar Matthew Franks was forced to abandon work on a book

"It seemed counterintuitive, but the higher-ups didn't know what they were doing."

about the Bay Of Pigs invasion after declassified documents proved nearly impossible to read.

"With all the highlighting in the documents I unearthed in the National Archives, it's really no wonder that the invasion failed," Franks said. "I don't see how the field operatives and commandos were expected to decipher their orders."

The inspector general's report cited in particular the damage black highlighting did to documents concerning the assassination of John F. Kennedy, thousands of pages of which "are completely highlighted, from top to bottom margin."

"It is unclear exactly why CIA bureaucrats sometimes chose to emphasize entire documents," the report read. "Perhaps the documents were extremely important in every detail, or the agents, not unlike college freshmen, were overwhelmed by the reading material and got a little carried away."

Also unclear is why black highlighters were chosen in the first place. Some blame it on the closed, elite culture of the CIA itself. A former CIA officer speaking on the condition of anonymity said highlighting documents with black pens was a common and universal practice.

"It seemed counterintuitive, but the higher-ups didn't know what they were doing," the ex-officer said. "I was once ordered to feed documents into a copying machine in order to make backups of some very important top-secret records, but it turned out to be some sort of device that cut the paper to shreds." ⊘

TOWN from page 303

case in point, the holiday garlands wound like strumpets' legs around lampposts on Wheaton's main drag. Or, even worse, that God-awful bunting that just hanged off the dais during the Wheaton High School wrestling-team banquet last weekend.

"We like to cut a rug," Johnson added. "Our recent library fundraiser dance raised over $4,000 for a new periodical wing. I heard they were still going well past midnight."

The outrages continue. According to city-hall sources, after Wheaton gained ISO certification in September, the local government has been sporting an ISO logo on all its papers and official documents, like it's some kind of an honor.

Media whore Mayor Ornblad has given interviews on several local-news shows, and has even gone so far as to brazenly broadcast town-hall meetings on local cable-access Channel 4.

According to Johnson, Wheaton's been trawling for company in some unusual places.

"Wheaton recently introduced a

Johnson seemed to be willfully turning a blind eye toward the discomfiting spectacle that is a small town held rapt by its own misguided vanity—case in point, the holiday garlands wound like strumpets' legs around lampposts on Wheaton's main drag.

website that provides potential visitors with a suggested itinerary," said Johnson, who seemed very comfortable with imparting intimate details on the World Wide Web. "Out-of-towners have said to me personally that our site is very helpful, and pointed out many interesting facts. Not very many towns of our size have their own ice rink, or a 70-year-old bandshell with its original aluminum exterior, for example. It feels good to let others know that."

Apparently, Wheaton exults in that sort of shameless notoriety.

"Wheaton's growth has not gone unnoticed nationally, either," panderer-in-chief Ornblad added. "Our Fall Hayride was featured in September's Travel Magazine as one of the top 20 little-known seasonal weekend getaways."

When asked his opinion of Wheaton's recent flowering, Clyde Heckert, mayor of nearby Rosholt, SD, gallantly took the high road.

"In the Midwest, we're starting to see a resurgence," Heckert said. "And like our farmers around here, the newcomers are bringing in a bountiful harvest of their own: jobs, revenue, and overall opportunity."

Asked what exactly he meant to imply when he said "bountiful harvest," Heckert demurred, in a show of modesty Wheaton would do well to emulate. ⊘

SUIT from page 302

cracked up when they saw me at Yeah Yeah Yeahs shows. If anything, they seemed to avoid me. One of my now ex-friends even called me a sellout. WTF? He worked for a fucking graphics design firm. I was standing right there in my goddamn suit, for Christ's sake. It's not my fault if some jerks can't handle the extreme and total "fuck you" of my next-level fashion statement.

I took it further. I moved out of my Williamsburg loft (so 10 years ago anyway) and put a down-payment on an Upper East Side co-op. Uniformed black doorman and everything. Hilarious! Then, on a lark, I applied for a job at this hysterical corporate law firm called Gorman, Gorman, Hensler, and Stein, and—this is the kicker—I actually got the job!

I figured I'd fake the law gag long enough to get my first paycheck, then totally blow off these cheese-asses and frame my uncashed check as an irony trophy. Well, I did that... But then, when people still failed to pick up the joke and more and more weeks went buy without me getting fired, the

One of my now ex-friends even called me a sellout. WTF? He worked for a fucking graphics design firm. I was standing right there in my goddamn suit, for Christ's sake. It's not my fault if some jerks can't handle the extreme and total "fuck you" of my next-level fashion statement.

paychecks started to pile up and I figured, "What the hell? Might as well cash these extra ones." I had to, really, to pay for all this expensive ironic shit.

But what good is all this hilarity if there's no one else hip enough to appreciate it? On the 8:12 a.m. commuter train, everybody just assumes I'm one of them. So does my secretary, my assistant, and every single one of my colleagues at the law firm, where I'm now a partner. I even married this clueless girl from Connecticut—loves shopping and everything—and we have two ironic kids. I swear, they look like something out of a creepy 1950s Dick And Jane reader—I even have these hilarious silver-framed pictures of them in my cheesy corner office. But still, the humor is lost on everybody but me. I'm probably the most fashionable guy on the planet at this point, but no one understands. God! Do you have any idea how difficult it is being so far ahead of your time? Some days, it's enough to make me want to embrace conformity like all the other sheep.

But who am I kidding? Living on the cutting edge of irony is in my blood, man! I couldn't go straight if I tried! ⊘

PINE NEEDLES from page 174

amounts of blood. Passersby were amazed by the unusually large amounts of blood. Passersby were amazed by the unusually large amounts of blood. Passersby were amazed by the unusually large amounts of blood. Passersby were amazed by the unusually large amounts of blood. Passersby were amazed by the unusually large amounts of blood. Passersby were amazed by the unusually large amounts of blood. Passersby were amazed by the unusually large amounts of blood. Passersby were amazed by the unusually large

Knives are not toys. Knife-toys are.

amounts of blood. Passersby were amazed by the unusually large amounts of blood. Passersby were amazed by the unusually large amounts of blood. Passersby were amazed by the unusually large amounts of blood. Passersby were amazed by the unusually large amounts of blood. Passersby were amazed by the unusually large amounts of blood. Passersby were amazed by the unusually large amounts of blood. Passersby were amazed by the unusually large amounts of blood. Passersby were amazed by the unusually large amounts of blood. Passersby were amazed by the unusually large amounts of blood. Passersby were amazed by the unusually large amounts of blood. Passersby were amazed by the unusually large amounts of blood. Passersby were amazed by the unusually large

see PINE NEEDLES page 223

SNAKISTAN from page 301

signing of the historic Buttermilk Compromise, which established bilateral chiplomacy and regulated trade flows by setting the international Rold Gold standard of currency.

"The only option besides bowing to Fritolaysia's demands is to begin trading with the extreme funyunmentalist people of Utzonia," Freedman said, referring to the Blandinavian nation that offers similar but less-satisfying goods for cheaper exchange rates.

Above: Fritolaysia's CORNCOM command center.

The dispute over increased prices and decreased serving sizes escalated when Snakistan, swayed by the influence of the nation's healthiest 1 percent, signed a historic fat-free-trade agreement with the Yogurtslavian nation of Colombo. Preparing for a long and grueling war of nutrition, Fritolaysia imposed trade snacktions and set up a blockade of Snakistan's major ports, cutting off their commerce with Yumen, Mmm-madagascar, and the Chex Republic.

According to internoshonal-relations expert Grady Freedman, Snakistan's reliance on, and craving for, Fritolaysia's delicious exports will likely force their chargé d'éclaires to re-establish ties with Fritolaysia's government and draw up a late-night treaty.

"The only option besides bowing to Fritolaysia's demands is to begin trading with the extreme funyunmentalist people of Utzonia," Freedman said, referring to the Blandinavian nation that offers similar but less-satisfying goods for cheaper exchange rates. "But deals with the Utzonians always leave a funny taste in your mouth."

With much of his country fearing that the rift with Snakistan could lead to a family-size conflict, Snakistan's President Ghulam Murtaza Pringle, whose pork-rind-barrel legislation and 2002 negotiations with international spambassadors earned him the Hormel Peace Prize, said his country cannot live without a strong, flavorful relationship with Snakistan.

"I am sending hundreds of chiplomats to Fritolaysia in the hopes that something can be worked out," Pringle said. "Even if we have to dig in and get our hands a little greasy, we aim to hunker down, preferably on a couch." ⌀

TERRORIST from page 301

eight men consulted the Muslim holy book the Quran, which proved unhelpful. Said Akhtar: "Even Umar Abd al-Malik, who interprets the ancient scripture more freely than the rest of us, could not find an instructive passage."

Morale was temporarily buoyed when cell member Dawoud Bishr, a former student at the Sorbonne in Paris, was found intently examining the exposed plutonium, which he had lifted from its protective lead footlocker. Two days later, however, the others had to bury Bishr in a landfill outside the city.

Akhtar, in hiding in a small, spartan cellar in one of Zahedan's poorer neighborhoods, said that the only use he's found for the encased lethal substance so far is as a flat surface on which to lay out a map of a government armory outside Islamabad and a large piece of paper to make a blueprint for transferring the plutonium to an effective delivery system.

"I drew a circle to represent the plutonium," Akhtar said. "Then I drew a line pointing to it, and beside it wrote 'plutonium.' After that, I just hit a wall."

Akhtar and his associates initially planned to create a "suitcase bomb," but soon after they obtained the plutonium, they learned that such bombs weigh over 700 pounds, and are therefore too heavy for any of them to lift alone.

Said Akhtar: "The only thing this weapon of mass destruction is destroying right now is our ability to kill infidels."

"I have heard many in the corrupt

Morale was temporarily buoyed when cell member Dawoud Bishr, a former student at the Sorbonne in Paris, was found intently examining the exposed plutonium, which he had lifted from its protective lead footlocker.

Western media say that Muslim terrorists have acquired harmful radioactive materials that can be readily deployed," al-Malik said. "Whoever this terrorist group is that's all but ready to strike America with a nuclear device, we sure could use their help."

Unable to search for bomb-making instructions on his laptop for fear of being monitored, Akhtar has been forced to send another of his sub-lieutenants, 23-year-old Ibraheem Jaalal, to a local Internet café in hopes of acquiring the necessary data. According to Jaalal, the process so far has proven "unbearably slow" and "outrageously expensive," claiming he can't believe the coffee shop charges $4.95 for an hour of dial-up-speed Internet use.

The cell's lack of contacts with professional scientists and engineers has also undermined their bomb-building efforts. "A friend of mine at university studied metallurgy," Jaalal said. "I have his e-mail address, but I can't just write him and say, 'Oh, hello, Suleymann, long time no see. Say, I'm a terrorist now, and I was wondering: How do you go about building a nuclear bomb?'"

After three days without progress, the plutonium, once a source of pride for Akhtar and the other men, has increasingly become a fountain of frustration.

"I guess we got carried away with the idea of making a nuclear weapon before thinking the whole thing

Unable to search for bomb-making instructions on his laptop for fear of being monitored, Akhtar has been forced to send another of his sub-lieutenants, 23-year-old Ibraheem Jaalal, to a local Internet café in hopes of acquiring the necessary data.

through," said Akhtar, who admitted that even if he "could bombard that plutonium nuclei with enough electrons, whatever those are," getting the bomb to North America would prove another logistical mess.

"I still believe in taking the lives of American civilians as revenge for the atrocities committed on our brothers, our wives, and our daughters," Akhtar said. "I'm just not entirely sure it's worth a headache this big." ⌀

At Least I Got My Ass Kicked By A Name-Brand Crowbar

Every day, people get the shit kicked out of them by cheap, second-rate implements. Be it discount baseball bats, flimsy aluminum pipes, or after-market non-waffle-head hammers, nearly everyone has at one time or another gone through the dehumanizing experience of being severely pummeled with a lesser-quality product. Well, I'm proud to say the crowbar that landed me in the hospital three weeks ago retails for $39.95, and is sold only in the better hardware stores.

By Brent Waldie

Let me tell you, this is the kind of crowbar you'd tell everyone about if your lower jaw hadn't been smashed to pieces.

Sure, it hurt my ego when the Titan SureGrip crowbar was first driven into the back of my head, and yes, I did cry about it for a couple of hours afterwards, but that night, I was hit by something even harder than that 18-inch, curved piece of high-carbon steel: the realization that there's no shame in being beaten down by the best crowbar money can buy.

While I originally harbored some resentment toward my assailant for

Even while choking on my vital fluids and drifting in and out of consciousness, it was hard to ignore Titan's superior quality and craftsmanship with each two-handed, overhead blow to my ribcage.

knocking out 17 of my teeth, all it took was one glance upward through a mist of blood at that blazing Titan logo arcing toward my face to realize I wouldn't have wanted it any other way.

Even while choking on my vital fluids and drifting in and out of consciousness, it was hard to ignore Titan's superior quality and craftsmanship with each two-handed, overhead blow to my ribcage. Pleading desperately for mercy, I was immediately struck by the crowbar's sturdy hexagonal cross-sectional structure, which prevented any bending of the shaft. Most of all, though, I was floored by how its cushioned SureGrip handle allowed my assailant to confidently pummel away at my helpless face-down frame without fear that it would slip loose.

No way. Not the SureGrip.

As far as durability goes, I'd proba-

Everybody says it must have been some psychopath who beat me and left me for dead. And while at first that seems to make sense, ask yourself this: Would a psychopath purchase the highest-quality crowbar on the market today?

bly have to rate the hardened and tempered Titan somewhere between "more durable" and "much more durable" than my skull.

The way I see it, if you're going to lose three pints of blood, you might as well lose it to the crowbar most trusted by demolition professionals the world over. After all, how many people can really say they were bludgeoned within an inch of their lives by the only crowbar to receive a perfect five-star rating in Hard Hat News magazine?

Everybody says it must have been some psychopath who beat me and left me for dead. And while at first that seems to make sense, ask yourself this: Would a psychopath purchase the highest-quality crowbar on the market today?

Never.

Sure, I may never be able to walk unassisted, but after months of physical therapy, I will be able to hold my head high. Things could have been a lot worse. For instance, I might have had to live out the remainder of my life with the humiliation of nearly dying at the hands of a mass-produced, stamp-steel-forged crowbar.

At the end of the day, after countless radiology exams and CAT scans, that's what separates me from the rest of the wimps in my ward. While it's possible that many of us will forget our names or what year it is again, I alone will always remember the brand name responsible for the debilitating trauma to my frontal lobe. ⌀

Your Horoscope

By Lloyd Schumner Sr.
Retired Machinist and
A.A.P.B.-Certified Astrologer

Aries: (March 21–April 19)
While it's possible that, one day, you'll be able to forgive your husband for walking out on your children, you will never forgive him for walking out on your children without you.

Taurus: (April 20–May 20)
According to the stars, a misguided attempt to prevent injury will instead result in a debilitating spinal-cord injury when you attempt to lift a 500-pound pallet of ball bearings with your knees, instead of using a forklift.

Gemini: (May 21–June 21)
For years you've thought of yourself as most resembling the Greek goddess Aphrodite, but the stars think that you are ready to know the truth: You're a mix between Teiresias, the Gorgon sisters, and Cerberus.

Cancer: (June 22–July 22)
You will feel let down by the historical inaccuracies at a nearby medieval-themed restaurant this week before paying a visit to its bathroom.

Leo: (July 23–Aug. 22)
Your attempt to play guitar under the bedroom window of your one true love will fail this week when you are denied flame-cannon permits.

Virgo: (Aug. 23–Sept. 22)
You will be forever labeled "quixotic" after mistaking a field of windmills for the solution to the world's energy crisis.

Libra: (Sept. 23–Oct. 23)
Sure, they may all be laughing at you now, but pretty soon they'll have to stop in order to catch their breath.

Scorpio: (Oct. 24–Nov. 21)
Despite there being over 50 different words for snow in Inuktitut, you will fail time after time to score cocaine while visiting the Yukon next week.

Sagittarius: (Nov. 22–Dec. 21)
Statistics say that nearly 78 percent of rapes are committed by someone the victim knew, but you'll insist next week that the more correct phrasing is "thought they knew."

Capricorn: (Dec. 22–Jan. 19)
While it's often true that two heads are better than one, the shattered skull of your adulterous wife will prove no help in coming up with a place to bury the body.

Aquarius: (Jan. 20–Feb. 18)
The stars say that birdwatchers from all over the world will congregate outside your home sometime next week to observe more than five distinct species of vultures.

Pisces: (Feb. 19–March 20)
You'll be forced to learn yet another lesson the hard way this week, but it's college-level differential calculus for engineers, and that's the way everyone learns.

BACON from page 72

amounts of blood. Passersby were amazed by the unusually large amounts of blood. Passersby were amazed by the unusually large amounts of blood. Passersby were amazed by the unusually large amounts of blood. Passersby were amazed by the unusually large amounts of blood. Passersby were amazed by the unusually large amounts of blood. Passersby were amazed by the unusually large amounts of blood. Passersby were amazed by the unusually large amounts of blood. Passersby were amazed by the unusually large amounts of blood. Passersby were amazed by the unusually large amounts of blood. Passersby were amazed by the unusually large amounts of blood. Passersby were amazed by the unusually large amounts of blood. Passersby were amazed by the unusually large amounts of blood. Passersby were amazed by the unusually large amounts of blood. Passersby were amazed by the unusually large

Those monks were assholes.

amounts of blood. Passersby were amazed by the unusually large amounts of blood. Passersby were amazed by the unusually large amounts of blood. Passersby were amazed by the unusually large amounts of blood. Passersby were amazed by the unusually large amounts of blood. Passersby were

see BACON page 95

NEWS

Motivational Poster Inspires 264 Layoffs

see BUSINESS page 2C

Silicon Breast Implants Perform Millions Of Calculations Per Second

see SCIENCE & TECHNOLOGY page 3E

New Medicare Program To Cost $724 Billion Per Person

see NATIONAL page 12F

STATshot

A look at the numbers that shape your world.

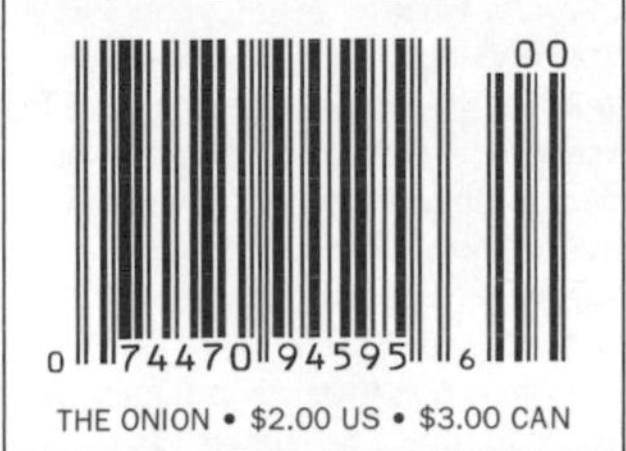

the ONION®

VOLUME 41 ISSUE 49 AMERICA'S FINEST NEWS SOURCE™ 8–14 DECEMBER 2005

Voice Of God Revealed To Be Cheney On Intercom

WASHINGTON, DC—Telephone logs recorded by the National Security Agency and obtained by Congress as part of an ongoing investigation suggest that the vice president may have used the Oval Office intercom system to address President Bush at crucial moments, giving categorical directives in a voice the president believed to be that of God.

While journalists and presidential historians had long noted Bush's deep faith and Cheney's powerful influence in the White House, few had drawn a direct correlation between the two until Tuesday, when transcripts of meetings that took place in March and April of 2002 became available.

In a transcript of an intercom exchange recorded in March 2002, a voice positively identified as the vice

see INTERCOM page 311

Left: President Bush sits at his desk in the Oval Office, where he received messages from an intercom voice identifying itself as "God" and thought to have been Vice President Cheney (inset).

Rest Of U2 Perfectly Fine With Africans Starving

SAN FRANCISCO—Rock band U2, currently on tour in North America, is well-known for its human-rights advocacy, particularly its ongoing campaign to eradicate poverty in Africa. Less known to fans of the Irish supergroup, however, is that the lion's share of these efforts are made by lead singer Bono. The three other U2 members are perfectly okay with the dismal plight of Africa's poor.

"Yeah, that Africa stuff is Bono's thing," The Edge said. "I don't mind if he pursues other interests, but I really try to focus on the guitar riffs that give U2 its characteristic sound."

Bassist Adam Clayton, while "not opposed" to Bono's tireless efforts to improve the quality of life for impoverished Third World citizens, is apparently too busy to spearhead an anti-poverty initiative of his own.

"I was happy to help out with the Live 8 thing," said

see U2 page 311

Above: The Edge, Larry Mullen Jr., and Adam Clayton.

Report: U.S. Coupon Wealth Largely Untapped

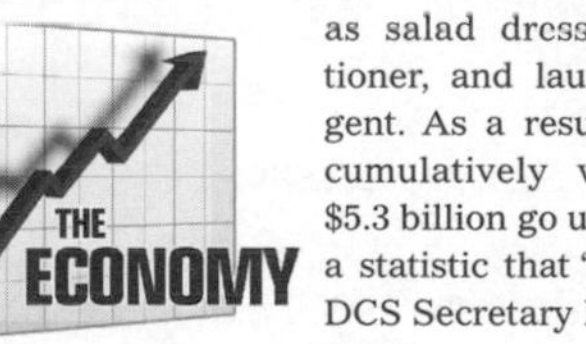

WASHINGTON, DC—Billions of dollars of coupon savings are wasted every year, and Americans are missing out on countless money-saving opportunities, according to a report issued by the federal Department Of Consumer Savings.

Despite the stagnating economy and the threat of inflation, Americans continue to pay full price for such items as salad dressing, conditioner, and laundry detergent. As a result, coupons cumulatively worth over $5.3 billion go unredeemed, a statistic that "concerned" DCS Secretary Edward Fellowes.

"Personal savings are down in fiscal 2005, primarily because Americans are unwilling to cash in on these amazing rebates," Fellowes said. "Simply purchasing any Boca-brand meatless product at a 75-cent discount could spur vast growth in other key economic areas such as cold-sore medication, halogen light bulbs, and the entire frozen-foods sector."

Although these coupons can easily be found in flyers tucked between the sections of a Sunday newspaper, in racks in front of retail stores, or even on the ground, the report revealed that as many as seven in 10 Americans have not redeemed a coupon in two years.

see COUPON page 310

Britain Recognizes Gay Unions

Gay "civil partnerships" will be legally recognized in Great Britain later this month. What do *you* think?

"Finally, Ian McKellen has no more excuses not to buy me a ring! Do you hear me, Sir Ian? I want a June wedding!!!"

Tom DiMenna
Waiter

"And the U.S. loses another ally from the closet of the willing."

Karla Strahl
Radiologist

"I'm already yelling supportive remarks at any likely gays I see."

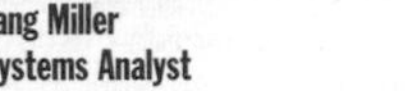

Yang Miller
Systems Analyst

"The British should never have allowed men to play the women's roles back in the Elizabethan theatre."

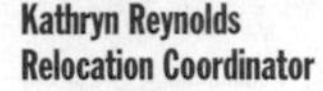

Kathryn Reynolds
Relocation Coordinator

"Who knew that the Cockney phrase 'bugger all' would be so prophetic?"

Drew Pisarra
Bus Driver

"Great. The next thing you know, they'll want taxation without representation."

Kurt Braunholler
Photo Editor

Human-Genome Patenting

According to a recent study, 20 percent of human genes have been patented in the U.S. Here are several of those that are registered, along with their holders:

Gene	Owner
Controls glandular response to folksy homilies	Reader's Digest
Deactivates "flight" aspect of fight-or-flight reflex	WWE
Allows human sweat glands to produce synthetic carbon-rubber	Goodyear Inc.
Regulates behaviors including small talk, walking, simple tool use, and colorblindness	Callaway Golf
Transfigures normal student into actual blue demon for one semester	DePaul University
Heightens interest in Tubgirl, the Egypt vote, and *Dragonball Z*	Google Inc.
Makes people naturally happy and content without use of medication	Pfizer

the ONION®
America's Finest News Source.™

Herman Ulysses Zweibel
Founder

T. Herman Zweibel
Publisher Emeritus
J. Phineas Zweibel
Publisher
Maxwell Prescott Zweibel
Editor-In-Chief

I'd Love This Product Even If I Weren't A Stealth Marketer

Like you, I'm bombarded every minute of every day with advertising. And having been misled more than a few times in my life, I'm immediately skeptical of any product I see on the side of a bus. That's why I was so surprised by the new Mountain Dew True Blue.

By Kyle Pafrath

It truly lives up to the hype: Crisp and tangy, refreshing and energizing, it reminds my jaded taste buds how good a soda can be. Sure, I may be a stealth marketer employed by a national conglomerate to imperceptibly push the product in public, but this beverage is so unbelievably great, I'd subliminally market it to perfect strangers for free!

Honestly, this awesome beverage packs such a punch, you'd practically have to pay me not to pretend to talk about it on my cell phone when I'm in earshot of consumers in the coveted 17-34 demographic.

Even if I weren't required by my employer to pull a six-pack off the shelf at my local grocery store while emitting a quiet but distinct "All right!" under my breath just loud enough for the other customers to hear, I'd do it anyway—just for the pleasure of furtively turning people on to this amazing thirst quencher.

Seriously, it's an honor to subtly plug something I actually believe in for once. I'm so in love with this one-of-a-kind soda, I want to shout its product name from the rooftops of a lower-to-middle-class neighborhood! Preferably one with an elementary school nearby.

In stealth-marketing parlance, this is what is known as "roach baiting," but I prefer to call it "the least I can do."

Seriously, it's an honor to subtly plug something I actually believe in for once. I'm so in love with this one-of-a-kind soda, I want to shout its product name from the rooftops of a lower-to-middle-class neighborhood! Preferably one with an elementary school nearby, where consumers are still young enough that their brand loyalty is not yet fully established. I know it sounds crazy, maybe even a little scary, but honestly, True Blue is just that good.

Honestly, this awesome beverage packs such a punch, you'd practically have to pay me not to pretend to talk about it on my cell phone when I'm in earshot of consumers in the coveted 17-34 demographic.

Don't tell my bosses, but I enjoy True Blue so much, I sometimes stealth market it well outside PepsiCo's target demographic. Maybe it's wrong of me to sit in on the senior center's weekly square-dance classes while chugging True Blue, but the rush I get from inconspicuously getting the word out about this tremendous new product is nearly impossible to find anywhere else. Come to think of it, the only other time I experience pure exhilaration like that is when I twist open a 20-oz. bottle of True Blue.

Also, I get it from drinking Mountain Dew Code Red and Mountain Dew Pitch Black.

Sure, the task of registering for nearly 30 different newsgroup accounts using fake names and e-mail addresses just to generate the honest word-of-mouth buzz this product deserves may sound like a lot of work to you, one of the few Americans who hasn't been bowled over by the no-holds-barred flavor of True Blue.

Normally, if I were hired to viral market a new beverage I wasn't particularly passionate about—for example, that new Coca-Cola drink, whatever it's called—I would just subliminally insert favorable comments in two dozen or so high-traffic chat rooms and be done with it. Only a very special product could make me devote a week of evenings to surfing literally hundreds of chat rooms, gaining the confidence of unwitting users by establishing a base of common interests before casually mentioning how I recently tried the most hardcore, carbonated pick-me-up the world has ever seen.

But hey, don't let me influence you. Try True Blue for yourself! Ø

LOCAL

Area Cherokee In Violation Of Indian Removal Act Of 1830

DAHLONEGA, GA—Authorities issued a warrant for the arrest and forced relocation of local carpenter and half-blooded Cherokee Indian Jonathan Silvers Monday, when he was found to be in violation of the federal Indian Removal Act of 1830.

> "When I told my wife that, under American federal law, we were going to have to leave everything behind and start over in Oklahoma, she was furious," Silvers said. "I blame myself: I totally blanked on the Indian Removal Act of 1830 when looking for a place to live."

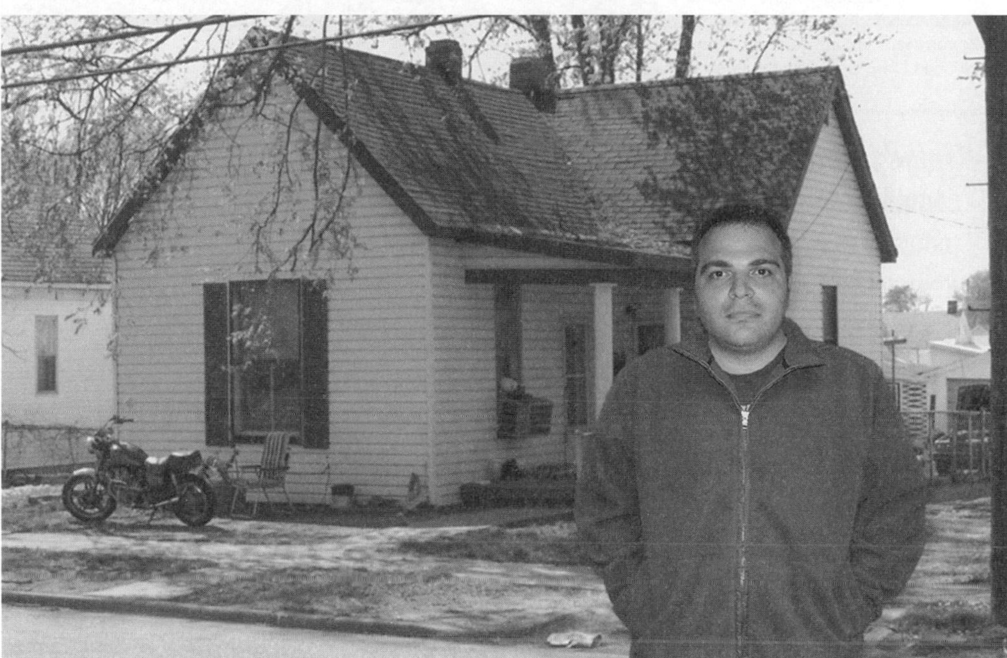

Above: Half-blood Cherokee Jonathan Silvers outside his soon-to-be-vacated home.

"Mr. Silvers is in violation of federal law," said Col. Jack Kippler, who is leading the Bureau of Indian Affairs case against Silvers. "For this reason, he was taken into custody, and he is currently awaiting forcible resettlement on a Cherokee reservation in Oklahoma by the U.S. Army."

Once in Oklahoma, Silvers and his wife and two children will be permanently housed in a trailer home.

According to Silvers' lawyers, the Cherokee Indian did not realize he was living in violation of the 175-year-old act signed into law by Andrew Jackson, the seventh president of the U.S.

"When I told my wife that, under American federal law, we were going to have to leave everything behind and start over in Oklahoma, she was furious," Silvers said. "I blame myself: I totally blanked on the Indian Removal Act of 1830 when looking for a place to live."

The BIA is currently fielding applications from families who would like to live on Silvers' former land. According to Kippler, the Silvers' two-story, 1,600-square-foot house, valued at $145,000, would make an excellent home for a white family.

"It's a nice house," Kippler said. "They've taken very good care of the place, really shown it a lot of love. It has one and a half baths and a very nice finished basement with a TV den."

Army personnel say the Silvers will be given sufficient time to pack their belongings into the trunk of a police cruiser before they are escorted to their new and federally mandated homeland. Additionally, the U.S. gov-

see CHEROKEE page 310

NEWS IN BRIEF

Goldfish Can't Stand Bowlmate

INNISKILL, RI—Sonny Jim, a 9-month-old goldfish, can no longer tolerate his bowlmate, 9-month-old goldfish Sally. "Always hanging out at the top of the bowl, looking for food, just waiting, blocking the light," Sonny Jim said Monday. "Never moves. Just eats and craps and does that annoying thing with his mouth. Unless I want to go in the castle. Then, bam! Sally's right there hogging the whole thing. Also, 'Sally?' A guy. What's with that?" The beleaguered miniature carp said he would prefer rooming with a "psychotic betta fish" and wouldn't care if Sally jumped out of the bowl.

Alcoholic Kindergarten Teacher Stretches Naptime To Three Hours

IRVING, TX—Following a tiring weekend, kindergarten teacher and self-described "party girl" Jeanie Rigby, 29, extended the naptime at Irving KinderKare to three hours Monday. "Let's get those nap pads out, kids," Rigby said in what her students described as "an extra-hushy indoor voice." "Quiet time now, so you get your rest and Ms. Rigby gets her juice." Kindergarteners who only pretended to sleep later said they were pretty sure that Rigby was not faking her own nap.

'Employees Must Wash Hands' Signs Top Iraqi Hospital Wish List

MAHMOUDIYA, IRAQ—As the tumultuous process of reconstruction continues throughout Iraq, healthcare workers are still lacking the basic necessities. "Before anything else at all, we need a supply of new, bilingual 'Employees Must Wash Hands' signs," said Youssef Al-Obaidi, director of Mahmoudiya Hospital. "We appreciate the bedding, laundry-sanitization equipment, window glass, penicillin, needles, wall-repair materials, and so on, but without clean hands, none of these mean anything." Al-Obaidi said the importance of hand-washing could not, unlike doctors and nurses, be overstressed.

New Book Written From Perspective Of Gargamel

NEW YORK—Gregory Maguire, author of *Wicked*, the story of Oz told from the Wicked Witch's perspective, has completed a novel told from the point of view of the Smurf-hating sorcerer Gargamel. "I thought this much-maligned man worthy of closer scrutiny, perhaps even sympathy," Maguire said. "His lust for the Smurfs' gold can't entirely explain his actions. His creation of Smurfette, his uneasy partnership with Azrael, his possibly forbidden feelings for his assistant Scruple—there's definitely more than meets the eye." HarperCollins will release *I Hate Those Smurfs...?* in February.

More Americans Falling For 'Get Rich Slowly Over A Lifetime Of Hard Work' Schemes

OMAHA, NB—A report released Monday by the Omaha-based public-interest group Aurora indicates that increasing numbers of Americans are being defrauded by schemes that offer financial reward for a lifetime of hard work. "People don't realize that long-term savings and loyalty to one company don't pan out," said Sylvia Girouard, the study's author. Girouard added that steady employment which claims to offer long-term financial gain in the form of a pension plan is nothing more than an elaborate Ponzi scheme. ⊘

COUPON from page 307

In a time in which personal debt is at a record high, Fellowes said that such financial lassitude is "America's shame."

"Twenty years ago, a 50-cent coupon for Mazola corn oil produced runs on supermarkets so large that rain checks had to be issued by the tens of thousands," Fellowes said. "Today, such a discount receives barely an acknowledgment from the public. Even two-thirds of all issued rain checks are unused."

"There's a myriad of complications with coupon use," FSI spokesperson Leslie Frye said. "Certain coupons are not valid with other offers, and participation among stores may vary. Also, if consumers do not hurry, there is a significant risk that the coupons will reach their expiration dates."

Above: Coupon users in a Grand Forks, ND grocery store.

The DCS report also connected the decline of take-home wages in the past five years to the public's reluctance to redeem a $1.50 rebate on Duracell AA-sized batteries in the fall of 1999.

To raise more awareness of the potential savings bonanzas available, the DCS has launched a campaign in which operatives hand coupons directly to consumers, often right in front of the establishment where they can be redeemed. The campaign, scheduled to last through the holiday season, will cost taxpayers an estimated $10 million, but the cost will be made up for as long as Americans use the coupons, Fellowes said.

"Brushing past the operatives or throwing their handouts in the trash only hurts the American consumer in the long run," Fellowes said. "After all, 30 cents off Downy fabric softener is 30 cents toward a new home."

Consumer advocacy groups such as the Foundation For Shoppers' Issues, however, contend that when it comes to coupon use, too many restrictions apply.

"There's a myriad of complications with coupon use," FSI spokesperson Leslie Frye said. "Certain coupons are not valid with other offers, and participation among stores may vary. Also, if consumers do not hurry, there is a significant risk that the coupons will reach their expiration dates."

Outgoing Federal Reserve Chairman Alan Greenspan appeared to side with the conclusions of the DCS report. A regular coupon clipper with a Sam's Club membership, Greenspan has warned against rash disregard of coupon use for years. In a statement reacting to the report's findings, he said that unless Americans start becoming "smart shoppers," families and possibly the country at large will experience a sharp economic downturn. He also called for retailers to offer more double-coupon days, and for coupon-issuing businesses to improve perforation standards, so coupons can be more easily separated from their promotional materials without tearing.

"Coupons need to be out of the kitchen drawer and into the cash register if this economy has any chance of turning around," Greenspan said. "I'd also like to draw particular attention to the recent two-for-$5 deal on all flavors of Doritos-brand chips, buy-two-get-one-free deals on Wizard air fresheners, and, perhaps most importantly, box-top proofs of purchase on many Betty Crocker products, which, when redeemed, raise funds for schools nationwide."

"Every little bit helps," Greenspan added. ⌀

The DCS report also connected the decline of take-home wages in the past five years to the public's reluctance to redeem a $1.50 rebate on Duracell AA-sized batteries in the fall of 1999.

CHEROKEE from page 309

ernment has taken responsibility for euthanizing the Silvers' dog, Spunky.

"I don't see the kids taking this too well," Silvers said. "Already, they're worrying about making new friends in Oklahoma... But what are you going to do? The law is the law."

"I've submitted Silvers' case to the Supreme Court, but it is very unlikely that they will add it to next term's docket," Twoblood said. "I have done what I can. I would like to wish him and his family good luck in their new home."

"They'll be in tears the whole car ride there, I expect," he added.

Silvers told reporters that his forcible ejection under armed guard could not have come at a worse time.

"We just ordered a new couch from Ikea," Silvers said. "Who's going to get that? The new white family? Maybe I can cancel the order."

Mark Twoblood, an attorney with the National Native American Bar Association, has reviewed Silvers' claim to the land and home he purchased in 1997, and he says there is little he can do under the existing law.

"I've submitted Silvers' case to the Supreme Court, but it is very unlikely that they will add it to next term's docket," Twoblood said. "I have done what I can. I would like to wish him and his family good luck in their new home."

Twoblood reportedly gave the Silvers a decorative dreamcatcher as a housewarming gift. ⌀

BAGEL BARN from page 99

amounts of blood. Passersby were amazed by the unusually large amounts of blood. Passersby were amazed by the unusually large amounts of blood. Passersby were amazed by the unusually large

She expected death to be less "deathy."

amounts of blood. Passersby were amazed by the unusually large amounts of blood. Passersby were amazed by the unusually large amounts of blood. Passersby were amazed by the unusually large amounts of blood. Passersby were amazed by the unusually large amounts of blood. Passersby were amazed by the unusually large amounts of blood. Passersby were amazed by the unusually large amounts of blood. Passersby were

see BAGEL BARN page 115

INTERCOM from page 307

president's identifies himself as "the Lord thy God" and promotes the invasion of Iraq, as well as the use of torture in prisoner interrogations.

A close examination of Bush's public statements and Secret Service time logs tracking the vice president reveals a consistent pattern, one which links Bush's belief that he had received word from God with Cheney's use of the White House's telephone-based intercom system.

Officials privately acknowledged that there is reason to believe that the vice president, as God, urged Bush to sign legislation benefiting oil companies in 2005.

"There's a lot of religious zeal in the West Wing," said a former White House staffer who spoke on the condition of anonymity. "It's possible that the vice president has taken advantage of that to fast-track certain administration objectives."

An ex-Treasury Department official and longtime friend of Cheney was asked to comment on the vice president's possible subterfuge. "I don't know. I certainly don't think it's something [Cheney] planned," he said. "I do know that Mr. Bush was unfamiliar with a phone based intercom,

A close examination of Bush's public statements and Secret Service time logs tracking the vice president reveals a consistent pattern, one which links Bush's belief that he had received word from God with Cheney's use of the White House's telephone-based intercom system.

and I suppose it is possible that Dick took advantage of that."

A highly placed NSA official who has reviewed the information released Tuesday said Cheney masked his clipped monotone, employing a deeper, booming voice.

Said the NSA source: "It sounded as though the speaker, who identified himself as God, stood away from the intercom to create an echo effect."

On Capitol Hill, sources are expressing surprise that Cheney, a vice president with more influence than any other in U.S. history, would have resorted to such deception.

"The vice president has a lot of sway in this administration," said a former White House aide. "But perhaps when President Bush was particularly resolute and resistant to mortal persuasion, the vice president chose to quickly resolve disputes in his favor with a half-decent God impression."

For many, the revelation explains Bush's confusion in the wake of Hurricane Katrina.

"I was very surprised by the president's slow response in New Orleans," political commentator Bill Kristol said. "The president told me that he was praying every day in his office, but had received no reply. I had no idea what he meant, but of course, it all makes sense now."

At the time of Katrina, Cheney was on a fly-fishing trip, from which he returned on Sept. 1.

According to highly placed White

"I was very surprised by the president's slow response in New Orleans," political commentator Bill Kristol said. "The president told me that he was praying every day in his office, but had received no reply."

House sources, Bush's senior advisers are trying to shield the president from the news. Aides are concerned that too harsh an awakening might shake Bush's faith, which has been a central part of his life for nearly 20 years.

"It's hard to tell the leader of the free world that he has been the butt of an elaborate and long-term ruse," a former staffer said. "Maybe it would be easier to take if it came from Cheney's God voice."

U2 from page 307

Clayton, referring to the July mega-concert benefit. "But ever since I discovered rock 'n' roll in the mid-'70s, music has been my passion, and I'd be lying if I said it was something different, like helping people."

Clayton added: "I don't have a problem with [Bono] trying to save Africa. Who knows, it might inspire some decent songs. But just as long as it doesn't interfere with the band."

In 2002, Bono started an organization called Debt, AIDS, Trade, Africa to raise awareness of the deep health and economic crises that cripple much of the continent. His fellow bandmates, however, do not lose any sleep over the debt crisis facing many African nations.

"If I could wave a magic wand and cure Africa's problems, I would do

In the rare moment they have free, Clayton, Mullen, and The Edge said they choose to relax and rejuvenate, without letting the plight of Africa's starving and disease-afflicted millions weigh too heavily on their minds.

that," drummer Larry Mullen Jr. said. "But someone has to take care of the more practical, day-to-day stuff that Bono doesn't really bother with. Like, for example, how's the next album going to sound? How're we going to keep our live act fresh? I can't tell you how many millions of decisions go into making one Elevation tour."

Mullen added: "You don't win 14 Grammys feeding Africans."

In the rare moment they have free, Clayton, Mullen, and The Edge said they choose to relax and rejuvenate, without letting the plight of Africa's starving and disease-afflicted millions weigh too heavily on their minds.

"I have a garden to tend to when we're not on the road," The Edge said. "There's nothing wrong with taking care of your own little corner of the world. I work very hard in my garden."

When asked their opinion about

During live concerts, U2 audiences are treated to a stunning audiovisual experience, with Bono periodically giving his opinion on social and world events between songs. During these interludes, the rest of U2 is often conspicuously silent.

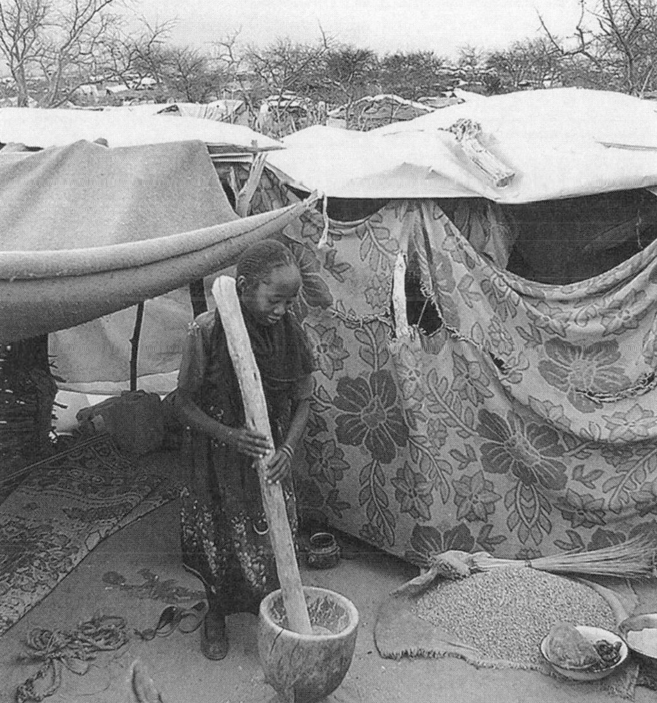

Above: A starving African, who is of little concern to the other members of U2.

Bono's prospects of being awarded the Nobel Peace Prize within the next year, the music-playing part of U2 could not stifle their groans.

"We had a big scare last year when [Bono's] name was put forward as the new president of the World Bank," Clayton said. "I mean, I have nothing against it, but it would just be more work for us, because we'd be left with the very challenging task of finding a new lead singer."

During live concerts, U2 audiences are treated to a stunning audiovisual experience, with Bono periodically giving his opinion on social and world events between songs. During these interludes, the rest of U2 is often conspicuously silent.

"When Bono starts telling the audience how messed up the world can be and how we should work together to make things better, I usually just zone out," Mullen said.

COMMUNITY VOICES

My Songs About Topsoil Say What I Can't

I'm not much of a talker. Never have been. But that doesn't mean I don't have a lot to say. It's just that, sometimes, I can't communicate what I'm trying to say with just words. I guess that's just how I am.

By Jack Richland

I was only 8 when we moved to the farm in North Dakota, but even then I had certain feelings about the topsoil—feelings that I did not know how to express. Back then, I didn't know where the emotions came from, much less how to put them into words. I was young, and had a lot to learn about myself, and even more about the chocolate brown soil that kept a whole mess of good people fed.

When I was a teenager, my feelings about the topsoil grew more intense. In my head, I saw just what I wanted to express as plain as day, but every time I tried to talk it out, it came out wrong. During this time, I hurt some people, but really I was only hurting myself. Without a way to channel my feelings, I spent most of my time brooding, stealing whiskey from my folks, getting into fights, and sometimes even cutting myself just to stop the pain inside.

When I was a teenager, my feelings about the topsoil grew more intense. In my head, I saw just what I wanted to express as plain as day, but every time I tried to talk it out, it came out wrong. During this time, I hurt some people, but really I was only hurting myself.

As I lie in bed at night, my feelings for the black, nitrogen-rich soil were so strong it seemed like they would burst out of my chest.

It wasn't until my cousin Jimmy came to live with us that I saw a new path. Cousin Jimmy didn't bring much with him but a sack half full of clothes and a battered old guitar. After a couple weeks of bugging him, he taught me a few chords, and before a week was out, I spent more time with that guitar than he did. Over the years, I picked up a few more things, but I didn't need a lot of fancy learning to say what I needed to say about soil so rich you could put it to seed pretty much forever, as long as you correctly rotate the crops.

And I just started to sing. I started to sing about the topsoil, what it means to me, what feelings I had when I weeded it, everything. I don't even remember the words. All I remember was that it was like the song was just pouring out of me and it wouldn't stop. It was scary, but it felt right.

I started to sing about the topsoil, what it means to me, what feelings I had when I weeded it, everything. I don't even remember the words. All I remember was that it was like the song was just pouring out of me and it wouldn't stop.

One of the pivotal moments of my life was the afternoon I played my first show at a Future Farmers of America convention. Some of the kids got it and some didn't, but I knew I was onto something when almost every single adult came up to me after the show with tears in their eyes, telling me, "You really said it." I had put into song something they'd felt their whole lives. One of those guys, Ned Rembach, even picked up his old banjo and started playing music again. He opens for me sometimes. He does a couple songs about detasseling corn that never leave a dry eye in the house.

It's funny when I look back at some of those early songs, like "Don't Blow Away (Don't Leave Me)," "Ten-Pound Fertilizer," and "Terra Cotta Planter (Alone In My Room)," I realize how simple the songs I was writing back then were. They had a certain charm, but as I've gotten older, my feelings toward topsoil have gotten more complex. So has my music. It used to be real simple folk and country blues stuff. The latest song, "Dirt Anchor," has a real jazzy feel to it with some complex horn charts that say more about my complex relationship with the dirt than anything else I've ever done.

Of course, I still struggle with my art. A couple of years ago, I was getting to the point where I thought I had said all I could say with music. Even so, my love for the soil still burned inside me. So I took a little break and went back to the family farm and started doing some abstract paintings. Two years and hundreds of dollars in burnt-umber acrylic paint later, I felt I had become pretty accomplished as a painter even though most people were more confused than excited by my richly textured, brown works.

The way I figure it, that's all a part of the creative process. Ever since that hiatus, I've come back to music feeling fully recharged, ready to dig deep and explore some feelings about topsoil I never even knew I had. I've had so much creative juice that I started a band just to perform my free-form, red-clay-soil compositions. We're called the Red Clay Rumblers, and we play Freddy's on Tuesdays, so come on out and see us. We've got T-shirts that sum up my ideology: When dirt is your muse, inspiration is only a few steps away. ⌀

I've had so much creative juice that I started a band just to perform my free-form, red-clay-soil compositions.

HOROSCOPES

Your Horoscope

By Lloyd Schumner Sr.
Retired Machinist and
A.A.P.B.-Certified Astrologer

Aries: (March 21–April 19)
Like that of human beings, the beauty of snowflakes lies in the fact that no two are exactly alike. Also, a big part of their beauty lies in the fact that every single one of them is white.

Taurus: (April 20–May 20)
The Sistine Chapel panel that depicts the creation of the sun and moon never fails to hold spectators captive with its beauty and vast scope, allowing you plenty of time to search through their purses and pockets for money.

Gemini: (May 21–June 21)
A signature lovingly practiced and perfected in youth, when there seemed to be nothing but time and dreaming, will be used to sign off on a shipment of new highlighter pens for the conference room this week.

Cancer: (June 22–July 22)
The stars will send you a special message this week, but sadly, you will be long dead by the time it reaches Earth.

Leo: (July 23–Aug. 22)
Satan will take the form of Excel spreadsheet cell G-14 this week and refuse to assume the proper formatting.

Virgo: (Aug. 23–Sept. 22)
Your brand-new goose-down jacket will be damaged beyond repair this week when you're shot 11 times in the chest.

Libra: (Sept. 23–Oct. 23)
To many, you're nothing more than an overly enthusiastic carpet salesman, which is unfortunate, really, considering the importance of your fight to rid the world of tap-dancing.

Scorpio: (Oct. 24–Nov. 21)
You're thankful that the governor keeps granting you last-minute reprieves, but your waistline is starting to reflect all those last meals.

Sagittarius: (Nov. 22–Dec. 21)
Certain people will never understand how you can be married to your job in the rare-book room of the Frick, but that's only because they think that what you do for a living is gay.

Capricorn: (Dec. 22–Jan. 19)
After years of conflict, your parents will finally accept that you're a picky eater this week and just begin serving you food at every meal.

Aquarius: (Jan. 20–Feb. 18)
A general sense of warm well-being will lead you to decide that prog-metal band Dream Theater should be killed painlessly and without torture, a decision you may later come to regret.

Pisces: (Feb. 19–March 20)
You've never been the sort to pat yourself on the back, but that was before you had a piece of steak lodged firmly in your windpipe. ⌀